ANTITRUST LAW IN PERSPECTIVE:

CASES, CONCEPTS AND PROBLEMS IN COMPETITION POLICY

Second Edition

By

Andrew I. Gavil

Professor of Law
Howard University

William E. Kovacic

Professor of Law
George Washington University (on leave)
and Chairman, Federal Trade Commission

Jonathan B. Baker

Professor of Law
Washington College of Law
American University

AMERICAN CASEBOOK SERIES®

THOMSON
™
WEST

Mat #40392396

American Casebook Series and West Group are trademarks
registered in the U.S. Patent and Trademark Office.

© West, Thomson business, 2002
© 2008 Thomson/West
      610 Opperman Drive
      St. Paul, MN 55123
      1–800–313–9378

Printed in the United States of America

ISBN: 978–0–314–16261–8

 TEXT IS PRINTED ON 10% POST CONSUMER RECYCLED PAPER

To my parents, Ruth and Irving, who gave me all they had to give,
and to my wife, Judy, and my children, Justin, Noah and
Zoe Ruth, who sustain me each day.

AIG

To my parents, Evan and Frances, and to my wife, Kathy.

WEK

To my sons, Danny and Alex, my wife, Susan, and my parents,
Beverly and David.

JBB

*

Preface to the Second Edition

In the more than five years since the first edition was published, antitrust law has continued to evolve rapidly and in important ways. In the United States, the Supreme Court and lower courts have continued to look increasingly to economic analysis to refine and narrow the substantive rules of antitrust law. Internationally, competition law and policies have expanded to more than 100 nations which now participate to varying degrees in a still developing global competition policy system. These developments have together created new challenges for antitrust professors, but also exciting opportunities for greater perspective and deeper understanding for both experienced and new students to the subject.

We are very pleased, therefore, to bring you this thoroughly updated second edition. The book's basic structure and contents will be familiar to prior adopters and we hope inviting to new ones. As with the first edition, we have strived to make the second edition a compelling introduction to how antitrust is practiced today. To accommodate different styles of teaching and different degrees of emphasis on economics, we hope you will find it both user-friendly and sophisticated. In addition to updating throughout to reflect the latest court decisions, enforcement actions, and commentary (including Supreme Court antitrust decisions through the 2006–07 term), several chapters have been revamped more substantially. The treatment of antitrust economics in Chapter 1 has been expanded and now includes an appendix on cost concepts for those teachers inclined to delve more deeply into antitrust law's economic underpinnings. To reflect major areas of change, Chapter 4 (Distributional Relationships) has been significantly revised to take full account of the Supreme Court's 2007 decision in *Leegin*. Likewise, Chapter 6 (Dominant Firm Behavior) has been significantly updated to reflect the considerable developments that have taken place with respect to the treatment of single firm conduct. Finally, we have added several "Comparative Perspective Sidebars" to facilitate classroom discussion of competition law developments in the rest of the world, especially the European Union. Additional and significantly revised Notes and Sidebars also have been interspersed throughout the book.

We are grateful for the many suggestions we received from adopters of the first edition which have helped us to improve the second. In particular, we express our appreciation to Professors Peter C. Carstensen, Alvin K. Klevorick, James C. May, and Peter P. Swire. For updating their Sidebars, we also thank Kathryn M. Fenton and Professor Spencer Weber Waller. A very special note of thanks and our deep appreciation goes to Professor Steven C. Salop, who provided us extensive comments, freely offered us the benefit of his extraordinary insights into antitrust economics and law, and even took up his pen on occasion to help us better frame some key issues.

We also thank the many students past and present who provided the research assistance and other support necessary to bring such a major undertaking to fruition. These include at Howard University, Nina R. Frant, Obinna C. Ihekweazu, Marques S. Johnson, and Michelle M. Yost, and at American University, Katherine Chesnut. We are especially grateful for the work at Howard of Kapil V. Pandit and Jack N.E. Pitts, Jr., who gave generously of their time, intellect, skill, and good spirits under often demanding deadlines to keep the book moving forward in the final months of preparation.

As with the first edition, a complete Teacher's Manual will be available to guide the use of the second and we encourage adopters to sign on to our Author's Forum in the West Education Network (TWEN), where we will post supplemental material and updates as needed. We look forward to hearing comments and reactions from established and new adopters, alike.

ANDREW I. GAVIL
WILLIAM E. KOVACIC
JONATHAN B. BAKER

Washington, D.C.
March 2008

Preface to the First Edition

In compiling and drafting this Casebook, our goal was to capture antitrust law as it is understood and practiced today. Hence, the book emphasizes the central role of concepts such as market power, efficiency, and entry across the full spectrum of competitively sensitive conduct. It does so in a flexible format that includes accessible narrative material, as well as charts, tables and figures that enable in-class teaching. We hope it will provide an engaging, contemporary, sophisticated and user-friendly vehicle for exploring the content and boundaries of modern "competition policy."

Reflecting our goals, the book has a number of distinctive features:

- **Immediate exposure to the core issues of antitrust law.** In a unique opening chapter, the book uses three case studies to introduce the core issues that shape competition policy. The case studies range from the hard core violations in the lysine and vitamin cartel cases, to the more complex Boeing-McDonnell Douglas merger. In addition, the chapter uses a hypothetical "Coffee Shop" problem to introduce the economics of "market power" and other fundamental economic concepts. The chapter also examines the Supreme Court's *Brunswick* decision to demonstrate at the outset how the analysis of "antitrust injury" has led modern courts increasingly to focus on broad economic concepts in defining anticompetitive effects. Through its case studies and case excerpts, the chapter quickly introduces the fundamentals of modern antitrust analysis, including the rich factual detail required to evaluate the reasonableness of most antitrust-sensitive conduct.

- **From categories to concepts.** Traditionally, antitrust rules and antitrust casebooks were organized by categories defined by the nature of the relationships among the parties (e.g., horizontal, vertical) and type of conduct at issue (e.g., concerted vs. unilateral). Although those categories continue to play a role in modern antitrust analysis, today's antitrust lawyers, enforcers and courts focus far more on the nature of the anticompetitive effects, and in private cases, the antitrust injuries, alleged. A major theme of the book, therefore, is that American antitrust law is evolving away from reliance on narrow doctrinal categories towards a more unitary analytical framework, driven by broad economic concepts such as market power, entry and efficiency. Reflecting that theme, the book separately groups conduct threatening collusive anticompetitive effects—including traditional horizontal agreements, vertical intrabrand agreements and horizontal mergers—and conduct threatening exclusionary effects—including dominant firm behavior, vertical interbrand restraints and vertical mergers.

- **Up-to-date and comprehensive treatment of horizontal merger analysis.** Because so much of the development of those concepts can be traced to modern merger practice, the casebook features one of the most comprehensive chapters on horizontal merger analysis to be found. It highlights the important lower court decisions that have supplanted older Supreme Court precedent in this important area, and is framed largely around the DOJ/FTC Horizontal Merger Guidelines.

- **New approaches to proving collusion.** In recognition of the renewed focus of courts, commentators and antitrust enforcers on domestic and international cartels, the book also includes one of the most comprehensive treatments available of the contemporary law and economics of proving collusion between rivals. Critical recent lower court decisions, such as *Blomkest* and *Toys-R-Us*, are excerpted and analyzed.

- **Contemporary approach to distribution practices.** Divided into two chapters, the book takes a sophisticated, yet practical and comprehensive approach to the antitrust issues that attend various distribution strategies.

- **Addresses role of antitrust in high-tech markets.** Our casebook recognizes the increasing importance of competitive effects involving innovation in antitrust analysis, and the contemporary ferment over the extent to which antitrust law can and should be harmonized with intellectual property law. The capstone chapter is devoted exclusively to antitrust in the new economy.

- **Fully integrates economic thinking.** Our casebook does not relegate modern economic analysis to occasional notes or to a discrete section on economics. Instead, we present the economics students need to know to practice antitrust today simply and clearly, and integrate economic thinking throughout the casebook. Differences between a Chicago school and post-Chicago perspective are noted where appropriate, as are other perspectives. On the other hand, we recognize that few students will have extensive backgrounds in economics, and that teachers, themselves, may have varying degrees of economic expertise. The economic content, therefore, is designed to be accessible, and adaptable to varying degrees of economic sophistication and varying styles of teaching.

- **Inclusive approach to the relevant cases.** Our casebook excerpts or discusses the traditional and familiar Supreme Court cases that have long been staples of the antitrust course. But the book also recognizes that much of the action in recent years has been in the lower courts. The casebook responds to that development by highlighting contemporary lower court decisions, especially with respect to mergers and the developing standards for proving market power and anticompetitive effects. Comprehensive treatment of the enduring aspects of the *Microsoft* litigation is also integrated throughout the book.

- **Beyond case law.** The sources of antitrust law encompass far more than just cases. The book relies upon a range of sources, not only to enhance its substantive content, but also to expose students to the full range of antitrust practice. Non-case materials include expert economic testimony, consent decrees, FTC Aids to Public Comment, business review letters, a complaint, and extensive treatment of government enforcement guidelines.

- **Sensitivity to antitrust's global context.** U.S. antitrust practitioners can no longer ignore developments in competition policy elsewhere in the world. Although comprehensive treatment of U.S. antitrust law remains the principal focus of the book, we provide an occasional counterpoint to the American approach by looking briefly at how other competition policy systems (primarily the E.U.) address similar issues. Moreover, beginning in the first chapter, we highlight the problems that the globalization of antitrust presents for firms that must manage compliance with multiple jurisdictions simultaneously.

• **Treatment of ethics.** Several Sidebars are specifically devoted to issues of ethics and professional responsibility in both the litigation and counseling context. These Sidebars allow interested teachers and students to explore how issues of professional responsibility can arise in and complicate antitrust practice.

In addition to these substantive features of the book, teachers and students alike will notice some important, and, we hope, productive characteristics of the presentation.

• **"Sidebars" and "Notes".** We have banned the typical "notes" sections typified by numbered paragraphs following cases. All too often, our collective experience suggests that these notes reflect a counterproductive "hide the ball" approach to teaching, and can obscure important cases and concepts. In their place, we have prepared extensive narrative interstitial material in the form of "Sidebars" and "Notes." This material is accessible, informative, challenging and flexible. It serves many possible functions, including coverage of live controversies in the field, the historical development of antitrust concepts and thought, discussion of trends in the law, discussion of particular economic and legal issues in greater depth, and thoughts on future directions in our field.

• **Visual Learning.** In addition to the network of interstitial material, the book includes over 80 tables, charts and figures. Some simply summarize relevant factors, while others visually present more complex ideas, including relationships among parties to a case or transaction.

• **Attention to lawyering skills and problem solving.** Almost every chapter concludes with problems and exercises that develop lawyering skills as well as deepen the understanding of antitrust principles. The skills exercises also offer the opportunity to socialize students to the wide range of functions of antitrust lawyers and involve various litigation, counseling and regulatory settings.

As is common in any multi-authored book of this kind, no individual author necessarily agrees with every statement the book makes, even when we do not present multiple points of view. Moreover, we have at times chosen to emphasize perspectives we may not share for pedagogical reasons.

We believe that we have presented antitrust in an accessible yet sophisticated way that is consonant with modern antitrust practice. We hope you will agree, and look forward to hearing your comments and reactions.

ANDREW I. GAVIL
WILLIAM E. KOVACIC
JONATHAN B. BAKER

Washington, D.C.
October 2002

*

Acknowledgments to the First Edition

On the day we received our contract offer from West Group, I called Bill Kovacic to report that there was "good news and bad news." The "good news"? We were on our way with our casebook concept. The "bad news"? He would be working with me on the casebook and updates for the rest of his life! I had no idea that the first phase of the rest of our working life together would take nearly six years! But here we finally are.

First and foremost, I want to thank my co-authors, Bill and Jon. All three of us share a true love for the subject, which I hope is revealed in the pages that follow. Those pages have been immeasurably enriched by the intellectual capital that Bill and Jon have brought to the book. Crossing paths with Bill Kovacic more than 15 years ago was one of the great fortunes of my life. He has been mentor, teacher, colleague, friend, and now co-author. I owe him a debt of gratitude that will be hard ever to repay. And Bill and I could not have been more delighted when Jon accepted our invitation to join the project after he left the FTC. The value he has added is incalculable in terms of the book's economic sophistication and clarity of presentation. It would not have been the same book without you, Jon. I have thoroughly enjoyed the many hours we three have spent dissecting and pondering antitrust's intricacies, and have learned so much from the both of you.

Bill, Jon and I also would like to collectively thank Kathryn M. Fenton, Steven C. Salop and Spencer Weber Waller, each of whom has made valuable contributions to the book that are noted in the text.

Of course, completing such a major project requires a great deal of support and research assistance. I am especially grateful to the Howard University School of Law for financial support over many years, and in particular to President H. Patrick Swygert and former Dean Alice Gresham Bullock for their consistent encouragement and support of my work. For the kind of unqualified and tireless encouragement one hopes to get from colleagues, I am also indebted to Professors Loretta C. Argrett, Rhea Ballard-Thrower, Cynthia Mabry, Laurence C. Nolan, Isiah Leggett, Okianer Christian Dark, Homer C. LaRue, Ziyad Motala, J. Clay Smith, Denise W. Spriggs, Andrew E. Taslitz and Frank H. Wu. A very special note of appreciation to the "other Andy"—to have found not only a colleague but a fellow Bronx traveler and best friend has been a source of persistent strength throughout our years together at Howard. Thanks, Taz!

Many students also have made significant contributions to the quality of the book. To my Howard students who, through the last several years, have cheerfully worked with earlier drafts of the manuscript, freely offering constructive comments, I thank you and hope the end product meets with your approval. To research assistants who have worked hard over the years, and frequently under tight deadlines, gratitude is also due. I want to especially thank Summeet Lall, Edrei Swanson, Darren P. Riley, Tyresse Horne, Sophiea C. Bailey, Esther R. Sailo, Nadine Jones-Francis, Natasha Yates and Charles W. Brumskine.

I have also been a very fortunate beneficiary of the wisdom and professionalism of some terrific antitrust lawyers in Chicago, Denver and Washington, D.C., who not only taught me a great deal, but encouraged my interest and enthusiasm for antitrust law. In particular, I want to express my gratitude to the late John T. ("Ted") Loughlin, and to Victor E. Grimm, John C. Christie, Jr., Michael Sennett, James E. Hartley, Larry R. Fullerton and Andrew J. Strenio, Jr..

To my "first fan," my sister Gale S. Wachs, boundless appreciation for a lifetime of confidence, encouragement and support. And finally, there is my family, to whom I dedicate it all. Without the unwavering support, love and encouragement of my wife, Judy Veis, and our children, Justin, Noah and Zoe Ruth, it could never have been done, and could hardly have been worth the effort.

ANDREW I. GAVIL

Washington, D.C.
October 2002

I want to express my gratitude to Andy and Jon. The vision for this book is first and foremost Andy's. In 1996 Andy and I traveled to Cairo to assist the Government of Egypt in developing a new competition law. Our Egyptian counterparts often pressed us to describe how academics, practitioners, and judges analyze antitrust issues in the United States and solicited our thoughts about the optimal design of competition policy institutions. Answering these questions required us to step back and reexamine competition policy in the United States and around the globe. On a day of tourism amid the pyramids at Giza, Andy said this introspection provided us an opportunity to develop a casebook that captured modern antitrust analysis. To Andy's wonderful concept Jon later added his unsurpassed appreciation of how economics has shaped contemporary antitrust doctrine and is likely to influence its future evolution. My gratitude for the chance to work with Andy and Jon is no less monumental than the antiquities that provided the setting for Andy's original proposal.

I also must note that Andy and Jon have borne the heaviest burdens in completing the casebook, especially after I came to the Federal Trade Commission in June 2001. This was not because they had idle time to occupy. Rather, it demonstrates their unbounded generosity. Their kindness did not surprise me. On countless occasions since I met them in the mid-1980s Andy and Jon have carried me, whether teaching me economics and law, providing career advice, or simply supplying encouragement. Broad minds and great hearts.

I got lots of help from the university communities at George Mason and George Washington. No academic prospers without astute research assistants. My deepest thanks to Eric Berman, Neil Graham, Robin Moore, and Tom Mila for doing research and editing that made this a much better casebook. I am also grateful to my antitrust students at George Washington who used early versions of the manuscript and provided countless helpful suggestions.

Finally, I dedicate my efforts to my Father, who died soon before we began the project, to my Mother, and to my wife, Kathy.

WILLIAM E. KOVACIC

Washington, D.C.
October 2002

Thanks first to Andy and Bill for inviting me to join them in this project. "Free riding" works best with co-authors as hard-working and talented as both of you. Thanks also to Dean Claudio Grossman and the Washington College of Law for supporting my work on this casebook; to the students who tried out the manuscript in draft; to the Dean's Fellows who provided research assistance, Alexandra Cornhill, Arturo DeCastro, Sharmalee Rajakumaran and Traci Tyers; and to my many mentors and colleagues in antitrust.

JONATHAN B. BAKER

Washington, D.C.
October 2002

*

Summary of Contents

*

Table of Contents

PART IV. CONSTRUCTING THE MODERN ANTITRUST CASE

Table of Figures

Table of Cases

The principal cases are in bold type. Cases cited or discussed in the text are roman type. References are to pages. Cases cited in principal cases and within other quoted materials are not included.

ANTITRUST LAW IN PERSPECTIVE:

CASES, CONCEPTS AND PROBLEMS IN COMPETITION POLICY

Second Edition

*

Part I

AN INTRODUCTION TO THE STUDY OF ANTITRUST LAW

Chapter 1

DEFINING COMPETITION POLICY FOR A GLOBAL ECONOMY

INTRODUCTION

What is "antitrust law" about? In important ways, the answer depends upon when we ask the question. The word "anti-trust" appeared in the United States in the late nineteenth century in connection with a movement to ban a form of business organization known as "the trust." Trusts combined in one enterprise the power to make pricing and output decisions for entire industries, such as oil, sugar, tobacco, and whiskey. Public officials, editorial writers, and small businesses denounced the trusts for raising prices and excluding rival firms that refused to cooperate in price-raising schemes. Popular opposition to the trusts culminated in the passage of state antitrust laws and in 1890 of the federal "Sherman Antitrust Law," which will occupy much of our attention in this Casebook.

Through the first half of the twentieth century, enforcement of antitrust law was predominantly an American endeavor. A few other jurisdictions—notably, Canada in 1889—also adopted antitrust laws, but they were largely ineffectual. As late as 1975, only a handful of other jurisdictions, such as the European Union, actively enforced antitrust laws. Indeed, most of the world's population lived in countries that curbed private enterprise, distrusted market-based competition, and depended chiefly on central planning to determine the price, type, and amount of goods and services their citizens could consume.

Developments in recent decades have been truly remarkable. To the generation that first studied antitrust in the 1970s and early 1980s, it is a source of continuing amazement. Today few jurisdictions do not rely extensively upon market-oriented policies to spur economic growth. With this transformation has come a stunning increase in the number of nations with antitrust laws. Over 100 jurisdictions have enacted antitrust laws, and many apply them with true force. In 2007 alone, the People's Republic of China adopted its first antitrust law, and India retooled an older, largely dormant measure.

As a consequence, the study of antitrust law today has a degree of significance that was inconceivable in the recent past. For business managers

2

and their legal advisors, global expansion in the number of antitrust laws and the enhancement of enforcement tools compel greater attention to antitrust concerns in carrying out mergers or other routine transactions. Yet these matters of considerable practical relevance are only the beginning. To a growing degree, the study of antitrust law has great and increasing intellectual vitality, for it provides a way to assess the role of public intervention in the economy, to understand the considerations that govern the design of administrative and law enforcement institutions, and to understand how nations with dissimilar legal systems and analytical approaches can achieve needed levels of integration, cooperation, and consistency.

More than may appear at first glance, antitrust's foundational principles will be strikingly familiar to the reader living in a market-driven economy. Many economic principles that provide the conceptual framework for modern antitrust law are evident in daily life in the multitude of nations which use markets to organize the production and sale of goods and services. In short, we can understand many antitrust ideas instinctively from our daily interactions with markets.

To introduce those ideas, this Chapter begins with two case studies. The first examines the prosecution in the 1990s of an international supplier cartel that fixed the prices of the food additive lysine. The second case study presents a hypothetical example involving retail sales of coffee. These case studies illustrate three themes of this casebook. First, they suggest how antitrust law is evolving away from an analytical model that depends on separating conduct into discrete categories towards reliance on a set of core concepts that have been greatly influenced by economic theory. Although we present and explain the traditional framework, it serves mainly as a stepping stone towards a more modern, concept-based vision of antitrust law. Critical to the practical operation of these economic concepts is their ability to serve as reliable means for distinguishing "anticompetitive" from "procompetitive" business conduct.

Second, the international cartel case illustrates the dramatic and still unfolding trend toward the globalization of antitrust law and its concepts. The food additive cartel was truly a global enterprise, and the successful prosecution of its participants demonstrates how anticompetitive conduct can fall within the jurisdiction of different national competition policy systems. The global expansion of competition regimes poses challenges of culturally integrating and adapting antitrust law to varying settings, coordinating investigations and prosecution efforts, and minimizing the burdens placed upon businesses subject to multiple competition law systems with sometimes dissimilar visions of the law and its purposes.

Finally, the case studies illustrate the skills demanded of the modern antitrust lawyer. From using sophisticated legal analysis of the likely treatment of a competitively sensitive transaction under the laws of multiple jurisdictions, to persuading government enforcement agencies not to challenge a particular transaction, to negotiating with enforcement officials and potential litigants, the antitrust lawyer must skillfully play a variety of roles. These include analyzing the application of antitrust rules—for an increasingly large range of behavior, the rules of two or more jurisdictions—to complex facts, working closely with economic consultants and witnesses, identifying economic and political trends that shape government decisions, and negotiating settlements with multiple antitrust enforcers. Paramount among the antitrust lawyer's associated skills is a basic knowledge of economics. The centrality of economic principles to evaluating the competitive significance of business behavior is emphasized through our retail coffee shop case study.

Before we begin, we would like to address a basic point of terminology. In this text we use the terms "antitrust law" or "antitrust policy" and "competition law" or "competition policy" somewhat interchangeably. A North American who practices in this field is likely to call herself an "antitrust lawyer"—a habit that reflects the vocabulary used in Canada and the United States since the late nineteenth century to describe the first laws. Specialists in other parts of the world tend to say that they practice "competition law," which is the phrase rooted in the experience of Europeans under the Treaty of Rome and in the laws of EU member states.

These terms sometimes are synonyms, but they also can have different meanings. The term "antitrust law and policy" sometimes is taken to mean the enforcement of prohibitions against certain conduct by private firms. By contrast, "competition law and policy" tends to embrace the larger range of intervention. For example, it might include scrutiny of public restrictions on entry into a market or suggestions for adjustments in the design of an intellectual property system, by which a jurisdiction determines the level of competition within its borders. It also comprehends and includes instruments other than law enforcement, *e.g.*, the issuance of guidelines, by which an agency responsible for antitrust enforcement makes policy. This Casebook focuses heavily on law enforcement and the cases that result from the prosecution of violations of antitrust laws, but it also draws attention to the broader array of public interventions that affect competition and emphasizes measures beyond law enforcement that government antitrust agencies use to implement competition policy.

This Chapter has three Sections. Section A presents the facts and background information needed to begin considering the competition issues raised in the international lysine cartel prosecution. Section B introduces four core issues that occupy our attention throughout the casebook and introduces the basic economic concepts of modern antitrust law through our second case study, which involves the retail sales of coffee. Section C concludes, providing an introduction to the forms of economic proof that figure so prominently in modern antitrust analysis and which will be evident in all of the Chapters to come.

A.   "HARVEST KING"—THE LYSINE CARTEL

Most systems of competition law deal severely with agreements by rival firms to suppress production, raise prices, or retard innovation. This section looks at one of the most notorious cartels in modern antitrust experience.

Most of the food we consume does not acquire its taste or composition without some degree of human intervention. Our meats often come from animals fattened with feed containing growth-enhancing additives. The producers of food additives participate in a vast global enterprise. They account for billions of dollars of sales annually and touch hundreds of millions of lives daily. Despite the nearly universal consumption of their products, the leading suppliers generally operate out of the public eye. It is the rare fast food restaurant customer who can say whose lysine may have fed the chicken that became a "chicken nugget" or the beef that produced a tasty hamburger.

For a time in the 1990s, the anonymity of food additives companies vanished. The transforming cause was not a public relations campaign, but the prosecution of the industry's leaders under a statute adopted a century earlier in part to assuage farmers complaining of exploitation by cartels that bought their livestock and produce. An encounter with the Sherman Act put the names of the leading producers on the front page of the newspaper. For reasons described below, the global competition policy community will never forget them.

———

Decatur, Illinois sits amid some of the most fertile land in North America. Since the 1920s, Decatur has been home to the headquarters of the Archer–Daniels–Midland Company (ADM), the world's largest manufacturer of food additives, oils, and fibers derived from grains, soybeans, and other farm staples. From 1991 to 1995, ADM helped orchestrate a global cartel to boost the price of lysine. With the help of a company insider, the Federal Bureau of Investigation (FBI) began a lengthy inquiry that ultimately spanned the globe. Recounted below by the U.S. Court of Appeals for the Seventh Circuit is the story of the case the FBI called "Harvest King."

UNITED STATES v. ANDREAS
United States Court of Appeals for the Seventh Circuit, 2000.
216 F.3d 645.

Before: KANNE, ROVNER, and EVANS, Circuit Judges.

KANNE, Circuit Judge.

For many years, Archer Daniels Midland Co.'s philosophy of customer relations could be summed up by a quote from former ADM President James Randall: "Our competitors are our friends. Our customers are the enemy." This motto animated the company's business dealings and ultimately led to blatant violations of U.S. antitrust law, a guilty plea and a staggering criminal fine against the company. It also led to the criminal charges against three top ADM executives that are the subject of this appeal. The facts involved in this case reflect an inexplicable lack of business ethics and an atmosphere of general lawlessness that infected the very heart of one of America's leading corporate citizens. Top executives at ADM and its Asian co-conspirators throughout the early 1990s spied on each other, fabricated aliases and front organizations to hide their activities, hired prostitutes to gather information from competitors, lied, cheated, embezzled, extorted and obstructed justice.

After a two-month trial, a jury convicted three ADM officials of conspiring to violate § 1 of the Sherman Antitrust Act, 15 U.S.C. § 1, which prohibits any conspiracy or combination to restrain trade. District Judge Blanche M. Manning sentenced defendants Michael D. Andreas and Terrance S. Wilson to twenty-four months in prison. They now appeal several issues related to their convictions and sentences, and the government counter-appeals one issue related to sentencing. We find no error related to the convictions, but agree with the government that the defendants should have received longer sentences for their leadership roles in the conspiracy.

I. History

The defendants in this case, Andreas and Wilson, were executives at Archer Daniels Midland Co., the Decatur, Illinois-based agriculture processing company. Mark E. Whitacre, the third ADM executive named in the indictment, did not join this appeal.[1] ADM, the self-professed "supermarket to the world," is a behemoth in its industry with global sales of $14 billion in 1999 and 23,000 employees. Its concerns include nearly every farm commodity, such as corn, soybeans and wheat, but also the processing of commodities into such products as fuel ethanol, high-fructose sweeteners, feed additives and various types of seed oils. ADM has a worldwide sales force and a global transportation network involving thousands of rail lines, barges and trucks. The company is publicly held and listed on the New York Stock Exchange.

The Andreas family has long controlled ADM. Dwayne Andreas is a director and the former CEO, G. Allen Andreas is the board chairman and president, and various other family members occupy other executive positions. Michael D. Andreas, commonly called "Mick," was vice chairman of the board of directors and executive vice president of sales and marketing. Wilson was president of the corn processing division and reported directly to Michael Andreas.

A. The Lysine Industry

Lysine is an amino acid used to stimulate an animal's growth. It is produced by a fermentation process in which nutrients, primarily sugar, are fed to microorganisms, which multiply and metabolize. As a product of that process, the microorganisms excrete lysine, which is then harvested and sold to feed manufacturers who add it to animal feed. Feed manufacturers sell the feed to farmers who use it to raise chickens and pigs. The fermentation process tends to be very delicate, and utmost care must be used to keep the fermentation plant sterile.

Until 1991, the lysine market had been dominated by a cartel of three companies in Korea and Japan, with American and European subsidiaries. Ajinomoto Co., Inc. of Japan, was the industry leader, accounting for up to half of all world lysine sales. Ajinomoto had 50 percent interests in two subsidiaries, Eurolysine, based in Paris, and Heartland Lysine, based in Chicago. The other two producers of lysine were Miwon Co., Ltd. (later renamed Sewon Co., Ltd.) of South Korea, and Kyowa Hakko, Ltd. of Japan. Miwon ran a New Jersey-based subsidiary called Sewon America, and Kyowa owned the American subsidiary Biokyowa, Inc., which is based in Missouri.

Lysine is a highly fungible commodity and sold almost entirely on the basis of price. Pricing depended largely on two variables: the price of organic

---

1. At his insistence, Whitacre was tried in absentia from the prison where he is serving a 108–month sentence for embezzlement. He was represented vigorously by counsel at trial and aided his defense through telephone communication with his lawyer. Kazutoshi Yamada, an employee of Ajinomoto Co. of Japan, was the fourth defendant named in the indictment. He has not been tried and remains a fugitive.

substitutes, such as soy or fish meal, and the price charged by other lysine producers. Together, the three parent companies produced all of the world's lysine until the 1990s, presenting an obvious opportunity for collusive behavior. Indeed the Asian cartel periodically agreed to fix prices, which at times reached as high as $3.00 per pound.

In 1989, ADM announced that it was building what would be the world's largest lysine plant. If goals were met, the Illinois facility could produce two or three times as much lysine as any other plant and could ultimately account for up to half of all the lysine produced globally. Even before the plant became operational, ADM embarked on an ambitious marketing campaign aimed at attracting large American meat companies, such as Tyson Foods, in part by capitalizing on anti-Asia sentiment prevalent at the time. Also around 1990, another South Korean company, Cheil Jedang Co., began producing lysine. Despite some early difficulties with the fermenting process, the ADM plant began producing lysine in 1991 and immediately became a market heavyweight, possibly even the industry leader. The two new producers created chaos in the market, igniting a price war that drove the price of lysine down, eventually to about 70–cents per pound. The Asian companies understandably were greatly concerned by developments in this once profitable field.

B.   Start of the Conspiracy

Against this background, Kyowa Hakko arranged a meeting with Ajinomoto and ADM in June 1992. Mexico City was chosen as the site in part because the participants did not want to meet within the jurisdiction of American antitrust laws. Ajinomoto was represented by Kanji Mimoto and Hirokazu Ikeda from the Tokyo headquarters, and Alain Crouy from its Eurolysine subsidiary. Masaru Yamamoto represented Kyowa Hakko, and Wilson and Whitacre attended for ADM. Mimoto, Ikeda, Crouy and Yamamoto testified as government witnesses at trial. At this meeting, the three companies first discussed price agreements and allocating sales volumes among the market participants. Wilson, who was senior to Whitacre in the corporate hierarchy, led the discussion on behalf of ADM. The price agreements came easily, and all present agreed to raise the price in two stages by the end of 1992. According to internal Ajinomoto documents prepared after the meeting, the cartel's goal was to raise the price to $1.05 per pound in North America and Europe by October 1992 and up to $1.20 per pound by December, with other price hikes for other regions. The companies agreed to that price schedule and presumed that Ajinomoto and Kyowa would convince Sewon and Cheil to agree as well.

The sales volume allocation, in which the cartel (now including ADM) would decide how much each company would sell, was a matter of strong disagreement. In ADM's view, ADM should have one-third of the market, Ajinomoto and its subsidiaries should have one-third and Kyowa and the Koreans should have the remaining third. Ajinomoto—the historical industry leader—disagreed vehemently and thought ADM did not deserve an equal portion of the market and could not produce that much lysine in any case. Wilson also suggested each company pick an auditor to whom sales volumes could be reported so that the cartel could keep track of each other's business. The meeting ended without a sales volume allocation agreement, but two months later, at the recommendation of Whitacre, the cartel raised prices anyway, and prices rose from $.70 to $1.05 per pound.

Still, the cartel considered a price agreement without allocating sales volume to be an imperfect scheme because each company would have an incentive to cheat on the price to get more sales, so long as its competitors continued to sell at the agreed price. With cheating, the price ultimately would drop, and the agreement would falter. An effort had to be made to get the parties to agree to a volume agreement, and to that end, Whitacre invited Ajinomoto officials to visit ADM's Decatur lysine facility to prove that it could produce the volume ADM claimed. Mimoto, Ikeda and other Ajinomoto officials, including an engineer named Fujiwara, visited the plant in September 1992. At a meeting before the tour, Whitacre and Mimoto confirmed the price schedule to which the parties had agreed in Mexico City.

The cartel met again in October 1992, this time in Paris. All five major lysine producers attended, along with representatives of their subsidiaries. Wilson and Whitacre again represented ADM. To disguise the purpose of the meeting, the parties created a fake agenda, and later a fictitious lysine producers trade association, so they could meet and share information without raising the suspicions of customers or law enforcement agencies. According to the agenda, the group was to discuss such topics as animal rights and the environment. In reality, they discussed something much dearer to their hearts—the price of lysine. According to internal Ajinomoto documents, the "purpose of the meeting" was to "confirm present price level and reaction of the market, and 2, future price schedule."

Shortly after this meeting, under circumstances explained below, Whitacre began cooperating with the FBI in an undercover sting operation aimed at busting the price-fixing conspiracy. As a result, most of the meetings and telephone conversations involving Whitacre and other conspirators after October 1992 were audiotaped or videotaped.

Despite the cartel's efforts to raise prices, the price of lysine dropped in 1993. According to executives of the companies who testified at trial, without a sales volume agreement, each company had an incentive to underbid the agreed price, and consequently each company had to match the lower bids or lose sales to its underbidding competitors. This resulted in the price of lysine falling in the spring of 1993. The group, calling itself "G–5" or "the club," met in Vancouver, Canada, in June 1993 to deal with the disintegrating price agreement. Wilson and Whitacre again represented ADM. At this meeting, the Asian companies presented a sales volume allocation that limited each company to a certain tonnage of lysine per year. ADM, through Wilson, rejected the suggested tonnage assignment because it granted ADM less than one-third of the market. Ajinomoto still considered ADM's demands too high.

That summer's strong commodities market permitted frequent increases in the lysine price, to which each of the companies agreed, despite the absence of a volume allocation. The cartel's continued strong interest in a volume allocation to support the price agreement led to another meeting in Paris in October 1993. The failure to reach a volume schedule in Paris finally led to a call for a meeting between the top management at Ajinomoto and ADM: Kazutoshi Yamada and Mick Andreas.

In October 1993, Andreas and Whitacre met with Yamada and Ikeda in Irvine, California. With Whitacre's assistance, the meeting was secretly video-taped and audiotaped. Andreas threatened Yamada that ADM would flood the market unless a sales volume allocation agreement was reached that would allow ADM to sell more than it had the previous year. The four discussed the dangers of competing in a free market and hammered out a deal on volume allocations, with Andreas accepting less than a one-third share of the market in exchange for a large portion of the market's growth. Specific prices were not discussed, but Andreas acknowledged the price deal that had already been negotiated. Yamada agreed to present ADM's proposal to the other three Asian producers.

A central concern to Andreas was the difficulty he expected the Asian producers to encounter in maintaining their agreed price level. As Andreas explained at some length, the Asian companies had a more decentralized sales system that depended on agents making deals with customers. ADM featured a very centralized system in which agents played a small role in overall sales and had no discretion over price. In such an environment, maintaining control over price was easy; for the Japanese, Andreas feared it would be difficult and suggested that Ajinomoto move to a more ADM-like centralized pricing system. Andreas also expressed concern that customers could "cheat" the producers by bargaining down the price, apparently by claiming to have received lower bids from competing producers. Ikeda and Yamada agreed that customer cheating was a problem, and the four briefly discussed a quick-response system that would allow the producers to verify with each other the prices offered to particular customers.

After the Irvine meeting, the cartel met in Tokyo to work out the details of the Andreas–Yamada arrangement. All the companies except for Cheil now agreed to both tonnage maximums and percentage market shares. The group excluded Cheil from this discussion because it considered Cheil's volume demand unreasonable. The cartel, expecting the lysine market to grow in 1994, thought it wise to agree on percentages of the market that each company could have since it was possible that all five producers could sell more than their allotted tonnage. With a total expected market of 245,000 tons for 1994, Ajinomoto was to sell 84,000 tons, ADM would sell 67,000 tons, Kyowa would sell 46,000 tons, Miwon would sell 34,000 tons and Cheil, if it eventually accepted the deal, would get 14,000 tons, according to the deal hammered out by Yamada and Andreas in Irvine.

As they had before the Andreas–Yamada meeting, Wilson and Whitacre attended these Tokyo meetings for ADM. In Tokyo, Wilson suggested, and the members agreed, that each producer report their monthly sales figures by telephone to Mimoto throughout the year, and if one producer exceeded its allocation, it would compensate the others by buying enough from the shorted members to even out the allocation. The producers also agreed on a new price of $1.20 for the United States market. The agreement to buy each other's unsold allocation cemented the deal by eliminating any incentive for a company to underbid the sales price. According to Mimoto: "Since there is an agreement on the quantity allocation, our sales quantity is guaranteed by other manufacturers of the lysine. So by matching the price, to us, lowering the price is very silly. We can just keep the price." With the agreement on prices and quantities in place, the lysine price remained at the agreed level for January and February 1994.

On March 10, 1994, the cartel met in Hawaii. At this meeting, attended by Wilson and Whitacre on behalf of ADM, the producers discussed the progress of the volume allocation agreement, reported their sales figures and agreed on prices. They also considered letting Cheil into the allocation agreement and agreed to grant the company a market share of 17,000 tons. Cheil accepted this arrangement at a meeting later that day, at which Wilson explained that the conspiracy would operate almost identically to the scheme used to fix prices in the citric-acid market. The cartel further agreed on prices for Europe, South America, Asia and the rest of the world, and discussed how the global allocations would work on a regional basis. According to the figures reported to Mimoto through May 1994, prices were maintained, and both ADM and Ajinomoto were on track to meet their sales volume limits.

In the summer of 1994, the producers met in Sapporo, Japan, for a routine cartel meeting. Whitacre represented ADM by himself. At this meeting, Sewon demanded a larger share of the market for 1995. This created a problem for the cartel, which necessitated another meeting between Andreas and Yamada. In October 1994, while on a separate business trip to the United States, Yamada met with Andreas in a private dining room at the Four Seasons Hotel in Chicago. Whitacre, Wilson and Mimoto also attended along with their bosses.

The cartel met in Atlanta in January 1995, using a major poultry exposition as camouflage for the producers being in the same place at the same time. The cartel, without the presence of Sewon, decided to cut Sewon out of the agreement for 1995 because of its unrealistic volume demand. Sewon then joined the meeting and agreed to abide by the set price, if not the volume. The group discussed the year-end sales figures for 1994, comparing them to each company's allocated volume, and discussed the new allotment for 1995. According to the 1994 numbers, each company finished fairly close to its allotted volume. The cartel met once more in Hong Kong before the FBI raided the offices of ADM in Decatur and Heartland Lysine in Chicago. These raids ended the cartel. Heartland Lysine immediately notified its home office in Japan of the search, and Ajinomoto began destroying evidence of the cartel housed in its Tokyo office. Mimoto overlooked documents stored at his home and later turned these over to the FBI. Included in these saved documents were copies of internal Ajinomoto reports of the Mexico and Paris meetings.

C.   The Investigation

Mark E. Whitacre joined ADM in 1989 as president of its bioproducts division. That year, ADM announced that it would enter the lysine market dominated by Asian producers. Whitacre, who held a Ph.D. in biochemistry from Cornell University and degrees in agricultural science, answered directly to Mick Andreas. Just 32 years old when he joined the company, Whitacre's star clearly was rising fast at ADM, and some industry analysts thought he could be the next president of ADM.

In 1992, Whitacre began working with Wilson, and the two attended the first meetings of the lysine producers in Mexico City. Also in 1992, Whitacre began embezzling large sums of money from ADM and eventually stole at least $9 million from the company by submitting to ADM phony invoices for work done by outside companies, who would then funnel the money to Whitacre's personal offshore and Swiss bank accounts. To cover up the embezzlement, Whitacre hatched a scheme in the summer of 1992 to accuse Ajinomoto of planting a saboteur in ADM's Decatur plant. Whitacre would accuse the saboteur of contaminating the delicate bacterial environment needed for the production of lysine, a story made believable because of the many early difficulties the ADM lysine plant encountered.

In accordance with the plot, Whitacre told Mick Andreas that an engineer at Ajinomoto named Fujiwara had contacted him at his home and offered to sell ADM the name of the saboteur in exchange for $10 million. The story was a lie. However, Dwayne Andreas believed it and feared it could jeopardize relations between the United States and Japan. He called the CIA, but the CIA, considering the matter one of federal law enforcement rather than national security, directed the call to the FBI, which sent agents out to ADM to interview Whitacre and other officials about the extortion. Whitacre apparently had not expected this and realized quickly that his lie would be discovered by the FBI, particularly after Special Agent Brian Shepard asked Whitacre if he could tap Whitacre's home telephone to record the next extortion demand. Whitacre knew that when the extortionist failed to call, Shepard would know Whitacre had invented the story. Whitacre confessed the scheme to Shepard, but to save himself, he agreed to become an undercover informant to help the FBI investigate price fixing at ADM. He did not come totally clean with the FBI, however; he failed to mention the millions he embezzled and in fact continued to embezzle after he began working for the government. For the next two-and-a-half years, Whitacre acted as an undercover cooperating witness—legally a government agent—and secretly taped hundreds of hours of conversations and meetings with Wilson, Mick Andreas and the other conspirators. In addition, the FBI secretly videotaped meetings of the lysine producers.

Whitacre made between 120 and 130 tapes for the FBI during the investigation, beginning with a November 9, 1992, conversation with Yamamoto, by using recording equipment, tapes and instruction provided by the government. FBI agents met with Whitacre more than 150 times during the investigation. The tapes were collected and reviewed usually within a day or two of the FBI receiving them, and Department of Justice (DOJ) attorneys regularly participated in reviewing the tapes and monitoring the supervision of Whitacre. However, the FBI's supervision of Whitacre was not flawless. Whitacre was, to say the least, a difficult cooperating witness to handle. Whitacre lied to the FBI during the probe, failed polygraph tests, bragged to his gardener about his role as an FBI mole, all while continuing to embezzle millions of dollars from the company. He even envisioned himself ascending to the ADM presidency as a hero once Andreas, Wilson and Randall were taken down in the FBI sting. In short, he was out of control, and the FBI struggled to keep him on track. Nonetheless, the FBI and the DOJ considered him the best opportunity to stop a massive price-fixing scheme.

* * *

Mark Whitacre, the high-level ADM executive featured so prominently in the Seventh Circuit's opinion, proved to be a vexing informant for the Department of Justice as it sought to pin down ADM's participation in the food additives cartel. Only gradually did the government learn that Whitacre aided the investigation to deflect attention from his embezzlement of ADM funds. Yet for all the trouble Whitacre's falsehoods caused the prosecutors, the information he provided was pure gold for building their case. *See generally* KURT EICHENWALD, THE INFORMANT (2000).

The most stunning evidence was contained in the videotapes that Whitacre helped the government obtain by alerting them to the time and location of meetings of the cartel members. Captured in grainy, black and white images were hours of discussions in which the world's lysine producers set output levels, argued over their individual quotas, and devised ways to audit compliance with their pact. In one memorable session in a hotel room in Atlanta, the competitors joked openly about the possibility that the FBI or the U.S. antitrust agencies might detect their behavior.

Seldom had U.S. antitrust prosecutors obtained such damning evidence of a flagrant crime. By early 1995, the Justice Department informed ADM's top management and its board of directors about its intention to prosecute the cartel participants and many of their top employees. At key points when company officials and their lawyers expressed doubts about the strength of the government's proof, the government's lawyers pulled out a video cassette called "the greatest hits" and played episodes of the cartel's meetings for all to see. Within months, ADM's board decided it was time to deal.

ADM agreed to pay a criminal fine of $100 million—at that time, the largest criminal recovery in the history of the Sherman Act. The Justice Department indicted ADM executives Michael Andreas, Terrence Wilson, and Mark Whitacre, the cooperating witness who provided prosecutors with vital evidence, but violated his cooperation agreement through a series of deceits. A jury convicted all three men, and Andreas and Wilson contested their conviction on appeal. In the excerpt from the *Andreas* opinion we just read, the Seventh Circuit upheld their convictions and concluded that the trial judge had erred by imposing excessively lenient (24 month) sentences. ADM later paid hundreds of millions of dollars in settlements to resolve private class action cases and matters initiated by foreign governments.

What do you suppose motivated ADM and its co-conspirators to undertake the price-fixing scheme described in *Andreas*? How might it benefit them? Are there reasons to object to such arrangements among competitors? Would it harm consumers? How? If "antitrust" law is intended to prohibit such conduct, how can it do so? What should the scope of the offense be? The punishment? Should the conspirators be permitted any defenses? What if they set "reasonable" prices that stabilized their industry and helped to keep employment in the industry high? What if the arrangement helped them lower their production costs? What if they had no defense save increasing their profits?

Also, what was the mechanism used to fix prices, and what steps did the conspirators have to undertake to implement their agreement? Why did they keep coming back to discussions of "quotas" and output allocations? How easy or hard is it to agree to fix prices? How often did the conspirators have to meet? Why did they meet *where* they met?

Sidebar 1–1:
"Vitamins, Inc."

During its investigation of the lysine bid-rigging scheme, the FBI enlisted Mark Whitacre's help in uncovering other products for which ADM and its rivals had agreed to restrict output and fix prices. Whitacre had heard conversations within ADM about arrangements to set production levels for another food additive, citric acid. Whitacre also knew that ADM executives met regularly with some of Europe's leading producers of food additives, including Hoffmann–La Roche (Roche). Whitacre correctly perceived that ADM was collaborating with Roche to orchestrate citric acid production, but he did not imagine the full state of play in Europe. On a scale that dwarfed the lysine cartel, Roche, BASF, and Rhone–Poulenc had formed their own covert consortium to control the production and pricing of vitamins. Observing ADM's success in boosting prices for food additives, the three European firms set out to replicate the model of industry-wide coordination for vitamins. They targeted the market for industrial quantities of Vitamins A, B, and C, which were purchased by food companies and blended into products consumed by hundreds of millions of individuals every day.

The resulting covert scheme, which the participants called "Vitamins, Inc.," was a marvel of organization. From the group's formation in 1991, the cartel members met regularly each year in elegant European resorts to identify global levels of demand, to set overall production levels, to allocate individual production quotas, and to arrange for producers who exceeded their quotas to pay firms whose sales had fallen below the cartel's projections. The cartel delegated implementation of its strategic plan to committees organized by geographic region and by product group. The committees scheduled their own meetings and reported periodically to the cartel's board, which met in Switzerland each year to set a budget for the entire undertaking.

At about the time it was closing in on the lysine conspirators, the Justice Department initiated a new policy designed to disrupt the operation of cartels. For a number of years, the department had promised to reduce the punishment for companies and individuals that revealed their participation in antitrust crimes such as price-fixing. The "leniency" program was successful in eliciting cooperation from cartel insiders, but only modestly. To do better, the government sweetened the prize. In August 1993, the Antitrust Division announced that it would grant full immunity from criminal prosecution for the first company (other than the cartel ringmaster) to notify the government of a cartel in which it had participated. In August 1994 the Antitrust Division expanded the new policy to include individuals engaged in criminal antitrust violations. The leniency polices are discussed at greater length in Sidebar 3–4, *infra*.

As it pursued the lysine and citric acid cartels, federal investigators began to suspect that other ingredients commonly used as inputs by food companies were the objects of price fixing schemes. Combined with tips from other sources, evidence gathered in the lysine and citric acid inquiries pointed toward a massive, European-based effort to set vitamin prices. Attacking Vitamins, Inc. shaped up as a more difficult endeavor. Each producer was located overseas, and the price fixing participants held all of their meetings in European countries that never had displayed the U.S. government's enthusiasm for prosecuting cartels.

Late in 1997, the business press reported that the Justice Department was investigating pricing patterns in the vitamins industry and was steadily accumulating evidence. The reports caught the attention of Rhone–Poulenc, the smallest Vitamins, Inc. member. Fearing that the walls might be closing in on the cartel, Rhone–Poulenc played the leniency card, and informed the Antitrust Division of the U.S. Department of Justice that it had a story to tell.

In return for full immunity from criminal prosecution for the company and its employees, Rhone–Poulenc revealed the details of the vitamins cartel and its operations. After sorting through a treasure trove of new information, the Justice Department confronted Roche and BASF. Compared to the lysine cartel, the vitamins scheme was staggering in its financial scale and organizational intricacy. In 1999, Roche and BASF agreed to pay the Justice Department massive criminal fines ($500 million and $225 million, respectively) for their role in colluding to set vitamin prices. At that time, the total payment of $725 million constituted the largest criminal fine ever recovered by the Justice Department for any violation of a U.S. criminal statute. In addition, private parties overcharged by the vitamin cartel recovered an estimated $3–4 billion in damages. Government fines paid as a consequence of public enforcement actions in the U.S. and elsewhere totaled nearly $1.8 billion. A number of foreign citizens also agreed to serve prison terms in the United States to resolve their participation in the illegal scheme. *See generally* JOHN M. CONNOR, GLOBAL PRICE FIXING (2d ed. 2007).

As we proceed through the material that follows in this Chapter, consider why the conduct of the lysine and vitamins cartels should be treated so harshly under antitrust laws. What effect did they have and on whom? What kinds of penalties are available to deter them, and others who might be considering similar conduct? What kinds of remedies are available for those who bought products from them at higher prices? Who institutionally, the government or the parties most injured by their practices, should have primary responsibility for prosecuting them?

In several parts of this Casebook, we will return to the issues of substantive doctrine and prosecutorial process that figured prominently in the lysine and vitamins cases. For now it is enough to underscore several features of these two episodes. First, the Sherman Act was among the earliest "white collar" criminal statutes, and today U.S. antitrust policy treats the behavior at issue—joint efforts by producers to restrict output as a means of raising prices—as so dangerous to the competitive process that it warrants prosecution as a felony. The modern U.S. antitrust system has relied on two interrelated strategies to detect and deter such cartels: enhance the leniency program to boost the prizes for cartel participants to report their own misconduct and increase the sanctions for corporate and individual violators, including the imposition of severe criminal sanctions (the maximum possible jail sentence for culpable individuals today is ten years). For data on the largest U.S. fine recoveries, see U.S. Dep't of Justice, Antitrust Division, *Sherman Act Violations Yielding a Corporate Fine of $10 Million or More*, *available at* http://www.usdoj.gov/atr/public/criminal/225540.htm. *See also* Scott D. Hammond, Deputy Assistant Attorney General for Criminal Enforcement, Antitrust Division, U.S. Dep't of Justice, *Recent Developments, Trends, and Milestones in the Antitrust Division's Criminal Enforcement Program* (Nov. 16, 2007), *available at* http://www.usdoj.gov/atr/public/speeches/227740.htm (discussing increased fines and jail sentences).

Second, much of the illegal activity took place outside the borders of the United States in jurisdictions that, until recently, have taken a more benign view of cartels. The global character of the conduct in question raises questions about the appropriate content of national and international competition principles and invites discussion about the proper scope of an antitrust system. The Justice Department's prosecution of the lysine and vitamins cartels helped catalyze major changes in the approach taken by the European Union and other jurisdictions to cartels. After decades of an indifferent commitment of resources to anti-cartel programs, many foreign authorities have declared cartel prosecutions to be their top enforcement priority. Like the U.S., foreign public authorities are increasingly likely to seek very substantial fines for cartel activity, which is one indication of the growing global acceptance of an anti-cartel norm. *See* Phillip Lowe, *Preventing and Sanctioning Anticompetitive Conduct: Effective Use of Administrative and Criminal Sanctions, Leniency Programmes and Private Action in the EU*, 2006 FORDHAM COMP. L. INST. 87 (B. Hawk ed. 2007).

Figure 1–1:
Ten Largest Industry Fines Worldwide

Industry	Year	Total Fines ($ Millions)	Jurisdiction
Elevators and Escalators	2007	1,400	EC
Vitamins	2001	1,100	EC
Gas Insulated Switchgear	2007	1,050	EC
Vitamins	1998-2000	915	U.S.
Synthetic Rubber	2006	732	EC
DRAM	2004-2006	729	U.S.
Plasterboard	2002	674	EC
Air Transportation	2007	600	U.S.
Hydrogen peroxide and perborate	2006	547	EC
Methacrylates	2006	486	EC

Third, the lysine and vitamins case studies underscore the value of achieving a better understanding of the operation and economic consequences of cartels and of the machinery needed to detect and deter them. These and other cartels required the participants to establish intricate administrative machinery and take elaborate measures to ensure the effective management of the cartel. *See* William E. Kovacic et al., *Bidding rings and the design of anti-collusive measures for auctions and procurements, in* HANDBOOK OF PROCUREMENT 381 (Nicola Dimitri et al., eds. 2006). One can ask what motivates business managers to take the risks associated with participation in these arrangements, what public harms they cause, and what enhancements to penalties and detection tools would discourage them from doing so. As the case studies indicate, solutions to the cartel problem are likely to benefit greatly from substantial cooperation among different nations.

B. IDENTIFYING THE CORE QUESTIONS OF ANTITRUST LAW

Like few other contemporary antitrust matters, the international cartel cases led the antitrust bar and government officials to revisit basic issues surrounding the operation of antitrust systems and to confront the consequences of the globalization of competition law. In this Section, we identify the core questions of antitrust law that were implicated in the cartel cases and that increasingly dominate the design and implementation of antitrust systems in the U.S. and abroad.

1. WHAT ARE THE PURPOSES OF COMPETITION LAW SYSTEMS?

A "system" of law has two basic elements: (1) *doctrinal principles* usually embodied in statutes, administrative regulations, and judicial interpretations, and (2) the *institutions* that implement legal commands. For any single jurisdiction, the institutional focal point of a competition law system tends to be the public authority entrusted with enforcing the competition law. The effectiveness of a competition law system depends on the contributions from a number of collateral public and private institutions. These include the courts in which cases or appeals are adjudicated; the provision (if any) for private rights of action; universities that teach courses in antitrust economics and law and hire researchers who write about the theory and practice of competition law; legal societies that provide a forum for discussion about competition law issues; and trade associations that provide channels through which information about the competition law is passed along to individual business operators.

A central question about any antitrust system is "what are its goals?" In this section, we explore the economic and non-economic goals that a competition law system might serve. For economic purposes, we look to what society expects to achieve through the operation of private markets. These economic purposes of competition law systems are particularly important for contemporary antitrust analysis, especially in the United States. On the non-economic side, we explore some of antitrust's more deeply embedded, historically persistent sub-themes, such as a fear of corporate bigness, a preference for commercial fairness, and a distrust of economic phenomena that threaten to undermine political stability.

a. What Economic Purposes Can They Serve?

A generation ago, Robert Bork underscored the importance of objectives to the operation of a competition policy system. "Antitrust policy," Bork wrote, "cannot be made rational until we are able to give a firm answer to one question: What is the point of the law—what are its goals? Everything else follows from the answer we give." ROBERT H. BORK, THE ANTITRUST PARADOX 50 (1978).

The primary economic aim of competition law is to prevent the acquisition or exercise of "market power," as the term is used in microeconomics. A firm or firms exercise market power when they reduce output or otherwise restrict competition in order to raise price above the competitive level. Yet market power is not the reason for every price increase. The price of any good or service can rise as a consequence of an increase in the costs of producing and selling it, or due to inflation. Such price increases reflect the natural operation of markets, not the exercise of market power, and although they may concern policy-makers, they are not the object of the antitrust laws. Below we present a hypothetical case that explains the economic underpinnings of antitrust's concern with market power—the relationship between a reduction in output and higher prices—and describe the economic effects that result. As you read the Coffee Shop case, ask yourself whether the higher prices the co-conspirators received in the lysine and vitamins cartels reflected the exercise of market power.

MARKET POWER AND ITS CONSEQUENCES:
THE CASE OF THE COFFEE SHOP

Stroll into any office complex and you are likely to find that one of the ground-floor tenants is a coffee shop. Customers stop by to choose from a selection of coffees and teas and at least to scan the display of freshly baked cookies, muffins, scones, and pastries. The shop owner is fond of her customers, but she also is fond of her income. As she sees patrons fill the shop every day, she asks herself whether she could charge more money for her products. She wonders if she could get her customers to pay more if she reduced the total amount she produces each day. Below we explore the question of whether our shop owner has, or can exercise "market power." Doing so allows us to introduce some basic ideas from microeconomics that are relevant to antitrust analysis.

i. Demand

If a reduction in output is to cause a price increase, the firm or firms cutting back on sales must face a downward-sloping demand function. A demand function is a schedule that describes the amount of a good or service buyers would be willing to purchase at varying prices in some time period. Figure 1–2 depicts the hypothetical demand for coffee in the morning at our coffee shop. At a price of $1 per cup, our coffee shop sells 100 cups in a typical morning. If the shop raised the price to $1.25 per cup without regard to what other coffee vendors nearby were doing, it would only sell 50 cups in a typical morning. If it lowered its price to 75 cents per cup it would sell 150 cups. How can we know the likely effect of a price change on the shop's coffee sales? Perhaps the coffee shop experimented with raising or lowering price. We might also survey customers, study the experience of coffee shops in other office complexes, ask an industry expert (such as our coffee shop owner) to share her business judgment based on her experience, or ask an expert economist to study the available data and provide an opinion.

Figure 1–2:
Demand for Coffee

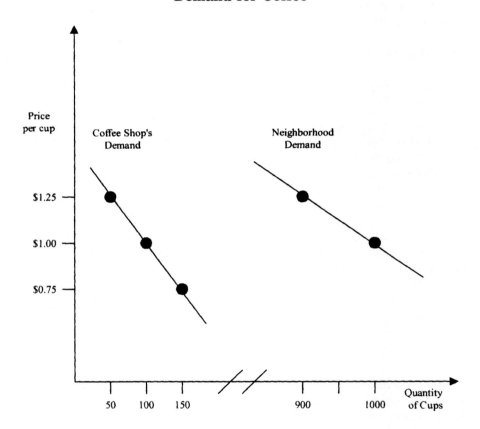

As the price rises, the quantity sold falls; this is what is meant by a "downward-sloping demand curve." Quantity falls because, as price rises, fewer buyers are willing to patronize the coffee shop. The demand function thus summarizes the economic force of *buyer substitution*. At the higher price, some buyers (half in the example) would continue to purchase coffee from the coffee shop before work. But the other half would not. Some may choose to purchase coffee from some other vendor; some may choose to make coffee in their office; some may choose to drink coffee at home before work; some may switch to drinking tea or other beverages; and some may do without a morning beverage entirely. As Figure 1–2 also indicates, if the coffee shop lowers price below $1 per cup, its sales would likely rise as buyers purchase more coffee at that location. Some might shift their purchases from other vendors to the coffee shop, or from other beverages to coffee, while others might decide that at the lower price they can now afford to buy coffee at work or afford occasionally to have a second cup.

Buyers can be more or less sensitive to changes in price. The more sensitive they are—the greater the change in quantity generated by a small change in price—the less steep the slope of the demand curve. If the quantity demanded is extremely responsive to a small change in price, the demand curve will be a horizontal line. Conversely, the less the change in quantity generated by a small change in price, the steeper the slope of the demand curve. Buyer sensitivity to changes in price can be computed in terms of the *percentage* change in quantity generated by a small *percentage* change in price. This degree to which buyers respond to price changes is termed the "elasticity of demand." In Figure 1–2 the elasticity of demand is –2 at the initial sales level (approximated by the percentage change in the quantity demanded, –50%, divided by the percentage change in the price, 25%).*

Demand curves characterized by various elasticities are depicted in Figure 1–3. If a small percentage change in price leads to a very large percentage change in quantity demanded, demand is said to be highly "elastic." The demand for coffee from our coffee shop might be elastic in a business district where most workers would respond to a price increase by putting small coffee makers in their offices or carrying a thermos of the beverage from home. If sellers would lose so many customers in response to a very small price increase as to make some or all of the demand curve a horizontal line, demand in the horizontal segment is said to be "perfectly elastic." For example, the demand for coffee sold in our coffee shop might be highly elastic if the same coffee were available for the same price from a coffee service that provided coffee machines for the offices of tenants in the office building. A demand curve might also vary in elasticity along its length. For example, the demand for coffee from our coffee shop might be perfectly elastic along some segment or segments along the demand curve, but not along a different segment, where price is higher or lower.

Conversely, if a small percentage change in price leads to only a small change in quantity demanded, demand is said to be highly "inelastic." Producers of a good or service facing inelastic demand can raise price without significantly reducing demand. For example, the demand for our coffee shop's variety of espresso might be relatively inelastic. This is because our owner has an unmatched skill at making a type of espresso viewed by coffee connoisseurs as so sublime that the price of the product becomes unimportant to them. If the quantity demanded is so unresponsive to price as to make the demand curve a vertical line, demand is said to be "perfectly inelastic."

---

* The mathematically inclined will recognize that the elasticity of a demand curve is not the same thing as its slope, though the two concepts are related. Think of the demand curve as relating the quantity of the product demanded (Q) to the price charged (P). Then the slope of the demand curve can be written as $\triangle Q/\triangle P$ (where $\triangle$ represents the change), and the elasticity is written $(\triangle Q/Q)/(\triangle P/P)$, or, equivalently, as $(\triangle Q/\triangle P)(P/Q)$.

Figure 1–3:
Demand Elasticities Compared

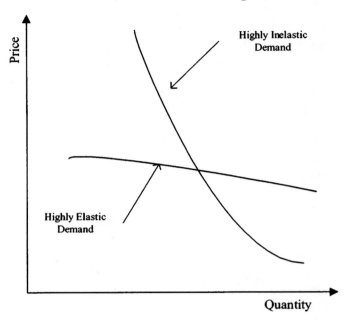

Notice that in each of the above examples, the demand curve relates to both a product and a geographic region. In the case of the cafeteria selling coffee, the extent of buyer substitution can depend upon the proximity of other coffee vendors to our coffee shop, the acceptability to consumers of other beverages in the coffee shop, or some combination of both. In the aggregate, buyer willingness to substitute these and other alternatives to purchasing coffee in the cafeteria will determine the degree of the coffee shop's market power, if any, over coffee. Defining the range of reasonable geographic and product substitutes is the goal of "market definition," which can play an important role in the identification of market power.

Figure 1–2 also depicts a second demand function, the demand for morning coffee collectively faced by all the coffee shops and restaurants in the neighborhood. It shows that at a price of $1 per cup—charged by all vendors simultaneously—1000 cups are sold in the typical morning. If the price were to rise to $1.25 per cup, 900 cups would instead be sold. Most buyers would continue to buy morning coffee, perhaps while grumbling about the price increase, but some would substitute other ways of getting coffee, switch to tea or other beverages, or forego a morning beverage. Note that the demand curve facing an individual *firm* is often more elastic than the demand curve facing the *industry* as a whole, a circumstance illustrated in Figure 1–2. If the coffee shop alone raises price by a small percentage, it will lose a significant percentage of its customers to rival coffee vendors. But if all of the coffee shops in the neighborhood raise price together, it will be able to retain many of those customers.

ii.   Supply and Perfect Competition

The demand curve describes how one important group of market partici-pants, buyers, will respond to changes in price. In order to understand what price is actually set in the market, it is also necessary to consider the behavior of the other important group of market participants, sellers.

Seller behavior generally depends both on each firm's costs and on the way the firms interact with each other. In a perfectly competitive market, the simplest case, each firm's supply decision depends only on its costs; it does not take into account the response of rivals in making its supply decisions. Such firms are sometimes termed "price-takers," because they decide how much output to supply based solely on comparing their costs to the market price.

In particular, a firm selling in a perfectly competitive market will produce an additional unit of output so long as the market price is at least as great as the cost of producing that incremental unit. The cost of producing an additional unit of output is termed the *marginal cost* of that unit. The key distinction is between costs that vary with the decision the firm is making (here, whether to produce additional output) and costs that do not. If the coffee shop has already rented retail space, installed brewing equipment, hired its staff, and advertised its presence, for example, the cost of producing and selling one more cup of coffee this morning is likely to be simply the cost of the extra beans, hot water, and electricity required to brew one more cup. The marginal cost of producing one more cup would be those *variable costs* (costs that vary with the decision, here whether to produce additional cups of coffee) associated with the incremental (additional) cup produced.

In many industries, the marginal cost of production increases with output (an upward sloping curve), as depicted for the firm in Figure 1–4. This might occur for the coffee shop, for example, if it costs more to buy coffee beans if they have to be purchased at the last minute, to serve a new customer. Marginal cost curves are often upward sloping, as drawn in the figure, but they do not have to be. In some industries, each additional unit can be produced at the same cost as the previous one, and in other industries, additional units can be produced for less.

Figure 1–4:

Supply Function for a Competitive Industry

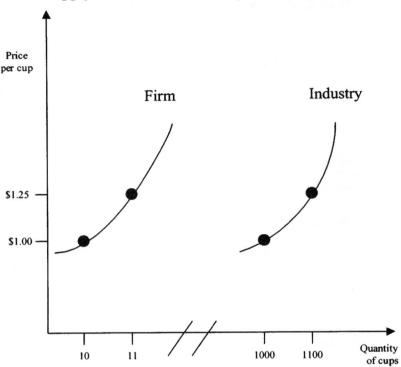

Costs that do not vary with producing additional cups of coffee are termed *fixed costs*. If the firm was making a different decision, for example whether to expand the business by doubling the size of the retail space, adding more equipment and increasing the staff, some of the costs that are considered fixed with respect to selling an additional cup in a given morning would become variable, and, consequently, would matter in making that decision. Hence, from an economic perspective, the "cost" of a product like a cup of coffee depends on what decision the firm is making: whether to brew an additional cup this morning with the existing facility, staff and equipment, or whether to expand the operation in order to be able to produce and sell more cups every day in the future. (We will discuss these cost concepts in more detail, along with additional cost concepts, in the Appendix at the end of this Chapter.)

In a perfectly competitive market, each firm produces every unit of output for which the price exceeds or equals its marginal cost of production, because every such unit adds to the firm's profit. Under such circumstances, the amount that the industry as a whole will supply at any price depends only on the marginal cost functions of the individual firms. Figure 1–4 depicts the derivation of the industry supply function from the marginal cost functions of an industry composed of one hundred identical firms. For the representative firm, marginal cost rises with output. The tenth unit costs $1 to produce, while the eleventh unit costs $1.25. If the market price were $1, therefore, each firm would choose to produce ten units and the industry as a whole (all one hundred firms) would supply 1000 units. Similarly, at a market price of $1.25, the industry would supply 1100 units.

Under perfect competition, the market price is determined by the intersection of the industry supply function and the industry demand function, as depicted in Figure 1–5. If price were lower, buyers would want to purchase more than the sellers would supply, and the price would be bid up until supply equals demand. Similarly, if the price were higher, sellers would see a shortfall of willing buyers; price would be bid down until supply equals demand.

Figure 1–5:
Supply, Demand & Equilibrium

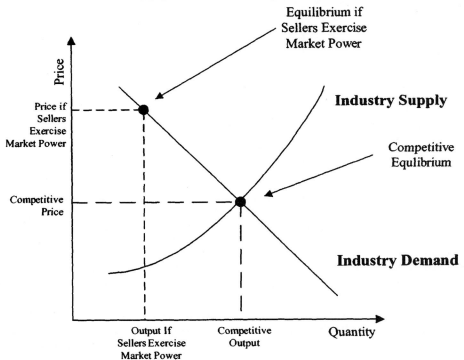

Price increases in a perfectly competitive model reflect higher seller costs. One reason the competitive price might rise is if the marginal costs of production increase for some or all firms. This might occur for the coffee shop, for example, if the price of coffee beans rises. Under such circumstances, firms will require a higher market price before they will produce the same amount of output as before. This is depicted graphically as a backward (or upward) shift in the industry supply function, and, as shown in Figure 1–6, it leads to a higher competitive price.

Figure 1–6:
Backward (Upward) Shift in Supply

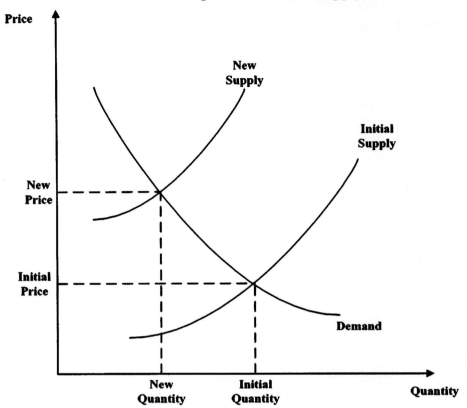

Another reason prices might rise in a competitive market is that buyers might increase their demand for coffee, desiring to purchase more than before at any price. This might occur, for example, if the number of office workers taking coffee breaks increased, or if a widely-reported study identified previously unknown health benefits to coffee drinking. This dynamic is depicted as an outward (or upward) shift in the demand curve. As shown in Figure 1–7, it leads to a higher price if the industry supply curve is rising. Here, the higher demand leads firms to expand output, and seller marginal costs rise as they do, leading to higher market prices.

Figure 1–7:
Outward (Upward) Shift in Demand

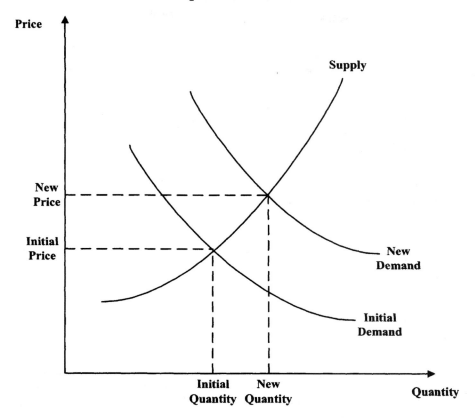

Both buyers and sellers benefit from participating in a competitive market. To see why, suppose, that the competitive price is $1 per cup, and at that price 1000 cups are sold by all firms participating in the market. Now consider the 500th unit produced and sold. Suppose that this unit is valued by its buyer at $2, and costs its producer only 50 cents to make. Pause on this point to marvel at the miracle of the market: it takes resources worth only 50 cents to the seller, and converts them into a product, here a cup of coffee, worth $2.00 to the buyer—for a gain to society of $1.50. If the competitive price is $1, then the buyer claims the majority of the total social gain: the buyer pays $1 for a product she values at $2, for a benefit of $1, and the seller receives $1 for producing something that costs it only 50 cents, for a benefit of 50 cents. This kind of calculation could be repeated for every unit produced and sold, as depicted in Figure 1–8. In the figure, the two shaded triangles collectively reflect the total social benefit of all the transactions in the market—the $1.50 benefit of the transaction involving the 500th unit, combined with the benefit to society of every other one of the 1000 units produced and sold. This area is termed the "aggregate surplus." It is divided into two parts: the "consumers' surplus" is the triangle above the market price, and the "producers' surplus" is the area below that triangle. The consumers'

surplus and the producers' surplus reflects the portion of the aggregate surplus that accrues to buyers and sellers, respectively.

Figure 1–8:

Consumers' and Suppliers' Surplus

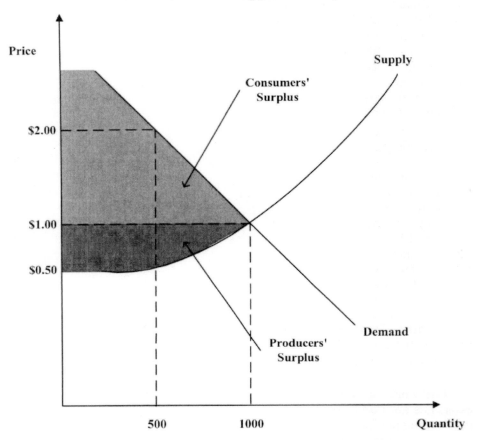

iii.   Market Power

When competition is not perfect, the firms participating in the market may be able to exercise what economists term "market power" by raising price above the competitive level. The neighborhood coffee vendors could exercise market power if they reduced their sales and raised price—but only if they act together. If they collectively agreed to cut back sales by 10% (from 1000 to 900) and raise price by 25% (from $1 to $1.25), they would likely increase their profits, assuming that the higher price did not attract new competition. Whether they actually would find this strategy profitable, assuming for the moment that it were legal, depends not just on how many sales they would lose (the slope of the industry demand curve) but also on the profit margin (price less unit cost) on those lost sales.

For example, if it costs these vendors 60 cents to make a cup of coffee, each cup sold at $1.00 contributes 40 cents to profit. Their gross profit on sales of coffee at $1.00 per cup is $400 (1000 cups x 40 cents). By collectively raising their price from $1.00 to $1.25 they can increase their profits by $185 to a total of $585, even though they will be selling 100 fewer cups of coffee per day. Here's why. At $1.25 a cup, the coffee vendors will sell only 900 cups of coffee a day, but as a result of the 25 cent price increase their total revenues on the sale of those 900 cups will increase by $225 (25 cents x 900 cups). This gain of $225 would be partially offset by a loss of the 40 cents per cup they would have made selling an additional 100 cups at $1.00, for a revenue loss of $40 (40 cents x 100). Raising price from $1.00 to $1.25, therefore, would yield a net profit increase of $185 ($225–$40). The unit cost relevant to this analysis is an "incremental" or "marginal" cost that does not take into account fixed costs (up-front expenditures) unrelated to the number of cups sold, like rent and kitchen equipment.

The more attractive the substitution alternatives buyers have—that is, the more elastic industry demand—the more sales sellers would lose by raising price and the less profitable this strategy would become. For this reason, it is more likely that the group of coffee vendors would find it profitable to raise price collectively than that our coffee shop would choose to do so on its own. Acting alone, our coffee shop would gain 25 cents per cup on the 50 cups it continues to sell by raising price to $1.25 per cup (25 cents x 50 cups = $12.50), but would lose 40 cents per cup on the 50 cups it no longer sells each morning at $1.00 (40 cents x 50 cups = $20), for a net loss of $7.50. So the coffee shop acting alone lacks market power. In contrast, the coffee shop may be able to exercise market power by colluding with other neighborhood sellers. This conclusion presumes that the coffee vendors could reach and implement an agreement to raise price, and that the higher price does not attract entry—for example, from restaurants adding a take-out counter. In later chapters, we will see ways in which firms, acting individually or collectively, can exercise market power, and the legal implications of that behavior.

It is worth noting that every firm, even a firm that exercises market power, has an incentive to change its output in response to shifts in marginal cost, leading to changes in price. If a firm's marginal cost increases, the firm will have an incentive not to sell as much as before, as the last units it previously sold would no longer be profitable to produce. The firm will cut back on output until the last unit sold becomes profitable again, as a result of a reduction in marginal cost (if marginal cost is less when the firm produces fewer units) or an increase in the market price (to the extent the reduction in firm output leads buyers to bid up the market price, along a downward sloping market demand curve) or both. If a firm's marginal cost of producing a product declines, similarly, the firm will have an incentive to produce and sell more, even if the addition to industry output leads to some decline in the market price. Indeed, even a monopolist, a firm without competition in its market, will find it profitable to lower price if its marginal cost declines (as might occur if input costs fall) and will raise price if its marginal cost increases.

iv.   The Consequences of the Exercise of Market Power

Figure 1–9 depicts the economic consequences of the exercise of market power. (To facilitate computations, this figure assumes that the marginal costs of production are not increasing with the number of units produced, the assumption made previously, but instead remain the same for all units produced.) If the neighborhood coffee vendors collectively raise price from $1 to $1.25, the 900 daily buyers who continue to purchase coffee in the typical morning lose even though they stay in the market. They must pay 25 cents more per cup. This is a transfer of wealth from buyers to sellers. As a group, these buyers previously paid $900 for their morning coffee; now they pay $1125. The $225 extra buyers pay to sellers is both a loss in consumers' surplus and an increase in producers's surplus. This transfer constitutes one effect of the exercise of market power.

Figure 1–9:
Consequences of the Exercise of Market Power

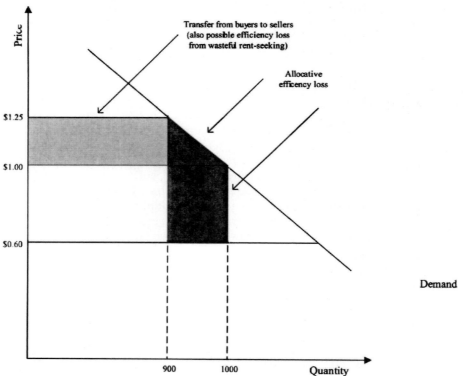

In addition, when price exceeds the competitive price, there is a loss to society termed an "allocative efficiency loss" or "deadweight loss." This loss is a reduction in aggregate surplus. It arises because some socially valuable purchases cannot be made. Some buyers—accounting for 100 daily coffee cups—were willing to pay at least $1 per cup, though less than $1.25 per cup, for a product that cost some seller only 60 cents to make. From a social point of view, the reduction in sales from 1000 cups to 900 thus means that society is not taking advantage of 100 opportunities to increase social welfare, by turning resources costing 60 cents per cup to a seller into a product worth at least $1 per cup to a buyer. These lost gains from trade cost society; it is as though society is throwing away at least 40 cents for each cup previously sold that is no longer sold. Put differently, resources such as coffee beans and labor that might have been used to make a product worth $1 will be put to some other use making something worth much less, and buyers willing to pay $1 for a cup of coffee will use that dollar to acquire something else worth less to them.

Moreover, under some circumstances most of the wealth transfer could represent a loss to society. The profit to producers from exercising market power is $185, the $225 transfer less the lost profit of $40 on the units the firms must forgo selling in order to raise price (40 cents on each of 100 units). To sustain their ability to collectively raise price, the incumbent coffee vendors would be willing to spend up to $185 in order to keep out new coffee sellers, who might undercut the $1.25 price. They might, for example, lobby the zoning commission to prevent new restaurants from opening. Such "rent-seeking" expenditures—if they are made—protect monopoly profits without helping the sellers produce cheaper or better coffee and represent an additional waste of social resources. Both the allocative efficiency loss and the possible efficiency loss from wasteful rent-seeking are depicted in Figure 1–9.*

Although the *exercise* of market power reduces social wealth and transfers resources from buyers to sellers, competition in the *pursuit* of market power can be beneficial. If a firm obtains market power, that situation presents an opportunity for rivals: if they can undersell the firm exercising market power slightly, they may be able to steal away most if its business, and earn much of the rewards sellers obtain from exercising market power. Of course, many firms may seek to follow this strategy, and the firm initially exercising market power may be led to protect its business by cutting price as well. Through competition among firms pursuing market power, the price could return to the competitive level, to the benefit of buyers and society as a whole. But this competitive dynamic, in which the pursuit of market power is beneficial, cannot occur unless existing rivals are able to expand output or new competitors are able to enter the market.

Similarly, the patent laws seek to enlist competition in the pursuit of a prize—the ability to exclude rivals, which may at times permit the patent holder to exercise market power—in order to spur innovation. Here again, the pursuit of market power could create a benefit to society. But, as we will examine in Chapter 10, this benefit is not unequivocal. The same patent laws which may generate a competitive race to innovate, may also discourage later innovation that builds upon the first new idea and may permit the owner of the intellectual property to exercise market power in pricing the product or process it patents.

v.   The Benefits of Competition

The previous discussion and Figures 1–2 to 1–9 simplify the dimensions on which competition takes place to two: price and output. In actual markets, market power can be manifested not just by a reduction in output and increase in price, but also in other ways, such as a reduction in product

---

* Richard Posner emphasized the possibility of an efficiency loss of monopoly from wasteful rent-seeking in Richard A. Posner, *The Social Costs of Monopoly and Regulation*, 83 J. POL. ECON. 807 (1975). Franklin Fisher clarified the conditions under which this might occur in Franklin M. Fisher, *The Social Costs of Monopoly and Regulation: Posner Reconsidered*, 93 J. POL. ECON. 410 (1985).

quality (in effect selling less at the same price, which can be understood as effectively an increase in price), loss of product variety, or decrease in the resources devoted to pursuing innovation. For example, the neighborhood coffee vendors might agree to maintain the price of a small, medium, and large cup, but to shrink each cup size by one ounce. They might agree collectively to use lower quality coffee beans to cut costs, or not to add espresso drinks to the menu because they are difficult to make. These agreements would not provide customers with less expensive or better products; rather each would increase profits by reducing output and raising price, broadly defined, and thus reflect the exercise of market power.

In older cases, the term market power is sometimes equated with a high market share. By "market share," the cases mean the percentage of aggregate sales, output or capacity accounted for by a firm in a particular, "defined" market. That is not how economists use the term market power today and not how we will do so in this book. Market power in economics refers to the ability to profit by circumscribing some dimension of competition, as by raising price above the competitive level without losing so many sales that the price increase will be unprofitable. We will see later when and how a high market share might constitute indirect proof that a firm or group of firms has or can exercise market power. But a high share in an industry characterized by highly elastic demand, for example, might not. We also will follow the contemporary convention in economics of not distinguishing between market power and monopoly power, though the older case law sometimes treated these terms differently. If there is a difference between market power and monopoly power, it is just a matter of degree.

The previous discussion has highlighted one efficiency benefit of competition relative to the exercise of market power: competition achieves allocative efficiency (avoids an allocative efficiency loss). Two other economic benefits of competition are worth highlighting, although they do not necessarily distinguish competitive industries from those exercising market power. First, competition ensures that goods are made by the firm which can produce them at lowest cost. Firms that can produce some units at high cost will be underbid, and find themselves unable to sell those units. Producers are driven, in consequence, to keep costs low. This outcome is termed "production efficiency."* The possible loss from wasteful rent-seeking, discussed above, can be understood as a type of production inefficiency, by which the firms are spending more than necessary to make the units they sell. Second, competition ensures that the buyers who most value the goods get them. The buyers with the highest valuation will find it worthwhile to bid up the price until prospective buyers who value the goods less drop out of the bidding. This result is termed "consumption efficiency." (Note that consumption efficiency ignores differences in the distribution of wealth across buyers, which could

---

* Some authors also refer to "transactional" efficiencies (ways of minimizing the cost of making transactions, as by lessening information costs or reducing the threat of opportunistic behavior or "hold ups") and "dynamic" efficiencies (ways of lowering the costs of, and thus stimulating, the development of new and improved products and better production processes). In general, this casebook does not distinguish these benefits from other aspects of production efficiency. However, transactional efficiencies will come up in Sidebar 7–6, *infra*, and dynamic efficiencies are the subject of Chapter 10. For a survey of efficiency concepts in antitrust that emphasizes the importance of transactional and dynamic efficiencies, see William J. Kolasky & Andrew R. Dick, *The Merger Guidelines and the Integration of Efficiencies into Antitrust Review of Horizontal Mergers*, 71 ANTITRUST L.J. 207 (2003).

affect how much those buyers are willing to bid for desired goods. Hence a competitive market, while ensuring consumption efficiency, may generate a distribution of goods across buyers that some may find undesirable.)

The allocative efficiency loss depicted in Figure 1–9 was computed relative to a starting point in which price was $1.00 and 1000 cups of coffee were sold each morning. Buyers and sellers *collectively* would, however, be even better off if coffee sold at a lower price, at coffee's marginal cost of 60 cents per cup, because a number of buyers willing to pay at least marginal cost went unserved at the price of $1.00. Indeed, buyers and sellers *as a group* do better for this reason in the economist's model of perfect competition.

Under perfect competition, no firm has the power to raise price by reducing output. Each firm sells as much as it can profitably produce at the market price. Accordingly, the firm produces every unit of output for which the price exceeds or equals its marginal cost of production, and the amount that the industry as a whole will supply at any price depends only on the marginal cost functions of the individual firms. As we have already discussed, Figure 1–4 depicts the derivation of the industry supply function from the marginal cost functions of an industry composed of one hundred identical firms. For the representative firm, marginal cost rises with output. The tenth unit costs $1 to produce, while the eleventh unit costs $1.25. If the market price were $1, therefore, each firm would choose to produce ten units and the industry as a whole (all one hundred firms) would supply 1000 units. Similarly, at a market price of $1.25, the industry would supply 1100 units.

Under perfect competition, the market price is determined by the intersection of the industry supply function and the industry demand function, as depicted in Figure 1–5. If price were lower, buyers would want to purchase more than the sellers would supply, and the price would be bid up until supply equals demand. Similarly, if the price were higher, sellers would see a shortfall of willing buyers; price would be bid down until supply equals demand. At this competitive equilibrium, every seller would produce all units of output for which price is at least marginal cost, guaranteeing production efficiency; the buyers who value the product the most would obtain it, guaranteeing consumption efficiency; and every buyer willing to pay more than the production costs of a seller will obtain the product, guaranteeing allocative efficiency. As Figure 1–5 also shows, if the sellers are able to exercise market power, for example by collectively acting at least in part as though they were a monopolist, price will be higher and output lower than under perfect competition.

In some circumstances, markets that do not match the model of perfect competition may be considered workably competitive. For example, in an industry with high fixed costs relative to the size of the market and low marginal costs (a situation which might describe movie theaters, hotels, or computer software), marginal cost pricing may be too low to keep the firms profitably in business. In the competitive benchmark for these industries, against which the exercise of market power may be compared, prices to at least some customers will exceed marginal cost. This situation may still be workably competitive when free entry by new competitors caps those prices and prevents the firms from achieving monopoly profits. (Figure 1–9 can be interpreted as depicting this situation, if $1.00 is the competitive price and a price of $1.25 reflects the exercise of market power.) We will revisit the meaning of "competition" in this setting in Chapter 10, when we consider antitrust issues raised by high technology markets.

————

The Coffee Shop case study highlights two economic consequences of the exercise of market power: a transfer of resources from buyers to sellers and an allocative efficiency loss. Standard welfare economics focuses on minimizing efficiency losses. An economy in which markets achieve allocative, production, and consumption efficiency can be thought of as maximizing aggregate wealth.* Thus, the allocative efficiency loss in Figure 1–9 is costly to society, and counts as an economic harm, because it reduces collective wealth. Welfare economics does not take a view on whether the consequences of wealth transfers from buyers to sellers create the kind of harms that ought to concern policy-makers and courts. Antitrust commentators dispute whether wealth transfers should count in antitrust policy-making. As will be discussed later in this Chapter, advocates of an "aggregate welfare standard" would not consider wealth transfers while advocates of a "consumer welfare standard" would.

b. What Non–Economic Purposes Can They Serve?

Thus far we have focused on the economic reasons to have antitrust laws, because today they dominate discussion of antitrust rules. The U.S. and other nations sometimes have used antitrust to promote non-economic goals, too, such as fairness, protection of small businesses, social justice, equity, and political stability. These goals are viewed as "non-economic" because they are concerned with values other than the economic well-being of consumers or the economy as a whole. For example, eliminating smaller firms in favor of larger ones may benefit consumers if the larger firms can realize economies of scale unavailable to smaller ones, *i.e.*, if the larger firms can lower their per unit costs by expanding their output, and the consequence is lower prices. An antitrust policy motivated by the economic goal of "efficiency," therefore, might permit conduct that allows firms to grow to achieve economies of scale, even if that growth also eliminates some smaller, less efficient competitors.

For non-economic reasons, one might prefer antitrust rules that preserve a market comprised of smaller firms. The reasons for such a preference might include the independent value placed on individual autonomy, entrepreneurship, local ownership and "quality of life" gains associated with the service and variety offered by large numbers of smaller firms, a belief that smaller businesses increase aggregate employment, the fear that elimination of some smaller firms will inevitably lead to the elimination of others, or the fear that highly concentrated wealth can facilitate the corruption of the political process. An antitrust policy motivated by these non-economic values might treat harshly all conduct that diminishes the number of firms in a market, regardless of the conduct's immediate impact on consumers. In pursuing non-

* Formal welfare economics is based on the concept of Pareto efficiency, which arises when there is no way to make any economic actor better off without making any other actor worse off. Pareto efficiency is not the same thing as wealth maximization, but the difference is not generally important for analyzing the welfare issues raised in this book.

economic values, one might sacrifice to some extent the promise of lower consumer prices and other benefits associated with efficient markets.

Although less likely to prove influential today, in the past these kinds of non-economic goals consistently found expression in the antitrust decisions of the federal courts. In the first decade following adoption of the Sherman Act, the Supreme Court invoked those purposes in a much-quoted passage from its decision in *Trans-Missouri Freight*:

> [The result of a combination of capital controlling the price of a commodity] * * * is unfortunate for the country, by depriving it of the services of a large number of small but independent dealers, who were familiar with the business, and who spent their lives in it, and who supported themselves and their families from the small profits realized therein. * * * [I]t is not for the real prosperity of any country that such changes should occur which result in transferring an independent business man, the head of his establishment, small though it might be, into a mere servant or agent of a corporation for selling the commodities which he once manufactured or dealt in, having no voice in shaping the business policy of the company and bound to obey orders issued by others.

United States v. Trans–Missouri Freight Ass'n, 166 U.S. 290, 324 (1897). A similarly famous expression of this perspective appeared in *United States v. Aluminum Co. of America,* 148 F.2d 416, 428–29 (2d Cir.1945), where Judge Learned Hand's opinion observed:

> We have been speaking only of the economic reasons which forbid monopoly; but * * * there are others, based upon the belief that great industrial consolidations are inherently undesirable, regardless of their economic results. * * * Throughout the history of [the federal antitrust laws] * * * it has been constantly assumed that one of their purposes was to perpetuate and preserve, for its own sake and in spite of possible cost, an organization of industry in small units which can effectively compete with each other.

There are many other examples in the older antitrust cases. But for the most part, modern U.S. antitrust jurisprudence has subordinated non-economic goals to the attainment of economic efficiency. Nevertheless, non-economic goals occasionally find expression in modern judicial decisions. In the following excerpt from *United States v. Brown University*, 5 F.3d 658 (3d Cir. 1993), the court of appeals assesses whether it should consider the diversity and social welfare goals of a university's scholarship program in analyzing antitrust claims.

UNITED STATES v. BROWN UNIVERSITY
United States Court of Appeals for the Third Circuit, 1993.
5 F.3d 658.

Before: MANSMANN, COWEN and WEIS, Circuit Judges.

COWEN, Circuit Judge.

The Antitrust Division of the United States Department of Justice ("Division") brought this civil antitrust action against appellant Massachusetts Institute of Technology ("MIT") and eight Ivy League colleges and universities. The Division alleged that MIT violated section one et seq. of the Sherman Anti–Trust Act by agreeing with the Ivy League schools to distribute financial aid exclusively on the basis of need and to collectively determine the amount of financial assistance commonly admitted students would be awarded.

The district court entered judgment in favor of the Division. * * * [W]e hold that the district court erred by failing to adequately consider the procompetitive and social welfare justifications proffered by MIT and by deciding the case on the basis of an abbreviated rule of reason analysis. * * *

I.   FACTUAL AND PROCEDURAL BACKGROUND

* * *

In 1958, MIT and the eight Ivy League schools formed the "Ivy Overlap Group" to collectively determine the amount of financial assistance to award to commonly admitted students. The facts concerning this Agreement are essentially undisputed. The Ivy Overlap Group expressly agreed that they would award financial aid only on the basis of demonstrated need. Thus, merit-based aid was prohibited. To ensure that aid packages would be comparable, the participants agreed to share financial information concerning admitted candidates and to jointly develop and apply a uniform needs analysis for assessing family contributions.

* * *

Although each Ivy Overlap institution employed the same analysis to compute family contributions, discrepancies in the contribution figures still arose. To eliminate these discrepancies, the Overlap members agreed to meet in early April each year to jointly determine the amount of the family contribution for each commonly admitted student. Prior to this conference, the Overlap schools independently determined the family contribution of each student they admitted, and transmitted this data to Student Aid Services. Student Aid Services then compiled rosters. A bilateral roster listed aid applicants who were admitted to two Ivy Overlap Group schools, and a multilateral roster compiled applicants admitted to more than two participating schools. For each student, the rosters showed each school's student budget, proposed student and parent contributions, self-help levels, and grant awards.

At the two-day spring Overlap conference, the schools compared their family contribution figures for each commonly admitted student. Family contribution differences of less than $500 were ignored. When there was a disparity in excess of $500, the schools would either agree to use one school's figure or meet somewhere in the middle. Due to time constraints, the schools spent only a few minutes discussing an individual and the agreed upon figures were more a result of compromise than of a genuine effort to accurately assess the student's financial circumstances.

All Ivy Overlap Group institutions understood that failing to comply with the Overlap Agreement would result in retaliatory sanctions. Consequently, noncompliance was rare and quickly remedied. * * *

In 1991, the Antitrust Division of the Justice Department brought this civil suit alleging that the Ivy Overlap Group unlawfully conspired to restrain trade in violation of section one of the Sherman Act, 15 U.S.C. § 1, by (1) agreeing to award financial aid exclusively on the basis of need; (2) agreeing to utilize a common formula to calculate need; and (3) collectively setting, with only insignificant discrepancies, each commonly admitted students' family contribution toward the price of tuition. The Division sought only injunctive relief. All of the Ivy League institutions signed a consent decree with the United States, and only MIT proceeded to trial. * * *

* * *

III.   RESTRAINT OF TRADE

* * *

MIT does not dispute that the stated purpose of Overlap is to eliminate price competition for talented students among member institutions. Indeed, the intent to eliminate price competition among the Overlap schools for commonly admitted students appears on the face of the Agreement itself. * * * Because the Overlap Agreement aims to restrain "competitive bidding" and deprive prospective students of "the ability to utilize and compare prices" in selecting among schools, it is anticompetitive "on its face." We therefore agree that Overlap initially "requires some competitive justification even in the absence of a detailed market analysis."

* * *

On appeal, MIT first contends that by promoting socio-economic diversity at member institutions, Overlap improved the quality of the education offered by the schools and therefore enhanced the consumer appeal of an Overlap education. The Supreme Court has recognized improvement in the quality of a product or service that enhances the public's desire for that product or service as one possible procompetitive virtue. The district court itself noted that it cannot be denied "that cultural and economic diversity contributes to the quality of education and enhances the vitality of student life." * * *

MIT also contends that by increasing the financial aid available to needy students, Overlap provided some students who otherwise would not have been able to afford an Overlap education the opportunity to have one. In this respect, MIT argues, Overlap enhanced consumer choice. The policy of allocating financial aid solely on the basis of demonstrated need has two obvious consequences. First, available resources are spread among more needy students than would be the case if some students received aid in excess of their need. Second, as a consequence of the fact that more students receive the aid they require, the number of students able to afford an Overlap education is maximized. In short, removing financial obstacles for the greatest number of talented but needy students increases educational access, thereby widening consumer choice. Enhancement of consumer choice is a traditional objective of the antitrust laws and has also been acknowledged as a procompetitive benefit.[10]

10. To the extent that increasing consumer choice and promoting socioeconomic diversity in the context of higher education reflect social as well as procompetitive values, the district

Finally, MIT argues that by eliminating price competition among participating schools, Overlap channeled competition into areas such as curriculum, campus activities, and student-faculty interaction. As the Division correctly notes, however, any competition that survives a horizontal price restraint naturally will focus on attributes other than price. This is not the kind of procompetitive virtue contemplated under the Act, but rather one mere consequence of limiting price competition.

MIT next claims that beyond ignoring the procompetitive effects of Overlap, the district court erroneously refused to consider compelling social welfare justifications. MIT argues that by enabling member schools to maintain a steadfast policy of need-blind admissions and full need-based aid, Overlap promoted the social ideal of equality of educational access and opportunity.

* * *

[Here the court of appeals discussed evidence that Congress sought to promote the "same ideal of equality of educational access and opportunity" and MIT's efforts in the district court to establish that Overlap promoted "similar social and educational policy objectives." It also pointed out that the district court was not persuaded that the social welfare values asserted by MIT could be equated with "procompetitive justifications," owing to the Supreme Court's decisions in *Nat'l Soc'y of Prof'l Eng'rs v. United States*, 435 U.S. 679 (1978)(Casebook, *infra*, Chapter 2) and *FTC v. Indiana Fed'n of Dentists*, 476 U.S. 447 (1986). In *Nat'l Soc'y of Prof'l Eng'rs*, the Court had rejected public safety concerns as a valid defense to a Sherman Act challenge to a ban on all competitive bidding that was contained in the Society's Code of Ethics; in *Indiana Fed'n of Dentists*, the Court similarly rejected a defense based on alleged public health concerns, proffered by the dentists to justify their ban on supplying insurance companies with dental x-rays. Eds.]

Both the public safety justification rejected by the Supreme Court in *Professional Engineers* and the public health justification rejected by the Court in *Indiana Dentists* were based on the defendants' faulty premise that consumer choices made under competitive market conditions are "unwise" or "dangerous." Here MIT argues that participation in the Overlap arrangement provided some consumers, the needy, with additional choices which an entirely free market would deny them. The facts and arguments before us may suggest some significant areas of distinction from those in *Professional Engineers* and *Indiana Dentists* in that MIT is asserting that Overlap not only serves a social benefit, but actually enhances consumer choice. Overlap is not an attempt to withhold a particular desirable service from customers, as was the professional combination in *Indiana Dentists*, but rather it purports only to seek to extend a service to qualified students who are financially "needy" and would not otherwise be able to afford the high cost of education at MIT. Further, while Overlap resembles the ban on competitive bidding at issue in *Professional Engineers*, MIT alleges that Overlap enhances competition by broadening the socio-economic sphere of its potential student body. Thus, rather than suppress competition, Overlap may in fact merely regulate

court should have considered the degree to which Overlap furthered these social objectives. * * *

competition in order to enhance it, while also deriving certain social benefits. If the rule of reason analysis leads to this conclusion, then indeed Overlap will be beyond the scope of the prohibitions of the Sherman Act.

* * *

The nature of higher education, and the asserted procompetitive and pro-consumer features of the Overlap, convince us that a full rule of reason analysis is in order here. It may be that institutions of higher education "require that a particular practice, which could properly be viewed as a violation of the Sherman Act in another context, be treated differently."

It is most desirable that schools achieve equality of educational access and opportunity in order that more people enjoy the benefits of a worthy higher education. There is no doubt, too, that enhancing the quality of our educational system redounds to the general good. To the extent that higher education endeavors to foster vitality of the mind, to promote free exchange between bodies of thought and truths, and better communication among a broad spectrum of individuals, as well as prepares individuals for the intellectual demands of responsible citizenship, it is a common good that should be extended to as wide a range of individuals from as broad a range of socio-economic backgrounds as possible. It is with this in mind that the Overlap Agreement should be submitted to the rule of reason scrutiny under the Sherman Act.

* * *

———————

Brown University is noteworthy on a number of fronts. In the passage reproduced above, we see the court attempting to distinguish earlier Supreme Court decisions that rejected attempts to justify trade restraints by arguing that competition itself was unreasonable. Is the effort persuasive? Is the Third Circuit's effort to effectuate the social and economic aims of the overlap policy consistent with the Supreme Court's teaching? Are you persuaded that the Overlap was "pro-competitive" in some economic sense?

In Sidebar 1–2, which follows, we consider some of the traditional arguments for and against giving weight to non-economic goals and their current status under U.S. antitrust law. We also note some of the various ways that non-economic goals continue to have influence outside of antitrust.

———————

Sidebar 1–2:
Non-Economic Values and Competition Policy

Trade Laws and Antitrust

Non-economic values can animate laws that appear to conflict with antitrust. Some nations, both developed and developing, might elect to use trade barriers to insulate domestic industries from foreign competition—even when the predictable result is higher domestic prices. Such a policy choice might reflect the belief that foreign competitors enjoy some unfair advantage over domestic firms, or that a policy of free trade will cause some domestic industry to falter, leading in turn to economic displacement, unemployment and ultimately political unrest.

Although a policy of free trade might increase a nation's aggregate wealth, it also may disrupt the distribution of wealth: while some citizens may benefit, others, like established businesses and displaced workers, may suffer uncompensated losses. The perceived benefits of barring imports or impeding their entry by raising tariffs, therefore, might be viewed as greater than the detriment of reduced domestic competition and higher domestic prices. But how much employment saved counterbalances what degree of lower prices to consumers? And what are the long term consequences for the competitiveness of domestic industries that rely on protection rather than competition? These are complex and challenging issues that often demand subtle political as well as economic judgments.

Exemptions

In the context of competition laws, non-economic goals most frequently receive expression today in the form of exemptions from competition law coverage. Exemptions can exist for industries, particular firms, or particular transactions, and are often justified on the ground that competition will produce undesirable consequences or that other policies could best be served by lifting the legal mandate that firms compete vigorously. Under U.S. antitrust law, for example, statutory exemptions exist for the activities of labor unions undertaken in the context of collective bargaining and the business of insurance. On occasion, the courts also have recognized exemptions, such as with the non-statutory labor exemption and a long-standing exemption for baseball. *See* Figure 8–8, *infra* (listing major statutory and non-statutory exemptions).

Recognizing the distinct role that the legislative process plays in establishing exemptions, the United States Supreme Court has on several occasions rejected defenses that amounted to "competition is destructive in our industry," characterizing them in one instance as a "frontal assault on the basic policy of the Sherman Act." *National Soc'y of Prof'l Eng'rs v. United States*, 435 U.S. 679, 695 (1978).

The mere availability of exemptions, or requirements that certain transactions receive government approval, either through legislative or administrative means, may create strong incentives for firms to pursue a government-bestowed dispensation from the usual mandate of competition. In some systems, this also can foster a threat that bribery or other means will corrupt the mechanisms for antitrust enforcement.

Other Laws and Regulatory Schemes

Non-economic concerns associated with competition also are addressed through other laws, such as tax, employment, and corporation laws, or by creating specialized administrative agencies. Such agencies can be charged with public purposes that include or ignore competition concerns. In the United States such specialized agencies include the Federal Communications Commission, the Federal Energy Regulatory

Commission, and the Federal Reserve Board. Congress has given these agencies concurrent authority with the Department of Justice and the FTC to review mergers or to police unfair and deceptive practices in specific sectors.

The Case Against Reliance on Non–Economic Goals as a Guide to Antitrust Policy

Defenders of an economic approach to antitrust assert that antitrust rules and exemptions guided by non-economic values are usually inconsistent with economic interests and impose significant aggregate costs on consumers. They also assert that such rules can be criticized for their tendency to be inflexible and prone to over-deterrence. If every reduction in the number of competitors is deemed undesirable, antitrust law would always condemn mergers of competitors, regardless of both the firms's ability to raise prices after the merger and the efficiency benefits that might result from the merger. Similarly, conduct that results in the elimination of even a single competitor, such as the decision by a firm to substitute one dealer for several, might constitute a violation. And if we charge courts with weighing economic versus non-economic values, we may be demanding too much of them institutionally: how can a court effectively weigh the social harm of eliminating one competitor (as in the case of a merger) against the social benefits that may flow from the merger if it leads to efficiencies and lower prices for consumers? Are small firms truly politically feeble, especially in an era where interest-group lobbying through trade associations is a common and seemingly influential practice? Some would argue that such decisions are better suited for the legislative process.

An additional argument against devising antitrust rules to pursue non-economic goals explicitly is that relying on economic rules of decision often may also serve non-economic goals, albeit indirectly or incompletely. A byproduct of blocking the merger of two substantial firms on economic grounds, for example, will be benefits for non-economic goals such as mitigating corporate concentration. In many instances, conduct barred on consumer welfare grounds will also serve in part to protect other interests, such as equity, social justice, and controlling sheer corporate size. The converse is less likely to be true. Giving primacy to non-economic goals in framing rules of decision would more likely lead to conflict with economic goals.

Reliance on non-economic goals does not necessarily yield more, rather than less, antitrust enforcement. A decision to approve an otherwise anticompetitive merger, for example, because it may produce a "national champion" better equipped to compete internationally, will be expressed in non-enforcement of the competition law.

Conclusion

It is important to realize at the outset of our study of antitrust law that contemporary U.S. antitrust analysis focuses almost solely on economic goals—preventing the creation or exploitation of market power. Although, as noted above, courts sometimes have articulated non-economic goals for U.S. antitrust law, their reliance on such goals as a source of useful guidance for deciding particular cases has consistently waned since the early 1970s. Non-economic goals frequently conflict with economic aims, provide too little guidance for antitrust decision makers, and arguably are ill-suited to decision-making processes that rely on adjudication and the adversary system. It is equally important to appreciate that this was not always the case in the United States, may still not be the case in some isolated circumstances, and may not be the case universally in the world today.

2. WHAT CONDUCT, PUBLIC OR PRIVATE, CAN IMPAIR THE PROPER FUNCTIONING OF MARKETS?

As discussed in Subsection B1, we expect competitive markets to yield production, allocative, and consumption efficiency, and we associate efficiency with the maximization of consumer welfare. "Competitive" markets in turn can take many forms, and competition often is a matter of degree. As a general matter, however, we associate "competitive markets" with certain structural features:

- Enough buyers and sellers to insure competitive pricing, features, quality, and innovation;

- Homogeneous (*i.e.*, undifferentiated) products or services;

- Easy entry, expansion, and exit by firms; and

- Relatively unhindered information and knowledge about market conditions on the part of sellers and buyers.

Markets are less likely to perform competitively if any of these features is lacking in whole or part, although markets also can be very competitive if all of these conditions are not "perfectly" present. More importantly, the significance to competition of each of these factors does not necessarily mean that antitrust law is concerned with them all. For example, deceptive advertising, a form of imperfect information, is usually addressed through consumer protection laws and the common law of fraud. And product differentiation is now widely accepted as a common feature of competitive markets, even though it can lead to some market power when consumers prove willing to spend more for a familiar or prestigious brand name. Efforts in the 1970s to challenge "brand proliferation" in the cereal industry, for example, were ultimately abandoned.

Antitrust law primarily is concerned with two of the features associated with perfect competition: the number of buyers and sellers and conditions of entry. Private conduct intended to or having the actual effect of eroding competition by directly manipulating either of these requirements of competition frequently attracts antitrust scrutiny. Although public sector conduct, particularly extensive regulation as in public licensing of trades and professions, can also directly impair the functioning of markets, U.S. antitrust law largely does not reach it for reasons related to the legislative history of the Sherman Act and constitutional issues associated with federalism. But public sector conduct is often within the scope of the antitrust laws of other nations.

With this core set of concerns in mind, this Subsection develops a framework for identifying what we mean by "anticompetitive conduct," and for evaluating such conduct in terms of its "anticompetitive effects."

a.   What Do We Mean by "Anticompetitive" Conduct?

"Anticompetitive" cannot be defined without answering the question: "What goals do the antitrust laws intend to promote?" In the U.S. today, the predominance of economic analysis necessarily creates a link between "anti-competitive" and economic goals. "Anticompetitive" means conduct likely to lead to the creation, maintenance, or enhancement of market power, or that involves the actual exercise of market power. As we learned in connection with the Coffee Shop hypothetical, "market power" in turn refers to the ability to raise price by reducing output, or by limiting some other dimension of competition, and typically is associated with a departure from the conditions necessary for the optimal functioning of a market: a sufficient number of buyers or sellers, relatively easy conditions of entry and exit, or readily accessible information on market conditions.

Figure 1–10:

Comparison of Characteristics of Competitive and Non–Competitive Markets

Characteristics of Competitive Markets	**Associated Benefits**
• numerous sellers and buyers	• marginal cost pricing (production efficiency)
• ease of entry	• societal resources are well-allocated (allocative efficiency)
• complete knowledge/information	• consumer welfare is maximized (consumption efficiency)
• competitive levels of innovation, quality, variety	

Possible Variations from Competitive Model	**Potential Anticompetitive Consequences**
• fewer buyers or sellers	• higher prices
• impediments to entry	• consumer deception
• limited access to information	• lower product quality, less consumer choice, and little product innovation
	• wealth transfer

As Figure 1–10 indicates, ample supply and competitive prices are but two of a wide range of characteristics associated with markets that redound to the benefit of consumers. The Supreme Court and enforcement officials in the U.S. have recognized, for example, that competitive markets should produce a variety of economic benefits: "The assumption that competition is the best method of allocating resources in a free market recognizes that all elements of a bargain—quality, service, safety and durability—and not just the immediate cost, are favorably affected by the free opportunity to select among alternative offers." *National Soc'y of Prof'l Eng'rs* v. *United States*, 435 U.S. 679, 695 (1978). So "anticompetitive effects" in the form of higher prices, lower quality or less innovation can flow from conduct that alters any of the characteristic features of markets. What sorts of conduct have been recognized as producing these varied effects?

i. Introducing the Concept of "Antitrust Injury"

The centrality of this question to the development of competition policy is highlighted in *Brunswick Corp. v. Pueblo Bowl–O–Mat, Inc.*, 429 U.S. 477, 97 S.Ct. 690 (1977). In *Brunswick*, the Supreme Court considered whether a competitor can use the anti-merger provisions of the antitrust laws to challenge the acquisition of its principal rival by an even larger rival for whom the acquisition is a means of entering the market. To answer the question, the Court had to ask two questions: (1) what makes acquisitions and mergers anticompetitive? and (2) who can be harmed by them? By focusing on these two questions, the Court in *Brunswick* sparked an era of more critical analysis of the core purposes of specific antitrust prohibitions that begins with an evaluation of their potential anticompetitive effects. Look for the answers to these two questions as you now read *Brunswick*.

BRUNSWICK CORPORATION v. PUEBLO BOWL–O–MAT, INC.

Supreme Court of the United States, 1977.
429 U.S. 477, 97 S.Ct. 690, 50 L.Ed.2d 701.

Mr. Justice MARSHALL delivered the opinion of the Court.

This case raises important questions concerning the interrelationship of the antimerger and private damages action provisions of the Clayton Antitrust Act.

I

Petitioner is one of the two largest manufacturers of bowling equipment in the United States. Respondents are three of the 10 bowling centers owned by Treadway Companies, Inc. Since 1965, petitioner has acquired and operated a large number of bowling centers, including six in the markets in which respondents operate. Respondents instituted this action contending that these acquisitions violated various provisions of the antitrust laws.

* * *

Respondents initiated this action in June 1966, alleging, *inter alia*, that these acquisitions might substantially lessen competition or tend to create a monopoly in violation of § 7 of the Clayton Act, 15 U.S.C. § 18. Respondents sought damages, pursuant to § 4 of the Act, 15 U.S.C. § 15, for three times "the reasonably expectable profits to be made [by respondents] from the operation of their bowling centers." Respondents also sought a divestiture order, an injunction against future acquisitions, and such "other further and different relief" as might be appropriate under § 16 of the Act, 15 U.S.C. § 26.

* * *

II

The issue for decision is a narrow one. Petitioner does not presently contest the Court of Appeals' conclusion that a properly instructed jury could have found the acquisitions unlawful. Nor does petitioner challenge the Court of Appeals' determination that the evidence would support a finding that had petitioner not acquired these centers, they would have gone out of business and respondents' income would have increased. Petitioner questions only whether antitrust damages are available where the sole injury alleged is that competitors were continued in business, thereby denying respondents an anticipated increase in market shares.

To answer that question it is necessary to examine the antimerger and treble-damages provisions of the Clayton Act. Section 7 of the Act proscribes mergers whose effect *"may be* substantially to lessen competition, or *to tend* to create a monopoly."* (Emphasis added.) It is, as we have observed many times, a prophylactic measure, intended "primarily to arrest apprehended consequences of intercorporate relationships before those relationships could work their evil. . . ."

Section 4, in contrast, is in essence a remedial provision. It provides treble damages to "[a]ny person who shall be injured in his business or property by reason of anything forbidden in the antitrust laws. . . ." Of course, treble damages also play an important role in penalizing wrongdoers and deterring wrongdoing, as we also have frequently observed. It nevertheless is true that the treble-damages provision, which makes awards available only to injured parties, and measures the awards by a multiple of the injury actually proved, is designed primarily as a remedy.[10]

Intermeshing a statutory prohibition against acts that have a potential to cause certain harms with a damages action intended to remedy those harms is not without difficulty. Plainly, to recover damages respondents must prove more than that petitioner violated § 7, since such proof establishes only that injury may result. Respondents contend that the only additional element they need demonstrate is that they are in a worse position than they would have been had petitioner not committed those acts. The Court of Appeals agreed, holding compensable any loss "causally linked" to "the mere presence of the violator in the market." Because this holding divorces antitrust recovery from the purposes of the antitrust laws without a clear statutory command to do so, we cannot agree with it.

Every merger of two existing entities into one, whether lawful or unlawful, has the potential for producing economic readjustments that adversely affect some persons. But Congress has not condemned mergers on that account; it has condemned them only when they may produce anticompetitive effects. Yet under the Court of Appeals' holding, once a merger is found to violate § 7, all dislocations caused by the merger are actionable, regardless of whether those dislocations have anything to do with the reason the merger was condemned. This holding would make § 4 recovery entirely fortuitous, and would authorize damages for losses which are of no concern to the antitrust laws.

10. Treble-damages antitrust actions were first authorized by § 7 of the Sherman Act. The discussions of this section on the floor of the Senate indicate that it was conceived of primarily as a remedy for "[t]he people of the United States as individuals," especially consumers. Treble damages were provided in part for punitive purposes, but also to make the remedy meaningful by counterbalancing "the difficulty of maintaining a private suit against a combination such as is described" in the Act.

When Congress enacted the Clayton Act in 1914, it "extend[ed] the remedy under section 7 of the Sherman Act" to persons injured by virtue of any antitrust violation. * * *

Both of these consequences are well illustrated by the facts of this case. If the acquisitions here were unlawful, it is because they brought a "deep pocket" parent into a market of "pygmies." Yet respondents' injury—the loss of income that would have accrued had the acquired centers gone bankrupt—bears no relationship to the size of either the acquiring company or its competitors. Respondents would have suffered the identical "loss"—but no compensable injury—had the acquired centers instead obtained refinancing or been purchased by "shallow pocket" parents as the Court of Appeals itself acknowledged. Thus, respondents' injury was not of "the type that the statute was intended to forestall."

But the antitrust laws are not merely indifferent to the injury claimed here. At base, respondents complain that by acquiring the failing centers petitioner preserved competition, thereby depriving respondents of the benefits of increased concentration. The damages respondents obtained are designed to provide them with the profits they would have realized had competition been reduced. The antitrust laws, however, were enacted for "the protection of *competition* not *competitors*," *Brown Shoe Co. v. United States*. It is inimical to the purposes of these laws to award damages for the type of injury claimed here.

* * *

We therefore hold that for plaintiffs to recover treble damages on account of § 7 violations, they must prove more than injury causally linked to an illegal presence in the market. Plaintiffs must prove *antitrust* injury, which is to say injury of the type the antitrust laws were intended to prevent and that flows from that which makes defendants' acts unlawful. The injury should reflect the anticompetitive effect either of the violation or of anticompetitive acts made possible by the violation. It should, in short, be "the type of loss that the claimed violations ... would be likely to cause."

* * *

In the Court's view in *Brunswick*, what is the essential "anticompetitive" characteristic of a merger? Brunswick's conduct consisted of acquiring some of Pueblo's local rivals, which otherwise were scheduled to close. What, then, was the essence of Pueblo's complaint about the acquisition?

Pueblo asked for the "damages" it would suffer from facing new competition from Brunswick, as compared to the market it would have faced if its local rivals had closed, ceding the market to Pueblo. As the Supreme Court explained, such "damages" were a consequence of *increased*, not decreased competition. Pueblo was implicitly arguing that but for Brunswick's acquisition of its local rivals, the rivals would have shut their doors, and Pueblo would have thereafter enjoyed some degree of market power. Increased competition from its larger, perhaps more efficient rival, Brunswick, eroded Pueblo's hoped for increased profitability. Asking for the difference between its pre-entry and post-entry profits was tantamount, therefore, to asking the Court to protect its hoped for market power—hence the Court's response that to do so would be "inimical" to the purposes of the antitrust laws.

We will revisit *Brunswick* and the concept of "antitrust injury" at several later points in the Casebook. For now, it is important to observe that *Brunswick* proved to be a watershed case. Afterwards, it became increasingly important in antitrust cases to articulate a clear theory of anticompetitive harm with any challenged conduct. For example, note how *Brunswick* itself forced the fundamental question: "what would make an acquisition or merger 'anticompetitive'?" For Brunswick's acquisitions to have been anticompetitive, they would have had to *decrease* competition.

Modern discourse between E.U. and U.S. government officials has featured many statements about the proper aims of competition law. The speeches of top agency leaders in both jurisdictions indicate broad agreement on the question of goals. Each jurisdiction accepts the broad proposition that the central aim of competition law is "the objective of benefitting consumers." Consistent with the single-minded focus on "consumer welfare," E.U. and U.S. antitrust officials routinely disavow any purpose of applying competition laws to safeguard individual competitors as an end in itself. E.U. officials also have grown accustomed to hearing, by direct quotation or paraphrase, the U.S. Supreme Court's admonition in *Brunswick* that the proper aim of antitrust law is " 'the protection of *competition*, not *competitors*.' " *Brunswick Corp. v. Pueblo Bowl–O–Mat, Inc.*, 429 U.S. 477, 488 (1977) (*quoting Brown Shoe Co. v. United States*, 370 U.S. 294, 320 (1962) (emphasis in original).

The habit of E.U. and U.S. officials to invoke consumer welfare and related expressions is a useful start to a larger and continuing discussion about the objectives of competition law. As we will see as our study of antitrust develops, by themselves, these phrases do not tell us much about the deeper levels of meaning that each jurisdiction attaches to them. Nor do the phrases deny each jurisdiction considerable discretion to achieve varied policy ends through the process of interpretation and application.

ii. Distinguishing Collusive From Exclusionary Anticompetitive Effects

Anticompetitive conduct today is generally divided into two broad categories, which are defined by the nature of the effects they can precipitate: *collusive* or *exclusionary*. The distinction flows not so much from the relationship between the parties as in the traditional cases, but from the *mechanism for producing anticompetitive effects*. "*Collusive*" effects directly impair markets and typically will involve coordinated action by competitors, which collectively possess market power and are attempting to emulate the behavior of a monopolist by restricting output and raising price.* Many of the boldest examples of conduct having collusive effects involve price fixing, as in the lysine and vitamins cartel cases. When substantial competitors decide to agree

---

* As described above in the Coffee Shop Hypothetical in Section B1, economic theory predicts that a monopolist will seek to maximize its profits by reducing output and raising price if it faces a downward sloping demand curve. If it does, such a strategy will maximize its profits. Nevertheless, for policy reasons explored in Chapter 6, Section 2 of the Sherman Act does not outlaw "monopoly;" instead it bars "monopolization," the active pursuit of monopoly through improperly exclusionary conduct. As a result, a firm that gains a monopoly through the superiority of its product may charge its profit maximizing price without interference under U.S. antitrust law—even though the economic effects (an allocative efficiency loss and a transfer of wealth from producers to consumers) are no different than those explained in the example of the coffee vendors colluding to raise price. In contrast, serious antitrust issues arise when firms try to achieve the same results by agreement or merger.

on prices, or in some circumstances to merge rather than compete, the consequence is more likely to be less output and higher prices for consumers.** Such conduct does not depend for its anticompetitive impact on any follow-on activity; its effects are immediate and direct: output is reduced; prices are inflated. Such conduct directly impairs the market's mechanisms for determining output, price, product quality and characteristics, and innovation. The analysis of collusive effects, therefore, tends to focus on the process of competition generally, and seeks to determine whether the conduct will result in the direct exercise of market power.

Figure 1–11:
Collusive Anticompetitive Effects

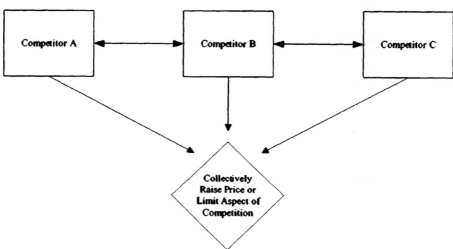

"Exclusionary" effects confer market power by raising a rival's costs (as by cutting it off from key inputs to its production) or limiting a rival's access to the market (as by cutting off its access to a key channel of distribution). Exclusionary effects can result from the act of a single firm, or arise as the product of agreement among firms. In the latter instance, the relationship of the agreeing firms can vary, and can include horizontal as well as vertical coordination.

Whether perpetrated by a single firm or more than one firm, the effects of exclusionary conduct are always *indirect*: by excluding a rival, or impairing its ability to compete effectively by, for example, raising its costs, the predator hopes to obtain power over price or influence some other dimension of competition. Exclusionary conduct will be condemned when, in restraining or excluding a rival, the conduct establishes conditions under which a firm or group of firms is able, or is very likely to be able, to exercise market power. Examples include unilateral efforts to exclude rivals through cost-raising

---

** As we will see in Chapter 5, we are not using "collusive" here the way "coordinated" is used in the Department of Justice/Federal Trade Commission Guidelines on Horizontal Mergers. "Coordinated" and "unilateral" anticompetitive effects, as those terms are used in the Guidelines, are both types of direct, "collusive" effects.

strategies or predatory pricing, as well as coordinated efforts to restrict a rival's competitive options, such as exclusive dealing agreements, tying arrangements, and refusals to deal. In each instance, the common *direct* effect of the exclusionary conduct is its impact on one or more rivals. If that effect is significant enough, it may, by substantially diminishing the sources of competition, *indirectly* permit the excluding firm to harm competition. As a consequence, exclusionary effects cases commence with an examination of the challenged conduct's tendency to exclude or impair rivals, and then move on to consider the consequences of that harm for competition more generally.

Figure 1–12:
Exclusionary Anticompetitive Effects

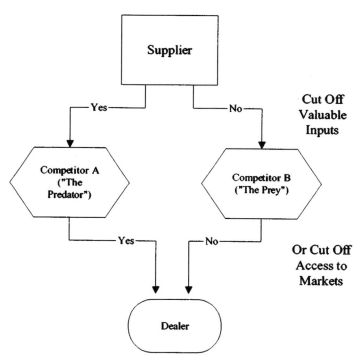

Firms, therefore, can directly or indirectly impede the operation of markets through conduct that produces *collusive* or *exclusionary effects*. Appreciating these two categories of anticompetitive effects is central to comprehending the operation of modern antitrust laws, driven as it is by economic goals, and the burdens of proof associated with differing antitrust offenses. The plaintiff in an antitrust case today, whether the government or a private party, will have to articulate a coherent theory of anticompetitive effects, and it will bear the burden of linking particular conduct to those effects. In response, the defense will attempt to link that same conduct to neutral or procompetitive effects. In either event, the parties will have to address whether the conduct was collusive or exclusionary and whether it was intended to incapacitate the competitive process directly or indirectly. The nature of the evidence adduced in each instance may greatly vary, as will the relative burdens of production.

Figure 1–13:

Comparing Collusive and Exclusionary Anticompetitive Effects

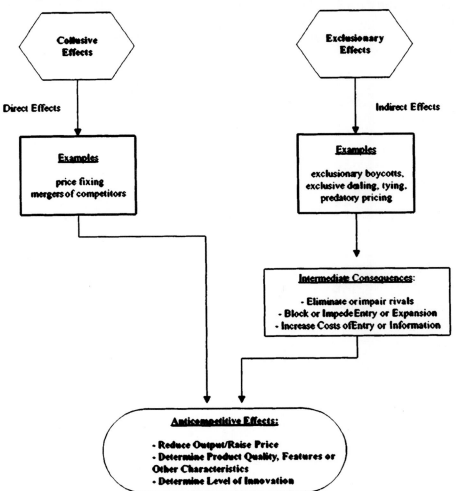

To apply the collusive-exclusionary distinction, let's first revisit the international cartel cases presented earlier in this Chapter. One anticompetitive hypothesis is that the two cartels would cause *collusive* anticompetitive effects. The participants in the lysine and vitamin cartels collectively had market power and acted in concert to curb the output of lysine and vitamins in order to raise prices. The impact of their conduct was *direct*: they restricted output and raised price.

At some point, however, the cartels might need to use concerted *exclusionary* strategies to ensure that the output restrictions boosted prices. Suppose an existing producer refused to go along with the cartel's plans or that there was a new entrant into the lysine or vitamins industry that refused to join the cartel. Such a "maverick" could destabilize the cartel. The existing cartel members might threaten to punish the maverick's customers or suppliers if the maverick undercut the cartel's prices in order to exclude it from the market entirely, or perhaps raise its costs just enough to neutralize its ability to undercut the cartel's preferred prices.

Anticompetitive strategies, therefore, may involve a mix of collusive and exclusionary effects. Consider the following case in which Chief Judge Richard A. Posner of the United States Court of Appeals for the Seventh Circuit examines a variant of the behavior at issue in the lysine and vitamins cases: agreements among competitors to suppress competition. The defendants in *JTC Petroleum* undertake a variety of means to implement a program to rig bids on road construction projects that have characteristics of several forms of behavior deemed illegal under the antitrust laws. They seek to set prices and divide markets, and they organize a group boycott directed at firms like the plaintiff, that could unravel the coordination. Notice how Judge Posner goes about analyzing the likely competitive effects of the challenged arrangement.

JTC PETROLEUM CO. v. PIASA MOTOR FUELS, INC.

United States Court of Appeals for the Seventh Circuit, 1999.
190 F.3d 775.

Before POSNER, Chief Judge, and EASTERBROOK and ROVNER, Circuit Judges.

POSNER, Chief Judge.

The plaintiff seeks damages for violations of section 1 of the Sherman Act arising out of the road-repair business in southern Illinois. There are two groups of defendants: the road contractors themselves, called "applicators," and producers of the emulsified asphalt that the applicators apply to the surface of the roads. After the plaintiff, itself an applicator, settled with all three of the producers and three of the six applicator defendants, the district court granted summary judgment for the remaining applicator defendants, who are the appellees in this court.

* * *

The plaintiff presented evidence both that the applicator defendants had agreed not to compete with one another in bidding on local government contracts and that the producers had agreed not to compete among each other either, both agreements being (if proved) per se violations of section 1 of the Sherman Act. There is a long history of bid-rigging and related practices of collusion in the road construction and road maintenance business. These are local markets, with a limited number of competitors, selling a rather standardized service to local governments constrained to give their business to the lowest bidder, a constraint that makes it easy for colluding bidders to determine whether one of their number is cheating on the agreement to divide markets. The conditions are thus ripe for effective collusion, making it unsurprising that there is evidence that the applicator defendants in fact colluded with one another to allocate the applicator business in their region.
* * *

As for the producers of the asphalt used by these applicators, the record contains evidence that the product is both heavy relative to value and prone to deteriorate when transported long distances, and that as a result the practical radius within which a plant can supply applicators is only about 70 miles. This has limited to three the number of producers that can supply applicators in the region served by the plaintiff and by the applicator defendants. The plants are specialized to the production of emulsified asphalt, meaning that they can't readily be switched to producing other products. This gives the producers an incentive to produce emulsified asphalt up to the capacity of their plants (because there is no profitable use of the plants other than producing this product), and, since it is a fungible product, about the only way of increasing output is by cutting price. But since the demand for emulsified asphalt is inelastic-that is, lower prices do not yield commensurate increases in volume-the effect of price competition would be to diminish profits. So the producers, like the applicators, have much to gain by eliminating competition among themselves. And since the product is standard and the number of competing producers few, an agreement not to compete should not be too difficult to enforce; that is, at the producer level as at the applicator level, cheating should be readily observable and hence quickly checked by a retaliatory price cut. Therefore a cartel agreement would not be quickly eroded by cheating, and so again the conditions for collusion are ripe and again the record contains evidence of such collusion.

* * *

* * * JTC has tried to show * * * that the applicators enlisted the producers in their conspiracy, assigning them the role of policing the applicators' cartel by refusing to sell to applicators who defied the cartel—such as JTC, which has bid for jobs that the cartel had assigned to other applicators. JTC, a maverick, was a threat to the cartel—but only if it could find a source of supply of emulsified asphalt. The claim is that the applicators got the producers to deny JTC this essential input into its business, and as a result injured it. The producer was the cat's paw; the applicators were the cat.

* * * [I]t might seem to make no sense from the producers' standpoint to shore up a cartel of their customers. Cartels * * * raise price above the competitive level and by doing so reduce the demand for their product. The less asphalt the members of the applicators' cartel sell (perhaps because the higher, cartel price induces municipalities to defer road maintenance), the less they will buy, and so the producers will be hurt. But if the producers have nowhere else to turn to sell their product, as may be the case here because of the specialized character of their plants and the limited radius within which they can ship their product from the plant, the applicator defendants may be able to coerce them into helping to police their cartel by threatening to buy less product from them or pay less for it * * *.

Alternatively, and more plausibly (at least on this record), the cartelists may have been paying the producers to perform the policing function, rather than coercing them, by threats, to do so. If by refusing to sell to mavericks the producers increase the profits of the applicators' cartel, they create a fund out of which the cartel can compensate them, in the form of a higher price for the purchase of the product, for their services to the cartel. The record contains evidence that one of the producers obtained from applicators in the cartel area prices that were 4 to 18 (or maybe even 28) percent higher than the prices it obtained from presumably noncolluding applicators in the adjacent region, though there is no suggestion that the producer's costs were any higher in that region. The evidence is contested by the defendants, but the resolution of the contest is for trial. There is also evidence (again contested, and again this is irrelevant to whether summary judgment was properly granted) that the reasons the producers gave for refusing to sell to JTC were pretextual, for example, that JTC was not a good credit risk, even though when JTC offered to pay cash the producers still refused to sell to it. This suggests that the real reason for the refusal was one that the producers didn't want to acknowledge—namely that they were being compensated by the cartel for refusing to sell to a customer whom otherwise they would have been happy to sell to. The combination of the price difference with the evidence of pretext supports an inference that the producers were being compensated by the applicators for shoring up the cartel by boycotting an applicator that was competing with the cartel. If so—if the producers were working for the cartel—they were part of the applicators' conspiracy, and for the injury that they inflicted on JTC as agents of the applicators' cartel by denying JTC a source of supply the members of the cartel, three of which are the remaining defendants, would be culpable under elementary principles of both conspiracy law and agency law.

There may be an innocent explanation for why producers would charge lower prices elsewhere or why they refused to sell to JTC. But the only issue for us, in reviewing the grant of summary judgment for these defendants, is whether a rational jury, having before it the evidence developed to date, could conclude * * * that the reason for the producers' refusal to deal with JTC was that they were in cahoots with the cartel to discourage competition in the applicator market. Given the evidence of cartelization at both the applicator and producer level, the suspicious producer price behavior (suggestive of the producers' having been "paid off" by the cartel to boycott JTC and other upstarts), and the pretextual character of the reasons the producers gave for the refusal to deal, a rational jury could conclude that JTC was indeed the victim of a producers' boycott organized by the applicator defendants.

* * *

Reversed.

———

Figure 1–14:
The Alleged JTC Conspiracy

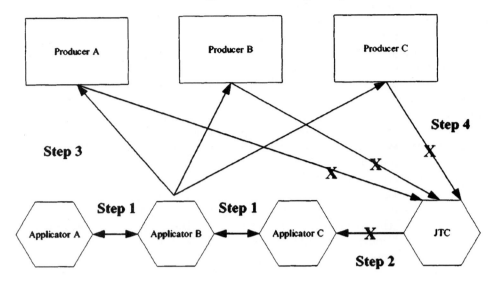

Step 1: Applicators Conspire to Fix Prices and Divide Territories

Step 2: JTC Refuses to Join Conspiracy

Step 3: Applicators "Compensate" Producers to Refuse to Deal With JTC

Step 4: Producers Refuse To Deal With JTC

Why is the conduct in *JTC* treated as categorically unlawful? The harsh treatment of the defendants' conduct in *JTC* appears to turn on the court of appeals' view that the applicators' conduct would have collusive effects, as with price fixing. Is there an argument, however, that the conduct could be viewed as exclusionary? How are the collusive and exclusionary effects, if any, inter-related?

JTC helps us to understand better the challenges that cartels must overcome to succeed. The first stage of a cartel involves formulating a consensus among its members. This is not always, or often, an easy task, as the participants must deal with the range of disagreements suggested in the lysine and vitamins case studies—for example, how to allocate shares of the cartel's output. Once the consensus is formed, the cartel not only must sustain the commitment of its own members, but it must deal with problems that arise from sources outside its membership, such as rivals and new entrants that refuse to join the cartel. It must also address pressure from suppliers, the threat of substitute products, and the possibility that powerful buyers may undermine the cartel by negotiating secretly with its members for better terms.

To deal with these second-stage problems, the cartel may resort to a variety of techniques that, we will see in Chapters 6 and 7, often arise in the analysis of monopolization or attempted monopolization. The cartel might try to deny a rival access to needed inputs or customers. It might drop its prices to compete for the hold-out's customers. If the maverick resides off-shore and exports its products to the location of the cartel, the cartel members might file an anti-dumping action within their own borders. Or one of the cartel members simply might acquire the maverick. *See* Randal D. Heeb et al., *Illuminating Section 2 Through Cartels* (Jan. 2007) (unpublished manuscript) (demonstrating how cartels use exclusionary tactics associated with single firm monopolization). *See also* Margaret C. Levenstein & Valerie Y. Suslow, *What Determines Cartel Success?*, 44 J. Econ. Lit. 43, 75–79 (2006).

The kinds of questions posed in this discussion of anticompetitive effects will occupy our attention throughout this Casebook.

b. *Justifying Intervention: When Can Markets Be "Self–Correcting"?*

Is all "anticompetitive conduct" worthy of condemnation? As with any area of government regulation, one must consider the costs and benefits of antitrust's legal rules. A competition law system, therefore, might aspire for its antitrust rules to: (1) minimize the likelihood of both under-deterrence of anticompetitive conduct and over-deterrence of aggressive, but competitive conduct; (2) establish clear, easily ascertainable rules; (3) authorize administrative or judicial law enforcement only under circumstances likely to produce results that are demonstrably superior to reliance on markets; and (4) create an enforcement scheme that is easy and cost effective to administer. But these aspirational goals for antitrust rules may not always be in alignment. A rule that fares well under one criteria may not fare well under another. Antitrust rules, like other legal rules, may require difficult trade-offs in the real world.

First, antitrust rules should be adequate to deter anticompetitive conduct, but should not unduly inhibit procompetitive conduct. Rules that sweep too broadly might result in condemning conduct that, while appearing "aggressive," may reflect nothing more than healthy, vigorous rivalry. Competition will always yield winners and losers. The vanquished may be inclined to attribute their failure to the competitive aggression of their rivals, but an antitrust law incapable of distinguishing such aggression from truly anticompetitive conduct will lead to the condemnation—and hence the inhibition—of desirable competitive instincts. Such "false positives" can be costly to consumers. Conduct that might lead to increased competition, lower prices, more services or other competitive benefits will be retarded due to antitrust enforcement—and consumers will be worse off. This was the accusation leveled forcefully by Robert H. Bork in a series of articles published in the 1960s and 1970s, culminating in his influential book, The Antitrust Paradox (1978). In Judge Bork's view the antitrust laws were paradoxically being interpreted in a way that actually hindered competition. "Certain of its doctrines," he wrote, "preserve competition, while others suppress it, resulting in a policy at war with itself." *Id.* at 7.

On the other hand, lax rules can have substantial adverse consequences. "False negatives," concluding that anticompetitive conduct does not constitute an antitrust violation, also can be damaging for consumers, especially if market imperfections keep the offending conduct from being naturally corrected. Permissive rules can lead to higher prices, diminished choice and a slower pace of product innovation. Discerning the appropriate line between over and under-deterrence, however, is difficult and is a source of much debate in antitrust circles.

Antitrust rules also should be reasonably certain and accessible. Firms that want to comply with the law should be able to do so without undue cost, delay, or uncertainty. Vague, unduly complex, or unwritten antitrust rules increase the costs of compliance, may provide inadequate guidance to business firms or judges, and necessarily increase the incidence of administrative and judicial intervention into private markets. Depending on their aversion to risk, some firms may forego procompetitive or otherwise desirable conduct for fear of antitrust liability, whereas others may be emboldened by a lack of clarity to undertake truly anticompetitive conduct either out of ignorance or in the hope of avoiding detection.

Finally, it is desirable that the cost of enforcement yield net benefits when compared to the cost of reliance on the market itself to provide a "cure" for the anticompetitive effects of conduct. As a general rule, some economists predict that market power invites entry, which in turn erodes market power. To the degree any particular market is viewed as producing extraordinary levels of profit, other firms will be attracted to and invest in that market. With entry, market power will quickly wither and competitive conditions will be restored. In this view, market power is an advertisement for entry, and will necessarily erode.

The conclusion that market power will naturally erode depends upon several preconditions that may not be present in all instances. For example, entry may not be "easy;" resources for expansion may not be readily available; and strategic behavior by the firm with market power may discourage or otherwise hinder the efforts of new entrants. Strategic responses to entry can impede entry as it happens. In addition, the mere threat of future strategic responses, if credible, may influence the decision to enter. A firm contemplating entry will try to anticipate and predict the incumbent rival's response to its entry before reaching a decision on whether entry will be profitable. If the potential new entrant becomes persuaded that it will be met by strategic behavior, perhaps because the incumbent firm has a past history of so meeting entrants, it may perceive its investment to be at risk and conclude that entry should not be attempted. This might especially be true when the entrant faces the prospect of incurring unrecoverable or "sunk" costs, which may be lost if exit becomes necessary as a consequence of strategic behavior. In these instances neither actual entry, nor the threat of entry, will be sufficient to deter the exercise of market power.

Moreover, even when markets function well, there will always be some "lag time" between the onset of market power and the emergence of new rivals. Strategic decisions about entry or expansion may take months, if not years. New or expanded plants and facilities may not be susceptible to rapid construction. Entry, if and when it comes, may not suffice to counteract the persistence of market power. These are difficult issues. As a matter of antitrust policy, we will need to decide whether a preference for market forces over government intervention justifies the risk associated with tolerating the exercise of market power for some period of time. If we choose the market as the best cure, how long are we willing to await correction through entry? And how can we know with some confidence that the entry, when it comes, will be adequate to mitigate the existing firm's market power?

If the alternative is litigation, however, it is important to assess its costs, as well, so they can be weighed against the price of leaving cures to the market. Litigation can be a slow and costly process. Although injunctive relief can quickly correct for a market problem that, if left to fester, could be difficult to undo, the full course of litigation from trial through appeals can be protracted. The *Matsushita* case (Chapter 3, *infra*), for example, alleged a conspiracy among Japanese consumer product manufacturers that began in 1953. The case was filed in 1974 and litigated vigorously and extensively until it was finally resolved on summary judgment in the U.S. Supreme Court in 1986. Even the government's 1998 case against Microsoft, remarkable for the pace at which it proceeded through discovery and trial, required enormous effort on the part of the parties and the court, and involved years of subsequent appeals and further proceedings. In both instances the cases demanded extensive evaluation of industry information and difficult judgments about the consequences of the alleged conduct.

Lag time also can permit the persistence of ultimately objectionable conduct, or it can delay and even deter conduct that after careful scrutiny may prove to be unobjectionable. Conversely, in the merger area, the mere announcement by the government of its intention to challenge a merger frequently prompts the parties to abandon the transaction, even if significant efficiencies may well be at stake.

Litigation also depends on the quality of advocates and judges, who may have little formal training in economic analysis. Although the use of experts can compensate for the lack of expertise, choosing between conflicting expert testimony can be a daunting task. There is also the risk of "error" and the costs associated with it. Injunctive remedies such as barring specified conduct or ordering the divestiture or restructuring of a firm can lead to more, rather than less competitive markets, and require the courts to oversee industry behavior for years, as was the case with the 1982 settlement that decreed the breakup of the American Telephone & Telegraph Company. The federal court in *AT & T* oversaw many aspects of the telecommunications industry for more than a decade after the decree was entered. Choosing between antitrust law enforcement and the market, therefore, is far from an easy task.

Many antitrust rules, even well settled ones, have faired poorly when carefully evaluated against these standards. When they have been so evaluated, the courts have either abandoned the rules, or amended them in various ways. Revisit the arguments outlined in this section when you read cases such as *Continental T.V., Inc. v. GTE Sylvania Inc.*, 433 U.S. 36 (1977) and *Leegin Creative Leather Prods., Inc. v. PSKS, Inc.*, ___ U.S. ___, 127 S.Ct. 2705 (2007) (Casebook, *infra* Chapter 4), and *Matsushita Elec. Indus. Co. v. Zenith Radio Corp.*, 475 U.S. 574 (1986) (Casebook, *infra* Chapter 3). We will revisit the significance of false positives, false negatives, and administrative costs associated with various alternative antitrust rules later in this Chapter in Sidebar 1–4, *Economics and the Development of Legal Rules*.

3. WHAT FORMS CAN COMPETITION LAW SYSTEMS TAKE?

The impact of a competition law also depends crucially on the mechanism for its implementation. Adopting nominally powerful commands without effective means to enforce them is not a harmless exercise. Establishing unenforceable or erratically applied laws can create significant risks for and impose substantial costs on businesses. For the public, hollow laws foster cynicism about the rule of law and raise doubts about the integrity of public administration. In Chapter 9, we will examine implementation questions in detail. Here we introduce some of the issues that a jurisdiction, such as a state or country, must address in designing a competition policy system.

A jurisdiction can use various institutional approaches to create and execute antitrust commands. Perhaps the Sherman Act's most important innovation in 1890 was to replace a passive competition policy mechanism, in which common law courts merely refused to enforce competition-suppressing private agreements, with a positive system of enforcement executed by public authorities and private entities. But that positive system of enforcement also relied on the common law model, as was reflected in the broadly drafted prohibitions of Sections 1 and 2 of the Sherman Act, and later in the provisions of the Clayton Act of 1914. As William F. Baxter, the Assistant Attorney General for Antitrust from 1981 to 1984, observed, this was by design:

> These provisions contain the kernel of antitrust law. They are broadly phrased—almost constitutional in quality—embracing fundamental concepts with a simplicity virtually unknown in modern legislative enactments. In failing to provide more guidance, the framers of our antitrust laws did not abdicate their responsibility any more than did the Framers of the Constitution. The antitrust laws were written with awareness of the diversity of business conduct and with the knowledge that the detailed statutes which would prohibit socially undesirable conduct would lack the flexibility needed to encourage (and at times even permit) desirable conduct. To provide flexibility, Congress adopted what is in essence enabling legislation that has permitted a common-law refinement of antitrust law through an evolution guided by only the most general statutory directions.

William F. Baxter, *Separation of Powers, Prosecutorial Discretion, and the "Common Law" Nature of Antitrust Law*, 60 TEX. L. REV. 661, 662–63 (1982). But such a system presumes the independence, competence, and integrity of both the judiciary and public enforcement agencies—elements frequently lacking to some degree in emerging markets that are seeking to establish competition policy systems. Moreover, common law competition systems repose significant autonomy with courts, which become the primary source of specific legal prohibitions. But assigning that level of discretion and autonomy to courts is an approach unique to common law countries, and is quite foreign to civil law ones accustomed to the supremacy of the legislature and the use of lengthy, detailed legislative enactments.

The need to understand the institutional foundations of competition policy has assumed ever greater significance for antitrust practice in today's increasingly market-dependent, global economy. Business conduct increasingly implicates several national antitrust regimes and requires counselors to understand the varied institutional mechanisms through which the older capitalist countries and newer emerging market ones, alike, enforce competition policy commands.

Although antitrust's roots run deep historically, two distinct models have greatly influenced its contemporary form. The U.S. model, originated with the passage of antitrust laws by a number of states and with the Sherman Act in 1890. For implementation, these antitrust laws relied upon a law enforcement model, originally implemented by state law enforcers and the Department of Justice, as well as private rights of action for individuals and businesses injured by anticompetitive conduct. For its content, the Sherman Act relied on a familiar common law method of interpretation to identify anticompetitive conduct. Thus, the federal statute charged the courts with developing and refining antitrust doctrine. This assigned a particularly important institutional role to the United States Supreme Court.

In contrast, the European model, which dates from the ratification of the Treaty of Rome in 1957, more particularly specifies conduct that is anticompetitive and vests greater authority for formulating competition policy with the European Commission ("EC"), a centralized, multi-national regulatory body. The EC implements the competition law provisions of the Treaty by both conducting enforcement proceedings and adopting regulations that cover specific sectors of the economy or categories of conduct, such as mergers. Widespread national-level enforcement of the competition laws and private rights of action have only recently begun to develop as a significant aspect of European competition policy system.

As we shall see, the U.S. and European models can differ in both substance and institutional design, and have had substantial influence on the more than 100 jurisdictions that today have competition law systems.

a.   The Structure of Legal Rules

When constructing antitrust precepts, legislatures, administrative agencies and courts first must decide how elaborate the rule should be. One method is to create general rules and rely chiefly on enforcement officials and courts to articulate the law's substance. The Sherman Act exemplifies this technique. As the Supreme Court emphasized in *State Oil Co. v. Khan*, 522 U.S. 3 (1997), the Sherman Act gives a pivotal role to the courts in adapting the statute to changing views of what constitutes sound policy:

> * * * "[S]tare decisis is not an inexorable command." In the area of antitrust law, there is a competing interest, well-represented in this Court's decisions, in recognizing and adapting to changed circumstances and the lessons of accumulated experience. Thus, the general presumption that legislative changes should be left to Congress has less force with respect to the Sherman Act in light of the accepted view that Congress "expected the courts to give shape to the statute's broad mandate by drawing on common-law tradition." As we have explained, the term "restraint of trade," as used in § 1, also "invokes the common law itself, and not merely the static content that the common law assigned to the term in 1890." Accordingly, this Court

has reconsidered its decisions construing the Sherman Act when the theoretical underpinnings of those decisions are called into serious question.

Id. at 20–21. As Justice O'Connor suggested, drafting antitrust rules in general terms gives courts and enforcement agencies much discretion to shape policy and makes the law flexible and adaptable. Some legislatures might regard this degree of flexibility suspiciously if they think prosecutors will misuse their discretion or that courts will ignore the legislature's intent in interpreting the law. The antidote to these possibilities is to draft highly specific commands that give courts and enforcement agencies a narrower role for elaboration. Congress did that to a limited degree when it drafted the Clayton Act in 1914. As we shall learn in Chapters 5 and 7, compared to the Sherman Act, the Clayton Act more particularly specifies conduct that may be anticompetitive.

Another example of a more particularized approach to specifying prohibited conduct is Article 81 of the Treaty of Rome, the European Union's counterpart to Section 1 of the Sherman Act. Although Article 81 addresses some of the same illicit acts that U.S. courts have condemned in applying Section 1's general ban against trade restraints, it does so more specifically. *See* Appendix A. Article 81's effort to more explicitly codify specific offenses is characteristic of civil law regimes. Compared to common law nations, civil law systems rely more upon elaborate statutory statements of the duties of affected parties and give judges less power to interpret statutes. The typical enforcement mechanism in civil law systems is the expert administrative commission, which exercises its authority subject to highly deferential review by the nation's courts. The EU competition system features a hybrid of civil law and common law approaches. The EU competition statute is comparatively detailed and entrusts enforcement to a directorate of the European Commission, but the EU's judicial tribunals—the Court of First Instance and the Court of Justice—have played an increasingly significant role in defining the competition statute's meaning.

b. *Design of the Enforcement Mechanism*

No less important than the choice of legal rules is the legislature's decision about who can enforce the law. The U.S. antitrust system decentralizes the decision to prosecute to an unparalleled degree. By statute and by judicial interpretation, potential prosecutors in the U.S. include an executive department (the Antitrust Division of the Department of Justice), an independent administrative agency (the Federal Trade Commission), the attorneys general of the 50 states and the District of Columbia, and aggrieved individuals, including consumers and competitors of the alleged violator.

Figure 1–15:

The Structure of the U.S. Antitrust Enforcement System

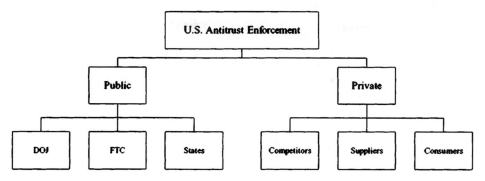

In cases involving regulated sectors such as telecommunications, other government bureaus, such as the Federal Communications Commission, exercise competition policy functions concurrently with the federal antitrust agencies. Mergers in the telecommunications industry, for example, can require the approval of the Department of Justice, the Federal Communications Commission, and state Public Service Commissions. No other antitrust system distributes the power to enforce the law and shape competition policy so broadly. What might justify such a decentralized system? Sidebar 1–3 explores that and related questions.

———

Sidebar 1–3:
Ramifications of Decentralized Enforcement

Each actor identified above has distinctive institutional traits. Consider the choice of an executive department, like the Department of Justice, or an independent agency, like the Federal Trade Commission. Giving an *executive* department enforcement power increases presidential control over the law's implementation and makes policy more responsive to presidential election results. Executive branch participation also tends to be imperative in countries, such as the U.S., which punish antitrust violations as crimes and, by a constitutional mandate, vest all criminal enforcement power in the executive.

Creating an independent agency, such as the FTC, gives the *legislature* more ability to shape competition policy and vests dispute resolution in an expert body. Compared to courts of general jurisdiction, administrative adjudication by an independent commission might expedite the decision of cases and build a more coherent, sensible body of competition doctrine. A tradition of relying on administrative enforcement complicates decisions about subjecting antitrust offenders to criminal sanctions. In systems modeled along civil law lines, criminal punishment would entail the novel step of dividing enforcement responsibilities between administrative bodies and executive ministries.

Diversifying prosecutorial power among two or more agents has three basic rationales. The first is to guard against default by any single prosecutorial agent. For example, a private right of action might ensure that the law is enforced if public officials, due to neglect, capture, inadequate resources, or a shift in the ideology in public enforcement bodies, do not attack behavior otherwise forbidden in the antitrust statute or by well-established judicial precedent. A second rationale involves the relative efficacy of private lawsuits. Compared to a government bureau, the victim of a price fixing cartel may be closer to the relevant information about a violation and may have stronger incentives to attack such conduct aggressively. The third rationale concerns the competitive benefits of diversification. Having two enforcement institutions, such as the Justice Department and the FTC "compete" against each other can induce each agency to improve law enforcement by, for example, developing more effective ways to detect and attack harmful behavior or minimize compliance burdens by giving companies better guidance about contemplated business ventures.

In the 1980s, the Reagan Administration significantly retrenched several of the federal government's antitrust programs. Among other areas, the federal antitrust agencies relaxed controls on mergers and reduced scrutiny of restrictions that manufacturers impose upon their retailers. As it reduced the federal government's presence in these areas, the Reagan White House also promoted the value of federalism. An unintended consequence of these policies was a dramatic increase in efforts by state governments to enforce the federal antitrust laws against behavior that the FTC and Justice Department refused to challenge. The state attorneys general assumed an active role in merger enforcement and in opposing various restrictive practices in the distribution sector.

Some observers point to experience in the 1980s as demonstrating the value of diversifying the field of potential antitrust plaintiffs. By allowing private individuals and companies to bring cases under the federal antitrust laws, the U.S. competition policy system contains an important safeguard against inadequate enforcement by the national antitrust authorities. Cases filed by state attorneys general and private class actions initiated on behalf of injured consumers or businesses constitute important elements of the U.S. enforcement scheme today.

Decentralizing prosecutorial power also entails costs. Where decentralization involves creating two or more public enforcers, the treasury must pay for some duplication in personnel and spend some resources to ensure that two public agencies do not extensively examine the same potential misconduct. This factor has largely precluded creation of dual enforcement systems in transition economies that recently have adopted antitrust laws.

Splintering authority across a number of prosecutorial agents also can reduce the clarity and predictability of competition law. If one agent's decision not to prosecute does not bind other agents, a firm must assume that the same conduct might still be investigated and/or challenged by other agents. This structure also limits the ability of any single agent to narrow the scope of antitrust prohibitions by declining to invoke overly expansive interpretations of the law. Identifying and responding to the preferences of multiple prosecutorial agents requires businesses to incur costs that would not be borne if all enforcement power was vested in a single authority. Possibilities for divergence among agents is evident in U.S. merger enforcement, where state governments at times have preferred tougher enforcement than the federal agencies.

Diversification also raises the question of whether each prosecutorial agent is motivated to bring cases that serve consumer interests. One company might use the antitrust laws to sue a rival for conduct, such as aggressive, non-predatory pricing, that benefits consumers, but cuts the plaintiff's sales. A state official might attack a competitively benign merger because the merging parties will close plants and eliminate jobs in her state. The rivalry that emerges between the Justice Department and the FTC might involve experiments with enforcement theories that raise each agency's visibility without improving antitrust policy.

The U.S. competition policy system relies heavily on the courts to rationalize doctrine and constrain the discretion of prosecutorial agents. Although individual agents may proceed on different theories, judicial decisions establish binding principles that apply to all agents, at least with respect to federal antitrust laws.

Figure 1–16:
Institutional Enforcement Models

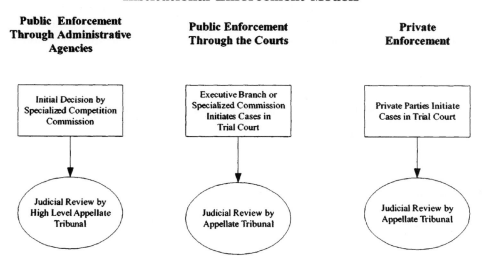

c. *Remedies*

A statute's impact often hinges on the nature of punishments for violations. The U.S. has adopted a singularly broad collection of remedies. Perhaps the most powerful is the Sherman Act's treatment of some violations as crimes. The 1890 statute condemned infractions as misdemeanors and was amended in 1974 to make offenses felonies. As noted earlier, the Sherman Act might be called the first prototype for the twentieth century practice of treating economic misdeeds as "white collar crimes."

Criminal enforcement has important institutional implications. Criminal sanctions ordinarily give a major prosecutorial role to the executive branch, as most countries treat criminal enforcement as an executive prerogative. The second major implication involves defining the zone of forbidden conduct. Criminal punishment such as imprisoning individuals can greatly affect company behavior and have tremendous political ramifications. To retain political support and perceived legitimacy in society, an antitrust system must subject only clearly harmful behavior to criminal scrutiny. In antitrust systems with criminal sanctions, criminal punishment ordinarily is reserved for well-defined categories of the most obviously pernicious conduct, such as price fixing by competitors or bid-rigging.

The more common remedies are civil sanctions. These include civil monetary penalties, such as fines and damages, limits on behavior, mandatory licensing of intellectual property, and the divestiture of assets. Many countries, including the United States, permit independent commissions or other administrative bodies to impose civil sanctions, subject to judicial review. Another major element of U.S. civil enforcement is the availability of treble damages in private cases and the reimbursement by the defendant of the attorneys fees and costs for prevailing private plaintiffs. 15 U.S.C. § 15. The U.S. government also can obtain treble damages where a federal purchasing authority (such as the General Services Administration) is the victim of a cartel. 15 U.S.C. § 15a. Unlike the United States, many foreign countries expressly allow the government to recover civil monetary penalties for illegal behavior. In recent years, the FTC has successfully recovered monetary penalties as restitution for violations of the federal antitrust laws. (Casebook, Chapter 9, *infra*.).

Figure 1–17:

Possible Remedies for Antitrust Violations

Criminal

- imprisonment
- fines (corporate and individual)
- asset forfeitures
- injunctive relief

Civil

- damages (double, treble or more)
- injunctive relief
  - conduct prohibitions
  - divestiture or other structural relief
- attorneys fees

d. *The Role of the Courts*

Competition laws usually give the courts a key role in developing antitrust principles. The role is most pronounced in the U.S., which relies heavily on judicial interpretation to elaborate antitrust rules. Countries that rely on administrative adjudication before agencies such as the FTC typically permit the affected parties to appeal the decisions of such tribunals to courts.

In both settings, the courts help shape doctrine. Particularly in systems that decentralize the power to prosecute, the courts become the chief means for clarifying doctrine and reconciling divergent impulses in the law. Since the late 1970s, the preeminence of the courts in the U.S. has diminished as government enforcers have relied more heavily on non-litigation strategies— such as issuing guidelines and negotiating settlements—to shape policy. *See* Appendix B (collecting U.S. Guidelines and Policy Statements since 1980).

e.   The Scope of the Law

Antitrust laws and the competition ethic they embody are not the sole legal commands governing business decisions that influence the intensity of economic rivalry in most economic systems. As we will see more fully in Chapter 8, antitrust laws coexist with many government policies that either suppress competition among private firms or supplant private enterprise by entrusting important economic functions to state-owned enterprises. *See also* Sidebar 1–2, *supra*. The history of antitrust law has featured a contest between those who would expand direct regulatory supervision and government ownership and those who would rely chiefly on private rivalry, policed with antitrust oversight, to organize the production of goods and services.

Adopting an antitrust law, by itself, does not determine how robustly a system of law promotes business rivalry. Many other elements of a nation's legal system determine the vitality of the competitive process. Key ingredients include rules that define rights in real and intangible property; contract doctrines that facilitate the buying and selling of goods and services; corporation, financial services, and securities laws that enable entrepreneurs to create business organizations and raise capital for them; bankruptcy laws that help revive temporarily ailing enterprises and ensure the orderly redeployment of assets of failed firms; employment laws that create a fluid market for labor and provide a basic level of social insurance for the unemployed; and trade laws that govern the flow of imports into the country. An antitrust regime's ability to promote competition depends greatly on the efficacy of all of these collateral legal commands.

4.   WHAT ROLE DOES IDEOLOGY PLAY IN ANSWERING THE CORE QUESTIONS OF COMPETITION POLICY?

In Section B1 we discussed economic and non-economic goals that competition laws might pursue. As was probably apparent, the choice among and between such goals frequently will be driven by "ideology." By "ideology" we mean *a priori* commitment to a set of specific assumptions about political or economic values. Antitrust, like many areas of public policy, has always been affected by ideology. In this section, we explore some of the principal schools of thought that have influenced antitrust doctrine and enforcement priorities in the last 50 years. To a large extent, that history reflects a clash of opposing, timeless views, and a classical choice that ultimately redounds to leaps of faith: to whose discretion should we entrust decisions about critical economic choices—the market or the government? What do we fear more, big government or big business? It also charts a course that has increasingly looked to economics for guidance in making some of antitrust's most fundamental choices.

a.   Ideological Origins

Classically American political themes such as "tyranny," "autonomy," and "freedom" have long been a part of antitrust discourse. In one of his more colorful speeches in support of the Sherman Act, the Act's namesake and supporter, Senator John Sherman (R-OH)* charged that the early trusts were governed only by "[t]he law of selfishness, uncontrolled by competition," which "compels [them] to disregard the interest of the consumer." The trust, he argued, "dictates terms to transportation companies, it commands the price of labor without fear of strikes...." He continued:

> If the concentrated powers of this combination are intrusted to a single man, it is a kingly prerogative, inconsistent with our form of government, and should be subject to strong resistance of the State and national authorities. If anything is wrong, this is wrong. If we will not endure a king as a political power, we should not endure a king over the production, transportation, and sale of any of the necessaries of life. If we would not submit to an emperor we should not submit to an autocrat of trade. * * *

21 CONG. REC. 2456–57 (1890)(statement of Sen. Sherman). His words rise in a crescendo from "dictate" and "command," to "kingly prerogatives" exercised by "emperors" and "autocrats." This early association of antitrust with populist themes has remained an enduring feature of public debate over antitrust policy, and remains an important source of the continuing popular appeal of antitrust enforcement, especially against very large firms. Periodically, these themes also have found expression in antitrust decisions:

> Antitrust laws in general, and the Sherman Act in particular, are the Magna Carta of free enterprise. They are as important to the preservation of economic freedom and our free enterprise system as the Bill of Rights is to the protection of our fundamental personal freedoms. And the freedom guaranteed each and every business, no matter how small, is the freedom to compete—to assert with vigor, imagination, devotion, and ingenuity whatever economic muscle it can muster.

United States v. Topco Assocs., Inc., 405 U.S. 596, 610 (1972).

> The Sherman Act was designed to be a comprehensive charter of economic liberty aimed at preserving free and unfettered competition as the rule of trade. It rests on the premise that the unrestrained interaction of competitive forces will yield the best allocation of our economic resources, the lowest prices, the highest quality and the greatest material progress, while at the same time providing an environment conducive to the preservation of our democratic, political and social institutions.

Northern Pac. Ry. Co. v. United States, 356 U.S. 1, 4 (1958).

> The purpose of the Sherman Anti–Trust Act is to prevent undue restraints of interstate commerce, to maintain its appropriate freedom in the public interest, to afford protection from the subversive or coercive influences of monopolistic endeavor. As a charter of freedom, the Act has a generality and adaptability comparable to that found to be desirable in constitutional provisions.

Appalachian Coals, Inc. v. United States, 288 U.S. 344, 359–60 (1933).

---

* Sherman came from a storied Ohio family and had a long and distinguished political career. In addition to serving in the Senate, he was a congressman, a Secretary of the Treasury, and after the time of the Sherman Act, a Secretary of State. *See* John Sherman—Biography, http://bioguide.congress.gov/scripts/biodisplay.pl?index=s000346. His brother, Maj. General William Tecumseh Sherman, was well-known for his role in the Civil War.

The ideology of antitrust slowly evolved, however, from a debate about *political economy* to one about *economic theory*.** This is not to say that economics and antitrust were distinct fields prior to the 1950s—quite to the contrary, economics has always played a role in the development of antitrust law. But by the 1950s, more defined schools of economic thought began to exert increasing influence on antitrust enforcers and lawyers. By absorbing the economic teaching of their time and incorporating it into their work before the courts, these enforcers and lawyers played an important role in launching a pronounced and continuing trend towards greater reliance on economics, and economists, in developing antitrust law.

b. *The Influence of Industrial Organization Economics*

In the 1950s and 1960s, the rise of industrial organization economics greatly influenced antitrust. Industrial organization economists focused on three characteristics of markets, which they believed to be interrelated: structure, conduct, and performance. Sometimes called "structuralists," these economists heavily weighted the structure of markets—the number of buyers and sellers and conditions of entry—in predicting the likelihood of competitive problems. Based on a skepticism for the ability of heavily concentrated markets to perform competitively, many industrial organization economists presumed that concentrated markets necessarily would spawn anticompetitive conduct, which in turn would lead to noncompetitive market performance. *See, e.g.*, CARL KAYSEN & DONALD F. TURNER, ANTITRUST POLICY: AN ECONOMIC AND LEGAL ANALYSIS (1959); REPORT OF THE ATTORNEY GENERAL'S NATIONAL COMMITTEE TO STUDY THE ANTITRUST LAWS (1955). They also maintained a skeptical view of assertions of efficiency, which they viewed as difficult to measure and prove, preferring the predictability of structural assumptions. *See, e.g.*, Derek C. Bok, *Section 7 of the Clayton Act and the Merging of Law and Economics*, 74 HARV. L. REV. 226 (1960).

The teachings of the industrial organization economists had a very significant impact on antitrust discourse and enforcement in the 1950s and 1960s, particularly in the area of mergers. As we will learn in Chapter 5, courts began to rely on "trends towards concentration" and "concentration ratios" as sufficient to make out a prima facie case for prohibiting mergers under Section 7 of the Clayton Act. Illustrative cases include *United States v. Philadelphia Nat'l Bank*, 374 U.S. 321, 362–63 (1963); *Brown Shoe Co. v. United States*, 370 U.S. 294, 315 (1962); *United States v. Von's Grocery Co.*, 384 U.S. 270 (1966); and *United States v. Pabst Brewing Co.*, 384 U.S. 546 (1966).

But, as we explore more fully in Chapter 5, the structuralist paradigm, and the decisions it spawned, came under increased criticism. Through reliance on concentration trends and aggregate concentration ratios, it encouraged condemnation of mergers of firms with relatively small market shares (less than 10% in *Von's*; less than 6% in *Pabst*) and no likely ability to affect prices. Critics argued that these mergers were motivated by a desire to achieve economic efficiencies, rather than the "anticompetitive" scenario painted by the courts. Condemnation might well have meant higher prices for

---

** For an additional discussion, *see* William E. Kovacic & Carl Shapiro, *Antitrust Policy: A* *Century of Economic and Legal Thinking*, 14 J. ECON. PERSP. 43 (2000).

consumers. Moreover, by focusing on "trends" towards concentration, the courts ignored the possibility that concentration might be a naturally occurring, inevitable and efficiency driven phenomenon. The stage was set for the rise of an alternative mode of analysis.

c. The Chicago School of Antitrust

One of the most significant developments affecting antitrust since the middle of the twentieth century was the emergence of the "law and economics" movement. Given the role that antitrust plays in regulating economic activity, it is not surprising that the movement found its early inspiration and focus in the analysis of antitrust law. Its most significant expression has come in the form of the "Chicago School of Antitrust," which evolved in part as a critical response to the principal tenets of industrial organization economics. *See generally* Richard A. Posner, *The Chicago School of Antitrust Analysis*, 127 U. Pa. L. Rev. 925 (1979).

The Chicago School emerged in the 1950s, but did not begin to influence significantly the course of antitrust doctrine and enforcement until the late 1970s. Its progenitors, Aaron Director, George Stigler, and Edward Levi of the University of Chicago, influenced a generation of advocates of a narrowly focused, economic approach to legal analysis, particularly antitrust analysis. Chicago School advocates, including Ward Bowman, Harold Demsetz, John McGee, Lester Telser, and later Judges Robert Bork, Richard Posner, and Frank Easterbrook, as well as William F. Baxter, who headed the Antitrust Division of the Department of Justice in the first Reagan Administration, have had a profound impact on the analysis of antitrust problems.

In contrast to the structuralists, the Chicago School sought to apply the insights of price theory to antitrust law. "Price theory" is comprised of a set of theoretical assumptions about how competitive markets and firms behave. Firms will act to maximize profits; markets left unfettered by regulation will lead to productive and allocative efficiency. Together, profit maximizing firms and efficient markets will produce maximum "consumer welfare," which should serve as the principal goal of antitrust law. With these theoretical tools in hand, its advocates authored a series of ultimately influential articles and books challenging many of the accepted antitrust mores of the times.

The Chicago School viewed industrial structure as far less significant a predictor of anticompetitive conduct and performance. In its view, trends towards concentration might reflect a natural progression towards more efficient, and therefore more desirable, market structures, induced by the desire to achieve economies of scale. As a consequence, they tended to conclude that most markets were competitive, even those with few firms, and that true monopoly, when it did arise, would generally be self-correcting. As discussed in Section B2, above, it would soon invite entry and erode. Chicago School advocates also took the position that market entry and exit generally are easy, and that government regulation is the likeliest source of true barriers to entry. Finally, Chicago School advocates took particular aim at antitrust prohibitions of various arrangements directed at the distribution of products and services that in their view were far more likely to promote efficient distribution than a reduction in competition.

Analyzed through the lens of price theory, few of the accepted prohibitions of the 1950s and 1960s appeared objectionable to the Chicago School. To the contrary, many prohibited types of conduct appeared upon microeconomic inspection to be driven by a firm's desire to maximize profits by achieving greater efficiencies, and, as a consequence, were likely to benefit consumers, not harm them. The Chicago School thus questioned many of antitrust's traditional prohibitions and urged a more narrow focus on cartels and horizontal mergers of truly substantial competitors.

Aided by a broad-based and growing conservative political tide, the consequent appointments of William Baxter as head of the Antitrust Division of the Department of Justice and conservative economist James C. Miller, III, as Chair of the FTC, and the confirmation of very substantial numbers of ideologically sympathetic judges to the federal bench, the Chicago School became very influential in antitrust enforcement circles and the courts by the late 1970s and the1980s. While falling short of the total restructuring of antitrust doctrine it sought, the Chicago School had by that time succeeded in reformulating antitrust rules in many areas, including most notably, mergers, vertical restrictions, and predatory pricing. The 1982 and 1984 federal Merger Guidelines, for example, reflected a major shift from the concentration concerns of the structuralist inspired 1968 Guidelines, to the market power and collusion focused Chicago School view.

Perhaps most importantly, the Chicago School altered the terms of antitrust debate. Many of their views, once controversial, are now well accepted. Many of the concepts they relied upon, such as market power, entry, and efficiency, are now essential to antitrust analysis. Critics are compelled to anticipate their positions and respond. Courts continue to adopt their views and use their analytical approach. This is not to say that the ascension of the Chicago School was uncontroversial. Quite to the contrary, it was accompanied first by intense criticism from defenders of the structuralist and populist approaches it challenged, and later by pointed economic criticisms based upon both theory and empirical evidence.

At the time Chicago emerged, critics charged that the Chicago School's models were exceedingly theoretical, ignored contrary evidence in particular cases, and imposed daunting burdens of proof on antitrust enforcers and plaintiffs. As the Chicago School's influence waxed, the fortunes of antitrust plaintiffs unmistakably waned. Of course, Chicago School proponents responded that this outcome was as it should be—that many plaintiffs, including the government, were bringing economically unjustifiable cases. Critics also charged that the Chicago School's operative definition of "consumer welfare" was narrow, normative, and ignored concerns about the distribution of wealth. Criticism too came from those who questioned the efficacy of all antitrust law on the ground that, even as conceived by the Chicago School, it was still too interventionist and too easily subject to manipulation by interest groups. *See generally* FRED S. MCCHESNEY & WILLIAM F. SHUGART II, Eds., THE CAUSES AND CONSEQUENCES OF ANTITRUST: THE PUBLIC-CHOICE PERSPECTIVE (1995).

d. *The Harvard School of Antitrust*

By the mid–1980s, economists began to develop theoretical models and empirical evidence that, while accepting many of the Chicago School's basic microeconomic assumptions, questioned some of its central conclusions about the likelihood of anticompetitive conduct. But before moving on to discuss this important response to the Chicago School, it is necessary to consider another identifiable group of antitrust commentators, who evolved out of the structuralist school, but who, influenced by the Chicagoans, offered an arguably more pragmatic and less ideologically-driven approach to antitrust analysis. These commentators, associated with the Harvard Law School, also had and continue to have substantial influence that is also likely to endure.

In the late 1950s, Professors Carl Kaysen and Donald Turner authored what was at the time the single most comprehensive and immediately authoritative treatise on antitrust law. Influenced in large part by the work of industrial organization economists, Kaysen & Turner's ANTITRUST POLICY (1959), sought to construct a coherent analytical framework for all areas of antitrust based upon the economic and legal teachings of the day. As a collaboration among economist and lawyer-economist the work was unique, and represented an important step forward in the evolution of antitrust analysis. Although it reflected far more of an interventionist bent than did the contemporaneous work of the Chicago School, it still departed from the arguably more populist antitrust of the pre and post-World War II period.

Near the close of the 1960s, Turner, as head of the Antitrust Division, successfully guided the drafting and adoption of the first Merger Guidelines in 1968, which reflected the industrial organization approach to merger analysis that developed from his work with Kaysen. As time went on, however, the views of Turner and his later co-author, Professor Phillip Areeda, began to evolve away from a rigid structuralist approach to include Chicago School perspectives, modified by their own insights. Together they produced the multi-volume treatise ANTITRUST LAW, which first appeared in 1978 and is today one of the most influential works on antitrust law every written. ANTITRUST LAW demonstrated their willingness to incorporate myriad perspectives into their analysis, including those of the Chicago School. Their reasoned approach to integrating antitrust law and economics produced balanced, practical solutions to the antitrust challenges of the time, although over time they became increasingly non-interventionist based on their concerns about the administrability of various antitrust rules and the costs of likely errors by generalist judges and juries trying to implement them. Today, in the hands of their successor, Professor Herbert Hovenkamp, the treatise continues that tradition, and remains a frequently cited source of thoughtful antitrust analysis.

One co-author of this Casebook has suggested that the intellectual DNA of modern U.S. antitrust doctrine can be understood as a double helix that consists of two intertwined chains of ideas, one drawn from the Chicago School of Robert Bork, Richard Posner, and Frank Easterbrook, and the other drawn from the Harvard School of Phillip Areeda, Donald Turner, and now Justice Stephen G. Breyer. *See* William E. Kovacic, *The Intellectual DNA of Modern U.S. Competition Law for Dominant Firm Conduct: The Chicago/Harvard Double Helix*, 2007 COLUM. BUS. L. REV. 1. From this perspective, the combination of Chicago School and Harvard School views features shared prescriptions about the appropriate substantive theories for antitrust enforcement (Chicago's main contribution to the double helix) and cautions about the administrability of legal rules and the capacity of the institutions entrusted with implementing them (Harvard's main contribution to the double helix).

For example, Professors Areeda and Turner believed that private rights of action, with mandatory treble damages and jury trials, created a serious danger of over-deterrence in the U.S. antitrust system. Professor Areeda played a formative role in devising the concept of antitrust injury that the Supreme Court endorsed in *Brunswick*. The Harvard strand in the double helix of ideas does not preclude enforcement, but it has supported the acceptance of presumptions that elevate the hurdles that antitrust plaintiffs must clear to prevail in the courts.

e. *Post–Chicago Antitrust Analysis*

Just as the Chicago School of antitrust evolved to challenge the dominant perspective of the industrial organization economics of the 1950s and 1960s, so too another school of thought emerged to challenge the antitrust views of Chicago commentators. The distinctive feature of this newer school, sometimes labeled "post-Chicago," is its concern with strategic conduct. This modern approach has been gaining influence among antitrust commentators, enforcers and courts in the U.S. and abroad since the mid–1980s.

Although the application to industrial organization economics of the modern economic theory of strategic behavior may be dated from the mid–1970s, particularly the work of economist A. Michael Spence, it has roots in the prior work of Joe S. Bain, Thomas Schelling, and others. Nineteenth century French economists Bertrand and Cournot developed models of industry conduct that recognized that oligopolists will take into account the responses of their rivals. Strategic considerations were important in Chicagoan George Stigler's analysis of collusion among oligopolists and Chicagoan Ronald Coase's path-breaking observation that a monopolist selling durable goods cannot price above competitive levels unless it can commit not to cut price in the future; otherwise buyers will expect prices to fall and delay purchases until then. Strategic considerations were also important to the Chicago view that price predation is unlikely because the predator generally cannot reasonably expect to recoup the lost profits from below-cost price through the later exercise of monopoly power. Nevertheless, strategic issues such as these played a lesser role in Chicago School economic analyses than they do in antitrust analysis today largely because the tools of game theory were not routinely used to facilitate their analysis before the final decades of the twentieth century.

"Game theory" is particularly suited to analyzing the conduct of oligopolists (firms facing a limited number of significant rivals), because it seeks to explain how economic actors interact when they recognize their interdependence. An atomistic competitor—a small wheat farmer in the Midwest, perhaps—knows that its output and price decisions will have no effect on the decisions of other sellers in the marketplace. In consequence, as we learned in the Coffee Shop hypothetical, it maximizes profits by producing and selling its product so long as the market price exceeds it's cost of bringing the last unit to market (that is, so long as price is greater than or equal to marginal cost).

Business decisions are not so simple for firms large enough to recognize their interdependence. Coca–Cola and Pepsi–Cola each must think about the way the other will respond when considering key business decisions. As with an atomistic wheat farmer, a firm like Coke might consider reducing prices closer to costs as a method of increasing sales. But unlike the farmer, Coke might refrain from doing so for fear that its price reduction will set off a price war with Pepsi. Game theory provides mathematical tools for analyzing this sort of strategic consideration, and is widely employed in contemporary industrial organization economics.

Post–Chicago commentators generally propose qualifying rather than supplanting Chicago views. (But not always, as with the critique of the "single monopoly profit" argument discussed in Sidebar 7–3, *The Economics of Tying*, and the *Note on Tying and the "Single Monopoly Profit" Theory*, Chapter 7, *infra*.) They tend to be more interventionist than Chicago School commentators, and question Chicago views that markets commonly self-correct, entry is commonly easy, firms cannot successfully, coordinate, and government intervention can rarely succeed. This difference of viewpoint and approach follows in part because the new economic models, derived in part from game theory and empirical research, often identify circumstances under which business practices can benefit firms by harming competition. Chicago-oriented scholars tended to focus their attention on explaining why the observed business practices could be efficient. But while the new models of strategic behavior tend to temper the pro-efficiency interpretations of business practices suggested by Chicago commentators, both schools rely on formal arguments from microeconomics and the post-Chicago School does not propose to demonstrate the logical fallacies of the Chicago School. In this respect, the new economic literature differs in spirit from the Chicago criticisms of the industrial organization economists of the structural school, whose prior dominance they challenged.

Post–Chicago economics has been reinforced by the development of new empirical tools for identifying the nature of strategic interactions among firms and measuring market power. This literature, sometimes called the "New Empirical Industrial Organization," originated in the work of Timothy Bresnahan and Robert Porter beginning in the early 1980s. In their antitrust applications, these new empirical tools have been particularly influential in shaping the analysis of mergers among sellers of differentiated products in branded consumer products industries because they can permit economists to determine whether the brands of the merging firms are particularly close substitutes.

Perhaps the greatest success of the post-Chicago school to date has been in persuading antitrust enforcement agencies in the U.S. and Europe, and to some extent the courts, to take seriously claims of anticompetitive harm from exclusion. Chicagoans had accepted the theoretical possibility that exclusion could harm competition, but generally argued that the cure was worse than the disease: anticompetitive exclusion was probably rare, while antitrust rules attempting to prevent it would be prone to error in application by nonspecialist judges and to misuse by rivals seeking to obtain inappropriate competitive advantage by chilling competition. In accordance with this perspective, the federal enforcement agencies during the 1980s brought few cases alleging harmful vertical practices or other exclusionary conduct.

In contrast, following the influential work of one leading post-Chicago antitrust commentator, Professor Steven C. Salop, and his co-authors, the federal enforcement agencies exhibited a new willingness to challenge exclusionary and vertical conduct in the 1990s. By the end of the decade, the government was involved in high profile cases challenging exclusionary conduct by Microsoft, Intel, Visa and Mastercard, and Toys–R–Us, for example— all of which will be mentioned in the materials that follow. But interest in exclusion cases at the federal enforcement agencies, especially the Department of Justice, may have waned since that time. From 2001 to 2007, the Antitrust Division in the administration of President George W. Bush brought none. Current and future perceptions about the relative success or failure of efforts in the 1990s to promote recognition of the anticompetitive consequences of strategic behavior, therefore, may well determine the legacy of Post–Chicago antitrust economics and its ultimate influence.

Post–Chicago influence is also apparent in the 1992 revisions to the federal horizontal merger guidelines, especially in the conceptual paradigms set forth for the analysis of unilateral competitive effects of mergers and the likelihood of entry. *See* Chapter 5C, *infra*. The government's approach to unilateral competitive effects shaped a large number of consent settlements with merging firms during the 1990s, and some commentators consider it to have been vindicated in the government's successful effort to block the proposed merger of Staples and Office Depot. *Federal Trade Comm'n v. Staples, Inc.*, 970 F.Supp. 1066 (D.D.C.1997) (Casebook, *infra* Chapter 5).

Finally, the 1992 Supreme Court decision in *Eastman Kodak Co. v. Image Tech. Servs., Inc.*, 504 U.S. 451 (1992) has been hailed by some as a post-Chicago decision because it recognized the possibility of market power arising from strategic conduct in a setting where buyers had imperfect information. But subsequent Supreme Court decisions, particularly *Brooke Group Ltd. v. Brown & Williamson Tobacco Corp.*, 509 U.S. 209 (1993) and *Weyerhaeuser Co. v. Ross–Simmons Hardwood Lumber Co., Inc.*, __ U.S. __, 127 S.Ct. 1069 (2007), appear consistent with the Chicago School perspective on exclusionary conduct.

Recall the *JTC Petroleum* decision, written by Judge Richard Posner, a leader of the Chicago School. In analyzing the conduct in that case, Judge Posner emphasized the possibility that the defendant applicators were colluding, and that the alleged conspiracy to exclude JTC was in part a way of preventing cheating on that cartel. In general, antitrust commentators associated with the Chicago School are more skeptical of exclusion cases than collusion cases, so it may be no accident that Judge Posner highlighted the possibility of collusion among applicators in his opinion. But suppose the defendant was a single, dominant firm rather than a group of firms, and that the defendant acted alone in soliciting the support of the producers for a refusal to deal with JTC. The exclusionary conduct in the case could still be understood as creating an "involuntary cartel"—allowing the defendant to maintain its market power by raising the cost of asphalt to a maverick firm that refused to go along with the defendant in keeping the price charged by applicators high. From a Chicago School perspective, the practical burden facing plaintiff in that case might be higher, for fear of discouraging pro-competitive conduct. But under a Post–Chicago view, which is more comfortable with exclusion cases than the Chicagoans, the exclusionary conduct would likely be viewed as equally troublesome regardless of whether the exclusion was secured by a cartel or single firm.

Antitrust will always be a product of the prevailing economic and political thinking of the times. This is no less true today than when Senator Sherman delivered his oratory on the floor of the Senate. The ubiquitous influence of political and economic thought throughout antitrust's history, combined with the longevity of some antitrust precedent, as well as the conflicting ideologies of contemporary federal judges and justices, guarantees that antitrust will continue to provide an arena for the clash of contemporary ideas on government and markets. The arena of that debate, however, is becoming increasingly global.

C. AN INTRODUCTION TO ECONOMIC PROOF

In modern antitrust, since the rise of the Chicago School, the core concepts of the field—including market power, anticompetitive effect, and procompetitive justifications—are understood to a great, even overwhelming extent as microeconomic concepts. As we observed in the Coffee Shop hypothetical, from an economic perspective, antitrust law aims to distinguish firm conduct that creates economic harms from benign or procompetitive conduct. In this Section of the Chapter, we more closely examine the theoretical and practical ramifications of integrating this perspective into antitrust law.

1. WHAT ARE THE EFFECTS OF BUSINESS CONDUCT ON ECONOMIC WELFARE?

The problem of economic proof arises because many of the practices subject to antitrust review can simultaneously create benefits and harms. An agreement among rivals, for example, can help the firms lower costs or improve products, but it also can help them to exercise market power by acting collectively more like a single firm. Mergers can create market power and efficiencies. Dominant firms can engage in conduct that enhances the quality of the product they sell to customers, while simultaneously making it more difficult for their rivals to market competing products. Much of antitrust analysis involves the resolution of tradeoffs between procompetitive and anticompetitive effects of business decisions.

The possibility that firm conduct can both harm and benefit competition is depicted below, in Figure 1–18, a diagram introduced into antitrust commentary by economist Oliver Williamson. The diagram depicts supply and demand within a market. (In Chapter 5 we will look at how "markets" are defined for antitrust purposes.) Using economic concepts we previously met in the coffee example, Figure 1–18 illustrates the effects on price, output, and economic welfare (efficiency) of firm conduct—whether unilateral or arising from agreement, whether collusive or exclusionary, whether merger or non-merger—that simultaneously raises price *and* generates cost savings.

Figure 1–18:
The Williamson Diagram

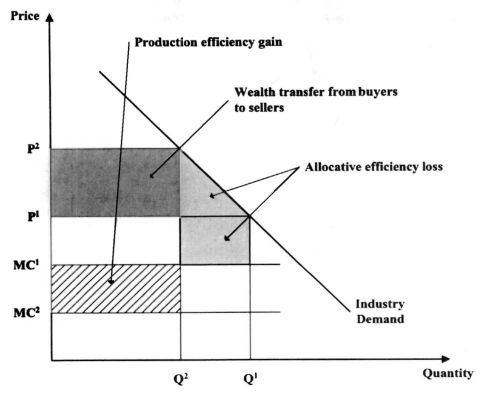

Initially, the industry was selling Q^1 units of output at a price P^1. This price was in excess of the previous industry marginal cost (MC^1), which can be thought of as the supply curve that would be observed if the market were characterized by perfect competition. (As with Figure 1–9, this figure assumes that the marginal costs of production are not increasing with the number of units produced, but instead remain the same for all units produced.) The conduct gives the firms in the market the ability to exercise market power by reducing output to Q^2, leading price to rise along the industry demand curve to the post-conduct price P^2. The conduct also generates cost savings, allowing the firms to reduce industry marginal cost to a lower level (MC^2). (Although the conduct leads to an increase in price in the figure, that need not always be the case.)

As Figure 1–18 suggests, many of the business practices reviewed under antitrust law may simultaneously generate opposing effects: (1) a higher price (or other harm to buyers) that may result from an increased ability to exercise market power; and (2) a lower price (or other benefit to buyers) that may derive from cost savings or other efficiencies. As a consequence, the market price may either rise or fall; the actual outcome will be based on the relative strength of these two incentives in particular cases.

Returning to Figure 1–18, the higher price creates a transfer from buyers to sellers (shaded rectangle in upper left), as buyers of Q^2 units who formerly paid P^1 are forced to pay P^2. (The figure and our discussion ignore the possibility that the transfer could be dissipated through wasteful rent-seeking, and thus that it also represents an efficiency loss.) The higher price also leads to an allocative efficiency loss (the shaded triangle and rectangle to the right of the transfer as indicated by the arrows), equal to the social gain no longer achieved after the exercise of market power. Before the business conduct under review, the market was able to convert resources that cost MC^1 into products worth as indicated on the demand curve to buyers; the exercise of market power denies society this benefit for $(Q^1\text{-}Q^2)$ units, generating an allocative efficiency loss.

But let us suppose that the business conduct also generates a production efficiency gain, depicted by the shaded rectangle in the lower left of the figure. The Q^2 units that are still produced and sold after the merger are produced with less resources, as marginal cost falls to a lower level, which generates an efficiency gain. Fixed cost savings resulting from the conduct under review (*e.g.*, a merger that reduces duplicative overhead expenditures like payroll) may also represent social resource savings but are not depicted.

As the Williamson diagram suggests, business conduct that raises price can simultaneously reduce social welfare (through the allocative efficiency loss) *and* increase it (as a result of the cost savings or other production efficiency gain). As drawn in Figure 1–18, the allocative efficiency loss exceeds the production efficiency gain arising from the cost savings, making the transaction objectionable on two grounds: (1) it will reduce aggregate social welfare; and (2) it will harm buyers by raising price. However, with different assumptions it is possible for the transaction simultaneously to increase aggregate social welfare (if the production efficiency gain exceeds the allocative efficiency loss) and harm buyers through higher prices (by generating a transfer from buyers to sellers).

In principle, this latter possibility may present a difficult policy tradeoff, even if competition law is understood as having an exclusively economic purpose. Some commentators argue that antitrust should be concerned with protecting the welfare of consumers (and other buyers). From this perspective, business conduct is harmful if it reduces consumers' surplus; this commonly is termed the "consumer welfare standard." This standard is defended primarily on grounds of distributional fairness to consumers.** Other commentators contend that antitrust should instead be concerned with protecting total surplus (consumers' and producers' surplus combined); this is commonly termed the "aggregate welfare standard" (or the "total welfare standard"). This standard is justified primarily as a means of increasing social wealth.*** The antitrust enforcement agencies have consistently favored the

---

** *See, e.g.*, Steven C. Salop, *Question: What is the Real and Proper Antitrust Welfare Standard? Answer: The* True *Consumer Welfare Standard* (November 2005), *available at* http://www.amc.gov/public_studies_fr28902/exclus_conduct_pdf/051104_Salop_Mergers.pdf; Robert H. Lande, *Chicago's False Foundation: Wealth Transfers (Not Just Efficiency) Should Guide Antitrust*, 58 Antitrust L.J. 631 (1989).

*** *See, e.g.*, Robert H. Bork, The Antitrust Paradox (1978); *cf.* Louis Kaplow & Steven Shavell, Fairness and Efficiency 29–38 (2002) (arguing that the policy analysis of legal rules outside those governing the tax and transfer system should generally focus on efficiency considerations rather than distributional ones). Bork uses the confusing terminology of "con-

consumer welfare standard, so a business practice that raises price can generally be expected to draw close scrutiny.

Conduct that harms consumer welfare often also harms aggregate welfare, and vice versa. The lysine and vitamins cartels, for example, raised prices while generating no cost savings or other efficiency benefits, so harmed competition under both standards. However, some business practices would be beneficial under one standard but harmful under the other. For example, suppose certain business conduct is likely to generate a small price increase but also lead to large cost savings (or other efficiencies) that are not passed through to consumers, but instead accrue largely to the benefit of shareholders. Should antitrust law prohibit or applaud that conduct? It would be deemed beneficial under the aggregate welfare standard but harmful under the consumer welfare standard.

Changes in market price or output are often looked to as a guide to whether the conduct at issue harms economic welfare. These tests are particularly useful for applying the consumer welfare standard. In Figure 1–18, consumers' surplus falls (as a result of both the wealth transfer and allocative efficiency loss), implying that competition is harmed, only if price increases. Similarly, consumers' surplus does not decline unless output decreases.

The analysis is somewhat more complicated for the aggregate welfare test. If price rises (thereby reducing consumer welfare), aggregate welfare could increase or decrease, and in particular may actually increase if cost savings are large. Those cost savings might arise from reductions in marginal cost, as are depicted in the figure, or from reductions in fixed cost, which are not. For similar reasons, even if output falls as a result of the business conduct under review, reducing consumer welfare, aggregate welfare could increase if the cost savings are large. The production efficiency gain from the cost savings would have to exceed the allocative efficiency loss arising from the output reduction. Moreover, aggregate welfare might fall even when consumer welfare rises. This could happen, for example, if a less efficient competitor enters the market. Its entry could lead prices to fall, but aggregate welfare may decrease if the shift of business from incumbents to the entrant leads to a sufficiently large increase in total industry production costs.

These conclusions are subject to a number of qualifications. First, the analysis with respect to both welfare standards is more complicated if the conduct under review affects product quality. For example, if quality is reduced, the business practice could lead to a lower price in the marketplace, while harming competition. (To an economist, this is actually a situation in which the "quality-adjusted" price increases. But the quality-adjusted price may not be observed directly but would have to be established through economic analysis, perhaps involving expert economic testimony.) Or if quality is improved, output could in principle be lower, even though consumers benefit from the quality improvement and even though aggregate welfare rises. (Here, the economist would say that output increased in quality-adjusted units.)

sumer welfare" to refer to what economists
would term an aggregate welfare standard.

Second, it is important to recognize that the "output" relevant for applying the output test is measured for the market as a whole, not just for the firm engaged in the practice under review. This point can be important particularly when the conduct at issue is exclusionary. If, for example, a dominant firm excludes one or more rivals, the result could be an increase in the market price resulting from a reduction in industry output—the exercise of market power. Yet the dominant firm could find that its own output has increased. Here, an output test based on the *dominant firm's* output would mislead, while an output test based on *market* output would not.

Third, some types of conduct may lessen economic welfare, however measured, in one market while reducing it in another. Commentators debate whether conduct likely to harm competition in one market may be saved by cost savings or other efficiencies benefitting buyers in other markets.

Finally, the comparisons between the aggregate welfare standard and the consumer welfare standard highlighted above focuses on short run considerations. Some advocates of the aggregate welfare standard argue that the short run benefits to producers recognized under the aggregate welfare standard, but excluded from consideration by the consumer welfare standard will turn out to benefit consumers in the long run, making the aggregate welfare standard the better approach for protecting consumers in situations where business conduct that generates both market power and costs savings increases aggregate welfare but reduces consumer welfare. This could happen in two ways, but will not necessarily occur in either manner. First, cost-savings that are not passed through to consumers initially may lead in the long run to lower prices or other buyer benefits, if firms are led to confer those benefits on buyers through competition among sellers. But this outcome is based on two assumptions unlikely to hold in general: that rivals rapidly and fully replicate the cost savings, and that competition works well in the market notwithstanding the ability of some firms to exercise market power in the short run. Second, the higher firm profits (both from the exercise of market power and from cost savings not passed through to buyers) could benefit buyers if they spur innovation. As will be discussed more fully in Chapter 10, this argument presumes, controversially, that the greater innovation incentives arising from the increased reward to a successful innovator outweighs the reduction in innovation incentives arising from the loss of competition. These possible long run dynamics are difficult to analyze in individual cases, so most commentators working within the economic approach to antitrust simply adopt either the consumer welfare standard or the aggregate welfare standard, and advocate application of that test across the board.

2. HOW CAN THE EFFECTS OF BUSINESS CONDUCT ON ECONOMIC WELFARE BE DEMONSTRATED?

Antitrust analysis would be a daunting task indeed if the determination of harm to competition requires the computation of consumers' surplus or aggregate surplus in every case, and a determination of how either of those measures of economic welfare changed as a result of the business practice under review. This could be done in theory, but courts and enforcers have developed ways of simplifying the task in practice.

One common approach is to employ legal rules that embody presumptions based on limited factual showings, sometimes rebuttable and sometimes conclusive, or shift burdens of production and persuasion. These kind of rules appear in many forms in antitrust practice, including "per se" rules, "quick look" rules, and "presumptions" and will be discussed in greater depth at various points throughout the book. For example, in Chapter 2, see *Note on the Development of the "Quick Look,"* and Sidebar 2–5: *The Contemporary Rule of Reason: Core Economic Concepts with Multiple Frameworks. See also* Chapter 5B on "The Emergence and Erosion of the Structural Presumption."

When a detailed economic analysis cannot be avoided, a wide range of economic evidence may be brought to bear. Even then, economic evidence need not be quantitative, though it could be. As will be evident from reading the cases, the testimony of fact witnesses and documentary evidence from firm files can often be used to reach conclusions about market power, efficiencies, and the like.

Economic evidence is often integrated into the decision-making process at agencies and courts through the testimony of economic experts. These experts may rely on qualitative and anecdotal evidence, as well as quantitative and systematic evidence. (We provide examples of expert testimony on market power from the *Microsoft* litigation in Chapter 8, and consider how judges evaluate the sufficiency and reliability of such evidence in Sidebar 8–7.)

Does antitrust law, with all its decision rules and with reliance on the adversarial process to test economic evidence, do a good job at evaluating the economic consequences of firm conduct? This is a lively subject of discussion in antitrust commentary and among economists.*

Before we conclude Chapter 1's introduction to the study of modern antitrust law, it is important to consider one other way in which economics and economic evidence influences antitrust-decision-making. Not only does it help us to evaluate market power, efficiencies, and the welfare effects of conduct, but it also provides a way of thinking about alternative legal standards that might be used when we integrate those concepts into a system of administrative or adversarial, litigation-based decision-making.

Sidebar 1–4:
Economics and the Development of Legal Rules**

Economics influences more today than just the substantive standards of antitrust laws. It also influences how courts and other policy-makers choose from among alternative legal standards. For example, what standard should be used to evaluate the legality under the Sherman Act of

---

* For a sample of the debate, compare Robert W. Crandall & Clifford Winston, *Does Antitrust Policy Improve Consumer Welfare? Assessing the Evidence*, 17 J. ECON. PERSPECTIVES 3 (2003) with Jonathan B. Baker, *The Case for Antitrust Enforcement*, 17 J. ECON. PERSPECTIVES 27 (2003).

** Portions of this Sidebar are adapted from Andrew I. Gavil, BURDEN OF PROOF IN U.S. ANTI-

TRUST LAW, *in* ABA Antitrust Section, ISSUES IN COMPETITION LAW AND POLICY __ (forthcoming 2008) and Andrew I. Gavil, *Exclusionary Distribution Strategies by Dominant Firms: Striking a Better Balance*, 72 ANTITRUST L.J. 3, 65–68 (2004).

conduct such as the lysine and vitamins price fixing cartels we learned about earlier in this chapter? One alternative would be to condemn such cartel activity "absolutely," under what is typically referred to as "per se" condemnation. As we will learn in the next chapter, with a per se rule, evidence of actual anticompetitive effects is not required of the plaintiff (they are presumed), and evidence from co-conspirators that might excuse their conduct is not permitted (such justifications are presumed to be unlikely sufficient to justify the conduct). To prove a violation under a per se approach, therefore, it is enough to establish that the defendants were rivals who fixed prices. That creates an "irrebuttable presumption" that the conduct was anticompetitive. *See* Sidebar 2–1, *Defining and Justifying the Contemporary Per Se Rule.*

Per se rules are used, therefore, to condemn conduct that experience has suggested is very likely to be anticompetitive and very unlikely to be justifiable in very many instances. What kind of conduct is likely to meet those criteria? If it does not, what alternative standards are possible? One alternative would be to require the plaintiff to present some kind of proof of anticompetitive effects. Such proof would then shift a burden of production to the defendant, who would then be permitted to introduce evidence of legitimate justifications. Which approach should be used for cartels? Which approach would be best for exclusionary conduct, such as that presented in *JTC Petroleum*, cooperative relationships, such as those at issue in *Brown University*, and mergers, which were the subject of *Brunswick*? For each sort of potentially anticompetitive conduct, often there is more than one possible standard for defining the line between the permissible and the impermissible. How can policy-makers and courts choose?

Drawing on economic reasoning and concepts, commentators have developed general models to assist in the choice of legal rules. These models have had particular appeal for antitrust, because as a general matter it is an area of law that has been increasingly receptive to economic teachings. In selecting "optimal" legal rules, an economic analysis focuses on two factors: (1) error costs; and (2) processing, information, and administrative costs, sometimes referred to as "direct" costs. It postulates that legal commands, here rules for competitive conduct, should be designed to minimize the costs of incorrect decisions, either false convictions (referred to as "false positives") or false acquittals (also known as "false negatives), while also taking into account the costs of gathering, presenting, and processing the information needed to decide cases. *See generally* C. Frederick Beckner, III & Steven C. Salop, *Decision Theory and Antitrust Rules*, 67 Antitrust L.J. 41 (1999) ("Decision Theory"); Frank H. Easterbrook, *The Limits of Antitrust*, 63 Tex. L. Rev. 1 (1984).***

What are the likely costs of "false positives?" If procompetitive or neutral conduct is condemned as anticompetitive, efficiencies may be lost to the economy and other firms considering similar conduct may be

---

*** This framework for economic analysis of legal rules has its roots in earlier writings on law and economics, especially the work of Judge Richard A. Posner. *See, e.g.*, Richard A. Posner, *The Behavior of Administrative Agencies*, 1 J. Leg. Studies 305 (1972); Richard A. Posner, *An Economic Approach to Legal Procedure and Judicial Administration*, 2 J. Leg. Studies 399 (1973) (hereafter "*Economic Approach to Procedure*"). *See also* William M. Landes, *An Economic Analysis of the Courts*, 14 J. Law & Econ. 61 (1971).

deterred from undertaking it. False negatives, on the other hand, may permit anticompetitive conduct to go un-checked, permitting some firms to exercise market power. And, as with false positives, false negatives may affect the conduct of firms that have not been charged with an antitrust violation. False negatives may encourage other firms to undertake similar conduct to the detriment of competition and require an increase in public and private resources being devoted to antitrust enforcement. Which kind of error is more costly, false positives or false negatives?

Typically, those arguing for more lenient antitrust rules (higher burdens of proof) argue that false positives are far more costly, because they result in immediate losses of efficiency. They also argue that even if market power is facilitated in some cases, it is likely to be temporary, because market power is quickly eroded by new competition absent government action to protect monopolists or cartels. In contrast, proponents of less lenient standards (lower burdens of proof, as with presumptions that can shift a burden of production to a defendant) argue that market power results in immediate harm to consumers and the exercise of market power is often long-lasting, even in private markets free from governmental interference.

Economic models for decision-making also must take into account the costs of administration associated with alternative legal rules, what have been labeled "direct costs." A "per se" rule, for example, might involve lower costs of administration than a more complete inquiry into effects and justifications, because less evidence must be discovered and presented than with a more expansive inquiry. It might be advantageous, therefore, from the point of view of direct costs. Yet if per se rules sometimes or even often falsely condemn conduct that is beneficial for competition (or is unlikely to affect it significantly), then a per se rule might involve increased error costs. In more economic terms, it might be necessary to ask for any given legal standard whether the marginal contribution to accuracy of outcome (reduction of error) derived from additional process would be outweighed by the costs required to gather, present, and evaluate additional information.****

There may often be a trade-off between reduction of error and direct costs. It is frequently argued, for example, that the cure for error is additional information. Often this is argued by proponents of more demanding standards of proof. More and better economic evidence, however, can almost always be imagined and hence demanded, and it increases the direct costs of decision-making. For example, it might require more extensive discovery, longer trials, and more complex fact-finding and appeals. Will the reduction of false positives and false negatives through additional economic data necessarily reduce overall error costs? If not, imposition of the additional direct costs may be difficult to justify.

This kind of economic analysis of alternative legal rules and standards can be seductive in its seeming promise of mathematical precision. But it has limits. Can antitrust policy-makers assess the relevant costs—

**** At one extreme, false positives could be eliminated through repeal of all prohibitions. Likewise, all false negatives could be eliminated through sole reliance on per se prohibitions. The challenge in antitrust law as elsewhere in law is to optimize antitrust rules, taking into account the judicial process used to implement them. For further discussion of this point, see Beckner & Salop, *Decision Theory*, at 50 & n.21.

both error and direct costs—with sufficient precision to identify appropriate legal rules? How well can courts, in developing rules, assess tradeoffs in costs? For example, if courts seek to reduce error costs by demanding additional information from the litigants, how well can they compare the benefits from increased correctness in their decisions with the costs imposed on the parties that must collect and present that evidence and the fact-finders that must evaluate it? Finally, if courts in developing legal rules focus only on economic costs, will litigants—especially losers in court—lose faith that the courts can produce fair and consistent results, what some commentators have labeled "procedural justice"? *See, e.g.,* John Thibault & Laurens Walker, *A Theory of Procedure*, 66 CAL. L. REV. 541 (1978); TOM R. TYLER, ED., PROCEDURAL JUSTICE (2005). Could the result be to undermine the political support for the existence of competition policy systems? *See* Jonathan B. Baker, *Competition Policy as a Political Bargain*, 73 ANTITRUST L.J. 483 (2006).

As you will see as this Casebook unfolds, this economic way of thinking about antitrust standards has been very influential. Beginning in the mid-to late—1970s, the U.S. Supreme Court became persuaded that harsh antitrust prohibitions likely were leading to a high incidence of false positives and that those false positives were costly for the American economy. What followed was a generation of reconstruction of the content of many U.S. antitrust rules, a process that continues today. As you learn more about today's antitrust, consider why the Court altered direction, largely under the influence of economic critiques of older antitrust rules of the sort discussed in this Chapter. Although there is general consensus that today's antitrust rules are superior to older rules that were more prone to produce false positives that were costly, consider also whether some of the newer standards have perhaps erred on the side of being prone to false negatives, in part because they are so demanding of economic proof.

D. CONCLUSION

This Chapter introduced the basic legal and economic concepts of modern antitrust law and sketched out the questions that antitrust policy is designed to ask; the remainder of the book seeks to answer those questions. One of the principal assumptions of this book is that antitrust has persistently evolved from an emphasis on categories of conduct to one focused on more ubiquitous concepts, greatly influenced by economics. Today, those concepts: market power and market definition, entry, efficiency, and anticompetitive effect, cut across a wide variety of antitrust offenses. To answer the core questions of antitrust, therefore, our ultimate goal will be to identify, understand and obtain a working knowledge of these core concepts. We have only begun!

Appendix to Chapter 1
Cost Concepts

Antitrust analysis often relies on economic concepts of cost, nowhere more than in predatory pricing cases, which we will study in Chapter 6. A number of the ways that economists classify costs are set forth below.[1]

One way to explain cost concepts is to consider a hypothetical example. Consider a small stand selling ice cream on the boardwalk in a beach town during the summer. The owner of the business leases the location from the town over the 100–day summer season for $1000, or a rate of $10 per day. The rent covers utilities, including electricity and water. The stand is open every day of the week, but only in the afternoon, for four hours daily. It is staffed by a single worker, hired month by month. The owner pays the worker $1200 per month, which works out to be a rate of $10 per hour. The stand has very little equipment—a freezer and an ice cream scoop. The owner of the business purchased them for $500 at the start of the summer and they are likely to last five summers (500 operating days), and thus will cost the owner $1 per day.[2] Each cone of ice cream uses raw materials (two scoops of ice cream and the cone) that cost $1.

On a typical day, the stand sells 100 cones of ice cream. Given the above information, an accountant might record its costs on a per-day basis like this[3]:

Rent	$ 10
Wages	40
Cost of goods sold (raw materials)	100
Equipment	1
Total:	$151

Whether these figures appropriately represent the ice cream stand's costs depends on what question is being asked. It could even mislead, as the ice cream stand owner cannot save $10 (the rent on a per day basis) by choosing not to open the stand for a day, nor save $10 (the wage on a per-hour basis) by closing an hour early one day.

Total Cost and Average Cost

The accounting records indicate that the daily *total cost* (TC) of producing the 100 cones of ice cream sold on the typical day is $151. This implies that the daily *average cost* (AC) per cone is $1.51 ($151 ÷ 10).

Fixed Costs, Variable Costs, and Average Variable Cost

In economic terms, the total costs of a business can be divided into *fixed costs*, which the firm is committed to pay even if it produces nothing, and *variable costs*, which the firm would avoid by not producing. Here, if the stand was open but the day was cold and stormy, so the stand sold no ice cream at all, the owner would continue to pay rent, wages, and the costs of equipment, but it would not use up any raw materials. Accordingly, its daily total fixed

---

1. These cost concepts are discussed in more detail—usually with graphs—in most microeconomics or industrial organization economics texts. *See, e.g.,* Dennis W. Carlton & Jeffrey M. Perloff, Modern Industrial Organization 29–47, 50–54 (4th ed. 2005).

2. There are a number of methods of accounting for the cost associated with the decline in value of the equipment, as it grows

more likely to break or becomes obsolete; this is the simplest.

3. In computing total cost, an economist (but probably not an accountant) would also include a "normal" or "competitive" return on capital to the owner of the business. To keep the example simple, this component of economic cost is ignored.

costs are $51 ($10 + $40 + $1). On days when the weather is more typical, the stand sells 100 cones and also has daily total variable costs (TVC) of $100. Given that the stand sold 100 cones, the average variable cost (AVC) per cone is $1.00 ($100 ÷ 10). The distinction between average variable cost and average cost often arises when discussing price-cost comparisons in predatory pricing cases (Casebook, *infra* Chapter 6).

The classification between fixed costs and variable costs depends on what is contemplated in the assumption that the firm would not produce. The above example presumed that the stand was open, but sold no ice cream. If instead the business owner planned to shut down for one month of the summer, he or she could avoid paying wages too. With that decision in mind, wages would become a variable cost. Then the total variable cost (measured on a daily basis) would be $140 ($100 + $40) and the average variable cost would be $1.40 ($140 ÷ 10). If the business owner planned not to open for an entire season, he or she could avoid paying rent, making rent a variable cost as well.[4]

Sunk Costs

Fixed costs can be classified further based on the extent to which they are *sunk costs*. Costs are sunk if they cannot be avoided by selling the asset or putting it to an alternative use. If the freezer could be sold for $500 used, then its costs are fixed but not sunk. If it has no resale value and cannot be shifted to use in some other business (like a coffee shop), then its costs are entirely sunk. If the business owner can recoup half its value in the event he or she exits the ice cream stand business, then its costs are half sunk. Similarly, if the stand shut down half-way through the season and the owner could not sublet the space to another business, then the rent would be a sunk cost. The distinction between fixed costs and sunk costs will arise when discussing committed and uncommitted entry in merger analysis (Casebook, *infra* Chapter 5).

Marginal Cost

The cost of producing an additional unit of output is termed the *marginal cost* of that unit. In the ice cream stand example, the 101st cone would cost the firm $1 (the cost of two scoops of ice cream and the cone), given the assumption that it is already making 100 units (and thus already has leased the stand for the summer and hired the worker for the month). In the example, marginal cost would also be $1 for every cone, whether the 20th unit or the 120th unit.

For some technologies, the magnitude of marginal cost instead could vary with the output level. For example, suppose the worker is more likely to spill ice cream and waste it when the stand is busy. Perhaps the worker never spills any ice cream when the stand sells 100 cones per day, but every tenth cone is wasted when the stand sells 150 or more cones per day, and the spillage rate is even greater (*e.g.*, 15%) when the stand sells 200 or more cones daily. Then marginal cost is an increasing function of output. It is $1 for the 100th unit sold, but $1.10 for the 150th unit ($1.00 plus 10% of $1.00), until 200 units are reached, at which point the marginal cost for the 200th unit

---

4. Although labor is treated as a fixed cost in this simple example, it is more common in antitrust applications for it to be considered a variable cost.

(and subsequent units) rises to $1.15.[5] This marginal cost function is depicted in Figure 1–19:

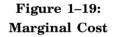

Figure 1–19:
Marginal Cost

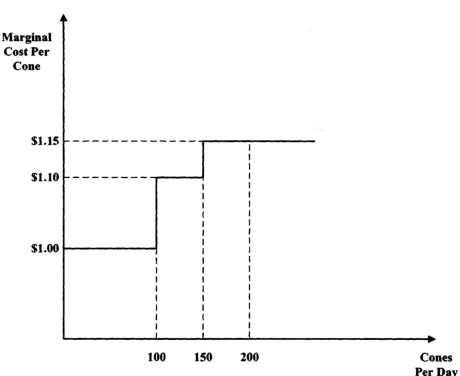

In the "textbook" model of perfect competition that beginning students of economics often learn, marginal cost is typically rising for individual firms, leading to an upward-sloping supply curve for the industry. This characterization of cost is plausible for an ice cream stand. In the oligopoly markets in which most antitrust enforcement arises, however, marginal cost can just as easily be constant or declining.

Even in the ice cream stand example, marginal cost could fall for larger levels of output, if, for example, the firm's ice cream supplier gives volume discounts. Perhaps the supplier would charge it $1.50 per cone for bulk ice cream if the stand bought only enough to sell up to 20 cones, but $1.00 per cone if the stand bought enough for 20 or more cones. Then marginal cost

5. Capacity constraints can be represented in terms of steeply increasing marginal costs. If the ice cream stand could not produce more than 250 cones per day without investing in additional production capacity (expanding its size, adding another worker, installing another freezer, etc.) then the marginal cost of the 251st unit would be much greater than the marginal cost of the 250th unit; its marginal cost would rise substantially when its output reached 250 cones per day, to include the costs of expansion. After expansion, though, marginal cost would fall.

would be $1.50 for the 20th unit but would fall to $1.00 for the 21st (or more) cone. Marginal cost can even fall in some range of firm output and rise in other ranges.

In this example, putting aside the wastage and the volume discount, the ice cream stand's marginal cost ($1.00) of producing output is equal to its average variable cost and less than its average total cost ($1.50). Average variable cost will always be less than or equal to average total cost (they can be identical only if there are no fixed costs). But marginal cost can be above, equal to, or below either measure of average cost. If the spillage rate increased as output rose, so that marginal cost increased with output, then there would be some number of cones sold such that marginal cost would equal average cost.[6]

Different Costs for Different Purposes

The economic concept of cost is always tied to a decision, in the above example a decision to produce one more unit of output. There are, as it is sometimes said, "different costs for different purposes."

When the ice cream stand's decision is whether to sell one more cone, it considers its marginal costs of $1 per cone. Selling one more unit would be profitable if the additional cone brought in more than $1 in revenue (that is, if the cone's price was more than $1).[7] For it to be profitable to open the stand for any period up to a month (the period after which the worker becomes a variable cost), the owner must expect to receive price in excess of $1.50 per cone (the average variable cost).

These measures no longer reflect cost well if the ice cream stand's decision is instead whether to extend its business hours by one more hour on holiday weekends. The cost of extending business hours would be just the costs of hiring a worker for an extra hour. If overtime is paid on an hourly basis (not contracted for monthly), and the ice cream stand owner pays the worker $20 per hour of overtime work, the cost for the typical holiday weekend day would be $20 per day. (This is the marginal cost of opening the stand for an extra hour.) If the stand expects to sell ten more ice cream cones during that extra hour, its average cost for those 10 extra cones is $3 ($1 per cone for the raw materials and $2 per cone for the worker). Accordingly, extending business hours would only be profitable if the price per cone exceeds $3.

The idea of focusing on different concepts of cost for different purposes often comes up when comparing a firm's decision to enter a business versus the decision to exit. In the ice cream stand example, if the issue is whether to open in the first place—purchase the freezer and scoops and lease the facility from the town—and the business expects to sell 100 cones per day (as it did in the example above), then its average cost would be $151 per day or $1.51 per cone. The firm would only enter the market if it anticipated being able to charge at least $1.51 per cone.

6. In the "textbook" model of perfect competition, where marginal cost is increasing, the number of firms in the industry adjusts so that marginal cost equals average cost for the last firm to enter.

7. This discussion assumes that the ice cream stand charges the same price to all buyers, thus ruling out the possibility that the ice cream stand faces a downward sloping demand curve or the possibility that it discriminates in price (Casebook, *infra* Chapter 7).

If the issue is instead whether to shut down the stand at the end of the first month of operation, and if the freezer cost is completely sunk and the owner could not sublease the stand, then the firm only would save the costs of the worker and the raw materials it no longer needs to purchase. Those saved costs are equal to $140 ($40 for the worker and $100 for the ice cream and the cone). Assuming that it would have sold 100 cones per day had it continued in business, the firm's relevant average cost would be $1.40 per cone ($140÷10), with respect to the shut down decision. That is, it would be profitable for the firm to stay in business so long as it anticipated that it could receive a price of at least $1.40 for the remainder of the season. This figure is less than the $1.51 minimum price that was needed to make entry profitable before any costs were sunk. If the ice cream stand knew that it could not charge more than $1.50 per cone (perhaps because that is what rival ice cream vendors charge), the business owner would not have chosen to enter in the first place. But if the ice cream stand entered and then the other stands reduced price to $1.45, the owner would do better to cut its price and remain in business, rather than exit halfway through the season.

Scale Economies and Diseconomies

A firm experiences *economies of scale* if its average cost declines with output. This occurs when marginal cost is declining as output increases. It also occurs when marginal cost is constant and there are fixed costs. Returning to the original ice cream stand example, where fixed costs are $51 and marginal costs are $1 per cone, if the stand sold only one cone in a day, its total costs would be $52, and its average cost would be $52 as well ($52 ÷ 1). If the stand sold ten cones, its total cost would be $62 and its average cost would fall to $6.20 ($62 ÷ 10). At 100 cones sold in a day, average cost declines to $1.51, as previously noted.

If average cost is constant, the firm is said to experience *constant returns to scale*. If average cost is rising as output increases, the firm experiences *diseconomies of scale*.

In industries in which firms experience substantial scale diseconomies, firms will likely be small relative to the size of the market—it is simply too expensive for them to grow large. As a result, such industries commonly have many firms, and tend to behave competitively. By contrast, industries in which firms experience substantial scale economies may have few firms, each with a high market share. Small firms in such industries often cannot compete effectively without a differentiated (niche) product that is particularly valuable to some group of buyers, as they do not have the size needed to keep average costs low. Accordingly, in a market in which large firms obtain substantial cost savings as a result of their size, small firms often must offer a differentiated product to succeed. Antitrust enforcement tends to be concentrated in oligopoly markets (those with a small number of large firms), where scale economies are often important. When rivals merge in such markets, they may seek to justify their transaction, which increases firm size, on the ground that it permits the firm to achieve greater economies of scale.[8]

---

8. When firms sell multiple products, they sometimes can lower the cost of producing one by increasing their output of the other. If this situation arises, it is said to reflect *economies of scope*. The concept of average cost can be difficult to define when firms sell multiple

Opportunity Cost

Suppose that a wealthy beach resident offers to rent the ice cream stand for a day for a private beach party. In order to decide whether to accept the offer (and at what price), the ice cream stand operator will need to consider and compare its options. If the stand is not rented for the party, it would likely serve 100 cones. The cost of giving up the daily business is the amount the stand owner would have received in revenue from selling those 100 cones less the variable costs of producing those costs. This difference is sometimes called the *contribution to profit*. If cones sell for $2.50, the contribution to profit from a regular day's operation would be $150 ($250 in revenues (100 x $2.50/cone) less $100 in costs of goods sold (100 x $1)). In order for the private party to be profitable, the wealthy resident would need to offer the stand owner more than $150 plus the cost of the ice cream needed to serve the private party guests. If the party guests would likely want only 50 cones, which cost $50 in raw materials (ice cream and cones), therefore, the wealthy resident would need to pay at least $200 ($150 + $50) to the ice cream stand owner.

As this example indicates, the cost of using the stand for a private party includes the foregone benefit from applying the resource in its best alternative use. That forgone benefit is termed an *opportunity cost*. Opportunity costs might be important in determining whether price is less than average cost or average variable cost, for the purpose of evaluating a predatory pricing claim. For example, if an airline has added a flight to a route, an economist would say that the cost of doing so includes the profits foregone by not employing the aircraft on its most profitable alternative route.

products, raising problems for determining whether price is less than average cost or average variable cost, as some legal rules for evaluating predatory pricing allegations require.

Part II

CONDUCT HAVING COLLUSIVE ANTICOMPETITIVE EFFECTS

Chapter 2

CONCERTED ACTION AMONG COMPETITORS ("HORIZONTAL" AGREEMENTS)

INTRODUCTION

Although some of the cases discussed in Chapter 1 involved efforts by competitors to cooperate in ways that were clearly anticompetitive and even nefarious, it would be a mistake at the start of a course on competition policy to assume that cooperative arrangements among competitors are predominantly anticompetitive. Partnerships, joint ventures, and strategic alliances among rivals are ubiquitous and rarely present serious competitive concerns. Quite to the contrary, they often provide a significant source of competitive vigor and product and service innovation. As one court has observed, "[c]ooperation is the basis of productivity. It is necessary for people to cooperate in some respects before they may compete in others, and cooperation facilitates efficient production." *Polk Bros., Inc. v. Forest City Enters., Inc.*, 776 F.2d 185, 188 (7th Cir. 1985). As a matter of perspective, therefore, it is important to recognize that a course on antitrust law will of necessity tend to focus on those types of arrangements that have invited scrutiny and resulted either in condemnation or at least in thoughtful evaluation.

This chapter provides an introduction to the evolution of the treatment of agreements among competitors, but with a particular emphasis on agreements involving actual or threatened collusive effects. As we initially explored in Chapter 1, conduct can be challenged as anticompetitive either for its "collusive" or direct effects on price, output, or innovation, or for its "exclusionary" or indirect effects. The task is to devise a set of legal commands that can effectively distinguish between arrangements that promise to invigorate competition, or at the least have little effect on it, and those that present a threat of serious anticompetitive harm. Ensuring that these commands neither over-deter desirable collaborations nor under-deter undesirable ones has proved to be a serious challenge, and achieving the right balance has been an elusive goal.

A. THE EVOLUTION OF "UNREASONABLENESS" UNDER SECTION 1 OF THE SHERMAN ACT

The Sherman Act of 1890 was the first federal antitrust statute in the United States. Section 1 of the Act declares "[e]very contract, combination in the form of trust or otherwise, or conspiracy, in restraint of trade" to be unlawful both civilly and criminally. *See* Appendix A, *infra.* An offense under Section 1, therefore, consists of two elements: (1) concerted action—a "contract, combination, or conspiracy," and (2) an anticompetitive effect—a "restraint of trade." In partial contrast, Section 2 of the Sherman Act alone addresses single firm conduct—usually the activities of actual or would-be monopolists. But it, too, places a great deal of emphasis on the evaluation of the market effects of allegedly anticompetitive conduct.

Chapter 3 focuses on the first requirement of Section 1, concerted action. This Chapter begins with the Supreme Court's earliest efforts to interpret the second requirement, "restraint of trade." In its first attempt to do so, the Court considered itself to be constrained by the seemingly plain meaning of the word "every" as it related to concerted action that restrained trade. Rejecting the defendants's assertion that a reasonableness qualification was inherent in "restraint of trade," the Court held:

> When * * * the body of an act pronounces as illegal every contract or combination in restraint of trade or commerce among the several states, etc., the plain and ordinary meaning of such language is not limited to that kind of contract alone which is in unreasonable restraint of trade, but all contracts are included in such language, and no exception or limitation can be added without placing in the act that which has been omitted by congress.

United States v. Trans–Missouri Freight Ass'n, 166 U.S. 290, 328 (1897). But even as the Court emphasized the seemingly unequivocal "every" in Section 1, it recognized that the English and American common law, from which the phrase "restraint of trade" had been taken by the Sherman Act's drafters, allowed for exceptions. *Id.* at 329. Justice Edward Douglass White, dissenting in *Trans-Missouri Freight*, urged the Court to recognize the full import of that common law history, by interpreting Section 1 as prohibiting only "unreasonable" restraints of trade. *Id.* at 343–74 (White, J., dissenting). *See also United States v. Joint-Traffic Ass'n*, 171 U.S. 505 (1898). As we will shortly see, the common law exceptions that led Justice White to advocate a broad reasonableness inquiry also provided the basis for another, far more narrow "reasonableness" framework just a year later in Judge William H. Taft's opinion in *United States v. Addyston Pipe & Steel Co.*, 85 F. 271 (6th Cir.1898), *aff'd*, 175 U.S. 211 (1899).

Trans-Missouri Freight's literal reading of the Sherman Act may have had the virtue of simplicity, but it also had the vice of over-inclusiveness. A prohibition of "every" agreement that restrained trade could encompass a full range of common, competitively insignificant or beneficial business arrangements, including most business partnerships and joint ventures, no matter how they affect competition. Not surprisingly, therefore, little more than a decade after *Trans-Missouri Freight*, the Court charted a new course for

Section 1 in its watershed decision in *Standard Oil Co. v. United States*, 221 U.S. 1 (1911).

Standard Oil was by far the most celebrated antitrust case yet to have been brought under the Sherman Act. Indeed the term "anti-trust" had been coined with trusts such as Standard Oil in mind. The trust was a form of business organization that permitted rival firms to delegate to a single decision-maker, a "trustee," the authority to make decisions about industry-wide output and pricing. Without effectuating a formal merger, it permitted rivals to coordinate their production and, in effect, act as a monopoly. Its invention is often credited to Samuel C.T. Dodd, an attorney for Standard Oil, who first used the device to organize the Standard Oil Trust in 1882, see RON CHERNOW, TITAN: THE LIFE OF JOHN D. ROCKEFELLER, SR. 226–27 (1998), but it spread to other industries such as whiskey, railroads, and sugar.

Pitting the determined antitrust enforcers of the time against the financial interests of John D. Rockefeller and other prominent industrialists, the government's case against Standard Oil marked the end of antitrust's adolescence in more ways than one. The record, reported the Court, "is inordinately voluminous, consisting of twenty-three volumes of printed matter, aggregating about 12,000 pages, containing a vast amount of confusing and conflicting testimony relating to innumerable, complex, and varied business transactions, extending over a period of nearly forty years." 221 U.S. at 30–31. Although the bulk and complexity of the record are greatly exaggerated by today's standards, the contemporary association of antitrust with complex litigation can be traced to *Standard Oil*.

At the conclusion of the case, one of the most extensive trusts to emerge from the late nineteenth century became a casualty of the twentieth, disassembled into its over thirty constituent parts. More importantly for current purposes, the Court did so after implying a reasonableness modification to the language of Section 1 of the Sherman Act. Now writing for the Court's majority and as its Chief Justice, White implemented the approach he had first outlined in his dissent in *Trans-Missouri Freight*: "the rule of reason." In so doing, the Court forever turned its back on the plain meaning approach of *Trans-Missouri Freight* and *Joint Traffic Ass'n*, emphasizing instead the link between the Sherman Act and the English and American common law of restraint of trade as it stood in 1890:

> [Section 1 of the Sherman Act] necessarily called for the exercise of judgment which required that some standard should be resorted to for the purpose of determining whether the prohibition contained in the statute had or had not in any given case been violated. Thus, not specifying, but indubitably contemplating and requiring a standard, it follows that it was intended that the standard of reason which had been applied at the common law and in this country in dealing with subjects of the character embraced by the statute was intended to be the measure used for the purpose of determining whether, in a given case, a particular act had or had not brought about the wrong against which the statute provided.

Standard Oil, 221 U.S. at 60.

The full import of *Standard Oil* was not apparent, however, until the Court's decision in *Bd. of Trade of Chicago v. United States*, 246 U.S. 231,

238–39 (1918), where the Court under the influence of Justice Louis Brandeis set out its most well known statement of the rule of reason:

> [T]he legality of an agreement or regulation cannot be determined by so simple a test, as whether it restrains competition. Every agreement concerning trade, every regulation of trade, restrains. To bind, to restrain, is of their very essence. The true test of legality is whether the restraint imposed is such as merely regulates and perhaps thereby promotes competition or whether it is such as may suppress or even destroy competition. To determine that question the court must ordinarily consider the facts peculiar to the business to which the restraint is applied; its condition before and after the restraint was imposed; the nature of the restraint and its effect, actual or probable. The history of the restraint, the evil believed to exist, the reason for adopting the particular remedy, the purpose or end sought to be attained, are all relevant facts. This is not because a good intention will save an otherwise objectionable regulation or the reverse; but because knowledge of intent may help the court to interpret facts and to predict consequences.

By emphasizing the need to evaluate a restraint's "purpose," "nature" and "effects," the Court set down the path of what today is referred to as the "unstructured" or "full-blown" rule of reason analysis. Many facts are relevant, none decisively so.

From a contemporary perspective, *Standard Oil* and *Chicago Bd. of Trade* can be read as echoing aspects of the approach embraced in Judge Taft's 1898 opinion in *Addyston Pipe*. There Judge Taft separated restraints of trade into two categories. In the first lay restraints that had no purpose save restraining trade. These were condemned absolutely at common law, and, he reasoned, should be similarly condemned under the Act. In this way *Addyston Pipe*, like *Trans-Missouri Freight*, introduced the concept of "absolutely" prohibited categories of conduct. But in contrast to *Trans-Missouri Freight*, Taft's approach followed from the restraint's plainly anticompetitive effect rather than any literal reading of the language of the Sherman Act. It can, therefore, fairly be identified as the point of origin for later per se rules (rules by which certain factual showings create a presumption, possibly irrebuttable, of anticompetitive effect).

In Taft's second category, however, were those restraints "ancillary" to an otherwise legitimate business venture, such as the sale of a business. Examples might include an agreement by the seller of an ongoing business, such as a bakery, not to enter into competition with the buyer for a period of three years after the purchase within a radius of five miles. Such ancillary restraints, in this case a "covenant not to compete," actually facilitated the underlying, legitimate transaction, and could be justified on the ground that they promoted trade—in this example the sale of a business. The sale would not sensibly go forward if the purchaser could not contractually protect against the possibility that the seller would promptly enter into a competing business proximate to that sold. Taft argued based on common law examples that these sorts of ancillary restraints ought to be assessed further for their reasonableness, but in a very specific fashion. They were deemed reasonable at common law when both integral to and no greater than necessary to facilitate the legitimate transaction. The duration of the covenant not to compete, as well as its geographic scope, would have to be assessed and found to be "reasonable."

Just as Taft's per se rule was distinct from the per se rule of *Trans-Missouri Freight*, so too his "rule of reason" was distinct from that enunciated in *Standard Oil*—in two important respects. First, in contrast to *Standard Oil*, "reasonableness" only entered into the analysis of *ancillary* restraints. Taft's approach would not entertain broadly conceived reasonableness defenses directed at arrangements that only restrained trade. Second, and more significantly, for Taft "reasonableness" was a limited inquiry under the Sherman Act, and mandated a disciplined approach. In his view, courts were ill equipped to evaluate unstructured, non-specific claims of reasonableness, such as those later approved in *Standard Oil*:

> But where the sole object of both parties in making the contract as expressed therein is merely to restrain competition, and enhance or maintain prices, it would seem that there was nothing to justify or excuse the restraint, that it would necessarily have a tendency to monopoly, and therefore would be void. In such a case there is no measure of what is necessary to the protection of either party, except the vague and varying opinion of judges as to how much, on principles of political economy, men ought to be allowed to restrain competition. There is in such contracts no main lawful purpose, to subserve which partial restraint is permitted, and by which its reasonableness is measured, but the sole object is to restrain trade in order to avoid the competition which it has always been the policy of the common law to foster.

Addyston Pipe, 85 F. at 282–83. Courts that entertained broader arguments for reasonableness, Taft argued, had in doing so "set sail on a sea of doubt." *Id.* at 284. As we shall explore in Sidebar 2–4, modern commentary also views *Addyston Pipe* as having heralded greater attention to economic values, especially "efficiency," which arguably is inherent to a degree in the concept of ancillarity.

So this chapter commences with a variety of approaches to applying Section 1 of the Sherman Act—only some of which remain relevant today. The expansive plain meaning rule of *Trans-Missouri Freight* was quickly abandoned, but the "per se rule" from *Addyston Pipe,* which abbreviates the analysis of reasonableness by triggering a presumption of unreasonable anticompetitive effect, has had an important impact on the development of Section 1 and remains highly relevant. The two approaches to the rule of reason reflected in *Standard Oil* and *Addyston Pipe* also have been influential and remain so today. Judge Taft's limited rule of reason permitted an inquiry into reasonableness, but only under limited circumstances, and even then only as to particular questions—economic necessity and duration of the restraint. The "rule of reason" of Justices White and Brandeis, in contrast, encouraged a fairly wide ranging inquiry in all cases. The case law continues to struggle today with the scope and breadth of the per se approach to unreasonableness and the strain of accommodating both the structured and the potentially unstructured rule of reason. We now turn to examine the development of these approaches in greater detail.

Figure 2–1:
Alternate Forms of Original Sherman Act Rules (1890–1927)

Two Approaches to Per Se Condemnation

Trans-Missouri Freight: **The Literal Per Se Rule**

- "every" restraint of trade is unlawful [*no longer relevant*]

Addyston Pipe: **Judge Taft's Per Se Rule**

- no purpose/effect other than restraint
- not related to any legitimate main purpose

Two Approaches to the Rule of Reason

Standard Oil/Chicago Bd. of Trade: **Unstructured Rule of Reason**

- look to purpose, nature, and effect of restraint

Addyston Pipe: **Judge Taft's Limited Rule of Reason**

- only ancillary restraints can be justified as reasonable

B. THE EVOLUTION OF THE PER SE BAN ON PRICE–FIXING BY COMPETITORS

Although the per se approaches outlined in *Trans-Missouri Freight* and *Addyston Pipe* proceeded in different ways, they shared a common hostility to agreements by competitors to fix prices. Such agreements did not require sophisticated economic analysis to warrant suspicion, particularly when they were undertaken by firms who appeared collectively to possess market power. The predictable motivation was profits above the competitive level; the predictable consequences included less output and higher prices for consumers, and a transfer of consumer wealth from consumers to producers, as we explored in Chapter 1.

As we shall see, hostility to price fixing by competitors became more formalized after *Standard Oil*, and is embodied in a per se rule that the Supreme Court began to create in 1927 and that became well-settled by 1945. This per se rule was then extended to variants of price fixing, such as agreements to restrict output, agreements to divide markets, and collusive group boycotts. Each of these will be examined, in turn.

1. FOUNDATION CASES: *TRENTON POTTERIES* AND *SOCONY-VACUUM OIL*

In *United States v. Trenton Potteries Co.*, 273 U.S. 392 (1927), the Supreme Court reviewed the criminal convictions under the Sherman Act of twenty-three producers and twenty individuals charged with fixing the prices of "sanitary pottery"—bathroom fixtures. There was no dispute that the producers had, through their trade association, fixed prices. Neither was there any dispute that they together accounted for 82% of the production of bathroom fixtures in the United States. While conceding these facts, the defendants responded that the prices they had set were "reasonable." Although the identical defense had been rejected in *Trans-Missouri Freight*, the defendants urged that *Standard Oil* and *Chicago Bd. of Trade* had reopened the door to broad based defenses based upon "reasonableness."

The Court rejected the approach, at least as it related to the treatment of price fixing under the Sherman Act:

> The aim and result of every price-fixing agreement, if effective, is the elimination of one form of competition. The power to fix prices, whether reasonably exercised or not, involves power to control the market and to fix arbitrary and unreasonable prices. The reasonable price fixed today may through economic and business changes become the unreasonable price of to-morrow. Once established, it may be maintained unchanged because of the absence of competition secured by the agreement for a price reasonable when fixed. Agreements which create such potential power may well be held to be in themselves unreasonable or unlawful restraints, without the necessity of minute inquiry whether a particular price is reasonable or unreasonable as fixed and without placing on the government in enforcing the Sherman Law the burden of ascertaining from day to day whether it has become unreasonable through the mere variation of economic conditions. Moreover, in the absence of express legislation requiring it, we should hesitate to adopt a construction making the difference between legal and illegal conduct in the field of business relations depend upon so uncertain a test as whether prices are reasonable—a determination which can be satisfactorily made only after a complete survey of our economic organization and a choice between rival philosophies.

Trenton Potteries, 273 U.S. at 397–98. Quoting from its previous opinion in *Standard Oil*, the Court then went on to reject the defendants's argument that *Standard Oil* had effectively overruled *Joint Traffic Ass'n*:

> That the opinions in the *Standard Oil* and *Tobacco* Cases were not intended to affect this view of the illegality of price-fixing agreements affirmatively appears from the opinion in the *Standard Oil* Case, where, in considering the *Freight Association* Case, the court said:

>> That as considering the contracts or agreements, their necessary effect and the character of the parties by whom they were made, they were clearly restraints of trade within the purview of the statute, they could not be taken out of that category by indulging in general reasoning as to the expediency or nonexpediency of having made the contracts or the wisdom or want of wisdom of the statute which prohibited their being made; that is to say, the cases but decided that the nature and character of the contracts, creating as they did a conclusive presumption which brought them within the statute, such result was not to be disregarded by the substitution of a judicial appreciation of what the law ought to be for the plain judicial duty of enforcing the law as it was made.

Id. at 399–400.

Although *Standard Oil* may have rejected *Trans-Missouri Freight's* literal reading of Section 1 of the Sherman Act, in the Court's view it had not altered *Trans-Missouri Freight's* underlying view that price fixing by competitors should be treated harshly. But does *Trenton Potteries* endorse use of a per se rule? If so, is the rule akin to that proposed in *Addyston Pipe*? Did the Court look merely to the fact of the agreement? Did it go further and consider evidence of its actual effects?

Consider the Court's statement that "[a]greements which *create such potential power* may well be held to be *in themselves* unreasonable or unlawful restraints." "In themselves" seems to be an endorsement of a per se rule against price fixing. Less clear until our next case, *Socony-Vacuum Oil*, was whether application of the per se rule was limited to cases of market power and actual anticompetitive effects. In addition to its reference to agreements creating "such potential power," the Court also stated that "uniform price fixing *by those controlling in any substantial manner a trade or business* in interstate commerce is prohibited by the Sherman Law, despite the reasonableness of the particular prices agreed upon." *Id.* at 398. If the per se rule applies only when the colluding firms possess market power and actually succeed in raising prices, how truly "per se" was the Court's approach? We will explore these questions in our next case, *Socony-Vacuum Oil*, after reflecting on the role of antitrust law during the Great Depression.

Note on Antitrust Law Developments During the Great Depression

Trenton Potteries appeared firmly to establish that price fixing by competitors was per se unlawful, and it did so by creating an irrebuttable presumption of unreasonableness. Evidence of the purported reasonableness of such agreements would simply not be heard. But just two years after the decision, the Nation's economy began its plunge into the Great Depression. Industry after industry experienced "distress" conditions, characterized by steep price cutting and shrinking production.

Perhaps not surprisingly, the Great Depression led to a number of developments relevant to antitrust. Critics of competition called for government intervention to stabilize prices and halt the continuing de-stabilization of the economy. Congress responded in June 1933 with the National Industrial Recovery Act, 48 Stat. 195 ("NIRA"), which led to the creation of codes of "fair competition" negotiated by the firms in many industries, and authorized the President to act in response to distress conditions in particular industries. Our next case, *Socony-Vacuum Oil*, arose directly from efforts to organize the petroleum industry under the NIRA during the short period before the entire Act was declared unconstitutional by the Supreme Court. *See A.L.A. Schecter Poultry Corp. v. United States,* 295 U.S. 495 (1935).

Even before the passage of the NIRA, however, some parties took matters into their own hands, often encouraged by state and local officials. In *Appalachian Coals, Inc. v. United States,* 288 U.S. 344 (1933), just six years after *Trenton Potteries* appeared to establish an inflexible rule against price fixing by competitors, the Supreme Court rejected the government's attempt to enjoin the creation of an exclusive, joint selling agency by 137 Appalachian producers of bituminous coal. The producers, in response to what the district court termed "deplorable conditions resulting from overexpansion, destructive competition, wasteful trade practices, and the inroads of competing industries," 288 U.S. at 359, sought the

Justice Department's approval of the creation of an exclusive, joint selling agent. The agent, which the producers had created, and through which they agreed to sell all of their production, would negotiate all sales on behalf of its shareholders, whose collective share of the market was reported to be somewhere between 12 and 74%, depending upon how broadly it was defined. *Id.* at 357. In structure, the sales agency looked much like the classic trusts—a new entity was created to handle all sales, and the defendant producers owned all of its capital stock in proportion to their production. *Id.* at 357–58.

According to the Supreme Court, the producers insisted that "the primary purpose of the formation of the selling agency was to increase the sale, and thus the production, of Appalachian coal through better methods of distribution, intensive advertising and research, to achieve economies in marketing, and to eliminate abnormal, deceptive, and destructive trade practices." *Id.* at 359. The Court continued:

> Defendants contend that the evidence establishes that the selling agency will not have the power to dominate or fix the price of coal in any consuming market; that the price of coal will continue to be set in an open and competitive market; and that their plan by increasing the sale of bituminous coal from Appalachian territory will promote, rather than restrain, interstate commerce.

Id. The government argued in response, and the district court agreed, that although the selling agency would not lead to "monopoly control of any market nor the power to fix monopoly prices," it nevertheless "will * * * have a tendency to stabilize prices and to raise prices to a higher level than would prevail under conditions of free competition." *Id.*

Nevertheless, the Supreme Court turned to *Chicago Bd. of Trade*, not *Trenton Potteries*, and upheld the agency agreement as reasonable. Noting that "wherever their selling agency operates, it will find itself confronted by effective competition backed by virtually inexhaustive sources of supply, and will also be compelled to cope with the organized buying power of large consumers," the Court appeared to differ with the district court regarding its prediction that the agency would "stabilize" and raise prices on two grounds. First, it noted that there was no "monopolistic menace." The high figure of 74% used to describe the defendants' market share was a measure of their share of bituminous coal production in Appalachia—but most of their sales were made elsewhere, which meant that their ability to control prices was limited. "The plan cannot be said either to contemplate or involve the fixing of *market* prices." 288 U.S. at 373 (emphasis added). On this ground, the Court distinguished *Trenton Potteries*, pointing out that there the defendants had the power to set market prices, because they "controlled 82 per cent. of the business of manufacturing and distributing vitreous pottery in the United States." *Id.* at 375.

Undeniably, however, the Court was also greatly influenced by the conditions in the industry. Appearing to concede that some effect on prices might result from the agreement, the Court concluded that "the evidence fails to show * * * that any effect will be produced *which in the circumstances of this industry* will be detrimental to fair competition." *Id.* (emphasis added). The Court explained:

> The evidence leaves no doubt of the existence of the evils at which defendants' plan was aimed. The industry was in distress. It suffered from overexpansion and from a serious relative decline through the growing use of substitute fuels. It was afflicted by injurious practices within itself-practices which demanded correction. If evil conditions could

not be entirely cured, they at least might be alleviated. The unfortunate state of the industry would not justify any attempt unduly to restrain competition or to monopolize, but the existing situation prompted defendants to make, and the statute did not preclude them from making, an honest effort to remove abuses, to make competition fairer, and thus to promote the essential interests of commerce. The interests of producers and consumers are interlinked. When industry is greviously [sic] hurt, when producing concerns fail, when unemployment mounts and communities dependent upon profitable production are prostrated, the wells of commerce go dry. So far as actual purposes are concerned, the conclusion of the court below was amply supported that defendants were engaged in a fair and open endeavor to aid the industry in a measurable recovery from its plight.

Id. at 372.

Is the Court's application of the rule of reason consistent with *Chicago Bd. of Trade*? Is it subject to the kind of criticisms Judge Taft leveled in *Addyston Pipe*? Was the Court now "setting sail on a sea of doubt"? How important was it to the Court's conclusion that the agency arrangement had yet to take effect? How did that fact affect the evidence it was able to consider? How important was the Court's perception that the producers lacked the ability seriously to affect market prices? Wasn't affecting market prices a critical goal of the arrangement in the first place? Do you find the Court's basis for distinguishing *Trenton Potteries* persuasive? Were there other grounds of distinction that could be argued?

————

Trenton Potteries and *Appalachian Coals* together appeared to hold that the per se rule was most appropriate when the defendants controlled "in any substantial manner a trade or business in interstate commerce," *i.e.*, they were in a position to exercise market power. But as we shall see in our next case, *Socony-Vacuum Oil*, just seven years after *Appalachian Coals* the Court appeared to reject any limitation on the per se rule for horizontal price fixing based on the effect of the agreement or the market share or market power of the firms involved, making the prohibition unequivocal.

UNITED STATES v. SOCONY–VACUUM OIL CO.

Supreme Court of the United States, 1940.
310 U.S. 150, 60 S.Ct. 811, 84 L.Ed. 1129.

[As noted in the text, *Socony-Vacuum Oil* also arose out of the economic upheaval of the Great Depression, but it was a more direct consequence of federal government efforts to organize industries and stabilize prices pursuant to the NIRA. After the authority to do so under NIRA was removed by the courts, the defendants, major oil companies, continued their organizing efforts through various means.

In a criminal indictment, the government charged that among those means were two concerted gasoline buying programs that were designed to and had the effect of limiting the output and raising the price of gasoline in the mid-western United States. Figure 2–2 depicts the levels of distribution in the industry. Gasoline production and sales involved four steps: (1) exploration and drilling; (2) refining; (3) distribution; and (4) retail sale. Only the major oil companies were fully integrated and performed all four functions. "Independents" were also engaged in refining, but sold their output to "jobbers," who acted as distributors. The major oil companies also sold to the jobbers, who supplied roughly 50% of the retail gasoline stations in the Mid-Western area.

Independents sold to jobbers at "spot" market prices that constantly fluctuated; in contrast, the integrated firms sold to jobbers pursuant to long term contracts, but those contracts tied sale prices to spot market prices through a negotiated formula. As a consequence, deteriorating spot market prices due to increased supply from independents had a downward effect on all wholesale pricing.

The challenged agreements focused on the purchase of this surplus ("distress") gasoline from independent refiners, who accounted for virtually all of the gasoline sold in tank car quantities on the "spot market" in the Mid-Western area. Such sales amounted to less than 5% of all gasoline marketed there, but they produced a significant downward pressure on prices. The agreements orchestrated by the integrated major oil companies set up an informal system, termed "gentlemen's agreements," whereby each of the majors would select one or more independents with distress gasoline as a "dancing partner." It would then assume responsibility for purchasing its partner's distress supply. Because the majors had more substantial storage facilities than the independents, they could then hold the purchased surplus gasoline off of the market. Doing so had the effect of raising spot market prices, and ultimately stabilizing and raising prices market-wide. There was evidence that the defendants collectively shared a very substantial share of the market and that as a consequence of their actions prices actually increased. Eds.]

Figure 2–2:

The Structure of the Gasoline Industry in *Socony-Vacuum Oil*

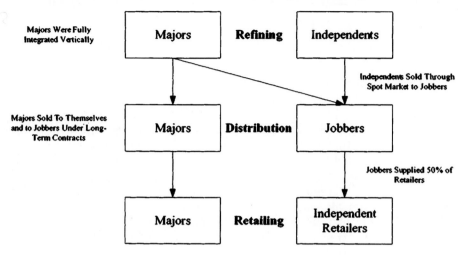

Mr. Justice DOUGLAS delivered the opinion of the Court.

* * *

III.   THE ALLEGED CONSPIRACY.

* * *

As a result of these buying programs it was hoped and intended that both the tank car and the retail markets would improve. The conclusion is irresistible that defendants' purpose was not merely to raise the spot market prices but, as the real and ultimate end, to raise the price of gasoline in their sales to jobbers and consumers in the Mid–Western area. Their agreement or plan embraced not only buying on the spot markets but also, at least by clear implication, an understanding to maintain such improvements in Mid–Western prices as would result from those purchases of distress gasoline. The latter obviously would be achieved by selling at the increased prices, not by price cutting. * * * In essence the raising and maintenance of the spot market prices were but the means adopted for raising and maintaining prices to jobbers and consumers.

* * *

V.   APPLICATION OF THE SHERMAN ACT.

* * *

The [district] court charged the jury that it was a violation of the Sherman Act for a group of individuals or corporations to act together to raise the prices to be charged for the commodity which they manufactured where they controlled a substantial part of the interstate trade and commerce in that commodity. The court stated that where the members of a combination had the power to raise prices and acted together for that purpose, the combination was illegal; and that it was immaterial how reasonable or unreasonable those prices were or to what extent they had been affected by the combination. It further charged that if such illegal combination existed, it did not matter that there may also have been other factors which contributed to the raising of the prices.

* * *

The Circuit Court of Appeals held this charge to be reversible error, since it was based upon the theory that such a combination was illegal *per se*. In its view respondents' activities were not unlawful unless they constituted an unreasonable restraint of trade. Hence, since that issue had not been submitted to the jury and since evidence bearing on it had been excluded, that court reversed and remanded for a new trial so that the character of those activities and their effect on competition could be determined. In answer to the government's petition respondents here contend that the judgment of the Circuit Court of Appeals was correct, since there was evidence that they had affected prices only in the sense that the removal of the competitive evil of distress gasoline by the buying programs had permitted prices to rise to a normal competitive level; that their activities promoted rather than impaired fair competitive opportunities; and therefore that their activities had not unduly or unreasonably restrained trade.

* * *

In *United States v. Trenton Potteries Co.*, this Court sustained a conviction under the Sherman Act where the jury was charged that an agreement on the part of the members of a combination, controlling a substantial part of an industry, upon the prices which the members are to charge for their commodity is in itself an unreasonable restraint of trade without regard to the reasonableness of the prices or the good intentions of the combining units. * * * This Court reviewed the various price-fixing cases under the Sherman Act and said " * * * it has since often been decided and always assumed that uniform price-fixing by those controlling in any substantial manner a trade or business in interstate commerce is prohibited by the Sherman Law, despite the reasonableness of the particular prices agreed upon." This Court pointed out that the so-called "rule of reason" announced in *Standard Oil* and in *American Tobacco* had not affected this view of the illegality of price-fixing agreements.

* * *

Respondents seek to distinguish the *Trenton Potteries* case from the instant one. They assert that in that case the parties substituted an agreed-on price for one determined by competition; that the defendants there had the power and purpose to suppress the play of competition in the determination of the market price; and therefore that the controlling factor in that decision was the destruction of market competition, not whether prices were higher or lower, reasonable or unreasonable. * * *

But we do not deem those distinctions material.

In the first place, there was abundant evidence that the combination had the purpose to raise prices. And likewise, there was ample evidence that the buying programs at least contributed to the price rise and the stability of the spot markets, and to increases in the price of gasoline sold in the Mid–Western area during the indictment period. * * * Proof that there was a conspiracy, that its purpose was to raise prices, and that it caused or contributed to a price rise is proof of the actual consummation or execution of a conspiracy under § 1 of the Sherman Act.

Secondly, the fact that sales on the spot markets were still governed by some competition is of no consequence. For it is indisputable that that competition was restricted through the removal by respondents of a part of the supply which but for the buying programs would have been a factor in determining the going prices on those markets.

* * *

The elimination of so-called competitive evils is no legal justification for such buying programs. The elimination of such conditions was sought primarily for its effect on the price structures. Fairer competitive prices, it is claimed, resulted when distress gasoline was removed from the market. But such defense is typical of the protestations usually made in price-fixing cases. Ruinous competition, financial disaster, evils of price cutting and the like appear throughout our history as ostensible justifications for price-fixing. If the so-called competitive abuses were to be appraised here, the reasonableness of prices would necessarily become an issue in every price-fixing case. In that event the Sherman Act would soon be emasculated; its philosophy would be supplanted by one which is wholly alien to a system of free competition; it would not be the charter of freedom which its framers intended.

The reasonableness of prices has no constancy due to the dynamic quality of the business facts underlying price structures. Those who fixed reasonable prices today would perpetuate unreasonable prices tomorrow, since those prices would not be subject to continuous administrative supervision and readjustment in light of changed conditions. Those who controlled the prices would control or effectively dominate the market. And those who were in that strategic position would have it in their power to destroy or drastically impair the competitive system. But the thrust of the rule is deeper and reaches more than monopoly power. Any combination which tampers with price structures is engaged in an unlawful activity. Even though the members of the price-fixing group were in no position to control the market, to the extent that they raised, lowered, or stabilized prices they would be directly interfering with the free play of market forces. The Act places all such schemes beyond the pale and protects that vital part of our economy against any degree of interference. Congress has not left with us the determination of whether or not particular price-fixing schemes are wise or unwise, healthy or destructive. It has not permitted the age-old cry of ruinous competition and competitive evils to be a defense to price-fixing conspiracies. It has no more allowed genuine or fancied competitive abuses as a legal justification for such schemes than it has the good intentions of the members of the combination. If such a shift is to be made, it must be done by the Congress.

* * *

Nor is it important that the prices paid by the combination were not fixed in the sense that they were uniform and inflexible. Price-fixing as used in the

Trenton Potteries case has no such limited meaning. * * * Hence, prices are fixed within the meaning of the *Trenton Potteries* case if the range within which purchases or sales will be made is agreed upon, if the prices paid or charged are to be at a certain level or on ascending or descending scales, if they are to be uniform, or if by various formulae they are related to the market prices. They are fixed because they are agreed upon. And the fact that, as here, they are fixed at the fair going market price is immaterial.

* * *

Under the Sherman Act a combination formed for the purpose and with the effect of raising, depressing, fixing, pegging, or stabilizing the price of a commodity in interstate or foreign commerce is illegal per se. Where the machinery for price-fixing is an agreement on the prices to be charged or paid for the commodity * * * the power to fix prices exists if the combination has control of a substantial part of the commerce in that commodity. Where the means for price-fixing are purchases or sales of the commodity in a market operation or, as here, purchases of a part of the supply of the commodity for the purpose of keeping it from having a depressive effect on the markets, such power may be found to exist though the combination does not control a substantial part of the commodity. In such a case that power may be established if as a result of market conditions, the resources available to the combinations, the timing and the strategic placement of orders and the like, effective means are at hand to accomplish the desired objective. But there may be effective influence over the market though the group in question does not control it. Price-fixing agreements may have utility to members of the group though the power possessed or exerted falls far short of domination and control. Monopoly power * * * is not the only power which the Act strikes down, as we have said. Proof that a combination was formed for the purpose of fixing prices and that it caused them to be fixed or contributed to that result is proof of the completion of a price-fixing conspiracy under § 1 of the Act.[59] The indictment in this case charged that this combination had that purpose and effect. And there was abundant evidence to support it. Hence the

---

59. Under this indictment proof that prices in the Mid–Western area were raised as a result of the activities of the combination was essential, since sales of gasoline by respondents at the increased prices in that area were necessary in order to establish jurisdiction. * * * But that does not mean that both a purpose and a power to fix prices are necessary for the establishment of a conspiracy under § 1 of the Sherman Act. * * * [I]t is well established that a person "may be guilty of conspiring, although incapable of committing the objective offense." In view of these considerations a conspiracy to fix prices violates § 1 of the Act though no overt act is shown, though it is not established that the conspirators had the means available for accomplishment of their objective, and though the conspiracy embraced but a part of the interstate or foreign commerce in the commodity. * * * Price-fixing agreements may or may not be aimed at complete elimination of price competition. The group making those agreements may or may

not have power to control the market. But the fact that the group cannot control the market prices does not necessarily mean that the agreement as to prices has no utility to the members of the combination. The effectiveness of price-fixing agreements is dependent on many factors, such as competitive tactics, position in the industry, the formula underlying price policies. Whatever economic justification particular price-fixing agreements may be thought to have, the law does not permit an inquiry into their reasonableness. They are all banned because of their actual or potential threat to the central nervous system of the economy. * * *

The existence or exertion of power to accomplish the desired objective * * * becomes important only in cases where the offense charged is the actual monopolizing of any part of trade or commerce in violation of § 2 of the Act. * * * An intent and a power to produce the result which the law condemns are then necessary.

existence of power on the part of members of the combination to fix prices was but a conclusion from the finding that the buying programs caused or contributed to the rise and stability of prices.

* * *

Socony-Vacuum Oil settled the status of price fixing by competitors as unlawful under Section 1 of the Sherman Act, definitively placing it in the per se category. It did not matter that the mechanism was restriction of output, as opposed to fixing a price, because, as we learned in Chapter 1, lower industry output and higher industry prices go hand in hand. Moreover, in famous footnote 59, the Court strongly suggested that price fixing by competitors should be treated harshly regardless of the market power of the price fixers, an apparent contradiction with its basis for distinguishing Trenton Potteries in Appalachian Coals.

The Court also declared that "[t]he elimination of so-called competitive evils is no legal justification for such buying programs." 310 U.S. at 220. Can this statement, coupled with the Court's view that the market power of the price fixers does not affect application of the per se rule, be reconciled with Appalachian Coals? Did it effectively overrule it? See Virginia Excelsior Mills, Inc. v. FTC, 256 F.2d 538, 541 (4th Cir.1958)(suggesting that Appalachian Coals was effectively overruled by Socony-Vacuum Oil and other subsequent pronouncements on price fixing).

Should Socony-Vacuum Oil be viewed narrowly, in part as a product of its historical context? Recall that just five years earlier, the Court had categorically rejected the National Industrial Recovery Act ("NIRA"), a cornerstone of the Roosevelt Administration's New Deal program, in A.L.A. Schechter Poultry Corp. v. United States, 295 U.S. 495 (1935). The NIRA sought to encourage the formation of industry "fair competition codes" in response to the Great Depression. Is the Court merely reemphasizing in Socony Vacuum Oil that it will not endorse efforts, either public or private, to create exceptions to competition? Could historical context also explain Appalachian Coals, which pre-dated adoption of the NIRA? Are the two decisions "irreconcilable"? Do they reflect shifting views on the Court about government and private efforts to regulate the economy?

Sidebar 2–1:
Defining and Justifying the Contemporary Per Se Rule

Having read about the foundation cases that endorsed abbreviated analysis of patently anticompetitive agreements, it is useful to pause and ask "what is the per se rule?" That question, which will be explored further as this Chapter unfolds, can be addressed from both *legal* and *economic* points of view.

What is the per se rule legally?

In its purest form, the per se rule reduces the Section 1 inquiry to whether the defendants engaged in a "contract, combination or conspiracy" and whether that agreement falls into a recognized per se category, such as price-fixing or market division. Once such an agreement is proved, if a per se rule applies the anticompetitive effect is presumed. At that point, all defenses, *i.e.*, attempts to demonstrate "reasonableness," are precluded.

One way to look at the per se rule is as a rule of evidence, as opposed to one of substantive antitrust law. When sufficient indicia of anticompetitive potential are present, they can give rise to an irrebuttable presumption of unreasonableness. But what are those indicia, and how much evidence must be established in order to trigger the presumption?

A more searching analysis of the per se cases reveals that, although the courts surely viewed themselves as applying a rule of facial invalidity—at least with respect to agreements among competitors—the cases themselves frequently involved well-developed records. Note for example that in *Trenton Potteries* the Court observed that the alleged conspirators had a very substantial market share, an indication that they were well able collectively to raise prices. In *Socony-Vacuum Oil*, too, the Court had very extensive evidence of the alleged practice's impact on industry output and price. Yet, in its famous footnote 59, the Court disavowed reliance on actual market effect as a prerequisite for invocation of the per se rule. These are not the only prominent cases in which the per se rule has been successfully invoked in the presence of some evidence of harm to competition beyond just the nature of the agreement itself.

Because of this reality, as well as many other anomalies in the cases, Professor Thomas Krattenmaker has argued that there are no truly per se "offenses" under the antitrust laws; instead, he maintained, antitrust has identified certain *defenses*, such as "reasonable prices," as per se inadmissable. *See* Thomas G. Krattenmaker, *Per Se Violations in Antitrust Law: Confusing Offenses With Defenses*, 77 GEO. L.J. 165 (1988). What is the practical consequence of characterizing the per se rule as one that precludes certain defenses, as opposed to one that identifies certain offenses as indefensible? Another commentator maintained that "in the modern context" the per se rule describes conduct that is "inherently suspect because it appears highly likely, absent an efficiency justification, to decrease the output of the collaborators or to increase their price." Timothy J. Muris, *The New Rule of Reason*, 57 ANTITRUST L.J. 859, 861 (1989). As you read the cases in this chapter, consider which of these approaches best describes the Court's actions, and what the consequences of the various approaches might be for allocating burdens of production and proof in the cases.

What is the per se rule economically?

The per se rule reflects a judgment that the costs of identifying exceptions to the general rule so far outweigh the costs of occasionally condemning conduct that might upon further inspection prove to be acceptable, that it is preferable not to entertain defenses to the conduct at all. Hence per se rules have long been justified on the ground that certain kinds of conduct are so likely to prove to be unreasonably anticompetitive that time spent considering defenses would be time wasted. From the point of view of administrative convenience and judicial efficacy, therefore, the search for the exceptional case—the truly "reasonable" instance of such conduct—is not worth the cost of investigation. Also, it was argued that per se rules provided unambiguous guidance to courts and the business community. Bright line rules meant, for better or worse, that the law was relatively clear and compliance was easy. As the Supreme Court put it in 1958:

> * * * [T]here are certain agreements or practices which because of their pernicious effect on competition and lack of any redeeming virtue are conclusively presumed to be unreasonable and therefore illegal without elaborate inquiry as to the precise harm they have caused or the business excuse for their use. This principle of per se unreasonableness not only makes the type of restraints which are proscribed by the Sherman Act more certain to the benefit of everyone concerned, but it also avoids the necessity for an incredibly complicated and prolonged economic investigation into the entire industry involved, as well as related industries, in an effort to determine at large whether a particular restraint has been unreasonable—an inquiry so often wholly fruitless when undertaken.

Northern Pac. Ry. Co. v. United States, 356 U.S. 1, 5 (1958).

Accordingly, per se rules make the most economic sense when factors like the following are present:

- if permitted, the prohibited conduct will likely harm competition severely;

- if the conduct is reviewed for reasonableness rather than held illegal per se, defendants will frequently claim that their conduct is reasonable, it will be costly and time-consuming to evaluate those claims, and in the end, few such claims will prove to be valid; and

- little pro-competitive conduct will be deterred by establishing a rule that denies defendants the ability to prove that their conduct was reasonable.

As the Supreme Court explained in *FTC v. Superior Court Trial Lawyers Ass'n*, 493 U.S. 411, 433–34 (1990):

> The *per se* rules in antitrust law serve purposes analogous to *per se* restrictions upon, for example, stunt flying in congested areas or speeding. Laws prohibiting stunt flying or setting speed limits are justified by the State's interest in protecting human life and property. Perhaps most violations of such rules actually cause no harm. No doubt many experienced drivers and pilots can operate much more safely, even at prohibited speeds, than the average citizen. * * * Yet the laws may nonetheless be enforced against these skilled persons without proof that their conduct was actually harmful or dangerous.

> In part, the justification for these *per se* rules is rooted in administrative convenience. They are also supported, however, by the observation that every speeder and every stunt pilot poses some threat to the community. * * *

* * * Every * * * horizontal arrangement among competitors [that falls within the per se prohibition] poses some threat to the free market. A small participant in the market is, obviously, less likely to cause persistent damage than a large participant. Other participants in the market may act quickly and effectively to take the small participant's place. For reasons including market inertia and information failures, however, a small conspirator may be able to impede competition over some period of time. Given an appropriate set of circumstances and some luck, the period can be long enough to inflict real injury upon particular consumers or competitors.

So it is with price fixing by competitors. The consequences can be quite severe, as we saw in Chapter 1 when we considered the behavior of the lysine and vitamin cartels and the coffee suppliers. Successful price fixing conspiracies can lead to very significant inefficiencies and transfers of wealth. On the other hand, truly "reasonable" instances of competitors fixing prices may be rare—but the cost of identifying them judicially could be substantial. In short, the social costs of condemning the rare instance of "reasonable" price fixing will likely be far outweighed by the benefits of a bright line prohibition. Those benefits include certainty—firms can readily discern the line between acceptable and unacceptable business behavior—and deterrence—instances of objectionable price fixing can be minimized. As one commentator has observed:

> From a law and economics perspective, per se rules may be preferred to a rule of reason when violations are expensive for a court to observe but are strongly correlated with observable behaviors that are cheaply observed, and when it would be expensive for a violator to break the law without engaging in the observable behavior. Under such circumstances, the judicial system would minimize enforcement costs by conditioning liability on the cheaply observable behavior, and the resulting enforcement errors, corporate compliance costs, and social costs of deterring socially beneficial actions, would not produce an efficiency loss.*

Hence, when the defendants in *Trenton Potteries* argued to the Court that the rates they had agreed to were "reasonable," the Court refused to entertain their argument as a defense to price fixing. That reflected a presumption that the benefits of permitting such a defense are far outweighed by their costs, because they will be difficult to verify and are so unlikely to prove to be valid.

As we proceed through the Chapter, consider how the "per se" rule has evolved. How is it used and when? How much and what kind of evidence is present when it is invoked? Under what circumstances is it triggered simply

---

* Jonathan B. Baker, *Per Se Rules in the Antitrust Analysis of Horizontal Restraints*, 36 ANTITRUST BULL. 733, 740 n.29 (1991). *See also* F.M. SCHERER & DAVID ROSS, INDUSTRIAL MARKET STRUCTURE AND ECONOMIC PERFORMANCE 335–39 (3d ed. 1990)(discussing rationale for per se prohibition of price fixing); C. Frederick Beckner III & Steven C. Salop, *Decision Theory and Antitrust Rules*, 67 ANTITRUST L.J. 41 (1999)(proposing decision theoretic model to guide process of fact-gathering, decision-making, and rule choice in antitrust cases).

by demonstrating the presence of a particular kind of pernicious agreement? Under what kinds of conditions has the Court declined to invoke it, and why?

2. RULE OF REASON OR PER SE: TENSIONS EMERGE IN THE MODERN TREATMENT OF PRICE–FIXING

The breadth of the Court's decision in *Socony–Vacuum Oil* and its seemingly unequivocal condemnation of all manner of price-fixing posed more challenging questions for antitrust doctrine. The discussion of price fixing in *Socony-Vacuum Oil* seemed to leave little room—and no rationale—for justifying common arrangements such as partnerships and joint ventures, that "fix" prices as an incident to their integration. Thereafter, proof of a price fixing agreement alone arguably was sufficient to establish an offense under Section 1, and the only practical hope of avoiding condemnation was to have the challenged conduct classified as something other than "price fixing." This could be a difficult task, as "price-fixing" was construed broadly. For example, in 1965 the FTC challenged an agreement among rivals to reduce product quality—which could have the effect of lowering the price that the firms paid for a key production input or raising the effective (quality-adjusted) price of their output—as being within the per se prohibition of *Socony*, even though the firms never discussed price. *Nat'l Macaroni Mfrs. Ass'n v. FTC*, 345 F.2d 421 (7th Cir.1965).

Socony-Vacuum Oil thus planted the seed of necessity that led nearly forty years later to our next case, which illustrates a very successful attempt to do just that—reclassify literal price fixing as something else. Consider carefully, however, the Court's reasons for doing so, and the prior cases that might support its departure from an arguably dogmatic approach to price fixing. What rationale prompts the Court to de-classify the blanket licensing arrangement challenged in *Broadcast Music, Inc. v. Columbia Broadcasting System, Inc.*, 441 U.S. 1 (1979) as "price-fixing" and what are its broader implications for antitrust analysis?

Another aspect of *Socony-Vacuum Oil*'s legacy is evident in the tension between *Broadcast Music* and the case that immediately follows it, *Arizona v. Maricopa County Medical Society*. There, just three years after *Broadcast Music*, the Court returned to seemingly harsh language condemning price fixing. The consequent tension between *Broadcast Music* and *Maricopa* persists to this day, and can be directly traced to *Socony-Vacuum Oil*. Can the three decisions be reconciled?

BROADCAST MUSIC, INC. v. COLUMBIA BROADCASTING SYSTEM, INC.

Supreme Court of the United States, 1979.
441 U.S. 1, 99 S.Ct. 1551, 60 L.Ed.2d 1.

Mr. Justice WHITE delivered the opinion of the Court.

This case involves an action under the antitrust and copyright laws brought by respondent Columbia Broadcasting System, Inc. (CBS), against petitioners, American Society of Composers, Authors and Publishers (ASCAP) and Broadcast Music, Inc. (BMI), and their members and affiliates. * * * The basic question presented is whether the issuance by ASCAP and BMI to CBS of blanket licenses to copyrighted musical compositions at fees negotiated by them is price fixing *per se* unlawful under the antitrust laws.

CBS operates one of three national commercial television networks, supplying programs to approximately 200 affiliated stations and telecasting approximately 7,500 network programs per year. Many, but not all, of these programs make use of copyrighted music recorded on the soundtrack. CBS also owns television and radio stations in various cities.

* * *

I

Since 1897, the copyright laws have vested in the owner of a copyrighted musical composition the exclusive right to perform the work publicly for profit * * * but the legal right is not self-enforcing. In 1914, Victor Herbert and a handful of other composers organized ASCAP because those who performed copyrighted music for profit were so numerous and widespread, and most performances so fleeting, that as a practical matter it was impossible for the many individual copyright owners to negotiate with and license the users and to detect unauthorized uses. * * * As ASCAP operates today, its 22,000 members grant it nonexclusive rights to license nondramatic performances of their works, and ASCAP issues licenses and distributes royalties to copyright owners in accordance with a schedule reflecting the nature and amount of the use of their music and other factors.

* * *

BMI, a nonprofit corporation owned by members of the broadcasting industry * * * was organized in 1939, [and] is affiliated with or represents some 10,000 publishing companies and 20,000 authors and composers, and operates in much the same manner as ASCAP. Almost every domestic copyrighted composition is in the repertory either of ASCAP, with a total of three million compositions, or of BMI, with one million.

Both organizations operate primarily through blanket licenses, which give the licensees the right to perform any and all of the compositions owned by the members or affiliates as often as the licensees desire for a stated term. Fees for blanket licenses are ordinarily a percentage of total revenues or a flat dollar amount, and do not directly depend on the amount or type of music used. Radio and television broadcasters are the largest users of music, and almost all of them hold blanket licenses from both ASCAP and BMI. Until this litigation, CBS held blanket licenses from both organizations for its television network on a continuous basis since the late 1940's and had never attempted to secure any other form of license from either ASCAP * * * or any of its members.

* * *

The complaint filed by CBS charged * * * that ASCAP and BMI are unlawful monopolies and that the blanket license is illegal price fixing, an unlawful tying arrangement, a concerted refusal to deal, and a misuse of copyrights. The District Court, though denying summary judgment to certain defendants, ruled that the practice did not fall within the *per se* rule. * * *

After an 8–week trial, limited to the issue of liability, the court dismissed the complaint, rejecting again the claim that the blanket license was price fixing and a *per se* violation of § 1 of the Sherman Act, and holding that since direct negotiation with individual copyright owners is available and feasible there is no undue restraint of trade. * * *

* * *

Though agreeing with the District Court's factfinding and not disturbing its legal conclusions on the other antitrust theories of liability * * * the Court of Appeals held that the blanket license issued to television networks was a form of price fixing illegal *per se* under the Sherman Act.

* * *

Because we disagree with the Court of Appeals' conclusions with respect to the *per se* illegality of the blanket license, we reverse its judgment and remand the cause for further appropriate proceedings.

II

In construing and applying the Sherman Act's ban against contracts, conspiracies, and combinations in restraint of trade, the Court has held that certain agreements or practices are so "plainly anticompetitive," and so often "lack ... any redeeming virtue," that they are conclusively presumed illegal without further examination under the rule of reason generally applied in Sherman Act cases. This *per se* rule is a valid and useful tool of antitrust policy and enforcement.[11] And agreements among competitors to fix prices on their individual goods or services are among those concerted activities that the Court has held to be within the *per se* category. But easy labels do not always supply ready answers.

A

To the Court of Appeals and CBS, the blanket license involves "price fixing" in the literal sense: the composers and publishing houses have joined together into an organization that sets its price for the blanket license it sells. But this is not a question simply of determining whether two or more potential competitors have literally "fixed" a "price." As generally used in the antitrust field, "price fixing" is a shorthand way of describing certain categories of business behavior to which the *per se* rule has been held applicable. The Court of Appeals' literal approach does not alone establish that this particular practice is one of those types or that it is "plainly anticompetitive" and very likely without "redeeming virtue." Literalness is overly simplistic and often overbroad. When two partners set the price of their goods or services they are literally "price fixing," but they are not *per se* in violation of the Sherman Act. *See United States v. Addyston Pipe & Steel Co.*, 85 F. 271, 280 (C.A.6 1898), *aff'd*, 175 U.S. 211, 20 S.Ct. 96, 44 L.Ed. 136 (1899). Thus, it is necessary to characterize the challenged conduct as falling within or

---

11. "This principle of per se unreasonableness not only makes the type of restraints which are proscribed by the Sherman Act more certain to the benefit of everyone concerned, but it also avoids the necessity for an incredibly complicated and prolonged economic investigation into the entire history of the industry involved, as well as related industries, in an effort to determine at large whether a particular restraint has been unreasonable—an inquiry so often wholly fruitless when undertaken." *Northern Pac. R. Co. v. United States.* * * *

without that category of behavior to which we apply the label *"per se* price fixing."* That will often, but not always, be a simple matter.

Consequently, * * * "[i]t is only after considerable experience with certain business relationships that courts classify them as *per se* violations...." We have never examined a practice like this one before. * * * And though there has been rather intensive antitrust scrutiny of ASCAP and its blanket licenses, that experience hardly counsels that we should outlaw the blanket license as a *per se* restraint of trade.

B

* * *

The Department of Justice first investigated allegations of anticompetitive conduct by ASCAP over 50 years ago. A criminal complaint was filed in 1934, but the Government was granted a midtrial continuance and never returned to the courtroom. In separate complaints in 1941, the United States charged that the blanket license, which was then the only license offered by ASCAP and BMI, was an illegal restraint of trade and that arbitrary prices were being charged as the result of an illegal copyright pool. The Government sought to enjoin ASCAP's exclusive licensing powers and to require a different form of licensing by that organization. The case was settled by a consent decree that imposed tight restrictions on ASCAP's operations. * * * [T]he 1941 decree was reopened and extensively amended in 1950.

Under the amended decree, which still substantially controls the activities of ASCAP, members may grant ASCAP only nonexclusive rights to license their works for public performance. Members, therefore, retain the rights individually to license public performances, along with the rights to license the use of their compositions for other purposes. ASCAP itself is forbidden to grant any license to perform one or more specified compositions in the ASCAP repertory unless both the user and the owner have requested it in writing to do so. ASCAP is required to grant to any user making written application a nonexclusive license to perform all ASCAP compositions either for a period of time or on a per-program basis. ASCAP may not insist on the blanket license, and the fee for the per-program license, which is to be based on the revenues for the program on which ASCAP music is played, must offer the applicant a genuine economic choice between the per-program license and the more common blanket license. * * *

The 1950 decree, as amended from time to time, continues in effect, and the blanket license continues to be the primary instrument through which ASCAP conducts its business under the decree. The courts have twice construed the decree not to require ASCAP to issue licenses for selected portions of its repertory. It also remains true that the decree guarantees the legal availability of direct licensing of performance rights by ASCAP members; and the District Court found, and in this respect the Court of Appeals agreed, that there are no practical impediments preventing direct dealing by the television networks if they so desire. Historically, they have not done so. Since 1946, CBS and other television networks have taken blanket licenses from ASCAP and BMI. It was not until this suit arose that the CBS network demanded any other kind of license.

* * * In these circumstances, we have a unique indicator that the challenged practice may have redeeming competitive virtues and that the search for those values is not almost sure to be in vain. Thus, although CBS is not bound by the Antitrust Division's actions, the decree is a fact of economic and legal life in this industry, and the Court of Appeals should not have ignored it completely in analyzing the practice. That fact alone might not remove a naked price-fixing scheme from the ambit of the *per se* rule, but * * * here we are uncertain whether the practice on its face has the effect, or could have been spurred by the purpose, of restraining competition among the individual composers.

* * *

III

* * *

As a preliminary matter, we are mindful that the Court of Appeals' holding would appear to be quite difficult to contain. If, as the court held, there is a *per se* antitrust violation whenever ASCAP issues a blanket license to a television network for a single fee, why would it not also be automatically illegal for ASCAP to negotiate and issue blanket licenses to individual radio or television stations or to other users who perform copyrighted music for profit? Likewise, if the present network licenses issued through ASCAP on behalf of its members are *per se* violations, why would it not be equally illegal for the members to authorize ASCAP to issue licenses establishing various categories of uses that a network might have for copyrighted music and setting a standard fee for each described use?

Although the Court of Appeals apparently thought the blanket license could be saved in some or even many applications, it seems to us that the *per se* rule does not accommodate itself to such flexibility and that the observations of the Court of Appeals with respect to remedy tend to impeach the *per se* basis for the holding of liability.[27]

CBS would prefer that ASCAP be authorized, indeed directed, to make all its compositions available at standard per-use rates within negotiated categories of use. But if this in itself or in conjunction with blanket licensing constitutes illegal price fixing by copyright owners, CBS urges that an injunction issue forbidding ASCAP to issue any blanket license or to negotiate any fee except on behalf of an individual member for the use of his own

---

27. * * * The Court of Appeals would apparently not outlaw the blanket license across the board but would permit it in various circumstances where it is deemed necessary or sufficiently desirable. It did not even enjoin blanket licensing with the television networks, the relief it realized would normally follow a finding of *per se* illegality of the license in that context. Instead, as requested by CBS, it remanded to the District Court to require ASCAP to offer in addition to blanket licensing some competitive form of per-use licensing. But per-use licensing by ASCAP, as recognized in the consent decrees, might be even more susceptible to the *per se* rule than blanket licensing.

The rationale for this unusual relief in a *per se* case was that "[t]he blanket license is not simply a 'naked restraint' ineluctably doomed to extinction." To the contrary, the Court of Appeals found that the blanket license might well "serve a market need" for some. *Ibid.* This, it seems to us, is not the *per se* approach, which does not yield so readily to circumstances, but in effect is a rather bobtailed application of the rule of reason, bobtailed in the sense that it is unaccompanied by the necessary analysis demonstrating why the particular licensing system is an undue competitive restraint.

copyrighted work or works. Thus, we are called upon to determine that blanket licensing is unlawful across the board. We are quite sure, however, that the *per se* rule does not require any such holding.

B

In the first place, the line of commerce allegedly being restrained, the performing rights to copyrighted music, exists at all only because of the copyright laws. Those who would use copyrighted music in public performances must secure consent from the copyright owner. * * * Furthermore, nothing in the Copyright Act of 1976 indicates in the slightest that Congress intended to weaken the rights of copyright owners to control the public performance of musical compositions. Quite the contrary is true. Although the copyright laws confer no rights on copyright owners to fix prices among themselves or otherwise to violate the antitrust laws, we would not expect that any market arrangements reasonably necessary to effectuate the rights that are granted would be deemed a *per se* violation of the Sherman Act. * * *

C

More generally, in characterizing this conduct under the *per se* rule[33] our inquiry must focus on whether the effect and, here because it tends to show effect, the purpose of the practice are to threaten the proper operation of our predominantly free-market economy—that is, whether the practice facially appears to be one that would always or almost always tend to restrict competition and decrease output, and in what portion of the market, or instead one designed to "increase economic efficiency and render markets more, rather than less, competitive."

The blanket license, as we see it, is not a "naked restrain[t] of trade with no purpose except stifling of competition," but rather accompanies the integration of sales, monitoring, and enforcement against unauthorized copyright use. As we have already indicated, ASCAP and the blanket license developed together out of the practical situation in the marketplace: thousands of users, thousands of copyright owners, and millions of compositions. Most users want unplanned, rapid, and indemnified access to any and all of the repertory of compositions, and the owners want a reliable method of collecting for the use of their copyrights. Individual sales transactions in this industry are quite expensive, as would be individual monitoring and enforcement, especially in light of the resources of single composers. Indeed, as both the Court of Appeals and CBS recognize, the costs are prohibitive for licenses with individual radio stations, nightclubs, and restaurants, and it was in that milieu that the blanket license arose.

A middleman with a blanket license was an obvious necessity if the thousands of individual negotiations, a virtual impossibility, were to be avoided. Also, individual fees for the use of individual compositions would presuppose an intricate schedule of fees and uses, as well as a difficult and expensive reporting problem for the user and policing task for the copyright owner. Historically, the market for public-performance rights organized itself

---

33. The scrutiny occasionally required must not merely subsume the burdensome analysis required under the rule of reason, or else we should apply the rule of reason from the start. That is why the *per se* rule is not employed until after considerable experience with the type of challenged restraint.

largely around the single-fee blanket license, which gave unlimited access to the repertory and reliable protection against infringement. * * *

With the advent of radio and television networks, market conditions changed, and the necessity for and advantages of a blanket license for those users may be far less obvious than is the case when the potential users are individual television or radio stations, or the thousands of other individuals and organizations performing copyrighted compositions in public. But even for television network licenses, ASCAP reduces costs absolutely by creating a blanket license that is sold only a few, instead of thousands, of times, and that obviates the need for closely monitoring the networks to see that they do not use more than they pay for. ASCAP also provides the necessary resources for blanket sales and enforcement, resources unavailable to the vast majority of composers and publishing houses. Moreover, a bulk license of some type is a necessary consequence of the integration necessary to achieve these efficiencies, and a necessary consequence of an aggregate license is that its price must be established.

D

This substantial lowering of costs, which is of course potentially beneficial to both sellers and buyers, differentiates the blanket license from individual use licenses. The blanket license is composed of the individual compositions plus the aggregating service. Here, the whole is truly greater than the sum of its parts; it is, to some extent, a different product. The blanket license has certain unique characteristics: It allows the licensee immediate use of covered compositions, without the delay of prior individual negotiations and great flexibility in the choice of musical material. * * * Thus, to the extent the blanket license is a different product, ASCAP is not really a joint sales agency offering the individual goods of many sellers, but is a separate seller offering its blanket license, of which the individual compositions are raw material.[40] ASCAP, in short, made a market in which individual composers are inherently unable to compete fully effectively.

E

Finally, we have some doubt—enough to counsel against application of the *per se* rule—about the extent to which this practice threatens the "central nervous system of the economy," that is, competitive pricing as the free market's means of allocating resources. Not all arrangements among actual or potential competitors that have an impact on price are *per se* violations of the Sherman Act or even unreasonable restraints. Mergers among competitors eliminate competition, including price competition, but they are not *per se* illegal, and many of them withstand attack under any existing antitrust standard. Joint ventures and other cooperative arrangements are also not usually unlawful, at least not as price-fixing schemes, where the agreement on price is necessary to market the product at all.

40. Moreover, because of the nature of the product—a composition can be simultaneously "consumed" by many users—composers have numerous markets and numerous incentives to produce, so the blanket license is unlikely to cause decreased output, one of the normal un- desirable effects of a cartel. And since popular songs get an increased share of ASCAP's revenue distributions, composers compete even within the blanket license in terms of productivity and consumer satisfaction.

Here, the blanket-license fee is not set by competition among individual copyright owners, and it is a fee for the use of any of the compositions covered by the license. But the blanket license cannot be wholly equated with a simple horizontal arrangement among competitors. ASCAP does set the price for its blanket license, but that license is quite different from anything any individual owner could issue. The individual composers and authors have neither agreed not to sell individually in any other market nor use the blanket license to mask price fixing in such other markets. Moreover, the substantial restraints placed on ASCAP and its members by the consent decree must not be ignored. The District Court found that there was no legal, practical, or conspiratorial impediment to CBS's obtaining individual licenses; CBS, in short, had a real choice.

With this background in mind, which plainly enough indicates that over the years, and in the face of available alternatives, the blanket license has provided an acceptable mechanism for at least a large part of the market for the performing rights to copyrighted musical compositions, we cannot agree that it should automatically be declared illegal in all of its many manifestations. Rather, when attacked, it should be subjected to a more discriminating examination under the rule of reason. It may not ultimately survive that attack, but that is not the issue before us today.

* * *

[The dissenting opinion of Mr. Justice Stevens is omitted. Eds.]

———————

What factors accounted for the Court's conclusion in *Broadcast Music* that the blanket license should be evaluated under the rule of reason, rather than the per se rule? Is its rationale convincing? Would the case have fallen comfortably into the per se category if ASCAP and Broadcast Music had together agreed on the prices each would charge for comparable blanket licenses?

Note that the Court remands the case for further proceedings under the rule of reason. Given the extent of the record in the case, as well as the Court's conclusions regarding the nature, purpose and effect of the blanket license, what was left for the Court of Appeals to do? Could it have reached any conclusion other than that the blanket license was reasonable? Justice Stevens concurred with the Court majority that the blanket license should not have been treated as per se unlawful. He dissented, however, arguing that in lieu of a remand the Court should have affirmed the Court of Appeals, albeit on different grounds—he would have reached the analysis of the blanket license and found it to be unreasonable under Section 1. 441 U.S. at 25–38 (Stevens, J., dissenting). In Stevens' view, ASCAP and Broadcast Music possessed market power, *id.* at 30, the blanket license resulted in higher prices for many licensees, *id.* at 31–32, and joint pricing did not appear to be reasonably necessary to their efforts to monitor use of the copyrighted compositions within their respective repertories. *Id.* at 33. Moreover, Stevens rejected the Court majority's assumption that licenses on a per-composition or per-use basis were too costly to negotiate, arguing that there was no support in the district court's findings for that conclusion. *Id.* at 34. Do you find

Justice Stevens' points to be persuasive? For the resolution on remand, see *CBS, Inc. v. ASCAP*, 620 F.2d 930 (2d Cir.1980).

In explaining the origins and purposes of the blanket license, the Supreme Court asserted at one point that "[i]ndividual sales transactions in this industry are quite expensive, as would be individual monitoring and enforcement, especially in light of the resources of single composers." (Casebook, *supra*, at 112.) Yet for purposes of assessing the blanket license's impact on competition, the Court also observes that "[t]he District Court found that there was no legal, practical, or conspiratorial impediment to CBS's obtaining individual licenses; CBS, in short, had a real choice." (Casebook, *supra*, at 114.) Are these two propositions consistent? Mutually exclusive? How critical was resolution of this question to the rule of reason inquiry? *See CBS, Inc.*, 620 F.2d at 936–38 (discussing feasibility of individual licenses and concluding: " * * * the District Court has found that CBS can feasibly obtain individual licenses from competing copyright owners and that it incurs no risk in endeavoring to do so. There is no basis in the record for concluding that these findings by the District Court are clearly erroneous.").

Broadcast Music has had significance well beyond the narrow "price fixing" pigeon hole, and will be discussed further later in this chapter as well as in Chapter 8. For purposes of price fixing, however, *Broadcast Music* appeared to open up the possibility of escaping per se treatment where its application would sweep too broadly. Much as *Standard Oil* had prompted litigants to test the limits of "reasonableness" in the context of price fixing, so too did *Broadcast Music*.

The Court promptly returned to its more basic price fixing criteria just a year later in *Catalano, Inc. v. Target Sales, Inc.*, 446 U.S. 643 (1980). *Catalano* struck down an agreement among competing wholesalers to refuse to sell on credit. Although there is no suggestion in *Catalano* that the colluding beer wholesalers had agreed upon set prices, they had collectively agreed to discontinue their prior practice of extending credit without interest for up to 30 to 42 days. The plaintiffs alleged that prior to their agreement to do so, there was vigorous competition among the wholesalers relating to terms of credit. For the retailers, these were just forms of discounts. After the agreement went into effect, all payments had to be made in advance of or upon delivery. In a per curiam opinion, the Court concluded that a collective refusal to compete on credit terms was indistinguishable from an agreement to fix prices. Quoting *Socony-Vacuum Oil*, the Court reasoned that such an agreement eliminated competition concerning one component of price and tended to stabilize pricing, and reiterated that " 'the machinery employed by a combination for price-fixing is immaterial.' " 446 U.S. at 647.

Catalano thus stands as a reminder that "price" is comprised of many components. Although it is possible to argue that eliminating competition as to just one component of price might not necessarily "fix prices" and might therefore be defensible, the Court's previous rejection of a "reasonable prices" defense in cases like *Trenton Potteries* precluded such an approach. Thus, after *Catalano*, to fix a component of price is to fix price.

Three years after *Broadcast Music*, the Court again reasserted the per se rule in our next case, *Maricopa*. In reading *Maricopa*, note particularly the majority's basis for distinguishing *Broadcast Music* and the dissent's response.

ARIZONA v. MARICOPA COUNTY MEDICAL SOCIETY

Supreme Court of the United States, 1982.
457 U.S. 332, 102 S.Ct. 2466, 73 L.Ed.2d 48.

Justice STEVENS delivered the opinion of the Court.

The question presented is whether § 1 of the Sherman Act has been violated by agreements among competing physicians setting, by majority vote, the maximum fees that they may claim in full payment for health services provided to policyholders of specified insurance plans. The United States Court of Appeals for the Ninth Circuit held that the question could not be answered without evaluating the actual purpose and effect of the agreements at a full trial. Because the undisputed facts disclose a violation of the statute, we granted certiorari, and now reverse.

* * *

II

The Maricopa Foundation for Medical Care is a nonprofit Arizona corporation composed of licensed doctors of medicine, osteopathy, and podiatry engaged in private practice. Approximately 1,750 doctors, representing about 70% of the practitioners in Maricopa County, are members.

The Maricopa Foundation was organized in 1969 for the purpose of promoting fee-for-service medicine and to provide the community with a competitive alternative to existing health insurance plans. The foundation performs three primary activities. It establishes the schedule of maximum fees that participating doctors agree to accept as payment in full for services performed for patients insured under plans approved by the foundation. It reviews the medical necessity and appropriateness of treatment provided by its members to such insured persons. It is authorized to draw checks on insurance company accounts to pay doctors for services performed for covered patients. In performing these functions, the foundation is considered an "insurance administrator" by the Director of the Arizona Department of Insurance. Its participating doctors, however, have no financial interest in the operation of the foundation.* * * [10]

* * *

The fee schedules limit the amount that the member doctors may recover for services performed for patients insured under plans approved by the foundations. To obtain this approval the insurers—including self-insured employers as well as insurance companies—agree to pay the doctors' charges up to the scheduled amounts, and in exchange the doctors agree to accept those amounts as payment in full for their services. The doctors are free to charge higher fees to uninsured patients, and they also may charge any

---

10. The parties disagree over whether the increases in the fee schedules are the cause or the result of the increases in the prevailing rate for medical services in the relevant mar-kets. There appears to be agreement, however, that 85–95% of physicians in Maricopa County bill at or above the maximum reimbursement levels set by the Maricopa Foundation.

patient less than the scheduled maxima. A patient who is insured by a foundation-endorsed plan is guaranteed complete coverage for the full amount of his medical bills only if he is treated by a foundation member. He is free to go to a nonmember physician and is still covered for charges that do not exceed the maximum-fee schedule, but he must pay any excess that the nonmember physician may charge.

The impact of the foundation fee schedules on medical fees and on insurance premiums is a matter of dispute. The State of Arizona contends that the periodic upward revisions of the maximum-fee schedules have the effect of stabilizing and enhancing the level of actual charges by physicians, and that the increasing level of their fees in turn increases insurance premiums. The foundations, on the other hand, argue that the schedules impose a meaningful limit on physicians' charges, and that the advance agreement by the doctors to accept the maxima enables the insurance carriers to limit and to calculate more efficiently the risks they underwrite and therefore serves as an effective cost-containment mechanism that has saved patients and insurers millions of dollars. * * *

* * *

III

The respondents recognize that our decisions establish that price-fixing agreements are unlawful on their face. But they argue that the *per se* rule does not govern this case because the agreements at issue are horizontal and fix maximum prices, are among members of a profession, are in an industry with which the judiciary has little antitrust experience, and are alleged to have procompetitive justifications. Before we examine each of these arguments, we pause to consider the history and the meaning of the *per se* rule against price-fixing agreements.

A

Section 1 of the Sherman Act of 1890 literally prohibits *every* agreement "in restraint of trade." * * * [S]ince *Standard Oil Co*, we have analyzed most restraints under the so-called "rule of reason." As its name suggests, the rule of reason requires the factfinder to decide whether under all the circumstances of the case the restrictive practice imposes an unreasonable restraint on competition.

The elaborate inquiry into the reasonableness of a challenged business practice entails significant costs. Litigation of the effect or purpose of a practice often is extensive and complex. Judges often lack the expert understanding of industrial market structures and behavior to determine with any confidence a practice's effect on competition. And the result of the process in any given case may provide little certainty or guidance about the legality of a practice in another context.

The costs of judging business practices under the rule of reason, however, have been reduced by the recognition of *per se* rules. Once experience with a particular kind of restraint enables the Court to predict with confidence that the rule of reason will condemn it, it has applied a conclusive presumption that the restraint is unreasonable. As in every rule of general application, the match between the presumed and the actual is imperfect. For the sake of business certainty and litigation efficiency, we have tolerated the invalidation of some agreements that a fullblown inquiry might have proved to be reasonable.

Thus the Court in *Standard Oil* recognized that inquiry under its rule of reason ended once a price-fixing agreement was proved, for there was "a conclusive presumption which brought [such agreements] within the statute." By 1927, the Court was able to state that "it has * * * often been decided and always assumed that uniform price-fixing by those controlling in any substantial manner a trade or business in interstate commerce is prohibited by the Sherman Law." *United States v. Trenton Potteries* . * * *

Thirteen years later, the Court could report that "for over forty years this Court has consistently and without deviation adhered to the principle that price-fixing agreements are unlawful *per se* under the Sherman Act and that no showing of so-called competitive abuses or evils which those agreements were designed to eliminate or alleviate may be interposed as a defense." *United States v. Socony–Vacuum Oil Co.* * * *

The application of the *per se* rule to maximum-price-fixing agreements in *Kiefer-Stewart Co. v. Joseph E. Seagram & Sons, Inc.*, followed ineluctably from *Socony–Vacuum*:

> For such agreements, no less than those to fix minimum prices, cripple the freedom of traders and thereby restrain their ability to sell in accordance with their own judgment. * * *

Over the objection that maximum-price-fixing agreements were not the "economic equivalent" of minimum-price-fixing agreements, *Kiefer-Stewart* was reaffirmed in *Albrecht v. Herald Co.*, 390 U.S. 145 (1968).*

We have not wavered in our enforcement of the *per se* rule against price fixing. * * *

B

Our decisions foreclose the argument that the agreements at issue escape *per se* condemnation because they are horizontal and fix maximum prices. *Kiefer-Stewart* and *Albrecht* place horizontal agreements to fix maximum prices on the same legal—even if not economic—footing as agreements to fix minimum or uniform prices.[18] The *per se* rule "is grounded on faith in price competition as a market force [and not] on a policy of low selling prices at the price of eliminating competition." In this case the rule is violated by a price restraint that tends to provide the same economic rewards to all practitioners regardless of their skill, their experience, their training, or their willingness to employ innovative and difficult procedures in individual cases. Such a restraint also may discourage entry into the market and may deter experimentation and new developments by individual entrepreneurs. It may be a masquerade for an agreement to fix uniform prices, or it may in the future take on that character.

---

* [*Albrecht* was later overruled in *State Oil Co. v. Khan*, 522 U.S. 3 (1997). Eds.]

18. It is true that in *Keifer-Stewart*, as in *Albrecht*, the agreement involved a vertical arrangement in which maximum resale prices were fixed. But the case also involved an agreement among competitors to impose the resale price restraint. In any event, horizontal restraints are generally less defensible than vertical restraints. * * *

Nor does the fact that doctors—rather than nonprofessionals—are the parties to the price-fixing agreements support the respondents' position. * * * The price-fixing agreements in this case * * * are not premised on public service or ethical norms. The respondents do not argue * * * that the quality of the professional service that their members provide is enhanced by the price restraint. The respondents' claim for relief from the *per se* rule is simply that the doctors' agreement not to charge certain insureds more than a fixed price facilitates the successful marketing of an attractive insurance plan. But the claim that the price restraint will make it easier for customers to pay does not distinguish the medical profession from any other provider of goods or services.

We are equally unpersuaded by the argument that we should not apply the *per se* rule in this case because the judiciary has little antitrust experience in the health care industry. The argument quite obviously is inconsistent with *Socony–Vacuum*. In unequivocal terms, we stated that, "[w]hatever may be its peculiar problems and characteristics, the Sherman Act, so far as price-fixing agreements are concerned, establishes one uniform rule applicable to all industries alike." 310 U.S., at 222, 60 S.Ct., at 843. We also stated that "[t]he elimination of so-called competitive evils [in an industry] is no legal justification" for price-fixing agreements, yet the Court of Appeals refused to apply the *per se* rule in this case in part because the health care industry was so far removed from the competitive model. Consistent with our prediction in *Socony–Vacuum*, the result of this reasoning was the adoption by the Court of Appeals of a legal standard based on the reasonableness of the fixed prices, an inquiry we have so often condemned. Finally, the argument that the *per se* rule must be rejustified for every industry that has not been subject to significant antitrust litigation ignores the rationale for *per se* rules, which in part is to avoid "the necessity for an incredibly complicated and prolonged economic investigation into the entire history of the industry involved, as well as related industries, in an effort to determine at large whether a particular restraint has been unreasonable—an inquiry so often wholly fruitless when undertaken." *Northern Pacific R. Co. v. United States.*

The respondents' principal argument is that the *per se* rule is inapplicable because their agreements are alleged to have procompetitive justifications. The argument indicates a misunderstanding of the *per se* concept. The anticompetitive potential inherent in all price-fixing agreements justifies their facial invalidation even if procompetitive justifications are offered for some. Those claims of enhanced competition are so unlikely to prove significant in any particular case that we adhere to the rule of law that is justified in its general application. Even when the respondents are given every benefit of the doubt, the limited record in this case is not inconsistent with the presumption that the respondents' agreements will not significantly enhance competition.

The respondents contend that their fee schedules are procompetitive because they make it possible to provide consumers of health care with a uniquely desirable form of insurance coverage that could not otherwise exist. The features of the foundation-endorsed insurance plans that they stress are a choice of doctors, complete insurance coverage, and lower premiums. The first two characteristics, however, are hardly unique to these plans. Since only about 70% of the doctors in the relevant market are members of either foundation, the guarantee of complete coverage only applies when an insured chooses a physician in that 70%. * * *

It is true that a binding assurance of complete insurance coverage—as well as most of the respondents' potential for lower insurance premiums[25]— can be obtained only if the insurer and the doctor agree in advance on the maximum fee that the doctor will accept as full payment for a particular service. Even if a fee schedule is therefore desirable, it is not necessary that the doctors do the price fixing. * * * [I]nsurers are capable not only of fixing maximum reimbursable prices but also of obtaining binding agreements with providers guaranteeing the insured full reimbursement of a participating provider's fee. * * * [I]t is not surprising that nothing in the record even arguably supports the conclusion that this type of insurance program could not function if the fee schedules were set in a different way.

The most that can be said for having doctors fix the maximum prices is that doctors may be able to do it more efficiently than insurers. The validity of that assumption is far from obvious, but in any event there is no reason to believe that any savings that might accrue from this arrangement would be sufficiently great to affect the competitiveness of these kinds of insurance plans. It is entirely possible that the potential or actual power of the foundations to dictate the terms of such insurance plans may more than offset the theoretical efficiencies upon which the respondents' defense ultimately rests.[29]

C

Our adherence to the *per se* rule is grounded not only on economic prediction, judicial convenience, and business certainty, but also on a recognition of the respective roles of the Judiciary and the Congress in regulating the economy. Given its generality, our enforcement of the Sherman Act has required the Court to provide much of its substantive content. By articulating the rules of law with some clarity and by adhering to rules that are justified in their general application, however, we enhance the legislative prerogative to amend the law. * * * Congress may consider the exception that we are not free to read into the statute.

IV

Having declined the respondents' invitation to cut back on the *per se* rule against price fixing, we are left with the respondents' argument that their fee schedules involve price fixing in only a literal sense. For this argument, the

---

25. We do not perceive the respondents' claim of procompetitive justification for their fee schedules to rest on the premise that the fee schedules actually reduce medical fees and accordingly reduce insurance premiums, thereby enhancing competition in the health insurance industry. Such an argument would merely restate the long-rejected position that fixed prices are reasonable if they are lower than free competition would yield. It is arguable, however, that the existence of a fee schedule, whether fixed by the doctors or by the insurers, makes it easier—and to that extent less expensive—for insurers to calculate the risks that they underwrite and to arrive at the appropriate reimbursement on insured claims.

29. In this case it appears that the fees are set by a group with substantial power in the market for medical services, and that there is competition among insurance companies in the sale of medical insurance. Under these circumstances the insurance companies are not likely to have significantly greater bargaining power against a monopoly of doctors than would individual consumers of medical services.

respondents rely upon *Broadcast Music, Inc. v. Columbia Broadcasting System, Inc.*, 441 U.S. 1, 99 S.Ct. 1551, 60 L.Ed.2d 1 (1979).

* * *

This case is fundamentally different. Each of the foundations is composed of individual practitioners who compete with one another for patients. Neither the foundations nor the doctors sell insurance, and they derive no profits from the sale of health insurance policies. The members of the foundations sell medical services. Their combination in the form of the foundation does not permit them to sell any different product. Their combination has merely permitted them to sell their services to certain customers at fixed prices and arguably to affect the prevailing market price of medical care.

The foundations are not analogous to partnerships or other joint arrangements in which persons who would otherwise be competitors pool their capital and share the risks of loss as well as the opportunities for profit. In such joint ventures, the partnership is regarded as a single firm competing with other sellers in the market. The agreement under attack is an agreement among hundreds of competing doctors concerning the price at which each will offer his own services to a substantial number of consumers. * * * If a clinic offered complete medical coverage for a flat fee, the cooperating doctors would have the type of partnership arrangement in which a price-fixing agreement among the doctors would be perfectly proper. But the fee agreements disclosed by the record in this case are among independent competing entrepreneurs. They fit squarely into the horizontal price-fixing mold.

The judgment of the Court of Appeals is reversed.

———

Maricopa was decided by a vote of 4–3. Justices Blackmun and O'Connor took no part in the consideration of the case and Justice Lewis Powell dissented from the majority's decision. He was joined in his dissent by Chief Justice Warren Burger and Justice William Rehnquist. *See Maricopa*, 457 U.S. at 357–67 (Powell, J., dissenting). Powell viewed the foundation's principal arguments far more favorably, especially their proffered business justifications. In his view, the challenged agreements were novel, arose in an industry with which the Court had little experience, and did not foreclose any competition. In short, they appeared to be reasonable efforts at cost containment. He argued that in the medical services field, insurance companies stand in the shoes of consumers and have every incentive to reduce costs. He found it significant that the insurance companies that had contracted with the Maricopa Foundation had no objections to the fees it set and concluded that the plans benefitted consumers.

Powell also was more receptive to the Foundation's arguments based on *Broadcast Music*:

The Court * * * is content simply to brand this type of plan as "price fixing" and describe the agreement in *Broadcast Music*— which also literally involved the fixing of prices—as "fundamentally different."

In fact, however, the two agreements are similar in important respects. Each involved competitors and resulted in cooperative pricing. Each arrangement also was prompted by the need for better service to the consumers. And each arrangement apparently makes possible a new product by reaping otherwise unattainable efficiencies. The Court's effort to distinguish *Broadcast Music* thus is unconvincing.

Id. at 364–65. Powell's dissent concluded with stern criticism of the majority:

I believe the Court's action today loses sight of the basic purposes of the Sherman Act. As we have noted, the antitrust laws are a "consumer welfare prescription." In its rush to condemn a novel plan about which it knows very little, the Court suggests that this end is achieved only by invalidating activities that *may* have some potential for harm. But the little that the record does show about the effect of the plan suggests that it is a means of providing medical services that in fact benefits rather than injures persons who need them.

In a complex economy, complex economic arrangements are commonplace. It is unwise for the Court, in a case as novel and important as this one, to make a final judgment in the absence of a complete record and where mandatory inferences create critical issues of fact.

Id. at 367.

How convincing a case does the majority make for use of the per se rule? Does the dissent make a better one for treating the maximum fee schedule under the rule of reason? Note that the plaintiff likened the fee schedule to naked price restraints, but the defendants analogized it to the blanket license in *Broadcast Music*. How did the majority distinguish *Broadcast Music*? What was the dissent's response? Which position did you find more persuasive and why? In Sidebar 2–2, which follows, we will discuss what the Court's internal papers reveal about the development of the Justices' positions and their final decision.

The majority asserts that its "adherence to the *per se* rule is grounded not only on economic prediction, judicial convenience, and business certainty, but also on a recognition of the respective roles of the Judiciary and the Congress in regulating the economy." *Id.* at 354. How does this stated rationale for the per se rule compare to the factors we discussed in Sidebar 2–1? Are they legal justifications? Economic? Why did the Court majority deem it necessary to offer such a justification for the per se rule? Consider that question as you read the next Sidebar.

Sidebar 2–2:
Maricopa as Seen Through The Marshall and Powell Papers

Maricopa is a noteworthy Supreme Court decision that nearly did not happen. The papers of Justices Thurgood Marshall and Lewis Powell reveal how a case destined for relative obscurity instead exposed a significant rift in the Justices' evolving views of the continued vitality of the per se rule. The skirmish, triggered by an unexpectedly sweeping draft opinion by Justice Powell, thus provides important insights into the Court's efforts in the 1970s and 1980s to delineate the respective roles of the rule of reason and the rule of per se illegality in antitrust analysis.

The procedural history of *Maricopa* provides an important backdrop to the Supreme Court's deliberations. In 1979, at the request of the State of Arizona Attorney General, the U.S. District Court for the District of Arizona granted a temporary restraining order to enjoin the defendant physicians' network from implementing a maximum fee-setting arrangement. After a number of months, the district court dissolved the injunction and denied the plaintiff's motion for summary judgment on the question of liability. That motion, filed by the Arizona Attorney General, was premised on the argument that the fee caps constituted a per se illegal horizontal price-fixing agreement.

A divided panel of the U.S. Court of Appeals for the Ninth Circuit affirmed the trial court's ruling. 643 F.2d 553 (9th Cir.1980). Relying on the Supreme Court's then recent decisions in *Nat'l Soc'y of Prof'l Eng'rs* and *Broadcast Music*, the court of appeals majority emphasized the need for a full trial to gather and evaluate evidence of the actual purpose and effect of the relatively novel fee-setting agreement. In a concurring opinion, Judge (later Supreme Court Justice) Anthony Kennedy maintained that a fuller factual record was necessary to permit a proper assessment of the challenged restraint, though he cautioned that such an assessment would not necessarily exculpate the arrangement. The dissenting member of the Ninth Circuit panel argued that the restriction fell squarely within the per se ban of *Socony-Vacuum Oil* and, notwithstanding the distinctive circumstances of the market for health care services, warranted condemnation without further inquiry.

The Arizona Attorney General petitioned the Supreme Court for a writ of certiorari, and in 1981 the Court granted the petition. Following briefing and oral argument, the Court met to discuss the case. According to the Marshall and Powell papers, several justices initially expressed second thoughts about having granted certiorari in the first place. Powell's papers indicate that Chief Justice Burger and Justice Marshall were initially "firm votes for a DIG"—the informal acronym for announcing that certiorari has been "dismissed as improvidently granted." They were not alone, however, in expressing concern that the record below provided a sparse factual basis for deciding which legal standard should apply.

With Justices Harry Blackmun and Sandra Day O'Connor recused, only seven remained to decide the case. According to Powell's records, Justices Stevens and Brennan favored reversal, which would reassert the vitality of the per se rule, whereas Justice White "would remand without deciding whether there has been a per se violation or whether the rule of reason is applicable." Powell further indicated that "[b]oth Bill Rehnquist and I expressed views generally similar to those of Byron [White]." A fourth vote was needed to establish a Court majority.

Powell believed that the Chief Justice, who had expressed some interest in the idea of a DIG, could be persuaded in the alternative to remand the case, and on November 21, 1981 Powell wrote to him seeking his support for that approach:

> As we have only a seven member Court, there would be no Court opinion, unless you revert to your alternative vote which—as recorded in my notes—was to remand. You stated that summary judgment had been granted prematurely, and that the record before us is inadequate, a view that appears to be similar to that of Byron [White], Bill Rehnquist and mine.

Justices White and Rehnquist promptly responded in writing that Powell had accurately stated their positions. On November 27, the Chief Justice responded, indicating his support for the approach and asking Powell "to draft a dispositive Per Curiam on this case." A hand written note memorializes a conversation between the Chief Justice and Justice Powell in which they agreed that it would not be a "full opinion." Powell was directed to "keep it short."

But as Powell set about the task of drafting the short opinion that would seal the four-vote pact, he developed concerns about the wisdom of the approach. It would provide little guidance to the district court, which would still have to parse the three opinions generated by the court of appeals. The draft opinion grew to what Powell himself described as a "rather full memorandum" of fifteen single-spaced pages. Although it still left the ultimate disposition of the case to the district court, it reviewed the Court's recent Section 1 jurisprudence and underscored how *Sylvania* and *Broadcast Music* had questioned the analytical rigidities of per se rules and demanded a more probing evaluation of business practices previously believed to be inimical to the competitive process.

The document appears to have startled several of Powell's colleagues. Justice John Paul Stevens called it a direct assault upon the per se rule against naked horizontal restraints. *Maricopa*, he said, was the place for the Court to decide whether the bright lines drawn in *Socony–Vacuum Oil* and nurtured by decades of judicial elaboration retained their vitality. Two days after Powell's draft was circulated, Stevens responded:

> The analysis in your memorandum is somewhat puzzling. If the maximum price fixing arrangement is illegal per se—as I believe it is—I do not understand how any of the three justifications can save it. If you are saying that an arrangement is not a "price fixing" agreement that deserves per se condemnation if the participants are motivated by any purpose except stifling competition, not much will remain of the per se doctrine. In any event, I intend to adhere to the position I took in Conference and will be writing in dissent as soon as I can.

What once seemed to be a case destined for an unremarkable dismissal of certiorari had become a pitched contest over the fundamentals of antitrust doctrine.

To Powell's seeming chagrin, both the Chief Justice and Justice White responded to Steven's promise of an alternate opinion by withholding their immediate support for Powell's draft. When completed, Stevens' "dissent" initially gained the support of Justices William Brennan and Thurgood Marshall. But on April 26, 1982, Justice Byron White (the author of *Broadcast Music*) wrote to Powell: "I have spent considerable time in this case and have decided, contrary to my conference vote, that the Court of Appeals should be reversed." Steven's "dissent" had become the majority opinion.

Not only did Stevens, Brennan, Marshall—and now White—oppose Powell's memorandum, but they believed the Court should decide the case on its merits and reverse the Ninth Circuit. As you have just read, by a 4–3 vote the Court condemned the fee setting arrangement and restated the value of per se rules. Joined by the Chief Justice and Justice William Rehnquist, Justice Powell wrote a dissent based largely upon the draft memorandum that had triggered the Court's internal debate. Four years later, in the context of preparing the majority opinion in *Matsushita* (Casebook, *infra*, Chapter 3), Powell would write to Justice Rehnquist that "the Court's 4–3 decision in [*Maricopa*] could well be the most erroneous antitrust decision the Court has ever made."

What do the Powell and Marshall papers tell us about *Maricopa*'s significance? Is the decision best understood as an idiosyncratic consequence of efforts by some of the Court's members to control apparent overreaching by one of their colleagues? As you read further in this Chapter and Chapter 4, consider whether the behind the scenes history suggests that the case is an anomaly in a landscape in which *Sylvania* (1977) (Casebook, *infra*, Chapter 4), *Broadcast Music* (1979), and *NCAA* (1984)(Casebook, *infra*, Chapter 2) provide the more reliable guideposts to the direction of the Court's Section 1 jurisprudence. Or is *Maricopa* simply an indication that the Court always will strive to preserve a well-delineated zone of per se illegality, even if doing so requires making debatable judgments about certain types of practices? Had Justice Powell simply drafted a one page notice identifying categories of facts for the trial court to consider on remand, would this case (or a case like it) subsequently have made its way back to the Supreme Court—with the same result?

While the Powell and Marshall papers may not give us clear answers to these questions, they do reinforce one point that arguably can be distilled from a reading of the Court's modern Section 1 decisions. A doctrinal framework that seeks to preserve both the substantive and administrative benefits of bright line rules, yet still makes discriminating judgments about the competitive significance of business conduct, is certain to generate continuing debate about whether the bright lines are correctly placed.

After reading *Socony-Vacuum Oil*, *Broadcast Music*, and *Maricopa*, how useful do you think the per se/rule of reason dichotomy is? Could you determine with confidence in any of the cases whether the per se rule would apply? If so, what distinguished those cases from the others?

The courts continue to face cases in which plaintiffs allege per se unlawful price fixing and defendants argue that they are instead engaged in legitimate "joint venture" type activity. *See, e.g., Freeman v. San Diego Ass'n of Realtors*, 322 F.3d 1133 (9th Cir. 2003) (summary judgment for defendants was reversed in suit by subscribers to real estate listing service alleging per se unlawful price fixing). Another interesting example is *Polygram Holding, Inc. v. FTC*, 416 F.3d 29 (D.C. Cir. 2005). *Polygram* involved a challenge by the FTC under Section 5 of the FTC Act to an agreement between two competing record producers to suspend advertising and promotion of each venturer's previously released recordings during the introductory phase of a new, jointly produced album by the same artists. The FTC concluded that although the agreement was not per se unlawful, it was "inherently suspect" and hence the defendant was required to come forward with evidence of a cognizable justification, something it failed to do. Even if it had done so, the FTC concluded that there was evidence of actual anticompetitive effects that outweighed the possible benefits of the proffered justification. In a unanimous decision by Chief Judge Douglas Ginsburg, a former head of the Antitrust Division of the Department of Justice, the D.C. Circuit affirmed. An excerpt from the decision appears later in this Chapter.

The Supreme Court placed significant restrictions on the use of the per se rule in the context of pricing by joint ventures in *Texaco Inc. v. Dagher*, 547 U.S. 1, 126 S.Ct. 1276 (2006). *Dagher* involved a joint venture between Texaco and Shell to refine and sell gasoline in the western United States. Pursuant to the joint venture agreement, the two previous rivals combined their refining and distribution networks in a new entity, Equilon, but sought to maintain their distinct brand names. Despite the fact that the FTC had earlier reviewed and declined to oppose the venture, a class of Texaco and Shell service station owners brought suit, alleging that the joint venturers' decision to permit Equilon to set joint prices for both brands constituted per se unlawful price fixing.

In an opinion authored by Justice Clarence Thomas, the Supreme Court reaffirmed the vitality of the per se ban on price-fixing, but concluded that application of the per se rule was inappropriate to the joint price setting. Citing to *Maricopa* and *Broadcast Music*, the Court reasoned:

> Price-fixing agreements between two or more competitors, otherwise known as horizontal price-fixing agreements, fall into the category of arrangements that are *per se* unlawful. * * * These cases do not present such an agreement, however, because Texaco and Shell Oil did not compete with one another in the relevant market—namely, the sale of gasoline to service stations in the western United States—but instead participated in that market jointly through their investments in Equilon. In other words, the pricing policy challenged here amounts to little more than price setting by a single entity—albeit within the context of a joint venture—and not a pricing agreement between competing entities with respect to their competing products. Throughout Equilon's existence, Texaco and Shell Oil shared in the profits of Equilon's activities in their role as investors, not competitors. When "persons who would otherwise be competitors pool their capital and share the risks of loss as well as the opportunities for profit ... such joint ventures [are] regarded as a single firm competing with other sellers in the market." *Arizona v. Maricopa County Medical Soc.*, 457 U.S. 332, 356 (1982). As such, though Equilon's pricing policy may be price fixing in a literal sense, it is not price fixing in the antitrust sense. *See Broadcast Music, Inc. v. Columbia Broadcasting System, Inc.*, 441 U.S. 1, 9 (1979) ("When two partners set the price of their goods or services they are literally 'price fixing,' but they are not *per se* in violation of the Sherman Act.").

547 U.S. at 5–6 (footnotes omitted). The Court found unpersuasive the plaintiff class's assertion that the venturers' decision to retain their distinct brand identities had any relevance to the antitrust analysis:

> * * * This conclusion is confirmed by respondents' apparent concession that there would be no *per se* liability had Equilon simply chosen to sell its gasoline under a single brand. We see no reason to treat Equilon differently just because it chose to sell gasoline under two distinct brands at a single price. As a single entity, a joint venture, like any other firm, must have the discretion to determine the prices of the products that it sells, including the discretion to sell a product under two different brands at a single, unified price. If Equilon's price unification policy is anticompetitive, then respondents should have challenged it pursuant to the rule of reason. But it would be inconsistent with this Court's antitrust precedents to condemn the internal pricing decisions of a legitimate joint venture as *per se* unlawful.

Id. (footnote omitted). Because the plaintiffs elected to pursue their claims under the per se rule or not at all, the Court ordered that judgment be entered for the defendants.

Although there has been little criticism of the Court's ultimate conclusion that the per se rule should not have been applied to the joint venture's pricing conduct, the Court's reasoning seems to sweep more broadly, strongly suggesting that the pricing practices of the joint venture did not raise *any* significant antitrust concerns. In that regard, commentators have questioned a number of elements of the Court's reasoning and noted its failure to mention some facts that were highlighted by the court of appeals. *See Dagher v. Saudi Refining, Inc.*, 369 F.3d 1108, 1111–13 (9th Cir. 2004). For example: (1) Equilon was not evenly owned by Shell and Texaco (Shell owned 56% whereas Texaco owned 44%); (2) the joint venture agreements permitted the two firms to dissolve Equilon at any time by mutual consent or, after an initial term of five years, unilaterally upon two years advance notice; (3) the specific decision to market both brands at the same price was not contained in the main venture agreements and there was some evidence that the two parties conceived of the joint pricing idea before the venture was formed; (4) there was some evidence that the joint pricing permitted Equilon to raise prices in at least two major metropolitan areas at a time when crude oil prices were low and stable; and (5) the alleged efficiencies of $800 million did not appear in any way related to the agreement on price. Do any of these facts alone or in combination suggest that the pricing provision could have been anticompetitive under a rule of reason analysis?

We will re-visit the seeming tension between *Maricopa* and *Broadcast Music* later in this Chapter when we read the Supreme Court's decision in *NCAA*. Although at the time it was decided *Maricopa* put into question whether *Broadcast Music* was an anomaly or had significantly altered the law of *Socony-Vacuum Oil*, *NCAA* and later cases like *Dagher* strongly suggest that *Broadcast Music* was no outlier. Instead, it signaled the beginning of important changes of attitude at the Court about the standards for judging cooperative conduct and, more generally, the role of economic analysis. Today, it is clear that *Broadcast Music* narrowed the traditional per se rule to limit it to naked price-fixing: an agreement among rivals on price with no plausible efficiency justification. Indeed, it is unclear whether today's Supreme Court would still endorse the 4–3 decision in *Maricopa*, or would find Justice Powell's dissent the more persuasive approach.

C. MARKET DIVISION BY COMPETITORS

Price fixing is not the only way competitors can emulate a monopolist—they can also do so by "dividing markets." When competitors divide markets they are agreeing to create monopolies of a sort for each other. They can do this geographically by agreeing not to compete in defined areas, by dividing up and assigning customers or customer categories, by agreeing not to solicit each other's customers, or by agreeing to divide product lines. The quid pro quo for Firm A staying away from the territory, customers or products of Firm B, is that Firm B will do the same. In this way, all of the colluding firms can obtain power over price and output—they can in effect insulate themselves from competition through collusion, thereby creating monopolies by agreement. Indeed, in some ways dividing markets can be more anticompetitive than price fixing. Price-fixing agreements may leave open the possibility of non-price competition, such as on quality, features or service, but dividing markets will generally limit *all* competition, price and non-price.

As in the case of price fixing, however, such a scheme could not effectively convey power over price unless the parties to the arrangement collectively possess market power. In the absence of collective market power, any agreement to divide markets is unlikely to confer power over price since the participants in the agreement will still face competition from other firms not party to the understanding.

In *Timken Roller Bearing Co. v. United States*, 341 U.S. 593 (1951), the Supreme Court appeared to move division of markets by competitors into the per se category along with price fixing. There the government charged that the defendants, the world's principal manufacturers of "antifriction bearings," had over a period of some 40 years established "comprehensive agreements providing for a territorial division of the world markets." The agreements included allocating trade territories, fixing the price of products of one affiliate that were sold in the territory of another, cooperating to hinder new entry, and restricting imports and exports from the United States. Although the facts were somewhat complicated by the cross-ownership of the principal defendants, Timken Roller Bearing (U.S.), British Timken and French Timken, the Court viewed the group as a cartel, and the arrangements as merely an alternate method of price fixing.

The principle established in *Timken* later spread to factual contexts arguably distinct from the one the Court faced in *Timken*. In two important cases that predate *Broadcast Music—United States v. Sealy, Inc.*, 388 U.S. 350 (1967) and *United States v. Topco Associates, Inc.*, 405 U.S. 596 (1972)—the Supreme Court treated arrangements that were less clearly "horizontal" as nevertheless subject to the per se rule that was implicit in *Timken*. Although both cases challenged conduct that clearly met a literal definition of "dividing markets," it was less clear that the parties doing the dividing were truly "competitors" and that the arrangement could facilitate the exercise of market power. As a consequence of the invocation of the per se rule in both, however, the Court bypassed opportunities to explore efficiency based defenses that were raised by the parties.

UNITED STATES v. TOPCO ASSOCIATES, INC.

Supreme Court of the United States, 1972.
405 U.S. 596, 92 S.Ct. 1126, 31 L.Ed.2d 515.

Mr. Justice MARSHALL delivered the opinion of the Court.

The United States brought this action for injunctive relief against alleged violation by Topco Associates, Inc. (Topco), of § 1 of the Sherman Act. Following a trial on the merits, the United States District Court * * * entered judgment for Topco and the United States appealed directly to this Court pursuant to § 2 of the Expediting Act as amended, 15 U.S.C. § 29. * * * [W]e now reverse the judgment of the District Court.

I

Topco is a cooperative association of approximately 25 small and medium-sized regional supermarket chains that operate stores in some 33 States. * * * Each of the member chains operates independently; there is no pooling of earnings, profits, capital, management, or advertising resources. No grocery business is conducted under the Topco name. Its basic function is to serve as a purchasing agent for its members.[2] In this capacity, it procures and distributes to the members more than 1,000 different food and related nonfood items, most of which are distributed under brand names owned by Topco.

* * *

All of the stock in Topco is owned by the members, with the common stock, the only stock having voting rights, being equally distributed. The board of directors, which controls the operation of the association, is drawn from the members and is normally composed of high-ranking executive officers of member chains.

* * *

Topco was founded in the 1940's by a group of small, local grocery chains, independently owned and operated, that desired to cooperate to obtain high quality merchandise under private labels in order to compete more effectively with larger national and regional chains.[3] With a line of canned, dairy, and

---

2. In addition to purchasing various items for its members, Topco performs other related functions: *e.g.*, it insures that there is adequate quality control on the products that it purchases; it assists members in developing specifications on certain types of products (*e.g.*, equipment and supplies); and it also aids the members in purchasing goods through other sources.

3. The founding members of Topco were having difficulty competing with larger chains. This difficulty was attributable in some degree to the fact that the larger chains were capable of developing their own private-label programs.

Private-label products differ from other brand-name products in that they are sold at a limited number of easily ascertainable stores. A & P, for example, was a pioneer in developing a series of products that were sold under an A & P label and that were only available in A & P stores. It is obvious that by using private-label products, a chain can achieve significant cost economies in purchasing, transportation, warehousing, promotion, and advertising. These economies may afford the chain opportunities for offering private-label products at lower prices than other brand-name products. This, in turn, provides many advan-

other products, the association began. It added frozen foods in 1950, fresh produce in 1958, more general merchandise equipment and supplies in 1960, and a branded bacon and carcass beef selection program in 1966. By 1964, Topco's members had combined retail sales of more than $2 billion; by 1967, their sales totaled more than $2.3 billion, a figure exceeded by only three national grocery chains.

* * *

Members of the association vary in the degree of market share that they possess in their respective areas. The range is from 1.5% to 16%, with the average being approximately 6%. While it is difficult to compare these figures with the market shares of larger regional and national chains because of the absence in the record of accurate statistics for these chains, there is much evidence in the record that Topco members are frequently in as strong a competitive position in their respective areas as any other chain. The strength of this competitive position is due, in some measure, to the success of Topco-brand products. Although only 10% of the total goods sold by Topco members bear the association's brand names, the profit on these goods is substantial and their very existence has improved the competitive potential of Topco members with respect to other large and powerful chains.

II

The United States charged that, beginning at least as early as 1960 and continuing up to the time that the complaint was filed, Topco had combined and conspired with its members to violate § 1 in two respects. First, the Government alleged that there existed:

"a continuing agreement, understanding and concert of action among the co-conspirator member firms acting through Topco, the substantial terms of which have been and are that each co-conspirator member firm will sell Topco-controlled brands only within the marketing territory allocated to it, and will refrain from selling Topco-controlled brands outside such marketing territory."

The division of marketing territories to which the complaint refers consists of a number of practices by the association.

Article IX, § 2, of the Topco bylaws establishes three categories of territorial licenses that members may secure from the association: * * * "Exclusive * * * Non-exclusive * * * [and] Coextensive * * *." When applying for membership, a chain must designate the type of license that it desires. Membership must first be approved by the board of directors, and thereafter by an affirmative vote of 75% of the association's members. If, however, the member whose operations are closest to those of the applicant, or any member whose operations are located within 100 miles of the applicant, votes against

tages of which some of the more important are: a store can offer national-brand products at the same price as other stores, while simultaneously offering a desirable, lower priced alternative; or, if the profit margin is sufficiently high on private-brand goods, national-brand products may be sold at reduced price. Other advantages include: enabling a chain to bargain more favorably with national-brand manufacturers by creating a broader supply base of manufacturers, thereby decreasing dependence on a few, large national-brand manufacturers; enabling a chain to create a "price-mix" whereby prices on special items can be lowered to attract customers while profits are maintained on other items; and creation of general goodwill by offering lower priced, higher quality goods.

approval, an affirmative vote of 85% of the members is required for approval. Bylaws, Art. I, § 5. Because, as indicated by the record, members cooperate in accommodating each other's wishes, the procedure for approval provides, in essence, that members have a veto of sorts over actual or potential competition in the territorial areas in which they are concerned.

Following approval, each new member signs an agreement with Topco designating the territory in which that member may sell Topco-brand products. No member may sell these products outside the territory in which it is licensed. Most licenses are exclusive, and even those denominated "coextensive" or "non-exclusive" prove to be *de facto* exclusive. * * * When combined with each member's veto power over new members, provisions for exclusivity work effectively to insulate members from competition in Topco-brand goods. Should a member violate its license agreement and sell in areas other than those in which it is licensed, its membership can be terminated.

* * *

The Government maintains that this scheme of dividing markets violates the Sherman Act because it operates to prohibit competition in Topco-brand products among grocery chains engaged in retail operations. The Government also makes a subsidiary challenge to Topco's practices regarding licensing members to sell at wholesale. Under the bylaws, members are not permitted to sell any products supplied by the association at wholesale, whether trademarked or not, without first applying for and receiving special permission from the association to do so. * * * Permission to wholesale has often been sought by members, only to be denied by the association. The Government contends that this amounts not only to a territorial restriction violative of the Sherman Act, but also to a restriction on customers that in itself is violative of the Act.

* * *

From the inception of this lawsuit, Topco accepted as true most of the Government's allegations regarding territorial divisions and restrictions on wholesaling, although it differed greatly with the Government on the conclusions, both factual and legal, to be drawn from these facts.

* * *

Topco essentially maintains that it needs territorial divisions to compete with larger chains; that the association could not exist if the territorial divisions were anything but exclusive; and that by restricting competition in the sale of Topco-brand goods, the association actually increases competition by enabling its members to compete successfully with larger regional and national chains.

The District Court, considering all these things relevant to its decision, agreed with Topco. It recognized that the panoply of restraints that Topco imposed on its members worked to prevent competition in Topco-brand products * * * but concluded that "(w)hatever anti-competitive effect these practices may have on competition in the sale of Topco private label brands is far outweighed by the increased ability of Topco members to compete both with the national chains and other supermarkets operating in their respective territories.''

The court held that Topco's practices were procompetitive and, therefore, consistent with the purposes of the antitrust laws. But we conclude that the District Court used an improper analysis in reaching its result.

III

* * *

While the Court has utilized the "rule of reason" in evaluating the legality of most restraints alleged to be violative of the Sherman Act, it has also developed the doctrine that certain business relationships are *per se* violations of the Act without regard to a consideration of their reasonableness.

* * * One of the classic examples of a *per se* violation of § 1 is an agreement between competitors at the same level of the market structure to allocate territories in order to minimize competition. Such concerted action is usually termed a "horizontal" restraint, in contradistinction to combinations of persons at different levels of the market structure, *e.g.*, manufacturers and distributors, which are termed "vertical" restraints. This Court has reiterated time and time again that "[h]orizontal territorial limitations ... are naked restraints of trade with no purpose except stifling of competition." Such limitations are *per se* violations of the Sherman Act. * * *

We think that it is clear that the restraint in this case is a horizontal one, and, therefore, a *per se* violation of § 1. The District Court failed to make any determination as to whether there were *per se* horizontal territorial restraints in this case and simply applied a rule of reason in reaching its conclusions that the restraints were not illegal. * * * In so doing, the District Court erred.

* * *

Whether or not we would decide this case the same way under the rule of reason used by the District Court is irrelevant to the issue before us. The fact is that courts are of limited utility in examining difficult economic problems.[10] Our inability to weigh, in any meaningful sense, destruction of competition in one sector of the economy against promotion of competition in another sector is one important reason we have formulated *per se* rules.

In applying these rigid rules, the Court has consistently rejected the notion that naked restraints of trade are to be tolerated because they are well intended or because they are allegedly developed to increase competition.

Antitrust laws in general, and the Sherman Act in particular, are the Magna Carta of free enterprise. They are as important to the preservation of economic freedom and our free-enterprise system as the Bill of Rights is to the protection of our fundamental personal freedoms. And the freedom guaranteed each and every business, no matter how small, is the freedom to compete-

---

10. * * * Without the *per se* rules, businessmen would be left with little to aid them in predicting in any particular case what courts will find to be legal and illegal under the Sherman Act. Should Congress ultimately determine that predictability is unimportant in this area of the law, it can, of course, make *per se* rules inapplicable in some or all cases, and leave courts free to ramble through the wilds of economic theory in order to maintain a flexible approach.

to assert with vigor, imagination, devotion, and ingenuity whatever economic muscle it can muster. Implicit in such freedom is the notion that it cannot be foreclosed with respect to one sector of the economy because certain private citizens or groups believe that such foreclosure might promote greater competition in a more important sector of the economy.

The District Court determined that by limiting the freedom of its individual members to compete with each other, Topco was doing a greater good by fostering competition between members and other large supermarket chains. But, the fallacy in this is that Topco has no authority under the Sherman Act to determine the respective values of competition in various sectors of the economy. On the contrary, the Sherman Act gives to each Topco member and to each prospective member the right to ascertain for itself whether or not competition with other supermarket chains is more desirable than competition in the sale of Topco-brand products. Without territorial restrictions, Topco members may indeed "[cut] each other's throats." But we have never found this possibility sufficient to warrant condoning horizontal restraints of trade.

* * *

* * * If a decision is to be made to sacrifice competition in one portion of the economy for greater competition in another portion this too is a decision that must be made by Congress and not by private forces or by the courts. Private forces are too keenly aware of their own interests in making such decisions and courts are ill-equipped and ill-situated for such decisionmaking. To analyze, interpret, and evaluate the myriad of competing interests and the endless data that would surely be brought to bear on such decisions, and to make the delicate judgment on the relative values to society of competitive areas of the economy, the judgment of the elected representatives of the people is required.

Just as the territorial restrictions on retailing Topco-brand products must fall, so must the territorial restrictions on wholesaling. The considerations are the same, and the Sherman Act requires identical results.

We also strike down Topco's other restrictions on the right of its members to wholesale goods. These restrictions amount to regulation of the customers to whom members of Topco may sell Topco-brand goods. Like territorial restrictions, limitations on customers are intended to limit intra-brand competition and to promote inter-brand competition. For the reasons previously discussed, the arena in which Topco members compete must be left to their unfettered choice absent a contrary congressional determination.

We reverse the judgment of the District Court and remand the case for entry of an appropriate decree.

* * *

Mr. Chief Justice BURGER, dissenting.

This case does not involve restraints on interbrand competition or an allocation of markets by an association with monopoly or near-monopoly control of the sources of supply of one or more varieties of staple goods. Rather, we have here an agreement among several small grocery chains to join in a cooperative endeavor that, in my view, has an unquestionably lawful principal purpose; in pursuit of that purpose they have mutually agreed to certain minimal ancillary restraints that are fully reasonable in view of the principal purpose and that have never before today been held by this Court to be *per se* violations of the Sherman Act.

In joining in this cooperative endeavor, these small chains did not agree to the restraints here at issue in order to make it possible for them to exploit an already established line of products through non-competitive pricing. There was no such thing as a Topco line of products until this cooperative was formed. The restraints to which the cooperative's members have agreed deal only with the marketing of the products in the Topco line, and the only function of those restraints is to permit each member chain to establish, within its own geographical area and through its own local advertising and marketing efforts, a local consumer awareness of the trademarked family of products as that member's "private label" line. The goal sought was the enhancement of the individual members' abilities to compete, albeit to a modest degree, with the large national chains which had been successfully marketing private-label lines for several years. The sole reason for a cooperative endeavor was to make economically feasible such things as quality control, large quantity purchases at bulk prices, the development of attractively printed labels, and the ability to offer a number of different lines of trademarked products. All these things, of course, are feasible for the large national chains operating individually, but they are beyond the reach of the small operators proceeding alone.

* * *

I do not believe that our prior decisions justify the result reached by the majority. Nor do I believe that a new *per se* rule should be established in disposing of this case, for the judicial convenience and ready predictability that are made possible by *per se* rules are not such overriding considerations in antitrust law as to justify their promulgation without careful prior consideration of the relevant economic realities in the light of the basic policy and goals of the Sherman Act.

* * *

II

With all respect, I believe that there are two basic fallacies in the Court's approach here. First, while I would not characterize our role under the Sherman Act as one of "rambl[ing] through the wilds," it is indeed one that requires our "examin[ation of] difficult economic problems." We can undoubtedly ease our task, but we should not abdicate that role by formulation of *per se* rules with no justification other than the enhancement of predictability and the reduction of judicial investigation. Second, from the general proposition that *per se* rules play a necessary role in antitrust law, it does not follow that the particular *per se* rule promulgated today is an appropriate one. Although it might well be desirable in a proper case for this Court to formulate a *per se* rule dealing with horizontal territorial limitations, it would not necessarily be appropriate for such a rule to amount to a blanket prohibition against all such limitations. More specifically, it is far from clear to me why such a rule should cover those division-of-market agreements that involve no price fixing and which are concerned only with trademarked products that are not in a monopoly or near-monopoly position with respect to competing brands. The instant case presents such an agreement; I would not decide it upon the basis of a *per se* rule.[11]

* * *

The issues presented by the antitrust cases reaching this Court are rarely simple to resolve under the rule of reason; they do indeed frequently require us to make difficult economic determinations. We should not for that reason alone, however, be overly zealous in formulating new *per se* rules, for an excess of zeal in that regard is both contrary to the policy of the Sherman Act and detrimental to the welfare of consumers generally. Indeed, the economic effect of the new rule laid down by the Court today seems clear: unless Congress intervenes, grocery staples marketed under private-label brands with their lower consumer prices will soon be available only to those who patronize the large national chains.

* * *

————

As we will explore later in Chapter 8, it is unlikely that the Court would decide *Topco* similarly today. As Chief Justice Burger correctly pointed out, in contrast to the Timken affiliates, the Topco members were not clearly competitors. In addition, the Topco brand was a product of cooperation that no individual member could have otherwise created and offered for sale, and the territorial restraints adopted by Topco were designed to permit its members to better compete against integrated national chains by offering a low cost house private label brand, *i.e.*, to expand market output. The competition that existed among Topco members for the Topco brand, therefore, only existed by virtue of their agreement collectively to create the brand. Should restraints on such new products be presumptively lawful, instead of per se unlawful, as they were in *Topco*?

The Supreme Court's later decisions in *Sylvania* (1977)(Casebook, *infra* Chapter 4) and *Broadcast Music* (1979) both demonstrated a far greater willingness to give weight to similar factors. Viewed in the light of these and other decisions subsequent to *Topco*, such as *Northwest Wholesale Stationers* (Casebook, *infra* Chapter 7) and *NCAA* (Casebook, *infra* Chapter 2), it is unlikely that the Court today would refuse as it did in *Topco* to consider Topco's defenses. Several appellate court decisions have made these arguments and treated *Topco* as having been effectively overruled, at least on similar facts. *See, e.g., Rothery Storage & Van Co. v. Atlas Van Lines, Inc.*, 792 F.2d 210, 229 (D.C.Cir.1986)(Bork, J.); *Polk Bros., Inc. v. Forest City Enters.*,

11. The national chains market their own private-label products, and these products are available nowhere else than in the stores of those chains. The stores of any one chain, of course, do not engage in price competition with each other with respect to their chain's private-label brands, and no serious suggestion could be made that the Sherman Act requires otherwise. I fail to see any difference whatsoev-er in the economic effect of the Topco arrangement for the marketing of Topco brand products and the methods used by the national chains in marketing their private-label brands. * * * The controlling consideration * * * should be that in neither case is the policy of the Sherman Act offended, for the practices in both cases work to the benefit, and not to the detriment, of the consuming public.

Inc., 776 F.2d 185, 188–89 (7th Cir.1985)(Easterbrook, J.). *See also General Leaseways, Inc. v. National Truck Leasing Ass'n.*, 744 F.2d 588 (7th Cir. 1984)(Posner, J.)(implicitly following same approach).

Nevertheless, as we see in the next case, the simple legal principle iterated in *Topco*—that division of markets by competitors is per se illegal— remains very much the law when the parties to the division are true competitors and the conduct evidences no apparent competitive benefits, such as efficiencies.

PALMER v. BRG OF GEORGIA

Supreme Court of the United States, 1990.
498 U.S. 46, 111 S.Ct. 401, 112 L.Ed.2d 349.

PER CURIAM.

In preparation for the 1985 Georgia Bar Examination, petitioners contracted to take a bar review course offered by respondent BRG of Georgia, Inc. (BRG). In this litigation they contend that the price of BRG's course was enhanced by reason of an unlawful agreement between BRG and respondent Harcourt Brace Jovanovich Legal and Professional Publications (HBJ), the Nation's largest provider of bar review materials and lecture services. The central issue is whether the 1980 agreement between respondents violated § 1 of the Sherman Act. * * *

HBJ began offering a Georgia bar review course on a limited basis in 1976, and was in direct, and often intense, competition with BRG during the period from 1977 to 1979. BRG and HBJ were the two main providers of bar review courses in Georgia during this time period. In early 1980, they entered into an agreement that gave BRG an exclusive license to market HBJ's material in Georgia and to use its trade name "Bar/Bri." The parties agreed that HBJ would not compete with BRG in Georgia and that BRG would not compete with HBJ outside of Georgia.[2] Under the agreement, HBJ received $100 per student enrolled by BRG and 40% of all revenues over $350. Immediately after the 1980 agreement, the price of BRG's course was increased from $150 to over $400.

On petitioners' motion for partial summary judgment as to the § 1 counts in the complaint and respondents' motion for summary judgment, the District Court held that the agreement was lawful. The United States Court of Appeals for the Eleventh Circuit, with one judge dissenting, agreed with the District Court that *per se* unlawful horizontal price fixing required an explicit agreement on prices to be charged or that one party have the right to be consulted about the other's prices. The Court of Appeals also agreed with the District Court that to prove a *per se* violation under a geographic market allocation theory, petitioners had to show that respondents had subdivided some relevant market in which they had previously competed. * * *

---

2. The 1980 agreement contained two provisions, one called a "Covenant Not to Compete" and the other called "Other Ventures." The former required HBJ not to "directly or indirectly own, manage, operate, join, invest, control, or participate in or be connected as an officer, employee, partner, director, indepen- dent contractor or otherwise with any business which is operating or participating in the preparation of candidates for the Georgia State Bar Examination." * * * The latter required BRG not to compete against HBJ in States in which HBJ currently operated outside the State of Georgia. * * *

In *United States v. Socony–Vacuum Oil Co.*, we held that an agreement among competitors to engage in a program of buying surplus gasoline on the spot market in order to prevent prices from falling sharply was unlawful, even though there was no direct agreement on the actual prices to be maintained. We explained that "[u]nder the Sherman Act a combination formed for the purpose and with the effect of raising, depressing, fixing, pegging, or stabilizing the price of a commodity in interstate or foreign commerce is illegal *per se.*"

The revenue-sharing formula in the 1980 agreement between BRG and HBJ, coupled with the price increase that took place immediately after the parties agreed to cease competing with each other in 1980, indicates that this agreement was "formed for the purpose and with the effect of raising" the price of the bar review course. It was, therefore, plainly incorrect for the District Court to enter summary judgment in respondents' favor. Moreover, it is equally clear that the District Court and the Court of Appeals erred when they assumed that an allocation of markets or submarkets by competitors is not unlawful unless the market in which the two previously competed is divided between them.

In *United States v. Topco Associates, Inc.* we held that agreements between competitors to allocate territories to minimize competition are illegal. * * * The defendants in *Topco* had never competed in the same market, but had simply agreed to allocate markets. Here, HBJ and BRG had previously competed in the Georgia market; under their allocation agreement, BRG received that market, while HBJ received the remainder of the United States. Each agreed not to compete in the other's territories. Such agreements are anticompetitive regardless of whether the parties split a market within which both do business or whether they merely reserve one market for one and another for the other. Thus, the 1980 agreement between HBJ and BRG was unlawful on its face.

The petition for a writ of certiorari is granted, the judgment of the Court of Appeals is reversed, and the case is remanded for further proceedings consistent with this opinion.

* * *

———

What justifies treating a division of markets by competitors as per se unlawful? How, economically, is it like price fixing? Under what circumstances might it have some justification worth evaluating? Should it be treated as per se unlawful even when there is a plausible efficiency-related justification for the conduct?

Can *BRG* be distinguished from *Topco*? Do both cases present equally compelling cases for imposition of a per se rule? In answering that question, how significant is the evidence cited by the Court in *BRG* that the price of bar review courses increased almost threefold after the agreement between the defendants was adopted? Does the rise in price suggest that BRG had market power? What evidence was there in *Topco* that the defendants had market power? Is the Court implicitly suggesting that market power should be a prerequisite to application of the per se rule, or is an inquiry into market power unnecessary if the restraint is "naked"? Is the division of markets in *BRG* fairly characterized as "naked," because the defendants had no plausible justification for their actions? Did the defendants in *Topco* offer a justification for their division of markets that would warrant different treatment?

D. GROUP BOYCOTTS HAVING COLLUSIVE EFFECTS

"Group Boycotts," also referred to as "concerted refusals to deal," have a long and unsettled history that has included outright per se condemnation, qualified per se condemnation and even treatment under the rule of reason. This Section briefly traces that history, and in keeping with the book's overall organizational approach, offers a framework for working with the relevant cases that turns on the nature of their alleged anticompetitive effect: collusive or exclusionary.*

All "concerted refusals to deal" are the product of "collusion," in the sense of "agreement." By "collusive group boycotts" we refer to concerted refusals to deal that result in collusive effects, *i.e.*, those that directly restrict output or raise price. Principal examples of collusive group boycotts include an agreement among competitors to boycott a supplier in order to coerce acceptance of a lower price than the supplier could charge in a competitive market, or one to boycott a purchaser in order to coerce acceptance of a higher price than the purchaser would pay in a competitive market. In these instances, the object of the boycott is a customer or supplier of the colluding firms, and the anticompetitive impact is a consequence of the boycotters' effort to affect output. Characterization of the conduct as a boycott instead of mere price fixing may turn on little more than the presence of evidence of express, coercive demands—"meet our price or we will refuse to deal with you." Its impact on output and price, therefore, as with all collusive anticompetitive effects, is *direct*.

The evidence relevant to a case of collusive group boycott will focus on the boycotters' demonstrated ability to secure their demanded price—their market power. This evidence might take the form of proof that the boycott actually led to higher prices, or circumstantial evidence, in the form of proof that the boycotters collectively command a significant share of a properly defined relevant market and that conditions of entry into that market are difficult. Justifications for the boycott may not prove convincing, and may not even be accepted into evidence.

* *See* Kenneth L. Glazer, *Concerted Refusals to Deal Under Section 1 of the Sherman Act*, 70 ANTITRUST L.J. 1 (2002).

Figure 2–3:

Typical Collusive Group Boycotts

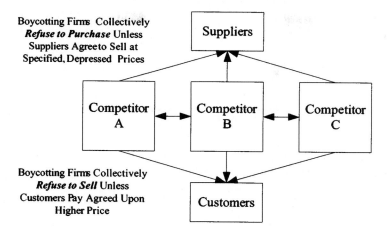

In contrast, *exclusionary* group boycotts most typically are directed at rivals of the colluding firms, rather than suppliers or customers, and seek to affect price only *indirectly*. Indirect power over price can be achieved, for example, by raising a rival's costs or limiting its revenues, limiting its access to a needed source of supply or to customers, or otherwise hindering its ability to expand or enter a market. While the ultimate goal of such a boycott may be the same as a collusive one—to obtain power over price—the mechanism for doing so, and the analysis of the boycott's effects, are different. The relevant evidence here will focus on the impact of the boycott on the rival, *i.e.*, the actual exclusionary effect of the refusal to deal, and on other evidence tending to support the prediction that the rival's exclusion will confer power over price on the colluding firms.

As a consequence, market power is likely to be relevant to a case of exclusionary group boycott, just as it is in the case of a collusive group boycott. Absent market power, it is unlikely that the boycotting firms will be able to significantly affect their rival. But there is an important difference in the character of the relevant evidence of market power. In the case of collusive group boycotts, direct evidence of market power will consist of evidence tending to establish the boycotters' actual ability to coerce a higher or lower price; in the case of an exclusionary group boycott, direct evidence of market power will consist of both evidence tending to demonstrate actual exclusion of the rival and evidence that the boycotting firms have the ability thereafter to maintain or raise price. Another difference in terms of relevant evidence relates to the boycotters' justifications for their conduct. For a variety of reasons, evidence of justifications is more likely to be considered in the case of an exclusionary group boycott than a collusive one. As you read the cases, consider the reasons for this important difference in the treatment of the two types of boycotts.

Figure 2–4:

Exclusionary Group Boycotts—Three Scenarios

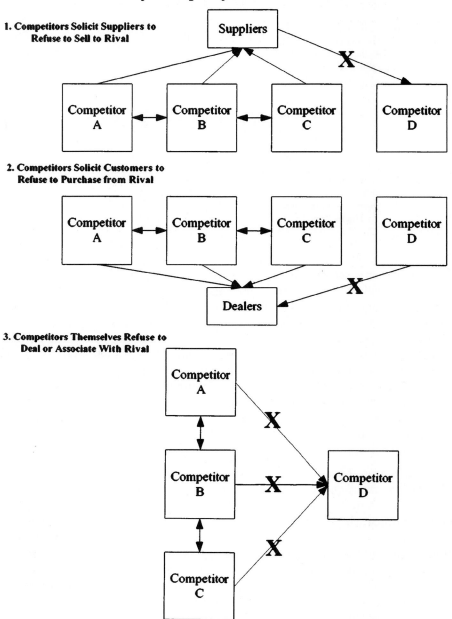

Exclusionary group boycotts may also be used to solve the "cheating" problem inherent in many conspiracies, which we will study in Chapter 3, *infra*. The colluders might be willing to share some of the excess profits obtained through price fixing with one or more suppliers willing to refuse to deal with a maverick rival that refuses to join in the price fixing scheme. In this scenario, illustrated in Figure 2–4(1), the boycott can be an effective tool for policing or enforcing an underlying agreement to fix prices or divide territories among the boycotting firms. If effective, the maverick will be forced to choose between joining the cartel and remaining free of the cartel while being forced to compete less aggressively. If it continues to compete, it will reduce output and raise price, because it must endure the higher costs associated with identifying alternative suppliers, if they are available at all. It will act as though it has joined the cartel, but its participation in the cartel's collective industry output reduction is "involuntary." The end result in terms of competitive effects is the same.

An exclusionary (cartel-policing) boycott is still distinguishable from a collusive one, however, because its target is a rival of the colluders, not a customer or supplier, and the crucial evidence will still turn on the tendency of the boycott to exclude the rival, and the likelihood that the exclusion will lead to higher prices. *See Hartford Fire Ins. Co. v. California*, 509 U.S. 764, 800–11 (1993)(Scalia, J.)(distinguishing between collective refusals to deal on specified terms—what we describe as refusals to deal having collusive effects—and "conditional boycotts," which have as their goal the coercion of another competing firm in order to alter its conduct—what we describe as a concerted refusal to deal having exclusionary effects, or an "involuntary cartel").

In this section of the Chapter we will examine the modern treatment of collusive boycotts. Further discussion of the analysis of exclusionary boycotts and the traditional Supreme Court boycott cases, many of which concerned exclusionary group boycotts, will await Chapter 7, which places them in context with other exclusionary conduct. In Sidebar 2–3, immediately below, we consider some additional issues that have complicated the legal treatment of conduct characterized as a "boycott."

Sidebar 2–3:
Use of the "Group Boycott" Label

Many of the problems associated with the placement of refusals to deal in the context of per se rules on horizontal agreements concern two factors. First, the terms "concerted refusal to deal" and "group boycott" can be used literally to describe a wide variety of benign and common business relationships. Every decision to purchase a good or service from one seller, for example, can be interpreted by another seller as an agreement between the buyer and seller NOT to deal with another seller.

Similarly, every decision to appoint a dealer as the representative of a particular manufacturer or to identify a sole source of supplies for a specific input, even when the selection follows a competitive bidding process, could too easily be labeled a "group boycott" of the firm or firms not chosen. If the per se rule on refusals to deal covered all such relationships, it would prove to be quite disruptive and costly. As one court observed in refusing to characterize an exclusive dealing agreement as a per se unlawful group boycott:

> * * * [P]er se condemnation is not visited on every arrange-
> ment that might, as a matter of language, be called a group

boycott or concerted refusal to deal. Rather, today that designation is principally reserved for cases in which competitors agree with each other not to deal with a supplier or distributor if it continues to serve a competitor whom they seek to injure. This is the "secondary boycott" device used in [some of the] * * * classic boycott cases. * * *

We doubt that the modern Supreme Court would use the boycott label to describe, or the rubric to condemn, a joint venture among competitors in which participation was allowed to some but not all * * * although such a restriction might well fall after a more complete analysis under the rule of reason. What is even more clear is that a purely vertical arrangement, by which (for example) a supplier or dealer makes an agreement exclusively to supply or serve a manufacturer, is not a group boycott. * * * Were the law otherwise, every distributor or retailer who agreed with a manufacturer to handle only one brand of television or bicycle would be engaged in a group boycott of other manufacturers.

U.S. Healthcare, Inc. v. Healthsource, Inc., 986 F.2d 589, 593–94 (1st Cir.1993). *See also Rothery Storage & Van Co. v. Atlas Van Lines, Inc.*, 792 F.2d 210, 215–16 (D.C.Cir.1986)(*citing* James A. Rahl, *Per Se Rules and Boycotts Under the Sherman Act: Some Reflections on the* Klor's *Case*, 45 Va. L. Rev. 1165, 1172 (1959)("All agreements to deal on specified terms mean refusal to deal on other terms;" hence any literal application of group boycott label would mean "that every restraint is illegal.").

The courts also have recognized that the label can be abused if applied to totally non-commercial boycotts, such as those used in the pursuit of civil rights causes. For example, in *NAACP v. Claiborne Hardware Co.*, 458 U.S. 886 (1982), discussed immediately below in *Superior Court Trial Lawyers Ass'n*, the Court overturned the Mississippi Supreme Court's imposition of civil, common law liability against a group of African–Americans engaged in a civil rights motivated boycott of white merchants. In the Court's view, the non-violent aspects of the boycott were constitutionally protected forms of association and speech. Damages for lost profits attributable to the boycott's success, therefore, could not provide a legitimate basis for antitrust liability.

Second, neither the term "group boycott," nor the Supreme Court's cases using it, distinguish between concerted refusals to deal that have collusive anticompetitive effects and those that have exclusionary effects. But that distinction may go a long way towards explaining why different analytical approaches might be used to assess different sorts of refusals to deal, and why some might be more readily condemned than others. As a general matter, for example, courts appear to view collusive boycotts as better candidates for per se condemnation, especially when there is evidence of an underlying agreement to fix prices or divide markets, as we will see in our next case, *Superior Court Trial Lawyers Ass'n*. In such instances it can be difficult to imagine a justification that would be worth considering.

The Court declined to use a per se approach, however, in *F.T.C. v. Indiana Fed'n of Dentists*, 476 U.S. 447 (1986), a case that involved a variation of a collusive group boycott, suggesting that use of the per se approach should be confined to certain *exclusionary* boycotts that are targeted at competitors. There the FTC challenged a dental association's policy of refusing to supply x-rays to third-party insurers, who used the x-rays to verify treatment decisions and to determine consequent payments to the dentists for services rendered to their insureds. The purpose of the refusal seemed clear: frustrate efforts at cost containment by the third-party payors. Nevertheless, both the FTC and the Court declined to apply the per se rule. The Court reasoned:

> The policy of the Federation with respect to its members' dealings with third-party insurers resembles practices that have been labeled "group boycotts": the policy constitutes a concerted refusal to deal on particular terms with patients covered by group dental insurance. Although this Court has in the past stated that group boycotts are unlawful per se, we decline to resolve this case by forcing the Federation's policy into the "boycott" pigeonhole and invoking the per se rule. * * * [T]he category of restraints classed as group boycotts is not to be expanded indiscriminately, and the per se approach has generally been limited to cases in which firms with market power boycott suppliers or customers in order to discourage them from doing business with a competitor-a situation obviously not present here. Moreover, we have been slow to condemn rules adopted by professional associations as unreasonable per se, and, in general, to extend per se analysis to restraints imposed in the context of business relationships where the economic impact of certain practices is not immediately obvious. Thus, as did the FTC, we evaluate the restraint at issue in this case under the Rule of Reason rather than a rule of per se illegality.

Id. at 458–59. In *Indiana Fed'n of Dentists*, the Court addressed a collusive group boycott "where the economic impact of [the challenged] ... practices [was] ... not immediately obvious," and for that reason, among others, it declined to extend per se treatment beyond the more familiar setting of exclusionary group boycotts arising in cases when firms with market power boycott their suppliers or customers to disadvantage their rivals. By the time the Court decided our next case, *Superior Court Trial Lawyers*, it recognized collusive group boycotts as a species of price-fixing and had more confidence that per se treatment would be appropriate.

The Supreme Court's fractured decision in *Hartford Fire Ins. Co. v. California*, 509 U.S. 764 (1993) presents the most comprehensive attempt to date by the Court to develop a taxonomy for refusals to deal. Justice Scalia traced the label to its origins—an organized effort in 1880 by tenants on various estates in Ireland to reduce their rents and rid themselves of Captain Charles Boycott, the managing agent of the estates. His opinion would confine the term "boycott" to its original context—coercive or "conditional" efforts to alter the conduct of another. Disagreement within the Court over use of "boycott," however, was largely influenced by the context of the narrow question before it—whether the defendants' conduct met the definition of a boycott as that term is used in Section 3(b) of the McCarren Ferguson Act. The Court's goal, therefore, was not specifically to synthesize and explain all of its prior decisions, something it may have occasion to do in the future.

In the section that follows, we will explore the more contemporary treatment by the Court of collusive group boycotts, starting with perhaps the most easily identifiable, and controversial, recent case of a very visible, collusive group boycott. We will return to the topic in Chapter 7, where we examine boycotts having exclusionary effects.

As noted above, most of the traditional Supreme Court cases, many of which are associated with the use of the per se rule, involved exclusionary, not collusive group boycotts. In our next case, *Superior Court Trial Lawyers Ass'n* (*SCTLA*), the Court focused on a collusive group boycott. As you read the case, reflect on the issues raised in Sidebar 2–3. Does the "group boycott" label add anything to the economic analysis of the conduct challenged in *SCTLA*? Note too how the Court struggles with the fact that some boycotts may contain an expressive component that may be protected in part by the First Amendment.

FEDERAL TRADE COMMISSION v. SUPERIOR COURT TRIAL LAWYERS ASS'N
Supreme Court of the United States, 1990.
493 U.S. 411, 110 S.Ct. 768, 107 L.Ed.2d 851.

Justice STEVENS delivered the opinion of the Court.

Pursuant to a well-publicized plan, a group of lawyers agreed not to represent indigent criminal defendants in the District of Columbia Superior Court until the District of Columbia government increased the lawyers' compensation. The questions presented are whether the lawyers' concerted conduct violated § 5 of the Federal Trade Commission Act and, if so, whether it was nevertheless protected by the First Amendment to the Constitution.

I

The burden of providing competent counsel to indigent defendants in the District of Columbia is substantial. During 1982, court-appointed counsel represented the defendant in approximately 25,000 cases. In the most serious felony cases, representation was generally provided by full-time employees of the District's Public Defender System (PDS). Less serious felony and misdemeanor cases constituted about 85 percent of the total caseload. In these cases, lawyers in private practice were appointed and compensated pursuant to the District of Columbia Criminal Justice Act (CJA).

Although over 1,200 lawyers have registered for CJA appointments, relatively few actually apply for such work on a regular basis. In 1982, most appointments went to approximately 100 lawyers who are described as "CJA regulars." These lawyers derive almost all of their income from representing indigents. * * *

In 1974, the District created a Joint Committee on Judicial Administration with authority to establish rates of compensation for CJA lawyers not exceeding the rates established by the federal Criminal Justice Act of 1964. After 1970, the federal Act provided for fees of $30 per hour for court time and $20 per hour for out-of-court time. * * * These rates accordingly capped the rates payable to the District's CJA lawyers, and could not be exceeded absent amendment to either the federal statute or the District Code.

Bar organizations began as early as 1975 to express concern about the low fees paid to CJA lawyers. Beginning in 1982, respondents, the Superior Court Trial Lawyers Association (SCTLA) and its officers, and other bar groups sought to persuade the District to increase CJA rates to at least $35 per hour. Despite what appeared to be uniform support for the bill, it did not pass. It is also true, however, that nothing in the record indicates that the low fees caused any actual shortage of CJA lawyers or denied effective representation to defendants.

* * *

At a SCTLA meeting [in the Summer of 1983], the CJA lawyers voted to form a "strike committee." The eight members of that committee promptly met and informally agreed "that the only viable way of getting an increase in fees was to stop signing up to take new CJA appointments, and that the boycott should aim for a $45 out-of-court and $55 in-court rate schedule."

On August 11, 1983, about 100 CJA lawyers met and resolved not to accept any new cases after September 6 if legislation providing for an increase in their fees had not passed by that date. Immediately following the meeting, they prepared (and most of them signed) a petition stating:

"We, the undersigned private criminal lawyers practicing in the Superior Court of the District of Columbia, agree that unless we are granted a substantial increase in our hourly rate we will cease accepting new appointments under the Criminal Justice Act."

On September 6, 1983, about 90 percent of the CJA regulars refused to accept any new assignments. Thereafter, SCTLA arranged a series of events to attract the attention of the news media and to obtain additional support. * * *

* * *

Within 10 days, the key figures in the District's criminal justice system "became convinced that the system was on the brink of collapse because of the refusal of CJA lawyers to take on new cases." On September 15, they hand-delivered a letter to the Mayor describing why the situation was expected to "reach a crisis point" by early the next week and urging the immediate enactment of a bill increasing all CJA rates to $35 per hour. The Mayor promptly met with members of the strike committee and offered to support an immediate temporary increase to the $35 level as well as a subsequent permanent increase to $45 an hour for out-of-court time and $55 for in-court time.

At noon on September 19, 1983, over 100 CJA lawyers attended an SCTLA meeting and voted to accept the $35 offer and end the boycott. The city council's Judiciary Committee convened at 2 o'clock that afternoon. The committee recommended legislation increasing CJA fees to $35, and the council unanimously passed the bill on September 20. On September 21, the CJA regulars began to accept new assignments and the crisis subsided.

II

The Federal Trade Commission (FTC) filed a complaint against SCTLA and four of its officers (respondents) alleging that they had "entered into an agreement among themselves and with other lawyers to restrain trade by refusing to compete for or accept new appointments under the CJA program beginning on September 6, 1983, unless and until the District of Columbia increased the fees offered under the CJA program." The complaint alleged that virtually all of the attorneys who regularly compete for or accept new appointments under the CJA program had joined the agreement. The FTC characterized respondents' conduct as "a conspiracy to fix prices and to conduct a boycott" and concluded that they were engaged in "unfair methods of competition in violation of Section 5 of the Federal Trade Commission Act."

After a 3–week hearing, the ALJ found that the facts alleged in the complaint had been proved, and rejected each of the respondents' three legal defenses—that the boycott was adequately justified by the public interest in obtaining better legal representation for indigent defendants; that as a method of petitioning for legislative change it was exempt from the antitrust laws under our decision in *Eastern Railroad Presidents Conference v. Noerr Motor Freight, Inc.*, 365 U.S. 127 (1961) and that it was a form of political action protected by the First Amendment under our decision in *NAACP v. Claiborne Hardware Co.*, 458 U.S. 886 (1982). The ALJ nevertheless concluded that the complaint should be dismissed because the District officials, who presumably represented the victim of the boycott, recognized that its net effect was beneficial. * * *

The ALJ's pragmatic moderation found no favor with the FTC. Like the ALJ, the FTC rejected each of respondents' defenses. It held that their "coercive, concerted refusal to deal" had the "purpose and effect of raising prices" and was illegal *per se*. Unlike the ALJ, the FTC refused to conclude that the boycott was harmless, noting that the * * * boycott forced the city government to increase the CJA fees from a level that had been sufficient to obtain an adequate supply of CJA lawyers to a level satisfactory to the respondents. * * *

The Court of Appeals vacated the FTC order and remanded for a determination whether respondents possessed "significant market power." The court began its analysis by recognizing that absent any special First Amendment protection, the boycott "constituted a classic restraint of trade within the meaning of Section 1 of the Sherman Act." * * * The Court of Appeals was not persuaded by respondents' reliance on *Claiborne Hardware* or *Noerr*, or by their argument that the boycott was justified because it was designed to improve the quality of representation for indigent defendants. It concluded, however, that "the SCTLA boycott did contain an element of expression warranting First Amendment protection." It noted that boycotts have historically been used as a dramatic means of expression and that respondents intended to convey a political message to the public at large. It therefore concluded that under *United States* v. *O'Brien*, 391 U.S. 367 (1968), a restriction on this form of expression could not be justified unless it is no greater than is essential to an important governmental interest. This test, the court reasoned, could not be satisfied by the application of an otherwise appropriate *per se* rule, but instead required the enforcement agency to "prove rather than presume that the evil against which the Sherman Act is directed looms in the conduct it condemns." * * *

* * *

III

* * * We may assume that the preboycott rates were unreasonably low, and that the increase has produced better legal representation for indigent defendants. Moreover, given that neither indigent criminal defendants nor the lawyers who represent them command any special appeal with the electorate, we may also assume that without the boycott there would have been no increase in District CJA fees at least until the Congress amended the federal statute. These assumptions do not control the case, for it is not our task to pass upon the social utility or political wisdom of price-fixing agreements.

As the ALJ, the FTC, and the Court of Appeals all agreed, respondents' boycott "constituted a classic restraint of trade within the meaning of Section 1 of the Sherman Act." As such, it also violated the prohibition against unfair methods of competition in § 5 of the FTC Act. Prior to the boycott CJA lawyers were in competition with one another, each deciding independently whether and how often to offer to provide services to the District at CJA rates. The agreement among the CJA lawyers was designed to obtain higher prices for their services and was implemented by a concerted refusal to serve an important customer in the market for legal services and, indeed, the only customer in the market for the particular services that CJA regulars offered. "This constriction of supply is the essence of 'price-fixing,' whether it be accomplished by agreeing upon a price, which will decrease the quantity demanded, or by agreeing upon an output, which will increase the price offered." The horizontal arrangement among these competitors was unquestionably a "naked restraint" on price and output.

* * *

The social justifications proffered for respondents' restraint of trade thus do not make it any less unlawful. The statutory policy underlying the Sherman Act "precludes inquiry into the question whether competition is good or bad." Respondents' argument * * * ultimately asks us to find that their boycott is permissible because the price it seeks to set is reasonable. But it was settled shortly after the Sherman Act was passed that it * * * is no excuse that the prices fixed are themselves reasonable. * * *

Our decision in *Noerr* in no way detracts from this conclusion. In *Noerr*, we "considered whether the Sherman Act prohibited a publicity campaign waged by railroads" and "designed to foster the adoption of laws destructive of the trucking business, to create an atmosphere of distaste for truckers among the general public, and to impair the relationships existing between truckers and their customers." Interpreting the Sherman Act in the light of the First Amendment's Petition Clause, the Court noted that "at least insofar as the railroads' campaign was directed toward obtaining governmental action, its legality was not at all affected by any anticompetitive purpose it may have had."

It of course remains true that "no violation of the Act can be predicated upon mere attempts to influence the passage or enforcement of laws," even if the defendants' sole purpose is to impose a restraint upon the trade of their competitors. But in the *Noerr* case the alleged restraint of trade was the intended *consequence* of public action; in this case the boycott was the *means* by which respondents sought to obtain favorable legislation. The restraint of trade that was implemented while the boycott lasted would have had precisely the same anticompetitive consequences during that period even if no legislation had been enacted. In *Noerr*, the desired legislation would have created the restraint on the truckers' competition; in this case the emergency legislative response to the boycott put an end to the restraint.

* * *

IV

SCTLA argues that if its conduct would otherwise be prohibited by the Sherman Act and the Federal Trade Commission Act, it is nonetheless protected by the First Amendment rights recognized in *NAACP v. Claiborne Hardware Co.*, 458 U.S. 886 (1982). That case arose after black citizens boycotted white merchants in Claiborne County, Mississippi. The white merchants sued under state law to recover losses from the boycott. We found that the "right of the States to regulate economic activity could not justify a complete prohibition against a nonviolent, politically motivated boycott designed to force governmental and economic change and to effectuate rights guaranteed by the Constitution itself." * * *

* * *

The activity that the FTC order prohibits is a concerted refusal by CJA lawyers to accept any further assignments until they receive an increase in their compensation; the undenied objective of their boycott was an economic advantage for those who agreed to participate. * * * Those who joined the *Claiborne Hardware* boycott sought no special advantage for themselves. They were black citizens in Port Gibson, Mississippi, who had been the victims of political, social, and economic discrimination for many years. They sought only the equal respect and equal treatment to which they were constitutionally entitled. * * * As we observed, the campaign was not intended "to destroy legitimate competition." * * * Equality and freedom are preconditions of the free market, and not commodities to be haggled over within it.

The same cannot be said of attorney's fees. * * * [O]ur reasoning in *Claiborne Hardware* is not applicable to a boycott conducted by business competitors who "stand to profit financially from a lessening of competition in the boycotted market." * * *

* * *

V
* * *

The Court of Appeals, however, crafted a new exception to the *per se* rules, and it is this exception which provoked the FTC's petition to this Court. The Court of Appeals derived its exception from *United States v. O'Brien*, 391

U.S. 367 (1968). In that case O'Brien had burned his Selective Service registration certificate on the steps of the South Boston Courthouse. He did so before a sizable crowd and with the purpose of advocating his antiwar beliefs. We affirmed his conviction. We held that the governmental interest in regulating the "nonspeech element" of his conduct adequately justified the incidental restriction on First Amendment freedoms. * * *

However, the Court of Appeals held that, in light of *O'Brien*, the expressive component of respondents' boycott compelled courts to apply the antitrust laws "prudently and with sensitivity," ... with a "special solicitude for the First Amendment rights" of respondents. The Court of Appeals concluded that the governmental interest in prohibiting boycotts is not sufficient to justify a restriction on the communicative element of the boycott unless the FTC can prove, and not merely presume, that the boycotters have market power. Because the Court of Appeals imposed this special requirement upon the government, it ruled that *per se* antitrust analysis was inapplicable to boycotts having an expressive component.

There are at least two critical flaws in the Court of Appeals' antitrust analysis: it exaggerates the significance of the expressive component in respondents' boycott and it denigrates the importance of the rule of law that respondents violated. Implicit in the conclusion of the Court of Appeals are unstated assumptions that most economic boycotts do not have an expressive component, and that the categorical prohibitions against price fixing and boycotts are merely rules of "administrative convenience" that do not serve any substantial governmental interest unless the price-fixing competitors actually possess market power.

It would not much matter to the outcome of this case if these flawed assumptions were sound. *O'Brien* would offer respondents no protection even if their boycott were uniquely expressive and even if the purpose of the *per se* rules were purely that of administrative efficiency. * * * The administrative efficiency interests in antitrust regulation are unusually compelling. The *per se* rules avoid "the necessity for an incredibly complicated and prolonged economic investigation into the entire history of the industry involved, as well as related industries, in an effort to determine at large whether a particular restraint has been unreasonable." If small parties "were allowed to prove lack of market power, all parties would have that right, thus introducing the enormous complexities of market definition into every price-fixing case." For these reasons, it is at least possible that the *Claiborne Hardware* doctrine, which itself rests in part upon *O'Brien*, exhausts *O'Brien's* application to the antitrust statutes.

In any event, however, we cannot accept the Court of Appeals' characterization of this boycott or the antitrust laws. Every concerted refusal to do business with a potential customer or supplier has an expressive component. At one level, the competitors must exchange their views about their objectives and the means of obtaining them. The most blatant, naked price-fixing agreement is a product of communication, but that is surely not a reason for viewing it with special solicitude. At another level, after the terms of the boycotters' demands have been agreed upon, they must be communicated to its target: "[W]e will not do business until you do what we ask." That expressive component of the boycott conducted by these respondents is surely not unique. On the contrary, it is the hallmark of every effective boycott.

At a third level, the boycotters may communicate with third parties to enlist public support for their objectives; to the extent that the boycott is newsworthy, it will facilitate the expression of the boycotters' ideas. But this level of expression is not an element of the boycott. * * *

In sum, there is thus nothing unique about the "expressive component" of respondents' boycott. A rule that requires courts to apply the antitrust laws "prudently and with sensitivity" whenever an economic boycott has an "expressive component" would create a gaping hole in the fabric of those laws. Respondents' boycott thus has no special characteristics meriting an exemption from the *per se* rules of antitrust law.

Equally important is the second error implicit in respondents' claim to immunity from the *per se* rules. In its opinion, the Court of Appeals assumed that the antitrust laws permit, but do not require, the condemnation of price fixing and boycotts without proof of market power. * * * The opinion further assumed that the *per se* rule prohibiting such activity "is only a rule of 'administrative convenience and efficiency,' not a statutory command." This statement contains two errors. The *per se* rules are, of course, the product of judicial interpretations of the Sherman Act, but the rules nevertheless have the same force and effect as any other statutory commands. Moreover, while the *per se* rule against price fixing and boycotts is indeed justified in part by "administrative convenience," the Court of Appeals erred in describing the prohibition as justified only by such concerns. The *per se* rules also reflect a longstanding judgment that the prohibited practices by their nature have "a substantial potential for impact on competition." * * *

* * *

The *per se* rules in antitrust law serve purposes analogous to *per se* restrictions upon, for example, stunt flying in congested areas or speeding. Laws prohibiting stunt flying or setting speed limits are justified by the State's interest in protecting human life and property. Perhaps most violations of such rules actually cause no harm. No doubt many experienced drivers and pilots can operate much more safely, even at prohibited speeds, than the average citizen.

If the especially skilled drivers and pilots were to paint messages on their cars, or attach streamers to their planes, their conduct would have an expressive component. High speeds and unusual maneuvers would help to draw attention to their messages. Yet the laws may nonetheless be enforced against these skilled persons without proof that their conduct was actually harmful or dangerous.

In part, the justification for these *per se* rules is rooted in administrative convenience. They are also supported, however, by the observation that every speeder and every stunt pilot poses some threat to the community. * * *

So it is with boycotts and price fixing.[16] Every such horizontal arrangement among competitors poses some threat to the free market. A small

---

16. "In sum, price-fixing cartels are condemned per se because the conduct is tempting to businessmen but very dangerous to society. The conceivable social benefits are few in prin-

participant in the market is, obviously, less likely to cause persistent damage than a large participant. Other participants in the market may act quickly and effectively to take the small participant's place. For reasons including market inertia and information failures, however, a small conspirator may be able to impede competition over some period of time. Given an appropriate set of circumstances and some luck, the period can be long enough to inflict real injury upon particular consumers or competitors.

* * *

Of course, some boycotts and some price-fixing agreements are more pernicious than others; some are only partly successful, and some may only succeed when they are buttressed by other causative factors, such as political influence. But an assumption that, absent proof of market power, the boycott disclosed by this record was totally harmless—when overwhelming testimony demonstrated that it almost produced a crisis in the administration of criminal justice in the District and when it achieved its economic goal—is flatly inconsistent with the clear course of our antitrust jurisprudence. Conspirators need not achieve the dimensions of a monopoly, or even a degree of market power any greater than that already disclosed by this record, to warrant condemnation under the antitrust laws.

* * *

[The opinion of Justices Brennan and Marshall, concurring in part, and dissenting in part, is omitted, as is the opinion of Mr. Justice Blackmun, also concurring in part and dissenting in part. Eds.]

What makes *SCTLA* a case of "collusive" group boycott? Note that it could easily be viewed as a price fixing agreement among competitors—the members of the SCTLA collectively agreed upon a specific hourly rate for their services and demanded it from their customer, the District of Columbia. Yet the mechanism chosen to implement the price fixing scheme was a boycott of the buyer, the D.C. government. This point was emphasized near the end of the majority's opinion in response to an argument made by Justice Brennan in his dissent. Brennan argued that in fact not all boycotts had been deemed per se unlawful by the Court. Justice Stevens replied for the majority:

> In response to Justice Brennan's opinion, and particularly to its observation that some concerted arrangements that might be characterized as "group boycotts" may not merit per se condemnation * * * we emphasize that this case involves not only a boycott but also a horizontal price-fixing arrangement-a type of conspiracy that has been consistently analyzed as a per se violation for many decades.

ciple, small in magnitude, speculative in occurrence, and always premised on the existence of price-fixing power which is likely to be exercised adversely to the public. Moreover, toleration implies a burden of continuous supervision for which the courts consider themselves ill-suited. And even if power is usually established while any defenses are not, litigation will be complicated, condemnation delayed, would be price-fixers encouraged to hope for escape, and criminal punishment less justified. Deterrence of a generally pernicious practice would be weakened. The key points are the first two. Without them, there is no justification for categorical condemnation." 7 P. Areeda, Antitrust Law ¶ 1509, pp. 412–413 (1986).

All of the "group boycott" cases cited in Justice Brennan's footnote involved nonprice restraints. There was likewise no price-fixing component in any of the boycotts listed [in] * * * Justice BRENNAN's opinion. Indeed, the text of the opinion virtually ignores the price-fixing component of respondents' concerted action.

493 U.S. at 436 n.19. Is the majority implicitly recognizing that collusive group boycotts should be treated as per se unlawful? Only those that function as a mechanism to enforce an underlying price fixing agreement?

You may recall that in the notes preceding *Maricopa*, we discussed the Supreme Court's 1980 decision in *Catalano, Inc. v. Target Sales, Inc.*, 446 U.S. 643 (1980), where the Court struck down as price fixing a collective agreement by beer wholesalers to refuse to continue offering short-term credit. Yet the mechanism chosen by the wholesalers to enforce the agreement could be characterized as a boycott: they refused to deal with any beer retailer that would not pay in full either in advance or upon delivery. Should *Catalano* be categorized as a "boycott" or as a "price-fixing" case? Should it matter? Are the economic consequences of the conduct the same whether it bears one label or the other?

Note that a significant portion of the Court's opinion in *SCTLA* has to do with the inter-relationship of the Sherman Act and the First Amendment. Why? Would the SCTLA have been immune from antitrust prosecution had its members simply lobbied the D.C. government for an increase in the statutory rate they were paid for their services as CJA lawyers? What is the majority's response to the fact that SCTLA's conduct involved, but went beyond simple lobbying?

The Majority's treatment of the First Amendment issue provoked a pointed dissent by Justices Brennan and Marshall. While concurring in the majority's conclusion that the SCTLA's actions were neither outside the scope of the Sherman Act, nor automatically immunized from antitrust regulation by the First Amendment, Justices Brennan and Marshall took issue with Part V of the majority's opinion—its discussion of *United States v. O'Brien*. In their view, the majority's endorsement of the FTC's use of the per se rule demonstrated insensitivity "to the venerable tradition of expressive boycotts as an important means of political communication." 493 U.S. at 782–83 (Brennan, J., dissenting).

Might the alignment of the justices in the decision have been affected by the injection of First Amendment issues? What fear regarding the First Amendment likely prompted Justices Brennan and Marshall to back away from the Court's application of the per se rule? Would that concern be relevant to all collusive group boycotts, or just those involving "expressive" components? Might the majority have viewed the case as an opportunity to contain the scope of First Amendment protections? Considering both opinions—is it possible that the views of the majority and the dissent concerning the First Amendment explain more about their positions in the case than their views on antitrust enforcement? Is there a tension for both the majority and the dissent between their views on the scope of antitrust enforcement and their views of the scope of protected speech under the First Amendment?

We will return to this difficult area of antitrust law in Chapter 9, when we will again see that conduct that would appear to fall within the scope of the First Amendment can have significant anticompetitive consequences.

Finally, note that the SCTLA also argued that it should be treated as a labor union, immune from antitrust scrutiny under the exemptions set forth in the Norris LaGuardia Act, 29 U.S.C. § 101, et. seq. Why should labor unions be exempt from the coverage of the Sherman Act for their collective bargaining efforts, including the threat of strike? Why didn't SCTLA succeed in invoking the Act? We will return to the issue of statutory exemptions in Chapter 8.

The next figure summarizes the general state of per se rules as it stands today. Consider the Court's evolution away from reliance on per se rules as we move on to our discussion of the rule of reason in the next section.

Figure 2–5:
Summary of Traditional Horizontal Per Se Rules

Price Fixing	Division of Markets	Concerted Refusals to Deal	
Foundation Cases:	Foundation Cases:	Foundation Cases:	
Trenton Potteries (1927) *Socony-Vacuum Oil* (1940)	*Timken* (1951) *Sealy* (1967) *Topco* (1972)	*Eastern States* (1914) *FOGA* (1941) *Klor's* (1959)	
Current Status:	Current Status:	Current Status:	
Operative under *Maricopa* (1982), but with *BMI* (1979), *NCAA* (1984), and *Dagher* (2006) qualifications.	Operative under *BRG* (1990); vitality of *Topco* eroded by *BMI* (1979), *Sylvania* (1977), and other decisions.	Collusive Operative under *SCTLA* (1990)	Exclusionary Operative as qualified by *Northwest Wholesale Stationers* (1985)

E. COLLUSIVE EFFECTS AND THE "RULE OF REASON"

To this point in the Chapter we have focused largely on the development of the Supreme Court's per se jurisprudence under Section 1 of the Sherman Act in cases involving agreements among competitors, examining cases from 1927 to 1990. We now turn the clock back to 1918, and focus our attention on the parallel development of the "rule of reason" during that time. After exploring its traditional origins, we will address contemporary developments in the use of the per se and rule of reason approaches.

1. ORIGINS OF THE TRADITIONAL "RULE OF REASON"

As discussed earlier in this Chapter, the Supreme Court read the "rule of reason" into Section 1 of the Sherman Act in its 1911 *Standard Oil* decision. Seven years later, Justice Brandeis set out what has become the prevailing statement of that rule and the earliest example of its practical operation in *Chicago Bd. of Trade.* As you read the case, try to answer the question: "what is the content of the rule of reason?" What factors does it identify as relevant to the rule of reason inquiry? How are those factors to be weighted? What defenses can be raised in rule of reason cases? How are burdens of production to be allocated among the plaintiffs and defendants in rule of reason cases?

BOARD OF TRADE OF CITY OF CHICAGO v. UNITED STATES
Supreme Court of the United States, 1918.
246 U.S. 231, 38 S.Ct. 242, 62 L.Ed. 683.

Mr. Justice BRANDEIS delivered the opinion of the Court.

Chicago is the leading grain market in the world. Its Board of Trade is the commercial center through which most of the trading in grain is done. * * * Its 1600 members include brokers, commission merchants, dealers, millers, maltsters, manufacturers of corn products and proprietors of elevators. * * * The standard forms of trading are: (a) Spot sales; that is, sales of grain already in Chicago in railroad cars or elevators for immediate delivery by order on carrier or transfer of warehouse receipt. (b) Future sales; that is, agreements for delivery later in the current or in some future month. (c) Sales 'to arrive'; that is, agreements to deliver on arrival grain which is already in transit to Chicago or is to be shipped there within a time specified. On every business day sessions of the Board are held at which all bids and sales are publicly made. Spot sales and future sales are made at the regular sessions of the Board from 9:30 a. m. to 1:15 p. m., except on Saturdays, when the session closes at 12 m. Special sessions, termed the 'call,' are held immediately after the close of the regular session, at which sales 'to arrive' are made. These sessions are not limited as to duration, but last usually about half an hour. At all these sessions transactions are between members only; but they may trade either for themselves or on behalf of others. Members may also trade privately with one another at any place, either during the sessions or after, and they may trade with nonmembers at any time except on the premises occupied by the Board.

* * *

In 1906 the Board adopted what is known as the 'call' rule. By it members were prohibited from purchasing or offering to purchase, during the period between the close of the call and the opening of the session on the next business day, any wheat, corn, oats or rye 'to arrive' at a price other than the closing bid at the call. The call was over, with rare exceptions, by 2 o'clock. The change effected was this: Before the adoption of the rule, members fixed their bids throughout the day at such prices as they respectively saw fit; after the adoption of the rule, the bids had to be fixed at the day's closing bid on the call until the opening of the next session.

In 1913 the United States filed in the District Court for the Northern District of Illinois, this suit against the Board and its executive officers and directors, to enjoin the enforcement of the call rule, alleging it to be in violation of the Anti–Trust Law of July 2, 1890 [the Sherman Act]. The defendants admitted the adoption and enforcement of the call rule, and averred that its purpose was not to prevent competition or to control prices, but to promote the convenience of members by restricting their hours of business and to break up a monopoly in that branch of the grain trade acquired by four or five warehousemen in Chicago. On motion of the government the allegations concerning the purpose of establishing the regulation were stricken from the record. The case was then heard upon evidence; and a decree was entered which declared that defendants became parties to a combination or conspiracy to restrain interstate and foreign trade and commerce "by adopting, acting upon and enforcing" the "call" rule; and enjoined them from acting upon the same or from adopting or acting upon any similar rule.

* * * The government proved the existence of the rule and described its application and the change in business practice involved. It made no attempt to show that the rule was designed to or that it had the effect of limiting the amount of grain shipped to Chicago; or of retarding or accelerating shipment; or of raising or depressing prices; or of discriminating against any part of the public; or that it resulted in hardship to any one. The case was rested upon the bald proposition, that a rule or agreement by which men occupying positions of strength in any branch of trade, fixed prices at which they would buy or sell during an important part of the business day, is an illegal restraint of trade under the Anti–Trust Law. But the legality of an agreement or regulation cannot be determined by so simple a test, as whether it restrains competition. Every agreement concerning trade, every regulation of trade, restrains. To bind, to restrain, is of their very essence. The true test of legality is whether the restraint imposed is such as merely regulates and perhaps thereby promotes competition or whether it is such as may suppress or even destroy competition. To determine that question the court must ordinarily consider the facts peculiar to the business to which the restraint is applied; its condition before and after the restraint was imposed; the nature of the restraint and its effect, actual or probable. The history of the restraint, the evil believed to exist, the reason for adopting the particular remedy, the purpose or end sought to be attained, are all relevant facts. This is not because a good intention will save an otherwise objectionable regulation or the reverse; but because knowledge of intent may help the court to interpret facts and to predict consequences. The District Court erred, therefore, in striking from the answer allegations concerning the history and purpose of the call rule and in later excluding evidence on that subject. But the evidence admitted makes it clear that the rule was a reasonable regulation of business consistent with the provisions of the Anti–Trust Law.

First. The nature of the rule: The restriction was upon the period of price-making. It required members to desist from further price-making after the close of the call until 9:30 a.m. the next business day; but there was no restriction upon the sending out of bids after close of the call. Thus it required members who desired to buy grain "to arrive" to make up their minds before the close of the call how much they were willing to pay during the interval before the next session of the Board. The rule made it to their interest to attend the call; and if they did not fill their wants by purchases there, to make the final bid high enough to enable them to purchase from country dealers.

Second. The scope of the rule: It is restricted in operation to grain "to arrive." It applies only to a small part of the grain shipped from day to day to Chicago, and to an even smaller part of the day's sales; members were left free to purchase grain already in Chicago from any one at any price throughout the day. It applies only during a small part of the business day; members were left free to purchase during the sessions of the Board grain "to arrive," at any price, from members anywhere and from nonmembers anywhere except on the premises of the Board. It applied only to grain shipped to Chicago; members were left free to purchase at any price throughout the day from either members or non-members, grain "to arrive" at any other market. Country dealers and farmers had available in practically every part of the territory called tributary to Chicago some other market for grain "to arrive."
* * *

Third. The effects of the rule: As it applies to only a small part of the grain shipped to Chicago and to that only during a part of the business day and does not apply at all to grain shipped to other markets, the rule had no appreciable effect on general market prices; nor did it materially affect the total volume of grain coming to Chicago. But within the narrow limits of its operation the rule helped to improve market conditions thus:

(a) It created a public market for grain "to arrive." Before its adoption, bids were made privately. Men had to buy and sell without adequate knowledge of actual market conditions. This was disadvantageous to all concerned, but particularly so to country dealers and farmers.

(b) It brought into the regular market hours of the Board sessions, more of the trading in grain "to arrive."

(c) It brought buyers and sellers into more direct relations; because on the call they gathered together for a free and open interchange of bids and offers.

(d) It distributed the business in grain "to arrive" among a far larger number of Chicago receivers and commission merchants than had been the case there before.

(e) It increased the number of country dealers engaging in this branch of the business; supplied them more regularly with bids from Chicago; and also increased the number of bids received by them from competing markets.

(f) It eliminated risks necessarily incident to a private market, and thus enabled country dealers to do business on a smaller margin. In that way the rule made it possible for them to pay more to farmers without raising the price to consumers.

(g) It enabled country dealers to sell some grain to arrive which they would otherwise have been obliged either to ship to Chicago commission merchants or to sell for "future delivery."

(h) It enabled those grain merchants of Chicago who sell to millers and exporters, to trade on a smaller margin and by paying more for grain or selling it for less, to make the Chicago market more attractive for both shippers and buyers of grain.

(i) Incidentally it facilitated trading "to arrive" by enabling those engaged in these transactions to fulfill their contracts by tendering grain arriving at Chicago on any railroad, whereas formerly shipments had to be made over the particular railroad designated by the buyer.

* * * Every Board of Trade and nearly every trade organization imposes some restraint upon the conduct of business by its members. Those relating to the hours in which business may be done are common; and they make a special appeal where, as here, they tend to shorten the working day or, at least, limit the period of most exacting activity. The decree of the District Court is reversed with directions to dismiss the bill.

Reversed.

————

If *Chicago Bd. of Trade* had arisen after *Socony-Vacuum Oil* solidified the per se ban on price-fixing, but before *Broadcast Music* limited its reach, would the Court have been more inclined to treat the Board of Trade's conduct as price-fixing and condemn it as illegal per se? Were the restrictions on trading imposed by the Board of Trade harmful to competition, pro-competitive, or competitively of little consequence?

What is the test of "reasonableness" announced by the Court in *Chicago Bd. of Trade*? What factors are deemed relevant to the inquiry? Consider the following summary:

Figure 2–6:
The *Chicago Board of Trade* Rule of Reason

Major Propositions:

(1) "true test of legality is whether the restraint imposed is such as merely regulates and perhaps thereby promotes competition or whether it is such as may suppress or even destroy competition."

(2) Three Categories of Factors to Consider: Nature; Scope; Effect

Relevant Factors:

- **facts peculiar to the business**
  - conditions of business before and after restraint was imposed
- **nature of restraint**
  - its effect, actual or probable
- **history and purposes of the restraint**
  - evil believed to exist
  - reason for adopting particular remedy
  - purpose or end sought to be attained
  - these are "all relevant factors"

———

Remarkably, from 1918 when *Chicago Bd. of Trade* was decided, until the late 1970s, the rule of reason received little in the way of further consideration or elaboration from the Supreme Court. During that time and continuing to today, *Chicago Bd. of Trade's* formulation of the rule of reason has proved to be an enduring source of controversy. Some commentators have criticized its formulation as "empty," *e.g.*, Thomas C. Arthur, *Farewell to the Sea of Doubt: Jettisoning the Constitutional Sherman Act*, 74 Cal. L. Rev. 263 (1986); Frank H. Easterbrook, *The Limits of Antitrust*, 63 Tex. L. Rev. 1 (1984), and it has spawned continuing debates about the meaning and utility of so general a test of lawfulness as "reasonableness." *See, e.g.*, Symposium: *The Future Course of the Rule of Reason*, 68 Antitrust L.J. 331 (2000); Peter C. Carstensen, *The Content of the Hollow Core of Antitrust: The* Chicago Board of Trade *Case and the Meaning of the "Rule of Reason" in Restraint of Trade Analysis*, 1992 J. Res. L. & Econ. 1 (1992). Why should that be so? What problems can you anticipate in applying the test as articulated in *Chicago Bd. of Trade*?

As we will study in greater depth later in this Chapter and again in Chapter 8, one of the enduring legacies of the rule of reason as described in *Chicago Bd. of Trade*, is its flexibility and adaptability. But those features also have led to considerable uncertainty. Three questions, in particular, remained unanswered after *Chicago Bd. of Trade*:

> (1) What factors matter to the rule of reason inquiry? Is the list provided in *Chicago Bd. of Trade* exhaustive or suggestive? Within its more general categories are there more specific ones?

> (2) How are competing factors to be weighted? *Chicago Bd. of Trade* says nothing, for example, about how courts are to weigh countervailing evidence. What if there is evidence that the "nature" of the agreement was anticompetitive, but that it also had some important and arguably procompetitive justifications? Is the agreement a reasonable or unreasonable restraint of trade?

> (3) How are burdens of production and proof to be allocated under the rule of reason? How much and what kind of evidence of "purpose, nature, and effect" will be sufficient to shift a burden of production to the defendant? How much and what kind of evidence can a defendant introduce to rebut?

As noted earlier in the Chapter, the Court's failure to specify these particulars may have been due in part to its increased reliance throughout that period on per se rules, which continued to be viewed favorably until the Supreme Court's watershed decision in *Continental T.V., Inc. v. GTE Sylvania Inc.*, 433 U.S. 36 (1977)(Casebook, *infra* Chapter 4.). *Sylvania* appeared to turn the tide, returning the Court's attention to the content of the rule of reason and the wisdom of expansive use of per se rules. Within two years of *Sylvania*, a vertical restraint case, the Court began to more carefully consider the tension between the per se and rule of reason approaches in horizontal cases, as well. In doing so, it began to focus the relevant inquiry more and more on competitive effects, just as it had done in *Sylvania*.

Broadcast Music, which we studied earlier in this Chapter, and our next case, *Nat'l Soc'y of Prof'l Eng'rs,* which was decided a year before *Broadcast Music,* evidence two important trends that materialized in the Supreme Court in the late 1970s. First, as we have already noted, the Court began to move away from heavy reliance on per se rules. In doing so it returned to *Chicago Bd. of Trade's* loose framework, but was compelled to confront its vagueness. That triggered a second trend—a still evolving effort by the Court to move the rule of reason towards greater certainty, particularity, and predictability. In this effort, as will be seen, the courts have developed a variety of "quick look" rules and structured inquiries for implementing the rule of reason. That process of evolution continues today, and will be evident in much of the material considered in the remainder of this Chapter and in Chapter 8.

NATIONAL SOCIETY OF PROFESSIONAL ENGINEERS v. UNITED STATES
Supreme Court of the United States, 1978.
435 U.S. 679, 98 S.Ct. 1355, 55 L.Ed.2d 637.

Mr. Justice STEVENS delivered the opinion of the Court.

This is a civil antitrust case brought by the United States to nullify an association's canon of ethics prohibiting competitive bidding by its members. The question is whether the canon may be justified under the Sherman Act, because it was adopted by members of a learned profession for the purpose of minimizing the risk that competition would produce inferior engineering work endangering the public safety. The District Court rejected this justification without making any findings on the likelihood that competition would produce the dire consequences foreseen by the association. The Court of Appeals affirmed. * * * Because we are satisfied that the asserted defense rests on a fundamental misunderstanding of the Rule of Reason frequently applied in antitrust litigation, we affirm.

I

Engineering is an important and learned profession. There are over 750,000 graduate engineers in the United States, of whom about 325,000 are registered as professional engineers. * * * They perform services in connection with the study, design, and construction of all types of improvements to real property—bridges, office buildings, airports, and factories are examples. * * *

The National Society of Professional Engineers (Society) was organized in 1935 to deal with the nontechnical aspects of engineering practice, including the promotion of the professional, social, and economic interests of its members. Its present membership of 69,000 resides throughout the United States and in some foreign countries. * * *

The charges of a consulting engineer may be computed in different ways. He may charge the client a percentage of the cost of the project, may set his fee at his actual cost plus overhead plus a reasonable profit, may charge fixed rates per hour for different types of work, may perform an assignment for a specific sum, or he may combine one or more of these approaches. Suggested fee schedules for particular types of services in certain areas have been promulgated from time to time by various local societies. This case does not, however, involve any claim that the National Society has tried to fix specific fees, or even a specific method of calculating fees. It involves a charge that the members of the Society have unlawfully agreed to refuse to negotiate or even to discuss the question of fees until after a prospective client has selected the engineer for a particular project. Evidence of this agreement is found in § 11(c) of the Society's Code of Ethics, adopted in July 1964.[3]

* * *

In 1972 the Government filed its complaint against the Society alleging that members had agreed to abide by canons of ethics prohibiting the submission of competitive bids for engineering services and that, in consequence, price competition among the members had been suppressed and customers had been deprived of the benefits of free and open competition. The complaint prayed for an injunction terminating the unlawful agreement.

In its answer the Society admitted the essential facts alleged by the Government and pleaded a series of affirmative defenses, only one of which remains in issue. In that defense, the Society averred that the standard set out in the Code of Ethics was reasonable because competition among professional engineers was contrary to the public interest. It was averred that it would be cheaper and easier for an engineer "to design and specify inefficient and unnecessarily expensive structures and methods of construction." * * * Accordingly, competitive pressure to offer engineering services at the lowest possible price would adversely affect the quality of engineering. Moreover, the practice of awarding engineering contracts to the lowest bidder, regardless of quality, would be dangerous to the public health, safety, and welfare. For these reasons, the Society claimed that its Code of Ethics was not an "unreasonable restraint of interstate trade or commerce."

* * *

II

* * *

A. *The Rule of Reason.*

One problem presented by the language of § 1 of the Sherman Act is that it cannot mean what it says. The statute says that "every" contract that restrains trade is unlawful. * * * But, as Mr. Justice Brandeis perceptively noted, restraint is the very essence of every contract; * * * read literally, § 1 would outlaw the entire body of private contract law. Yet it is that body of law that establishes the enforceability of commercial agreements and enables competitive markets—indeed, a competitive economy—to function effectively.

Congress, however, did not intend the text of the Sherman Act to delineate the full meaning of the statute or its application in concrete situations. The legislative history makes it perfectly clear that it expected the courts to give shape to the statute's broad mandate by drawing on common-

---

3. That section, which remained in effect at the time of trial, provided:

"Section 11—The Engineer will not compete unfairly with another engineer by attempting to obtain employment or advancement or

professional engagements by competitive bidding. * * *

c. He shall not solicit or submit engineering proposals on the basis of competitive bidding. * * *

law tradition. The Rule of Reason, with its origins in common-law precedents long antedating the Sherman Act, has served that purpose. It has been used to give the Act both flexibility and definition, and its central principle of antitrust analysis has remained constant. Contrary to its name, the Rule does not open the field of antitrust inquiry to any argument in favor of a challenged restraint that may fall within the realm of reason. Instead, it focuses directly on the challenged restraint's impact on competitive conditions.

* * *

The Rule of Reason * * * has been regarded as a standard for testing the enforceability of covenants in restraint of trade which are ancillary to a legitimate transaction, such as an employment contract or the sale of a going business. Judge (later Mr. Chief Justice) Taft so interpreted the Rule in his classic rejection of the argument that competitors may lawfully agree to sell their goods at the same price as long as the agreed-upon price is reasonable. *United States v. Addyston Pipe & Steel Co.* That case, and subsequent decisions by this Court, unequivocally foreclose an interpretation of the Rule as permitting an inquiry into the reasonableness of the prices set by private agreement.

The early cases also foreclose the argument that because of the special characteristics of a particular industry, monopolistic arrangements will better promote trade and commerce than competition. That kind of argument is properly addressed to Congress and may justify an exemption from the statute for specific industries, but it is not permitted by the Rule of Reason. * * *

The test prescribed in *Standard Oil* is whether the challenged contracts or acts "were unreasonably restrictive of competitive conditions." Unreasonableness under that test could be based either (1) on the nature or character of the contracts, or (2) on surrounding circumstances giving rise to the inference or presumption that they were intended to restrain trade and enhance prices. * * * Under either branch of the test, the inquiry is confined to a consideration of impact on competitive conditions.

In this respect the Rule of Reason has remained faithful to its origins. From Mr. Justice Brandeis' opinion for the Court in *Chicago Board of Trade,* to the Court opinion written by Mr. Justice Powell in *Continental T. V., Inc.,* the Court has adhered to the position that the inquiry mandated by the Rule of Reason is whether the challenged agreement is one that promotes competition or one that suppresses competition. "The true test of legality is whether the restraint imposed is such as merely regulates and perhaps thereby promotes competition or whether it is such as may suppress or even destroy competition." [*Chicago Bd. of Trade,*] 246 U.S. at 238.

There are, thus, two complementary categories of antitrust analysis. In the first category are agreements whose nature and necessary effect are so plainly anticompetitive that no elaborate study of the industry is needed to establish their illegality—they are "illegal *per se*." In the second category are agreements whose competitive effect can only be evaluated by analyzing the facts peculiar to the business, the history of the restraint, and the reasons why it was imposed. In either event, the purpose of the analysis is to form a judgment about the competitive significance of the restraint; it is not to decide whether a policy favoring competition is in the public interest, or in the interest of the members of an industry. Subject to exceptions defined by statute, that policy decision has been made by the Congress.

B.   The Ban on Competitive Bidding

Price is the "central nervous system of the economy," and an agreement that "interfere[s] with the setting of price by free market forces" is illegal on its face. In this case we are presented with an agreement among competitors to refuse to discuss prices with potential customers until after negotiations have resulted in the initial selection of an engineer. While this is not price fixing as such, no elaborate industry analysis is required to demonstrate the anticompetitive character of such an agreement. It operates as an absolute ban on competitive bidding, applying with equal force to both complicated and simple projects and to both inexperienced and sophisticated customers. As the District Court found, the ban "impedes the ordinary give and take of the market place," and substantially deprives the customer of "the ability to utilize and compare prices in selecting engineering services." On its face, this agreement restrains trade within the meaning of § 1 of the Sherman Act.

The Society's affirmative defense confirms rather than refutes the anticompetitive purpose and effect of its agreement. The Society argues that the restraint is justified because bidding on engineering services is inherently imprecise, would lead to deceptively low bids, and would thereby tempt individual engineers to do inferior work with consequent risk to public safety and health.[19] The logic of this argument rests on the assumption that the agreement will tend to maintain the price level; if it had no such effect, it would not serve its intended purpose. The Society nonetheless invokes the Rule of Reason, arguing that its restraint on price competition ultimately inures to the public benefit by preventing the production of inferior work and by insuring ethical behavior. As the preceding discussion of the Rule of Reason reveals, this Court has never accepted such an argument.

It may be, as petitioner argues, that competition tends to force prices down and that an inexpensive item may be inferior to one that is more costly. There is some risk, therefore, that competition will cause some suppliers to market a defective product. Similarly, competitive bidding for engineering projects may be inherently imprecise and incapable of taking into account all the variables which will be involved in the actual performance of the project. Based on these considerations, a purchaser might conclude that his interest in quality—which may embrace the safety of the end product—outweighs the

19.   The Society also points out that competition, in the form of bargaining between the engineer and customer, is allowed under its canon of ethics once an engineer has been initially selected. It then contends that its prohibition of competitive bidding regulates only the *timing* of competition, thus making this case analogous to *Chicago Board of Trade.* * * * We find this reliance on *Chicago Board of Trade* misplaced for two reasons. First, petitioner's claim mistakenly treats negotiation between a single seller and a single buyer as the equivalent of competition between two or more potential sellers. Second, even if we were to accept the Society's equation of bargaining with price competition, our concern with *Chicago Board of Trade* is in its formulation of the proper test to be used in judging the legality of an agreement; that formulation unquestionably stresses impact on competition. Whatever one's view of the application of the Rule of Reason in that case, the Court considered the exchange's regulation of price information as having a positive effect on competition. The District Court's findings preclude a similar conclusion concerning the effect of the Society's "regulation."

advantages of achieving cost savings by pitting one competitor against another. Or an individual vendor might independently refrain from price negotiation until he has satisfied himself that he fully understands the scope of his customers' needs. These decisions might be reasonable; indeed, petitioner has provided ample documentation for that thesis. But these are not reasons that satisfy the Rule; nor are such individual decisions subject to antitrust attack.

The Sherman Act does not require competitive bidding; it prohibits unreasonable restraints on competition. Petitioner's ban on competitive bidding prevents all customers from making price comparisons in the initial selection of an engineer, and imposes the Society's views of the costs and benefits of competition on the entire marketplace. It is this restraint that must be justified under the Rule of Reason, and petitioner's attempt to do so on the basis of the potential threat that competition poses to the public safety and the ethics of its profession is nothing less than a frontal assault on the basic policy of the Sherman Act.

The Sherman Act reflects a legislative judgment that ultimately competition will produce not only lower prices, but also better goods and services. "The heart of our national economic policy long has been faith in the value of competition." The assumption that competition is the best method of allocating resources in a free market recognizes that all elements of a bargain— quality, service, safety, and durability—and not just the immediate cost, are favorably affected by the free opportunity to select among alternative offers. Even assuming occasional exceptions to the presumed consequences of competition, the statutory policy precludes inquiry into the question whether competition is good or bad.

* * *

* * * We adhere to the view * * * that, by their nature, professional services may differ significantly from other business services, and, accordingly, the nature of the competition in such services may vary. Ethical norms may serve to regulate and promote this competition, and thus fall within the Rule of Reason. But the Society's argument in this case is a far cry from such a position. We are faced with a contention that a total ban on competitive bidding is necessary because otherwise engineers will be tempted to submit deceptively low bids. Certainly, the problem of professional deception is a proper subject of an ethical canon. But, once again, the equation of competition with deception, like the similar equation with safety hazards, is simply too broad; we may assume that competition is not entirely conducive to ethical behavior, but that is not a reason, cognizable under the Sherman Act, for doing away with competition.

In sum, the Rule of Reason does not support a defense based on the assumption that competition itself is unreasonable. Such a view of the Rule would create the "sea of doubt" on which Judge Taft refused to embark in *Addyston*, and which this Court has firmly avoided ever since.

* * *

———

[Justice Brennan took no part in the consideration or decision of the case. The opinion of Mr. Justice Blackmun, with whom Mr. Justice Rehnquist joined, concurring in part and concurring in the judgment, is omitted, as is the opinion of Mr. Chief Justice Burger, concurring in part and dissenting in part. Eds.]

————

Suppose the NSPE had evidence that when engineers engaged in competitive bidding the buildings and bridges they helped to build were more likely to have safety problems. For example, suppose—contrary to fact—that the NSPE only had members in half of the states, and it proffered an expert witness prepared to testify that in the 50% of states where the Society's Code of Ethics did not apply engineering services were lower in quality as well as lower in price. Should the NSPE have been permitted to introduce the expert's testimony? Why or why not?

Note on the Rule of Reason After Nat'l Soc'y Prof'l Eng'rs and Broadcast Music

The bipolar analytical framework described in *Nat'l Soc'y Prof'l Eng'rs* ("*NSPE*") had a significant impact on the allocation of the burdens of production and proof in antitrust cases. For cases falling under the per se rule, plaintiffs needed only to establish concerted action of a kind that fell within one of the recognized per se categories, like price-fixing, division of markets, or certain group boycotts. The courts would then presume that such conduct had the requisite unreasonable anticompetitive effect. As we have already noted, in evidentiary terms, the per se rule created an irrebuttable presumption of unreasonableness.

Under the rule of reason, *Chicago Bd. of Trade*'s approach called for a thorough-going, multi-factored analysis to prove that a given restraint was in fact unreasonable. When *Chicago Bd. of Trade* was combined with *NSPE*, it appeared that in a rule of reason case (in contrast to the per se approach), the plaintiff would have to introduce evidence of likely or actual adverse competitive effects and the defendants would be permitted to introduce evidence to rebut the plaintiff's case. The scope of the defendant's rebuttal would not be restricted, provided it was directed at the issue of effects. The Court made clear that "ruinous competition," like "reasonable prices," would not constitute a cognizable defense. But beyond this limitation, the specific requirements of burden shifting remained to be addressed.

In practice, plaintiffs found it much easier to prove cases under the per se rule than the rule of reason. In consequence, a court's determination as to whether the alleged conduct fell within or outside a category of per se conduct—a decision often termed "categorization" of the case—often was outcome determinative. The Court in *NSPE* twice emphasized, however, that whether the per se or rule of reason is applied, "the purpose of the analysis is to form a judgment about the competitive significance of the restraint." Even though the "rule of reason" and "per se rule" were specified as distinct modes of analysis, therefore, the Court made clear that they represented two paths to implementing the same underlying standard, the standard of "reasonableness." Accordingly, the "per se rule" can fairly be viewed as just an abbreviated method of applying the rule of reason.

Additional guidance in applying the rule of reason came a year after *NSPE* in the Court's decision in *Broadcast Music*. *Broadcast Music* appeared to mandate consideration of efficiencies, both in characterizing the conduct to determine whether a per se rule would apply and, if a per se rule was inapplicable, in determining whether competition would be harmed. In so doing, the Court provided important guidance about what kinds of defenses would be cognizable in a rule of reason case. The Court concluded in *Broadcast Music* that the presence of plausible efficiencies—cost reducing and output expanding tendencies—could justify moving a case out from under the per se label.

NSPE and *Broadcast Music*, together with other Supreme Court decisions of the period, combined to reframe antitrust rules around core economic concepts of anticompetitive effect, market power, and efficiencies: (1) the core issue for antitrust (especially Section 1 of the Sherman Act) was anticompetitive effects; (2) such effects are unlikely to arise absent significant interbrand market power; and (3) before condemning conduct, consideration must also be given to its potential to generate efficiencies—lower costs and increased output. This constituted a more focused and economically-grounded framework than had existed before.

We will return to these issues later in this Chapter when we consider modern trends in application of the rule of reason. Before doing so, however, it is necessary to revisit the "second" rule of reason, Judge Taft's ancillary restraint formulation.

2.   ANCILLARY RESTRAINT ANALYSIS—AN ALTERNATIVE APPROACH TO DEFINING REASONABLENESS

As was noted above, Judge Taft's 1898 opinion in *Addyston Pipe* proceeded from a different view of the common law than did *Standard Oil* (1911) and *Chicago Bd. of Trade* (1918), and consequently proposed an arguably more limited approach to the integration of reasonableness into Section 1 of the Sherman Act. Owing in part to both criticism of the unstructured nature of *Chicago Bd. of Trade*-style rule of reason analysis and the kind of focus on anticompetitive effects reflected in cases like *Nat'l Soc'y of Prof'l Eng'rs* and *Broadcast Music*, *Addyston Pipe* has enjoyed something of a revival among both commentators and the courts.

Interest in *Addyston Pipe* may also have endured in part because of Taft, himself. He served as Solicitor General of the United States under President Benjamin Harrison, who signed the Sherman Act into law, and later served for eight years on the United States Court of Appeals for the Sixth Circuit, during which time he authored *Addyston Pipe*. In 1908 he was elected President, and in 1921 he became the only president ever also to serve as Chief Justice of the United States Supreme Court. As evidence of his persistent interest in antitrust law, he also authored one of the earliest monographs in the field. WILLIAM H. TAFT, THE ANTI-TRUST ACT AND THE SUPREME COURT (1914).

Here is a longer excerpt from the opinion he authored in 1898 in *Addyston Pipe*. Together with the earlier excerpt from *Broadcast Music*, consider what, if anything "ancillary restraint" analysis adds to our understanding of the rule of reason, as initially defined in *Chicago Bd. of Trade*. Consider as well its significance for defining the scope of any per se rule.

UNITED STATES v. ADDYSTON PIPE & STEEL CO.

United States Court of Appeals for the Sixth Circuit, 1898.
85 F. 271, *aff'd*, 175 U.S. 211 (1899).

Before HARLAN, Circuit Justice, and TAFT and LURTON, Circuit Judges.

TAFT, Circuit Judge.

* * *

From early times it was the policy of Englishmen to encourage trade in England, and to discourage those voluntary restraints which tradesmen were often induced to impose on themselves by contract. Courts recognized this public policy by refusing to enforce stipulations of this character. The objections to such restraints were mainly two. One was that by such contracts a man disabled himself from earning a livelihood with the risk of becoming a public charge, and deprived the community of the benefit of his labor. The other was that such restraints tended to give the covenantee, the beneficiary of such restraints, a monopoly of the trade, from which he had thus excluded one competitor, and by the same mean might exclude others.

* * *

The inhibition against restraints of trade at common law seems at first to have had no exception. After a time it became apparent to the people and the courts that it was in the interest of trade that certain covenants in restraint of trade should be enforced. It was of importance, as an incentive to industry and honest dealing in trade, that, after a man had built up a business with an extensive good will, he should be able to sell his business and good will to the best advantage, and he could not do so unless he could bind himself by an enforceable contract not to engage in the same business in such a way as to prevent injury to that which he was about to sell. It was equally for the good of the public and trade, when partners dissolved, and one took the business, or they divided the business, that each partner might bind himself not to do anything in trade thereafter which would derogate from his grant of the interest conveyed to his former partner. Again, when two men became partners in a business, although their union might reduce competition, this effect was only an incident to the main purpose of a union of their capital, enterprise, and energy to carry on a successful business, and one useful to the community. Restrictions in the articles of partnership upon the business activity of the members, with a view of securing their entire effort in the common enterprise, were, of course, only ancillary to the main end of the union, and were to be encouraged. Again, when one in business sold property with which the buyer might set up a rival business, it was certainly reasonable that the seller should be able to restrain the buyer from doing him an injury which, but for the sale, the buyer would be unable to inflict. This was not reducing competition, but was only securing the seller against an increase of competition of his own creating. Such an exception was necessary to promote the free purchase and sale of property. Again, it was of importance that business men and professional men should have every motive to employ the ablest assistants, and to instruct them thoroughly; but they would naturally be reluctant to do so unless such assistants were able to bind themselves not to set up a rival business in the vicinity after learning the details and secrets of the business of their employers.

* * *

For the reasons given, then, covenants in partial restraint of trade are generally upheld as valid when they are agreements (1) by the seller of property or business not to compete with the buyer in such a way as to derogate from the value of the property or business sold; (2) by a retiring partner not to compete with the firm; (3) by a partner pending the partnership not to do anything to interfere, by competition or otherwise, with the business of the firm; (4) by the buyer of property not to use the same in competition with the business retained by the seller; and (5) by an assistant, servant, or agent not to compete with his master or employer after the expiration of his time to service. Before such agreements are upheld, however, the court must find that the restraints attempted thereby are reasonably necessary (1, 2, and 3) to the enjoyment by the buyer of the property, good will, or interest in the partnership bought; or (4) to the legitimate ends of the existing partnership; or (5) to the prevention of possible injury to the business of the seller from use by the buyer of the thing sold; or (6) to protection from the danger of loss to the employer's business caused by the unjust use on the part of the employee of the confidential knowledge acquired in such business.

* * *

It would be stating it too strongly to say that these five classes of covenants in restraint of trade include all of those upheld as valid at the common law; but it would certainly seem to follow from the tests laid down for determining the validity of such an agreement that no conventional restraint of trade can be enforced unless the covenant embodying it is merely ancillary to the main purpose of a lawful contract, and necessary to protect the covenantee in the full enjoyment of the legitimate fruits of the contract, or to protect him from the dangers of an unjust use of those fruits by the other party.

* * *

This very statement of the rule implies that the contract must be one in which there is a main purpose, to which the covenant in restraint of trade is merely ancillary. The covenant is inserted only to protect one of the parties from the injury which, in the execution of the contract or enjoyment of its fruits, he may suffer from the unrestrained competition of the other. The main purpose of the contract suggests the measure of protection needed, and furnishes a sufficiently uniform standard by which the validity of such restraints may be judicially determined. In such a case, if the restraint exceeds the necessity presented by the main purpose of the contract, it is void for two reasons: First, because it oppresses the covenantor, without any corresponding benefit to the covenantee; and, second, because it tends to a monopoly. But where the sole object of both parties in making the contract as expressed therein is merely to restrain competition, and enhance or maintain prices, it would seem that there was nothing to justify or excuse the restraint, that it would necessarily have a tendency to monopoly, and therefore would be void. In such a case there is no measure of what is necessary to the protection of either party, except the vague and varying opinion of judges as to how much, on principles of political economy, men ought to be allowed to restrain competition. There is in such contracts no main lawful purpose, to subserve which partial restraint is permitted, and by which its reasonableness is measured, but the sole object is to restrain trade in order to avoid the competition which it has always been the policy of the common law to foster.

* * * [Cases cited in support of the proposition that the common law's harsh treatment of restraints of trade was relaxed] all involved contracts in which the covenant in restraint of trade was ancillary to the main and lawful purpose of the contract, and was necessary to the protection of the covenantee in the carrying out of the main purpose. They do not manifest any general disposition on the part of the courts to be more liberal in supporting contracts having for their sole object the restraint of trade than did the courts of an earlier time. It is true that there are some cases in which the courts, mistaking, as we conceive, the proper limits of the relaxation of the rules for determining the unreasonableness of restraints of trade, have set sail on a sea of doubt, and have assumed the power to say, in respect to contracts which have no other purpose and no other consideration on either side than the mutual restraint of the parties, how much restraint of competition is in the public interest, and how much is not.

The manifest danger in the administration of justice according to so shifting, vague, and indeterminate a standard would seem to be a strong reason against adopting it. * * *

* * *

Ironically, given the importance associated with it today, Taft's entire discussion of ancillary restraints and their treatment at common law is *dicta*. *Addyston Pipe* involved an alleged price fixing scheme among competing producers of cast iron pipe. (The facts are described in greater detail in Sidebar 8–5.) They defended on several grounds, most significantly arguing that: (1) but for the agreement setting prices, the defendants would have been "subjected to ruinous competition" from each other; (2) the prices set by agreement were "reasonable" ones; and (3) the prices agreed to had to be reasonable, because the defendants accounted for only 30% of the market for cast iron pipe in the United States (although as is discussed in Sidebar 8–5, the evidence was compelling that the defendants collectively had a much greater market share and exercised market power in more local markets). These arguments were similar to those made in *Trans-Missouri Freight* and *Joint Traffic Ass'n*, and, were revived in *Trenton Potteries* as a consequence of a broader than intended reading of the Court's reasonableness message in *Standard Oil*. As was true in *Trenton Potteries*, under Taft's approach none of these "defenses" were admissible. The agreement to fix prices involved nothing but restraint, and therefore did not qualify for any limited inquiry into reasonableness based on his ancillary restraint framework. He viewed such agreements as "per se" unlawful. Taft's approach to reasonableness, however, was quickly overshadowed by *Standard Oil*. That his approach was different from that taken by the Court is evidenced by the separate opinion of Justice Harlan in *Standard Oil*. Harlan was member of the *Addyston Pipe* panel before he was elevated to the Supreme Court. Although he concurred in the result in *Standard Oil*, he wrote separately to dissent specifically from the Court's formulation of the "rule of reason," but to no avail. *Standard Oil*, 221 U.S., at 98–99 (Harlan, J., concurring in part and dissenting in part).

Addyston Pipe's framework lay dormant for many years, only to be dusted off in the 1970s by critics of the broader rule of reason that derived from *Standard Oil* and *Chicago Bd. of Trade*. As we have now learned, under the broader approach it is more difficult to articulate the reasons why some agreements are subject to per se condemnation, whereas others can be defended under the rule of reason.

Broadcast Music and *Nat'l Soc'y of Prof'l Eng'rs* together heralded the rebirth of *Addyston Pipe*'s framework for dealing with that issue. Before moving on, therefore, you should review Section III C, D, and E of the Court's decision in *Broadcast Music*. Look particularly for evidence of Taft's ancillary restraint framework, then read Sidebar 2–4.

Figure 2–7:

Ancillary Restraint Analysis Under *Addyston Pipe*

**Two Categories of Horizontal
Agreements Under Section 1 of
the Sherman Act**

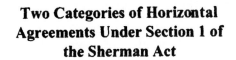

Not Subject to Reasonableness Inquiry	Subject to Reasonableness Inquiry
• "sole object" is "merely to restrain competition" • enhance or maintain prices • no justification • no basis for assessing reasonableness	• procompetitive "main purpose" • restraint is *"ancillary"* to that main purpose *and "necessary"* • but restraint is *no greater than necessary* to facilitate procompetitive purpose

Note that embedded in *Addyston Pipe*'s formulation of ancillary restraint analysis is the idea that restraints should be no greater than necessary to achieve the restraint's legitimate, procompetitive purposes, and that if they exceed the necessary, they become suspect and potentially "unreasonable." As a policy matter, this interest that restraints among rivals be the "least restrictive" necessary to achieve their legitimate purposes can be understood as an effort to accommodate concerns about anticompetitive effects and the desire to protect restraints that have sufficiently procompetitive virtues as to justify their use. It can also be understood in evidentiary terms.

A plaintiff challenging an agreement that restrains trade must first demonstrate that it indeed "restrains" trade in some significant way. This might be the product of proof of actual effects or presumption. In the case of per se rules, such as the prohibition of "naked" price-fixing by competitors, the presumption is irrebuttable, although under *Broadcast Music* it might be necessary to first rule out the presence of a plausible efficiency explanation before invoking the presumption. In the case of non-per se cases, however, a showing of anticompetitive effects creates a rebuttable presumption of unreasonableness, and the burden of production will shift to the defendant.

When the burden shifts to the defendant, and the defendant can demonstrate that the restraint is ancillary to a legitimate underlying transaction, the presumption of unreasonableness is rebutted, and the burden of production shifts back to the plaintiff. At that point the plaintiff might still prevail by demonstrating that, although ancillary, the restraint is more restrictive than necessary, and is, therefore unreasonable. The reasoning might be that either (1) the "legitimate" reasons given for the restraint were pretext, as is evidenced by the choice of a restraint greater than necessary, or (2) that the "excess" restraint alone is the source of unreasonableness. Resting a finding on one or the other of these grounds might greatly affect the choice of remedy: in the first instance, the restraint might be totally prohibited; whereas in the second, it might be permitted, but narrowed.

Such an evidentiary framework for evaluating agreements under Section 1 of the Sherman Act raises a number of issues. Should the law in effect impose a duty on the defendant to adopt the *very least* restrictive means of accomplishing its goals? Should the duty be imposed regardless of cost? For example, what if a marginally less restrictive restraint is available, but only at significantly higher cost to the firm? What if the least restrictive restraint would be somewhat less effective than the restraint preferred by the firm? Or should it be sufficient that the means chosen were practical and reasonably designed to achieve the desired end, even if not the very least restrictive?

Finally, in theory, the burden of demonstrating that there are less restrictive means ample to serve the legitimate purposes of the defendant could be allocated to either the plaintiff or the defendant, and it could be imposed at different stages of the decision making process. One court framed the approach in this way:

> The final step of the rule of reason involves determining whether the challenged agreement is necessary to achieve its purported goals. * * * Even if an anticompetitive restraint is intended to achieve a legitimate objective, the restraint only survives a rule of reason analysis if it is reasonably necessary to achieve the legitimate objectives proffered by the defendant. To determine if a restraint is reasonably necessary, courts must examine first whether the restraint furthers the legitimate objectives, and then whether comparable benefits could be achieved through a substantially less restrictive alternative. Once a defendant demonstrates that its conduct promotes a legitimate goal, the plaintiff, in order to prevail, bears the burden of proving that there exists a viable less restrictive alternative.

United States v. Brown University, 5 F.3d 658, 678–79 (3d Cir. 1993). Note how the court of appeals closely integrated the issue of less restrictive means with the language of ancillary restraint analysis.

In 2000, the FTC and the Antitrust Division of the Department of Justice issued joint ANTITRUST GUIDELINES FOR COLLABORATIONS AMONG COMPETITORS. Section 3.36(b) of the Guidelines provides that in assessing whether a restraint is "reasonably necessary" to a competitor collaboration, the agencies will assess whether the participants "could have achieved or could achieve similar efficiencies by practical, significantly less restrictive means." If they could have, "the Agencies conclude that the relevant agreement is not reasonably necessary to their achievement." Are the Collaboration Guidelines consistent with *Brown University*? With *Addyston Pipe* and *Broadcast Music*? Do they utilize less restrictive means in the same fashion? As we shall see in Chapter 7, less restrictive means may also be relevant in the analysis of vertical exclusionary agreements.

Sidebar 2–4:
"Efficiency" and the *Addyston Pipe* Revival Movement

Judge Taft's careful analysis of the common law restraint of trade cases, and his formulation of the "ancillarity" approach to judging the reasonableness of restraints of trade, was unique in its time. Taft repeated and expanded the analysis some fifteen years later in his monograph, WILLIAM H. TAFT, THE ANTI-TRUST ACT AND THE SUPREME COURT (1914)(Fred B. Rothman & Co. 1993), which was one of the first early treatises on antitrust law. But his approach was neither cited nor relied upon in either of the Supreme Court's subsequent and formative decisions on the rule of reason—*Standard Oil* and *Chicago Bd. of Trade*—and thus had little immediate impact on antitrust analysis generally. It was simply overshadowed by *Standard Oil* and *Chicago Bd. of Trade*, the Supreme Court's principal rule of reason decisions. Why has it taken on greater importance today?

As a purely legal construct—which was how it was offered by Taft—ancillarity had two critical features. First, by implication, it distinguished pure or "naked" restraints from ancillary ones. When nothing but restraint was apparent, as was the case in *Addyston Pipe*, little analysis was needed. But where the restraint appeared to be derivative—ancillary and necessary to support some broader purpose—further inquiry into reasonableness was indicated. In its typical context of covenants not to compete, therefore, ancillary restraint analysis consisted of a series of pointed inquiries: (1) Was the restraint ancillary to a proper or legitimate purpose? (2) How necessary was it? (3) Was it no more restrictive than necessary to facilitate the proper purpose?

Taft, therefore, was thinking purely in terms of the common law and its operation, not necessarily to the economic implications of ancillary restraint analysis. But, to the extent the common law's approach to ancillary restraints sought to facilitate legitimate commerce, it clearly had economic consequences. "Reasonableness," it could be argued, was defined by the line separating agreements that functioned solely to restrict output, from those that served to expand it, a very contemporary approach that could be viewed as promoting efficiency and consumer welfare. By making the formation of a partnership, the sale of a shop or an apprenticeship possible, an ancillary restraint actually facilitated the expansion of supply, even though it ostensibly also involved the restriction of some rivalry. Only restraints on someone's trade, with no corresponding benefit to general output, were readily condemned. Restraints on rivalry that served to promote economic expansion were "reasonable," for they restrained trade only as a means of expanding it. Ancillarity as a legal construct thus served to promote the integration of resources that typifies and often facilitates greater economic activity and a more efficient allocation of resources.

This more economic interpretation of *Addyston Pipe* proved very appealing to some commentators, especially proponents of the Chicago School of antitrust, who sought support in historical antitrust for their approach to antitrust analysis. As Robert Bork wrote in 1978, referring to Judge Taft's invocation of the partnership example:

> This insight is, or should be, central to modern antitrust. It is useful, therefore, to put Taft's reasoning in modern terms and to generalize it. The integration of economic activities, which is indispensable to productive efficiency, always involves the implicit elimination of actual or potential competition. We allow it—indeed, should encourage it—because the integration creates wealth for the community. We should equally encourage those explicit and ancillary agreed-upon eliminations of rivalry that make the basic integration more efficient.

ROBERT H. BORK, THE ANTITRUST PARADOX 28 (1978). *See also* Thomas C. Arthur, *Farewell to the Sea of Doubt: Jettisoning the Constitutional Sherman Act*, 74 CAL. L. REV. 263 (1986). As Judge Easterbrook reasoned in *Polk Bros., Inc. v. Forest City Enterprises, Inc.*, 776 F.2d 185, 189 (7th Cir.1985):

> The evaluation of ancillary restraints under the Rule of Reason does not imply that ancillary agreements are not real horizontal restraints. They are. A covenant not to compete following employment does not operate any differently from a horizontal market division among competitors—not at the time the covenant has its bite, anyway. The difference comes at the time people enter beneficial arrangements. A legal rule that enforces covenants not to compete, even after an employee has launched his own firm, makes it easier for people to cooperate productively in the first place. Knowing that he is not cutting his own throat by doing so, the employer will train the employee, giving him skills, knowledge, and trade secrets that make the firm more productive. Once that employment ends, there is nothing left but restraint-but the aftermath is the wrong focus.
>
> A court must ask whether an agreement promoted enterprise and productivity at the time it was adopted. * * *

The challenge in embracing any vision of antitrust, of course, is in identifying a legal rule that can successfully implement an articulated economic or other goal. The Supreme Court's apparent reliance on *Addyston Pipe* in *Broadcast Music*, therefore, was quite significant.

Broadly, it heralded a welcome, greater focus on economic efficiency in antitrust analysis. Narrowly, it signaled the rebirth of Judge Taft's analysis. Moreover, it arguably suggested that ancillary restraint analysis might be the appropriate legal vehicle for implementing a more efficiency oriented analysis of cooperative agreements among rivals. Then recently appointed federal judges associated with the Chicago School, including Judge Bork, wasted no time in reading *Addyston Pipe*, as reborn in *Broadcast Music*, for all it was worth—an invitation to the use of ancillary restraint analysis to evaluate agreements among rivals for their tendency to promote output and productive efficiency. *See, e.g., Rothery Storage & Van Co. v. Atlas Van Lines, Inc.*, 792 F.2d 210 (D.C.Cir. 1986), *cert. denied*, 479 U.S. 1033 (1987)(Judge Bork); *Polk Bros., Inc. v. Forest City Enterprises, Inc.*, 776 F.2d 185 (7th Cir. 1985)(Judge Easterbrook). In both cases, the courts were willing to view *Broadcast Music* broadly, as an invitation to jettison prior decisions such as *Topco*, in favor of a more structured, and economic framework derived from *Addyston Pipe*. By aggressively extending *Broadcast Music* from the price-fixing context to division of markets, these influential appellate judges were promoting antitrust's movement away from narrowly tailored legal categories—like "price-fixing" and "division of markets"—towards more economically-grounded core concepts, such as "efficiency."

The trend towards placing greater weight on critical, *economic* analysis of a horizontal restraint's impact on productive efficiency, signaled by *Broadcast Music*, has proved durable and is now a widely accepted tenet of antitrust law. But the election to implement that economic analysis through *Addyston Pipe's* ancillary restraint framework has been more controversial. As we shall see through the remaining materials in this chapter, although ancillary restraint analysis retains proponents, it has not emerged as the sole means for implementing an economic efficiency goal. Consider carefully why that might be so. Would Taft's framework uniformly predict reasonable horizontal agreements? Could it be over or under-inclusive in some circumstances? Are there criteria other than ancillarity that might lead to the conclusion that an agreement to reduce rivalry can enhance productivity?

Note on the Supreme Court's Decision in Dagher (2006)

The Supreme Court arguably injected some confusion into the operation and role of ancillary restraint analysis in *Texaco Inc. v. Dagher*, 547 U.S. 1, 126 S.Ct. 1276 (2006). As noted, *supra*, in *Dagher* the Court reversed the Ninth Circuit's decision to apply the per se rule to the pricing conduct of a joint venture. In criticizing that court's decision, it argued:

> The court below reached the opposite conclusion by invoking the ancillary restraints doctrine. That doctrine governs the validity of restrictions imposed by a legitimate business collaboration, such as a business association or joint venture, on nonventure activities. Under the doctrine, courts must determine whether the nonventure restriction is a naked restraint on trade, and thus invalid, or one that is ancillary to the legitimate and competitive purposes of the business association, and thus valid. We agree with petitioners that the ancillary restraints doctrine has

no application here, where the business practice being challenged involves the core activity of the joint venture itself—namely, the pricing of the very goods produced and sold by Equilon. And even if we were to invoke the doctrine in these cases, Equilon's pricing policy is clearly ancillary to the sale of its own products. Judge Fernandez, dissenting from the ruling of the court below, put it well:

> "In this case, nothing more radical is afoot than the fact that an entity, which now owns all of the production, transportation, research, storage, sales and distribution facilities for engaging in the gasoline business, also prices its own products. It decided to price them the same, as any other entity could. What could be more integral to the running of a business than setting a price for its goods and services?"

[Here the Court cited *Broadcast Music* for the proposition that "[j]oint ventures and other cooperative arrangements are ... not usually unlawful, at least not as price-fixing schemes, where the agreement on price is necessary to market the product at all." Eds.]

547 U.S. at 8. At least two things are noteworthy about the Court's discussion of ancillary restraint analysis. First, its statement of the approach is arguably incomplete and imprecise. As noted in *Addyston Pipe*, a restraint can be analyzed under the ancillary restraint approach—and hence subject to rule of reason analysis as opposed to per se analysis—if it is (1) *ancillary* to a main legitimate activity, (2) *necessary* to achieve the legitimate purposes of that activity, and (3) *no greater than necessary* to achieve that purpose. In its statement of the ancillary restraint approach, the Court does not mention the second and third steps.

Perhaps more importantly, the Court claims that ancillary restraint analysis only applies to the "non-venture" activities of a joint venture. This was an argument advocated by the United States as Amicus Curiae. *See* Brief of the United States as Amicus Curiae Supporting Petitioners, at 21–28, *Texaco Inc. v. Dagher*, 547 U.S. 1 (2006) (Nos. 04–805, 04–814). Here the implication is quite clear: there can be no liability for the internal restraints of a joint venture, such as the decision to price jointly produced products. The Court's concern appears to be with antitrust challenges that subject the legitimate internal decisions of joint ventures to antitrust scrutiny.

But is it true that ancillary restraint analysis has historically been applied solely to the "non-venture" activities of joint ventures? The Court approvingly cites *Broadcast Music* at the end of its discussion, but the blanket license in *Broadcast Music* certainly does not appear to have been a "non-venture" activity. Some of the Court's other citations in *Dagher* are also debatable.

It is worth asking whether the "within the venture" vs. "non-venture" distinction has economic and therefore antitrust relevance. The Court's quotation from *Broadcast Music* appears to belie its own distinction. A price agreement "necessary to market the product at all" would be within the venture, yet the question of whether it was in fact necessary to that venture is part of the traditional ancillary restraint analysis and would seem to be a part of reasonableness analysis whether the restraint was within or without the venture. Moreover, the Court's distinction would create a per se legal status for all restraints adopted by joint ventures so long as they are deemed to be "within the venture." Is there a danger that such an approach will invite parties to form joint ventures that are less than fully legitimate efforts to integrate their assets in order to secure a kind of antitrust immunity? Will parties who have formed legitimate joint ventures seek to overreach in adopting anticompetitive restraints that are arguably "within" the venture, yet are not really necessary to achieve their legitimate aims? *Dagher's* approach, which had never before been articulated by the Court, would seem to elevate form over substance in terms of the economic analysis of specific restraints and creates some additional uncertainty on the role of ancillary restraint analysis.

F. MODERN TRENDS: THE SEARCH FOR A MORE STRUCTURED AND OPERATIONAL RULE OF REASON

Beginning with the Supreme Court's decision in *Nat'l Soc'y of Prof'l Eng'rs*, a third path to unreasonableness began to evolve in the Court's decisions. Proceeding from the assumption that not all cases literally falling into the per se category warrant per se treatment—a conclusion that was apparent in the 1979 decision in *Broadcast Music*, the Court also appeared to recognize that not all cases excused from per se treatment deserved or required "full blown" rule of reason analysis under the *Chicago Bd. of Trade* standard. As a consequence, it began scouting out a middle ground between abrupt per se condemnation and full rule of reason inquiry—a development that has continued.

The Supreme Court and the lower courts also began to address the legacy of *Chicago Bd. of Trade's* rule of reason, searching for ways to better specify the facts most relevant to a rule of reason inquiry and the allocation of burdens among plaintiffs and defendants. This development also continues, especially as the cost of complex litigation such as antitrust cases has become an increasing concern of courts, commentators, and enforcers.

As you read the next case and the note that follows, consider how each of the cases discussed easily could have been pigeon-holed under the traditional horizontal per se categories—but to what end? Perhaps they are better considered as a group that suggests a unified framework for analyzing competitor conduct allegedly having collusive effects. Consider too whether Taft's ancillary restraints approach, as utilized in *Broadcast Music*, played a role in this developing framework.

NATIONAL COLLEGIATE ATHLETIC ASS'N v. BOARD OF REGENTS OF THE UNIVERSITY OF OKLAHOMA

Supreme Court of the United States, 1984.
468 U.S. 85, 104 S.Ct. 2948, 82 L.Ed.2d 70.

Justice STEVENS delivered the opinion of the Court.

The University of Oklahoma and the University of Georgia contend that the National Collegiate Athletic Association has unreasonably restrained trade in the televising of college football games. After an extended trial, the District Court found that the NCAA had violated § 1 of the Sherman Act and granted injunctive relief. The Court of Appeals agreed that the statute had been violated but modified the remedy in some respects. We granted certiorari, and now affirm.

I

The NCAA

Since its inception in 1905, the NCAA has played an important role in the regulation of amateur collegiate sports. It has adopted and promulgated playing rules, standards of amateurism, standards for academic eligibility, regulations concerning recruitment of athletes, and rules governing the size of athletic squads and coaching staffs. * * * With the exception of football, the NCAA has not undertaken any regulation of the televising of athletic events.

The NCAA has approximately 850 voting members. The regular members are classified into separate divisions to reflect differences in size and scope of their athletic programs. * * *

Some years ago, five major conferences together with major football-playing independent institutions organized the College Football Association (CFA). The original purpose of the CFA was to promote the interests of major football-playing schools within the NCAA structure. The Universities of Oklahoma and Georgia, respondents in this Court, are members of the CFA.

* * *

The Current Plan

The [television] plan adopted in 1981 for the 1982–1985 seasons is at issue in this case. This plan * * * recites that it is intended to reduce, insofar as possible, the adverse effects of live television upon football game attendance. * * * The plan recites that the television committee has awarded rights to negotiate and contract for the telecasting of college football games of members of the NCAA to two "carrying networks." * * *

In separate agreements with each of the carrying networks, ABC [the American Broadcasting Cos.] and the Columbia Broadcasting System (CBS), the NCAA granted each the right to telecast the 14 live "exposures" described in the plan, in accordance with the "ground rules" set forth therein. Each of the networks agreed to pay a specified "minimum aggregate compensation to the participating NCAA member institutions" during the 4–year period in an amount that totaled $131,750,000. In essence the agreement authorized each network to negotiate directly with member schools for the right to televise their games. The agreement itself does not describe the method of computing the compensation for each game, but the practice that has developed over the years and that the District Court found would be followed under the current agreement involved the setting of a recommended fee by a representative of the NCAA for different types of telecasts, with national telecasts being the most valuable, regional telecasts being less valuable, and Division II or Division III games commanding a still lower price. The aggregate of all these payments presumably equals the total minimum aggregate compensation set forth in the basic agreement. * * * [T]he amount that any team receives does not change with the size of the viewing audience, the number of markets in which the game is telecast, or the particular characteristic of the game or the participating teams. Instead, the "ground rules" provide that the carrying networks make alternate selections of those games they wish to televise, and thereby obtain the exclusive right to submit a bid at an essentially fixed price to the institutions involved.

The plan also contains "appearance requirements" and "appearance limitations" which pertain to each of the 2–year periods that the plan is in effect. The basic requirement imposed on each of the two networks is that it must schedule appearances for at least 82 different member institutions during each 2–year period. Under the appearance limitations no member institution is eligible to appear on television more than a total of six times and more than four times nationally, with the appearances to be divided equally between the two carrying networks. The number of exposures specified in the contracts also sets an absolute maximum on the number of games that can be broadcast.

Thus * * * the current plan * * * limits the total amount of televised intercollegiate football and the number of games that any one team may televise. No member is permitted to make any sale of television rights except in accordance with the basic plan.

Background of this Controversy

Beginning in 1979 CFA members began to advocate that colleges with major football programs should have a greater voice in the formulation of football television policy than they had in the NCAA. CFA therefore investigated the possibility of negotiating a television agreement of its own, developed an independent plan, and obtained a contract offer from the National Broadcasting Co. (NBC). This contract, which it signed in August 1981, would have allowed a more liberal number of appearances for each institution, and would have increased the overall revenues realized by CFA members.

In response the NCAA publicly announced that it would take disciplinary action against any CFA member that complied with the CFA–NBC contract. * * * On September 8, 1981, respondents commenced this action in the United States District Court for the Western District of Oklahoma and obtained a preliminary injunction preventing the NCAA from initiating disciplinary proceedings or otherwise interfering with CFA's efforts to perform its agreement with NBC. Notwithstanding the entry of the injunction, most CFA members were unwilling to commit themselves to the new contractual arrangement with NBC in the face of the threatened sanctions and therefore the agreement was never consummated.

* * *

[Here the Court described in detail the proceedings in the district court and the court of appeals. Although the district court had condemned the NCAA's plan, it did so after a lengthy trial, and it considered each of the NCAA's defenses. In contrast, the Court of Appeals held that the plan should have been treated as per se unlawful price fixing and that, in any event, the procompetitive justifications urged by the NCAA were not supported by the evidence. Eds.]

II

There can be no doubt that the challenged practices of the NCAA constitute a "restraint of trade" in the sense that they limit members' freedom to negotiate and enter into their own television contracts. In that sense, however, every contract is a restraint of trade, and as we have repeatedly recognized, the Sherman Act was intended to prohibit only unreasonable restraints of trade.

It is also undeniable that these practices share characteristics of restraints we have previously held unreasonable. * * * By participating in an association which prevents member institutions from competing against each other on the basis of price or kind of television rights that can be offered to broadcasters, the NCAA member institutions have created a horizontal restraint—an agreement among competitors on the way in which they will compete with one another. A restraint of this type has often been held to be unreasonable as a matter of law. Because it places a ceiling on the number of games member institutions may televise, the horizontal agreement places an artificial limit on the quantity of televised football that is available to broadcasters and consumers. By restraining the quantity of television rights available for sale, the challenged practices create a limitation on output; our cases have held that such limitations are unreasonable restraints of trade. Moreover, the District Court found that the minimum aggregate price in fact operates to preclude any price negotiation between broadcasters and institutions, thereby constituting horizontal price fixing, perhaps the paradigm of an unreasonable restraint of trade.

Horizontal price fixing and output limitation are ordinarily condemned as a matter of law under an "illegal *per se*" approach because the probability that these practices are anticompetitive is so high. * * * In such circumstances a restraint is presumed unreasonable without inquiry into the particular market context in which it is found. Nevertheless, we have decided that it would be inappropriate to apply a *per se* rule to this case. This decision is not based on a lack of judicial experience with this type of arrangement,[21] on the fact that the NCAA is organized as a nonprofit entity,[22] or on our respect for the NCAA's historic role in the preservation and encouragement of intercollegiate amateur athletics.[23] Rather, what is critical is that this case involves an industry in which horizontal restraints on competition are essential if the product is to be available at all.

* * * What the NCAA and its member institutions market in this case is competition itself—contests between competing institutions. Of course, this would be completely ineffective if there were no rules on which the competitors agreed to create and define the competition to be marketed. * * * Moreover, the NCAA seeks to market a particular brand of football—college football. The identification of this "product" with an academic tradition differentiates college football from and makes it more popular than professional sports to which it might otherwise be comparable, such as, for example, minor league baseball. * * * Thus, the NCAA plays a vital role in enabling college football to preserve its character, and as a result enables a product to be marketed which might otherwise be unavailable. In performing this role,

21. While judicial inexperience with a particular arrangement counsels against extending the reach of *per se* rules, the likelihood that horizontal price and output restrictions are anticompetitive is generally sufficient to justify application of the *per se* rule without inquiry into the special characteristics of a particular industry. * * *

22. There is no doubt that the sweeping language of § 1 applies to nonprofit entities. * * *

23. While as the guardian of an important American tradition, the NCAA's motives must be accorded a respectful presumption of validity, it is nevertheless well settled that good motives will not validate an otherwise anticompetitive practice.

its actions widen consumer choice—not only the choices available to sports fans but also those available to athletes—and hence can be viewed as procompetitive.

Broadcast Music squarely holds that a joint selling arrangement may be so efficient that it will increase sellers' aggregate output and thus be procompetitive. Similarly, as we indicated in *Continental T.V., Inc. v. GTE Sylvania Inc.* [Casebook, *infra* Chapter 4], a restraint in a limited aspect of a market may actually enhance marketwide competition. Respondents concede that the great majority of the NCAA's regulations enhance competition among member institutions. Thus, despite the fact that this case involves restraints on the ability of member institutions to compete in terms of price and output, a fair evaluation of their competitive character requires consideration of the NCAA's justifications for the restraints.

Our analysis of this case under the Rule of Reason, of course, does not change the ultimate focus of our inquiry. Both *per se* rules and the Rule of Reason are employed "to form a judgment about the competitive significance of the restraint." *National Society of Professional Engineers.* * * *

Per se rules are invoked when surrounding circumstances make the likelihood of anticompetitive conduct so great as to render unjustified further examination of the challenged conduct. But whether the ultimate finding is the product of a presumption or actual market analysis, the essential inquiry remains the same-whether or not the challenged restraint enhances competition.[26] Under the Sherman Act the criterion to be used in judging the validity of a restraint on trade is its impact on competition.

III

Because it restrains price and output, the NCAA's television plan has a significant potential for anticompetitive effects.[28] The findings of the District Court indicate that this potential has been realized. The District Court found that if member institutions were free to sell television rights, many more games would be shown on television, and that the NCAA's output restriction has the effect of raising the price the networks pay for television rights.[29] Moreover, the court found that by fixing a price for television rights to all games, the NCAA creates a price structure that is unresponsive to viewer demand and unrelated to the prices that would prevail in a competitive

26. Indeed, there is often no bright line separating *per se* from Rule of Reason analysis. *Per se* rules may require considerable inquiry into market conditions before the evidence justifies a presumption of anticompetitive conduct. * * *

28. In this connection, it is not without significance that Congress felt the need to grant professional sports an exemption from the antitrust laws for joint marketing of television rights. *See* 15 U.S.C. §§ 1291–1295. The legislative history of this exemption demonstrates Congress' recognition that agreements among league members to sell television rights in a cooperative fashion could run afoul of the Sherman Act. * * *

29. "It is clear from the evidence that were it not for the NCAA controls, many more college football games would be televised. This is particularly true at the local level. * * * The evidence establishes the fact that the networks are actually paying the large fees because the NCAA agrees to limit production. If the NCAA would not agree to limit production, the networks would not pay so large a fee. Because NCAA limits production, the networks need not fear that their broadcasts will have to compete head-to-head with other college football telecasts, either on the networks or on various local stations. * * * "

market.[30] And, of course, since as a practical matter all member institutions need NCAA approval, members have no real choice but to adhere to the NCAA's television controls.[31]

The anticompetitive consequences of this arrangement are apparent. Individual competitors lose their freedom to compete. Price is higher and output lower than they would otherwise be, and both are unresponsive to consumer preference. This latter point is perhaps the most significant, since "Congress designed the Sherman Act as a 'consumer welfare prescription.' " A restraint that has the effect of reducing the importance of consumer preference in setting price and output is not consistent with this fundamental goal of antitrust law. Restrictions on price and output are the paradigmatic examples of restraints of trade that the Sherman Act was intended to prohibit. At the same time, the television plan eliminates competitors from the market, since only those broadcasters able to bid on television rights covering the entire NCAA can compete. Thus, as the District Court found, many telecasts that would occur in a competitive market are foreclosed by the NCAA's plan.

Petitioner argues, however, that its television plan can have no significant anticompetitive effect since the record indicates that it has no market power—no ability to alter the interaction of supply and demand in the market.[38] We must reject this argument for two reasons, one legal, one factual.

As a matter of law, the absence of proof of market power does not justify a naked restriction on price or output. To the contrary, when there is an agreement not to compete in terms of price or output, "no elaborate industry analysis is required to demonstrate the anticompetitive character of such an agreement." *Professional Engineers*, 435 U.S., at 692.[39] * * * We have never required proof of market power in such a case. This naked restraint on price and output requires some competitive justification even in the absence of a detailed market analysis.[42]

30. "Turning to the price paid for the product, it is clear that the NCAA controls utterly destroy free market competition. NCAA has commandeered the rights of its members and sold those rights for a sum certain. In so doing, it has fixed the minimum, maximum and actual price which will be paid to the schools appearing on ABC, CBS and TBS. * * * Because of the NCAA controls, the price which is paid for the right to televise any particular game is responsive neither to the relative quality of the teams playing the game nor to viewer preference." * * *

31. Since, as the District Court found, NCAA approval is necessary for any institution that wishes to compete in intercollegiate sports, the NCAA has a potent tool at its disposal for restraining institutions which require its approval. * * *

38. Market power is the ability to raise prices above those that would be charged in a competitive market. * * *

39. "The fact that a practice is not categorically unlawful in all or most of its manifestations certainly does not mean that it is univer-

sally lawful. * * * The essential point is that the rule of reason can sometimes be applied in the twinkling of an eye." P. Areeda, The "Rule of Reason" in Antitrust Analysis: General Issues 37–38 (Federal Judicial Center, June 1981). * * *

42. The Solicitor General correctly observes:

"There was no need for the respondents to establish monopoly power in any precisely defined market for television programming in order to prove the restraint unreasonable. Both lower courts found not only that NCAA has power over the market for intercollegiate sports, but also that in the market for television programming—no matter how broadly or narrowly the market is defined—the NCAA television restrictions have reduced output, subverted viewer choice, and distorted pricing. Consequently, unless the controls have some countervailing procompetitive justification, they should be deemed unlawful regardless of whether petitioner has substantial market power over advertising dollars. While the 'reasonableness' of a particular

As a factual matter, it is evident that petitioner does possess market power. The District Court employed the correct test for determining whether college football broadcasts constitute a separate market—whether there are other products that are reasonably substitutable for televised NCAA football games. Petitioner's argument that it cannot obtain supracompetitive prices from broadcasters since advertisers, and hence broadcasters, can switch from college football to other types of programming simply ignores the findings of the District Court. It found that intercollegiate football telecasts generate an audience uniquely attractive to advertisers and that competitors are unable to offer programming that can attract a similar audience. These findings amply support its conclusion that the NCAA possesses market power. Indeed, the District Court's subsidiary finding that advertisers will pay a premium price per viewer to reach audiences watching college football because of their demographic characteristics is vivid evidence of the uniqueness of this product. * * *[49] It inexorably follows that if college football broadcasts be defined as a separate market—and we are convinced they are—then the NCAA's complete control over those broadcasts provides a solid basis for the District Court's conclusion that the NCAA possesses market power with respect to those broadcasts. * * *

Thus, the NCAA television plan on its face constitutes a restraint upon the operation of a free market, and the findings of the District Court establish that it has operated to raise prices and reduce output. Under the Rule of Reason, these hallmarks of anticompetitive behavior place upon petitioner a heavy burden of establishing an affirmative defense which competitively justifies this apparent deviation from the operations of a free market. We turn now to the NCAA's proffered justifications.

IV

Relying on *Broadcast Music*, petitioner argues that its television plan constitutes a cooperative "joint venture" which assists in the marketing of broadcast rights and hence is procompetitive. While joint ventures have no immunity from the antitrust laws * * * a joint selling arrangement may "mak[e] possible a new product by reaping otherwise unattainable efficiencies." The essential contribution made by the NCAA's arrangement is to define the number of games that may be televised, to establish the price for each exposure, and to define the basic terms of each contract between the network and a home team. The NCAA does not, however, act as a selling

alleged restraint often depends on the market power of the parties involved, because a judgment about market power is the means by which the effects of the conduct on the market place can be assessed, market power is only one test of 'reasonableness.' And where the anticompetitive effects of conduct can be ascertained through means short of extensive market analysis, and where no countervailing competitive virtues are evident, a lengthy analysis of market power is not necessary." Brief for United States as *Amicus Curiae* 19–20. * * *

49. For the same reasons, it is also apparent that the unique appeal of NCAA football telecasts for viewers means that "from the standpoint of the consumer—whose interests the statute was especially intended to serve," there can be no doubt that college football constitutes a separate market for which there is no reasonable substitute. Thus we agree with the District Court that it makes no difference whether the market is defined from the standpoint of broadcasters, advertisers, or viewers. [The dissent took issue with the majority's conclusion on this point, arguing that the competitive effect of the NCAA's plan should have been judged in a broader "entertainment" market. He also urged the Court to consider the non-economic nature of the NCAA's program of self regulation. 468 U.S. at 131–33 (White, J., dissenting). Eds.]

agent for any school or for any conference of schools. * * * Thus, the effect of the network plan is not to eliminate individual sales of broadcasts, since these still occur, albeit subject to fixed prices and output limitations. Unlike *Broadcast Music's* blanket license covering broadcast rights to a large number of individual compositions, here the same rights are still sold on an individual basis, only in a noncompetitive market.

The District Court did not find that the NCAA's television plan produced any procompetitive efficiencies which enhanced the competitiveness of college football television rights; to the contrary it concluded that NCAA football could be marketed just as effectively without the television plan. There is therefore no predicate in the findings for petitioner's efficiency justification. Indeed, petitioner's argument is refuted by the District Court's finding concerning price and output. If the NCAA's television plan produced procompetitive efficiencies, the plan would increase output and reduce the price of televised games. The District Court's contrary findings accordingly undermine petitioner's position. In light of these findings, it cannot be said that "the agreement on price is necessary to market the product at all." *Broadcast Music*, 441 U.S., at 23, 99 S.Ct., at 1564. In *Broadcast Music*, the availability of a package product that no individual could offer enhanced the total volume of music that was sold. Unlike this case, there was no limit of any kind placed on the volume that might be sold in the entire market and each individual remained free to sell his own music without restraint. Here production has been limited, not enhanced. No individual school is free to televise its own games without restraint. The NCAA's efficiency justification is not supported by the record.

Neither is the NCAA's television plan necessary to enable the NCAA to penetrate the market through an attractive package sale. Since broadcasting rights to college football constitute a unique product for which there is no ready substitute, there is no need for collective action in order to enable the product to compete against its nonexistent competitors.[55] * * *

V

Throughout the history of its regulation of intercollegiate football telecasts, the NCAA has indicated its concern with protecting live attendance. This concern, it should be noted, is not with protecting live attendance at games which *are* shown on television; that type of interest is not at issue in this case. Rather, the concern is that fan interest in a televised game may adversely affect ticket sales for games that will not appear on television.

* * * [T]he District Court found that there was no evidence to support that theory in today's market. Moreover, as the District Court found, the television plan has evolved in a manner inconsistent with its original design to protect gate attendance. Under the current plan, games are shown on television during all hours that college football games are played. The plan simply does not protect live attendance by ensuring that games will not be shown on television at the same time as live events.

---

55. If the NCAA faced "interbrand" competition from available substitutes, then certain forms of collective action might be appropriate in order to enhance its ability to compete. Our conclusion concerning the availability of substitutes in Part III, *supra*, forecloses such a justification in this case, however.

There is, however, a more fundamental reason for rejecting this defense. The NCAA's argument that its television plan is necessary to protect live attendance is not based on a desire to maintain the integrity of college football as a distinct and attractive product, but rather on a fear that the product will not prove sufficiently attractive to draw live attendance when faced with competition from televised games. At bottom the NCAA's position is that ticket sales for most college games are unable to compete in a free market. The television plan protects ticket sales by limiting output—just as any monopolist increases revenues by reducing output. By seeking to insulate live ticket sales from the full spectrum of competition because of its assumption that the product itself is insufficiently attractive to consumers, petitioner forwards a justification that is inconsistent with the basic policy of the Sherman Act. * * *

VI

* * *

Our decision not to apply a *per se* rule to this case rests in large part on our recognition that a certain degree of cooperation is necessary if the type of competition that petitioner and its member institutions seek to market is to be preserved. * * * The specific restraints on football telecasts that are challenged in this case do not, however, fit into the same mold as do rules defining the conditions of the contest, the eligibility of participants, or the manner in which members of a joint enterprise shall share the responsibilities and the benefits of the total venture.

The NCAA does not claim that its television plan has equalized or is intended to equalize competition within any one league. The plan is nation-wide in scope and there is no single league or tournament in which all college football teams compete. * * * The interest in maintaining a competitive balance that is asserted by the NCAA as a justification for regulating all television of intercollegiate football is not related to any neutral standard or to any readily identifiable group of competitors.

The television plan is not even arguably tailored to serve such an interest. It does not regulate the amount of money that any college may spend on its football program, nor the way in which the colleges may use the revenues that are generated by their football programs, whether derived from the sale of television rights, the sale of tickets, or the sale of concessions or program advertising. The plan simply imposes a restriction on one source of revenue that is more important to some colleges than to others. There is no evidence that this restriction produces any greater measure of equality throughout the NCAA than would a restriction on alumni donations, tuition rates, or any other revenue-producing activity. * * *

Perhaps the most important reason for rejecting the argument that the interest in competitive balance is served by the television plan is the District Court's unambiguous and well-supported finding that many more games would be televised in a free market than under the NCAA plan. The hypothesis that legitimates the maintenance of competitive balance as a procompetitive justification under the Rule of Reason is that equal competition will maximize consumer demand for the product. The finding that consumption will materially increase if the controls are removed is a compelling demonstration that they do not in fact serve any such legitimate purpose.

* * *

Affirmed.

[The dissenting opinion of Mr. Justice White, with whom Justice Rehnquist joined, is omitted. Eds.]

————

Why does the Court in *NCAA* decline to apply the per se rule to the Association's television plan? In applying the rule of reason, how elaborate an inquiry does it make? What factors does it weigh? How does it allocate the burden of proof as between the parties? Why did the plaintiffs prevail? Why was it so readily convinced from that evidence that the television plan was unreasonable? Was it the strength of the plaintiff's evidence? The weakness of the NCAA's defense? These questions have recurred in the NCAA's later encounters with the Sherman Act. *See Law v. NCAA*, 134 F.3d 1010 (10th Cir. 1998)(applying rule of reason to conclude that NCAA's limit on compensation of college basketball coaches was unlawful restraint of trade).

Consider as well whether ancillary restraint analysis could be used to explain the Court's approach in *NCAA*, even though the Court did not expressly refer to it. The Court appeared to accept that as a general matter producing collegiate football contests was a legitimate underlying reason for the members of the NCAA to cooperate. In terms of ancillary restraint analysis, would that alone justify removing the television rights issues from treatment under the per se standard? Did the Court then effectively conclude that the television contract was an unreasonable restraint of trade because it was not ancillary and necessary to the legitimate purposes of the more general cooperation among the members of the NCAA?

When approaching arrangements such as those in NCAA that have many components of cooperation, should the courts consider the effects of the various components individually or as a whole? Would application of ancillary restraint analysis clarify whether it should look to the whole or evaluate each individually? What if no single restraint has a very significant impact on competition, but collectively they do? Should all be enjoined? Some?

In footnote 26 the Court says "there is often no bright line separating *per se* from Rule of Reason analysis." Is that proposition inconsistent with the Court's assertion in *Nat'l Soc'y of Prof'l Eng'rs* that Section 1 cases fall into "two categories," per se or rule of reason? What does the Court mean when in footnote 39 it quotes Professor Areeda for the proposition that "the rule of reason can sometimes be applied in the twinkling of an eye"? If that is true, what then distinguishes per se from rule of reason treatment? What implication does the statement have for the cases we have studied to this point in the Chapter? In the Note that follows, we explore the meaning of the Court's various references to abbreviated rule of reason analysis.

Note on the Development of the "Quick Look"

What did the Court mean in *NCAA* when it said "the absence of proof of market power does not justify a naked restriction on price or output"? "Naked restrictions" would typically be treated as per se unlawful, yet here the Court had already decided to evaluate the *NCAA* television contracts under the rule of reason. In footnote 38 the Court defined "market power" as "the ability to raise prices above those that would be charged in a competitive market." Wouldn't such power tend to be a prerequisite for any proof of anticompetitive effects? And how would a plaintiff prove such power on the part of the defendants? The statement on its face thus seems to be a bit incomplete and confusing. What distinction is the Court trying to draw?

The Court clarified its meaning in two later cases, that together with *NCAA* endorsed what has become known as the "quick look" or the "structured" or "truncated" rule of reason. *See FTC v. Indiana Fed'n of Dentists*, 476 U.S. 447 (1986)("*IFD*") and *California Dental Ass'n v. FTC*, 526 U.S. 756 (1999). With origins in Professor Philip Areeda's famed "twinkling of an eye" allusion cited by *NCAA* in its footnote 39, the quick look acknowledges that there are alternatives to the bipolar extremes of per se condemnation and "full-blown" rule of reason analysis. Just as efficiencies in cases like *Broadcast Music* demonstrated that rote application of the per se rule can be unwarranted, *NCAA* held that harm to competition can be so evident that a court will be justified in shifting the burden of production to the defendants to justify their conduct without undertaking any "elaborate industry analysis," an allusion to the full-blown rule of reason, which has become associated with lengthy, costly, and complex litigation.

In *IFD*, first discussed in Sidebar 2–3, the FTC challenged a dentists' federation's policy of refusing to supply x-rays to third-party insurers, who used the x-rays to verify treatment decisions and to determine consequent payments to the dentists for services rendered to their insureds. Although the Federation argued that its actions were justified to ensure quality dental care, the FTC argued, and the Court found, that the refusal frustrated efforts at cost containment by the third-party payors. The Federation also argued that it lacked market power, and that the FTC should have been required to define the relevant markets in which its members competed and demonstrate that it had market power in each of those markets.

As in *NCAA*, the Court rejected the Federation's position, specifically its demand that the FTC prove "market power." Building on *NCAA's* assertion that "the absence of proof of market power does not justify a naked restriction on price or output," the *IFD* Court further explained its reasoning:

> Since the purpose of the inquiries into market definition and market power is to determine whether an arrangement has the potential for genuine adverse effects on competition, "proof of actual detrimental effects, such as reduction of output," can obviate the need for an inquiry into market power, which is but a "surrogate for detrimental effects." In this case, we conclude that the finding of actual, sustained adverse effects on competition in those areas where IFD dentists predominated, viewed in light of the reality that markets for dental services tend to be relatively localized, is legally sufficient to support a finding that the challenged restraint was unreasonable even in the absence of elaborate market analysis.

IFD, 476 U.S. at 460–61 (citations omitted).

Taken together, *NCAA* and *IFD* added important pieces to the rule of reason puzzle. In both cases the Court re-emphasized its holding in *NSPE* that the focus of all Section 1 inquiries is on proof of "anticompetitive effects." But it recognized that such effects can be proven in two ways: direct or circumstantial evidence. Circumstantial evidence—what was being demanded by the NCAA and the Federation—would consist of market definition, a calculation of market shares, and an inference from high market shares that the defendants had the capacity to harm competition, *i.e.*, market power. Direct evidence—what the plaintiffs proffered in both—was evidence of actual anticompetitive effects, of the exercise of market power, such as reduced output, higher prices, or diminished quality. Such direct evidence, because it is responsive to the ultimate question under Section 1, obviates the need for an inquiry into market power as evidenced circumstantially by market shares.

The Court's suggestion that "market power" is an alternative to proof of actual detrimental effects is sometimes the source of confusion. Another way to understand the Court's insight in the two cases is that market power is the source of the ability to inflict competitive harm, but in direct evidence cases like *NCAA* and *IFD* the evidence demonstrates the actual exercise of that power, whereas in circumstantial evidence cases it is inferred. Hence, when direct evidence of actual effects is presented, there is no need for "elaborate industry analysis" in the form of market definition and market share calculations. Direct evidence is qualitatively superior to circumstantial evidence. Of course, a plaintiff could offer both, but it should not have to do so. *See generally* Andrew I. Gavil, Copperweld *2000: The Vanishing Gap Between Sections 1 and 2 of the Sherman Act*, 68 ANTITRUST L.J. 87 (2000).

The two cases also provided important guidance on how burdens should be allocated in rule of reason cases under Section 1. Like the per se rule, the "quick look" can be understood in evidentiary terms as a burden-shifting device: evidence of actual harm to competition gives rise to a presumption that the challenged conduct was an unreasonable restraint of trade and shifts the burden of production to the defendant to offer evidence that the conduct can otherwise be justified. In contrast to the traditional per se rule, however, the quick look creates a rebuttable, not an irrebuttable, presumption of unreasonableness. The quick look also narrowed the range of cognizable rebuttal evidence.

As an alternative to forcing plaintiffs to offer circumstantial evidence to corroborate their direct evidence, in both cases the defendants sought to rebut the plaintiff's direct evidence of market power by offering evidence of their own allegedly diminutive market shares—and the Court twice rejected the approach. Whether reliance on direct evidence is implemented by rejecting the defendant's demand that the plaintiff bear the burden of proving high market shares in a properly defined relevant market or by refusing to credit the defendant's circumstantial evidence as rebutting direct evidence, the consequence is the same: proof of market power drawn from direct evidence is given greater weight than circumstantial evidence based on market shares. Actual adverse effects evidence creates a presumption that cannot easily be rebutted by circumstantial, market share evidence. To rebut the direct evidence of market power, a defendant must challenge the direct evidence on its own terms. The Supreme Court reiterated the reasoning of *NCAA* and *IFD* in *Eastman Kodak Co. v. Image Technical Services, Inc.*, 504 U.S. 451, 469 & n.15 (1992), a case that involved claims of exclusionary conduct under both Sections 1 and 2. *See also Toys "R" Us, Inc. v. FTC*, 221 F.3d

928 (7th Cir. 2000). *But see Republic Tobacco Co. v. North Atlantic Trading Co.*, 381 F.3d 717 (7th Cir. 2004)(declining to apply direct evidence approach in non-horizontal case).

Some very important questions remained unanswered after *NCAA* and *IFD* and the "quick look" approach was not uniformly welcomed by commentators. The two decisions had three common characteristics: (1) a "quick" review of the challenged conduct indicated harm to competition; (2) the defendants articulated a plausible efficiency defense that was sufficient to justify abandoning the per se rule, but (3) condemnation followed when it appeared that the defense was not supported by evidence. The two cases did not specify, however, what kind and how much evidence of actual effects would be sufficient to warrant a burden shift. Actual price effects, for example, could be relatively minor or substantial, and evidence of such effects may be relatively more persuasive or conjectural. Moreover, developing proof of actual detrimental effects to competition is not necessarily any "quicker" than presenting a fully developed circumstantial case based on market definition and market share analysis. It might be, but not necessarily. Finally, the approach could be faulted if it too readily permits a burden shift, even on the slightest bit of "actual effects" evidence. "Too quick" of a look could lead to more challenges based on relatively weak evidence in contexts where anticompetitive effects seem very unlikely. These issues required further consideration and development and remain somewhat unsettled. For additional discussion of these and other questions regarding the import of direct evidence of actual effects, see Andrew I. Gavil, *A Comment on the Seventh Circuit's* Republic Tobacco *Decision: On the Utility of "Direct Evidence of Anticompetitive Effects,"* ANTITRUST, Spring 2005, at 59.

In Chapter 8 we will take another look at the enduring meaning of *NCAA* and *IFD*. In our next case, *California Dental ("CDA")*, note how the two cases continued to evolve, and became recognized as establishing a more structured and focused approach to applying the rule of reason. What if anything does *CDA* add to that approach beyond recognizing it? Although the Court reaffirmed its commitment to the quick look concept, does it place any limitations on its use? If so, is the end result greater or lesser clarity in the use of the rule of reason?

CALIFORNIA DENTAL ASSOCIATION v. FEDERAL TRADE COMMISSION
Supreme Court of the United States, 1999.
526 U.S. 756, 119 S.Ct. 1604, 143 L.Ed.2d 935.

Justice SOUTER delivered the opinion of the Court.

There are two issues in this case: whether the jurisdiction of the Federal Trade Commission extends to the California Dental Association (CDA), a nonprofit professional association, and whether a "quick look" sufficed to justify finding that certain advertising restrictions adopted by the CDA violated the antitrust laws. We hold that the Commission's jurisdiction under the Federal Trade Commission Act (FTC Act) extends to an association that, like the CDA, provides substantial economic benefit to its for-profit members, but that where, as here, any anticompetitive effects of given restraints are far from intuitively obvious, the rule of reason demands a more thorough enquiry into the consequences of those restraints than the Court of Appeals performed.

I

The CDA is a voluntary nonprofit association of local dental societies to which some 19,000 dentists belong, including about three-quarters of those practicing in the State. The CDA is exempt from federal income tax * * * although it has for-profit subsidiaries that give its members advantageous access to various sorts of insurance, including liability coverage, and to financing for their real estate, equipment, cars, and patients' bills. The CDA lobbies and litigates in its members' interests, and conducts marketing and public relations campaigns for their benefit.

The dentists who belong to the CDA through these associations agree to abide by a Code of Ethics (Code) including the following § 10:

> "Although any dentist may advertise, no dentist shall advertise or solicit patients in any form of communication in a manner that is false or misleading in any material respect. In order to properly serve the public, dentists should represent themselves in a manner that contributes to the esteem of the public. Dentists should not misrepresent their training and competence in any way that would be false or misleading in any material respect."

The CDA has issued a number of advisory opinions interpreting this section,[1] and through separate advertising guidelines intended to help members comply with the Code and with state law the CDA has advised its dentists of disclosures they must make under state law when engaging in discount advertising.[2]

* * *

1. The advisory opinions, which substantially mirror parts of the California Business and Professions Code, include the following propositions:

> "A statement or claim is false or misleading in any material respect when it:
>
> > "a. contains a misrepresentation of fact;
> >
> > "b. is likely to mislead or deceive because in context it makes only a partial disclosure of relevant facts;
> >
> > "c. is intended or is likely to create false or unjustified expectations of favorable results and/or costs;
> >
> > "d. relates to fees for specific types of services without fully and specifically disclosing all variables and other relevant factors;
> >
> > "e. contains other representations or implications that in reasonable probability will cause an ordinarily prudent person to misunderstand or be deceived.
>
> "Any communication or advertisement which refers to the cost of dental services shall be exact, without omissions, and shall make each service clearly identifiable, without the use of such phrases as 'as low as,' 'and up,' 'lowest prices,' or words or phrases of similar import.

> "Any advertisement which refers to the cost of dental services and uses words of comparison or relativity-for example, 'low fees'-must be based on verifiable data substantiating the comparison or statement of relativity. The burden shall be on the dentist who advertises in such terms to establish the accuracy of the comparison or statement of relativity."

> "Advertising claims as to the quality of services are not susceptible to measurement or verification; accordingly, such claims are likely to be false or misleading in any material respect." * * *

2. The disclosures include:

> "1. The dollar amount of the nondiscounted fee for the service[.]
>
> "2. Either the dollar amount of the discount fee or the percentage of the discount for the specific service[.]
>
> "3. The length of time that the discount will be offered[.]
>
> "4. Verifiable fees[.]
>
> "5. [The identity of] [s]pecific groups who qualify for the discount or any other terms and conditions or restrictions for qualifying for the discount."

The Commission brought a complaint against the CDA, alleging that it applied its guidelines so as to restrict truthful, nondeceptive advertising, and so violated § 5 of the FTC Act. The complaint alleged that the CDA had unreasonably restricted two types of advertising: price advertising, particularly discounted fees, and advertising relating to the quality of dental services. An Administrative Law Judge (ALJ) * * * found that, although there had been no proof that the CDA exerted market power, no such proof was required to establish an antitrust violation under *In re Mass. Bd. of Registration in Optometry*, 110 F.T.C. 549 (1988), since the CDA had unreasonably prevented members and potential members from using truthful, nondeceptive advertising, all to the detriment of both dentists and consumers of dental services. He accordingly found a violation of § 5 of the FTC Act.

The Commission adopted the factual findings of the ALJ except for his conclusion that the CDA lacked market power, with which the Commission disagreed. The Commission treated the CDA's restrictions on discount advertising as illegal *per se*. In the alternative, the Commission held the price advertising (as well as the nonprice) restrictions to be violations of the Sherman and FTC Acts under an abbreviated rule-of-reason analysis. * * *

The Court of Appeals for the Ninth Circuit affirmed, sustaining the Commission's assertion of jurisdiction over the CDA and its ultimate conclusion on the merits. The court thought it error for the Commission to have applied *per se* analysis to the price advertising restrictions, finding analysis under the rule of reason required for all the restrictions. But the Court of Appeals went on to explain that the Commission had properly [applied an abbreviated version of the Rule of Reason]. * * *

The Court of Appeals thought truncated rule-of-reason analysis to be in order for several reasons. As for the restrictions on discount advertising, they "amounted in practice to a fairly 'naked' restraint on price competition itself." The CDA's procompetitive justification, that the restrictions encouraged disclosure and prevented false and misleading advertising, carried little weight because "it is simply infeasible to disclose all of the information that is required," and "the record provides no evidence that the rule has in fact led to increased disclosure and transparency of dental pricing." As to non-price advertising restrictions, the court said that

> "[t]hese restrictions are in effect a form of output limitation, as they restrict the supply of information about individual dentists' services. The restrictions may also affect output more directly, as quality and comfort advertising may induce some customers to obtain nonemergency care when they might not otherwise do so. * * * Under these circumstances, we think that the restriction is a sufficiently naked restraint on output to justify quick look analysis."

* * *

II

[In Part II of its opinion, the Court affirmed the view of both the Commission and the Court of Appeals that the FTC Act provides the FTC with jurisdiction over not-for-profit associations like the CDA when they engage in activities that significantly enhance their members' "profits." Eds.]

III

The Court of Appeals treated as distinct questions the sufficiency of the analysis of anticompetitive effects and the substantiality of the evidence supporting the Commission's conclusions. Because we decide that the Court of Appeals erred when it held as a matter of law that quick-look analysis was appropriate (with the consequence that the Commission's abbreviated analysis and conclusion were sustainable), we do not reach the question of the substantiality of the evidence supporting the Commission's conclusion.[8]

In *National Collegiate Athletic Assn. v. Board of Regents of Univ. of Okla.*, we held that a "naked restraint on price and output requires some competitive justification even in the absence of a detailed market analysis." Elsewhere, we held that "no elaborate industry analysis is required to demonstrate the anticompetitive character of" horizontal agreements among competitors to refuse to discuss prices, *National Soc. of Professional Engineers v. United States*, or to withhold a particular desired service, *FTC v. Indiana Federation of Dentists*. In each of these cases, which have formed the basis for what has come to be called abbreviated or "quick-look" analysis under the rule of reason, an observer with even a rudimentary understanding of economics could conclude that the arrangements in question would have an anticompetitive effect on customers and markets. * * * As in such cases, quick-look analysis carries the day when the great likelihood of anticompetitive effects can easily be ascertained.

The case before us, however, fails to present a situation in which the likelihood of anticompetitive effects is comparably obvious. Even on Justice Breyer's view that bars on truthful and verifiable price and quality advertising are *prima facie* anticompetitive, * * * and place the burden of procompetitive justification on those who agree to adopt them, the very issue at the threshold of this case is whether professional price and quality advertising is sufficiently verifiable in theory and in fact to fall within such a general rule. Ultimately our disagreement with Justice Breyer turns on our different responses to this issue. Whereas he accepts, as the Ninth Circuit seems to have done, that the restrictions here were like restrictions on advertisement of price and quality generally, it seems to us that the CDA's advertising restrictions might plausibly be thought to have a net procompetitive effect, or possibly no effect at all on competition. The restrictions on both discount and nondiscount advertising are, at least on their face, designed to avoid false or deceptive advertising[9] in a market characterized by striking disparities between the information available to the professional and the patient. * * *

The explanation proffered by the Court of Appeals for the likely anticompetitive effect of the CDA's restrictions on discount advertising began with the unexceptionable statements that "price advertising is fundamental to price competition," and that "[r]estrictions on the ability to advertise prices normally make it more difficult for consumers to find a lower price and for dentists to compete on the basis of price." The court then acknowledged that,

---

8. We leave to the Court of Appeals the question whether on remand it can effectively assess the Commission's decision for substantial evidence on the record, or whether it must remand to the Commission for a more exten-

sive rule-of-reason analysis on the basis of an enhanced record.

9. That false or misleading advertising has an anticompetitive effect, as that term is customarily used, has been long established. * * *

according to the CDA, the restrictions nonetheless furthered the "legitimate, indeed procompetitive, goal of preventing false and misleading price advertising." The Court of Appeals might, at this juncture, have recognized that the restrictions at issue here are very far from a total ban on price or discount advertising, and might have considered the possibility that the particular restrictions on professional advertising could have different effects from those "normally" found in the commercial world, even to the point of promoting competition by reducing the occurrence of unverifiable and misleading across-the-board discount advertising. Instead, the Court of Appeals confined itself to the brief assertion that the "CDA's disclosure requirements appear to prohibit across-the-board discounts because it is simply infeasible to disclose all of the information that is required," followed by the observation that "the record provides no evidence that the rule has in fact led to increased disclosure and transparency of dental pricing."

But these observations brush over the professional context and describe no anticompetitive effects. Assuming that the record in fact supports the conclusion that the CDA disclosure rules essentially bar advertisement of across-the-board discounts, it does not obviously follow that such a ban would have a net anticompetitive effect here. * * * [T]he CDA's rule appears to reflect the prediction that any costs to competition associated with the elimination of across-the-board advertising will be outweighed by gains to consumer information (and hence competition) created by discount advertising that is exact, accurate, and more easily verifiable (at least by regulators). As a matter of economics this view may or may not be correct, but it is not implausible, and neither a court nor the Commission may initially dismiss it as presumptively wrong.[12]

In theory, it is true, the Court of Appeals neither ruled out the plausibility of some procompetitive support for the CDA's requirements nor foreclosed the utility of an evidentiary discussion on the point. The court indirectly acknowledged the plausibility of procompetitive justifications for the CDA's position when it stated that "the record provides no evidence that the rule has in fact led to increased disclosure and transparency of dental pricing." But because petitioner alone would have had the incentive to introduce such evidence, the statement sounds as though the Court of Appeals may have thought it was justified without further analysis to shift a burden to the CDA to adduce hard evidence of the procompetitive nature of its policy; the court's aversion to empirical evidence at the moment of this implicit burden-shifting underscores the leniency of its enquiry into evidence of the restrictions' anticompetitive effects.

12. Justice Breyer suggests that our analysis is "of limited relevance," because "the basic question is whether this ... theoretically redeeming virtue in fact offsets the restrictions' anticompetitive effects in this case." He thinks that the Commission and the Court of Appeals "adequately answered that question," but the absence of any empirical evidence on this point indicates that the question was not answered, merely avoided by implicit burden-shifting of the kind accepted by Justice Breyer. The point is that before a theoretical claim of anticompet- itive effects can justify shifting to a defendant the burden to show empirical evidence of procompetitive effects, as quick-look analysis in effect requires, there must be some indication that the court making the decision has properly identified the theoretical basis for the anticompetitive effects and considered whether the effects actually are anticompetitive. Where, as here, the circumstances of the restriction are somewhat complex, assumption alone will not do.

The Court of Appeals was comparably tolerant in accepting the sufficiency of abbreviated rule-of-reason analysis as to the nonprice advertising restrictions. The court began with the argument that "[t]hese restrictions are in effect a form of output limitation, as they restrict the supply of information about individual dentists' services." Although this sentence does indeed appear as cited, it is puzzling, given that the relevant output for antitrust purposes here is presumably not information or advertising, but dental services themselves. The question is not whether the universe of possible advertisements has been limited (as assuredly it has), but whether the limitation on advertisements obviously tends to limit the total delivery of dental services. * * * If quality advertising actually induces some patients to obtain more care than they would in its absence, then restricting such advertising would reduce the demand for dental services, not the supply; and it is of course the producers' supply of a good in relation to demand that is normally relevant in determining whether a producer-imposed output limitation has the anticompetitive effect of artificially raising prices.[13]

Although the Court of Appeals acknowledged the CDA's view that "claims about quality are inherently unverifiable and therefore misleading," it responded that this concern "does not justify banning all quality claims without regard to whether they are, in fact, false or misleading." As a result, the court said, "the restriction is a sufficiently naked restraint on output to justify quick look analysis." The court assumed, in these words, that some dental quality claims may escape justifiable censure, because they are both verifiable and true. But its implicit assumption fails to explain why it gave no weight to the countervailing, and at least equally plausible, suggestion that restricting difficult-to-verify claims about quality or patient comfort would have a procompetitive effect by preventing misleading or false claims that distort the market. It is, indeed, entirely possible to understand the CDA's restrictions on unverifiable quality and comfort advertising as nothing more than a procompetitive ban on puffery.

The point is not that the CDA's restrictions necessarily have the procompetitive effect claimed by the CDA; it is possible that banning quality claims might have no effect at all on competitiveness. * * * And it is also of course possible that the restrictions might in the final analysis be anticompetitive. The point, rather, is that the plausibility of competing claims about the effects of the professional advertising restrictions rules out the indulgently abbreviated review to which the Commission's order was treated. The obvious anticompetitive effect that triggers abbreviated analysis has not been shown.

In light of our focus on the adequacy of the Court of Appeals's analysis, Justice Breyer's thorough-going, *de novo* antitrust analysis contains much to impress on its own merits but little to demonstrate the sufficiency of the Court of Appeals's review. The obligation to give a more deliberate look than

---

13. Justice Breyer wonders if we "mea[n] this statement as an argument against the anticompetitive tendencies that flow from an agreement not to advertise service quality." But as the preceding sentence shows, we intend simply to question the logic of the Court of Appeals's suggestion that the restrictions are anticompetitive because they somehow "affect output," presumably with the intent to raise prices by limiting supply while demand remains constant. We do not mean to deny that an agreement not to advertise service quality might have anticompetitive effects. We merely mean that, absent further analysis of the kind Justice Breyer undertakes, it is not possible to conclude that the net effect of this particular restriction is anticompetitive.

a quick one does not arise at the door of this Court and should not be satisfied here in the first instance. Had the Court of Appeals engaged in a painstaking discussion in a league with Justice Breyer's (compare his 14 pages with the Ninth Circuit's 8), and had it confronted the comparability of these restrictions to bars on clearly verifiable advertising, its reasoning might have sufficed to justify its conclusion. Certainly Justice Breyer's treatment of the antitrust issues here is no "quick look." Lingering is more like it, and indeed Justice Breyer, not surprisingly, stops short of endorsing the Court of Appeals's discussion as adequate to the task.

Saying here that the Court of Appeals's conclusion at least required a more extended examination of the possible factual underpinnings than it received is not, of course, necessarily to call for the fullest market analysis. Although we have said that a challenge to a "naked restraint on price and output" need not be supported by "a detailed market analysis" in order to "requir[e] some competitive justification," *National Collegiate Athletic Assn.,* 468 U.S., at 110, 104 S.Ct. 2948, it does not follow that every case attacking a less obviously anticompetitive restraint (like this one) is a candidate for plenary market examination. The truth is that our categories of analysis of anticompetitive effect are less fixed than terms like *"per se," "quick look,"* and "rule of reason" tend to make them appear. We have recognized, for example, that "there is often no bright line separating *per se* from Rule of Reason analysis," since "considerable inquiry into market conditions" may be required before the application of any so-called *"per se"* condemnation is justified. *Id.* at 104, n.26, 104 S.Ct. 2948. "[W]hether the ultimate finding is the product of a presumption or actual market analysis, the essential inquiry remains the same—whether or not the challenged restraint enhances competition." *Id.,* at 104, 104 S.Ct. 2948. * * * As the circumstances here demonstrate, there is generally no categorical line to be drawn between restraints that give rise to an intuitively obvious inference of anticompetitive effect and those that call for more detailed treatment. What is required, rather, is an enquiry meet for the case, looking to the circumstances, details, and logic of a restraint. The object is to see whether the experience of the market has been so clear, or necessarily will be, that a confident conclusion about the principal tendency of a restriction will follow from a quick (or at least quicker) look, in place of a more sedulous one. And of course what we see may vary over time, if rule-of-reason analyses in case after case reach identical conclusions. For now, at least, a less quick look was required for the initial assessment of the tendency of these professional advertising restrictions. Because the Court of Appeals did not scrutinize the assumption of relative anticompetitive tendencies, we vacate the judgment and remand the case for a fuller consideration of the issue.

It is so ordered.

Justice BREYER, with whom Justice STEVENS, Justice KENNEDY, and Justice GINSBURG join, concurring in part and dissenting in part.

I agree with the Court that the Federal Trade Commission has jurisdiction over petitioner, and I join Parts I and II of its opinion. I also agree that in a "rule of reason" antitrust case "the quality of proof required should vary with the circumstances," that "[w]hat is required ... is an enquiry meet for the case," and that the object is a "confident conclusion about the principal tendency of a restriction." But I do not agree that the Court has properly applied those unobjectionable principles here. In my view, a traditional application of the rule of reason to the facts as found by the Commission requires affirming the Commission—just as the Court of Appeals did below.

I

The Commission's conclusion is lawful if its "factual findings," insofar as they are supported by "substantial evidence," "make out a violation of Sherman Act § 1." To determine whether that is so, I would not simply ask whether the restraints at issue are anticompetitive overall. Rather, like the Court of Appeals (and the Commission), I would break that question down into four classical, subsidiary antitrust questions: (1) What is the specific restraint at issue? (2) What are its likely anticompetitive effects? (3) Are there offsetting procompetitive justifications? (4) Do the parties have sufficient market power to make a difference?

A

The most important question is the first: What are the specific restraints at issue? Those restraints do *not* include merely the agreement to which the California Dental Association's (Dental Association or Association) ethical rule literally refers, namely, a promise to refrain from advertising that is " 'false or misleading in any material respect'." Instead, the Commission found a set of restraints arising out of the way the Dental Association implemented this innocent-sounding ethical rule in practice, through advisory opinions, guidelines, enforcement policies, and review of membership applications. As implemented, the ethical rule reached beyond its nominal target, to prevent truthful and nondeceptive advertising. In particular, the Commission determined that the rule, in practice:

> (1) "precluded advertising that characterized a dentist's fees as being low, reasonable, or affordable,"

> (2) "precluded advertising . . . of across the board discounts," and

> (3) "prohibit[ed] all quality claims."

Whether the Dental Association's basic rule as *implemented* actually restrained the truthful and nondeceptive advertising of low prices, across-the-board discounts, and quality service are questions of fact. * * * [B]oth the ALJ and the Commission ultimately found against the Dental Association in respect to these facts. And the question for us—whether those agency findings are supported by substantial evidence—is not difficult.

* * *

B

Do each of the three restrictions mentioned have "the potential for genuine adverse effects on competition"? I should have thought that the anticompetitive tendencies of the three restrictions were obvious. An agreement not to advertise that a fee is reasonable, that service is inexpensive, or that a customer will receive a discount makes it more difficult for a dentist to inform customers that he charges a lower price. If the customer does not know about a lower price, he will find it more difficult to buy lower price service. That fact, in turn, makes it less likely that a dentist will obtain more customers by offering lower prices. And that likelihood means that dentists will prove less likely to offer lower prices. * * * The Commission thought this fact sufficient to hold (in the alternative) that the price advertising restrictions were unlawful *per se*. For present purposes, I need not decide whether the Commission was right in applying a *per se* rule. I need only assume a rule of reason applies, and note the serious anticompetitive tendencies of the price advertising restraints.

The restrictions on the advertising of service quality also have serious anticompetitive tendencies. This is not a case of "mere puffing." * * * [S]ome parents may still want to know that a particular dentist makes a point of "gentle care." Others may want to know about 1–year dental work guarantees. To restrict that kind of service quality advertisement is to restrict competition over the quality of service itself, for, unless consumers know, they may not purchase, and dentists may not compete to supply that which will make little difference to the demand for their services. That, at any rate, is the theory of the Sherman Act. And it is rather late in the day for anyone to deny the significant anticompetitive tendencies of an agreement that restricts competition in any legitimate respect, let alone one that inhibits customers from learning about the quality of a dentist's service.

Nor did the Commission rely solely on the unobjectionable proposition that a restriction on the ability of dentists to advertise on quality is likely to limit their incentive to compete on quality. Rather, the Commission pointed to record evidence affirmatively establishing that quality-based competition is important to dental consumers in California. Unsurprisingly, these consumers choose dental services based at least in part on "information about the type and quality of service." * * *

The FTC found that the price advertising restrictions amounted to a "naked attempt to eliminate price competition." It found that the service quality advertising restrictions "deprive consumers of information they value and of healthy competition for their patronage." It added that the "anticompetitive nature of these restrictions" was "plain." The Court of Appeals agreed. I do not believe it possible to deny the anticompetitive tendencies I have mentioned.

C

We must also ask whether, despite their anticompetitive tendencies, these restrictions might be justified by other procompetitive tendencies or redeeming virtues. This is a closer question—at least in theory. The Dental Association argues that the three relevant restrictions are inextricably tied to a legitimate Association effort to restrict false or misleading advertising. The Association, the argument goes, had to prevent dentists from engaging in the kind of truthful, nondeceptive advertising that it banned in order effectively to stop dentists from making unverifiable claims about price or service quality, which claims would mislead the consumer.

The problem with this or any similar argument is an empirical one. Notwithstanding its theoretical plausibility, the record does not bear out such a claim. The Commission, which is expert in the area of false and misleading advertising, was uncertain whether petitioner had even *made* the claim. It characterized petitioner's efficiencies argument as rooted in the (unproved) factual assertion that its ethical rule "challenges *only* advertising that is false or misleading." Regardless, the Court of Appeals wrote, in respect to the price restrictions, that "the record provides no evidence that the rule has in fact led to increased disclosure and transparency of dental pricing." With respect to quality advertising, the Commission stressed that the Association "offered no convincing argument, let alone evidence, that consumers of dental services have been, or are likely to be, harmed by the broad categories of advertising it restricts." * * *

With one exception, my own review of the record reveals no significant evidentiary support for the proposition that the Association's members must agree to ban truthful price and quality advertising in order to stop untruthful claims. The one exception is the obvious fact that one can stop untruthful advertising if one prohibits all advertising. But since the Association made virtually no effort to sift the false from the true, that fact does not make out a valid antitrust defense.

In the usual Sherman Act § 1 case, the defendant bears the burden of establishing a procompetitive justification. And the Court of Appeals was correct when it concluded that no such justification has been established here.

D

I shall assume that the Commission must prove one additional circumstance, namely, that the Association's restraints would likely have made a real difference in the marketplace. The Commission, disagreeing with the ALJ on this single point, found that the Association did possess enough market power to make a difference. In at least one region of California, the mid-Peninsula, its members accounted for more than 90% of the marketplace; on average they accounted for 75%. In addition, entry by new dentists into the market place is fairly difficult. Dental education is expensive * * * as is opening a new dentistry office. And Dental Association members believe membership in the Association is important, valuable, and recognized as such by the public.

These facts, in the Court of Appeals' view, were sufficient to show "enough market power to harm competition through [the Association's] standard setting in the area of advertising." And that conclusion is correct. Restrictions on advertising price discounts * * * may make a difference because potential patients may not respond readily to discount advertising by a handful (10%) of dentists who are not members of the Association. And that fact, in turn, means that the remaining 90% will prove less likely to engage in price competition. Facts such as these have previously led this Court to find market power—unless the defendant has overcome the showing with strong contrary evidence. I can find no reason for departing from that precedent here.

II

In the Court's view, the legal analysis conducted by the Court of Appeals was insufficient, and the Court remands the case for a more thorough application of the rule of reason. But in what way did the Court of Appeals fail? I find the Court's answers to this question unsatisfactory—when one divides the overall Sherman Act question into its traditional component parts and adheres to traditional judicial practice for allocating burdens of persuasion in an antitrust case.

Did the Court of Appeals misconceive the anticompetitive tendencies of the restrictions? * * *

* * * [T]he Court of Appeals * * * *rejected* the legal "treatment" customarily applied "to classic horizontal agreements to limit output or price competition"—*i.e.*, the FTC's (alternative) *per se* approach. It did so because the Association's "policies do not, on their face, ban truthful nondeceptive ads"; instead, they "have been enforced in a way that restricts truthful advertising." It added that "[t]he value of restricting false advertising ... counsels some caution in attacking rules that purport to do so but merely sweep too broadly."

Did the Court of Appeals misunderstand the nature of an anticompetitive effect? * * *

* * * An agreement not to advertise, say, "gentle care" is anticompetitive because it imposes an artificial barrier against each dentist's independent decision to advertise gentle care. That barrier, in turn, tends to inhibit those dentists who want to supply gentle care from getting together with those customers who want to buy gentle care. There is adequate reason to believe that tendency present in this case.

Did the Court of Appeals inadequately consider possible procompetitive justifications? * * *

The Commission found that the defendant did not make the necessary showing that a redeeming virtue existed in practice. The Court of Appeals, asking whether the rules, as enforced, "augment[ed] competition and increase[d] market efficiency," found the Commission's conclusion supported by substantial evidence. * * *

The majority correctly points out that "petitioner alone would have had the incentive to introduce such evidence" of procompetitive justification. But despite this incentive, petitioner's brief in this Court offers nothing concrete to counter the Commission's conclusion that the record does not support the claim of justification. Petitioner's failure to produce such evidence itself "explain[s] why [the lower court] gave no weight to the ... suggestion that restricting difficult-to-verify claims about quality or patient comfort would have a procompetitive effect by preventing misleading or false claims that distort the market."

* * * With respect to any of the three restraints found by the Commission, whether "net anticompetitive effects" follow is a matter of how the Commission, and, here, the Court of Appeals, have answered the questions I laid out at the beginning. Has the Commission shown that the restriction has anticompetitive tendencies? It has. Has the Association nonetheless shown offsetting virtues? It has not. Has the Commission shown market power sufficient for it to believe that the restrictions will likely make a real world difference? It has.

The upshot, in my view, is that the Court of Appeals, applying ordinary antitrust principles, reached an unexceptional conclusion. It is the same legal conclusion that this Court itself reached in *Indiana Federation*—a much closer case than this one. * * *

I would note that the form of analysis I have followed is not rigid; it admits of some variation according to the circumstances. The important point, however, is that its allocation of the burdens of persuasion reflects a gradual evolution within the courts over a period of many years. That evolution represents an effort carefully to blend the procompetitive objectives of the law of antitrust with administrative necessity. It represents a considerable advance, both from the days when the Commission had to present and/or refute every possible fact and theory, and from antitrust theories so abbreviated as to prevent proper analysis. The former prevented cases from ever reaching a conclusion, and the latter called forth the criticism that the "Government always wins." I hope that this case does not represent an abandonment of that basic, and important, form of analysis.

For these reasons, I respectfully dissent from Part III of the Court's opinion.

* * *

———

NCAA was decided by a vote of 7–2, with Justices White and Rehnquist dissenting. Justice White later authored the unanimous opinion of the Court in *IFD*. What explains the fracturing of the Court in *CDA*? Did the dissenters disagree with Justice Souter's conclusion that the case was ill-suited for treatment under a quick look? Is Justice Breyer's four step framework just a variation of the quick look approach? An alternate form of structured rule of reason analysis?

CDA posed the question whether the combination of economic reasoning based on prior judicial experience with conduct and some circumstantial evidence, as opposed to actual effects evidence, can justify the burden shift associated with the quick look. The FTC had not relied on actual effects evidence such as would typically be presented through expert economic testimony, but rather on its view that the anticompetitive effects of the advertising restrictions at issue were relatively obvious, so much so that a burden shift to the CDA that would require it to come forward with evidence of the procompetitive justifications for the restrictions was warranted. *See* Timothy J. Muris, California Dental Association v. Federal Trade Commission: *The Revenge of Footnote 17*, 8 Sup. Ct. Econ. Rev. 265 (2000)(arguing that the empirical literature concerning the consequences of restraining professional advertising should have been sufficient to support the conclusion that CDA's restraints on advertising were likely to lead to increased prices without any improvement in quality).

Imbedded in this formulation of the arguments is an important additional question: should quick look analysis apply retrospectively or can it also apply prospectively? Actual effects evidence will likely be available only after conduct has been implemented. Hence, if *CDA* is read to permit a burden shift only based on actual effects evidence, it might only apply retrospectively, based on the observable effects of conduct. Can a facial review of conduct before any effects have accrued ever substitute for actual effects evidence? That appears to be the point being urged by Professor Muris. Experience with similar practices in the past can substitute for actual effects evidence because it makes the prediction of those effects especially sound. Similarly, perhaps economic reasoning alone could in some circumstances justify the prediction of anticompetitive effects. These approaches would permit quick look analysis to be applied prospectively.

Significantly, all members of the Court endorsed quick look analysis, but by a narrow majority the Court rejected its use under the facts of *CDA*. What made use of the quick look appropriate in *NCAA* and *IFD* (which Justice Breyer describes as "a much closer case"), but inappropriate in *CDA*? What might the answer to that question tell us about the focus and function of the "quick look"? Is the quick look a distinct alternative to both per se and rule of reason analysis?

One possible explanation for the majority's position lies in the comparative strength of the evidence of actual anticompetitive effects in both *NCAA* and *IFD*. Initially, the Court observed that "quick look analysis carries the day when the great likelihood of anticompetitive effects can easily be ascertained." (Casebook, *supra*, at 190). After reviewing the evidence of both anticompetitive effects and procompetitive justifications, it further concluded that "[t]he obvious anticompetitive effect that triggers abbreviated analysis has not been shown." (Casebook, *supra*, at 192). And in footnote 12, the Court states: "before a theoretical claim of anticompetitive effects can justify shifting to a defendant the burden to show empirical evidence of procompetitive effects, as quick-look analysis in effect requires, there must be some indication that the court making the decision has properly identified the theoretical basis for the anticompetitive effects *and considered whether the effects actually are anticompetitive*." (Emphasis added).

Justice Souter's opinion for the majority thus suggests that the focus of "quick look" analysis is anticompetitive effects, and that its function is to cut to the quick of cases where the defendant's conduct has obvious anticompetitive consequences. In such cases, the burden of production should shift to the defendants to determine whether or not they have any supportable procompetitive justifications. If not, the case can be brought to conclusion.

Two factors in *CDA* that suggest limitations on the use of quick look analysis are: (1) the presence of plausible efficiency claims by the defendant; and (2) the absence of evidence of actual anticompetitive effects, such as that present in *NCAA* and *IFD*. As to actual effects, however, the Court's opinion equivocates. In praising Justice Breyer's separate opinion concurring and dissenting in part, the Court appeared to leave open the possibility of a quick look burden shift based on economic reasoning alone. It simply did not find the economic reasoning supplied by the court of appeals in the specific case it was reviewing to be adequate to the task. In our final case in the Chapter, *Polygram Holding, Inc. v. FTC*, 416 F.3d 29 (D.C. Cir. 2005), we will see an example of reliance on economic reasoning to shift a burden to the defendant. There the FTC successfully claimed that it should not have to present actual effects evidence in order to justify an initial burden shift to the defendant. In its view, only if the defendant met its burden of production with regard to its claimed efficiencies would the burden shift back to the FTC, and only then should it be required to come forward with effects evidence, which it claimed was in fact available.

The majority and the dissent reached different conclusions about the sufficiency of the FTC's theoretical economic case against advertising restrictions to meet its burden of production and shift that burden to the CDA to support its assertions of procompetitive justifications. As the Court observed, "the Court of Appeals may have thought it was justified without further analysis to shift a burden to the CDA to adduce hard evidence of the procompetitive nature of its policy; the court's adversion to empirical evidence at the moment of this implicit burden shifting underscores the leniency of its enquiry into evidence of the restrictions' anticompetitive effects." *California Dental Ass'n.*, 526 U.S. at 776. In dissent, Justice Breyer saw no reason to be cautious given the nature of CDA's restraints. In his view, the anticompetitive effects were likely enough to warrant a burden shift. Do you agree with the majority or the dissent? How obvious was the anticompetitive effect of the CDA's restrictions? At least obvious enough to warrant a burden shift that would have required CDA to support its assertions of procompetitive justifications?

If the FTC had met its initial burden of production as described by the Court, and the burden had shifted to CDA, what kind of evidence would CDA have needed to produce in order to shift the burden of production back to the FTC?

Although both opinions in *CDA* appeared uniformly to endorse the quick look in theory, one commentator has argued that the case "will certainly be characterized as a setback" for the "quick look movement." Stephen Calkins, California Dental Association: *Not a Quick Look But Not the Full Monty*, 67 ANTITRUST L.J. 495 (2000)("*Full Monty*"). After *CDA*, can a plaintiff confidently predict whether it will be able to win on a quick look without need to prove actual effects? If not, can plaintiff afford to limit discovery and limit testimony in litigating its case? Does *CDA* have the practical effect of endorsing the quick look while simultaneously removing its advantages in giving guidance to firms and reducing the transaction costs of litigation?

The Court concluded its opinion in *CDA* by trying to locate the "quick look" within the larger context of Section 1—and here an opportunity for clarification of the rule of reason was arguably lost. The Court explained that the analysis under Section 1 involves a range of choices, not three distinct approaches, per se and "full blown rule of reason," with "quick look" lying somewhere between. "What is required * * * is an enquiry meet for the case, looking to the circumstances, details, and logic of a restraint." Does this approach provide any clarity to the rule of reason? What options were available to the court of appeals on remand to resolve the case in light of this standard? *See California Dental Ass'n v. FTC*, 224 F.3d 942 (9th Cir. 2000) (concluding that the FTC failed to demonstrate the anticompetitive effect of the CDA's advertising restrictions and was not entitled to remand to further develop the record).

While perhaps theoretically defensible, the Court's "enquiry meet for the case" standard can be faulted on the ground that it provides no more guidance than the unstructured rule of reason of *Chicago Bd. of Trade*. The Court even made the per se rule sound like less of a bright line test, observing that " 'considerable inquiry into market conditions' may be required before the application of any so-called 'per se' condemnation is justified.' "* It is simply not responsive to the exigencies of litigation and hardly provides any notice to parties of how much and what kind of evidence will be required to shift a burden of production or satisfy a burden of proof. One commentator has criticized the majority's "requirement that the plaintiff prove everything" as a "throwback to the unstructured rule of reason of the early twentieth century." HERBERT HOVENKAMP, THE ANTITRUST ENTERPRISE: PRINCIPLE AND EXECUTION 147 (2005). He continues:

> * * * As a matter of pure logic, the Court was certainly right when it said that competitor-created restraints on advertising could increase, decrease, or have no impact at all on the output of dental services. As a matter of evidence and history, however, that position is myopic. * * * [A] fox going into a hen house at night might be intending to kill chickens, to take a harmless nap, or to gather eggs and clean cages. But the farmer, knowing the history of foxes in hen houses, need not wait until the fox's intentions are clear.

Id. at 147–48.

Justice Breyer, concurring in part and dissenting in part, sought to articulate a more structured approach to implementing the rule of reason by presenting four questions that should guide the inquiry. (Casebook, *supra*, at 194.) Identifying the right questions to ask certainly can focus an inquiry, and it might even aid an enforcement agency in deciding whether to challenge a particular restraint. But like the majority, Justice Breyer did not undertake to specify how his questions could be integrated into the relative burdens of the parties. We will further examine Justice Breyer's four questions in Sidebar 2–5. For another effort to structure the rule of reason inquiry through use of a series of questions, see HOVENKAMP, THE ANTITRUST ENTERPRISE, *supra*, at 149–50.

Note on Antitrust and the Professions

How important is it to an understanding of *CDA* that it concerned self-regulation by a trade association of professionals? As we have already seen, the application of the antitrust laws to the professions has a long and contentious history. Cases like *Nat'l Soc'y of Prof'l Eng'rs, Maricopa, Indiana Fed'n of Dentists,* and *CDA* all involved application of the antitrust laws to efforts by professions to regulate their own competitive activities.

In virtually all of these cases the defendants urged the Supreme Court to acknowledge that there were differences in the nature of competition among professionals that warranted departures from traditional antitrust rules applied in other industries. These arguments typically sought either relief from the per se

---

* The Court's observation provides some useful insight into cases like *Socony-Vacuum Oil.* Despite the Court's stated position in footnote 59 that extensive market power evidence was unnecessary to support application of the per se rule, the Court clearly considered the case on a fairly well-developed record that included evidence of actual anticompetitive price increases. And although *NSPE* has been read as a per se case, in some ways it reads more like a quick look case, because the Court considered and then rejected the engineers' proffered justifications before reaching its ultimate conclusion. In retrospect, these and other cases can perhaps be fairly analyzed as progenitors of the quick look used in *NCAA* and *IFD.*

rule, or special consideration under the rule of reason, but for the most part they failed—until *CDA*. And there is a well-established line of cases harshly condemning obviously anticompetitive arrangements among professionals. *See, e.g., Goldfarb v. Virginia State Bar*, 421 U.S. 773 (1975)(minimum fee schedules adopted by Bar Association per se unlawful). Indeed, a wide range of economic benefits and harms can come from various forms of professional industry self-regulation. *See, e.g.*, Marina Lao, Comment: *The Rule of Reason and Horizontal Restraints Involving Professionals*, 68 ANTITRUST L.J. 499, 520–23 (2000).

What characteristics of professions might distinguish them from other trades or industries? Professor Lao observes that "[d]emands for special antitrust rules pertaining to the professions are usually based on information asymmetries between professionals and their clients or patients." *Id.* at 512. What does she mean by "information asymmetries"? How might such asymmetries warrant treating industry self-regulating restraints, such as the advertising restraints in *CDA*, differently from similar restraints among other industries? Is there any question in your mind that an agreement between General Motors and Ford to refuse to advertise quality or price information to consumers would be unlawful? What arguments related to the professional context of the CDA's advertising regulations did the Court appear to accept in *CDA*? How might they explain the outcome of the case? What kinds of authority did it cite in support of its position?

Some commentators have sought to limit the scope of *CDA* by confining it to its "professional" context. These commentators cite the Court's long-evident animosity towards professional advertising, and its tolerance of efforts to curb it. *See, e.g.,,* Calkins, *Full Monty*, 67 ANTITRUST L.J. at 518 ("The Court majority's unhappiness with professional advertising is essential to an understanding of its opinion in CDA."). Do you agree? Is the opinion relevant only to agreements within professions relating to advertising? Does it relate to all professional self-regulation whether directed at advertising or otherwise? Or does it have general applicability to all horizontal cases? For a broader discussion of the FTC's efforts over time to police the professions, see John E. Kwoka, Jr., *The Federal Trade Commission and the Professions: A Quarter Century of Accomplishment and Some New Challenges*, 72 ANTITRUST L.J. 997 (2005) (including an analysis of *CDA*).

Sidebar 2–5:
The Contemporary Rule of Reason:
Core Economic Concepts With
Multiple Frameworks

As should be clear at this point, the rule of reason and the per se rule were designed to answer the same question under Section 1 of the Sherman Act: did the defendants undertake conduct that unreasonably restrained trade? In terms of burdens of proof, they represented two contrasting models—at least theoretically. The per se rule reduced the plaintiff's burden of proving a Section 1 offense to a finding of "agreement." If agreement was proved, and it fell into one of the per se categories, it was swiftly condemned. On the other hand, if a given restraint fell outside of the per se categories, the parties would have to sift through potentially voluminous and complex data, but with little in the way of firm guidance.

Many antitrust rules began to change at the Supreme Court and in the lower courts beginning in the mid–1970s to focus antitrust analysis on core economic concepts. As a consequence, the seemingly bright line dichotomy between the rule of reason and the per se rules began to erode. Per se rules began to take on aspects of the rule of reason by requiring at least some analysis of competitive effects and lack of justifications before conduct would be characterized as illegal per se. Likewise, rule of reason inquiries began to take on aspects of per se rules, by incorporating burden-shifting elements or "quick look" decision rules to structure the factual inquiry. The analytical framework is no longer entirely settled, but, as we shall see, modern courts and the federal enforcement agencies have been moving toward a consistent approach for determining whether horizontal agreements violate Section 1 of the Sherman Act.

The Core Economic Concepts of Antitrust Take Shape in the Courts

By the mid–1980s, it was evident that antitrust analysis had become focused on several core economic concepts.

Anticompetitive Effects. Starting with the Court's decision in *Nat'l Soc'y Prof'l Eng'rs* ("*NSPE*") in 1978, Section 1 analysis was more firmly tied to anticompetitive effects. Cases like *NCAA* in turn helped to define the kinds of anticompetitive effects that should be of concern, particularly highlighting output restriction, which is associated with higher prices. *NSPE* also noted that an unreasonable reduction of competition could manifest itself in lower "quality, service, safety, and durability." The Court continued to emphasize the centrality of anticompetitive effects through *California Dental Ass'n* ("*CDA*"), and it continues to do so today.

Market Power. Contemporary commentators argued that absent market power, or the prospect of securing it, conduct was unlikely to result in significant anticompetitive effects. In fact, any effort to exercise market power by a firm that lacked it could only result in an unprofitable loss of sales as other rivals stepped in to compete away its customers. Market power can only be successfully exercised when the increased profits on sales made at the higher price exceed the profits lost on sales no longer made. The Court implicitly recognized the importance of market power in its *Sylvania* decision in 1977, as well as in *Broadcast Music* and *NCAA*.

Some contemporary commentators urged courts to use the *absence* of market power as a screen for filtering out and dismissing antitrust challenges to conduct that was unlikely to lead to any objectionable anticompetitive effects. *See, e.g.*, Frank H. Easterbrook, *The Limits of Antitrust*, 63 TEX. L. REV. 1 (1984). The Supreme Court agreed that market power was an important component of Section 1 analysis, but it reflected that observation in a different way: by developing the direct/circumstantial evidence framework endorsed in *NCAA*, *IFD*, and *CDA*. As was discussed in the Note following *NCAA*, anticompetitive effects could be proved by direct evidence of actual effects—of the exercise of market power, or circumstantially—through inferences drawn from high market shares in defined markets. Because a high market share suggests the absence of rivalry, it may justify the inference that a firm or firms can profitably charge prices above marginal cost, and hence a *presumption* that a firm possess market power.* Both approaches—the filter approach

---

* The ability to do so, however, will depend on the elasticity of demand. The greater the elasticity of demand (loosely, the flatter the demand curve), the less likely it is that a firm

and the direct/circumstantial framework—recognize the core significance of market power. The filter approach is not precluded by the direct/circumstantial framework, and some lower courts have pursued it.

Efficiencies. *Sylvania* and *Broadcast Music* both injected a concern for efficiencies, defined as pro-competitive effects. If output restriction is the key to anticompetitive effects, output expansion is a window into likely pro-competitive effects. Hence lower costs of production or distribution, as well as other conduct that boosts output, came to characterize the "cognizable defenses" to allegations of violation under Section 1.

Conditions of Entry. Although we have only alluded to it at this point, the importance of analyzing conditions of entry also emerged in this period as a fourth core concept that was essential to judging anticompetitive effects. We will study the analysis of entry at length in Chapters 5 (mergers) and 6 (monopolization). It is easy to understand its importance. The success of any effort to exercise market power may be undermined by the ability of rivals, current or new, to respond to a price increase by increasing the supply of goods or services to a market. Increased supply from new entrants, or from incumbents not involved in exercising market power who instead expand their output, can defeat any effort to increase price. To the degree the firms that seek to exercise market power are aware that entry responses will be swift and substantial, moreover, the incentive to try can be reduced. Conversely, the presence of "barriers to entry" helps to facilitate the exercise of market power, because they reduce the likelihood of supply responses from rivals.

Figure 2–8 summarizes these core concepts of antitrust.

with a high market share can restrict output and raise price without losing so many sales that it will prove to be an unprofitable strategy. *See, e.g.*, DENNIS W. CARLTON & JEFFREY M. PERLOFF, MODERN INDUSTRIAL ORGANIZATION 93 (4th ed. 2005) ("[T]he key element in an investigation of market power is the price elasticity of demand.").

Figure 2–8:
The Core Economic Concepts of Antitrust Analysis

- Anticompetitive Effects
  - reduced output/supra-competitive prices
  - reduced quality or service (effectively a higher price)
  - reduced innovation
  - diminished buyer choice

- Market Power (Used to Infer Anticompetitive Effects)
  - Circumstantial Evidence
    - define relevant market
    - calculate market shares
    - infer market power from high market shares
  - Direct Evidence
    - measure demand elasticities
    - price/cost ratios
    - econometric analysis
    - actual exclusion of rivals

- Efficiencies
  - output expansion/lower costs
  - improved quality or service
  - enhanced innovation

- Conditions of Entry
  - ability of rivals and/or new entrants to expand output in response to price increases

Toward a Modern Analytical Framework

The task that remained for courts, commentators, and enforcement agencies was to harness these concepts, drawn largely from the economics literature, and combine them with the law that had developed over the prior decades to establish an integrated framework that could facilitate economically-informed legal decision-making. In doing so, it would be necessary to take into account access to evidence, as well as burdens of pleading, production, and proof. The most important challenge was to calibrate application of the rule of reason: must it be applied swiftly through clear and simple rules (risking errors of over-inclusion or under-inclusion) or applied carefully, through painstaking, detailed analysis (making it more difficult for firms to know in advance what rules would apply to their conduct and more time-consuming and expensive for courts and parties)? In short, how could the rule of reason be made reasonably administrable by courts and predictable for businesses and enforcers?

The erosion of the rigid per se/rule of reason dichotomy through development of the "quick look" was an advance in that effort. Conceptually, the quick look serves as a method for identifying conduct that on the one hand falls outside of the traditional per se rules owing to plausible efficiencies, but that nevertheless raises some relatively significant competitive concerns. Because it functions to shift the burden of production from the plaintiff to the defendant, it can be thought of as a "pro-enforcement" plaintiff's device, offering a way for plaintiffs to win a rule of reason case more quickly. But the quick look also invites early consideration of plausible efficiencies, and in that sense it can also benefit defendants by ameliorating the harsh consequences of hasty invocation of traditional per se rules. Many commentators agree that courts should not be bound to full-blown rule of reason requirements in cases where there are other, more readily available and reliable indicators of anticompetitive effects. But critics argue that the quick look provides plaintiffs with too easy a means of shifting their burden to defendants and demanding of them evidence of justification, effectively shifting the burden of *proof* under the rule of reason. *See generally* Alan J. Meese, *Farewell to the Quick Look: Redefining the Scope and Content of the Rule of Reason*, 68 Antitrust L.J. 461, 464 (2000)(describing quick look as "an artifact of a bygone Populist era").

As a practical matter, the policy goals involved in structuring the rule of reason could lead to three kinds of "quick look" analysis: (a) private plaintiffs and public enforcers want courts to condemn conduct without detailed analysis of market power and likely effects when it is facially objectionable or has actual adverse effects; (b) private plaintiffs and public enforcers also want courts to condemn conduct when it would be in a traditional per se category but for plausible efficiencies, and on review the efficiencies do not actually appear substantial; and (c) defendants want courts to exonerate conduct without analysis of effects or efficiencies if the parties involved collectively lack market power. *NCAA*, *IFD*, and *CDA* involved only the first of these three approaches, and can usefully be viewed as establishing the parameters of a "quick look to condemn." The second approach is also a form of quick look to condemn. The third approach, urged by some commentators, amounts to a "quick look to exonerate"—a method for more readily filtering out cases that are unlikely to present a serious competitive threat. *See, e.g.,* Frank H. Easterbrook, *The Limits of Antitrust*, 63 Tex. L. Rev. 1 (1984). The Court's extensive treatment of the first type of quick look to condemn, however, makes it the most well-established form of quick look analysis.

The erosion of the per se/rule of reason dichotomy has led lower courts and commentators to propose a number of general frameworks for applying Section 1 to varied circumstances. These approaches seek to combine the benefits of filters and burden-shifting devices into a single framework, often utilizing presumptions. The FTC made an important contribution to the effort in *In re Massachusetts Bd. of Registration in Optometry*, 110 F.T.C. 549 (1988), which later served as the basis for its approach in other cases. For a sampling of the responses to these early efforts, see Stephen Calkins, California Dental Association: *Not a Quick Look But Not the Full Monty*, 67 Antitrust L.J. 495, 542–43 (2000);

Joseph Kattan, *The Role of Efficiency Considerations in the Federal Trade Commission's Antitrust Analysis*, 64 ANTITRUST L.J. 613 (1996); Timothy J. Muris, *The Federal Trade Commission and the Rule of Reason: In Defense of* Massachusetts Board, 66 ANTITRUST L.J. 773 (1998); Timothy J. Muris, *The Rule of Reason After* California Dental, 68 ANTITRUST L.J. 527 (2000).

The lower courts have also sought to synthesize the prior case law and adapt it for use in litigation. The result has been something of an emerging consensus on a more structured rule of reason that specifically addresses burden shifting.

One frequently cited example of the typical judicial framework can be found in the Tenth Circuit's decision in *Law v. NCAA*, 134 F.3d 1010 (10th Cir. 1998). *See also Gregory v. Fort Bridger Rendezvous Ass'n*, 448 F.3d 1195, 1205 (10th Cir. 2006) (reaffirming *Law* framework). *Law* itself drew upon a variety of lower court cases and other authorities. It can be viewed as setting forth a four-step approach:

> [1]. . . . [T]he plaintiff bears the initial burden of showing that an agreement had a substantially adverse effect on competition. [2] If the plaintiff meets this burden, the burden shifts to the defendant to come forward with evidence of the procompetitive virtues of the alleged wrongful conduct. [3] If the defendant is able to demonstrate procompetitive effects, the plaintiff then must prove that the challenged conduct is not reasonably necessary to achieve the legitimate objectives or that those objectives can be achieved in a substantially less restrictive manner. [4] Ultimately, if these steps are met, the harms and benefits must be weighed against each other in order to judge whether the challenged behavior is, on balance, reasonable.

Law, 134 F.3d at 1019 (citations omitted).

As should be evident, *Law's* framework draws upon and seeks to synthesize elements from many different previous decisions and commentators. It is consistent with *NSPE's* direction that the core purpose of the Section 1 inquiry is to determine whether the challenged conduct caused anticompetitive effects and it incorporates the essential teaching of *NCAA*. *Id.* at 1019 ("A plaintiff may establish anticompetitive effect indirectly by proving that the defendant possessed the requisite market power within a defined market or directly by showing actual anticompetitive effects, such as control over output or price."). Although it is arguable that ancillary restraint analysis is not a good fit for every case of competitor collaboration, a number of other circuits have incorporated it into their framework, as does *Law*. Perhaps most importantly, today commentators and courts equate *Addyston Pipe* with the priority of addressing concerns for promoting economic efficiency.

Finally, the *Law* framework suggests that in cases where both plaintiffs and defendants have met their respective burdens of production, courts, and presumably juries, should "balance" the relative negative effects and benefits. Such "rule of reason balancing" is perhaps the greatest myth in all of U.S. antitrust law. It is almost always described as the final step in the rule of reason analysis, yet there are few if any reported decisions that turned on a true balancing of pro-and anticompetitive effects. Instead, most cases turn on the strength and weight of the evidence of effects or efficiencies. *See, e.g.*, Michael A. Carrier, *The Rule of Reason: Bridging the Disconnect*, 1999 B.Y.U. L. REV. 1265 (concluding that "in an astonishing 96% of Rule of Reason cases, courts do not balance anything").

The *Law* framework appears to accommodate the call by private plaintiffs and public enforcers for courts to condemn conduct without detailed analysis of market power and likely effects when it is facially objectionable or has resulted in actual adverse effects. Such evidence would presumably satisfy the plaintiff's initial burden, and in consequence would be sufficient to ground a judgment in the plaintiff's favor unless the defendant could provide an efficiency justification (as required by the second step). It is less clear that the *Law* framework accommodates the call by private plaintiffs and public enforcers for courts to condemn conduct when it would be in a traditional per se category but for plausible efficiencies, and on review the efficiencies do not actually appear substantial. Do the second and third steps proposed by the *Law* court permit a court to scrutinize the proffered justification beyond assessing its plausibility and the reasonableness of the means chosen to accomplish the claimed procompetitive end? If not, should they? Finally, the *Law* framework does not appear to accommodate the call by defendants for courts to exonerate conduct without analysis of effects or efficiencies if the parties involved collectively lack market power. Should the *Law* court have added another step, perhaps just prior to the final balancing test, to do so?

The analytical frameworks developed by *Law* and other lower federal courts are similar to what the FTC and DOJ jointly proposed in their *Antitrust Guidelines for Competitor Collaborations* (2000) ("*Collaboration Guidelines*"). But not all of the frameworks are identical. *See, e.g.*, *Expert Masonry, Inc. v. Boone County, KY*, 440 F.3d 336, 343 (6th Cir. 2006); and *United States v. Visa U.S.A., Inc.*, 344 F.3d 229, 238 (2d Cir. 2003) (Casebook, *infra*, Chapter 7).

Like *Law* and other lower court decisions, the Collaboration Guidelines seek to synthesize the per se rule, the traditional rule of reason, and the quick look, as well as the ancillary restraint model of *Addyston Pipe*. Although they use the traditional per se/rule of reason dichotomy as an organizational tool, they clearly mean to recognize that the range of antitrust inquiry under Section 1 is flexible, not fixed, and will depend upon the circumstances of each case. *Collaboration Guidelines*, § 3.1 & n.15 (citing *CDA*). But they go well beyond *Law* by describing in greater detail the kinds of facts that might be relevant to the various steps in the analysis, making them the most comprehensive statement of a framework that could be applied to all competitor collaborations.

Endorsing use of the traditional per se rule where appropriate, the Guidelines also embrace *Addyston Pipe*'s ancillary restraint approach as a method of distinguishing "naked" restraints from those warranting more elaborate analysis, "even if [they are] of a type that might otherwise be considered per se illegal." *Collaboration Guidelines*, § 3.2 ("If * * * participants in an efficiency-enhancing integration of economic activity enter into an agreement that is reasonably related to the integration and reasonably necessary to achieve its procompetitive benefits, the Agencies analyze the agreement under the rule of reason * * *.").

Once an agreement* falls outside the per se rule, the Guidelines turn to the rule of reason. According to the Guidelines:

> Rule of reason analysis focuses on the state of competition with, as compared to without, the relevant agreement. The central question is whether the relevant agreement likely harms competition by increasing the ability or incentive profitably to raise price above or reduce output, quality, service, or innovation below what likely would prevail in the absence of the relevant agreement.

Collaboration Guidelines, § 1.2. The benchmark for judging the competitive effects of agreements, therefore, is the price and competitive conditions that would have prevailed absent the collaboration. By implication, an agreement that had the effect of maintaining a monopoly price that might otherwise have fallen owing to competition, or that harmed some other dimension of competition, as by having the effect of reducing quality or inhibiting innovation, could be condemned.

The rule of reason as set forth in the Guidelines incorporates the quick look, both as a filter and burden-shifter:

> If the nature of the agreement and the absence of market power together demonstrate the absence of anticompetitive harm, the Agencies do not challenge the agreement. * * * Alternatively, where the likelihood of anticompetitive harm is evident from the nature of the agreement, or anticompetitive harm has resulted from an agreement already in operation, then, absent overriding benefits that could offset the anticompetitive harm, the agencies challenge such agreements without a detailed market analysis.

Collaboration Guidelines, § 3.3 (footnotes omitted).

If an agreement raises some competitive concerns, but there is also evidence of justification, such as efficiencies, the Guidelines move on to the next step: detailed market analysis, including defining relevant markets, and evaluating circumstantial evidence of market power. Absent either evidence of actual anticompetitive effects or circumstantial evidence of market power, the Guidelines conclude that the Agencies will "end the investigation without considering procompetitive benefits." In evidentiary terms, they in effect would conclude that the burden of production has not shifted to the defendant warranting any showing of justifications. (Like other government guidelines, however, the Collaboration Guidelines specifically disclaim any intention to specify burdens of production or proof).

Only agreements that present actual evidence of anticompetitive effect and/or circumstantial evidence of market power continue onto the next step: a consideration of procompetitive justifications. Here the Guidelines outline the parameters of the modern "full blown" rule of reason investigation that seeks to assess competitive harms and benefits

---

* A collaboration may be formalized through one or more agreements. The Guidelines indicate that the agencies will assess the overall competitive impact of a collaboration, as well as "any individual agreement or set of agreements within the collaboration that may harm competition." *Collaboration Guidelines*, § 2.3.

and reach a judgment about the overall reasonableness of the agreement. *Collaboration Guidelines*, §§ 3.31–37. A final step incorporates consideration of less restrictive means of achieving the procompetitive benefits. *Id.* at § 3.36(b), which we considered earlier in this Chapter in connection with *Addyston Pipe*.

Are the Collaboration Guidelines entirely consistent with the law? Do they make accommodation for all three kinds of quick looks, described above in this Note? Consider Figure 2–9, which summarizes the various approaches.

Figure 2–9
The Unreasonable Restraint of Trade Continuum Under Section 1 of the Sherman Act

	Per Se Rule	Quick Look to Condemn Type 1	Quick Look to Condemn Type 2	Quick Look to Exculpate	Comprehensive Rule of Reason
Anticompetitive Effects Plaintiff's Burden (if met, shifts burden of production to defendant)	*Naked restraint* Obviously anticompetitive Anticompetitive effects presumed <u>Examples</u>: *ADM, Socony, BRG, SCTLA*	*Facial analysis* *Inherently suspect*, because anticompetitive effect is *intuitively obvious* based on economic analysis. Plaintiff need not prove actual anticompetitive effects or market power. <u>Example</u>: *Polygram*	*Actual anticompetitive effects* Plaintiff need not prove market power. <u>Examples</u>: *NCAA, Indiana Fed'n, CDA* (theory endorsed, but rejected on facts)	*No anticompetitive effects* Infer absence of anticompetitive effects from absence of market power when defendants collectively have a low market share.	*Market power analysis* Anticompetitive effects shown by direct evidence or inferred from proof of market power.
Efficiencies Defendant's burden (if met, shifts burden of production back to plaintiff)	*No plausible efficiencies* Presumption of anticompetitive effects irrebuttable; justification evidence inadmissible If plausible efficiencies, or restraints necessary, per se rule inapplicable – move on to other approaches. (*BMI, NCAA*)	*Plausible efficiencies* (could have been the basis for removing from per se category) Justification evidence admissible If efficiencies are plausible, evaluate evidence; may still be condemned if efficiency evidence is unsupported or insufficient. Hard to rebut, but not as hard as with evidence of actual effects (Quick Look to Condemn #2).	*Plausible efficiencies* (could have been the basis for removing from per se category) Justification evidence admissible With actual anticompetitive effects having been demonstrated by plaintiff, difficult in practice for defendant to rebut.	*Efficiencies presumed* With no shift of a burden of production to defendants, no need for defendant to introduce evidence of efficiencies. <u>Possible Example</u>: Competitor Collaboration Guidelines Example 8	*Plausible efficiencies* (could have been the basis for removing from per se category) Justification evidence admissible Rebut presumption of anticompetitive effects by showing (a) *cognizable efficiency*, or (b) restraint is reasonably necessary to achieve a legitimate objective. <u>Possible Example</u>: Competitor Collaboration Guidelines Example 10
Ultimate Disposition	*Condemn* If not condemned under this quick look rule, analyze under more comprehensive rule of reason.	*Likely condemn* If not condemned under this quick look rule, analyze under more comprehensive rule of reason.	*Very likely condemn* If not condemned under this quick look rule, analyze under more comprehensive rule of reason.	*Do not condemn* If not exculpated under this quick look rule, analyze under more comprehensive rule of reason.	*Plaintiff has burden of persuasion* Condemn only if (a) efficiency shown is *insufficient to offset anticompetitive effects* or (b) restraint was *greater than necessary*.

Conclusion

The various frameworks described in the second half of this Sidebar seek to incorporate the core economic concepts described in the first half. They also try to redress a reality of the current state of rule of reason jurisprudence at the Supreme Court: nearly a century after *Standard Oil* first embraced the "rule of reason," the Supreme Court has not fully developed an operative model for applying it consistently through judicial process.

The frameworks developed in the Collaboration Guidelines and cases like *Law* summarize much of what we have learned in this Chapter about the analysis of agreements among rivals that threaten collusive effects and provide a roadmap for that analysis. How much of that roadmap is specifically authorized or supported by Supreme Court case law? Do you think the Collaboration Guidelines make good policy sense? Will they work as effectively as tools for exercising prosecutorial discretion as they will for litigating in private civil actions? In the final section of this Chapter, which looks more specifically at joint ventures, we will examine one last example of an effort to structure the rule of reason inquiry in the decision of the D.C. Circuit in *Polygram*. *Polygram* does not track either *Law* or the Collaboration Guidelines in every respect, but as we shall see, it has important affinities with both.

Finally, recall what has motivated the courts, commentators, and enforcers to refine the content of the rule of reason by moving towards greater reliance on core economic concepts and seeking to establish a clear framework for applying them to varied cases. Per se rules have the clear advantages of being administrable, less expensive to implement, and a ready source of guidance for firms' primary conduct. But as the Supreme Court acknowledged in its cases in the late 1970s and into the 1980s, easy answers do not necessarily provide the best antitrust rules. The per se rules of the past likely increased error costs, particularly by over-deterring beneficial or competitively insignificant conduct resulting in systemic inefficiencies in the economy. At the same time, the full-blown rule of reason was seen by many as an unattractive alternative, because of the costs and time involved in its application and the lack of guidance it provides to firms seeking to comply with the antitrust laws. The structured inquiries set forth in quick look rules can be understood as an attempt to find the optimal rule: one that minimizes false positives, false negatives, and costs of administration. How well have the courts and agencies succeeded in doing so?

G. JOINT VENTURES AND STRATEGIC ALLIANCES

To this point in the Chapter we have examined many kinds of arrangements among competing firms. Some, the Court concluded, warranted relatively swift condemnation, like price-fixing, dividing markets and collusive group boycotts. But others, such as the blanket license in *Broadcast Music*, the call rule in *Chicago Bd. of Trade*, and the advertising restrictions in *CDA* survived the Court's scrutiny. As other antitrust commentators have observed, many of these undertakings could be labeled "joint ventures" if that term were defined expansively and without regard to possible legal status. The Chicago Board of Trade, the NCAA, ASCAP and Broadcast Music, and Topco can all be viewed as joint ventures—agreements formed among rival firms to achieve specified purposes, purposes that none of the participants could have realized on its own. But if "joint venture" is to be associated with certain kinds of procompetitive cooperative relationships, they must be distinguished from simple agreements among rivals to restrain trade.

This Chapter would not be complete, therefore, without a brief overview of the nature, scope and legal status of joint ventures. As even a brief overview will reveal, however, the analysis of joint ventures can be complex and there is a great deal of current controversy about the role joint ventures can play in fast-moving, technology-driven industries, a topic we consider in Chapter 10.

1. CATEGORIZING JOINT VENTURES BY FUNCTION

Of course, the examples of joint ventures we have observed thus far in the Casebook far from exhaust the range of cooperative relationships that can be formed among firms, be they rivals or not. Cooperative arrangements are ubiquitous and infinitely variable. Nevertheless, they generally fall into one of three basic categories: (1) research and development joint ventures; (2) production joint ventures; and (3) distribution (marketing) joint ventures. Any given venture may fall exclusively into one of these categories, or combine features of more than one.

Research and Development ("R & D") Joint Ventures. Perhaps the best known of contemporary joint ventures is the "R & D Venture." R & D ventures pool the intellectual and financial resources of firms—often rivals—to pursue the development of new products, processes, or even basic scientific or technical knowledge. They may entail the sharing of an existing facility or funding the creation of a new one. Often, the cost of undertaking such research is daunting for a single firm, and a single firm may lack all of the know-how to pursue the research. Indeed, R & D ventures frequently involve the cross-licensing of intellectual property, such as patents or copyrights, and can lead to the creation of new intellectual property. Such ventures can accelerate the pace of innovation and lead to significant technological breakthroughs.

Production Joint Ventures. Production joint ventures are exactly what they sound like—an undertaking jointly to produce something, typically a new product. As with R & D ventures, production joint ventures may involve sharing production facilities or know-how, or, in combination with R & D, the joint development of new production methods. Production joint ventures may also facilitate the combination of complementary know-how or distribution capabilities. To further encourage R & D joint ventures, and some production ones, Congress has provided some limited exemptions from antitrust coverage in the National Cooperative Research and Production Act of 1993, 15 U.S.C. § 4301.

Distribution Joint Ventures. Distribution or marketing joint ventures combine the capabilities of firms to bring new or existing products or services to market. They may combine, improve upon or expand existing capabilities, or lead to the creation of new capabilities or methods.

All joint ventures share certain critical characteristics that illustrate their procompetitive potential. First, they involve an integration of assets, know-how or both to produce something that none of the venturers could produce on its own, at least not as cost-effectively. Second, they involve efficiencies—cost savings or product improvements that flow from combining efforts and sharing risks and costs. Finally, they typically require contractual restraints to ensure that the fruits of the venture are not exploited by one or more of the venturers.

For some of these same reasons, joint ventures can pose serious antitrust issues. Frequently, they arise between and among rivals. And because they almost always substitute some degree of cooperation for competition, the possibility exists that they will be used directly or indirectly to facilitate anticompetitive coordination of the sort we have examined in this Chapter. Characterizing the conduct under examination in each case as a "joint venture," therefore, does not help to answer the question whether it is anticompetitive. Indeed, the Court has reminded firms engaged in coordination that the joint venture label offers no immunity from antitrust scrutiny where competitive concerns are raised. *See, e.g., Timken,* 341 U.S. at 597–98.

Evaluating joint ventures thus requires an appreciation for the kinds of anticompetitive effects associated with different kinds of collaborations and the legal framework necessary to distinguish the legitimate from the illegitimate. As we have been learning, anticompetitive conduct can be usefully categorized as collusive or exclusionary. This is true as well for joint ventures.

2. POSSIBLE ANTICOMPETITIVE EFFECTS OF JOINT VENTURES

In applying the collusive/exclusionary framework to joint ventures, it is useful to separately consider joint venture *formation* and *operation.* As is illustrated in Figure 2–10, the formation alone of a joint venture can lead to collusive or exclusionary effects. By combining the research, production, or marketing capabilities of competing firms that collectively possess market power, a joint venture substitutes joint for individual action, cooperation for competition. It can serve, therefore, as just another vehicle for setting prices, reducing innovation, or restricting some other dimension of competition. Competition among multiple joint ventures could be sufficient to protect buyers from non-competitive prices, however, even if each venture sets its own price.

Joint ventures also can involve a risk of harmful "spill over" effects. Ventures with entirely laudable goals can produce anticompetitive effects that surface as the rivals engage in direct conversation and cooperation. It may be difficult to confine such conversation to the legitimate aims of the venture. Specific practices and structural protections may be needed to insure that operation of the joint venture will not facilitate unrelated and unnecessary cooperation. For example, membership on the joint venture's board of directors could be limited and officers of the venture could be given real autonomy to make pricing and output decisions. Important information concerning the venture, such as costs, pricing, product and R & D plans, might also be limited to specified persons, or circulated only in summary form to prevent sensitive data from being discussed jointly by the rival owners. There are many other examples of devices commonly used to keep joint ventures from wandering beyond their legitimate purposes.

Another critical issue will be *inclusiveness*—the broader the scope of the venture in terms of its membership, the greater the risk that it will attain market power. Can you think of any cases we have studied in this Chapter that would fit that description? If so, how would they be treated? As per se unlawful? Would it depend on the nature of their proposed actions? On the other restraints agreed to my members? How did the government's Collaboration Guidelines treat such ventures? *See* Sidebar 2–5.

Another concern is *exclusion*. By including some, but excluding others, the formation of a joint venture can cause exclusionary effects. Under what circumstances might those effects give raise to significant competitive concerns? When would an excluded rival complain and why? Under what circumstances would such complaints signal significant concern about antitrust violations? In Chapter 7 we will examine the Supreme Court's 1985 *Northwest Wholesale Stationers* decision, which raised some of these issues in the context of a group boycott having exclusionary effects, as well as the Second Circuit's decision in *United States v. VISA U.S.A., Inc.*, 344 F.3d 229 (2d Cir. 2003).

The *operation* of joint ventures also raises questions of both collusive and exclusionary effects. Here we have seen many examples—the call rule in *Chicago Bd. of Trade*, the blanket license in *Broadcast Music*, the television contract in *NCAA*, the Code of Ethics in *Nat'l Soc'y of Prof'l Eng'rs*, and the refusal to supply x-rays in *Indiana Fed'n of Dentists* were all examples of operational rules adopted by the organizations after they were formed. Given this Chapter's focus on conduct having collusive effects, the anticompetitive effects at issue in these cases were collusive, but in Chapter 7 we will also examine operational rules of collaborative ventures that could be exclusionary.

Figure 2–10 summarizes some of the common competitive concerns associated with joint ventures. How would you use the chart to go about analyzing one? What cases from this Chapter would be most relevant? How would you use the Collaboration Guidelines? What role, if any, would ancillary restraint analysis play? What other conditions would have to be present to make a case for *anticompetitive* exclusion? Should exclusion only be a concern when it is likely to create or enhance market power?

Figure 2–10:
Anticompetitive Theories Associated with Joint Ventures

Stage of Operations	Collusive Effects	Exclusionary Effects
Formation	• are co-venturers rivals? • will they together be able to raise prices or restrict some aspect of competition? • are there protections in the formation papers that will prevent such actions?	• is the venture exclusive to its members? • how competitively significant will access to the venture be? • will members enjoy advantages not reasonably obtainable by non-members?
Operation	• how do the venture documents contemplate operation of the venture? • will the venturers divide markets? • are there ancillary restrictions that will prevent or facilitate collusive effects?	• do the venture documents contemplate exclusive dealing, licensing, or tying? • are there features of the venture that in operation likely will impair or exclude non-members from access to input suppliers or dealers?

In our next and final case of this chapter, *Polygram Holding*, we consider the intersection of joint ventures and the analysis generally of agreements among rivals that threaten collusive effects. As we discussed above in Sidebar 2–5, courts, commentators, and enforcers continue to work at developing a satisfactory and operable framework for distinguishing reasonable from unreasonable restraints of trade under Section 1. Joint ventures have presented the courts with opportunities to do just that. As you read *Polygram*, focus particularly on the FTC's suggested framework and the court's response to it.

POLYGRAM HOLDING, INC. v. FEDERAL TRADE COMMISSION

United States Court of Appeals for the District of Columbia Circuit, 2005.
416 F.3d 29.

Before: GINSBURG, Chief Judge, and EDWARDS and ROGERS, Circuit Judges.

GINSBURG, Chief Judge.

PolyGram Holding, Inc. and several of its affiliates petition for review of an order of the Federal Trade Commission holding PolyGram violated § 5 of the Federal Trade Commission Act, 15 U.S.C. § 45. As detailed below, PolyGram entered into an agreement with Warner Communications, Inc. to distribute the recording of a concert to be given by "The Three Tenors" in 1998. The two companies later entered into a separate agreement to suspend, for ten weeks, advertising and discounting of two earlier Three Tenors concert albums, one distributed by PolyGram and the other by Warner. The Commission held the latter agreement unlawful and prohibited PolyGram from entering into any similar agreement in the future. We agree with the

Commission that, although not a *per se* violation of antitrust law, the agreement was presumptively unlawful and PolyGram failed to rebut that presumption. We therefore deny PolyGram's petition for review.

I.   BACKGROUND

* * * The Three Tenors—José Carreras, Placido Domingo, and Luciano Pavarotti—put on spectacular concerts coinciding with the World Cup soccer finals in 1990, 1994, and 1998. PolyGram distributed the recording of the 1990 concert, which became one of the best-selling classical albums of all time. Warner distributed the 1994 concert album, which also met with great success. Both albums remained on the top-ten classical list throughout 1994, 1995, and 1996.

In late 1997 PolyGram and Warner agreed jointly to distribute the recording of The Three Tenors' July 1998 concert. Warner, which had the worldwide rights, retained the United States rights but licensed to PolyGram the exclusive right to distribute the 1998 album outside the United States, and the companies agreed to share equally the worldwide profit or loss on the project. The agreement also obligated PolyGram and Warner to consult with one another on all "marketing and promotional activities" for the 1998 concert album, but each company was free ultimately to pursue its own marketing strategy and to continue exploiting its earlier Three Tenors concert album without limitation. * * *

Representatives of PolyGram and Warner first met in January 1998 to discuss "marketing and operational issues." One of PolyGram's representatives voiced concern about the effect of marketing the earlier Three Tenors albums upon the prospects for the 1998 concert album and suggested the two companies impose an "advertising moratorium" surrounding the 1998 release, which was scheduled for August 1. According to notes of their next meeting (in March) PolyGram and Warner representatives agreed that "a big push" on the earlier albums "shouldn't take place before November 15." After that meeting, each company instructed its affiliates to cease all promotion of the 1990 and 1994 Three Tenors albums for approximately six weeks, beginning in late July or early August.

Apparently Warner's overseas division did not get the message because in May it announced an aggressive marketing campaign, scheduled to run through December, to discount and to promote the 1994 album throughout Europe. When PolyGram learned of this, it threatened to "retaliate" by cutting the price of its 1990 album. Accusations then flew between the two companies about which had started the imminent price war. Meanwhile, in June the promoter of The Three Tenors concert informed PolyGram and Warner that the repertoire for the 1998 concert would substantially overlap those of the 1990 and 1994 concerts, which in the view of both PolyGram and Warner executives jeopardized the commercial viability of the forthcoming concert album.

By the time The Three Tenors performed in Paris on July 10, PolyGram and Warner had exchanged letters reaffirming their commitment to suspend advertising and discounting the 1990 and 1994 concert albums and agreeing the moratorium would run from August 1 through October 15. About a week later, however, PolyGram's Senior Marketing Director, who had passed on the details of the agreement to PolyGram's General Counsel, sent a memorandum around the company stating, "Contrary to any previous suggestion, there has been no agreement with [Warner] in relation to the pricing and marketing of the previous Three Tenors albums." Warner followed suit on August 10, sending a letter to PolyGram repudiating any pricing or advertising restrictions relative to its 1994 album. At the same time, however, PolyGram and Warner executives privately assured one another their respective companies intended to honor the agreement, and in fact the companies did substantially comply with the agreement through October 15, 1998.

* * *

II. ANALYSIS
* * *

The Commission's findings of fact are conclusive if supported by substantial evidence. *See* 15 U.S.C. § 45(c). The legal issues are "for the courts to resolve, although even in considering such issues the courts are to give some deference to the Commission's informed judgment that a particular commercial practice is to be condemned as 'unfair.' " *FTC v. Ind. Fed'n of Dentists*, 476 U.S. 447, 454 (1987) (*IFD*).

The Supreme Court's approach to evaluating a § 1 claim has gone through a transition over the last twenty-five years, from a dichotomous categorical approach to a more nuanced and case-specific inquiry. In 1978, just before the transition began, the Court summarized its doctrine as follows:

> There are . . . two complimentary categories of antitrust analysis. In the first category are agreements whose nature and necessary effect are so plainly anticompetitive that no elaborate study of the industry is needed to establish their illegality—they are "illegal per se." In the second category are agreements whose competitive effect can only be evaluated by analyzing the facts particular to the business, the history of the restraint, and the reasons why it was imposed.

Nat'l Soc'y of Prof'l Eng'rs v. FTC, 435 U.S. 679, 692 (1978).

Courts and commentators have recognized the trade-offs inherent in each category. *Per se* analysis, which requires courts to generalize about the utility of a challenged practice, reduces the cost of decision-making but correspondingly raises the total cost of error by making it more likely some practices will be held unlawful in circumstances where they are harmless or even procompetitive. The converse—increased litigation cost but reduced cost of error—obtains under the rule of reason, which requires an exhaustive inquiry into all the myriad factors "bearing on whether the conduct is on balance anticompetitive or procompetitive."

Since *Professional Engineers* the Supreme Court has steadily moved away from the dichotomous approach—under which every restraint of trade is either unlawful *per se,* and hence not susceptible to a procompetitive justification, or subject to full-blown rule-of-reason analysis—toward one in which the extent of the inquiry is tailored to the suspect conduct in each particular case. * * * [Here the court cited as examples *NCAA v. Board of Regents,* 468 U.S. 85 (1984) and *Indiana Federation of Dentists*, contrasting them with earlier cases that favored the per se approach, such as *United States v. Socony–*

Vacuum Oil Co., 310 U.S. 150 (1940) and *Klor's, Inc. v. Broadway–Hale Stores, Inc.*, 359 U.S. 207 (1959). Eds.]

At the same time, however, in *NCAA* and *IFD* the Court did not insist upon the elaborate market analysis ordinarily required under the rule of reason to prove the defendant had market power and the restraint it imposed had an anticompetitive effect. The Court instead adopted an intermediate inquiry, since dubbed the "quick look," to evaluate horizontal restraints of trade.

It would be somewhat misleading, however, to say the "quick look" is just a new category of analysis intermediate in complexity between *"per se "*condemnation and full-blown "rule of reason" treatment, for that would suggest the Court has moved from a dichotomy to a trichotomy, when in fact it has backed away from any reliance upon fixed categories and toward a continuum. The Court said as much in *California Dental Association v. FTC*:

> The truth is that our categories of analysis of anticompetitive effect are less fixed than terms like *"per se,"* "quick look," and "rule of reason" tend to make them appear. We have recognized, for example, that there is often no bright line separating *per se* from Rule of Reason analysis, since considerable inquiry into market conditions may be required before the application of any so-called *"per-se"* condemnation is justified.

526 U.S. 756, 779 (1999).

Rather than focusing upon the category to which a particular restraint should be assigned, therefore, the Court emphasized the basic point that under § 1 the essential inquiry is "whether ... the challenged restraint enhances competition. In order to make that determination, a court must make "an enquiry meet for the case, looking to the circumstances, details, and logic of a restraint," which in some cases may not require a full-blown market analysis. The Court continued:

> The object is to see whether the experience of the market has been so clear, or necessarily will be, that a confident conclusion about the principle tendency of a restriction will follow from a quick (or at least quicker) look, in place of a more sedulous one. And of course what we see may vary over time, if rule-of-reason analyses in case after case reach identical conclusions.

In this case * * * the Commission analyzed PolyGram's conduct under the legal framework it had devised in [*In re Massachusetts Board of Optometry,* 110 F.T.C. 549 (1988)], which it maintains is consistent with the Supreme Court's teaching of more than a decade later in *California Dental* (1999). The *Mass. Board* analysis proceeds in several distinct steps: First, the Commission must determine whether it is obvious from the nature of the challenged conduct that it will likely harm consumers. If so, then the restraint is deemed "inherently suspect" and, unless the defendant comes forward with some plausible (and legally cognizable) competitive justification for the restraint, summarily condemned. "Such justifications," the Commission explained, "may consist of plausible reasons why practices that are competitively suspect as a general matter may not be expected to have adverse consequences in the context of the particular market in question, or they may consist of reasons why the practices are likely to have beneficial effects for consumers.''

If the defendant does offer such an explanation, then the Commission "must address the justification" in one of two ways. First, the Commission may explain why it can confidently conclude, without adducing evidence, that the restraint very likely harmed consumers. Alternatively, the Commission may provide the tribunal with sufficient evidence to show that anticompetitive effects are in fact likely. If the Commission succeeds in either way, then the evidentiary burden shifts to the defendant to show the restraint in fact does not harm consumers or has "procompetitive virtues" that outweigh its burden upon consumers.

PolyGram argues the Commission's framework conflicts with Supreme Court precedent by condemning a restraint that is not *per se* illegal without the Commission having to prove the restraint actually harms competition. According to PolyGram, "proof of actual anticompetitive effect (or market power as its surrogate) is required in *any* Rule of Reason case.''

* * * [W]e reject PolyGram's attempt to locate the appropriate analysis, and the concomitant burden of proof, by reference to the vestigial line separating *per se* analysis from the rule of reason. At bottom, the Sherman Act requires the court to ascertain whether the challenged restraint hinders competition; the Commission's framework, at least as the Commission applied it in this case, does just that.

We therefore accept the Commission's analytical framework. If, based upon economic learning and the experience of the market, it is obvious that a restraint of trade likely impairs competition, then the restraint is presumed unlawful and, in order to avoid liability, the defendant must either identify some reason the restraint is unlikely to harm consumers or identify some competitive benefit that plausibly offsets the apparent or anticipated harm. That much follows from the caselaw * * *

Although the Commission uses the term "inherently suspect" to describe those restraints that judicial experience and economic learning have shown to be likely to harm consumers, we note that, under the Commission's own framework, the rebuttable presumption of illegality arises not necessarily from anything "inherent" in a business practice but from the close family resemblance between the suspect practice and another practice that already stands convicted in the court of consumer welfare. The Commission appears to acknowledge, as it must, that as economic learning and market experience evolve, so too will the class of restraints subject to summary adjudication.

That said, we have no difficulty with the Commission's conclusion that PolyGram's agreement with Warner in all likelihood had a deleterious effect upon consumers—unless, that is, PolyGram comes forward with some plausible explanation to the contrary. An agreement between joint venturers to restrain price cutting and advertising with respect to products not part of the joint venture looks suspiciously like a naked price fixing agreement between competitors, which would ordinarily be condemned as *per se* unlawful. The Supreme Court has recognized time and again that agreements restraining autonomy in pricing and advertising impede the "ordinary give and take of the market place.''

PolyGram's fate in this case therefore rests upon the plausibility of the sole competitive justification it proffered for the moratorium agreement, namely, that the restrictions on discounting and advertising enhanced the long-term profitability of all three concert albums and promoted the "Three Tenors" brand. According to PolyGram, each company was concerned the other would "free ride" on the promotional activities of the joint venture by promoting its own earlier concert album; as a result fewer Three Tenors albums would be sold overall and the joint venture would be less likely to create future products, such as a "greatest hits" album or a boxed set. Thus, PolyGram likens the moratorium agreement here to the restraint at issue in *Polk Brothers, Inc. v. Forest City Enterprises*, 776 F.2d 185 (7th Cir. 1985), where two potential retail competitors collaborated to build a store offering some of each company's products but agreed not to sell competing products at the new store. Because the restraint arguably promoted productivity and output by controlling each participant's ability to free-ride on the other's promotional efforts, the court, rather than condemning the restraint summarily, went on to evaluate it under the rule of reason.

At first glance PolyGram's contention has some force; the moratorium appears likely to have mitigated the "spillover" effects that could be expected to follow an aggressive launch of the 1998 album. Absent the moratorium, that is, a consumer, after learning of the new album through the joint venture's advertising, might decide that he would be just as happy with an older concert album, especially if the older album were then available at a discount. The "free-riding" to be eliminated by the moratorium agreement, however, was nothing more than the competition of products that were not part of the joint undertaking. Why not an agreement by which PolyGram and Warner would eliminate advertising and price competition on all their records for a time while they focused exclusively upon promoting the new Three Tenors album? The "procompetitive" justification PolyGram offers is "nothing less than a frontal assault on the basic policy of the Sherman Act." *Nat'l Soc'y of Prof'l Engineers*, 435 U.S. at 695.

To take the Commission's example, if General Motors were vigorously to advertise the release of a new model SUV, other SUV manufacturers would no doubt reap some of the benefit of GM's efforts. But that would not mean General Motors and its competitors could lawfully agree to restrict prices and advertising on existing SUV models in return for General Motors giving its rivals a share of its profit on the new model. Nor would an agreement to restrain prices and advertising on existing SUVs be lawful if General Motors were to release the new model SUV as a joint venture with one of its competitors. A restraint cannot be justified solely on the ground that it increases the profitability of the enterprise that introduces the new product, regardless whether that enterprise is a joint venture or a solo undertaking. And it simply does not matter whether the new SUV would have been profitable absent the restraint; if the only way a new product can profitably be introduced is to restrain the legitimate competition of older products, then one must seriously wonder whether consumers are genuinely benefitted by the new product. As the Supreme Court said in *Catalano, Inc. v. Target Sales, Inc.*, 446 U.S. 643, 649 (1980),

> in any case in which competitors are able to increase the price level
> or to curtail production by agreement, it could be argued that the

agreement has the effect of making the market more attractive to potential new entrants. If that potential justifies horizontal agreements among competitors imposing one kind of voluntary restraint or another on their competitive freedom, it would seem to follow that the more successful an agreement is in raising the price level, the safer it is from antitrust attack. Nothing could be more inconsistent with our cases.

In sum, because PolyGram has failed to identify any competitive justification for its agreement with Warner to refrain from advertising or discounting their competitive Three Tenors products, we hold it violated § 5 of the FTC Act. Hence, we need not go on to determine whether the Commission's findings of fact concerning actual competitive harm are supported by substantial evidence.

Finally, we hold the remedy ordered by the Commission was reasonable. The Commission found there was a significant risk that, if not prohibited from doing so, PolyGram would enter into similar arrangements in the future. That determination is supported by substantial evidence. The record shows the condition that gave rise to the moratorium agreement—namely, the company "fear[ed] that a new release by one of [its] recording artists may lose sales to the artist's older albums owned by a competitor"—is a recurrent one in the record industry; therefore, PolyGram would have the same incentive in the future to enter into other agreements to restrain advertising and price discounting. * * *

* * *

————

What was it about Polygram and Warner's conduct that made it "inherently suspect"? Why in the FTC and the court's view was it so likely to be anticompetitive? If that was true, why wasn't it deemed *per se* unlawful?

The FTC applied a framework developed years earlier in *In re Massachusetts Bd. of Optometry*, 110 F.T.C. 549 (1988), which the court discusses. Does the court clearly endorse that approach? What does it mean when it states that it "accept[s] the Commission's analytical framework"? Are there other frameworks it might also "accept"? What components would they have to share with the *Mass. Board* framework in order also to be acceptable to the D.C. Circuit?

Recall that in *NCAA* and *IFD* the Supreme Court concluded that evidence of actual anticompetitive effects was sufficient to warrant a shift of burden to the defendant, who at that point had to present a justification—*i.e.*, meet a burden of production. That was the import of the "quick look": when actual anticompetitive effects are present, the plaintiff's initial burden of production is satisfied and the defendant must respond. As we discussed in the notes following *CDA*, *CDA* appeared to suggest that the quick look could only be applied when there is evidence of actual anticompetitive effect.

Does *Polygram* effectively expand the use of quick look analysis to cases where there may not be evidence of actual effects, but there is a high likelihood of them? Polygram and Warner objected to the "inherently suspect" approach, in part on the ground that it was inconsistent with the Supreme Court's "quick look" jurisprudence, which they claimed required proof of actual anticompetitive effects. The FTC maintained that there was in fact evidence of actual anticompetitive effect, but it took the position—and the D.C. Circuit agreed—that it did not have to present that evidence. Why? What was its rationale? Having agreed that the conduct was inherently suspect, the D.C. Circuit concluded that there was no need to examine that additional evidence. Should it have? What would have been the significance of doing so?

How does the D.C. Circuit reconcile *Polygram* with *CDA*? Recall that near the conclusion of the majority opinion in *CDA*, the Court said "there is generally no categorical line to be drawn between restraints that give rise to an *intuitively obvious inference of anticompetitive effect* and those that call for more detailed treatment." In using the phrase "intuitively obvious inference," was the Court leaving open the possibility that some kinds of conduct— perhaps conduct such as the promotional moratorium at issue in *Polygram*— could be sufficient to warrant a shift of burden even in the absence of evidence of actual anticompetitive effects? Are "intuitively obvious" and "inherently suspect" two ways of describing the same kind of restraint? Note that the D.C. Circuit expressed its support for shifting a burden of production to the defendants conduct appears anticompetitive "based upon economic learning and the experience of the market." Would *CDA* have been decided the same way if the Supreme Court had utilized the D.C. Circuit's approach?

What justification for the advertising moratorium did Polygram and Warner offer? Why did the FTC and the court agree that it was insufficient to shift a burden back to the FTC and force it to establish actual anticompetitive effects? The court declines to accept the parties' free-riding justification, although it acknowledges that absent the condemned practice, free riding of some sort could occur. On what basis does the court distinguish free riding that a joint venture may prohibit from free riding that it cannot lawfully prevent?

Finally, note that the FTC's remedy was to enjoin the defendants from entering into similar agreements in the future. Was the remedy adequate to solve the competitive problem? Could someone who purchased the 1998 CD during the period of the ban on promotions of the 1990 and 1994 CDs bring suit against Polygram and Warner under the antitrust laws? What would be their theory of antitrust injury?

3.   THE VARIEGATED LEGAL FRAMEWORK FOR ANALYZING JOINT VENTURES

Given the range of conduct that can be categorized as a joint venture, as well as their potential for both collusive and exclusionary effects, it will come as no surprise that the legal context in which joint ventures are evaluated is complex. Moreover, with increasing frequency, joint ventures are taking on international dimensions, which implicates the laws of multiple jurisdictions. Assessing the antitrust risk of joint ventures for clients today, therefore, frequently involves application of the statutes, regulations and guidelines of more than one competition policy system.

In one of the significant, traditional U.S. cases concerning joint ventures, for example, the Supreme Court observed that joint ventures can be analyzed as "agreements" under Section 1 of the Sherman Act, or, when they involve the acquisition of assets, as mergers under Section 7 of the Clayton Act. *See United States v. Penn–Olin Chemical Co.*, 378 U.S. 158, 177 (1964) and Casebook, Chapter 5.

As we have already noted, for the most part joint ventures are viewed in a positive light given their significant potential to facilitate greater production and innovation. From time to time, however, industries have maintained that the antitrust standards applied to joint ventures are too stringent to the point of inhibiting firms from pursuing legitimate and pro-competitive collaborations. Although that perception is less true today, it has produced several amendments to the antitrust laws designed to remove any impediments antitrust enforcement might pose to the use of joint ventures. Typically, these amendments allowed for pre-notification of some ventures, which conferred limited immunity from government and private challenges. There is little evidence to suggest, however, that these amendments triggered any greater level of joint venture activity, which at least raises the question whether antitrust enforcement was truly hindering their creation in the first place. These statutes are listed in Figure 2–11, below.

Finally, it is important to consider the role of government regulations and guidelines in assessing joint ventures. In Sidebar 2–5, we introduced perhaps the most significant, the 2000 Guidelines for Collaborations Among Competitors. Joint ventures might also be subject to analysis under other statutes and guidelines, however, which are collected in Figure 2–11. The sheer number and scope of these is a reminder of the ubiquity of practices that can fall within the label "joint venture."

Figure 2–11:

U.S. Statutes and Guidelines Potentially Applicable to Joint Ventures

Statutes:

- Section 1 of the Sherman Act
- Section 2 of the Sherman Act
- Section 3 of the Clayton Act
- Section 7 of the Clayton Act
- Export Trading Company Act of 1982
- National Cooperative Research and Production Act of 1993

Guidelines:

- Antitrust Guidelines for Collaborations Among Competitors (2000)
- Antitrust Enforcement Guidelines for International Operations (1995)
- Antitrust Guidelines for the Licensing of Intellectual Property (1995)
- Horizontal Merger Guidelines (1982–1997)
- Statements on Antitrust Enforcement Policy in Health Care (1996)

H. CONCLUSION

Welcome to the study of antitrust law! Although it may not yet be apparent, you have already been exposed to some of the most enduring challenges of competition policy, and many of the core concepts that are used to resolve them. But this Chapter focused solely on arrangements among rivals having collusive effects. Antitrust also has been traditionally concerned with relationships among suppliers and their customers, so called "vertical" agreements, which can have collusive or exclusionary effects. Chapter 4 examines vertical arrangements having collusive effects, whereas treatment of vertical conduct having exclusionary effects awaits Chapter 7. Before proceeding, however, take advantage of the Problems and Exercises that follow to reinforce and further refine your appreciation for the material we have covered thus far.

I. PROBLEMS AND EXERCISES

Problem 2–1:
Mountain Medical

a. The Facts

Mountain is the largest city in a rural Western state. Its 150,000 residents are served by two hospitals and 250 physicians, including general practitioners and a variety of sub-specialists, such as surgeons, cardiologists, gastroenterologists, and nephrologists. The nearest hospital outside of Mountain is located in a small town some 30 miles away. Roughly half of the doctors in Mountain are members of a single multi-specialty physician practice, which is owned by one of the two hospitals.

Most of the remaining, independent doctors formed an association, Mountain Medical (MM). The physicians in MM created a common practice name. They jointly marketed their availability to insurers and employers seeking to provide health insurance to their employees, but did not merge their practices, or share profits and financial risks. Were MM to contract with a health insurer or employer, each of its physician members would charge that doctor's individual fees, and those fees might differ. In contrast, the hospital-owned multi-specialty physician practice charged common fees based upon a schedule adopted by the hospital. MM forbade its members from negotiating individually with health insurers, like an HMO, and employers.

MM was approached by More Care, a Health Maintenance Organization ("HMO"), that had previously not served Mountain, and that wanted to sign up doctors in order to enter the Mountain market. MM and More Care engaged in extended, but ultimately fruitless negotiations. More Care never entered the Mountain market. MM also collected detailed fee information from member doctors, and used that information to suggest that some doctors seek higher fees from a health plan that wanted a group contract.

b. The Problem

In light of the cases we have studied in Chapter 2, have the physicians who are members of MM reached any agreement that should be deemed illegal per se under Section 1 of the Sherman Act? If not, have they reached any agreement that otherwise would be deemed an unreasonable restraint of trade?

c. *Skills Exercise*

You are an associate at Mountain's premier law firm, which has been retained to provide antitrust counseling advice to Mountain Medical. Assume for purposes of this exercise that MM is still negotiating with More Care, but is about to terminate those negotiations. MM seeks the firm's advice on the likelihood that the Federal Trade Commission would initiate an investigation of its activities and conclude that they were unlawful under Section 1 of the Sherman Act.

Your task is to prepare a memorandum of no more than five (5) pages evaluating the antitrust risks associated with MM's conduct, including, but not limited to its interactions with More Care. In doing so, you should pay particular attention to relevant case law, as well as the *Antitrust Guidelines for Collaborations Among Competitors* (2000), and the *Department of Justice & Federal Trade Commission Statements of Antitrust Enforcement Policy in Health Care* (1996). Draft the memorandum.

Problem 2–2:
Midwest Truck Leasing

a. *The Facts*

Midwest Truck Leasing ("MTL") is a company engaged in the business of leasing trucks. It is also a member of the North American Truck Leasing Association ("NATLA"). The roughly 150 members of NATLA, including MTL, lease trucks to businesses on a "full service" basis. This means that the lessor rather than the lessee is responsible for maintaining the trucks and for repairing them if they break down. The leases are short term or long term, local or "over the road," which means that the lessee may drive the truck anywhere in the country. Over-the-road customers demand full service, nation-wide.

NATLA members, however, are local companies, none of which owns service facilities outside of its local area, nor could any afford to do so. NATLA was created in order to set up and administer a reciprocal service arrangement that would enable each member to lease trucks on a full-service over-the-road basis and thus compete with the national truck-leasing companies, which have their own service depots all over the United States. NATLA requires each member to give the trucks of the other members prompt and efficient repair service, but it does not regulate the price of the service. NATLA also collects and disseminates information on prices, services, and other issues of interest to its members, and operates a joint fuel purchasing program on behalf of its members. By aggregating their fuel requirements, they can usually negotiate more favorable prices from fuel suppliers.

Each NATLA member operates under a franchise from NATLA that designates the particular location at which it may conduct business as a "National franchisee"—and it specifically forbids each member from doing business as a National franchisee at any other location. NATLA rules also forbid each member/franchisee to affiliate with any other full-service truck-leasing enterprise or association. Typically, authorized locations are placed more than 25 miles apart. NATLA members can open an outlet at an unauthorized location under a different name, but trucks rented under that name would not be entitled to reciprocal service; and even if the member were willing to forgo that advantage, it still could not open an outlet under license from another full-service truck-leasing enterprise without violating NATLA rules and risking expulsion. Because markets for full-service commercial truck leases are local—to facilitate regular maintenance on their vehicles lessees typically lease trucks from a firm having an outlet within a few miles (no more than 25) of the lessee's place of business—the overall effect of NATLA's rules is to severely limit over-the-road leasing competition between its members.

MTL decided to defy both the location and non-affiliation restrictions. Upon discovering those facts, NATLA gave MTL notice that it would be expelled from NATLA immediately.

b. The Problem

In light of the cases we have studied in Chapter 2, has NATLA reached any agreement that should be deemed illegal per se under Section 1 of the Sherman Act? If not, has it reached any agreement that otherwise would be deemed an unreasonable restraint of trade?

c. Skills Exercise

You are an associate at the law firm that has been retained as antitrust counsel to NATLA. NATLA seeks the firm's advice on the likelihood that the Federal Trade Commission would initiate an investigation of its activities and conclude that they were unlawful under Section 1 of the Sherman Act.

Your task is to prepare a memorandum of no more than five (5) pages evaluating the antitrust risks associated with NATLA's conduct, including, but not limited to its expulsion of MTL. Pay particular attention to the relevant case law, as well as the *Antitrust Guidelines for Collaborations Among Competitors* (2000). Draft the memorandum.

Chapter 3

DISTINGUISHING CONCERTED FROM UNILATERAL ACTION

INTRODUCTION

Many competition laws, including Section 1 of the Sherman Act and Article 81 of the EU Treaty, attach special significance to conduct involving "concerted action." Section 1 of the Sherman Act prohibits "[e]very contract, combination . . . or conspiracy" in restraint of trade, and imposes no liability on firms that act alone. Single firm conduct is addressed instead under Section 2, but only when it concerns monopolization or attempt to monopolize. Similarly, Article 81 only applies to "all agreements between undertakings, decisions by associations of undertakings and concerted practices," whereas Article 82 is directed at single-firm conduct, but only when it concerns a "dominant firm."

As we will see in Chapter 6, a monopolist operates outside the Sherman Act's reach when it cuts its own output and boosts prices above competitive levels, even though the economic effects can be the same as when rival firms form a price-fixing cartel. But if a cartel is detected, its participants risk the same fate that befell the ADM executives we observed in Chapter 1 in *Andreas*–imprisonment as felons and payment of substantial fines.

Recall also from Chapter 2 that concerted action alone does not offend Section 1 of the Sherman Act. To violate Section 1, a "contract, combination . . . or conspiracy" must unreasonably restrain trade. In the cases we studied in Chapter 2, the fact of agreement, of "concerted action," usually was conceded, leaving only the conduct's competitive effects to be evaluated. In *Socony Vacuum Oil* and *Maricopa*, the defendants acknowledged they had acted in concert and focused their defense on proving the "reasonableness" of their joint conduct. Similarly, in *Topco*, *Nat'l Soc'y Prof'l Eng'rs*, and *NCAA*, the defendants' concerted conduct was apparent and even took the form of formal contracts and bylaws.

By contrast, the *Andreas* defendants vigorously contested the existence of an agreement. In this and similar cases, plaintiffs, prosecutors, and courts alike have had to develop an analytical framework for defining what constitutes concerted action. In this Chapter we study why competition laws have viewed concerted action more skeptically than unilateral action, and how courts and enforcement authorities have sought to distinguish collective conduct from independent action, especially when direct evidence of agreement is lacking in whole or part.

Implementing this distinction has given rise to two sets of issues in the law of conspiracy. The first stemmed from the development of harsh prohibitions against concerted trade restraints and concerns about the impact of such prohibitions on firm behavior. In early Sherman Act cases such as *Addyston Pipe* (Casebook, *supra*, Chapter 2), courts rarely faced difficult "agreement" issues, as defendants felt no urgency to depict their conduct as being unilateral rather than concerted. Over time, courts interpreted Section 1 to condemn certain agreements categorically–as "per se" unlawful. Because such cases presumed unreasonableness, the fact of agreement became the focal point for litigating Section 1 offenses. Proving agreement meant establishing a violation. *See* Sidebar 2–1.

Aggressive Sherman Act enforcement against some forms of concerted action drove many cartels underground. Cartel members exercised greater precautions to shield illicit collaboration from detection, or they sought other ways to facilitate coordination without agreement–so called "tacit collusion." In turn, prosecutors and courts alike strove to: (1) formulate policies that would help to flush out direct evidence, such as testimony from a cartel insider or documents that show an agreement existed; and (2) develop analytical methods for establishing agreement without express or direct evidence.

To obtain direct evidence of collusion today, prosecutors rely on informants, as in *Andreas*, corporate leniency programs, and offers of immunity for cooperative witnesses. Yet direct evidence is frequently unavailable, so governmental and private plaintiffs also rely heavily on circumstantial evidence to establish the fact of agreement.

The second set of issues resulted from increased reliance on circumstantial evidence and inference to establish conspiracy. When plaintiffs used circumstantial proof extensively, the courts faced an apparent economic anomaly: the Sherman Act did not reach unilateral conduct having the same economic effects as similar, but concerted conduct. Judges felt bound by Section 1 to reject challenges to rivals that used coordination and facilitation devices falling short of the law's definition of agreement. Economic models that demonstrated the common nature of the effects of tacit and express coordination triggered vigorous debate among commentators and courts, but ultimately proved inadequate to bring informal coordination within Section 1's ambit.

Section A begins with the Supreme Court's *Copperweld* decision, which offers some traditional explanations for why U.S. antitrust law treats collective action more harshly than unilateral behavior. As we shall see, those explanations flow from two goals that sometimes conflict: (1) preserving the incentive of individual firms to compete aggressively–specifically by guarding their autonomy over pricing decisions; and (2) protecting against the effects of combined economic power–as when firms coordinate their competitive behavior.

Section B explores the modern economic framework for understanding how firms collude. Starting with some pioneering Chicago School commentary, antitrust policy gradually has embraced a more economically-grounded framework for analyzing the formation, maintenance, and detection of cartels. Although Chicago School commentary typically concluded that durable cartels were difficult to form and maintain, and were therefore rare, later commentary–and enforcement experiences such as the lysine and vitamins cases–have raised doubts about that skepticism. Nevertheless, economic analysis that builds on the Chicago School's earlier work continues to lead the vanguard in analyzing cartel problems today.

Section C examines how the prohibition of certain concerted acts induced firms to alter their methods for coordinating output decisions, and how antitrust conspiracy law tried to neutralize and provide legal means for exposing those efforts. We present the traditional framework for inferring conspiracy from circumstantial evidence, including the "hub and spoke" and "plus factor" conspiracy models. Section C also examines information exchanges and other means of facilitating price and output coordination, which often fall short of "agreement." We conclude the traditional framework with the *Matsushita* decision, which illustrates how the Supreme Court today relies heavily on modern economic theories concerning cartel formation and maintenance.

The central challenge in contemporary antitrust conspiracy law is to integrate the economic insights we see in Section B into the traditional legal framework presented in Section C. In Section D we focus on modern judicial efforts to address this challenge. The Chapter concludes with an overview of "incipient" conspiracy–the treatment of practices falling short of agreement, yet arguably designed to achieve the same economic effects.

A. ANTITRUST'S SPECIAL SCRUTINY OF COLLECTIVE ACTION

Antitrust rules seldom interfere with decisions to raise prices by firms acting alone. As we will see in Chapter 6, dominant firms usually are free to set prices as high as they wish to exploit the market power inherent in a superior product or process. Public utility price controls for natural monopolies and occasional European Commission attacks on exploitative pricing under Article 82 are rare exceptions to the rule that monopolists may restrict output unilaterally to raise prices.

The main cases in Chapters 2 and 4 show that the rules can change dramatically when firms act together. A monopolist legally can curb output to raise prices, but rival business executives risk criminal sanctions if they agree to pursue the same result in concert, regardless of whether their agreement raises prices in fact. A vertically integrated company incurs no liability when it sets the price its wholly-owned retail outlets may charge for products made in its own factories. But, as we will learn in Chapter 4, a manufacturer may commit a Section 1 offense if it agrees with an independent retailer to set a minimum price for the resale of its goods if the agreement unreasonably restrains competition.

In *Copperweld Corp. v. Independence Tube Corp.*, 467 U.S. 752 (1984), the Supreme Court addressed the rationale for this distinction in U.S. antitrust law. *Copperweld* treated the different standards for unilateral and concerted action in analyzing whether acts by firms subject to common ownership might satisfy Section 1's collective action requirement. In ruling that a parent corporation and its wholly-owned subsidiary constitute but a single economic actor, and therefore lack the capacity to conspire for Sherman Act Section 1 purposes, the Court examined the basis for subjecting concerted behavior to more demanding scrutiny.

COPPERWELD CORP. v. INDEPENDENCE TUBE CORP.
United States Supreme Court, 1984.
467 U.S. 752, 104 S.Ct. 2731, 81 L.Ed.2d 628.

Chief Justice BURGER delivered the opinion of the Court.

[Independence Tube Corporation ("Independence") initiated a private, treble damage antitrust civil action under Section 1 of the Sherman Act against Copperweld Corporation ("Copperweld"), its wholly-owned subsidiary, the Regal Tube Corporation ("Regal"), and the Yoder Company ("Yoder"). Regal, a manufacturer of steel tubing, had been acquired by Copperweld from Lear Siegler, where it had been an unincorporated division. It was thereafter separately incorporated as a wholly-owned subsidiary of Copperweld. Independence alleged that Copperweld and Regal had induced Yoder, a mill supplier, to breach a contract it had with Independence to supply a tubing mill, thus delaying Independence's entry into the steel tubing business by nine months. Copperweld also was accused of taking steps to dissuade banks and real estate firms from doing business with Independence.

The jury returned a verdict for Independence, but found that only Copperweld and Regal had conspired—Yoder had not. As a consequence, Independence's Section 1 claim rested solely on the proposition that a parent and wholly-owned subsidiary could provide the "plurality of actors" necessary to satisfy Section 1's concerted action requirement. The Court of Appeals for the Seventh Circuit affirmed. Eds.]

* * *

II

Review of this case calls directly into question whether the coordinated acts of a parent and its wholly owned subsidiary can, in the legal sense contemplated by § 1 of the Sherman Act, constitute a combination or conspiracy. The so-called "intra-enterprise conspiracy" doctrine provides that § 1 liability is not foreclosed merely because a parent and its subsidiary are subject to common ownership. The doctrine derives from declarations in several of this Court's opinions.

* * *

III

Petitioners, joined by the United States as amicus curiae, urge us to repudiate the intra-enterprise conspiracy doctrine. The central criticism is that the doctrine gives undue significance to the fact that a subsidiary is separately incorporated and thereby treats as the concerted activity of two entities what is really unilateral behavior flowing from decisions of a single enterprise.

We limit our inquiry to the narrow issue squarely presented: whether a parent and its wholly owned subsidiary are capable of conspiring in violation of § 1 of the Sherman Act. We do not consider under what circumstances, if any, a parent may be liable for conspiring with an affiliated corporation it does not completely own.

A

The Sherman Act contains a "basic distinction between concerted and independent action." Monsanto Co. v. Spray–Rite Service Corp., 465 U.S. 752, 761, 104 S.Ct. 1464, 1469 (1984). The conduct of a single firm is governed by § 2 alone and is unlawful only when it threatens actual monopolization. It is not enough that a single firm appears to "restrain trade" unreasonably, for even a vigorous competitor may leave that impression. For instance, an efficient firm may capture unsatisfied customers from an inefficient rival, whose own ability to compete may suffer as a result. This is the rule of the marketplace and is precisely the sort of competition that promotes the consumer interests that the Sherman Act aims to foster. In part because it is sometimes difficult to distinguish robust competition from conduct with long-run anti-competitive effects, Congress authorized Sherman Act scrutiny of single firms only when they pose a danger of monopolization. Judging unilateral conduct in this manner reduces the risk that the antitrust laws will dampen the competitive zeal of a single aggressive entrepreneur.

Section 1 of the Sherman Act, in contrast, reaches unreasonable restraints of trade effected by a "contract, combination ... or conspiracy" between separate entities. It does not reach conduct that is "wholly unilateral." Concerted activity subject to § 1 is judged more sternly than unilateral activity under § 2. Certain agreements, such as horizontal price fixing and market allocation, are thought so inherently anticompetitive that each is illegal per se without inquiry into the harm it has actually caused. Other combinations, such as mergers, joint ventures, and various vertical agreements, hold the promise of increasing a firm's efficiency and enabling it to compete more effectively. Accordingly, such combinations are judged under a rule of reason, an inquiry into market power and market structure designed to assess the combination's actual effect. Whatever form the inquiry takes, however, it is not necessary to prove that concerted activity threatens monopolization.

The reason Congress treated concerted behavior more strictly than unilateral behavior is readily appreciated. Concerted activity inherently is fraught with anticompetitive risk. It deprives the marketplace of the independent centers of decisionmaking that competition assumes and demands. In any conspiracy, two or more entities that previously pursued their own interests separately are combining to act as one for their common benefit. This not only reduces the diverse directions in which economic power is aimed but suddenly increases the economic power moving in one particular direction. Of course, such mergings of resources may well lead to efficiencies that benefit consumers, but their anticompetitive potential is sufficient to warrant scrutiny even in the absence of incipient monopoly.

B

The distinction between unilateral and concerted conduct is necessary for a proper understanding of the terms "contract, combination . . . or conspiracy" in § 1. Nothing in the literal meaning of those terms excludes coordinated conduct among officers or employees of the same company. But it is perfectly plain that an internal "agreement" to implement a single, unitary firm's policies does not raise the antitrust dangers that § 1 was designed to police. The officers of a single firm are not separate economic actors pursuing separate economic interests, so agreements among them do not suddenly bring together economic power that was previously pursuing divergent goals. Coordination within a firm is as likely to result from an effort to compete as from an effort to stifle competition. In the marketplace, such coordination may be necessary if a business enterprise is to compete effectively. For these reasons, officers or employees of the same firm do not provide the plurality of actors imperative for a § 1 conspiracy.

[Here the Court observed that the operations of a corporate enterprise organized into unincorporated divisions similarly would not provide the plurality of economic actors contemplated by Section 1 and that parent corporations and their wholly-owned subsidiaries should not be treated any differently. Parent corporations always share a common purpose with their divisions and wholly-owned subsidiaries, and the firm should be left free to select the organizational structure that best advances that purpose, unencumbered by formalistic distinctions lacking competitive significance. Eds.]

* * *

D

Any reading of the Sherman Act that remains true to the Act's distinction between unilateral and concerted conduct will necessarily disappoint those who find that distinction arbitrary. It cannot be denied that § 1's focus on concerted behavior leaves a "gap" in the Act's proscription against unreasonable restraints of trade. An unreasonable restraint of trade may be effected not only by two independent firms acting in concert; a single firm may restrain trade to precisely the same extent if it alone possesses the combined market power of those same two firms. Because the Sherman Act does not prohibit unreasonable restraints of trade as such–but only restraints effected by a contract, combination, or conspiracy–it leaves untouched a single firm's anticompetitive conduct (short of threatened monopolization) that may be indistinguishable in economic effect from the conduct of two firms subject to § 1 liability.

We have already noted that Congress left this "gap" for eminently sound reasons. Subjecting a single firm's every action to judicial scrutiny for reasonableness would threaten to discourage the competitive enthusiasm that the antitrust laws seek to promote. Moreover, whatever the wisdom of the distinction, the Act's plain language leaves no doubt that Congress made a purposeful choice to accord different treatment to unilateral and concerted conduct. Had Congress intended to outlaw unreasonable restraints of trade as such, § 1's requirement of a contract, combination, or conspiracy would be superfluous, as would the entirety of § 2. Indeed, this Court has [long] recognized that § 1 is limited to concerted conduct * * *

Although we recognize that any "gap" the Sherman Act leaves is the sensible result of a purposeful policy decision by Congress, we also note that the size of any such gap is open to serious question. Any anticompetitive activities of corporations and their wholly owned subsidiaries meriting antitrust remedies may be policed adequately without resort to an intra-enterprise conspiracy doctrine. A corporation's initial acquisition of control will always be subject to scrutiny under § 1 of the Sherman Act and § 7 of the Clayton Act, 38 Stat. 731, 15 U.S.C. § 18. Thereafter, the enterprise is fully subject to § 2 of the Sherman Act and § 5 of the Federal Trade Commission Act, 38 Stat. 719, 15 U.S.C § 45. That these statutes are adequate to control dangerous anticompetitive conduct is suggested by the fact that not a single holding of antitrust liability by this Court would today be different in the absence of an intra-enterprise conspiracy doctrine. It is further suggested by the fact that the Federal Government, in its administration of the antitrust laws, no longer accepts the concept that a corporation and its wholly owned subsidiaries can "combine" or "conspire" under § 1. [The Solicitor General filed an amicus brief in the case urging the Court to abandon the intra-enterprise conspiracy doctrine. Eds.] Elimination of the intra-enterprise conspiracy doctrine with respect to corporations and their wholly owned subsidiaries will therefore not cripple antitrust enforcement. It will simply eliminate treble damages from private state tort suits masquerading as antitrust actions.

IV

We hold that Copperweld and its wholly owned subsidiary Regal are incapable of conspiring with each other for purposes of § 1 of the Sherman Act. To the extent that prior decisions of this Court are to the contrary, they are disapproved and overruled. Accordingly, the judgment of the Court of Appeals is reversed.

Justice WHITE took no part in the consideration or decision of this case.

Justice STEVENS, BRENNAN, and MARSHALL dissented (opinion omitted).

Copperweld's narrow holding was that a parent and its wholly-owned subsidiary could not provide the plurality of economic actors necessary to satisfy the concerted action requirement of Section 1. In later decisions, the courts of appeals expanded *Copperweld's* principles to encompass the acts of parents and their less than wholly-owned subsidiaries, to sister corporations controlled by the same parent, and to other forms of intra-enterprise conduct. Does *Copperweld's* rationale apply equally in all of those circumstances? Is it never true that the actions of sister corporations, for example, might involve the joining together of "separate economic actors"? Did Regal bring anything to the relationship with Copperweld that it lacked before? Was the "whole" greater than the sum of its parts? If so, how might that affect application of the *Copperweld* analysis?

Copperweld is also significant for its description of the relationship between Sections 1 and 2 of the Sherman Act. The Court emphasizes that only Section 2 covers unilateral firm conduct and that the standards for condemning unilateral conduct should be more lenient (*i.e.*, require proof of more than an "unreasonable restraint of trade") than the standards for condemning concerted conduct. In doing so, the case sheds some light on the underlying rationale for the concerted conduct requirement of Section 1–a common feature of many competition law statutes throughout the world– which singles out concerted action, especially among rivals, for greater scrutiny. That rationale is further explored in the following Note.

Note on the Rationale for Scrutinizing Concerted Action

Fear of the anticompetitive effects of "collusion,"especially by competing firms, has long preoccupied economists and competition laws. One of the earliest reported accounts of competition-type law enforcement, Lysias's "Against the Grain Dealers," concerned the prosecution of a grain buying cartel in ancient Greece, which sought to depress the prices paid to grain importers, and raise the prices charged to Atticans for their grain. *See* Lambros E. Kotsiros, *An Antitrust Case in Ancient Greek Law*, 22 INT'L LAW. 451 (1988). And students of economics are well acquainted with Adam Smith's classic admonition that "People of the same trade seldom meet together, even for merriment and diversion, but the conversation ends in a conspiracy against the public, or in some contrivance to raise prices." ADAM SMITH, THE WEALTH OF NATIONS 144 (E. CANNON, ED. 1976) (1776). The broader dilemma, of course, is both conceptual and linguistic. We recognize that "cooperation" is essential to economic progress, but seek to distinguish the positive, "cooperation," from the nefarious, "conspiracy." Both involve "concerted action," but only one potentially warrants condemnation.

It is also well settled that Section 1 of the Sherman Act prohibits the act of conspiring, alone, and the offense is complete even though no party to the conspiracy ever undertakes "an overt act *in furtherance* of the conspiracy." The only essential "overt act" is the act of conspiring, itself. Moreover, venue can be proper in an antitrust conspiracy case in any district in which an overt act in furtherance of a conspiracy has occurred, even though no overt act is required to establish the offense. In a non-antitrust case, the Supreme Court recently reiterated these two long established propositions relevant to conspiracy under the Sherman Act and other federal conspiracy statutes that are modeled on the Sherman Act. *See Whitfield v. U.S.*, 543 U.S. 209 (2005). *See also United States v. Socony–Vacuum Oil Co.*, 310 U.S. 150, 224 n.59 (1940).

The Sherman Act sets forth a particular, compound formula in an attempt to distinguish cooperation from conspiracy, condemning any "contract, combination in the form of trust or otherwise, or conspiracy." *See* James A. Rahl, *Conspiracy and the Anti-trust Laws*, 44 ILL. L. REV. 743 (1950). Why did the drafters choose such a seemingly redundant formulation? Some scholars have suggested that it was designed to capture the full range of arrangements, and progresses from the "tightest" to the loosest of "agreements." It can also be viewed as a continuum, leading from the most "formal" to the most "informal" of arrangements, or from the "express" to the tacit or illicit. *See, e.g.*, Robert H. Bork, *Legislative Intent And The Policy Of The Sherman Act*, 9 J. L. & ECON. 7, 21–22 (1966). As we noted in the introduction to this Chapter, however, formal and express agreements rarely pose any serious questions of proof. Much of this Chapter, therefore, is instead concerned with the standards for proving "conspiracy," the illicit. In any event, the courts increasingly have come to view the Sherman Act's terms as coextensive, rarely attributing any significance to its precise words.

More broadly, what accounts for this suspicion of what *Copperweld* labeled "concerted action"? *Copperweld*'s explanation for Section 1's treatment of concerted action is based upon the view that when separate economic actors combine, the threat to competition is often greater than when single firms act. Hence, we invoke a higher level of scrutiny, *i.e.*, a lower burden of proof, for concerted action.

This rationale recognizes a link between the finding of concerted action and the substantive test for determining liability (and, perhaps, the remedy imposed for violations). It has major implications for how courts define the agreement requirement under a statute—such as Section 1—which demands a plurality of actors. In deciding whether the requisite agreement exists, a court might take account of how readily a finding of plurality will lead to a finding of liability and the imposition of sanctions. If a court doubted the wisdom of the substantive standard or feared that sanctions for violations of a well-conceived standard were excessive, the tribunal consciously or unconsciously might strengthen the tests that plaintiffs must satisfy to prove an agreement.

Consider the interplay of the agreement requirement and the substantive rules of liability in the horizontal restraints cases you read in Chapter 2 and in the vertical restraints cases you will study in Chapter 4. Do the courts perceive different or similar competitive dangers from concerted action in horizontal and vertical cases? Do they account for differences by adjusting the agreement requirement, the substantive liability standard, or both?

We want to raise one other question regarding *Copperweld*'s observation about the relative hazards of unilateral and concerted action. As you reflect upon the cases in Chapters 2 and 4 (concerted action) and Chapter 6 (unilateral action), consider whether and when courts today scrutinize concerted action more thoroughly than, or to the same degree as, all forms of unilateral action. Do you agree with *Copperweld*'s assumption that concerted action poses a greater competitive threat than unilateral action?

We will return to and test *Copperweld's* proposition that unilateral and concerted action are treated differently in terms of proof of anticompetitive effects in Chapter 8. The remainder of this Chapter focuses on the rationale for singling out, and the standards for proving, "concerted action."

B. THE MODERN ECONOMICS OF COLLUSION

Much antitrust law is concerned with the possibility that firms may choose not to compete aggressively, but may instead collude, acting collectively more as though they were a monopolist. Yet collusion may not be easy to accomplish, whether it involves an express exchange of assurances or tacit understandings. Economists have explained that successful coordination in an oligopoly requires that the firms solve three "cartel problems:"

- reaching consensus;
- deterring deviation (*i.e.*, "cheating") through detection of cheating and a credible threat of punishment for cheating; and
- preventing new competition.

These three economic problems incident to the formation and successful operation of a cartel must be solved regardless of whether the collusive conduct is express or tacit. For this reason, the legal differences between express and tacit collusion are generally unimportant economically, and economists today frequently employ the terms "coordination" or "collusion" to encompass both possibilities, without distinction. Indeed, throughout this casebook, the terms "collusion" (whether tacit or express), "cartel" and "coordination" are used interchangeably, although these concepts are technically distinct. For a discussion of the differences among them, see Jonathan B. Baker, *Two Sherman Act Section 1 Dilemmas: Parallel Pricing, the Oligopoly Problem, and Contemporary Economic Theory*, 38 ANTITRUST BULL. 143 (1993).

In this Section, we explore the economic problems of collusion from three perspectives. We begin with three case studies that illustrate the economic obstacles that firms must surmount to collude. We then consider the situation in which firms coordinate their conduct imperfectly.

The case studies in this section will examine ways that coordinating firms might act to overcome the three cartel problems. As will be seen, coordinating firms can solve their first problem, of reaching consensus, by identifying terms of coordination, such as the prices each firm will charge (or the rule the firms will apply to select prices), the reduction in output each firm will undertake, or the way the firms will allocate customers or territories. Coordinating firms can solve their second problem, of deterring deviation, if they have or can create a method of detecting firms that cheat on the consensus, and a means of punishing cheaters. Cheating is more likely to be deterred as its detection becomes more swift and certain and the punishment to cheaters becomes more severe. This assumes that the punishment threat is credible in the eyes of the potential cheater: not so costly to the punishing firms as to make the cheating firms reasonably question whether the punishing firms would be willing to carry it out. If the punishment threat is not credible, cheating will not be deterred. The third problem, preventing new competition, is solved by making entry difficult. It is not necessary for the coordinating firms to take steps to do so, however, if entry barriers are already high. Moreover, coordination may succeed even if some new competition occurs, so long as the addition to industry output is not so great as to make coordination unprofitable.

1. THE PROBLEMS OF COLLUSION AND THEIR SOLUTIONS: THREE CASE STUDIES*

We present three case studies to illuminate the problems inhibiting collusion and to suggest how colluding firms may act to overcome them. The first case study looks at the history of the international oil cartel, the Organization of Petroleum Exporting Countries (OPEC). OPEC is an express cartel: its members regularly meet face to face and reach agreements to alter their collective output and set price. The second case study is a hypothetical and involves tacit collusion among nearby gas stations. The third, also a hypothetical, concerns the conduct of a group of rival delicatessens. The insights developed through these case studies form the basis for identifying features of market structure that facilitate or frustrate collusion.

* An additional, numerical example is posted on the Casebook's Author's Forum on The West Education Network ("TWEN"). The numerical example provides a deeper examination of the economic issues at stake in coordination, and highlights the significance of repeated interaction for facilitating coordination.

CASE STUDY I:
THE RISE AND FALL OF OPEC

To understand the economic problems that colluding firms must solve, it is useful to consider a famous modern cartel. The Organization of Petroleum Exporting Countries (OPEC) was formed in the early 1960s by many of the major oil producing nations. OPEC is an express cartel: it sets prices and assigns production levels to its members at face-to-face meetings. Shortly after OPEC's formation, the price of oil rose dramatically. The resulting transfer of resources to oil producers from oil buyers made many oil producing nations, particularly the Persian Gulf States, wealthy and caused some of the economic malaise experienced by the United States and other industrial nations during the mid-and late–1970s.

OPEC members faced three types of problems in seeking to create and sustain their cartel; these are the problems facing every cartel, whether express (as with OPEC) or tacit. First, they had to *reach consensus*. The cartel members agreed that industry output should be reduced in order to raise the industry price, but each would have preferred that the others do the bulk of the cutting back. As a result, negotiations among OPEC members over production quotas are sometimes difficult. Second, OPEC members had to *deter cheating*. At times, some member nations would produce more than their assigned quota, resulting in less than the expected reduction in industry output (and less than the expected increase in the industry price). Similarly, over time countries may expand drilling in their existing oil fields and raise their production capacity and production rate. Actions like these might be profitable for the nation that increased output, but they tended to undermine the cartel as a whole. Third, OPEC members had to *prevent new competition*, whether from oil-producing nations that chose not to join OPEC (such as the United States) or from entrants discovering and developing new oil fields throughout the world.

The cartel overcame these difficulties in the 1970s and was extremely successful for nearly a decade. As time went by, the cartel continued to meet, but with decreasing effectiveness. By the mid–1980s, OPEC no longer appeared able to solve its cartel problems, and oil prices fell to levels comparable to what prevailed before the OPEC cartel began (adjusted for the cost of living), and oil prices stayed low during the 1990s. Crude oil prices began to rise again in 2001, however. In Chapter 9 we will revisit OPEC and evaluate whether its conduct could be effectively challenged under the Sherman Act. (*See* Sidebar 9–1).

CASE STUDY II:
TACIT COORDINATION—A GASOLINE
STATION HYPOTHETICAL

The OPEC example emphasizes the difficulties that an express cartel, with all the advantages of direct communication, faces in overcoming its cartel problems. A hypothetical example involving gas stations highlights a point that goes the opposite way: even firms colluding tacitly, without reaching an express agreement, can overcome those problems and successfully reach a coordinated outcome.*

Suppose four gasoline stations are located at four corners of a busy intersection, with no other stations for miles. Assume that the zoning laws do not permit any other gas stations to enter nearby. The latter assumption puts aside the cartel problem of deterring new competition to focus on reaching consensus and deterring cheating.

Each gasoline station pays $1.00 per gallon for gas, and the typical industry markup between the wholesale price and retail pricing is 5¢ per gallon. Each of the four stations thus charges $1.05 per gallon when they are competing aggressively. Each posts that price on a large sign where it can be seen by motorists coming from all directions, as well as viewed by its competitors.

One day, one station raises its posted price to $1.10 per gallon, although neither its costs nor those of its rivals have increased. The other three stations see the new price and match it. If the new price sticks, the four rivals will have found a price in excess of the competitive level; they will be exercising market power.

Will any of the gas stations find it in its interest to cheat on the new, higher price? Quite possibly not. Consider the alternatives each firm faces. On the one hand, it can stick with the $1.10 price, and earn an extra 5¢ per gallon on all the gasoline it sells, well into the future. This could be very profitable. On the other hand, it could cheat, perhaps by deciding to sell gasoline at $1.09 per gallon. Will price-cutting be more profitable to the firm than cooperating? In order to get more business by lowering price, the firm will need to post its lower price on its sign. Then drivers will see that it sells gasoline for less, and will fill up at its pumps, rather than those of its rivals. Its sales will go up.

But the profitability of price-cutting depends on how its rivals respond. They will see the lower price of $1.09 per gallon too, and can be expected to cut their own price to match before very many drivers learn about the discounting station and switch to the cheater. Because price-cutting will be rapidly detected and responded to by its rivals, the price-cutting firm will get very little additional business by lowering price. Against this small benefit, it will give up 1¢ per gallon on all its future gasoline sales. Based on this comparison, cheating appears less profitable than cooperation. Accordingly, each firm will most likely stick with the $1.10 price, and not undercut it. Thus, the cartel problem of deterring cheating may not be a problem for these firms: with rapid detection of cheating by rivals, and rapid response by rivals, the gains from cheating may be so limited as to make continued cooperation more attractive than cheating for all firms.

The incentive to cheat on a coordinated outcome is the economic force that generates competition. If the goal is to get the nations of the world to cooperate on arms control, cheating is a bad thing. But if the goal is to ensure low prices and high output, cheating is good. Some readers may recognize this incentive as arising in the "game theory" model of a prisoner's dilemma (*See infra*, Sidebar 3–1).

---

* The antitrust implications of a similar example are considered in Dennis W. Carlton, Robert H. Gertner & Andrew M. Rosenfield, *Communication Among Competitors: Game Theory and Antitrust*, 5 GEO. MASON L. REV. 423 (1997).

The cartel problem of deterring cheating is not insoluble, even though the firms cannot write an enforceable contract to cut output and raise price. Cheating can be made unprofitable if a firm's rivals find out quickly, and respond rapidly to impose costs on the cheating firm (commonly referred to in the economics literature as "punishment"). The more rapid detection and punishment of cheating, and the more severe the likely punishment, the greater the likelihood that a firm will decide not to cheat in the first place.

Repeated interaction among firms can make cheating less likely. If firms interact only a short, finite time and have no future interactions to worry about, cheating is likely more profitable for each than cooperation. But repeated interaction can make continued cooperation more profitable than cheating by increasing the likely punishment that the cheater's rivals can impose.** Simply by declining to cooperate in the future, they can deny the cheater the profits it would otherwise have obtained from a long period of coordination.

Even with repeated interaction among the firms, coordination will not always be more profitable than cheating. In particular, with less rapid and less severe punishment—a less steep price reduction or a punishment response that does not last forever—cheating might not be deterred and the cartel might not survive (or might never form in the first place). The greater the opportunity for secret cheating—cheating that would likely last a long time before detection by rivals—the more likely a cartel will be unstable and not form in the first place. For similar reasons, if cheating would occur on a large scale before its rivals would respond—if the cheater takes most of the market, for example, by making a long-term deal with a few large customers— the more likely cheating will be profitable, notwithstanding the repeated interaction among sellers.

What about the remaining cartel problem of reaching consensus? After all, firms invariably have divergent interests as well as a common interest in obtaining a higher price. While each wants price to rise, each also wants to increase its market share at the higher price. Moreover, the firms may differ in ways that affect their views about these matters. One may have a much larger number of self-service pumps than the rest and, uniquely, a convenience store. This station might prefer higher automobile traffic than its rivals, and thus prefer a lower cartel price (and higher industry sales) than they would.

Notwithstanding the possibility of divergent views, price leadership may suffice to solve the cartel problem of reaching consensus. The firms could settle on a number of cartel prices in excess of $1.05 per gallon. By selecting $1.10, the firm that raised price first establishes that price as one for its rivals to match. Each rival knows that if all the firms go along with $1.10, that price is likely to stick—they can go through the same analysis of incentives to cheat that we have undertaken. Nor do any of the firms take much financial risk in raising price before knowing whether the others will go along. The first firm to raise its prices will lose business while its rivals consider whether to raise

---

** According to what economists refer to as the "folk theorem" for oligopoly interaction with repeated play, repeated interaction creates a more congenial environment for successful coordination than a one time interaction when the firms expect to interact infinitely, or, more to the point, when they expect to interact for a finite time with an uncertain ending point.

price as well, but the rivals are likely to respond quickly. If some rivals do not match the price increase, the firm which first boosted prices knows that it can back down before much time has gone by. So once the first firm raises price to $1.10 per gallon, the other firms are likely to follow.

As this example suggests, reaching a consensus on the collective output reduction, the collusive price, and the allocation of production and profits among the firms may be facilitated by communication among the firms. That is why price-fixing conspirators often meet face-to-face. Communication is dangerous, however, because it makes it more likely that the firms will be found to have violated Sherman Act § 1. Absent such conversations, the firms may be able to reach a consensus by making some price or customer allocation "focal" (natural and obvious), in ways that do not necessarily violate the antitrust laws–such as the use of posted gasoline prices by the gas stations in this example. In other cases, customer allocations may plausibly be focal. Firms may see some customers as naturally theirs and other customers as belonging to their rivals. If so they may reach a market allocation along the lines "I won't solicit your historical customers if you don't solicit mine" or "I won't do business on your side of town if you don't do business on mine."

If raising price is so easy, and cheating so unlikely, why would the firms ever stop? Why wouldn't price rise to $100 per gallon? Because the industry demand curve is not perfectly inelastic. At a high enough price for gasoline, enough people will cut back on their driving, or drive to neighboring cities to buy gas, as to make continued price increases unprofitable. Indeed, even a monopolist will stop raising its prices eventually.

CASE STUDY III:
FACTORS FACILITATING OR FRUSTRATING COORDINATION—
A DELICATESSEN HYPOTHETICAL

How do firms solve their cartel problems? And what factors affect their ability to do so?

We focus here on the first two cartel problems, reaching consensus and deterring cheating; ease of entry is analyzed in later chapters. Recall that we first visited some of these issues in Chapter 1 in connection with our reading of *Andreas*, and the hypothetical neighborhood coffee shop conspiracy.

To frame the discussion, consider the following hypothetical example. A number of office buildings are clustered in one downtown neighborhood in a large city. These buildings house, among other things, several large law firms, various business offices, and a law school. The neighborhood has a number of restaurants that are popular lunch time spots, as well as several delicatessens. Take-out food is available only from the delis. We assume that deli takeout is a relevant product market, and the neighborhood is a relevant geographic market. Were it otherwise, the delicatessens as a group would not find it profitable to raise prices; a deli cartel would fail as buyers responded to higher prices by shifting their purchases elsewhere.

What economic factors would affect the ability of the delicatessens to collude, whether tacitly or expressly? A list of factors facilitating or frustrating collusion is a staple of textbooks in industrial organization economics, and we discuss some possibilities below. A similar list appears in the U.S. Horizontal Merger Guidelines (§§ 2.11, 2.12), which we will study in Chapter 5. The factors sketched below are not comprehensive. Some of these factors make collusion more likely, others make collusion less likely, and still others could go either way. We caution that we are not presenting a checklist. The issue in determining whether collusion is likely is not how many factors are present and how many are not; it is whether the firms can reasonably expect to reach a consensus and deter deviation. For this reason, it is important to understand why each factor might be relevant to evaluating whether the firms participating in a market could reasonably be expected to solve their cartel problems, and we will highlight the explanation in our discussion below.

Number of Firms

It is commonly thought that the greater the number of firms, the more difficult it will be for them to collude successfully.* As the number of firms grows, reaching consensus and deterring deviation both may become more difficult. If there are only two or three delis in the neighborhood, their ability to work out a mutually acceptable arrangement (reach a consensus) will likely be easier than if there are a dozen delis, much as it is generally easier for a few friends to coordinate their calendars and arrange to meet for dinner at a restaurant than it is for a large group to do so. Moreover, the larger the number of firms seeking to coordinate their pricing or other actions, the more likely one will prefer cheating rather than cooperating. It may also be more likely that a cheater will be able to do so for a while, secretly—without its rivals noticing and responding. This possibility will increase each firm's temptation to cheat or compete rather than collude.

The empirical relationship between the number of firms and the likelihood that they will overcome their cartel problems and successfully coordinate is widely accepted, but it is hardly the only relevant factor. Tacit or express collusion has occurred even in markets with a large number of firms, and collusion may be unsuccessful even with as few as two firms in a market. Moreover, there is no fixed "critical" number of firms below which coordinated conduct becomes more likely or more effective. These caveats are discussed in more detail in Chapter 5 with respect to horizontal mergers, as this is the context in which the significance of the number of firms for the likelihood of collusion has undergone the most analysis and elaboration. (*See* Sidebar 5–6.)

Product Heterogeneity and Complex, Changing Products

It is plausible that the delicatessens have different menus, and each firm's menu includes a large number of products. The delis may have different locations, some may be a longer walk for most of the workers and students looking for lunch, they may differ in perceived quality, and they may vary on features such as image, ambience, and helpfulness of staff. The resulting product heterogeneity may create problems for both reaching consensus and deterring cheating from it. The sheer complexity of negotiating a price for every menu item may be hard for the firms to overcome. In addition, product heterogeneity may create opportunities for cheating that is hard for

---

* Relatedly, the conditions of entry matter to whether collusion can succeed. If new competitors can easily appear, and have entered in a way that would lead them to expand output, prices may fall back to the competitive level unless the new rivals are brought into the collusive arrangement. Accordingly, the relevant number of firms may include potential entrants as well as incumbents. Entry conditions and the role of new competition are discussed in more detail in Chapter 5 with respect to mergers and, more generally, in Chapter 8.

rivals to detect quickly. For example, a deli could effectively cut price for a sandwich while leaving the list price on its menu unchanged by giving away drinks and cookies for free. These problems of reaching consensus and deterring cheating are likely exacerbated if products are changing. A deli that frequently refreshes its menu by altering the special sandwiches on it can come up with variants that are outside the price consensus and take business away from rivals. Thus, a successful delicatessen cartel may need to develop a mechanism to incorporate new products into its coordinated arrangement. This may be difficult, especially if the agreement is only tacit.

While product heterogeneity is commonly thought to frustrate collusion, and similarity among firms and homogeneous products are often thought to facilitate coordination, these are at best general tendencies. Even similar firms selling identical products may have divergent interests, and they may not be able to reach a consensus or successfully deter cheating. Indeed, more similar firms may at times have a greater temptation to cheat than firms that are differentiated, because the former may have a greater ability to attract business from their rivals through price cuts.

Moreover, coordination can succeed notwithstanding the complexity and range of products offered by sellers. The firms may facilitate collusion by developing ways of *exchanging information* to help reach a consensus and deter cheating by avoiding secret transactions, making detection of cheating easier. (*See* Sidebar 3–6, which discusses most favored customer provisions, one practice firms could adopt to facilitate information exchange.) Alternatively, the firms could *follow simple, obvious rules* (also termed "focal" rules) to simplify their coordination task. For example, the delis could allocate the office buildings among themselves, so that each deli would market the delivery of catered lunches exclusively to specified buildings. Or they could grandfather in the variation in prices and products on their current menus, and merely agree to raise all prices by 5% across the board, without altering product definitions. The resulting coordinated outcome may fall short of what a delicatessen monopolist would choose to do, but it may nevertheless involve prices substantially in excess of what would be expected from a competitive industry.

Excess Capacity

A Firm's Own Excess Capacity. Some of the delicatessens may be very busy at lunch time, have lines out the door, and find themselves unable to serve many more customers within the confines of their retail space, even if they were to add workers. These delicatessens are operating at nearly full capacity. In contrast, other delicatessens might readily be able to serve more customers; they may have a great deal of excess capacity. Cheating on a cartel may be more tempting for a firm with substantial excess capacity than for a firm with limited or no excess capacity. The gains from cheating typically come from diverting a great deal of business away from rivals; a firm that cannot serve many more customers than it handles already may not find price-cutting a tempting strategy.

Moreover, any other feature of the industry that allows a firm to expand output rapidly operates much like a firm's own excess capacity in terms of its influence on the likelihood of successful coordination. Thus, under some circumstances, *vertical integration* or the sale of *complementary products* may encourage cartel cheating. For example, if one of the delicatessens (and only one) was affiliated with a chain of coffee shops, it might have a unique ability to expand, and thus cheat on a cartel, by preparing sandwiches in the morning and stocking a refrigerator at the coffee shops with food for sale during lunch.

Excess Capacity in the Hands of Multiple Firms. While a firm's own excess capacity may encourage it to cheat, excess capacity in the hands of rival firms may discourage it from cheating. At some point, those rivals will discover that the price-cutter has been cheating. When they do, their excess capacity gives them the ability to punish that price-cutting severely: they can cut price deeply themselves, without fear that they will find themselves unable to serve the higher demand that will predictably flow from a lower price. Because excess capacity in the hands of rivals represents a threat to punish cheating severely, the firm may be discouraged from cheating in the first place.** Recall from *Andreas* in Chapter 1, that ADM was accused of just so using the threat of its excess capacity to discourage other lysine cartel members from cheating.

Moreover, any feature of the industry that leads cheating firms to expect that a severe price war will result from the breakdown of a cartel operates much like excess capacity in the hands of rivals in terms of its influence on the likelihood of successful coordination. Thus, under some circumstances, *inelastic market demand* or *low marginal costs* relative to market prices may discourage cheating on a cartel.

Public vs. Private Transactions

The delicatessens post the prices for the items on their take out menu and advertise those prices in flyers distributed to the nearby offices and law school. Transactions are public and open, in the sense that the delis could not change the prices they charge their walk-in customers without their rivals finding out. However, transactions are not completely open. The number of customers served remains private information, unavailable to rivals. Nevertheless, if one deli decides to cheat on a cartel by cutting price, its rivals will detect that cheating rapidly, perhaps within the day, and can respond by lowering their own prices rapidly, as soon as they can print new flyers and change prices on their posted in-store displays. Open transactions may thus facilitate collusion by discouraging cheating.

The delicatessens in the neighborhood sell to the walk-in crowd at lunch, and to this point we have emphasized that aspect of their business in our analysis. But now suppose that much of their business takes a second form, catering lunch time meetings at law firms and other neighborhood businesses. The delis may give the law firms their take out menus, but they may also give the law firms discounts. A deli may tell an office manager: "If you let us cater all your meetings, we will give you a 10% discount off our regular prices." These discounts are private. A savvy office manager may tell a second deli: "Your rival is offering us a 10% discount; you'll need to give us 15% off to get

---

** This discussion presumes that the rivals would find it profitable to follow through to punish the cheating firm severely were they to observe cheating. If a severe punishment is not a credible threat, the threat of a less severe punishment that is credible may still be sufficient to foster incomplete coordination, as discussed below in Section B2 of this chapter.

us to switch," but the rival need not believe the office manager, as her information may be inaccurate or strategically exaggerated.

If the delis have historically offered businesses 10% off, and one of the delis decides to raise its discount to 15% in order to cheat, it may take a while for its rivals to catch on. They may notice they are losing some business, and hear more law firm administrators than usual tell them that they must offer a larger discount to win their business, but they may not rapidly figure out that all the lost business is going to one particular price-cutting rival. Thus, when transactions are private, cheating is more likely to succeed for a while, firms are more likely to cheat on a cartel, and, recognizing this, cartels are less likely to form in the first place. Private or confidential transactions are thus a factor tending to frustrate collusion.***

Predictable vs. Unpredictable Demand

As the last example suggests, the delicatessens may learn about the possibility of rival cheating from what happens to their own business. If they are losing more customers than usual, they may suspect that cheating is the reason, and investigate further. That inference is facilitated by stable demand, or more generally by predictable demand. Thus, if deli demand always falls in the summer, when law school classes are out and many office workers take vacation, colluding delicatessens are unlikely to interpret a July falloff in sales as cheating by a rival unless they seem to be losing more sales than past experience would suggest.

But catering demand may instead be characterized by "background noise"—*i.e.*, in the past demand may often have fluctuated for no obvious reason, and been unusually low for a couple of months at a time. This "background noise" means that it may take several months before a cartel member discovers that something is amiss. Its law firm catering business may be down, but the deli may think nothing of it until much time has passed. This possibility means that a cheating firm can expect to get away with its price-cutting undetected for a longer period than if demand were more stable, encouraging cheating and discouraging cartel formation.

"Lumpy" Sales and Large Buyers

Suppose now that the bulk of each delicatessen's business is law firm and business lunch catering rather than walk-in lunch time sales. Suppose further that two large law firms together account for three-quarters of the catering business in the neighborhood, and that law firm catering is negotiated annually, resulting in a year-long contract. A successful delicatessen cartel will presumably need to fix the price of catering services, perhaps in the form of an agreement not to discount more than 10% off of the "list" price on the menu.

In this market, buyers are large and sales are "lumpy" in the sense that the business comes up for renewal only annually. Transactions are thus

---

*** The relevant dimension on which privacy of transactions tends to frustrate collusion depends on the nature of the collusive agreement. If the delis had colluded by dividing markets (allocating customers) rather than by agreeing on price—for example, through an agreement that each deli was responsible for catering in specific office buildings, and would not deliver outside its assigned territory—then the degree of transparency of pricing for catering services would not affect incentives to cheat. All that would matter would be whether a deli could secretly deliver lunch to customers in office buildings assigned to its rivals.

aggregated due to the nature of contracting practices and the demands of larger buyers. As a consequence, a cheating firm, by making only two deals, one with each large law firm, can attract a full year's worth of business accounting for three-quarters of the largest market segment. Even if its rivals detect what has happened, they cannot rapidly punish the cheating firm by cutting price and stealing the business back, as most of the market is tied up for a year. A firm considering cheating in such an industry will realize that it can take a large chunk of business easily, and do so free from the threat of rapid punishment. This opportunity will encourage firms to cheat, and its threat will discourage cartel formation in the first instance. So industries in which rival firms vie for a few, large, and long-term contracts may be less prone to collusion.

Conversely, if the great majority of deli sales are individual sandwiches sold to walk-in customers, each deli will realize that it cannot obtain very much additional business through cheating before that act is detected by its rivals and they respond. When sales are small and frequent, cheating may thus be less attractive a strategy, facilitating coordination.

Figure 3–1 summarizes the factors we have just outlined. As previously noted, analysis of the ability of firms successfully to coordinate is not a matter of counting the factors in each column and reaching a conclusion based on which side predominates. Instead, all the factors must be considered as a whole.

Figure 3–1:
Factors Facilitating or Frustrating Coordination

Facilitating	Frustrating
Few firms	Many firms
Product homogeneity	Product heterogeneity
Simple products	Complex, changing products
Excess capacity (multiple firms)	Excess capacity (individual firm)
Inelastic market demand	Vertical integration
Low marginal costs relative to price	Sale of complementary products
Open transactions	Private transactions
Predictable demand	Unpredictable demand
Small transactions	"Lumpy" sales
Small buyers	Large buyers

2. INCOMPLETE COORDINATION

As the above examples suggest, coordination may be partly successful, but nevertheless fall short of replicating the price a monopolist would charge and the output a monopolist would produce for a number of reasons, including the following four.

First, coordinating firms may not be able to punish cheating rivals as strongly as would be necessary to induce every cartel member to charge the full monopoly price. In some industries, for example, the necessary punishment may require that the punishing firms charge prices below their marginal costs, yet this strategy may require that the cartel absorb substantial losses, so it may not be credible. On the other hand, colluding firms may well be willing to engage in punishment that merely returns price to the competitive level—as would happen in any event were the cartel to break down—and this response to cheating may be sufficient to induce all the firms to charge a price substantially in excess of the competitive level without cheating.

Second, coordinating firms may not be able to allocate the monopoly profits they achieve in a manner satisfactory to all the participants, because they may be unable to compensate each other directly. For example, in Case Study II, the gas station hypothetical, if the competitive price is $1.00 per gallon and most firms want a cartel price of $1.30, a firm that instead prefers that the cartel stop raising price at $1.10 would be able to insist on that price. In theory, the other firms could still get price up to $1.30 by paying off the latter seller to accept a price in excess of $1.10; if $1.30 were much more profitable for them than $1.10, they may earn enough extra monopoly profits to make such a payment advantageous. In practice, however, such payments, termed "side payments" by economists, could be difficult to negotiate and impossible to enforce given the risk that a prosecutor and court would infer an unlawful (even criminal) agreement to fix price.

Third, firms sometimes are uncertain about the strategies their rivals are pursuing, and have difficulty inferring cheating from marketplace observations (*i.e.*, against a "noisy" background in which prices frequently fall for other reasons like unexpected declines in demand, as discussed in Case Study III, the delicatessen hypothetical, under the heading "Predictable vs. Unpredictable Demand"). Here the coordinating firms may find it necessary to undertake expensive strategies for deterring cheating. For example, they may reduce the gains to cheating by setting price below the level a monopolist would charge, or they may respond to the mere possibility of cheating by engaging in a price war for some time before returning to higher prices. Indeed, one of the surprising discoveries of the modern economic theory of coordinated behavior is that occasional price wars—on their face, the essence of competition—are not inconsistent with coordination and indeed may be part of the mechanism by which cheating is deterred during high price periods.

Fourth, the firms may have difficulty in identifying the price that a monopolist would set, especially when they must coordinate pricing and output over a large number of products or markets without communicating. As has previously been noted, however, under such circumstances, firms may employ simple rules like a common percentage or dollar price increase applied to a large class of products, rather than fine-tuning price changes product by product to maximize joint profits.

These difficulties do not necessarily make coordination impossible. They may instead lead to occasional price reductions or price wars in response to shock, and to pricing that is maintained above competitive levels but short of monopoly levels. Indeed, perfect coordination—in which the firms act collectively like a monopolist, then split the joint profits—is likely rare, and imperfect coordination—in which the firms earn some monopoly profits but fall short of replicating how a monopolist would behave—is likely the general rule when coordination is at all successful.

3. SOLVING CARTEL PROBLEMS IN PRACTICE

How do firms solve their cartel problems in practice? Recall our case study on the lysine and vitamin cartels, set forth in Chapter 1. What steps did the firms involved in that cartel take to reach consensus, deter cheating, and prevent entry?

A second possible example of cartel problem-solving appears below in the Seventh Circuit's opinion in the *Brand Name Prescription Drugs* case. The excerpt below focuses on the possibility that tacitly colluding drug manufacturers might enlist drug wholesalers to help police a manufacturers' cartel. Note how the appeals court conducts a careful economic analysis of the defendants' conduct and recognizes that real-world coordination may be incomplete. Recall, too, that Judge Posner conducted a similar analysis in *JTC Petroleum*, (Casebook, Chapter 1, *supra*), focusing on both the mechanics and economics of collusion.

IN RE BRAND NAME PRESCRIPTION DRUGS ANTITRUST LITIGATION

United States Court of Appeals for the Seventh Circuit, 1997.
123 F.3d 599.

POSNER, Chief Judge.

We have consolidated for decision four appeals * * * from rulings in a huge price-fixing litigation that the Judicial Panel on Multidistrict Litigation has consolidated * * * for pretrial proceedings. The consolidation covers hundreds of separate cases (a number of them class actions) brought under section 1 of the Sherman Act * * * by retail pharmacies against manufacturers and wholesalers of prescription drugs. The pharmacies complain that the defendants have conspired among themselves to deny all pharmacies, including chains and buying groups, discounts off the list price of brand-name drugs that the manufacturers sell to the wholesalers and that the wholesalers in turn resell to the pharmacies. A brief sketch of the operation of the alleged conspiracy will provide the essential background to understanding the issues presented by these appeals.

While refusing to give pharmacies any discounts, the defendants give steep discounts to favored classes of customers, including hospitals, health maintenance organizations, nursing homes, and mail-order companies. The defendants maintain this differential pricing through a "chargeback" system. Under that system, the manufacturer makes a contract with the favored customer establishing a discounted price at which the customer is entitled to buy from wholesalers; the wholesaler sells to the favored customer at that price; and the manufacturer then reimburses the wholesaler for the difference between the regular wholesale price and the discounted price. So if the manufacturer's regular price to the wholesaler for some drug is $100 and the contractually agreed upon discounted price for a favored customer is $75, the wholesaler will pay the manufacturer $100 for the drug but resell it to the favored customer at $75 and the[n] bill the manufacturer $25. The plaintiffs claim that the purpose of the chargeback system is to make it difficult for the favored customers to engage in arbitrage, that is, to buy more than they need and resell the surplus to pharmacies at a price between the discounted price that the favored customers pay and the higher, undiscounted wholesale price that nonfavored customers pay. The chargeback system permits the wholesalers to buy cheap only when they are reselling to someone whom the manufacturer wants to be given a discount.

* * *

In the extensive pretrial proceedings that have been conducted to date in this litigation, the plaintiffs have presented evidence that the defendant manufacturers agreed among themselves, and also with the defendant wholesalers, to refuse discounts to pharmacies and to make this refusal stick by adopting the chargeback system in order to prevent arbitrage. * * * The plaintiffs' objection is to having to pay high prices that, but for the defendants' alleged conspiracy, would be brought down by competition.

One might have supposed that if the defendants were going to collude on price, they would go the whole hog and agree not to provide discounts to the hospitals and other customers favored by the discriminatory system. But the defendants' cartel—if that is what it is—may not be tight enough to prevent hospitals and other bulk purchasers with power to shift demand among different manufacturers' drugs from whipsawing the members of the cartel for discounts; or maybe these purchasers could shift demand to manufacturers that are not members of the cartel. If, for whatever reason, the elasticity of demand for a cartel's product differs among groups of purchasers, a single cartel price will not be profit-maximizing unless a discriminatory price scheme cannot be enforced at reasonable cost.

The manufacturers moved for summary judgment, arguing that there wasn't enough evidence of collusion to warrant a trial. The district judge denied the motion. The correctness of his ruling is not before us. And whether it was correct or not, the reader should bear in mind that the manufacturers have not been found to have violated the Sherman Act; the only determination is that there is enough evidence of a violation to require that the case be allowed to proceed to trial.

* * * The judge * * * granted summary judgment to the wholesaler defendants because he thought there was insufficient evidence of their participation in the manufacturers' conspiracy to warrant a trial. That * * * ruling [is] appealed from.

* * *

* * * [W]e move on to the question whether the wholesalers should have been dropped as defendants. Pretrial discovery included the taking of a thousand depositions and the production of *fifty million* pages of documents, and from this indigestible mass the plaintiffs have plucked a number of tasty morsels to garnish their briefs. We shall not extend this opinion with quotations. Suffice it to say that the record discloses a number of instances in which officers of the defendant wholesalers urge manufacturers to hold the line against discounting to pharmacies and their buying groups, and pledge to adhere to the chargeback system. The defendants argue that each of these "smoking guns" is susceptible of an innocent interpretation. But the issue before us is not whether the wholesalers were in fact participants in the price-fixing conspiracy; it is whether there is sufficient evidence of this to create a jury issue. In deciding this question we must construe the evidence as favorably to the plaintiffs as the record permits, not as favorably to the defendants as it permits. The defendants' interpretations may be correct; they are not inevitable.

But they argue, pointing to *Matsushita* and other decisions by the Supreme Court and this court, that summary judgment for a defendant is proper, even if there is some evidence of an antitrust violation, if the plaintiff's theory of violation makes no economic sense. *Matsushita Electric Industrial Co. v. Zenith Radio Corp.*, 475 U.S. 574, 587, 106 S.Ct. 1348, 1356 (1986); *Eastman Kodak Co. v. Image Technical Services, Inc.*, 504 U.S. 451, 467–69, 112 S.Ct. 2072, 2082–83 (1992). This has to be the right rule, given the potential for jury confusion in litigation as enormous and esoteric as a billion-dollar antitrust damages action. The wholesalers argue that it would have been contrary to their economic self-interest for them to have joined a conspiracy that prevents them from selling at discounted prices to the pharmacies. The lower the price at which they sell to the pharmacies, the larger their volume of sales, and if their markup is unaffected this will translate into larger gross and probably net revenues.

But this misconceives the plaintiffs' theory of the wholesalers' violation. The theory is that the wholesalers were the manufacturers' cats-paws. There is nothing new about the idea that a cartel might "hire" a customer to help police the cartel. See Elizabeth Granitz & Benjamin Klein, "Monopolization by 'Raising Rivals' Costs': The Standard Oil Case," 39 *J. Law & Econ.* 1 (1996). The theory is especially plausible in the circumstances of the present case. (That doesn't mean it's correct; that's not the issue.) Drug wholesalers appear to be an endangered commercial species. Before the chargeback system was adopted, the manufacturers would often sell directly to hospitals, HMOs, and other favored customers, bypassing the wholesalers, since by selling directly they could monitor each customer's purchases and so try to identify instances in which a customer was purchasing for purposes of arbitrage rather than for its own use. The pharmacies were trying to get into the act by forming buying groups. Buying groups frequently act as their members' wholesaler, buying directly from the manufacturer and thus cutting out independent wholesalers. Desiring a piece of the action with the favored customers, who were proliferating, the wholesalers agreed to implement a chargeback system that would shore up the manufacturers' system of price discrimination, an integral component of the price-fixing conspiracy. And desiring to discourage buying groups they joined with the manufacturers to hold the line against granting any discounts to such groups and so discourage their formation by reducing the advantages of membership.

The picture that we have just sketched may not be true, but there is enough evidence supporting it to preclude summary judgment; and our main point for the present is merely that the defendants are wrong to argue that it would make no sense for the wholesalers to conspire with them to fix the prices of pharmaceutical drugs. It would make perfectly good sense, and so the "smoking gun" evidence cannot be dismissed as being obviously misunderstood, empty boasting, or idle corporate gossip.

The wholesalers point to their wafer-thin profit margins. The margins might be even thinner if the wholesalers had refused to play their appointed role as agents of a manufacturers' cartel–in fact they might be out of business. And absence of monopoly profits is not inconsistent with monopoly (collusive or single-firm), since firms may transform monopoly profits into costs in their efforts to engross a larger share of them. The wholesalers point to instances in which they did engage in arbitrage, sought permission to give discounts to pharmacies, and even helped to organize buying groups of pharmacies. This evidence does not erase the factual question of whether the wholesalers joined the conspiracy. It is just evidence to be weighed in the balance by the trier of fact. There are inherent strains in a cartel. A member can do better by undercutting the cartel slightly and obtaining enormously increased volume at a slight sacrifice of unit profit than by honoring the cartel price and suffering an erosion of sales because of cheating by less scrupulous members. George J. Stigler, "A Theory of Oligopoly," in Stigler, *The Organization of Industry* 39 (1968). That is why cartels tend to collapse of their own weight. And if as the plaintiffs argue the wholesalers were tools of the manufacturers–reluctant accomplices, yet not the less liable for that, * * * rather than principals– naturally they would be restive. As for the wholesalers' sponsorship of buying groups, it did not begin until after this litigation commenced, and may be strategic. And no significance can be attached to the fact that some of the wholesalers sued the manufacturers. *Illinois Brick** entitles them to do so. One virtue of the rule of that case is that it creates an incentive for middlemen to break out of a cartel and sue the supplier members; it sows dishonor among thieves; they still may *be* thieves.

* * *

The four rulings appealed from are thus REVERSED.

―――――

Judge Posner's *Prescription Drug* opinion is also interesting because it addressed price discrimination, a topic we consider in Chapter 7. (*See* Sidebar 7–8). For purposes of the agreement questions, notice how Judge Posner assesses each element of evidence by its potential to aid the defendants' efforts to solve the problems of cartel coordination. As Judge Posner empha-sizes, the court of appeals is not being asked here to determine whether the defendants actually coordinated their conduct and violated the law. The question posed here is whether the plaintiffs have offered enough evidence to defeat the defendants' motion for summary judgment and proceed to trial on their allegations. In deciding whether the plaintiffs have cleared that hurdle, Judge Posner dwells extensively on whether the proffered evidence of conspir-acy might be consistent with the defendants' efforts to solve the cartel problems of reaching consensus, deterring cheaters, and forestalling new competition.

---

* [The reference here is to *Illinois Brick Co. v. Illinois*, 431 U.S. 720 (1977), in which the Court held that indirect purchasers were barred under Section 4 of the Clayton Act from suing cartel members for the damages that may have been passed-on to them by direct purchasers. One reason the Court gave for its decision was that it would enhance deterrence of cartel behavior by providing the direct pur-chasers with the incentive to detect and pursue claims against cartels. For further discussion, see Chapter 9, *infra*. Eds.]

After this decision the case returned to district court, which again awarded summary judgment to the wholesalers. That decision was affirmed on appeal. *In re Brand Name Prescription Drugs Antitrust Litigation*, 288 F.3d 1028 (7th Cir. 2002) (Posner, J.). In his later opinion, Judge Posner agreed that the record evidence was insufficient to permit a reasonable jury to infer the wholesalers' guilt on the only theory on which the wholesalers could be liable: that they had joined a conspiracy of the manufacturers. Posner concluded that the absence of evidence that the wholesalers knew that the manufacturers' price discrimination was collusive rather than individual was dispositive, without need to address whether there actually was a manufacturers' conspiracy or whether, if there was one, the wholesalers had joined it.

Sidebar 3–1:
The Prisoner's Dilemma

One of the most basic and widely-studied models in game theory is that of the prisoner's dilemma. In addition to suggesting how the police can get suspects to confess—the setting in which the story is usually told—the model also explains why firms compete even though they would jointly profit from collusion. After describing the prisoner's dilemma in its original setting, we will sketch its application to competition.

Two hard cases, Biff and Rocky, are suspects in a bank robbery. The investigating police officers are virtually certain that the two committed the crime, as in fact they did. But the police know this in part through inadmissible evidence, and do not think they can secure a conviction without at least one confession.

Biff and Rocky are questioned separately. Each knows that if they both hang tough, and do not confess, they will be interrogated in jail for a while, then allowed to go free. If both confess, they will both go to jail. And if one confesses while the other does not, the cooperating prisoner will be freed immediately, while the prosecutor will throw the book at the non-cooperating one. As a result the non-cooperating prisoner will likely receive a much longer jail term than if both were to confess.

These outcomes ("payoffs" in game theoretic language) are sketched in the following chart.

	Rocky does not confess	Rocky confesses
Biff does not confess	Biff and Rocky are jailed for a short while, then go free	Rocky goes free immediately; long jail term for Biff
Biff confesses	Biff goes free immediately; long jail term for Rocky	Medium jail sentence for both Biff and Rocky

Recall that the prisoners are separated. Each must make a decision about whether to confess without communicating with his partner. What strategy would we expect Biff to pursue?

We could begin by analyzing the outcomes from the point of view of the partnership between Biff and Rocky. The best outcome for the two together is if neither confesses, as their aggregate jail time together is small. The worst outcome for the two together is if both confess, as they then both stay in jail for a medium term.

But now look at the outcomes from Biff's individual point of view. Biff may think this way: "Rocky will either confess or not confess. If Rocky is going to confess, the best thing for Biff to do is confess too; that way Biff will avoid a long jail sentence in favor of a medium jail sentence. If Rocky is instead going to hang tough, confession is still the best strategy for Biff to follow; that way Biff will go free immediately." In short, whichever strategy Rocky follows, the best strategy for Biff is to confess. Confession is thus a "dominant" strategy for Biff, in game theory language. Rocky will think the same way, and conclude that no matter what Biff does, the best strategy for Rocky is to confess. Accordingly, the most likely outcome is that both confess and both go to jail for a medium term, even though a better outcome (a short jail time during interrogation) was available to both. The two suspects are led by individual self-interest to confess.

The analogy to competition among firms can quickly be sketched. Biff Co. and Rocky, Inc. are the only two firms competing in a relevant market. The management team at each must decide whether to cooperate (collude) or compete. Collusion is attractive: if both firms decide to collude, and charge a high price, they each earn substantial profits. If both instead compete, and expand output while charging a low price, they earn zero economic profits (no profits in excess of what is required to keep the assets in the market). A firm makes out best by cheating, charging a low price when its rival's price is high, but then its rival loses money. These outcomes are set forth in the table below.

	Rocky Inc. cooperates	Rocky Inc. competes
Biff Co. cooperates	Biff: $10 million profit Rocky: $10 million profit	Biff: $5 million loss Rocky: $20 million profit
Biff Co. competes	Biff: $20 million profit Rocky: $5 million loss	Biff : $0 profit Rocky: $0 profit

As before, joint profits are maximized when both cooperate–they then split $20 million–and joint profits are the least when both compete. Nevertheless, each has a powerful incentive to compete. Biff reasons: "Rocky can either cooperate or compete. If Rocky cooperates, I do best by competing; I make $20 million rather than $10 million. If Rocky instead competes, I do best by competing also; at least I break even rather than losing money. Either way, I want to compete." Rocky reasons the same way, and both are led to compete rather than cooperate. Both would do better if they could find a way to cooperate, but competition is nevertheless the marketplace outcome.

Note that this discussion assumes that Rocky Inc. and Biff Co. have only one decision to make, whether to cooperate or compete, just like Rocky and Biff. In the language of game theory, the prisoner's dilemma problem set forth above is a "one-shot" game. Repeated interaction (or "repeated play" in the language of game theory) can alter the outcome, and make it more likely that the firms will choose to cooperate in any period. This point is discussed in Case Study III, above.

A final word: from the point of view of the firms in this example, cooperation is the goal, not competition. Cooperation leads to the greatest profits to split between the firms. But don't forget that from the point of view of buyers and economic efficiency, competition, not cooperation is the goal. Antitrust law enforcement can be understood as designed to discourage tacit collusion by making it less profitable.

C. THE DEVELOPMENT OF TRADITIONAL CONSPIRACY LAW

In Section B we learned that the members of a cartel must do three basic things to raise prices by restricting output. They must reach consensus on the terms of their collaboration, deter cheating by detecting and punishing deviations from the agreement, and forestall or co-opt new competition. The adoption of competition statutes does not change the importance to successful cartel coordination of executing these tasks, but antitrust laws can dramatically affect *how* firms go about accomplishing them.

Consider the legal environment confronting business managers in the United States before the passage of state antitrust laws in the 1880s and the Sherman Act in 1890. Many common law contract cases had decided that a rule of reason governed agreements by competitors to fix prices or allocate markets. At worst, a common law court might refuse to enforce the terms of a collusive undertaking. Damage awards to cartel victims or criminal sanctions for cartel members were out of the question. Business rivals met openly to coordinate their production and pricing decisions. Newspapers announced the time and place for firms in an industry to meet to discuss possibilities for creating cartels. *See* Louis Galambos, *Loose Combinations and Their Public Control Over Time*, in National Competition Policy: Historians' Perspectives on Antitrust and Business Relationships in the United States 143, 149–50 (FTC, Aug. 1981).

The culture of open cooperation often tolerated by the common law was slow to change even after the passage of the first antitrust statutes. In early Section 1 cases, the courts rarely confronted the question of whether challenged conduct resulted from concerted action or unilateral behavior. For example, the pipe manufacturers in *Addyston Pipe* did not dispute the Justice Department's contention that they coordinated their production and sales activities.

Why did the defendants in early Section 1 cases feel no urgency to show that they had acted independently? Three explanations come to mind. The first is uncertainty created by judicial efforts to define the rules for competitor collaboration from 1890 until the late 1930s. Not until 1940 in *Socony-Vacuum Oil* (Casebook, Chapter 2, *supra*), did the Supreme Court make absolutely clear that some types of behavior would be prohibited categorically.

A second factor is the periodic U.S. ambivalence about the value of competition as an organizing principle for the economy. As we discussed in Chapter 2, in the first term of Franklin Roosevelt's presidency, various statutes and regulations sought to promote recovery from the Depression by relying on central planning and other forms of extensive cooperation between producers in the same industry. Government programs to displace or suppress competition probably led companies to question the intensity of the country's commitment to enforce the Sherman Act's controls on concerted behavior that restrains trade.

The third factor has been the growth in the power of sanctions for Sherman Act violations. Consider the case of criminal penalties. In 1890, Congress made Sherman Act offenses punishable as misdemeanors and established a maximum criminal fine of $50,000. The Sherman Act's original menu of criminal sanctions remained largely unchanged until the early 1970s. Today individual violators can be punished with prison terms of up to ten years and fines of up to $1 million. Corporate entities can be fined $100 million per offense or can pay significantly higher fines under the standards set forth in the Federal Sentencing Guidelines. *See* Federal Sentencing Guidelines, § 2R1.1. The two principal defendants in the vitamins price fixing cartel (Hoffmann–La Roche and BASF) paid a total of $725 million in fines to the Justice Department and saw several of their executives serve prison terms.

1. COLLUSION IN THE SHADOW OF ANTITRUST: COORDINATION STRATEGIES FOR THE FIRMS AND PROOF STRATEGIES FOR PLAINTIFFS

As the implementation of an antitrust regime creates greater dangers for certain agreements, firms desiring to coordinate output and pricing decisions with their rivals are likely to reconsider their strategies for collaboration. Recall how we used the example of a coffee shop owner in Chapter 1 to identify the basic economic purposes of antitrust law. Suppose that our coffee shop owner and four of her rivals wished to cooperate to collectively reduce output and increase prices. How might our coffee shop entrepreneurs accomplish their aims? The firms would have several options.

Form Immunized Overt Agreements with Competitors. Serious exposure for criminal and civil liability makes it hazardous for competitors to create readily observable cartel agreements. Today companies would pursue this course only if authorization by federal or state government bodies provided Sherman Act immunity. The ability of foreign, federal and state governments to immunize collective business conduct from antitrust prohibitions is discussed further in Chapter 9.

Form Overt Agreements Supported by Reasonable Business Justifications. Firms use overt agreements when they believe that their behavior conforms with antitrust standards and does not constitute a per se violation. Joint ventures, which we examined in Chapter 2, frequently are created by means of elaborate contractual documents, and their formation routinely is announced to the public. The fact of overt cooperation obviates the need for a court to devote attention to proof of concerted action.

Form Illegal Agreements Covertly with Competitors. Firms seeking to engage in forbidden concerted behavior could cooperate covertly and take precautions to avoid detection by law enforcement officials or private antitrust plaintiffs. The participants in the food additives and vitamins cartels we examined in Chapter 1 took this path. If they are careful, creative, and loyal, the cartel members can minimize the creation of direct evidence, in the form of documents or testimony by insiders, with which a plaintiff could establish the fact of collusion.

Even with precautions, cartel participants still must make difficult decisions about whether to make records of their understandings and about how to ensure that each conspirator remains faithful to the cause. The tasks of organizing and managing a cartel may be so complex that the members must make covert written records concerning the scheme's operation. Moreover, designing and implementing covert understandings can involve extensive contact among the cartel members.

Frequent communication and recourse to written records can create two nightmares for the cartel—that a prosecutor will obtain its written records, or that a disaffected cartel participant (or, perhaps, a participant's employee) will inform prosecutors and perhaps testify in court about its existence. These forms of documentary and testimonial proof, usually referred to as *direct evidence*, have sufficed in many instances to prove a conspiracy. The logic for public prosecutors to adopt amnesty, leniency, and other forms of immunity programs is to exploit the intuition of the "Prisoner's Dilemma" game, described in Sidebar 3–1 above, and induce cartel members to defect and provide direct evidence of conspiracy.

Skillful, well-disciplined cartels minimize the creation of incriminating written records and strive to hide their illicit activities from employees within their own firms. They also seek to defuse discontent among cartel members that could lead a disgruntled participant to divulge the cartel's existence. If a cartel adopts these safeguards, an antitrust plaintiff may be forced to rely entirely on *circumstantial* proof of concerted action.

In sum, when rivals have reached a covert agreement, a public prosecutor or a private plaintiff can take alternative paths to establish the existence of an illegal arrangement. The first relies on direct evidence. In *Andreas* in Chapter 1, an ADM insider (Mark Whitacre) voluntarily supplied the information that helped the Justice Department uncover the food additives cartel. Or, as Sidebar 3–4 suggests below, the public prosecutor can try to induce cartel participants to supply direct evidence of conspiracy by providing something of benefit to an informer.

Second, the plaintiff can rely on circumstantial evidence from which the finder of fact might infer concerted action. The rise of harsh penalties for cartel formation has driven would-be cartel participants to greater secrecy. This development has challenged antitrust policy to define the types of circumstantial proof that permit the finder of fact to infer that the defendants acted collectively.

Collectively Adopt "Facilitating Practices." Firms intent on coordinating their behavior might identify forms of coordinated activity that fall outside the zone of behavior that courts have denominated as per se offenses, yet which still "facilitate" coordination. Thus, firms might agree, perhaps in the guise of a trade association, to share current information about prices, production levels, costs, or inventories. They might do so in the hope that a court would (1) not deem an agreement to share such information to be a form of per se unlawful "price fixing;" (2) not permit an information-sharing agreement to serve as circumstantial evidence from which a fact finder could infer that the participants were engaging in a covert agreement to set prices themselves; and (3) not find the agreement unlawful as an unreasonable restraint on competition. The information exchange cases, which we study later in this Chapter, seek to address the third possibility.

Engage in "Conscious Parallelism." If there are sufficiently few suppliers in the industry, firms might try to coordinate their behavior and achieve higher than competitive prices simply by anticipating and responding to the moves of their rivals. In this scenario, the competitors do not form overt or covert agreements to restrict output, and they need not form overt or covert agreements to adopt facilitating practices. Instead, the oligopolists recognize and act upon their interdependence. They select strategies on the assumption that each industry member realizes that its counterparts will observe and be affected by each of its moves. They do so in the expectation that no firm will have incentives to compete more aggressively and the hope that courts will not treat the sequence of action and reaction as a form of "agreement."

For example, one firm, perhaps the largest, might act as a "price leader," while its rivals observe and quickly copy the leader's price increases. Under such circumstances, all firms may raise prices in parallel to a higher than competitive level. The result may be "parallel pricing," by which all firms raise and lower prices nearly simultaneously, and prices end up above the competitive price. Whether this conduct should be deemed an unlawful agreement on price has bedeviled antitrust for decades, as will be discussed further in Section C3, below.

Unilaterally Adopt Facilitating Practices. In a concentrated industry, a firm might try to enhance the quality of tacit coordination by unilaterally adopting a practice that signals to other industry members that the actor either is seeking to curb its discretion or is willing to punish rivals who compete too aggressively. The initial adopter of the practice may hope that its competitors will mimic its moves by embracing the practice as well. For example, a company might establish a widely known practice of promising to give its largest customers the benefit of any price cut given to any single customer. Because such a commitment may force a supplier to cut prices for a broad swath of its customer base if it reduces prices for any single buyer, using a "most favored nations" or "most favored customers" clause can be a way for a firm to tell its rivals that it will try to refrain from cutting prices. (*See* Sidebar 3–6.) Because unilateral facilitating practices can be implemented without an agreement, they cannot be challenged under Section 1 of the Sherman Act. Legal strategies for scrutinizing such conduct are considered in Section E2 of this Chapter, which discusses the *Ethyl* case.

In the balance of this Chapter, we turn to how the legal system and case law have responded to the range of coordination strategies that firms have adopted in trying to avoid antitrust liability.

2. INFERRING CONSPIRACY FROM CIRCUMSTANTIAL EVIDENCE: *INTERSTATE CIRCUIT*

In the second term of Franklin Roosevelt's presidency, the Justice Department undertook an ambitious expansion of antitrust enforcement, including a commitment to prosecute cartels aggressively. The new wave of cartel cases yielded several Supreme Court decisions that confronted the issue of identifying agreements where the plaintiff relied mainly on proof of circumstantial evidence to establish conspiracy. We will look at one of the first, *Interstate Circuit.*

Interstate Circuit involves inferring an agreement from circumstantial evidence that includes parallel price increases. In this respect it addresses an issue that courts have confronted repeatedly in the many decades since. The decision appears animated by a common concern of courts during antitrust's structuralist era, which began in the late 1930s and extended through the Chicago School revolution of the late 1970s: the fear that covert cartels and other anticompetitive conduct would go unpunished if the courts became overly cautious in identifying antitrust violations. Today *Interstate Circuit* is commonly viewed as marking the outer limits of how far courts will go to infer an agreement from circumstantial evidence that includes parallel conduct. But the decision retains vitality, as shown by the Seventh Circuit's decision in *Toys "R" Us, Inc. v. FTC,* 221 F.3d 928 (7th Cir. 2000), which is discussed in the notes following the case.

The agreement found in *Interstate Circuit* has an unusual structure, sometimes called a "hub and spoke" conspiracy, in which a single firm is said to have acted as a cartel manager, orchestrating an agreement among its suppliers (as in this case) or customers. The defendants conceded that they had formed vertical agreements linking film exhibitors and distributors. The legal issue was whether the distributors agreed with each other, horizontally, by making identical agreements in parallel.

As you read this decision, consider why the Court found an agreement among the distributors. What factors permitted this inference?

INTERSTATE CIRCUIT, INC. v. UNITED STATES

Supreme Court of the United States, 1939.
306 U.S. 208, 59 S.Ct. 467, 83 L.Ed. 610.

Mr. Justice STONE delivered the opinion of the Court.

[This case grew out of a government lawsuit challenging the conduct of a number of firms involved in the motion picture industry in Texas during the 1930s. Two types of firms, distributors and exhibitors, were defendants. The distributors owned or controlled the copyrights for movies, and accounted for 75% of the "first-class feature films exhibited in the United States." Exhibitors, who owned local theaters, would show the films pursuant to license agreements with the distributors. Local theaters, in turn, could be divided into two groups: "first-run" theaters (that showed a film during its first exhibition in a given locality) and "second-run" theaters (that showed a film during a subsequent exhibition in that locality).

At the time of the events giving rise to this litigation, Interstate Circuit operated forty-three first-run and second-run theaters located in six Texas cities. It had a complete monopoly of first-run theaters in these cities (excepting one theater in Houston). Although Interstate operated twenty-two second-run theaters, its only second-run theater monopoly was in Galveston. In most cities, Interstate competed with other second-run theaters. Texas Consolidated operated sixty-six theaters, both first-run and second-run, all in cities different from those served by Interstate. In six leading cities, Texas

Consolidated faced no competing first-run theaters. Interstate and Texas Consolidated dominated the exhibition business in the cities in which their theaters were located, together contributing more than 74% of all license fees paid by exhibitors in their territories to the leading distributors. Interstate and Texas Consolidated were both affiliated with each other and with Paramount, one of the distributor defendants. Interstate and Consolidated were run by the same senior managers: Hoblitzell (president of both) and O'Donnell (general manager of both). First-run theaters typically charged an admission price for adults of at least 40 cents, while second-run theaters typically charged 15 cents. Eds.]

* * *

On July 11, 1934, following a previous communication on the subject to the eight branch managers of the distributor appellants, O'Donnell, the manager of Interstate and Consolidated, sent to each of them a letter on the letterhead of Interstate, each letter naming all of them as addressees, in which he asked compliance with two demands as a condition of Interstate's continued exhibition of the distributors' films in its 'A' or first-run theatres at a night admission of 40 cents or more.[4] One demand was that the distributors "agree that in selling their product to subsequent runs, that this 'A' product will never be exhibited at any time or in any theatre at a smaller admission price than 25 cents for adults in the evening". The other was that "on 'A' pictures which are exhibited at a night admission of 40 cents or more—they shall never be exhibited in conjunction with another feature picture under the so-called policy of double features". The letter added that with respect to the "Rio Grande Valley situation", with which Consolidated alone was concerned, "We must insist that all pictures exhibited in our 'A' theatres at a maximum night admission price of 35 cents must also be restricted to subsequent runs in the Valley at 25 cents".

* * *

The local representatives of the distributors, having no authority to enter into the proposed agreements, communicated the proposal to their home offices. Conferences followed between Hoblitzelle and O'Donnell, acting for Interstate and Consolidated, and the representatives of the various distributors. In these conferences each distributor was represented by its local branch manager and by one or more superior officials from outside the state of Texas. In the course of them each distributor agreed with Interstate for the 1934–35 season to impose both the demanded restrictions upon their subsequent-run licensees in the six Texas cities served by Interstate, except Austin and Galveston. While only two of the distributors incorporated the agreement to impose the restrictions in their license contracts with Interstate, the evidence establishes, and it is not denied, that all joined in the agreement, four of them after some delay in negotiating terms other than the restrictions and not now material. These agreements for the restrictions—with the immaterial exceptions noted—were carried into effect by each of the distributors' imposing

---

4. A Class 'A' picture is a 'feature picture' having five reels or more of film each approximately 1,000 feet in length, shown in theatres of the specified Texas cities charging 40 cents or more for adult admission at night. Approximately fifty percent of the pictures released by the distributor defendants in the Texas cities in 1934–1935 were Class 'A' pictures.

them on their subsequent-run licensees in the four Texas cities during the 1934–35 season. One agreement, that of Metro–Goldwyn–Mayer Distributing Corporation, was for three years. The others were renewed in the two following seasons and all were in force when the present suit was begun.

None of the distributors yielded to the demand that subsequent runs in towns in the Rio Grande Valley served by Consolidated should be restricted. One distributor, Paramount, which was affiliated with Consolidated, agreed to impose the restrictions in certain other Texas and New Mexico cities.

* * *

THE AGREEMENT AMONG THE DISTRIBUTORS.

Although the films were copyrighted, appellants do not deny that the conspiracy charge is established if the distributors agreed among themselves to impose the restrictions upon subsequent-run exhibitors. * * * As is usual in cases of alleged unlawful agreements to restrain commerce, the government is without the aid of direct testimony that the distributors entered into any agreement with each other to impose the restrictions upon subsequent-run exhibitors. In order to establish agreement it is compelled to rely on inferences drawn from the course of conduct of the alleged conspirators.

* * *

The O'Donnell letter named on its face as addressees the eight local representatives of the distributors, and so from the beginning each of the distributors knew that the proposals were under consideration by the others. Each was aware that all were in active competition and that without substantially unanimous action with respect to the restrictions for any given territory there was risk of a substantial loss of the business and good will of the subsequent-run and independent exhibitors, but that with it there was the prospect of increased profits. There was, therefore, strong motive for concerted action, full advantage of which was taken by Interstate and Consolidated in presenting their demands to all in a single document.

There was risk, too, that without agreement diversity of action would follow. Compliance with the proposals involved a radical departure from the previous business practices of the industry and a drastic increase in admission prices of most of the subsequent-run theatres. Acceptance of the proposals was discouraged by at least three of the distributors' local managers. Independent exhibitors met and organized a futile protest which they presented to the representatives of Interstate and Consolidated. While as a result of independent negotiations either of the two restrictions without the other could have been put into effect by any one or more of the distributors and in any one or more of the Texas cities served by Interstate, the negotiations which ensued and which in fact did result in modifications of the proposals resulted in substantially unanimous action of the distributors, both as to the terms of the restrictions and in the selection of the four cities where they were to operate.

One distributor, it is true, did not agree to impose the restrictions in Houston, but this was evidently because it did not grant licenses to any subsequent-run exhibitor in that city, where its own affiliate operated a first-run theatre. The proposal was unanimously rejected as to Galveston and

Austin, as was the request that the restrictions should be extended to the cities of the Rio Grande Valley served by Consolidated. We may infer that Galveston was omitted because in that city there were no subsequent-run theatres in competition with Interstate. But we are unable to find in the record any persuasive explanation, other than agreed concert of action, of the singular unanimity of action on the part of the distributors by which the proposals were carried into effect as written in four Texas cities but not in a fifth or in the Rio Grande Valley. Numerous variations in the form of the provisions in the distributors' license agreements and the fact that in later years two of them extended the restrictions into all six cities, do not weaken the significance or force of the nature of the response to the proposals made by all the distributor appellants. It taxes credulity to believe that the several distributors would, in the circumstances, have accepted and put into operation with substantial unanimity such far-reaching changes in their business methods without some understanding that all were to join, and we reject as beyond the range of probability that it was the result of mere chance.

* * *

This inference [that the distributors acted in concert and in common agreement] was supported and strengthened when the distributors, with like unanimity, failed to tender the testimony, at their command, of any officer or agent of a distributor who knew, or was in a position to know, whether in fact an agreement had been reached among them for concerted action. When the proof supported, as we think it did, the inference of such concert, the burden rested on appellants of going forward with the evidence to explain away or contradict it. They undertook to carry that burden by calling upon local managers of the distributors to testify that they had acted independently of the other distributors, and that they did not have conferences with or reach agreements with the other distributors or their representatives. The failure under the circumstances to call as witnesses those officers who did have authority to act for the distributors and who were in a position to know whether they had acted in pursuance of agreement is itself persuasive that their testimony, if given, would have been unfavorable to appellants. The production of weak evidence when strong is available can lead only to the conclusion that the strong would have been adverse.

While the District Court's finding of an agreement of the distributors among themselves is supported by the evidence, we think that in the circumstances of this case such agreement for the imposition of the restrictions upon subsequent-run exhibitors was not a prerequisite to an unlawful conspiracy. It was enough that, knowing that concerted action was contemplated and invited, the distributors gave their adherence to the scheme and participated in it. Each distributor was advised that the others were asked to participate; each knew that cooperation was essential to successful operation of the plan. They knew that the plan, if carried out, would result in a restraint of commerce, which, we will presently point out, was unreasonable within the meaning of the Sherman Act, and knowing it, all participated in the plan. The evidence is persuasive that each distributor early became aware that the others had joined. With that knowledge they renewed the arrangement and carried it into effect for the two successive years.

It is elementary that an unlawful conspiracy may be and often is formed without simultaneous action or agreement on the part of the conspirators. * * * Acceptance by competitors, without previous agreement, of an invitation to participate in a plan, the necessary consequence of which, if carried out, is restraint of interstate commerce, is sufficient to establish an unlawful conspiracy under the Sherman Act. * * *

* * *

We think the conclusion is unavoidable that the conspiracy and each contract between Interstate and the distributors by which those consequences were effected are violations of the Sherman Act and that the District Court rightly enjoined enforcement and renewal of these agreements, as well as of the conspiracy among the distributors.

Affirmed.

Mr. Justice FRANKFURTER took no part in the consideration or decision of this case.

Justices ROBERTS, McReynolds, and Butler dissented (opinion omitted).

————

In *Interstate Circuit*, the Department of Justice relied entirely on circumstantial evidence to prove its case. What facts led the Supreme Court to conclude that the behavior in question was the result of a conspiracy? Is it possible to identify what evidence, in the Court's eyes, was crucial to the government's case? Imagine the finding of conspiracy to be a platform resting on a series of pillars, with each pillar representing one piece of circumstantial evidence. Which pillars, if removed, would have caused the allegation of conspiracy to collapse?

Figure 3–2:
Interstate Circuit–The Hub and Spoke Conspiracy

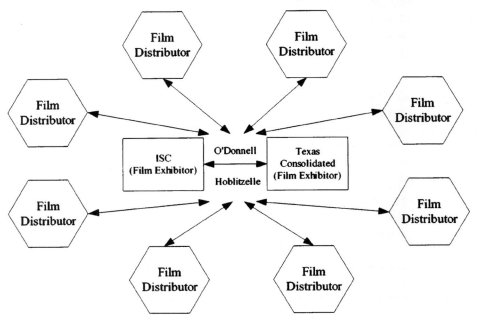

Interstate Circuit endorsed the theory that a series of *overt* agreements between a common dealer and its various suppliers could be used as circumstantial evidence of a *covert* horizontal agreement among the suppliers. That theory was invoked by the Federal Trade Commission in *Toys "R" Us, Inc. v. FTC*, 221 F.3d 928 (7th Cir. 2000), where the FTC alleged that Toys "R" Us ("TRU") had used a series of vertical agreements with each of ten leading toy suppliers to orchestrate a horizontal agreement among the suppliers to boycott discounting retailers. According to the court, faced with new, low-priced competition from warehouse club stores, TRU proposed a set of policies that limited the ability of the warehouse club stores to compete on an equal footing with TRU and to discount. In reaching the agreement with each of its suppliers:

> TRU was careful to meet individually with each of its suppliers to explain its new policy. Afterwards, it then asked each one what it intended to do. Negotiations between TRU and the manufacturers followed, as a result of which each manufacturer eventually agreed that it would sell to the clubs only highly differentiated products (either unique individual items or combo packs) that were not offered to anything but a club (and thus of course not to TRU). As the Commission put it, "[t]hrough its announced policy and the related agreements discussed below, TRU sought to eliminate the competitive threat the clubs posed by denying them merchandise, forcing the clubs' customers to buy products they did not want, and frustrating customers' ability to make direct price comparisons of club prices and TRU prices."

> The agreements between TRU and the various manufacturers were, of course, vertical agreements, because they ran individually from the supplier/manufacturer to the purchaser/retailer. The Commission found that TRU reached about 10 of these agreements. After the agreements were concluded, TRU then supervised and enforced each toy company's compliance with its commitment.
>
> But TRU was not content to stop with vertical agreements. Instead, the Commission found, it decided to go further. It worked for over a year and a half to put the vertical agreements in place, but "the biggest hindrance TRU had to overcome was the major toy companies' reluctance to give up a new, fast-growing, and profitable channel of distribution." The manufacturers were also concerned that any of their rivals who broke ranks and sold to the clubs might gain sales at their expense, given the widespread and increasing popularity of the club format. To address this problem, the Commission found, TRU orchestrated a horizontal agreement among its key suppliers to boycott the clubs. The evidence on which the Commission relied showed that, at a minimum, Mattel, Hasbro, Fisher Price, Tyco, Little Tikes, Today's Kids, and Tiger Electronics agreed to join in the boycott *"on the condition that their competitors would do the same."*

221 F.3d at 932. Focusing specifically on the FTC's conclusion that the manufacturers had formed a horizontal conspiracy, the court affirmed:

> The Commission's theory, stripped to its essentials, is that this case is a modern equivalent of the old *Interstate Circuit* decision. That case too involved actors at two levels of the distribution chain, distributors of motion pictures and exhibitors. * * * The trial court there drew an inference of agreement from the nature of the proposals, from the manner in which they were made, from the substantial unanimity of action taken, and from the lack of evidence of a benign motive; the Supreme Court affirmed. The new policies represented a radical shift from the industry's prior business practices, and the Court rejected as beyond the range of probability that such unanimity of action was explainable only by chance.
>
> The Commission is right. Indeed, as it argues in its brief, the TRU case if anything presents a more compelling case for inferring horizontal agreement than did *Interstate Circuit,* because not only was the manufacturers' decision to stop dealing with the warehouse clubs an abrupt shift from the past, and not only is it suspicious for a manufacturer to deprive itself of a profitable sales outlet, but the record here included the direct evidence of communications that was missing in *Interstate Circuit.* Just as in *Interstate Circuit,* TRU tries to avoid this result by hypothesizing independent motives. * * * [But the] evidence showed that * * * each manufacturer was afraid to curb its sales to the warehouse clubs alone, because it was afraid its rivals would cheat and gain a special advantage in that popular new market niche. The Commission was not required to disbelieve the testimony of the different toy company executives and TRU itself to the effect that the only condition on which each toy manufacturer

would agree to TRU's demands was if it could be sure its competitors were doing the same thing.

221 F.3d at 935.

Do you agree with the Seventh Circuit that the evidence of conspiracy adduced in *Toys "R" Us* is even more compelling than the evidence in *Interstate Circuit*? What is the economic role of the vertical agreements in supporting horizontal coordination among the toy suppliers? Did they help the suppliers solve one or more of their "cartel problems"? In particular, did they help the suppliers reach consensus, deter cheating, or limit entry? We will return to *Toys "R" Us* to consider its significance for proving anticompetitive effects in Chapter 8.

3. THE DEVELOPMENT AND EVOLUTION OF THE "PARALLELISM PLUS" DOCTRINE

Seven years after *Interstate Circuit*, the Supreme Court again considered the concerted action issue in the context of reviewing conspiracy to monopolize charges brought under Section 2 of the Sherman Act against the country's leading producers of tobacco products. Here again the basis for the government's proof of conspiracy was circumstantial evidence. The Court's decision provides an important basis for requiring evidence of factors which, when added to the fact of parallel conduct by the defendant, can sustain a finding of conspiracy. These additional factors have come to be known as "plus factors." What plus factors did the Court rely upon in *American Tobacco*?

The Court notes that the major tobacco firms implemented identical cigarette price increases on June 23, 1931, with no economic justification. Does the Court believe that this fact rules out the possibility that the cigarette price increases came about through an oligopoly interaction short of agreement, or does it not care, on the view that such an interaction would constitute an unlawful conspiracy?

AMERICAN TOBACCO CO. v. UNITED STATES

Supreme Court of the United States, 1946.
328 U.S. 781, 66 S.Ct. 1125, 90 L.Ed. 1575.

Mr. Justice BURTON delivered the opinion of the Court.

The petitioners are The American Tobacco Company, Liggett & Myers Tobacco Company, R. J. Reynolds Tobacco Company, American Suppliers, Inc., a subsidiary of American, and certain officials of the respective companies who were convicted by a jury, in the District Court of the United States for the Eastern District of Kentucky, of violating §§ 1 and 2 of the Sherman Anti–Trust Act * * * pursuant to an information filed July 24, 1940, and modified October 31, 1940.

* * * The conspiracy to monopolize and the monopolization charged here do not depend upon proof relating to the old tobacco trust [which was dissolved in 1911—Eds.] but upon a dominance and control by petitioners in recent years over purchases of the raw material and over the sale of the finished product in the form of cigarettes. The fact, however, that the purchases of leaf tobacco and the sales of so many products of the tobacco

industry have remained largely within the same general group of business organizations for over a generation, inevitably has contributed to the ease with which control over competition within the industry and the mobilization of power to resist new competition can be exercised. A friendly relationship within such a long established industry is, in itself, not only natural but commendable and beneficial, as long as it does not breed illegal activities. Such a community of interest in any industry, however, provides a natural foundation for working policies and understandings favorable to the insiders and unfavorable to outsiders. The verdicts indicate that practices of an informal and flexible nature were adopted and that the results were so uniformly beneficial to the petitioners in protecting their common interests as against those of competitors that, entirely from circumstantial evidence, the jury found that a combination or conspiracy existed among the petitioners from 1937 to 1940, with power and intent to exclude competitors to such a substantial extent as to violate the Sherman Act as interpreted by the trial court.

* * * [A]lthough American, Liggett and Reynolds gradually dropped in their percentage of the national domestic cigarette production from 90.7% in 1931 to 73.3%, 71% and 68%, respectively, in 1937, 1938 and 1939, they have accounted at all times for more than 68%, and usually for more than 75%, of the national production. The balance of the cigarette production has come from six other companies. No one of those six ever has produced more than the 10.6% once reached by Brown & Williamson in 1939. * * *

* * *

With this background of a substantial monopoly, amounting to over two-thirds of the entire domestic field of cigarettes, and to over 80% of the field of comparable cigarettes, and with the opposition confined to several small competitors, the jury could have found from the actual operation of the petitioners that there existed a combination or conspiracy among them not only in restraint of trade, but to monopolize a part of the tobacco industry. * * *

* * *

II.

The verdicts show * * * that the jury found that the petitioners conspired to fix prices and to exclude undesired competition in the distribution and sale of their principal products. The petitioners sold and distributed their products to jobbers and to selected dealers who bought at list prices, less discounts. Almost all of the million or more dealers who handled the respective petitioners' products throughout the country consisted of such establishments as small storekeepers, gasoline station operators and lunch room proprietors who purchased the cigarettes from jobbers. The jobbers in turn derived their profits from the difference between the wholesale price paid by them and the price charged by them to local dealers. A great advantage therefore accrued to any dealer buying at the discounted or wholesale list prices. Selling to dealers at jobbers' prices was called 'direct selling' and the dealers as well as the jobbers getting those prices were referred to as being on the 'direct list.' The list prices charged and the discounts allowed by petitioners have been practically identical since 1923 and absolutely identical since 1928. Since the latter date, only seven changes have been made by the three companies and those have been identical in amount. The increases were first announced by Reynolds. American and Liggett thereupon increased their list prices in identical amounts.

The following record of price changes is circumstantial evidence of the existence of a conspiracy and of a power and intent to exclude competition coming from cheaper grade cigarettes. During the two years preceding June, 1931, the petitioners produced 90% of the total cigarette production in the United States. In that month tobacco farmers were receiving the lowest prices for their crops since 1905. The costs to the petitioners for tobacco leaf, therefore, were lower than usual during the past 25 years, and their manufacturing costs had been declining. It was one of the worst years of financial and economic depression in the history of the country. On June 23, 1931, Reynolds, without previous notification or warning to the trade or public, raised the list price of Camel cigarettes, constituting its leading cigarette brand, from $6.40 to $6.85 a thousand. The same day, American increased the list price for Lucky Strike cigarettes, its leading brand, and Liggett the price for Chesterfield cigarettes, its leading brand, to the identical price of $6.85 a thousand. No economic justification for this raise was demonstrated. The president of Reynolds stated that it was 'to express our own courage for the future and our own confidence in our industry.' The president of American gave as his reason for the increase, 'the opportunity of making some money.' He further claimed that because Reynolds had raised its list price, Reynolds would therefore have additional funds for advertising and American had raised its price in order to have a similar amount for advertising. The officials of Liggett claimed that they thought the increase was a mistake as there did not seem to be any reason for making a price advance but they contended that unless they also raised their list price for Chesterfields, the other companies would have greater resources to spend in advertising and thus would put Chesterfield cigarettes at a competitive disadvantage. This general price increase soon resulted in higher retail prices and in a loss in volume of sales. Yet in 1932, in the midst of the national depression with the sales of the petitioners' cigarettes falling off greatly in number, the petitioners still were making tremendous profits as a result of the price increase. Their net profits in that year amounted to more than $100,000,000. This was one of the three biggest years in their history.

* * *

III.

It was on the basis of such evidence that the Circuit Court of Appeals found that the verdicts of the jury were sustained by sufficient evidence on each count. * * *

It is not the form of the combination or the particular means used but the result to be achieved that the statute condemns. It is not of importance whether the means used to accomplish the unlawful objective are in themselves lawful or unlawful. Acts done to give effect to the conspiracy may be in themselves wholly innocent acts. Yet, if they are part of the sum of the acts which are relied upon to effectuate the conspiracy which the statute forbids, they come within its prohibition. No formal agreement is necessary to constitute an unlawful conspiracy. Often crimes are a matter of inference deduced from the acts of the person accused and done in pursuance of a criminal purpose. Where the conspiracy is proved, as here, from the evidence of the action taken in concert by the parties to it, it is all the more convincing proof of an intent to exercise the power of exclusion acquired through that conspiracy. The essential combination or conspiracy in violation of the Sherman Act may be found in a course of dealings or other circumstances as well as in any exchange of words. Where the circumstances are such as to warrant a jury in finding that the conspirators had a unity of purpose or a common design and understanding, or a meeting of minds in an unlawful arrangement, the conclusion that a conspiracy is established is justified. Neither proof of exertion of the power to exclude nor proof of actual exclusion of existing or potential competitors is essential to sustain a charge of monopolization under the Sherman Act.

* * *

In the present cases, the petitioners have been found to have conspired to establish a monopoly and also to have the power and intent to establish and maintain the monopoly. To hold that they do not come within the prohibition of the Sherman Act would destroy the force of that Act. Accordingly, the instructions of the trial court under § 2 of the Act are approved and the judgment of the Circuit Court of Appeals is affirmed.

Justices REED and JACKSON took no part in the consideration or decision of these cases.

Mr. Justice RUTLEDGE, concurring (opinion omitted).

———

The Supreme Court provided the capstone to this formative period of agreement decisions in *Theatre Enters., Inc. v. Paramount Film Distrib. Corp.*, 346 U.S. 537 (1954). In this private treble damage action, the Court considered the conduct of movie distributors who had refused to allow an exhibitor access to first-run films for showing in a suburban theater. The defendant distributors denied that they had acted in concert and offered economic justifications showing why each had chosen independently to follow the same course of action. Most importantly, suburban theaters were served by limited public transportation facilities and had a much smaller drawing area than downtown theaters. Accordingly, "[t]he downtown theaters offer[ed] far greater opportunities for the widespread advertisement and exploitation of newly released features, which is thought necessary to maximize the overall return from subsequent runs as well as first-runs." *Id.* at 540. After trial, the jury returned a verdict for the defendants. On appeal, the suburban exhibitor urged that the trial judge should have directed a verdict in its favor. In sustaining the jury's verdict, the Supreme Court cautioned that "[c]ircumstantial evidence of consciously parallel behavior may have made heavy inroads into the traditional judicial attitude toward conspiracy; but 'conscious parallelism' has not read conspiracy out of the Sherman Act entirely." *Id.* at 541.

As a group, the Supreme Court agreement decisions beginning with *Interstate Circuit* and ending with *Theatre Enterprises* established three points of reference for antitrust conspiracy jurisprudence. First, courts would apply the label of "concerted action" to interfirm coordination accomplished by means other than a direct exchange of assurances. Second, courts would allow agreements to be inferred from circumstantial proof suggesting that the challenged behavior more likely than not was the result of a jointly determined course of action. Third, courts would not find concerted action where the plaintiff showed only that the defendants recognized their interdependence and simply mimicked their competitors' conduct. Additional evidence beyond parallel conduct, today termed "plus factors," was required.

Sidebar 3–2:
The Turner/Posner Debate on Conscious Parallelism

The progression from *Interstate Circuit* to *Theatre Enterprises* inspired a famous debate in the 1960s about the application of Section 1 to oligopoly behavior. The contestants were Donald F. Turner, a Harvard Law School professor who served as Assistant Attorney General for Antitrust in the mid–1960s, and Richard A. Posner, a professor at the University of Chicago Law School and subsequently a court of appeals judge. Endorsing the approach of *Theatre Enterprises,* Turner argued that interdependent behavior should not be interpreted as an illegal conspiracy under Section 1. Donald F. Turner, *The Definition of Agreement Under the Sherman Act: Conscious Parallelism and Refusals to Deal*, 75 HARV. L. REV. 655 (1962). Turner argued that an oligopolist behaves exactly as a seller in a competitive industry, except that it also accounts for its rivals' reactions. From this he concluded that it would be unreasonable to interpret the Sherman Act to condemn rational and unavoidable unilateral behavior, even though the economic consequences mirrored those of conspiracy.

Even if oligopoly behavior were held illegal, Turner doubted that any remedy available under Section 1 would prove effective. Injunctive relief that directed defendants to ignore their rivals would be anomalous, for it would order them to make irrational price and output decisions. Commanding firms to price their goods at their marginal costs (*i.e.*, as if the market were competitive) would involve the courts in continuous regulation for which they are ill-equipped. Nor would dissolution or other structural solutions seem appropriate since the essence of the Section 1 offense would be the interdependence theory, and this relies on the seller's conduct (interdependent pricing) rather than market structure as ultimately being responsible for the result. In a separate paper, Turner contended that the proper solution to the oligopoly problem would be to restructure oligopolists into smaller units, either by charging them with joint monopolization under Section 2 or by adopting special legislation. *See* Donald F. Turner, *The Scope of Antitrust and Other Economic Regulatory Policies*, 82 HARV. L. REV. 1207, 1217–31 (1969).

In contrast, Judge Posner suggested that these analytical difficulties might be overcome by an alternative theory. *See* Richard A. Posner, *Oligopoly and the Antitrust Laws: A Suggested Approach*, 21 STAN. L. REV.

1562 (1969). Posner argued that oligopoly markets involve concerted action in that they manifest a tacit output agreement among sellers. In a concentrated market, sellers must act voluntarily to translate their mutual dependence into oligopoly prices. This constitutes a meeting of the minds even though there is no overt communication among sellers. Each seller communicates its offer to the others by restricting output (and thereby maintains its prices above marginal cost). If oligopoly pricing is to succeed, the seller's rivals must cooperate by curbing their output, as well. Therefore Posner argued that since "tacit collusion or non-competitive pricing is not inherent in an oligopolist market structure but, like conventional cartelizing, requires additional, voluntary behavior by the sellers," it violates Section 1. *Id.* at 1578. Nor did Posner find the problem of formulating an effective remedy under Section 1 insoluble. Posner believed that there were specific forms of behavior beyond the mere fact of interdependence that could be enjoined in a practical way. For an updated presentation of his critique of Turner, see RICHARD A. POSNER, ANTITRUST LAW 55–60 (2d ed. 2001).

The Turner/Posner debate arguably reflects a difference in judgment about the relative "error costs" of not finding agreement when firms are acting in ways that harm competition (false acquittals), versus finding agreement when firms are not harming competition or competition is harmed but there is no practical remedy (false convictions). From this perspective, Posner's view makes sense if firms that are able to solve their cartel problems (reaching consensus, deterring cheating and preventing new competition) to achieve higher than competitive prices through coordination almost invariably engage in explicit communication or other forms of conduct that can be enjoined. Turner's view makes sense if, in industries where firms can readily solve their cartel problems, high prices frequently result from leader-follower behavior that cannot practically be enjoined. For further discussion of the implications of the latter view, see Sidebar 3–5 (What is an Agreement?).

On the whole, Turner's position in the debate has prevailed in subsequent judicial treatments of the agreement issue in Section 1 litigation involving oligopolies. Courts consistently have held that conscious parallelism alone does not support an inference of agreement. It bears repeating, however, that judges enjoy substantial discretion to define the elements of behavior that, when added to conscious parallelism, permit the fact finder to conclude that an agreement existed. After reciting the *Theatre Enterprises* admonition that conscious parallelism is not enough, some decisions have gone to great lengths to identify additional behavior from which an inference of agreement might be inferred. And Judge Posner, himself, reignited this debate by reaffirming his views in *In re High Fructose Corn Syrup Antitrust Litigation*, 295 F.3d 651 (7th Cir. 2002)(Posner, J.).

The doctrinal framework established in the progression from *Interstate Circuit* to *Theatre Enterprises*, and in the early information sharing cases discussed in Section C4, *infra*, governed most analysis of agreement issues through the early 1980s and continues to shape counseling and litigation in important respects. In this segment we examine refinements of these analytical approaches in the modern era. The main ingredients of this review are two Supreme Court decisions from the mid–1980s, *Monsanto* and *Matsushita*. In returning to the agreement question in these matters, the Supreme Court reflected both an awareness of developments in the economic literature concerning efforts by competitors to coordinate their activities and a heightened concern about the potential overinclusiveness of certain antitrust rules that forbade agreements as illegal per se. We first examine *Monsanto* and *Matsushita* and then review several recent cases that revisit issues posed in agreement cases from the earlier era.

As we will see in Chapter 4, *Monsanto Co. v. Spray–Rite Service Corp.*, 465 U.S. 752 (1984) reaffirmed the proposition–since abandoned by the Court–that an agreement between a manufacturer and a distributor or retailer to set a minimum price for the resale of its products is illegal per se. More importantly, it focused on the standard of proof that plaintiffs must satisfy when they seek to establish the fact of such an agreement. In a highly influential passage, the Supreme Court observed:

> The correct standard is that there must be evidence that tends to exclude the possibility of independent action by the [parties]. That is, there must be direct or circumstantial evidence that reasonably tends to prove that [the parties] had a conscious commitment to a common scheme designed to achieve an unlawful objective.

465 U.S. at 768.

The *Monsanto* Court was seeking to protect the principle of *Sylvania* (Casebook, Chapter 4, *infra*) that non-price vertical agreements must be judged by a rule of reason. With this aim in mind, the Court attempted to frame the agreement standard in a manner that would preclude courts from inferring unlawful minimum resale price maintenance ("RPM") arrangements, which were illegal per se at the time, when a manufacturer and its retailers exchanged information that arguably was relevant to the adoption of non-price restraints, which are judged by a rule of reason standard. *Monsanto* rejected the view, adopted by the court of appeals, that an unlawful RPM agreement could be inferred from proof of a sequence that consisted simply of complaints from a retailer about a discounting competitor followed by the manufacturer's termination of the discounter. Although the Court found that the plaintiff (Spray–Rite) had satisfied its elevated standard of proof, *Monsanto* enhanced the burden that future plaintiffs would face in proving minimum RPM agreements. *Monsanto* will be discussed again in Chapter 4. At this juncture it is important to consider its holding briefly in order to appreciate its influence on our next case, *Matsushita*, which was decided two years later. In *Matsushita*, the Court extended *Monsanto*'s formulation of the agreement requirement to certain horizontal arrangements. The majority opinion was authored by Justice Lewis F. Powell, who also authored the Court's opinion in *Monsanto*.

MATSUSHITA ELECTRIC INDUSTRIAL CO. v. ZENITH RADIO CORP.
United States Supreme Court, 1986.
475 U.S. 574, 106 S.Ct. 1348, 89 L.Ed.2d 538.

Justice POWELL delivered the opinion of the Court.

This case requires that we again consider the standard district courts must apply when deciding whether to grant summary judgment in an antitrust conspiracy case.

I

* * *

A.

Petitioners, defendants below, are 21 corporations that manufacture or sell "consumer electronic products" (CEPs)–for the most part, television sets. Petitioners include both Japanese manufacturers of CEPs and American firms, controlled by Japanese parents, that sell the Japanese-manufactured products. Respondents, plaintiffs below, are Zenith Radio Corporation (Zenith) and National Union Electric Corporation (NUE). Zenith is an American firm that manufactures and sells television sets. NUE is the corporate successor to Emerson Radio Company, an American firm that manufactured and sold television sets until 1970, when it withdrew from the market after sustaining substantial losses. Zenith and NUE began this lawsuit in 1974, claiming that petitioners had illegally conspired to drive American firms from the American CEP market. According to respondents, the gist of this conspiracy was a " 'scheme to raise, fix and maintain artificially *high* prices for television receivers sold by [petitioners] in Japan and, at the same time, to fix and maintain *low* prices for television receivers exported to and sold in the United States.' " These "low prices" were allegedly at levels that produced substantial losses for petitioners. The conspiracy allegedly began as early as 1953, and according to respondents was in full operation by sometime in the late 1960's. * * *

After several years of detailed discovery, petitioners filed motions for summary judgment on all claims against them. The District Court directed the parties to file, with preclusive effect, "Final Pretrial Statements" listing all the documentary evidence that would be offered if the case proceeded to trial. Respondents filed such a statement, and petitioners responded with a series of motions challenging the admissibility of respondents' evidence. In three detailed opinions, the District Court found the bulk of the evidence on which Zenith and NUE relied inadmissible.

The District Court then turned to petitioners' motions for summary judgment. In an opinion spanning 217 pages, the court found that the admissible evidence did not raise a genuine issue of material fact as to the existence of the alleged conspiracy. * * *

B.

The Court of Appeals for the Third Circuit reversed. * * *

We granted certiorari to determine (i) whether the Court of Appeals applied the proper standards in evaluating the District Court's decision to grant petitioners' motion for summary judgment, and (ii) whether petitioners could be held liable under the antitrust laws for a conspiracy in part compelled by a foreign sovereign. We reverse on the first issue, but do not reach the second.

II

We begin by emphasizing what respondents' claim is *not*. Respondents cannot recover antitrust damages based solely on an alleged cartelization of the Japanese market, because American antitrust laws do not regulate the competitive conditions of other nations' economies. Nor can respondents recover damages for any conspiracy by petitioners to charge higher than competitive prices in the American market. Such conduct would indeed violate the Sherman Act, *United States v. Trenton Potteries Co.*, 273 U.S. 392, 47 S.Ct. 377 (1927); *United States v. Socony–Vacuum Oil Co.*, 310 U.S. 150, 223, 60 S.Ct. 811, 844 (1940), but it could not injure respondents: as petitioners' competitors, respondents stand to gain from any conspiracy to raise the market price in CEPs. Finally, for the same reason, respondents cannot recover for a conspiracy to impose nonprice restraints that have the effect of either raising market price or limiting output. Such restrictions, though harmful to competition, actually *benefit* competitors by making supracompetitive pricing more attractive. * * *

Respondents nevertheless argue that these supposed conspiracies, if not themselves grounds for recovery of antitrust damages, are circumstantial evidence of another conspiracy that *is* cognizable: a conspiracy to monopolize the American market by means of pricing below the market level. The thrust of respondents' argument is that petitioners used their monopoly profits from the Japanese market to fund a concerted campaign to price predatorily and thereby drive respondents and other American manufacturers of CEPs out of business. Once successful, according to respondents, petitioners would cartelize the American CEP market, restricting output and raising prices above the level that fair competition would produce. The resulting monopoly profits, respondents contend, would more than compensate petitioners for the losses they incurred through years of pricing below market level.

The Court of Appeals found that respondents' allegation of a horizontal conspiracy to engage in predatory pricing, if proved, would be a *per se* violation of § 1 of the Sherman Act. Petitioners did not appeal from that conclusion. The issue in this case thus becomes whether respondents adduced sufficient evidence in support of their theory to survive summary judgment. We therefore examine the principles that govern the summary judgment determination.

III

To survive petitioners' motion for summary judgment, respondents must establish that there is a genuine issue of material fact as to whether petitioners entered into an illegal conspiracy that caused respondents to suffer a cognizable injury. Fed.Rule Civ.Proc. 56(e). * * * This showing has two components. First, respondents must show more than a conspiracy in violation of the antitrust laws; they must show an injury to them resulting from the illegal conduct. Respondents charge petitioners with a whole host of conspiracies in restraint of trade. Except for the alleged conspiracy to monopolize the American market through predatory pricing, these alleged conspiracies could not have caused respondents to suffer an "antitrust injury," * * * because they actually tended to benefit respondents. Therefore, unless, in context, evidence of these "other" conspiracies raises a genuine issue concerning the existence of a predatory pricing conspiracy, that evidence cannot defeat petitioners' summary judgment motion.

Second, the issue of fact must be "genuine." Fed.Rules Civ.Proc. 56(c), (e). * * * Where the record taken as a whole could not lead a rational trier of fact to find for the non-moving party, there is no "genuine issue for trial."

It follows from these settled principles that if the factual context renders respondents' claim implausible—if the claim is one that simply makes no economic sense—respondents must come forward with more persuasive evidence to support their claim than would otherwise be necessary. * * *

Respondents correctly note that "[o]n summary judgment the inferences to be drawn from the underlying facts ... must be viewed in the light most favorable to the party opposing the motion." But antitrust law limits the range of permissible inferences from ambiguous evidence in a § 1 case. Thus, in *Monsanto Co. v. Spray–Rite Service Corp.*, 465 U.S. 752, 104 S.Ct. 1464 (1984), we held that conduct as consistent with permissible competition as with illegal conspiracy does not, standing alone, support an inference of antitrust conspiracy. To survive a motion for summary judgment or for a directed verdict, a plaintiff seeking damages for a violation of § 1 must present evidence "that tends to exclude the possibility" that the alleged conspirators acted independently. 465 U.S., at 764, 104 S.Ct., at 1471. Respondents in this case, in other words, must show that the inference of conspiracy is reasonable in light of the competing inferences of independent action or collusive action that could not have harmed respondents.

Petitioners argue that these principles apply fully to this case. According to petitioners, the alleged conspiracy is one that is economically irrational and practically infeasible. Consequently, petitioners contend, they had no motive to engage in the alleged predatory pricing conspiracy; indeed, they had a strong motive *not* to conspire in the manner respondents allege. Petitioners argue that, in light of the absence of any apparent motive and the ambiguous nature of the evidence of conspiracy, no trier of fact reasonably could find that the conspiracy with which petitioners are charged actually existed. This argument requires us to consider the nature of the alleged conspiracy and the practical obstacles to its implementation.

IV

A.

A predatory pricing conspiracy is by nature speculative. Any agreement to price below the competitive level requires the conspirators to forgo profits that free competition would offer them. The forgone profits may be considered an investment in the future. For the investment to be rational, the conspirators must have a reasonable expectation of recovering, in the form of later monopoly profits, more than the losses suffered. * * * [T]he success of such schemes is inherently uncertain: the short-run loss is definite, but the long-run gain depends on successfully neutralizing the competition. Moreover, it is not enough simply to achieve monopoly power, as monopoly pricing may breed quick entry by new competitors eager to share in the excess profits. The success of any predatory scheme depends on *maintaining* monopoly power for long enough both to recoup the predator's losses and to harvest some additional gain. Absent some assurance that the hoped-for monopoly will materialize, *and* that it can be sustained for a significant period of time, "[t]he predator must make a substantial investment with no assurance that it will pay off." For this reason, there is a consensus among commentators that predatory pricing schemes are rarely tried, and even more rarely successful.

These observations apply even to predatory pricing by a *single firm* seeking monopoly power. In this case, respondents allege that a large number of firms have conspired over a period of many years to charge below-market prices in order to stifle competition. Such a conspiracy is incalculably more difficult to execute than an analogous plan undertaken by a single predator. The conspirators must allocate the losses to be sustained during the conspiracy's operation, and must also allocate any gains to be realized from its success. Precisely because success is speculative and depends on a willingness to endure losses for an indefinite period, each conspirator has a strong incentive to cheat, letting its partners suffer the losses necessary to destroy the competition while sharing in any gains if the conspiracy succeeds. The necessary allocation is therefore difficult to accomplish. Yet if conspirators cheat to any substantial extent, the conspiracy must fail, because its success depends on depressing the market price for *all* buyers of CEPs. If there are too few goods at the artificially low price to satisfy demand, the would-be victims of the conspiracy can continue to sell at the "real" market price, and the conspirators suffer losses to little purpose.

Finally, if predatory pricing conspiracies are generally unlikely to occur, they are especially so where, as here, the prospects of attaining monopoly power seem slight. In order to recoup their losses, petitioners must obtain enough market power to set higher than competitive prices, and then must sustain those prices long enough to earn in excess profits what they earlier gave up in below-cost prices. Two decades after their conspiracy is alleged to have commenced, petitioners appear to be far from achieving this goal: the two largest shares of the retail market in television sets are held by RCA and respondent Zenith, not by any of petitioners. * * * Moreover, those shares, which together approximate 40% of sales, did not decline appreciably during the 1970's. Petitioners' collective share rose rapidly during this period, from one-fifth or less of the relevant markets to close to 50%. Neither the District Court nor the Court of Appeals found, however, that petitioners' share presently allows them to charge monopoly prices; to the contrary, respondents contend that the conspiracy is ongoing—that petitioners are still artificially *depressing* the market price in order to drive Zenith out of the market. The data in the record strongly suggest that that goal is yet far distant.

The alleged conspiracy's failure to achieve its ends in the two decades of its asserted operation is strong evidence that the conspiracy does not in fact exist. Since the losses in such a conspiracy accrue before the gains, they must be "repaid" with interest. And because the alleged losses have accrued over the course of two decades, the conspirators could well require a correspondingly long time to recoup. Maintaining supracompetitive prices in turn depends on the continued cooperation of the conspirators, on the inability of other would-be competitors to enter the market, and (not incidentally) on the conspirators' ability to escape antitrust liability for their *minimum* price-fixing cartel.[16] Each of these factors weighs more heavily as the time needed to

16. The alleged predatory scheme makes sense only if petitioners can recoup their loss- es. In light of the large number of firms involved here, petitioners can achieve this only

recoup losses grows. If the losses have been substantial—as would likely be necessary in order to drive out the competition[17]—petitioners would most likely have to sustain their cartel for years simply to break even.

Nor does the possibility that petitioners have obtained supracompetitive profits in the Japanese market change this calculation. Whether or not petitioners have the *means* to sustain substantial losses in this country over a long period of time, they have no *motive* to sustain such losses absent some strong likelihood that the alleged conspiracy in this country will eventually pay off. The courts below found no evidence of any such success, and—as indicated above—the facts actually are to the contrary: RCA and Zenith, not any of the petitioners, continue to hold the largest share of the American retail market in color television sets. More important, there is nothing to suggest any relationship between petitioners' profits in Japan and the amount petitioners could expect to gain from a conspiracy to monopolize the American market. In the absence of any such evidence, the possible existence of supracompetitive profits in Japan simply cannot overcome the economic obstacles to the ultimate success of this alleged predatory conspiracy.[18]

B.

In *Monsanto*, we emphasized that courts should not permit factfinders to infer conspiracies when such inferences are implausible, because the effect of such practices is often to deter procompetitive conduct. Respondents, petitioners' competitors, seek to hold petitioners liable for damages caused by the alleged conspiracy to cut prices. Moreover, they seek to establish this conspiracy indirectly, through evidence of other combinations * * * whose natural tendency is to raise prices, and through evidence of rebates and other price-cutting activities that respondents argue tend to prove a combination to suppress prices.[19] But cutting prices in order to increase business often is the very essence of competition. Thus, mistaken inferences in cases such as this one are especially costly, because they chill the very conduct the antitrust

by engaging in some form of price fixing *after* they have succeeded in driving competitors from the market. Such price fixing would, of course, be an independent violation of § 1 of the Sherman Act. *United States v. Socony–Vacuum Oil Co.,* 310 U.S. 150, 60 S.Ct. 811 (1940).

17. The predators' losses must actually *increase* as the conspiracy nears its objective: the greater the predators' market share, the more products the predators sell; but since every sale brings with it a loss, an increase in market share also means an increase in predatory losses.

18. The same is true of any supposed excess production capacity that petitioners may have possessed. The existence of plant capacity that exceeds domestic demand does tend to establish the ability to sell products abroad. It does not, however, provide a motive for selling at prices lower than necessary to obtain sales; nor does it explain why petitioners would be willing to *lose* money in the United States

market without some reasonable prospect of recouping their investment.

19. Respondents also rely on an expert study suggesting that petitioners have sold their products in the American market at substantial losses. The relevant study is not based on actual cost data; rather, it consists of expert opinion based on a mathematical construction that in turn rests on assumptions about petitioners' costs. The District Court analyzed those assumptions in some detail and found them both implausible and inconsistent with record evidence. Although the Court of Appeals reversed the District Court's finding that the expert report was inadmissible, the court did not disturb the District Court's analysis of the factors that substantially undermine the probative value of that evidence. We find the District Court's analysis persuasive. Accordingly, in our view the expert opinion evidence of below-cost pricing has little probative value in comparison with the economic factors * * * that suggest that such conduct is irrational.

laws are designed to protect. "[W]e must be concerned lest a rule or precedent that authorizes a search for a particular type of undesirable pricing behavior end up by discouraging legitimate price competition."

In most cases, this concern must be balanced against the desire that illegal conspiracies be identified and punished. That balance is, however, unusually one-sided in cases such as this one. As we earlier explained, predatory pricing schemes require conspirators to suffer losses in order eventually to realize their illegal gains; moreover, the gains depend on a host of uncertainties, making such schemes more likely to fail than to succeed. These economic realities tend to make predatory pricing conspiracies self-deterring: unlike most other conduct that violates the antitrust laws, failed predatory pricing schemes are costly to the conspirators. Finally, unlike predatory pricing by a single firm, *successful* predatory pricing conspiracies involving a large number of firms can be identified and punished once they succeed, since some form of minimum price-fixing agreement would be necessary in order to reap the benefits of predation. Thus, there is little reason to be concerned that by granting summary judgment in cases where the evidence of conspiracy is speculative or ambiguous, courts will encourage such conspiracies.

V

* * * [P]etitioners had no motive to enter into the alleged conspiracy. To the contrary, as presumably rational businesses, petitioners had every incentive *not* to engage in the conduct with which they are charged, for its likely effect would be to generate losses for petitioners with no corresponding gains. The Court of Appeals did not take account of the absence of a plausible motive to enter into the alleged predatory pricing conspiracy. It focused instead on whether there was "direct evidence of concert of action." The Court of Appeals erred in two respects: (i) the "direct evidence" on which the court relied had little, if any, relevance to the alleged predatory pricing conspiracy; and (ii) the court failed to consider the absence of a plausible motive to engage in predatory pricing.

The "direct evidence" on which the court relied was evidence of *other* combinations, not of a predatory pricing conspiracy. Evidence that petitioners conspired to raise prices in Japan provides little, if any, support for respondents' claims: a conspiracy to increase profits in one market does not tend to show a conspiracy to sustain losses in another. Evidence that petitioners agreed to fix *minimum* prices * * * for the American market actually works in petitioners' favor, because it suggests that petitioners were seeking to place a floor under prices rather than to lower them. The same is true of evidence that petitioners agreed to limit the number of distributors of their products in the American * * *. That practice may have facilitated a horizontal territorial allocation, see *United States v. Topco Associates, Inc.*, 405 U.S. 596, 92 S.Ct. 1126, but its natural effect would be to raise market prices rather than reduce them. Evidence that tends to support any of these collateral conspiracies thus says little, if anything, about the existence of a conspiracy to charge below-market prices in the American market over a period of two decades.

That being the case, the absence of any plausible motive to engage in the conduct charged is highly relevant to whether a "genuine issue for trial" exists within the meaning of Rule 56(e). Lack of motive bears on the range of permissible conclusions that might be drawn from ambiguous evidence: if petitioners had no rational economic motive to conspire, and if their conduct is consistent with other, equally plausible explanations, the conduct does not give rise to an inference of conspiracy. Here, the conduct in question consists largely of (i) pricing at levels that succeeded in taking business away from respondents, and (ii) arrangements that may have limited petitioners' ability to compete with each other (and thus kept prices from going even lower). This conduct suggests either that petitioners behaved competitively, or that petitioners conspired to *raise* prices. Neither possibility is consistent with an agreement among 21 companies to price below-market levels. Moreover, the predatory pricing scheme that this conduct is said to prove is one that makes no practical sense: it calls for petitioners to destroy companies larger and better established than themselves, a goal that remains far distant more than two decades after the conspiracy's birth. Even had they succeeded in obtaining their monopoly, there is nothing in the record to suggest that they could recover the losses they would need to sustain along the way. In sum, in light of the absence of any rational motive to conspire, neither petitioners' pricing practices, nor their conduct in the Japanese market, nor their agreements respecting prices and distribution in the American market, suffice to create a "genuine issue for trial." Fed.Rule Civ.Proc. 56(e).[21]

On remand, the Court of Appeals is free to consider whether there is other evidence that is sufficiently unambiguous to permit a trier of fact to find that petitioners conspired to price predatorily for two decades despite the absence of any apparent motive to do so. The evidence must "ten[d] to exclude the possibility" that petitioners underpriced respondents to compete for business rather than to implement an economically senseless conspiracy. *Monsanto,* 465 U.S., at 764, 104 S.Ct., at 1471. In the absence of such evidence, there is no "genuine issue for trial" under Rule 56(e), and petitioners are entitled to have summary judgment reinstated.

* * *

[Dissenting opinion of Justices WHITE, BRENNAN, BLACKMUN, and STEVENS omitted.]

———

As in *Monsanto*, the Court's analysis of the agreement issue in *Matsushita* tried to reduce error costs associated with overly broad application of substantive liability standards. In *Matsushita* the alleged horizontal conspiracy consisted of a two-part concerted scheme by Japanese producers of consumer electronic equipment to price above costs in Japan, to use supra-competitive profits from the cartel in Japan to cross-subsidize collusive efforts to set prices at predatorily low levels in the United States, and later to raise prices above competitive levels in the United States once U.S. manufacturers had

---

21. We do not imply that, if petitioners had had a plausible reason to conspire, ambiguous conduct could suffice to create a triable issue of conspiracy. Our decision in *Monsanto Co. v. Spray–Rite Service Corp.,* 465 U.S. 752, 104 S.Ct. 1464 (1984), establishes that conduct that is as consistent with permissible competition as with illegal conspiracy does not, without more, support even an inference of conspiracy. *Id.,* at 763–764, 104 S.Ct., at 1470.

left the market. In such a setting, the Court emphasized that mistaken inferences of conspiracy could injure consumers by deterring firms from offering low prices.

At first glance, *Matsushita* might seem to have relatively limited application for Section 1 agreement jurisprudence. Few horizontal conspiracy cases allege that the defendants conspired to set prices below cost. The common horizontal restraint claim, as in the lysine and vitamins cartel prosecutions, argues that the defendants colluded to raise prices or restrict output–conduct that, unlike the asserted below cost pricing cartel in *Matsushita*, offers consumers fewer benefits and therefore might be subject to more lenient standards of proof. The caution mandated by *Matsushita* might not be warranted where the challenged behavior poses greater dangers to the competitive process and enforcement false positives are less likely to harm society. But *Matsushita*, as we will see later in this Chapter in *Blomkest*, (Casebook, *infra* at 311) has not been limited to its facts and instead has been read broadly in subsequent lower court decisions and by the Supreme Court, as is discussed in the Note following Sidebar 3–3. Sidebar 3–3 provides some additional insight into *Matsushita*.

Sidebar 3–3:
Matsushita–Perspectives From the
Marshall Papers

The papers of Justice Thurgood Marshall reveal that *Matsushita*, one of the most important pro-defendant Supreme Court decisions of the 1980s, very nearly was a plaintiff's victory.

After the Third Circuit reversed the district court's grant of summary judgment in 1983, the defendants filed a petition for certiorari with the Supreme Court. On April 1, 1985, the Court granted certiorari, but soon had second thoughts. The dispute's factual complexity and voluminous record–circumstances ultimately detailed in Justice Powell's majority opinion, excerpted above–daunted several members of the Court. By mid-June 1985, several justices seemed to conclude that the case was "factbound"–a decision so heavily dependent on idiosyncratic facts that it was poorly suited to serve as a vehicle for the Court to state principles of general application for future disputes. During a meeting on June 13, 1985, and in correspondence among the justices, the Court considered whether to "dismiss certiorari as improvidently granted" (or, in the Court's jargon, "DIG" the case). Fearing that a decision to DIG the case might create confusion about why the Court changed direction, the Court proceeded to hear argument and decide the matter.

Oral argument took place on November 12, 1985. The Marshall papers indicate that, soon after oral argument, five members of the court (Justices Blackmun, Brennan, Marshall, Stevens, and White) voted either to affirm the decision of the Third Circuit or to dismiss the original grant of certiorari as improvidently granted. Either outcome would have vindicated the plaintiffs by leaving in place the decision of the court of appeals. By the week's end, however, the alignment had changed. In a letter of November 15, 1985, Justice Marshall told Chief Justice Burger that "I have reexamined my position in this case and would like to change my vote from Affirm to Reverse." Informed of the switch in Justice Marshall's vote, Justice Powell proceeded to draft the majority opinion that would be joined by the Chief Justice and Justices Marshall, O'Connor, and Rehnquist.

Why did Justice Marshall change his vote and transform what had shaped up as a 5–4 plaintiff's victory into a 5–4 defendant's triumph? Perhaps it was simply the second thoughts of a Justice whose past decisions occasionally had revealed skepticism about the proper scope of antitrust private treble damage actions. Justice Marshall, after all, previously had authored the *Brunswick* decision (Casebook, Chapter 1, *supra*) and constructed the modern antitrust injury test for private cases. Maybe it was the interaction with colleagues who believed the Third Circuit's decision was misguided. A further possibility, indicated in the Marshall papers, is that one of Justice Marshall's law clerks played a major role in persuading him to change his vote. Justice Marshall's papers contain a bench memorandum prepared by his clerk for oral argument. The bench memorandum presents the argument that ultimately formed the core of Justice Powell's opinion. It is conceivable that the clerk continued to discuss the matter with his boss and finally persuaded him that the defendants had the better argument.

The Marshall papers on *Matsushita* raise interesting questions about what motivates a jurist's exercise of discretion in deciding cases. Is the dominant force a world view shaped by education and experience? Is it the quality of advocacy by the parties, especially their skill in writing briefs that assemble strong arguments and authorities for a favored proposition? For multi-member courts, is it the interaction with colleagues and the persuasiveness and personal appeal of individual tribunal members? Or is it the perspectives of the clerks whom the judge hires to assist in handling the tasks of chambers? The Marshall papers suggest that answering the larger question of why judges decide cases as they do can be terribly be complicated, and the solution may appear from directions that are hardly obvious to the observer who focuses solely on published decisions for clues.

Note on the Evolution of Attitudes at the Supreme Court About Burdens of Pleading and Production in Antitrust Cases: From Conley and Poller to Matsushita and Twombly

Matsushita invited district court judges to conduct a preliminary assessment of the economic plausibility of a plaintiff's evidence of conspiracy at the summary judgment stage of litigation. If the plaintiff is incapable of producing evidence that would "tend to exclude the possibility" of unilateral conduct, the Court indicates that summary judgment is warranted.

Before *Matsushita*, the Court had long held that "summary procedures should be used sparingly in complex antitrust litigation where motive and intent play leading roles, the proof is largely in the hands of the alleged conspirators, and hostile witnesses thicken the plot." *Poller v. Columbia Broadcasting System, Inc*, 368 U.S. 464, 473 (1962). *Poller* thus viewed summary judgment as a disfavored procedure. *Matsushita* marked a clear departure from this attitude and in effect abrogated *Poller*.

As one of three landmark summary judgment cases decided by the Court during its 1985–86 term, *Matsushita* reflected the Court's general interest in re-invigorating use of summary judgment under Federal Rule of Civil Procedure 56, especially by defendants. *See also Celotex Corp. v. Catrett*, 477 U.S. 317 (1986); *Anderson v. Liberty Lobby, Inc.*, 477 U.S. 242 (1986). Collectively, these three cases evidenced serious concern on the part of the Court with increased case loads, increased litigation costs, *in terrorem* settlements, and inadequately aggressive case management by district court judges. In the antitrust area, *Matsushita* greatly expanded the use of summary judgment, which in turn focused a great deal of the effort that goes into antitrust litigation on preparation for and possible disposition of the case through summary judgment.

The Supreme Court has now extended *Matsushita*'s plausibility screen backwards to the pleading stage of litigation. *See Bell Atlantic Corp. v. Twombly*, ___ U.S. ___, 127 S.Ct. 1955 (2007). The defendants in *Twombly* were five large local telephone companies, all once part of AT & T before that company was broken up in 1984, which collectively accounted for the vast majority of local telephone service in the United States. Under the terms of the Telecommunications Act of 1996, the defendants are sometimes termed "Incumbent Local Exchange Carriers" (ILECs). To foster competition, the Act compelled ILECs to open their previously government-sanctioned monopolies over local telephone service to competition from so-called "Competitive Local Exchange Carriers" (CLECs) by allowing CLECs to connect to their local networks in various ways. ILECs could themselves become CLECs by entering the territory of another ILEC.

The proposed plaintiff class of consumers alleged that the ILECs conspired in two ways that had the effect of inflating the charges for local telephone and high-speed Internet access services. First, they acted in parallel to impede entry and expansion of services by CLECs, as by making it costly and cumbersome for them to interconnect with the ILECs' telephone networks and providing them with poor quality connections. Second, the ILECs allegedly entered into agreements not to compete with one another in their historical territories (a market division agreement). The complaint alleged that such agreements could be inferred from the ILECs' failure to pursue attractive business opportunities in contiguous markets where they had "substantial competitive advantages," and from the public statement of an ILEC officer "that competing in the territory of another ILEC 'might be a good way to turn a quick dollar but that doesn't make it right.' " 127 S. Ct. at 1962 (quoting the complaint). The lengthy complaint culminated in the following allegation:

> In the absence of any meaningful competition between the [ILECs] in one another's markets, and in light of the parallel course of conduct that each engaged in to prevent competition from CLECs within their respective local telephone and/or high speed internet services markets and the other facts and market circumstances alleged above, Plaintiffs allege upon information and belief that [the ILECs] have entered into a contract, combination or conspiracy to prevent competitive entry in their respective local telephone and/or high speed internet services markets and have agreed not to compete with one another and otherwise allocated customers and markets to one another.

127 S. Ct. at 1962–63.

The district court dismissed the plaintiffs' complaint for failure to state a claim of conspiracy pursuant to Federal Rule of Civil Procedure 12(b)(6), primarily because in its view the complaint alleged only conscious parallelism and did not include allegations of sufficient "plus factors" to permit the inference of an agreement from circumstantial evidence. The appellate court reversed on the ground that the Federal Rules do not impose a heightened pleading standard on claims of antitrust conspiracy, as they do for fraud under Federal Rule 9(b). All that is needed, according to the circuit court, is "a short and plain statement of the claim showing that the pleader is entitled to relief." Fed. R. Civ. P. 8(a). In the case of claims of antitrust conspiracy, the appellate court held, "the factual predicate that is pleaded does need to include conspiracy among the realm of plausible possibilities," *Twombly v. Bell Atlantic Corp.*, 425 F.3d 99, 111 (2d Cir. 2005), but it does not require that the plaintiff also plead specific plus factors. *Id.* at 114. The appeals panel also concluded that in requiring the plaintiff to allege more, the district court had improperly applied the standard developed in *Matsushita* for reviewing a motion for summary judgment to decide whether a claim of conspiracy had been properly alleged. The district court also ignored the possibility that the plaintiff may not be required to establish plus factors at all at trial if, for example, it can prove conspiracy directly. *Id.*

In a 7–2 decision, the Supreme Court reversed, and in doing so modified the longstanding interpretation of one of the rules of civil procedure. For fifty years before *Twombly*, the Court had interpreted the "short and plain statement" language of Rule 8(a)(2) of the Federal Rules of Civil Procedure very permissively, as did the court of appeals. The Rule, in the Court's view, embodied the policy of "notice pleading" and contemplated that complete development of the plaintiff's allegations should be reserved for discovery. In its watershed decision in *Conley v. Gibson*, 355 U.S. 41 (1957), the Court had held that "a complaint should not be dismissed for failure to state a claim unless it appears beyond doubt that the plaintiff can prove no set of facts in support of his claim which would entitle him to relief." *Id.* at 45–46. Although *Conley* was a civil rights, not an antitrust case, *Conley* had the general effect of discouraging motions to dismiss for failure to state a claim under Federal Rule 12(b)(6), just as *Poller* had discouraged summary judgment in antitrust cases.

In an opinion authored by Justice David Souter, the majority reversed, specifically abrogating *Conley's* "no set of facts" standard. 127 S. Ct. at 1968–69. It reiterated the principle that conscious parallelism alone is insufficient to establish antitrust conspiracy, expressly extending *Matsushita's* plausibility test to the pleading stage. *Id.* at 1964–65. At the pleading stage, it explained, the plausibility standard "simply calls for enough fact to raise a reasonable expectation that discovery will reveal evidence of illegal agreement." *Id.* at 1965. "[A]n allegation of parallel conduct and a bare assertion of conspiracy will not suffice." *Id.* at 1966. The Court concluded by insisting that it was not requiring particularized pleadings: "we do not require heightened fact pleading of specifics, but only enough facts to state a claim to relief that is plausible on its face. Because the plaintiffs here have not nudged their claims across the line from conceivable to plausible, their complaint must be dismissed." *Id.* at 1974.

Justice Stevens, joined by Justice Ginsburg, dissented from the majority's opinion. Agreeing that parallel conduct alone is insufficient to establish antitrust conspiracy, Stevens nevertheless concluded that under the Court's "well-settled" procedural law the plaintiff's complaint was adequate to state a claim for conspiracy. *Id.* at 1975. Rather than accepting those allegations as true, the dissent emphasized, the majority dismissed the complaint in advance of the filing of an answer, even though the allegations of agreement have "not even been denied." *Id.* at 1974. The Court's "dramatic departure from settled procedural law" was driven by its concerns with (1) the expense of private antitrust litigation, and (2) the potential that jurors will mistakenly equate parallel conduct for conspiracy. *Id*. at 1975. In the dissent's view, however,

> Those concerns merit careful case management, including strict control of discovery, careful scrutiny of evidence at the summary judgment stage, and lucid instructions to juries; they do not, however, justify the dismissal of an adequately pleaded complaint without even requiring the defendants to file answers denying a charge that they in fact engaged in collective decisionmaking. More importantly, they do not justify an interpretation of Federal Rule of Civil Procedure 12(b)(6) that seems to be driven by the majority's appraisal of the plausibility of the ultimate factual allegation rather than its legal sufficiency.

Id. Stevens concluded, expressing his "fear that the unfortunate result of the majority's new pleading rule will be to invite lawyers' debates over economic theory to conclusively resolve antitrust suits in the absence of any evidence." *Id*. at 1988.

As a policy matter, lower pleading standards might be favored because they allow plaintiffs to obtain the information they need to pursue claims they reasonably believe to be meritorious, thus encouraging lawsuits that would vindicate the antitrust laws, compensate victims, and deter anticompetitive conduct. In the specific case of conspiracy, such an approach also recognizes that the best evidence of conspiracy is likely to lie in the hands of the defendants. In contrast, the value of a higher pleading standard lies in weeding out meritless suits that may never uncover plus factors or direct evidence of agreement before they risk generating costly discovery and debilitating diversion of management time, and in reducing the threat that plaintiffs may file suit simply in order to extract settlements (to the extent those suits are not already discouraged by the summary judgment standards). Whereas the two dissenting justices embraced the former argument, the majority of seven viewed the latter arguments as more persuasive. What will be the likely result of encouraging district court judges to differentiate between the "conceivable" and the "plausible"? Does the Court provide much guidance in applying such a distinction?

The combination of *Twombly* and *Matsushita* makes the pursuit of an antitrust claim a costly and challenging undertaking for plaintiffs. Indeed, it is already clear that *Twombly* will not be confined to allegations of conspiracy any more than *Matsushita* was confined to claims of predatory pricing conspiracies. *Twombly* is being invoked by defendants and lower courts to demand more elaborate allegations of all elements of an antitrust claim and is even spreading quickly outside of antitrust.

Do the two cases go too far in responding to the argument that antitrust cases can be very costly for defendants, difficult to comprehend by juries, and hence subject to abuse by plaintiffs seeking unwarranted settlements? Does it seem likely that plaintiffs, enticed by the promise of treble damages and attorneys fees, will lightly undertake the pursuit of a potentially years-long antitrust litigation in the hope of procuring a favorable settlement? Doesn't discovery have significant costs for plaintiffs as well as defendants? And is it very likely that especially weak cases will pose a sufficiently credible threat to extract large settlements given the increasingly favorable standards of substantive antitrust law that have evolved over the last thirty years? It is at least arguable that in the current atmosphere— as opposed to the atmosphere that prevailed until the late 1970s when the per se rule was far more commonly endorsed by the Court—truly innocent defendants are far less likely to be paying out large settlements to avoid the prospect of facing a jury.

The *Twombly* majority presumed that the alleged excesses of antitrust litigation are real, but the citations it offers to support these views are unimpressive from an empirical point of view. There is, in fact, little if any empirical evidence to support these assumptions about antitrust litigation. Neither is there any reason to assume that antitrust cases are any more complex and costly to process than any other kind of major federal litigation. Justice Stevens thus repeatedly faults the majority for relying on "lawyers' arguments" made in briefs and papers in a case where no answer denying conspiracy had even been filed and no evidence had been collected. Do you agree with his argument that even if these concerns are truly acute, Congress or the Federal Rules Advisory Committee are in a better position institutionally to gather objective evidence to assess and address those risks through revisions to the Rules than is the Court?

4. INFORMATION EXCHANGE: AN INTRODUCTION TO FACILITATING PRACTICES

When courts interpret an antitrust law to forbid horizontal agreements to set prices, firms seeking to coordinate their behavior may experiment with "second best" devices that fall short of reaching a consensus on output and prices but that help approximate the result of an express price-fixing arrangement. A number of Sherman Act decisions in the 1920s dealt with agreements by competitors to engage in what commentators later would call "facilitating practices." The era's most prevalent practice consisted of agreements, often reached in the context of a trade association, to share information on matters such as pricing, costs, inventories, and the terms of specific sales transactions. A combination of factors, notably the *Chicago Bd. of Trade* decision in 1918 (Casebook, Chapter 2, *supra*) and encouragement from the Department of Commerce in the early 1920s for the development of information-sharing programs, led companies and entire industries to engage in various forms of cooperation that seemed to stop short of achieving an agreement on prices.

In a series of decisions beginning with two from that era, *American Column & Lumber Co. v. United States*, 257 U.S. 377 (1921) and *Maple Flooring Mfrs.' Ass'n v. United States*, 268 U.S. 563 (1925), the Supreme Court sought to define how Section 1 of the Sherman Act applied to these arrangements. As we shall see, because agreements to share information typically were express, these cases presented what appeared to be two distinct questions: (1) whether an express agreement to share information can provide a basis for inferring an illicit agreement to fix prices (potentially per se unlawful); and (2) whether an express agreement among rivals to exchange information could itself constitute an unreasonable restraint of trade under Section 1 of the Sherman Act (judged under the rule of reason). This seemingly clear differentiating line, however, became blurred in the cases and we will examine why that might be so.

American Column & Lumber involved a trade association comprised of 400 firms with hardwood lumber mills concentrated in the hardwood producing territory of the southwest United States. Although the members operated only 5% of the U.S. mills engaged in hardwood production, they produced one-third of the total national hardwood output. 257 U.S. at 391. Under the association's Open Competition Plan, to which 90% of its members subscribed, the firms were required to provide the association with extensive, detailed data about their businesses. For example, each firm was required to make daily reports to the association's secretary "of all sales actually made, with the name and address of the purchaser, the kind, grade and quality of lumber sold and all special agreements of every kind, very or written with respect thereto" and "a daily shipping report," "with exact copies of all the invoices, special agreements as to terms, grade, etc." *Id.* at 394. Firms were also required to submit monthly production and inventory reports, and current price lists. The reports were subject to audit by association representatives, and the association inspected the stocks of member firms from time to time to ensure consistency of grading across firms. "Plainly" according to the Supreme Court, "it would be very difficult to devise a more minute disclosure of everything connected with one's business than is here provided for by this Plan. * * * " *Id.* at 395.

The association assembled and digested this information, and provided reports to the members in a condensed and interpreted form. Members received weekly reports indicating the prices and sales in every individual transaction of all firms, and all shipments, and monthly reports indicating price lists, production and inventory holdings of all firms. Monthly meetings supplemented these extensive reports. In advance of the meetings, an association statistician compiled and distributed the results of a monthly survey of members indicating the expected future production of all firms. The association also suggested future prices and production levels to each firm every month. These reports went only to hardwood sellers. The information was not made available to buyers.

From the point of view of contemporary economic theory, these reports could be understood as helping the firms reach a consensus on price (as by suggesting prices) and deterring cheating on that consensus (by making secret price-cutting difficult). Moreover, the fact that the information went to sellers (and not to buyers) undermined many possible business justifications for the sharing of information. The Supreme Court majority saw the Open Competition Plan similarly, concluding that the members of the association had indeed "conspired" to fix prices:

> The Plan is, essentially, simply an expansion of the gentleman's agreement of former days, skillfully devised to evade the law. To call it open competition, because the meetings were nominally open to the public, or because some voluminous reports were transmitted to the Department of Justice, or because no specific agreement to restrict trade or fix prices is proved, cannot conceal the fact that the fundamental purpose of the Plan was to procure 'harmonious' individual action among a large number of naturally competing dealers with respect to the volume of production and prices, without having any specific agreement with respect to them * * *.

Id. at 410–11. *See also United States v. American Linseed Oil Co.,* 262 U.S. 371, 389–90 (1923).

In separate dissents, Justices Holmes and Brandeis asked an important question. How can competition be prevented without a binding agreement, *id.* at 412–13 (Holmes, J., dissenting), or without coercion, *id.* at 413–19 (Brandeis, J., dissenting)? Modern economic theory provides an answer. When firms know that their rivals will rapidly detect cheating and respond by also cutting price and expanding output, they may prefer not to compete aggressively, and thus collude tacitly. Justice Brandeis also suggested that the plan benefitted competition by placing small and isolated backwoods producers on a comparable informational footing with larger mills against whom they competed. *Id.* at 416 (Brandeis, J., dissenting).

Four years later, in *Maple Flooring*, the Supreme Court reviewed another information sharing agreement implemented by a trade association. In contrast to *American Column & Lumber*, the Court's analysis did not focus narrowly on the question of "agreement." In part because the government appeared to present its case in the alternative—either the information sharing facilitated an illicit agreement to fix uniform prices or it had undesirable effects itself—the Court did not carefully differentiate the two points. In its view, the case failed for want of proof of uniform pricing, which undermined both of the government's theories. 268 U.S. at 567–68.

The defendants were 22 members of a trade association of lumber and flooring manufacturers, with mills mainly located in Michigan, Minnesota, and Wisconsin. Although there were a number of competing manufacturers who were not members of the association, association members accounted for 70% of the total U.S. production of certain types of wood flooring in one of the subject years. *Id.* at 565–66.

The association's many activities "admittedly beneficial to the industry and to consumers," according to the Court, *id.* at 566, included cooperative advertising and the standardization and improvement of products. The government challenged other activities, however, including the computation and dissemination of aggregated information on price, inventory, and quantity sold, information on average cost of producing all dimensions and grades of flooring, and a booklet showing freight rates on flooring from Cadillac, MI to more than five thousand points of shipment in the United States. The flooring trade association held monthly meetings at which market conditions and input prices were discussed, but not past or future output prices. *Id.* at 566–67.

But unlike the trade association in *American Column & Lumber*, the Court noted that the flooring association did not identify the seller or customer when sharing information on past transactions, did not share current price quotations or information on future plans, and did not make recommendations as to future prices. *Id.* at 573–74. Moreover, the Court observed that the industry statistics gathered and disseminated by the trade association did not "differ in any essential respect from trade or business statistics which are freely gathered and publicly disseminated in numerous branches of industry producing a standardized product.* * * "*Id.* at 574. The Court concluded, therefore, that the agreement to share prices did not violate the Sherman Act, but its analysis did not rest solely on the absence of a price-fixing agreement. It also discussed at length what it viewed as the competitively legitimate purposes of the information exchange and the absence of evidence that it affected costs or prices. *Id.* at 579–86.

As we shall discuss at greater length below, an economist's inquiry about information sharing today would focus on its impact on competition, not on any formal distinction regarding whether it provides circumstantial evidence of a price-fixing agreement or is unreasonable itself. Figure 3–3 below thus compares the key traits of the information-sharing arrangements in *American Column & Lumber* and *Maple Flooring* from a modern economic perspective. Viewed in that way, the information exchange in *Maple Flooring* appears likely to have been substantially less effective in deterring cheating than the information shared in *American Column & Lumber*, notwithstanding that the association members accounted for a much larger share of the market in the flooring case (70% as compared with 33% in the lumber case). Detection of cheating would be more difficult after the information exchange, as the flooring firms would have to infer cheating by rivals from aggregated industry-wide information. In theory, however, the shared information about average costs and freight rates might help the firms reach a consensus by making one set of prices natural and obvious ("focal") in the event actual freight rates varied substantially from firm to firm. Although the government made this argument, *see* 268 U.S. at 572, the Supreme Court found instead that the firms had a legitimate business justification for sharing freight rate information:

> * * * [T]here were delays in securing quotations of freight rates from the local agents of carriers in towns in which the factories of defendants are located, which seriously interfered with prompt quotations of delivered prices to customers; that the actual aggregate difference between local freight rates for most of defendants' mills and the rate appearing in defendants' freight rate book based on rates at Cadillac, Mich., were so small as to be only nominal, and that the freight rate book served a useful and legitimate purpose in enabling members to quote promptly a delivered price on their product by adding to their mill price a previously calculated freight rate which approximated closely to the actual rate from their own mill town.

Id. at 571.

The Court also defended the exchange of accurate information about business conditions among industry participants, sellers and buyers, as likely to facilitate the efficient adjustment of production levels to market conditions:

> * * * [T]he making available of such information tends to stabilize trade and industry, to produce fairer price levels and to avoid the waste which inevitably attends the unintelligent conduct of economic enterprise. 'Free competition' means a free and open market among both buyers and sellers for the sale and distribution of commodities. Competition does not become less free merely because the conduct of commercial operations becomes more intelligent through the free distribution of knowledge of all the essential factors entering into the commercial transaction.

Id. at 583.

Had the information exchange in this case been shown to be "the basis of agreement or concerted action to lessen production arbitrarily or to raise prices beyond the levels of production and price which would prevail if no such agreement or concerted action ensued," as in *American Column & Lumber*, it would have been enjoined. *Id.* at 587. But, as noted above, the

Court held that the practices of the flooring trade association did not meet the requirements set out in *American Column & Lumber* and other decisions of the Court. *See also Sugar Inst., Inc. v. United States,* 297 U.S. 553, 598 (1936); *Cement Mfrs.' Protective Ass'n v. United States,* 268 U.S. 588, 602–03, 606 (1925).

Figure 3–3:

**Information Sharing: *American Column Lumber*
and *Maple Flooring* Compared**

***American Column & Lumber* (1921)**	***Maple Flooring* (1925)**
• Members' market share: 33%	• Members' market share: 70%
• Type of information disseminated by Association (monthly or weekly):	• Type of information disseminated by Association (at least monthly):

• Current price lists
   • Output data
   • Inventory data
   • Data for each sale, including quantity, price, and buyer
	• Past sales (no current prices)
	   • Output data
	   • Inventory data
	   • No data on purchasers

• Form in which data was disseminated: Company by company.	• Form in which data was disseminated: Aggregated on Association-wide basis (specific sellers not identified).
• Distribution of data: To Association members only.	• Distribution of data: Made available to public.
• Commentary on trends: Reports to members proposed future output and pricing levels.	• Commentary on trends: No effort to propose future output or pricing levels.
• Meetings: Members met monthly or weekly by area for "discussion of all subjects of interest."	• Meetings: Members met regularly, but no record evidence that meetings were occasions to fix prices.
• Effects Evidence: Information exchanges raised prices.	• Effects Evidence: No evidence that information exchanges raised prices.
	• Freight book: Provided rates on shipment of flooring from Cadillac, MI to over 5000 destinations in United States.
	• No evidence in record that rate book was used to fix prices.

American Column & Lumber, and to a significant extent *Maple Flooring,* both focused on whether the information exchanges at issue could provide a reasonable basis for inferring an illicit agreement to fix prices. Courts continue to face that question, *i.e.,* whether the exchange of certain types of information by rivals can fairly be viewed as circumstantial evidence—a "plus factor"—that tends to prove the existence of an agreement to fix prices. If proven, such an agreement to fix prices likely would be treated as per se unlawful.

In our next case, the plaintiff pointed to a number of alleged plus factors in an attempt to prove that the principal U.S. cigarette manufacturers conspired to fix prices. The excerpt focuses solely on the court's discussion of an information exchange plan that they collectively implemented. As you read the excerpt from the court's opinion, consider whether the court correctly analyzes the information exchange evidence from contemporary legal and economic perspectives. In particular, consider whether the court considers how information exchanges can help rivals to solve their cartel problems. Also note (1) the influence of the Supreme Court's *Matsushita* decision; and (2) the court's treatment of the testimony proffered by the plaintiff through its economic expert.

WILLIAMSON OIL CO., INC. v. PHILIP MORRIS USA
United States Court of Appeals for the Eleventh Circuit, 2003.
346 F.3d 1287.

MARCUS, Circuit Judge:

This is an antitrust action brought pursuant to section 1 of the Sherman Act * * * by a class of several hundred cigarette wholesalers ("the class" or "the wholesalers") against Philip Morris, Inc. ("PM"), R.J. Reynolds Tobacco Co. ("RJR"), Brown & Williamson Tobacco Corp. ("B & W") and Lorillard Tobacco Co. ("Lorillard") (collectively "the manufacturers"). The class alleges that the manufacturers conspired between 1993 and 2000 to fix cigarette prices at unnaturally high levels, and that this collusion resulted in wholesale list price overcharges of nearly $12 billion. The district court ultimately entered summary judgment in favor of the manufacturers. It reasoned that the wholesalers had failed to demonstrate the existence of a "plus factor," as is necessary to create an inference of a price fixing conspiracy, and that even if the class had shown that a plus factor was present, the manufacturers were able to rebut fully the inference of collusion, as the economic realities of the 1990s cigarette market rendered the class's conspiracy theory untenable. Rather, the district court held that the manufacturers' pricing behavior evidenced nothing more than "conscious parallelism," a perfectly legal phenomenon commonly associated with oligopolistic industries.

On appeal, the wholesalers say that the district court misapplied the summary judgment standard, that they presented sufficient evidence to withstand the manufacturers' motions, and that the court erred by excluding portions of the testimony proffered by their primary expert witness. In the end, we conclude that none of the class's arguments are compelling and that the district court's treatment of the wealth of complicated issues in this case was nuanced, insightful and, ultimately, correct. Accordingly, we affirm the court's entry of final summary judgment in favor of PM, RJR, B & W and Lorillard.

I

The modern American tobacco industry is a classic oligopoly. Between 1993 and 1999, appellees-the nation's four largest cigarette manufacturers-along with Liggett Group, Inc. [which was not a party to the action] manufactured more than 97% of the cigarettes sold in the United States. Moreover, the composition of the industry has been remarkably stable over time, a condition that has resulted largely from the fact that during the twentieth century the major tobacco players engaged in minimal price competition. Because price fluctuations were relatively rare, smokers typically had no reason to change brands, brand loyalties were solidified and sizable market share shifts were uncommon.

During the early 1990s, however, a price gap widened between premium brands like Marlboro, Newport and Camel and discount and deep discount brands such as GPC, Basic and Doral. This price differential was the result of extremely competitive pricing of the non-premium brands, especially by B & W and RJR, which focused a large percentage of their competitive efforts on the discount and deep discount markets. This led some "premium smokers" to shift to one of the non-premium brands, and by 1993 these brands had captured over 40% of the United States market. At that time, there were 10 different wholesale list price points, *i.e.*, cigarette price tiers.

Although this trend toward the discount and deep discount brands benefitted RJR and B & W, it was extremely undesirable from the perspective of premium-intensive manufacturers like PM and Lorillard. As such, PM—which at the time was (and remains) the market leader, with a market share that ranged from 42% to 50% during the period of the alleged conspiracy—sought in April, 1992 to raise the price of its lowest tier products by $4 per thousand. This effort was unsuccessful, however, because RJR, B & W and Lorillard did not follow suit, and PM was forced to rescind its price increase. Although PM again attempted to increase its deep discount prices in March, 1993, this effort similarly was rebuffed by its competitors.

Though temporarily unsuccessful, PM continued looking for ways to reverse the trend toward discount cigarettes, and roughly one year after its failed $4 per thousand price increase it found one. On April 2, 1993, PM decided to take what appellants refer to as "the single boldest commercial move in U.S. cigarette market history": it announced that it was cutting the retail price of Marlboro cigarettes—which were by far the single best selling brand in America, enjoying a 21% market share—by 40 cents per pack and foregoing price increases on other premium brands "for the foreseeable future." April 2, 1993 subsequently became widely known throughout the industry as "Marlboro Friday." This highly competitive pricing decision was extremely significant for several reasons. First, it left no doubt that PM was willing to take drastic competitive measures (indeed, to sacrifice profits) in order to protect the market share of its flagship brand. Second and quite importantly, it slimmed the price gap between premium and discount cigarettes. Because this price differential was constricted, consumers suddenly had less of an economic incentive to purchase discount cigarettes, and as a result premium brands like Marlboro regained some of market share they had lost prior to Marlboro Friday.

Finally, it set off a price war among appellees, as RJR, B & W and Lorillard were immediately confronted with a need to respond in some way to PM's bold action. In order to remain competitive, these manufacturers matched PM's retail price reductions. Although these pricing actions cut into the market share held by discount brands generally, and thus led to a reduction in the overall share held by RJR and B & W, which, as stated, were more heavily invested in these brands, the decision to match PM's price reduction meant that no manufacturer suffered unduly large market share losses.

However, this vast decrease in cigarette prices was disastrous for PM, RJR, B & W and Lorillard alike in terms of profits, and appellees were forced to rethink their profitability strategies. Indeed, appellants recognize that this economic landscape became especially difficult in light of increasing regulation of the industry and the surge of health-related litigation. To exacerbate its competitors' predicament, on July 20, 1993, PM announced that its Marlboro Friday price reduction would be made permanent and expanded to all of its premium brands, *e.g.*, Parliament and Virginia Slims. Moreover, PM simultaneously lowered the wholesale price of its discount cigarettes and raised the wholesale price of its deep discount brands by 10 cents per pack, thereby consolidating the prices of these brand categories. This action reduced what had been 10 price points in the American cigarette market to four * * *. Again, PM's competitors promptly matched these newly announced prices. What's more, the very next day RJR announced that it would collapse the prices of its regular and 100 mm cigarettes, thereby reducing the price tiers to two: premium and discount. PM, B & W and Lorillard quickly followed suit.

Appellants contend that it is only at this point that PM, RJR, B & W and Lorillard began conspiring to fix and steadily increase prices to make up for the tremendous financial losses they suffered as a consequence of this price war. The class says that PM's actions on Marlboro Friday constructively informed its competitors that price discounting to gain market share would no longer be tolerated, and that only when such efforts were abandoned, and the premium/discount price gap narrowed, could prices again rise. By appellants' account, the manufacturers' conspiracy began in earnest when appellees began using trade press—*i.e.*, tobacco industry financial analysts * * * to "signal" each other regarding their willingness to comply with PM's implicit demands so as to facilitate price increases. For example, the class points to a statement made by * * * Martin Broughton, the CEO and Deputy Chairman of British American Tobacco ("BAT"), B & W's parent company, that "BAT may be one of those who started the price war in the U.S., but we have no wish to escalate it."[5] Appellants argue that this statement somehow was a signal sent by B & W to its competitors that B & W was willing to reduce or end price competition. The class alleges that RJR conveyed a similar message on November 2, 1993 by publicly announcing that it would no longer sacrifice profitability for market share.

Appellants say that PM signaled its acceptance of its competitors' overtures by putting its distributors on "permanent allocation"—that is, limiting the quantities of product the distributors could order—on November 5, 1993. Historically, this practice had been implemented as a temporary measure prior to a price increase, with the purpose being to prevent the wholesalers from engaging in "trade loading," *i.e.*, stocking up on cigarettes before the increase so as to deprive appellees of the benefit of their price adjustment. The class says that PM's placement of its wholesalers on permanent allocation actually was a signal that the price increase sought by RJR, B & W and Lorillard was coming.

---

5. As the district court recognized * * * this statement is taken out of context. Broughton's full statement was that "BAT may be one of those who started the price war in the U.S., but we have no wish to escalate it. *But we shall be ready to respond tactically where necessary.*"

Appellants suggest that RJR responded to PM's signal on November 8, 1993 with one last signal of its own. Specifically, the class argues that by announcing an increase of $2 per thousand cigarettes (4¢ per pack) in both the premium and discount categories, and thus maintaining the constricted discount/premium price gap, RJR indicated that it was acceding to PM's conditions for increasing prices. By November 22, 1993, PM, B & W and Lorillard had matched RJR's increase. * * *

This initial RJR-led price increase was followed by eleven more parallel increases between May 4, 1995 and January 14, 2000. * * *

[Here the court described additional details of the plaintiffs' allegations and evidence and the defendants' arguments in response. Eds.]

* * *

Appellants also argue PM, RJR, B & W and Lorillard furthered their collusive enterprise by exchanging sales data through a common consultant, Management Science Associates ("MSA"), which allegedly enabled appellees to ensure that all were adhering to their allocation programs and to detect and punish what plaintiffs' expert Franklin M. Fisher termed "defections from an industry understanding on price." The MSA system tracks shipments from the manufacturers to wholesalers and from the wholesalers to retailers and provides reports to each appellee regarding the shipments of its competitors. Appellants allege that although in 1994 PM began collecting sales data on RJR, B & W and Lorillard through MSA, and thereby incurred a great competitive advantage, in 1995 it inexplicably began sharing this system with its competitors. Moreover, the class posits, over time the MSA system has been modified to make the cigarette market more transparent, and all of these alterations have been implemented with the unanimous consent of PM, RJR, B & W and Lorillard.

* * *

II

* * *

1. Appellants' Alleged Plus Factors

After articulating the summary judgment standard in an antitrust case, the district court delineated eleven distinct factors that appellants had denominated "plus factors." These are: "(1) signaling of intentions; (2) permanent allocations programs; (3) monitoring of sales; (4) actions taken contrary to economic self-interest, including (a) little analysis of whether to follow price increases, (b) B & W and RJR pulling away from the discount cigarette market, (c) the May 1995 price increase lead by RJR and followed by Philip Morris, (d) Philip Morris' agreement to base the initial [Management Science Associates] ... payments on market capitalization rather than market share, and (e) 'excessive' price increases after the MSA; (5) nature of the market; (6) strong motivation; (7) reduction in the number of price tiers; (8) opportunities to conspire; (9) pricing decisions made at high levels; (10) the smoking and health conspiracy; and (11) foreign conspiracies." * * * The district court ultimately concluded that none of them actually tended to exclude the possibility of independent behavior, and the class contests the correctness of the court's conclusions as to each factor. * * *

* * *

Appellants * * * raise two arguments related to the exchange by each appellee of wholesale-to-retail sales information through Management Science Associates. Around 1993–94, PM developed with MSA a system for tracking wholesale to retail shipments of its products, which it believed would afford it a great competitive advantage. Subsequently, in 1995, PM permitted MSA to share this service with its competitors. In exchange for their acceptance of the service, RJR, B & W and Lorillard agreed to share their own sales information.

Appellants first argue that PM's decision to share this service cannot be seen as being in its economic interest, and instead must be viewed as a means of facilitating the monitoring of the conspiracy by all of the conspirators. PM responds that by sharing the MSA service it shifted the financial burden of gathering sales and market share data for its competitors to RJR, B & W and Lorillard, and that as a result it actually realized an annual savings of millions of dollars. Viewed in the light most favorable to appellants, both explanations are plausible, and thus, at the most, this action by PM stands in equipoise; that is, it is equally consistent with collusion as with lawful competition, and accordingly * * * it cannot represent a plus factor. Second, appellants argue that the participation by all appellees in the MSA data sharing system was contrary to their respective interests.

Preliminarily (and quite significantly), we note that the evidence establishes that appellees exchanged only sales, *not pricing,* information through MSA. Simply put, it is far less indicative of a *price fixing* conspiracy to exchange information relating to sales as opposed to prices. Moreover, it plainly was economically beneficial for each individual appellee to keep tabs on the commercial activities of its competitors, so the receipt of information concerning their sales does not tend to exclude the possibility of independent action or to establish anticompetitive collusion. Indeed, as RJR argues, "[e]ven if one assumes that, all else being equal, RJR would prefer that data about its products not be available to its rivals . . . , that does not tell us that RJR acts irrationally if it concludes that the competitive benefit of obtaining its rivals' data outweighs whatever preference it has against sharing its own data."

Thus, although the sharing of information can be seen as suggesting conspiracy, as appellants allege, it also can be seen equally as a necessary means to the receipt of its competitors' information. If a particular manufacturer ceased providing its own information, its entitlement to that of its competitors would similarly end. To draw an analogy, each company's willingness to give its own information can be viewed as the ante in a poker game. To ante is irrational only if there is no legitimate reason why one would be playing the game; yet here, the game is oligopolistic competition, which everyone concedes is lawful, and the ante is perfectly consonant with the desire to play. For both of these reasons, the delivery of wholesale-to-retail sales information to MSA does not tend to exclude the possibility of independent action (or tend to establish a price fixing conspiracy), and thus cannot constitute a plus factor.

* * *

IV

Besides arguing that the district court erred by rejecting their arguments concerning plus factors, the class further contends that the court erroneously excluded the expert testimony of Professor Fisher on some of these points. Specifically, appellants say that the district court improperly excluded Fisher's conclusion that the manufacturers engaged in activities beyond mere conscious parallelism, which he expressed in the context of several of the particular actions on which appellants base their claims.[21]

[Here the court discussed the standards for the admissibility of expert economic testimony under Federal Rule of Evidence 702 and the Supreme Court's line of cases following *Daubert v. Merrell Dow Pharmaceuticals, Inc.*, 509 U.S. 579 (1993). Eds.]

* * * Expert testimony may be admitted into evidence if: (1) the expert is qualified to testify competently regarding the matters he intends to address; (2) the methodology by which the expert reaches his conclusions is sufficiently reliable as determined by the sort of inquiry mandated in *Daubert*; and (3) the testimony assists the trier of fact, through the application of scientific, technical, or specialized expertise, to understand the evidence or to determine a fact in issue. * * *

In this case, the district court held that Fisher's opinions that collusive price fixing was afoot should be excluded because they were unhelpful and thus irrelevant, *i.e.*, they did not tend to make it any more probable that appellees were (or were not) engaged in a price fixing conspiracy. Additionally, the court held in at least one case that Fisher's testimony was unhelpful because he had misunderstood the evidence. More specifically, the district court excluded Fisher's ultimate opinion that there was an illegal price fixing conspiracy as irrelevant because Fisher did not differentiate between lawful, conscious parallelism and collusive price fixing. Accordingly, the court held, these conclusions were of absolutely no use to a factfinder.

* * *

Simply stated, we can perceive no abuse of discretion in the district court's decision to exclude some of Fisher's testimony. Fisher's conclusion was that plaintiffs participated in an illegal price fixing conspiracy, and he expressed this opinion in the context of several aspects of appellants' evidence, *e.g.*, by saying that the manufacturers' participation in the MSA information sharing system created an inference of collusion. However, Fisher defined "collusion" to include conscious parallelism. Put differently, he did not differentiate between legal and illegal pricing behavior, and instead simply grouped both of these phenomena under the umbrella of illegal, collusive price fixing. This testimony could not have aided a finder of fact to determine

---

21. Specifically, the district court excluded Fisher's testimony that appellees' alleged signaling was indicative of collusive price fixing; that their adoption of permanent allocation programs was indicative of price fixing; and that their exchange of information through MSA was part of a price fixing conspiracy.

whether appellees' behavior was or was not legal, and the district court properly excluded it. * * *

* * *

V

Because appellants cannot demonstrate the existence of a plus factor, they cannot establish an inference of conspiracy, as they must to carry the burden imposed on them at the summary judgment stage of a collusive price fixing case. Moreover, appellees would have rebutted any inference that they conspired to fix prices by demonstrating that the class's conspiracy theory is utterly implausible. In addition, the court's exclusion of several portions of Fisher's testimony was in no sense an abuse of discretion, *i.e.*, did not constitute manifest error. Accordingly, we affirm in all respects the district court's final summary judgment in favor of the manufacturers.

———

Do you agree with the Eleventh Circuit's analysis of the MSA information sharing system? Could the exchange help to facilitate an agreement on prices among the defendants? Also, do you agree with the court's observation that the information sharing here was equally consistent with unilateral and conspiratorial conduct, and hence insufficient to satisfy *Matsushita's* "tending to exclude the possibility" standard?

Cartel Problems, Courts and Economists

The *Williamson* court does not seem to consider how sharing historical information about quantities sold could facilitate collusion. Consider the following line of reasoning: Sales volume or market share data might serve as a useful surrogate for pricing data to identify cheating given that a firm that cheats on a collusive arrangement expands its output (and market share), resulting in a decline in the market price. In other words, if prices are not transparent—and wholesale prices may not be even if retail prices are—one way to tell if a firm is cheating on a price fixing agreement is to observe a significant increase in its share of sales. Even if retail prices are transparent, moreover, a firm might cheat secretly, *i.e.*, in ways that do not lead to a lower retail price, perhaps by giving retailers promotional incentives to display its brands more attractively or in better store locations. In either event, the firm's cheating will likely be observable in the form of increased sales volume or a higher market share. (Recall from the lysine cartel in Chapter 1 that the conspiring producers conferred to check sales volume and market shares at the end of each year).

Contrary to the court's conclusion, therefore, the exchange of historical sales information could facilitate cartel formation by helping the participants to solve their problem of deterring cheating through rapid detection and response. If that is true, might the exchange of such information also be circumstantial evidence of an underlying agreement on price? The testimony of the plaintiff's economist, Dr. Franklin M. Fisher (who also testified for the Department of Justice as an expert witness in the government's 1998 case against *Microsoft*; *see Microsoft*, Chapter 8, *infra*) appeared to be focused on some of these very points. What was the court's response and why did the court exclude his testimony?

The court's treatment of Dr. Fisher's testimony highlights another challenge in addressing cases of alleged price-fixing in oligopolistic industries: because the Sherman Act only condemns "agreement," courts reviewing firm conduct in oligopolistic industries must differentiate between parallel conduct attributable simply to leader-follower behavior that has historically not been considered unlawful and "conspiracy." How can they do so, and what is the role of the economist in such a case?

Noting that "the definition of what qualifies as an 'agreement' is ultimately a question of law and driven by policy considerations," Professor Herbert Hovenkamp has suggested that, "nevertheless, an economist can contribute many observations relevant to the fact finder's determination." Herbert Hovenkamp, *Economic Experts in Antitrust Cases*, in 3 DAVID L. FAIGMAN ET AL., MODERN SCIENTIFIC EVIDENCE: THE LAW AND SCIENCE OF EXPERT TESTIMONY § 10.12 (2006). According to Hovenkamp, these observations include: (1) whether the market structure would make an agreement rational or worthwhile; (2) whether the market structure makes an agreement unnecessary; (3) whether a firm's actions are contrary to self-interest except on the supposition of an agreement; and (4) whether the degree of parallelism is sufficient that, when coupled with other factors, a fact inference of agreement is warranted. *Id*. Hovenkamp observes, however, "that much of what the economists have to say on the matter is theoretical and not subject to empirical falsification at all." *Id*. Do all four of his listed factors seem equally appropriate subjects of an economist's testimony? Doesn't the fourth factor seem to invite the economist to offer an opinion on the ultimate legal question at issue, whereas the first three seem to leave that issue to the fact-finder?

The problem remains that all of these factors—legal and economic—might facilitate parallel pricing in an oligopolistic industry, but still not add up to the legal requirement of "agreement." Did the evidence and testimony in *Williamson* try to go further? Is Hovenkamp overlooking the role of facilitating practices? Might an economist be well-positioned to judge whether specific kinds of conduct—such as information sharing—are likely to facilitate cartel formation by solving cartel problems? Or was the court correct that Dr. Fisher's testimony still failed to differentiate between leader-follower behavior and "conspiracy"? As an economic matter, can an economist differentiate between the two situations? If not, what should an economist be permitted to say about the fact of "conspiracy"? We will discuss more about the concept of "agreement" in Sidebar 3–5, *infra*.

The Impact of the Matsushita Standard

One of the *Williamson* court's penultimate observations is that sharing of past sales volume information was equally consistent with both unilateral and conspiratorial conduct. Invoking *Matsushita*, the court reasoned:

If a particular manufacturer ceased providing its own information, its entitlement to that of its competitors would similarly end. To draw an analogy, each company's willingness to give its own information can be viewed as the ante in a poker game. To ante is irrational only if there is no legitimate reason why one would be playing the game;

yet here, the game is oligopolistic competition, which everyone concedes is lawful, and the ante is perfectly consonant with the desire to play.

Casebook, *supra* at 292. Is the court conceding too much to oligopoly here? Is it accurate to describe a coordinated, cooperative effort to share information by rival oligopolists as "unilateral" conduct in any sense? In fact, doesn't that characterization ignore the cartel-facilitating theory presented by the plaintiffs?

Recall the Turner–Posner debate about the Sherman Act's ability to condemn "conscious parallelism." Sidebar 3–2, *supra*. One of Turner's most persuasive points related to remedy. He argued that leader-follower behavior is difficult to remedy without disrupting normal strategic decision-making in an oligopolistic industry, arguing that there was in fact nothing to enjoin. Is that true in the case of coordinated facilitating practices, such as information exchanges? Couldn't the court in *Williamson* have enjoined the MSA information-sharing system, potentially frustrating the defendants' ability to detect cheating? By dismissing the information sharing as normal oligopolistic behavior, is the court leaving open any rationale for condemning facilitating conduct? Is it reading *Matsushita* beyond its reasonable limits in doing so? We will revisit the impact of *Matsushita* on the burden of proving price-fixing conspiracies when we read the *Blomkest* decision later in this Chapter.

Although the court's analysis of information sharing can thus be critically examined, it is not clear that its ultimate conclusion was incorrect. Information sharing, alone, may not be sufficient to infer a conspiracy. In *Williamson*, it was only one factor addressed by the court, and as the court argues in other portions of its opinion, it did not agree with the plaintiffs that the tobacco industry defendants had gone beyond the kind of unilateral conduct one would expect from an oligopoly.

The Tobacco Industry and Antitrust.

As the court in *Williamson* describes, the American tobacco industry is recognized as an oligopoly that is prone to parallel behavior, especially with regard to pricing. That has long been the case, as you will recall from *American Tobacco*.

In the late 1990s, massive civil actions for damages were brought against the firms in the tobacco industry by various states to recover the costs of health care to their citizens for tobacco-related illnesses. In connection with the first proposed settlement of the cases, which would have required Congressional action, the FTC prepared a report to Congress in September, 1997 on the conduct of the industry. Specifically, it discussed whether the industry structure was conducive to coordination and whether the proposed settlement would make coordination more likely or more effective. (The report became moot when the states and the firms reached an alternative settlement that did not require Congressional intervention). The press release stated: "[the Report] identifies several features of the industry's past history and current structure that suggest why the industry is susceptible to coordinated price rises, including the tendency for price increases to consistently outpace cost increases, the small number of significant firms in the market, and the historical insulation of the cigarette industry from entry by new firms." *See Press Release, Substantial Profits for Tobacco Companies Could Result from Tobacco Settlement, Says FTC Staff, available at* http://www.ftc.gov/opa/1997/

09/tobrep.shtm. Do these findings tend to support the court or the plaintiffs in *Williamson*?

Note that the FTC Staff looked at some of the same factors identified by both Dr. Fisher and Professor Hovenkamp in concluding that the tobacco industry was "susceptible" to price-fixing. But as a matter of proof, should such evidence ever be enough to prove that in fact an agreement was reached? We will revisit the challenges of evaluating competitively significant conduct in the tobacco industry in Chapter 6 in the Supreme Court's decision in *Brooke Group*.

Note on Information Sharing as an Independent Sherman Act Violation

As was noted above at the beginning of this section of the Chapter, agreements to share information often are express, leaving no question that the parties have reached an "agreement" for purposes of Section 1. The treatment of information sharing under the Sherman Act, therefore, has sometimes been viewed by courts and commentators as falling into two distinct categories: (1) cases in which the express information sharing agreement provides a basis for inferring an illicit agreement to fix prices; and (2) cases in which the agreement to share information is itself challenged as a stand alone unreasonable restraint if trade. Although the two questions can be separated in theory, the line between them can be and historically has been blurred. In this Note, we further explore both the cases and some relevant economic commentary that illuminates the tension between these two seemingly distinct approaches, focusing on information sharing as a stand alone violation.

Cases like *American Column & Lumber* and, more recently, *Williamson*, illustrate how information sharing agreements can be analyzed as circumstantial evidence of illicit agreements to fix prices. As one contemporary court has observed, however, "[t]here is a closely related but analytically distinct type of claim, also based on § 1 of the Sherman Act, where the violation lies in the information exchange itself—as opposed to merely using the information exchange as evidence upon which to infer a price-fixing agreement. This exchange of information is not illegal *per se*, but can be found unlawful under a rule of reason analysis." *Todd v. Exxon Corp.*, 275 F.3d 191, 198 (2d Cir. 2001). One way to understand the differing results in *American Column & Lumber* and *Maple Flooring* is to see them as addressing these two distinct issues: *American Column & Lumber* more clearly involved the inference of a price-fixing agreement, whereas *Maple Flooring's* greater focus on effects and justifications arguably suggests that it was evaluating information sharing as a stand alone antitrust issue.

As *Todd* observes, it was not until the late 1960s, in *United States v. Container Corp.*, 393 U.S. 333 (1969), that the Supreme Court returned to the issues it first addressed in *American Column & Lumber* and *Maple Flooring*, and more clearly separated the two issues when it held that an information exchange could itself constitute a violation of Section 1. The information exchange in *Container Corp.* was limited to price verification on demand. The defendants, who were rivals, would periodically request of each other verification of the prices they had been charging. The data was furnished by each defendant on the expectation that its rivals would comply with its requests for similar data, when made. 393 U.S. at 335. The Court barely paused to consider whether there was an agreement. It saw the case as "obviously quite different from the parallel business behavior condoned in *Theatre Enterprises, Inc. v. Paramount Film Distributing Corp.*" 393 U.S. at 335 n.2.

The concerted action identified by the Court in *Container* is best understood as an agreement to exchange price information. With an agreement established, the question was whether that agreement harmed competition. Writing for the Court, Justice Douglas analyzed the effect of the agreement this way:

> The result of this reciprocal exchange of prices was to stabilize prices though at a downward level. Knowledge of a competitor's price usually meant matching that price. The continuation of some price competition is not fatal to the Government's case. The limitation or reduction of price competition brings the case within the ban, for as we held in United States v. Socony–Vacuum Oil Co., interference with the setting of price by free market forces is unlawful per se. Price information exchanged in some markets may have no effect on a truly competitive price. But the corrugated container industry is dominated by relatively few sellers. The product is fungible and the competition for sales is price. The demand is inelastic, as buyers place orders only for immediate, short-run needs. The exchange of price data tends toward price uniformity. For a lower price does not mean a larger share of the available business but a sharing of the existing business at a lower return. Stabilizing prices as well as raising them is within the ban of § 1 of the Sherman Act. As we said in United States v. Socony–Vacuum Oil Co., 'in terms of market operations stabilization is but one form of manipulation.' The inferences are irresistible that the exchange of price information has had an anticompetitive effect in the industry, chilling the vigor of price competition. The agreement in the present case, though somewhat casual, is analogous to those in American Column & Lumber Co. v. United States. * * *

393 U.S. at 336–38.

Justice Douglas appeared to find the Agreement's vice to be price stabilization without regard to whether the agreement harmed consumers through higher prices. A concurring opinion by Justice Fortas suggested a more modern analysis focused on how information exchange can facilitate coordination on prices by helping the firms deter cheating. Justice Fortas concluded that the agreement led to higher prices than would have otherwise occurred and that therefore application of a per se approach was unnecessary:

> * * * In summary, the record shows that the defendants sought and obtained from competitors who were part of the arrangement information about the competitors' prices to specific customers. '[I]n the majority of instances,' the District Court found, that once a defendant had this information he quoted substantially the same price as the competitor, although a higher or lower price would 'occasionally' be quoted. Thus the exchange of prices made it possible for individual defendants confidently to name a price equal to that which their competitors were asking. The obvious effect was to 'stabilize' prices by joint arrangement—at least to limit any price cuts to the minimum necessary to meet competition. In addition, there was evidence that, in some instances, during periods when various defendants ceased exchanging prices exceptionally sharp and vigorous price reductions resulted.

> On this record, taking into account the specially sensitive function of the price term in the antitrust equation, I cannot see that we would be

justified in reaching any conclusion other than that defendants' tacit agreement to exchange information about current prices to specific customers did in fact substantially limit the amount of price competition in the industry. That being so, there is no need to consider the possibility of a per se violation.

393 U.S. at 339–40 (Fortas, J., concurring).

Justice Marshall's dissent argued that the government had not proved its case with evidence of anticompetitive effect, notwithstanding that the government "presented a convincing argument in theoretical terms." 393 U.S. at 345 (Marshall, J., dissenting). He emphasized that "The trial judge found that price decisions were individual decisions, and that defendants frequently did cut prices in order to obtain a particular order." In his view, "the absence of any price parallelism or price uniformity and the downward trend in the industry undercut the conclusion that price information was used to stabilize prices." 393 U.S. at 346 (Marshall, J., dissenting).

With *Container Corp.* and other antitrust decisions, it often is difficult to determine how specific judicial rulings actually affect business behavior. But in 1982 the Federal Trade Commission published a report on petroleum industry mergers that suggested how *Container Corp.* might have complicated efforts by direct rivals to coordinate pricing decisions. The FTC study quoted an undated document prepared by a petroleum industry company commenting on *Container Corp.*'s influence on the behavior of major integrated oil firms:

> It is difficult to over-estimate the significance of this [the *Container Corp.* decision] development. Previously, with price verification, the individual majors knew the price levels of the other majors and some stability and order was possible. Today, the only information available is the actual pump price at the station which is set by some relatively irresponsible dealers, and when instability sets in, a single major does not know if this is a move by the supplier or by a few dealers.

Federal Trade Commission, *Mergers in the Petroleum Industry* 291–92 (Sept. 1982). As this passage suggests, *Container Corp.* appears to have forced the petroleum firms to resort to more cumbersome methods—actually examining prices posted at individual retail outlets—to monitor pricing decisions of their competitors.

Justice Fortas's suggestion that application of the per se rule was not essential to the result in *Container* was later influential in persuading the Court that information exchanges in and of themselves should not be subject to per se condemnation. *See United States v. Citizens & Southern National Bank,* 422 U.S. 86, 113 (1975) ("the dissemination of price information is not itself a *per se* violation of the Sherman Act."). The Court explained its reasoning in *Citizens & Southern* several years later in *United States v. United States Gypsum Co.,* 438 U.S. 422 (1978):

> The exchange of price data and other information among competitors does not invariably have anticompetitive effects; indeed such practices can in certain circumstances increase economic efficiency and render markets more, rather than less, competitive. For this reason, we have held that such exchanges of information do not constitute a *per se* violation of the Sherman Act. A number of factors including most prominently the structure of the industry involved and the nature of the information exchanged are generally considered in divining the procom-

petitive or anticompetitive effects of this type of interseller communication.

Id. at 441 n.16. Citing to *American Column & Lumber, American Linseed,* and *Container,* the Court also observed, however, that "[e]xchanges of current price information, of course, have the greatest potential for generating anticompetitive effects and although not *per se* unlawful have consistently been held to violate the Sherman Act." *Id. See also Todd,* 275 F.3d at 199 (discussing the evolution of the cases in the Supreme Court).

In the wake of the information-sharing decisions discussed above, two generalizations can be made concerning the Sherman Act's application to agreements by competitors to share information about their operations. First, the case law is interpreted today as indicating that an agreement merely to share information– even information about current prices–is not illegal per se and would be judged by a reasonableness standard. From a contemporary perspective, this conclusion may be understood as consistent with the legal rule established in *Broadcast Music, Inc.* (Casebook, Chapter 2, *supra*) and with the rule as articulated in *Gypsum.* 438 U.S. at 441 n. 16. It is also consistent with how economists tend to view information sharing. From an economic point of view, Section 1's "agreement" requirement is far less important than the effects and justifications for information sharing. *See, e.g.,* Dennis W. Carlton, et al., *Communication Among Competitors: Game Theory and Antitrust,* 5 GEO. MASON L. REV. 423, 424 (1997) ("There is, in general, no economic theory of the meaning of 'agreement' wherein one may determine easily when communication leads to anticompetitive results irrespective of the context of the events. Nor do we think this is the right problem to solve."). Moreover, some commentators have argued that information sharing by rivals can promote competition in a variety of settings. *Id. See also* David J. Teece, *Information Sharing, Innovation, and Antitrust,* 62 ANTITRUST L.J. 465, 466 (1994)(arguing that "information collection, dissemination, and exchange among 'competitors' . . . [in] dynamic environments where markets are experiencing rapid change, often induced by technological innovation," can promote innovation and hence competition); Richard A. Posner, *Information and Antitrust: Reflections on the* Gypsum *and* Engineers *Decisions,* 67 GEO. L.J. 1187, 1194 (1979) ("producers must be well informed about competitors' prices and plans if resources are to be allocated efficiently.").

Second, the validity of an information sharing program depends heavily on several variables. Courts are more likely to approve information sharing arrangements if the participants:

- Collectively hold a relatively modest share of total sales in the relevant market;
- Share information concerning past, rather than current or future, transactions;
- Avoid exchanging information about prices or key cost elements that determine prices; and
- Share information that aggregates activities of all participants rather than transaction-specific and firm-specific data.

Todd, which involved the appeal of a district court's dismissal of plaintiff's claim that the defendant employers shared information concerning compensation arrangements for purpose of setting salaries at artificially low levels, illustrates this kind of synthesis of the previous cases. Relying in significant part on *Gypsum,* the court concluded that the complaint should not have been dismissed. In doing so, it evaluated the allegations of the plaintiff's complaint by looking at factors such as market definition, market power, evidence of actual effects, the susceptibility of the market to collusion, the nature of the information exchanged. *Todd*, 275 F.3d at 199–214.

We will revisit the antitrust treatment of practices that might facilitate collusion. Sidebar 3–6 later in this Chapter discusses the antitrust treatment of "most favored nations" or "most favored customer clauses," in connection with the FTC's *Ethyl* litigation.

D. INTEGRATING TRADITIONAL LEGAL ANALYSIS AND MODERN ECONOMICS: CONTEMPORARY AGREEMENT ISSUES

In this Section we examine how modern judicial decisions have addressed longstanding questions about distinguishing concerted from unilateral conduct. As you read these decisions, consider the range of factors that may influence judicial decision-making. Some of the most important factors are academic and doctrinal: modern courts are beginning to be influenced by the contemporary economic analysis of coordination set forth in Section B of this Chapter, and by the lessons of *Monsanto* and *Matsushita* discussed immediately above in Section C.

Yet courts also are concerned with the interplay of doctrinal standards, standards of proof, and remedies. For example, the emergence of per se liability rules and the enhancement of sanctions can converge to cause judges to impose a more demanding standard of proof when defining what constitutes concerted action. Courts might manipulate the agreement standard to correct what they regard as imperfections in the substantive liability tests and sanctions, themselves. Judges uncomfortable with the potential overinclusiveness of a per se prohibition, which reflects a basic judgment that some conduct is so routinely pernicious that one can forego the elaborate factual inquiry that might exculpate defendants in those rare instances where the behavior is benign, may impose greater evidentiary demands on plaintiffs to prove collective action, because finding such action, by itself, establishes guilt. Similarly, a judge who believes the antitrust remedial scheme is too severe— for example, in commanding that damages in private actions be trebled—also might increase the plaintiff's burden of pleading or proving agreement to diminish the likelihood that disfavored remedies might be applied.

As you read the modern appellate decisions highlighted in this section, consider the extent to which the courts are influenced by modern economic thinking, contemporary Supreme Court guidance, and a desire to modify what they perceive to be rough edges in antitrust substantive rules and remedies.

1. INCREASING ACCESS TO DIRECT EVIDENCE

One frontier of the agreement battle in modern practice is to undermine covert collusive schemes by providing greater incentives for cartel participants to disclose the fact of their unlawful collaboration. In our treatment of the lysine and vitamins cartels in Chapter 1, we observed the Justice Department's success in using information provided by cartel insiders to prove the fact of agreement. For example, in the *Andreas* case, Mark Whitacre assisted the Justice Department in preparing audio recordings and videotapes of conversations in which the cartel participants formulated and implemented their agreement. In Sidebar 3–4 below, we explore one of the most important recent efforts by public prosecutors to gather direct evidence of collusion.

Sidebar 3–4:
Leniency Programs

Precaution-taking by cartel members to avoid detection and the emergence of doctrinal limits upon the use of circumstantial evidence to establish concerted action have inspired antitrust enforcement agencies to improve tools for detecting covert arrangements and generating direct evidence of unlawful agreements. Since the early 1980s, U.S. enforcement officials have pursued a number of initiatives to increase their ability to obtain direct evidence of collusion. The U.S. Department of Justice ("DOJ") has resorted more frequently to investigation techniques such as wire-tapping and electronic surveillance and broadened cooperation with other law enforcement entities and government bureaus in the U.S. and abroad. These steps have increased the likelihood that efforts by competitors to coordinate their behavior through a direct exchange of assurances will be detected.

In 1993 and 1994, the DOJ expanded leniency programs that provide incentives for cartel participants to inform the government about episodes of collusion. *See* U.S. Department of Justice, Antitrust Division, *Corporate Leniency Policy* (Aug. 10, 1993), *available at* http://www.usdoj. gov/atr/public/guidelines/0091.htm; U.S. Department of Justice, Antitrust Division, *Individual Leniency Policy* (Aug. 10, 1994), *available at* http:// www.usdoj.gov/atr/public/guidelines/0092.htm. These mechanisms essentially offer immunity from criminal prosecution to the first individual or organization to inform the government about the cartel's existence. Although the second party to inform might obtain some attenuation of punishment, the leniency program confers enormous advantages on the first to disclose the cartel.

In June 2004, the Sherman Act was amended to increase the penalties for criminal violations. Individuals now face up to 10 years in prison (up from three years) and fines of up to $1 million (up from $350,000); corporations can be fined up to $100 million (up from $10 million). At the same time, the law expanded the Department of Justice's discretion with respect to its leniency program. Under Section 213 of Title II of the law, which are set out as notes to Section 16 of the Sherman Act, a cooperating individual's damage exposure for any subsequent private treble damage litigation can be "de-trebled" and limited to that individual's share of the affected commerce. In light of the prospect of treble damages and joint and several liability, the new provision, which will remain in effect until 2009, is intended to increase the incentives of cartel participants to report cartel activity to the government.

In effect, leniency exploits the tensions among cartel members suggested in our discussion of the Prisoner's Dilemma in Sidebar 3–1, above. Recent experience with leniency has yielded some dramatic successes. In the Vitamins, Inc. prosecution detailed in Chapter 1, the Leniency Program motivated one of the cartel members (Rhone Poulenc) to disclose the operation of the cartel and greatly accelerated the Justice Department's negotiation of guilty pleas with the corporations and culpable individuals. The Leniency Program also played a key role in providing the Justice Department with evidence of a conspiracy between the world's two leading art auction houses, Christie's International and Sotheby's Holdings, to set commission rates. In return for an abatement of her own punishment, the former Sotheby's chief executive officer provided testimony against Sotheby's chairman of the board, who was convicted of price-fixing. *See United States v. Taubman*, 2002 WL 548733 (S.D.N.Y. 2002), *aff'd*, 297 F.3d 161 (2d Cir.2002).

Leniency is the latest of a series of anti-cartel information-gathering mechanisms that seek to obtain the assistance of cartel insiders. Cooperation by insiders—such as a disgruntled employee or a cartel member that feels betrayed by other cartel participants—is vital to many successful efforts to unmask covert coordination among rivals. By providing an incentive for such informants to come forward, DOJ's leniency program has demonstrated the benefits of using decentralized monitoring to enforce antitrust laws. Inspired by the success of the DOJ program, a number of other jurisdictions, including Canada, the European Union, and the United Kingdom, have instituted leniency programs.

To date, antitrust enforcement agencies have enlisted informants chiefly by offering leniency or immunity to offenders, or simply by relying on voluntary disclosures by non-culpable individuals (such as a sales manager who objects to a supervisor's instructions not to fulfill orders from a loyal customer) who are upset by what they perceive to be improper conduct. Beyond offering dispensations from criminal sanctions and encouraging pure volunteerism, the U.S. antitrust system provides no further incentives to gain the assistance of informers. An interesting question is whether offering additional rewards, such as the payment of bounties, might elicit still greater detection of cartels. *See* William E. Kovacic, *Private Monitoring and Antitrust Enforcement: Paying Informants to Reveal Cartels*, 69 GEO. WASH. L. REV. 766 (2001).

Leniency, both corporate and individual, may be conditional, granted by the government in return for certain representations about the cartel participants' past conduct, or perhaps for promises of future cooperation. What happens, however, when in the government's view the conditions have not been satisfied? In *Stolt-Nielsen, S.A. v. United States*, 442 F.3d 177 (3d Cir. 2006), the court reversed a district court's order enjoining the Department of Justice from indicting a company and one of its officers, despite their having previously entered into leniency agreements. In the view of the government, they had breached the conditions of those agreements and were therefore subject to prosecution for their participation in criminal antitrust violations. In the Third Circuit's view, although a prior grant of immunity may be a defense to conviction, it was not a defense to indictment. Moreover, it was a violation of principles of separation of powers for the court to enjoin the indictment. *But see U.S. v. Stolt–Nielsen S.A.*, 524 F. Supp. 2d 586 (E.D. Pa. 2007) (concluding after an evidentiary hearing that Stolt–Nielsen and individual defendants did not breach their leniency agreements and dismissing the DOJ's indictment).

Cartel enforcement and the use of leniency programs is an area in which E.U. practice in the past decade has converged substantially upon U.S. norms by a process of voluntarily opting in. Both the E.U. and the U.S. treat cartels harshly. Speeches of E.U. and U.S. Antitrust Division officials today depict cartels as the most serious form of anticompetitive behavior and both institutions have devoted substantial effort to prosecuting offenders and to devising new techniques for detecting covert arrangements. Recoveries in the hundreds of millions of dollars occur today with some regularity. The modern trend in sanctions in both jurisdictions has been to increase punishments for violators, and two E.U. member states (Ireland and the United Kingdom) have adopted policies, like that of the U.S., of seeking incarceration for individual offenders. There is a continuing debate within the European Commission and in the member states about the desirability of relying to a greater degree on criminal sanctions.

2. CIRCUMSTANTIAL PROOF OF AGREEMENT: REVISITING PARALLELISM AND PLUS FACTORS AS A BASIS FOR INFERRING AGREEMENT

Success in obtaining greater access to direct evidence of cartel coordination has not eliminated the importance of circumstantial proof in many horizontal restraints cases. This is particularly true in civil matters that do not "piggyback" upon a Justice Department investigation of possible criminal misconduct. The most significant recent cases analyzing agreement issues have been private civil suits, where the proof of agreement was largely circumstantial.

Since *Matsushita*, courts have struggled with whether parallel conduct that seems to flow from the recognition of interdependence should suffice, without more, to support an inference of agreement. Courts continue to hold, as the Supreme Court did in *Theatre Enterprises* in 1954, that mere conscious parallelism or oligopolistic interdependence does not permit an inference of conspiracy. Courts require plaintiffs to supplement proof of parallel conduct with additional facts ("plus factors") to justify an inference of agreement. *See Bell Atlantic Corp. v. Twombly*, ___ U.S. ___, 127 S.Ct. 1955 (2007).

Historically, communication among the firms, or the opportunity to communicate prior to an increase in industry prices, has been the most important plus factor relied upon by the courts to infer an agreement on price in a parallel pricing case. If firm representatives meet for dinner one day, and all raise price the next, courts may conclude that the firms reached an unlawful price-fixing deal over dessert. The significance of this plus factor is emphasized by a pre-*Matsushita* case, *United States v. Foley*. In *Foley* the court of appeals reviewed the criminal price-fixing conviction of ten leading suburban Washington D.C. realtors, who raised commission rates in the months following a dinner meeting at a country club.

UNITED STATES v. FOLEY
Unites States Court of Appeals for the Fourth Circuit, 1979.
598 F.2d 1323.

Before WINTER, Circuit Judge, COWEN, Senior Judge and PHILLIPS, Circuit Judge.

PHILLIPS, Circuit Judge:

Six corporate and three individual defendants appeal their felony convictions for conspiracy to fix real estate commissions in Montgomery County, Maryland in violation of § 1 of the Sherman Act, 15 U.S.C. § 1. Finding no error, we affirm.

During the critical period in question all the defendants were realtors engaged as competitors in the business of "reselling" houses. When a person desired to sell his house in Montgomery County he listed it with a realtor, provided he did not decide to attempt to sell it directly. The listing provided that when the house was sold a fixed percentage of the sales price would be paid as a commission to the realtor. This commission was divided among the firms involved in the sale, a portion going to the firm that obtained the listing, another portion to the firm that produced the buyer. To facilitate the operation of this shared commission arrangement, each of the defendants belonged to the Montgomery County Board of Realtors, a trade association that operated a multiple listing service. In the case of almost all houses listed with a member realtor, the member sent a card to the listing service containing a picture of the house and certain pertinent information, including the commission. Thus all member realtors had available a fairly comprehensive list of houses on the market in the county.

During the summer of 1974, and for some time before, the prevailing commission rate in Montgomery County was six percent of the sales price. A few houses were listed at seven percent, but additional services were apparently provided for the higher rate. At this time the real estate brokerage business in the county was in difficult straits. While the number of houses listed with brokers for resale had continued to rise as it had for several previous years, the number of sales had fallen, mortgage funds were in short supply and increasing costs of stationery, telephone service, advertising and gasoline had reduced the profit margin.

On September 5, 1974, defendant John Foley, the president of defendant Jack Foley Realty, Inc., hosted a dinner party at the Congressional Country Club in Bethesda, Maryland. The guests were nine of the leading realtors in Montgomery County, including each of the three individual defendants and one representative of each of the corporate defendants in this appeal. Following the meal, Foley arose and, after making some other remarks, announced that his firm was raising its commission rate from six percent to seven percent. A discussion about the rate change ensued. Within the following months each of the corporate defendants substantially adopted a seven percent commission rate.

A United States grand jury for the district of Maryland indicted the nine defendants on April 1, 1977. Following a number of preliminary motions, the only one of which is of interest to this appeal being the denial of a motion to dismiss for lack of subject matter jurisdiction, a nine day jury trial was held in September 1977 before Judge Stanley Blair. All defendants were found guilty and this appeal ensued.

* * *

II. CONSPIRACY AND PARTICIPATION

Defendants * * * contend that there was insufficient evidence, although considered in the light most favorable to the government, to allow a jury to find the existence of a conspiracy and the participation of each defendant in it beyond a reasonable doubt. * * *

A. *The Evidence of Conspiracy*

Proof of a § 1 conspiracy need not be direct. "Acceptance by competitors of an invitation to participate in a plan, the necessary consequence of which, if carried out, is a restraint of commerce, is sufficient to establish an unlawful conspiracy under the Sherman Act, where each competitor knew that cooperation was essential to successful operation of the plan." While such evidence does not compel a finding of conspiracy, *Theatre Enterprises*, it does permit such a finding, *Interstate Circuit*. Within this principle, we find ample evidence to permit the finding of a conspiracy involving each of the defendants.

In the months preceding the September 5 dinner, several of the defendants were contemplating a change in commission rate, but were concededly afraid to undertake such a move for fear that they would be unable successfully to compete with firms still at six percent. Schick & Pepe had previously attempted to go to a seven percent rate and had failed because of competition. It was in this general climate of concern about competitive constraints that Foley called the meeting of September 5. At the dinner Foley rose, made some prefatory remarks and then stated that his firm was in dire financial condition. Saying that he did not care what the others did, he then announced that his firm was changing its commission rate from six percent to seven percent. Testimony as to what was said by various persons in the ensuing discussion is greatly in conflict, but there was evidence from which the jury could find that each of the individual defendants and a representative of each corporate defendant not represented by one of the individual defendants expressed an intention or gave the impression that his firm would adopt a similar change. The discussion also included reference to the earlier unsuccessful effort by Schick & Pepe to adopt a seven percent policy, from which the jury could conclude that defendants knew that their cooperation was essential. Evidence presented in the form of detailed charts with explanation by an economist qualified as expert witness showed that in the months following each defendant did in fact begin to take substantial numbers of seven percent listings. Moreover, the jury heard testimony of a number of instances in which members of the conspiracy sought after the September 5 dinner to hold their fellows to the "agreement." * * *

B. *Connection of Each Defendant to the Conspiracy*

(1) *Jack Foley Realty, Inc. and John P. Foley, Jr.*

Jack Foley hosted the September 5 dinner, inviting in addition to a few realtors who were close personal friends, those he regarded as the most active members of his profession. He had previously announced the commission change to his staff and on September 15 mailed a notice concerning it to all local realtors. By early October, Foley, Inc. had thirty percent of its listings at the higher rate; by December, the figure was in excess of seventy percent and remained in that neighborhood throughout 1975.

Allyn Rickman, vice president of Schick & Pepe and a guest at the September 5 dinner, testified that after Schick & Pepe took some six percent listings, Foley called him and told him that was a "mistake" because if they all did not hold the line none of them could get seven percent. Before the policy change, Foley's firm had accepted a house at a six percent listing. When the listing was renewed after the policy change, still at six percent, Foley, Inc. sent a card to the listing service which was in turn distributed to all the local realtors. A listing card was then received anonymously in the mail by Foley with a question mark on it. When the house was again relisted, the contract and the listing with the service were both at seven percent. John O'Keefe, a vice president at Foley, Inc., however, wrote a letter to the homeowner/seller informing him that Foley would reimburse him for the extra one percent. The letter contained the following explanation: "The reason I don't want (the listing) to go through showing 6% is our Firm was one of the leading Firms in changing from 6% to 7% and with Mr. Foley being the President of the Board of Realtors, I just don't want any unjust criticism of him or our Company for taking your listing at less than 7%."

(2) Colquitt–Carruthers, Inc. and John T. Carruthers, Jr.

John T. Carruthers of Colquitt–Carruthers, Inc. attended the dinner. The testimony conflicts on whether he said he was already at seven percent, or whether he was going to go to seven percent. His accountant testified that a policy change occurred between September 10 and September 24. Effective September 24, all listings other than at seven percent had to be accompanied by explanation; after November 1, they would not be accepted at less than seven percent. By October 1974, Colquitt–Carruthers had sixty percent of its listings at the new rate and through the end of 1975 the figure was generally in excess of eighty percent.

There was testimony that Carruthers made several attempts to ensure the cooperation of other firms. William Ellis, vice president of Shannon & Luchs Co., a firm that delayed implementation of the seven percent policy, testified that Carruthers called him on three occasions. Around January 1, 1975, Carruthers called and asked about Ellis' "considerations." Ellis replied "You know I can't make the decision." Carruthers then offered to call the man who could make the decision. Later in January, Carruthers again called, this time explicitly asking about the change. Upon being told that Shannon & Luchs had adopted a seven percent policy, but had set no date for its implementation, Carruthers "threatened" Ellis with the loss of his job. In April when Shannon & Luchs' Gaithersburg, Maryland office took some six percent listings, Carruthers again called Ellis to complain.

Allyn Rickman, vice president of Schick & Pepe Realty, Inc., also testified that Carruthers called him to complain about some six percent listings that Schick & Pepe had accepted. He quoted Carruthers as saying "if we do not stay at seven percent, then it would be a slide back and . . . no one could get seven percent, because the competition would hurt us." There was also testimony that Carruthers complained to Robert Dorsey, a vice president at Bogley, Inc., about that firm having taken more six than seven percent listings.

* * *

(5) Shannon & Luchs Co.

Shannon & Luchs did not officially adopt a seven percent policy until January 1975. At the dinner, its vice president, William Ellis, stated that they should not be discussing a rate increase and said that his firm was always the first to be investigated when something like this happened as it was the county's largest. He also stated that Shannon & Luchs would probably go to seven percent at a later date; Allyn Rickman remembered a possible mention of the first of the year. On September 9, Ellis told his managers not to turn down any seven percent listings they had an opportunity to get. In fact, the percentage of seven percent listings taken by Shannon & Luchs crept toward thirty percent by January 1975. Early in January, John T. Carruthers called Ellis and asked about his "considerations." Ellis told him that he, Ellis, did not make those decisions and Carruthers then offered to telephone the man who did; Ellis replied that he did not need help. On January 15, at Ellis' suggestion, Shannon & Luchs adopted a policy of taking seven percent listings unless some other rate were beneficial to the firm or otherwise appropriate. Although the new policy was not implemented until March 1, by that time forty percent of Shannon & Luchs' listings were at seven percent. By early April, the figure was about sixty-five percent and throughout 1975 it stood between eighty and ninety. In response to a comment from Carruthers in April, Ellis acknowledged that he had a "problem" in his Gaithersburg, Maryland office in implementing the policy. Shannon & Luchs did not adopt a seven percent policy for its offices in northern Virginia because of the threat of competition.

* * *

C. Conclusion

We conclude that this evidence, here merely summarized and highlighted from a much more detailed body of proof adduced by the Government, was sufficient to permit the jury to find as it did against each of the defendants on the conspiracy issue. Defendants of course offered explanatory and exculpatory evidence, and on this appeal urge that the proper inferences to be drawn from all the evidence relieve their actions of criminal implications. Among these arguments is the interesting one that only by graceless refusals to accept Foley's invitation to dinner or by equally graceless withdrawals from it once its purpose was revealed could they have avoided the factual inferences required to implicate them in the conspiracy, and that to sustain their convictions will impose intolerable burdens on businessmen confronted with like dilemmas. This, with other arguments about the proper inferences to be drawn from the evidence, was undoubtedly presented to the jury by able counsel for the defendants. A properly composed jury of defendants' peers rejected this factual argument as well as others in reaching its verdict of guilty. That to sustain the jury finding on this issue may have the inhibitory effect on the conduct of others that is urged by defendants does not speak to the force of the evidence supporting the jury's finding in this case.

* * *

What plus factors did the court rely upon to infer an agreement from the parallel increase in real estate commission rates beyond the fact that the realtors had the opportunity to reach an agreement at a dinner meeting where, they admit, prices were discussed? Is it easy to come up with an innocent explanation for the later complaint calls, during which some realtors raised questions about price-cutting by others?

Suppose the only evidence of an agreement was statements at the dinner that simply restate the obvious, like "We're all better off with high prices. If the rest of you match our commission rate, we'll all make money." Could a court reasonably infer that the subtext of those statements was the message "Please raise your rates to match"? If a court concluded that the firms had reached an unlawful agreement on price based solely on this evidence, what would the court enjoin as the remedy?

In the real estate industry, the seller and the buyer often have different agents, which must cooperate in a house sale and would then share the commission. What does this fact suggest about the likelihood that rivals would detect a realtor cutting the commission rate below an agreed-upon level? Would it have been possible for one of the realtors to cheat by signing up homeowners with a nominal 7% commission reported on the multiple listing service, but secretly rebating 1% back to the homeowner? Or would this practice likely get out before the cheating realtor increased its business significantly? What does the need for cooperation between realtors suggest about the ability of colluding firms to punish a discounter? If secret cheating was feasible, should that possibility have counted against the inference of an agreement in *Foley*?

The growth of the Internet has been changing the real estate industry. In 2005, the Justice Department sued the National Association of Realtors, an association of real estate brokers, alleging that association rules prevented the growth of brokers with Internet-based business models by restricting their access to the information about houses for sale available on multiple listing services. *United States v. National Association of Realtors*, No. 05C–5140 (N.D.Ill. filed Sept. 8, 2005). The Federal Trade Commission has also reached consent settlements with several local associations of real estate brokers involving similar practices.

Figure 3–4 summarizes the principal plus factors that courts use to illuminate the source of parallel conduct, starting with communication, such as was described in *Foley*. Many of these factors are derived from the Supreme Court's opinions in *Interstate Circuit* and *American Tobacco*.

For example, in addition to communication, Section 1 cases often seek to analyze whether defendants had a rational motive to engage in a conspiracy. Here courts may point to inelastic market demand and difficult conditions of entry, for example. When demand is inelastic, the firms in a market can increase revenues and, almost surely, profit by collectively reducing output and raising price. (*See* Chapter 1, *supra*.) Under such circumstances, if the firms are not already colluding, they can profit by doing so. If instead they are already colluding, they may be earning substantial profits from the exercise of market power, as demand may have been even more inelastic when the market price was lower, before their cartel was formed. But if market demand is inelastic, any existing coordination is imperfect, and the firms could increase their anticompetitive profits by making coordination more effective.

In a closely related inquiry, other decisions consider whether the disputed conduct would have contradicted the defendants' self-interest if pursued unilaterally. In applying the "motive to conspire" and "contrary to self-interest" factors, many cases have dismissed claims that rest chiefly on the fact of parallelism without a showing that defendants could expect to gain from concerted action.

Plus factors that have supported an inference of conspiracy include proof that defendants priced uniformly where price uniformity was improbable without an agreement; committed past antitrust violations involving collective action; directly communicated with competitors, and then made simultaneous, identical changes in their behavior; or agreed to adopt common practices, such as product standardization, whose implementation helped achieve pricing uniformity. Some of these plus factors can be understood as suggesting that the firms have found ways to solve the economic "cartel problems" of reaching consensus, deterring deviation, and preventing new competition. Defendants have rebutted an inference of concerted action where they have demonstrated that their conduct either was consistent with independent choice or accomplished procompetitive or competitively neutral objectives.

Figure 3–4 organizes the plus factors into three groups. Those in the first group are related to the economic question of whether the firms can successfully reach a coordinated outcome by reaching consensus on the terms of coordination, deterring deviation from those terms, and preventing new competition. Those in the second group are more closely related to the legal question of distinguishing between consciously parallel conduct and conduct that would be deemed an agreement under the antitrust laws. (See the discussion of the Turner/Posner debate in Sidebar 3–2 and the discussion of what constitutes an agreement in Sidebar 3–5). The plus factors in the third group have also been cited by courts. Should they have been placed in either of the previous categories? Is it appropriate for courts to employ them unless they can be construed as falling into either of the previous categories?

Figure 3–4:
Synthesizing the "Plus Factors" for Proving Conspiracy

Parallel Pricing +

Factors Suggesting the Industry is Conducive to Coordination (ability to solve "cartel problems" of reaching consensus, deterring cheating, and preventing new competition)

- *industry structure*

(*e.g.*, oligopolistic market structure, homogeneous products, difficult entry conditions, large numbers of purchasers, information asymmetries, frequent transactions)

- *past history of industry collaboration*

(*e.g.*, historic evidence of successful interdependent or collusive action)

- *rational motive to behave collectively*

  (*e.g.*, inelastic demand, difficult conditions of entry)

Factors Tending to Distinguish Agreement from Conscious Parallelism

- *communication or opportunity to communicate*

  (*e.g.*, meetings, trade association conferences)

- *conduct too complicated to be explained by mere parallel behavior*

  (*e.g.*, conduct that appears irrational absent agreement)

- *conduct lacking an evident efficiency explanation*

  (*e.g.*, failure to price based on relative cost advantages)

Other Factors Sometimes Cited by Courts

- *industry performance*

(*e.g.*, stability of market shares over time, sustained and substantial profitability, persistently supra-competitive pricing, prices rise when costs fall)

- *actions contrary to self-interest unless pursued collectively*

  (*e.g.*, failure to alter price based on changes in supply and demand)

- *facilitating practices*

(*e.g.*, pre-announcement of price increases, other information exchange)

As we shall see below in *Blomkest*, decisions analyzing plus factors generally have failed to establish a clear boundary between tacit agreements—to which Section 1 applies—and parallel pricing stemming from oligopolistic interdependence, which *Theatre Enterprises* regards as insufficient to support an inference of agreement. Courts seldom rank plus factors by their probative value or specify the minimum critical mass of plus factors that will sustain an inference of concerted conduct. This condition makes judgments about future litigation outcomes unpredictable. The following decision, which involved allegations of a horizontal conspiracy to raise prices (unlike *Matsushita*, which involved allegations of a conspiracy to price below costs), highlight judicial disagreement over what type of evidence, when combined with conscious parallelism, ought to suffice to support an inference of agreement. Sidebar 3–5, following *Blomkest*, offers one attempt at such a synthesis, framed around the question "What is an agreement?".

BLOMKEST FERTILIZER, INC. v. POTASH CORP. OF SASKATCHEWAN, INC.

United States Court of Appeals for the Eighth Circuit, 2000.
203 F.3d 1028.

BEAM, Circuit J.

A certified class of potash consumers appeals the district court's grant of summary judgment in favor of defendants (collectively "the producers") in this action for conspiracy in restraint of trade under section 1 of the Sherman Act. We affirm.

I. BACKGROUND

This case involves the production and sale of potash, a mineral essential to plant growth and therefore used in fertilizer. The certified class includes all of those persons who directly purchased potash from one of the producers between April 1987 and July 1994. The class named six Canadian potash companies and two American companies.[2]

Both parties agree that the North American potash industry is an oligopoly.[3] Prices in an oligopolistic market tend to be higher than those in purely competitive markets, and will fluctuate independently of supply and demand. Furthermore, "price uniformity is normal in a market with few sellers and homogeneous products." *E.I. Du Pont de Nemours & Co. v. Federal Trade Comm'n,* 729 F.2d 128, 139 (2d Cir.1984). This is because all producers in an oligopoly must charge roughly the same price or risk losing market share.

The Canadian province of Saskatchewan is the source of most potash consumed in the United States. The province founded defendant Potash Corporation of Saskatchewan (PCS), which holds thirty-eight percent of the North American potash production capacity. As a governmental company, PCS had no mandate to maximize profits and was not accountable to private owners. Instead, the company was primarily concerned with maintaining employment and generating money for the local economy. Not surprisingly, PCS suffered huge losses as it mined potash in quantities that far outstripped global demand. These policies impacted the entire potash industry: during the 1980's, the price of potash fell to an historic low. In 1986, Saskatchewan voters elected a provincial government which had promised to privatize PCS. New management was appointed to PCS after the elections. Thereafter, PCS significantly reduced its output and raised its prices.

Also in 1986, New Mexico Potash Corporation (NMPC) and another American potash producer (who is not a named defendant) filed a complaint with the United States Department of Commerce. Frustrated with low potash prices, the petitioners alleged that Canadian producers had been dumping their product in the United States at prices below fair market value. In 1987, the Department issued a preliminary determination that the Canadian producers were dumping potash and ordered the companies to post bonds on all exports to the United States. These bonds were set according to each firm's calculated "dumping margin." Eventually, the Department negotiated a Suspension Agreement with each of the Canadian producers. The agreement raised the price of Canadian potash in the United States by setting a

---

2. (1) Potash Corporation of Saskatchewan, Inc. and Potash Corporation of Saskatchewan Sales, Ltd. (collectively "PCS"); (2) Cominco, Ltd. and Cominco American, Inc. (collectively "Cominco"); (3) IMC Global, Inc.; (4) Kalium Chemicals, Ltd., Kalium Canada, Ltd. and its former owner and operator, PPG Industries, Inc. and PPG Canada, Ltd. (collectively "Kalium"); (5) Noranda Mineral, Inc., Noranda Sales Corporation Ltd. and Central Canada Potash Co. (collectively "Noranda"); (6) Potash Corporation of America, Inc. and its owner Rio Algom, Ltd. (collectively "PCA"); (7) New Mexico Potash Corporation (NMPC) and its affiliate, (8) Eddy Potash Inc. (Eddy).

3. An oligopoly is an "[e]conomic condition where only a few companies sell substantially similar or standardized products." *Black's Law Dictionary* 1086 (6th ed.1990).

minimum price at which each Canadian producer could sell in the United States. That agreement remains in effect today. When the Canadian producers entered into the Suspension Agreement, PCS announced that it was raising its prices by eighteen dollars per ton. Other producers quickly followed suit. The price of potash has remained markedly higher after the Suspension Agreement, although prices have slowly but steadily declined for the most part since the agreement was signed by the producers on January 8, 1988.

The class alleges that between April 1987 and July 1994 the producers colluded to increase the price of potash. The producers, in turn, maintain that the price increase was the product of the interdependent nature of the industry and its reaction to the privatization of PCS and the Suspension Agreement. The district court granted the producers's motions for summary judgment and the class appeals.

II. DISCUSSION

The class asserts that if we affirm the district court, we will "stand alone in holding that circumstantial evidence, even if overwhelming, cannot be used to defeat a summary judgment motion in anti-trust cases." We make no such legal history here, however, because the class's proffered evidence, far from overwhelming, fails to establish the elements of a prima facie case.

Section 1 prohibits concerted action by two or more parties in restraint of trade. The Supreme Court in *Monsanto Co. v. Spray–Rite Service Corp.,* 465 U.S. 752, 764 & 768, 104 S.Ct. 1464 (1984) and *Matsushita Electric Industrial Co. v. Zenith Radio Corp.,* 475 U.S. 574, 588, 106 S.Ct. 1348 (1986), provided the standard used to determine whether the plaintiffs's evidence of a section 1 violation survives a summary judgment motion. In order to state a section 1 case, plaintiffs must present evidence that "tends to exclude the possibility of independent action" by the defendants. *Monsanto,* 465 U.S. at 768, 104 S.Ct. 1464. This means that conduct that is "as consistent with permissible [activity] as with illegal conspiracy does not, standing alone, support an inference of antitrust conspiracy." *Matsushita,* 475 U.S. at 588, 106 S.Ct. 1348. We are among the majority of circuits to apply *Monsanto* and *Matsushita,* broadly, and in both horizontal and vertical price fixing cases. Applied in this case, the standard requires that if it is as reasonable to infer from the evidence a price-fixing conspiracy as it is to infer permissible activity, then the plaintiffs's claim, without more, fails on summary judgment.

The class's price-fixing claim is based on a theory of conscious parallelism. Conscious parallelism is the process "not in itself unlawful, by which firms in a concentrated market might in effect share monopoly power, setting their prices at a profit-maximizing, supracompetitive level by recognizing their shared economic interests." *Brooke Group Ltd. v. Brown & Williamson Tobacco Corp.,* 509 U.S. 209, 227, 113 S.Ct. 2578 (1993). The class points out that the producers's prices were roughly equivalent during the alleged conspiracy, despite differing production costs. It further points out that price changes by one producer were quickly met by the others. This establishes only that the producers consciously paralleled each other's prices.

Evidence that a business consciously met the pricing of its competitors does not prove a violation of the antitrust laws. *See Theatre Enter., Inc. v. Paramount Film Distrib. Corp.,* 346 U.S. 537, 540–41, 74 S.Ct. 257 (1954).

Particularly when the product in question is fungible, as potash is, courts have noted that parallel pricing lacks probative significance. An agreement is properly inferred from conscious parallelism only when certain "plus factors" exist. *See In re Baby Food Antitrust Litigation,* 166 F.3d 112, 122 (3d Cir.1999). * * * A plus factor refers to " 'the additional facts or factors required to be proved as a prerequisite to finding that parallel [price] action amounts to a conspiracy.' " *In re Baby Food,* 166 F.3d at 122 (quoting 6 Phillip E. Areeda, *Antitrust Law* § 1433(e) (1986)).

A plaintiff has the burden to present evidence of consciously paralleled pricing *supplemented with* one or more plus factors. However, even if a plaintiff carries its initial burden, a court must still find, based upon all the evidence before it, that the plaintiff's evidence tends to exclude the possibility of independent action. *See Monsanto,* 465 U.S. at 764 & 768, 104 S.Ct. 1464; *Matsushita,* 475 U.S. at 588, 106 S.Ct. 1348; *see also In re Baby Food,* 166 F.3d at 122. As noted, the class identified parallel pricing. The class also asserts that it has established the existence of three plus factors: (1) interfirm communications between the producers; (2) the producers's acts against self-interest; and (3) econometric models which purport to prove that the price of potash would have been substantially lower in the absence of collusion. The evidence underlying these assertions, however, does not bear the weight the class places upon it.

A. Interfirm Communications

The class alleges a high level of interfirm communications between the producers and complains most vociferously about price verification information. Courts have held that a high level of communications among competitors can constitute a plus factor which, when combined with parallel behavior, supports an inference of conspiracy. However, the evidence presented by the class here is far too ambiguous to support such an inference. Considering the proof as a whole, the evidence of interfirm communications does not tend to exclude the possibility of independent action, as required under *Monsanto* and *Matsushita,* since other significant events strongly suggest independent behavior. The fundamental difficulty with the class's argument regarding price verifications is that it assumes a conspiracy first, and then sets out to "prove" it. However, a litigant may not proceed by first assuming a conspiracy and then explaining the evidence accordingly.

The class's evidence shows that the communications include meetings at trade shows and conventions, price verification calls, discussions regarding a Canadian potash export association, and the like. Taking the class's evidence as true, roughly three dozen price verifications occurred between employees, including high-level sales employees, of different companies, over at least a seven-year period. In large part, these contacts involved the verification of prices the companies had already charged on particular sales. The impotence of this circumstantial evidence is that it bears no relationship to the price increases most in question because it lacks the logical link necessary to infer such a relationship.

The class alleges that the price-fixing conspiracy began "at least as early as April, 1987." In 1987, the price for potash was at historically low levels, such that producers were losing millions of dollars. Then, a sudden and dramatic increase in price by PCS occurred on September 4, 1987, and approximately a week later the remaining producers followed suit.[6] The class argues that the large and parallel price increases together with nearly simultaneous price verifications create an inference sufficient to survive summary judgment.

The problem with this theory, as indicated, is that the price verification communications only concerned charges on particular completed sales, not future market prices. There is no evidence to support the inference that the verifications had an impact on price increases. The only evidence is that prices were possibly cut as a result. "[T]o survive summary judgment, there must be evidence that the exchanges of information had an impact on pricing decisions." *In re Baby Food,* 166 F.3d at 125. There is no evidence here that price increases resulted from any price verification or any specific communication of any kind. *Subsequent* price verification evidence on particular sales cannot support a conspiracy for the setting of a broad market price on September 4, 1987.

Even if we were to find the price verification evidence relevant, when considered with all the facts, it does not tend to exclude the possibility of independent action. To the contrary, there is strong evidence of independent action. Just before and concurrent with the suspect price increases, the following occurred: the price of potash was at historic lows and the producers were losing millions; potash companies in the United States complained to the United States Department of Commerce that the Canadian producers were dumping potash at well-below market value; the Department of Commerce made a preliminary determination that the Canadian producers were dumping and required expensive bonds for all imports; the industry leader, the government-founded PCS, hired new management and began privatization with the goal of becoming profitable; legislation was passed in the province of Saskatchewan—the source of nearly all United States potash—that provided for the setting and prorating of potash production; potash producers reached a Suspension Agreement with the Department of Commerce that set price floors for potash; and PCS was finally privatized and significantly reduced its output. In the face of these circumstances and with the price leadership of PCS in this oligopolistic industry, it would have been ridiculous for the remaining companies to not also raise their prices in a parallel fashion. Thus, we find the class's weak circumstantial evidence that the dramatic increases were the result of a price-fixing agreement is not sufficient to survive summary judgment.

This leaves only the question whether there is sufficient evidence to support an agreement to stabilize and maintain prices in violation of section 1 of the Sherman Act. The class's evidence of an agreement to maintain the price of potash at an artificially high level after the initial price increases is again the parallel pricing and price verifications. Parallel pricing has been conceded, leaving the burden once again on the verifications. Common sense dictates that a conspiracy to fix a price would involve one company communicating with another company *before* the price quotation to the customer. Here,

---

6. This price increase was rescinded in the wake of the Suspension Agreement. In its place came a much smaller increase by PCS on January 11, 1988—three days after the Suspension Agreement created a price floor—which pricing decision was followed thereafter by the remaining producers.

however, the class's evidence consists solely of communications to verify a price on a *completed* sale. The price verifications relied upon were sporadic and testimony suggests that price verifications were not always given. The fact that there were several dozen communications is not so significant considering the communications occurred over at least a seven-year period in which there would have been tens of thousands of transactions. Furthermore, one would expect companies to verify prices considering that this is an oligopolistic industry and accounts are often very large. We find the evidence falls far short of excluding the possibility of independent action.

In re Baby Food, 166 F.3d at 112, aptly illustrates why the communications complained about here are inadequate to exclude the possibility of independent action by the producers. The defendants, nationally prominent corporations with ninety-eight percent of the baby food business, were Gerber, H.J. Heinz, and Beech–Nut. It is true that the numerous intercompany pricing communications found by the Third Circuit to be *insufficient* to support a section 1 violation were characterized in one part of the opinion as price discussions among low-level employees. *See id.* at 125. However, deposition testimony in that case revealed that district sales employees and district sales managers of Heinz "were required to submit competitive activity reports to their superiors concerning baby food sales from information they picked up from competitor sales representatives." *Id.* at 118–19. This same line of testimony revealed that supervising managers for Heinz informed district managers "on a regular basis before any announcement to the trade as to when Heinz's competitors were going to increase [their] wholesale list prices." *Id.* at 119. The president of Beech–Nut "testified that it was [Beech–Nut's] policy for sales representatives to gather *and report* pricing information of [Beech–Nut's] competitors." *Id.* (emphasis added). Indeed, the *In re Baby Food* case is replete with evidence that pricing information was systematically obtained and directed to high-level executives of Gerber (including Gerber's vice president of sales), Beech–Nut and Heinz, the principal national competitors in the baby food industry.

The evidence in the case shows that a carefully conceived and effective system of price information gathering for the benefit of corporate executives was at all relevant times alive and well in the baby food industry. Notwithstanding communications that far surpassed any information exchanges established in this case, the Third Circuit applied *Matsushita* and granted summary judgment to the defendants, in large part because there was no evidence that the exchanges of information had an impact on pricing decisions. *See In re Baby Food*, 166 F.3d at 125. As earlier stated, there likewise is absolutely no such evidence in this litigation, only speculation.

The class directs our attention to *In re Brand Name Prescription Drugs Antitrust Litigation*, 123 F.3d 599, 614 (7th Cir.), *cert. denied*, 522 U.S. 1153, 118 S.Ct. 1178 (1998), in which the plaintiffs, like the class, searched through an enormous quantity of discovery material and culled out a number of suspicious interfirm communications. The court in *Brand Name* described these documents produced as "smoking guns." *Id.* By contrast, the communications here are facially innocent contacts which are, at most, ambiguous on the question of whether the producers schemed to set prices.

The class argues that a memorandum issued by Canpotex, a lawful Canadian cartel that sets prices for potash sold outside of the United States, is the class's "smoking gun." This memorandum, dated January 8, 1988, and directed to its "agents and offices" reads in pertinent part:

"FYI Canadian potash producers have reached agreement with the United States Department of Commerce and all dumping action has been suspended for minimum 5 years. It is rumoured that the USD 35.00 per metric ton increase posted by Canadian producers in 1987 to cover possible tariff payments to the U.S. Govt will be refunded in full or part. In the meantime new price lists are being issued on Monday Jan. 11 at:

Standard Grade	USD 80.00
Coarse Grade	USD 84.00
Granular Grade	USD 86.00"

Appellants's Joint App. at 910.

The class asserts that this memorandum establishes an agreement to fix prices. The class argues that the people who received the January 8, 1988, memorandum were all high-ranking officials in the producers's companies who were on the Board of Directors of Canpotex, and therefore, the memorandum is evidence that tends to exclude an inference that the producers acted independently.

The magistrate judge disagreed that this memorandum was sufficient evidence to exclude the possibility that the producers acted independently. The magistrate judge first noted that PCS had also announced the same prices in a telex to its customers on January 8, 1988, and thus the possibility that Canpotex learned of the price list from a customer of PCS could not be excluded. Further, the magistrate judge discovered that while most of the Canadian defendants had matched the prices in the memorandum by January 22, 1988, they did not uniformly issue price lists matching those prices on January 11, 1988, and one producer, Kalium, did not match those prices at all. However, as the magistrate judge pointed out, "evidence that the alleged conspirators were aware of each other's prices, before announcing their own prices, 'is nothing more than a restatement of conscious parallelism,' which is not enough to show an antitrust conspiracy." * * * *See also Weit v. Continental Ill. Nat'l Bank and Trust Co.*, 641 F.2d 457, 462 (7th Cir. 1981) (mere opportunity to conspire even in context of parallel business conduct not necessarily probative evidence of price-fixing conspiracy).

We agree with the magistrate judge's finding that this document was not sufficient evidence to exclude an inference that the producers acted independently. First, the memorandum was written by R.J. Ford and directed to "agents and offices." It is not at all clear who this memorandum was sent to or received by, and a thorough review of the appellants's voluminous joint appendix has not clarified this point. Dozens of these high ranking officials were deposed during pretrial discovery, and according to the documents submitted by the class in its joint appendix, only one person, Dave Benusa, was asked if he received "any document dated the 8th of January 1988 concerning pricing." Benusa was manager of marketing for Cominco American in 1988. Benusa stated in his deposition that he did not receive any document dated January 8, 1988, concerning pricing. The class apparently did not depose the author of the memorandum, R.J. Ford, nor did they make any further attempt that we can find to identify who received this "smoking gun" piece of evidence. Another document produced by Canpotex, an inter-office memorandum dated September 8, 1993, is actually directed to "Members of the Board of Directors of Canpotex Limited." We assume that had the January 8, 1988, memorandum been intended for the members of the board of directors, it likewise would have so stated.

Furthermore, even if, as the class asserts, the memorandum had been received by high-ranking officials in the producers's companies, we agree with the magistrate judge's reasoning that the memorandum does not assist the class in proving the existence of a conspiracy. As the magistrate judge pointed out, the producers did not uniformly increase prices to match the memorandum on January 11, 1988, and furthermore, one producer, Kalium, did not match the memorandum price at all. The fact that most of the producers did increase prices to match the PCS price increase of January 11, 1988, is not surprising in a market where conscious parallelism is the norm. Despite submitting a five-volume joint appendix, the class has failed to present evidence about this memorandum which tends to exclude the possibility of independent action by the producers. As it turns out, the "smoke" from this gun is barely, if at all, discernible.

Finally, the class asserts that the producers signaled pricing intentions to each other through advance price announcements and price lists. The Supreme Court has held, however, that "the dissemination of price information is not itself a per se violation of the Sherman Act." *United States v. Citizens & S. Nat'l Bank,* 422 U.S. 86, 113, 95 S.Ct. 2099 (1975).

As we noted at the outset, the class may not proceed by first assuming a conspiracy and then setting out to prove it. If the class were to present independent evidence tending to exclude an inference that the producers acted independently, then, and only then, could it use these communications for whatever additional evidence of conspiracy they may provide. As the record stands, we find these contacts far too ambiguous to defeat summary judgment.

B. Actions Against Self-interest

Evidence that defendants have acted against their economic interest can also constitute a plus factor. *See, e.g., Petruzzi's IGA Supermarkets, Inc. v. Darling–Delaware Co.,* 998 F.2d 1224, 1243–45 (3d Cir.1993) (denying defendants's motion for summary judgment where defendants refrained from bidding aggressively on accounts already serviced by other defendants). However, where there is an independent business justification for the defendants's behavior, no inference of conspiracy can be drawn.

The only evidence of actions against interest that the class has identified is the producers's uniform participation in the Suspension Agreement.[7] The class argues that those producers with low dumping margins could have

---

7. The class also asserts that PCS acted against its self-interest when it agreed to supply potash to PCA when PCA's mine flooded. This agreement occurred in February 1987, before the class contends the conspiracy ever began. It is, therefore, of little relevance to this case.

undercut other producers's prices and gained market share while still maintaining prices at profitable levels. Instead, the low tariff producers joined the Suspension Agreement. The class further posits that NMPC's[8] failure to object to the agreement was an action against self-interest.

In response, the producers point out that Department of Commerce investigations are unpredictable, and participation in the agreement reduced uncertainty. Furthermore, without the Suspension Agreement, even low tariff producers would have been required to post substantial bonds which would have caused considerable capital drain on corporate coffers. Like the Canadian producers, NMPC was uncertain about the ultimate outcome of the Department of Commerce's investigation. Under the Suspension Agreement, NMPC obtained certainty and a higher price for potash sold in the American market. This is the relief NMPC initially sought, and it is unsurprising that NMPC would not oppose such an outcome.

The class has thus failed to carry its burden to rebut the producers's independent business justification for their actions. There is nothing in this record that contradicts the conclusion that ending the dumping investigation with a settlement that required unreasonably low potash prices to rise was a legitimate business decision for the low tariff producers. They benefitted from increased revenues, while avoiding the cost of litigation and the risk of penalties. This cannot be construed as an act against self-interest.

C. Expert Testimony

Finally, the class argues that its expert's econometric model provided crucial confirmation that the prevailing potash prices during the alleged conspiracy were above those expected in the absence of collusion. While their expert concedes that the prices have primarily steadily decreased[9] since January 8, 1988, he asserts that prices would have been much lower absent an agreement to fix prices. We need not decide whether such evidence, in a proper case, could constitute a plus factor, because we find the report in this case is not probative of collusion.

The class's expert evidence is lacking in two crucial respects. First, the expert admits that his model fails to take into account the dramatic events of 1986. In his deposition, the class's expert confirmed that his model considers neither the privatization of PCS nor the anti-dumping proceedings. It is

---

8. The class also asserts that failure to object to the Suspension Agreement was contrary to Eddy's self-interest. This argument is puzzling because Eddy was not in existence at the time of the agreement and thus could hardly have objected to it.

9. It has been suggested that in the context of a price-fixing agreement among several producers in an oligopoly, the price actually would decrease somewhat over time because individual producers would attempt to "cheat" on the agreement by slightly lowering prices. Our review of the learned treatises on oligopolies and antitrust law does not seem to bear this theory out. First, there is very little discussion of the phenomenon of steadily *lowering* prices in an alleged price-fixing conspiracy. Second, several commentators have suggested that the incentive to lower prices while other oligopolists maintain prices deters collusion in the first place. *See* Jonathan B. Baker, *Two Sherman Act Section 1 Dilemmas: Parallel Pricing, the Oligopoly Problem, and Contemporary Economic Theory,* 38 Antitrust Bull. 143, 151 (1993) (analyzing George Stigler's 1964 article, *A Theory of Oligopoly,* 72 J.Pol.Econ. 44 (1964) and recognizing that "the unilateral incentive to deviate on a cooperative arrangement to fix price ... is the very market force by which competition insures low prices and high output"); *see also* Donald F. Turner, *The Definition of Agreement Under the Sherman Act: Conscious Parallelism and Refusals to Deal,* 75 Harv.Law Rev. 655, 660 (1962) (noting that *without* an agreement among oligopolists, the pressure to cut prices is irresistible).

beyond dispute that even without collusion, those events would have led to higher potash prices. A model that does no more than report that prices did, indeed, rise after these events tells us nothing about the existence of industry collusion.

A second flaw in the expert's report, as the magistrate judge noted, is that it relies almost exclusively on evidence (such as the producers's common membership in trade associations and their publication of price lists to customers) that is not probative of collusion as a matter of law. Under Federal Rule of Evidence 703, the facts underlying an expert's opinion need not be admissible if they are "of a type reasonably relied upon by experts in a particular field." The rule, however, contemplates that there will be "sufficient facts already in evidence or disclosed by the witness as a result of his or her investigation to take such expert opinion testimony out of the realm of guesswork and speculation." In this case, the expert's model is fundamentally unreliable because of his heavy (if not exclusive) reliance on evidence that is not probative of conspiracy, coupled with his failure to consider significant external forces that served to raise the price of potash.

III. Conclusion

We have carefully considered each of the class's other arguments and find them to be without merit. The class has failed to present evidence of collusion sufficient to create a genuine issue of material fact. The producers are therefore entitled to summary judgment. For the foregoing reasons, the decision of the district court is affirmed.

JOHN R. GIBSON, Circuit Judge, dissenting, with whom HEANEY, McMILLIAN, RICHARD S. ARNOLD, and MURPHY, Circuit Judges, join.

I dissent.

The Court today rejects circumstantial evidence of conspiracy and requires direct evidence to withstand summary judgment in an antitrust case. The court's requirement of direct evidence is contrary to *Monsanto v. Spray–Rite Service Corp.*, 465 U.S. 752, 768, 104 S.Ct. 1464 (1984), which only required "direct *or circumstantial* evidence that reasonably tends to prove . . . a conscious commitment to a common scheme designed to achieve an unlawful objective." (Emphasis added). Because conspirators cannot be relied upon either to confess or to preserve signed agreements memorializing their conspiracies, the court's requirement for direct evidence will substantially eliminate antitrust conspiracy as a ground for recovery in our circuit.

The potash industry is an oligopoly in which the producers ended a price war and raised prices dramatically. The question is whether the class has shown that the new prices resulted from an agreement among the producers to raise and stabilize prices, rather than from independent reactions to market conditions combined with actions of the United States and Canadian governments. I believe that the class has satisfied the existing standards for circumstantial proof that the prices resulted from collusion.

* * *

I.

* * *

Even though oligopoly pricing harms the consumer in the same way monopoly does, interdependent pricing that occurs *with no actual agreement* does not violate the Sherman Act, for the very good reason that we cannot order sellers to make their decisions without taking into account the reactions of their competitors. *See* Turner, *supra,* at 665–68. As then-Judge Breyer explained:

> "Courts have noted that the Sherman Act prohibits *agreements,* and they have almost uniformly held, at least in the pricing area, that such individual pricing decisions (even when each firm rests its own decision upon its belief that competitors will do the same) do *not* constitute an unlawful agreement under section 1 of the Sherman Act. That is not because such pricing is desirable (it is not), but because it is close to impossible to devise a judicially enforceable remedy for "interdependent" pricing. How does one order a firm to set its prices *without regard* to the likely reactions of its competitors?"

Clamp-All, 851 F.2d at 484 (emphases in original) (citations omitted).

Although interdependent pricing tends to happen naturally in an oligopoly, there are good reasons for competitors to enter into an actual agreement to fix prices. First, successful price coordination requires accurate predictions about what other competitors will do; it is easier to predict what people mean to do if they tell you. In the absence of express agreements, oligopolists "must rely on uncertain and ambiguous signals to achieve concerted action. The signals are subject to misinterpretation and are a blunt and imprecise means of ensuring smooth cooperation, especially in the context of changing or unprecedented market circumstances. This anticompetitive minuet is most difficult to compose and to perform, even for a disciplined oligopoly." *Brooke Group Ltd. v. Brown & Williamson Tobacco Corp.*, 509 U.S. 209, 227–28, 113 S.Ct. 2578 (1993). Second, competitors may have different preferences on decisions such as pricing and therefore may not be willing just to follow a leader's decision; words (or word substitutes) may be necessary to negotiate a common course of action. * * *

While the oligopoly market structure naturally facilitates supra-competitive pricing, that same market structure also makes cooperative arrangements unstable, for this reason: It is in the best interest of each individual competitor for his competitors to charge high prices, while he charges somewhat less when that will help him steal customers from his competitors. *See* George J. Stigler, *A Theory of Oligopoly,* 72 J.Pol.Econ. 44, 46 (1964) ("Let us assume that the collusion has been effected, and a price structure agreed upon. It is a well-established proposition that if any member of the agreement can secretly violate it, he will gain larger profits than by conforming to it."). The temptation to shade prices secretly is just as inherent in the oligopoly market structure as the temptation to collude to raise prices. *See* [HERBERT HOVEN-KAMP, FEDERAL ANTITRUST POLICY: THE LAW OF COMPETITION AND ITS PRACTICE 140–41 (1994)]; Jonathan B. Baker, *Two Sherman Act Section 1 Dilemmas: Parallel Pricing, the Oligopoly Problem, and Contemporary Economic Theory,* 38 Antitrust Bulletin 143, 154 (1993). Of course, if the competitors know about the undercutting, they will match it. *See* Stigler, *supra,* at 46. Therefore, price-shading and secrecy must go hand in hand. While publicly announced prices discourage the sellers from cutting prices because they know that their price cuts will be matched, thus eliminating any competitive advantage, conversely, secretly negotiated discounts encourage price-cutting, since each seller hopes to steal customers without suffering retaliation from its competitors. *See* Hovenkamp, *supra,* at 141. As a result, a cartel can only succeed for any period of time if it has the ability to detect cheating and punish it effectively.

If the oligopolists agree, either tacitly or expressly, to coordinate price increases, they have committed a per se violation of section 1 of the Sherman Act. *See United States v. Socony–Vacuum Oil Co.,* 310 U.S. 150, 212–18, 60 S.Ct. 811 (1940) (agreement to fix prices per se illegal); *American Tobacco Co. v. United States,* 328 U.S. 781, 809–10, 66 S.Ct. 1125 (1946) (agreement need not be express as long as there is unity of purpose or "common design and understanding"). From the outside, however, the conspirators' actions may look the same as innocent oligopoly pricing. Although parallel pricing evidence is *consistent* with illegal conduct, it is *equally consistent* with lawful conduct, and thus does not tend to exclude the possibility of independent action, as required by *Monsanto Co. v. Spray–Rite Service Corp.,* 465 U.S. 752, 764, 104 S.Ct. 1464 (1984). Therefore, parallel pricing in a concentrated market cannot make a submissible section one case, although it may set the groundwork for such a case. * * *

In a rather primitive way, the "plus factors" test incorporates the economic principles outlined above as a way to distinguish between innocent interdependence and illegal conspiracy. Under this test, plaintiffs can establish a prima facie case of conspiracy by showing parallel prices together with "plus factors" that increase the likelihood that the parallel prices resulted from conspiracy. * * *

We must, of course, take care to interpret the "plus factors" test in a way that is consistent with *Monsanto*. With *Monsanto* in mind, it is useful to distinguish between "plus factors" that establish a background making conspiracy likely and "plus factors" that tend to exclude the possibility that the defendants acted without agreement. For instance, "motive to conspire" and "high level of interfirm communications," are often cited as "plus factors" because they make conspiracy possible. Background facts showing a situation conducive to collusion do not tend to exclude the possibility of independent action, but they nevertheless form an essential foundation for a circumstantial case. In *Matsushita Electric Industrial Co. v. Zenith Radio Corp.,* 475 U.S. 574, 593–98, 106 S.Ct. 1348 (1986), the Supreme Court held that a conspiracy case based on circumstantial evidence must be economically plausible. The background "plus factors" of market structure, motivation and opportunity play an important role in establishing such plausibility. Generally, these background "plus factors" are necessary but not sufficient to prove conspiracy.[13]

On the other hand, acts that would be irrational or contrary to the defendant's economic interest if no conspiracy existed, but which would be

13. It is possible that some types of evidence not logically inconsistent with innocence, such as a high level of interfirm communications, could become so unusual that they suffice to make a prima facie case. *See City of* *Tuscaloosa v. Harcros Chems., Inc.,* 158 F.3d 548, 570–73 (11th Cir. 1998) (incumbency rate on new contracts so high it was inconsistent with independent action), *cert. denied,* 528 U.S. 812, 120 S.Ct. 309 (1999).

rational if the alleged agreement existed, do tend to exclude the possibility of innocence. * * *

A.

Of the "plus factors" that merely make conspiracy possible, such as motive and opportunity to conspire, the class has adduced abundant evidence. Within this category some "plus factors" are purely situational, involving no action on the part of the defendant, and some are volitional; while the former are important, the latter begin to make the required showing of collusion.

The purely situational factors in this case are the market structure and the crisis in the potash industry. The structure of the potash market was conducive to collusion, featuring an oligopoly, barriers to new sellers entering the market, inelastic demand, and a standardized product. *See JTC Petroleum,* 190 F.3d at 777 (market with these features is ripe for collusion). However, there was excess production capacity, which spurs competition, and a price war, which shows the producers had not been able to achieve a stable interdependent equilibrium. Individual attempts in 1986 by Noranda, Kalium, PCA, and PCS to initiate a price rise had failed. The producers were losing millions of dollars. The producers had good reason to wish for a truce.

The volitional background "plus factors" are also very strong in this case. At least one of the defendants actively considered the possibility of joint action, as is stated in the PCS "Corporate Plan" document dated September 25, 1986: "It is not possible for a single producer to affect [sic] a turn-around; however, joint action by a group of producers or governments could achieve this." Then there was a break in pattern, as the market went from price-war to profitability. *See* Turner, *supra,* at 672 ("Even in markets with few sellers, a fairly sudden change in pricing patterns is ground for suspicion.").

The class has introduced significant evidence of solicitations to enter a price-fixing agreement. Most, but not all, of the solicitations were by PCS. For instance, PCS freely complained to Kalium about Kalium's failure to adhere to pricing cut-offs. It was the custom in the industry to give lower prices at times of year when there was no immediate need for fertilizer, but to raise prices during high-use periods. Kalium published price lists announcing the pricing cut-off pattern, but in fact often shipped at the lower price after the cut-off date when it did not get orders filled before the cut-off date. PCS sales chief William Doyle repeatedly upbraided Kalium's vice president Robert Turner for shipping at the lower price after the cut-off date. Turner responded "something to the effect" that he would run his own business. Another time, Doyle called Turner and advised him that neither PCS, IMC, nor Cominco planned to accede to a certain customer's request to delay filling an order—that is, to ship at the old price after the cut-off. Turner answered that Kalium would try to ship by a certain date, as it had already said it would do in a letter to its customers. In the same vein, Doyle approached Turner about a certain bid and told Turner that Kalium's action was "wrong." John Ripperger, vice president of PCA, also testified that Doyle asked him if PCA was going to institute a price increase and not carry over product at the old price; Ripperger interpreted this question to mean that Doyle "would prefer that we don't make sales at the old price." Also, Doyle complained to Ripperger that PCA's pricing was undermining prices in Florida. Ripperger reported a conversation in which Gary Snyder of PCS asked a PCA salesman if he had sold at a certain price, and then said, "We [PCS] will take it [price] down and bury you [PCA] if that's what you want."

In 1988, after the sale of Kalium, Charles Childers, the CEO of PCS, called on Jay Proops, one of Kalium's new owners, armed with a chart showing that PCS was losing market share and that Kalium and other producers were gaining. Childers said Kalium was undercutting the price. Proops did some research and concluded that the chart had incorrect information and that Kalium was not undercutting. Therefore, Proops took no action in response to Childers's visit. In August 1990, Childers telephoned Joseph Sullivan, the other owner of Kalium. Childers told Sullivan that PCS's "price leadership was not working, despite major efforts" and that Childers "wanted to discuss this issue" with Sullivan. Sullivan declined to discuss prices.

Another time, a PCS employee took advantage of a trade meeting to apologize to Kalium's Turner about a low bid PCS had made by mistake. The PCS employee testified that he explained the mistake to Turner because he had "some concern that [the low price] may spread in the marketplace," and that he "was hopeful that it wouldn't go any darn further." Turner testified that Kalium matched the bid, but the reaction was "pretty much confined to that account. It did not go beyond that."

Though PCS made most of these overtures, on isolated occasions others did the same. Kalium's Turner called Ripperger of PCA to complain about a salesman who was cutting prices in Wisconsin. Similarly, Kip Williams of IMC complained to Ripperger about price-cutting in Florida.

Despite evidence that various defendants invited others to join in stabilizing prices, the class was not able to adduce direct evidence that the people on the receiving end of these solicitations accepted them and formed a deal. The evidence of solicitation is relevant, however, because it shows conspiratorial state of mind on the part of the solicitor and may also indicate that the solicitor was acting upon an earlier agreement. *See* 6 Phillip E. Areeda, *Antitrust Law* § 1419c (1986) ("Besides serving as direct evidence of a particular agreement, a solicitation might be circumstantial evidence of an ongoing conspiracy. Although no favorable response to the solicitation is shown, the solicitation itself might be the product of a prior agreement.").

B.

The stage was clearly set for conspiracy in this case. The question is whether the additional evidence tends to exclude the possibility that the producers acted independently. I believe that it does.

First, the class has produced evidence that the producers cooperated in disclosing prices they had charged on particular sales. The industry practice was that each producer published a price list stating its price, the dates for which that price would be available, and any discounts that the producer would extend. The price lists were widely distributed to customers and certainly were no secret. However, actual prices sometimes deviated from the lists. When Childers and Doyle came to PCS, a key aspect of their program to raise industry prices was to insist on the list price. Doyle stated in an industry publication: "When I first came on board in the spring of 1987, the first word I put out to our sales force was that the price list was our price, stick to that price and no bending. Anybody who bends was out of here.'' Despite published price lists with the high follow-the-leader price, the producers continued to undercut each other in privately negotiated deals. (This is what one would expect even from a cartel operating under an illegal agreement.) When word of the discounting got around to PCS, PCS executives, particularly sales chief Doyle, were quite active in contacting the discounter and asking for verification of the rumored price. Significantly, Doyle testified that he never made any such price verification calls before 1987. The number of these verification communications is difficult to pin down, but Doyle estimated he initiated or received three to four calls per year with PCA, five to six per year with IMC, three to four per year with Cominco, five to six total with Kalium, "a few" with NMPC, and one to two total with Noranda. Doyle was by no means the only person making such calls on behalf of PCS, and there is evidence that the other defendants called each other as well (except that there is no evidence of others calling Noranda).

These exchanges were often between high-level executives who were responsible for pricing decisions for their companies or who conveyed the price information to those who did set prices. For instance, Dale Massie, vice president of marketing for Cominco, testified that he had price verification communications with Doyle, head of sales at PCS. Massie testified that he made up the Cominco price lists, and the evidence shows that Doyle had a key role in determining PCS pricing policy. Charles Hoffman at IMC reported price information from Doyle to his superiors to inform them that "we would have to meet" PCS's price. Similarly, John Ripperger, vice president of PCA, had price verification discussions with Doyle, and Doyle said he had obtained price information from John Huber, Kalium's vice president of sales.

Price verification communications can either violate section 1 directly or they can be evidence of a violation. An agreement to exchange such communications can constitute an unreasonable restraint of trade under the rule of reason if the anticompetitive effect of the agreement outweighs its beneficial effects. In price fixing cases, the exchange of sensitive price information can sometimes be circumstantial evidence of the existence of a *per se* violation. * * * It is this second theory that the class pursues in this case.

Again, acts that would be contrary to the actor's self-interest in the absence of a conspiracy, but which make economic sense as part of a conspiracy, provide the crucial type of "plus factor" evidence necessary to exclude the possibility of independent action. The class contends that "the price verification calls were inconsistent with the 'pricing secrecy' sought by participants in oligopolistic industries because in such industries 'each producer would like to secretly "shade" price[s], thereby gaining sales and avoiding retaliation.' " The class's argument finds support in the reasoning of *United States v. United States Gypsum Co.,* 438 U.S. 422, 98 S.Ct. 2864 (1978), which stated: "Price concessions by oligopolists generally yield competitive advantages only if secrecy can be maintained; when the terms of the concession are made publicly known, other competitors are likely to follow and any advantage to the initiator is lost in the process. Thus, if one seller offers a price concession for the purpose of winning over one of his competitor's customers, it is unlikely that the same seller will freely inform its competitor of the details of the concession so that it can be promptly matched and diffused." *Id.* at 456, 98 S.Ct. 2864 (citations omitted). Therefore, if there were no reciprocal agreement to share prices (and the producers certainly do not argue that there was), an individual seller who revealed to his competitors the amount of his privately negotiated discounts would have been shooting himself in the foot. On the other hand, if there were a cartel, it would be crucial for the cartel members to cooperate in telling each other about actual prices charged in order to prevent the sort of widespread discounting that would eventually sink the cartel.

Nor is there any legitimate business purpose which would make it desirable for the producers to reveal their pricing concessions notwithstanding the disadvantage of helping their competitors compete more effectively. These private communications between competitors had no redeeming effect of informing customers of prices, such as the advance announcements of price increases in *Reserve Supply Corp. v. Owens–Corning Fiberglas Corp.,* 971 F.2d 37, 54 (7th Cir.1992), or the advertisement of fees in *Wallace v. Bank of Bartlett,* 55 F.3d 1166, 1169 and n. 5 (6th Cir.1995). *Cf. Market Force, Inc. v. Wauwatosa Realty Co.,* 906 F.2d 1167, 1173 (7th Cir.1990) (defendant broker announced intent to pay reduced commission to buyer's brokers; legitimate business reason was that other brokers needed to know in advance what commissions defendant was willing to pay). *See also United States v. Citizens & S. Nat'l Bank,* 422 U.S. 86, 113–14, 95 S.Ct. 2099 (1975) (correspondent bank program legitimate reason for "intimate and continuous cooperation and consultation on interest rates"). To the contrary, the prices stated here were discounts from the published price lists that reflected the prices the producers wanted to charge. The producers had no interest in publicizing these discounts to the market as a whole. Nor is there any evidence of special necessity for horizontal price communications, such as the customer fraud which justified the producers' practices in *Cement Manufacturers Protective Ass'n v. United States,* 268 U.S. 588, 595–96, 45 S.Ct. 586 (1925). The price communications in this case are more like those in *In re Coordinated Pretrial Proceedings,* 906 F.2d at 448, which served "little purpose" other than facilitating price coordination.

The Court today concludes that voluntarily revealing secret price-cutting to one's competitors is not probative of conspiracy, for three reasons, each of which is unsound. First, the price verification communications involved completed sales, not future sales. The Court states: "Common sense dictates that a conspiracy to fix a price would involve one company communicating with another company *before* the price quotation to the customer." This misconceives the purpose for which the price communications are being offered. The communications are not supposed to be direct evidence of a one-time mini-conspiracy to fix the price on one sale. Rather, they are circumstantial evidence of a type of behavior one would not expect in the absence of an agreement to cooperate. If no cartel was in place, each competitor would seek to benefit from high prices generally, while secretly shading prices when it would gain a customer without provoking retaliation. Confessing price-cutting when one needn't do so would only invite retaliation and guarantee that one's competitors could match the discounted price exactly next time. This is contrary to self-interest. On the other hand, if the producers were cooperating in a cartel, a necessary feature of their arrangement would be some way to determine who was discounting. Thus, confessing price-cutting to competitors makes no economic sense for independent actors, but makes perfect economic sense for cartel members. The Court has rejected circumstantial evidence of an agreement because it is not direct evidence.

The Court's second reason for dismissing the price verification evidence is that "[t]here is no evidence to support the inference that the verifications had an impact on price increases." The class points to the price verifications as circumstantial evidence of a broader conspiracy. Parallel price increases are the starting point for the class's case, so that if the conspiracy is proved, effect on prices has been proved at the first step. The Court argues that prices eventually went down, but this glosses over the fact that they first rose dramatically, then remained above both the forecasted price based on market factors and the suspension agreement price until 1992 (with the exception of the two-month dip caused by the PCS "market correction program"). If, to prove collusion, a plaintiff has to prove that there was no cheating, thus no downward pressure on prices, cartels will be quite safe from the Sherman Act.

To support its proposition that there is nothing suspicious about oligopolists exchanging non-public price information, the Court relies on *In re Baby Food Antitrust Litigation,* where the Third Circuit stated: "No evidence . . . shows that any executive of any defendant exchanged price or market information with any other executive." 166 F.3d at 135. The court held that price discussions among low level employees did not show a conspiracy. *Id.* at 137. This reasoning implies that if high-level executives had been involved, it would have constituted evidence of conspiracy (if, indeed, the plaintiffs had been able to prove parallel pricing, which they did not in *In re Baby Food.*) In our case there is a wealth of evidence that high level executives, who were in a position to respond to what they learned, were directly involved in exchanging secret price information. Citing *In re Baby Food* in a case with this kind of evidence vitiates the distinction on which the Third Circuit relied.

* * *

The Court's third reason for dismissing the price verifications is that the verifications were "sporadic." The evidence indicates that the producers called each other when they had reason to think their competitors were cutting prices, and that they responded to each other's inquiries. The total number of such inquiries is difficult to set, but the defendants characterize it as "no more than several dozen"—surely more than a scintilla. *Cf. Container Corp.,* 393 U.S. at 335, 89 S.Ct. 510 (liability where "all that was present was a request by each defendant of its competitor[s] for information as to the most recent price charged or quoted, whenever it needed such information" . . . ; "[t]here was to be sure an infrequency and irregularity of price exchanges").

This "sporadic" argument seems to be directed to the quantum of proof, rather than the quality of it. In other words, it is an argument that more proof should exist, rather than an argument that the existing proof is not probative. If the plaintiff adduces evidence of the kind that tends to prove the existence of a conspiracy, I do not believe that *Monsanto* and *Matsushita* give a justification for rejecting it. *Monsanto* and *Matsushita* lay out a test for the kind of proof necessary in antitrust cases, not the quantity of it. *Compare Monsanto,* 465 U.S. at 764, 104 S.Ct. 1464; and *Matsushita,* 475 U.S. at 587–88, 106 S.Ct. 1348 ("antitrust law limits the range of permissible inferences from ambiguous evidence"; if claim makes no economic sense, plaintiff's evidence must be "more persuasive" than would otherwise be necessary) *with Anderson v. Liberty Lobby, Inc.,* 477 U.S. 242, 254–55, 106 S.Ct. 2505 (1986) (where substantive law imposes a heightened standard of proof, as in libel cases, a higher quantum of proof is required to survive summary judgment). There is no heightened "clear and convincing" standard of proof in civil antitrust conspiracy cases, requiring a greater quantum of proof than the ordinary "preponderance of the evidence" standard. The plaintiff's evidence must amount to more than a scintilla, but the plaintiff does not have to outweigh the defendant's evidence item by item.

* * *

The Court states in this case that the fact that there were "several dozen communications" among competitors is not "significant." *Supra.* I would hold that evidence of several dozen communications of the type that tends to prove conspiracy creates a genuine issue of material fact.

In addition to the price verification practices, evidence concerning PCS's "market correction program" in December 1989 also tends to exclude the hypothesis of independent action. On December 18, 1989, PCS cut its prices by $18 a ton for five days. PCS's Carlos Smith stated that the purpose (and effect) of the program was to stabilize prices in the industry:

Q. [W]as it an attempt to stabilize prices?

A. Yes.

* * *

Q. And did it work?

A. It leveled them.

A high-level Kalium executive, John Huber, wrote the following notes: "Program was a market correction. Weren't trying to teach other people—only got tired of people who kept chipping away. Program was reasonable one— checked with people.... People started *cheating*.... *We* wanted to get their attention. Program to be short, very specific." (Emphasis added.) Huber said he did not recall to whom he had been talking when he made these notes, but the use of the phrase, "We wanted to get their attention," suggests he was taking dictation from someone at PCS.[14]

The wording of Huber's notes implies that the "market correction" program was a way of disciplining producers who had breached an earlier agreement. In plain English, the use of the word "cheating" denotes the breach of an agreement or convention, not independent action. Without an agreement, price cutting would be called "competing," not "cheating."

Moreover, the Huber notes suggest PCS's action was not lonely price leadership, but rather that PCS "checked with people" before cutting prices. Apparently, PCS did not want to risk sparking another price war by letting other producers misunderstand the intent behind the "market correction

---

14. Another memorandum in the same time frame prepared by a Noranda employee states: "Casual conversation at the SMA meeting with a fairly senior PCS guy got quite pointed about 'market correction plan' and he was happy to indicate that they could do it again.... I don't think the conversation was idle." The similarity of the messages lends additional weight to the inference that PCS was the source of information for the Kalium memo.

program." These notes illustrate a situation in which smoke signals were just too ambiguous and dangerous to be trusted, so that competitors had to resort to explicit communications to coordinate prices. *See Brooke Group Ltd. v. Brown & Williamson Tobacco Corp.*, 509 U.S. 209, 227–28, 113 S.Ct. 2578 (1993) ("anticompetitive minuet" difficult to compose and perform). The notes, taken together with the successful "market correction" program, tend to exclude the possibility of independent action.

The class also points to another piece of evidence that tends to exclude the hypothesis of independent action. This is the Canpotex memorandum of Friday, January 8, 1988, which stated:

> "FYI Canadian potash producers have reached agreement with the United States Department of Commerce and all dumping action has been suspended for a minimum of 5 years. It is rumored that the USD per metric ton increase posted by Canadian producers in 1987 to cover possible tariff payments to the U.S. Govt will be refunded in full or part. *In the meantime new price lists are being issued on Monday Jan. 11 at: Standard Grade USD 80.00; Coarse Grade USD 84.00; Granular Grade USD 86.00.*"

(emphasis added). Canpotex is the Canadian producers' cartel organized for sales outside the United States.

Again, the Court misconceives the import of this evidence, rejecting it as direct evidence of an attempt to reach an agreement, when the class offers it as circumstantial evidence of an agreement that already existed. The Court considers it crucial to establish who received the Canpotex memorandum, apparently reasoning that if the memorandum was meant to negotiate an agreement, only people who got the memorandum could respond to it. Instead, the class offers this memorandum as circumstantial evidence tending to show that Canpotex knew on Friday, January 8, of an existing agreement to raise prices. The prophecy by Canpotex that its members would issue new "price lists" with particular prices does indeed tend to show the price increase was coordinated, because otherwise it would have been impossible to know in advance what the individual producers would do.

In sum, the class has adduced evidence of a market structure ripe for collusion, a sudden change from price war to supra-competitive pricing, price-fixing overtures from one competitor to another, voluntary disclosure of secret price concessions, an explicitly discussed cheater punishment program, and advance knowledge of other producers' price moves. Taken together, this list of "plus factors" adds up to evidence that satisfies the *Monsanto* standard.

II.

As I understand our previous cases, it is still necessary to take into account the producers' explanation of their conduct in order to ascertain whether their theory deprives the plaintiffs' case of its probative value. In this case, the producers' theory is that the price rises are explained entirely by the suspension agreement and the spectre of Saskatchewan prorationing legislation. In light of the evidence adduced by Professor Rausser and the Commerce Department correspondence indicating that the industry price far exceeded the price floors set by the suspension agreement, I cannot see that the producers' explanation deflates the class's price-fixing theory. I fully understand that the producers dispute Rausser's understanding of the suspension agreement price levels. Moreover, there is absolutely no dispute that prices had to rise above the price-war levels to comply with the suspension agreement. However, the producers make no attempt to identify a price floor required by the suspension agreement or to show that the producers actually set their prices, * * * by reference to the suspension agreement floor. Indeed, their expert William Barringer argued that it was actually impossible to ascertain whether a given price would satisfy the agreement. Instead, the producers' expert Andrew Rosenfield opined that the defendants needed only to set their prices "well above" suspension agreement floor prices. Under these experts' testimony, the suspension agreement did not dictate the actual prices charged; therefore, the existence of the suspension agreement does not explain away the facts supporting the class's theory that the actual prices were set by illegal collusion.

Not only were the January 1988 prices higher than the prices required by the suspension agreement, but there is evidence tending to prove that the producers felt free to dip below the suspension agreement prices when it served their purposes. Professor Rausser's price chart shows that during PCS's "market correction" program in January and February 1990, prices dipped below the suspension agreement floor. Deliberately taking prices below the suspension agreement floor to punish price-cutters is not a convincing sign of industry devotion to the suspension agreement, and the fact that it happened discredits the producers' argument that their prices were compelled by the suspension agreement.

The producers have not made a showing that the governmental intervention so explains their actual behavior as to take away the probative power of the class's case. This case should therefore proceed to trial. Accordingly, I dissent.

Variation in judicial analyses of plus factors suggests that decisions sometimes may depend on the court's unarticulated intuition about the likely cause of observed parallel behavior. Judges seem to vary in their acceptance of the proposition in *Theatre Enterprises* that conscious parallelism does not necessarily indicate concerted action. Courts that appear to regard pricing uniformity as a sign of collaboration and market failure tend to expand the range and reduce the quantum of conduct that, when added to parallel behavior, can support a finding of agreement. Thus, some decisions go to great lengths to characterize proof as suggesting collective activity. On the other hand, judges who see parallelism as benign—*e.g.*, a natural result of the tendency of supplier prices to converge in competitive markets—implicitly hold the plaintiff to more rigorous standards of proof and display a greater reluctance to infer an agreement on the basis of asserted plus factors.

Blomkest was decided by a 6–5 vote of the Eighth Circuit, sitting en banc. The *Blomkest* majority considered the three types of "plus factors" alleged by the plaintiffs to be sufficient to allow the district court to infer an unlawful agreement on price in a parallel pricing setting: (1) interfirm communication, including price verification calls; (2) action against self-interest; and (3) expert testimony that prices exceeded competitive levels. The majority found these proposed plus factors ambiguous or insufficient, individually and collectively. For example, the price verification communications were dismissed as a plus factor primarily on the ground that the calls were infrequent and not made before the price quotation to the customer. Moreover, the majority observed, price may have risen naturally as the result of governmental actions in the United States and the Canadian province of Saskatchewan limiting industry output. Accordingly, the majority upheld the district court's award of summary judgment to defendants.

The dissent took a different approach, using the plus factors to explain how the firms solved their cartel problems to make tacit collusion successful. According to the dissent, deterring cheating formed the key impediment to successful tacit collusion. Many "situational" plus factors—the dissent's term for important aspects of potash industry structure—were conducive to tacit collusion, but the evidence that excess capacity led to price wars suggested to the dissent that the firms were initially unable to deter cheating. The dissent then examined other plus factors with the problem of deterring cheating in mind. This framework led the dissent to understand the price verification calls, for example, differently from the analysis proffered by the majority. According to the dissent, these calls were not efforts to solve the cartel problem of reaching consensus; that was not the central difficulty facing the potash producers. Rather, the calls helped the firms deter cheating, and thus solve the cartel problem that had previously impeded tacit collusion. In plus factor terms, the dissent found that these calls were acts contrary to self-interest absent a conspiracy, and that they lacked a legitimate business purpose. The dissent rejected the alternative explanation for price increases as resulting from governmental actions to limit industry output on the primary ground that the price increase substantially exceeded what would be expected from the governmental intervention alone.

Figure 3–5:
Contrasting the *Blomkest* Majority and Dissenting Opinions

The *Blomkest* Majority	The *Blomkest* Dissent
• interfirm communications 　—few in number; 　—lack connection with price increases; 　—do not exclude possibility of unilateral decision-making	"Situational Factors" • structure of the potash industry • crisis in the potash industry "Volitional Factors"
• absence of direct evidence of agreement	• sudden change in pricing patterns • solicitations to collude
• no actions against self-interest 　—independent business justifications	• voluntary disclosure and exchange of information on pricing • communications among rivals
• expert testimony flawed	• cheater punishment program • advance knowledge of price moves

The *Blomkest* Majority	The *Blomkest* Dissent
	Defendants' Response
	• governmental intervention fails to explain pricing behavior

Which opinion has the more convincing analysis of the *economic* consequences of industry conduct: the dissent, which concludes that the industry participants raised price through coordinated conduct, or the majority, which concludes that higher industry prices may have had a non-conspiratorial explanation?

Which opinion does a better job of integrating the traditional legal framework for inferring agreement with modern economics?

Which opinion's approach to analyzing the plus factors is the more convincing: the dissent's effort to integrate the plus factors into an economic analysis of tacit collusion, or the majority's category-by-category plus factor analysis?

Given the majority's seemingly skeptical approach to the circumstantial evidence, could the plaintiffs ever have convinced the majority to infer an agreement from circumstantial evidence alone, without direct evidence of an agreement from "hot documents" or informants?

Suppose the dissent is correct in its conclusion that the conduct under review was coordinated, and that potash prices were higher than they would otherwise have been as a result (including that they would have declined farther or more quickly after their initial increase absent that conduct). Was it necessary that the firms reach an agreement in order to achieve that outcome? Can the firms make arguments that Sidebar 3–5 suggests should insulate them from the inference of an agreement, namely: "Even if we are coordinating—which, of course, we do not admit—we did not need to agree in order to do so" and "We acknowledge that we each pay attention to our rival's prices when we make our own pricing decisions—we often follow the leader. But we make our decisions independently, and neither negotiate with our competitors nor exchange assurances with them about our prices."?

Could the dissent be correct in concluding that the firms' conduct facilitated coordination by deterring cheating, while the majority is also correct in concluding that the firms had not reached an agreement on price? If the firms had not reached an agreement on price, would it be reasonable to infer that they had reached an agreement to engage in a facilitating practice of verifying prices on demand? Could the plaintiffs have proven such an agreement from circumstantial evidence, and then gone on to show that the agreement was unreasonable, relying on information exchange cases such as *Container*?

If the dissent had prevailed, sending the case back to the district court for trial, and if the lower court had gone on to find an agreement on price, that agreement would almost surely have been considered an antitrust violation given the dissent's view that price rose in excess of what should have been expected to result from the leading non-conspiratorial interpretation, governmental intervention. Indeed, the agreement on price may well have been treated as illegal per se. Does this observation explain the passion with which the majority and dissent fought over the conspiracy issue?

The *Blomkest* majority states:

> We are among the majority of circuits to apply *Monsanto* and *Matsushita,* broadly, and in both horizontal and vertical price fixing cases. Applied in this case, the standard requires that if it is as reasonable to infer from the evidence a price-fixing conspiracy as it is to infer permissible activity, then the plaintiffs's claim, without more, fails on summary judgment.

203 F.3d at 1032. Compare the following paragraph from a Seventh Circuit opinion by Judge Posner:

> The alternative hypothesis is that the manufacturers [have reached an agreement]. * * * As there is neither an a priori reason nor direct evidence to suppose this hypothesis more likely than the first, and as the plaintiffs bore the burden of persuasion, it was necessary for them to present economic evidence that would show that the hypothesis of collusive action was more plausible than that of individual action. *Matsushita Electric Industrial Co. v. Zenith Radio Corp.* * * * They did not, however, as the defendant manufacturers rather absurdly argue, have to exclude all possibility that the manufacturers' [conduct] was unilateral rather than collusive. That would imply that the plaintiff in an antitrust case must prove a violation of the antitrust laws not by a preponderance of the evidence, not even by proof beyond a reasonable doubt (as indeed is required in criminal antitrust cases), but to a 100 percent certainty, since any lesser degree of certitude would leave a possibility that the defendant was innocent.

In re Brand Name Prescription Drugs Antitrust Litigation, 186 F.3d 781, 787 (7th Cir. 1999) (Posner, C.J.) (An earlier opinion from the same litigation was excerpted earlier in this Chapter.) How, if at all, does the *Blomkest* majority's "broad" view of *Matsushita* differ from the defendants' interpretation dismissed by Judge Posner? In practice, does the *Blomkest* majority require of plaintiffs an elevated burden of proof, seemingly contrary to their own formulation and the view of Judge Posner that *Matsushita's* elevated proof standard should be limited in application to economically implausible conspiracies, such as those to lower price to predatory levels, but not applied when rivals seek to raise prices through collusion?

Before *Matsushita*, courts rarely struggled with economic evidence when considering whether to infer an agreement to fix prices when prices rose in parallel. This has changed, as is suggested by the extensive discussion of economic evidence by both the majority and dissent in *Blomkest*. Other recent appellate decisions on inferring agreement also include extensive treatments of economic evidence. The circuits differ in their willingness to infer conspiracy when evidence points both ways.

In *In re High Fructose Corn Syrup Antitrust Litigation*, 295 F.3d 651 (7th Cir. 2002), the Seventh Circuit overturned a district court's award of summary judgment to defendants in an opinion written by Judge Richard Posner. According to the court, "all of [the] evidence is consistent with the hypothesis that [defendants] had a merely tacit agreement, which at least for purposes of this appeal the plaintiffs concede is not actionable under section 1 of the Sherman Act." *Id.* at 661. Yet the Seventh Circuit nevertheless found enough evidence for a reasonable jury to find an agreement to fix prices: "The evidence is not conclusive by any means—there are alternative interpretations of every bit of it—but it is highly suggestive of the existence of an explicit though of course covert agreement to fix prices." *Id.* at 663.

Recall that in *Williamson Oil Co. v. Philip Morris USA*, 346 F.3d 1287 (11th Cir. 2003), the appeals court affirmed a district court's entry of summary judgment in favor of defendants. The Eleventh Circuit held that the evidence, taken as a whole, did not distinguish between a conspiracy to fix prices and lawful "conscious parallelism." "Because [the plaintiffs] cannot demonstrate the existence of a plus factor," the Eleventh Circuit held, "they cannot establish an inference of conspiracy," as would be necessary to overturn the award of summary judgment to the defendants. *Id.* at 1323. Moreover, the defendants "would have rebutted any inference that they conspired to fix prices by demonstrating that the [plaintiff] class's conspiracy theory is utterly implausible." *Id. See also In re Flat Glass Antitrust Litigation*, 385 F.3d 350 (3d. Cir. 2004) (reversing district court award of summary judgment to plaintiffs, on the ground that the evidence was ambiguous as to whether the firms had agreed and, consequently, insufficient legally to support the inference of conspiracy).

The latest word on inferring agreement from circumstantial evidence comes from the Supreme Court. As was discussed in the *Note on the Evolution of Attitudes at the Supreme Court about Burdens of Pleading and Production in Antitrust Cases: From Conley and Poller to Matsushita and Twombly*, in *Bell Atlantic Corp. v. Twombly*, ___ U.S. ___, 127 S.Ct. 1955 (2007), the Court held that an allegation of parallel conduct without further factual support is insufficient to state a claim. "[S]tating such a claim requires a complaint with enough factual matter (taken as true) to suggest that an agreement was made. Asking for plausible grounds to infer an agreement does not impose a probability requirement at the pleading stage; it simply calls for enough fact to raise a reasonable expectation that discovery will reveal evidence of an illegal agreement." *Id.* at 1965. When agreement is alleged based on evidence of parallel conduct, this holding effectively imports to the *pleading* stage of litigation the evidentiary sufficiency standard for summary judgment (*Matsushita*), or equivalently for judgment as a matter of law (*Monsanto*), in conspiracy cases: that the allegations tend to exclude the possibility that the alleged conspirators acted independently.

What are the likely consequences of imposing such a requirement at the pleading stage? Will it discourage plaintiffs with suspicions of conspiracy, but little evidence, from attempting to initiate private treble damage actions that are likely without merit, as the Court hopes? Or will it discourage potentially meritorious claims, which, owing to the fact that the critical evidence of conspiracy is almost always likely to be in the hands of the alleged conspirators, will now not survive motions to dismiss? In concluding its opinion, the majority states that "[b]ecause the plaintiffs here have not nudged their claims across the line from conceivable to plausible, their complaint must be dismissed." *Id.* at 1974. What will distinguish the "conceivable" from the "plausible" at the pleading stage?

Sidebar 3–5:
What is an Agreement?

What is an agreement under the antitrust laws? In one view an agreement is best understood as a process, involving negotiation and the exchange of assurances, not an outcome. This sidebar summarizes the argument for this perspective.*

It is tempting but ultimately unpersuasive to identify an agreement under the antitrust laws from circumstantial evidence in parallel pricing cases by applying common judicial definitions that sound in contract, like a "meeting of the minds" or "conscious commitment to a common scheme." The reason: a court conscientiously applying these definitions would be led to mistakenly infer an agreement merely from the consciously parallel interaction among oligopolists. When one firm in an oligopoly raises its price, and each of the others follows that lead, the definitions are satisfied: the first price increase is an offer; those that follow are acceptances; as each observes the other's actions, they reach a common understanding.

Yet accepting this result by inferring an agreement whenever oligopolists price in parallel would be a mistake. As we learned in Sidebar 3–2, it would permit a finding of unlawful conspiracy in situations where courts would very likely be unable to craft any effective remedy—there would be nothing practical that a court could order the parties to do to correct it. If agreement is evidenced by something beyond merely parallel price behavior, then a court can, in principle, enjoin that extra "something." But absent that extra "something," the only remedy is judicial price regulation—objectionable on a number of grounds. That is why, to paraphrase the Supreme Court, conscious parallelism has not read "agreement" out of the Sherman Act.

The need to frame a satisfactory remedy generates other limits on the application of the antitrust laws. A firm or oligopoly that happens to charge prices above the competitive level does not for that reason alone violate Sherman Act Section 1. Moreover, mere leader-follower behavior is not illegal even if supracompetitive prices result. Consider the Gas Station Hypothetical (Case Study II in section B of this chapter) with this issue in mind. Under contract law, a court could arguably find an implied-in-fact contract. Yet, at least in the Turner tradition, the gas stations would not be deemed to have reached an agreement under the antitrust laws.

An agreement under antitrust law is better defined by what the courts actually do in parallel pricing cases than by the words of the common legal definitions. Rather than deeming mere conscious parallelism an "agreement," courts look for certain additional features of firm behavior called "plus factors" to support an inference of agreement. Plus factors are best thought of as evidence that the alleged conspirators have

---

* This sidebar is adapted from Jonathan B. Baker, *Identifying Horizontal Price Fixing in the Electronic Marketplace*, 65 ANTITRUST L. J. 41, 47–51 (1996). *See also* Jonathan B. Baker, *Two Sherman Act Section 1 Dilemmas: Parallel Pricing, the Oligopoly Problem, and Contemporary Economic Theory*, 38 ANTITRUST BULL. 143 (1993).

gone through a process of negotiation and exchange of assurances in addition to, or as the reason for, their parallel price behavior. They support a conclusion based on the totality of the circumstantial evidence that the parties have done more than merely watch each other's market behavior and respond to it independently, as leaders and followers, and, consequently, that the firms could have behaved differently.

This judicial methodology carries with it an important point: the legal idea of an agreement does not describe a result or equilibrium, but one particular process of reaching supracompetitive marketplace outcomes—what may be termed the "forbidden process" of negotiation and exchange of assurances. The forbidden process consists of behavior that can be enjoined. Thus, if the oligopoly reaches a high price equilibrium through the forbidden process that the law calls an agreement, Sherman Act Section 1 has been violated. If the same result were reached through leader-follower behavior, no agreement on price will be found.

Historically, the most important plus factors involved evidence suggesting that the firms were a hidden cartel, as the court appeared to believe in *Foley*. For example, secret and direct communications among the sellers just before prices rose suggest a cartel denied by its members and pushed underground by the Sherman Act. The list of plus factors has expanded as the critical task of determining whether firms pricing in parallel have engaged in the forbidden process has increasingly become an economic question. Recall that the Supreme Court in *Matsushita*, refused to permit an inference of conspiracy that did not make "economic sense."

In two situations, *Matsushita's* "economic sense" requirement should shield firms from claims of conspiracy. First, if the industry structure is not conducive to coordination—perhaps because entry is easy or because a firm could cut prices in secret and steal business from rivals—then a court should recognize that it would be irrational for a firm to risk prosecution by engaging in the forbidden process without any hope of gaining market power. Under such circumstances the inference of agreement from parallel pricing might not make economic sense. But a past history of coordination, or evidence, as in *American Tobacco*, that prices rose with no plausible economic justification would tend to suggest that coordination is feasible after all. Several of the plus factors listed in Figure 3–4 address whether coordination would be feasible, including the rational motive to behave collectively, past history of industry collaboration, and aspects of industry structure and industry performance.

Second, if the industry structure is conducive to coordination, a court should consider whether it was necessary for the firms to engage in the forbidden process to reach a coordinated, high-price equilibrium, or whether they could achieve the same outcome through leader-follower behavior that does not carry the risk of liability. In the latter case, the firms can argue that "even if we are coordinating—which, of course, we do not admit—we did not need to agree in order to do so." In a parallel pricing case, the firms might also contend: "We acknowledge that we each pay attention to our rival's prices when we make our own pricing decisions—we often follow the leader. But we make our decisions independently, and neither negotiate with our competitors nor exchange assurances with them about our prices." If the facts support this argument, here, too, the inference of agreement would not make economic sense.

Under other circumstances, however, the inference of conspiracy could make economic sense. In particular, a court should be willing to infer an agreement in a parallel pricing case in an industry where entry and discounting are discouraged if the firms appear to have been doing more than merely following each other's market moves. Three indicators could help courts infer that firms have selected a coordinated equilibrium by engaging in the forbidden process of negotiation and exchange of assurances. First, firm behavior might be more complex than would be plausible if the outcomes had been reached absent the forbidden process, as through mere leader-follower behavior. A focal point or rule that developed from historic precedent or clear business imperatives would be expected to be obvious and straightforward—such as "we raise all our prices by a common percentage," or "we don't solicit each other's customers or in each other's territories." More complex relationships and rules might imply that the parties had engaged in active negotiation to reach an agreement. Second, the inference of agreement would be strengthened if the explanations offered by the parties about the putative legitimate business purposes are weak or even pretextual. Third, the inference of agreement would be strengthened if the rivals had an opportunity to communicate, and strengthened even more if their conduct includes overt communications spurring immediate responses, even if those communications and responses are not binding on the parties. These three indicators are reflected in some of the plus factors listed in Figure 3–4, particularly communication or opportunity to communicate, and market conduct that appears irrational absent agreement.

Two plus factors listed in Figure 3–4 are more difficult to understand as evidence that the firms have engaged in the forbidden process of negotiation and exchange of assurances, because they are also consistent with leader-follower behavior. One is actions contrary to self-interest unless pursued collectively. The other is facilitating practices, which often make it more likely that the firms can reach a consensus on high prices through leader-follower behavior without engaging in the forbidden process. Moreover, repeated interaction among firms does not make leader-follower conduct more suspect. Leader-follower behavior may make it possible for firms to achieve higher than competitive prices without engaging in negotiations, particularly when the firms interact repeatedly, as emphasized in Case Study IV in section B of this chapter. But firms that interact repeatedly might raise price even if they are not coordinating, for example if they learn over time that costs or demand are high.

Recall the Turner/Posner debate discussed in Sidebar 3–2. Would you agree that the views expressed in this Sidebar generally coincide with those of Turner? If so, how would Posner respond? *See* RICHARD A. POSNER, ANTITRUST LAW 60–100 (2d ed. 2001).

E. POLICING INCIPIENT DANGERS

The renewed attention to the problems of collusion in the wake of high profile express cartel cases like *Andreas* (Casebook, *supra* Chapter 1), highlights limitations in the legal approach to inferring an agreement on price from circumstantial evidence. Most importantly, mere leader-follower conduct will not supply the plus factors necessary to infer an agreement from parallel pricing, even if higher than competitive prices result. Accordingly, antitrust policy relies upon additional techniques to defeat inter-firm coordination that serves to restrict output and raise prices.

One such technique is to act to prevent the formation of the kind of oligopolistic market structures that might be prone to consciously parallel pricing. Historically, the danger of tacit collusion, and the need to prevent market structures likely to lead to coordinated conduct, was one justification for a tough anti-merger policy that was skeptical of all significant increases in market concentration. (The evolving role of market concentration in horizontal merger analysis is surveyed in Chapter 5, *supra*.) Professor Areeda's treatise describes this approach to addressing the danger of supracompetitive oligopoly pricing as pursuing a "containment" policy that obstructs mergers threatening to create oligopolistic market structures. 6 PHILLIP E. AREEDA, ANTITRUST LAW ¶ 1432d (1986).

This section examines two possibilities for attacking the danger of high prices in oligopolies that go beyond agreement jurisprudence: the prosecution of invitations to collude and an attack on unilateral facilitating practices.

1. INVITATIONS TO COLLUDE

One approach to preventing tacit collusion is to take measures that increase the hazards of even inviting a competitor to engage in a collusive scheme. Although Section 1 of the Sherman Act only reaches actual agreements, the Justice Department in the mid–1980s sought to use Section 2's prohibition against attempted monopolization to attack an unaccepted invitation to collude where the offeror and the offeree together accounted for a substantial share of market activity.

UNITED STATES v. AMERICAN AIRLINES, INC.
United States Court of Appeals for the Fifth Circuit, 1984.
743 F.2d 1114.

W. EUGENE DAVIS, Circuit Judge:

The question presented in this antitrust case is whether the government's complaint states a claim of attempted monopolization under section 2 of the Sherman Act against the defendants, American Airlines, and its president Robert L. Crandall, for Crandall's proposal to the president of Braniff Airlines that the two airlines control the market and set prices. * * *

I.

In February 1982, American Airlines (American) and Braniff Airlines (Braniff) each had a major passenger airline complex, or "hub" at the Dallas–Fort Worth International Airport (DFW).[1] These hubs enabled American and

---

1. Many airlines structure their services around major airports in network complexes termed hubs. The term derives from the fact that the routes of an airline maintaining a hub operation resemble the hub and spokes of a wheel, with the major airport, for example,

Braniff to gather passengers from many cities, concentrate them at DFW, and then arrange connections for them on American and Braniff flights to other cities. The hub systems gave American and Braniff a marked competitive advantage over other airlines that served or might wish to serve DFW. In addition, the limitations on arrivals imposed by the Federal Aviation Administration (FAA) after the 1981 air traffic controllers' strike impeded any significant expansion or new entry by airlines into service at DFW. These limitations helped enable American and Braniff to maintain their high market shares in relation to other competitors.

In February 1982, American and Braniff together enjoyed a market share of more than ninety percent of the passengers on non-stop flights between DFW and eight major cities, and more than sixty percent of the passengers on flights between DFW and seven other cities. The two airlines had more than ninety percent of the passengers on many flights connecting at DFW, when no non-stop service was available between the cities in question. Overall, American and Braniff accounted for seventy-six percent of monthly enplanements at DFW.

For some time before February 1982, American and Braniff were competing fiercely for passengers flying to, from and through DFW, by offering lower fares and better service. During a telephone conversation between Robert Crandall, American's president, and Howard Putnam, Braniff's president, the following exchange occurred:

Crandall: I think it's dumb as hell for Christ's sake, all right, to sit here and pound the * * * out of each other and neither one of us making a * * * dime.

Putnam: Well—

Crandall: I mean, you know, goddamn, what the * * * is the point of it?

Putnam: Nobody asked American to serve Harlingen. Nobody asked American to serve Kansas City, and there were low fares in there, you know, before. So—

Crandall: You better believe it, Howard. But, you, you, you know, the complex is here—ain't gonna change a goddamn thing, all right. We can, we can both live here and there ain't no room for Delta. But there's, ah, no reason that I can see, all right, to put both companies out of business.

Putnam: But if you're going to overlay every route of American's on top of over, on top of every route that Braniff has—I can't just sit here and allow you to bury us without giving our best effort.

Crandall: Oh sure, but Eastern and Delta do the same thing in Atlanta and have for years.

Putnam: Do you have a suggestion for me?

Crandall: Yes. I have a suggestion for you. Raise your goddamn fares twenty percent. I'll raise mine the next morning.

Putnam: Robert, we—

Crandall: You'll make more money and I will too.

DFW, as the hub and the routes to other cities radiating like spokes.

Putnam: We can't talk about pricing.

Crandall: Oh bull * * *, Howard. We can talk about any goddamn thing we want to talk about.

Putnam did not raise Braniff's fares in response to Crandall's proposal; instead he presented the government with a tape recording of the conversation. * * *

II.

The language of the Sherman Act, its legislative history, the general criminal law relating to attempt and the jurisprudence relating to attempt specifically under the Sherman Act, lead us to the same conclusion: the government need not allege or prove an agreement to monopolize in order to establish an attempted joint monopolization under section 2 of the Sherman Act.

* * *

* * * The offense of attempted monopolization * * * has two elements: (1) specific intent to accomplish the illegal result; and (2) a dangerous probability that the attempt to monopolize will be successful. When evaluating the element of dangerous probability of success, we do not rely on hindsight but examine the probability of success at the time the acts occur.

The government unequivocally alleged that Crandall proposed to enlist his chief competitor in a cartel so that American and Braniff, acting together, could control prices and exclude competition at DFW; as Crandall explained to Putnam, "we can both live here and there ain't no room for Delta." As a result of the monopolization, Braniff would "make more money and I will too."

Both Crandall and Putnam were the chief executive officers of their airlines; each arguably had the power to implement Crandall's plan. The airlines jointly had a high market share in a market with high barriers to entry. American and Braniff, at the moment of Putnam's acceptance, would have monopolized the market. Under the facts alleged, it follows that Crandall's proposal was an act that was the most proximate to the commission of the completed offense that Crandall was capable of committing. Considering the alleged market share of American and Braniff, the barriers to entry by other airlines, and the authority of Crandall and Putnam, the complaint sufficiently alleged that Crandall's proposal had a dangerous probability of success.

The requirement that an accused's conduct have a dangerous probability of success expresses a significant antitrust principle that the antitrust laws protect competition, not competitors, and its related principle that the Sherman Act does not reach practices only unfair, impolite, or unethical.

* * *

* * * We note * * * both that dangerous probability remains an element of attempted monopolization in this circuit and that in concluding that the government here stated a claim we do not retreat from its proof requirements. We see Crandall's alleged conduct as uniquely unequivocal and its potential,

given the alleged market conditions, as being uniquely consequential. In sum, our decision that the government has stated a claim does not add attempt to violations of Section 1 of the Sherman Act or lower the incipiency gate of Section 2.

Finally, we note one final consequence of our reasoning. If a defendant had the requisite intent and capacity, and his plan if executed would have had the prohibited market result, it is no defense that the plan proved to be impossible to execute. As applied here, if Putnam from the beginning never intended to agree such fact would be of no aid to Crandall and American.

* * *

* * * We * * * conclude that the better reasoned authorities support the view that a highly verbal crime such as attempted monopolization may be established by proof of a solicitation along with the requisite intent.

III.

Our decision that the government's complaint states a claim of attempted monopolization is consistent with the Act's language and purpose. * * * If section 2 liability attaches to conduct such as that alleged against Crandall, naked proposals for the formation of cartels are discouraged and competition is promoted.

* * *

Appellees argue that price fixing is an offense under section 1 of the Sherman Act and since the government charges that Crandall sought to have American and Braniff fix prices, the government's complaint in reality seeks to have us write an attempt provision into section 1. This argument is meritless. Appellees confuse the section 1 offense of price fixing with the power to control price following acquisition of monopoly power under section 2. Under the facts alleged in the complaint, Crandall wanted both to obtain joint monopoly power and to engage in price fixing. That he was not able to price fix and thus, has no liability under section 1, has no effect on whether his unsuccessful efforts to monopolize constitute attempted monopolization.

* * *

Conclusion

We hold that an agreement is not an absolute prerequisite for the offense of attempted joint monopolization and that the government's complaint sufficiently alleged facts that if proved would permit a finding of attempted monopolization by defendants. * * *

———

The court evaluated whether the "dangerous probability of success" element of the attempt to monopolize offense was satisfied by examining the aggregate market shares of American and Braniff, not the market share of the defendant alone. Was this a creative approach and sensible approach for reaching egregious conduct? Or the court stretch the offense of attempted monopolization to cover this case because there is no attempted collusion offense under the Sherman Act?

How far does the *American Airlines* precedent extend? Suppose four airlines, not two, were significant competitors for airline travel out of Dallas, each accounting for about 25% of passengers and enplanements, and that the president of American Airlines made his price-fixing suggestion at a meeting at which the heads of all four carriers were present. Assuming that the other carriers did not go along with that suggestion, would the *American Airlines* precedent permit the government to bring an attempted monopolization case against American under such circumstances?

Since *American Airlines* was decided, the Justice Department has preferred to challenge attempted price-fixing or attempted bid rigging as violations of the wire fraud or mail fraud statutes rather than as attempts to monopolize. *See, e.g., United States v. Ames Sintering Co.*, 927 F.2d 232 (6th Cir. 1990).

The Federal Trade Commission can also reach invitations to collude under the broad unfair competition prohibition of the statute it enforces, Section 5 of the Federal Trade Commission Act. For example, in *In re Stone Container Corp.*, 63 Fed. Reg. 10,628 (FTC Mar. 4, 1998) (analysis of proposed consent order to aid public comment), the FTC settled by consent allegations that the leading U.S. manufacturer of linerboard had invited its rivals to join it in a strategy to raise the price of linerboard by reducing production and inventory levels. According to the FTC, Stone had previously attempted to raise price, but was forced to back down when its rivals did not follow. Stone concluded that the rivals did not support its earlier price increase because many held excess inventory, tempting them to cheat rather than join in charging higher coordinated prices. Stone's new strategy to raise price, the FTC alleged, was to suspend production (take "downtime") at five of its nine North American linerboard mills, and simultaneously to arrange to purchase excess inventory from several of its competitors. According to the FTC:

> Stone Container subsequently communicated to competitors its intention to take mill downtime and to draw down industry inventory levels, and its belief that these actions would support a price increase. The methods of communication included public statements—press releases and published interviews. Stone Container also communicated its scheme through direct, private conversations with high level executives of its competitors that were outside of the ordinary course of business. Senior officers of Stone Container contacted their counterparts at competing linerboard manufacturers to inform them of the extraordinary planned downtime and Stone Container's plan to make substantial linerboard purchases from its competitors. In the course of these communications, Stone Container arranged and agreed to purchase a significant volume of linerboard from each of several competitors.

> Stone Container's intent was to coordinate an industry-wide price increase; there was no independent legitimate business justification for the company's actions. The unprecedented mill downtime was not a response to the company's own inventory build-up. Further, it would have been less costly for the company to self-manufacture linerboard (at its idled mills) than to purchase inventory from its competitors. Mill downtime and linerboard acquisitions were

mechanisms that enabled Stone Container to be seen by competitors as incurring significant costs in order to manipulate industry supply conditions. These, together with other public and private communications, were a signal to rival firms to join in a coordinated price increase.

The Chairman and Chief Executive Officer of Stone Container has stated that the cost to the company of taking massive mill downtime was approximately $26 million, but that this investment was beneficial for the company and the linerboard industry. He has characterized the company's strategy as an "unqualified success" that helped to "jump start" an industry-wide price increase in October of 1993.

63 Fed. Reg. at 10,629.

A dissenting Commissioner questioned the majority's view that it would have been more economical for Stone Container to keep its plants open than to purchase inventory. He instead saw mill downtime and inventory reductions as a normal competitive response to general industry conditions. He noted that industry prices and sales were low by historical standards, and a number of firms were experiencing financial difficulties.

Should Stone Container be able to defend by demonstrating that it was wrong in viewing rivals' incentive to cheat arising from their excess inventories as the only serious impediment to successful industry coordination? That is, in determining whether Stone Container's actions were invitations to collude, should it matter whether industry coordination was in fact feasible?

2. UNILATERAL FACILITATING PRACTICES

Firms can make unilateral decisions that help them and their rivals solve the "cartel problems" of reaching a consensus, deterring cheating, and preventing entry. One example of how firms can solve their cartel problems unilaterally, without agreement, comes from the experience of two large sellers of electrical equipment, General Electric and Westinghouse, during the 1960s. At the beginning of the decade, the two firms had been convicted of price-fixing (along with a third firm who later exited the market) in a famous scandal that sent executives to jail, and subjected the firms to expensive private lawsuits for treble damages. After the collapse of the price-fixing scheme, firm profitability fell. The companies wanted higher prices, but they did not want to risk another price-fixing conviction.

The two firms independently, but similarly, took several steps to restore profitability; we will focus on two. These steps can be understood as efforts to change the structure of the market to facilitate tacit collusion. First, the firms standardized their product definitions, and published price books setting forth list prices for the wide range of variants. These acts could simplify the coordination task by facilitating price leadership, much in the way simple, obvious rules did so in the hypothetical delicatessen example. The firms would no longer have to work out prices product-by-product in order to collude successfully; they could merely raise prices on all products across-the-board. Moreover, published price lists may make each firm's transactions more apparent to its rivals, creating more "open" pricing and thus discouraging cartel cheating.

Second, GE and Westinghouse promised customers that if any other electrical equipment customer got a lower price, the firm would retroactively give that lower price to the original customer, by refunding the difference. This practice is a type of "most favored nations" or "most favored customer" provision, and is discussed in more detail below in Sidebar 3–6. In brief, although such contractual agreements may appear favorable to individual buyers, their widespread use may be harmful to buyers as a group because they may facilitate coordination by discouraging cheating. Each firm that makes such a promise raises its own costs of cutting price. It effectively ties its own hands so that it won't have an incentive to cheat, making a price war less likely.

With these practices in place, prices and profits rose. Because the firms adopted these practices unilaterally, and neither was a monopolist, the Justice Department did not challenge them under the Sherman Act. But in the unique circumstances of this industry, the Justice Department was able to bring a case as a violation of the decree settling the earlier price-fixing convictions. *See* Proposed Modification of Existing Judgments, *United States v. General Electric Co.*, 42 Fed. Reg. 17,005 (1977); *see also* MICHAEL PORTER, CASES IN COMPETITIVE STRATEGY 102–18 (1983).

Unilateral facilitating practices among oligopolists cannot be challenged under Sherman Act § 1. Unlike the information exchange cases we read earlier, they were not adopted through agreement. Neither can they be reached under Sherman Act § 2, so long as the industry lacks a dominant seller. At least this is the prevailing view today. During the 1970s, as part of a broad attack on market concentration discussed in Sidebar 6–2, the federal enforcement agencies explored the possibility of deconcentrating markets through "shared monopoly" cases. During the 1980s, the Federal Trade Commission saw the problem of unilateral facilitating practices among oligopolists as a gap in the Sherman Act that could potentially be filled through application of FTC Act § 5. Section 5 has long been recognized to reach conduct beyond Sherman and Clayton Act violations, including acts that violate the "spirit" of those antitrust statutes and even conduct that offends public values beyond the letter or spirit of the antitrust laws. *See, e.g., FTC. v. Indiana Federation of Dentists*, 476 U.S. 447, 454 (1986); *FTC v. Sperry & Hutchinson Co.*, 405 U.S. 233, 244 (1972); *FTC v. Brown Shoe Co.*, 384 U.S. 316, 320–21 (1966); *FTC v. Motion Picture Advertising Service Co.*, 344 U.S. 392, 394–95 (1953).

But in the *Du Pont (Ethyl)* case, decided in 1984, the Second Circuit held that FTC Act § 5 did not reach the challenged practices. *E.I. Du Pont De Nemours & Co. v. Federal Trade Commission (Ethyl)*, 729 F.2d 128 (2d Cir. 1984). The practices at issue in *Ethyl* included "most favored nations" clauses; the anticompetitive potential and procompetitive justifications for these provisions are considered in Sidebar 3–6. In its opinion, the appellate panel addressed both the scope of the FTC Act and the competitive effects of the practices that the FTC had held unlawful.

E.I. DU PONT DE NEMOURS & CO. v. FEDERAL TRADE COMMISSION

United States Court of Appeals for the Second Circuit, 1984.
729 F.2d 128.

MANSFIELD, Circuit Judge:

E.I. Du Pont De Nemours and Company ("Du Pont") and Ethyl Corporation ("Ethyl"), the nation's two largest manufacturers of lead antiknock gasoline additives, petition this court pursuant to § 5(c) of the Federal Trade Commission Act, 15 U.S.C. § 45(c), to review and set aside a final order of the Federal Trade Commission ("FTC") * * *. The FTC held that Du Pont, Ethyl and two other antiknock compound manufacturers, PPG Industries, Inc. ("PPG") and Nalco Chemical Company ("Nalco"), had engaged in unfair methods of competition in violation of § 5(a)(1) when each firm independently and unilaterally adopted at different times some or all of three business practices * * * : (1) the sale of the product by all four firms at a delivered price which included transportation costs, (2) the giving by Du Pont and Ethyl of extra advance notice of price increases, over and above the 30 days provided by contract, and (3) the use by Du Pont and Ethyl (and infrequently by PPG) of a "most favored nation" clause under which the seller promised that no customer would be charged a higher price than other customers. The Commission reasoned that, although the petitioners' adoption of these practices was non-collusive, they collectively had the effect, by removing some of the uncertainties about price determination, of substantially lessening competition by facilitating price parallelism at non-competitive levels higher than might have otherwise existed. The order is set aside.

* * *

These characteristics of the industry—high concentration, small likelihood of new entries because of a sharply declining market, inelastic demand, and homogeneity of product—led to a natural oligopoly with a high degree of pricing interdependence in which there was far less incentive to engage in price competition than if there had been many sellers in an expanding market. * * *

Notwithstanding the highly concentrated structure of the industry, there was substantial price and non-price competition during the 1974–1979 period that is the subject of the complaint. * * *

* * *

When a business practice is challenged by the Commission, even though, as here, it does not violate the antitrust or other laws and is not collusive, coercive, predatory or exclusionary in character, standards for determining whether it is "unfair" within the meaning of § 5 must be formulated to discriminate between normally acceptable business behavior and conduct that is unreasonable or unacceptable. Otherwise the door would be open to arbitrary or capricious administration of § 5; the FTC could, whenever it believed that an industry was not achieving its maximum competitive potential, ban certain practices in the hope that its action would increase competition. * * *

In our view, before business conduct in an oligopolistic industry may be labeled "unfair" within the meaning of § 5 a minimum standard demands that, absent a tacit agreement, at least some indicia of oppressiveness must exist such as (1) evidence of anticompetitive intent or purpose on the part of the producer charged, or (2) the absence of an independent legitimate business reason for its conduct.[10] If, for instance, a seller's conduct, even absent identical behavior on the part of its competitors, is contrary to its independent self-interest, that circumstance would indicate that the business practice is "unfair" within the meaning of § 5. In short, in the absence of proof of a violation of the antitrust laws or evidence of collusive, coercive, predatory, or exclusionary conduct, business practices are not "unfair" in violation of § 5 unless those practices either have an anticompetitive purpose or cannot be supported by an independent legitimate reason. To suggest, as does the Commission in its opinion, that the defendant can escape violating § 5 only by showing that there are "countervailing procompetitive justifications" for the challenged business practices goes too far.

In the present case the FTC concedes that the petitioners did not engage in the challenged practices by agreement or collusively. Each acted independently and unilaterally. There is no evidence of coercive or predatory conduct. If the petitioners nevertheless were unable to come forward with some independent legitimate reason for their adoption of these practices, the Commission's argument that they must be barred as "unfair" when they have the effect of facilitating conscious price parallelism and interdependence might have some merit. But the evidence is overwhelming and undisputed, as the ALJ found, that each petitioner independently adopted its practices for legitimate business reasons which we have described.

The tenuousness of the Commission's finding that the challenged practices are "unfair" is illustrated by the fact that it does not tell us when the practices became unlawful: at the time of their original adoption by Ethyl when it was the sole manufacturer of antiknock compounds, when Du Pont entered the market in 1948, when PPG entered in 1961, when Nalco appeared on the scene in 1964, or at some other time. The matter is of some importance for the reason that during the period from 1948 (when Du Pont entered) to 1974 Ethyl's share of the market fell from 100% to 33%. Du Pont's share likewise fell from 50% in 1961, the time of PPG's entry, to 38% in 1974. In the meantime PPG and Nalco, using aggressive competitive measures, captured substantial shares of the market.

* * *

In short, we do not find substantial evidence in this record as a whole that the challenged practices significantly lessened competition in the anti-

---

10. The requirement is comparable to the principle that there must be a "plus factor" before conscious parallelism may be found to be conspiratorial in violation of the Sherman Act. The "plus factor" may be conduct that is contrary to the defendants' independent self-interest, the presence or absence of a strong motive on a defendants' part to enter an alleged conspiracy, or the artificial standardization of products. In United States v. General

Electric Co., 565 F.2d 208 (E.D.Pa.1977), for instance, General Electric in addition to announcing that it would adhere to its published prices and grant no discounts, adopted a "price-protection" policy under which, if it offered a discount to a customer, it obligated itself to give the same discount retroactively to all other customers who had bought the product within the previous six months, thus voluntarily penalizing itself for price-discounting.

knock industry or that the elimination of those practices would improve competition. * * * [E]ven if the Commission has authority under § 5 to forbid legitimate, non-collusive business practices which substantially lessen competition, there has not been a sufficient showing of lessening of competition in the instant case to permit the exercise of that power.

* * *

[The concurring and dissenting opinion of Circuit Judge Lumbard has been omitted. Eds.]

———

After the Second Circuit's *Ethyl* opinion, what room is left for the FTC to challenge unilateral facilitating practices under FTC Act § 5? To challenge facilitating practices under § 5, what showing must the FTC make before the defendant is required to present offsetting justifications? Were you persuaded that the challenged practices were innocuous? Could the FTC have brought *Ethyl* as an agreement case by adopting Judge Posner's views about inferring agreement from parallel conduct (see Sidebar 3–2)?

Sidebar 3–6:
The Economic Effect of "Most Favored Customer" Provisions*

A most-favored-customer clause, also called an "antidiscrimination" or "most-favored-nation" provision, is a promise by one party, for example a supplier, to treat a buyer as well as the supplier treats its best, "most-favored" customer. These provisions can be retroactive (a commitment to treat a buyer as well as the supplier treated its best customer in the recent past) or contemporaneous (a commitment to treat buyer as well as the supplier treats its best customer today). In some cases, the clause appears as an express provision in a supply contract. In other cases a seller will establish a most-favored-customer policy for all its buyers across-the-board. In general, it is unusual to find such provisions established by agreement among rivals. When these commitments are not the product of a horizontal agreement, they may well result from a vertical agreement between a firm and its customer or supplier. Accordingly, one author has suggested that antitrust law attack this practice, when anticompetitive, as an unlawful vertical agreement under Sherman Act § 1, rather than treating it as a unilateral practice beyond the reach of the Sherman Act, as the FTC did in *Ethyl*. Joseph Simons, *Fixing Price with Your Victim: Efficiency and Collusion with Competitor–Based Formula Pricing Clauses*, 17 Hofstra L. Rev. 599 (1989).

Most-favored customer provisions can have anticompetitive or procompetitive effects. One anticompetitive possibility is that they may be employed to facilitate tacit collusion, by helping a cartel deter deviation. A firm that has agreed to offer most-favored-customer treatment in its

* Adapted from Jonathan B. Baker, *Vertical Restraints with Horizontal Consequences: Com-* *petitive Effects of "Most–Favored–Customer" Clauses*, 64 Antitrust L.J. 517 (1996).

contracts has reduced its incentive to deviate from a coordinated horizontal arrangement, because if it offers a discount to a single customer—if it "cheats" on the cartel price—it will be compelled to offer that discount to all customers. The seller's reduced incentive to negotiate price cuts to individual buyers is complemented by a lessening of buyer efforts to drive a hard bargain. After all, a buyer likely has less incentive to invest in negotiating with a seller who will find it expensive to discount. To facilitate horizontal coordination among sellers, it may be enough for a firm to offer most-favored-customer protection only to major customers, or even a single large customer. The facilitating coordination effects of most-favored customer clauses were one object of the FTC's *Ethyl* litigation.

Most-favored-customer provisions can also harm competition through a second route: exclusion or raising rivals' costs. Firms that demand and obtain most-favored-customer treatment from important input suppliers are assured that new entrants and existing competitors will not be able to secure lower costs by getting better prices from those suppliers. By reducing the ability of entrants or rivals to lower their costs, firms can achieve or maintain prices above competitive levels. A number of antitrust cases have considered threats of this kind in the context of large health insurance plans demanding most-favored-customer protection in contracts with hospitals or doctors.

The economic literature also suggests a third route by which most-favored-customer provisions may harm competition: by dampening competition without facilitating tacit collusion (that is, without coordination among rivals). Under this theory, a firm may choose not to discriminate against its customers as a means of committing to less aggressive conduct, as the provision effectively obligates the firm to pay a substantial penalty if it lowers price to any individual customer. In a setting in which rivals can be expected to respond by acting less aggressively as well, the result may be higher prices. (Similar possibilities will be considered in the casebook discussion of the economics of resale price maintenance, Casebook, Chapter 4, *infra*.) This possibility has not yet appeared in the case law, however.

Two types of efficiencies are often cited as justification for most-favored-customer provisions. First, some courts and commentators have described the provisions as standard devices by which buyers bargain for low prices. *E.g.*, *Blue Cross & Blue Shield United of Wisconsin v. Marshfield Clinic*, 65 F.3d 1406, 1415 (7th Cir. 1995) (Posner, C.J.). If the provisions are desired by some or many individual buyers, how can they not be procompetitive? This theory has been criticized, however, on the ground that there is no justification for assuming that a practice desired by buyers individually is in the best interests of buyers collectively. The provision might help a buyer that expects to make many future purchases lower its costs of search, but once one buyer discovers this way of shopping at low cost, other buyers may be led by competition to seek most-favored-customer status as well. Once the provision proliferates, seller discounting will be discouraged and the clauses may no longer help buyers obtain the product for less.

A second efficiency justification applies when firms must write long term contracts with their customers knowing that supply and demand conditions might change unpredictably. For example, natural gas pipelines must contract with well owners without knowing the future demand for gas. A long-term fixed-price contract is unattractive because it would not lead production to respond efficiently to changes in demand. Yet, the well owners would not be willing to agree to renegotiate the price every year because doing so puts them in a difficult bargaining position: once they drill, they would find themselves at the mercy of a single pipeline buyer in future years. One solution is to sign a long-term contract that contemplates annual price changes, but to constrain the pipeline's ability to exploit individual well owners with a most-favored-customer provision.

F. CONCLUSION

In this Chapter, we have examined both the law and economics of cartel theory, from both an historical and contemporary perspective. As we noted at the outset, the Sherman Act's distinction of unilateral and concerted action, combined with the impact of harsh treatment of price-fixing, has led to two sets of challenges. First, it became necessary to develop a framework for relying on circumstantial evidence of agreement to infer conspiracy. Second, even once such a framework developed, it remained essential to integrate that legal framework with modern economic concepts and principles. Doing so remains an ongoing challenge that continues to divide courts and commentators alike.

G. PROBLEMS AND EXERCISES
Problem 3–1:
Durab*

a. The Facts

Many consumer electronics devices, such as radios and portable tape and compact disc players, are powered by small batteries, typically sold in different size categories, such as "D," "C," "A," "AA," and "AAA." The small battery industry is comprised of three main firms: Durab, Allthere, and Batteron. These firms account for approximately 90% of U.S. sales of small batteries. Durab and Allthere have 35% each and Batteron has 20%. These relative shares have been fairly stable for the past five years.

Recently a major camera company, Caman, entered the small battery market, but its sales have been limited due to its inability to gain sufficient retail distribution. A large Japanese battery company, Nisobat, has recently begun to import batteries from Japan. Nisobat's prospects for success are uncertain. The Nisobat brand name is well-regarded by consumers in general, and many of the firm's other products are sold through the same retailers that handle batteries, but the transportation costs of importing batteries are high.

---

* This exercise is based on a problem created by Professor Steven C. Salop, and is used with his permission.

Around 20% of all retail sales of batteries in the United States are made through Elec–City, a national chain of retail electronics stores. Most of the rest are made through large electronics and appliance superstores, department stores, and warehouse discounters. Some of these retailers, including Elec–City, also purchase private label batteries from the three major U.S. firms, and sell them side-by-side with the leading brands. Private label products carry the retailer's brand name (*e.g.*, "Elec–City"), not the manufacturer's brand name (*e.g.*, Durab). Private label batteries account for 5% of batteries sold nationwide. Retailers buy private label brands from battery manufacturers at a substantial discount below the standard wholesale list price for batteries carrying the manufacturer's brand name. (The wholesale price is the price a manufacturer charges for the product to the retailer. The retail price (usually higher) is the price the retailer charges to the consumer.)

Last December, the CEO of Durab gave a speech before securities analysts and the business press. The CEO's prepared remarks were followed by a question and answer session. A reporter for Consumer Electronics Daily, a leading trade publication, asked the Durab CEO about reports that wholesale battery prices would be rising soon. The CEO replied that costs had risen, and he thought prices should rise across-the-board, for all battery sizes. When asked how much he thought prices should rise, he replied "10–12%." This range was reported the next day in several news stories about the speech.

During January, the same reporter interviewed the CEO of Batteron and asked her about the Durab CEO's statement. She replied that she thought a 10% across-the-board price increase would be appropriate, except for size D batteries, which should go up 15%. That interview was reported in the January 24 edition of the Consumer Electronics Daily. On January 25, Durab announced that effective February 1, the wholesale price of batteries would rise by 10%, except that the price of size D batteries would increase by 12%. Two days later, on January 26, Batteron and Allthere announced similar wholesale price increases (10% for most batteries, 12% for size D), effective immediately. On February 1, Durab increased its wholesale price in accordance with its announcement. Nisobat and Caman did not announce price increases.

b. The Problem

In response to complaints from various consumer groups, the Justice Department has undertaken a preliminary investigation of this episode. Initially, the question before the Division staff is whether a full-scale investigation of possible collusion in the small battery industry is warranted.

c. Skills Exercise

You are a member of the team assigned to evaluate the above facts and determine whether further investigation is warranted. In light of the material we have studied in this Chapter, draft a brief memorandum (no more than five (5) pages) setting forth the *best arguments in favor* of pursuing a complete investigation of this conduct as an antitrust violation, and the *best arguments against* doing so. In drafting the memorandum, indicate whether you find any of the facts provided above to be significant, one way or the other, and explain why. Also discuss any significant facts about the conduct or the industry that you don't have, but will need to complete your evaluation.

Chapter 4

DISTRIBUTION RELATIONSHIPS HAVING COLLUSIVE EFFECTS (VERTICAL INTRABRAND AGREEMENTS)

INTRODUCTION

The cases and issues addressed in Chapters 2 and 3 primarily involved coordination among competitors. Such agreements among or between competing firms traditionally have been referred to as "horizontal" restraints to emphasize the fact that the firms involved market *substitute* products or services. This Chapter focuses on coordination among firms that do not directly compete, but that nevertheless have reason to cooperate in order to bring a product or service to market. Typically these firms perform distinct functions at different stages of a chain or channel of distribution. Coordination agreements between such firms traditionally have been referred to as "vertical" to emphasize the fact that they involve *complementary* products or services.

Figure 4–1:
Horizontal and Vertical Relationships Compared

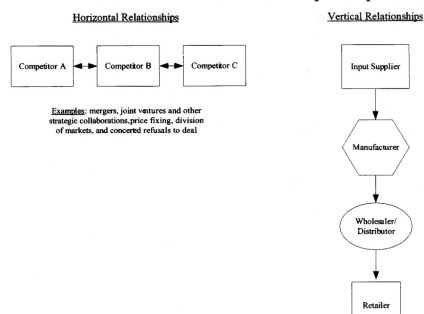

As was true of horizontal agreements, vertical restraints can have collusive or exclusionary anticompetitive effects, but traditionally they have not been grouped by type of effect. Instead, they have been divided into two principal categories: those that restrict "int*r*abrand" competition, and those that restrict "int*er*brand" competition.

Intrabrand restraints affect competition between sellers of the same brand—such as rival Chevrolet dealers, ExxonMobil gasoline stations, or Burger King franchises. Often, these single brand sellers are authorized to sell only from specified locations, or within a specific geographic area, which may tend to diminish competition between them while at the same time intensifying competition with their interbrand rivals. Figure 4–2, for example, illustrates an exclusive distributorship at the wholesale level, and restricted territories at the dealer level. As long as interbrand competition is robust, these kinds of restrictions on intrabrand competition raise few significant antitrust concerns. They could, however, be used by a group of competing dealers or manufacturers to help facilitate price coordination—all *collusive* effects. Less clear today is whether a dominant manufacturer or supplier could use vertical intrabrand restraints to protect or enhance its own market power simply by reducing intrabrand competition, another *collusive* effect. As is discussed in the Supreme Court's 2007 decision in *Leegin*, which we will read later in the Chapter, they could also be used to facilitate efforts by a dominant dealer or manufacturer to exclude rivals—both *exclusionary* effects.

Figure 4–2:
Vertical Intrabrand Restraints—Examples

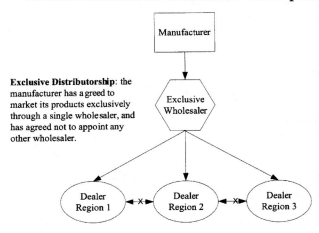

Exclusive Distributorship: the manufacturer has agreed to market its products exclusively through a single wholesaler, and has agreed not to appoint any other wholesaler.

Territorial Restrictions (with or without exclusive distributorships): Each dealer has agreed to concentrate its sales efforts within an assigned region, and each is prohibited from selling the wholesaler's products outside of that region. The wholesaler may remain free to appoint additional retailers in each region, depending upon whether it has also agreed to make each dealer an exclusive distributor. Restrictions might also apply to customers or sales locations.

In contrast, interbrand restraints limit competition between competing brands, such as Chevrolet and Ford, ExxonMobil and Shell, or Burger King and McDonald's. Often, single brand sellers of these sorts of branded products are prohibited by their suppliers from carrying competing brands, perhaps through "exclusive dealing" arrangements. As a consequence, we do not expect to find Ford automobiles for sale at a Chevrolet dealer, Shell gasoline at an ExxonMobil station, or a Burger King "Whopper" at a McDonald's. Interbrand restraints like exclusive dealing raise concerns about *exclusion* when it could lead to higher prices.

Similarly, "tying," which requires a dealer or consumer to purchase a second, generally unwanted product or service (the "tied" product) as a condition of purchasing a desired item (the "tying" product), can affect interbrand competition in the market for the "tied" product. Examples could include a manufacturer of laser printers requiring that its customers purchase toner as a condition of sale of the printer, or a photocopier manufacturer only offering its photocopiers for sale on the condition that the customer purchase all of its photocopier paper from the manufacturer, as well. In circumstances we discuss at greater length in Chapter 7, like exclusive dealing, tying can raise concerns about *exclusion* that can lead to higher prices or other anticompetitive harms.

Figure 4–3:
Vertical Interbrand Restraints—Examples

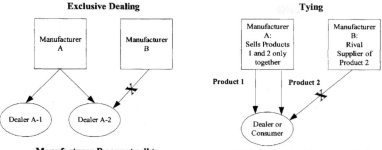

Addressing the competitive issues posed by these various types of arrangements demands a discriminating eye. First, vertical restraints and horizontal restraints traditionally have been distinguished and analyzed under different standards. Second, once a restraint is properly characterized as "vertical," assessing its economic effects can range from being a rather simple matter to being extremely complex. Intrabrand restraints tend to raise concerns about collusive effects, whereas interbrand restraints primarily raise exclusionary effect concerns. Further complexity arises from the legal fact that vertical intrabrand restraints are generally addressed under Section 1 of the Sherman Act, whereas vertical interbrand restraints can be addressed under Section 1 and/or Section 3 of the Clayton Act, which has legally distinct standards of proof. Because interbrand restraints pose the threat of exclusionary effects, they can also be relevant to claims of monopolization or attempted monopolization under Section 2 of the Sherman Act. Finally, some categories of vertical restraints were associated with the "per se" label for a very long time, whereas others are judged under the rule of reason, or some variant of it, although today only tying remains formally per se in limited circumstances.

Our exploration of vertical restraints, however, moves beyond the traditional. As we look towards integrating our understanding of vertical restraints into the broader picture of modern antitrust, it is necessary to take from the cases an understanding of when and how vertical restraints can be efficient, and when they can lead to collusive or exclusionary anticompetitive effects. We will begin in this Chapter with intrabrand restraints, then move on to interbrand restraints in Chapter 7.

It is important to realize at the outset that vertical restraints—both intra-and interbrand—are ubiquitous in the United States, owing in part to a pronounced trend in antitrust law towards increased acceptance of their economic utility. Vertical restraints can provide solutions for many of the practical problems that arise in the course of producing, distributing, and selling products and frequently present the parties to the restraint with a more flexible and cost effective alternative to vertical integration through expansion, formal mergers, or acquisitions. As in Chapter 2, then, the principal challenge we face in Chapters 4 and 7 is to develop legal standards that can effectively distinguish between efficient and anticompetitive distribution strategies.

A. VERTICAL PRICE AND NON–PRICE RESTRAINTS: *SYLVANIA* AND *LEEGIN*

1. A BRIEF HISTORY OF THE ANTITRUST TREATMENT OF VERTICAL INTRABRAND RESTRAINTS

The antitrust treatment of agreements imposing vertical intrabrand restraints has varied significantly over the past century. At times, such practices have faced very harsh, even per se treatment. Today, by contrast, they are seen as largely benign and far more likely to promote than restrict competition. In this introductory note we outline some of the critical case developments that provide the historical foundation for the two modern pillars in this area, *Sylvania* and *Leegin*, which follow. In following the narrative, it will be important to keep in mind the distinction between vertical agreements concerning price, often referred to as resale price maintenance ("RPM"), and vertical nonprice restraints.

At times over the last century of antitrust history, the courts and Congress have taken different views of these two practices, most often exhibiting less tolerance of RPM than vertical agreements not involving price. It will also be useful to keep in mind the business context in which these issues arise: the relationship between manufacturers or suppliers and dealers (distributors). Although vertical intrabrand restraints are agreements between firms at different positions on the distribution chain, antitrust analysis of those restraints focuses on the impact of these practices on final consumers.

Vertical restraint doctrine began with the Supreme Court's 1911 decision in *Dr. Miles Medical Co. v. John D. Park & Sons Co.*, 220 U.S. 373 (1911), concerning vertical price restraints. Although *Dr. Miles* did not itself use the "per se" label, over time the Court, as well as lower courts and commentators, consistently recognized the decision as holding that vertical price restraints are per se unlawful.

After *Dr. Miles*, minimum resale price maintenance was treated as per se unlawful just as any price fixing agreement—at least until the 1930s. The per se approach of *Dr. Miles* did not follow from an elaborate economic analysis of RPM's consequences. Rather, it arose from the Court's conclusion that the restraints were not "fairly necessary" to "the protection of the covenantee," and were therefore "unreasonable." Its reasoning thus echoed the ancillary restraint analysis developed in *Addyston Pipe*, which the Court cited in its opinion. *Dr. Miles's* "per se" rule, therefore, derived more from its perception of the absence of any underlying legitimate purpose, than from a clear conclusion about likely competitive effects. That, in turn, prompted Justice Holmes' well-known dissent, in which he took the majority to task for failing to focus on the competitive impact of resale price maintenance and for protecting "knaves" (discounting dealers) who would cut prices for their own purposes. The Court also referred to traditional principles of property law, relying upon the common law's prohibition of general restraints on alienation. To the extent the Court provided any competition-related rationale for using a per se rule in such cases, it suggested that RPM could be used to facilitate either a dealer-organized or manufacturer-organized cartel. In today's economic terms, RPM could be used to help solve cartel problems of reaching consensus and detecting cheating, either among dealers or among manufacturers, most importantly because it makes it easier for industry participants to coordinate and reach a consensus to set retail prices and to identify price-cutting.

The seeds of contemporary debate over the scope and wisdom of *Dr. Miles's* per se rule were sown soon after. Eight years following *Dr. Miles*, the Supreme Court generated a tension in the case law by holding in *Colgate* that a firm seeking to impose minimum RPM was free to do so "unilaterally," provided it was not a monopolist:

> The purpose of the Sherman Act is to prohibit monopolies, contracts and combinations which probably would unduly interfere with the free exercise of their rights by those engaged, or who wish to engage, in trade or commerce—in a word to preserve the right of freedom of trade. In the absence of any purpose to create or maintain a monopoly, the act does not restrict the long recognized right of trader or manufacturer engaged in an entirely private business, freely to exercise his own independent discretion as to parties with whom he will deal; and, of course, he may announce in advance the circumstances under which he will refuse to sell. * * *

United States v. Colgate & Co., 250 U.S. 300, 307 (1919). The Court's conclusion was animated by two factors: Section 1's requirement of "agreement," and a presumption of manufacturer freedom of contract, similar to the property rights concepts at work in *Dr. Miles*. So the "*Colgate* Doctrine," as it later became known, led RPM law to place a premium on the first element of a Section 1 Sherman Act charge based on RPM—evidence of agreement, usually between a manufacturer or supplier and its dealer. Resale price maintenance was illegal per se, but a manufacturer could accomplish a similar end by simply announcing that it would not sell to price-cutting dealers—so long as the manufacturer did not take other steps that would lead a court to infer that it was doing more than merely adhering to that stated policy and had in fact reached an agreement on the resale price with a dealer. This in effect was viewed as "unilateral resale price maintenance." But the *Colgate* Court did not delve deeply into the question of how much and what kind of evidence of dealer compliance with supplier demands is necessary to establish proof of agreement.

Bolstered by the Court's later harsh pronouncements on price fixing generally, as in horizontal cases like *Trenton Potteries*, *Dr. Miles* remained in full force until the late 1930s. But, in response to the economic strain of the Great Depression, many believed that permitting firms to place a floor under resale pricing would help to stabilize the economy by providing a remedy for rapid deflation. It was also believed that enforceable price floors would help small businesses in their struggle to compete with large discounting retailers, who were just starting to emerge. As a consequence, Congress passed the

Miller–Tydings Fair Trade Amendments in 1937, ch. 690, 50 Stat. 693 (1937), which authorized states, in their own discretion, to establish "fair trade" pricing, *i.e.*, resale price maintenance agreements, on an industry by industry basis.

In response to the Supreme Court's narrow reading of Miller–Tydings in *Schwegmann Bros. v. Calvert Distillers Corp.*, 341 U.S. 384 (1951), Congress broadened the states's authority to authorize resale price maintenance in the McGuire Act of 1952, ch. 745, 66 Stat. 632 (1952). The combination of the Miller–Tydings Amendment and the McGuire Act seriously limited the impact of *Dr. Miles* through the mid–1970s. In 1975, however, *Dr. Miles* was fully restored, when Congress repealed Miller–Tydings and the McGuire Act in the Consumer Goods Pricing Act, Pub. L. No. 94–145, 89 Stat. 80 (1975). In the interim, the Supreme Court had extended the per se rule to cover vertical intrabrand *non*-price restraints, see *United States v. Arnold, Schwinn & Co.*, 388 U.S. 365 (1967), as well as maximum resale price maintenance, see *Albrecht v. Herald Co.*, 390 U.S. 145 (1968). *Schwinn* represented something of an unexplained departure from earlier Supreme Court treatments of vertical non-price agreements, particularly *White Motor Co. v. United States*, 372 U.S. 253 (1963), but it was consistent with the rising tide of per se rules that characterized the period from 1940 to 1972.

Almost immediately after the per se rule of *Dr. Miles* was fully restored in 1975, however, a second tension developed in the law, this one focused on the restraint of trade component of Section 1. Whereas *Dr. Miles* and *Colgate* led to a "unilateral-concerted" axis of tension that placed a premium on the importance of evidence of "agreement" in analyzing vertical conduct, the Supreme Court's 1977 decision in *Continental T.V., Inc. v. GTE Sylvania Inc.*, 433 U.S. 36 (1977) added another tension that divided vertical agreements on price from those affecting non-price restraints.

2. THE COURT CHARTS A NEW COURSE FOR INTRABRAND NON–PRICE RESTRAINTS: THE *SYLVANIA* DECISION

Sylvania, our next case, involved a challenge to vertical, intrabrand non-price restraints. Sylvania's dealer agreements limited the locations from which its dealers were authorized to sell its televisions. Location restraints are a variant of territorial restraints, such as those at issue in cases like *Schwinn*. But by 1977, when *Sylvania* came before the Court, virtually all vertical intrabrand restraints were treated as per se unlawful under *Dr. Miles*, *Albrecht*, and *Schwinn*, and horizontal territorial allocations had been declared per se unlawful in *Topco* (1972). To abandon the per se rule for vertical intrabrand non-price restraints, therefore, the Court in *Sylvania* had to distinguish vertical agreements to allocate territories from horizontal agreements to do so (*Sylvania* from *Topco*), and distinguish vertical agreements involving price from non-price vertical intrabrand restraints (*Schwinn* from *Dr. Miles*).

As you read the case, focus on how those distinctions were made. Are the reasons for abandoning the per se rule for vertical intrabrand non-price restraints persuasive? Are they economic? Are they legal? If they are persuasive, are the reasons for distinguishing vertical non-price from vertical price and horizontal territorial allocations also persuasive? Finally, consider the implications of *Sylvania* for cases like *Dr. Miles* and *Topco*—did it undermine the rationale for maintaining the per se rule in those cases?

CONTINENTAL T.V., INC. v. GTE SYLVANIA INCORPORATED

United States Supreme Court, 1977.
433 U.S. 36, 97 S.Ct. 2549, 53 L.Ed.2d 568.

Mr. Justice POWELL delivered the opinion of the Court.

Franchise agreements between manufacturers and retailers frequently include provisions barring the retailers from selling franchised products from locations other than those specified in the agreements. This case presents important questions concerning the appropriate antitrust analysis of these restrictions under § 1 of the Sherman Act and the Court's decision in *United States v. Arnold, Schwinn & Co.*, 388 U.S. 365 (1967).

I

Respondent GTE Sylvania Inc. (Sylvania) manufactures and sells television sets. * * * Prior to 1962, like most other television manufacturers, Sylvania sold its televisions to independent or company-owned distributors who in turn resold to a large and diverse group of retailers. Prompted by a decline in its market share to a relatively insignificant 1% to 2% of national television sales,[1] Sylvania conducted an intensive reassessment of its marketing strategy, and in 1962 adopted the franchise plan challenged here. Sylvania phased out its wholesale distributors and began to sell its televisions directly to a smaller and more select group of franchised retailers. An acknowledged purpose of the change was to decrease the number of competing Sylvania retailers in the hope of attracting the more aggressive and competent retailers thought necessary to the improvement of the company's market position. To this end, Sylvania limited the number of franchises granted for any given area and required each franchisee to sell his Sylvania products only from the location or locations at which he was franchised. * * * The revised marketing strategy appears to have been successful during the period at issue here, for by 1965 Sylvania's share of national television sales had increased to approximately 5%, and the company ranked as the Nation's eighth largest manufacturer of color television sets.

This suit is the result of the rupture of a franchiser-franchisee relationship that had previously prospered under the revised Sylvania plan. Dissatisfied with its sales in the city of San Francisco,[4] Sylvania decided in the spring of 1965 to franchise Young Brothers, an established San Francisco retailer of televisions, as an additional San Francisco retailer. The proposed location of the new franchise was approximately a mile from a retail outlet operated by petitioner Continental T. V., Inc. (Continental), one of the most successful Sylvania franchisees. Continental protested that the location of the new

---

1. RCA at that time was the dominant firm with as much as 60% to 70% of national television sales in an industry with more than 100 manufacturers.

4. Sylvania's market share in San Francisco was approximately 2.5%, half its national and northern California average.

franchise violated Sylvania's marketing policy, but Sylvania persisted in its plans. Continental then canceled a large Sylvania order and placed a large order with Phillips, one of Sylvania's competitors.

During this same period, Continental expressed a desire to open a store in Sacramento, Cal., a desire Sylvania attributed at least in part to Continental's displeasure over the Young Brothers decision. Sylvania believed that the Sacramento market was adequately served by the existing Sylvania retailers and denied the request.[6] In the face of this denial, Continental advised Sylvania in early September 1965, that it was in the process of moving Sylvania merchandise from its San Jose, Cal., warehouse to a new retail location that it had leased in Sacramento. Two weeks later, allegedly for unrelated reasons, Sylvania's credit department reduced Continental's credit line from $300,000 to $50,000. In response to the reduction in credit and the generally deteriorating relations with Sylvania, Continental withheld all payments owed to * * * Sylvania. * * * Shortly thereafter, Sylvania terminated Continental's franchises. * * *

The antitrust issues before us originated in cross-claims brought by Continental against Sylvania. * * * Most important for our purposes was the claim that Sylvania had violated § 1 of the Sherman Act by entering into and enforcing franchise agreements that prohibited the sale of Sylvania products other than from specified locations.[8] At the close of evidence in the jury trial of Continental's claims, Sylvania requested the District Court to instruct the jury that its location restriction was illegal only if it unreasonably restrained or suppressed competition. Relying on this Court's decision in *United States v. Arnold, Schwinn & Co.* * * * the District Court rejected the proffered instruction.* * *

In answers to special interrogatories, the jury found that Sylvania had engaged "in a contract, combination or conspiracy in restraint of trade in violation of the antitrust laws with respect to location restrictions alone," and assessed Continental's damages at $591,505, which was trebled pursuant to 15 U.S.C. § 15 to produce an award of $1,774,515.

On appeal, the Court of Appeals for the Ninth Circuit, sitting en banc, reversed by a divided vote. The court acknowledged that there is language in *Schwinn* that could be read to support the District Court's instruction but concluded that *Schwinn* was distinguishable on several grounds.* * *

We granted Continental's petition for certiorari to resolve this important question of antitrust law. * * *

II

We turn first to Continental's contention that Sylvania's restriction on retail locations is a *per se* violation of § 1 of the Sherman Act as interpreted in *Schwinn*. The restrictions at issue in *Schwinn* were part of a three-tier distribution system comprising, in addition to Arnold, Schwinn & Co. (Schwinn), 22 intermediate distributors and a network of franchised retailers.

---

6. Sylvania had achieved exceptional results in Sacramento, where its market share exceeded 15% in 1965.

8. Although Sylvania contended in the District Court that its policy was unilaterally enforced, it now concedes that its location restriction involved understandings or agreements with the retailers.

Each distributor had a defined geographic area in which it had the exclusive right to supply franchised retailers. Sales to the public were made only through franchised retailers, who were authorized to sell Schwinn bicycles only from specified locations. In support of this limitation, Schwinn prohibited both distributors and retailers from selling Schwinn bicycles to nonfranchised retailers. At the retail level, therefore, Schwinn was able to control the number of retailers of its bicycles in any given area according to its view of the needs of that market.

* * *

Schwinn came to this Court on appeal by the United States from the District Court's decision. Abandoning its per se theories, the Government argued that Schwinn's prohibition against distributors' and retailers' selling Schwinn bicycles to nonfranchised retailers was unreasonable under § 1.
* * *

The Court acknowledged the Government's abandonment of its *per se* theories and stated that the resolution of the case would require an examination of "the specifics of the challenged practices and their impact upon the marketplace in order to make a judgment as to whether the restraint is or is not 'reasonable' in the special sense in which § 1 of the Sherman Act must be read for purposes of this type of inquiry." Despite this description of its task, the Court proceeded to articulate the following "bright line" *per se* rule of illegality for vertical restrictions: "Under the Sherman Act, it is unreasonable without more for a manufacturer to seek to restrict and confine areas or persons with whom an article may be traded after the manufacturer has parted with dominion over it." * * *

* * *

In the present case * * * the *Schwinn per se* rule applies unless Sylvania's restriction on locations falls outside Schwinn's prohibition against a manufacturer's attempting to restrict a "retailer's freedom as to where and to whom it will resell the products." As the Court of Appeals conceded, the language of *Schwinn* is clearly broad enough to apply to the present case. Unlike the Court of Appeals, however, we are unable to find a principled basis for distinguishing *Schwinn* from the case now before us.

Both Schwinn and Sylvania sought to reduce but not to eliminate competition among their respective retailers through the adoption of a franchise system. * * * [The location] restrictions [adopted by both] allowed Schwinn and Sylvania to regulate the amount of competition among their retailers by preventing a franchisee from selling franchised products from outlets other than the one covered by the franchise agreement. To exactly the same end, the Schwinn franchise plan included a companion restriction, apparently not found in the Sylvania plan, that prohibited franchised retailers from selling Schwinn products to nonfranchised retailers. In *Schwinn* the Court expressly held that this restriction was impermissible under the broad principle stated there. In intent and competitive impact, the retail-customer restriction in *Schwinn* is indistinguishable from the location restriction in the present case. In both cases the restrictions limited the freedom of the retailer to dispose of the purchased products as he desired. The fact that one restriction was addressed to territory and the other to customers is irrelevant to functional anti-trust analysis, and indeed, to the language and broad thrust of the opinion in *Schwinn*. * * *

III

Sylvania argues that if *Schwinn* cannot be distinguished, it should be reconsidered. Although *Schwinn* is supported by the principle of *stare decisis*, we are convinced that the need for clarification of the law in this area justifies reconsideration. *Schwinn* itself was an abrupt and largely unexplained departure from *White Motor Co. v. United States*, 372 U.S. 253 (1963), where only four years earlier the Court had refused to endorse a *per se* rule for vertical restrictions. Since its announcement, *Schwinn* has been the subject of continuing controversy and confusion, both in the scholarly journals and in the federal courts. The great weight of scholarly opinion has been critical of the decision, and a number of the federal courts confronted with analogous vertical restrictions have sought to limit its reach.[14] In our view, the experience of the past 10 years should be brought to bear on this subject of considerable commercial importance.

The traditional framework of analysis under § 1 of the Sherman Act is familiar and does not require extended discussion. Section 1 prohibits "[e]very contract, combination ... , or conspiracy, in restraint of trade or commerce." Since the early years of this century a judicial gloss on this statutory language has established the "rule of reason" as the prevailing standard of analysis. Under this rule, the factfinder weighs all of the circumstances of a case in deciding whether a restrictive practice should be prohibited as imposing an unreasonable restraint on competition. *Per se* rules of illegality are appropriate only when they relate to conduct that is manifestly anticompetitive. As the Court explained in *Northern Pac. R. Co. v. United States*, 356 U.S. 1, 5 (1958), "there are certain agreements or practices which because of their pernicious effect on competition and lack of any redeeming virtue are conclusively presumed to be unreasonable and therefore illegal without elaborate inquiry as to the precise harm they have caused or the business excuse for their use."[16]

In essence, the issue before us is whether *Schwinn's* per se rule can be justified under the demanding standards of *Northern Pac.* * * * The Court's refusal to endorse a per se rule in *White Motor Co.* was based on its uncertainty as to whether vertical restrictions satisfied those standards. * * *

The market impact of vertical restrictions[18] is complex because of their potential for a simultaneous reduction of intrabrand competition and stimu-

---

14. Indeed, as one commentator has observed, many courts "have struggled to distinguish or limit *Schwinn* in ways that are a tribute to judicial ingenuity." * * *

16. *Per se* rules thus require the Court to make broad generalizations about the social utility of particular commercial practices. The probability that anticompetitive consequences will result from a practice and the severity of those consequences must be balanced against its pro-competitive consequences. Cases that do not fit the generalization may arise, but a *per se* rule reflects the judgment that such cases are not sufficiently common or important to

justify the time and expense necessary to identify them. Once established, *per se* rules tend to provide guidance to the business community and to minimize the burdens on litigants and the judicial system of the more complex rule-of-reason trials but those advantages are not sufficient in themselves to justify the creation of *per se* rules. If it were otherwise, all of antitrust law would be reduced to *per se* rules, thus introducing an unintended and undesirable rigidity in the law.

18. As in *Schwinn*, we are concerned here only with nonprice vertical restrictions. The *per se* illegality of price restrictions has been

lation of interbrand competition.[19] Significantly, the Court in *Schwinn* did not distinguish among the challenged restrictions on the basis of their individual potential for intrabrand harm or interbrand benefit. Restrictions that completely eliminated intrabrand competition among Schwinn distributors were analyzed no differently from those that merely moderated intrabrand competition among retailers. The pivotal factor was the passage of title: All restrictions were held to be per se illegal where title had passed, and all were evaluated and sustained under the rule of reason where it had not. The location restriction at issue here would be subject to the same pattern of analysis under *Schwinn*.

It appears that this distinction between sale and nonsale transactions resulted from the Court's effort to accommodate perceived intrabrand harm and interbrand benefit of vertical restrictions. The *per se* rule for sale transactions reflected the view that vertical restrictions are "so obviously destructive" to intrabrand competition that their use would "open the door to exclusivity of outlets and limitation of territory further than prudence permits."[21] Conversely, the continued adherence to the traditional rule of reason for nonsale transactions reflected the view that the restrictions have too great a potential for promotion of interbrand competition to justify complete prohibition. The Court's opinion provides no analytical support for these contrasting positions. Nor is there even an assertion in the opinion that the competitive impact of vertical restrictions is significantly affected by the form of the transaction. Non-sale transactions appear to be excluded from the *per se* rule,

established firmly for many years and involves significantly different questions of analysis and policy. * * * [S]ome commentators have argued that the manufacture's motivation for imposing vertical price restrictions may be the same as for nonprice restrictions. There are, however, significant differences that could easily justify different treatment. * * * [U]nlike nonprice restrictions, "[r]esale price maintenance is not only designed to, but almost invariably does in fact, reduce price competition not only *among* sellers of the affected product, but quite as much *between* that product and competing brands." * * * Professor Posner also recognized that "industry-wide resale price maintenance might facilitate cartelizing." * * * Furthermore, Congress recently has expressed its approval of a *per se* analysis of vertical price restrictions by repealing those provisions of the Miller–Tydings and McGuire Acts allowing fair trade pricing at the option of the individual States. Consumer Goods Pricing Act of 1975, 89 Stat. 801, amending 15 U.S.C. §§ 1, 45(a). No similar expression of congressional intent exists for nonprice restrictions.

19. Interbrand competition is the competition among the manufacturers of the same generic product, television sets in this case, and is the primary concern of antitrust law. The extreme example of a deficiency of interbrand competition is monopoly, where there is only one manufacturer. In contrast, intrabrand competition is the competition between the distributors, wholesale or retail, of the product of a particular manufacturer.

The degree of intrabrand competition is wholly independent of the level of interbrand competition confronting the manufacturer. Thus, there may be fierce intrabrand competition among the distributors of a product produced by a monopolist and no intrabrand competition among the distributors of a product produced by a firm in a highly competitive industry. But when interbrand competition exists, as it does among television manufacturers, it provides a significant check on the exploitation of intrabrand market power because of the ability of consumers to substitute a different brand of the same product.

21. The Court also stated that to impose vertical restrictions in sale transactions would "violate the ancient rule against restraints on alienation." The isolated reference has provoked sharp criticism from virtually all of the commentators on the decision, most of whom have regarded the Court's apparent reliance on the "ancient rule" as both a misreading of legal history and a perversion of antitrust analysis. We quite agree with Mr. Justice Stewart's dissenting comment in *Schwinn* that "the state of the common law 400 or even 100 years ago is irrelevant to the issue before us: the effect of the antitrust laws upon vertical distributional restraints in the American economy today." * * * Competitive economies have social and political as well as economic advantages, but an antitrust policy divorced from market considerations would lack any objective benchmarks. * * *

not because of a greater danger of intrabrand harm or a greater promise of interbrand benefit, but rather because of the Court's unexplained belief that a complete *per se* prohibition would be too "inflexibl[e]."

Vertical restrictions reduce intrabrand competition by limiting the number of sellers of a particular product competing for the business of a given group of buyers. Location restrictions have this effect because of practical constraints on the effective marketing area of retail outlets. Although intrabrand competition may be reduced, the ability of retailers to exploit the resulting market may be limited both by the ability of consumers to travel to other franchised locations and, perhaps more importantly, to purchase the competing products of other manufacturers. None of these key variables, however, is affected by the form of the transaction by which a manufacturer conveys his products to the retailers.

Vertical restrictions promote interbrand competition by allowing the manufacturer to achieve certain efficiencies in the distribution of his products. These "redeeming virtues" are implicit in every decision sustaining vertical restrictions under the rule of reason. Economists have identified a number of ways in which manufacturers can use such restrictions to compete more effectively against other manufacturers.[23] For example, new manufacturers and manufacturers entering new markets can use the restrictions in order to induce competent and aggressive retailers to make the kind of investment of capital and labor that is often required in the distribution of products unknown to the consumer. Established manufacturers can use them to induce retailers to engage in promotional activities or to provide service and repair facilities necessary to the efficient marketing of their products. Service and repair are vital for many products, such as automobiles and major household appliances. The availability and quality of such services affect a manufacturer's goodwill and the competitiveness of his product. Because of market imperfections such as the so-called "free rider" effect, these services might not be provided by retailers in a purely competitive situation, despite the fact that each retailer's benefit would be greater if all provided the services than if none did.

Economists also have argued that manufacturers have an economic interest in maintaining as much intrabrand competition as is consistent with the efficient distribution of their products. Although the view that the manufacturer's interest necessarily corresponds with that of the public is not universally shared, even the leading critic of vertical restrictions concedes that *Schwinn's* distinction between sale and nonsale transactions is essentially unrelated to any relevant economic impact. Indeed, to the extent that the form of the transaction is related to interbrand benefits, the Court's distinction is inconsistent with its articulated concern for the ability of smaller firms to compete effectively with larger ones. Capital requirements and administrative expenses may prevent smaller firms from using the exception for nonsale transactions.[24]

---

23. Marketing efficiency is not the only legitimate reason for a manufacturer's desire to exert control over the manner in which his products are sold and serviced. As a result of statutory and common-law developments, society increasingly demands that manufacturers assume direct responsibility for the safety and quality of their products. * * *

24. "Generally a manufacturer would prefer the lowest retail price possible, once its price to dealers has been set, because a lower retail price means increased sales and higher

We conclude that the distinction drawn in *Schwinn* between sale and nonsale transactions is not sufficient to justify the application of a *per se* rule in one situation and a rule of reason in the other. The question remains whether the *per se* rule stated in *Schwinn* should be expanded to include nonsale transactions or abandoned in favor of a return to the rule of reason. We have found no persuasive support for expanding the *per se* rule. * * *

We revert to the standard articulated in *Northern Pac. R. Co.*, and reiterated in *White Motor*, for determining whether vertical restrictions must be "conclusively presumed to be unreasonable and therefore illegal without elaborate inquiry as to the precise harm they have caused or the business excuse for their use." Such restrictions, in varying forms, are widely used in our free market economy. As indicated above, there is substantial scholarly and judicial authority supporting their economic utility. There is relatively little authority to the contrary.[28] Certainly, there has been no showing in this case, either generally or with respect to Sylvania's agreements, that vertical restrictions have or are likely to have a "pernicious effect on competition" or that they "lack . . . any redeeming virtue."[29] Accordingly, we conclude that the *per se* rule stated in *Schwinn* must be overruled. In so holding we do not foreclose the possibility that particular applications of vertical restrictions might justify *per se* prohibition under *Northern Pac. R. Co.* But we do make clear that departure from the rule-of-reason standard must be based upon demonstrable economic effect rather than—as in *Schwinn*—upon formalistic line drawing.

* * * When anticompetitive effects are shown to result from particular vertical restrictions they can be adequately policed under the rule of reason, the standard traditionally applied for the majority of anticompetitive practices challenged under § 1 of the Act. * * *

[Justice Rehnquist did not take part in the consideration or decision of the case. Justice White's concurring opinion is omitted. Eds.]

Sylvania's significance cannot be over-emphasized. On its most narrow terms, *Sylvania* initiated a major change of course for the law of vertical restraints. The Supreme Court embraced the notion that interbrand competi-

manufacturer revenues." Note, 88 HARV. L. REV. 636, 641 (1975). In this context, a manufacturer is likely to view the difference between the price at which it sells to its retailers and their price to the consumer as his "cost of distribution," which it would prefer to minimize.

28. We also note that *per se* rules in this area may work to the ultimate detriment of the small businessmen who operate as franchisees. To the extent that a *per se* rule prevents a firm from using the franchise system to achieve efficiencies that it perceives as important to its successful operation, the rule creates an incentive for vertical integration into the distribution system, thereby eliminating to that extent the role of independent businessmen.

29. The location restriction used by Sylvania was neither the least nor the most restrictive provision that it could have used. But we agree with the implicit judgment in *Schwinn* that a *per se* rule based on the nature of the restriction is, in general, undesirable. Although distinctions can be drawn among the frequently used restrictions, we are inclined to view them as differences of degree and form. We are unable to perceive significant social gain from channeling transactions into one form or another. Finally, we agree with the Court in *Schwinn* that the advantages of vertical restrictions should not be limited to the categories of new entrants and failing firms. Sylvania was faltering, if not failing, and we think it would be unduly artificial to deny it the use of valuable competitive tools.

tion was the "primary concern of antitrust law." (footnote 19). That represented a remarkable turn about from the position taken by the Court just five years earlier in *Topco*, where the majority refused in the horizontal context to "ramble through the wilds of economic theory" by entertaining the assertion that reductions in intrabrand competition might be reasonable if they benefitted interbrand competition. (Casebook, Chapter 2, *supra*) In liberating the law of vertical restraints from *Schwinn's* per se rule, it also ushered in a period of far more lenient treatment of distribution restraints that provided suppliers with significantly greater discretion in structuring their distribution practices. Indeed, it endorsed the view that manufacturer's and consumer interests are generally aligned when it comes to maximizing the efficiency of distribution systems. What factors did it find so persuasive? And how might those factors guide firms considering the use of vertical restraints? Consider Figure 4–4.

Figure 4–4:
Justifications for Vertical Non–Price Intrabrand Restrictions Recognized in *Sylvania*

- induce competent retailers to carry new products
- induce retailers to promote existing products
- defeat market imperfections, such as free riding
- insulate manufacturer from product liability exposure by ensuring safety
- protect manufacturer's reputation by assuring quality

More broadly, despite fifty years of almost uninterrupted expansion in the scope of per se rules, the *Sylvania* Court declared that the rule of reason was "the rule," and that per se rules were "the exception" under Section 1 of the Sherman Act. "Departure from the rule of reason," it declared, could only be justified by "demonstrable economic effects." In doing so, it implicitly rejected reliance on non-economic goals as a guide to antitrust analysis, especially the kinds of concerns for protecting property rights and dealer autonomy that had animated *Schwinn*, *Colgate*, and *Dr. Miles*. Justice White took note of this change of direction in his concurring opinion:

> After summarily rejecting this concern, reflected in our interpretations of the Sherman Act, for "the autonomy of independent businessmen," [*Sylvania*, *supra*, at n.21], the majority not surprisingly finds "no justification" for *Schwinn's* distinction between sale and nonsale transactions because the distinction is "essentially unrelated to any relevant economic impact." But while according some weight to the businessman's interest in controlling the terms on which he trades in his own goods may be anathema to those who view the Sherman Act as directed solely to economic efficiency, this principle is without question more deeply embedded in our cases than the notions of "free rider" effects and distributional efficiencies borrowed by the majority from the "new economics of vertical relationships."

Sylvania, 433 U.S. at 68–69 (White, J., concurring).

Sylvania's seemingly abrupt turn towards economic analysis, particularly the preservation and promotion of economically efficient business practices, ushered in a period of rapid evolution for all antitrust doctrine. Thereafter, the Court systematically went about the task of dismantling many of the per se rules it had created in the prior fifty years, and increasingly turned to modern economic theory to inform its interpretation and application of the Sherman Act. The trend was evident two years after *Sylvania* in *Broadcast Music* (1979) (Casebook, Chapter 2, *supra*), and in many other subsequent cases. It is a trend that continues today, and to which we shall return in Chapter 8.

Second, *Sylvania* also marked the re-emergence of the rule of reason as the guiding force of antitrust law. Largely dormant since its origins in *Standard Oil* and *Chicago Board of Trade*, the rule once again began to evolve in the courts in both vertical cases owing to *Sylvania*, and horizontal cases because of *Broadcast Music*, decided two years later. Perhaps more so than in its original form, however, the Court emphasized that the rule of reason had to be grounded in economic principles. Sylvania's location clauses had no doubt reduced intrabrand competition—they literally "restrained trade." But the evidence indicated that they also helped Sylvania expand its output by reducing its distribution costs, attracting aggressive retailers, and strengthening its ability to compete on the interbrand level with other, more successful television brands. In short, the object and effect of its marketing plan was to abate impediments to its entry and expansion by reducing costs— hallmarks of economic efficiency. Again, in decided contrast with the views expressed in *Topco*, the Court's rationale implicitly acknowledged that courts applying the Sherman Act must indeed be willing and able to "ramble through the wilds of economic theory" in order to identify and protect such arrangements from successful challenge under rigid, formalistic, and economically unsophisticated analysis.

Third, *Sylvania* introduced two critical distinctions in antitrust law—one that has now been abandoned and one that continues to challenge courts and legal counselors. First, because it left *Dr. Miles* undisturbed, the Court drew a distinction between vertical, intrabrand price restraints, which remained per se unlawful, and vertical, intrabrand, *non*-price restraints, like the location clauses at issue in *Sylvania*, which were thereafter judged under the rule of reason. The distinction between price and non-price vertical restraints led to persistent controversy, owing in large part to the fact that the effects of price and non-price vertical intrabrand restraints, and the justifications for their use, can be so alike. This was almost immediately apparent as the lower courts began to grapple with *Sylvania's* meaning. *See, e.g., Eastern Scientific Co. v. Wild Heerbrugg Instruments, Inc.*, 572 F.2d 883, 885–86 (1st Cir. 1978).

Noting this tension in his concurring opinion, Justice White predicted that *Sylvania* would increase pressure on the Court to overrule *Dr. Miles*:

> * * * It is common ground among the leading advocates of a purely economic approach to the question of distribution restraints that the economic arguments in favor of allowing vertical nonprice restraints generally apply to vertical price restraints as well.[10] Although the

---

10. Professor Posner writes, for example:

"There is no basis for choosing between (price fixing and market division) on social grounds. If resale price maintenance is like dealer price fixing, and therefore bad, a man-

ufacturer's assignment of exclusive territories is like market division, and therefore bad too. . . .

"(If helping new entrants break into a market) is a good justification for exclusive

majority asserts that "the per se illegality of price restrictions ... involves significantly different questions of analysis and policy," [*Sylvania, supra* n.18], I suspect this purported distinction may be as difficult to justify as that of Schwinn under the terms of the majority's analysis. Thus Professor Posner, in an article cited five times by the majority, concludes: "I believe that the law should treat price and nonprice restrictions the same and that it should make no distinction between the imposition of restrictions in a sale contract and their imposition in an agency contract." Indeed, the Court has already recognized that resale price maintenance may increase output by inducing "demand-creating activity" by dealers (such as additional retail outlets, advertising and promotion, and product servicing) that outweighs the additional sales that would result from lower prices brought about by dealer price competition. These same output-enhancing possibilities of nonprice vertical restraints are relied upon by the majority as evidence of their social utility and economic soundness, and as a justification for judging them under the rule of reason. The effect, if not the intention, of the Court's opinion is necessarily to call into question the firmly established *per se* rule against price restraints.

Sylvania, 433 U.S. at 69–70 (White, J., concurring). Do you agree with the Court's stated assumption that price restraints are more inherently anticompetitive than non-price restraints? Do you think Justice White's concerns are well-taken? Could non-price restraints actually be more anticompetitive in practice than price restraints because they can eliminate all forms of intrabrand competition, not just price? As we shall see in our next case, *Leegin*, Justice White's prediction has come true, although it took longer than he perhaps would have predicted at the time.

Finally, *Sylvania* also drew a distinction between *vertical* and *horizontal* non-price restrictions. *Vertical* restrictions—supplier limitations on the geographic areas or classes of customers to which a downstream supplier is authorized to sell, or, as in *Sylvania*, the locations from which it is authorized to sell, were to be evaluated under the rule of reason. Yet *horizontal* non-price restrictions remained per se unlawful under *Topco*. As a consequence, in cases where the restraints were deemed vertical, the reduction of intrabrand competition could be weighed against enhanced interbrand competition. But the same would not be permitted if the restraints were deemed horizontal. Whereas before *Sylvania* all such restraints, price and non-price, vertical and horizontal, were condemned under the per se rule, afterwards how a restraint was characterized had grave consequences—vertical price restraints remained per se unlawful; horizontal territorial, customer or location restraints also remained per se unlawful. Other vertical/horizontal disparities also developed.

We will return to these challenges created by *Sylvania's* categorization scheme later in this Chapter. The next Sidebar looks at the practical consequences of the decision for supplier-dealer relations.

---

territories, it is an equally good justification for resale price maintenance, which as we have seen is simply another method of dealing with the free-rider problem....

In fact, any argument that can also be made on behalf of exclusive territories can also be made on behalf of resale price maintenance."

Sidebar 4–1:
Dealer Relations After *Sylvania*

The most critical unanswered question of *Sylvania* was "what does the rule of reason really mean"? What would make vertical intrabrand non-price restraints "unreasonable"? Although the decision expounded upon the reasons why vertical restraints might be reasonable, it offered little guidance for identifying those that would not.

Since *Sylvania*, there have been only two or three instances in which the plaintiff has prevailed in attacking such arrangements, and virtually no government enforcement actions have been brought. In one plaintiff's victory, *Graphic Products Distributors, Inc. v. ITEK Corp.*, 717 F.2d 1560 (11th Cir. 1983), the court found that the defendant had a market share of over 70%. With a market share of 70% the defendant in *Graphic Products* arguably faced little significant interbrand competition. Building on the Supreme Court's reasoning in *Sylvania*, the court of appeals in *Graphic Products* concluded that intrabrand competition provided the most significant source of downward pressure on price. So one answer to the question left unanswered by *Sylvania*, "when can vertical, intrabrand, non-price restraints be unreasonable," may be "when intrabrand competition represents a substantial source of downward pressure on price, *i.e.*, when the firm imposing the restraint has interbrand market power." But that general proposition provides little guidance as to difficult questions of degree and, as we shall see, may have been implicitly rejected by the Supreme Court in our next case, the Court's 2007 decision in *Leegin*.

In another early case, *Eiberger v. Sony Corp.*, 622 F.2d 1068 (2d Cir. 1980), the defendants adopted vertical, intrabrand, non-price restraints and enforced them rather brutally. Although there was little evidence that the defendant possessed interbrand market power, there was almost no apparent evidence that the defendant had any of the kinds of pro-competitive purposes cited in *Sylvania* as justifications for its actions. There were, in effect, no pro-competitive, interbrand effects that mitigated the restraining effect the arrangements had on intrabrand competition. One explanation for the decision, therefore, is that even small negative effects on intrabrand competition may be unreasonable if there is no justification for the restraint.

Since *Sylvania*, vertical, intrabrand, non-price restraints have become even more common for firms engaged in multi-level distribution, particularly franchising. In large part, the paucity of successful challenges to these common arrangements may reflect what critics of *Schwinn* had asserted—that vertical, intrabrand, non-price restraints are almost always pro-competitive in the interbrand market. As a practical matter, therefore, they have become almost per se *lawful. See, e.g.*, Douglas H. Ginsburg, *Vertical Restraints: De Facto Legality Under the Rule of Reason*, 60 Antitrust L.J. 67 (1991). This was a specific goal of commentators that heralded *Sylvania*, but urged the Court to go even further in authorizing all vertical restraints. *See, e.g.*, Richard A. Posner, *The Next Step in the Antitrust Treatment of Restricted Distribution: Per Se Legality*, 48 U. Chi. L. Rev. 6 (1981). They provide manufacturers with invaluable flexibility in shaping their distribution systems, and a potentially cost-effective alternative to vertical integration.

That is not to say, however, that *Sylvania* is without critics. The "free rider" rationale so important to the Court's reasoning in *Sylvania* may simply be inapplicable to many products that involve no significant point of sale services or promotional activities. Some suspect, therefore, that vertical, intrabrand, non-price restraints are over-used, *i.e.*, permitted in circumstances where they are unlikely to offer consumers any significant benefits in terms of intensified interbrand competition. Critics argue that intrabrand competition can provide significant downward pressure on price in addition to that provided by interbrand competition, and that it is ill-advised to permit its total elimination in circumstances that promise little in the way of benefits. *See, e.g.,* Robert L. Steiner, *Sylvania Economics—A Critique,* 60 ANTITRUST L.J. 41 (1991). And as one court has observed, compensation from the supplier to dealers that supply services can neutralize the negative effect of "free riding" dealers who do not receive any payments because they do not supply the services. *See Toys "R" Us, Inc. v. FTC,* 221 F.3d 928, 937–38 (7th Cir. 2000). We will return to some of these issues in Sidebar 4–2 following *Leegin*.

A final consequence of *Sylvania* has been the re-channeling of disputes between dealers and their suppliers into state courts. Many disputes that focused on the competitive effects of dealer restraints were in fact prompted by a variety of deeper tensions typical among suppliers and their customers, typically retailers. These underlying tensions were not eliminated by *Sylvania*, they were simply shunted to other areas of law that affect supplier-dealer relations. With the possibility of treble damages and attorney's fees removed, disheartened or injured dealers redirected their efforts to redress grievances with their suppliers to state courts and state law remedies, such as those provided by franchise, contract, state unfair competition and commercial tort laws. *See, e.g.,* Jean Wegman Burns, *Vertical Restraints, Efficiency and the Real World,* 62 FORDHAM L. REV. 597 (1993). Awareness of the scope and protection provided by state law, therefore, has become a significant and integral part of the practice of competition law, particularly with respect to supplier-dealer relations.

3. CLOSING THE CIRCLE: RECONCILING *SYLVANIA* AND *DR. MILES*

After *Sylvania*, the Court continued to erode the rule of *Dr. Miles* both directly and indirectly by addressing the tension between *Dr. Miles* and *Colgate* (the different standards governing concerted and unilateral RPM) and the tension newly created by *Sylvania* (the different standards governing price and non-price vertical agreements).

In the pre-*Sylvania* cases following *Colgate*, the Court consistently sought to protect *Colgate's* core holding that a manufacturer can decline to sell to a dealer that refuses to adhere to the manufacturer's specified resale prices provided its policy is truly unilateral, *i.e.*, in the absence of evidence of "agreement." But, in deference to *Dr. Miles*, the Court also recognized that

Colgate's protections could be forfeited if the manufacturer undertakes efforts to cajole or coerce a resisting dealer into adhering to the specified prices, through, for example, threats to terminate sales. Such "negotiations" between the supplier and dealer—supplier threats, followed by dealer adherence—would establish "agreement." *See, e.g., United States v. Parke, Davis & Co.,* 362 U.S. 29 (1960). Trying to toe this line between *Colgate* and *Dr. Miles,* however, highlighted the tension between them. *See generally* Edward H. Levi, *The Parke, Davis–Colgate Doctrine: The Ban on Resale Price Maintenance,* 1960 SUP. CT. REV. 258.

Colgate stands for the proposition, quoted above, that a manufacturer does not enter into any "agreement" with its dealer if it simply "announces" the conditions on which it will agree to sell—including that the product must be resold at prices determined by the manufacturer—and then refuses to sell to dealers who purchase, but do not adhere to those conditions. But what legal significance should attach when a distributor, informed of the manufacturer's conditions, asks to purchase the product? Has it thereby entered into an "agreement" with the manufacturer? Here is the distinction that *Colgate* endorses:

> (1) A manufacturer who announces to its dealer: "I only sell to dealers who resell at the prices I determine in advance," and then asks "will you agree to my terms?," has invited a resale price maintenance agreement. If the dealer responds "yes, I accept your terms," the dealer and the manufacturer have entered into an agreement to fix minimum resale prices.

> (2) On the other hand, if the manufacturer announces: "I only sell to dealers that resell at the prices I determine in advance," but then asks only "would you like to place an order?," it can arguably assert that no "agreement" has been reached, even if the sale is made, and even if the evidence discloses that the dealer thereafter adhered to the mandated price.

This technical and artificial legal fiction is unrelated to economic analysis. If minimum RPM is economically objectionable in the first example, shouldn't it be equally objectionable in the second? To what extent should the "agreement" requirement of Section 1 of the Sherman Act alter that consequence?

Other problems arose when the manufacturer used multiple dealers with whom it had developed complex relationships, for example involving the distribution of multiple products, credit terms, returns, product allocations in times of shortage, or service. When a discounting dealer was terminated by the manufacturer—the most common way a resale price maintenance case would arise—a court would have to parse the details of the relationship carefully to determine whether the manufacturer was simply adhering to a stated policy (legal under *Colgate*), or instead had cut off the discounter in order to implement a resale price maintenance agreement reached with rival distributors (illegal per se under *Dr. Miles*).

In 1984, the Court appeared poised to overrule *Dr. Miles* when it granted review in *Monsanto Co. v. Spray–Rite Service Corp.,* 465 U.S. 752 (1984). The narrow question presented in the case was whether a terminated discounter could establish an unlawful RPM agreement if it alleged and proved only that rival dealers complained about its discounting to their common supplier and the supplier responded by terminating all sales to the dealer. Because of the per se rule of *Dr. Miles*, the answer to this question could be outcome determinative: if an agreement was found, a violation had occurred. Both the Department of Justice and *Monsanto* urged the Court to use the case to overrule *Dr. Miles*, thus harmonizing the treatment of price and non-price vertical restraints.

The Court declined this invitation, instead confining itself to the narrow question presented, ostensibly because the defendant had not preserved the issue by failing to object to the per se instruction proffered to the jury, but also because Congress had intervened as the case was pending before the Court to express its approval of the per se rule. To formally preserve *Dr. Miles*, but protect *Sylvania*, the Court elevated the burden of proving an RPM agreement:

> Thus, something more than evidence of complaints is needed. There must be evidence that tends to exclude the possibility that the manufacturer and nonterminated distributors were acting independently. * * * [T]he antitrust plaintiff should present direct or circumstantial evidence that reasonably tends to prove that the manufacturer and others "had a conscious commitment to a common scheme designed to achieve an unlawful objective."

Monsanto, 465 U.S. at 764. It then went on to hold that the evidence was sufficient under its newly announced and heightened standard to support the jury's verdict against *Monsanto*. *Id*. at 765–68.

Colgate and *Monsanto* together served as a counterbalance to the harsh per se rule of *Dr. Miles*. By providing a safety valve, *Colgate* arguably diminished the per se rule's full impact. *Sylvania* made clear the need for such a safety valve, because characterization of a vertical restraint as involving price could trigger much harsher treatment—a per se prohibition—than would characterization of the restraint as non-price, which would lead to review under the rule of reason, afar more lenient standard. *Colgate's* fiction of "no agreement," as a way of evading the harsh per rule, arguably would become unnecessary if minimum RPM were also to be judged under the rule of reason.

Colgate also created a challenge for antitrust counselors and firms that sought to take advantage of its safe harbor. The client that asks "can I determine resale prices," can be stunned by the explanation from its antitrust counselor that follows: "only if you announce your policy in advance of making any sale, undertake no effort to discipline or cajole customers who fail to comply with your stated policy, and promptly terminate any non-compliant customers." It is simply unnatural to expect a sales force to be so disciplined that it will never attempt to coax its customers into adhering to the suggested prices rather than risk the loss of a sale.

Four years after *Monsanto*, the Court again visited the burden of proof question in the context of dealer terminations involving allegations of minimum resale price maintenance. In *Business Electronics Corp. v. Sharp Electronics Corp.*, 485 U.S. 717 (1988), the Court reaffirmed *Monsanto's* holding that dealer complaints about a rival dealer's low prices, followed by termination of the price cutting dealer, were alone insufficient to establish a per se unlawful vertical price maintenance agreement. An elevated standard of proof was necessary, the Court maintained, to prevent *Dr. Miles* from encroaching upon *Sylvania* and *Colgate*. 485 U.S. at 724–26. But the Court went further, arguably adding yet another requirement:

> Our approach to the question presented in the present case is guided by the premises of *GTE Sylvania* and *Monsanto*: that there is a presumption in favor of a rule-of-reason standard; that departure from that standard must be justified by demonstrable economic effect, such as the facilitation of cartelizing, rather than formalistic distinctions; that interbrand competition is the primary concern of the antitrust laws; and that rules in this area should be formulated with a view towards protecting the doctrine of *GTE Sylvania*. * * *

> There has been no showing here that an agreement between a manufacturer and a dealer to terminate a "price cutter," *without a further agreement on the price or price levels to be charged by the remaining dealer*, almost always tends to restrict competition and reduce output. Any assistance to cartelizing that such an agreement might provide cannot be distinguished from the sort of minimal assistance that might be provided by vertical nonprice agreements like the exclusive territory agreement in *GTE Sylvania*, and is insufficient to justify a *per se* rule. Cartels are neither easy to form nor easy to maintain. Uncertainty over the terms of the cartel, particularly the prices to be charged in the future, obstructs both formation and adherence by making cheating easier. Without an agreement with the remaining dealer on price, the manufacturer both retains its incentive to cheat on any manufacturer-level cartel (since lower prices can still be passed on to consumers) and cannot as easily be used to organize and hold together a retailer-level cartel.

> * * * Any agreement between a manufacturer and a dealer to terminate another dealer who happens to have charged lower prices can be alleged to have been directed against the terminated dealer's "price cutting." In the vast majority of cases, it will be extremely difficult for the manufacturer to convince a jury that its motivation was to ensure adequate services, since price cutting and some measure of service cutting usually go hand in hand. * * *

> We cannot avoid this difficulty by invalidating as illegal *per se* only those agreements imposing vertical restraints that contain the word "price," or that affect the "prices" charged by dealers. Such formalism was explicitly rejected in *GTE Sylvania*. As the above discussion indicates, all vertical restraints, including the exclusive territory agreement held not to be *per se* illegal in *GTE Sylvania*, have the potential to allow dealers to increase "prices" and can be characterized as intended to achieve just that. In fact, vertical nonprice restraints only accomplish the benefits identified in *GTE Sylvania* because they reduce intrabrand price competition to the point where the dealer's profit margin permits provision of the desired services. * * *

Id. at 726–28 (emphasis added). The combination of *Monsanto* and *Business Electronics* made it very difficult for terminated discounters to prove that their termination was pursuant to an agreement to fix minimum resale prices.

See, e.g., Miles Distributors, Inc. v. Specialty Const. Brands, Inc., 476 F.3d 442 (7th Cir. 2007).

What does the emphasized language in the excerpt from *Business Electronics* add to the test set forth in *Monsanto*? Did *Monsanto* and *Business Electronics* modify the per se rule against minimum resale price maintenance as conceived in *Dr. Miles*? If so, how? Why does the Court refer to the fear of "cartelization"? Would you agree or disagree with the proposition that *Business Electronics* attempted to fashion a per se rule limited to those circumstances where minimum RPM is most likely to prove anticompetitive? If that is true, is such an approach really a per se rule at all?

The papers of Justices Thurgood Marshall concerning *Business Electronics*, and Lewis Powell concerning *Monsanto*, reveal that the Supreme Court of the 1980s was committed to preserving at least the formality of the per se ban on minimum resale price maintenance announced in *Dr. Miles* and reiterated in *Sylvania* and *Monsanto*, but that support for the per se rule was waning. One way of interpreting *Monsanto* and *Business Electronics*, therefore, is that, while restating the nominal rule of *Dr. Miles*, the decisions together indirectly eroded the precedent by making it more difficult for the plaintiff to prove the sort of RPM agreement that triggers the application of the per se rule.

On February 29, 1988, while *Business Electronics* was still pending, Justice Scalia wrote a note to Justice Brennan, who had expressed some concern about the likely effect of an early draft of the Court's opinion on *Dr. Miles*, that "[i]t was not my intent to use this opinion to call *Dr. Miles* into question." For example, to assuage Justice Brennan's concerns, Justice Scalia replaced a passage reading "Particularly in the context of vertical restraints, we have recognized that the scope of *per se* illegality should be narrow" with a sentence reading "Although vertical agreements on resale prices have been *per se* illegal since *Dr. Miles Medical Co. v. John D. Park & Sons Co.*, 220 U.S. 373 (1911), we have recognized that the scope of *per se* illegality should be narrow in the context of vertical restraints."

But although the Court in *Monsanto* and *Business Electronics* remained formally respectful of *Dr. Miles*, the respect was grudging. Indeed, the papers of Justice Lewis Powell, the author of the Court's opinions in *Sylvania* and *Monsanto*, indicate that he was inclined to overrule *Dr. Miles* in *Monsanto*, but ultimately felt constrained from doing so because (1) the issue had not been preserved by the parties, and (2) there was apparent Congressional support for *Dr. Miles*. In a perhaps unique incident in the history of public antitrust enforcement, after the Department of Justice had filed an amicus brief urging the Court to overrule *Dr. Miles*, Congress intervened with a bill that precluded the Justice Department from expending any of its appropriation to argue its position before the Court. Although the brief was not formally withdrawn, at oral argument in the case the spokesperson for the Department could say only that the Department stood by its brief. *See Monsanto*, 465 U.S. at 761 n.7.

Only the first of these two reasons is reflected in the Court's final opinion, *see* Monsanto, 465 U.S. at 761 n.7, but it appears that the second, which the Court only alluded to in the same footnote, was the more influential within the Court. In a December 5, 1983 memorandum to the file, Justice Powell elaborated on his views:

These old cases [*Dr. Miles* and *Colgate*] are not easily reconciled with my opinion in *Sylvania*, in which I emphasized the importance of economic considerations.

Although both parties here accepted these cases (naturally), the issue is purely one of law and is of great importance. We therefore can address it.

It is true that Congress apparently has accepted—if not approved—the *per se* rule. Only last week a bill was signed by the President that bars the Justice Department from spending any funds "to overturn or alter the *per se* prohibition on resale price maintenance in effect under federal antitrust laws." See respondent's supplemental brief at p. 2. The legislative history endorses the *per se* rule. As much as I would like to decide the issue here (and it is to be remembered that the rule is one made by this Court), my guess is that the majority of the Court will want to leave this to the Congress.

Powell's hand-written notes from the December 7, 1983 conference leave little doubt as to his personal views: "I'd like to over-rule Dr. Miles & perhaps construe others—but not before us."

The papers of Justices Marshall and Powell thus unveil the dynamics of the divisions on the Court during a crucial period in the development of modern antitrust doctrine. Although the Marshall papers offer no sign that Justices Brennan and Marshall perceived themselves as merely preserving form over substance in joining Justice Scalia's opinion for the six-member majority in *Business Electronics*, Powell's *Monsanto* papers suggest that he and perhaps others, frustrated by their inability to confront *Dr. Miles*, set about the task of confining it as best they could. Perhaps Brennan and Marshall, sensing that the tide had turned, envisioned a time when the Court would reexamine its agreement jurisprudence and loosen the requirements plaintiffs must satisfy. They were content to sustain the principle of per se illegality for minimum RPM. On the other hand, perhaps Powell and others thought that a restricted and narrowed *Dr. Miles* could some day more readily be overruled.

The Court returned to consideration of *Dr. Miles* in our next case, *Leegin Creative Leather Products, Inc. v. PSKS, Inc.*, ___ U.S. ___, 127 S.Ct. 2705 (2007), where it completed the work it had begun in *Sylvania* thirty years earlier. By a 5–4 margin it abandoned the rule of *Dr. Miles*. As we have explained, by this time, the Court had elevated the burden of proving minimum RPM agreements in *Monsanto* and *Business Electronics*. It also had abandoned the per se rule for *maximum* resale price maintenance, endorsed in *Albrecht v. Herald Co.*, 390 U.S. 145 (1968), which was overruled nearly three decades later in *State Oil Co. v. Khan*, 522 U.S. 3 (1997). Given this history of erosion of *Dr. Miles*, perhaps the biggest surprise when *Leegin* was announced was how close the vote was. As you read the decision, consider what prompted the dissenters to mount a defense of *Dr. Miles* at this late date.

LEEGIN CREATIVE LEATHER PRODUCTS, INC. v. PSKS, INC.
United States Supreme Court, 2007.
127 S.Ct. 2705, 168 L.Ed.2d 623.

Justice Kennedy delivered the opinion of the Court.

* * *

I

Petitioner, Leegin Creative Leather Products, Inc. (Leegin), designs, manufactures, and distributes leather goods and accessories. In 1991, Leegin began to sell belts under the brand name "Brighton." The Brighton brand has now expanded into a variety of women's fashion accessories. It is sold across the United States in over 5,000 retail establishments, for the most part independent, small boutiques and specialty stores. Leegin's president, Jerry Kohl, also has an interest in about 70 stores that sell Brighton products. Leegin asserts that, at least for its products, small retailers treat customers better, provide customers more services, and make their shopping experience more satisfactory than do larger, often impersonal retailers. Kohl explained: "[W]e want the consumers to get a different experience than they get in Sam's Club or in Wal–Mart. And you can't get that kind of experience or support or customer service from a store like Wal–Mart."

Respondent, PSKS, Inc. (PSKS), operates Kay's Kloset, a women's apparel store in Lewisville, Texas. Kay's Kloset buys from about 75 different manufacturers and at one time sold the Brighton brand. It first started purchasing Brighton goods from Leegin in 1995. Once it began selling the brand, the store promoted Brighton. For example, it ran Brighton advertisements and had Brighton days in the store. Kay's Kloset became the destination retailer in the area to buy Brighton products. Brighton was the store's most important brand and once accounted for 40 to 50 percent of its profits.

In 1997, Leegin instituted the "Brighton Retail Pricing and Promotion Policy." Following the policy, Leegin refused to sell to retailers that discounted Brighton goods below suggested prices. The policy contained an exception for products not selling well that the retailer did not plan on reordering. * * * Leegin adopted the policy to give its retailers sufficient margins to provide customers the service central to its distribution strategy. It also expressed concern that discounting harmed Brighton's brand image and reputation.

A year after instituting the pricing policy Leegin introduced a marketing strategy known as the "Heart Store Program." It offered retailers incentives to become Heart Stores, and, in exchange, retailers pledged, among other things, to sell at Leegin's suggested prices. Kay's Kloset became a Heart Store soon after Leegin created the program. After a Leegin employee visited the store and found it unattractive, the parties appear to have agreed that Kay's Kloset would not be a Heart Store beyond 1998. Despite losing this status, Kay's Kloset continued to increase its Brighton sales.

In December 2002, Leegin discovered Kay's Kloset had been marking down Brighton's entire line by 20 percent. Kay's Kloset contended it placed Brighton products on sale to compete with nearby retailers who also were undercutting Leegin's suggested prices. Leegin, nonetheless, requested that Kay's Kloset cease discounting. Its request refused, Leegin stopped selling to the store. The loss of the Brighton brand had a considerable negative impact on the store's revenue from sales.

PSKS sued Leegin in the United States District Court for the Eastern District of Texas. It alleged, among other claims, that Leegin had violated the antitrust laws by "enter[ing] into agreements with retailers to charge only those prices fixed by Leegin." Leegin planned to introduce expert testimony describing the procompetitive effects of its pricing policy. The District Court excluded the testimony, relying on the *per se* rule established by *Dr. Miles*. At trial PSKS argued that the Heart Store program, among other things, demonstrated Leegin and its retailers had agreed to fix prices. Leegin responded that it had established a unilateral pricing policy lawful under § 1, which applies only to concerted action. See *United States v. Colgate & Co.,* 250 U.S. 300, 307, 39 S. Ct. 465, 63 L.Ed. 992 (1919). The jury agreed with PSKS and awarded it $1.2 million. Pursuant to 15 U.S.C. § 15(a), the District Court trebled the damages and reimbursed PSKS for its attorney's fees and costs. It entered judgment against Leegin in the amount of $3,975,000.80.

The Court of Appeals for the Fifth Circuit affirmed. On appeal Leegin did not dispute that it had entered into vertical price-fixing agreements with its retailers. Rather, it contended that the rule of reason should have applied to those agreements. The Court of Appeals rejected this argument. It was correct to explain that it remained bound by *Dr. Miles* "[b]ecause [the Supreme] Court has consistently applied the *per se* rule to [vertical minimum price-fixing] agreements." On this premise the Court of Appeals held that the District Court did not abuse its discretion in excluding the testimony of Leegin's economic expert, for the *per se* rule rendered irrelevant any procompetitive justifications for Leegin's pricing policy. We granted certiorari to determine whether vertical minimum resale price maintenance agreements should continue to be treated as *per se* unlawful.

II

[In part II of its opinion, the Court reiterated that Section 1 only prohibits unreasonable restraints of trade and that the rule of reason is the "accepted standard for testing whether a practice restrains trade in violation of § 1." The inquiry under the rule of reason requires an evaluation of "all of the circumstances of a case," such as the history, nature, and effect of the restraint, as well as industry structure and the defendant's market power. In the Court's view, "[i]n its design and function the rule [of reason] distinguishes between restraints with anticompetitive effect that are harmful to the consumer and restraints stimulating competition that are in the consumer's best interest."

The *per se* rule provides more clear guidance and "eliminates the need to study the reasonableness of an individual restraint in light of the real market forces at work," but [r]esort to *per se* rules is confined to restraints * * * "that would always or almost always tend to restrict competition and decrease output." Such restraints must be "manifestly anticompetitive" and "lack any redeeming virtue." Quoting *Sylvania*, the Court emphasized that a "departure from the rule-of-reason standard must be based upon demonstrable economic effect rather than . . . upon formalistic line drawing." Eds.]

* * *

III

The Court has interpreted *Dr. Miles Medical Co. v. John D. Park & Sons Co.,* 220 U.S. 373, 31 S.Ct. 376, 55 L.Ed. 502 (1911), as establishing a *per se* rule against a vertical agreement between a manufacturer and its distributor to set minimum resale prices. In *Dr. Miles* the plaintiff, a manufacturer of medicines, sold its products only to distributors who agreed to resell them at set prices. The Court found the manufacturer's control of resale prices to be unlawful. It relied on the common-law rule that "a general restraint upon alienation is ordinarily invalid." The Court then explained that the agreements would advantage the distributors, not the manufacturer, and were analogous to a combination among competing distributors, which the law treated as void.

The reasoning of the Court's more recent jurisprudence has rejected the rationales on which *Dr. Miles* was based. By relying on the common-law rule against restraints on alienation, the Court justified its decision based on "formalistic" legal doctrine rather than "demonstrable economic effect," *GTE Sylvania, supra,* at 58–59, 97 S.Ct. 2549. The Court in *Dr. Miles* relied on a treatise published in 1628, but failed to discuss in detail the business reasons that would motivate a manufacturer situated in 1911 to make use of vertical price restraints. Yet the Sherman Act's use of "restraint of trade" "invokes the common law itself, . . . not merely the static content that the common law had assigned to the term in 1890." * * * We reaffirm that "the state of the common law 400 or even 100 years ago is irrelevant to the issue before us: the effect of the antitrust laws upon vertical distributional restraints in the American economy today." *GTE Sylvania,* 433 U.S., at 53, n. 21, 97 S.Ct. 2549 (internal quotation marks omitted).

Dr. Miles, furthermore, treated vertical agreements a manufacturer makes with its distributors as analogous to a horizontal combination among competing distributors. In later cases, however, the Court rejected the approach of reliance on rules governing horizontal restraints when defining rules applicable to vertical ones. Our recent cases formulate antitrust principles in accordance with the appreciated differences in economic effect between vertical and horizontal agreements, differences the *Dr. Miles* Court failed to consider.

The reasons upon which *Dr. Miles* relied do not justify a *per se* rule. As a consequence, it is necessary to examine, in the first instance, the economic effects of vertical agreements to fix minimum resale prices, and to determine whether the *per se* rule is nonetheless appropriate.

A

Though each side of the debate can find sources to support its position, it suffices to say here that economics literature is replete with procompetitive justifications for a manufacturer's use of resale price maintenance. Even those more skeptical of resale price maintenance acknowledge it can have procompetitive effects.

The few recent studies documenting the competitive effects of resale price maintenance also cast doubt on the conclusion that the practice meets the criteria for a *per se* rule.

The justifications for vertical price restraints are similar to those for other vertical restraints. Minimum resale price maintenance can stimulate interbrand competition—the competition among manufacturers selling different brands of the same type of product—by reducing intrabrand competition-the competition among retailers selling the same brand. The promotion of interbrand competition is important because "the primary purpose of the antitrust laws is to protect [this type of] competition." A single manufacturer's use of vertical price restraints tends to eliminate intrabrand price competition; this in turn encourages retailers to invest in tangible or intangible services or promotional efforts that aid the manufacturer's position as against rival manufacturers. Resale price maintenance also has the potential to give consumers more options so that they can choose among low-price, low-service brands; high-price, high-service brands; and brands that fall in between.

Absent vertical price restraints, the retail services that enhance interbrand competition might be underprovided. This is because discounting retailers can free ride on retailers who furnish services and then capture some of the increased demand those services generate. Consumers might learn, for example, about the benefits of a manufacturer's product from a retailer that invests in fine showrooms, offers product demonstrations, or hires and trains knowledgeable employees. Or consumers might decide to buy the product because they see it in a retail establishment that has a reputation for selling high-quality merchandise. If the consumer can then buy the product from a retailer that discounts because it has not spent capital providing services or developing a quality reputation, the high-service retailer will lose sales to the discounter, forcing it to cut back its services to a level lower than consumers would otherwise prefer. Minimum resale price maintenance alleviates the problem because it prevents the discounter from undercutting the service provider. With price competition decreased, the manufacturer's retailers compete among themselves over services.

Resale price maintenance, in addition, can increase interbrand competition by facilitating market entry for new firms and brands. "[N]ew manufacturers and manufacturers entering new markets can use the restrictions in order to induce competent and aggressive retailers to make the kind of investment of capital and labor that is often required in the distribution of products unknown to the consumer." New products and new brands are essential to a dynamic economy, and if markets can be penetrated by using resale price maintenance there is a procompetitive effect.

Resale price maintenance can also increase interbrand competition by encouraging retailer services that would not be provided even absent free riding. It may be difficult and inefficient for a manufacturer to make and enforce a contract with a retailer specifying the different services the retailer must perform. Offering the retailer a guaranteed margin and threatening termination if it does not live up to expectations may be the most efficient way to expand the manufacturer's market share by inducing the retailer's performance and allowing it to use its own initiative and experience in providing valuable services.

B

While vertical agreements setting minimum resale prices can have pro-competitive justifications, they may have anticompetitive effects in other cases; and unlawful price fixing, designed solely to obtain monopoly profits, is an ever present temptation. Resale price maintenance may, for example, facilitate a manufacturer cartel. An unlawful cartel will seek to discover if some manufacturers are undercutting the cartel's fixed prices. Resale price maintenance could assist the cartel in identifying price-cutting manufacturers who benefit from the lower prices they offer. Resale price maintenance, furthermore, could discourage a manufacturer from cutting prices to retailers with the concomitant benefit of cheaper prices to consumers.

Vertical price restraints also "might be used to organize cartels at the retailer level." A group of retailers might collude to fix prices to consumers and then compel a manufacturer to aid the unlawful arrangement with resale price maintenance. In that instance the manufacturer does not establish the practice to stimulate services or to promote its brand but to give inefficient retailers higher profits. Retailers with better distribution systems and lower cost structures would be prevented from charging lower prices by the agreement.

A horizontal cartel among competing manufacturers or competing retailers that decreases output or reduces competition in order to increase price is, and ought to be, *per se* unlawful. To the extent a vertical agreement setting minimum resale prices is entered upon to facilitate either type of cartel, it, too, would need to be held unlawful under the rule of reason. This type of agreement may also be useful evidence for a plaintiff attempting to prove the existence of a horizontal cartel.

Resale price maintenance, furthermore, can be abused by a powerful manufacturer or retailer. A dominant retailer, for example, might request resale price maintenance to forestall innovation in distribution that decreases costs. A manufacturer might consider it has little choice but to accommodate the retailer's demands for vertical price restraints if the manufacturer believes it needs access to the retailer's distribution network. A manufacturer with market power, by comparison, might use resale price maintenance to give retailers an incentive not to sell the products of smaller rivals or new entrants. As should be evident, the potential anticompetitive consequences of vertical price restraints must not be ignored or underestimated.

C

Notwithstanding the risks of unlawful conduct, it cannot be stated with any degree of confidence that resale price maintenance "always or almost always tend[s] to restrict competition and decrease output." Vertical agreements establishing minimum resale prices can have either procompetitive or anticompetitive effects, depending upon the circumstances in which they are formed. And although the empirical evidence on the topic is limited, it does not suggest efficient uses of the agreements are infrequent or hypothetical. As the rule would proscribe a significant amount of procompetitive conduct, these agreements appear ill suited for *per se* condemnation.

Respondent contends, nonetheless, that vertical price restraints should be *per se* unlawful because of the administrative convenience of *per se* rules. That argument suggests *per se* illegality is the rule rather than the exception. This misinterprets our antitrust law. *Per se* rules may decrease administrative costs, but that is only part of the equation. Those rules can be counterproductive. They can increase the total cost of the antitrust system by prohibiting procompetitive conduct the antitrust laws should encourage. They also may increase litigation costs by promoting frivolous suits against legitimate practices. The Court has thus explained that administrative "advantages are not sufficient in themselves to justify the creation of *per se* rules," and has relegated their use to restraints that are "manifestly anticompetitive." Were the Court now to conclude that vertical price restraints should be *per se* illegal based on administrative costs, we would undermine, if not overrule, the traditional "demanding standards" for adopting *per se* rules. Any possible reduction in administrative costs cannot alone justify the *Dr. Miles* rule.

Respondent also argues the *per se* rule is justified because a vertical price restraint can lead to higher prices for the manufacturer's goods. Respondent is mistaken in relying on pricing effects absent a further showing of anticompetitive conduct. For, as has been indicated already, the antitrust laws are designed primarily to protect interbrand competition, from which lower prices can later result. The Court, moreover, has evaluated other vertical restraints under the rule of reason even though prices can be increased in the course of promoting procompetitive effects. And resale price maintenance may reduce prices if manufacturers have resorted to costlier alternatives of controlling resale prices that are not *per se* unlawful.

Respondent's argument, furthermore, overlooks that, in general, the interests of manufacturers and consumers are aligned with respect to retailer profit margins. The difference between the price a manufacturer charges retailers and the price retailers charge consumers represents part of the manufacturer's cost of distribution, which, like any other cost, the manufacturer usually desires to minimize. A manufacturer has no incentive to overcompensate retailers with unjustified margins. The retailers, not the manufacturer, gain from higher retail prices. The manufacturer often loses; interbrand competition reduces its competitiveness and market share because consumers will "substitute a different brand of the same product." As a general matter, therefore, a single manufacturer will desire to set minimum resale prices only if the "increase in demand resulting from enhanced service ... will more than offset a negative impact on demand of a higher retail price."

The implications of respondent's position are far reaching. Many decisions a manufacturer makes and carries out through concerted action can lead to higher prices. A manufacturer might, for example, contract with different suppliers to obtain better inputs that improve product quality. Or it might hire an advertising agency to promote awareness of its goods. Yet no one would think these actions violate the Sherman Act because they lead to higher prices. The antitrust laws do not require manufacturers to produce generic goods that consumers do not know about or want. The manufacturer strives to improve its product quality or to promote its brand because it believes this conduct will lead to increased demand despite higher prices. The same can hold true for resale price maintenance.

Resale price maintenance, it is true, does have economic dangers. If the rule of reason were to apply to vertical price restraints, courts would have to be diligent in eliminating their anticompetitive uses from the market. This is a realistic objective, and certain factors are relevant to the inquiry. For example, the number of manufacturers that make use of the practice in a given industry can provide important instruction. When only a few manufacturers lacking market power adopt the practice, there is little likelihood it is facilitating a manufacturer cartel, for a cartel then can be undercut by rival manufacturers. Likewise, a retailer cartel is unlikely when only a single manufacturer in a competitive market uses resale price maintenance. Interbrand competition would divert consumers to lower priced substitutes and eliminate any gains to retailers from their price-fixing agreement over a single brand. Resale price maintenance should be subject to more careful scrutiny, by contrast, if many competing manufacturers adopt the practice.

The source of the restraint may also be an important consideration. If there is evidence retailers were the impetus for a vertical price restraint, there is a greater likelihood that the restraint facilitates a retailer cartel or supports a dominant, inefficient retailer. If, by contrast, a manufacturer adopted the policy independent of retailer pressure, the restraint is less likely to promote anticompetitive conduct. A manufacturer also has an incentive to protest inefficient retailer-induced price restraints because they can harm its competitive position.

As a final matter, that a dominant manufacturer or retailer can abuse resale price maintenance for anticompetitive purposes may not be a serious concern unless the relevant entity has market power. If a retailer lacks market power, manufacturers likely can sell their goods through rival retailers. And if a manufacturer lacks market power, there is less likelihood it can use the practice to keep competitors away from distribution outlets.

The rule of reason is designed and used to eliminate anticompetitive transactions from the market. This standard principle applies to vertical price restraints. A party alleging injury from a vertical agreement setting minimum resale prices will have, as a general matter, the information and resources available to show the existence of the agreement and its scope of operation. As courts gain experience considering the effects of these restraints by applying the rule of reason over the course of decisions, they can establish the litigation structure to ensure the rule operates to eliminate anticompetitive restraints from the market and to provide more guidance to businesses. Courts can, for example, devise rules over time for offering proof, or even presumptions where justified, to make the rule of reason a fair and efficient way to prohibit anticompetitive restraints and to promote procompetitive ones.

For all of the foregoing reasons, we think that were the Court considering the issue as an original matter, the rule of reason, not a *per se* rule of unlawfulness, would be the appropriate standard to judge vertical price restraints.

IV

We do not write on a clean slate, for the decision in *Dr. Miles* is almost a century old. So there is an argument for its retention on the basis of *stare decisis* alone. Even if *Dr. Miles* established an erroneous rule, "[s]tare decisis reflects a policy judgment that in most matters it is more important that the applicable rule of law be settled than that it be settled right." And concerns about maintaining settled law are strong when the question is one of statutory interpretation.

Stare decisis is not as significant in this case, however, because the issue before us is the scope of the Sherman Act. From the beginning the Court has treated the Sherman Act as a common-law statute. Just as the common law adapts to modern understanding and greater experience, so too does the Sherman Act's prohibition on "restraint[s] of trade" evolve to meet the dynamics of present economic conditions. The case-by-case adjudication contemplated by the rule of reason has implemented this common-law approach. Likewise, the boundaries of the doctrine of *per se* illegality should not be immovable. For "[i]t would make no sense to create out of the single term 'restraint of trade' a chronologically schizoid statute, in which a 'rule of reason' evolves with new circumstance and new wisdom, but a line of *per se* illegality remains forever fixed where it was."

A

Stare decisis, we conclude, does not compel our continued adherence to the *per se* rule against vertical price restraints. As discussed earlier, respected authorities in the economics literature suggest the *per se* rule is inappropriate, and there is now widespread agreement that resale price maintenance can have procompetitive effects. It is also significant that both the Department of Justice and the Federal Trade Commission—the antitrust enforcement agencies with the ability to assess the long-term impacts of resale price maintenance—have recommended that this Court replace the *per se* rule with the traditional rule of reason. In the antitrust context the fact that a decision has been "called into serious question" justifies our reevaluation of it.

Other considerations reinforce the conclusion that *Dr. Miles* should be overturned. Of most relevance, "we have overruled our precedents when subsequent cases have undermined their doctrinal underpinnings." The Court's treatment of vertical restraints has progressed away from *Dr. Miles'* strict approach. We have distanced ourselves from the opinion's rationales. This is unsurprising, for the case was decided not long after enactment of the Sherman Act when the Court had little experience with antitrust analysis. Only eight years after *Dr. Miles,* moreover, the Court reined in the decision [in *Colgate*] by holding that a manufacturer can announce suggested resale prices and refuse to deal with distributors who do not follow them.

In more recent cases the Court, following a common-law approach, has continued to temper, limit, or overrule once strict prohibitions on vertical restraints. [Here the Court discussed its subsequent decisions in *Sylvania, Monsanto, Business Electronics,* and *Khan,* which it characterized as collectively "limiting of the reach of" *Dr. Miles.* Eds.]

The *Dr. Miles* rule is also inconsistent with a principled framework, for it makes little economic sense when analyzed with our other cases on vertical restraints. If we were to decide the procompetitive effects of resale price maintenance were insufficient to overrule *Dr. Miles,* then cases such as *Colgate* and *GTE Sylvania* themselves would be called into question. These later decisions, while they may result in less intrabrand competition, can be justified because they permit manufacturers to secure the procompetitive benefits associated with vertical price restraints through other methods. The other methods, however, could be less efficient for a particular manufacturer to establish and sustain. The end result hinders competition and consumer welfare because manufacturers are forced to engage in second-best alternatives and because consumers are required to shoulder the increased expense of the inferior practices.

The manufacturer has a number of legitimate options to achieve benefits similar to those provided by vertical price restraints. A manufacturer can exercise its *Colgate* right to refuse to deal with retailers that do not follow its suggested prices. The economic effects of unilateral and concerted price setting are in general the same. The problem for the manufacturer is that a jury might conclude its unilateral policy was really a vertical agreement, subjecting it to treble damages and potential criminal liability. The increased costs these burdensome measures generate flow to consumers in the form of higher prices.

Furthermore, depending on the type of product it sells, a manufacturer might be able to achieve the procompetitive benefits of resale price maintenance by integrating downstream and selling its products directly to consumers. *Dr. Miles* tilts the relative costs of vertical integration and vertical agreement by making the former more attractive based on the *per se* rule, not on real market conditions. This distortion might lead to inefficient integration that would not otherwise take place, so that consumers must again suffer the consequences of the suboptimal distribution strategy. And integration, unlike vertical price restraints, eliminates all intrabrand competition.

There is yet another consideration. A manufacturer can impose territorial restrictions on distributors and allow only one distributor to sell its goods in a given region. Our cases have recognized, and the economics literature confirms, that these vertical nonprice restraints have impacts similar to those of vertical price restraints; both reduce intrabrand competition and can stimulate retailer services. The same legal standard (*per se* unlawfulness) applies to horizontal market division and horizontal price fixing because both have similar economic effect. There is likewise little economic justification for the current differential treatment of vertical price and nonprice restraints. Furthermore, vertical nonprice restraints may prove less efficient for inducing desired services, and they reduce intrabrand competition more than vertical price restraints by eliminating both price and service competition.

In sum, it is a flawed antitrust doctrine that serves the interests of lawyers-by creating legal distinctions that operate as traps for the unwary-more than the interests of consumers-by requiring manufacturers to choose second-best options to achieve sound business objectives.

B

[In the final portion of the majority opinion, the Court rejected several additional arguments urged by the respondent in support of *stare decisis*. First, the Court rejected the argument that Congress over time had approved of the per se rule in several previous acts. In the Court's view, none of the cited acts specifically approved of *Dr. Miles*. And it reiterated its view that Congress gave the Court wide discretion in interpreting the Sherman Act so it might evolve over time to reflect economic learning. Second, the Court rejected the argument that reliance interests justified continued adherence to the *per se* rule of *Dr. Miles*, asserting that "reliance interests * * * cannot justify an inefficient rule." Finally, the Court noted that even when resale price maintenance was specifically authorized for a time, few manufacturers embraced it as a regular practice. Hence overruling *Dr. Miles* would not in fact result in any major changes in most manufacturers' distribution practices. Eds.]

* * *

For these reasons the Court's decision in *Dr. Miles Medical Co. v. John D. Park & Sons Co.*, 220 U.S. 373, 31 S.Ct. 376, 55 L.Ed. 502 (1911), is now overruled. Vertical price restraints are to be judged according to the rule of reason.

Justice BREYER, with whom Justice STEVENS, Justice SOUTER, and Justice GINSBURG join, dissenting.

* * * This Court has consistently read *Dr. Miles* as establishing a bright-line rule that agreements fixing minimum resale prices are *per se* illegal. That *per se* rule is one upon which the legal profession, business, and the public have relied for close to a century. Today the Court holds that courts must determine the lawfulness of minimum resale price maintenance by applying, not a bright-line *per se* rule, but a circumstance-specific "rule of reason." And in doing so it overturns *Dr. Miles*.

The Court justifies its departure from ordinary considerations of *stare decisis* by pointing to a set of arguments well known in the antitrust literature for close to half a century. Congress has repeatedly found in these arguments insufficient grounds for overturning the *per se* rule. And, in my view, they do not warrant the Court's now overturning so well-established a legal precedent.

I

* * *

The case before us asks which kind of approach the courts should follow where minimum resale price maintenance is at issue. Should they apply a *per se* rule (or a variation) that would make minimum resale price maintenance always (or *almost* always) unlawful? Should they apply a "rule of reason"? Were the Court writing on a blank slate, I would find these questions difficult. But, of course, the Court is not writing on a blank slate, and that fact makes a considerable legal difference.

To best explain why the question would be difficult were we deciding it afresh, I briefly summarize several classical arguments for and against the use of a *per se* rule. The arguments focus on three sets of considerations, those involving: (1) potential anticompetitive effects, (2) potential benefits, and (3) administration. The difficulty arises out of the fact that the different sets of considerations point in different directions.

On the one hand, agreements setting minimum resale prices may have serious anticompetitive consequences. *In respect to dealers:* Resale price maintenance agreements, rather like horizontal price agreements, can diminish or eliminate price competition among dealers of a single brand or (if practiced generally by manufacturers) among multibrand dealers. In doing so, they can prevent dealers from offering customers the lower prices that many customers prefer; they can prevent dealers from responding to changes in demand, say falling demand, by cutting prices; they can encourage dealers to substitute service, for price, competition, thereby threatening wastefully to attract too many resources into that portion of the industry; they can inhibit expansion by more efficient dealers whose lower prices might otherwise attract more customers, stifling the development of new, more efficient modes of retailing; and so forth.

In respect to producers: Resale price maintenance agreements can help to reinforce the competition-inhibiting behavior of firms in concentrated industries. In such industries firms may tacitly collude, *i.e.,* observe each other's pricing behavior, each understanding that price cutting by one firm is likely to trigger price competition by all. Where that is so, resale price maintenance can make it easier for each producer to identify (by observing retail markets) when a competitor has begun to cut prices. And a producer who cuts wholesale prices *without* lowering the minimum resale price will stand to gain little, if anything, in increased profits, because the dealer will be unable to stimulate increased consumer demand by passing along the producer's price cut to consumers. In either case, resale price maintenance agreements will tend to prevent price competition from "breaking out"; and they will thereby tend to stabilize producer prices.

Those who express concern about the potential anticompetitive effects find empirical support in the behavior of prices before, and then after, Congress in 1975 repealed the Miller–Tydings Fair Trade Act, 50 Stat. 693, and the McGuire Act, 66 Stat. 631. Those Acts had permitted (but not required) individual States to enact "fair trade" laws authorizing minimum resale price maintenance. At the time of repeal minimum resale price maintenance was lawful in 36 States; it was unlawful in 14 States. Comparing prices in the former States with prices in the latter States, the Department of Justice argued that minimum resale price maintenance had raised prices by 19% to 27%.

After repeal, minimum resale price maintenance agreements were unlawful *per se* in every State. The Federal Trade Commission (FTC) staff, after studying numerous price surveys, wrote that collectively the surveys "indicate[d] that [resale price maintenance] in most cases increased the prices of products sold with [resale price maintenance]." Most economists today agree that, in the words of a prominent antitrust treatise, "resale price maintenance tends to produce higher consumer prices than would otherwise be the case."

On the other hand, those favoring resale price maintenance have long argued that resale price maintenance agreements can provide important consumer benefits. The majority lists two: First, such agreements can facilitate new entry. For example, a newly entering producer wishing to build a product name might be able to convince dealers to help it do so—if, but only if, the producer can assure those dealers that they will later recoup their investment. * * * The result might be increased competition at the producer level, *i.e.,* greater *inter*-brand competition, that brings with it net consumer benefits.

Second, without resale price maintenance a producer might find its efforts to sell a product undermined by what resale price maintenance advocates call "free riding." Suppose a producer concludes that it can succeed only if dealers provide certain services, say, product demonstrations, high quality shops, advertising that creates a certain product image, and so forth. Without resale price maintenance, some dealers might take a "free ride" on the investment that others make in providing those services. Such a dealer would save money by not paying for those services and could consequently cut its own price and increase its own sales. Under these circumstances, dealers might prove unwilling to invest in the provision of necessary services.

Moreover, where a producer and not a group of dealers seeks a resale price maintenance agreement, there is a special reason to believe some such benefits exist. That is because, other things being equal, producers should want to encourage price competition among their dealers. By doing so they will often increase profits by selling more of their product. And that is so, even if the producer possesses sufficient market power to earn a super-normal profit. That is to say, other things being equal, the producer will benefit by charging his dealers a competitive (or even a higher-than-competitive) whole-sale price while encouraging price competition among them. Hence, if the producer is the moving force, the producer must have some special reason for wanting resale price maintenance; and in the absence of, say, concentrated producer markets (where that special reason might consist of a desire to stabilize wholesale prices), that special reason may well reflect the special circumstances just described: new entry, "free riding," or variations on those themes.

The upshot is, as many economists suggest, sometimes resale price maintenance can prove harmful; sometimes it can bring benefits. But before concluding that courts should consequently apply a rule of reason, I would ask such questions as, how often are harms or benefits likely to occur? How easy is it to separate the beneficial sheep from the antitrust goats?

Economic discussion, such as the studies the Court relies upon, can *help* provide answers to these questions, and in doing so, economics can, and should, inform antitrust law. But antitrust law cannot, and should not, precisely replicate economists' (sometimes conflicting) views. That is because law, unlike economics, is an administrative system the effects of which depend upon the content of rules and precedents only as they are applied by judges and juries in courts and by lawyers advising their clients. And that fact means that courts will often bring their own administrative judgment to bear, sometimes applying rules of *per se* unlawfulness to business practices even when those practices sometimes produce benefits.

I have already described studies and analyses that suggest (though they cannot prove) that resale price maintenance can cause harms with some regularity-and certainly when dealers are the driving force. But what about benefits? How often, for example, will the benefits to which the Court points occur in practice? I can find no economic consensus on this point. There is a consensus in the literature that "free riding" takes place. But "free riding" often takes place in the economy without any legal effort to stop it. * * * The question is how often the "free riding" problem is serious enough significantly to deter dealer investment.

* * *

All this is to say that the ultimate question is not whether, but *how much,* "free riding" of this sort takes place. And, after reading the briefs, I must answer that question with an uncertain "sometimes."

How easily can courts identify instances in which the benefits are likely to outweigh potential harms? My own answer is, *not very easily.* For one thing, it is often difficult to identify *who*—producer or dealer—is the moving force behind any given resale price maintenance agreement. Suppose, for example, several large multibrand retailers all sell resale-price-maintained products. Suppose further that small producers set retail prices because they fear that, otherwise, the large retailers will favor (say, by allocating better shelf-space) the goods of other producers who practice resale price maintenance. Who "initiated" this practice, the retailers hoping for considerable insulation from retail competition, or the producers, who simply seek to deal best with the circumstances they find? For another thing, as I just said, it is difficult to determine just when, and where, the "free riding" problem is serious enough to warrant legal protection.

I recognize that scholars have sought to develop check lists and sets of questions that will help courts separate instances where anticompetitive harms are more likely from instances where only benefits are likely to be found. But applying these criteria in court is often easier said than done. The Court's invitation to consider the existence of "market power," for example, invites lengthy time-consuming argument among competing experts, as they seek to apply abstract, highly technical, criteria to often ill-defined markets. And resale price maintenance cases, unlike a major merger or monopoly case, are likely to prove numerous and involve only private parties. One cannot fairly expect judges and juries in such cases to apply complex economic criteria without making a considerable number of mistakes, which themselves may impose serious costs.

Are there special advantages to a bright-line rule? Without such a rule, it is often unfair, and consequently impractical, for enforcement officials to bring criminal proceedings. And since enforcement resources are limited, that loss may tempt some producers or dealers to enter into agreements that are, on balance, anticompetitive.

Given the uncertainties that surround key items in the overall balance sheet, particularly in respect to the "administrative" questions, I can concede to the majority that the problem is difficult. And, if forced to decide now, at most I might agree that the *per se* rule should be slightly modified to allow an exception for the more easily identifiable and temporary condition of "new entry." But I am not now forced to decide this question. The question before us is not what should be the rule, starting from scratch. We here must decide whether to change a clear and simple price-related antitrust rule that the courts have applied for nearly a century.

II

We write, not on a blank slate, but on a slate that begins with *Dr. Miles* and goes on to list a century's worth of similar cases, massive amounts of advice that lawyers have provided their clients, and untold numbers of business decisions those clients have taken in reliance upon that advice. Indeed a Westlaw search shows that *Dr. Miles* itself has been cited dozens of times in this Court and hundreds of times in lower courts. Those who wish this Court to change so well-established a legal precedent bear a heavy burden of proof. I am not aware of any case in which this Court has overturned so well-established a statutory precedent. Regardless, I do not see how the Court can claim that ordinary criteria for over-ruling an earlier case have been met. *See, e.g., Planned Parenthood of Southeastern Pa. v. Casey*, 505 U.S. 833, 854–855, 112 S.Ct. 2791, 120 L.Ed.2d 674 (1992). *See also Federal Election Comm'n v. Wisconsin Right to Life, Inc.*, ___ U.S. ___, at 19–21, 127 S. Ct. 2652, 168 L.Ed.2d 329, 2007 WL 1804336 (SCALIA, J., concurring in part and concurring in judgment).

A

I can find no change in circumstances in the past several decades that helps the majority's position. In fact, there has been one important change that argues strongly to the contrary. In 1975, Congress repealed the McGuire and Miller–Tydings Acts. And it thereby consciously *extended Dr. Miles' per se* rule. Indeed, at that time the Department of Justice and the FTC, then urging application of the *per se* rule, discussed virtually every argument presented now to this Court as well as others not here presented. And they explained to Congress why Congress should reject them. Congress fully understood, and consequently intended, that the result of its repeal of McGuire and Miller–Tydings would be to make minimum resale price maintenance *per se* unlawful

Congress did not prohibit this Court from reconsidering the *per se* rule. But enacting major legislation premised upon the existence of that rule constitutes important public reliance upon that rule. And doing so aware of the relevant arguments constitutes even stronger reliance upon the Court's keeping the rule, at least in the absence of some significant change in respect to those arguments.

Have there been any such changes? There have been a few economic studies, described in some of the briefs, that argue, contrary to the testimony of the Justice Department and FTC to Congress in 1975, that resale price maintenance is not harmful. One study, relying on an analysis of litigated resale price maintenance cases from 1975 to 1982, concludes that resale price maintenance does not ordinarily involve producer or dealer collusion. But this study equates the failure of plaintiffs to *allege* collusion with the *absence* of collusion-an equation that overlooks the superfluous nature of allegations of horizontal collusion in a resale price maintenance case and the tacit form that such collusion might take.

The other study provides a theoretical basis for concluding that resale price maintenance "need not lead to higher retail prices." But this study develops a theoretical model "under the assumption that [resale price maintenance] is efficiency-enhancing." Its only empirical support is a 1940 study that the authors acknowledge is much criticized.

Regardless, taken together, these studies at most may offer some mild support for the majority's position. But they cannot constitute a major change in circumstances.

Petitioner and some *amici* have also presented us with newer studies that show that resale price maintenance sometimes brings consumer benefits. But the proponents of a *per se* rule have always conceded as much. What is remarkable about the majority's arguments is that *nothing* in this respect *is new*. The only new feature of these arguments lies in the fact that the most current advocates of overruling *Dr. Miles* have abandoned a host of other not-very-persuasive arguments upon which prior resale price maintenance proponents used to rely.

The one arguable exception consists of the majority's claim that "even absent free riding," resale price maintenance "may be the most efficient way to expand the manufacturer's market share by inducing the retailer's performance and allowing it to use its own initiative and experience in providing valuable services." I cannot count this as an exception, however, because I do not understand how, in the absence of free-riding (and assuming competitiveness), an established producer would need resale price maintenance. Why, on these assumptions, would a dealer not "expand" its "market share" as best that dealer sees fit, obtaining appropriate payment from consumers in the process? There may be an answer to this question. But I have not seen it. And I do not think that we should place significant weight upon justifications that the parties do not explain with sufficient clarity for a generalist judge to understand.

No one claims that the American economy has changed in ways that might support the majority. Concentration in retailing has increased. That change, other things being equal, may enable (and motivate) more retailers, accounting for a greater percentage of total retail sales volume, to seek resale price maintenance, thereby making it more difficult for price-cutting competitors (perhaps internet retailers) to obtain market share.

Nor has anyone argued that concentration among manufacturers that might use resale price maintenance has diminished significantly. And as far as I can tell, it has not. Increased concentration among manufacturers increases the likelihood that producer-originated resale price maintenance will prove more prevalent today than in years past, and more harmful. At the very least, the majority has not explained how these, or other changes in the economy could help support its position.

In sum, there is no relevant change. And without some such change, there is no ground for abandoning a well-established antitrust rule.

B

With the preceding discussion in mind, I would consult the list of factors that our case law indicates are relevant when we consider overruling an earlier case. Justice SCALIA, writing separately in another of our cases this Term, well summarizes that law. See *Wisconsin Right to Life, Inc.,* ___ U.S. at ___, 19–21, 127 S. Ct. 2652, 2007 WL 1804336. (opinion concurring in part and concurring in judgment). And every relevant factor he mentions argues against overruling *Dr. Miles* here.

[Here Justice Breyer discussed the six factors discussed in *Wisconsin Right to Life*: (1) *stare decisis* is applied more rigidly in statutory than constitutional cases, (2) the Court has more leeway in overruling cases that it deems were wrongly decided when those decisions are relatively recent; (3)

previous cases may lend themselves to being overruled if they established what proved to be "an unworkable legal regime;" (4) the fact that a decision "unsettles" the law may argue in favor of overruling it; (5) the fact that a case involves property rights or contract rights, where reliance interests are involved, argues against overruling it; and (6) the fact that a rule of law has become "embedded" in our "national culture" argues strongly against overruling it. Justice Breyer argued that all of these factors leaned in favor of retaining *Dr. Miles*. Eds.]

* * *

The only contrary *stare decisis* factor that the majority mentions consists of its claim that this Court has "[f]rom the beginning ... treated the Sherman Act as a common-law statute," and has previously overruled antitrust precedent. It points in support to *State Oil Co. v. Khan*, 522 U.S. 3, 118 S.Ct. 275, 139 L.Ed.2d 199 (1997), overruling *Albrecht v. Herald Co.*, 390 U.S. 145, 88 S.Ct. 869, 19 L.Ed.2d 998 (1968), in which this Court had held that *maximum* resale price agreements were unlawful *per se*, and to *Sylvania*, overruling *United States v. Arnold, Schwinn & Co.*, 388 U.S. 365, 87 S.Ct. 1856, 18 L.Ed.2d 1249 (1967), in which this Court had held that producer-imposed territorial limits were unlawful *per se*.

The Court decided *Khan*, however, 29 years after *Albrecht*—still a significant period, but nowhere close to the century *Dr. Miles* has stood. The Court specifically noted the *lack* of any significant reliance upon *Albrecht*. *Albrecht* had far less support in traditional antitrust principles than did *Dr. Miles*. And Congress had nowhere expressed support for *Albrecht's* rule.

In *Sylvania*, the Court, in overruling *Schwinn*, explicitly distinguished *Dr. Miles* on the ground that while Congress had "recently ... expressed its approval of a *per se* analysis of vertical price restrictions" by repealing the Miller–Tydings and McGuire Acts, "[n]o similar expression of congressional intent exists for nonprice restrictions." Moreover, the Court decided *Sylvania* only a decade after *Schwinn*. And it based its overruling on a generally perceived need to avoid "confusion" in the law, a factor totally absent here.

The Court suggests that it is following "the common-law tradition." But the common law would not have permitted overruling *Dr. Miles* in these circumstances. Common-law courts rarely overruled well-established earlier rules outright. Rather, they would over time issue decisions that gradually eroded the scope and effect of the rule in question, which might eventually lead the courts to put the rule to rest. One can argue that modifying the *per se* rule to make an exception, say, for new entry, could prove consistent with this approach. To swallow up a century-old precedent, potentially affecting many billions of dollars of sales, is not.

Moreover, a Court that rests its decision upon economists' views of the economic merits should also take account of legal scholars' views about common-law overruling. Professors Hart and Sacks list 12 factors (similar to those I have mentioned) that support judicial "adherence to prior holdings." They all support adherence to *Dr. Miles* here. See H. Hart & A. Sacks, The Legal Process 568–569 (W. Eskridge & P. Frickey eds. 1994). Karl Llewellyn has written that the common-law judge's "conscious reshaping" of prior law "must so move as to hold the degree of movement down to the degree to which need truly presses." The Bramble Bush 156 (1960). Where here is the pressing need? The Court notes that the FTC argues here in favor of a rule of reason. But both Congress and the FTC, unlike courts, are well-equipped to gather empirical evidence outside the context of a single case. As neither has done so, we cannot conclude with confidence that the gains from eliminating the *per se* rule will outweigh the costs.

In sum, every *stare decisis* concern this Court has ever mentioned counsels against overruling here. It is difficult for me to understand how one can believe both that (1) satisfying a set of *stare decisis* concerns justifies over-ruling a recent constitutional decision, *Wisconsin Right to Life, Inc.,* ___ U.S., at ___–___, 19–21, 127 S. Ct. 2652, 2007 WL 1804336 (SCALIA, J., joined by KENNEDY and THOMAS, JJ., concurring in part and concurring in judgment), but (2) failing to satisfy any of those same concerns nonetheless permits overruling a longstanding statutory decision. Either those concerns are relevant or they are not.

* * *

The only safe predictions to make about today's decision are that it will likely raise the price of goods at retail and that it will create considerable legal turbulence as lower courts seek to develop workable principles. I do not believe that the majority has shown new or changed conditions sufficient to warrant overruling a decision of such long standing. All ordinary *stare decisis* considerations indicate the contrary. For these reasons, with respect, I dissent.

———

Recall that from 1967–77 the treatment of vertical price and non-price restraints was briefly aligned under *Dr. Miles* and *Schwinn*: all vertical intrabrand restraints were per se unlawful. *Sylvania* created disequilibrium and tension by differentiating vertical intrabrand non-price restraints. *Sylvania* and *Leegin* together, therefore, established a new equilibrium, one far more tolerant of all vertical intrabrand restraints. What arguments persuaded the majority that it was time to abandon *Dr. Miles* despite its near-century reign?

How persuasive a case do the dissenters make for invoking *stare decisis* to save *Dr. Miles*? What was the majority's response? Note in particular, the authorities cited by Justice Breyer in support of his argument for *stare decisis*. Some commentators have suggested that the selection of cases reveals deeper concerns among the dissenters for the fate of non-antitrust precedents, especially *Roe v. Wade*, 410 U.S. 113 (1973).

Sidebar 4–2:
After *Leegin*

One might think that harmonizing the treatment of vertical price and non-price intrabrand restraints under the rule of reason would equate with greater certainty and predictability. But *Leegin* raises many questions that will be have to be answered in the coming years. In this

Sidebar we pose some of the more important ones, dividing them into political, legal, and economic.

Political. Amicus briefs were filed in the Court by consumer groups and 37 states, all of whom favored preservation of the rule of *Dr. Miles*. Like the dissenters, they questioned the basis for abandoning *Dr. Miles* after so long and feared that doing so would lead to higher prices and little consumer benefit. An important and obvious question, therefore, is whether Congress will act to overrule or otherwise limit *Leegin*. Likewise, it is possible that some of the states that joined the brief will continue to challenge minimum RPM as per se unlawful under state antitrust laws.

Although federal legislative action seems unlikely as of this writing, some states that generally follow federal law might seek to amend their state statutes to preserve *Dr. Miles*. The antitrust statutes of other states already appear to include express statutory per se prohibitions and may not need to respond to *Leegin*. The Supreme Court has given the states wide discretion to fashion their own antitrust rules, even when those rules supplement federal antitrust prohibitions. *See California v. ARC America Corp.*, 490 U.S. 93 (1989). So it seems likely that such efforts would withstand legal challenge based on any inconsistency with *Leegin* unless the Court were to view state level per se rules as creating conflicting and incompatible substantive standards, as opposed to a merely supplemental remedy. If major states like New York, California, Texas, and Florida re-assert *Dr. Miles*, the impact of *Leegin* may be limited, as nationwide manufacturers would not be able to impose RPM across-the-board. On the other hand, state enforcers may be influenced by *Leegin*. Prosecutors in states that formally retain the rule of *Dr. Miles* might recognize the concerns of the *Leegin* majority and choose, as a matter of prosecutorial discretion, to prioritize cases that are consistent with its discussion of circumstances that might render RPM unreasonable.

Another potentially political dimension is international in scope. The competition laws of jurisdictions such as Canada and the European Union and many other countries have long prohibited minimum RPM as did the United States under *Dr. Miles*. It seems unlikely that these jurisdictions will all abandon their more strict treatment of minimum RPM in immediate response to *Leegin*. A division of approaches will further complicate the marketing practices decisions of international suppliers and could lead to some tension between different national enforcement agencies.

Legal. *Leegin* implicitly and explicitly raises a host of legal questions that the Supreme Court in effect remanded to the lower courts for development, which is likely to take many years.

First, and perhaps foremost, when, if ever, will minimum RPM warrant condemnation under the rule of reason? Although *Leegin* sought to harmonize the treatment of minimum RPM with the treatment of intrabrand non-price restraints under *Sylvania*, as noted above *Sylvania* offered almost no guidance as to how the rule of reason should be applied to vertical restraints beyond declaring that interbrand competition is the "primary concern of antitrust law." One message of *Sylvania* appeared to be that restraints on intrabrand competition can promote interbrand competition and are of little competitive significance provided the supplier imposing them faces significant interbrand competition. In such cases, interbrand competition should provide a significant source of competition, such as downward pressure on price. Another message of *Sylvania* left open the possibility that the elimination of intrabrand competition by a firm possessing significant market power could pose a threat to competition, because in such cases intrabrand competition may be the primary source of downward pressure on price. Will the courts apply this logic in the wake of *Leegin* by significantly limiting the use of minimum RPM by dominant firms? As is discussed below, *Leegin* does not mention this scenario among its examples of anticompetitive uses of minimum RPM.

Very little additional guidance can be gleaned from the lower courts post-*Sylvania*. As noted in Sidebar 4–1, plaintiffs have had substantial difficulty succeeding in rule of reason challenges to non-price vertical restraints and as a practical matter vertical intrabrand non-price restraints have become virtually *per se lawful* since *Sylvania*. Now that vertical restraints on price are also to be tested under the rule of reason, will the lower courts be equally lenient in reviewing them?

The relaxed review of non-price vertical restraints following *Sylvania* was predicted by proponents of the rule of reason, precisely because the rule of reason lacked a robust analytical framework. *See, e.g.*, Richard A. Posner, *The Rule of Reason and the Economic Approach: Reflections on the* Sylvania *Decision*, 45 U. Chi. L. Rev. 1, 14 (1977) ("The content of the Rule of Reason is largely unknown; in practice, it is little more than a euphemism for nonliability. Before *Schwinn*, restrictions on distribution were tested under the Rule of Reason, meaning: they were lawful."). The *Leegin* majority also appeared to recognize that the rule of reason remains somewhat undeveloped. In three ways, therefore, it sought to provide guidance to the lower courts and firms considering use of minimum RPM. First, it described four situations in which minimum RPM is more likely to be anticompetitive. Second, it also listed three factors that could be relevant to a rule of reason analysis of minimum RPM. Finally, it discussed those recognized ways in which minimum RPM might be procompetitive or competitively neutral.

Anticompetitive Uses of RPM

Leegin recognizes that although it might not warrant per se condemnation, minimum RPM can in fact be anticompetitive. It described four examples: (1) when minimum RPM is used to facilitate a manufacturer's cartel; (2) when minimum RPM is used to facilitate a dealer cartel; (3) when minimum RPM is used by a manufacturer with market power to protect that power by providing its dealers with an incentive not to sell the products of the manufacturer's smaller rivals or new entrants; and (4) when a dealer with market power solicits minimum RPM in order to forestall innovation in distribution that decreases costs. 127 S.Ct. at 2716–17.

Manufacturers' Cartel

Since *Dr. Miles*, courts and commentators have expressed the concern that RPM could be used to facilitate a manufacturer's cartel by making the policing of agreed upon prices easier. Assume, for example, that a group of rival manufacturers have agreed to coordinate prices. RPM may help them do so because it provides a means of detecting cheating: it will be easier to identify cartel members who cut price to dealers, because those dealers will in turn promote the product by lowering the retail price. Maintaining resale prices thus provides a method for policing cheating, and, in doing so, neutralizes the incentive to cheat in the first place.

For this theory to make sense, the tacitly colluding firms must be capable of exercising market power by reducing output collectively. Thus, their products as a group will likely comprise much of the sales in a relevant market protected against entry; if only a fraction of the manufacturers impose RPM, the practice may not help much in facilitating collusion. In addition, we would expect RPM to be a cost-effective way to stop cartel cheating by those firms that employ it, relative to the alternatives. Thus, RPM may not be a good tool to deter cheating unless rival manufacturers find it difficult to observe reductions in each others' wholesale price directly or to infer them from fluctuations in the retail price, which may arise from shifts in retailing costs. In addition, the dealers must not be able to substitute non-price promotions that are as attractive to customers but more difficult for rival manufacturers to observe. Moreover, all the competing manufacturers must employ RPM, or else those that do not must be free from the temptation or ability to cheat through other means, perhaps because they are capacity constrained.

Dealers' Cartel

Second, as arguably suggested by *Dr. Miles,* and emphasized in *Business Electronics* and *Leegin,* minimum RPM could be used by a group of colluding dealers to police and enforce a horizontal price fixing agreement among themselves. Picture a number of dealers who would like to collude, but are unable to do so because they are each too tempted to cheat. One or more manufacturers could help make dealer collusion successful, and make price-cutting impossible, by insisting upon a resale price and threatening to reduce the quantity of product they will ship to discounting retailers. They could even threaten to cut off discounting dealers from access to their products altogether. Recall the economic issues involved in facilitating successful collusion, which were discussed more fully in Chapter 3.

The simple-sounding "dealers' cartel" theory appears more complex upon analysis, however, although there are indeed circumstances under which such an arrangement could work. To begin with, the goods over which the dealers would like to collude must themselves be sufficiently free of competition to make a dealer cartel profitable. Collusion could probably not be limited to some models of a product, for example, if most buyers would respond by substituting other models.* In addition, entry into retailing of the product cannot be easy; otherwise some or all of the manufacturers who would not benefit from a dealers' cartel would avoid selling through the colluding dealers merely by shifting their distribution to new retailers coming into the market.

Finally, the theory must explain why a manufacturer would be willing to police the dealer cartel. If a manufacturer were a monopolist, it

---

* On the other hand, it may not be necessary for all manufacturers to employ RPM in order for dealer cheating to be deterred. For example, those manufacturers that do not employ RPM may be limited in their ability to expand output or attract the customers of those that do through lower prices, or those that employ RPM may be willing to terminate dealers who cut the prices of goods produced by manufacturers who do not impose RPM.

could earn greater profits by setting a monopoly wholesale price and allowing retailers to compete than by enforcing a dealer cartel. Enforcing the cartel would require the monopolist to share some of its market power gains with the retailers. If there are multiple, competing manufacturers of the product, and the manufacturers are not colluding themselves, the colluding dealers are likely extending their cartel to multiple, competing products. Doing so would permit the dealers collectively to earn monopoly profits in the retailing of the products generally if they can convince some, most, or all of the manufacturers to impose RPM, and thus perform the "service" of making the cartel viable by preventing dealer cheating.

Assuming that manufacturers are unlikely to have a direct interest in facilitating such a dealer cartel, the issue becomes how the dealers can persuade their suppliers to do so? The dealers can induce the manufacturers to impose RPM with either a carrot or a stick. The carrot would be compensation to the manufacturers, for example if the dealers were to accede to a higher wholesale price or accept lower manufacturer payments into a cooperative advertising fund. The stick would involve a threat to harm the manufacturer, as by denying the manufacturer access to the retail market through a "group boycott." The latter possibility presumes significant dealer market power. Moreover, for the latter alternative to make sense, it must be easier for the dealers to police cheating on a group boycott than to police cheating on collusion in retail sales. Finally, for a dealers' cartel to succeed, the costs of using the carrot or stick must not exceed the monopoly profits earned by the dealer cartel.

Exclusionary Strategies by a Manufacturer or Dealer with Market Power

Whereas the first two anticompetitive scenarios described by the Court in *Leegin* focused on the role RPM can play in facilitating cartel behavior, the third and fourth related to exclusionary conduct.

First, the Court posits that a manufacturer with market power might adopt minimum RPM to impair its rivals' access to dealers. For this strategy to work, several conditions would have to be satisfied. For the dealer, RPM must result in higher profits than would obtain if it agreed to carry the products of the manufacturer's rivals. The manufacturer would in effect use RPM to pay the dealer for its agreement not to carry the products of the manufacturer's rivals, creating a larger margin between the wholesale price and the manufacturer's required resale price. One way to view this scenario is as a form of compensated exclusive dealing. (Exclusive dealing is examined in Chapter 7, *infra*.) For the manufacturer, the exclusionary benefits of the strategy must outweigh its costs. The manufacturer would have to believe, therefore, that impairing its rivals' access to dealers will raise their costs and thereby confer, or insulate from erosion, its own market power.

Second, the Court suggested that a dealer with market power might induce minimum RPM to forestall innovation in distribution that could reduce costs. In this scenario, a dominant dealer fearful that it might lose significant sales to an innovative dealer with lower costs might solicit minimum RPM from a common supplier. RPM could reduce the incentive of the rival dealer to develop more efficient distribution strategies, because it will prevent it from fully exploiting those strategies by reducing prices in an effort to compete with the dominant dealer. Although its own greater efficiency might still increase its profitability, minimum RPM would prevent the rival dealer from expanding its market share through lower prices. Normally, one would presume that the manufacturer has an interest in promoting more efficient methods of distribution and therefore would resist the use of RPM under these circumstances. So the dominant dealer's ability to induce the RPM is a critical assumption of this scenario.

Interestingly, the Court in *Leegin* did not address two additional situations in which RPM could be anticompetitive. Because they are not discussed at all, it is difficult to say whether the Court would recognize them if they arose.

Dampening Competition

The Court in *Leegin* did not discuss a fifth anticompetitive possibility, which is suggested by some contemporary economic models of strategic interaction among firms that are *not* coordinating (tacitly colluding). Under some circumstances, manufacturers may impose RPM on dealers as a way of making a commitment to compete less aggressively with each other. This would lead to higher retail prices in settings in which rivals would be expected to respond by becoming less aggressive as well. *See* Daniel P. O'Brien & Greg Shaffer, *Vertical Control with Bilateral Contracts*, 23 RAND J. Econ. 299 (1992); Greg Shaffer, *Slotting Allowances and Resale Price Maintenance: A Comparison of Facilitating Practices*, 22 RAND J. Econ. 120 (1991). RPM is likely to have more power in generating higher prices through this mechanism if adopted by multiple, competing manufacturers. Dampening competition theories of this sort represent something of a frontier for antitrust enforcement. The theory makes sense, but enforcers and courts have yet to confront the litigation challenges that will arise in demonstrating that a commitment to less-aggressive behavior has led, or likely will lead, rivals to act likewise.

Monopoly Pricing

Neither did the *Leegin* Court discuss the possibility that RPM could enhance a monopoly manufacturer's ability to engage in monopoly, or "supra-competitive" pricing. This theory requires an answer to the "single monopoly profit" theory (discussed at greater length in Chapter 7, *infra*)—an explanation as to how the monopolist can extract more monopoly profits from consumers than it could obtain merely by charging an appropriate (high) wholesale price, or by charging a high lump-sum "franchise" fee, or both. As we shall see later in this Chapter in *E & L Consulting, Ltd. v. Doman Indus. Ltd.*, 472 F.3d 23 (2d Cir. 2006), acceptance of the single monopoly profit theory can lead to the conclusion that interbrand competition is not merely the "primary concern of antitrust law," as the Court held in *Sylvania*, but the *only* concern of antitrust law. Under this view, neither RPM nor any non-price restraint can really enhance that power.

The Supreme Court seemed implicitly to reject the single monopoly profit idea in *Sylvania*. By declaring interbrand competition to be the "primary concern of antitrust law," the Court seemed to preserve the possibility that in the absence of significant interbrand competition, antitrust law might intervene to protect at least some degree of intrabrand competition, which could serve as the only source of downward pressure on price. This idea was evident in *Graphic Products Distributors, Inc. v. ITEK Corp.*, 717 F.2d 1560 (11th Cir.1983), discussed *supra* in Sidebar 4–1. Such an intervention, it could be argued, might be justifiable if a restraint by a dominant firm eliminated intrabrand competition, but did not appear to significantly promote interbrand competition. Justice Stevens made this point in his dissent in *Business Electronics*, where he accused the majority of failing "to attach any weight to the value of intrabrand competition." *Business Electronics.*, 485 U.S. at 748 (Stevens, J., dissenting). Stevens continued:

> In *Continental T.V., Inc. v. GTE Sylvania Inc.*, we correctly held that a demonstrable benefit to interbrand competition will outweigh the harm to intrabrand competition that is caused by the imposition of vertical nonprice restrictions on dealers. But we also expressly reaffirmed earlier cases in which the illegal conspiracy affected only intrabrand competition. Not a word in the *Sylvania* opinion implied that the elimination of intrabrand competition could be justified as reasonable without any evidence of a purpose to improve interbrand competition.

Id. at 748–49.

The *Note on Intrabrand Competition and the "Single Monopoly Profit" Theory*, which appears later in this Chapter after *E & L Consulting*, explains how a reduction in intrabrand competition could allow a monopolist to increase its market power. Resale price maintenance (RPM) could be used as part of such a scheme if the discount distributors (which would be unwilling to agree to fix the resale price) are also the distributors likely to carry the products of the fringe rivals. RPM could also be employed to allow a monopolist to discriminate in the price it charges various groups of buyers. For example, a toaster monopolist could require that dealers with stores in affluent neighborhoods, where the buyers are willing to pay the most, set a high minimum resale price. The issues involved in determining whether price discrimination benefits or harms consumers are taken up in Sidebar 7–3, *infra*.

One way to account for these anticompetitive possibilities would allow the demonstration by plaintiff of substantial restrictions on intrabrand competition by a firm with significant market power to shift a burden of production to that firm to demonstrate that the restraints in fact promoted interbrand competition in some way. This is what Justice Stevens appeared to be suggesting in *Business Electronics*. Would such an approach be appropriate? Would it be difficult for suppliers to prove specific benefits to interbrand competition that flow from intrabrand restraints? If so, what does that suggest about the Court's assumption in *Sylvania* and *Leegin* that intrabrand restraints can improve interbrand competition? Figure 4–5 summarizes the anticompetitive theories discussed in the two decisions.

Figure 4-5:
Anticompetitive Theories Associated with Vertical Intrabrand Restraints Recognized by the Supreme Court in *Sylvania* and *Leggin*

Sylvania	*Leegin*
Collusive Effects	Collusive Effects
• facilitate the exercise of market power by a dominant firm by eliminating the	• facilitate manufacturer cartel • facilitate dealer cartel

downward pressure on price created by intrabrand competition	Exclusionary Effects
• Criticism: Single Monopoly Profit Theory	• facilitate exclusion of rivals to • dominant firm • facilitate exclusion of rivals to dominant dealer
• RPM could facilitate cartelizing (fn. 18)	

Excess Services

Finally, not all consumers will need or want to pay for the same services, yet under a system of RPM they will all be treated alike. The studious consumer, for example, who researches major purchases and obtains information that is publicly available, may be ready to purchase when she enters the retailer. She neither needs nor wants to pay for the point-of-sale services it offers. Yet, under a system of RPM, she is forced to do so, since all consumers pay the same price. This can actually lead to a diminution in consumer welfare, especially when the manufacturer over-estimates the actual consumer demand for point of sale services.**

The Rule of Reason After Leegin

In addition to identifying four anticompetitive uses of minimum RPM, the Court described three factors that would be relevant to a rule of reason analysis of the practice: (1) the scope of use of minimum RPM in a market; (2) the source of the restraint, i.e. whether it originated with the supplier or dealer; and (3) the market power of the supplier and the dealer. 127 S. Ct. at 2719–20.

These factors, however, can be difficult to interpret and apply. Widespread use of minimum RPM, for example, could suggest that the practice has anticompetitive potential, for example, by facilitating a dealer or manufacturer cartel. But it also could suggest that it is widely perceived to be an efficient marketing practice by many firms in an industry and that courts should be hesitant to condemn the practice. Second, while it may be easy to discern in some cases whether the idea for the practice originated with dealers as opposed to suppliers, in others the evidence may be more ambiguous. Litigating the question of "whose idea was it" might well divert attention and litigation resources from the more central question of evaluating the competitive effects of the practice. Finally, market power can be an enticing screening device: if the supplier (or retailer demanding RPM) lacks it, the case can be terminated; but if the supplier (or retailer demanding RPM) possesses it, the potential for anticompetitive harm increases and the burden of production should shift to the defendants to justify its use. But market power assessments can themselves be subtle and require extensive discovery and expert elucidation before a reliable judgment can be reached.

Each of these scenarios and factors, moreover, has the potential to impose significant burdens on a plaintiff, public or private, making it difficult for many plaintiffs to mount a successful challenge to minimum RPM. Does this reflect the Court majority's belief that such challenges

---

** For a discussion of these arguments, see William S. Comanor, *Vertical Price–Fixing, Vertical Market Restrictions, and the New Antitrust Policy*, 98 HARV. L. REV. 983 (1985). In evaluating these arguments, it is worth noting that even in competitive markets, product variety may be limited and, in consequence, some customers may be forced to accept undesirable features in a similar sense.

should in fact be few, because the practice is so likely to be pro-competitive or benign? The Court does seem to acknowledge at one point that this kind of "full-blown rule of reason" analysis could lead to costly and protracted proceedings that would task both plaintiffs and defendants. In a potentially important passage, it states:

> The rule of reason is designed and used to eliminate anti-competitive transactions from the market. This standard principle applies to vertical price restraints. A party alleging injury from a vertical agreement setting minimum resale prices will have, as a general matter, the information and resources available to show the existence of the agreement and its scope of operation. As courts gain experience considering the effects of these restraints by applying the rule of reason over the course of decisions, they can establish the litigation structure to ensure the rule operates to eliminate anticompetitive restraints from the market and to provide more guidance to businesses. Courts can, for example, devise rules over time for offering proof, or even presumptions where justified, to make the rule of reason a fair and efficient way to prohibit anticompetitive restraints and to promote procompetitive ones.

127 S.Ct. at 2720. While this passage invites lower courts to consider such potentially litigation-shortening devices as market power screens, burden-shifting based on actual effects evidence (such as that endorsed in *NCAA*, *Indiana Fed'n of Dentists*, and *California Dental*), inferences of harm to competition from the absence of a legitimate business justification, and efficiency reasons for disqualifying use of the per se rule (as the Court did in *Broadcast Music*), it provides no specific suggestions to guide their inquiries.

What then will it take for a plaintiff to succeed in shifting a burden of production to the defendant? And what kinds of justifications might warrant a shift of the burden back to the plaintiff? The Court is less specific on this point, although again some guidelines can be gleaned from its discussion of the pro-competitive uses of minimum RPM. The Court says these are "similar to those for other vertical restraints" and include various ways that they can stimulate interbrand competition, such as by: (1) providing means to encourage dealers to invest in tangible and intangible services or promotional efforts; (2) facilitating efforts by new firms to enter or expand into a market; (3) providing consumers with more options, such as goods that are low price/low service, high price/high service, or a range of options in between; (4) addressing market imperfections such as free riding; and (5) providing a more efficient means of contractually requiring dealers to provide certain levels of performance. 127 S.Ct. at 2715–16.

Procompetitive Justifications for RPM

The intellectual roots of *Leegin*, including criticism of the per se rule of *Dr. Miles*, was long-standing and rooted in some specific scholarship associated with the Chicago School. Justice Breyer's dissent, however, gave voice to some responses to that criticism that have also developed over time. In considering these justifications, it is important to appreciate the paradox of RPM. All of the justifications for its use—both pro-and anticompetitive—lead to higher absolute prices. What arguably differentiates them is that the procompetitive instances provide value to consumers that can justify the higher price. The challenge for critics of the per se rule was to identify and evaluate that value.

The Chicago School Critique

The per se treatment of RPM that originated in *Dr. Miles* came under attack from Lester G. Telser in *Why Should Manufacturers Want Fair Trade*, 3 J. L. & Econ. 86 (1960). Telser, a contributor to Chicago School antitrust analysis, challenged the "monopoly prices" hypothesis, openly doubted the ubiquity of dealer cartels, and, perhaps most importantly, suggested another, *pro*-competitive, explanation for manufacturers's use of minimum RPM—one that in fact was evident in *Dr. Miles*. *See* 221 U.S. at 374 (Statement by Mr. Justice Hughes). Indeed, he asserted that this pro-competitive explanation for RPM was far more plausible than any anticompetitive explanation of RPM, making the per se rule ill-suited for use with RPM.***

Telser observed that a product sold at retail can usefully be viewed in two component parts: (1) the actual product; and (2) the point-of-sale services associated with the product, such as product information, promotion and instructions on its use. A manufacturer might price its product on the assumption that the dealer will provide such services. Indeed, it may view those services as essential to promoting its product adequately and competing against rival suppliers. It must, therefore, provide its dealers with an incentive to undertake such services. It can do so by lowering its price or otherwise "compensating" the dealers for the services. If the strategy proves successful, the dealers, and the manufacturer will be rewarded through higher output. In this respect, Telser observed, the manufacturer's desire to profit through expanded output was consistent with the consumers' interest, as reflected in increased demand for its products. Deferring to the manufacturer's wishes was for Telser presumptively likely to best serve consumers.

But what if some dealers do not offer the same level of services as others? Why would they not do so? Picture an electronics retailer on one side of "Main Street, USA." Pursuant to guidelines received from the manufacturer, it has fully outfitted its store, complete with display space, demonstration products, an adequate inventory of all models in each line, promotional literature, and salespeople hired and trained to be knowledgeable and available to demonstrate the products and answer all customer questions. It also takes out weekly advertisements in the town newspaper, and pays for occasional advertisements through other media. And the strategy works—demand for the manufacturer's products begins to increase.

Now look to the other side of the street. There we find a simple store front with a simple sign: "BUY IT HERE FOR LESS." On this side of the street there are no displays or trained salespeople, and the owner seldom advertises. Inside the store there are only stacked boxes of the identical merchandise available across the street, but at prices that are 25 percent less. It can charge so much less, because it has not incurred many of the

---

*** Telser's arguments were later elaborated by other Chicago School proponents. *See, e.g.,* Robert H. Bork, *The Rule of Reason and the* *Per Se Concept: Price Fixing and Market Division*, 75 YALE L.J. 373 (1966).

costs shouldered by its across-the-street rival—no advertising, no big inventory, no space for displays, and no helpful salespeople. A pattern quickly develops. Shoppers drawn to the fully outfitted store by its advertisements, attractive displays, and first rate service start there, obtain the necessary demonstrations, literature and information, and then cross the street, model number in hand, and purchase the merchandise at a lower price. The "no-frills" operation thus can be said to be taking a "free ride" on the promotional and other efforts of the fully outfitted store. It can do so, indeed *it has an incentive to do so*, because its profits will rise. It can actually increase its profits owing to its much lower costs and increased volume. Yet it can do so only as long as the fully outfitted store continues to attract new customers that can be diverted.

How long will the fully outfitted store persist in its promotional strategy? If the diverted sales are significant, it will quickly abandon the plan, and the manufacturer may see its sales decline. The manufacturer might respond simply by raising its prices to the dealer who refused to supply adequate services. But, as we shall see in Chapter 7, the price discrimination laws generally prohibit a manufacturer from selling its product at different prices to competing dealers. Moreover, without the point-of-sale services, sales may decline anyway, frustrating the manufacturer's marketing strategy.

Telser posited that minimum RPM could be a solution for the manufacturer.**** By being able to set minimum resale prices, the manufacturer can eliminate the free rider's advantage in selling to consumers. To increase sales, it too must now offer services—and it can afford to do so because its price-cost margins are now guaranteed to be higher. In fact, as *Leegin* acknowledged, the two dealers may compete with each other to provide the best services, which could result in increased sales for the manufacturer.

The "Buy It Here for Less" scenario, however, may be something of a caricature. As discussed in Sidebar 4–1, many products simply do not require much in the way of point-of-sale information or services. They are sold off the shelf, frequently contain all the information the consumer needs either on or in the packaging, and rarely require post-sale service. For other products, the manufacturer pays the retailer to perform point-of-sale services, so there is no possibility of one dealer free riding off another dealer's expenditures. Moreover, the "no frills" store may be a very innovative, lower cost (*i.e.*, more efficient) retailer, not a "free rider." In truth it may offer all of the services consumers need, but at lower cost. The fully outfitted store may simply represent a more expensive method for selling a product given the tastes and needs of consumers. If so, RPM can stifle innovative, discount retailing and lead to higher prices, as noted above.

In addition, even if the manufacturer was concerned about free-riding, RPM might not be the most cost-effective way to prevent it. The manufacturer might instead require the dealers to perform point-of-sale

**** Justice Holmes's dissent in *Dr. Miles* seemed to make a related point, although it may not have been for the same reasons discussed here, when he derided the Court for allowing "knaves," *i.e.*, discounters, to interfere with the marketing strategies of manufacturers, who knew best how to market their products. *Dr. Miles*, 221 U.S. at 412 (Holmes, J., dissenting).

services; this would accomplish the same end if the manufacturer can cheaply monitor compliance with that contractual provision.

The dissenters thus accept that free-riding can easily be "imagined," but question how common a problem it is. *See Leegin,* 127 S. Ct. at 2730 (Breyer, J., dissenting). Perhaps more importantly, they question how easy it will be to differentiate reasonable from unreasonable instances of RPM purportedly used to eliminate free-riding. *Id.*

Economists writing after Telser have provided additional efficiency explanations for RPM, some of which were also discussed in *Leegin. See, e.g.,* Pauline M. Ippolito, *Resale Price Maintenance: Economic Evidence From Litigation* 18 (FTC, April 1986). These go beyond preventing free riding on point-of-sale services to include preventing free riding on post-sale services that influence product quality, such as rapid, high quality repairs or advice on product upgrades, or inducing greater dealer inventory holdings through shifting risk of overstocking from the dealers to the manufacturer. A related issue can arise in markets where consumers infer high quality from a good's high relative price. Some clothing manufacturers, for example, may sell through upscale department stores, but not through discount chains, in order to protect their quality image against price-cutting. RPM could allow such manufactures to expand their distribution and sales without undermining consumer perceptions of product quality.

This overview of *Leegin's* roots returns us to a basic question about its meaning: can *Leegin* fairly be characterized as holding that vertical price and non-price restraints should both be treated under the rule of reason because they are competitively identical? It might be more accurate to say that whereas all vertical intrabrand restraints share common justifications, minimum RPM still presents some distinct possibilities for anti-competitive results, but that those possibilities can be adequately policed, in the Court's view, under the rule of reason. What if Justice Breyer is correct, however, when he argues that the classic "free rider" rationale for vertical restraints is likely not a frequent justification for vertical restraints and, in any event, that it can be very difficult to evaluate as a matter of proof? *See* 127 S. Ct. at 2730 (Breyer, J., dissenting).

Other Ramifications of Leegin

In addition to the questions *Leegin* raises with regard to the application of the rule of reason to minimum RPM, it also poses a range of challenges owing to the elaborate legal framework that was constructed around *Dr. Miles* and *Colgate.* While the Court relieved the tension that had been generated for thirty years between *Dr. Miles* and *Sylvania,* it did not specifically address the fate of the long line of cases addressing the fact of an RPM "agreement" from *Colgate* to *Business Electronics.* These decisions narrowed the factual bases under which vertical agreements on price could be inferred, in part to ameliorate the harsh treatment of those agreements under the old per se rule. With *Dr. Miles* overruled, will those decisions come under pressure? At one point the majority acknowledged that *Monsanto* and *Business Electronics* accommodated the interests expressed in *Colgate* and *Sylvania* and "limit[ed] the reach" of *Dr. Miles'* per se rule, see 127 S.Ct. at 2721–22, but the Court stopped short of overruling those decisions as no longer necessary in light of its decision to abandon the per se rule. Are they gone? Gone only in some cases? Both the majority and the dissent seem to presume that at the very least *Colgate* lives and would now excuse even a demonstrably unreasonable use of RPM. *Id*. at 2722; *see also id.* at 2735 (Breyer, J., dissenting) (". . . *Colgate* would remain good law with respect to *unreasonable* price maintenance").

Other practices that tested the limits of *Dr. Miles* also developed. Three pricing strategies in particular received a great deal of attention in the case law and at the federal enforcement agencies and at times have been deemed "reasonable" despite *Dr. Miles'* seeming inflexibility: (1) *cooperative advertising programs*, which typically condition manufacturer financial support for advertising on the dealers' agreement not to advertise discounted prices;***** (2) *minimum advertised pricing programs* ("MAP"), which similarly restricted a dealer's ability to advertise discounted prices;****** and (3) *discount pass through programs*, whereby manufacturers agreed to specific discounts to dealers on the condition that the dealer pass-on the discount to its customers.******* When squarely confronted by these apparent examples of procompetitive, *reasonable* minimum RPM, courts and agencies frequently resorted to "characterization" mechanisms to circumvent the per se rule. As the Supreme Court did in *Broadcast Music* with respect to horizontal price agreements, they argued that such agreements are only "literal" price fixing, or that they lack the necessary evidence of "agreement." After *Leegin*, these kinds of practices can be judged more squarely on the merits by federal courts under the rule of reason without resort to forced characterizations. The federal cases interpreting these various doctrines may well remain relevant, however, in states that continue to endorse the per se rule of *Dr. Miles*.

Neither did the Court address the many other ways that firms and courts tried to work around *Dr. Miles*. For example, one consequence of the prohibition of minimum RPM was the common practice of utilizing "manufacturer's *suggested* retail prices" ("MSRP"), an effort to avoid allegations of "agreement." Another was the use of "consignment" sales, which do not involve passage of title or risk from the manufacturer to the

***** *See, e.g., In re Nissan Antitrust Litigation*, 577 F.2d 910 (5th Cir.1978)(approving use of rule of reason to analyze and approve cooperative advertising program where the evidence indicated that dealers were free to advertise at their own expense, at any price, without any limitations from Nissan). The FTC further developed standards for judging cooperative advertising in *In the Matter of Advertising Checking Bureau, Inc.,* 109 F.T.C. 146 (1987); *In the Matter of U.S. Pioneer Electronics Corp.,* 115 F.T.C. 446, 453 (1992); and *In the Matter of American Cyanamid,* 123 F.T.C. 1257, 1265 (1997).

****** MAP programs often are integrated into cooperative advertising programs and are unlikely to have any significant anticompetitive effects if dealers remain free to determine their actual resale prices and to advertise their prices outside of the supplier supported cooperative advertising program. But MAP can run afoul of the antitrust laws when the necessary

autonomy has not been protected. *See, e.g., In the Matter of Sony Music Entertainment, Inc.,* 2000 WL 689147 (F.T.C. May 10, 2000) (MAP was unreasonable when imposed simultaneously by music distributors who together accounted for some 85% of the industry's domestic sales and evidence indicated that MAP was adopted in response to complaints from the existing retailers about increased competition, particularly price competition, from new, lower priced, retailers, that offered services equal to or better than the incumbent dealers). *See also Analysis to Aid Public Statement on Proposed Consent Order,* 65 FR 31319, 31320 (May 17, 2000).

******* *See, e.g., Jack Walters & Sons Corp. v. Morton Bldg., Inc.,* 737 F.2d 698 (7th Cir. 1984); *Lewis Service Center, Inc. v. Mack Trucks, Inc.,* 714 F.2d 842 (8th Cir.1983); and *AAA Liquors, Inc. v. Joseph E. Seagram and Sons, Inc.,* 705 F.2d 1203 (10th Cir.1982).

consignee. True consignment arrangements might not qualify for condemnation as RPM on the theory that there can be no "agreement" between a manufacturer and a consignee, who merely acts as its agent. *See Simpson v. Union Oil*, 377 U.S. 13 (1964) (rejecting reliance on consignment label where the consignee assumed significant risks and costs and where the defendant appeared to invoke the label in an attempt to circumvent the per se rule). Firms might still utilize either of these approaches to minimize the risk of being ensnared in disputes about RPM.

Finally, the Court declined to address the plaintiff's assertion that the agreements at issue were not "vertical" at all. Because *Leegin* was a dual distributor, both supplying the plaintiff and other retailers and competing with them through its own, company-owned retail establishments, PSKS alleged in the Supreme Court (but not the lower courts) that "Leegin participated in an unlawful *horizontal* cartel with competing retailers." 127 S. Ct. at 2725 (emphasis added). The degree to which a per se rule might still be viable in such circumstances, however, is seriously in doubt, given a well established line of cases in the lower courts dealing with non-price restraints under *Sylvania*. Those cases rejected the argument that vertical restraints adopted by a supplier who was also a competitor of some of its dealers should be treated as horizontal and hence per se unlawful. *See, e.g., Electronics Commc'ns Corp. v. Toshiba Am. Consumer Products, Inc.*, 129 F.3d 240, 243–44 (2d Cir. 1997) (collecting authorities). *Leegin* invites additional arguments about the justifications for RPM in these and other arguably horizontal circumstances.

Economics. Leegin leaves open a number of important questions about the economics and economic effects of minimum RPM. The majority and the dissent openly disagreed about the lessons to be drawn from the existing empirical literature about RPM. The majority marginalizes the studies and seems to think overruling *Leegin* is unlikely to have any significant impact on prices. 127 S. Ct. at 27117–18. The dissent seems more concerned that minimum RPM will be widely used and that significant price increases will result, especially in concentrated industries. *Id.* at 2732–34 (Breyer, J., dissenting). If some states permit, while others prohibit, minimum RPM in the wake of *Leegin*, natural experiments may develop which will facilitate further empirical observation and study of its use and possible abuse. This may also be true owing to the continued adherence to strict prohibitions of minimum RPM outside of the United States.

Finally, as we have learned, today economics not only informs the analysis of the competitive effects and justifications for conduct, but also provides a way to think about and develop rules of conduct through decision-theoretic models. These models call for an evaluation of the incidence and likely effects of false positives and false negatives in selecting specific rules, as well as the costs of administering them. The majority, and especially the dissent, offer some interesting observations about how economic teaching informs the choice of legal rule for minimum RPM, and those portions of the Court's decision are also likely to influence lower courts and spark debate. Contrast *Leegin*, 127 S. Ct. at 2718; 2722–23, with *Leegin*, 127 S. Ct. at 2729; 2737 (Breyer, J., dissenting).

Conclusion

As should be evident, the lower courts, antitrust enforcers, and antitrust counselors will be working to sort out the practical implications of *Leegin* for some time to come. Ironically, as Justice Breyer predicted at the close of his dissent, the Court's desire to eliminate antitrust risk and antitrust litigation might well result in greater uncertainty and hence more litigation, at least for some period of time.

More broadly, *Leegin* illustrates some of the core concerns that currently motivate the Court in establishing antitrust rules. First, as the Court maintained in its decision a decade earlier in *Khan*, which over-ruled the per se rule against maximum RPM, "stare decisis is not an inexorable command" in antitrust cases interpreting the restraint of trade language of Section 1 of the Sherman Act. *State Oil Co. v. Khan,* 522 U.S. 3, 20 (1997). In addition, although expressed more explicitly in other recent decisions, the Court seems pro-occupied with the costs and risks of private treble damage actions, and appears willing to adjust the burdens of pleading, production, and in the case of *Leegin*, proof, upward to nullify the incentive to bring less-meritorious suits. The influence of economic thinking about the development of antitrust rules is quite evident in this analysis, which seems to lead to progressively higher burdens and fewer antitrust cases. These themes will recur as we proceed with our consideration of other areas of antitrust law.

4. RESALE PRICE MAINTENANCE AND ANTITRUST INJURY

As we have discussed throughout the Casebook, today anticompetitive effects largely come in two varieties—collusive and exclusionary—and these two categories of effects can be used to align much of antitrust analysis. Recall from Chapter 1, that cases like *Brunswick* introduced and advanced the use of "antitrust injury" as a vehicle for further defining those effects. Antitrust injury also has come to play a role in connection with private efforts to enforce the prohibitions of RPM.

In *Atlantic Richfield Co. v. USA Petroleum Co.*, 495 U.S. 328 (1990), the Supreme Court invoked *Brunswick* to reject an antitrust challenge by an independent gasoline retailer (USA Petroleum) to an alleged *maximum* resale price maintenance policy maintained by its competitors and their exclusive supplier, Atlantic Richfield ("ARCO"). The dealer was a low-overhead, high-volume discounter, that competed with brand-name retail gasoline stations, including ARCO retailers. According to USA, ARCO utilized maximum RPM to facilitate vigorous head-to-head competition between its retailers and discounting retailers, like USA. By forcing its own dealers to keep their prices lower than they otherwise would have, ARCO "injured" USA.

At that time, maximum RPM was per se unlawful under *Albrecht*, which was not overruled until the Court's 1997 decision in *Khan*. Indeed, in reaching its decision to overrule *Albrecht*, the Court in *Khan* referred back to *Atlantic Richfield*, in which it had first cast doubt on the continued vitality of *Albrecht*. *Atlantic Richfield*, itself, however, did not need to reach the question of *Albrecht's* wisdom, because it rested instead on USA's inability to assert any antitrust injury.

Relying on *Albrecht*, the Court reasoned that maximum RPM was declared unlawful as a consequence of its collusive anticompetitive effects on consumers and restrained dealers—not for its exclusionary effects on competitors of restrained dealers, such as USA. Provided the maximum prices set by ARCO were not predatory, USA simply could not suffer any "antitrust injury," i.e. injury "of the type the antitrust laws," i.e. *Albrecht*, were designed to prevent.

Atlantic Richfield thus suggested that like all private plaintiffs since *Brunswick*, private plaintiffs challenging RPM policies would have to allege and prove antitrust injury. To do so, they would first have to establish the nature of the anticompetitive effect associated with the conduct they were challenging, and then demonstrate that they suffered the kind of harm that justified the prohibition. Based on what we have learned thus far about the law and economics of minimum RPM, how would you answer those questions? What is the nature of the anticompetitive effect that justifies the prohibition of minimum RPM? Who are its victims?

Recall that in Sidebar 4–2 we evaluated the four possible anticompetitive theories associated with minimum RPM that were identified by the Court in Leegin, as well as a few others. Of the four theories specifically recognized by the Court, two are generally associated with collusive effects (manufacturer and dealer cartels) and the other two were based on theories of exclusion (manufacturer or dealer seeking to exclude rivals). Where do dealers who refuse to agree to manufacturer-imposed RPM fall in this analytical framework? Do they suffer any "antitrust injury" if they are terminated? Should it matter if the RPM is imposed pursuant to a dealer cartel that the dealer refused to join?

As you have seen in this Chapter, in older cases like *Dr. Miles* and *Schwinn*—both of which are now abandoned—the Supreme Court has invoked the preservation of property and contract rights, often couched as concerns for the preservation of "dealer freedom" as an independent aim of antitrust laws. As you read the following excerpts from *Pace*, which pre-dates *Leegin*, and thus was decided at a time when RPM was still per se illegal, consider how the court incorporates some of these distinct, traditional goals of the prohibition of minimum resale price maintenance into its analysis of antitrust injury to a restrained dealer. Also consider what impact, if any, *Leegin* should have on the kind of reasoning embraced by the court.

PACE ELECTRONICS, INC. v. CANON COMPUTER SYSTEMS, INC.

United States Court of Appeals for the Third Circuit, 2000.
213 F.3d 118.

Before: McKEE, RENDELL and ROSENN, Circuit Judges.

ROSENN, Circuit Judge.

The issue in this appeal is whether the termination of a wholesale dealer's contract for its refusal to acquiesce in an alleged vertical minimum price fixing conspiracy constitutes an antitrust injury that will support an action for damages under section 4 of the Clayton Act. The United States District Court for the District of New Jersey reasoned that a dealer terminated under these circumstances does not suffer an antitrust injury unless it can demonstrate that its termination had an actual, adverse economic effect on a relevant market. After concluding that the plaintiff's complaint in the instant case failed to allege such an effect, the District Court dismissed the complaint for failure to state a claim upon which relief may be granted. Because we believe the court misconstrued the antitrust injury requirement, we will reverse.

I

The plaintiff, Pace Electronics, Inc. ("Pace"), a New Jersey corporation, is engaged in the business of distributing various electronic products, including computer printers and related accessories. Pace purchases these products from manufacturers and wholesale distributors and then resells them to smaller retailers, who operate in the New Jersey and New York region.

In April of 1996, Pace entered into a nonexclusive dealer agreement with defendant Canon Computer Systems, Inc. ("Canon"), a California corporation. Under this agreement, Pace obtained the right to purchase Canon-brand ink-jet printers and related accessories from Canon at "dealer prices." In consideration for the right to purchase these products at "dealer prices," Pace agreed to purchase certain minimum quantities of the products.

The dealer agreement between Pace and Canon remained in effect for approximately one year and three months. Thereafter, on July 1, 1997, Canon terminated the agreement with Pace on the stated ground that Pace failed to purchase the minimum quantities of Canon-brand products required of it under the dealer agreement. Although Pace concedes that it did not purchase the amount of Canon-brand products called for under the dealer agreement, Pace contends that it was unable to do so because Canon ignored its purchase orders. Pace further contends that Canon ignored its purchase orders because Pace refused to acquiesce in a vertical minimum price fixing agreement designed and implemented by Canon and defendant Laguna Corporation ("Laguna"), Pace's direct competitor in the New Jersey and New York region.

* * *

Pace alleges that it has suffered financial losses as a result of its termination as an authorized Canon-brand dealer. Specifically, Pace avers that "[a]s a direct and proximate result of the actions of Defendants ... Pace has suffered significant financial detriment, consisting of, but not necessarily limited to, lost profits. Pace's losses result directly and proximately from the efforts of Canon and Laguna to limit price competition in the market ... for which both Laguna and Pace were competing." Appellant's App. at 77. Although these allegations of loss appear somewhat vague and conclusory, we accept them as true, as we must, for the purposes of this appeal.

Pace also alleges that its termination as an authorized dealer of Canon-brand products has harmed competition in two respects. First, it contends that its termination as a dealer has reduced price competition in the wholesale market for Canon-brand ink-jet printers (an intrabrand market) because

Laguna no longer faces price competition from Pace in selling these products to smaller retailers. Second, Pace asserts that its termination as a dealer has reduced price competition in the wholesale market for all brands of ink-jet printers (an interbrand market). In this connection, Pace alleges that: (1) Canon-brand ink-jet printers enjoy an inherent competitive price advantage over the ink-jet printers of other manufacturers; (2) until Canon permits its distributors to take advantage of this price advantage, other manufacturers will not attempt to reduce their production costs; and, (3) until an unrestrained free competitive market requires other manufacturers to reduce their production costs, the price of all brands of ink-jet printers will remain at an artificially high level.

II

To state a claim for damages under section 4 of the Clayton Act, 15 U.S.C. § 15, a plaintiff must allege more than that it has suffered an injury causally linked to a violation of the antitrust laws. *See Brunswick Corp. v. Pueblo Bowl–O–Mat, Inc.,* 429 U.S. 477, 489, 97 S.Ct. 690, 50 L.Ed.2d 701 (1977). In addition, it must allege antitrust injury, "which is to say injury of the type the antitrust laws were intended to prevent and that flows from that which makes defendants' acts unlawful." *Id.* This is so even where, as in the instant case, the alleged acts of the defendants constitute a per se violation of the antitrust laws.[2] *See also Atlantic Richfield Co. v. USA Petroleum Co.,* 495 U.S. 328, 341, 110 S.Ct. 1884, 109 L.Ed.2d 333 (1990). In applying the antitrust injury requirement, the Supreme Court has inquired whether the injury alleged by the plaintiff "resembles any of the potential dangers" which led the Court to label the defendants' alleged conduct violative of the antitrust laws in the first instance. *Id.* at 336, 110 S.Ct. 1884; *see also* II AREEDA & HOVENKAMP, ANTITRUST LAW, AN ANALYSIS OF ANTITRUST PRINCIPLES AND THEIR APPLICATION ¶ 362a. (Revised ed.1995) [hereinafter AREEDA & HOVENKAMP] ("The [antitrust injury requirement] forces . . . courts to connect the alleged injury to the purposes of the antitrust laws. Compensation for that injury must be consistent with . . . the rationale for condemning the particular defendant.").

* * *

* * * [W]e think it appropriate to ask whether Pace's alleged injury resembles any of the dangers which have led the Supreme Court to condemn vertical minimum price fixing agreements under the antitrust laws. Pace alleges that it has suffered antitrust injury because it was terminated as a wholesale dealer after it sold Canon-brand products at prices below the minimum resale price allegedly fixed by Canon and Laguna. Pace further alleges that its termination as a wholesale dealer has caused it to suffer lost profits because it may no longer obtain profits from selling Canon-brand products at "dealer prices." Under the Supreme Court's jurisprudence, these allegations suffice to establish antitrust injury.

On this point, *Simpson v. Union Oil,* 377 U.S. 13, 84 S.Ct. 1051, 12 L.Ed.2d 98 (1964) is instructive. * * *

---

2. Vertical minimum price fixing is, of course, *per se* unlawful under section 1 of the Sherman Act * * *.

[*Simpson* involved an ultimately successful challenge by a terminated dealer, who had entered into a consignment agreement with Union Oil, its supplier. Under the agreement, Union Oil required the dealer to adhere to specified minimum resale prices. When the dealer failed to do so, it was terminated. Quoting from *Simpson*, the *Pace* court observed that the Supreme Court in *Simpson* "placed primary focus on the consignment agreement's restriction on the ability of dealers such as the plaintiff to make independent pricing decisions." Eds.]

* * *

Thus, the Supreme Court considered a restriction on dealer independence with respect to pricing decisions to be an anticompetitive aspect of vertical minimum price fixing agreements, and one that the antitrust laws have an interest in forestalling. Accordingly, we think that a maverick dealer, such as Pace, which is terminated for charging prices less than those set under a vertical minimum price fixing agreement, suffers the type of injury which the antitrust laws are designed to prevent and may recover damages, such as lost profits, which flow from that termination. *See generally* AREEDA & HOVEN-KAMP, *supra,* ¶¶ 382a. and 382c. (discussing dealer standing to challenge various vertical restraints and noting that a terminated dealer which "can reasonably show that he would have been able to profit in a market free of the illegal arrangements has presumably suffered both injury-in-fact and antitrust injury."); *see also Simpson,* 377 U.S. at 16, 84 S.Ct. 1051 ("There is an actionable wrong whenever the restraint of trade has an impact on the market; and it matters not that the complainant may be only one merchant.").

Naturally, the defendants argue that the above analysis misses the mark. In essence, they contend that *Simpson* is no longer good law in light of the Supreme Court's decision in *Atlantic Richfield*. Furthermore, they urge, and the district court agreed, that a terminated dealer seeking to establish that it has suffered antitrust injury must allege facts demonstrating that its termination as an authorized dealer resulted in an actual, adverse economic effect on competition in a relevant interbrand market. In support of their position, the defendants primarily rely on the Supreme Court's statement in *Atlantic Richfield* that a plaintiff can recover damages under section 4 of the Clayton Act "only if [its] loss[es] stem[ ] from a competition-reducing aspect or effect of the defendant's behavior." *Atlantic Richfield,* 495 U.S. at 344, 110 S.Ct. 1884. On the basis of this brief statement, the defendants then argue that to be "competition-reducing" a defendant's challenged conduct must have had an actual adverse effect on a relevant interbrand market. Although the defendants' syllogism may have some allure, we decline to construe the antitrust injury requirement as suggested by the defendants for the following reasons.

First, we believe that requiring a plaintiff to demonstrate that an injury stemming from a *per se* violation of the antitrust laws caused an actual, adverse effect on a relevant market in order to satisfy the antitrust injury requirement comes dangerously close to transforming a *per se* violation into a case to be judged under the rule of reason. The *per se* standard is reserved for certain categories of conduct which experience has shown to be "manifestly anticompetitive." That standard, which is based on considerations of "business certainty and litigation efficiency," allows a court to presume that certain limited classes of conduct have an anticompetitive effect without engaging in the type of involved, market-specific analysis ordinarily necessary to reach such a conclusion. Were we to accept the defendants' construction of the antitrust injury requirement, we would, in substance, be removing the presumption of anticompetitive effect implicit in the *per se* standard under the guise of the antitrust injury requirement.[4]

Second, we do not believe that the Supreme Court's statement in *Atlantic Richfield* that a plaintiff can recover for losses only if they stem "from a competition-reducing aspect or effect of the defendant's behavior," when viewed in the context of the Court's entire opinion, can be fairly read to require a terminated dealer to prove that its termination caused an actual, adverse economic effect on a relevant market. In this connection, we note that in determining that the plaintiff in *Atlantic Richfield* failed to satisfy the antitrust injury requirement, the Supreme Court simply did not focus on whether the challenged conduct of the defendant had an actual, adverse economic effect on a relevant market. Rather, * * * the Court focused on whether the plaintiff's injury stemmed from any of the potential anticompetitive dangers which led the Court to label vertical maximum price fixing unlawful in the first instance. Implicit in the Court's approach is that a plaintiff who had suffered loss as a result of an anticompetitive aspect of a *per se* restraint of trade agreement would have suffered antitrust injury, without demonstrating that the challenged practice had an actual, adverse economic effect on a relevant market. The issue, thus, is not whether the plaintiff's alleged injury produced an anticompetitive result, but, rather, whether the injury claimed resulted from the anticompetitive aspect of the challenged conduct.

* * *

———

Are *Atlantic Richfield* and *Pace* irreconcilable? If so, why? Do they reflect incompatible views of the justification for the rule of *Dr. Miles*? Or do you accept the *Pace* court's distinction of *Atlantic Richfield*?

Perhaps more importantly, does *Pace* survive *Leegin*? Would a dealer terminated for refusing to abide by RPM that is deemed unreasonable under any one of the four scenarios outlined by the Court in *Leegin* presumptively be able to allege antitrust injury? Is the "injury" of diminished autonomy invoked in *Pace* simply a remnant of the *Dr. Miles* era and now effectively overruled, as well?

B. EXCLUSIVE DISTRIBUTORS AND SUPPLIERS

To this point, our discussion of vertical, intrabrand non-price restraints has focused exclusively on *Sylvania*-style restraints that limit the discretion of

---

4. We recognize that various scholars have taken issue with the Supreme Court's *per se* treatment of vertical minimum price fixing agreements and argued that these agreements may have significant, procompetitive attrib-utes. But, academic commentary, even if persuasive, does not permit us to expand the antitrust injury requirement to a point which undermines the Court's categorical disapproval of vertical minimum price fixing.

the dealer or downstream firm by, for example, limiting the territory in which it can sell, the customers to whom it can sell, or the locations from which it is can sell. But there are economically related kinds of vertical intrabrand non-price restraints that constrain the upstream firm.

The most typical example is the "exclusive distributorship." Exclusive distributorships take the form of commitments by a supplier not to appoint more than one or some limited number of dealers within a certain geographic area, or with authority to sell to a specified class or classes of customers. By limiting the number of dealers that might directly compete with each other in the sale of the same brand or line of products, exclusive distributorships limit intrabrand competition, just like territorial and customer restraints. Why would a dealer want such protections? Why would a supplier agree to provide them?

The economic justification for exclusive distributorships is indistinguishable from that identified in *Sylvania* to justify vertical intrabrand non-price restraints generally: to entice a dealer to undertake its best efforts to promote the supplier's brand of product. To do that, the dealer must know that it will not face free-riding dealers who will refrain from promoting the product, thereby minimizing their own costs, and then steal away customers persuaded to buy the product by the dealer's promotional efforts. In fact, it is likely that the reason Sylvania objected to Continental T.V.'s efforts to expand into Sacramento was that it had another dealer already serving that area successfully.

Exclusive distributorships are ubiquitous and rarely present any serious antitrust concerns. Examples include gasoline retailers, automobile dealerships, and many franchises. Indeed, recognition of their utility and legality under the Sherman Act long pre-dates *Sylvania*, and they never underwent a period of harsh treatment as did *Sylvania* type restraints. *See, e.g., Packard Motor Car. Co. v. Webster Motor Car Co.*, 243 F.2d 418 (D.C. Cir.), *cert. denied*, 355 U.S. 822 (1957); *United States v. Bausch & Lomb Optical Co.*, 45 F.Supp. 387 (S.D.N.Y. 1942), *aff'd by an equally divided court*, 321 U.S. 707 (1944). Even *Schwinn* singled them out as warranting leniency. *Schwinn*, 388 U.S. at 376.

At the outset, exclusive distributorships should be distinguished from "exclusive dealing," which we will discuss in Chapter 7. An exclusive distributorship typically limits the upstream supplier's ability to appoint other competing distributors or to distribute its own products. In contrast, exclusive dealing involves commitments by the dealer not to carry the products of its supplier's rivals. Whereas exclusive distributorships thus limit in*tra*brand competition, exclusive dealing restricts in*ter*brand competition, limiting the dealer's access to rival supplies and rival suppliers' access to dealers. Although some supplier-dealer arrangements can include both kinds of restraints, as we shall learn, the economic analysis of these two kinds of restraints is different, because they involve different kinds of competitive effects.

In *E&L Consulting*, which follows, we look at a modern example of the practice. As you read *E & L Consulting*, note the impact of *Sylvania* on the court's analysis. Note too the role that economic analysis plays today in evaluating the anticompetitive potential of vertical restraints. Consider whether that analysis is focused on the threat of collusive or exclusionary anticompetitive effects.

E & L CONSULTING, LTD. v. DOMAN INDUSTRIES LTD.

United States Court of Appeals for the Second Circuit, 2006.
472 F.3d 23.

Before WINTER, POOLER, and SOTOMAYOR, Circuit Judges.

WINTER, Circuit Judge.

E & L Consulting, Ltd. ("E & L"), which does business under the name C.B.C. Lumber, Co., and C.B.C. Wood Products, Inc. appeal from [the district court's] * * * dismissal of their complaint against a Canadian lumber company and its exclusive distributor. The complaint asserts, among other things, that a distribution agreement between appellees violates Section 1 of the Sherman Act * * *. We affirm principally because appellants have failed to allege facts that, if proven, would demonstrate harm to competition.

BACKGROUND

* * *

From 1990 until 2004, E & L was the distributor of green hem-fir lumber in New York, New Jersey, and Pennsylvania for appellees Doman Industries Limited ("Doman") and Eacom Timber Sales Ltd., a Doman subsidiary. The termination of that distribution arrangement gave rise to the present dispute.

Green hem-fir lumber is an inexpensive, durable wood that is "often utilized for homebuilding," particularly in the northeast. There is no hem-fir or green hem-fir tree; the product is a manufactured combination of different woods. Doman and Eacom together supply 95 percent of the green hem-fir lumber sold in New York, New Jersey, Connecticut, Rhode Island, Maryland, Delaware, and Pennsylvania.

Beginning in 1990, E & L had an arrangement with Doman under which E & L "would take delivery, but not ownership, of the green hem-fir lumber products at its port facility in Red Hook, Brooklyn, New York." E & L sold the lumber on Doman's behalf at prices set by Doman, and Doman provided E & L with set monthly payments and commissions. E & L had arrangements with two other green hem-fir distributors, Atlantic Coast Lumber Co. in Rhode Island and Futter Lumber in Delaware.

By 1998, Doman had severed its relationship with Atlantic Coast Lumber. To replace Atlantic Coast, Doman contracted with appellee Sherwood Lumber Corp., a New York corporation that sells lumber-including green hem-fir-and finished wood products. Under its agreement with Doman, Sherwood purchased green hem-fir lumber from Doman and resold it out of the port in New London, Connecticut. Doman prohibited E & L from selling lumber in the area served by Sherwood.

In 2003, Doman cancelled its agreement with Futter Lumber and replaced it with Sherwood. Doman continued to prohibit E & L from selling green hem-fir lumber in states served by Sherwood.

* * *

On January 30, 2004, Doman terminated its distribution agreement with E & L. On February 1, 2004, Doman notified its customers that Sherwood had become the exclusive distributor of Doman green hem-fir lumber in areas previously served by E & L, Futter, and Atlantic Coast.

E & L alleges that there are no commercially feasible alternative sources of green hem-fir lumber. Only one other company beside Doman supplies green hem-fir lumber-Timber West-and it supplies very little. Furthermore, no shipping carriers operate a route from the western United States to Brooklyn, and, consequently, the only way to get lumber from Timber West is by rail. This increases the cost of the lumber by "more than 10 percent," rendering it "uncompetitive for resale." In addition, the only ocean shipping line transporting lumber from Canada to New York told E & L that "no shipments [of non-Doman lumber products] could be made for an indefinite period of time." E & L alleges that Doman's reservation of all potential shipping methods was intended to prevent E & L and other distributors from obtaining an alternative source of supply.

E & L asserts that only a handful of other types of lumber are suitable for the framing of homes, and they cost 25 percent more than green hem-fir, which "precludes these products from being adequate substitutions." Once Sherwood obtained exclusive distribution rights in the northeast, it raised the price of green hem-fir lumber by, in some cases, "over 20 percent."

* * *

The district court concluded that plaintiffs' federal antitrust claims failed because the complaint did not adequately allege a relevant product market, or injury cognizable under the antitrust laws. With no remaining federal questions, [the district court] * * * declined to exercise supplemental jurisdiction over the state law claims. The present appeal ensued.

DISCUSSION

a) Standard of Review

We review a district court's grant of a motion to dismiss under Rule 12(b)(6) de novo. For purposes of such a review, we accept as true all allegations in the complaint and draw all reasonable inferences in favor of the non-moving party.[2] * * *

* * *

b) Section 1 Claim

Appellants' Sherman Act Section 1 claim, based on the Doman–Sherwood distribution agreement, fails because they have not alleged an injury to

---

2. We indulge in this assumption despite seeming anomalies in some factual allegations. For example, the complaint alleges that a 10% increase in transportation costs when rail is used renders green hem-fir lumber from another producer "uncompetitive for resale" because of the elasticity of demand for the product while also alleging that Sherwood has raised prices by over 20% and that alternative kinds of suitable lumber sell for 25% more than green hem-fir. Moreover, the complaint alleges that Doman has sold green hem-fir lumber at a discount to Sherwood to allow the latter to sell green hem-fir lumber at lower prices than E & L and to tie the sale of that product to Sherwood's sale of finished wood products, conduct that hardly benefits Doman.

competition, an element of a *prima facie* Section 1 claim.[3]

* * *

The complaint alleges a vertical restraint between a supplier (Doman) and a distributor (Sherwood).[4] The agreement between Doman and Sherwood designating the latter as the exclusive distributor of Doman green hem-fir in the northeast, like any commercial agreement, restrains trade. But, critically, nothing in the complaint suggests that this agreement results in either a "predictable and pernicious" (*per se* violation) or "unreasonable" (rule of reason violation) effect on competition. It is not "a violation of the antitrust laws, without a showing of actual adverse effect on competition market-wide, for a manufacturer to terminate a distributor . . . and to appoint an exclusive distributor."

Doman is alleged to have a market share in green hem-fir lumber amounting to 95% in the northeastern United States. Appellants do not assert that Doman's market share is somehow an illegal monopoly and seek no relief on that ground. But, they allege, the exclusive distributorship with Sherwood further harms competition. However, appellants' hypothesizing of an unreasonable effect on competition fails because such a vertical arrangement provides no monopolistic benefit to Doman that it does not already enjoy and would not continue to enjoy if the exclusive distributorship were enjoined. To put it another way, had Doman established its own in-house distribution system with the same monopoly that Sherwood is alleged to possess, there would have been no increase in the restriction of output of green hem-fir lumber and in the resultant misallocation of resources.

Indeed, an exclusive distributorship would be counterproductive so far as any monopolization goal of Doman is concerned. A monopolist manufacturer of a product restricts output of the product in order to maximize its profits. The power to restrict output to maximize profit is complete in the manufacturing monopoly, and there is no additional monopoly profit to be made by creating a monopoly in the retail distribution of the product. On the contrary, a firm with a monopoly at the retail distribution level will further reduce output to maximize *its* profits, thereby reducing the sales and profit of the monopoly manufacturer. *See Cont'l T.V., Inc. v. GTE Sylvania Inc.*, 433 U.S. 36, 56 (1977) * * *. Like any seller of a product, a monopolist would prefer multiple competing buyers unless an exclusive distributorship arrangement

3. One basis on which the district court dismissed the complaint was its conclusion that plaintiffs had not alleged "antitrust injury," because they had failed to "allege some type of harm to competition market-wide." We agree with the district court that the plaintiffs' failure to proffer allegations of harm to competition is fatal to their antitrust claims. However, the failure to allege harm to competition is analytically distinct from failure to plead antitrust injury. Antitrust injury is "injury of the type the antitrust laws were intended to prevent and that flows from that which makes defendants' acts unlawful." *Brunswick Corp. v. Pueblo Bowl–O–Mat, Inc.*, 429 U.S. 477, 489 (1977). An antitrust plaintiff "must show not only injury-in-fact, but also that [the injury] constitutes . . . the kind that the antitrust laws are designed to prevent and that [is] congruent with the rationale for finding an antitrust violation in the first place." It should go without saying, therefore, that a party cannot establish antitrust injury without establishing a violation of the antitrust laws, which, under Section 1, must involve an injury to competition.

4. "Restraints imposed by agreement between competitors have traditionally been denominated as horizontal restraints, and those imposed by agreement between firms at different levels of distribution as vertical restraints." *Business Elecs. Corp. v. Sharp Elecs. Corp.*, 485 U.S. 717, 730 (1988).

provides other benefits in the way of, for example, product promotion or distribution. *See Cont'l T.V.*, 433 U.S. at 54–56. In fact, we have explicitly noted that "a vertically structured monopoly can take only one monopoly profit."

The only detriment to competition alleged to result from the Doman–Sherwood agreement is that "end-users of lumber and finished wood products have fewer options to purchase their required supplies and are now required to pay artificially inflated prices." This, by itself, is not a sufficient allegation of harm to competition caused by the exclusive distributorship, again, because the alleged single source and price increase, even if monopolistic, is something Doman can achieve without the aid of a distributor.

Thus, we have noted that "exclusive distributorship arrangements are presumptively legal." To be sure, we have never held that all exclusive arrangements are reasonable as a matter of law. In *Geneva Pharmaceuticals*, for example, we vacated a grant of summary judgment on a Section 1 claim that was based on an exclusive supply agreement between a drug-maker and a supplier of the active ingredient in the drug. *Geneva Pharms. Tech. Corp. v. Barr Labs. Inc.*, 386 F.3d 485 (2d Cir. 2004). We acknowledged the general rule that "it usually does not further harm competition for a monopolist in one market to leverage its advantage into a monopoly in a downstream market." However, in that case there was a "window of monopoly opportunity [that] is unique." *Geneva* involved an allegation of two temporary, related monopolies in different products, a drug and its active ingredient. Moreover, the two firms, which had overlapping ownership, were jointly involved in predatory practices designed to extend their respective temporary monopolies by deterring entry by competitors. * * *

The facts in *Geneva*, therefore, were quite different from the claim in a typical exclusive distribution case, like the present one, where it is alleged only that a monopolist manufacturer is trying to extend its monopoly into the distribution or sale of its product. Unlike *Geneva*, the present case is a "run-of-the-mill exclusive distributorship controversy, where a former exclusive distributor is attempting to protect its competitive position vis a vis its supplier." The complaint simply does not allege, therefore, "that the challenged action has had an *actual* adverse effect on competition as a whole in the relevant market."

* * *

———

Do you agree with the court's economic reasoning in *E & L*? With its statement that exclusive distributorships are "presumptively legal"? Is the court's analysis consistent with the reasoning of *Sylvania*? Under this reasoning, when, if ever, could an exclusive distributorship—or any other vertical intrabrand restraint—raise any significant antitrust concerns?

What might be the consequence if the court had reached a different result? Consider, for example, how Doman could have responded if the court had concluded that the exclusive distributorship was unreasonable because it eliminated all intrabrand competition in a market defined (as the plaintiff asserted) for "green hem-fir lumber in the Northeastern United States." Such intrabrand competition, it might have reasoned, would provide the only downward pressure on price, and hence its elimination through exclusive territories, customers, or, as in this case, through an exclusive distributorship, unreasonably restrained trade. In effect, such a result would amount to ordering Doman to create intrabrand competition among dealers. Would it likely do so? Or would it, as the court intimates, simply switch to direct distribution? After *Leegin*, if it chose the route of selling to more dealers, might it also consider using minimum RPM to defeat discounting? Could it lawfully do so under *Leegin*? The court's line of reasoning invokes the "single monopoly profit" critique of older vertical restraint doctrine. We first discussed it above in Sidebar 4–2, and elaborate in the next note.

Note on Intrabrand Competition and the "Single Monopoly Profit" Theory

Can a monopolist manufacturer have an anticompetitive motive in eliminating intrabrand competition among its dealers, as by selecting one as its exclusive distributor? The argument against is the "single monopoly profit" theory, discussed above in Sidebar 4–2 and again in Chapter 7. Under that view, if there are multiple dealers, the manufacturer can extract the entire monopoly profit simply by raising the wholesale price. Exclusivity then confers no additional anticompetitive advantage on the manufacturer, so it must be motivated by the manufacturer's desire to achieve an efficiency (for example, inducing the dealer to offer more point-of-sale services by eliminating dealer free-riding).

But the single monopoly profit theory does not necessarily apply to eliminate the possibility of anticompetitive effect when a monopolist consolidates distribution in one dealer. The monopolist can earn greater profits by shifting to exclusive distribution if doing so reduces the competition the monopolist faces from fringe rivals or potential entrants, as in the hypothetical example below, by reducing the competition the monopolist faces from sellers of substitute products (which might constrain the monopolist from raising price further above the competitive level), or if doing so facilitates anticompetitive price discrimination (*see* Sidebar 7–3, *infra*).*

    Suppose that water heaters are distributed in metropolitan area markets by plumbing supply houses. The typical city has three such distributors. Suppose further that Heat, Inc. is the dominant seller of water heaters, with a 90% share in the typical city, and that its products are carried by virtually all plumbing supply houses. In addition, suppose that the cost of holding inventory is a major concern for plumbing supply houses, and that this cost is low if the distributor has a high volume of water heater business, but high otherwise. If Heat decides to select one supply house in the typical city to be its exclusive dealer, then its fringe rivals and potential entrants can only distribute through the remaining two distributors. But those other distributors will now have high inventory holding costs, making it uneconomic for them to price aggressively against the Heat line and helping Heat to obtain or maintain the ability to exercise market power. In an extreme case, the remaining two distributors may be forced to exit from the water

---

* A dominant manufacturer would accomplish the same end through vertical integration, which would eliminate all intrabrand competition, but that might not be cost-effective relative to an exclusive distribution contract (for example if the distributor deals in a wide range of products).

heater distribution business entirely, ending all possibility of competition by the fringe rivals or potential entrants.

———

The court in *Paddock Publ'ns, Inc. v. Chicago Tribune Co.*, 103 F.3d 42 (7th Cir. 1996), rejected an antitrust suit brought by Chicago's number three newspaper, The Herald, challenging a system of exclusive distributorship arrangements that had developed over time between what it alleged were "the best" news services and its two larger rivals, the Chicago Tribune and the Chicago Sun–Times. The plaintiff did not allege either that its two larger rival papers conspired with each other or that the news services had conspired with each other. According to the court, it therefore conceded that "each has adopted its method of doing business independently; they take the same approach to distribution because each has discovered that it is the most profitable way to do business." *Id*. at 44. In the court's view, "Competition-for-the-contract is a form of competition that antitrust laws protect rather than proscribe, and it is common." *Id*. at 45. The court then examined how an exclusive distributorship could be anticompetitive:

> In what way could the news services' practices harm consumers? Tacit collusion (economists' term for "shared monopoly") could be a source of monopoly profits and injury to consumers even if none of the stages of production is monopolized. Some distribution arrangements might be objectionable because they facilitate tacit collusion. But collusion, tacit or express, requires some horizontal cooperation, or at least forbearance from vigorous competition among rivals. * * * Although the newspaper market is concentrated on the readers' side, the inputs to newspaper production are unconcentrated and therefore do not facilitate tacit collusion in the more concentrated market. * * * The *Herald* does not argue that the practices at hand facilitate tacit collusion.

> What the *Herald* does argue is that a mixture of fewness of firms, exclusive contracts, and relations between suppliers and users of news that endure despite short contract terms, hampers the growth of small rivals even though each market is competitive. Such an argument does not come within any of the economic approaches to tacit collusion * * *.

Id. The court concluded: " . . . The *Herald* has never tried to make a better offer, and we conclude that it has come to the wrong forum. It should try to outbid the *Tribune* and *Sun-Times* in the marketplace, rather than to outmaneuver them in court." *Id*. at 47.

What kind of anticompetitive effects might flow from an exclusive distributorship, collusive, exclusionary, or both? What conditions would have to be present before those effects would become likely and substantial? On the other side of the scale, what efficiency-related justifications for exclusive distributorships are discussed by the court? How are those justifications to be weighed against the adverse impact the arrangements might have on aspiring entrants, like the Daily Herald? How realistic is it to suggest, as does the court, that the Herald should simply try to outbid the established incumbents? Do the exclusive arrangements perpetuate their dominance in the local newspaper market? If so, does it pose the threat of being a serious anticompetitive effect?

Sidebar 4–3:
Antitrust, Dealer Relations and Arbitration

For much of the Casebook thus far, we have focused on only two vehicles for resolving antitrust disputes—litigation and negotiation. Litigation, of course, has produced all of the judicial decisions we have examined, whereas negotiation has been evident in government prosecutions resolved through the entry of consent decrees and in connection with government application of various enforcement Guidelines. Negotiations will be especially relevant when we turn to merger enforcement in Chapter 5.

Manufacturer-dealer relations, however, have long been the focal point of debates about the use of other methods of dispute resolution, especially arbitration. This Sidebar looks at the history and current status of the use of arbitration to resolve antitrust disputes, especially those arising between dealers and their suppliers. Recall from Sidebar 4–1 that managing disputes that arise in the context of these relationships has become more challenging since *Sylvania*.

The American Safety Doctrine

For nearly twenty years, from 1968 to 1985, the courts expressed a decided hostility towards the use of arbitration in antitrust cases. That hostility can be traced *to American Safety Equip. Corp. v. J.P. Maguire & Co.*, 391 F.2d 821 (2d Cir. 1968), where the court refused to enforce an arbitration clause in connection with an antitrust dispute between a trademark licensor and licensee:

> A claim under the antitrust laws is not merely a private matter. The Sherman Act is designed to promote the national interest in a competitive economy; thus, the plaintiff asserting his rights under the Act has been likened to a private attorney-general who protects the public interest. Antitrust violations can affect hundreds of thousands—perhaps millions—of people and inflict staggering economic damage. * * * We do not believe that Congress intended such claims to be resolved elsewhere than in the courts. * * *

> * * * [I]n addition, the issues in antitrust cases are prone to be complicated, and the evidence extensive and diverse, far better suited to judicial than to arbitration procedures.

391 F.2d at 826–27. *American Safety* proved to be influential and was quickly followed by other circuits. The arbitration of antitrust disputes, despite contractual commitments to do so, was thereafter viewed as void as against public policy.

How persuasive are the Second Circuit's arguments in favor of refusing to enforce arbitration clauses in antitrust challenges? Would they be true of other areas typically subject to arbitration? Are antitrust cases really any more "complicated" than other kinds of large-scale litigation? Does the court's characterizations of typical antitrust litigation apply fully to dealer relations cases? Would they apply more persuasively to arbitration clauses contained in consumer contracts and invoked to block nationwide antitrust class actions?

Mitsubishi Motors Corp. v. Soler Chrysler–Plymouth

The *American Safety* doctrine faced its most significant challenge in 1985, in *Mitsubishi Motors Corp. v. Soler Chrysler–Plymouth*, 473 U.S. 614 (1985). *Mitsubishi* squarely placed the question of the arbitrability of antitrust claims before the Supreme Court—but solely in the context of international transactions. Mitsubishi's sales and distribution contract with Soler, one of its U.S. dealers, contained a clause requiring for arbitration of all disputes arising out of the sales relationship by the Japan Commercial Arbitration Association. When relations between Mitsubishi and Soler soured, Mitsubishi filed suit in federal district court under the Federal Arbitration Act and the Convention on the Recognition and Enforcement of Foreign Arbitral Awards to enforce the arbitration clause. Soler filed an answer and counterclaim asserting that certain provisions of the underlying sales agreement violated the Sherman Act.

The district court ordered the parties to arbitration, reasoning that the international context of the case distinguished it from *American Safety*. After rejecting several other points raised by Soler, the Supreme Court agreed. 473 U.S. at 628–40, reserving the question of *American Safety's* vitality in the purely domestic context.

The Revitalization of Arbitration of Domestic Antitrust Disputes

Not surprisingly, *Soler* provided some encouragement for manufacturers and suppliers intent on controlling the future costs of dispute resolution by providing for arbitration of all dealer disputes. Arbitration clauses became more common as a "forum selection" device, and the inevitable question was put to the courts: should *Soler* be extended to the domestic context and *American Safety* abandoned?

With increasing frequency, the Courts of Appeals are answering that question in the affirmative. *See, e.g., Seacoast Motors of Salisbury, Inc. v. DaimlerChrysler Motors Corp.*, 271 F.3d 6 (1st Cir. 2001); *Kotam Electronics, Inc. v. JBL Consumer Products, Inc.*, 93 F.3d 724 (11th Cir. 1996)(abandoning *American Safety* doctrine in domestic context in light of *Soler*); *Nghiem v. NEC Electronic, Inc.*, 25 F.3d 1437 (9th Cir. 1994)(*American Safety* doctrine did not preclude arbitration of antitrust dispute between employer and employee). The First Circuit's reasoning in *Seacoast* is typical:

> * * * This circuit once adopted *American Safety*, but the Supreme Court reversed, at least in the context of antitrust claims arising from international transactions. *Mitsubishi Motors Corp. v. Soler ChryslerPlymouth* * * *

> Since then, several circuits have abandoned the *American Safety* doctrine in its entirety. Others have expressed doubt whether it remains good law. It is time to lay it to rest.

> *American Safety* rested on the basic premise that the public interest in antitrust enforcement, the complexity of the antitrust

laws, and the inadequacy of arbitral tribunals make arbitration of private antitrust claims inappropriate. This premise has since been rejected by the Supreme Court with respect to a variety of other statutory claims no less important or complex.

There is no question here of an advance waiver of antitrust claims; arbitration clauses do not eliminate substantive rights but submit them for resolution in an arbitral, rather than a judicial forum. *Mitsubishi*, 473 U.S. at 628, 105 S.Ct. 3346. And while some antitrust cases do involve large issues in which the public has an interest, others are essentially business quarrels peculiar to the parties. For those in the former category, government agencies remain free to pursue the defendant regardless of private actions, whether before courts or arbitrators. We think time has passed by the *American Safety* doctrine and so hold.

271 F.3d at 10–11.

How persuasive is the critique of *American Safety*? Are there any factors peculiar to the international context that make abandonment of the *American Safety* doctrine more appropriate there then in the domestic context? Do you concur with Judge Boudin's opinion in *Seacoast*, that many antitrust disputes are "essentially business quarrels peculiar to the parties"?

Arbitration clauses come in many forms and can pose a number of additional issues. For example, in *Kristian v. Comcast Corp.*, 446 F.3d 25 (1st Cir. 2006), the court reversed a district court's conclusion that an arbitration clause in a cable provider's customer contract could not be enforced retroactively, but it went on to invalidate provisions of the arbitration agreement that purported to bar class actions as well as the recovery of treble damages and attorney's fees.

Conclusion

The trend in the courts suggests that antitrust claims are more likely to be subject to arbitration in the near future, especially in the context of domestic contractual dealer arrangements. Do you view that as a positive or negative development? Is it a matter of perspective? Why in each of the cases were the dealers resisting and the suppliers pressing for arbitration? And how will the trend toward arbitration affect the advice provided to suppliers and dealers by their antitrust counselors? What would you recommend to a supplier or franchisor? To a dealer or franchisee?

Finally, how far should this trend go toward facilitating the arbitration of antitrust claims? Assume, for example, that a consumer products manufacturer routinely included an arbitration clause in the fine print of its product packaging, should that be sufficient to commit a consumer class action for industry-wide price fixing to arbitration? What issues might such a clause pose? Similarly, what if arbitration clauses were inserted into software licenses for popular computer programs, should all antitrust claims arising between the manufacturer and end-users be subject to arbitration? What public policy arguments from *American Safety* might resurface in these two examples? What exceptions alluded to by the Court in *Mitsubishi*? These issues are very likely to challenge the courts in short order.

C. CHARACTERIZATION CHALLENGES

Recall that while *Dr. Miles* and *Sylvania* co-existed, the characterization of a vertical intrabrand restraint as "price" or "non-price" became very important, because price restraints were subject to per se prohibition. We now turn to another area where characterization issues have led to some confusion in the courts, although here the characterization problem was vertical vs. horizontal and concerned use of the "boycott" label, which we first encountered in Chapter 2 and will revisit in Chapter 7. You may want to read the introductory material in Chapter 7A1 at this time as background for our next case.

The typical scenario here involves the substitution by a supplier of one exclusive distributor for another. The combination of the exclusivity and the substitution lends itself to the charge that the supplier and its new distributor have engaged in a horizontal "concerted refusal to deal"—"horizontal," because it affected competition between the distributors. Indeed, there may even be evidence that one distributor sought to harm the other by replacing it as the supplier's representative. The typical defense, however, emphasized the *vertical* nature of all dealer relations, and the general legality of exclusive distributorships. So, once again the cases could turn on characterizations—concerted refusals to deal can be per se unlawful; exclusive distributorships are judged leniently under the rule of reason. The Supreme Court seems to have put to rest efforts to invoke the per se rule in such cases, however, with its decision in *NYNEX*.

NYNEX CORP. v. DISCON, INC.
United States Supreme Court, 1998.
525 U.S. 128, 119 S.Ct. 493, 142 L.Ed.2d 510.

Justice BREYER delivered the opinion of the Court.

In this case we ask whether the antitrust rule that group boycotts are illegal *per se* as set forth in *Klor's, Inc. v. Broadway–Hale Stores, Inc.*, 359 U.S. 207 (1959), applies to a buyer's decision to buy from one seller rather than another, when that decision cannot be justified in terms of ordinary competitive objectives. We hold that the *per se* group boycott rule does not apply.

I

Before 1984 American Telephone and Telegraph Company (AT & T) supplied most of the Nation's telephone service and, through wholly owned subsidiaries such as Western Electric, it also supplied much of the Nation's telephone equipment. In 1984 an antitrust consent decree took AT & T out of the *local* telephone service business and left AT & T a long-distance telephone service provider, competing with such firms as MCI and Sprint. The decree transformed AT & T's formerly owned local telephone companies into independent firms. At the same time, the decree insisted that those local firms help assure competitive *long-distance* service by guaranteeing long-distance companies physical access to their systems and to their local customers. To guarantee that physical access, some local telephone firms had to install new call-switching equipment; and to install new call-switching equipment, they often had to remove old call-switching equipment. This case involves the business of removing that old switching equipment (and other obsolete telephone equipment)—a business called *"removal services."*

Discon, Inc., the respondent, sold removal services used by New York Telephone Company, a firm supplying local telephone service in much of New York State and parts of Connecticut. New York Telephone is a subsidiary of NYNEX Corporation. NYNEX also owns Materiel Enterprises Company, a purchasing entity that bought removal services for New York Telephone. Discon * * * alleged that the NYNEX defendants * * * engaged in unfair, improper, and anticompetitive activities in order to hurt Discon and to benefit Discon's removal services competitor, AT & T Technologies, a lineal descendant of Western Electric. The Federal District Court dismissed Discon's complaint for failure to state a claim. The Court of Appeals for the Second Circuit affirmed that dismissal with an exception, and that exception is before us for consideration.

The Second Circuit focused on one of Discon's specific claims, a claim that Materiel Enterprises had switched its purchases from Discon to Discon's competitor, AT & T Technologies, as part of an attempt to defraud local telephone service customers by hoodwinking regulators. According to Discon, Materiel Enterprises would pay AT & T Technologies more than Discon would have charged for similar removal services. It did so because it could pass the higher prices on to New York Telephone, which in turn could pass those prices on to telephone consumers in the form of higher regulatory-agency-approved telephone service charges. At the end of the year, Materiel Enterprises would receive a special rebate from AT & T Technologies, which Materiel Enterprises would share with its parent, NYNEX. Discon added that it refused to participate in this fraudulent scheme, with the result that Materiel Enterprises would not buy from Discon, and Discon went out of business.

These allegations, the Second Circuit said, state a cause of action under § 1 of the Sherman Act, though under a "different legal theory" from the one articulated by Discon. The Second Circuit conceded that ordinarily "the decision to discriminate in favor of one supplier over another will have a pro-competitive intent and effect." But, it added, in this case, "no such pro-competitive rationale appears on the face of the complaint." Rather, the complaint alleges Materiel Enterprises' decision to buy from AT & T Technologies, rather than from Discon, was intended to be, and was, "anti-competitive." Hence, "Discon has alleged a cause of action under, at least, the rule of reason, and possibly under the *per se* rule applied to group boycotts in *Klor's*, if the restraint of trade 'has no purpose except stifling competition.' " * * *

* * * We granted certiorari in order to consider the applicability of the *per se* group boycott rule where a single buyer favors one seller over another, albeit for an improper reason.

II

* * *

The Court has found the *per se* rule applicable in certain group boycott cases. Thus, in *Fashion Originators' Guild of America, Inc. v. FTC*, 312 U.S.

457 (1941), this Court considered a group boycott created by an agreement among a group of clothing designers, manufacturers, suppliers, and retailers. The defendant designers, manufacturers, and suppliers had promised not to sell their clothes to retailers who bought clothes from competing manufacturers and suppliers. The defendants wanted to present evidence that would show their agreement was justified because the boycotted competitors used "pira[ted]" fashion designs. But the Court wrote that "it was not error to refuse to hear the evidence offered"—evidence that the agreement was reasonable and necessary to "protect ... against the devastating evils" of design pirating—for that evidence "is no more material than would be the reasonableness of the prices fixed" by a price-fixing agreement.

In *Klor's* the Court also applied the *per se* rule. The Court considered a boycott created when a retail store, Broadway–Hale, and 10 household appliance manufacturers and their distributors agreed that the distributors would not sell, or would sell only at discriminatory prices, household appliances to Broadway–Hale's small, nearby competitor, namely, Klor's. The defendants had submitted undisputed evidence that their agreement hurt only one competitor (Klor's) and that so many other nearby appliance-selling competitors remained that competition in the marketplace continued to thrive. The Court held that this evidence was beside the point. The conspiracy was "not to be tolerated merely because the victim is just one merchant." The Court thereby inferred injury to the competitive process itself from the nature of the boycott agreement. And it forbade, as a matter of law, a defense based upon a claim that only one small firm, not competition itself, had suffered injury.

The case before us involves *Klor's*. The Second Circuit did not forbid the defendants to introduce evidence of "justification." To the contrary, it invited the defendants to do so, for it said that the "*per se* rule" would apply only if no "pro-competitive justification" were to be found. Thus, the specific legal question before us is whether an antitrust court considering an agreement by a buyer to purchase goods or services from one supplier rather than another should (after examining the buyer's reasons or justifications) apply the *per se* rule if it finds no legitimate business reason for that purchasing decision. We conclude no boycott-related *per se* rule applies and that the plaintiff here must allege and prove harm, not just to a single competitor, but to the competitive process, *i.e.*, to competition itself.

Our conclusion rests in large part upon precedent, for precedent limits the *per se* rule in the boycott context to cases involving horizontal agreements among direct competitors. The agreement in *Fashion Originators' Guild* involved what may be called a group boycott in the strongest sense: A group of competitors threatened to withhold business from third parties unless those third parties would help them injure their directly competing rivals. Although *Klor's* involved a threat made by a *single* powerful firm, it also involved a horizontal agreement among those threatened, namely, the appliance suppliers, to hurt a competitor of the retailer who made the threat. * * *

This Court subsequently pointed out specifically that *Klor's* was a case involving not simply a "vertical" agreement between supplier and customer, but a case that also involved a "horizontal" agreement among competitors. *See Business Electronics* * * *. And in doing so, the Court held that a "vertical restraint is not illegal *per se* unless it includes some agreement on price or price levels." This precedent makes the *per se* rule inapplicable, for the case before us concerns only a vertical agreement and a vertical restraint, a restraint that takes the form of depriving a supplier of a potential customer.

We have not found any special feature of this case that could distinguish it from the precedent we have just discussed. We concede Discon's claim that the petitioners' behavior hurt consumers by raising telephone service rates. But that consumer injury naturally flowed not so much from a less competitive market for removal services, as from the exercise of market power that is *lawfully* in the hands of a monopolist, namely, New York Telephone, combined with a deception worked upon the regulatory agency that prevented the agency from controlling New York Telephone's exercise of its monopoly power.

To apply the *per se* rule here—where the buyer's decision, though not made for competitive reasons, composes part of a regulatory fraud—would transform cases involving business behavior that is improper for various reasons, say, cases involving nepotism or personal pique, into treble-damages antitrust cases. And that *per se* rule would discourage firms from changing suppliers—even where the competitive process itself does not suffer harm.

The freedom to switch suppliers lies close to the heart of the competitive process that the antitrust laws seek to encourage. At the same time, other laws, for example, "unfair competition" laws, business tort laws, or regulatory laws, provide remedies for various "competitive practices thought to be offensive to proper standards of business morality." Thus, this Court has refused to apply *per se* reasoning in cases involving that kind of activity.

Discon points to another special feature of its complaint, namely, its claim that Materiel Enterprises hoped to drive Discon from the market lest Discon reveal its behavior to New York Telephone or to the relevant regulatory agency. That hope, says Discon, amounts to a special anticompetitive motive.

We do not see how the presence of this special motive, however, could make a significant difference. That motive does not turn Materiel Enterprises' actions into a "boycott" within the meaning of this Court's precedents. Nor, for that matter, do we understand how Discon believes the motive affected Materiel Enterprises' behavior. Why would Discon's demise have made Discon's employees less likely, rather than more likely, to report the overcharge/rebate scheme to telephone regulators? Regardless, a *per se* rule that would turn upon a showing that a defendant not only knew about but also hoped for a firm's demise would create a legal distinction—between corporate knowledge and corporate motive—that does not necessarily correspond to behavioral differences and which would be difficult to prove, making the resolution of already complex antitrust cases yet more difficult. We cannot find a convincing reason why the presence of this special motive should lead to the application of the *per se* rule.

Finally, we shall consider an argument that is related tangentially to Discon's *per se* claims. The complaint alleges that New York Telephone (through Materiel Enterprises) was the largest buyer of removal services in New York State, and that only AT & T Technologies competed for New York Telephone's business. One might ask whether these accompanying allegations are sufficient to warrant application of a *Klor's*-type presumption of consequent harm to the competitive process itself.

We believe that these allegations do not do so, for, as we have said, antitrust law does not permit the application of the *per se* rule in the boycott context in the absence of a horizontal agreement. The complaint itself explains why any such presumption would be particularly inappropriate here, for it suggests the presence of other potential or actual competitors, which fact, in the circumstances, could argue against the likelihood of anticompetitive harm. * * *

IV

Petitioners ask us to reach beyond the *"per se"* issues and to hold that Discon's complaint does not allege anywhere that their purchasing decisions harmed the competitive process itself and, for this reason, it should be dismissed. They note that Discon has not pointed to any paragraph of the complaint that alleges harm to the competitive process. This matter, however, lies outside the questions presented for certiorari. Those questions were limited to the application of the *per se* rule. For that reason, we believe petitioners cannot raise that argument in this Court.

V

For these reasons, the judgment of the Court of Appeals is vacated, and the case is remanded for further proceedings consistent with this opinion.

Note on Discon Remand

The Supreme Court's opinion in *Discon* concludes with the customary "the case is remanded for further proceedings consistent with this opinion." But on remand to the Second Circuit the parties sharply divided on what proceedings would be "consistent" with the Court's opinion. *Discon, Inc. v. NYNEX Corp.,* 184 F.3d 111, 112 (2d Cir.1999). The Supreme Court certainly made clear that Discon's complaint could not proceed under a per se theory. Less clear was whether the Court's opinion left open the possibility that it could proceed under the rule of reason.

The Court of Appeals concluded that the Supreme Court's principal focus was on the inapplicability of the per se rule, and that its opinion did not necessarily foreclose the plaintiff from establishing competitive harm under a rule of reason inquiry. *Id.* at 114. While observing that "[i]t may well be difficult for Discon to resist a motion by NYNEX for summary judgment on the issue of lack of an adequate showing of injury to competition," the court nevertheless concluded that Discon should be afforded the opportunity to do so. It therefore remanded the action to the district court with directions to permit Discon to amend its complaint and attempt to make "the requisite showing" of harm to competition, as opposed to harm to itself. *Id.*

D. DISTRIBUTIONAL RELATIONSHIPS IN THE EUROPEAN UNION: THE ARTICLE 81 APPROACH

Article 81 of the Treaty of Rome is the European Union's rough equivalent of Section 1 of the Sherman Act. (*See* Appendix A.) In reading Article 81, note that, like Section 1 of the Sherman Act, it is focused on concerted action (single firm conduct is addressed under Article 82). But in at least three important ways, it is quite distinct from Section 1. First, in contrast to Section 1's all-encompassing language, Article 81 specifies more particular categories of agreements that are prohibited. Second, under Article 81(3), the Commission is empowered to exempt individual agreements, or categories of agreements, from the reach of Article 81(a), on the ground that they either do not pose a threat to competition *or that they serve other enumerated goals.* Finally, for most of the Treaty's history, Article 81's prohibitions have been interpreted more broadly than Section 1's, especially in the area of vertical restraints.

Vertical territorial restraints, like those at issue in *Sylvania*, were for a long time treated harshly under European competition laws. Dividing distribution along national lines, for example, as would typically be permitted by state in the United States, was prohibited, but not for reasons related to their narrowly defined economic consequences. Rather, competition enforcement officials recognized that vertical territorial restrictions could be used to segment European markets based on the geographic boundaries of its member states, undermining the broader integration goals of the Treaty of Rome. Thus, in a real sense the goal of encouraging "efficiency" in distribution, gave way to the broader goal of creating union. As we discussed in Chapter 1, this is a good example of how other countries have integrated different goals into the interpretation of competition laws.

More recently, however, with the goal of union increasingly realized, the European Commission has turned greater concern towards efficiency, and has signaled that the law of vertical restraints in Europe is converging to some extent with U.S. law. In December, 1999, the Commission promulgated a new regulation, No, 2790/1999, concerning the application of Article 81(3) to categories of vertical agreements and concerted practices. *See* http://ec.europa.eu/comm/competition/antitrust/legislation/vertical.html. This "Block Exemption" became effective June 1, 2000 and a set of Vertical Restraint Guidelines were adopted prior to the implementation date. The block exemption and accompanying guidelines were an important component of broader efforts to modernize the EC's rules on competition, and were intended to give greater weight to economic efficiency.

Not surprisingly, therefore, the exemption and guidelines suggest that the Commission's views on vertical restraints are now moving much closer to those prevalent in the United States since *Sylvania*. Despite some convergence, however, the EC rules remain less permissive than those that have evolved under *Sylvania*. To illustrate—the exemption emphasizes that vertical non-price restraints "can improve economic efficiency * * * by facilitating better coordination" between firms in a chain of distribution absent market power. It therefore provides a "safe harbor" for non-price restraints, but the safe harbor is limited to restraints adopted by a supplier with less than a 30% market share—a very low threshold by U.S. standards. Restraints adopted by a supplier with more than a 30% market share are not presumed to be unlawful, however. Rather, such agreements merely do not qualify for automatic safe harbor treatment and require further analysis. The Commission also preserves the authority to declare the exemption inapplicable to "parallel networks of vertical agreements * * * which cover more than 50% of a given market," a situation unlikely to give raise to equally heightened concern in the U.S. *See* EC, *Guidelines on Vertical Restraints*, *available at* http://eur-lex. europa.eu/LexUriServ/site/en/oj/2000/c_291/c_29120001013en00010044.pdf.

For some purposes the exemption distinguishes "passive" from "active" sales. Although producers can contractually limit their dealers from actively pursuing certain classes of customers, they cannot restrict them from accepting unsolicited, or "passive" orders—particularly on the Internet. Producers utilizing a "selective distribution system," however, are prohibited from restraining either passive or active sales by their "authorized distributors." What concerns do these provisions reveal? Would they also be of concern to U.S. antitrust enforcers? Under what circumstances?

The exemption expressly does not apply to vertical minimum price agreements, which are labeled "severely anti-competitive," a characterization that would not likely be used by many today in the United States, especially after *Leegin*. But the exemption does embrace *Khan*, treating maximum price agreements more leniently than minimum. "Suggested" minimum prices are also permitted. Would you agree that minimum RPM should be characterized as "severely anti-competitive"? Is the use of such a characterization tantamount to embracing a per se rule?

The EC's block exemption for vertical restraints, and the Guidelines that accompany it, provide a comprehensive analysis of all vertical restraints, not only the intrabrand ones which we have summarized here. They also cover "interbrand" restraints, such as tying and exclusive dealing, which we will examine in Chapter 7.

E. CONCLUSION

In this Chapter we have explored a range of vertical relationships that can under some circumstances produce collusive anticompetitive effects. All such relationships are today treated leniently in recognition of their pro-competitive potential, particularly with respect to interbrand competition. Although the categorization scheme that evolved over time generated a variety of fault lines that complicated the analysis of these kinds of arrangements and triggered disputes, cases like *Sylvania*, *Leegin*, and *Nynex* have alleviated much of those tensions. Characterizing restraints as vertical or horizontal, concerted or unilateral price or non-price, and minimum or maximum resale price maintenance may still have ramifications in terms of the conduct's treatment in some instances, but greater reliance on economic concepts has brought greater clarity and some continuing challenges for the contemporary antitrust counselor.

F. PROBLEMS & EXERCISES

Problem 4–1:
Pomegranate Apparel

a. *The Facts*

Pomegranate Apparel Company of Oak Park, Illinois ("Pomegranate") sells sports apparel from several retail stores in and around Chicago, Illinois. One of its principal suppliers is M. Scott Reubens Sportswear, Inc. ("Reubens"), one of only three apparel manufacturers in the United States licensed by the Federal Football League ("FFL") to manufacture and sell clothing bearing the official colors, emblems and logos of FFL member teams. Total sales of authorized FFL clothing in the United States totaled $100 million in 2006, and Reubens' annual sales exceeded $50 million.

Reubens is the FFL's exclusive authorized distributor in seven Midwestern states, including Illinois and Wisconsin, where it distributes the apparel through a small group of hand-picked dealers, such as Pomegranate. All of Reubens's dealers sign written dealer agreements with Reubens. Those agreements provide, in pertinent part:

Uniform Dealership Agreement

* * *

15. Dealer agrees that it shall not, without the prior written consent of Reubens, sell authentic FFL satin jackets (hereafter "the licensed goods") from any location other than that specified in paragraph 29 of this Agreement;

16. Reubens agrees that it will not appoint any other dealer of the licensed goods within a five (5) mile radius of the location specified in paragraph 29 of this agreement;

17. Dealer also agrees:

    (a) to maintain adequate displays of the licensed goods at the specified location;

    (b) to hire sales personnel that are knowledgeable of the licensed goods and adequately trained in the fitting of the licensed goods at the specified location; and

    (c) to advertise and promote said goods through local media including, but not limited to, newspapers, radio and television.

18. Dealer agrees that it will not sell the licensed goods to any person other than a retail customer.

19. Dealer agrees that it will promptly report the appearance in its assigned territory of any unlicensed, pirated or copied version of the licensed goods to Reubens.

* * *

Paragraph 29 of Pomegranate's agreement reads:

    29. The authorized location for purposes of this agreement shall be: Pomegranate Apparel Company, 112 Jenny Place, Oak, Park, Illinois.

Reubens now believes that Pomegranate may be in violation of paragraphs 15 and 18 of the Uniform Dealership Agreement. That view is based on correspondence Reubens has received from two of its other authorized FFL apparel dealers, one in downtown Chicago, the other in nearby Milwaukee, Wisconsin. The letter from the Chicago dealer accused Pomegranate of selling satin jackets bearing FFL logos from Pomegranate's downtown Chicago store, which was located across the street from another Reubens dealer. A complaint from Reubens's licensed dealer in Wisconsin accuses Pomegranate of transhipping satin jackets from Illinois to an unlicensed retailer in Milwaukee, Wisconsin, where they were sold in direct competition with Reubens's licensed dealer.

Although Pomegranate does not contest Reubens's accusations, it asserts that the real reason for the complaints from the Chicago and Milwaukee dealers is the prices it charged, which were significantly below Reubens's suggested retail prices. According to Pomegranate, since it refurbished and expanded its two stores and installed a state of the art computerized inventory control and accounting system, its costs decreased by almost 20%, allowing it to reduce its prices on all of its apparel, including the satin jackets. Pomegranate also maintains that none of the twelve other Reubens dealers it contacted in the midwest since its termination would agree to sell officially licensed satin jackets to it. A random investigation of Reubens's dealers in three metropolitan areas in the midwest finds that, during the football season, the satin jackets typically sell at a price equal to or greater than the manufacturer's suggested retail price approximately 85% of the time.

b. *Problem & Skills Exercise*

You are an associate at the law firm that has been retained by Reubens, who is considering various courses of action with respect to Pomegranate. Reubens has provided you with two letters, one from its Chicago dealer and one from its Milwaukee dealer, complaining about competition from Pomegranate. Both letters comment at length on the "low prices" at which the jackets were being sold. They also question whether the jackets are "authentic." One is captioned "Notice of Incident of Design Piracy Pursuant to Paragraph 19 of the Uniform Dealership Agreement." Both dealers assert they assumed that Pomegranate was selling unlicensed merchandise, because each was "the only dealer authorized to sell the jackets" in its specified territories. Reubens also mentions that Pomegranate's stores never lived up to paragraph 17 of the Uniform Dealer Agreement. The letters also state, in almost identical language, that "these problems could be eliminated if you would just set the minimum prices for all of us."

Reubens has now asked you to prepare a letter advising it of the antitrust risks associated with two possible courses of action: (1) terminating Pomegranate as a Reubens dealer. Draft the letter; and/or (2) adopting a uniform set of resale prices for all FFL merchandise sold by Reubens to its Midwestern dealers, including Pomegranate. Draft the letter.

Chapter 5

MERGERS AMONG COMPETITORS ("HORIZONTAL MERGERS")

INTRODUCTION

When a firm buys some or all of the stock or assets of another, the transaction is termed an "acquisition." If all of a firm is acquired, the two companies are said to have "merged." Mergers and acquisitions among rivals can reduce competition because they alter the structure of markets by changing the number, identity, size and other characteristics of firms. As of the end of 2007, a substantial majority of the more than 100 competition enforcement authorities in the world had adopted some form of merger control mechanism as part of their antitrust laws. As a consequence, acquisitions involving multinational corporations with significant worldwide operations commonly are subject to review by more than one jurisdiction, and sometimes by dozens.

Mergers and acquisitions commonly are categorized as "horizontal," "vertical," or "conglomerate." Like horizontal agreements (the subject of Chapter 2), horizontal mergers and acquisitions involve sellers of substitutes, *i.e.*, competitors; like vertical agreements (the subject of Chapters 4 and 7), vertical mergers and acquisitions involve firms and their suppliers, customers, or other sellers of complements; and conglomerate mergers involve firms that sell neither substitutes nor complements. Typically, a conglomerate is engaged in many unrelated lines of business. This chapter focuses on horizontal mergers and emphasizes "collusive" rather than "exclusionary" competitive concerns. Because vertical mergers more commonly may raise exclusionary concerns, they are discussed along with other conduct having exclusionary effects in Chapter 7. Conglomerate merges are discussed in Sidebar 5–2.

As will be evident in both the organization and content of this chapter, the development of merger law in the U.S. illustrates the antitrust field's shift in perspective from narrow doctrinal categories to broad, overarching concepts like market power, entry and efficiency. Indeed, under the influence of government Merger Guidelines, the shift toward a more concept-oriented approach to antitrust analysis coalesced and accelerated in the merger area, especially since the early 1980s. That influence has been more pronounced owing in part to the fact that the Supreme Court has not decided a substantive merger case since the mid–1970s. Although we will begin our study with a review of those early cases, therefore, much of the chapter focuses on how merger law, and merger lawyers, operate today—by applying economic concepts to make often complex judgments about the likely performance of markets affected by mergers.

A.   A PRIMER ON MERGER
ANALYSIS IN THE U.S.

1.   INTRODUCTION TO THE STATUTORY FRAMEWORK

Most mergers are reviewed under Section 7 of the Clayton Act, 15 U.S.C. § 18. *See* Appendix A, *infra*. The original version, enacted in 1914, was restricted to stock acquisitions. Congress closed the resulting loophole in 1950, amending the section so that it also covered asset acquisitions. The 1950 amendments also removed earlier language that had arguably limited the text to anticompetitive horizontal mergers, thus making clear that the statute applied equally to horizontal, vertical, and conglomerate mergers. *See generally Brown Shoe Co. v. United States*, 370 U.S. 294 (1962) (excerpted later in this Chapter).

Mergers also can be challenged under two other federal statutes. They may violate the Sherman Act, as Section 1 agreements in restraint of trade or as monopolization or attempts to monopolize under Section 2. They may also be viewed as unfair methods of competition in violation of Section 5 of the FTC Act. Interlocking directorates—the presence of common directors on the boards of rival firms—can also be an antitrust violation under Section 8 of the Clayton Act, 15 U.S.C. § 19. The distinguishing characteristic of the anti-merger prohibitions of the Clayton Act is its objection to mergers that "*may* * * * substantially * * * lessen competition*"* (emphasis added). As we shall see when we read *Brown Shoe* later in this Chapter, in the wake of the 1950 Amendments, this language was seized upon by the Supreme Court as "authority" for going beyond the Sherman Act by "arresting mergers at a time when the trend to a lessening of competition in a line of commerce was still in its *incipiency*." The "may" language also provides a basis for challenging mergers before they lead to actual anticompetitive effects, *i.e.*, before they are consummated.

The Clayton Act, like the Sherman Act (but not the FTC Act), may be enforced by states and private parties, as well as by the federal antitrust enforcement agencies. Private plaintiffs in merger litigation, as with other claims under the federal antitrust laws, must demonstrate that they are harmed as a result of the practice they challenge as anticompetitive. We first encountered this "antitrust injury" requirement in Chapter 1, when we read *Brunswick*, itself a private merger challenge. In practice, most merger enforcement is conducted by the federal antitrust agencies.

Some mergers in certain industries, mainly those currently or previously subject to extensive federal regulation, also may be reviewed on competition grounds by federal agencies other than the Justice Department and Federal Trade Commission, although typically with their input. In some cases, the transaction may be reviewed concurrently by an antitrust agency and by an industry regulator. Examples include railroads (Surface Transportation Board), communications (Federal Communications Commission), energy producers (Federal Energy Regulatory Commission), and banking (Federal Reserve Board). Mergers involving national security interests are subject to antitrust review and to an additional regulatory regime under the Exon–Florio Amendment to the Defense Production Act of 1950 ("Exon–Florio"), 50 U.S.C. App. § 2170.

Largely owing to the passage of the Hart–Scott–Rodino Antitrust Improvements Act in 1976, which created a system of pre-merger notification, mergers today commonly are challenged upon their announcement, before any possible adverse competitive effects can occur. *See* Sidebar 5–3. Before 1976, it was more common for acquisitions to be challenged only after consummation. But retrospective merger review often made remedy a difficult problem, because it required a court to unscramble integrated business assets and activities. Moreover, challenges after consummation created uncertainty for the merged entity and its employees for a substantial period of time. On the other hand, retrospective review in theory permitted courts to judge mergers based upon their actual effects. In practice, however, courts often discounted favorable post-transaction evidence on the ground that the firm's managers were aware that government investigation and judicial review were pending.

Prospective merger review requires enforcers and courts to make a prediction about the likely competitive effects of the deal. How might they do so? One traditional solution has been the "structural presumption," which predicts anticompetitive effects based on significant increases in market concentration. This presumption, the subject of the first cases we study in the next section, can be understood as a legal device for making predictions about the competitive effects of mergers in an environment of uncertainty. As you read the cases and learn of the law's evolution, consider the advisability of structuring merger review this way, and the different choices that have been made by courts in different eras. Also consider whether the various factors highlighted in those decisions—including high post-merger market concentration, a sizeable increase in concentration, and a trend toward concentration— are likely to serve as reliable indicators of future adverse competitive effects.

Although most merger challenges today occur before consummation, the legal authority for post-consummation challenges was unaffected by the enactment of pre-merger notification. The federal enforcement agencies occasionally undertake post-consummation challenges, either with respect to transactions that were not reportable under the pre-merger notification regime (perhaps because they were too small), or to mergers and acquisitions that may not have appeared to present competitive problems at the time they were reported, but raise concerns later. *See, e.g., Chicago Bridge & Iron Co. v. FTC*, 515 F.3d 447 (5th Cir. 2008).

2. MOTIVES FOR MERGER AMONG RIVALS

Before we begin our study of the cases, we examine why firms might seek to merge or to acquire each other's assets. Firms commonly seek to make acquisitions for a number of reasons that do not raise antitrust concerns, including these:

- to reduce costs or improve products in ways unavailable to the merger partners individually;

- to improve the profitability of the acquired assets by replacing ineffective management;

- to obtain tax advantages in some situations; and
- to satisfy the "hubris" of some managers, who obtain personal satisfaction from controlling large corporate empires.

The vast majority of mergers and acquisitions have motives such as these, and are commonly considered benign from an antitrust standpoint. Indeed, in a recent year, the federal antitrust enforcement agencies identified no antitrust problem in nearly all of the mergers and acquisitions that they reviewed, as indicated in Sidebar 5–3. Although this chapter looks at the antitrust law issues that arise in mergers and acquisitions, such transactions may also raise other legal issues, including tax, securities, and corporate law questions. Accordingly, legal counseling for merging firms commonly draws upon the expertise of attorneys practicing in all these fields.

Some mergers do raise antitrust concerns, and may be motivated in whole or part by the desire to obtain market power. An acquisition may permit the merger partners to obtain market power in three ways:

- *Coordinated Competitive Effects.* By reducing the number of competitors, a merger may make it easier for rivals in a market to collude tacitly or achieve higher prices through consciously parallel conduct after the merger. Such mergers would raise the same kind of concern about "collusive" conduct that might also arise, for example, in agreements among rivals to fix price or divide markets.

- *Unilateral Competitive Effects.* If the merging firms are the only two participants in the relevant market, their "merger to monopoly" could result in "unilateral competitive effects," because once merged they could together raise price without needing to coordinate with any other firms. A merger also may allow two merging firms that sell products that are close substitutes to coordinate their business strategies, lessening the competitive constraint the sellers pose for each other and leading to higher prices even if other sellers in the market do not change their strategies. Higher prices may spread beyond the merging firms to other sellers participating in the market. These "unilateral" competitive effects may also be understood as reflecting a "collusive" competitive concern (as opposed to an exclusionary competitive concern).*

- *Exclusionary Anticompetitive Effects.* A merger may allow firms to obtain market power by impairing rivals' access to key inputs or distribution channels.

Mergers that generate antitrust scrutiny may simultaneously permit the exercise of market power and allow the merging firms to lower costs or otherwise achieve efficiencies. This observation raises a frequent challenge in the antitrust analysis of mergers, and, indeed, in antitrust generally: how to

---

* Although this terminology should by now be familiar to students who have read our earlier chapters, it may be confusing to other readers steeped in the Merger Guidelines who look at this chapter first. In brief, this casebook distinguishes between "collusive" and "exclusionary" competitive concerns. Anticompetitive conduct is termed "collusive" if it harms competition directly, and termed "exclu-sionary" if it does so indirectly, as a result of the elimination or impairment of rivals. We do not use the term "collusive" synonymously with "coordinated" competitive effects. Rather, we describe the two types of competitive effects set forth in the Merger Guidelines, "coordinated" and "unilateral," as different types of "collusive" competitive effects.

evaluate conduct that appears likely to generate both anticompetitive harm and procompetitive efficiencies. One policy tradeoff that may result in the merger context is depicted in Figure 5–1. This type of figure originated with economist Oliver Williamson and is sometimes referred to as the "Williamson diagram."**

Figure 5–1:

The Williamson Diagram

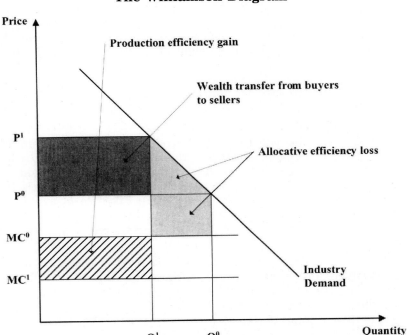

Figure 5–1 illustrates the effects on price, output, and economic welfare (efficiency) of a merger that simultaneously raises price *and* generates cost savings, using economic concepts we previously met in the coffee example in Chapter 1. Initially, the industry was selling Q^0 units of output at a price P^0. This price was in excess of pre-merger industry marginal cost (MC^0). The merger gives the firms participating in the market the ability to exercise market power by reducing output to Q^1, leading price to rise along the industry demand curve to the post-merger price P^1. Although the merger leads to an increase in price in the figure, that need not always be the case.

As Figure 5–1 suggests, a merger may create opposing incentives for the merging firms: (1) an incentive to raise price that may result from an

---

** Economics students will recognize that Figure 5–1 incorporates a number of assumptions that are made to simplify the graph and that do not qualify the general observations made in the text. For example, the possibility of product differentiation is ignored; marginal cost is assumed not to vary with output; and the industry is assumed to price in excess of marginal cost pre-merger. Note as well that the only costs depicted in the figure are variable (marginal) costs; fixed costs are not shown. (In this aspect, the figure differs from Williamson's original presentation, which worked with average costs.) The figure also does not show how the monopolist's price and output are determined (marginal revenue is not depicted).

increased ability to exercise market power; and (2) an incentive to lower price that may derive from efficiencies (here depicted as marginal cost savings). As a consequence, the post-merger price may either rise or fall; the actual outcome will be based on the relative strength of these two incentives in particular cases. If the post-merger price is likely to fall, the merger may be deemed procompetitive, making the antitrust enforcer's job easy. A merger likely to raise price, in contrast, can be expected to draw enforcer scrutiny, and may raise some of the policy issues sketched below.

Returning to Figure 5–1, the higher price creates a transfer from buyers to sellers (shaded rectangle in upper left), as buyers of Q^1 units who formerly paid P^0 are forced to pay P^1.*** It also leads to an allocative efficiency loss (the shaded triangle and rectangle to the right of the transfer as indicated by the arrows), equal to the social gain achieved pre-merger but no longer achieved after the exercise of market power. Before the merger, the market was able to convert resources that cost MC^0 into products worth as indicated on the demand curve to buyers; the exercise of market power denies society this benefit for $(Q^0\text{-}Q^1)$ units, generating an allocative efficiency loss.

But the merger also will generate a production efficiency gain. This gain arises from the cost savings depicted by the shaded rectangle in the lower left of the figure. In particular, the Q^1 units that are still produced and sold after the merger are produced with fewer resources, as marginal cost falls to a lower level, which generates an efficiency gain. Fixed cost savings resulting from the merger (*e.g.*, from the reduction in duplicative overhead expenditures like payroll) may also represent social resource savings but are not depicted in Figure 5–1.

As the Williamson diagram suggests, a merger that raises price can simultaneously reduce social welfare (through the allocative efficiency loss) *and* increase it (through the production efficiency gain). As drawn in Figure 5–1, the allocative efficiency loss exceeds the production efficiency gain, making the transaction objectionable on two grounds: (1) it will reduce aggregate social welfare; and (2) it will harm buyers by raising price. However, with different assumptions it is possible for the transaction simultaneously to increase aggregate social welfare (if the production efficiency gain exceeds the allocative efficiency loss) and harm buyers through higher prices (by generating a transfer from buyers to sellers).

In principle, this latter possibility may present a difficult policy tradeoff. Commentators and courts debate whether a merger likely to generate a small price increase may be saved by large cost savings (or other efficiencies) when those savings are not passed through to consumers but instead accrue largely to the benefit of shareholders. They also debate whether a merger likely to raise price in one market may be saved by cost savings or other efficiencies benefitting consumers in other markets. We will return to these issues when efficiencies are considered later in this chapter.

3. HISTORICAL PERSPECTIVES ON MERGER ENFORCEMENT

While mergers and acquisitions are routine in a dynamic economy, mergers sometimes come in waves. The U.S. is commonly thought to have

---

*** The figure and our discussion ignores the possibility, suggested in Chapter 1, that the transfer could be dissipated through wasteful rent-seeking, and thus also represents an efficiency loss.

experienced unusual clusters of mergers around 1900, during the late 1920s, during the late 1960s, during the 1980s, and during the late 1990s through 2000. Although merger waves seem largely unpredictable, it is noteworthy that these were all periods of economic expansion and strong stock market performance.

The characteristics of merging firms have varied from one era to the next. Many of the "trusts" that give "antitrust" law its name—including the Standard Oil and American Tobacco trusts that were the subject of high profile monopolization cases in the early twentieth century—were formed through mergers among rivals. During the 1990s, certain sectors of the economy—defense, energy, financial services, health care, pharmaceuticals, and telecommunications—accounted for a substantial proportion of the mergers that occurred, particularly the largest transactions. These sectors were buffeted by outside forces such as deregulation, technological change, and the end of the Cold War—leading firms to alter their business strategies and, in consequence, to reconfigure their assets.

In a recent year, around 1,700 mergers and acquisitions were reported to the federal enforcement agencies pursuant to the premerger notification requirements of the Hart–Scott–Rodino Antitrust Improvements Act, discussed in Sidebar 5–3. The number can vary substantially from year to year.

B.   THE EMERGENCE AND EROSION OF THE STRUCTURAL PARADIGM

1.   GUIDE TO THE CASES

Before the 1970s, the "oligopoly problem" loomed large in the thinking of courts and commentators concerned with the review of horizontal mergers under the antitrust laws. Coordination, and supracompetitive pricing, was commonly thought to be nearly inevitable when an industry had only a small number of firms, but frequently unreachable under Sherman Act § 1 because it could be accomplished through price leadership or other methods that might not constitute an "agreement." Economists schooled in the "structure-conduct-performance" paradigm emphasized the way market structure—primarily concentration of sellers, but also entry conditions, product differentiation, vertical integration and other factors—affected firm conduct (the pricing, advertising, investment, product variety, research and development, and other behavior of firms) and market performance (firm profits, economic welfare, and other measures).

In this intellectual environment, antitrust law accepted a strong presumption of economic harm from high market concentration, and identified competitive concerns at concentration levels that were low by today's standards. These views, combined with non-economic concerns to protect small business and avoid the adverse political consequences thought to arise from the aggregation of economic power, led Congress and the courts to look to merger law as a vehicle for preventing increased market concentration in its incipiency. These concerns are highlighted by the Supreme Court in *Brown*

Shoe, in its discussion of the legislative history of the 1950 amendments to the Clayton Act. The Court's decision in *United States v. Philadelphia Nat'l Bank*, 374 U.S. 321 (1963), which we will read after *Brown Shoe*, codified them doctrinally by setting forth a legal presumption of anticompetitive effect from a horizontal merger that would increase market concentration.

The legislative concern to prevent the growth of harmful concentration in its incipiency changed the focus of the antitrust review of mergers away from an *ex post* review of their actual effects, to an *ex ante* review of their likely future effects. Antitrust law's focus on future effects was heightened by the pre-merger notification requirements enacted in 1976, and discussed below in Sidebar 5–3.

The modern era in merger analysis can be dated from the Justice Department's 1982 Merger Guidelines, which accepted the structural presumption from *Philadelphia Nat'l Bank* and other controlling Supreme Court precedent, but also endorsed the idea from *United States v. General Dynamics Corp.*, 415 U.S. 486, 94 S.Ct. 1186, 39 L.Ed.2d 530 (1974), that the presumption can be rebutted by also considering factors that might facilitate or frustrate the anticompetitive effects of mergers such as entry and efficiencies. These are factors that must be assessed in making a predictive determination about likely competitive effects. The new approach went beyond the existing cases, however, and also reflected new thinking about oligopoly among economists, influenced importantly by the Nobel Prize-winning Chicago economist George Stigler. Stigler and others no longer saw coordination as inevitable in an oligopoly, but instead sought to analyze whether the firms in the market could overcome the difficulties of reaching a consensus and deterring deviation (cheating) from it, as was discussed in Chapter 3 of this casebook.

Although the Merger Guidelines were conceived as a guide to the exercise of prosecutorial discretion, the conceptual framework they adopt has greatly influenced merger analysis in the courts. The courts of appeals thus took the lead in working through the implications of the new Chicago-school economic perspective for horizontal merger law, under the framework set forth in the Merger Guidelines. In *United States v. Waste Management, Inc.*, 743 F.2d 976 (2d Cir.1984), excerpted later in this Chapter, the Second Circuit allowed ease of entry to rebut the structural presumption of harm to competition derived from concentration statistics. In *FTC v. University Health*, 938 F.2d 1206 (11th Cir.1991), discussed briefly in Section C of this chapter, the Eleventh Circuit suggested that efficiencies could do so as well.

The final two horizontal merger cases excerpted in this section are from the U.S. Court of Appeals for the D.C. Circuit. Both *United States v. Baker Hughes, Inc.*, 908 F.2d 981 (D.C. Cir. 1990) and *FTC v. H.J. Heinz Co.*, 246 F.3d 708 (D.C. Cir. 2001), reaffirm that the structural presumption set forth in *Philadelphia Nat'l Bank* remains controlling precedent. While *Baker Hughes* emphasizes how that presumption can be rebutted, *Heinz* highlights its importance when market concentration is very high. As you read these decisions, ask yourself whether they are consistent, or whether they suggest different answers to one of the central doctrinal questions in horizontal merger analysis today: how far has the structural presumption eroded in the years since *Philadelphia Nat'l Bank*?

2. THE EMERGENCE OF THE STRUCTURAL PRESUMPTION

BROWN SHOE CO. v. UNITED STATES

Supreme Court of the United States, 1962.
370 U.S. 294, 82 S.Ct. 1502, 8 L.Ed.2d 510.

[This case involved the proposed merger of two firms in the shoe business: Brown Shoe Company, Inc. proposed to acquire the G.R. Kinney Company, Inc. Both companies were vertically integrated, participating in both shoe manufacturing and shoe retailing.

Brown was the fourth largest shoe manufacturer in the country, accounting for about 4% of total domestic production and 6% of wholesale shoes sold nationally. It was also the Nation's third largest shoe retailer, controlling 1,230 retail shoe outlets. Of these, 470 were company owned and operated, and the rest were mainly independently-owned stores operating under the Brown franchise program. Most retail shoe stores were independent of any manufacturer: the 1,230 retail shoe outlets controlled by Brown accounted for only 20% of the firm's approximately 6,000 retail customers.

Kinney was primarily in the retail business, though it also was the twelfth largest domestic shoe manufacturer, with about a 0.5% share. Kinney was the country's eighth largest retailer, with over 350 retail outlets, accounting for 1.2% of shoes sold (and 2% of children's shoes sold). Kinney-manufactured products accounted for about one fifth of the company's retail sales. Brown was the largest outside supplier of the shoes sold in Kinney's retail outlets, supplying nearly 8% of those products.

After the merger, the four leading shoe manufacturers in the U.S. would account for about 23% of domestic production, and the 24 leading manufacturers would produce about 35% of the Nation's shoes. The district court found a "definite trend" among shoe manufacturers to acquire retail outlets, and for vertically integrated firms to supply an ever-increasing percentage of the retail outlets' needs, thereby foreclosing other manufacturers from effectively competing for the retail accounts. In consequence, the available outlets for independent shoe producers were "drying up" and the number of firms manufacturing shoes was falling, from 1,077 in 1947 to 970 by 1954. Brown had a history of acquiring independent retail outlets, purchasing seven over the previous five years, and then changing their product mix to favor Brown shoes.

The district court enjoined the merger, and the Supreme Court affirmed. In analyzing the vertical aspects of the merger, the Court concluded that the "trend toward vertical integration in the shoe industry, when combined with Brown's avowed policy of forcing its own shoes upon its retail subsidiaries, may foreclose competition from a substantial share of the markets for men's, women's, and children's shoes, without producing any countervailing competitive, economic, or social advantages." Accordingly, it held that the shoe industry "is being subjected to * * * a cumulative series of vertical mergers which, if left unchecked, will be likely 'substantially to lessen competition.' " The excerpts below describe the Court's analysis of the legislative history of the Clayton Act, and its analysis of the horizontal aspects of the merger. Eds.]

Mr. Chief Justice WARREN delivered the opinion of the court.

* * *

III.

LEGISLATIVE HISTORY.

This case is one of the first to come before us in which the Government's complaint is based upon allegations that the appellant has violated § 7 of the Clayton Act, as that section was amended in 1950. * * *

The dominant theme pervading congressional consideration of the 1950 amendments was a fear of what was considered to be a rising tide of economic concentration in the American economy. Apprehension in this regard was bolstered by the publication in 1948 of the Federal Trade Commission's study on corporate mergers. Statistics from this and other current studies were cited as evidence of the danger to the American economy in unchecked corporate expansions through mergers. Other considerations cited in support of the bill were the desirability of retaining 'local control' over industry and the protection of small businesses. Throughout the recorded discussion may be found examples of Congress' fear not only of accelerated concentration of economic power on economic grounds, but also of the threat to other values a trend toward concentration was thought to pose. * * *

* * * [I]t is apparent that a keystone in the erection of a barrier to what Congress saw was the rising tide of economic concentration, was its provision of authority for arresting mergers at a time when the trend to a lessening of competition in a line of commerce was still in its incipiency. Congress saw the process of concentration in American business as a dynamic force; it sought to assure the Federal Trade Commission and the courts the power to brake this force at its outset and before it gathered momentum. * * *

* * * [A]t the same time that it sought to create an effective tool for preventing all mergers having demonstrable anti-competitive effects, Congress recognized the stimulation to competition that might flow from particular mergers. When concern as to the Act's breadth was expressed, supporters of the amendments indicated that it would not impede, for example, a merger between two small companies to enable the combination to compete more effectively with larger corporations dominating the relevant market, nor a merger between a corporation which is financially healthy and a failing one which no longer can be a vital competitive factor in the market. The deletion of the word 'community' in the original Act's description of the relevant geographic market is another illustration of Congress' desire to indicate that its concern was with the adverse effects of a given merger on competition only in an economically significant 'section' of the country. Taken as a whole, the legislative history illuminates congressional concern with the protection of competition, not competitors, and its desire to restrain mergers only to the extent that such combinations may tend to lessen competition. * * *

* * * Congress used the words '*may* be substantially to lessen competition' (emphasis supplied), to indicate that its concern was with probabilities, not certainties. Statutes existed for dealing with clear-cut menaces to competition; no statute was sought for dealing with ephemeral possibilities. Mergers with a probable anticompetitive effect were to be proscribed by this Act. * * *

* * *

V.

The Horizontal Aspects of the Merger.

In an industry as fragmented as shoe retailing, the control of substantial shares of the trade in a city may have important effects on competition. If a merger achieving 5% control were now approved, we might be required to approve future merger efforts by Brown's competitors seeking similar market shares. The oligopoly Congress sought to avoid would then be furthered and it would be difficult to dissolve the combinations previously approved. Furthermore, in this fragmented industry, even if the combination controls but a small share of a particular market, the fact that this share is held by a large national chain can adversely affect competition. Testimony in the record from numerous independent retailers, based on their actual experience in the market, demonstrates that a strong, national chain of stores can insulate selected outlets from the vagaries of competition in particular locations and that the large chains can set and alter styles in footwear to an extent that renders the independents unable to maintain competitive inventories. A third significant aspect of this merger is that it creates a large national chain which is integrated with a manufacturing operation. The retail outlets of integrated companies, by eliminating wholesalers and by increasing the volume of purchases from the manufacturing division of the enterprise, can market their own brands at prices below those of competing independent retailers. Of course, some of the results of large integrated or chain operations are beneficial to consumers. Their expansion is not rendered unlawful by the mere fact that small independent stores may be adversely affected. It is competition, not competitors, which the Act protects. But we cannot fail to recognize Congress' desire to promote competition through the protection of viable, small, locally owned business. Congress appreciated that occasional higher costs and prices might result from the maintenance of fragmented industries and markets. It resolved these competing considerations in favor of decentralization. We must give effect to that decision.

Other factors to be considered in evaluating the probable effects of a merger in the relevant market lend additional support to the District Court's conclusion that this merger may substantially lessen competition. One such factor is the history of tendency toward concentration in the industry. As we have previously pointed out, the shoe industry has, in recent years, been a prime example of such a trend. Most combinations have been between manufacturers and retailers, as each of the larger producers has sought to capture an increasing number of assured outlets for its wares. Although these mergers have been primarily vertical in their aim and effect, to the extent that they have brought ever greater numbers of retail outlets within fewer and fewer hands, they have had an additional important impact on the horizontal plane. By the merger in this case, the largest single group of retail stores still independent of one of the large manufacturers was absorbed into an already substantial aggregation of more or less controlled retail outlets. As a result of this merger, Brown moved into second place nationally in terms of retail stores directly owned. Including the stores on its franchise plan, the merger placed under Brown's control almost 1,600 shoe outlets, or about 7.2% of the Nation's retail 'shoe stores' as defined by the Census Bureau, and 2.3% of the Nation's total retail shoe outlets. We cannot avoid the mandate of Congress that tendencies toward concentration in industry are to be curbed in their incipiency, particularly when those tendencies are being accelerated through giant steps striding across a hundred cities at a time. In the light of the trends in this industry we agree with the Government and the court below that this is an appropriate place at which to call a halt.

* * *

Brown Shoe arguably sets forth inconsistent themes. On the one hand, the Court notes congressional recognition of "the stimulation to competition that might flow from particular mergers," such as a merger of two small firms that would allow those sellers "to compete more effectively with larger corporations dominating the relevant market." When pursuing this theme, the Court emphasizes congressional concern with "the protection of competition, not competitors." On the other hand, the Supreme Court's focus on preventing a trend toward concentration in an industry could be understood as a mandate to protect competitors, particularly small businesses, against the possibility that they would be swallowed up in what has more recently been termed the "market for corporate control," even at the price of an efficiency loss to the economy. The Court explains that "Congress appreciated that occasional higher costs and prices might result from the maintenance of fragmented industries and markets." In the past, some commentators have read the passages pursuing the latter theme as suggesting that mergers could harm competition by *lowering* costs. As we shall see, however, modern courts and commentators no longer view an "efficiency offense" as a viable basis for a claim under the antitrust laws.

Philadelphia Nat'l Bank, which was handed down one year after *Brown Shoe*, highlights the second theme in creating the structural presumption that has since framed horizontal merger analysis in the courts. *Philadelphia Nat'l Bank*'s approach to merger analysis was also consistent with influential commentary by Derek Bok published two years before *Brown Shoe*. Derek C. Bok, *Section 7 of the Clayton Act and the Merging of Law and Economics*, 74 HARV. L. REV. 226 (1960). Bok had emphasized the conflict between the desire to make an accurate economic analysis of probable competitive effect and the need to adopt simple and predictable rules to facilitate workable judicial administration. To resolve that conflict, he proposed a simple standard for merger review based on market concentration.

UNITED STATES v. PHILADELPHIA NATIONAL BANK
Supreme Court of the United States, 1963.
374 U.S. 321, 83 S.Ct. 1715, 10 L.Ed.2d 915.

[The Philadelphia National Bank, the second largest commercial bank in the four-county Philadelphia metropolitan area, proposed to merge with the Girard Trust Corn Exchange Bank, the third largest in the region. The

United States challenged the transaction. After a district court decision in favor of the merging banks, the government appealed to the Supreme Court.

The Supreme Court analyzed this merger within a product market consisting of "the cluster of products (various kinds of credit) and services (such as checking accounts and trust administration) denoted by the term 'commercial banking' ." The Court explained that the services in the cluster were insulated from effective competition, some because they were "so distinctive," others because of "cost advantages," and the rest because they enjoy a "settled consumer preference." The Court defined a geographic market consisting of the four-county Philadelphia metropolitan area, notwithstanding its observation that some banking services were "more local in nature than others." Eds.]

Mr. Justice BRENNAN delivered the opinion of the Court.

I.   The Facts and Proceedings Below.

* * *

* * * Were the proposed merger to be consummated, the resulting bank would be the largest in the four-county area, with (approximately) 36% of the area banks' total assets, 36% of deposits, and 34% of net loans. It and the second largest (First Pennsylvania Bank and Trust Company, now the largest) would have between them 59% of the total assets, 58% of deposits, and 58% of the net loans, while after the merger the four largest banks in the area would have 78% of total assets, 77% of deposits, and 78% of net loans.

The present size of both PNB and Girard is in part the result of mergers. Indeed, the trend toward concentration is noticeable in the Philadelphia area generally, in which the number of commercial banks has declined from 108 in 1947 to the present 42. Since 1950, PNB has acquired nine formerly independent banks and Girard six * * *. During this period, the seven largest banks in the area increased their combined share of the area's total commercial bank resources from about 61% to about 90%.

* * *

The Government's case in the District Court relied chiefly on statistical evidence bearing upon market structure and on testimony by economists and bankers to the effect that, notwithstanding the intensive governmental regulation of banking, there was a substantial area for the free play of competitive forces; that concentration of commercial banking, which the proposed merger would increase, was inimical to that free play; that the principal anticompetitive effect of the merger would be felt in the area in which the banks had their offices, thus making the four-county metropolitan area the relevant geographical market; and that commercial banking was the relevant product market. The defendants, in addition to offering contrary evidence on these points, attempted to show business justifications for the merger. They conceded that both banks were economically strong and had sound management, but offered the testimony of bankers to show that the resulting bank, with its greater prestige and increased lending limit,[9] would be better able to compete

---

9. See 12 U.S.C. § 84 ***. The resulting bank would have a lending limit of $15,000,000, of which $1,000,000 would not be attributable to the merger but to unrelated accounting factors.

with large out-of-state (particularly New York) banks, would attract new business to Philadelphia, and in general would promote the economic development of the metropolitan area.[10]

* * *

III. The Lawfulness of the Proposed Merger Under Section 7.

The statutory test is whether the effect of the merger 'may be substantially to lessen competition' 'in any line of commerce in any section of the country.' We analyzed the test in detail in *Brown Shoe Co. v. United States*, 370 U.S. 294, 82 S.Ct. 1502, 8 L.Ed.2d 510, and that analysis need not be repeated or extended here, for the instant case presents only a straightforward problem of application to particular facts.

* * *

Having determined the relevant market, we come to the ultimate question under § 7: whether the effect of the merger 'may be substantially to lessen competition' in the relevant market. Clearly, this is not the kind of question which is susceptible of a ready and precise answer in most cases. It requires not merely an appraisal of the immediate impact of the merger upon competition, but a prediction of its impact upon competitive conditions in the future; this is what is meant when it is said that the amended § 7 was intended to arrest anticompetitive tendencies in their 'incipiency.' Such a prediction is sound only if it is based upon a firm understanding of the structure of the relevant market; yet the relevant economic data are both complex and elusive. See generally Bok, Section 7 of the Clayton Act and the Merging of Law and Economics, 74 Harv.L.Rev. 226 (1960). And unless businessmen can assess the legal consequences of a merger with some confidence, sound business planning is retarded. So also, we must be alert to the danger of subverting congressional intent by permitting a too-broad economic investigation. And so in any case in which it is possible, without doing violence to the congressional objective embodied in § 7, to simplify the test of illegality, the courts ought to do so in the interest of sound and practical judicial administration. This is such a case.

We noted in *Brown Shoe Co.* that '[t]he dominant theme pervading congressional consideration of the 1950 amendments [to § 7] was a fear of what was considered to be a rising tide of economic concentration in the American economy.' This intense congressional concern with the trend toward concentration warrants dispensing, in certain cases, with elaborate proof of market structure, market behavior, or probable anticompetitive effects. Spe-

---

10. There was evidence that Philadelphia, although it ranks fourth or fifth among the Nation's urban areas in terms of general commercial activity, ranks only ninth in terms of the size of its largest bank, and that some large business firms which have their head offices in Philadelphia must seek elsewhere to satisfy their banking needs because of the inadequate lending limits of Philadelphia's banks; First Pennsylvania and PNB, currently the two largest banks in Philadelphia, each have a lending limit of $8,000,000. Girard's is $6,000,000. Appellees offered testimony that the merger would enable certain economies of scale, specifically, that it would enable the formation of a more elaborate foreign department than either bank is presently able to maintain. But this attempted justification, which was not mentioned by the District Court in its opinion and has not been developed with any fullness before this Court, we consider abandoned.

cifically, we think that a merger which produces a firm controlling an undue percentage share of the relevant market, and results in a significant increase in the concentration of firms in that market is so inherently likely to lessen competition substantially that it must be enjoined in the absence of evidence clearly showing that the merger is not likely to have such anticompetitive effects.

Such a test lightens the burden of proving illegality only with respect to mergers whose size makes them inherently suspect in light of Congress' design in § 7 to prevent undue concentration. Furthermore, the test is fully consonant with economic theory. That '[c]ompetition is likely to be greatest when there are many sellers, none of which has any significant market share,' is common ground among most economists, and was undoubtedly a premise of congressional reasoning about the antimerger statute.

The merger of appellees will result in a single bank's controlling at least 30% of the commercial banking business in the four-county Philadelphia metropolitan area. Without attempting to specify the smallest market share which would still be considered to threaten undue concentration, we are clear that 30% presents that threat. Further, whereas presently the two largest banks in the area (First Pennsylvania and PNB) control between them approximately 44% of the area's commercial banking business, the two largest after the merger (PNB–Girard and First Pennsylvania) will control 59%. Plainly, we think, this increase of more than 33% in concentration must be regarded as significant.[42]

* * *

There is nothing in the record of this case to rebut the inherently anticompetitive tendency manifested by these percentages. There was, to be sure, testimony by bank officers to the effect that competition among banks in Philadelphia was vigorous and would continue to be vigorous after the merger. We think, however, that the District Court's reliance on such evidence was misplaced. This lay evidence on so complex an economic-legal problem as the substantiality of the effect of this merger upon competition was entitled to little weight, in view of the witnesses' failure to give concrete reasons for their conclusions.[43]

Of equally little value, we think, are the assurances offered by appellees' witnesses that customers dissatisfied with the services of the resulting bank may readily turn to the 40 other banks in the Philadelphia area. In every case short of outright monopoly, the disgruntled customer has alternatives; even in tightly oligopolistic markets, there may be small firms operating. A fundamental purpose of amending § 7 was to arrest the trend toward concentration, the

42. It is no answer that, among the three presently largest firms (First Pennsylvania, PNB, and Girard), there will be no increase in concentration. If this argument were valid, then once a market had become unduly concentrated, further concentration would be legally privileged. On the contrary, if concentration is already great, the importance of preventing even slight increases in concentration and so preserving the possibility of eventual deconcentration is correspondingly great.

43. The fact that some of the bank officers who testified represented small banks in competition with appellees does not substantially enhance the probative value of their testimony. * * * In an oligopolistic market, small companies may be perfectly content to follow the high prices set by the dominant firms, yet the market may be profoundly anticompetitive.

tendency to monopoly, before the consumer's alternatives disappeared through merger, and that purpose would be ill-served if the law stayed its hand until 10, or 20, or 30 more Philadelphia banks were absorbed. This is not a fanciful eventuality, in view of the strong trend toward mergers evident in the area; and we might note also that entry of new competitors into the banking field is far from easy.[44]

* * *

We turn now to three affirmative justifications which appellees offer for the proposed merger. The first is that only through mergers can banks follow their customers to the suburbs and retain their business. This justification does not seem particularly related to the instant merger, but in any event it has no merit. There is an alternative to the merger route: the opening of new branches in the areas to which the customers have moved–so-called de novo branching. Appellees do not contend that they are unable to expand thus, by opening new offices rather than acquiring existing ones, and surely one premise of an antimerger statute such as § 7 is that corporate growth by internal expansion is socially preferable to growth by acquisition.

Second, it is suggested that the increased lending limit of the resulting bank will enable it to compete with the large out-of-state banks, particularly the New York banks, for very large loans. We reject this application of the concept of 'countervailing power.' If anticompetitive effects in one market could be justified by procompetitive consequences in another, the logical upshot would be that every firm in an industry could, without violating § 7, embark on a series of mergers that would make it in the end as large as the industry leader. For if all the commercial banks in the Philadelphia area merged into one, it would be smaller than the largest bank in New York City. This is not a case, plainly, where two small firms in a market propose to merge in order to be able to compete more successfully with the leading firms in that market. Nor is it a case in which lack of adequate banking facilities is causing hardships to individuals or businesses in the community. The present two largest banks in Philadelphia have lending limits of $8,000,000 each. The only business located in the Philadelphia area which find such limits inadequate are large enough readily to obtain bank credit in other cities.

This brings us to appellees' final contention, that Philadelphia needs a bank larger than it now has in order to bring business to the area and stimulate its economic development. We are clear, however, that a merger the effect of which 'may be substantially to lessen competition' is not saved because, on some ultimate reckoning of social or economic debits and credits, it may be deemed beneficial. A value choice of such magnitude is beyond the ordinary limits of judicial competence, and in any event has been made for us already, by Congress when it enacted the amended § 7. Congress determined to preserve our traditionally competitive economy. It therefore proscribed anticompetitive mergers, the benign and the malignant alike, fully aware, we must assume, that some price might have to be paid.

* * *

44. Entry is, of course, wholly a matter of governmental grace. In the 10–year period ending in 1961, only one new bank opened in the Philadelphia four-county area. That was in 1951. At the end of 10 years, the new bank controlled only one-third of 1% of the area's deposits.

Note on Von's Grocery and Pabst Brewing

Two Supreme Court cases decided in 1966, three years after *Philadelphia Nat'l Bank*, represent the high water mark of judicial efforts to halt the rising tide of industrial concentration. In both *United States v. Von's Grocery Co.*, 384 U.S. 270, 86 S.Ct. 1478, 16 L.Ed.2d 555 (1966) and *United States v. Pabst Brewing Co.*, 384 U.S. 546, 86 S.Ct. 1665, 16 L.Ed.2d 765 (1966), the Court prohibited mergers among firms which, by present-day standards, had small market shares in largely unconcentrated markets.

Von's involved the acquisition of one grocery store chain serving Los Angeles, Shopping Bag Food Stores, by another, Von's Grocery Company. In 1958, the year before the merger, the largest chain in the metropolitan area had 8% of retail sales, Von's was third largest with 4.7% and Shopping Bag was sixth with 4.2%. In 1960, the merging firms together accounted for only 7.5% of the total. But these chain stores were growing rapidly and the number of single grocery stores in Los Angeles decreased from 5,365 in 1950 to 3,590 in 1963. In an opinion written by Justice Black, the Court majority observed:

> * * * While the grocery business was being concentrated into the hands of fewer and fewer owners, the small companies were continually being absorbed by the larger firms through mergers. * * * Moreover, * * * acquisitions and mergers in the Los Angeles retail grocery market have continued at a rapid rate since the merger. These facts alone are enough to cause us to conclude contrary to the District Court that the Von's-Shopping Bag merger did violate § 7. Accordingly, we reverse.
>
> * * *
>
> The facts of this case present exactly the threatening trend toward concentration which Congress wanted to halt.

384 U.S. at 273–74, 277. Justice Stewart responded in dissent:

> I believe that even the most superficial analysis of the record makes plain the fallacy of the Court's syllogism that competition is necessarily reduced when the bare number of competitors has declined. In any meaningful sense, the structure of the Los Angeles grocery market remains unthreatened by concentration. Local competition is vigorous to a fault, not only among chain stores themselves but also between chain stores and single-store operators. * * * And, most important of all, the record simply cries out that the numerical decline in the number of single-store owners is the result of transcending social and technological changes that positively preclude the inference that competition has suffered because of the attrition of competitors.
>
> Section 7 was never intended by Congress for use by the Court as a charter to roll back the supermarket revolution. Yet the Court's opinion is hardly more than a requiem for the so-called 'Mom and Pop' grocery stores—the bakery and butcher shops, the vegetable and fish markets— that are now economically and technologically obsolete in many parts of the country.

* * *

In a single sentence and an omnibus footnote at the close of its opinion, the Court pronounces its work consistent with the line of our decisions under § 7 since the passage of the 1950 amendment. The sole consistency that I can find is that in litigation under § 7, the Government always wins.

384 U.S. at 287–88, 301 (Stewart, J. dissenting).

The *Pabst* case, decided during the same Court term, involved the merger of what was in 1958 the Nation's tenth largest brewer, Pabst, and its eighteenth largest brewer, Blatz. The Supreme Court reversed a district court judgment in favor of the merging firms, in an opinion also written by Justice Black:

> * * * [The] facts show a very marked thirty-year decline in the number of brewers and a sharp rise in recent years in the percentage share of the market controlled by the leading brewers. If not stopped, this decline in the number of separate competitors and this rise in the share of the market controlled by the larger beer manufacturers are bound to lead to greater and greater concentration of the beer industry into fewer and fewer hands. The merger of Pabst and Blatz brought together two very large brewers competing against each other in 40 States. In 1957 these two companies had combined sales which accounted for 23.95% of the beer sales in Wisconsin, 11.32% of the sales in the three-state area of Wisconsin, Illinois, and Michigan, and 4.49% of the sales throughout the country. In accord with our prior cases, we hold that the evidence as to the probable effect of the merger on competition in Wisconsin, in the three-state area, and in the entire country was sufficient to show a violation of § 7 in each and all of these three areas.

384 U.S. at 551–52.

Rapid consolidation was a key feature of the industries in which the structural presumption was developed: banking *(Philadelphia Nat'l Bank)*, supermarkets *(Von's Grocery)* and beer *(Pabst)*. But was it driven by a desire to create a monopoly, and tending to result in higher prices, as the Court predicted?

One alternative explanation for industry trends toward concentration has been suggested by economist John Sutton. Technological developments that lower the costs of transportation and communication lead some markets to grow in size. For example, as automobile ownership became widespread, food consumers were no longer limited to the corner grocery. Sometimes larger markets facilitate the entry of new sellers; under such circumstances, concentration may fall. But in other cases, when firms find themselves in expanding markets, they find it profitable to make large investments in advertising or research and development, for example by developing regional or national brand names or new and better products, in order to attract a larger share of the growing market demand. In such industries, Sutton finds, markets become more concentrated as they grow in size. Increasing industry output suggests that prices will decline (see the discussion of demand in Chapter 1), even though the number of firms is shrinking. Sutton finds this pattern in a wide range of industries, highlighting many examples from the food and drink sector. John Sutton, Sunk Costs and Market Structure: Price Competition, Advertising and the Evolution of Concentration (1991).

3. THE EROSION OF THE STRUCTURAL PRESUMPTION

A Supreme Court case decided in 1974, *United States v. General Dynamics Corp.*, 415 U.S. 486, 94 S.Ct. 1186, 39 L.Ed.2d 530 (1974), foreshadowed a change in direction for merger analysis toward taking factors beyond market concentration into account. After years of litigation under Clayton Act § 7 in which, as Justice Stewart wrote in dissent in *Von's Grocery*, "the Government always wins," the Supreme Court decided a merger case in favor of allowing the acquisition, with Justice Stewart writing the majority opinion. By a 5–4 vote, the Supreme Court in *General Dynamics* made clear that the presumption of anticompetitive effect derived from concentration is rebuttable.

UNITED STATES v. GENERAL DYNAMICS CORPORATION

Supreme Court of the United States, 1974.
415 U.S. 486, 94 S.Ct. 1186, 39 L.Ed.2d 530.

Mr. Justice STEWART delivered the opinion of the Court.

[In 1959, Materials Service Corp., which was later itself purchased by General Dynamics, acquired the United Electric Coal Co. Both firms produced and sold coal in the state of Illinois, and in the Eastern Interior Coal Province Sales Area, a coal distribution area recognized by the industry comprising Illinois, Indiana, and parts of six neighboring states. The government challenged the acquisition based on evidence showing that in both markets, the coal industry was concentrated among a small number of leading producers and that the trend had been toward increasing concentration. For example, the top four firms accounted for 43% of the Eastern Interior Coal Province market in 1957, and nearly 63% in 1967. Over the same ten year period, the share accounted for by the top four firms in Illinois rose from 55% to 75%. The Supreme Court noted that the statistics on the degree of concentration in the two coal markets, and the percentage increase in concentration, were roughly comparable to those found in *Von's Grocery*. Eds.]

II

* * *

In prior decisions involving horizontal mergers between competitors, this Court has found prima facie violations of § 7 of the Clayton Act from aggregate statistics of the sort relied on by the United States in this case. * * *

The effect of adopting this approach to a determination of a 'substantial' lessening of competition is to allow the Government to rest its case on a showing of even small increases of market share or market concentration in those industries or markets where concentration is already great or has been recently increasing, since 'if concentration is already great, the importance of preventing even slight increases in concentration and so preserving the possibility of eventual deconcentration is correspondingly great.' *United States v. Aluminum Co. of Am.*, 377 U.S. 271 (1964)(citing *United States v. Philadelphia Nat'l Bank*, 374 U.S. at 365 n.42).

While the statistical showing proffered by the Government in this case, the accuracy of which was not discredited by the District Court or contested by the appellees, would under this approach have sufficed to support a finding of 'undue concentration' in the absence of other considerations, the question before us is whether the District Court was justified in finding that other pertinent factors affecting the coal industry and the business of the appellees mandated a conclusion that no substantial lessening of competition occurred or was threatened by the acquisition of United Electric. We are satisfied that the court's ultimate finding was not in error.

In *Brown Shoe v. United States*, we cautioned that statistics concerning market share and concentration, while of great significance, were not conclusive indicators of anticompetitive effects * * *.

Much of the District Court's opinion was devoted to a description of the changes that have affected the coal industry since World War II. On the basis of more than three weeks of testimony and a voluminous record, the court discerned a number of clear and significant developments in the industry. First, it found that coal had become increasingly less able to compete with other sources of energy in many segments of the energy market. * * *

Second, the court found that to a growing extent since 1954, the electric utility industry has become the mainstay of coal consumption. * * *

Third, and most significantly, the court found that to an increasing degree, nearly all coal sold to utilities is transferred under long-term requirements contracts, under which coal producers promise to meet utilities' coal consumption requirements for a fixed period of time, and at predetermined prices. * * *

* * * In markets involving groceries or beer, as in *Von's Grocery*, and *Pabst*, statistics involving annual sales naturally indicate the power of each company to compete in the future. Evidence of the amount of annual sales is relevant as a prediction of future competitive strength, since in most markets distribution systems and brand recognition are such significant factors that one may reasonably suppose that a company which has attracted a given number of sales will retain that competitive strength.

In the coal market, as analyzed by the District Court, however, statistical evidence of coal production was of considerably less significance. The bulk of the coal produced is delivered under long-term requirements contracts, and such sales thus do not represent the exercise of competitive power but rather the obligation to fulfill previously negotiated contracts at a previously fixed price. The focus of competition in a given time frame is not on the disposition of coal already produced but on the procurement of new long-term supply contracts. In this situation, a company's past ability to produce is of limited significance, since it is in a position to offer for sale neither its past production nor the bulk of the coal it is presently capable of producing, which is typically already committed under a long-term supply contract. A more significant indicator of a company's power effectively to compete with other companies lies in the state of a company's uncommitted reserves of recoverable coal. A company with relatively large supplies of coal which are not already under contract to a consumer will have a more important influence upon competition in the contemporaneous negotiation of supply contracts than a firm with small reserves, even though the latter may presently produce a greater tonnage of coal. In a market where the availability and price of coal are set by long-term contracts rather than immediate or short-term purchases and sales, reserves rather than past production are the best measure of a company's ability to compete.

The testimony and exhibits in the District Court revealed that United Electric's coal reserve prospects were 'unpromising.' United's relative position of strength in reserves was considerably weaker than its past and current ability to produce. While United ranked fifth among Illinois coal producers in terms of annual production, it was 10th in reserve holdings, and controlled less than 1% of the reserves held by coal producers in Illinois, Indiana, and western Kentucky. Many of the reserves held by United had already been depleted at the time of trial, forcing the closing of some of United's midwest mines. Even more significantly, the District Court found that of the 52,033,-304 tons of currently mineable reserves in Illinois, Indiana, and Kentucky controlled by United, only four million tons had not already been committed under long-term contracts. United was found to be facing the future with relatively depleted resources at its disposal, and with the vast majority of those resources already committed under contracts allowing no further adjustment in price. In addition, the District Court found that 'United Electric has neither the possibility of acquiring more (reserves) nor the ability to develop deep coal reserves,' and thus was not in a position to increase its reserves to replace those already depleted or committed.

Viewed in terms of present and future reserve prospects—and thus in terms of probable future ability to compete—rather than in terms of past production, the District Court held that United Electric was a far less significant factor in the coal market than the Government contended or the production statistics seemed to indicate. While the company had been and remained a 'highly profitable' and efficient producer of relatively large amounts of coal, its current and future power to compete for subsequent long-term contracts was severely limited by its scarce uncommitted resources. Irrespective of the company's size when viewed as a producer, its weakness as a competitor was properly analyzed by the District Court and fully substantiated that court's conclusion that its acquisition by Material Service would not 'substantially ... lessen competition....' * * *

———

General Dynamics was decided in 1974, before Supreme Court decisions like *GTE Sylvania* (1977) (Casebook, Chapter 4, *supra*) and *Broadcast Music* (1979) (Casebook, Chapter 2, *supra*) that appeared to embrace the Chicago School perspective, and before the 1982 Merger Guidelines. In part for this reason, it appears more like a modern merger decision in retrospect than it likely did at the time. Although the case made clear that the structural presumption was rebuttable, the successful rebuttal was arguably on narrow grounds: that concentration was measured incorrectly, using the wrong units in an unusual case in which market shares based upon production capacity (here, coal reserves) differed markedly from market shares computed in terms of past sales. These are, as Judge Posner has observed, "highly unusual facts." *Hospital Corp. of Am. v. Federal Trade Comm'n*, 807 F.2d 1381, 1385 (7th Cir.1986)(Posner, J.). Accordingly, Posner continued, this decision could be understood as "carv[ing] only a limited exception[] to the broad holdings of some of the merger decisions of the 1960s." *Id.* As you read the appeals court decisions that follow, notice how they instead read *General Dynamics* more broadly, to permit a wide-ranging analysis of whether market shares accurately reflect the merging firms' ability to compete.

Note on the Structural Presumption and the 1982 Merger Guidelines

The Justice Department's first merger guidelines were promulgated in 1968, before *General Dynamics*. Assistant Attorney General Donald Turner, who issued the 1968 Guidelines, chose to set enforcement standards at concentration levels less stringent than those *Pabst* and *Von's Grocery* might have permitted, though at levels that were still exceedingly strict by modern standards. In 1982, the U.S. Department of Justice, under the leadership of Assistant Attorney General William F. Baxter, issued merger guidelines that replaced Turner's guidelines. In doing so, and in many other ways, Baxter led the way in revising antitrust enforcement in light of Chicago School views, which the Supreme Court had just begun to incorporate into the case law. Because the Court had not issued a major merger decision since *General Dynamics* (and, since the 1982 Guidelines, still has not done so),* Baxter had to devise a way to harmonize the old precedents, rooted in antitrust's structural era, with the economic approach of the Chicago School. The 1982 Guidelines accomplished this task by declaring that concentration was highly influential but not outcome-determinative in evaluating acquisitions among rivals. In taking this view, Baxter was undoubtedly aware that economists had questioned the inevitability of tacit collusion in concentrated markets, as we learned in Chapter 3, and that the empirical groundings of the structural presumption had also been challenged (see Sidebar 5–6).

In the two decades since the 1982 Merger Guidelines were issued, they have been revised multiple times. (The current government Horizontal Merger Guidelines can be accessed at http://www.usdoj.gov/atr/public/guidelines/hmg.htm and are discussed in more detail in Section C of this chapter.) But the problem they address—harmonizing the older structural era decisions with contemporary economic thinking—remains central to horizontal merger analysis today. Although the Supreme Court has not revisited the question, several appeals courts have done so. The D.C. Circuit opinion that we shall read next, in *United States v. Baker Hughes*, may be the most authoritative, as it was written by one future Supreme Court justice and joined in by another (and the two are from opposite wings of many Court splits). Footnote 12 and the accompanying text expressly frame the *Baker Hughes* decision as harmonizing *General Dynamics* and *Philadelphia Nat'l Bank* with the newer economic thinking endorsed by the Supreme Court in other antitrust decisions. (We will discuss the *Baker Hughes* court's analysis of entry later in this Chapter.)

Sidebar 5–1:
The Sound of Silence: The Supreme Court and Merger Policy Since 1975

Imagine that a lawyer born and trained outside of the United States was asked to write a paper summarizing the current state of federal merger law in the United States. How should the foreign observer describe U.S. merger doctrine and policy today? The answer would depend on where she looks.

---

* Although the Supreme Court issued substantive antitrust merger decisions in three bank cases shortly after *General Dynamics*, in *United States v. Marine Bancorporation*, 418 U.S. 602 (1974), *United States v. Connecticut Nat'l Bank*, 418 U.S. 656 (1974) and *United States v. Citizens & Southern Nat'l Bank*, 422 U.S. 86 (1975), *General Dynamics* is generally treated as the last major Supreme Court interpretation of Clayton Act § 7.

The standard research methodology for tackling a question like this would follow the traditional hierarchy of authority in the U.S. legal system. The researcher would focus first upon statutes enacted by Congress and decisions of the Supreme Court interpreting those statutes. Like most of the U.S. antitrust laws, Section 7 of the Clayton Act is "open textured." Section 7's key operative terms—"may be substantially to lessen competition"—are not self-defining. This characteristic gives the judiciary considerable discretion to give specific substantive meaning to the statute and to determine the outcome of specific cases through interpretation of Section 7's relatively open-ended language. As seen thus far in Chapter 5, the trail of Supreme Court decisions interpreting the amended Section 7 begins with *Brown Shoe* in 1962 and effectively ends with *General Dynamics* in 1974 (formally ending one year later with *Citizens & Southern*). It has been decades since the Court commented upon the anti-merger provision's substantive liability standard.

A research project ruthlessly confined to analyzing the Supreme Court's Section 7 horizontal merger jurisprudence from 1962 through 1975 would reveal a strict set of limits on combinations involving rival firms. To such a reader, the Court's rulings might be distilled into three core principles:

- The plaintiff in a Section 7 case can create a presumption of illegality by demonstrating a trend toward concentration, a significant increase in concentration, and that post-acquisition market shares have exceeded a specific level. *See Philadelphia National Bank*. The relevant threshold of concern may be as low as 4.49 percent. *See Pabst*.

- The presumption of illegality created by market share data is virtually conclusive. In unusual circumstances, however, the defendant can rebut the presumption of illegality by showing that the plaintiff has calculated market shares based upon a measure of commercial activity that fails to give an accurate picture of the merging parties' capability to compete for future sales. *See General Dynamics*.

- Courts should subordinate efficiency considerations in favor of attaining a more decentralized commercial environment. *See Brown Shoe*.

In offering this restatement, a counselor would have to caution that the more recent Supreme Court decisions, such as *General Dynamics* (1974) and *Marine Bancorporation* (1974), had shown a tendency to favor defendants after a long, previously unbroken string of government victories that started with *Brown Shoe* (1962).

A second exercise would ignore the Supreme Court's jurisprudence and instead focus solely on the merger decisions of the lower courts and on government merger policy, especially as articulated in the federal merger guidelines. As you will see in decisions such as *Baker Hughes*, *infra*, the lower courts have not adhered closely to the letter or spirit of the Supreme Court's merger jurisprudence. Lower court decisions since 1975 hardly have blessed all horizontal mergers, but they (a) have raised the market share thresholds for presuming illegality and (b) have shown that the nominal opportunity, suggested in *Philadelphia Nat'l Bank*, for defendants to rebut the presumption can be exercised successfully. In addition, discussions of the political and social values of preferring economic decentralization at the possible cost of economic efficiency have vanished from the district court and court of appeals decisions.

In taking these steps, our researcher might observe, the courts often have relied on the framework presented in the federal merger guidelines issued in 1982 and modified in 1984, 1992 and 1997. The federal guidelines use the structural presumption of *Philadelphia Nat'l Bank*, but with several vital qualifications. The federal guidelines emphasize that the examination of market shares only starts the inquiry. The guidelines underscore the need to assess other variables that shed light on whether the merging parties, acting alone or coordinating their conduct with rivals, could raise prices. The federal guidelines also set the threshold of concern well above the 4.49 percent that the Supreme Court found sufficient in *Pabst*.

In applying their guidelines since 1982, DOJ and the FTC have tended to sue only when a merger reduces the number of companies in the market to fewer than four. The cases we study later in this Chapter—matters such as *Staples* and *Heinz* (both three-to-two mergers) and *Cardinal Health* (a four-to-two deal)—suggest where the federal agencies, in effect, have drawn the line when they go to court. This is a great distance from *Brown Shoe* where, as we saw earlier in Chapter 5, the Justice Department challenged a merger that would yield a combined market share of five percent.

Should our hypothetical researcher conclude that merger decisions of the lower federal courts and the enforcement policies of the federal antitrust agencies constitute civil disobedience that ignores the commands of Supreme Court Section 7 decisions? Two considerations suggest not. The first is that Congress has not amended Section 7 to forestall the drift away from the tenets of the Court's merger cases. Congressional committees responsible for antitrust issues pay close attention to merger policy. Congress could have embedded the precepts of 1960s Supreme Court merger analysis in the Clayton Act if it disapproved of the move by lower courts and enforcement bodies since 1975 to accept more permissive approaches. That Congress has not acted to arrest this development may suggest general acceptance with modern trends in interpreting and applying Section 7.

A second reason comes from reading Supreme Court antitrust decisions in non-merger matters since 1975. As a whole, these decisions provide grounds for inferring that the Court approves the evolution of lower court merger jurisprudence and agency enforcement practice. *GTE Sylvania*, *Matsushita*, and other tributes to efficiency since 1975 make it difficult to imagine today's Court endorsing the views it embraced in *Brown Shoe*, *Von's Grocery*, and *Pabst*. When U.S. antitrust lawyers tell their clients to attempt mergers at thresholds well above levels condemned in *Von's Grocery* and *Pabst*, the Court's non-merger cases support the common prediction that "the Court would decide those cases differently today."

The prediction is almost certainly correct. After all, two members of the unanimous *Baker Hughes* court of appeals panel—Ruth Bader Ginsburg and Clarence Thomas—now sit on the Supreme Court. No member

> of today's Court participated in any of the tribunal's previous merger decisions, and all have seemingly acquiesced, with varied degrees of enthusiasm, in the efficiency-oriented perspective that governs the Court's non-merger decisions. Still, the Court has never directly repudiated the teaching of its merger decisions. A researcher familiar with the hierarchy of authority in the U.S. legal system could be forgiven for being perplexed that the foundations of modern U.S. merger policy rest upon the assumption, without the benefit of the Court's own direct guidance, that the Court no longer means what it once said.

UNITED STATES v. BAKER HUGHES, INC.

United States Court of Appeals for the District of Columbia Circuit, 1990.
908 F.2d 981.

Before RUTH B. GINSBURG, SENTELLE, and THOMAS, Circuit Judges.

CLARENCE THOMAS, Circuit Judge:

Appellee Oy Tampella AB, a Finnish corporation, through its subsidiary Tamrock AG, manufactures and sells hardrock hydraulic underground drilling rigs (HHUDRs) in the United States and throughout the world. Appellee Baker Hughes Inc., a corporation based in Houston, Texas, owned a French subsidiary, Eimco Secoma, S.A. (Secoma), that was similarly involved in the HHUDR industry. In 1989, Tamrock proposed to acquire Secoma.

The United States challenged the proposed acquisition, charging that it would substantially lessen competition in the United States HHUDR market in violation of section 7 of the Clayton Act, 15 U.S.C. § 18. * * *

The basic outline of a section 7 horizontal acquisition case is familiar. By showing that a transaction will lead to undue concentration in the market for a particular product in a particular geographic area,[2] the government establishes a presumption that the transaction will substantially lessen competition. The burden of producing evidence to rebut this presumption then shifts to the defendant. If the defendant successfully rebuts the presumption, the burden of producing additional evidence of anticompetitive effect shifts to the government, and merges with the ultimate burden of persuasion, which remains with the government at all times.

By presenting statistics showing that combining the market shares of Tamrock and Secoma would significantly increase concentration in the already highly concentrated United States HHUDR market, the government established a prima facie case of anticompetitive effect.[3] The district court, however, found sufficient evidence that the merger would not substantially

---

2. The parties in this case do not seriously contest the district court's definition of the relevant markets. The court defined the geographic market as the entire United States, and the relevant product as three types of HHUDRs: face drills ("jumbos"), long-hole drills, and roof-bolting drills, as well as associated spare parts, components, and accessories, and used drills. * * *

3. From 1986 through 1988, Tamrock had an average 40.8% share of the United States

HHUDR market, while Secoma's share averaged 17.5%. In 1988 alone, the two firms enjoyed a combined share of 76% of the market. * * * The acquisition thus has brought about a dramatic increase in the Herfindahl–Hirschman Index (HHI)—a yardstick of concentration—for this market. * * * This acquisition has increased the HHI in this market from 2878 to 4303.

lessen competition to conclude that the defendants had rebutted this prima facie case. The government did not produce any additional evidence showing a probability of substantially lessened competition, and thus failed to carry its ultimate burden of persuasion.

In this appeal, * * * [t]he government's key contention is that the district court * * * failed to apply a sufficiently stringent standard. The government argues that, as a matter of law, section 7 defendants can rebut a prima facie case *only by a clear showing that entry into the market by competitors would be quick and effective.* Because the district court failed to apply this standard, the government submits, the court erred in concluding that the proposed acquisition would not substantially lessen future competition in the United States HHUDR market.

We find no merit in the legal standard propounded by the government. It is devoid of support in the statute, in the case law, and in the government's own Merger Guidelines. Moreover, it is flawed on its merits in three fundamental respects. First, it assumes that ease of entry by competitors is the only consideration relevant to a section 7 defendant's rebuttal. Second, it requires that a defendant who seeks to show ease of entry bear the onerous burden of proving that entry will be "quick and effective." Finally, by stating that the defendant can rebut a prima facie case only by a clear showing, the standard in effect shifts the government's ultimate burden of persuasion to the defendant. Although the district court in this case did not expressly set forth a legal standard when it evaluated the defendants' rebuttal, we have carefully reviewed the court's thorough analysis of competitive conditions in the United States HHUDR market, and we are satisfied that the court effectively applied a standard faithful to section 7. Concluding that the court applied this legal standard to factual findings that are not clearly erroneous, we affirm the court's denial of a permanent injunction and its dismissal of the government's section 7 claim.

I.

It is a foundation of section 7 doctrine, disputed by no authority cited by the government, that evidence on a variety of factors can rebut a prima facie case. These factors include, but are not limited to, the absence of significant entry barriers in the relevant market. In this appeal, however, the government inexplicably imbues the entry factor with talismanic significance. If, to successfully rebut a prima facie case, a defendant *must* show that entry by competitors will be quick and effective, then other factors bearing on future competitiveness are all but irrelevant. The district court in this case considered at least two factors in addition to entry: the misleading nature of the statistics underlying the government's prima facie case and the sophistication of HHUDR consumers. These non-entry factors provide compelling support for the court's holding that Tamrock's acquisition of Secoma was not likely to lessen competition substantially. We have concluded that the court's consideration of these factors was crucial, and that the government's fixation on ease of entry is misplaced.

Section 7 involves *probabilities*, not certainties or possibilities.[5] The Supreme Court has adopted a totality-of-the-circumstances approach to the

---

5. See *Brown Shoe Co. v. United States*, ("Congress used the words '*may* be substan-   tially to lessen competition' (emphasis supplied), to indicate that its concern was with

statute, weighing a variety of factors to determine the effects of particular transactions on competition. That the government can establish a prima facie case through evidence on only one factor, market concentration, does not negate the breadth of this analysis. Evidence of market concentration simply provides a convenient starting point for a broader inquiry into future competitiveness; the Supreme Court has never indicated that a defendant seeking to rebut a prima facie case is restricted to producing evidence of ease of entry. Indeed, in numerous cases, defendants have relied entirely on non-entry factors in successfully rebutting a prima facie case.

* * *

Indeed, that a variety of factors other than ease of entry can rebut a prima facie case has become hornbook law. * * *

It is not surprising, then, that the Department of Justice's own Merger Guidelines contain a detailed discussion of non-entry factors that can overcome a presumption of illegality established by market share statistics. According to the Guidelines, these factors include changing market conditions (§ 3.21), the financial condition of firms in the relevant market (§ 3.22), special factors affecting foreign firms (§ 3.23), the nature of the product and the terms of sale (§ 3.41), information about specific transactions and buyer market characteristics (§ 3.42), the conduct of firms in the market (§ 3.44), market performance (§ 3.45), and efficiencies (§ 3.5).*

Given this acknowledged multiplicity of relevant factors, we are at a loss to understand on what basis the government has decided that "[t]o rebut the government's prima facie case, the defendants were *required* to show that *entry* would be both quick and effective in preventing supracompetitive prices." Brief for Appellants at 11–12 (emphasis added). * * *

The district court's analysis of this case is fully consonant with precedent and logic. The court reviewed the evidence proffered by the defendants as part of its overall assessment of future competitiveness in the United States HHUDR market. As noted above, the court gave particular weight to two non-entry factors: the flawed underpinnings of the government's prima facie case and the sophistication of HHUDR consumers. The court's consideration of these factors was not only appropriate, but imperative, because in this case these factors significantly affected the probability that the acquisition would have anticompetitive effects.

With respect to the first factor, the statistical basis of the prima facie case, the court accepted the defendants' argument that the government's statistics were misleading. Because the United States HHUDR market is minuscule, market share statistics are "volatile and shifting," and easily skewed. In 1986, for instance, only 22 HHUDRs were sold in the United States. In 1987, the number rose to 43, and in 1988 it fell to 38. Every HHUDR sold during this period, thus, increased the seller's market share by two to five percent. A contract to provide multiple HHUDRs could catapult a

---

probabilities, not certainties. Statutes existed for dealing with clear-cut menaces to competition; no statute was sought for dealing with ephemeral possibilities. Mergers with a *probable* anticompetitive effect were to be proscribed by this Act.") (footnote omitted) (emphasis added).

* [The court's references here are to the 1984 version of the Merger Guidelines. Eds.]

firm from last to first place. * * * High concentration has long been the norm in this market. For example, only four firms sold HHUDRs in the United States between 1986 and 1989. Nor is concentration surprising where, as here, a product is esoteric and its market small. Indeed, the trial judge found that "[c]oncentration has existed for some time [in the United States HHUDR market] but there is no proof of overpricing, excessive profit or any decline in quality, service or diminishing innovation."

The second non-entry factor that the district court considered was the sophistication of HHUDR consumers. HHUDRs currently cost hundreds of thousands of dollars, and orders can exceed $1 million. These products are hardly trinkets sold to small consumers who may possess imperfect information and limited bargaining power. HHUDR buyers closely examine available options and typically insist on receiving multiple, confidential bids for each order. This sophistication, the court found, was likely to promote competition even in a highly concentrated market.

* * * These findings provide considerable support for the district court's conclusion that the defendants successfully rebutted the government's prima facie case. Because the defendants also provided compelling evidence on ease of entry into this market, we need not decide whether these findings, without more, are sufficient to rebut the government's prima facie case. The foregoing analysis of non-entry factors is intended merely to underscore that, contrary to the government's assumption, these factors are relevant, and can even be dispositive, in a section 7 rebuttal analysis.

II.

The existence and significance of barriers to entry are frequently * * * crucial considerations in a rebuttal analysis. In the absence of significant barriers, a company probably cannot maintain supracompetitive pricing for any length of time. The district court in this case reviewed the prospects for future entry into the United States HHUDR market and concluded that, overall, entry was likely, particularly if Tamrock's acquisition of Secoma were to lead to supracompetitive pricing. The government attacks this conclusion, asserting that, as a matter of law, the court should have required the defendants to show clearly that entry would be "quick and effective." We reject this novel and unduly onerous standard. The district court's factual findings amply support its determination that future entry into the United States HHUDR market is likely. This determination, in turn, supports the court's conclusion that the defendants successfully rebutted the government's prima facie case.

As authority for its "quick and effective" entry test, the government relies primarily on *United States v. Waste Management, Inc.*, 743 F.2d 976, 981–84 (2d Cir.1984). This reliance is misplaced. Neither *Waste Management* nor any other case purports to establish a categorical "quick and effective" entry requirement. The Second Circuit in *Waste Management* simply noted that the defendant had successfully rebutted the government's prima facie case by showing that entry into the Dallas/Fort Worth trash collection market was "easy." That a defendant *may* successfully rebut a prima facie case by showing quick and effective entry does not mean that successful rebuttal *requires* such a showing. We are at a loss to understand how the government derived from *Waste Management* (where, lest the irony be missed, the government lost) the proposition that "a defendant arguing supposed ease of entry can rebut the government's prima facie case *only* by clearly showing that entry will be both quick and effective at preventing supracompetitive pricing."

That the "quick and effective" standard lacks support in precedent is not surprising, for it would require of defendants a degree of clairvoyance alien to section 7, which, as noted above, deals with probabilities, not certainties. Although the government disclaims any attempt to impose upon defendants the burden of proving that entry actually will occur, we believe that an inflexible "quick and effective" entry requirement would tend to impose precisely such a burden. A defendant cannot realistically be expected to prove that new competitors will "quickly" or "effectively" enter unless it produces evidence regarding specific competitors and their plans. Such evidence is rarely available; potential competitors have a strong interest in downplaying the likelihood that they will enter a given market. When the government sarcastically "wonders how slow and ineffective entry rebuts a prima facie case," it misses a crucial point. If the totality of a defendant's evidence suggests that entry will be slow and ineffective, then the district court is unlikely to find the prima facie case rebutted. This is a far cry, however, from insisting that the defendant must invariably show that new competitors will enter quickly and effectively.

Furthermore, the supposed "quick and effective" entry requirement overlooks the point that a firm that *never* enters a given market can nevertheless exert competitive pressure on that market. If barriers to entry are insignificant, the *threat* of entry can stimulate competition in a concentrated market, regardless of whether entry ever occurs. If a firm that *never* enters a market can keep that market competitive, a defendant seeking to rebut a prima facie case certainly need not show that any firm *will* enter the relevant market.

* * *

Having rejected the "quick and effective" entry standard itself, we turn briefly to the government's more general argument that the district court's findings regarding ease of entry failed to support its conclusion that the defendants had rebutted the prima facie case. The district court in this case discussed a number of considerations that led it to conclude that entry barriers to the United States HHUDR market were not high enough to impede future entry should Tamrock's acquisition of Secoma lead to supracompetitive pricing. First, the court noted that at least two companies, Cannon and Ingersoll–Rand, had entered the United States HHUDR market in 1989, and were poised for future expansion. Second, the court stressed that a number of firms competing in Canada and other countries had not penetrated the United States market, but could be expected to do so if Tamrock's acquisition of Secoma led to higher prices.[9] Because the market is small, "[i]t is inexpensive to develop a separate sales and service network in the United States." Third, these firms would exert competitive pressure on the United

---

9. Some of these firms have already tried, but failed, to penetrate the United States HHUDR market. As the district court correctly noted, however, failed entry in the past does not necessarily imply failed entry in the future: if prices reach supracompetitive levels, a company that has failed to enter in the past could become competitive.

States HHUDR market even if they never actually entered the market. Finally, the court noted that there had been tremendous turnover in the United States HHUDR market in the 1980s. Secoma, for example, did not sell a single HHUDR in the United States in 1983 or 1984, but then lowered its price and improved its service, becoming market leader by 1989. Secoma's growth suggests that competitors not only can, but probably will, enter or expand if this acquisition leads to higher prices. The district court, to be sure, also found some facts suggesting difficulty of entry,[10] but these findings do not negate its ultimate finding to the contrary.

In sum, we see no error–legal or factual–in the district court's determination that entry into the United States HHUDR market would likely avert anticompetitive effects from Tamrock's acquisition of Secoma. The court's determination on entry, considered along with the findings discussed in section I of this opinion, suffices to rebut the government's prima facie case.

III.

Finally, we consider the strength of the showing that a section 7 defendant must make to rebut a prima facie case. The district court simply reviewed the evidence that the defendants presented and concluded that the acquisition was not likely to substantially lessen competition. The government argues that the court erred by failing to require the defendants to make a "clear" showing. The relevant precedents, however, suggest that this formulation overstates the defendants' burden. We conclude that a "clear" showing is unnecessary, and we are satisfied that the district court required the defendants to produce sufficient evidence.

The government's "clear showing" language is by no means unsupported in the case law. In the mid–1960s, the Supreme Court construed section 7 to prohibit virtually any horizontal merger or acquisition. At the time, the Court envisioned an ideal market as one composed of many small competitors, each enjoying only a small market share; the more closely a given market approximated this ideal, the more competitive it was presumed to be.

This perspective animated a series of decisions in which the Court stated that a section 7 defendant's market share measures its market power, that statistics alone establish a prima facie case, and that a defendant carries a heavy burden in seeking to rebut the presumption established by such a prima facie case. The Court most clearly articulated this approach in *Philadelphia Bank* * * *.

In *United States v. Von's Grocery Co.*, the Court further emphasized the weight of a defendant's burden. * * *

Although the Supreme Court has not overruled these section 7 precedents, it has cut them back sharply. In *General Dynamics*, the Court affirmed a district court determination that, by presenting evidence that undermined the government's statistics, section 7 defendants had successfully rebutted a

---

10. The court, for instance, noted that HHUDRs are custom-made, and thus are not readily interchangeable or replaceable. Buyers, therefore, tend to return to sellers from whom they have purchased in the past. The court also found that HHUDR customers typically place great importance on assurances of product quality and reliable future service–considerations that may handicap new entrants. It also noted the significant economies of scale involved in manufacturing HHUDRs.

prima facie case. In so holding, the Court did not expressly reaffirm or disavow *Philadelphia Bank*'s statement that a company must "clearly" show that a transaction is not likely to have substantial anticompetitive effects. The Court simply held that the district court was justified, based on all the evidence, in finding that "no substantial lessening of competition occurred or was threatened by the acquisition."

General Dynamics began a line of decisions differing markedly in emphasis from the Court's antitrust cases of the 1960s. Instead of accepting a firm's market share as virtually conclusive proof of its market power, the Court carefully analyzed defendants' rebuttal evidence.[12] These cases discarded *Philadelphia Bank*'s insistence that a defendant "clearly" disprove anticompetitive effect, and instead described the rebuttal burden simply in terms of a "showing." Without overruling *Philadelphia Bank*, then, the Supreme Court has at the very least lightened the evidentiary burden on a section 7 defendant.

In the aftermath of *General Dynamics* and its progeny, a defendant seeking to rebut a presumption of anticompetitive effect must show that the prima facie case inaccurately predicts the relevant transaction's probable effect on future competition. The more compelling the prima facie case, the more evidence the defendant must present to rebut it successfully. A defendant can make the required showing by affirmatively showing why a given transaction is unlikely to substantially lessen competition, or by discrediting the data underlying the initial presumption in the government's favor.

By focusing on the future, section 7 gives a court the uncertain task of assessing probabilities. In this setting, allocation of the burdens of proof assumes particular importance. By shifting the burden of producing evidence, present law allows both sides to make competing predictions about a transaction's effects. If the burden of production imposed on a defendant is unduly onerous, the distinction between that burden and the ultimate burden of persuasion—always an elusive distinction in practice—disintegrates completely. A defendant required to produce evidence "clearly" disproving future anticompetitive effects must essentially persuade the trier of fact on the ultimate issue in the case—whether a transaction is likely to lessen competition substantially. Absent express instructions to the contrary, we are loath to depart from settled principles and impose such a heavy burden.

Imposing a heavy burden of production on a defendant would be particularly anomalous where, as here, it is easy to establish a prima facie case. The government, after all, can carry its initial burden of production simply by presenting market concentration statistics. To allow the government virtually to rest its case at that point, leaving the defendant to prove the core of the

---

12. Judge Posner has elucidated this point: The most important developments that cast doubt on the continued vitality of such cases as *Brown Shoe* and *Von's* are found in other cases, where the Supreme Court, echoed by the lower courts, has said repeatedly that the economic concept of competition, rather than any desire to preserve rivals as such, is the lodestar that shall guide the contemporary application of the antitrust laws, not excluding the Clayton Act.... Applied to cases brought under Section 7, this principle requires the district court ... to make a judgment whether the challenged acquisition is likely to hurt consumers, as by making it easier for the firms in the market to collude, expressly or tacitly, and thereby force price above or farther above the competitive level.

Hospital Corp. of Am. v. FTC, 807 F.2d 1381, 1386 (7th Cir.1986), cert. denied, 481 U.S. 1038 (1987).

dispute, would grossly inflate the role of statistics in actions brought under section 7. The Herfindahl–Hirschman Index cannot guarantee litigation victories.[13] Requiring a "clear showing" in this setting would move far toward forcing a defendant to rebut a probability with a certainty.

* * *

The appellees in this case presented the district court with considerable evidence regarding the United States HHUDR market. The court credited the evidence concerning the sophistication of HHUDR consumers and the insignificance of entry barriers, as well as the argument that the statistics underlying the government's prima facie case were misleading. This evidence amply justified the court's conclusion that the prima facie case inaccurately depicted the probable anticompetitive effect of Tamrock's acquisition of Secoma. Because the government did not produce sufficient evidence to overcome this successful rebuttal, the district court concluded that "it is not likely that the acquisition will substantially lessen competition in the United States either immediately or long-term." 731 F. Supp. at 12. The government has given us no reason to reverse that conclusion.

For the foregoing reasons, the judgment of the district court is

Affirmed.

Note on Buyer Power

The appeals court in *Baker Hughes* cited "the sophistication of HHUDR consumers" as a non-entry factor tending to rebut the government's prima facie case and observes that the government's Merger Guidelines in force at the time recognize "information about specific transactions and buyer market characteristics" as among the "non-entry factors that can overcome a presumption of illegality established by market share statistics." How could powerful, large, or sophisticated buyers make anticompetitive effects from merger unlikely? There are at least two possible scenarios.

First, recall from Chapter 3 that when buyers are large and sales are "lumpy," coordination may be frustrated. A firm considering cheating in such an industry may realize that it can take a large chunk of business easily, and do so free from the threat of rapid punishment. This opportunity may encourage firms to cheat, and its threat may discourage cartel formation in the first instance. Second, a large buyer may be able to take advantage of its scale of purchases to integrate vertically into the upstream industry, creating new upstream rivalry that undermines the post-merger exercise of market power. Similarly, a large buyer may be able to help a small upstream seller become a substantial, low cost rival to the merged firm. Here the role of the large buyer is to facilitate entry or expansion upstream, creating additional rivalry for the merged firm.

---

13. We refer the government to its own Merger Guidelines, which recognize that "[i]n a variety of situations, market share and market concentration data may either understate or overstate the likely future competitive significance of a firm or firms in the market." Although the Guidelines disclaim "slavish[] ad- here[nce]" to such data, we fear that the Department of Justice has ignored its own admonition. The government does not maximize scarce resources when it allows statistics alone to trigger its ponderous enforcement machinery.

In each of these scenarios, one question that arises is whether the large buyer would simply protect itself, or whether the creation of these alternatives would benefit other buyers as well. When the court in *Baker Hughes* discusses the role of sophisticated buyers, does it have either of these possibilities in mind?

––––––

Eleven years after *Baker Hughes*, the D.C. Circuit revisited the structure of horizontal merger analysis in *Heinz*.* In reading this decision, consider the extent to which the court's approach to merger analysis is consistent with that of *Baker Hughes*.

FEDERAL TRADE COMMISSION v. H.J. HEINZ CO.
United States Court of Appeals for the District of Columbia Circuit, 2001.
246 F.3d 708.

Before: HENDERSON, RANDOLPH and GARLAND, Circuit Judges.

KAREN LeCRAFT HENDERSON, Circuit Judge.

On February 28, 2000 H.J. Heinz Company (Heinz) and Milnot Holding Corporation (Beech–Nut) entered into a merger agreement. The Federal Trade Commission (Commission or FTC) sought a preliminary injunction pursuant to section 13(b) of the Federal Trade Commission Act (FTCA), to enjoin the consummation of the merger. The injunction was sought in aid of an FTC administrative proceeding which was subsequently instituted by complaint to challenge the merger as violative of, *inter alia*, section 7 of the Clayton Act. The district court denied the preliminary injunction and the FTC appealed to this court. For the reasons set forth below, we reverse the district court and remand for entry of a preliminary injunction against Heinz and Beech–Nut.

I.   BACKGROUND

* * * The baby food market is dominated by three firms, Gerber Products Company (Gerber), Heinz and Beech–Nut. Gerber, the industry leader, enjoys a 65 per cent market share while Heinz and Beech–Nut come in second and third, with a 17.4 per cent and a 15.4 per cent share respectively. The district court found that Gerber enjoys unparalleled brand recognition with a brand loyalty greater than any other product sold in the United States. Gerber's products are found in over 90 per cent of all American supermarkets.

By contrast, Heinz is sold in approximately 40 per cent of all supermarkets. Its sales are nationwide but concentrated in northern New England, the Southeast and Deep South and the Midwest. * * * Heinz lacks Gerber's brand recognition; it markets itself as a "value brand" with a shelf price several cents below Gerber's.

Beech–Nut has a market share (15.4%) comparable to that of Heinz (17.4%) * * * Beech–Nut maintains price parity with Gerber, selling at about one penny less. It markets its product as a premium brand. Consumers generally view its product as comparable in quality to Gerber's. Beech–Nut is

––––––

* Two of the authors of this casebook, Jonathan B. Baker and William E. Kovacic, were involved in the *Heinz* litigation, both on the side of the merging firms.

carried in approximately 45 per cent of all grocery stores. Although its sales are nationwide, they are concentrated in New York, New Jersey, California and Florida.[3]

* * *

II. ANALYSIS

* * *

'Whenever the Commission has reason to believe that a corporation is violating, or is about to violate, Section 7 of the Clayton Act, the FTC may seek a preliminary injunction to prevent a merger pending the Commission's administrative adjudication of the merger's legality.' Section 13(b) provides for the grant of a preliminary injunction where such action would be in the public interest—as determined by a weighing of the equities and a consideration of the Commission's likelihood of success on the merits. * * *

To determine likelihood of success on the merits we measure the probability that, after an administrative hearing on the merits, the Commission will succeed in proving that the effect of the Heinz/Beech–Nut merger "may be substantially to lessen competition, or to tend to create a monopoly" in violation of section 7 of the Clayton Act. This court and others have suggested that the standard for likelihood of success on the merits is met if the FTC "has raised questions going to the merits so serious, substantial, difficult and doubtful as to make them fair ground for thorough investigation, study, deliberation and determination by the FTC in the first instance and ultimately by the Court of Appeals." * * *

In *United States v. Baker Hughes Inc.*, we explained the analytical approach by which the government establishes a section 7 violation. First the government must show that the merger would produce "a firm controlling an undue percentage share of the relevant market, and [would] result[ ] in a significant increase in the concentration of firms in that market." *Philadelphia Nat'l Bank*. Such a showing establishes a "presumption" that the merger will substantially lessen competition. To rebut the presumption, the defendants must produce evidence that "show[s] that the market-share statistics [give] an inaccurate account of the [merger's] probable effects on competition" in the relevant market. *United States v. Citizens & S. Nat'l Bank*, 422 U.S. 86, 120, 95 S.Ct. 2099, 45 L.Ed.2d 41 (1975).[7] "If the defendant successfully rebuts the presumption [of illegality], the burden of producing additional evidence of anticompetitive effect shifts to the government, and merges with the ultimate burden of persuasion, which remains with the government at all times." Although *Baker Hughes* was decided at the merits

---

3. Although Heinz and Beech–Nut introduced evidence showing that in areas that account for 80% of Beech–Nut sales, Heinz has a market share of about 2% and in areas that account for about 72% of Heinz sales, Beech–Nut's share is about 4%, the FTC introduced evidence that Heinz and Beech–Nut are locked in an intense battle at the wholesale level to gain (and maintain) position as the second brand on retail shelves.

7. To rebut the defendants may rely on "[n]onstatistical evidence which casts doubt on the persuasive quality of the statistics to predict future anticompetitive consequences" such as "ease of entry into the market, the trend of the market either toward or away from concentration, and the continuation of active price competition." * * * In addition, the defendants may demonstrate unique economic circumstances that undermine the predictive value of the government's statistics. *See United States v. General Dynamics Corp.* * * *.

stage as opposed to the preliminary injunctive relief stage, we can nonetheless use its analytical approach in evaluating the Commission's showing of likelihood of success. Accordingly, we look at the FTC's prima facie case and the defendants' rebuttal evidence.

Merger law "rests upon the theory that, where rivals are few, firms will be able to coordinate their behavior, either by overt collusion or implicit understanding, in order to restrict output and achieve profits above competitive levels." * * * Increases in concentration above certain levels are thought to "raise[ ] a likelihood of 'interdependent anticompetitive conduct.' " * * *

[The court then examined market concentration, employing the Herfindahl–Hirschman Index (HHI), a measure set forth in the Horizontal Merger Guidelines. It found that the baby food industry was "highly concentrated" pre-merger and that the merger would increase that concentration in excess of a threshold set forth in the Guidelines.—Eds.][10] * * * This creates, by a wide margin, a presumption that the merger will lessen competition in the domestic jarred baby food market.[11] * * * Here, the FTC's market concentration statistics[12] are bolstered by the indisputable fact that the merger will eliminate competition between the two merging parties at the wholesale level, where they are currently the only competitors for what the district court described as the "second position on the supermarket shelves." * * *

Finally, the anticompetitive effect of the merger is further enhanced by high barriers to market entry. * * *

As far as we can determine, no court has ever approved a merger to duopoly under similar circumstances.

In response to the FTC's prima facie showing, the appellees make three rebuttal arguments, which the district court accepted in reaching its conclusion that the merger was not likely to lessen competition substantially. For the reasons discussed below, these arguments fail and thus were not a proper basis for denying the FTC injunctive relief. * * *

[The three rebuttal arguments cited by the court involved claims that (1) "there is little competitive loss from the merger" because "Heinz and Beech-Nut do not really compete against each other at the retail level;" (2) "the anticompetitive effects of the merger will be offset by efficiencies resulting from the union of the two companies, efficiencies which they assert will be used to compete more effectively against Gerber;" and (3) "the merger is required to enable Heinz to innovate, and thus to improve its competitive position against Gerber." With respect to the second of these arguments, the appeals court noted that the district court had identified "substantial cost savings" from consolidating baby food product in Heinz' underutilized production plant and had accepted that Heinz would obtain quality improvements from recipe consolidation.—Eds.]

---

10. To determine the HHI score the district court first had to define the relevant market. The court defined the product market as jarred baby food and the geographic market as the United States. The parties do not challenge the court's definition.

11. The FTC argues that this finding alone—that it is certain to establish a prima facie case—entitles it to preliminary injunctive relief * * *. We disagree * * *.

12. The Supreme Court has cautioned that statistics reflecting market share and concentration, while of great significance, are not conclusive indicators of anticompetitive effects. *See General Dynamics* * * *.

In a footnote the district court dismissed the likelihood of collusion derived from the FTC's market concentration data. "[S]tructural market barriers to collusion" in the retail market for jarred baby food, the court said, rebut the normal presumption that increases in concentration will increase the likelihood of tacit collusion. The court's sole citation, however, was to testimony by the appellees' expert, Jonathan B. Baker, a former Director of the Bureau of Economics at the FTC, who testified that in order to coordinate successfully, firms must solve "cartel problems" such as reaching a consensus on price and market share and deterring each other from deviating from that consensus by either lowering price or increasing production. He opined that after the merger the merged entity would want to expand its market share at Gerber's expense, thereby decreasing the likelihood of consensus on price and market share. In his report, Baker elaborated on his theory, explaining that the efficiencies created by the merger will give the merged firm the ability and incentive to take on Gerber in price and product improvements. He also predicted that policing and monitoring of any agreement would be more difficult than it is now, due in part to a time lag in the ability of one firm to detect price cuts by another. But the district court made no finding that any of these "cartel problems" are so much greater in the baby food industry than in other industries that they rebut the normal presumption. * * *

The combination of a concentrated market and barriers to entry is a recipe for price coordination. * * * The creation of a durable duopoly affords both the opportunity and incentive for both firms to coordinate to increase prices. * * * Because the district court failed to specify any 'structural market barriers to collusion' that are unique to the baby food industry, its conclusion that the ordinary presumption of collusion in a merger to duopoly was rebutted is clearly erroneous. * * *

* * *

* * * The FTC demonstrated that the merger to duopoly will increase the concentration in an already highly concentrated market; that entry barriers in the market make it unlikely that any anticompetitive effects will be avoided; that pre-merger competition is vigorous at the wholesale level nationwide and present at the retail level in some metropolitan areas; and that post-merger competition may be lessened substantially. These substantial questions have not been sufficiently answered by the appellees. As we said in *Baker Hughes*, "[t]he more compelling the prima facie case, the more evidence the defendant must present to rebut it successfully." In concluding that the FTC failed to make the requisite showing, the district court erred in a number of respects. Regarding the contention of lack of pre-merger competition, it made a clearly erroneous factual finding and misunderstood the law with respect to the import of competition at the wholesale level. Regarding the proffered efficiencies defense, the court failed to make the kind of factual findings required to render that defense sufficiently concrete to rebut the government's prima facie showing. Finally, as to the contention that the merger is necessary for innovation, the court clearly erred in relying on evidence that does not support its conclusion. Because the district court incorrectly assessed the merits of the appellees' rebuttal arguments, it improperly discounted the FTC's showing of likelihood of success.

* * *

The *Heinz* panel expressly rejected the FTC's contention that high concentration in a market with entry barriers alone entitles the government to a preliminary injunction, and accepted that a successful rebuttal requires evidence showing that market share statistics provide "an inaccurate account of the [merger's] probable effects on competition." In both respects, the decision was consistent with *Baker Hughes*. But can these two cases be fully reconciled?

In *Baker Hughes*, the court stated "Evidence of market concentration simply provides a convenient starting point for a broader inquiry into future competitiveness." Consistent with that observation, the *Heinz* court approached its inquiry into the likely competitive effects of the baby food industry merger by beginning with concentration. But in doing so, the *Heinz* panel gave the concentration evidence substantial weight. The court treated the proposed transaction as reducing the number of firms from three to two ("a merger to duopoly"), and viewed the resulting high concentration as creating a strong presumption that the merger would harm competition. It observed: "[t]he combination of a concentrated market and barriers to entry is a recipe for price coordination. * * * The creation of a durable duopoly affords both the opportunity and incentive for both firms to coordinate to increase prices."

Moreover, the *Heinz* panel arguably incorporated its view of the likely consequences of a merger to duopoly into the legal standard it applied to test the defendants' rebuttal evidence. To successfully rebut the government's *prima facie* case with evidence that the industry participants were unlikely to successfully solve their "cartel problems," and thus that post-merger tacit collusion would be unlikely, the defense in *Heinz* was required to make a specific showing not specifically mentioned in *Baker Hughes*: that "these 'cartel problems' are so much greater in the baby food industry than in other industries that they rebut the normal presumption" that collusion is likely in a merger to duopoly.

In giving concentration such great weight, did the court in *Heinz* merely conduct a "totality-of-the-circumstances" analysis, as called for by *Baker Hughes*? Or did the *Heinz* court strengthen the structural presumption, relative to how the presumption was treated in *Baker Hughes*, even to the point of making it unrebuttable in practice when a merger reduces the number of firms to as few as two? Would *Baker Hughes*, in which post-merger market concentration was also high, have come out the same way had the court in that case adopted the approach suggested in *Heinz*, and explicitly inquired as to whether entry conditions were less congenial to the exercise of market power in the hardrock hydraulic underground drilling rig industry than in other industries?

The burden shifting framework developed in *Baker Hughes* and *Heinz* is arguably artificial, because it suggests a stilted approach in which each side introduces limited evidence intended solely to meet its burden of production. " 'In practice * * * the government usually introduces all of its evidence at one time, and the defendant responds in kind.' " *Chicago Bridge & Iron Co. v.*

FTC, 515 F.3d 447, 459 (5th Cir. 2008) (*quoting FTC v. University Health, Inc.*, 938 F.2d 1206 (11th Cir. 1991)). What are the implications of this practice for sorting out the parties' relative burdens of production and proof? According to *Chicago Bridge & Iron*, to accommodate the "practical difficulties in separating the burden to persuade and the burdens to produce" in such cases, courts use a more flexible approach, which "allows the Commission to preserve the prima facie presumption if the respondent * * * fails to satisfy the burden of production in light of contrary evidence in the prima facie case." 515 F.3d at 460. Is the court in *Chicago Bridge & Iron* confusing the burden of production with a totality of the circumstances approach to evaluating the government's ability ultimately to satisfy its burden of persuasion?

Relying on *Baker Hughes*, the *Heinz* court held that " '[t]he more compelling the prima facie case, the more evidence the defendant must present to rebut it successfully.' " *Heinz*, 246 F.3d at 725. With reference to this "sliding scale" language, *Chicago Bridge & Iron* adds that to the extent the government anticipates the merging firms' likely rebuttal evidence and responds to it in its case-in-chief, "the prima facie case is very compelling and significantly strengthened." 515 F.3d. at 461. Is this a reasonable interpretation of *Heinz*? Does *Heinz* stand for the proposition that the defendant must proffer more evidence to satisfy its initial burden on rebuttal the stronger the government's prima facie case? Or is the court in *Chicago Bridge & Iron* again confusing the respondent's burden of production with a totality of the circumstances approach to evaluating the government's ability ultimately to satisfy its burden of persuasion?

Sidebar 5–2:
Beyond Horizontal and Vertical: Conglomerate Mergers and Potential Competition

Conglomerate and Market Extension Mergers—Traditional Treatment

Conglomerate mergers—which involve firms not related either horizontally or vertically—were a significant enforcement concern at the height of antitrust's structural era. These then-frequent transactions attracted a great deal of attention during the late 1960s, the heyday of businesses like Gulf & Western Industries, Ling–Temco–Vought (LTV), and International Telephone & Telegraph (ITT), which grew through conglomerate acquisitions to be among the largest industrial corporations in the nation. "Although they added little to horizontal concentration, these transactions produced large conglomerate enterprises whose existence suggested that antitrust policy was seriously deficient in dealing with sheer corporate size." William E. Kovacic, *Failed Expectations: The Troubled Past and Uncertain Future of the Sherman Act as a Tool for Deconcentration*, 74 Iowa L. Rev. 1105, 1122–23 (1989).

Conglomerate merger enforcement played a role in the Watergate scandal. The Antitrust Division of the Justice Department brought several conglomerate merger cases during the first two years of the Nixon Administration, in 1969 and 1970, including four against ITT. These enforcement actions—and the Justice Department's determination to pursue an expedited appeal of a district court loss to the Supreme

Court—led to a furious lobbying effort by ITT to persuade Congress to repeal the Expediting Act (currently 15 U.S.C. § 29), which would have aided ITT by helping it delay or possibly avoid Supreme Court review. ITT also attempted to persuade the Nixon White House to instruct the Department of Justice to drop the appeal or settle the case. Evidence from that period established that President Nixon called Deputy Attorney General Richard Kleindienst and ordered the Justice Department to back off from pursuing conglomerate merger challenges. ITT's case was eventually settled.

A connection between that settlement and ITT's contemporaneous offer to help finance the 1972 Republican convention was alleged and given credence by some because of the overlap in the officials involved. But it was never conclusively demonstrated. Nonetheless, the antitrust dispute became enmeshed in scandal. A cover-up of White House contacts with Justice Department officials over the disposition of the case led to one of the Watergate-related impeachment counts against President Nixon and the conviction of Kleindienst after his elevation to Attorney General for false testimony before a congressional committee.* *See generally* ROBERT M. GOOLRICK, PUBLIC POLICY TOWARD CORPORATE GROWTH: THE ITT MERGER CASES (1978); FRANK MANKEWICZ, U.S. v. RICHARD M. NIXON: THE FINAL CRISIS 47–49, 70–72, 161–63 207, 261 (1975); J. ANTHONY LUKAS, NIGHTMARE: THE UNDERSIDE OF THE NIXON YEARS 130–34, 182–85 (1976).

Historically, the Supreme Court distinguished a fourth category of mergers that are "neither horizontal, vertical nor conglomerate" involving what is termed a product or market extension merger. *FTC v. Procter & Gamble Co.*, 386 U.S. 568, 578 (1967). In that case, a laundry detergent's acquisition of a producer of bleach was considered a "product extension merger" because the two products are "complementary:" they may be produced in the same facilities, distributed through the same channels, advertised by the same media, and marketed to the same ultimate consumer. A "market extension merger" occurs when the merging firms sell the same product in different geographic markets.

Conglomerate and Market Extension Mergers Today

From a more contemporary perspective, market and product extension mergers generate a potential for collusive competitive effects similar to the traditional concern about horizontal mergers. To the extent either firm is a potential competitor in the market in which its merger partner participates, as may be plausible given that its involvement in complementary activities may give it a "leg up" on entry unavailable to other potential entrants, the merger may harm competition. These transactions may also give rise to exclusionary competitive effects similar to the traditional concern about vertical mergers. To the extent the merged firm can exploit its control of complementary products to impair or eliminate access to those complements by an unintegrated rival or the rival's

---

* The President is entitled to instruct Justice Department officials on the disposition of individual cases handled by that Executive Branch agency, but Presidents invariably refrain from doing so for fear of being seen to "politicize" law enforcement. Accordingly, there would have been no legal problem had Nixon decided that Justice should settle or dismiss any particular case (only a possible political problem for the President). The congressional and criminal investigations instead focused on whether the settlement of ITT's antitrust case was connected to its offer to finance the Republican convention and on whether senior government officials lied under oath about President Nixon's role.

customers, the merger may lessen competition. In addition, these types of mergers create the potential for cost savings similar to the efficiencies often available from vertical integration. Product and market extension mergers have nevertheless historically been viewed as closer to conglomerate mergers than to horizontal and vertical acquisitions.

Since the 1970s, government challenges to conglomerate mergers and product or market extension mergers have become rare. Still the legal theories that were important historically in the review of conglomerate mergers have some resonance today. The major themes in this area of antitrust jurisprudence are sketched below. The emphasis is on potential competition theories, which generate the most current attention, most likely because they are closely related to horizontal merger analysis.

Potential Competition Theories

The acquisition of a potential horizontal rival could harm competition in much the same way as could the acquisition of an actual horizontal rival. Potential competition cases were divided into two categories. Under the "perceived potential competition" theory, the perceived threat of entry by a firm not now in the market limits anticompetitive behavior by incumbent sellers, so the acquisition of that outsider by an incumbent might harm competition because it relaxes that constraint. Under the "actual potential competition" or "actual potential entrant" theory, the acquisition involves a firm that would otherwise have entered and made the market more competitive. The categories differ in their evidentiary focus: perceived potential competition is concerned with the incumbent's expectations, while the actual potential competition theory is concerned with the entrant's actual plans.

The "perceived potential competition" theory was endorsed by the Supreme Court during the late 1960s and early 1970s. *United States v. Marine Bancorporation,* 418 U.S. 602, 639–40 (1974); *United States v. Falstaff Brewing Corp.,* 410 U.S. 526, 532–34 & n. 13 (1973); *FTC v. Procter & Gamble Co.,* 386 U.S. 568, 581 (1967). While the Supreme Court reserved judgment on the "actual potential competition" theory, *see Marine Bancorporation,* 418 U.S. at 625, 639; *Falstaff,* 410 U.S. at 537–38, some lower courts and the FTC accepted that theory in principle, at least if stringent factual predicates for its application are satisfied.

Potential competition theories are recognized by the 1992 Horizontal Merger Guidelines to the extent the potential competitor is an "uncommitted entrant," able to come into a market in response to a price increase quickly and with little sunk costs. As will be discussed later in this Casebook, such a firm is treated as a market participant—and thus effectively presumed to constrain existing rivalry—and assigned a market share based upon the capacity it could profitably shift into the production of goods that would be sold in the relevant market in response to a small price increase. Although the 1992 Guidelines do not recognize potential competition theories involving committed entrants, such possibilities are incorporated in the non-horizontal sections of the 1984 Department of Justice Merger Guidelines, which remain in force; only the horizontal merger standards of the 1984 Guidelines were superseded by the 1992 Merger Guidelines. In general, the 1984 Guidelines limit the application of the potential competition theory to concentrated markets where no more than two other outside firms have an entry advantage comparable to that ascribed to the potential competitor involved in a merger. They indicate that a challenge is more likely the greater the increase in market concentration and the fewer the number of other potential entrants with comparable entry advantages as the acquired firm. In recent years, government enforcers have occasionally mounted investigations of mergers involving a potential competition theory, but such cases are rare.

Other Theories

Conglomerate mergers have been attacked on a variety of grounds other than potential competition. One such ground is that the transaction would allow the merged firm to coerce suppliers or customers, as by facilitating tying, *see In re Heublein, Inc.*, 96 F.T.C. 385, 597–98 (1980), or reciprocal buying, *FTC v. Consolidated Foods Corp.*, 380 U.S. 592 (1965). (Reciprocal buying occurs when a firm purchases only from other firms that buy from it. A computer manufacturer, for example, may purchase components only from firms that use its computers in their offices.) A related concern, termed "entrenchment," is that a firm, dominant in its market, could obtain significant competitive advantages through merger with a large acquiring firm, because the transaction may raise entry barriers and disadvantage small rivals. *See In re Heublein, Inc.*, 96 F.T.C. 385, 593–96 (1980); *Emhart Corp. v. USM Corp.*, 527 F.2d 177, 181 (1st Cir. 1975). Today, it is likely that these possibilities would be analyzed similarly to other potential exclusionary effects of mergers, as will be discussed in Chapter 7 in connection with vertical mergers.

A final concern about conglomerate mergers in the case law relates to their potential for facilitating oligopolistic coordination through multi-market contact. For example, the government unsuccessfully argued in a 1974 bank merger case that the acquisition, and others it would likely trigger, would result in a market structure in which a few large statewide banks would face each other in a network of local, oligopolistic banking markets, and that this market structure would enhance the possibility of supracompetitive pricing through parallel, standardized conduct. *United States v. Marine Bancorporation*, 418 U.S. 602, 620, 623 (1974). This collusive theory would likely be analyzed today as a possible instance of coordinated competitive effects of horizontal mergers.

Acquisitions by Private Equity Firms—The New "Conglomerates"

During the first decade of the 21st century, private equity firms grew in size and importance as financial market participants. These firms often purchase, in whole or part, businesses in many industries. Many of their investments are more than passive financial interests; the private equity buyer may appoint management to run the firm with the hope of improving operations or cutting costs, and later selling the business at a profit. These financial entities can be thought of as conglomerates. Their acquisitions have only rarely drawn scrutiny from the antitrust enforcement agencies. Those transactions are most likely to draw such attention when the private equity buyer already owns or controls a rival firm. *E.g.*, *In re TC Group*, File No. 061 0197; Docket No. C–4183 (F.T.C. Jan. 27, 2007), available at http://www.ftc.gov/os/caselist/0610197/index.shtm) (analysis of proposed agreement containing consent orders to aid public comment) (acquisition of interests in Kinder Morgan by private equity funds managed and controlled by The Carlyle Group and Riverside Holdings).

C. MERGER ANALYSIS UNDER THE DOJ/FTC MERGER GUIDELINES

The Merger Guidelines promulgated by the federal antitrust enforcement agencies are designed to describe how the Justice Department and Federal Trade Commission will exercise their prosecutorial discretion in evaluating mergers, not to articulate the applicable legal standard that should or would be applied by a court. They bind the agencies, but not the courts. The Guidelines are nevertheless influential with judges, as we will see in the case excerpts below, because they set forth a systematic approach to the analysis of mergers that has been informed by the case law and contemporary economic thinking and because the Supreme Court has not decided a merger case on the merits since the mid–1970s.

The first Justice Department Merger Guidelines were issued in 1968. They have been revised several times since in response to experience and broad policy challenges. The 1982 Merger Guidelines were developed out of a need to harmonize the then-ascendant Chicago School economic learning with the pre-existing case law, which was rooted in prior, structural era thinking. The 1984 Merger Guidelines sought to resolve a national political debate over the Justice Department's handling of politically-sensitive mergers among large steel producers faced with foreign competition. The revision clarified geographic market definition analysis for firms competing with foreign rivals and expressed more sympathy toward an efficiency justification for acquisitions.

The 1992 Horizontal Merger Guidelines, issued for the first time jointly by the Justice Department and the FTC, followed a series of Antitrust Division losses in the courts (including *Baker Hughes*). After study, the Justice Department concluded that those losses were a consequence of over-emphasis by the government on market structure in litigation rather than on articulating a compelling competitive effects story, and from its lack of success in explaining the distinction between committed and uncommitted entry. These deficiencies were addressed by the revisions. The 1992 Guidelines also educated the bar, economic consultants, judges, and agency staff alike on new methods of analysis that the enforcement agencies had begun to employ internally, most notably involving the analysis of unilateral competitive effects, that were stimulated by then-contemporary developments in microeconomics. Agency interest in clarifying the role of efficiencies in merger analysis, the subject of the 1997 revisions, followed FTC hearings on Competition Policy in the New High–Tech, Global Marketplace and the resulting recognition that courts were becoming increasingly receptive to the possibility of an efficiency defense.

The 1992 Guidelines, as revised in 1997 to address efficiencies, are limited to the analysis of horizontal mergers and remain in operation today. In March 2006, the agencies supplemented them with a *Commentary on the Horizontal Merger Guidelines*. The *Commentary* aims to provide a more detailed explication of how the agencies apply the guidelines, mainly through detailed case illustrations. *See* http://www.usdoj.gov/atr/public/guidelines/215247.htm. Earlier Justice Department guidelines also addressed vertical mergers; the sections of the 1984 guidelines dealing with that subject remain in force at that agency. However, as discussed in Chapter 7, challenges to vertical mergers are less common than regulatory opposition to horizontal mergers.

The great influence of the federal Merger Guidelines has prompted the development of similar guidelines by other regulatory entities, including the National Association of Attorneys General and foreign regulators,* and led the federal agencies to develop guidelines for other areas of antitrust practice. The reasons for the success of the 1982 Merger Guidelines are explored in William Blumenthal, *Clear Agency Guidelines: Lessons from 1982*, 68 ANTI-TRUST L.J. 5 (2000).

Agency practice in merger analysis is also important because few merger challenges are litigated. As a consequence, judicial decisions concerning mergers are rare. To these matters one can add a small number of merger cases brought by state governments or by private parties that yielded judicial decisions. With so little merger litigation, merger law is primarily shaped by federal agencies through the government's negotiation of consent decrees and promulgation of guidelines.

Consideration of factors such as trends toward industry concentration or the loss of small businesses, that are prominent in older Supreme Court decisions like *Brown Shoe*, is absent from the analysis of the federal enforcement agencies today. The Merger Guidelines instead focus on market power as the source of concern about mergers under the antitrust laws: the possibility that a merger will "create or enhance market power, or * * * facilitate its exercise," resulting in "a transfer of wealth from buyers to sellers or a misallocation of resources." *Horizontal Merger Guidelines* § 0.1. In adopting this approach, the Guidelines are consistent with the modern case law, which interprets Clayton Act § 7's concern with acquisitions that "substantially . . . lessen competition" as tethering the statute to the economic concept of market power.

The Horizontal Merger Guidelines set forth a five-step analytical process for determining whether a merger is likely to harm competition:

(1) defining relevant markets and determining market concentration;

(2) assessing potential adverse competitive effects;

---

* The European Commission adopted its first Merger Regulation in 1989 and a significantly amended one in 2004. *See* Council Regulation (EC) No 139/2004 of 20 January 2004 on the control of concentrations between undertakings. O.J. L. 24, 29.01.2004, *available at* http://ec.europa.eu/comm/competition/mergers/legislation/regulations.html#merger_reg. Because the competition prohibitions of the Treaty of Rome did not include a separate merger provision like Section 7 of the Clayton Act in the U.S., the EC Merger Regulation is anchored to Article 82's prohibition of the abuse of dominant position. Shortly after the adoption of the revised EC Merger Regulation, the Commission also adopted Horizontal Merger Guidelines. *See* Guidelines on the assessment of horizontal mergers under the Council Regulation on the control of concentrations between undertakings, O.J. L.C 31, 05.02.2004, *available at* http://eur-lex.europa.eu/LexUriServ/site/en/oj/2004/c_031/c_03120040205en00050018.pdf. The Commission also adopted guidelines for non-horizontal mergers in 2007, which are discussed in Sidebar 7–7, *infra*.

(3) assessing whether entry would deter or counteract adverse effects;

(4) assessing potential procompetitive efficiencies; and

(5) determining whether one of the merging firms is in such severe financial distress as to qualify as failing.

The Guidelines "are designed primarily to articulate the analytical framework the Agency applies in determining whether a merger is likely substantially to lessen competition, not to describe how the Agency will conduct the litigation of cases that it decides to bring." *Horizontal Merger Guidelines* § 0.1. Thus, the Guidelines do not "attempt to assign the burden of proof, or the burden of coming forward with evidence, on any particular issue." *Horizontal Merger Guidelines* § 0.1. As in *Baker Hughes* and *Heinz*, the government could rely upon the *Philadelphia Nat'l Bank* presumption when challenging a merger in court. Moreover, steps three through five encompass analyses that have often historically been raised first by defendants seeking to rebut a prima facie case based on step 1, market concentration.

Sidebar 5–3:
Pre-Merger Notification and the Merger Enforcement Process in the U.S.

The Hart–Scott–Rodino Antitrust Improvements Act, enacted in 1976 and amended most recently in 2000, requires that merging firms provide the FTC and Justice Department with information about planned transactions that exceed a certain size threshold. 15 U.S.C. § 18a. Merging firms falling within those thresholds also must delay consummation to permit prior agency review. More than 1,700 transactions were reported during fiscal year 2006.

The statute responded to two problems limiting the effectiveness of antitrust enforcement. First, most mergers and acquisitions do not generate headlines, even in the industry trade press, and therefore do not come to the attention of the FTC or Justice Department prior to consummation. Second, before 1976, most mergers were consummated before an enforcement agency investigation was complete, and before any possible court case. As a result, even if the agency successfully challenged a merger, the assets of the merging firms would often have been scrambled, increasing the likelihood that a divestiture remedy would be impractical.

The statute generally requires that firms report all stock or asset acquisitions, including those involved in the formation of a joint venture, above certain thresholds based on the size of the transaction and the size of the parties. The thresholds are indexed for inflation. As of 2007, acquisitions of voting securities or assets worth more than $59.8 million but no more than $239.2 million were reportable if one party has at least $11.3 million and the other at least $119.6 million in annual sales or assets, and all transactions valued above $239.2 million must be reported regardless of the size of the parties. Acquisitions of goods and real estate in the ordinary course of business, stock purchases solely for the purpose of investment, and mere intracorporate transfers are exempted. Filing parties must pay a fee that varies between $45,000 and $280,000, depending on the value of the transaction. Failure to file may result in penalties. Extensive regulations dictate the form, timing, and procedure of HSR filings. 16 C.F.R. § 801 *et seq.*

Once a merger is reported to government antitrust enforcers, the transaction may not be closed and joint operations may not begin for several weeks (see Figure 5–2). During that period, the Justice Department and FTC undertake an initial review of the acquisition, decide whether a more extensive inquiry is called for, and, if so, determine which agency will conduct the investigation. When the agencies negotiate "clearance," historical expertise plays a major role. The resulting industry allocations can seem arbitrary: the FTC tends to investigate soft drink and cable television mergers, whereas the Justice Department tends to review beer and telephone mergers. In some industries, such as health care and defense, both agencies have extensive expertise and either may review the transaction.

Figure 5–2:

Stages of Merger Review at the Federal Antitrust Agencies

1. *Filing*: Transaction filed with the FTC and DOJ.

2. *Clearance*: DOJ and FTC decide which agency (if any) will investigate. If neither agency wishes to investigate, and early termination has been requested by the parties, it will generally be granted.

3. *Initial waiting period*: the investigating agency decides whether to issue a "second request." The merging firms cannot close (consummate) their transaction for 30 days following the date of their filing (15 days for a cash tender offer or an acquisition in bankruptcy), unless early termination of the waiting period is granted. The waiting period is extended if there is a second request.

4. *Second Request*: the investigating agency may request additional information. The second request is typically extensive, although it may be reduced by mutual agreement, and parties may take weeks or sometimes months to comply with it.

5. *Second waiting period*: the investigating agency decides whether to challenge the deal. The parties may not close their transaction until they have substantially complied with the second request and a second waiting period of thirty (30) days (ten (10) days for a cash tender offer or an acquisition in bankruptcy) is complete. If the agency brings a court challenge, it will typically seek a temporary restraining order (or negotiate one with the parties) to prevent consummation of the transaction while the preliminary injunction hearing is pending.

The vast majority of reported transactions are not investigated beyond the initial waiting period. (*See* Figure 5–3). Indeed, most filing parties request and are granted "early termination," or agency notification that its investigation has closed before the initial waiting period has ended. The agencies can, however, extend their review beyond the initial waiting period by issuing a request for additional information—commonly referred to as a "second request"—to both parties to the acquisition. The second request typically includes extensive interrogatories and document requests, though its scope is often modified in negotiations with the parties in order to satisfy the agencies' information needs at less burden to the merging firms. Party responses to the second request are confidential, although some information may be made public if presented as evidence in a judicial proceeding and not then covered by a court-issued protective order. Once the parties have complied substantially with the second request, the parties may consummate their transaction after a second waiting period is complete, unless doing so is enjoined by a court. This prevents the agencies from scuttling the transaction by delaying their review.

Figure 5–3:

Premerger Notification and Merger Enforcement
at the Federal Antitrust Agencies, FY 2006

Most Transactions Proceed Without Substantial Agency Review

	Number of Transactions	Percent of Transactions
Transactions reported	1768	100%
Early termination requested and granted	1098	61%
Second request issued	45	2.5%

Source: Federal Trade Commission & Dep't of Justice, Hart-Scott-Rodino Annual Report FY 2006, Appendix A *available at* http://www.ftc.gov/os/2007/07/P110014hsrreport.pdf

Most Agency Concerns Are Resolved Without Litigation

	Number of Transactions	Percent of Transactions
Second request issued	45	100%
Restructured to avoid agency concerns	12*	27%
Abandoned after agency challenge announced	9	20%
Settled by consent	17	38%
Litigated	0	0%
Transaction proceeds unchallenged	7*	16%

Source: Federal Trade Commission & Dep't of Justice, Hart-Scott-Rodino Annual Report FY 2006, at 3, *available at* http://www.ftc.gov/os/2007/07/P110014hsrreport.pdf.

* The DOJ specifically reports the number of transactions that were restructured to avoid agency concerns, but the FTC does not. The estimates in the Table assume that the same number of transactions were restructured after FTC review as were restructured after DOJ review.

After reviewing the merging firms' response to a second request, the agencies may identify competitive concerns. When they do, as indicated in the second table of Figure 5–3, agency concerns are generally not resolved through litigation. Sometimes the parties will withdraw their filing, restructure their transaction to avoid agency concerns, and refile. More often, the agency and parties will negotiate a limited divestiture of some of the merged firm's assets to resolve the agency's competitive concerns. That divestiture agreement is usually formalized in a consent decree, accepted by a district court or the Federal Trade Commission after public comment. Although the agencies prepare complaints and typically provide an analysis to aid public comment, the factual record is not developed as it would be in a litigated case. Merging firms often have an incentive to settle in order to avoid delay in consummating the merger, particularly when agency concerns relate to a small part of a large transaction.

In cases where the enforcement agency has competitive concerns, but a settlement cannot be reached, the agencies typically file a complaint to enjoin the merger preliminarily in federal district court (generally along with a request for a temporary restraining order to preserve the firms as separate entities). Often the merging firms will choose not to litigate, in part to avoid the associated delay and expense. The two federal enforcement agencies at most litigate only a handful of merger challenges in a typical year. In the event the matter proceeds beyond a preliminary injunction to a trial on the merits, that trial would be before an FTC administrative law judge in an FTC case and before the federal court in a Justice Department case (where it may be consolidated with the preliminary injunction hearing). As the data presented in Figure 5–3 indicates, consent settlements are much more common than litigated challenges; for this reason, some commentators view merger control in the U.S. as more a regulatory activity than a judicial one.

State attorneys general and private parties may also challenge mergers in court, though such actions are also rare. But the states in particular are active in merger review, often investigating a transaction simultaneously with the federal investigation (often coordinating their efforts with the relevant federal agency). The states can also participate as an amicus or party in the event of a federal challenge. States also may challenge transactions on their own if the federal agencies choose not to (*e.g., New York v. Kraft Gen. Foods, Inc.*, 926 F.Supp. 321 (S.D.N.Y. 1995), or even after a federal agency has resolved its concerns by consent order. *California v. American Stores Co.*, 495 U.S. 271 (1990). Private parties may also challenge mergers regardless of the outcome of federal enforcement agency review.

In planning a transaction or cooperating to complete the HSR premerger review process, the parties to a proposed consolidation must exercise care not to coordinate their affairs in a manner that assumes the deal is an accomplished fact. Until the transaction is closed, the parties retain the legal status of independent entities and therefore are bound by restrictions that Section 1 of the Sherman Act imposes upon relations between competitors. For example, efforts by the merging parties to set prices jointly or allocate common customers before the transaction is consummated is considered to be "gun-jumping" and, if discovered, is likely to be challenged by the federal antitrust agencies as illegal horizontal collusion, a violation of the mandatory HSR waiting periods, or both. Antitrust doctrine permits the purchaser to gather information from the seller to perform "due diligence" tasks necessary to verify the seller's financial condition, but well-counseled companies generally enlist corporate outsiders (such as law firms and accounting firms) to perform these tasks and take precautions to ensure that company insiders who receive due diligence information are precluded from transmitting such data to other company insiders.

Recall that the Merger Guidelines undertake horizontal merger analysis in five steps, examining market concentration, adverse competitive effects, entry, efficiencies, and the possibility that one of the firms is failing. We now turn to examine how each step proceeds at the enforcement agencies and in the courts.

1. MARKET DEFINITION, MARKET PARTICIPANTS, AND MARKET CONCENTRATION (HORIZONTAL MERGER GUIDELINES § 1.0)

Since the creation of the pre-merger notification program, the competitive consequences of mergers have generally been evaluated prospectively, i.e. prior to consummation. As we saw in *Brown Shoe, Philadelphia Nat'l Bank, General Dynamics, Baker Hughes*, and *Heinz*, to make these predictions about a merger's likely competitive effects, the courts and Merger Guidelines have relied upon inferences drawn from evidence of market power, such as market shares and market concentration. We will study market definition in detail below, but before we do so it is important to reiterate that this approach— defining markets and determining market shares—is not the only way to demonstrate market power, and that measurement of market power is not the only way to prove anticompetitive effect in antitrust analysis. These issues are only sketched here and are considered at greater length in Chapter 8.

To understand the role of market concentration in antitrust analysis, we begin by reconsidering the Supreme Court decision in *NCAA* (Casebook, Chapter 2, *supra*). *NCAA* was not a merger case, but it is instructive as to the evidentiary role of market shares in proving market power, and of market power in proving anticompetitive effect. As you will recall, the Court reached its conclusion that the television agreement at issue in *NCAA* harmed competition through two independent routes. The first involved *direct* evidence of actual anticompetitive effect on competition: the district court had found that due to the agreement, less college football was televised, and more was charged per televised game. The second route involved *circumstantial* evidence of anticompetitive effect, through proof of market power. If firms have market power—the ability to profit by reducing output (or some other dimension of competition) in order to raise price—then courts will often infer that they have acted to harm competition, or could do so in the future. *See Note on the Development of the "Quick Look,"* Casebook, Chapter 2, *supra*.

In traveling the second route for identifying harm to competition, by assessing the NCAA's market power, the Court did not rely on *direct* evidence of *market power,* such as evidence involving demand elasticities or evidence of exclusion by means other than efficiency. Rather, the Court looked to *circumstantial* evidence of *market power,* namely that the colleges collectively accounted for a high share (100 percent) of college football in the U.S., the relevant market. From such high market shares, market power can be inferred, and from market power, anticompetitive effects can be inferred. Some leading methods of proving market power, direct and circumstantial, are set forth in Figure 5–4 below. Regardless of how market power is demonstrated, it bears repeating that proof of market power is relevant because it provides circumstantial evidence of *anticompetitive effect.*

Figure 5–4:
Some Methods of Proving Substantial Market Power

Direct Evidence	**Circumstantial Evidence**
• Measure demand elasticities	• Persistently high market shares in properly defined relevant markets
• Exclusion by means other than efficiency	• Currently high profits or price-cost ratios

As indicated in Figure 5–4, the principal *direct* technique for identifying substantial market power, employed in other cases but not in *NCAA*, is to measure the elasticity of demand for the products of the firm believed to possess a monopoly. A relatively less elastic demand would indicate considerable power to raise prices above competitive levels and hold them there without experiencing a significant loss of customers. There are a variety of ways to approach assessing the response of buyers to changes in price (the elasticity of demand), some involving quantitative evidence and others involving qualitative evidence. In fact, all of the types of evidence of buyer substitution listed below in connection with market definition can be understood as ways of gauging the elasticity of demand. But it may be important (and difficult) to account for the *Cellophane* fallacy, discussed in Sidebar 5–4 in connection with market definition, before inferring market power directly from evidence as to the elasticity of demand.

A second direct measurement method is evidence of the alleged monopolist's actual responses to the entry and expansion of rivals. If the incumbent supplier routinely and successfully uses business methods other than superior performance to exclude its rivals from competing against it, one might presume that the incumbent has substantial market power. But it may be difficult to distinguish between conduct that excludes competitors through superior performance (*e.g.*, quality improvements or price cuts resulting from a reduction in costs) and conduct that does not. It may also be difficult to assess how much the incumbent's success in excluding rivals has resulted from its superior skill, or simply the independent failings of its competitors, rather than from exclusion by means other than efficiency. And it is possible using this method to mistake sheer animus for market power, if a firm harms a hated rival in a market under circumstances where it could not reasonably expect in consequence to raise price (or prevent an anticipated price decline).

Problems in implementing direct evidentiary techniques for proving the existence of monopoly power elevate the importance of circumstantial methods of doing so. Historically, circumstantial methods have been more common than direct methods of proving market power in litigated cases, especially those involving mergers. From the earliest days of the Sherman Act, courts have for the most part used the defendant's share of market-wide sales (or other measure of firm size, such as share of industry capacity) as the principal circumstantial measure of market power.

As a general rule, antitrust plaintiffs tend to advocate more narrow markets than antitrust defendants. The reason is simple: the more narrow the market, typically, the higher the defendants' market share, and thus the stronger the inference of market power and anticompetitive effect. In *NCAA*, for example, the Supreme Court majority defined the product market as college football broadcasts. In this market, the NCAA members collectively controlled a 100% share, providing a basis for the Court to infer market power. Had a broad entertainment market instead been defined (as the NCAA suggested and the dissenting Justices would have preferred), then the NCAA members' market share would have been much lower, and would probably not have provided a basis for inferring market power.

As we have previously seen in analyzing horizontal agreements (Chapter 2), and will see further in analyzing monopolization (Chapter 6), courts and agencies often rely on market concentration as circumstantial evidence of market power. In the absence of actual effects evidence, which is unavailable when a merger is challenged before consummation, the court must use evidence such as this to make a prediction as to the likely competitive effects of the transaction. In order to determine market concentration, it is necessary to define the *relevant market* and identify the *firms participating in the market*, as well as their individual *market shares*. In every case there is both a product market and a geographic market, consistent with the requirement in Clayton Act § 7 that the acquisition be found likely to harm competition "in any line of commerce * * * in any section of the country." When price discrimination is possible, a relevant market is also described by a class of targeted buyers, as will be discussed below in Sidebar 5–5.

The probative value of market shares as a proxy for measuring market power, however, depends importantly on various assumptions about the soundness of the market definition exercise. Has the court correctly decided which products customers regard as acceptable substitutes for the defendant's products? Has it properly identified, and assigned proper market shares to, all suppliers who serve the relevant market? Does a modest market share conclusively establish the lack of substantial market power, and does the presence of a high share invariably prove that the defendant is a monopolist? If so, how high a share suggests how strong an inference? Other possible sources of circumstantial evidence of market power, such as high profit levels or high price-cost margins have been more important in past cases than they are today, for reasons discussed in Chapter 8. Note, for example, how the government sought to raise such evidence in our next case, *du Pont (Cellophane)*, and how the Court responded.

a. The Evolution of Market Definition Standards

We begin our review of the evolution of market definition standards in the aftermath of *Alcoa*, a monopolization case decided in 1945, which we will examine in more detail in Chapter 6. The Justice Department's success in achieving a finding of liability in *Alcoa* inspired a new wave of efforts to enforce Section 2 of the Sherman Act. One of the most important was a challenge to du Pont's position as the leading supplier of cellophane. In a complaint filed in 1947, the government charged du Pont with monopolization, attempted monopolization, and conspiracy to monopolize. The trial court ruled for the defendant on all issues, and the government appealed to the Supreme Court.

The pivotal issue before the Court was whether du Pont possessed monopoly power. The company defended itself by arguing that buyers of cellophane routinely turned to other flexible packaging materials when du Pont attempted to raise the price of cellophane. Because cellophane appeared to face numerous close substitutes, du Pont proposed that the Court define a relevant market consisting of a wide range of flexible wrapping materials, of which cellophane would be only one element. In such a market, du Pont's market share would fall well below the threshold of concern articulated in cases such as *Standard Oil* (1911) and *Alcoa* (1945). *See Note on the Origins of Alcoa's Market Share Benchmarks*, Casebook, Chapter 6, *infra*. Both the trial court and the Supreme Court found du Pont's view persuasive. Although the Court's analysis of the evidence concerning the flexible packaging materials sector has attracted extensive criticism, its doctrinal formula for defining the relevant market remains the basic test that courts and enforcement agencies use today in merger and non-merger cases.

UNITED STATES v. E. I. DU PONT DE NEMOURS & CO.
United States Supreme Court, 1956.
351 U.S. 377, 76 S.Ct. 994, 100 L.Ed. 1264.

Mr. Justice REED delivered the opinion of the Court

* * *

* * * The appeal, as specifically stated by the Government, 'attacks only the ruling that du Pont has not monopolized trade in cellophane.' At issue for determination is only this alleged violation by du Pont of § 2 of the Sherman Act.

During the period that is relevant to this action, du Pont produced almost 75% of the cellophane sold in the United States, and cellophane constituted less than 20% of all 'flexible packaging material' sales. * * *

The Government contends that, by so dominating cellophane production, du Pont monopolized a 'part of the trade or commerce' in violation of § 2. Respondent agrees that cellophane is a product which constitutes 'a 'part' of commerce within the meaning of Section 2.' But it contends that the prohibition of § 2 against monopolization is not violated because it does not have the power to control the price of cellophane or to exclude competitors from the market in which cellophane is sold. The court below found that the 'relevant market for determining the extent of du Pont's market control is the market for flexible packaging materials,' and that competition from those other materials prevented du Pont from possessing monopoly powers in its sales of cellophane.

The Government asserts that cellophane and other wrapping materials are neither substantially fungible nor like priced. For these reasons, it argues that the market for other wrappings is distinct from the market for cellophane and that the competition afforded cellophane by other wrappings is not strong enough to be considered in determining whether du Pont has monopoly powers. Market delimitation is necessary under du Pont's theory to determine whether an alleged monopolist violates Section 2. The ultimate consideration in such a determination is whether the defendants control the price and competition in the market for such part of trade or commerce as they are charged with monopolizing. Every manufacturer is the sole producer of the particular commodity it makes but its control in the above sense of the relevant market depends upon the availability of alternative commodities for buyers: *i.e.*, whether there is a cross-elasticity of demand between cellophane and the other wrappings. This interchangeability is largely gauged by the purchase of competing products for similar uses considering the price, characteristics and adaptability of the competing commodities. The court below found that the flexible wrappings afforded such alternatives. This Court must determine whether the trial court erred in its estimate of the competition afforded cellophane by other materials.

The burden of proof, of course, was upon the Government to establish monopoly. This the trial court held the Government failed to do, upon findings of fact and law stated at length by that court. For the United States to succeed in this Court now, it must show that erroneous legal tests were applied to essential findings of fact or that the findings themselves were 'clearly erroneous' * * *.

I. *Factual Background.*—For consideration of the issue as to monopolization, a general summary of the development of cellophane is useful.

In the early 1900's, Jacques Brandenberger, a Swiss chemist, attempted to make tablecloths impervious to dirt by spraying them with liquid viscose (a cellulose solution available in quantity from wood pulp) and by coagulating this coating. His idea failed, but he noted that the coating peeled off in a transparent film. This first 'cellophane' was thick, hard, and not perfectly transparent, but Brandenberger apparently foresaw commercial possibilities in his discovery. By 1908 he developed the first machine for the manufacture of transparent sheets of regenerated cellulose. The 1908 product was not satisfactory, but by 1912 Brandenberger was making a saleable thin flexible film used in gas masks. He obtained patents to cover the machinery and the essential ideas of his process.

* * *

In 1917 Brandenberger assigned his patents to La Cellophane Societe Anonyme and joined that organization. Thereafter developments in the production of cellophane somewhat paralleled those taking place in artificial textiles. Chemical science furnished the knowledge for perfecting the new products. The success of the artificial products has been enormous. Du Pont was an American leader in the field of synthetics and learned of cellophane's successes through an associate, Comptoir des Textiles Artificiel.

In 1923 du Pont organized with La Cellophane an American company for the manufacture of plain cellophane. The undisputed findings are that:

> 'On December 26, 1923, an agreement was executed between duPont Cellophane Company and La Cellophane by which La Cellophane licensed duPont Cellophane Company exclusively under its United States cellophane patents, and granted duPont Cellophane Company the exclusive right to make and sell in North and Central America under La Cellophane's secret processes for cellophane manufacture. DuPont Cellophane Company granted to La Cellophane exclusive

rights for the rest of the world under any cellophane patents or processes duPont Cellophane Company might develop.'

* * *

Sylvania, an American affiliate of a Belgian producer of cellophane * * *, began the manufacture of cellophane in the United States in 1930. * * * Since 1934 Sylvania has produced about 25% of United States cellophane.

An important factor in the growth of cellophane production and sales was the perfection of moistureproof cellophane, a superior product of du Pont research and patented by that company through a 1927 application. Plain cellophane has little resistance to the passage of moisture vapor. Moisture-proof cellophane has a composition added which keeps moisture in and out of the packed commodity. This patented type of cellophane has had a demand with much more rapid growth than the plain.

In 1931 Sylvania began the manufacture of moistureproof cellophane under its own patents. After negotiations over patent rights, du Pont in 1933 licensed Sylvania to manufacture and sell moistureproof cellophane produced under the du Pont patents at a royalty of 2% of sales. These licenses with the plain cellophane licenses, from the Belgian company, made Sylvania a full cellophane competitor, limited on moistureproof sales by the terms of the licenses to 20% of the combined sales of the two companies of that type by the payment of a prohibitive royalty on the excess. There was never an excess production. The limiting clause was dropped on January 1, 1945, and Sylvania was acquired in 1946 by the American Viscose Corporation with assets of over two hundred million dollars.

Between 1928 and 1950, du Pont's sales of plain cellophane increased from $3,131,608 to $9,330,776. Moistureproof sales increased from $603,222 to $89,850,416, although prices were continuously reduced. It could not be said that this immense increase in use was solely or even largely attributable to the superior quality of cellophane or to the technique or business acumen of du Pont, though doubtless those factors were important. The growth was a part of the expansion of the commodity-packaging habits of business, a by-product of general efficient competitive merchandising to meet modern demands. The profits, which were large, apparently arose from this trend in marketing, the development of the industrial use of chemical research and production of synthetics, rather than from elimination of other producers from the relevant market. * * *

* * *

III. *The Sherman Act, § 2.* * * * If cellophane is the 'market' that du Pont is found to dominate, it may be assumed it does have monopoly power over that 'market.' Monopoly power is the power to control prices or exclude competition. It seems apparent that du Pont's power to set the price of cellophane has been limited only by the competition afforded by other flexible packaging materials. Moreover, it may be practically impossible for anyone to commence manufacturing cellophane without full access to du Pont's technique. However, du Pont has no power to prevent competition from other wrapping materials. The trial court consequently had to determine whether competition from the other wrappings prevented du Pont from possessing monopoly power in violation of Section 2. Price and competition are so intimately entwined that any discussion of theory must treat them as one. It is inconceivable that price could be controlled without power over competition or vice versa. This approach to the determination of monopoly power is strengthened by this Court's conclusion in prior cases that, when an alleged monopolist has power over price and competition, an intention to monopolize in a proper case may be assumed.

If a large number of buyers and sellers deal freely in a standardized product, such as salt or wheat, we have complete or pure competition. Patents, on the other hand, furnish the most familiar type of classic monopoly. As the producers of a standardized product bring about significant differentiations of quality, designed, or packaging in the product that permit differences of use, competition becomes to a greater or less degree incomplete and the producer's power over price and competition greater over his article and its use, according to the differentiation he is able to create and maintain. A retail seller may have in one sense a monopoly on certain trade because of location, as an isolated country store or filling station, or because no one else makes a product of just the quality or attractiveness of his product, as for example in cigarettes. Thus one can theorize that we have monopolistic competition in every nonstandardized commodity with each manufacturer having power over the price and production of his own product. However, this power that, let us say, automobile or soft-drink manufactures have over their trademarked products is not the power that makes an illegal monopoly. Illegal power must be appraised in terms of the competitive market for the product.

Determination of the competitive market for commodities depends on how different from one another are the offered commodities in character or use, how far buyers will go to substitute one commodity for another. For example, one can think of building materials as in commodity competition but one could hardly say that brick competed with steel or wood or cement or stone in the meaning of Sherman Act litigation; the products are too different. This is the interindustry competition emphasized by some economists. On the other hand, there are certain differences in the formulae for soft drinks but one can hardly say that each one is an illegal monopoly. Whatever the market may be, we hold that control of price or competition establishes the existence of monopoly power under Section 2. Section 2 requires the application of a reasonable approach in determining the existence of monopoly power just as surely as did Section 1. This of course does not mean that there can be a reasonable monopoly. Our next step is to determine whether du Pont has monopoly power over cellophane: that is, power over its price in relation to or competition with other commodities. The charge was monopolization of cellophane. The defense, that cellophane was merely a part of the relevant market for flexible packaging materials.

IV. *The Relevant Market.*—When a product is controlled by one interest, without substitutes available in the market, there is monopoly power. Because most products have possible substitutes, we cannot, as we said in *Times-Picayune Pub. Co. v. United States,* * * * give 'that infinite range' to the definition of substitutes. Nor is it a proper interpretation of the Sherman Act to require that products be fungible to be considered in the relevant market.

The Government argues:

'we do not here urge that in no circumstances may competition of substitutes negative possession of monopolistic power over trade in a product. The decisions make it clear at the least that the courts will not consider substitutes other than those which are substantially fungible with the monopolized product and sell at substantially the same price.'

But where there are market alternatives that buyers may readily use for their purposes, illegal monopoly does not exist merely because the product said to be monopolized differs from others. If it were not so, only physically identical products would be a part of the market. To accept the Government's argument, we would have to conclude that the manufactures of plain as well as moistureproof cellophane were monopolists, and so with films such as Pliofilm, foil, glassine, polyethylene, and Saran, for each of these wrapping materials is distinguishable. These were all exhibits in the case. New wrappings appear, generally similar to cellophane, is each a monopoly? What is called for is an appraisal of the 'cross-elasticity' of demand in the trade. The varying circumstances of each case determine the result. In considering what is the relevant market for determining the control of price and competition, no more definite rule can be declared than that commodities reasonably interchangeable by consumers for the same purposes make up that 'part of the trade or commerce', monopolization of which may be illegal. As respects flexible packaging materials, the market geographically is nationwide.

* * * In determining the market under the Sherman Act, it is the use or uses to which the commodity is put that control. The selling price between commodities with similar uses and different characteristics may vary, so that the cheaper product can drive out the more expensive. Or, the superior quality of higher priced articles may make dominant the more desirable. Cellophane costs more than many competing products and less than a few. But whatever the price, there are various flexible wrapping materials that are bought by manufacturers for packaging their goods in their own plants or are sold to converters who shape and print them for use in the packaging of the commodities to be wrapped.

Cellophane differs from other flexible packaging materials. From some it differs more than from others. The basic materials from which the wrappings are made * * * are aluminum, cellulose acetate, chlorides, wood pulp, rubber hydrochloride, and ethylene gas. It will adequately illustrate the similarity in characteristics of the various products by noting here * * * glassine. Its use is almost as extensive as cellophane, and many of its characteristics equally or more satisfactory to users.

It may be admitted that cellophane combines the desirable elements of transparency, strength and cheapness more definitely than any of the others. * * *

But, despite cellophane's advantages it has to meet competition from other materials in every one of its uses. * * * Food products are the chief outlet, with cigarettes next. The Government makes no challenge to [the trial court's finding] that cellophane furnishes less than 7% of wrappings for bakery products, 25% for candy, 32% for snacks, 35% for meats and poultry, 27% for crackers and biscuits, 47% for fresh produce, and 34% for frozen foods. Seventy-five to eighty percent of cigarettes are wrapped in cellophane.

Thus, cellophane shares the packaging market with others. The over-all result is that cellophane accounts for 17.9% of flexible wrapping materials, measured by the wrapping surface.

Moreover a very considerable degree of functional interchangeability exists between these products * * *. It will be noted * * * that except as to permeability to gases, cellophane has no qualities that are not possessed by a number of other materials. Meat will do as an example of interchangeability. Although du Pont's sales to the meat industry have reached 19,000,000 pounds annually, nearly 35%, this volume is attributed 'to the rise of self-service retailing of fresh meat.' In fact, since the popularity of self-service meats, du Pont has lost 'a considerable proportion' of this packaging business to Pliofilm. Pliofilm is more expensive than cellophane, but its superior physical characteristics apparently offset cellophane's price advantage. While retailers shift continually between the two, the trial court found that Pliofilm is increasing its share of the business. One further example is worth noting. Before World War II, du Pont cellophane wrapped between 5 and 10% of baked and smoked meats. The peak year was 1933. Thereafter du Pont was unable to meet the competition of Sylvania and of greaseproof paper. Its sales declined and the 1933 volume was not reached again until 1947. It will be noted that greaseproof paper, glassine, waxed paper, foil and Pliofilm are used as well as cellophane. * * *

An element for consideration as to cross-elasticity of demand between products is the responsiveness of the sales of one product to price changes of the other. If a slight decrease in the price of cellophane causes a considerable number of customers of other flexible wrappings to switch to cellophane, it would be an indication that a high cross-elasticity of demand exists between them; that the products compete in the same market. The court below held that the '(g)reat sensitivity of customers in the flexible packaging markets to price or quality changes' prevented du Pont from possessing monopoly control over price. The record sustains these findings.

We conclude that cellophane's interchangeability with the other materials mentioned suffices to make it a part of this flexible packaging material market.

The Government stresses the fact that the variation in price between cellophane and other materials demonstrates they are noncompetitive. As these products are all flexible wrapping materials, it seems reasonable to consider, as was done at the trial, their comparative cost to the consumer in terms of square area. * * *. Cellophane costs two or three times as much, surface measure, as its chief competitors for the flexible wrapping market, glassine and greaseproof papers. Other forms of cellulose wrappings and those from other chemical or mineral substances, with the exception of aluminum foil, are more expensive. The uses of these materials * * * are largely to wrap small packages for retail distribution. The wrapping is a relatively small proportion of the entire cost of the article. Different producers need different qualities in wrappings and their need may vary from time to time as their products undergo change. But the necessity for flexible wrappings is the central and unchanging demand. We cannot say that these differences in cost gave du Pont monopoly power over prices in view of the findings of fact on that subject.

It is the variable characteristics of the different flexible wrappings and the energy and ability with which the manufacturers push their wares that determine choice. A glance at 'Modern Packaging,' a trade journal, will give, by its various advertisements, examples of the competition among manufacturers for the flexible packaging market. The trial judge visited the 1952 Annual Packaging Show at Atlantic City, with the consent of counsel. He observed exhibits offered by 'machinery manufacturers, converters and manufacturers of flexible packaging materials.' He stated that these personal observations confirmed his estimate of the competition between cellophane and other packaging materials. * * *

The facts above considered dispose also of any contention that competitors have been excluded by du Pont from the packaging material market. That market has many producers and there is no proof du Pont ever has possessed power to exclude any of them from the rapidly expanding flexible packaging market. The Government apparently concedes as much, for it states that 'lack of power to inhibit entry into this so-called market (i.e., flexible packaging materials), comprising widely disparate products, is no indicium of absence of power to exclude competition in the manufacture and sale of cellophane.' The record shows the multiplicity of competitors and the financial strength of some with individual assets running to the hundreds of millions. Indeed, the trial court found that du Pont could not exclude competitors even from the manufacture of cellophane, an immaterial matter if the market is flexible packaging material. Nor can we say that du Pont's profits, while liberal (according to the Government 15.9% net after taxes on the 1937—1947 average), demonstrate the existence of a monopoly without proof of lack of comparable profits during those years in other prosperous industries. Cellophane was a leader over 17%, in the flexible packaging materials market. There is no showing that du Pont's rate of return was greater or less than that of other producers of flexible packaging materials.

The 'market' which one must study to determine when a producer has monopoly power will vary with the part of commerce under consideration. The tests are constant. That market is composed of products that have reasonable interchangeability for the purposes for which they are produced—price, use and qualities considered. While the application of the tests remains uncertain, it seems to us that du Pont should not be found to monopolize cellophane when that product has the competition and interchangeability with other wrappings that this record shows.

On the findings of the District Court, its judgment is affirmed.

[Justice FRANKFURTER's concurring opinion is omitted].

[The dissenting opinion of Mr. Chief Justice WARREN, with whom Mr. Justice BLACK and Mr. Justice DOUGLAS joined, is omitted.]

––––––

The outcome in *du Pont (Cellophane)* hinged on the definition of the relevant market. If the market was limited to cellophane, du Pont held a market share of nearly 75 percent, and the Supreme Court would have deemed it to have monopoly power. In a market defined as all flexible packaging materials, du Pont's market share was less than 20 percent—far below the threshold earlier cases had associated with dominance. The Supreme Court majority chose the second of these definitions and absolved the company of Section 2 liability.

Although the Court majority's ultimate conclusion has been sharply disputed, its basic methodology has become a staple element of antitrust analysis. In beginning its discussion of du Pont's market significance, Justice Reed provided what remains the most frequently cited definition of monopoly power in Sherman Act jurisprudence. "Monopoly power," the Court stated, "is the power to control prices or exclude competition." As the Court's analysis of du Pont's position in the wrapping materials sector indicates, this formula anticipates the use of market shares and other forms of circumstantial evidence to infer the existence of power to control prices. The Court's definition also reminds us that market shares are not the sole means for identifying monopoly power. It remains open for the plaintiff to offer other forms of proof that the defendant possesses substantial market power, perhaps by introducing evidence showing how the defendant has excluded rivals from the market.

To define the relevant market, the Court stated that "no more definite rule can be declared than that commodities reasonably interchangeable by consumers for the same purposes make up that 'part of the trade or commerce', monopolization of which may be illegal." This doctrinal test focuses upon *buyer substitution* possibilities. As it suggests, market definition seeks to identify the products (and geographic locations) that encompass the practical alternatives available to buyers, considering the price, use and qualities of those choices. The Court highlights the economic concept of buyer substitution by equating its "reasonably interchangeable" in demand formulation for market definition doctrine with "cross-elasticity of demand between products," an economic concept (discussed further below) which, the Court explains, relates to "the responsiveness of the sales of one product to price changes of the other." *Accord Brown Shoe Co. v. United States*, 370 U.S. 294, 325 (1962). The Court reiterated its emphasis on buyer substitution possibilities as the linchpin of market definition in 1964, when it issued a merger decision placing insulated copper conductor and insulated aluminum conductor in separate markets because of insufficient demand substitution, over a vigorous dissent that highlighted extensive supply substitution (production flexibility) between the two. *United States v. Aluminum Co. of Am.*, 377 U.S. 271 (1964) (*Rome Cable*). This demand-side orientation—delineating the product market according to the customer's view of which products (or geographic locations) are acceptable substitutes for each other—continues to provide the basic framework for delineating relevant markets today.*

Some contemporary courts follow the lead of the *Rome Cable* dissent, and expand markets to account for supply substitution as well as demand substitution. *See, e.g., Menasha Corp. v. News America Marketing In–Store, Inc.,* 354 F.3d 661 (7th Cir. 2004) (Easterbrook, J.). Deviation from an exclusive demand-side focus is rarely employed when markets are defined for the

---

*In defining antitrust markets in both merger and monopolization settings, courts have historically treated as relevant authority cases decided under Sherman Act § 2 (*Cellophane*) and those decided under Clayton Act § 7 (*Rome Cable, Brown Shoe*). Doing so is consistent with the concept-oriented perspective of modern antitrust, and we follow that practice here.

purpose of analyzing mergers, however. (*Menasha* was decided under the Sherman Act, as were the two monopolization cases discussed in the first paragraph of Sidebar 8–6, below, where markets were also broadened to account for the possibility of supply substitution.) For a defense of the demand-side orientation of market definition, see Jonathan B. Baker, *Market Definition: An Analytical Overview*, 74 Antitrust L.J. 129, 132–38 (2007).

Note on Cross–Price Elasticity of Demand

The elasticity of demand discussed in Chapter 1 is what economists term the *own*-price elasticity of demand. It asks how responsive a product's buyers are, in the aggregate, to changes in the product's own price. If price rises, do buyers tend to stick with the product (making demand relatively inelastic) or do they tend to reduce their purchases (making demand relatively elastic)? As the coffee discussion in Chapter 1 suggested, if the demand for a product is highly elastic (extremely responsive to changes in its own price), even a monopolist of that product would find it unprofitable to exercise market power. This economic insight underlies the market definition formula of the Merger Guidelines, which we will meet shortly.

The *cross*-price elasticity of demand asks a different question: how responsive are a product's buyers to changes in the price of a *different* product. If the quantity of brown paper wrapping sold, for example, increases when the price of cellophane rises, the two products are *substitutes* in demand.* Quantitatively, the cross-price elasticity of demand between products A and B can be expressed as the percentage change in quantity for product A, divided by the percentage change in price for product B. Cross-elasticities need not be symmetric: it is possible, for example, that cellophane sales increase a great deal when the price of brown paper wrapping rises (high cross-elasticity), but, simultaneously, that the quantity of brown paper wrapping sold does not rise very much in response to an increase in the price of cellophane (low cross-elasticity). If a product outside a proposed relevant market has a high cross-elasticity with the products included in the market, that observation suggests that the excluded product provides a relatively close substitute to buyers of the included products, and thus that the excluded product is a candidate for inclusion by expanding the market. (Demand cross-elasticities are also relevant to the analysis of unilateral effects among sellers of differentiated products, as will be discussed below in section C.2.b of this chapter.)

Sidebar 5–4:
The *Cellophane* Fallacy

The Court majority's conclusion in *Cellophane* that other flexible packaging materials such as glassine and pliofilm significantly constrained du Pont in setting cellophane prices aroused considerable criticism. The Court majority reasoned that, because du Pont's efforts to raise cellophane prices induced users to switch to other products, the company

---

* Products could instead be *complements* in demand. If peanut butter and jelly are usually used together to make sandwiches, one might expect that peanut butter sales would fall when the price of jelly rises (as would jelly sales). In short: if the price of one good rises, that will lead to an increase in quantity sold for substitute products and a decrease in quantity sold for demand complements.

lacked substantial market power. The flaw in this analysis is that the switching to other products may have taken place after du Pont already had set cellophane prices at monopoly levels and was trying to boost them still further. The fact of substitution by itself tells us relatively little about the effectiveness of the substitute products in curbing du Pont's power to control prices. At some price, virtually all products confront substitutes. If prices for trans-Atlantic airline tickets rose enough, larger numbers of travelers would begin crossing the ocean by ship. An increase in purchases of steamship tickets would not negate the possibility that the airlines had market power. It would merely show that the airlines' power over price is not infinite and that there is a price at some level at which prospective passengers seek alternative means of transit. Later commentary on *du Pont* would refer to the Court majority's conclusion that the presence of substitution precluded a finding of monopoly power as the "*Cellophane* fallacy."

The lesson of this controversy is in the importance of relating market definition to the allegation of harm to competition. When the allegations concern *past* exercise of market power, as they did in *Cellophane*, the market definition question should be whether buyer substitution would have made it unprofitable for firms to raise price from the original, lower and more competitive level. Evidence about likely buyer substitution in the event of a *further* price increase does not necessarily bear on this question; this is what the Supreme Court failed to recognize.

What if it is not practical to assess the profitability of a price increase from a competitive price? For example, what if the last price that both sides of the antitrust dispute would agree was competitive had been charged a long time in the past, and information about the extent of buyer substitution at that time is no longer available? It may still be possible to reduce the potential for error in assessing the constraint posted by substitute products or locations by investigating buyer responses to a hypothetical price *decrease* from the current level (rather than analyzing buyer responses to a price increase, as is common when the allegations concern a prospective exercise of market power).

In contrast, when the allegations concern likely *future* exercise of market power, as they generally do when mergers are proposed before consummation, it is typically appropriate to define markets by asking whether buyer substitution would make it unprofitable for firms to raise price from the *current* price level. The importance of relating the approach to market definition to the allegations of anticompetitive harm in this and other contexts is highlighted in Steven C. Salop, *The First Principles Approach to Antitrust,* Kodak, *and Antitrust at the Millennium,* 68 ANTITRUST L.J. 187 (2000).

b. *Market Definition Under the Merger Guidelines*

The goal of market definition is to facilitate a prediction as to whether a given merger or acquisition is likely to result in the exercise of market power in an industry. As we will learn later in this Chapter, the exercise of such market power might be a result of coordination among the merging firms and other firms in the industry ("coordinated effects") or a result of efforts by the merging firms alone to raise price or otherwise restrict competition ("unilateral effects").

For market definition to serve the goal of aiding in the prediction of such anticompetitive effects, it is first necessary to identify the products or services sold by the merging firms, the geographic areas in which they are offered for sale, and the collection of substitute products or services available to buyers from other sellers. Substitutes must be considered in terms of the products ("relevant product market") and geographic locations ("relevant geographic market") to which a buyer could turn for substitutes. Over or under-inclusive market definitions may not provide a reliable basis for making predictions about a merger's likely competitive effects.

Under the modern Merger Guidelines approach to merger analysis, the market definition step takes into account the economic force of demand (or buyer) substitution: the possibility that buyers would defeat an attempt by sellers to exercise market power by purchasing alternative products in place of those for which price has risen. Through this approach to market definition, market concentration statistics are connected to the economic concept of market power, for which concentration is a surrogate. Thus, for example, it would probably make no sense to define a geographic market for restaurants limited to one block in a large city, and stop a merger of the only two restaurants in that block on the ground that their combination would create a firm with a 100% market share. Many diners probably would be willing to substitute restaurants in the next block, or go out to eat in a different part of town, in the event lunch and dinner prices were to rise on the block where the merging restaurants were located. As a consequence, it would be unlikely that the post-merger price increase would be profitable, which calls into question whether it was appropriate to define the city block as a relevant geographic market.

Other economic forces relevant to merger analysis are accounted for at other steps of the Guidelines' approach. In particular, supply substitution (also called production flexibility) is examined in the identification of market participants and in the analysis of entry, and the nature of rivalry among the firms in the market is addressed in competitive effects analysis.

The Guidelines' focus on demand substitution as the basis of market definition is consistent with the Supreme Court's doctrinal formulation in *Cellophane* that product markets are collections of goods with "reasonable interchangeability" in demand. The Guidelines go beyond the case law by suggesting a metric–a conceptual answer to the question of "how much buyer substitution would be sufficient to preclude a proposed market definition." In particular, the Merger Guidelines define a market as a collection of product or services, and a geographic region that would form a valuable monopoly. Were a hypothetical monopolist of the products and region in the market to raise price, that act would likely be profitable, as most buyers would pay more rather than respond by substituting alternatives outside the market. *Horizontal Merger Guidelines* §§ 1.0, 1.11, and 1.21.

The approach to market definition under the Merger Guidelines can also be understood as an algorithm. It begins by specifying as a candidate market each product sold by either merging firm and the location at which it is sold. A candidate market is recognized as a relevant antitrust market if a hypothetical monopolist pursuing maximum profits would increase the price of some or all of the products, at some or all of the locations, by a "small but significant and nontransitory" amount (sometimes referred to as a "SSNIP") relative to the prices that would likely prevail but-for the merger under review (usually pre-merger prices). If the hypothetical monopolist would not find a SSNIP profitable, the candidate market is expanded by adding the next-best substitute, the new candidate market is tested to determine whether it constitutes a relevant antitrust market, and so on until a market is identified. More simply, if it would not be profitable to monopolize the candidate market, the market is expanded by adding products or regions until it would be profitable to do so.

In most contexts, the SSNIP is a price increase of five percent lasting for the foreseeable future. This 5% figure is a benchmark for a conceptual experiment defining markets, not a tolerance level. A merger within a relevant market would be considered anticompetitive if it appears likely to lead to any increase in price, no matter how small. Thus, potential substitutes that would not become available in time to prevent a hypothetical monopolist from raising price profitably in the short run would be excluded from the market. *See United States v. Microsoft Corp.*, 253 F.3d 34, 53–54 (D.C. Cir. 2001) (market definition requires that a court "consider only substitutes that constrain pricing in the reasonably foreseeable future, and only products that can enter the market in a relatively short time can perform this function").

The market definition approach of the Horizontal Merger Guidelines generally begins with the prevailing prices of the products of the merging firms and possible substitutes for those products. This approach grandfathers in any existing market power in the industry, and focuses the competitive effects analysis on the question of whether the merger will likely make the exercise of market power worse. It does not emphasize the possibility that the merger would prevent the erosion of market power and a decline in price. The Guidelines thus choose not to address the possibility of committing the *Cellophane* fallacy (see Sidebar 5–4), other than with two exceptions that are rarely employed in practice. First, when "changes in the prevailing prices can be predicted with reasonable reliability," the Guidelines begin the analysis with "likely future prices, absent the merger." Second, when "premerger circumstances are strongly suggestive of coordinated interaction," the Guidelines begin the analysis with "a price more reflective of the competitive price." *Horizontal Merger Guidelines* § 1.11.

Although some have criticized the Guidelines' approach to market definition as difficult to implement in practice, the federal enforcement agencies have become adept at developing evidence related to answering the Guidelines' central "hypothetical monopolist" question. An example of how a disputed market definition might be resolved will suggest some types of evidence that might be brought to bear. When the Federal Trade Commission sought a preliminary injunction against Coca–Cola's proposed acquisition of the Dr Pepper soft drink brand in the mid–1980s, the FTC staff proposed an "all carbonated soft drink" product market, in which the merging firms would have a combined market share of 42%, while Coke proposed a broader product market consisting of "all beverages," in which the merger partners would have a much lower combined market share, and the transaction would not appear likely to raise a competitive problem.* As this example suggests, plaintiffs in merger cases typically ask courts to define more narrow markets than those proposed by defendants, in order to make markets appear highly concentrated. Occasionally, however, a defendant will propose a market so narrow as to make the merging firms' products appear to lie in different markets, and thus make the transaction not appear to affect horizontal competition.

To decide between alternatives such as these, the Merger Guidelines focus on whether a hypothetical collusive price increase among sellers of a product would be profitable, or whether it would be made unprofitable by buyers responding to the high price by switching their purchases to other products or consuming less. Direct evidence of demand substitution might be obtained from examining buyer responses to price increases in the past or a survey of their likely responses in the future. The survey approach is simple. Buyers might be asked directly: "Would a 5% or 10% increase in the price of the merging firms lead you to switch to another product? For what fraction of your purchases?"

Evidence about the response of buyers to price changes could be anecdotal or systematic (*e.g.*, from an econometric (statistical) analysis of pricing data collected from sellers of the product). It may include studies of the elasticity of demand (*see* Casebook, Chapter 1) or a comparison of the price in monopolized markets with the price in otherwise similar markets thought to perform competitively (see the discussion of *Staples* later in this Chapter).

How much demand substitution would be too much to make a price increase unprofitable? Evidence about the extent of demand substitution in response to a price increase (the elasticity of demand) is often calibrated in relationship to accounting measures of price-cost margins. *See generally* Gregory J. Werden, *Demand Elasticities in Antitrust Analysis*, 66 ANTITRUST L. J. 363 (1998). But there is a debate as to what can be learned from this comparison. It is often observed that if price is well in excess of variable cost, then lost sales are very costly to the firms (in the form of foregone profits). Under such circumstances, even a small degree of buyer substitution in response to a price increase could make unprofitable the exercise of market power, and thus could suggest that the proposed market is defined too narrowly. Similarly, this logic runs, if industry price-cost margins are narrow, it may be appropriate to define a relevant market even if a small price increase would lead to a substantial amount of buyer substitution (that is, even if industry demand is fairly elastic). But this logic is not the only way to relate price-cost margins and buyer substitution. If industry price-cost margins are high, the reason may be that firms have learned that buyers do not readily substitute away from the product in response to price increases, suggesting that a narrow market is appropriate. Similarly, narrow price-cost margins may suggest that the firms believe that buyer substitution would be extensive, suggesting that a broader market should be appropriate.

---

* Although the district court that reviewed the FTC's preliminary injunction request did not report concentration estimates for the market alleged by Coke, it did observe that carbonated soft drinks accounted for less than one fourth (approximately 22.3%) of per capita beverage consumption in the U.S. at the time of the litigation. *FTC v. Coca-Cola Co.*, 641 F.Supp. 1128, 1133 (D.D.C. 1986), *vacated and remanded mem.*, 829 F.2d 191 (D.C. Cir. 1987).

If buyer substitution patterns are known to depend on the characteristics of products or geographic locations (perhaps because that relationship is widely recognized in the industry), indirect evidence about the extent of demand substitution might be obtained from examining the distribution of product or locational characteristics. For example, if a large group of soft drink buyers were known to consider carbonation a very important product attribute, then sparkling water might be a more plausible substitute, and thus a more plausible candidate for inclusion in the market, than fruit juices. In other industries, information about the nature and distribution of buyer switching costs might permit a similar inference.

Indirect evidence on the extent of likely buyer substitution might also be obtained from the views and actions taken by sellers, who have an economic interest in understanding buyer substitution patterns. Such evidence may appear in marketing documents of the merging firms or testimony of their marketing executives that shows whether the firms track and respond to the prices of beverages other than soft drinks. The focus is on identifying which rivals the firms routinely monitor and respond to, as a guide to seller views about likely buyer substitution responses to price increases. This may differ from the scope of the "market" identified by the sellers in their documents, as the relevant market for antitrust purposes need not be the same as what firms and their executives call the market for different purposes. Indirect evidence as to likely buyer substitution patterns in the event prices were to rise may also be found in the testimony of industry experts, in this case perhaps experienced soft drink merchandisers at grocery stores or other beverage firms. Moreover, if a product's costs rise but its prices do not, that observation suggests that sellers view product demand as highly elastic.

Evidence of similarities or differences in product prices is generally not indicative of likely buyer substitution responses. After all, in many settings, buyers may choose between high-price/high-quality products and low-price/low-quality products. For example, some buyers of high-priced custom suits might respond to a price increase for that product by switching to less expensive suits sold off-the-rack (or vice versa, responding to higher department store prices by switching to a custom tailor). Under such circumstances, it would not be correct to use high price (or low price) as a basis for market definition. However, if other evidence (not involving product price points) demonstrates that buyers of high-priced/high-quality pens, for example, would not switch to low-priced/low-quality pens in the event the price of high-quality pens were to rise, high-quality pens might constitute a product market—and the bounds of that market might conveniently be described in terms of fountain pens priced above a certain level. *See United States v. Gillette Co.*, 828 F.Supp. 78, 81–83 (D.D.C.1993)(defining market for premium writing instruments priced between $50 and $400).

Typically, no one type of evidence is dispositive, and a wide range of other information not listed here may also bear on the market definition question. Moreover, the probative value of direct and indirect evidence may vary from case to case; the classification scheme presented here is an aid to understanding, not a ranking indicating the types of evidence that are to be preferred. For a more detailed survey of market definition issues, see Jonathan B. Baker, *Market Definition: An Analytical Overview*, 74 ANTITRUST L.J. 129 (2007).

When the 1986 Coke/Dr Pepper merger case was tried, the district court agreed with the FTC on a carbonated soft drink product market, and enjoined the merger. In support of its product market definition, the court noted that the major soft drink producers "make pricing and marketing decisions based primarily on comparisons with rival carbonated soft drink products, with little if any concern about possible competition from other beverages such as milk, coffee, beer or fruit juice." *FTC v. Coca–Cola Co.*, 641 F.Supp. 1128, 1133 (D.D.C.1986), *vacated and remanded mem.*, 829 F.2d 191 (D.C. Cir. 1987).

The soft drink merger example focuses on product market definition. The same kinds of evidence are equally relevant to geographic market definition. Is the Washington, D.C. metropolitan area a relevant geographic market for analyzing a merger among soft drink producers? Under the Merger Guidelines' approach to answering this question, a court would be led to ask whether a hypothetical soft drink monopoly in Washington would be made unprofitable by consumers traveling to Baltimore to buy soft drinks. (The possibility that Baltimore firms would respond by opening soft drink stands in Washington is a supply substitution response that is relevant to analyzing the competitive effects of the merger, but would not be accounted for in the market definition step of the analysis under the Guidelines' approach.) Evidence of demand substitution away from Washington in response to a price rise could come from many sources, including the following: buyer responses to past price increases in Washington (where the price in Baltimore did not change); a survey of likely buyer responses to a price hike in Washington; information about the distribution of buyer and product characteristics (*e.g.*, what fraction of Washington area residents live very close to Baltimore area retailers?); evidence concerning the locations sellers monitor and respond to (*e.g.*, do Washington area sellers pay attention to what Baltimore sellers charge for soft drinks); and views of industry experts.

Sidebar 5–5:
Controversies in Market Definition:
Submarkets, Price Discrimination Markets,
and Cluster Markets

This Sidebar examines three controversies involving market definition: submarkets, price discrimination markets, and cluster markets.

Submarkets

One early list of evidence potentially relevant to market definition was provided by the Supreme Court in *Brown Shoe*, in connection with the Court's endorsement of the possibility of "submarkets" within a broader market:

> The outer boundaries of a product market are determined by the reasonable interchangeability of use or the cross-elasticity of demand between the product itself and substitutes for it. However, within this broad market, well-defined submarkets may exist which, in themselves, constitute product markets for antitrust purposes. The boundaries of such a submarket may be determined by examining such practical indicia as industry or public

recognition of the submarket as a separate economic entity, the product's peculiar characteristics and uses, unique production facilities, distinct customers, distinct prices, sensitivity to price changes, and specialized vendors. Because § 7 of the Clayton Act prohibits any merger which may substantially lessen competition "in *any* line of commerce" (emphasis supplied), it is necessary to examine the effects of a merger in each such economically significant submarket to determine if there is a reasonable probability that the merger will substantially lessen competition. If such a probability is found to exist, the merger is proscribed.

Brown Shoe, 370 U.S. at 325 (footnotes and citation omitted). Several of the seven *Brown Shoe* "practical indicia" appear related to the identification of buyer substitution patterns. Others appear related to the possibility of seller substitution, accounted for in the contemporary Merger Guidelines in the identification of market participants or the analysis of entry. Still others relate to the possibility of "price discrimination" markets (discussed later in this Sidebar) or unilateral adverse competitive effects of mergers (discussed later in this chapter).

In addition to its value in pointing lower courts toward potentially relevant evidence of buyer substitution patterns, this paragraph from *Brown Shoe* was influential in its endorsement of "submarkets." Submarkets continue to be defined by lower courts, as we will see later in this Chapter when we read *FTC v. Staples*, where the court defined a product market with reference to a particular distribution channel ("the sale of consumable office supplies through office supply superstores"). But this practice has been criticized. Critics emphasize that when the *Brown Shoe* practical indicia are applied blindly, without reference to the economic goal of identifying buyer substitution possibilities, they may allow courts to define inappropriately narrow submarkets within the outer bounds of markets properly defined with reference to substitution possibilities. For a survey of the uses and abuses of antitrust submarkets, see Jonathan B. Baker, *Stepping Out in an Old Brown Shoe: In Qualified Praise of Submarkets*, 68 ANTITRUST L.J. 203 (2000).

Price Discrimination Markets

The Merger Guidelines employ the term "price discrimination market" to describe the situation where a hypothetical monopolist of a group of products and geographic locations would likely charge different prices to different groups of buyers, and in consequence raise prices to a class of targeted buyers. *Horizontal Merger Guidelines* §§ 1.12, 1.22. For example, if a passenger airline monopolist would find it profitable to raise fares to business passengers (buying unrestricted tickets) on city-pair routes by a small but significant amount, then business fares (unrestricted tickets) on those routes would constitute a relevant market. This market could be described as a price discrimination market: the product market would be passenger air travel; the geographic market would be the city pairs, and business travelers would constitute the set of targeted buyers.

In order for price discrimination to be successful, the airline must be able to distinguish reliably between those buyers willing to pay a high price (here business travelers) and those that are not. The introduction of tickets with fare restrictions might be a way of sorting out leisure travelers from business passengers, for example. If doing so is impossible, the ability of leisure travelers to substitute connecting flights or driving for non-stop travel on a city-pair route might make it unprofitable for the airline to raise fares on that route. In addition, the buyers charged a low price must be unable to resell the product cheaply to the buyers charged a high price. In the airline industry, the necessary prohibition on buyer arbitrage is enforced by the requirement that passengers present identification at the airport consistent with the name on their ticket. (For further discussion of the economics of price discrimination, see Sidebar 7–8.)

Targeted buyers are often distinguished by their uses or locations. For example, one court limited a product market to latex condoms sold through retail outlets in the United States, excluding condom sales to the U.S. Agency for International Development (USAID) for distribution free of charge in third-world countries. *Ansell Inc. v. Schmid Laboratories, Inc.*, 757 F.Supp. 467 (D.N.J.), *aff'd*, 941 F.2d 1200 (3d Cir.1991). Another court upheld a market defined as the sale of new components for automotive electrical units to production-line rebuilders, excluding sales to repair shops. *Avnet, Inc. v. FTC*, 511 F.2d 70, 78–79 (7th Cir.), *cert. denied*, 423 U.S. 833 (1975).

Cluster Markets

In several bank merger cases in the 1960s and 1970s, beginning with *Philadelphia Nat'l Bank*, the Supreme Court employed a different approach to market definition, collecting into one product market the commercial banking "cluster of services." The Court determined that commercial banking activity—including loans and other types of credit, deposit accounts, checking services, and trust administration—constituted a unique cluster of products and services, distinct from those offered by savings and loans, finance companies, credit unions and other financial institutions. According to the Court in *Philadelphia Nat'l Bank*, banking services were clustered because distinctiveness, cost advantages, and "a settled consumer preference" insulated each commercial banking product from competition.

Lower courts have applied the cluster concept to define markets in a handful of other industry settings, including traditional grocery supermarkets, department stores, and "acute inpatient care" hospital services. The hospital example is instructive: courts have defined cluster markets in order to analyze hospital mergers even though the individual services that comprise the cluster are commonly recognized as relevant product markets in non-merger antitrust cases involving medical services provided by hospitals, as with anesthesiology services in *Jefferson Parish* (Casebook, Chapter 7, *infra*). The cluster market concept deviates from the demand substitution approach of the main line of Supreme Court market definition precedents and the Merger Guidelines because it includes in the same market products or services that are not substitutes from the standpoint of buyers.

All products are in a sense combinations of products that are not substitutes. In an appropriate case, automobiles could constitute a product market for antitrust analysis (perhaps, for example, if GM were accused of monopolization or if GM and Ford were to propose to merge), even though a car combines a chassis, engine, radio, etc. In fact, automobiles could be an appropriate product market for analyzing some allegations even though tires are relevant markets for analyzing other allegations (an agreement between Michelin and Goodyear to exchange information, perhaps). An automobile product market would be appropriate notwithstanding that it aggregates products that are not substitutes because the buyers alleged to have been harmed by the conduct under review purchase the aggregated product. Cluster markets are not defined by what buyers purchase, however; they are defined by the group of products that multi-product sellers offer.

Some commentators view cluster markets as merely a matter of analytic convenience: why bother to define separate markets for a large number of individual services when market shares and entry conditions are similar for each (or when data limitations will effectively require that the same proxy, such as number of hospital beds, be employed to estimate the market share for each individual service)? Other commentators suggest greater continuity with the judicial focus on demand substitution, and argue that clusters are properly defined when a seller can offer buyers substantial transactions costs savings from "one-stop shopping." *See* Ian Ayres, *Rationalizing Antitrust Cluster Markets*, 95 Yale L.J. 109 (1985). From either perspective, a proposed cluster market is called into question when competition from sellers of a partial line of products or services can constrain the pricing of the full line sellers offering the cluster.

c. *Identifying Market Participants*

After defining product and geographic markets, it is necessary to determine what firms sell in those markets before market concentration can be calculated. The Merger Guidelines count as firms participating in the market all firms that currently produce or sell in the market. *Horizontal Merger Guidelines* § 1.31. Although this step sounds straightforward, it involves a number of issues whose resolution may affect the concentration figures that result.

The Guidelines include vertically integrated firms as market participants "to the extent that such inclusion accurately reflects their competitive significance in the relevant market prior to the merger." To the extent that the market definition analysis indicates that used, reconditioned, or recycled goods should be included in the relevant market, firms selling such products are identified as market participants.

In addition, other firms not currently producing or selling the relevant product in the relevant geographic area may be counted as participating in the market if they could enter the market quickly, and enter without the prospect of incurring significant capital costs upon exit. *Horizontal Merger Guidelines* § 1.32. Specifically, an entrant is termed "uncommitted" by the Merger Guidelines if it would likely enter within one year, and without significant sunk expenditures, in response to a small but significant price increase. Sunk expenditures are investments that would not be recoverable in the event the firm were later to exit the market. Investments in office equipment might not be sunk, at least to the extent the firm could recover some or all of those expenditures were it to sell the equipment in the used market. But investments in tools and dyes specific to the firm's production process would be sunk to the extent they cannot be used by other firms, or by this firm in other plants selling to other markets. The significance of sunk expenditures is discussed more fully later in this chapter in connection with the analysis of entry. A firm that can enter quickly and without substantial sunk expenditures is more likely to enter the market in response to a short term profit opportunity. It can be thought of, therefore, as a "hit and run" entrant—available nimbly to come into the market in response to even a small increase in price, and ready to leave the market in the event that supply increases so much that price returns to its lower, pre-merger level.

As previously noted, some courts deviate from the Merger Guidelines approach to market definition by expanding markets to reflect seller substitution (production flexibility). In the Merger Guidelines, this important economic force is not addressed in market definition but is divided in two and treated in two places: the identification of market participants, a subject of this section, and the analysis of entry, which will be discussed in a later section of this chapter.

d. *Measuring Market Concentration*

With a market defined and market participants identified—including both incumbent sellers and uncommitted entrants—the stage is set to measure market concentration. A variety of units may be employed, including sales, shipments, production, capacity, or reserves—measured either in dollars or physical units. The choice of units does not usually make much difference to the picture of concentration that emerges, though the Guidelines suggest circumstances under which particular units of measurement may be the best indicator of the merging firms' future competitive significance. *Horizontal Merger Guidelines* § 1.41. *See generally* Gregory J. Werden, *Assigning Market Shares*, 70 ANTITRUST L. J. 67 (2002).

The Guidelines do not include a firm's sales or capacity in measuring its market share to the extent that the firm's capacity is committed or so profitably employed outside the relevant market that it would not be able to respond to an increase in price in the relevant market. By implication, uncommitted entrants are assigned a market share based on the capacity they would profitably divert to the relevant market in the event of a small but significant price increase. This approach accounts for the "opportunity cost" of diverting capacity: the profit or other benefit of using the resource in its next opportunity that must be forgone to put it to its present use. Assume, for example, that a widget producer currently sells widgets in San Francisco, but it is contemplating shifting some of its capacity to producing widgets for sale in New York City. The cost of selling a widget in the New York City market may be more than just the cost of producing and shipping the widget: if the widget could otherwise have been sold at a profit in the San Francisco market, the "lost" profit from the forgone opportunity to sell the widget in San Francisco is also part of the cost of selling the widget in New York.

Market concentration is examined using the Herfindahl–Hirschman Index (HHI). The HHI takes into account both the number and relative size of the firms in the market. It is computed by squaring the market share of each firm, and summing the resulting numbers. Thus, in a three firm market, in which firms have market shares a, b, and c, the HHI equals $a^2 + b^2 + c^2$. In the first example presented in Figure 5–5, markets 1 and 2 have a different number of firms and a different structure—one with three similarly-sized firms and two smaller sellers, the other with one firm twice the size of the next largest sellers—but their market concentration is summarized by the same HHI number. In contrast, markets 3 and 4 have the same number of firms, but very different HHIs. In reviewing these examples, ask yourself whether antitrust law should treat markets 1 and 2 as similarly structured, and markets 3 and 4 as differently structured, for the purpose of reviewing the likely competitive consequences of a horizontal merger.

One difference between the HHI and the leading prior approach to measuring concentration, the four-firm concentration ratio, is that the HHI takes into account the size distribution of the largest firms. The four-firm concentration ratio (C4) is the sum of the market shares of the four firms with the greatest market shares. Note that markets 3 and 4 in Figure 5–5 would be represented by the identical C4 (of 95%), but would have very different HHIs. Which index seems to you to capture best the extent of similarity or differences between these market structures?

Figure 5–5:
Understanding the HHI

Market 1

Firm	Market Share	Market Share Squared
A	30%	900
B	30%	900
C	25%	625
D	10%	100
E	5%	25
Total	**100%**	**HHI =2550**

Market 2

Firm	Market Share	Market Share Squared
A	40%	1600
B	20%	400
C	20%	400
D	10%	100
E	5%	25
F	5%	25
Total	**100%**	**HHI =2550**

Market 3

Firm	Market Share	Market Share Squared
A	80%	6400
B	5%	25
C	5%	25
D	5%	25
E	5%	25
Total	**100%**	**HHI =6500**

Market 4

Firm	Market Share	Market Share Squared
A	25%	625
B	25%	625
C	25%	625
D	20%	400
E	5%	25
Total	100%	HHI =2300

Calculating the Effect of a Merger on the HHI: Two Examples from Market 1

Example 1: Firm C acquires Firm D

Firm	Pre-Merger Market Share	Pre-Merger Market Share Squared	Post-Merger Market Share	Post-Merger Market Share Squared
A	30%	900	30%	900
B	30%	900	30%	900
C	25%	625	35%	1225
D	10%	100	--	--
E	5%	25	5%	25
Total	100%	HHI =2550	100%	HHI = 3050

Change in HHI from merger (also called "delta HHI" or "Δ HHI"): 3050-2550 = 500

Alternate calculation method for change in HHI (double the product of the merging firms' market shares): 2(25)(10) = 500.

Example 2: Firms A and B Merge

Firm	Pre-Merger Market Share	Pre-Merger Market Share Squared	Post-Merger Market Share	Post-Merger Market Share Squared
A	30%	900	60%	3600
B	30%	900	--	--
C	25%	625	25%	625
D	10%	100	10%	100
E	5%	25	5%	25
Total	**100%**	**HHI =2550**	**100%**	**HHI = 4350**

Change in HHI from merger (also called "delta HHI" or "Δ HHI"): 4350-2550 = 1800

Alternate calculation method for change in HHI (double the product of the merging firms' market shares): 2(30)(30) = 1800.

Note on Mathematical Properties of the HHI

The concentration standards in the Merger Guidelines concern (1) the post-merger HHI and (2) the change (increase) in the HHI resulting from the merger. The increase in the HHI (also termed the "delta HHI") can be computed by calculating the HHI based upon the pre-merger market structure and the HHI based upon the post-merger market structures, and subtracting the former from the latter. This process is illustrated in the final table in Figure 5–5. In the example, the merger of firms C and D raises the HHI from 2550 to 3050. Thus, the post-merger HHI is 3050, and the change in the HHI is 500. The change in the HHI can also be calculated from the pre-merger market shares of the merger partners, without need for determining the pre-merger or post-merger HHI. This is possible because, mathematically, the HHI has the property that the increase from merger equals double the product of the two market shares, as illustrated in the example.[*]

The HHI ranges from 0 to 10,000. An atomistic industry, with no firm having as much as 1% of the market, would have an HHI near zero. A monopolist, with 100% of the market, would have an HHI of 10,000. ($100^2 = 10,000$). If all firms in an industry were identically sized, the HHI would equal 10,000 divided by the number of firms. For example, a market with five identical firms, each holding 20%, would be characterized by an HHI of 2000. ($20^2 + 20^2 + 20^2 + 20^2 + 20^2 = 2000 = 10,000/5$). This mathematical property suggests that each HHI can be interpreted as a *numbers equivalent*: 10,000 divided by the HHI equals the number of identically-sized firms that would produce the same degree of market concentration measured by the HHI. For example, an HHI of 2550 has a numbers equivalent of 3.9 ($10,000/2550 = 3.9$), suggesting that the various market structures producing that HHI are roughly equivalent to an industry with slightly less than four equally-sized firms.

[*] This is an algebraic property of the HHI. The Horizontal Merger Guidelines (§ 1.51 n.18) explain:

In calculating the HHI before the merger, the market shares of the merging firms are squared individually: $(a)^2 + (b)^2$. After the merger, the sum of those shares would be squared: $(a + b)^2$, which equals $a^2 + 2ab + b^2$. The increase in the HHI therefore is represented by $2ab$.

Sidebar 5–6:
Inferring Market Power From Market Concentration:
The Economics of the Structural Presumption*

Economists have long attempted to identify empirically the relationship between market concentration and market power. Those efforts provide some justification for the structural presumption, but the relationship between concentration and market power is no longer thought to be as strong as was believed at the time of *Philadelphia Nat'l Bank*.

The original efforts at identifying the relationship, mainly published during the 1960s, sought to relate market concentration to firm profits. But these studies were subject to devastating criticism. The most important problem was emphasized by economist Harold Demsetz: if firms with high market shares have high price-cost margins (and thus high profits), is it because the large firms are able to exercise market power or because the large firms have obtained efficiencies that allow them to lower both costs and prices relative to their rivals? Harold Demsetz, *Two Systems of Belief About Monopoly, in* INDUSTRIAL CONCENTRATION: THE NEW LEARNING 164 (H.J. Goldschmid, H.M. Mann, and J.F. Weston, eds., 1974). Accordingly, a modern review of the studies finds: "The relation, if any, between seller concentration and profitability is weak statistically, and the estimated concentration effect is usually small. The estimated relation is unstable over time and space and vanishes in many multivariate studies." Richard Schmalensee, *Inter-Industry Studies of Structure and Performance, in* 2 HANDBOOK OF INDUSTRIAL ORGANIZATION 976 (R. Schmalensee and R. Willig, eds., 1989) (Stylized Fact 4.5).

In response, empirical economists led by Leonard Weiss sought to address these problems by relating market concentration to price. This approach had some success, particularly in analyses of different markets within the same industry. Critics of these studies emphasize two problems: it may be difficult to measure market concentration and to account adequately for the reverse effect of price on concentration. Still, the studies appear to find a relationship between market concentration and industry price. Thus, a modern survey concluded that "[i]n cross-section comparisons involving markets in the same industry, seller concentration is positively related to the level of price." Schmalensee, *Inter-Industry Studies, supra*, at 988 (Stylized Fact 5.1).

More recent studies, using empirical methodologies and data unavailable to Weiss, have reinforced his conclusion and made clear that increases in concentration, particularly substantial ones, may generate large increases in prices. For example, the results reported in Timothy F. Bresnahan & Valerie Y. Suslow, *Oligopoly Pricing with Capacity Constraints*, 15/16 ANNALES D'ECONOMIE ET DE STATISTIQUE 267 (1989), suggest that a merger in the North American aluminum industry during the 1960s and 1970s would have led to a price increase of 2.7% during cyclical downturns, when the firms were operating at excess capacity, for every

* This Sidebar was adapted from Jonathan B. Baker, *Mavericks, Mergers, and Exclusion: Proving Coordinated Competitive Effects Under the Antitrust Laws*, 77 N.Y.U. L. REV. 135 (2002).

100–point increase in the Herfindahl–Hirschman Index (HHI) of market concentration. Similarly, the FTC's econometric evidence showed that the proposed merger between Staples and Office Depot—which would have reduced the number of firms from three to two in some markets and two to one in others—would have raised price on average by about 8%. Jonathan B. Baker, *Econometric Analysis in* FTC v. Staples, 18 J. Pub. Pol'y & Marketing 11 (1999). These studies make careful efforts to account for differences in the competitive roles played by various firms, and distinguish between high costs and market power as the explanation for high prices.

But the empirical economic evidence does not support the structuralist view that high market concentration makes tacit collusion inevitable. While market concentration appears related to price, and improved prospects for tacit collusion offer one possible explanation, concentration is far from the only factor relevant to the assessment of whether the disappearance of a firm, through merger or exclusion, will facilitate coordination. The economic studies make it clear that other industry-specific and market-specific factors beyond concentration (such as the elasticity of market demand, the ability of firms to solve cartel problems, and the ease of entry and rival repositioning) are also important in determining price and the competitive effects of mergers. Moreover, the empirical research does not reliably identify any particular concentration level common across industries at which price increases kick in or raise particular competitive concerns. That is, there is no well-established "critical" concentration ratio.

The Merger Guidelines specify safe harbors for mergers in relatively unconcentrated markets or for mergers in more concentrated markets that do not increase concentration very much. *Horizontal Merger Guidelines* § 1.51. In particular, mergers are unlikely to be challenged if the post-merger HHI is below 1000 (unconcentrated markets); if the post-merger HHI is between 1000 and 1800 (moderately concentrated markets) and the HHI rises by no more than 100 points; or if the post-merger HHI is above 1800 (highly concentrated markets) and the HHI rises by no more than 50 points. Based on the numbers equivalent approach discussed above, these standards suggest that a market with at least the equivalent of ten equally-sized firms is regarded as unconcentrated, and that a market with less than the equivalent of five to six equally-sized firms (actually, a numbers equivalent of 5.56) is regarded as highly concentrated.

These concentration levels are not closely tied to empirical economic studies relating market concentration to price, though they are not inconsistent with such studies. (*See* Sidebar 5–1.). Rather, they appear to have been chosen to rationalize, in a rough way, the case law prior to the 1982 Justice Department Merger Guidelines, where the HHI was first adopted for merger analysis. One pair of commentators have suggested that "Had the HHI standards set forth in the [1982] Guidelines been applied during the Warren Court era, most of the leading merger cases would have reached the same result." Donald I. Baker & William Blumenthal, *The 1982 Guidelines and Preexisting Law*, 71 Cal. L. Rev. 311, 334 (1983). They recognize *Von's Grocery*, however, as an exception. *Id.* at 334 n.90.

For mergers that do not fall within safe harbors based on low market concentration, the Merger Guidelines call for further competitive analysis, with market shares taken into account to the extent they bear on the likely competitive effects of the transaction. The Guidelines recognize, consistent with the teaching of *General Dynamics*, that under some circumstances the historical market share of a firm may overstate its competitive significance. *Horizontal Merger Guidelines* § 1.521. Such circumstances are considered in interpreting market concentration and market share data.

The role of market definition and market concentration in modern-day merger analysis is highlighted by the district court opinion in *Cardinal Health*. The case was unusual because the government was simultaneously challenging two different mergers among leading firms in the same industry that had been proposed in close succession. Indeed, the first merger may have triggered the second, in recognition of the practical likelihood that the FTC and the court would analyze their competitive consequences in the same way if the two deals were reviewed simultaneously. The excerpt below focuses on product market definition issues, and the significance of market concentration in predicting the future competitive effects of a merger. In reading this case, notice how the court defines the relevant markets, identifies the firms that participate in them, and determines market concentration. What analytical issues did the court confront in undertaking each step?

FEDERAL TRADE COMMISSION v. CARDINAL HEALTH, INC.

United States District Court for the District of Columbia, 1998.
12 F. Supp. 2d 34.

SPORKIN, District Judge.

The Plaintiff Federal Trade Commission ("FTC") seeks to enjoin the proposed mergers of Defendants Cardinal Health, Inc. ("Cardinal") with Bergen–Brunswig Corp. ("Bergen") and McKesson Corp. ("McKesson") with AmeriSource Health Corp. ("AmeriSource"). * * * After careful consideration of all of the facts presented, this Court grants Plaintiff's motion for the reasons set forth below. * * *

I. BACKGROUND

The Defendants are Fortune 500 corporations listed on the New York Stock Exchange whose principal business is the nationwide wholesale distribution of prescription drugs. The four Defendants are the largest of the forty plus wholesale drug distributors in the United States. * * *

* * *

In the United States, the pharmaceutical industry is one of the most dynamic and important segments of the national economy. Due to the advances in medical science, there are a staggering number of prescription drugs for nearly every kind of health condition. Prescription drugs have become an essential elemental of modern health care. In 1997 alone, 94 billion dollars worth of prescription drugs were dispensed in the United States. Today, an individual can fill a prescription almost immediately, for there is a pharmacy around the corner in nearly every neighborhood in the United

States. Most pharmacies can fill a prescription on the spot, or at least guarantee next day delivery. The ease with which people can obtain their prescriptions requires an industry capable of delivering the needed drugs from the national manufacturers to the local dispensers. The dispensers of prescription drugs include the neighborhood independent pharmacies; chain pharmacies such as CVS, Rite–Aid, and Walgreens; hospitals; nursing homes; and alternate care sites.

The distribution and delivery of prescription drugs from the manufacturer to the dispenser is not an easy task. It involves not only the quick and efficient transportation of drugs on a daily basis, but also large facilities to keep a constant inventory of over 18,000 different brands of drugs in stock. Most of the retail outlets and institutions that dispense prescription drugs do not have the ability to store the large number and variety of drugs that they sell. In order to fill prescriptions on the spot each and every day, dispensers must be able to obtain the requested drugs on a continuous basis from the manufacturers as quickly as possible. Thus, the fast and efficient distribution of prescription drugs is a critical component of the pharmaceutical industry.

* * *

Of the 94 billion dollars in prescription drugs dispensed in 1997, 55 billion dollars (58.5% of the total) was distributed by wholesalers including the four Defendants. The other 39 billion dollars (41.5% of the total) was distributed through the other three channels, principally by direct delivery from the manufacturer. * * *

* * *

Traditionally, wholesalers bought the drugs from manufacturers, took ownership of the drugs in their own warehouses, and then in turn, resold them to the dispensers and delivered the goods direct to their individual stores and institutions. This traditional service is called "direct store delivery." In light the growing trend in the industry to self-warehouse, wholesalers have included in addition to this traditional delivery system "dock-to-dock" delivery and "drop shipment" charging. "Dock-to-dock" involves the wholesaler obtaining drugs in bulk from the manufacturer for direct delivery to a dispenser's own warehouse without taking the drugs into its own inventory. "Drop shipments" refer to when the manufacturer delivers the product directly to the customer, but the order and payment is made through the wholesaler. The combination of "drop ship" and "dock-to-dock" is known in the wholesaling industry as "brokerage."

Along with the delivery of pharmaceuticals, the wholesalers have a broad range of value added services that they can provide to their dispensing customers. These services are often not provided by the manufacturer and would be difficult and costly for the dispenser to reproduce them. Wholesalers have sophisticated ordering systems that allow customers to electronically order and confirm their purchases, as well as to confirm the availability and prices of wholesalers' stock. Wholesalers' inventory management systems help customers minimize inventory, customers can reduce inventory carrying costs while maintaining adequate inventory to meet patients' needs. Generic source programs enable wholesalers to combine the purchase volumes of customers and negotiate the cost of goods with generic manufacturers. Other services available from wholesalers include marketing and advertising programs, pharmacy networks for managed care plans, and software to assist with manufacturer bidding. * * *

* * *

Defendants contend that the proposed mergers are * * * their response to the mounting pressures to reduce cost, increase efficiency, and lower prices. After the mergers, the Defendants intend to begin an immediate plan of reorganization to lower cost and increase efficiency. Cardinal and Bergen announced that they plan to shut down and consolidate their combined 54 distribution centers into 29. This would include the opening of a few new facilities. Similarly, McKesson and AmeriSource publicly announced that they intend to consolidate their 54 distribution centers into 33, primarily by closing most of AmeriSource's existing facilities.

* * *

II.　ANALYSIS
* * *

For this Court to consider the likely competitive effects of the transactions, it must first define the relevant product and geographic boundaries of the markets in question. * * *

Defining the relevant market is critical in an antitrust case because the legality of the proposed mergers in question almost always depends upon the market power of the parties involved.[8]

In this case, the parties dispute the nature and scope of the relevant product market. The parties concede that in 1997, the total of all of the pharmaceutical sales in the United States was 94 billion dollars, 54 billion dollars of which was distributed through drug wholesalers. The other 39 billion dollars was distributed either directly by the manufacturers, through self-distribution, or through other alternative means such as mail order distribution. The FTC contends that the relevant product market is limited to the 54 billion dollar industry which specializes in the wholesale distribution of prescription drugs. The Defendants allege that the market as defined by the FTC is far too narrow. They claim that the relevant market in which to assess the likely competitive effects of the proposed mergers is the larger, 94 billion dollar prescription drug industry. In 1997, the wholesalers combined distributed only 57% of the total to be distributed. Upon careful consideration of all of the evidence presented in this case, the Court finds that the relevant product market is the wholesale distribution of prescription drugs, as advanced by the FTC.

In defining the relevant market, the Court is guided by the Supreme Court's leading opinion in *Brown Shoe Co. v. United States*, 370 U.S. 294, 82 S.Ct. 1502, 8 L.Ed.2d 510 (1962): "The outer boundaries of a product market are determined by the reasonable interchangeability of use or the cross-

---

8. This is because under Section 7 of the Clayton Act, enforcement of the anti-merger provisions proceeds from the premise that when a small group of firms occupies a large share of the relevant market, the firms can more easily coordinate sales policies in order to raise prices above competitive levels.

elasticity of demand between the product itself and substitutes for it." *Id.* at 325, 82 S.Ct. 1502. In other words, when one product is a reasonable substitute for the other, it is to be included in the same relevant product market even though the products themselves are not the same. * * * The degree to which a similar product may be substituted for the product in question–in this case, wholesale drug distribution–is said to measure the cross-elasticity of demand, while the capability of other production facilities to be converted to produce a substitute product is referred to as the cross-elasticity of supply. The higher these cross-elasticities, the more likely it is that the alternative products are to be counted in the relevant market. In other words, the relevant market consists of all of the products that the Defendants' customers view as substitutes to those supplied by the Defendants. Thus, in this case, if enough customers view other forms of prescription drug delivery methods as acceptable substitutes to the services provided by the Defendants, then the relevant market should include these alternative methods. On the other hand, if customers do not view the other methods of distribution as viable substitutes, then the relevant product market should be limited to the wholesalers' services. * * * Accordingly, the Court must determine whether, based upon the evidence presented at trial, there is reason to find that if the Defendants were to raise prices after the proposed mergers, their customers would switch to alternative sources of supply to defeat the price increase.

* * *

In this case, the FTC characterizes the wholesale drug industry as a "unique cluster of products and services" provided only by the wholesalers, for which the FTC claims there are no reasonable substitutes. To support this argument, the FTC at trial presented evidence demonstrating the uniqueness of the drug wholesale industry and highlighting the differences between the services provided by wholesalers and the other sources of supply. Based upon this evidence, the FTC contends that the distribution of prescription drugs by means other than wholesalers, including direct purchases from manufacturers, mail orders, and self-warehousing, should be excluded from the relevant product market because they are not alternative sources that customers reasonably could turn to in response to the Defendants' exercise of its increased market power.

Defendants presented evidence at trial to rebut the contention that wholesale drug distribution is a distinct market. Defendants describe themselves as "middlemen" who take delivery of pharmaceutical products in bulk from manufacturers, warehouse the products, and then deliver them to various dispensers. While they admit that they provide valuable services to their customers, Defendants argue that their function in the delivery chain can easily be substituted by other wholesalers, manufacturers, or by customers themselves. According to the Defendants, wholesale distribution does not involve any scarce resource, input, or expertise that would distinguish it from the other channels of drug distribution. According to the Defendants, the other forms of distribution perform the same basic function as they do, and as such, are "reasonably interchangeable" substitutes. The potential for substitution, Defendants claim, serves as a constraint upon them, thereby justifying that the relevant product market include manufacturers and self-warehousers as viable competitors.

While the additional services provided may vary from one form of distribution to another, this Court finds that the actual function of drug delivery from manufacturers to dispensers is basically the same regardless of the distributor. The parties cannot deny that various methods of distribution exist within the pharmaceutical industry. Thus, the Court recognizes that there is, in fact, a broader market encompassing the delivery of prescription drugs by all forms of distribution. All the forms of distribution must, at some level, compete with one another. However, "the mere fact that a firm may be termed a competitor in the overall marketplace does not necessarily require that it be included in the relevant product market for antitrust purposes." *Federal Trade Commission v. Staples, Inc.*, 970 F. Supp. 1066, 1075–1076 (D.D.C.1997). "The Supreme Court has recognized that within a broad market, 'well-defined submarkets may exist which, in themselves, constitute product markets for antitrust purposes.'" *Id.* (quoting *Brown Shoe Co. v. United States*, 370 U.S. 294, 325, 82 S.Ct. 1502, 8 L.Ed.2d 510 (1962)) * * *.

After carefully considering all of the evidence presented at trial, this Court finds that the services provided by wholesalers in fact comprise a distinct submarket within the larger market of drug delivery. The business of wholesale drug delivery is considerably more sophisticated than merely "picking and packing" as suggested by the Defendants throughout the trial. The evidence presented by the FTC clearly demonstrates that wholesalers provide customers with an efficient way to obtain prescription drugs through centralized warehousing, delivery, and billing services that enable the customers to avoid carrying large inventories, dealing with a large number of vendors, and negotiating numerous transactions. The value of this service is underscored by the additional services offered by the Defendants, which the evidence overwhelmingly shows are provided only by certain wholesalers. According to the FTC, if the Defendants were to merge and engage in anti-competitive practices, a large segment of Defendants' customers—namely hospitals and independent pharmacies—would have no reasonable substitutes.

On the other hand, Defendants contend that the FTC's definition of the relevant product market fails to take into account the economic realities of the larger 94 billion dollar drug industry. According to the Defendants, the FTC's definition of the relevant market inflates the Defendants' supposed market shares by "assuming away nearly half the market–the self-distribution portion." * * * The Defendants presented evidence at trial to show that chain pharmacies now frequently substitute self-distribution for the services of the wholesalers and would do so to an even greater extent in the event of a future price increase. Thus, the Defendants contend that self-warehousing and distribution by chain pharmacies present a significant competitive challenge to the wholesalers and should properly be included within the relevant market.

The Court is persuaded that within the overall industry, different classes of customers have varied ability to substitute the services currently provided by wholesalers. Whereas the FTC is correct in pointing out that hospitals and independent pharmacies continue to rely on wholesalers for a significant portion of their delivery needs, the Court also finds merit to the Defendants' position that a certain, yet significant, portion of the large retail chains can themselves reasonably provide a substitute for Defendants' services. Evidence shows that, in recent years, a growing number of retail pharmacy chains substituted the services provided by wholesalers through self distribution. Accordingly, this suggests to the Court that the large chain pharmacies not only play a part in the smaller 54 billion dollar market defined by the FTC, but that they also have access to the larger, 94 billion dollar market as defined by the Defendants. Courts have generally recognized that when a customer can replace the services of a wholesaler with an internally-created delivery system, this "captive output" (i.e. the self-production of all or part of the relevant product) should be included in the same market.

However, with regard to hospitals, independent pharmacies, and non-warehousing retail chains, the Court finds that the alternatives suggested by the Defendants such as captive production cannot be included within the relevant product market. As the Merger Guidelines state, although captive production can be considered by the Court, it can only be considered to the extent that "such inclusion reflects [its] competitive significance in the relevant market prior to the merger." Guidelines § 1.31 * * *. Numerous customers testified at trial that they would not increase their direct purchases from manufacturers or consider self-distribution in the event of anti-competitive practices. The evidence reflects that the majority of customers have increasingly relied on the services of wholesalers, moving away from direct purchases from manufacturers and self-distribution. For example, evidence presented at trial shows that as of 1997, independent pharmacies and hospitals relied on wholesalers for over 80% of their drug delivery needs, which was a substantial increase from ten years ago. * * * Hospitals purchased only 14.7% of their total dollar volume directly from the manufacturers and warehoused virtually no portion of that demand. Similarly, independent pharmacies directly purchased only 4.4% of their total dollar volume, and self-warehoused less than 1% of their total prescription drug sales. Based on this evidence, it does not appear plausible that the other methods of drug distribution that are not currently perceived as real substitutes for the Defendants' services would suddenly become so in the event of a merger and subsequent exercise of market power.

Business and economic realities of this industry demonstrate that the other forms of distribution lack the practical availability to be included within the relevant product market. Evidence presented at trial shows that most customers are not vertically-integrated. Dispensers who self-warehouse are overwhelmingly limited to a small segment of retail chain pharmacies. Thus, this Court finds that the majority of Defendants' customers cannot replicate the wholesalers' services themselves nor obtain them from any other source or supplier. Clearly, the independent pharmacy does not have access to the major retail chain's warehouse.

Moreover, it should be noted that internal documents presented at trial reveal that the Defendants themselves do not view the other forms of distribution to be viable competitors or substitutes. The Defendants' documents show that the merging parties clearly viewed their economic competition to be from their fellow drug wholesalers, and not from the other sources as suggested by the Defendants at trial.[10] Based on this evidence, it is clear to this Court that while there is no denying that the actions of manufacturers and retail chains affect the scope and size of the Defendants' market share on some level, the Defendants clearly operate within an economically distinct submarket of the larger, overall industry. In light of the economic realities of the industry, this Court finds that the 54 billion dollar wholesale market is the relevant product market in which to assess the likely competitive effects of the proposed mergers.

* * *

[The court found that the United States is a relevant geographic market for the drug wholesale industry. It also concluded that the Los Angeles, San Francisco, and Seattle regions were relevant geographic markets, and that those regions are "particularly concentrated and would be vulnerable to anti-competitive practices." The court also observed that "Given the existence of * * * competitive regional wholesalers, this Court finds that even with the mergers, the eastern part of the United States will likely remain more competitive than the western half of the United States." Eds.]

* * *

* * * The Supreme Court announced in *United States v. Philadelphia Nat'l Bank*, 374 U.S. 321, 363, 83 S.Ct. 1715, 10 L.Ed.2d 915 (1963), that a merger which significantly increases the share and concentration of firms in the relevant market is "so inherently likely to lessen competition" that it must be considered presumptively invalid and enjoined in the absence of clear evidence to the contrary. Specifically, the Court held that a post-merger market share of 30% or more could establish a prima facie case of the lack of competition. Subsequent cases have lowered the presumption somewhat to even 25% or less.

In this case, the market shares resulting from the proposed mergers would clearly cross the 30% threshold. According to the most recent data provided in 1997, McKesson had a 24.9% share of the drug wholesale market; Bergen had 22.4%; Cardinal had 17.5%; and AmeriSource had 12.3%. The next largest drug wholesaler, Bindley Western, had only a 4.35% share; followed by Neuman with 2.66%; Morris & Dickson with 1.69%; C.D. Smith Drug with 1.41%; D & K Wholesale Drug with 1.07%; and Kinray with 1.03%. None of the remaining wholesalers had a market share greater than 0.88%. Based on this data, after the proposed mergers, the two firms clearly would dominate the competition with close to 80% of the pharmaceutical wholesale market. * * *

* * * Including only the wholesalers' sales to independent pharmacies, McKesson in 1997 had a 30% share; Bergen had 14%; Cardinal had 9%; and AmeriSource had 11%. Post-merger, the two remaining firms would control

---

10. For example, an internal document from Amerisource shows a pie chart depicting "Industry Composition: Strong Dominance in Established Markets," and includes in the chart only McKesson, Cardinal, Bergen, Amerisource, and "Others" as the relevant players in the defined product market. * * * Similarly an internal document from Cardinal Corp. reveals a pie chart defining the "U.S. Pharmaceutical Wholesale Market," and includes in that relevant market only McKesson, Bergen, Cardinal Health, Amerisource and Others. * * * An internal document from McKesson defines the relevant product market as "Leading U.S. Wholesale Distributors," and refers to that market therein as its "business." * * *

63% of the wholesale market to independent pharmacies. Including only sales to institutional facilities, McKesson in 1997 had a 13% share; Bergen had 18%; Cardinal had 19%; and Amerisource had 13%. After the merger, the two firms together would have an 63% share of that market. Regardless of how one were to define the relevant drug wholesale market, whether it would include business to all or only some of its customers, the merged firms would control a significant share of all of the markets.

In addition to market share, the level of concentration in the relevant market is the other factor to be considered under *Philadelphia Nat'l Bank*, 374 U.S. at 363 * * *. To measure market concentration more accurately than in the past, economists devised a statistical measure called the Herfindahl–Hirschman Index (HHI), which calculates market concentration by summing the squares of the share of each participant in the market. * * *

* * *

If the mergers were to be approved by this Court, the level of concentration in the market would increase dramatically according the HHI. Using the last set of complete data in 1996, the FTC calculated that the current pharmaceutical wholesale market was only moderately concentrated, with an HHI of approximately 1648. * * * The Cardinal/Bergen merger alone would create a highly concentrated market, with an approximately 802 point increase in the HHI, raising the total market index from 1648 to 2450. * * * Similarly, the McKesson/AmeriSource merger alone would increase the HHI by approximately 629 points, from 1648 to approximately 2277. * * * If both of the mergers were consummated, the level of concentration in the market would almost double, from an HHI of approximately 1648 to 3079. * * * Not only would this be a significant increase in the HHI, but it would also raise the HHI to a level far beyond that of a highly concentrated market. Given the projected increases in the HHI, the Court must presume that the proposed mergers pose a risk to competition.

Even if this Court were to exclude from the market the wholesale business to retail chains, taking into account their ability to self-substitute, the post-merger levels of concentration in the market would still be high enough to trigger the presumption. Using the full set of data from 1996, the HHI index for the hospital and institutional drug wholesale market would increase from approximately 1774 to 3507–from a moderately concentrated market to a highly concentrated one. * * * Similarly, for the wholesale market to independent pharmacies, the HHI index would rise from approximately 1341 to 2224 if both of the mergers were to be approved. * * * The total market share and substantial increase in market concentration that would be produced by the proposed transactions far exceed the threshold limit that the Supreme Court established as raising a presumption of illegality under Section 7 of the Clayton Act. *See Philadelphia Nat'l Bank*, 374 U.S. at 364 * * *. Given the projected measures of market share and market concentration after the mergers, this Court finds that the Commission has made out a prima case of anti-competition.

* * *

Despite the shifting burdens of production in an anti-trust case, the ultimate burden of persuasion always rests with the Government. * * * While the Defendants presented credible evidence in this case to rebut the FTC's presumption of anti-competitiveness,* this Court ultimately finds on the record that the Government's case is more persuasive. In particular, this Court finds that the Government at trial presented three compelling examples of the way in which significant anti-competitive effects would likely occur if the mergers were to be approved. (1) The FTC at trial showed, through Defendants' own internal documents and public statements, that they perceived that the excess capacity currently in the marketplace was the primary factor fueling so-called "irrational" pricing. (2) With data supplied by the Defendants, the Government showed that continued competition in the industry after the FTC rejected a previous attempt by McKesson to acquire AmeriSource in 1988 led to a significant reduction in prices benefitting the American customer. (3) Lastly, the FTC presented evidence to suggest that Defendants, even without the mergers, have the ability to engage in collusive pricing practices. In light of this evidence, the Court finds that the Government has clearly shown the likelihood of success on the merits and met its burden under the law.

* * *

III. CONCLUSION
* * *

The current proposed mergers would * * * reduce the number of national wholesalers from four to two, giving them control of over 80% of the wholesale market. This tremendous concentration of business is the key obstacle that Defendants have been unable to overcome in this case.

While the Defendants have presented a formidable defense attempting to rationalize these latest proposed consolidations, they simply have been unable to overcome the FTC's charge that going from four to two national firms would reduce the competitive balance beyond that which is legally permissible. Defendants have made persuasive arguments that the market at issue is much broader than the 54 billion dollar wholesale market. They argue that the relevant market should include pharmaceutical products directly sold by the manufacturer and self-warehoused by the large drug store chains and others. Their argument fails because while self-warehousing acts as a buffer to price increases by those who self-warehouse, not all distributors self-warehouse, making them vulnerable to price increases. * * *

———

How important was market concentration in the district court's analysis of the likely competitive effects of the acquisitions in the drug wholesaling industry?

Concentration is an important determinant of merger enforcement at the Federal Trade Commission, according to statistics released by the FTC. Federal Trade Commission, *Horizontal Merger Investigation Data, Fiscal Years 1996–2005 (available at* <http://www.ftc.gov/os/2007/01/P035603 horizmergerinvestigationdata1996–2005.pdf>). (The Justice Department like-

---

* [This evidence related to entry and efficiencies. Eds.]

ly behaves similarly to the FTC, but DOJ has not released comparable data.) All the data are for horizontal merger investigations in which a "second request" was issued (see Sidebar 5–3). The study looks at the frequency with which such investigations resulted in enforcement actions—a term which includes consent settlements, litigation, or abandonment of the transaction once agency concerns are made evident. In the study, the FTC reports separately on its treatment of horizontal mergers in the grocery, oil, chemicals, and pharmaceutical industries, and aggregates the rest of the data into a category called "other" markets. Some of the industries broken out for separate reporting have been treated differently on occasion, so the data for the "other" category, when available, suggests the normal decision-making process at the FTC.

The importance of concentration is evident whether concentration is measured by the HHI or the number of firms. In "other" markets, the vast majority of both second requests and enforcement actions occurred in markets where the post-merger HHI was at least 2400 and rose by at least 300. Between 2001 and 2005, 81% percent of all second requests and 99% of all enforcement actions in "other" markets involved these very high concentration levels, according to Table 3.6 of the FTC report. (All of the FTC's enforcement actions involving post-merger HHI's less than 1800 during those years were in oil industry markets.) Are these statistics consistent with what you would expect given the general standards on concentration set forth in the Horizontal Merger Guidelines?

The FTC also provided data looking at market concentration not in terms of how the HHI changed, but in terms of how the merger affected the number of significant competitors remaining in the market. A significant competitor was measured as a firm with roughly a 10% or greater market share. The data for "other markets" reported in Table 4.6 for the 2001 through 2005 period show that in the most highly concentrated markets (mergers that reduce the number of significant firms from 3 to 2 or from 2 to 1), 91% of second requests led to enforcement actions. In mergers that reduced the number of significant firms from 5 to 4 or from 4 to 3, half (50%) of second requests led to enforcement actions. Only 8% of second requests led to enforcement actions in the small fraction of second request investigations involving less concentrated markets, namely those with five or more significant firms remaining post-merger (about 8% of all investigations).

The FTC's study also examined the effect of two types of information that might be uncovered in the investigation on the agency's decision to challenge. The first is "hot documents"—such as an internal memorandum of the merging firm that states "this merger will permit us to raise prices." The presence of such documents is commonly thought to improve the agency's litigation prospects in the event of a court challenge. The second is strong customer complaints. (The use and significance of customer views is discussed below in Sidebar 5–9.) The reported data (Tables 6.1, 6.2, 8.1, and 8.2), which cover all markets between 1996 and 2005, show that if the market is highly concentrated post merger, enforcement is likely regardless of the presence or absence of hot documents or strong customer complaints. But for cases that appear close based on concentration—particularly mergers in which the number of significant competitors falls from four to three—hot documents or strong customer complaints move the case from a close call to one in which enforcement was likely.

2. COMPETITIVE EFFECTS

The first steps in the Merger Guidelines—defining markets, identifying market participants, assigning market shares and determining the post-merger HHI and the increase in HHI from merger–can be thought of as identifying how the merger alters market structure. The Merger Guidelines go on to suggest a number of ways that the change in market structure resulting from merger among rivals might reduce competition; these are termed "competitive effects" theories. The competitive effects theories considered in the Merger Guidelines are grouped into two classes: "coordinated" and "unilateral." We follow that division in this Casebook, and discuss coordinated competitive effects in the first subsection below. It is possible for a merger to raise both unilateral and coordinated effects issues simultaneously, for example unilateral effects in a narrow market and coordinated effects in a broader one. In appropriate cases, therefore, both possibilities would have to be analyzed.

The Guidelines focus on collusive mergers; they do not consider ways in which a merger among rivals might lead to the exercise of market power through the exclusion of rivals. We discuss harmful exclusionary effects of mergers in connection with vertical mergers in Chapter 7 and conglomerate mergers in Sidebar 5–2. We note here without further analysis that it is possible for horizontal mergers to harm competition by making it easier for the merged firm to exclude rivals. For example, a horizontal merger might create a dominant firm and confer on it the bargaining leverage it needs to obtain exclusive contracts from key input suppliers. This could harm competition by making it more difficult for fringe rivals to expand output inexpensively and compete aggressively.

This chapter follows the Merger Guidelines by emphasizing the possibility that sellers with enhanced market power through merger would exercise that power by raising price. But, as the Guidelines note, "[s]ellers with market power also may lessen competition on dimensions other than price, such as product quality, service or innovation." *Horizontal Merger Guidelines* § 0.1 n.6. As one former, senior government official has emphasized:

> * * * [E]ven if antitrust analysis *appears* to focus on price effects, this can and should be understood as *synecdoche*: the part standing for the whole. That is, there are reasons to expect competitive effects in different dimensions (innovation, quality, price), and their net effect, usually to go together. The shifts in incentives that are fundamental in antitrust economics apply quite broadly, so that a price analysis can often proxy for a fuller competitive analysis.

Joseph Farrell, *Thoughts on Antitrust and Innovation* (January 25, 2001), *available at* http://www.usdoj.gov/atr/public/speeches/7402.htm. Examples of government enforcement actions against mergers thought to reduce competition in the development of new products are presented in Chapter 10.

Firms may also exercise market power as buyers, by depressing the price they pay for an input. This possibility is termed the exercise of "monopsony" power by economists (as opposed to the "monopoly" power firms exercise when raising the price they sell to their customers). Firms exercise monopsony power by reducing their purchases of an input, driving down the price paid to suppliers. The reduction in quantity below the competitive level makes the harm to the suppliers exceed the gain to the buyers, creating an efficiency loss in the market. If a merger permits the firms in an industry to exercise monopsony power, the lower input prices the merging firms pay do not necessarily benefit the consumers who buy the merging firms' products. First, firms may have buying power in dealing with their suppliers, but may sell in competitive markets; if so, their exercise of monopsony power may not affect the price they charge downstream.

Professor Marius Schwartz, formerly a senior economic official in the Antitrust Division, has made this point using the example of a merger of two textile producers that are major employers in a small town. The merged firm may be able to drive down local wages, but the price of textiles to consumers may remain unchanged if it is determined in a world market by the decisions of numerous other textile producers. Second, lower input prices resulting from the exercise of monopsony power typically mean that the input quantity utilized falls, inducing the merged firm to *contract* the output of the good it sells to consumers and *raise* its price. In contrast, lower production costs that arise from efficiencies are likely to benefit consumers of the merging firms' products, to the extent the reduction in production costs induces the merged firm to *expand* output of the good it sells to consumers and *lower* its price. Even without harm to consumers, Professor Schwartz contends, antitrust enforcement is warranted because of the harm to suppliers and loss in overall welfare (efficiency loss). He sees little economic basis for opposing the exercise of market power against individuals in their capacity as buyers of products but not as sellers of their resources. Marius Schwartz, *Buyer Power Concerns and the Aetna–Prudential Merger* (Oct. 20, 1999), *available at* http://www. usdoj.gov/atr/public/speeches/3924.htm.

a. Coordinated Competitive Effects

The Merger Guidelines recognize that a merger "may diminish competition by enabling the firms selling in the relevant market more likely, more successfully, or more completely to engage in coordinated interaction that harms consumers." *Horizontal Merger Guidelines* § 2.1. The term "coordinated" competitive effects refers to the threat that the firms in a market might act together to harm competition, as with tacit or express collusion (*e.g.,* price-fixing or market division) among rivals that recognize their interdependence.

However, coordinated competitive effects also include the threat of higher prices resulting from "conscious parallelism" and price leadership which, as we saw in Chapter 3, can have the same economic consequences as price-fixing without involving conduct that would satisfy the "agreement" requirement of Sherman Act § 1. Indeed, antitrust enforcement against horizontal mergers has at times been defended on the ground that it prevents the development of oligopoly market structures that might facilitate higher prices through conduct that falls short of violating the Sherman Act and could not therefore be challenged post-merger. This is sometimes called the "containment" justification for merger enforcement. Sidebar 5–7 considers what can be learned from criminal cartel prosecutions for the analysis of the coordinated competitive effects of horizontal mergers.

Sidebar 5–7:
Criminal Cartel Prosecutions and Coordinated Competitive Effects

The Department of Justice prosecutes operational criminal cartels and reviews mergers for their potential to facilitate coordination. Not surprisingly, therefore, government enforcers have evaluated their experiences detecting and prosecuting criminal cartels to determine whether those experiences can aid them in predicting the likelihood of future coordination as a consequence of mergers of competitors. Careful analysis of the factors that allowed cartel participants to solve their "cartel problems," might help to identify markets and mergers more susceptible to future coordination.

In the following excerpted speech, then Deputy Assistant Attorney General William J. Kolasky offered some "Lessons Learned from Criminal Cartel Prosecutions" to inform the prediction of future coordinated effects in horizontal mergers.* One such lesson drawn from the mere incidence of cartels is that coordination is perhaps more easily achieved than had previously been thought. If true, that "lesson" might suggest that a higher level of scrutiny would be in order for mergers in industries that possess some of the same coordination-facilitating characteristics as those found in the cartel cases.

As you read the speech, consider whether factual or legal differences between cartel prosecutions and mergers might nevertheless diminish to some degree the value of the lessons drawn. For example, as we saw in Chapters 1 and 3, the kinds of cartels that qualify for criminal prosecution are often express. Tacit coordination, alone, might not rise to the level of agreement that would justify even a civil prosecution. Yet, as we shall shortly see, evidence that a post-merger market will be significantly more susceptible to tacit collusion might warrant a prediction of probable future coordinated effects, satisfying the standards of Section 7 of the Clayton Act. Should this difference in legal standards limit the relevance of the cartel experience for mergers? Would you agree with Kolasky's assertion that "whether cartels are express or tacit, they have to reach a consensus and deter cheating, so what we learn from them can inform merger analysis, where the concern is as much about tacit collusion as express"? Might efforts to refocus merger analysis on the kinds of evidence found in the cartel cases perhaps unintentionally tend to elevate, rather than simply inform, the standards for predicting coordinated effects? What impact might it have on the continued vitality of the *Philadelphia Nat'l Bank* presumption?

---

* William J. Kolasky, *Coordinated Effects in Merger Review: From Dead Frenchmen to Beautiful Minds and Mavericks* (April 24, 2002), *available at* http://www.usdoj.gov/atr/public/speeches/11050.htm.

"For those who may be tempted to argue that coordination is too difficult to occur in the real world, I should not have to do more than to point to the large number of multinational cartels we've successfully prosecuted in [the] last seven years to show why such arguments will fall on deaf ears. Beyond that, I think there are at least ten important lessons to be drawn from those cases that should help inform our review of future mergers. While our criminal cartel cases involve express cartels, whether cartels are express or tacit, they have to reach a consensus and deter cheating, so what we learn from them can inform merger analysis, where the concern is as much about tacit collusion as express.

First, cartels can involve a fairly large number of firms. The number of participants in several of the cartels we prosecuted were surprisingly high. Five or six members were not uncommon and occasionally we have uncovered cartels with 10 or more members. This appears to be due in part at least to fringe players in the market feeling they will profit more by going along with the cartel than by trying to take share away from the larger firms by undercutting their prices.

Second, industry concentration matters. As expected, the industries in which we have detected cartels are usually highly concentrated with the largest firms acting as ringleaders and the fringe players following along. In one case, there was evidence that the industry had attempted unsuccessfully to coordinate prices for several years before the cartel finally got off the ground after the industry consolidated down to approximately six players.

Third, cartels often use multiple tools to enforce compliance. Just as Stigler observed, cartels can take many forms, with the choice of form being determined in part at least by balancing the comparative cost of reaching and enforcing the collusive agreement against the risk of detection. Past empirical studies of price-fixing cases found that multiple instruments of coordination are frequently employed. Our multinational cartel cases over the last seven years found that this pattern continues. The vitamin cartel of the 1990s (whose prosecution led to the largest Sherman Act fines in history), for example, included price-fixing, bid-rigging, customer and territorial allocations, and coordinated total sales.

Fourth, the ability of large sophisticated buyers to defeat cartel activity may be overrated. In merger analysis, some assume that large purchasers in the market will provide sufficient discipline to prevent cartels. Our experience shows to the contrary that many successful cartels sell to large, sophisticated buyers. In the lysine cartel, the buyers included Tysons Foods and Con Agra; in citric acid, the buyers included Coca–Cola and Procter & Gamble; and in graphite electrodes, the victims included every major steel producer in the world. What is particularly ironic is that the perpetrators and victims of the citric acid cartel included some of the very same firms that the district court found were unlikely to engage in or be vulnerable to cartel activity in refusing to enjoin an acquisition by ADM of one of its leading rivals in the high fructose corn syrup market back in 1991.[28]

Fifth, excess capacity in the hands of leading firms can be an effective tool for punishing cheating and thereby enforcing collusive agreements. In

---

28. U.S. v. Archer–Daniels–Midland Co., 781 F.Supp. 1400. (S.D. Iowa, 1991).

lysine, ADM, which had substantial excess capacity, repeatedly threatened to flood the market with lysine if the other producers refused to agree to a volume allocation agreement proposed by ADM. In another case where competitors bought from one another, the cartel member with the extra capacity threatened to not sell to a competitor who was undercutting the cartel.

Sixth, cartels are more durable than sometimes thought. After the ADM plea, the Wall Street Journal stated "If colluders push prices too high, defectors and new entrants will set things right." Our experience has shown that this is not the case. Several of the cartels we prosecuted had been in existence for over ten years, including one (sorbates) that lasted 17 years, from 1979 to 1996.

Seventh, large, publicly traded companies are not immune from the temptation to engage in cartel activity. Our cases have turned up hardcore cartel activity by top management at some of the world's largest corporations and most respected corporations including Christies/Sotheby's, ADM, Hoffmann–La Roche, BASF, ABB, and a host of others. We have repeatedly found that even the largest companies have become sloppy about their antitrust compliance programs and that they are not doing all they should to educate managers about the risks at which they put themselves and their companies by engaging in cartel activity.

Eighth, trade associations and industry publications that report detailed market information are important in facilitating cartel activity. Cartel members will often use trade associations as a cover for their cartel meetings. In both lysine and citric acid, the conspirators created a working group within a legitimate trade association. This group's sole purpose was to provide false, but facially legitimate, explanations as to why they were meeting. Similarly, in some of our chemical investigations, a widely read weekly newspaper was used as the way of announcing price increases to other cartel members, which they were to follow. Other investigations have turned up a one-time agreement to incorporate a public index into a formula; so, as a newspaper announces a commodity price index change, the conspirators do not need to communicate again.

Ninth, cartel participants tend to be recidivists. The most notorious example is Hoffmann–La Roche, which continued its participation in the vitamin conspiracy even as it was entering into a plea agreement for its participation in the citric acid cartel.

Tenth, and finally, while product homogeneity and high entry barriers may facilitate cartel behavior, they are not essential to it. While the products in our cartel cases tend to be fungible, there are sometimes exceptions. One case we prosecuted involved bid rigging on school bus bodies. School bus bodies have many options, but the conspirators were able to work out a formula that incorporated the options and trade-in value to determine a price at or below which the designated winning bidder was supposed to bid. Similarly, while most of our cartel cases involve industries in which entry tends to be difficult, there are notable exceptions, such as in the Division's many bid-rigging cases in the road building industry. The road building industry, at least at the time of the conspiracies, was not difficult to enter, yet the Division turned up numerous cartels."

With respect to coordinated competitive effects, the Guidelines focus on analyzing whether the post-merger market structure is one in which firms can likely overcome two key impediments to successful coordination: (1) reaching a consensus on the terms of coordination (such as price and market shares), and (2) discouraging cheating on those terms (as through rapid detection and punishment of deviation). The factors that might bear on whether coordination could be successful in an industry have been considered previously in Chapter 3, and are the primary focus of the excerpt from Judge Posner's *Hosp. Corp. of Am.* opinion, set forth below.

The Merger Guidelines recognize that the change in market structure resulting from merger could make coordination more likely or more effective. The reduction in the number of firms could make it easier for the remaining sellers to work out any differences over the terms of coordination, or make it easier for the remaining firms to identify rapidly a firm that attempts to cheat on the consensus (and thus make punishment for cheating more likely). From this perspective, which was also adopted by Judge Posner in *Hosp. Corp. of Am.*, the probability that a merger will diminish competition is the greatest when post-merger concentration is high and concentration has increased markedly.

HOSPITAL CORPORATION OF AMERICA v. FEDERAL TRADE COMMISSION

United States Court of Appeals for the Seventh Circuit, 1986.
807 F.2d 1381.

Before POSNER and FLAUM, Circuit Judges, and CAMPBELL, Senior District Judge.

POSNER, Circuit Judge.

Hospital Corporation of America, the largest proprietary hospital chain in the United States, asks us to set aside the decision by the Federal Trade Commission that it violated section 7 of the Clayton Act * * * by the acquisition in 1981 and 1982 of two corporations, Hospital Affiliates International, Inc. and Health Care Corporation. * * *

* * *

If all the hospitals brought under common ownership or control by the two challenged acquisitions are treated as a single entity, the acquisitions raised Hospital Corporation's market share in the Chattanooga area from 14 percent to 26 percent. This made it the second largest provider of hospital services in a highly concentrated market where the four largest firms together had a 91 percent market share compared to 79 percent before the acquisitions. * * * Nor would expressing the market shares in terms of the Herfindahl index alter the impression of a highly concentrated market.

* * *

* * * Hospital Corporation has argued the case to us as if we were the FTC, which assuredly we are not. Our only function is to determine whether the Commission's analysis of the probable effects of these acquisitions on

hospital competition in Chattanooga is so implausible, so feebly supported by the record, that it flunks even the deferential test of substantial evidence.

* * *

When an economic approach is taken in a section 7 case, the ultimate issue is whether the challenged acquisition is likely to facilitate collusion. In this perspective the acquisition of a competitor has no economic significance in itself; the worry is that it may enable the acquiring firm to cooperate (or cooperate better) with other leading competitors on reducing or limiting output, thereby pushing up the market price. * * * There is plenty of evidence to support the Commission's prediction of adverse competitive effect in this case; whether we might have come up with a different prediction on our own is irrelevant.

The acquisitions reduced the number of competing hospitals in the Chattanooga market from 11 to 7. True, this calculation assumes that the hospitals that came under the management although not ownership of Hospital Corporation should be considered allies rather than competitors of Hospital Corporation; but the Commission was entitled to so conclude. The manager (Hospital Corporation) sets the prices charged by the managed hospitals, just as it sets its own prices. Although the pricing and other decisions that it makes in its management role are subject to the ultimate control of the board of directors of the managed hospital, there is substantial evidence that the board usually defers to the manager's decisions. If it were not inclined to defer, it would not have a management contract; it would do its own managing, through officers hired by it. A hospital managed by Hospital Corporation is therefore unlikely to engage in vigorous or perhaps in any price competition with Hospital Corporation—or so at least the Commission was entitled to conclude.

The reduction in the number of competitors is significant in assessing the competitive vitality of the Chattanooga hospital market. The fewer competitors there are in a market, the easier it is for them to coordinate their pricing without committing detectable violations of section 1 of the Sherman Act, which forbids price fixing. This would not be very important if the four competitors eliminated by the acquisitions in this case had been insignificant, but they were not; they accounted in the aggregate for 12 percent of the sales of the market. As a result of the acquisitions the four largest firms came to control virtually the whole market, and the problem of coordination was therefore reduced to one of coordination among these four.

Moreover, both the ability of the remaining firms to expand their output should the big four reduce their own output in order to raise the market price (and, by expanding, to offset the leading firms' restriction of their own output), and the ability of outsiders to come in and build completely new hospitals, are reduced by Tennessee's certificate-of-need law. Any addition to hospital capacity must be approved by a state agency. The parties disagree over whether this law, as actually enforced, inhibits the expansion of hospital capacity. * * * Should the leading hospitals in Chattanooga collude, a natural consequence would be the creation of excess hospital capacity, for the higher prices resulting from collusion would drive some patients to shorten their hospital stays and others to postpone or reject elective surgery. If a noncolluding hospital wanted to expand its capacity so that it could serve patients driven off by the high prices charged by the colluding hospitals, the colluders would have not only a strong incentive to oppose the grant of a certificate of need but also substantial evidence with which to oppose it—the excess capacity (in the market considered as a whole) created by their own collusive efforts. At least the certificate of need law would enable them to delay any competitive sally by a noncolluding competitor. Or so the Commission could conclude (a refrain we shall now stop repeating). We add that at the very least a certificate of need law forces hospitals to give public notice, well in advance, of any plans to add capacity. The requirement of notice makes it harder for the member of a hospital cartel to "cheat" on the cartel by adding capacity in advance of other members; its attempt to cheat will be known in advance, and countermeasures taken.

All this would be of little moment if, in the event that hospital prices in Chattanooga rose above the competitive level, persons desiring hospital services in Chattanooga would switch to hospitals in other cities, or to nonhospital providers of medical care. But this would mean that the Chattanooga hospital market, which is to say the set of hospital-services providers to which consumers in Chattanooga can feasibly turn, * * * includes hospitals in other cities plus nonhospital providers both in Chattanooga and elsewhere; and we do not understand Hospital Corporation to be challenging the Commission's market definition, which is limited to hospital providers in Chattanooga. Anyway, these competitive alternatives are not important enough to deprive the market shares statistics of competitive significance. Going to another city is out of the question in medical emergencies; and even when an operation or some other hospital service can be deferred, the patient's doctor will not (at least not for reasons of price) send the patient to another city, where the doctor is unlikely to have hospital privileges. Finally, although hospitals increasingly are providing services on an out-patient basis, thus competing with nonhospital providers of the same services (tests, minor surgical procedures, etc.), most hospital services cannot be provided by nonhospital providers; as to these, hospitals have no competition from other providers of medical care.

In showing that the challenged acquisitions gave four firms control over an entire market so that they would have little reason to fear a competitive reaction if they raised prices above the competitive level, the Commission went far to justify its prediction of probable anticompetitive effects. Maybe it need have gone no further. *See United States v. Philadelphia Nat'l Bank*, supra, 374 U.S. at 362–63, 83 S.Ct. at 1740–41. * * * But it did. First it pointed out that the demand for hospital services by patients and their doctors is highly inelastic under competitive conditions. This is not only because people place a high value on their safety and comfort and because many of their treatment decisions are made for them by their doctor, who doesn't pay their hospital bills; it is also because most hospital bills are paid largely by insurance companies or the federal government rather than by the patient. The less elastic the demand for a good or service is, the greater are the profits that providers can make by raising price through collusion. A low elasticity of demand means that raising price will cause a relatively slight fall in demand, with the result that total revenues will rise sharply. * * *

Second, there is a tradition, well documented in the Commission's opinion, of cooperation between competing hospitals in Chattanooga. Of course, not all forms of cooperation between competitors are bad. *See, e.g., Broadcast Music, Inc. v. Columbia Broadcasting System, Inc.*, 441 U.S. 1, 99 S.Ct. 1551, 60 L.Ed.2d 1 (1979). But a market in which competitors are unusually disposed to cooperate is a market prone to collusion. The history of successful cooperation establishes a precondition to effective collusion—mutual trust and forbearance, without which an informal collusive arrangement is unlikely to overcome the temptation to steal a march on a fellow colluder by undercutting him slightly. That temptation is great. A seller who makes a profit of $10 on each sale at the cartel price, and then cuts price by $1 and thereby (let us suppose) doubles his output, will increase his total profits by 180 percent.

The management contracts between Hospital Affiliates (itself an owner as well as manager of hospitals) and two other hospitals in Chattanooga—contracts that when taken over by Hospital Corporation gave it virtual control over the pricing and other decisions of two of its competitors, at least for a time—illustrate the unusual degree of cooperation in this industry; imagine Ford's signing a management contract with General Motors whereby General Motors installed one of its officers (who would remain an officer of GM) as Ford's manager. Hospitals routinely exchange intimate information on prices and costs in connection with making joint applications to insurers for higher reimbursement schedules. Such cooperation may be salutary but it facilitates collusion and therefore entitles the Commission to worry even more about large horizontal acquisitions in this industry than in industries where competitors deal with each other at arm's length.

Third, hospitals are under great pressure from the federal government and the insurance companies to cut costs. One way of resisting this pressure is by presenting a united front in negotiations with the third-party payors—which indeed, as we have just said, hospitals in Chattanooga have done. * * *

All these considerations, taken together, supported—we do not say they compelled—the Commission's conclusion that the challenged acquisitions are likely to foster collusive practices, harmful to consumers, in the Chattanooga hospital market. Section 7 does not require proof that a merger or other acquisition has caused higher prices in the affected market. All that is necessary is that the merger create an appreciable danger of such consequences in the future. A predictive judgment, necessarily probabilistic and judgmental rather than demonstrable * * * is called for. Considering the concentration of the market, the absence of competitive alternatives, the regulatory barrier to entry (the certificate of need law), the low elasticity of demand, the exceptionally severe cost pressures under which American hospitals labor today, the history of collusion in the industry, and the sharp reduction in the number of substantial competitors in this market brought about by the acquisition of four hospitals in a city with only eleven (one already owned by Hospital Corporation), we cannot say that the Commission's prediction is not supported by substantial evidence.

But of course we cannot just consider the evidence that supports the Commission's prediction. We must consider all the evidence in the record. We must therefore consider the significance of the facts, pressed on us by Hospital Corporation, that hospital services are complex and heterogeneous, that the sellers in this market are themselves heterogeneous because of differences in the services provided by the different hospitals and differences in the corporate character of the hospitals (some are publicly owned, some are proprietary, and some are private but nonprofit), that the hospital industry is undergoing rapid technological and economic change, that the payors for most hospital services (Blue Cross and other insurance companies, and the federal government) are large and knowledgeable, and that the FTC's investigation which led to this proceeding was touched off by a complaint from a competitor of Hospital Corporation. Most of these facts do detract from a conclusion that collusion in this market is a serious danger, but it was for the Commission—it is not for us—to determine their weight.

The first fact is the least impressive. It is true that hospitals provide a variety of different services many of which are "customized" for the individual patient, but the degree to which this is true seems no greater than in other markets. Although collusion is more difficult the more heterogeneous the output of the colluding firms, there is no established threshold of complexity beyond which it is infeasible and Hospital Corporation made no serious effort to show that hospital services are more complex than products and services in other markets, such as steel, building materials, and transportation, where collusion has been frequent.

The heterogeneity of the sellers has two aspects: the hospitals in Chattanooga offer different mixtures of services; and they have different types of ownership—private for-profit ("proprietary"), private not-for-profit, public. The significance of these features is unclear. Concerning the first, if one assumes that collusion is practiced on a service-by-service basis, the fact that hospitals provide different mixtures of service seems irrelevant to the feasibility of collusion. True, since different types of service may not be substitutable—open-heart surgery is not a substitute for setting a broken leg—specialized hospitals might not compete with one another. But that is not Hospital Corporation's argument. Its argument is that the different mixture of services in the different hospitals would make it difficult for their owners to fix prices of competing services, and this we don't understand.

Different ownership structures might reduce the likelihood of collusion but this possibility is conjectural and the Commission was not required to give it conclusive weight. The adoption of the nonprofit form does not change human nature, * * * as the courts have recognized in rejecting an implicit antitrust exemption for nonprofit enterprises. * * *

* * *

The economic and technological ferment in the hospital industry may make collusion more difficult, but also more urgent, since risk-averse managers may be strongly inclined to stabilize, if necessary through collusion, whatever features of an uncertain environment they are able to bring under their control. Regarding the weighing of such imponderables as this, much must be left to the judgment of the Commission.

The concentration of the buying side of a market does inhibit collusion. The bigger a buyer is, the more easily and lucratively a member of the cartel can cheat on his fellows; for with a single transaction, he may be able to increase his sales and hence profits dramatically. But with all the members thus vying for the large orders of big buyers, the cartel will erode. * * * Hospital Corporation argues that the effective buyers of most hospital services are large and knowledgeable institutions rather than the patients who are the nominal buyers. But the role of the third-party payor is not quite that of a large buyer. * * * [A]s a practical matter Blue Cross could not tell its subscribers in Chattanooga that it will not reimburse them for any hospital services there because prices are too high. As a practical matter it could not, if the four major hospital owners in the city, controlling more than 90 percent of the city's hospital capacity, raised their prices, tell its subscribers that they must use the remaining hospitals–whose aggregate capacity would be completely inadequate and, for reasons discussed earlier, could not readily, or at least rapidly, be expanded—if they want to be reimbursed. * * *

Hospital Corporation's most telling point is that the impetus for the Commission's complaint came from a competitor—a large nonprofit hospital in Chattanooga. A rational competitor would not complain just because it thought that Hospital Corporation's acquisitions would facilitate collusion. Whether the competitor chose to join a cartel or stay out of it, it would be better off if the cartel were formed than if it were not formed. For the cartel would enable this seller to raise its price, whether or not to the cartel level. By staying out of the cartel and by pricing just below the cartel price, the competitor might, as we noted earlier, do even better than by joining the cartel.

The hospital that complained to the Commission must have thought that the acquisitions would lead to lower rather than higher prices—which would benefit consumers, and hence, under contemporary principles of antitrust law, would support the view that the acquisitions were lawful. But this is just one firm's opinion. It was not binding on the Commission, which having weighed all the relevant facts concluded that the acquisitions had made collusion in this market significantly more likely than before. Since, moreover, the complainant was a nonprofit hospital, in attributing the complaint to fear of lower prices Hospital Corporation is contradicting its argument that the non-profit sector of the hospital industry does not obey the laws of economic self-interest.

* * *

The Commission's order is affirmed and enforced.

As you reflect on Judge Posner's analysis of coordinated competitive effects in *Hosp. Corp. of Am.*, recall the discussion of tacit collusion in Chapter 3. If the firms in an oligopoly are able to achieve high prices without reaching an agreement, for example reaching a consensus through price leadership, they may exercise market power without violating Sherman Act § 1. "Conscious parallelism" is not a violation of the antitrust laws. But an acquisition that appears likely to facilitate tacit collusion violates Clayton Act § 7, even if the coordinated behavior that results would not itself be subject to attack under the antitrust laws. From this perspective, the merger laws are prophylactic, intended to limit the spread of coordinated pricing.

Coordinated competitive effects analysis in merger review is closely related to the problem of identifying price-fixing studied in Chapter 3, because the underlying economic problem is the same. Successful collusion, whether tacit or express, requires that the firms solve their "cartel problems" of reaching a consensus, deterring cheating, and preventing entry; these economic problems were discussed in that chapter. Accordingly, it is no surprise that Judge Posner, in his opinion in *Hosp. Corp. of Am.*, pays a great deal of attention to the range of factors that might bear on whether industry participants could reasonably be expected to collude tacitly. Posner's factors are listed in Figure 5–6; how does his list match up with the factors discussed in Chapter 3? With those discussed by Kolasky in Sidebar 5–7?

Figure 5–6:

Factors Urged by the Parties as Facilitating and Frustrating Tacit Collusion in *HCA*

Facilitating Tacit Collusion (FTC)

- reduction in numbers of competitors, leading to a market controlled by four (4) firms;
- absence of competitive alternatives within the relevant geographic market;
- regulatory limitations on output expansion or entry by non-merging firms (state certificate of need law);
- highly inelastic demand under competitive conditions;
- tradition of cooperation among rival sellers, including routine exchange of information on prices and costs; and
- sellers understand that cooperation would permit them to resist external pressures to lower price (motive to coordinate).

Frustrating Tacit Collusion (HCA)

- hospital services are complex and heterogeneous;
- sellers are heterogeneous;
- industry is undergoing rapid technological and economic change;
- buyers are large and sophisticated; and
- FTC investigation was triggered by competitor complaint.

In order to conclude that coordinated competitive effects are likely to result from merger, it is necessary to make two showings. The first is to demonstrate that the post-merger market is conducive to coordination (that is, that the firms likely can reach a consensus on terms of coordination and deter cheating on those terms). This issue was the focus of the coordinated effects sections of the Merger Guidelines and was emphasized by Judge Posner in *Hosp. Corp. of Am.*. The second is to show that the merger makes a difference (that is, that the merger increases the likelihood that firms in the market can successfully raise price through coordination or that the merger makes it likely that ongoing coordination would become more effective). The Merger Guidelines allude to the latter issue when they point out that a merger may enable firms "more likely, more successfully, or more completely" to engage in coordinated interaction. *Horizontal Merger Guidelines* § 2.1.

The latter issue—the incremental impact of the merger on coordinated conduct—can be addressed in various ways. A substantial increase in market concentration is generally thought to raise the odds that firms can reach consensus and deter cheating. In addition, the merger may alter certain factors facilitating or frustrating coordination to improve the prospects of coordination. For example, if a merger leads to greater symmetry among the firms in the market, as by reducing differences among sellers in the attributes of their products or seller costs, the odds of successful coordination may increase. Andrew R. Dick, *Coordinated Interaction: Pre–Merger Constraints and Post–Merger Effects*, 12 GEO. MASON L. REV. 65 (2003). In some cases, moreover, a merger may make coordination more likely or more effective by leading a "maverick" firm in the relevant market to compete less aggressively. The Merger Guidelines point out that when coordinated interaction in the pre-merger market is prevented or limited by a "maverick," a firm that has a greater incentive to keep prices low or otherwise deviate from the terms of coordination than its rivals, the acquisition of that maverick firm could make coordinated interaction more likely, more successful or more complete. Indeed, one reason a firm may acquire a maverick is to facilitate coordination. These issues are explored further in Sidebar 5–8.

Sidebar 5–8:
Mavericks and the Coordinated Competitive Effects of Mergers*

Maverick firms can play an important role in the analysis of the likely coordinated competitive effects of mergers. This Sidebar explains first, why mavericks commonly constrain coordination; second, how mavericks can be identified; and third, the significance of mavericks for merger analysis. It concludes by asking what to do if the maverick cannot be identified reliably, or if the effect of the merger on the maverick's incentives cannot be determined with precision.

Incomplete Coordination Leads Naturally to Mavericks

Although some commentators have argued that coordination among rivals is unlikely to be successful or last for long, modern economists generally accept that it can and does occur. When coordination does occur, moreover, it is likely to be imperfect and incomplete (relative to what a monopolist could achieve). This is because coordinating firms may have difficulty punishing cheating rivals severely, allocating joint profits in a way satisfactory to all without "side payments" to recalcitrant rivals, detecting cheating when prices decline frequently for reasons like unexpected declines in demand, and identifying the joint-profit maximizing outcome when firms must coordinate pricing and output over multiple products or markets without communicating.

When coordination is imperfect or incomplete, it is likely that some firms would be nearly indifferent between coordination and cheating, while others strongly prefer the coordinated outcome. From this perspective, a "maverick" firm is one that is nearly indifferent between coordination and cheating, and in consequence constrains coordination from

---

* This Sidebar has been adapted from Jonathan B. Baker, *Mavericks, Mergers, and Exclusion: Proving Coordinated Competitive Effects* *Under the Antitrust Laws*, 77 N.Y.U. L. REV. 135, 177–88 (2002).

becoming more effective. A maverick is likely to play a more significant role than its rivals in constraining the effectiveness of coordination. In theory, there could be more than one maverick in a market, particularly in markets where it is impossible for firms to reach consensus or deter cheating. But in the oligopoly markets in which most serious merger investigations arise, it is often plausible that firms can coordinate to some extent and unlikely that there will be more than one maverick unless the maverick firms are nearly identical.

The term "maverick" may mislead to the extent it suggests that the firm must be a price-cutter. The maverick could indeed be an observably disruptive force, taking the lead in starting price wars or sales. But it also could keep price from rising merely by refusing to follow rival attempts to raise price. In fact, it is possible that the maverick would not be recognizable as a holdout to the outside observer, as rivals would be expected not to attempt to increase price unless they had reason to think that industry conditions had changed in a way that would lead the maverick to go along.

Identifying Mavericks

Three strategies are available to antitrust enforcers and courts for identifying the maverick in an industry in which firms are coordinating, though none is guaranteed to succeed. First, a maverick firm might be identified based on past conduct showing that the firm has actually constrained industry pricing. The second approach looks for "natural experiments" that identify the firm that constrains industry pricing. These are events that would be expected to lead a maverick to alter price but not affect the pricing of non-maverick firms. For example, one natural experiment might involve changes in a firm's marginal costs related to the nature or location of its production processes but not paralleled by cost changes affecting its rivals. If that firm is a maverick, the market price will change; if another firm is the maverick, the market price will not. This idea can potentially be exploited to "test" which firm is the maverick, if the necessary data are available and sufficiently numerous natural experiments occur within the sample period.

The third approach looks for features of market structure that tend to suggest that a firm would prefer a lower coordinated price than would its rivals. For example, documentary evidence cited by the district court in *FTC v. Cardinal Health, Inc.*, 12 F. Supp. 2d 34, 63–64 (D.D.C.1998) indicated that in the drug wholesaling industry, excess capacity creates price pressure. If this is indeed the driving force behind firm preferences as to the industry price in that industry, and the firms are coordinating, a firm with substantially greater excess capacity than most of its rivals (either absolutely or relative to sales) is likely to be the industry maverick.

A variety of structural characteristics might give a firm a greater economic incentive to prefer a lower coordinated price than do its rivals (or to otherwise deviate from terms of coordination when its rivals would not), such as low costs and excess capacity, a low market share, or an unusual ability to expand sales by increasing captive production for a downstream affiliate. *See Horizontal Merger Guidelines* § 2.12.

The Significance of Mavericks for Merger Analysis

A focus on identifying the maverick explains why the loss of a firm through merger or exclusion will improve coordination. Moreover, the concept of a maverick can operate as sword or shield in merger review, helping distinguish anticompetitive mergers from procompetitive ones.

Mergers Involving the Maverick. A merger involving the maverick may harm competition by removing the maverick from the marketplace. Absent cognizable efficiencies from the transaction, the merged firm would most likely prefer higher prices than the maverick. If so, the merger could remove a constraint on more effective coordination, and lead to higher prices in the market. *See, e.g., United States v. Premdor, Inc.,* 66 Fed. Reg. 45,326, 45,336–37 (Aug. 28, 2001) (competitive impact statement); *In re Mahle,* 62 Fed. Reg. 10,566, 10,567 (F.T.C. Mar. 7, 1997) (Analysis to Aid Public Comment); *In re B.F. Goodrich,* 110 F.T.C. 207, 329–85 (1988); *United States v. Aluminum Co. of America,* 377 U.S. 271, 281 (1964) (*Rome Cable*).

In these instances, the concept of a maverick could operate as a sword, explaining why the prospective increase in market concentration generated by merger is likely to lead to higher prices. Because the acquisition of a maverick appears substantially more likely to harm competition than to promote it, the courts might plausibly develop a rebuttable presumption that such a transaction would harm competition.

Mergers Involving Non–Mavericks. In the most straightforward scenario involving a merger of non-mavericks, the transaction may have no effect on competition. The industry maverick may continue to constrain prices after the merger much as it did before. If so, the concept of a maverick would operate as a shield, to undermine an antitrust challenge to a merger that increases market concentration. *See, e.g., New York v. Kraft General Foods, Inc.,* 926 F.Supp. 321, 364–65 (S.D.N.Y.1995) (coordinated competitive effects allegation rejected on the ground that the acquired firm did not constrain more effective coordination); *FTC v. Arch Coal, Inc.,* 329 F. Supp. 2d 109 (D.D.C. 2004) (coordinated effects found unlikely, in part because the acquired firm was the high cost producer and likely to stay that way, so did not constrain coordination).

In order for the loss of a non-maverick firm to make coordination more effective, the merger must affect the maverick's incentives.* For example, a merger not involving the maverick could harm competition by excluding the maverick (as by raising its costs or reducing its access to customers), thus forcing the maverick to compete less aggressively. Moreover, a merger among non-mavericks could affect the severity of the punishment response the merged firm would be expected to employ in the event any rival, including the maverick, cheated on the coordinated outcome.

A merger involving non-mavericks could instead promote competition by creating a new industry maverick. In particular, the acquisition could confer such large efficiencies on the merging parties as to lead them to prefer a much lower price than either did before the transaction, and below the price desired by the current industry maverick. *Horizontal*

---

* Alternatively, there may be some chance that one of the non-maverick merged firms would become the industry maverick in the future. If the merger removes this possibility, it would, with probability, harm competition much as would the merger of a maverick.

Merger Guidelines § 4 ("In a coordinated interaction context . . ., marginal cost reductions may make coordination less likely or effective by enhancing the incentive of a maverick to lower price or by creating a new maverick firm"). This possibility was suggested by the district court's decision in *FTC v. H.J. Heinz Co.*, 116 F.Supp.2d 190 (D.D.C. 2000), *rev'd* 246 F.3d 708 (D.C. Cir. 2001).

Coordinated Competitive Effects Analysis Without a Maverick

It will not always be possible to identify the maverick with precision or to determine with confidence how the loss of a firm through merger affects the maverick's incentives. For example, the difference between the district court and the appellate court in *Heinz* can be understood as a dispute about whether the record in that case reasonably permitted identification of a maverick.

When courts and enforcers cannot identify a maverick in a market conducive to coordination they tend to have difficulty explaining why the particular merger under review matters. After all, any merger raises concentration but not every merger necessarily makes coordination more likely or more effective. Yet when a maverick cannot be identified (or the effect of the merger on the maverick's incentives cannot reliably be assessed), courts routinely rely on changes in market structure, particularly the structural presumption, to explain the incremental impact of a merger on coordinated conduct.

The maverick analysis helps justify that common practice, as it provides a theoretical connection between market concentration and more effective coordination: In the absence of specific evidence identifying a maverick or tending to suggest that any particular firm is likely to play that role, the fewer the number of significant sellers, the more likely it will be that the loss of any one would involve the loss of a firm that constrains the effectiveness of coordinated conduct. If, in addition, the merger narrows differences in product attributes across firms or differences in seller costs, the odds that the merger involves a maverick will increase. From this perspective, changes in market structure provide a basis for inferring that the merger makes a difference to the likelihood or effectiveness of coordinated conduct when they suggest that it is probable that the merger involves the loss of a maverick firm.

Conclusion

Increased awareness of the role of mavericks may offer important insights into the analysis of the expected coordinated effects of mergers. But can such awareness also be relevant in other areas of antitrust analysis? Reflect on that question further when we proceed to Part III of the Casebook to consider the motives for, and methods used to, exclude rivals.

As was no doubt evident from your reading of *HCA*, antitrust enforcers, and courts reviewing their actions, may rely on a wide variety of evidence in reaching their conclusions about a mergers likely effects, and that evidence may come from a variety of sources. Of course, in most instances the bulk of the evidence will come from the merging firms, themselves, through disclosures required through the HSR process, and the formal discovery that follows in the form of Second Requests and other follow-on discovery. Two other critical sources of information, however are rival firms and customers of the merging firms. Sidebar 5–9 evaluates the utility and issues that arise in connection with reliance on such information.

Sidebar 5–9:
Competitor vs. Customer Complaints

In *Hosp. Corp. of Am.*, Judge Posner observed that the merging firms' "most telling point" was that the impetus for the government investigation came from a competitor. Judge Posner explained that the very fact of a competitor complaint is inconsistent with the government's anticompetitive theory. If the merger would facilitate tacit collusion, the competitor should expect to share in the gains from higher market prices, and thus would not be expected to object to the deal. Only if the merger would promote competition and lead to lower prices, would rivals lose profits and be expected to oppose the deal. Judge Posner is suggesting, therefore, that competitor complaints should be discounted or ignored.

On the other hand, customer views normally would be aligned with the public interest. If the merger would raise price, customers should object; if it would lower price, they should favor the transaction. When coordinated anticompetitive effects are alleged, Judge Posner implies, the enforcement agency should always do what the customers suggest, and the opposite of what competitors recommend! Judge Easterbrook similarly proposes that courts employ the identity of the plaintiff as a filter for screening out unpromising cases, and "dismiss outright" some lawsuits brought by rivals. Frank H. Easterbrook, *The Limits of Antitrust*, 63 TEX. L. REV. 1, 35 (1984). This way of thinking also underlies the "antitrust injury" doctrine, which we met in Chapter 1 in reading *Brunswick*.

This analysis helps explain why the antitrust enforcement agencies are often more interested in customer views than rival views when reviewing a horizontal merger. In investigating a transaction, the agencies routinely talk to rivals to learn about the industry and confirm factual assertions about the market made by the merging firms—but such information may be discounted to the extent the rivals are seen as interested parties (just as information provided by the merging firms is often not accepted without testing).

Customers and suppliers may be less informed about the market than rivals, but their interests may generally be more aligned with the public interest that the agency hopes to vindicate. "Customers" in this context need not be consumers. Many goods are "intermediate goods," sold by one set of firms to large and sophisticated businesses who use them in their own production. For example, automobile manufacturers are customers whose views might be consulted in the event of horizontal mergers in a wide range of supplier markets, including steel, car radios, tires, and the like. In sum, the enforcement agencies are more likely to view information provided by customers as disinterested, and they are more likely to see customer complaints as a reason to launch an investigation.

It is one thing to approach the views of competitors with skepticism; it is quite another to draw an opposite inference from their complaints, as would Judges Posner and Easterbrook. First, in some important respects, the enforcement agency is in a better position to learn about competitive conditions in the market than is any firm involved in it, customer or competitor. No single firm will have access to the confidential marketing analyses and plans of every seller, for example, but the agency, with its subpoena power, does. Second, sometimes customers may be poor guides to likely competitive effects of the transaction. Small customers may not understand the industry in which their sellers participate. If the product whose sellers are merging is an intermediate good, the immediate customers may not pay much attention to the price they are charged by some suppliers: the intermediate product may only account for a small share of the cost of the final downstream product (as the car radio is to the automobile), and if the downstream industry has a relatively inelastic demand, the sellers may be able to pass through most of any increase in the costs of inputs to end use consumers (such as the automobile buyer). Under such circumstances, moreover, the end use consumer may have little understanding of the upstream markets subject to merger, and thus little basis for providing an informed opinion to antitrust enforcers.

Third, the inference that a merger is procompetitive from rival complaints presumes that the anticompetitive harm is collusive, not exclusionary. If the merger would harm competition by excluding competitors (*see* discussion of vertical mergers, Chapter 7C, *infra*), the complaints of the excluded rivals are consistent with the anticompetitive theory, and so should be heeded by antitrust enforcers. (A similar qualification arises in the discussion of antitrust injury in Chapter 9.) Some antitrust commentators would advise antitrust enforcers to ignore this possibility, however logical, on the view that anticompetitive exclusionary conduct is either rare or difficult for enforcers to attack without chilling procompetitive conduct. Others take the possibility of exclusion more seriously, and would welcome competitor complaints about anticompetitive exclusionary conduct as a guide to identifying harmful mergers.

Some of those who are most enthusiastic about making inferences about the likely competitive effects of a merger by evaluating its effect on rivals propose doing so based on the effect of merger announcements on share prices in the stock market. If the stock market price of rival firms rises upon the announcement of the merger (or falls when the investment community learns that antitrust enforcers have launched an investigation), some would infer that the transaction is likely to harm competition; if the stock market price of rival firms falls on the merger announcement (or rises in response to information about increased enforcer concern), the transaction is thought likely to promote competition. Because this methodology makes inferences from the stock market response to outside events, it is often termed an "event study" methodology. *See* Serdar Dalkir & Frederick R. Warren–Boulton, *Prices, Market Definition, and the Effects of Merger: Staples–Office Depot* (1997), *in* John E. Kwoka, Jr. and Lawrence J. White, eds., The Antitrust Revolution 153 (3d ed.1999).

Critics of the event study methodology make several points. First, they point to technical difficulties in identifying when the relevant "events" occurred (when did the news actually get out?) and controlling for other factors that might have affected share prices (like the general trend of the stock market as a whole). Second, they note that the key inference—lower stock market prices for rival shares suggesting that the merger creates efficiencies rather than anticompetitive harm—is only correct on its own terms if the anticompetitive theory involves collusive rather than exclusionary effects. Third, they suggest that notwithstanding the way that the stock market aggregates information from throughout the economy, antitrust enforcers have more information in important respects than is reflected in share values. Unlike investors and Wall Street analysts, enforcers can read the marketing documents of all the firms. Finally, they point out that when investors forecast the likely financial consequences of a merger proposal, they must consider not only the competitive effects of the deal but also the likelihood that the transaction will be challenged by antitrust enforcers. If investors believe that the merger would likely harm competition by facilitating tacit collusion, they should bid up the stock market price of rival shares. But if the resulting increase in the stock market price would make a government challenge to the deal likely, investors would not want to increase the stock price after all. Under such circumstances, it is far from clear what, if anything, the antitrust agencies could reliably infer by analyzing the stock market response to merger announcements.

Similar issues about the trustworthiness of competitor or customer evidence arise when executives from those firms provide evidence as to likely buyer substitution in connection with market definition or assessing unilateral effects of a merger among sellers of differentiated products. Before trusting customer views, a fact-finder can be expected to assess whether they are informed, representative, and reliable. In *United States v. Oracle Corp.*, 331 F. Supp. 2d 1098, 1131 (N.D. Cal. 2004), for example, the court declined to consider customer views it considered inadequately supported. When the issue is not market definition or unilateral effects, but the likelihood of coordinated effects, moreover, a court may be even more inclined to question the reliability of customer views. After all, buyers are unlikely to have special expertise as to how *seller* behavior would change after a merger, which is the competitive effects issue in a coordinated effects case. *See FTC v. Arch Coal, Inc.*, 329 F. Supp. 2d 109 (D.D.C. 2004).

b. *Unilateral Competitive Effects*

Traditionally, merger enforcement was focused on coordinated competitive effects. That theory was implicitly or explicitly behind the decisions in the major cases we have read to this point, from *Philadelphia Nat'l Bank* to *Hosp. Corp. of Am..* But mergers among rivals may diminish competition even if they do not make coordination among the market participants more likely or more successful; they may instead harm competition "unilaterally" by making it possible for the merged firm to raise price on its own, without consideration of the likely responses of non-merging rivals. This possibility is most clear in a "merger to monopoly," where the merger creates a firm with sufficient market power to raise price on its own. As we shall see, however, the Guidelines' concept of unilateral effects extends beyond the setting of mergers to monopoly.

The many unilateral competitive effects possibilities have long been known to industrial organization economists, but they have taken on increased importance in antitrust practice, particularly at the federal enforcement agencies, since economists developed ways to quantify the magnitude of the possible anticompetitive effects, beginning with the work of Jonathan B. Baker and Timothy F. Bresnahan in the mid–1980s, and when these theories appeared in the 1992 revisions to the Merger Guidelines.

The Merger Guidelines set forth two main unilateral competitive effects theories, one for markets in which products are differentiated (*Horizontal Merger Guidelines* § 2.21), and one for markets in which products are homogeneous (*Horizontal Merger Guidelines* § 2.22). These do not exhaust the range of possible unilateral theories, but they are the ones most commonly employed within the federal enforcement agencies—particularly the analysis of markets with differentiated products. This chapter will take a close look at the primary unilateral competitive effects theory, the one that applies when products are differentiated.

Goods and services may differ along a wide range of physical and non-physical characteristics, including features, colors, styles, geographic location, point-of-sale or post-sale services (like demonstrations and warranties), seller reputations for quality, delivery time, defect rate, and non-physical attributes, such as "brand" recognition or an image related to lifestyle (like "cool," "young," or "cutting-edge"). *See* Thomas J. Campbell, *Predation and Competition in Antitrust: The Case of Nonfungible Goods*, 87 COLUM. L. REV. 1625 (1987).

Differentiation is common in branded consumer products industries, such as soft drinks and breakfast cereals; in markets where buyers see important differences in the nature or quality of services offered by potential suppliers, such as automotive steel or the auditing services provided by accounting firms; and in industries where differences in seller locations are important to buyers, such as supermarkets or hospitals. In such markets, competition may be "localized," in the sense that buyers view some products within the market as closer substitutes to each other, and individual sellers compete more directly with those rivals selling the closest substitutes.

Although the analysis of unilateral effects among sellers of differentiated products had become routine at the federal enforcement agencies by the early 1990s, the courts have taken longer to address the topic, in part because merger litigation is rare. One early judicial effort to consider unilateral effects was *New York v. Kraft General Foods, Inc.*, 926 F.Supp. 321 (S.D.N.Y 1995), which involved a challenge to an acquisition in the breakfast cereal industry. The challenge was initiated by the New York State Attorney General, who alleged both coordinated and unilateral competitive effects; here we focus on the unilateral competitive effects issue.

The case involved a November 1992 transaction in which Kraft, the owner of Post cereals, acquired the ready-to-eat ("RTE") cereal assets of Nabisco. The Federal Trade Commission reviewed the transaction and declined to challenge it. At that time, over 200 RTE cereal products were available for sale to consumers. RTE cereals differ from one another in important respects, including type of grain, degree of sweetness, product form (*e.g.*, flake, nugget, shredded, etc.), texture, flavor, complexity, type of additional ingredients (*e.g.*, nuts and fruit), and perceived health benefits. Even the most popular RTE cereals accounted for only a small percentage of total RTE cereal sales. The best-selling RTE cereal, Kellogg's Corn Flakes, had a share only slightly above 5%.

Kellogg and General Mills were the two largest manufacturers, together accounting for 60% of RTE cereal products sold in the U.S. Kraft, the third largest manufacturer with about 12% of sales, produced and sold 28 RTE cereal products, most under the "Post" name. Grape Nuts was one of Post's most successful products. Nabisco, with a market share of less than 3%, was sixth largest. Its main strength was its shredded wheat line of cereals.

The district court rejected New York's unilateral effects claim because it concluded that "Grape Nuts and Nabisco Shredded Wheat compete with many other products and are not the first and second choices of a significant number of consumers." 926 F.Supp. at 352. One notable feature of the decision is the wide range of evidence the court relied upon in reaching this conclusion. At least five different types of evidence were analyzed.

First, the court looked at the extent to which the two brands had similar physical characteristics and images. It found that Grape Nuts and Nabisco Shredded Wheat differed in physical characteristics and that the two brands emphasized different attributes in their advertising. (Grape Nuts was marketed first as "healthy" and later as "energy sustaining;" Nabisco Shredded Wheat was marketed as "pure," with no added sugar or salt. Many other cereal brands were also promoted as healthy, plain cereals, such as Corn Flakes, Cheerios, Chex, Special K, Total, and Rice Krispies.

Second, the court also relied upon customer testimony about the extent of buyer substitution between the brands. It noted that executives of two large grocery retailers testified that they did not consider Grape Nuts and Nabisco Shredded Wheat to be particularly close competitors, and that they set the retail price for the two brands independently.

Third, the court relied upon marketing survey data about the characteristics of each brand's customers. It found that Grape Nuts consumers tended to be "upscale," younger, and more educated, while Nabisco Shredded Wheat consumers tended to be "downscale," older, and less educated.

Fourth, the district court examined the extent to which the merging firms monitored and responded to key marketing decisions of each other. The evidence in this category was mixed, according to the court. Some Post documents indicated that the two brands were viewed as at or near the top of each other's list of most direct competitors. But the evidence also showed that Post generally looked to Kellogg products, not Nabisco Shredded Wheat, as a benchmark in pricing Grape Nuts and that the evidence did not support plaintiff's assertion that Post tracked Nabisco Shredded Wheat's pricing, advertising, and promotional activities to determine expenditures for Grape Nuts.

Finally, the court relied upon an econometric study of buyer demand conducted by defendant's expert economist. The expert found low cross-price elasticities of demand between Grape Nuts and Nabisco Shredded Wheat, and that cross-price elasticities of demand were higher between Grape Nuts and a number of other cereals, including Cheerios, Kellogg's Raisin Bran, Kellogg's Frosted Mini–Wheats, the Kellogg's Nutri–Grain line, and Ralston Chex.

When turning to the law, the district court recognized that unilateral effects cases were at the time novel in the courts, and relied upon the Merger Guidelines as persuasive authority.

> The State contends that, even absent any consideration of coordinated effects, the Acquisition is unlawful because it promotes anticompetitive unilateral effects, i.e., by placing Shredded Wheat and Grape Nuts under one roof, the Acquisition diminishes the likelihood that there will be competition between the two brands, which the State contends are very close substitutes for one another. The Merger Guidelines recognize the danger of anticompetitive unilateral effects, pointing out (put most simply) that a merged firm may be able to raise the price of one product and capture any sales lost due to that price rise, if buyers will switch to another product that is now sold by the merged firm. As the Merger Guidelines note, a firm can wield such power (i.e., achieve substantial unilateral price elevation) in a market for differentiated products only if there is "a significant share of sales in the market accounted for by consumers who regard the products of the merging firms as their first and second choices, and that repositioning of the non-parties' product lines to replace the localized competition lost through the merger [is] unlikely."

> Although courts do not invariably concern themselves with unilateral effects in Section 7 cases, I will assume, arguendo, that the Merger Guidelines' concern for this effect is valid. * * *

> * * *

> The foregoing demonstrates that it would not be profitable for Kraft to raise the price of Grape Nuts in the expectation that a substantial portion of its lost sales would go to Nabisco Shredded Wheat, because it is likely that the lost sales would be dispersed among a wide variety of products, and that Nabisco Shredded Wheat would gain only a small percentage of those losses. The State has failed to prove its claim of adverse unilateral effects.

926 F.Supp. at 365–66.

Note that in analyzing unilateral effects, the *Kraft* court examined the same types of evidence that courts look to in defining markets under the Merger Guidelines. This is not a coincidence. Both market definition (under the Guidelines approach) and unilateral effects among sellers of differentiated products turn on the same economic force: demand (buyer) substitution. Would *Kraft* have come out differently had the plaintiff instead framed the unilateral effects allegation as a merger to monopoly within a narrow market or submarket (perhaps limited to "healthy" cereals)? After reading the Crunchies/Fruities illustration, which explicates the economic logic of unilateral effects among sellers of differentiated products, consider what if anything in the economics analysis turns on the scope of the product market.

Note on the Economics of Unilateral Effects:
The Merger of Crunchies and Fruities*

To understand the unilateral competitive effects theory analyzed in *Kraft*, consider a merger in a hypothetical, and much simplified, breakfast cereal industry. Suppose the Crunchy Cereal Co. which makes the Crunchies brand, seeks to acquire the Fruity Cereal Co., maker of Fruities. Assume further, at variance with the real breakfast cereal industry, that each firm sells only one brand and that firms promote their brands exclusively through national advertising, not by discounting prices at supermarkets. The example set forth in the following paragraphs is also summarized below in tables.

Before the merger, Crunchies sells for $2.00 per standard-sized box. An additional cereal box costs $1.10 to produce and sell. Assume that if Crunchies were to raise the price of a box of its product by 5%, to $2.10, Crunchies would lose 10 out of every 100 unit sales, or 10% of its sales. (If a 5% price increase induces a 10% reduction in the quantity sold, the own price elasticity of demand is –2.) Quantity sold declines because some customers buy fewer Crunchies than before, some substitute other breakfast cereals, and some do without cereal altogether, much as we saw in discussing the coffee hypothetical in Chapter 1.

With these assumptions, the manufacturer would not be able to increase profits by raising the Crunchies price. In making that determination, the company balances the projected costs of lost sales against the gain from higher price-cost margins. On the cost side, the company would lose a contribution margin (price less marginal cost) of $0.90 on the 10 out of every 100 premerger sales that it no longer makes, for a total loss of $9.00. Against that loss, Crunchies would gain an additional $0.10 profit on the 90 out of 100 sales it still makes at the higher price, for a gain of $9.00 per 100 units sold premerger. Because the gain from raising price ($9.00) does not exceed the cost (also $9.00), the firm will not attempt to increase its price.**

Figure 5–7:
A Price Increase Would Not Increase Crunchies Profits Pre–Merger

Types of Gains and Losses		Gain or Loss (per 100 buyers)
Gain from higher price-cost margin, per 100 customers	+ $0.10 x 90 customers	+ $9.00
Loss from losing contribution margin on sales, per 100 customers.	– $0.90 x 10 customers	– $9.00
Net gain or loss		$0

The merger of Crunchies and Fruities can alter this calculus, making an increase in the Crunchies price profitable. Three of the 10 unit sales lost (out

---

* This example is adapted from Jonathan B. Baker, *Unilateral Competitive Effects Theories in Merger Analysis*, ANTITRUST, Spring 1997, at 21, 23.

** Nothing of consequence in the example would change were the variable costs of production $1.099 per box, so that the price of $2.00 is strictly more profitable than the price of $2.10.

of every 100 lost sales) represent customers switching from Crunchies to Fruities as a consequence of the Crunchies price increase. (This figure—three lost Crunchies customers out of every ten go to Fruities—has been termed a "diversion ratio." It is related to the cross-price elasticity of demand between the brands.) For those 3 lost customers, Fruities is the closest substitute for Crunchies at current prices.

Suppose further that Fruities already sells for $2.10—the new Crunchies price—and that the next box of Fruities would cost $1.30 to produce and distribute. If Crunchies acquires Fruities and then raises the price of Crunchies to $2.10, Crunchies will avoid some of the losses it would otherwise have sustained by diverting some Crunchies sales to what is now its other brand, Fruities. On the 3 out of every 100 Crunchies units sold premerger that become Fruities sales, the merged firm earns a profit of $0.80 per unit ($2.10—$1.30), for a total gain of $2.40 per 100 Crunchies units sold premerger. That is, selling 90 units of Crunchies at $2.10 and 3 units of Fruities at $2.10 would be more profitable than selling 100 units of Crunchies alone at $2.00. Accordingly, as a consequence of the merger, it is now profitable to increase the Crunchies price to $2.10.

Figure 5–8:

A Price Increase Would Increase Crunchies Profits Post–Merger

Types of Gains and Losses		Gain or Loss (per 100 buyers)
Gain from higher price-cost margin, per 100 customers	+ $0.10 x 90 customers	+ $9.00
Loss from losing contribution margin on sales, per 100 customers.	- $0.90 x 10 customers	- $9.00
Gain in added profits to Fruities	+ $0.80 x 3 customers	+ $2.40
Net gain or loss		**+$2.40**

The profitability of a unilateral increase in the price of Crunchies thus may constitute a motive for merger. Before the merger, the Crunchies price was held in check by the collective presence of competition from rival brands, including Fruities, that were the second choice for a significant fraction of consumers. But with the merger, Crunchies no longer is concerned about the diversion of some buyers to Fruities. Thus, the merger removes Fruities as a constraint on Crunchies pricing. For similar reasons, the merger may also give the merged firm an incentive to increase the price of Fruities.

Fruities need not be the most preferred alternative among the buyers who switch away from Crunchies in response to a price rise in order for the merger to create harmful unilateral effects, so long as Fruities is the preferred alternative for a substantial group of those buyers. To see this, note that it does not matter in the example which brand was chosen by the remaining 7 of every 10 lost Crunchies customers that did not select Fruities as their second choice, or whether or not those lost customers continue to buy breakfast cereal. (Perhaps, for example, 6 out of every 10 lost Crunchies customers switched to Oaties.) So long as a substantial fraction of lost Crunchies customers (here 3 out every 10 lost customers) selected Fruities as their second choice, the merged firm will profit by raising the Crunchies price. In other words, Fruities must be the closest substitute for a substantial group of Crunchies buyers, but it is not necessary that Fruities be the closest substitute for the largest group of Crunchies buyers.

Moreover, the higher price of the merged firm's products may make it profitable for non-merging rivals like Oaties to raise the prices for their products. In this way, the adverse consequences of mergers creating unilateral effects may spread beyond the products of the merged firms.

The example also can be used to illustrate two kinds of defenses Crunchies and Fruities might offer to the claim that their merger will harm competition by reducing localized competition among sellers of differentiated products. The first involves expansion of output by rival suppliers, as through entry of new products (either by new or established firms), or the "repositioning" of existing products by competing firms (modifying product or brand attributes, or extending brands by adding variants to the product line). For example, Oaties, a third cereal brand, may respond to the Crunchies price rise by adding Crunchy Oaties and Fruity Oaties to its product line, or by stepping up promotion of these brands if they already exist. This repositioning response by Oaties might lead more than 10 out of 100 Crunchies customers to switch away in response to a Crunchies price increase, and lead most of the switchers who formerly saw Fruities as their second choice to select an Oaties product instead. If so, it may no longer be profitable to increase the price of Crunchies after the merger. A second defense possibility is that efficiencies from the merger may counteract the incentive to raise price. For example, Crunchies and Fruities together may be able to achieve substantial cost savings from their increased scale of promotion and distribution. If the marginal cost of producing Crunchies were to decline sufficiently, the post-merger price could fall notwithstanding the loss of direct competition between the two brands. Efficiencies are considered in more detail later in this chapter.

What element of the unilateral competitive effects theory sketched in this note did the district court find lacking in rejecting New York's challenge to Kraft's acquisition of Nabisco? Would the court agree that "it is not necessary that Fruities be the most preferred alternative among the buyers who switch away from Crunchies in response to a price rise" in order for the merger of Crunchies and Fruities to harm competition?

Economists analyzing unilateral effects have developed sophisticated simulation tools for predicting the post-merger price based on the kind of information used in the example in this note. These tools can be particularly valuable when the agency must assess the net effect of opposing forces, such as an incentive to raise price resulting from the loss of direct competition and the incentive to reduce price resulting from efficiencies. Simulation modeling is also sometimes employed by expert economists as a basis for the testimony in merger cases. For a technical survey by two leading proponents of the approach, see Gregory J. Werden & Luke M. Froeb, *Unilateral Competitive*

Effects of Horizontal Mergers, in HANDBOOK OF ANTITRUST ECONOMICS (Paolo Buccirossi, ed.) (forthcoming 2008) (working paper available at http://ssrn.com/abstract=927913).

———

The *Staples* case, which we will read next, involves an FTC challenge to a proposed merger of two of the three leading office supply superstore chains, Staples and Office Depot. As you read the case, consider how the economic principles explored in the previous Note on the Crunchies–Fruities merger could explain the FTC's theory of anticompetitive effects.

FEDERAL TRADE COMMISSION v. STAPLES, INC.

United States District Court for the District of Columbia, 1997.
970 F.Supp. 1066.

THOMAS F. HOGAN, District Judge.

Plaintiff, the Federal Trade Commission ("FTC" or "Commission"), seeks a preliminary injunction pursuant to Section 13(b) of the Federal Trade Commission Act, 15 U.S.C. § 53(b), to enjoin the consummation of any acquisition by defendant Staples, Inc., of defendant Office Depot, Inc., pending final disposition before the Commission of administrative proceedings to determine whether such acquisition may substantially lessen competition in violation of Section 7 of the Clayton Act, 15 U.S.C. § 18, and Section 5 of the Federal Trade Commission Act, 15 U.S.C. § 45. The proposed acquisition has been postponed pending the Court's decision on the motion for a preliminary injunction, which is now before the Court for decision after a five-day evidentiary hearing and the filing of proposed findings of fact and conclusions of law. For the reasons set forth below, the Court will grant the plaintiff's motion. This Memorandum Opinion constitutes the Court's findings of fact and conclusions of law.

BACKGROUND

* * *

Defendants are both corporations which sell office products–including office supplies, business machines, computers and furniture–through retail stores, commonly described as office supply superstores, as well as through direct mail delivery and contract stationer operations. Staples is the second largest office superstore chain in the United States with approximately 550 retail stores located in 28 states and the District of Columbia, primarily in the Northeast and California. In 1996 Staples' revenues from those stores were approximately $4 billion through all operations. Office Depot, the largest office superstore chain, operates over 500 retail office supply superstores that are located in 38 states and the District of Columbia, primarily in the South and Midwest. Office Depot's 1996 sales were approximately $6.1 billion. OfficeMax, Inc., is the only other office supply superstore firm in the United States.

* * *

DISCUSSION

I. Section 13(B) Standard for Preliminary Relief

* * *

In order to determine whether the Commission has met its burden with respect to showing its likelihood of success on the merits, that is, whether the FTC has raised questions going to the merits so serious, substantial, difficult and doubtful as to make them fair ground for thorough investigation, study, deliberation and determination by the FTC in the first instance and ultimately by the Court of Appeals and that there is a "reasonable probability" that the challenged transaction will substantially impair competition, the Court must consider the likely competitive effects of the merger, if any. Analysis of the likely competitive effects of a merger requires determinations of (1) the "line of commerce" or product market in which to assess the transaction, (2) the "section of the country" or geographic market in which to assess the transaction, and (3) the transaction's probable effect on competition in the product and geographic markets. * * *

II. The Geographic Market

One of the few issue about which the parties to this case do not disagree is that metropolitan areas are the appropriate geographic markets for analyzing the competitive effects of the proposed merger. * * *

III. The Relevant Product Market

In contrast to the parties' agreement with respect to the relevant geographic market, the Commission and the defendants sharply disagree with respect to the appropriate definition of the relevant product market or line of commerce. As with many antitrust cases, the definition of the relevant product market in this case is crucial. In fact, to a great extent, this case hinges on the proper definition of the relevant product market.

The Commission defines the relevant product market as "the sale of consumable office supplies through office superstores," * * * with "consumable" meaning products that consumers buy recurrently, i.e., items which "get used up" or discarded. For example, under the Commission's definition, "consumable office supplies" would not include capital goods such as computers, fax machines, and other business machines or office furniture, but does include such products as paper, pens, file folders, post-it notes, computer disks, and toner cartridges. The defendants characterize the FTC's product market definition as "contrived" with no basis in law or fact, and counter that the appropriate product market within which to assess the likely competitive consequences of a Staples–Office Depot combination is simply the overall sale of office products, of which a combined Staples–Office Depot accounted for 5.5% of total sales in North America in 1996. In addition, the defendants argue that the challenged combination is not likely "substantially to lessen competition" however the product market is defined. After considering the arguments on both sides and all of the evidence in this case and making evaluations of each witness's credibility as well as the weight that the Court should give certain evidence and testimony, the Court finds that the appropriate relevant product market definition in this case is, as the Commission has argued, the sale of consumable office supplies through office supply super-stores.

* * *

The Court recognizes that it is difficult to overcome the first blush or initial gut reaction of many people to the definition of the relevant product market as the sale of consumable office supplies through office supply super-stores. The products in question are undeniably the same no matter who sells them, and no one denies that many different types of retailers sell these products. After all, a combined Staples–Office Depot would only have a 5.5% share of the overall market in consumable office supplies. Therefore, it is logical to conclude that, of course, all these retailers compete, and that if a combined Staples–Office Depot raised prices after the merger, or at least did not lower them as much as they would have as separate companies, that consumers, with such a plethora of options, would shop elsewhere.

The Court acknowledges that there is, in fact, a broad market encompass-ing the sale of consumable office supplies by all sellers of such supplies, and that those sellers must, at some level, compete with one another. However, the mere fact that a firm may be termed a competitor in the overall marketplace does not necessarily require that it be included in the relevant product market for antitrust purposes. The Supreme Court has recognized that within a broad market, "well-defined submarkets may exist which, in themselves, constitute product markets for antitrust purposes." *Brown Shoe Co. v. United States*, 370 U.S. 294, 325, 82 S.Ct. 1502, 1524, 8 L.Ed.2d 510 (1962). * * * There is a possibility, therefore, that the sale of consumable office supplies by office superstores may qualify as a submarket within a larger market of retailers of office supplies in general.

The Court in *Brown Shoe* provided a series of factors or "practical indicia" for determining whether a submarket exists. * * *

* * * [T]he FTC focused on what it termed the "pricing evidence," which the Court finds corresponds with *Brown Shoe's* "sensitivity to price changes" factor. First, the FTC presented evidence comparing Staples' prices in geo-graphic markets where Staples is the only office superstore, to markets where Staples competes with Office Depot or OfficeMax, or both. Based on the FTC's calculations, in markets where Staples faces no office superstore competition at all, something which was termed a one firm market during the hearing, prices are 13% higher than in three firm markets where it competes with both Office Depot and OfficeMax. * * * Similarly, the evidence showed that Office Depot's prices are significantly higher—well over 5% higher, in Depot-only markets than they are in three firm markets.

* * *

The FTC also pointed to internal Staples documents which present price comparisons between Staples' prices and Office Depot's prices and Staples' prices and OfficeMax's prices within different price zones.[9] * * * Using Staples' data, but organizing it differently to show which of those zones were

---

9. It was established at the hearing that Staples and Office Depot do not maintain na-tionally uniform prices in their stores. Instead, both companies currently organize their stores into price zones which are simply groups of one or more stores that have common prices.

one, two, or three firm markets, the FTC showed once again that Staples charges significantly higher prices, more than 5% higher, where it has no office superstore competition than where it competes with the two other superstores. * * *

This evidence all suggests that office superstore prices are affected primarily by other office superstores and not by non-superstore competitors such as mass merchandisers like Wal–Mart, Kmart, or Target, wholesale clubs such as BJ's, Sam's, and Price Costco, computer or electronic stores such as Computer City and Best Buy, independent retail office supply stores, mail orders firms like Quill and Viking, and contract stationers. Though the FTC did not present the Court with evidence regarding the precise amount of non-superstore competition in each of Staples' and Office Depot's one, two, and three firm markets, it is clear to the Court that these competitors, albeit in different combinations and concentrations, are present in every one of these markets. * * *

* * * Staples' own pricing information shows that warehouse clubs have very little effect on Staples' prices. For example, Staples' maintains a "warehouse club only" price zone, which indicates a zone where Staples exists with a warehouse club but without another office superstore. The data presented by the Commission on Staples' pricing shows only a slight variation in prices (1%–2%) between "warehouse club only" zones and one superstore markets without a warehouse club. * * *

There is also consistent evidence with respect to computer and/or consumer electronics stores such as Best Buy. For example, Office Depot maintains a separate price zone, which it calls "zone 30," for areas with Best Buy locations but no other office supply superstores. However, the FTC introduced evidence * * * that prices in Office Depot's "zone 30" price zone are almost as high as in its "non-competitive" price zone, the zone where it does not compete with another office superstore.

There is similar evidence with respect to the defendants' behavior when faced with entry of another competitor. The evidence shows that the defendants change their price zones when faced with entry of another superstore, but do not do so for other retailers. * * * There are numerous additional examples of zones being changed and prices falling as a result of superstore entry. There is no evidence that zones change and prices fall when another non-superstore retailer enters a geographic market.

* * * [T]he Court finds this evidence a compelling showing that a small but significant increase in Staples' prices will not cause a significant number of consumers to turn to non-superstore alternatives for purchasing their consumable office supplies. * * *

Turning back to the other *Brown Shoe* "practical indicia" of submarkets that the Commission offered in this case, the Commission presented and the Court heard a great deal of testimony at the hearing and through declarations about the uniqueness of office superstores and the differences between the office superstores and other sellers of office supplies such as mass merchandisers, wholesale clubs, and mail order firms as well as the special characteristics of office superstore customers. In addition, the Court was asked to go and view many of the different types of retail formats. That evidence shows that office superstores are, in fact, very different in appearance, physical size, format, the number and variety of SKU's offered, and the type of customers targeted and served than other sellers of office supplies. * * * [SKUs, or stock-keeping units, are finely defined product categories, such as blue medium-point Bic pens. Eds.]

In addition to the differences in SKU numbers and variety, the superstores are different from many other sellers of office supplies due to the type of customer they target and attract. The superstores' customer base overwhelmingly consists of small businesses with fewer than 20 employees and consumers with home offices. * * *

* * * Based on the Court's observations, the Court finds that the unique combination of size, selection, depth and breadth of inventory offered by the superstores distinguishes them from other retailers. * * * No one entering Staples or Office Depot would mistakenly think he or she was in Best Buy or CompUSA. You certainly know an office superstore when you see one. * * *

Another of the "practical indicia" for determining the presence of a submarket suggested by *Brown Shoe* is "industry or public recognition of the submarket as a separate economic entity." * * * The Commission offered abundant evidence on this factor from Staples' and Office Depot's documents which shows that both Staples and Office Depot focus primarily on competition from other superstores. The documents reviewed by the Court show that the merging parties evaluate their "competition" as the other office superstore firms, without reference to other retailers, mail order firms, or independent stationers. In document after document, the parties refer to, discuss, and make business decisions based upon the assumption that "competition" refers to other office superstores only. * * *

* * * In a monthly report entitled "Competitor Store Opening/Closing Report" which Office Depot circulates to its Executive Committee, Office Depot notes all competitor store closings and openings, but the only competitors referred to for its United States stores are Staples and OfficeMax.

While it is clear to the Court that Staples and Office Depot do not ignore sellers such as warehouse clubs, Best Buy, or Wal–Mart, the evidence clearly shows that Staples and Office Depot each consider the other superstores as the primary competition. For example, Office Depot has a Best Buy zone and Staples has a warehouse club zone. However, each still refers to its one firm markets with no other office superstore as "non-competitive" zones or markets. In addition, it is clear from the evidence that Staples and Office Depot price check the other office superstores much more frequently and extensively than they price check other retailers such as BJ's or Best Buy, and that Staples and Office Depot are more concerned with keeping their prices in parity with the other office superstores in their geographic areas than in undercutting Best Buy or a warehouse club.

* * *

IV. *Probable Effect on Competition*

After accepting the Commission's definition of the relevant product market, the Court next must consider the probable effect of a merger between Staples and Office Depot in the geographic markets previously identified. One way to do this is to examine the concentration statistics and HHIs within the geographic markets. * * * If the relevant product market is defined as the sale of consumable office supplies through office supply superstores, the HHIs in many of the geographic markets are at problematic levels even before the merger. * * * The average increase in HHI caused by the merger would be 2,715 points. The concentration statistics show that a merged Staples–Office Depot would have a dominant market share in 42 geographic markets across the country. The combined shares of Staples and Office Depot in the office superstore market would be 100% in 15 metropolitan areas. It is in these markets the post-merger HHI would be 10,000. In 27 other metropolitan areas, where the number of office superstore competitors would drop from three to two, the post-merger market shares would range from 45% to 94%, with post-merger HHIs ranging from 5,003 to 9,049. Even the lowest of these HHIs indicates a "highly concentrated" market.

* * * With HHIs of this level, the Commission certainly has shown a "reasonable probability" that the proposed merger would have an anti-competitive effect. * * *

The HHI calculations and market concentration evidence, however, are not the only indications that a merger between Staples and Office Depot may substantially lessen competition. Much of the evidence already discussed with respect to defining the relevant product market also indicates that the merger would likely have an anti-competitive effect. The evidence of the defendants' own current pricing practices, for example, shows that an office superstore chain facing no competition from other superstores has the ability to profitably raise prices for consumable office supplies above competitive levels. The fact that Staples and Office Depot both charge higher prices where they face no superstore competition demonstrates that an office superstore can raise prices above competitive levels. The evidence also shows that defendants also change their price zones when faced with entry of another office superstore, but do not do so for other retailers. Since prices are significantly lower in markets where Staples and Office Depot compete, eliminating this competition with one another would free the parties to charge higher prices in those markets, especially those in which the combined entity would be the sole office superstore. In addition, allowing the defendants to merge would eliminate significant future competition. Absent the merger, the firms are likely, and in fact have planned, to enter more of each other's markets, leading to a deconcentration of the market and, therefore, increased competition between the superstores.

In addition, direct evidence shows that by eliminating Staples' most significant, and in many markets only, rival, this merger would allow Staples to increase prices or otherwise maintain prices at an anti-competitive level.[14]

14. There has been tremendous argument regarding whether the FTC actually contends that prices will go up after the merger. The Court understands that is not precisely the Commission's contention. Rather, the Commission argues that the merger will have an anti-competitive effect such that the combined firm's prices will be higher after the merger than they would be absent the merger. This does not necessarily mean that prices would rise from the levels they are now. Instead, according to the Commission, prices would simply not decrease as much as they would have on their own absent the merger. It is only in this sense that the Commission has contended that prices would go up–prices would go up compared to where they would have been absent the merger. It is only in this sense that consumers would be faced with "higher" prices. Therefore, when the Court discusses "raising" prices it is also with respect to raising prices with respect to where prices would

The merger would eliminate significant head-to-head competition between the two lowest cost and lowest priced firms in the superstore market. Thus, the merger would result in the elimination of a particularly aggressive competitor in a highly concentrated market, a factor which is certainly an important consideration when analyzing possible anti-competitive effects. * * * It is based on all of this evidence as well that the Court finds that the Commission has shown a likelihood of success on the merits and a "reasonable probability" that the proposed transaction will have an anti-competitive effect.

* * *

[The excerpt from *Staples* presented here includes the following section, which addresses the efficiency arguments urged on the court by the merging firms. Examination of this section of the decision can be delayed until later in this Chapter, when we more specifically explore efficiencies in merger analysis. Eds.]

VI. *Efficiencies*

Whether an efficiencies defense showing that the intended merger would create significant efficiencies in the relevant market, thereby offsetting any anti-competitive effects, may be used by a defendant to rebut the government's prima facie case is not entirely clear. The newly revised efficiencies section of the *Merger Guidelines* recognizes that, "mergers have the potential to generate significant efficiencies by permitting a better utilization of existing assets, enabling the combined firm to achieve lower costs in producing a given quality and quantity than either firm could have achieved without the proposed transaction." *See Merger Guidelines* § 4. This coincides with the view of some courts that "whether an acquisition would yield significant efficiencies in the relevant market is an important consideration in predicting whether the acquisition would substantially lessen competition.... [T]herefore, ... an efficiency defense to the government's prima facie case in section 7 challenges is appropriate in certain circumstances." *FTC v. University Health*, 938 F.2d 1206, 1222 (11th Cir.1991). The Supreme Court, however, in *FTC v. Procter & Gamble Co.*, 386 U.S. 568, 579, 87 S.Ct. 1224, 1230, 18 L.Ed.2d 303 (1967), stated that "[p]ossible economies cannot be used as a defense to illegality in section 7 merger cases." There has been great disagreement regarding the meaning of this precedent and whether an efficiencies defense is permitted. * * * Assuming that it is a viable defense, however, the Court cannot find in this case that the defendants' efficiencies evidence rebuts the presumption that the merger may substantially lessen competition or shows that the Commission's evidence gives an inaccurate prediction of the proposed acquisition's probable effect.

The Court agrees with the defendants that where, as here, the merger has not yet been consummated, it is impossible to quantify precisely the efficiencies that it will generate. In addition, the Court recognizes a difference between efficiencies which are merely speculative and those which are based on a prediction backed by sound business judgment. * * * [L]ike all rebuttal evidence in Section 7 cases, the defendants must simply rebut the presumption that the merger will substantially lessen competition by showing that the

have been absent the merger, not actually an
increase from present price levels. * * *

Commission's evidence gives an inaccurate prediction of the proposed acquisition's probable effect. * * * Defendants, however, must do this with credible evidence, and the Court with respect to this issue did not find the defendants' evidence to be credible.

Defendants' submitted an "Efficiencies Analysis" which predicated that the combined company would achieve savings of between $4.9 and $6.5 billion over the next five years. In addition, the defendants argued that the merger would also generate dynamic efficiencies. For example, defendants argued that as suppliers become more efficient due to their increased sales volume to the combined Staples–Office Depot, they would be able to lower prices to their other retailers. Moreover, defendants argued that two-thirds of the savings realized by the combined company would be passed along to consumers.

Evaluating credibility, as the Court must do, the Court credits the testimony and Report of the Commission's expert, David Painter, over the testimony and Efficiencies Study of the defendants' efficiencies witness, * * * [the] Senior Vice President of Integration at Staples. Mr. Painter's testimony was compelling, and the Court finds, based primarily on Mr. Painter's testimony, that the defendants' cost savings estimates are unreliable. First, the Court notes that the cost savings estimate of $4.947 billion over five years which was submitted to the Court exceeds by almost 500% the figures presented to the two Boards of Directors in September 1996, when the Boards approved the transaction. The cost savings claims submitted to the Court are also substantially greater than those represented in the defendants' Joint Proxy Statement/Prospectus "reflecting the best currently available estimate of management," and filed with the Securities and Exchange Commission on January 23, 1997, or referenced in the "fairness opinions" rendered by the defendants' investment bankers which are contained in the Proxy Statement.

The Court also finds that the defendants' projected "Base Case" savings of $5 billion are in large part unverified, or at least the defendants failed to produce the necessary documentation for verification. One example of this is the estimated cost savings from the Goods and Services category which projects cost savings of $553 million, about 10% of the total cost savings attributed to the merger by the defendants. * * * [Staples' Vice President for Integration] admitted that the entire backup, source, and the calculations of the Goods and Services' cost savings were not included in the Efficiencies Analysis. In addition, * * * [she] was unable to explain the methods used to calculate many of the cost savings. Similarly, the projected distribution cost savings, $883 million or 17% of the projected total cost savings, are problematic. Defendants' consultant A.T. Kearney estimated the savings, and * * * [Staples' Vice President for Integration] admitted the Efficiency Analysis did not show that Kearney had deducted the projected Staples stand-alone savings from the new Hagerstown and Los Angeles full line distribution centers.

As with the failure to deduct the Staples stand-alone savings from the new Hagerstown and Los Angeles full line distribution centers from the projected distribution cost savings, the evidence shows that the defendants did not accurately calculate which projected cost savings were merger specific and which were, in fact, not related to the merger. For example, defendants' largest cost savings, over $2 billion or 40% of the total estimate, are projected as a result of their expectation of obtaining better prices from vendors.

However, this figure was determined in relation to the cost savings enjoyed by Staples at the end of 1996 without considering the additional cost savings that Staples would have received in the future as a stand-alone company. Since Staples has continuously sought and achieved cost savings on its own, clearly the comparison that should have been made was between the projected future cost savings of Staples as a stand-alone company, not its past rate of savings, and the projected future cost savings of the combined company. Thus, the calculation in the Efficiencies Analysis included product cost savings that Staples and Office Depot would likely have realized without the merger. In fact, Mr. Painter testified that, by his calculation, 43% of the estimated savings are savings that Staples and Office Depot would likely have achieved as stand-alone entities. * * *

In addition to the problems that the Court has with the efficiencies estimates themselves, the Court also finds that the defendants' projected pass through rate–the amount of the projected savings that the combined company expects to pass on to customers in the form of lower prices–is unrealistic. The Court has no doubt that a portion of any efficiencies achieved through a merger of the defendants would be passed on to customers. Staples and Office Depot have a proven track record of achieving cost savings through efficiencies, and then passing those savings to customers in the form of lower prices. However, in this case the defendants have projected a pass through rate of two-thirds of the savings while the evidence shows that, historically, Staples has passed through only 15–17%. Based on the above evidence, the Court cannot find that the defendants have rebutted the presumption that the merger will substantially lessen competition by showing that, because of the efficiencies which will result from the merger, the Commission's evidence gives an inaccurate prediction of the proposed acquisition's probable effect. * * *

* * *

———

The merger analysis in *Staples* was framed by the district court judge as primarily a question of market definition. In particular, the court employed the *Brown Shoe* practical indicia to define a submarket consisting of the sale of consumable office supplies through superstores within a broader product market involving the sale of such products through all distribution methods (including stationary stores, mass merchandisers, warehouse club stores, mail order and contract vendors, and others). Within the narrow submarket, the merger meant that the number of sellers would fall from three to two in some metropolitan areas, and from two to one in others, if the merger was permitted. If the transaction can be characterized as a merger to monopoly, as the court concluded was true in a number of geographic markets, there is little need to engage in a detailed economic analysis of competitive effects.

But the court's submarket definition can also be understood as an expositional tool for highlighting the potential loss of localized competition within the broader market (though this frame was not suggested by the district court judge). That is, the court in effect concluded that Staples and Office Depot were first and second choices for a substantial number of office supply customers, giving the merged firm an incentive to raise prices after the merger without regard to the presence of Wal–Mart and other non-superstore rivals in the market. One way a merged firm could exercise market power unilaterally under such circumstances is to do what the merged Crunchies/Fruities firm planned to do in the hypothetical breakfast cereal example: raise the price of one or both products. In some cases, a merged firm might do even better by altering some of the product or brand attributes. In *Staples*, the litigation proceeded under the assumption that post-merger, Staples would keep stores at the Office Depot locations, but change their name to Staples. Those locations would presumably remain the second choice for many shoppers who patronized the pre-merger Staples locations. If so, the competitive effects theory in the case can be understood as a variant of the unilateral effect theory for differentiated products set forth in the Merger Guidelines: by acquiring Office Depot, Staples could recapture many of the customers that would have been diverted by higher prices at its original stores to previously Office Depot stores, thus making the increased prices more likely to be profitable.

As this discussion suggests, if the loss of head-to-head competition among merger partners would permit the firms to raise price regardless of the response by other sellers in the market, the competitive concern can be described equivalently as a unilateral competitive effect within a broad market, or as a merger to near monopoly within a narrow submarket. Framing the case in the latter terms may make it more appealing, at least if the submarket definition can be simply stated, so as not to appear to reflect result-driven market gerrymandering. The lead attorney for the FTC when the case was tried, George Cary, has taken the view that *Staples* is best interpreted as a unilateral competitive effects case:

> I do think of *Staples* as a unilateral effects case. ... Ultimately, I think it has to be viewed as a unilateral effects case because the proof that was put forward in defining the product market was the closeness of competition between Staples and Office Depot and the effect of that competition on prices, without regard to competition from other firms.

Roundtable Discussion: *Unilateral Effects Analysis After* Oracle, ANTITRUST, Spring 2005, at 8, 9. By contrast, another senior FTC insider, then-Chairman Robert Pitofsky, has emphasized the market definition interpretation of the decision. Robert Pitofsky, *Staples and Boeing: What They Say About Merger Enforcement at the FTC* (Sept. 23, 1997), *available at* http://www.ftc.gov/speeches/pitofsky/STAPLESspc.shtm.

Which interpretation of *Staples* do you find more persuasive? What kind of evidence did the FTC and the court rely upon to demonstrate competitive effects? How (if at all) does that evidence differ from the evidence that the court relied upon to define the market?

As noted above, we will return to *Staples* to consider the court's analysis of efficiencies later in this Chapter.

———

In the wake of the 1992 Merger Guidelines, the unilateral competitive effects analysis of mergers among sellers of differentiated products became "the predominant theory of economic harm pursued in government merger investigations and challenges." Charles A. James, *Rediscovering Coordinated Effects* (Aug. 13, 2002), *available at* http://www.usdoj.gov/atr/public/speeches/200124.htm. By 2002, however, senior government antitrust enforcers began to question whether their agencies were relying too heavily on unilateral competitive effects analysis. *Id.* These officials and other critics of over-reliance on the unilateral approach did not question its theoretical soundness. They instead raised several concerns about its practical implementation.

First, critics pointed out that the unilateral approach may render market definition unnecessary, as harm can be found without regard to whether market shares are large or small. Indeed, market definition may appear "reverse engineered," defined by the set of customers likely to be harmed by the merger. Yet the Clayton Act's "in any line of commerce" and "any section of the country" language appears to require market definition. In contrast, some defenders of the unilateral approach embrace this feature, arguing that indirect evidence of market power derived from market share should take a back seat to direct evidence of likely competitive effects in these cases, and that if harm to competition can be demonstrated directly, some market in which competition can be harmed must exist and it is not important to specify the bounds of that market with precision. (The relative importance of direct and indirect evidence will be considered more fully in Chapter 8.) Consider the decision in *Staples* in light of these criticisms: Was the market definition reverse engineered? Did the court reach the right outcome?

Second, a number of econometric and conceptual issues may arise when attempting to assess quantitatively, through analysis of historical pricing data, the unilateral incentive to raise price arising from a given merger. Daniel Hosken, Daniel P. O'Brien, David Scheffman, and Michael Vita, *Demand System Estimation and its Application to Horizontal Merger Analysis*, F.T.C. Working Paper No. 246 (April 2002), *available at* http://www.ftc.gov/be/workpapers/wp246.pdf.

Third, anticompetitive harm will always be found, to at least some degree, if efficiencies, repositioning, and entry cannot be taken explicitly into account. In practice, critics contend, this unilateral competitive effects approach may tend to make all mergers among sellers of differentiated products appear harmful, especially to the extent that the devaluation of market shares precludes appeal to the Guidelines' safe harbors, which are based on low concentration. To address this concern, the Merger Guidelines incorporate a "safe harbor" provision that was intended to bar challenge to mergers among sellers of differentiated products on a unilateral competitive effects theory unless the merging firms have a combined market share in excess of 35 percent. The language chosen by the Guidelines' drafters, however, arguably restricts the application of this safe harbor provision to those rare cases in which the likely harm to competition (closeness of substitutes) is inferred solely from market shares. *Horizontal Merger Guidelines* § 2.211. Some defenders of the unilateral approach question the need for the 35% safe harbor, arguing that it unnecessarily forces the government to define a narrow market, and could impede the government from successfully challenging harmful mergers.

Do the results in *Staples* and *Kraft*—one a successful merger challenge, one an unsuccessful challenge—bear out these concerns? Or do they give you confidence that unilateral competitive effects analysis can successfully be employed to identify anticompetitive transactions without sweeping in procompetitive ones? Consider two subsequent efforts by the federal enforcement agencies to challenge mergers based on theories of anticompetitive unilateral effects in the next Note.

Note on the Merger Challenges in Oracle and Whole Foods

Although the unilateral theory of competitive effects among sellers of differentiated products is well established at the federal enforcement agencies, merger litigation framed around this theory is rare and the judicial reaction has been mixed. In 2004, the Justice Department was unsuccessful in persuading a federal district court to block the merger of Oracle and PeopleSoft under a unilateral effects theory. *United States v. Oracle Corp.*, 331 F. Supp. 2d 1098 (N.D. Cal. 2004). In many respects, the district court sided with the critics of unilateral effects theory.

Oracle and PeopleSoft both produced enterprise resource planning software, packaged software used by large and complex enterprises to integrate data across most of the firm's activities. The Justice Department alleged that the merger harmed competition within a product market of high function software used for financial management systems and human relations management. According to Justice, three firms dominated this category of business software, the merging firms and SAP. The government further claimed that Oracle and PeopleSoft were the leading choices for many customers. The merging firms argued for a broader market in which several other firms also participated, including Lawson, AMS and Microsoft. The district court declined to enjoin the merger primarily on the ground that the Justice Department had failed to prove the product market it alleged.

In deciding the case for defendants, the district court stated a controversial legal standard for proving unilateral effects among sellers of differentiated products. The court held that "[t]o prevail on a differentiated products unilateral effects claim, a plaintiff must prove a relevant market in which the merging parties would have essentially a monopoly or dominant position," 331 F. Supp. 2d at 1123. Critics charge that this standard is inconsistent with the economic analysis of unilateral effects. Recall that in the Crunchies–Fruities example, it was neither necessary nor helpful to define a product market limited to the Crunchies and Fruities products. In that example, the products of the merging firms were the first and second choice for many customers, but more customers of each could have picked a different brand as their second choice. In consequence, Oaties could have been a closer substitute to both Crunchies and Fruities than those two products were to each other. (After all, nothing in the example precludes the possibility that more lost Crunchies customers could have switched to Oaties than to Fruities.) Indeed, as previously noted, some economists have argued that market definition is unimportant or unnecessary in order to prove unilateral effects, as the same evidence about demand substitution would be analyzed in the same way regardless of how the claim is framed legally. Does any aspect of the economic logic demonstrating the harm to competition from the Crunchies–

Fruities merger turn on whether the market is narrow or broad? What legal purpose might be served by the *Oracle* court's requirement that plaintiff prove a merger to monopoly or near monopoly in a challenge based on unilateral effects? Look again at the language of Section 7 of the Clayton Act.

Moreover, while insisting that the government prove a narrow market in order to prevail on a unilateral effects claim, the *Oracle* district court simultaneously expressed skepticism about whether narrow markets could ever be defined in a principled way. The court noted the difficulty of defining narrow markets when products are differentiated, because it may be hard to identify clear breaks in the chain of substitutes. The court also emphasized "the potential for 'localized competition' analysis to devolve into an unstructured submarket-type analysis" in which courts could improperly identify narrow groupings as markets on the basis of noneconomic criteria unrelated to the ability of firms to exercise market power. 331 F. Supp. 2d at 1119. (The controversy over submarkets is discussed in Sidebar 5–5.) In practical effect, the district court's approach would likely turn unilateral effects into a competitive effects possibility that plaintiffs can hardly ever prove, in which narrow markets have to be defined in theory but can rarely be defined in practice. Is the court's approach a sensible one for reining in the interventionist potential of unilateral effects analysis among sellers of differentiated products, or does it create a gap in the law by permitting mergers creating harmful unilateral effects to escape challenge except in the rare case that the government can prove a merger to monopoly or near-monopoly without defining a narrow market?

These issues were explored in Roundtable Discussion: *Unilateral Effects Analysis After* Oracle, Antitrust, Spring 2005, at 8. Many resurfaced in 2007, when the FTC challenged the acquisition of the Wild Oats organic supermarket chain by rival Whole Foods. *FTC v. Whole Foods Market, Inc.*, 502 F.Supp.2d 1 (D.D.C.2007), *appeal pending*. In that case, the FTC alleged that the transaction harmed competition in the "premium natural and organic supermarkets" product market in twenty-two localities (regions no larger than a metropolitan area); in seventeen regions the FTC claimed the acquisition was a merger to monopoly. The district court denied the FTC's request for a preliminary injunction. It broadened the relevant product market to include at least all supermarkets, and found that many other supermarkets have been increasing their offerings of natural and organic products. The district court also found that the merging firms' pricing practices did not differ depending on the presence or absence of each other in the area, and that the two firms did not significantly constrain each other's pricing.

Sidebar 5–10:
Comparative Perspectives: Merger Enforcement in the U.S. and E.U.

Similarities Predominate

The European Commission ("EC"), the E.U.'s regulatory body, adopted its first Merger Regulation in 1989 and amended the regulation significantly in 2004. *See* Council Regulation (EC) No 139/2004 of 20 January 2004 on the control of concentrations between undertakings, O.J. L. 24, 29.01.2004, *available at* http://ec.europa.eu/comm/competition/mergers/legislation/regulations.html#merger_reg. Because the competition prohibitions of the Treaty of Rome did not include a separate merger provision like Section 7 of the U.S. Clayton Act, the EC Merger Regulation is anchored to Article 82's prohibition of the abuse of dominant position. *See* Sidebar 6–5: *Comparative Perspectives: The Treatment of Anticompetitive Single Firm Conduct in the U.S. and E.U.* Soon after issuing its revised Merger Regulation, the EC adopted Horizontal Merger Guidelines. *See Guidelines on the assessment of horizontal mergers under the Council Regulation on the control of concentrations between undertakings,* O.J. L.C 31, 05.02.2004, *available at* http://eur-lex.europa.eu/LexUri Serv/site/en/oj/2004/c_031/c_03120040205en00050018.pdf. In 2007, the Commission also adopted guidelines for non-horizontal mergers, which are discussed in Sidebar 7–7, *infra.*

Today horizontal merger policy in the E.U. and the U.S. share many significant features. In terms of process, both jurisdictions require pre-merger notifications of certain large transactions and impose mandatory waiting periods. In both jurisdictions, the enforcement agencies rely principally on information provided by the merging parties and by interested third parties, including customers and rivals. The informational demands imposed by the U.S. process through Hart–Scott–Rodino Second Requests tend to be more taxing than the information required by the EC. Unlike the U.S. system of dual enforcement, the EC has a single competition policy entity (DG Comp), and there is no uncertainty about which instrumentality will review a deal with community-wide importance. Thus, parties in the E.U. need not await the results of a U.S.-style "clearance" process, and pre-filing discussions often provide a way for DG Comp and the parties to identify issues before the formal premerger notice (the "Form CO") is filed.

The elaboration and revision of merger guidelines in both jurisdictions in the past 20 years has yielded extensive convergence on the analytical framework. In particular, the horizontal merger guidelines of the two jurisdictions share a largely common intellectual vision. Since 2000, judicial decisions in the E.U. and the U.S. have pressed both sets of public enforcement authorities to satisfy more demanding evidentiary standards and withstand closer judicial scrutiny of proof offered to demonstrate likely anticompetitive effects. Noteworthy losses in the courts in merger challenges in the two jurisdictions have included Case T–342/99, *Airtours plc v. Commission* [2002] E.C.R. II–2585, 5 C.M.L.R. 7, Case T–310/01, *Schneider Electric SA v. Commission,* [2002] E.C.R. II–4071, and Case T–5/02, *Tetra Laval BV v. Comm'n,* [2002] E.C.R. II–4381, *aff'd in part,* Cases C–12/03 P & C–13/03 P, *Comm'n v. Tetra Laval BV,* OJ 2005 C82/1 in the E.U. and *United States v. Sungard Data Sys.,* 172 F. Supp. 2d 172 (D.D.C. 2001), *FTC v. Arch Coal,* 329 F. Supp. 2d 109 (D.D.C. 2004), *U.S. v. Oracle Corp.,* 331 F. Supp. 2d 1098 (N.D. Cal. 2004), *FTC v. Foster,* 2007 WL 1793441 (D.N.M.2007)("Giant/Western"), and *FTC v. Whole Food Market, Inc.,* 502 F. Supp. 2d 1 (D.D.C. 2007) in the U.S. Cases such as *AirTours* and *Arch Coal* are strikingly similar in their insistence that prosecutors show how the collaboration among firms in a coordinated effects case will unfold after the merger is completed.

The adverse results noted above have motivated the E.U. and U.S. enforcement agencies to strengthen internal quality control mechanisms. For example, the 2002 "trilogy" of *Airtours, Schneider,* and *Tetra Laval* helped inspire major reforms inside DG Comp, including the establishment of a more robust process of peer review for individual cases and the creation of the position of Chief Economist, who reports to the Director

General and to the Commissioner for Competition. *See* Jonathan B. Baker, *My Summer Vacation at the European Commission*, ANTITRUST SOURCE (Sept. 2005) (comparing merger enforcement in the U.S. and E.U.), *available at* http://www.abanet.org/antitrust/at-source/05/09/Sep05–Baker9=27.pdf. By early 2008, the Chief Economist's Team had grown to twenty Ph.D. economists and had come to play an increasingly influential role in the examination of merger and non-merger matters.

Some Important Differences

Against a backdrop of substantial convergence, significant differences between the E.U. and U.S. systems are also apparent. Recent decisions of the European Court of First Instance underscore some noteworthy dissimilarities.

First, in Case No. T–464/04, *Independent Music Publishers and Labels Association v. Commission*, OJ 2006 C224/39 ("Impala"), DG Comp was criticized by the Court of First Instance for *declining* to challenge a merger. In the U.S., a decision not to challenge is not subject to judicial review. By contrast, in transactions subject to review in the E.U., third parties can appeal a decision of the Commission not to intervene or to resolve competitive concerns with remedies that a third party believes to be inadequate. Moreover, unlike U.S. practice, DG Comp is compelled to provide a written opinion explaining all decisions to intervene and not to intervene. In *Impala* the CFI agreed with third party complainants that the EC had provided an inadequate basis for deciding not to challenge the transaction in question (a merger of Sony and BMG's music businesses) and ordered the Commission to undertake a further review of the transaction. The analysis of factors facilitating or frustrating tacit collusion played a prominent role in the court's decision.

The availability of judicial review for decisions not to prosecute has important implications for a competition agency. In merger control, for example, the U.S. agencies have greater latitude to rely on qualitative, subjective judgments about the strength of efficiency arguments that would weigh in favor of permitting a merger to take place. If it relies on efficiency arguments to withhold a challenge, the EC would be required to spell out those arguments and to offer evidence to substantiate them. This procedural requirement, coupled with the availability of judicial review for decisions not to prosecute, limits the freedom of EC decision makers to rely on relatively subjective considerations for which quantitative verification might be impossible. By comparison, the U.S. agencies would have more leeway to give effect to such considerations.

Second, on July 11, 2007, the Court of First Instance ordered DG Comp to pay damages to Schneider Electric in connection with its proceeding to block Schneider's acquisition of one of its rivals, Legrand SA, in 2001. *See* Case No. T–351/03, *Schneider Electric SA v. Comm'n.*, OJ 2007 C199/29. Although the CFI rejected Schneider's request for an award of more than $2 billion, it ordered further proceedings which could still result in payment of significant damages measured by the difference between what Schneider paid for Legrand and the far lower amount it received when it was forced to sell it in response to the Commission's order, which was later overturned. U.S. agencies would not be liable for damages even if their decisions were overruled by reviewing courts.

Before the 2002 trilogy and later cases such as *Impala* and the *Schneider* opinion on the availability of damages against the E.U., many observers believed that the EC faced no realistic prospect of judicial rebuke in merger cases. The EC, with an administrative model that permitted the Commission to forbid combinations and forced the merger parties to overturn the prohibition on appeal, was said to enjoy much greater latitude to block deals than the U.S. antitrust agencies, which lacked the power independently to forestall a consolidation and required an order from a federal district court to enjoin transactions. The adversarial model of the U.S. system, which required judicial approval for merger prohibitions, was believed to impose more demanding evidentiary burdens on the U.S. agencies and therefore induced greater caution when deciding to challenge a transaction.

As you have gathered from the examples discussed in this Sidebar, judicial oversight of EC merger decisions can be a powerful constraint on the EC's discretion. At the same time, it remains the case that the U.S. adversarial model continues to give the U.S. agencies comparatively less latitude to block mergers than the European Commission. This difference in process may continue, in occasional cases, to generate different outcomes.

Occasional Conflict

A small number of high-profile transnational mergers sometimes have triggered tensions between E.U. and U.S. enforcers, owing to their differing assessments of the merger's likely competitive effects. In 1997, Boeing sought to acquire McDonnell–Douglas Corporation ("MDC") for $14 billion. For over a decade, MDC's share of sales of new commercial airliners had sagged and the firm believed its civil aircraft operations would atrophy and die. By acquiring MDC, Boeing could preserve MDC's remaining capability to design and produce passenger airliners and assure MDC's existing customers that Boeing would fulfill MDC's previous commitments to provide spare parts and service. By acquiring MDC's large portfolio of defense contracts, Boeing also expected to bolster its ability to supply high-quality weapon systems to the U.S. Department of Defense ("DOD").

But the acquisition would give Boeing 70 percent of the market for large commercial aircraft and reduce to two, along with Europe's Airbus consortium, the number of firms that build such vehicles. It might also significantly reduce competition in the U.S. for various weapons systems sold to the DOD. Critics in both the E.U. and the U.S. voiced concern that the competition agencies might act out of a desire to protect and promote a "national champion" in the industry. This led to speculation that the U.S. would permit the deal to assist Boeing and that the E.U. would oppose it to protect Airbus.

The FTC declined to challenge the merger and allowed it to proceed without imposing any conditions. In a statement issued by the FTC Chairman and three concurring Commissioners, the Commission specifically denied that it was approving the merger to fortify a "national champion." Instead, they asserted, they were persuaded that, although it was not failing, MDC no longer constituted a "meaningful competitive force in the commercial aircraft market." They also found no significant threat to competition for military weapons systems. *See Statement of*

Chairman Robert Pitofsky and Commissioners Janet D. Steiger, Roscoe B. Starek III and Christine A. Varney in the Matter of The Boeing Company/McDonnell Douglas Corporation, available at http://www.ftc.gov/opa/1997/07/boeingsta.shtm.

But the EC opposed the deal as originally proposed. U.S. government officials, including President Bill Clinton and Vice President Al Gore, warned that an E.U. decision to block the transaction would elicit U.S. retaliation against European manufacturers. The U.S. Department of Defense notified the EC competition policy directorate that it viewed approval of the merger to be vital to the health of the U.S. defense industry and urged the EC not to impede the transaction. The U.S. government sent the Acting Assistant Attorney General for Antitrust in the Department of Justice to meet with the Commissioner for Competition of the European Commission, to urge that the EC follow the lead of the U.S. FTC.

The EC backed away from prohibiting the deal outright or mandating a divestiture of MDC's commercial operations. Yet the Commission obtained a settlement that, among other conditions, forced Boeing to modify the contracts that bound three major airlines (American, Continental, and Delta) to purchase Boeing aircraft exclusively over the next twenty years. *See* Case No. IV/M.877, *Boeing–McDonnell Douglas,* 1997 O.J. (L 336) 16. Officials and commentators in the U.S. criticized even these limited measures as addressing competitive concerns unrelated to the acquisition.

A second difference in perspective between E.U. and U.S. antitrust enforcers arose with respect to the economic significance of "range," "portfolio," or "conglomerate" effects in connection with General Electric's proposed acquisition of Honeywell. Although the U.S. Department of Justice declined to challenge the transaction, the E.U.'s opposition, made public in 2001, led the parties to abandon the deal. The E.U. reportedly had concerns that the merged firm could entrench a dominant position in the sale of certain aircraft components by bundling GE products with those of Honeywell. Although the issue was couched in terms of bundling rather than range effects, the underlying concerns of the European Commission appear to have been similar.

In December 2005, the Court of First Instance affirmed the Commission's conclusion that the GE/Honeywell merger would have created or strengthened a dominant position in specific markets and hence was properly blocked. However, the CFI also concluded that the EC committed "errors of assessment" in its analysis of conglomerate effects. According to the court, the evidence was insufficient to support the EC's conclusion that conglomerate effects from either vertical integration or product bundling would have harmed competition. *See* Case T–210/01, *General Electric Co. v. Commission,* 2005 WL 3429326, [2006] 4 C.M.L.R. 15 (Dec. 14, 2005).

Conclusion

Differences of opinion over cases like *Boeing-McDonnell Douglas* and *General Electric/Honeywell* are likely inevitable and will continue to arise. Such differences, however, should not obscure the fact that, as discussed in this Sidebar, on the whole merger analysis in the E.U. and the U.S.

> today shares a great deal of common ground and has been moving towards producing consistent results across jurisdictions.

3. SUPPLY SUBSTITUTION AND ENTRY

Under the Merger Guidelines, once market concentration is found to exceed safe harbor levels and a plausible threat of unilateral or coordinated competitive effects is demonstrated, the inquiry turns to two factors that can mitigate competitive concerns: entry and efficiencies. This section looks at entry, and the following section considers efficiencies. Chapter 8 will look at how these concepts are employed in antitrust today in contexts other than horizontal merger analysis.

During antitrust's structural era, around the time of *Philadelphia Nat'l Bank*, *Von's Grocery*, and *Pabst*, the Supreme Court issued a decision in *Rome Cable*, a merger case that seemed to foreclose the argument that a merger should be permitted on the ground that the prospect of new competition would prevent harm to competition. In that case, the Court placed insulated copper conductor and insulated aluminum conductor in separate markets, notwithstanding a strong dissent highlighting the extensive manufacturing interchangeability (supply substitution) between the two. *United States v. Aluminum Co. of Am.*, 377 U.S. 271 (1964) (*Rome Cable*). Nevertheless, in the wake of *General Dynamics*, but even before the adoption of the 1982 Merger Guidelines, lawyers considering the role of entry under Clayton Act § 7 began to ask how supply substitution and ease of entry can be used to rebut the inference of anticompetitive effect derived from high and increasing market concentration. There were two main possibilities: easy entry might merely dilute or weaken the inference of anticompetitive effect; or ease of entry might trump everything else. Under the latter view, unless the *plaintiff* can prove that entry is *not easy*, the plaintiff must lose regardless of any other evidence including the level of market concentration. The "ease of entry is a trump" approach made sense as a matter of economics, but seemed hard to reconcile with *Rome Cable*. Could it be reconciled with the governing legal framework after *General Dynamics*?

A judicial response came during the mid–1980s. In 1984, the Second Circuit embraced the latter view, in the *Waste Management* decision, by deciding to treat ease of entry as a trump. In doing so the court relied on *General Dynamics*, and also asserted that it was merely holding the government to the terms of its own Merger Guidelines. The decision was quickly followed by a district court opinion and a Federal Trade Commission opinion taking a similar view. *United States v. Calmar Inc.*, 612 F.Supp. 1298 (D.N.J. 1985); *In re Echlin Mfg. Co.*, 105 F.T.C. 410 (1985). This approach to adjudication is consistent with the economic perspective on market power: if the threat of entry would prevent price from rising after a merger, the merger would not make coordinated or unilateral price increases more likely, or otherwise generate market power.

UNITED STATES v. WASTE MANAGEMENT, INC.
United States Court of Appeals for the Second Circuit, 1984.
743 F.2d 976.

Before VAN GRAAFEILAND, WINTER and PRATT, Circuit Judges.

WINTER, Circuit Judge.

Appellants Waste Management, Inc. ("WMI") and EMW Ventures Incorporated ("EMW") appeal from Judge Griesa's decision, * * * after a bench trial, that WMI's acquisition of EMW violated section 7 of the Clayton Act * * *.

We reverse.

BACKGROUND

* * *

We summarize those facts that are not in dispute. WMI is in the solid waste disposal business. It provides services in twenty-seven states and had revenues of approximately $442 million in 1980. At the time of the acquisition, EMW was a diversified holding company that owned a subsidiary by the name of Waste Resources, which was in the waste disposal business in ten states and had revenues of $54 million in 1980.

WMI and Waste Resources each had subsidiaries that operated in or near Dallas. WMI has one subsidiary, American Container Service ("ACS") in Dallas * * *. Waste Resources had a Dallas subsidiary called Texas Industrial Disposal, Inc. ("TIDI"). * * *

* * *

* * * The district court adopted a definition of the relevant product market that differed from the positions of both parties. Judge Griesa concluded that the product market included all trash collection, except for collection at single-family or at multiple family residences or small apartment complexes. Rejecting WMI's contentions as to the relevant geographic market, the district court excluded Tarrant County, which includes Fort Worth, thus limiting the market to Dallas County plus a small fringe area.

Based on revenue data, Judge Griesa found that the combined market share of TIDI and ACS was 48.8%. He viewed that market share as prima facie illegal under *United States v. Philadelphia National Bank*, 374 U.S. 321, 364–66, 83 S.Ct. 1715, 1742–43, 10 L.Ed.2d 915 (1963). Agreeing with appellants that entry into the product market is easy–indeed, individuals operating out of their homes can compete successfully "with any other company"–Judge Griesa nevertheless held that proof of ease of entry did not rebut the prima facie showing of illegality. The district court therefore ordered WMI to divest itself of TIDI. Because we conclude that potential entry into the relevant Dallas market by new firms or by firms now operating in Fort Worth is so easy as to constrain the prices charged by WMI's subs, we reverse on the grounds that the merged firm does not substantially lessen competition.

DISCUSSION

* * *

B. *WMI's Rebuttal*

A post-merger market share of 48.8% is sufficient to establish prima facie illegality under *United States v. Philadelphia National Bank*, 374 U.S. 321, 83

S.Ct. 1715, 10 L.Ed.2d 915 (1963), and its progeny.* That decision held that large market shares are a convenient proxy for appraising the danger of monopoly power resulting from a horizontal merger. Under its rationale, a merger resulting in a large market share is presumptively illegal, rebuttable only by a demonstration that the merger will not have anticompetitive effects. Thus in *United States v. General Dynamics Corp.*, 415 U.S. 486, 94 S.Ct. 1186, 39 L.Ed.2d 530 (1974), the Court upheld a merger of two leading coal producers because substantially all of the production of one firm was tied up in long-term contracts and its reserves were insubstantial. Since that firm's future ability to compete was negligible, the Court reasoned that its disappearance as an independent competitor could not affect the market.

WMI does not claim that 48.8% is too small a share to trigger the *Philadelphia National Bank* presumption. Rather, it argues that the presumption is rebutted by the fact that competitors can enter the Dallas waste hauling market with such ease that the finding of a 48.8% market share does not accurately reflect market power. WMI argues that it is unable to raise prices over the competitive level because new firms would quickly enter the market and undercut them.

* * *

The Supreme Court has never directly held that ease of entry may rebut a showing of *prima facie* illegality under *Philadelphia National Bank*. However, on several occasions it has held that appraisal of the impact of a proposed merger upon competition must take into account potential competition from firms not presently active in the relevant product and geographic markets. * * *

Moreover, under *General Dynamics*, a substantial existing market share is insufficient to void a merger where that share is misleading as to actual future competitive effect. * * * In the present case, a market definition artificially restricted to existing firms competing at one moment may yield market share statistics that are not an accurate proxy for market power when substantial potential competition able to respond quickly to price increases exists.

Finally, the Merger Guidelines issued by the government itself not only recognize the economic principle that ease of entry is relevant to appraising the impact upon competition of a merger but also state that it may override all other factors. * * * We conclude, therefore, that entry by potential competitors may be considered in appraising whether a merger will "substantially lessen competition."

Turning to the evidence in this case, we believe that entry into the relevant product and geographic market by new firms or by existing firms in the Fort Worth area is so easy that any anti-competitive impact of the merger before us would be eliminated more quickly by such competition than by litigation. * * * Judge Griesa specifically found that individuals operating out of their homes can acquire trucks and some containers and compete success-

---

* [Based on data reported in the district court opinion in this proceeding, the HHI for commercial trash collection in Dallas would have risen by 1184 points to 2678 as a result of the proposed transaction. *United States v. Waste Management, Inc.*, 588 F. Supp. 498, 512 (S.D.N.Y.1983). Eds.]

fully "with any other company." The government's response to this factual finding is largely to the effect that economies of scale are more important than Judge Griesa believed. As with his other findings of fact, however, this one is not clearly erroneous, as there are examples in the record of such entrepreneurs entering and prospering.

In any event, entry by larger companies is also relatively easy. At existing prices most Fort Worth and Dallas haulers operate within their own cities, but it is clear from the record that Fort Worth haulers could easily establish themselves in Dallas if the price of trash collection rose above the competitive level. Although it may be true that daily travel from Fort Worth to Dallas and back is costly, there is no barrier to Fort Worth haulers' acquiring garage facilities in Dallas permitting them to station some of their trucks there permanently or for portions of each week. The risks of such a strategy are low since substantial business can be assured through bidding on contracts even before such garage facilities are acquired, as one Fort Worth firm demonstrated by winning such a contract and then opening a facility in a Dallas suburb. That example can hardly be ignored by WMI or other Dallas haulers (not to mention their customers) in arriving at contract bids. The existence of haulers in Fort Worth, therefore, constrains prices charged by Dallas haulers * * *.

The fact that such entry has not happened more frequently reflects only the existence of competitive, entry-forestalling prices * * *.

* * *

Judge Griesa's conclusion that "there is no showing of any circumstances, related to ease of entry or the trend of the business, which promises in and of itself to materially erode the competitive strength of [the merged firms]" is consistent with our decision. [The merged firms] may well retain their present market share. However, in view of the findings as to ease of entry, that share can be retained only by competitive pricing. Ease of entry constrains not only WMI, but every firm in the market. Should WMI attempt to exercise market power by raising prices, none of its smaller competitors would be able to follow the price increases because of the ease with which new competitors would appear. WMI would then face lower prices charged by all existing competitors as well as entry by new ones, a condition fatal to its economic prospects if not rectified.

The government argues that consumers may prefer WMI's services, even at a higher price, over those of a new entrant because of its "proven track record." We fail to see how the existence of good will achieved through effective service is an impediment to, rather than the natural result of, competition. The government also argues that existing contracts bind most customers to a particular hauler and thereby prevent new entrants from acquiring business. If so, they also prevent the price increases until new entrants can submit competitive bids.

Given Judge Griesa's factual findings, we conclude that the 48.8% market share attributed to WMI does not accurately reflect future market power. Since that power is in fact insubstantial, the merger does not, therefore, substantially lessen competition in the relevant market and does not violate Section 7.

Reversed.

Waste Management drew a great deal of attention when it was decided. The case signaled that the government would be held to its own Merger Guidelines in court, and that the courts of appeals were willing to allow merger law to embrace modern economic thinking even without further guidance from the Supreme Court.

Do you agree with the court's rationale? What kind of evidence did the Second Circuit rely upon? Who had the burden of proof, according to the court? Should the mere possibility of entry be enough to rebut the *Philadelphia Nat'l Bank* presumption? Is that what *Waste Management* holds, or does the decision depend on a more extensive factual showing by defendant?

In determining whether entry would deter or counteract competitive harm from merger, evidence of the history of entry, without further analysis, is double-edged. If entry occurred in the past, that fact is consistent both with low entry barriers in the past (which permitted the entry to occur) and with the exercise of market power in the past (which induced that entry). Similarly, if entry did not occur in the past, that fact is consistent both with a competitive market in the past (which made entry unattractive even though it was possible) or with the presence of entry barriers (which made entry impractical or unprofitable). On the other hand, past episodes of successful or unsuccessful entry may provide insight into the types of actions entrants must take and the problems entrants must surmount for entry to succeed—which in turn may inform a judgment about the likelihood that entry after merger would address concerns about the exercise of market power. How was the history of entry employed by the court in *Waste Management*?

The role of entry also was at issue in the D.C. Circuit's 1990 decision in *United States v. Baker Hughes, Inc.*, 908 F.2d 981 (D.C. Cir. 1990), which we read earlier in this Chapter. As we saw, *Baker Hughes* set forth the modern interpretation of the *Philadelphia Nat'l Bank* presumption in light of *General Dynamics*, the Chicago School critique of structural merger policy, and contemporary developments in economics. As in *Waste Management*, the appeals court deciding *Baker Hughes* also concluded that the evidence of ease of entry was fatal to the Justice Department's efforts to challenge a proposed acquisition. The D.C. Circuit opinion is noteworthy for its strong rhetoric, suggesting that in bringing and litigating *Baker Hughes*, the Justice Department was willfully ignoring the teaching of *Waste Management*. Review that portion of the opinion now and consider whether, on the facts recounted in the opinion, this charge was warranted.

Recall that in concluding that evidence of ease of entry sufficiently rebutted the government's prima facie case, the court specifically rejected the government's position that the merging firms should have been required to "show clearly" that entry would be "quick and effective." Casebook, *supra*, at 458-62. The requirement in the current Merger Guidelines, that committed entry be "timely, likely, and sufficient" in order to undermine inferences drawn from market concentration statistics, had not been developed when *Baker Hughes* was litigated. Why did the court reject application of the standard advocated by the Justice Department? Why did it conclude that entry would likely solve any competitive problem from the acquisition? Were similar facts demonstrated in *Waste Management*? Had the government's competitive effects theory in *Baker Hughes* been unilateral rather than coordinated anticompetitive effects, would entry analysis likely have proceeded differently?

In 1992, shortly after *Baker Hughes*, and *United States v. Syufy Enterprises*, 903 F.2d 659 (9th Cir.1990), another appellate decision rejecting a Justice Department challenge to a merger in part on grounds of ease of entry, the Justice Department and Federal Trade Commission revised the Merger Guidelines. The section on entry promulgated in 1992 and discussed in the following note remains in force today.

Note on Entry Analysis in the Merger Guidelines

The 1992 Merger Guidelines provided a more detailed explanation of the role of conditions of entry in horizontal merger analysis. First, they adopted a three part test, which, as noted above, requires that entry be "timely, likely, and sufficient" to solve any competitive harms of the merger. In addition, the 1992 Guidelines drew a distinction that was not clear in the prior case law (including *Baker Hughes*) between what is called "uncommitted" entry and "committed" entry. The Merger Guidelines' concept of uncommitted entry, which was discussed earlier in this chapter in connection with the identification of market participants, generalizes the idea of supply substitution. Uncommitted entry is hit-and-run. Uncommitted entrants are firms that (1) can enter quickly (within one year) and (2) do so with little in the way of unrecoverable or "sunk" costs—expenditures that would be unrecoverable in the event the firm later chooses to exit the market. They take advantage of any short-run profit opportunities that anticompetitive behavior by incumbent firms might offer, and leave the market rapidly and inexpensively if those opportunities disappear. A metal stamping firm producing hubcaps, for example, might be an uncommitted entrant into the mailbox market. Or a firm producing no. 2 lead pencils might be an uncommitted entrant into the production of lead-based artists' sketching pencils.

In contrast, committed entrants are in for the long haul. Once they enter a market, they expect to stay, because to abandon the market would mean walking away from a substantial sunk investment. A firm that needs to build a new production facility to enter a market is likely a committed entrant. In deciding whether it would be profitable to enter a market, an uncommitted entrant considers the current price in the market while a committed entrant must instead consider what competition and prices will look like after it enters.

The latter point is key to the Merger Guidelines' approach to the analysis of likelihood (profitability) of committed entry. In deciding whether to enter the market, a new competitor expecting to stay for the long term—a committed entrant—must consider the effect of its entry on the price it will receive and the profits it can expect to make. Entry may depress the market price for two reasons. First, the entrant adds output to the market, causing the industry outcome to move along the demand curve in the direction of a lower price. Second, incumbent firms may react to the competition from the new entrant with an aggressive competitive response (price war) of their own. That is, entry will be discouraged by the fear of post-entry competition.

To analyze entry likelihood, the Merger Guidelines observe that a committed entrant would not find such entry profitable if it has a large "minimum viable scale," measured by break-even annual sales at pre-merger prices, as a percent of the total market. The Guidelines suggest that the merger analyst assess entry likelihood by estimating the minimum viable scale of an entrant–considering the planning, production, marketing other activities the entrant must undertake–and compare that estimate against a 5% benchmark for assessing the magnitude of a minimum viable scale calculation. As a general rule, both higher fixed costs and higher variable costs of entry would increase the minimum viable scale. For example, if it is very costly for an entrant to satisfy governmental regulations, or to acquire the necessary patent licenses (or invent around the intellectual property of rivals), those factors would tend to raise entrant costs and in consequence increase the minimum viable scale.

The Guidelines go on to indicate that the benchmark can be modified if called for by an examination of factors affecting the "sales opportunities" available to the committed entrant, including market growth, the extent to which buyers are locked in to incumbent sellers through long term contracts or vertical integration, and the anticipated response of incumbent firms to new entry. *Horizontal Merger Guidelines* § 3.3. For example, if the market is growing, there may be more room for entry to occur without depressing prices. Also, sales opportunities would also increase to the extent large customers would respond to higher prices by sponsoring upstream entry (as by guaranteeing business to the entrant).

The Merger Guidelines also require an analysis of whether committed entry would be "timely"—that is, whether it would achieve significant market impact within two years—and "sufficient" in magnitude, character, and scope to solve the competitive problem. *Horizontal Merger Guidelines* §§ 3.2, 3.4. In practice, timeliness is typically the easiest consideration to assess. The sufficiency inquiry might consider whether some potential entrants are better situated than others, for example, or whether entry into one niche of a market characterized by product differentiation would solve a competitive problem that arises largely in some other part of the market. It might also consider whether the increased capacity brought to the market by the most likely new entrants would be enough to offset the output-restricting result of a price increase by the merging firms. Committed entry is considered easy, and likely to deter or counteract an anticompetitive problem from merger, only if that entry satisfies all three tests; that is, only if it is "timely, likely, and sufficient."

How does the Merger Guidelines framework differ from the approach set forth in *Waste Management* and *Baker Hughes*? Although the Guidelines disclaim any effort to allocate burdens of proof, some have criticized them for implicitly placing too great a burden on defendants. Do you agree? We will revisit the significance of entry and the standards for evaluating it in Chapter 8.

———

Are the 1992 Merger Guidelines consistent with what Clayton Act § 7 requires, according to the D.C. Circuit in *Baker Hughes*? Note that the D.C. Circuit rejected the government's argument that entry must be "quick and effective" in order to count as easy and thus be used to rebut the government's prima facie case based on market concentration. Yet just two years later, the government published Merger Guidelines requiring that committed entry be something quite similar—"timely, likely, and sufficient"—in order to count. Is the Justice Department willfully ignoring the dictates of the appeals court? Or did Justice view the entry possibilities in *Baker Hughes* as committed while the D.C. Circuit instead saw the entry possibilities in that case as uncommitted, and so viewed the Justice Department's appeal as a misguided effort to overturn *Waste Management*?

District courts in the D.C. Circuit, where government merger challenges are often filed, have not interpreted *Baker Hughes* as inconsistent with the entry framework of the Merger Guidelines. In *Staples*, the district court highlighted language from *Baker Hughes* indicating that defendants must show that entry into the market "would likely avert" anticompetitive effects in order to rebut the government's *prima facie* case with evidence about entry. *FTC v. Staples, Inc.*, 970 F.Supp. 1066, 1086 (D.D.C. 1997) (*quoting United States v. Baker Hughes Inc.*, 908 F.2d 981, 987 (D.C. Cir.1990)). The *Staples* court relied in part on evidence of high sunk costs to conclude that the merging firms had failed to meet this standard, thus making clear that the court saw the relevant entry possibilities in that case as committed. Similarly, in *Cardinal Health* the district court directly applied the "timely, likely, and sufficient" framework of the Merger Guidelines for analyzing committed entry and treated its approach as consistent with *Baker Hughes*. *FTC v. Cardinal Health, Inc.*, 12 F. Supp. 2d 34, 54–58 (D.D.C. 1998).

Sidebar 5–11:
The Ethics of Taking Discovery From One Client in Connection With Another Client's Proposed Merger*

[Thus far we have examined cases involving proof of market concentration, competitive effects and conditions of entry. Typically, at least some of the evidence necessary to establish each of these elements of merger analysis—and often some of the crucial evidence—comes not from the merging parties, but from other firms in the industry, such as suppliers, customers and rivals of the merging firms. This Sidebar considers some of the ethical issues that can arise when counsel defending a merger for one of the merging firms uses civil discovery techniques to obtain information from other industry participants—and she represents those parties in other, unrelated matters. Eds.]

In defending your corporate client in a federal district court lawsuit brought by the U.S. Department of Justice seeking to block the client's proposed merger, you conclude that it is necessary for the client's defense to seek third-party discovery from a number of other companies that compete with your client. It turns out that your law firm represents at least two of these companies on matters completely unrelated to the relevant product or issues raised by the DOJ merger challenge. Do you face any ethical issues if you file discovery demands seeking deposition testimony and the production of documents from these current clients on behalf of the client you represent in the DOJ merger case? What if you need to file motions to compel to enforce the subpoenas?

Under many circumstances, seeking discovery from a firm client to benefit another client may create a situation in which client interests are

---

* This Sidebar was prepared by Kathryn M. Fenton, and is adapted from *Ask the Ethics*   *Experts*, Antitrust, Summer 2000, at 50.

"directly adverse," thus triggering a conflict of interest that requires the consent of both clients for the law firm to proceed. Merely sending a civil subpoena for documents or information, on its own, may not create direct adversity. But once a discovery recipient has indicated an objection to the discovery or expressed concerns with its burden, it is hard to characterize the situation as anything but directly adverse. Thus, a lawyer's examining a client as a hostile witness or seeking to enforce third-party discovery demands of a client ordinarily will present a conflict of interest.

ABA Formal Opinion 92–367 succinctly captures the ethical concerns presented in seeking discovery or testimony from a current client:

> [A]s a general matter examining one's own client as an adverse witness on behalf of another client, or conducting third party discovery of one client on behalf of another client, is likely (1) to pit the duty of loyalty to each client against the duty of loyalty to the other; (2) to risk breaching the duty of confidentiality to the client-witness; and (3) to present a tension between the lawyer's own pecuniary interest in continued employment by the client-witness and the lawyer's ability to effectively represent the litigation client.

While emphasizing that the degree of direct adversity presented will depend on the particular circumstances in which the question arises, the ABA Formal Opinion concluded that the specifics of the inquiry prompting its opinion—cross-examination of a doctor client as an adversary's expert witness—was directly adverse and thus disqualifying under ABA Model Rule 1.7(a).

Similarly, once the recipient of the discovery demand manifests an unwillingness to comply, and it becomes necessary to resort to a motion to compel or other means to enforce compliance with the subpoena, the threshold of direct adversity is likely to be crossed. Certainly a motion for sanctions against a current client because of a discovery dispute would likely be found directly adverse. *See In re Suard Barge Services, Inc.,* 1997 WL 703000 (E.D.La.1997) (law firm disqualified from pursuing motions to compel and for discovery sanctions against current firm client). In most instances, however, reviewing courts have limited conflicts arising out of discovery matters to the discovery dispute only, and not granted disqualification motions with respect to the underlying litigation.

Making appropriate disclosures and obtaining the consent of both clients to waive the conflict and allow the law firm to proceed with discovery is one way to address this conflict. Such consent is often obtained based on the law firm's commitment to implement screening procedures and similar measures to preserve client confidences. In the absence of such consent, another way of resolving such conflicts is to have a separate law firm (co-defendant's counsel, local counsel, or a law firm retained particularly for this purpose) initiate and pursue discovery against or examination of the firm client. *See, e.g.,* ABA Comm. on Ethics & Professional Responsibility, Formal Opin. 92–367 (1992)("a satisfactory solution may be the retention of another lawyer solely for the purpose of examining the principal lawyer's client"). The general rule is that a co-counsel relationship generally does not, in and of itself, result in any imputed disqualification, and so the separate law firm is free to seek discovery without triggering conflict of interest concerns.

Are all forms of discovery from the existing client likely to be viewed as directly adverse to the client? What ethical issues, if any, are posed by seeking discovery from a former client? Can you deal with concerns about possible misuse of client confidences or secrets by having another firm attorney conduct the discovery and implementing an ethical screen? If your firm represents a party in underlying litigation, but a separate law firm is conducting third party discovery, can your firm then represent another firm client receives a third party discovery demand in the litigation?

4. EFFICIENCIES

Mergers and other cooperative relationships, such as joint ventures, can benefit the economy by allowing firms to reduce costs or develop better products. They "have the potential to generate significant efficiencies by permitting a better utilization of existing assets, enabling the combined firm to achieve lower costs in producing a given quantity and quality than either firm could have achieved without the proposed transaction." *Horizontal Merger Guidelines* § 4.0. As one court has observed, "Cooperation is the basis of productivity. It is necessary for people to cooperate in some respects before they may compete in others, and cooperation facilitates efficient production." *Polk Bros., Inc. v. Forest City Enters., Inc.*, 776 F.2d 185, 188 (7th Cir. 1985).

Yet Supreme Court merger cases from antitrust's structural era questioned whether cost savings or other efficiencies from merger should ever count in favor of a transaction that increased market concentration substantially. For example, in *FTC v. Procter & Gamble Co.*, 386 U.S. 568, 580 (1967), the Court stated that "[p]ossible economies cannot be used as a defense to illegality." Absent competition to prevent the exercise of market power, one argument for this position runs, consumers will not receive the benefits of any efficiencies in the form of lower prices or otherwise. Recall as well the Court's observation in *Philadelphia Nat'l Bank* that an otherwise anticompetitive merger "is not saved because, on some ultimate reckoning of social or economic debits and credits, it may be deemed beneficial." *United States v. Philadelphia Nat'l Bank*, 374 U.S. 321, 370–71 (1963). The Court explained that "[a] value choice of such magnitude is beyond the ordinary limits of judicial competence, and in any event has been made for us already, by Congress. * * * "*Id.*

Although these older decisions remain formally controlling, they have not been interpreted as foreclosing all consideration of efficiencies in the analysis of horizontal mergers. Professors Areeda and Turner observed that in *Procter & Gamble* "the court referred only to 'possible' economies and to economies that 'may' result from mergers that lessen competition. To reject an economies defense based on mere possibilities does not mean that one should reject such a defense based on more convincing proof." 4 PHILLIP AREEDA & DONALD TURNER, ANTITRUST LAW ¶ 941b, at 154 (1980). Moreover, *Procter & Gamble* was decided during an era in which merger law was thought to vindicate non-economic concerns such as halting trends toward market concentration in their incipiency and protecting small business, as well as preventing the exercise of market power. Consideration of efficiencies from merger may have been inconsistent with advancing these non-economic goals. (Indeed, some older decisions could be read to create an "efficiency offense," by which efficiencies from merger would count against the deal because the creation of a large firm with low costs would accelerate the demise of small business rivals.) But the judicial hostility to efficiencies has steadily decreased as such concerns have come to take a back seat to economic concerns across much of antitrust.

Accordingly, beginning in the early 1990s, some lower courts indicated that efficiencies are a relevant consideration in merger analysis. In 1991, an appeals court cited efficiencies as one factor that may be used to rebut the plaintiff's *prima facie* case based on market concentration. *FTC v. University Health, Inc.*, 938 F.2d 1206 (11th Cir. 1991). Efficiencies from merger also have played a role in successful defenses by the merging firms against government challenges to two hospital mergers, although they were not the primary reason for the failure of the government's cases. *FTC v. Butterworth Health Corp.*, 946 F.Supp. 1285 (W.D. Mich. 1996), *aff'd*, 121 F.3d 708 (6th Cir.1997); *United States v. Long Island Jewish Med. Center*, 983 F.Supp. 121 (E.D.N.Y. 1997). More generally, the D.C. Circuit observed that "the trend among lower courts is to recognize the defense." *FTC v. H.J. Heinz Co.*, 246 F.3d 708, 720 (D.C. Cir. 2001).

In 1991, when *University Health* was decided, the then-current Merger Guidelines recognized an efficiencies defense but made clear that it would rarely succeed. Those Guidelines required that the merging firms establish "by clear and convincing evidence" that their merger was "reasonably necessary to achieve significant net efficiencies," and indicated that the necessary level of expected net efficiencies would be greater, the more significant the competitive risks arising from the transaction. In 1997, the government's Merger Guidelines were revised to articulate an approach for taking efficiencies into account in evaluating the likely competitive effects of a merger. The revisions were prompted by a Federal Trade Commission staff report, issued in 1996, that discussed whether and how competition policy should be modified to account for the "new high-tech, global marketplace."

Under the revised Guidelines, efficiencies can be the basis for allowing a merger to go forward even though it otherwise appears likely to be anticompetitive. Such efficiencies must be "cognizable" as that term is defined in the Guidelines. Efficiencies are not "cognizable" unless they are (1) substantiated and verified, and (2) merger-specific, *i.e.*, they could not practically be achieved through some reasonable alternative that presents less risk to competition. In addition, efficiencies are not cognizable if they constitute harms to competition in disguise; they must (3) not arise from anticompetitive reductions in output or service. *Horizontal Merger Guidelines* § 4.0

The Guidelines go on to suggest that certain types of efficiencies are more likely to be cognizable and substantial than others. For example, "efficiencies resulting from shifting production among facilities formerly owned separately, which enable the merging firms to reduce the marginal cost of production" are said to have promise; efficiencies relating to research and development are considered potentially substantial but less susceptible to verification; and efficiencies relating to procurement, management, or capital cost are questioned as less likely to be cognizable or substantial. *Horizontal Merger Guidelines* § 4.0. If a merger affects not whether, but only when, an efficiency would be achieved, only the timing advantage is a merger-specific efficiency. *Id.* at § 4.0 n.35. For a summary of the efficiencies more or less likely to be deemed cognizable under the Guidelines, see Figure 8–7, *infra*.

The Guidelines indicate that a merger will not be challenged if the cognizable efficiencies are of a character and magnitude such that the merger is not likely to be anticompetitive in any relevant market. The efficiencies must reverse the merger's potential to harm competition, as by preventing pricing increases in that market.

Recall that efficiencies were asserted by the merging parties in Staples as a basis for rebutting the government's case. Review now that portion of the opinion that addressed, and rejected, the merging firms' effort to assert an efficiency defense.

FEDERAL TRADE COMMISSION v. STAPLES, INC.

United States District Court for the District of Columbia, 1997.
970 F.Supp. 1066.

[The relevant excerpt can be found *supra*, at 542. Eds.]

––––––––––

The discussion of efficiencies from *Staples* illustrates the influence of the Merger Guidelines on the federal courts and provides an example of how the cognizability criteria are applied in practice. The Guidelines do not discuss how to allocate the relevant burdens of going forward and persuasion, as they were conceived only as a guide for enforcement decisions. To the extent they do suggest an allocation of burdens, however, they are ambiguous. On the one hand, the Guidelines ask whether cognizable efficiencies "likely would be sufficient to reverse the merger's potential to harm consumers in the relevant market, *e.g.*, by preventing price increases in that market." *Horizontal Merger Guidelines* § 4. The emphasis here on rebutting the case for anticompetitive effects recalls the shifting burden of production concept associated procedurally with "defenses." On the other hand, the cognizability requirement that firms substantiate efficiency claims, along with the statement that "[e]fficiency claims will not be considered if they are vague or speculative or otherwise cannot be verified by reasonable means," suggests that the firms asserting efficiencies bear a burden of proof, not merely one of production, and thus that efficiencies should be understood as providing an "affirmative defense" to an otherwise unlawful merger. *Id.* This effort to speak with two procedural voices may create confusion for those courts that look to the Guidelines for guidance in analyzing efficiencies. Should courts analyze efficiencies as an "affirmative defense" (carrying with it a burden of proof) or as a "defense" (requiring the merging firms to meet only a burden of production)? Which approach did the court take in *Staples*? The distinction also has implications for the choice of welfare standard, as is explored in the next Note.

Note on Efficiencies and Consumer Welfare

Under the Merger Guidelines, if a merger creates cognizable efficiencies, the agency then asks whether they "likely would be sufficient to reverse the merger's potential to harm consumers in the relevant market, *e.g.,* by preventing price increases in that market." *Horizontal Merger Guidelines* § 4. As this quotation suggests, the Merger Guidelines are generally read as concerned primarily with an anticompetitive merger's potential to harm competition by shifting wealth from sellers to buyers (the "transfer" in the Williamson diagram, Figure 5–1) within a market, not with efficiency losses to the economy. If so, the Guidelines focus on consumer welfare rather than aggregate economic welfare, as these terms were used in the discussion of the goals of antitrust in Chapter 1.

The primary focus of the Merger Guidelines on consumer welfare arguably makes consideration of efficiencies part of the competitive effects analysis—part of the determination of whether the merger will likely raise price—rather than an analysis conducted in defense of an otherwise anticompetitive acquisition. Under such circumstances, whether and how the efficiencies will "reverse" the merger's potential to harm competition will depend on the nature of the harm alleged, *i.e.,* whether the concern is with coordinated interaction or some type of unilateral competitive effects. In a coordinated effects case, for example, the Guidelines suggest that the merger might promote competition by creating a maverick firm with an incentive to expand output and lower price.* In a unilateral effects case, the merger might reduce the merged firm's variable costs, giving it an incentive to lower price that outweighs any incentive to increase price resulting from the loss of localized competition. Moreover, a focus on competitive effects means that variable cost savings matter more than reductions in fixed costs, as only the former have the potential to provide incentives for the merged firm to lower price in the relevant market. Fixed cost savings do not affect a firm's pricing decisions directly in any particular market. If they lead to higher than competitive profits and entry is easy, however, they may be competed away through reductions in the price of some or all of the full line of firm products.

Although the Guidelines emphasize a concern with the welfare of buyers, this is not their exclusive concern. The Guidelines do not insist that cost savings or other efficiencies be passed through to consumers in order to count, although that requirement is to some extent implicit in the suggestion that efficiencies must prevent price increases or otherwise reverse a merger's anticompetitive potential.** In practice, the agencies have usually viewed their charge as focusing on

---

* On the other hand, a cost-reducing merger in a coordinated competitive effects setting could in theory actually harm competition. For example, if a merger among imperfectly coordinating firms lowers the costs of a non-maverick firm, its competitive effect may instead be to deter price-cuts by an existing maverick who fears a deeper price war, making coordination more effective and leading to higher prices.

** One footnote to the Guidelines' efficiency section permits consideration of cost savings "with no short-term, direct effect on prices in the relevant market"—that is, fixed cost reductions that represent real resource savings. *Horizontal Merger Guidelines* § 4, n.37. In addition, the Guidelines indicate in another foot-

note that efficiencies from the merger accruing in some *other* relevant market might save a merger likely to raise price in a given market, if the two effects "are so inextricably linked * * * that a partial divestiture or other remedy could not feasibly eliminate the anticompetitive effect in the relevant market without sacrificing the efficiencies in the other market." *Horizontal Merger Guidelines* § 4, n.36. To the extent these footnotes allow consideration of fixed cost savings and efficiencies outside the relevant market along with variable cost savings within the relevant market, they effectively convert what is said to be a consumer welfare analysis into an aggregate economic welfare analysis. It remains to be seen, howev-

the welfare of consumers rather than aggregate welfare. They do not commonly refrain from challenging a merger likely to raise price to consumers in one market on the ground that consumers in some other market would benefit, or refrain from challenging a merger likely to raise price on the ground that the transaction also produces large fixed cost savings, unlikely to benefit consumers in the relevant market. The debate over the appropriate economic goal for antitrust may, however, be largely an academic one—a minor area of disagreement within a broad consensus in favor of an economic approach to antitrust. A former FTC Commissioner has suggested that the fine distinction between aggregate social welfare and consumer welfare may be difficult to make in practice, as "virtually all cases worthy of prosecution have both wealth transfers and [aggregate economic] welfare losses." Terry Calvani, *Rectangles & Triangles: A Response to Mr. Lande*, 58 ANTITRUST L.J. 657 (1989).

The U.S. is not the only jurisdiction that has grappled with the question of the goals of the antitrust laws in connection with determining the proper role of efficiencies in merger analysis. *See, e.g., Canada (Commissioner of Competition) v. Superior Propane, Inc.*, 7 C.P.R. (4th) 385, [2000] Carswell Nat 3449, ¶¶ 426–32 (Competition Trib.), *rev'd in part*, 199 D.L.R. (4th) 130, [2001] Carswell Nat 702 (Fed. C.A.), *appeal refused*, [2001] Carswell Nat 1905 (Can.). Moreover, the competition policy adopted by countries with small economies is often more accommodating to efficiencies than the approach adopted by large economies. Michal S. Gal, *Size Does Matter: The Effects of Market Size on Optimal Competition Policy*, 74 S. CAL. L. REV. 1437, 1459–60 (2001).

The efficiency revisions to the Merger Guidelines explain that "[t]he greater the potential adverse competitive effects of a merger * * * the greater must be cognizable efficiencies" in order to conclude that the merger will not harm competition. *Horizontal Merger Guidelines* § 4. A similar approach was adopted by the D.C. Circuit in *FTC v. H.J. Heinz Co.*, 246 F.3d 708, 720–21 (D.C. Cir. 2001). *See also Baker Hughes*, 908 F.2d at 991 ("The more compelling the prima facie case, the more evidence the defendant must present to rebut it successfully."). Is this "sliding scale" approach an unreasonable interpretation of the *Philadelphia Nat'l Bank* presumption, inconsistent with the outcome in *Baker Hughes* and likely to discourage procompetitive acquisitions? Or is it a sensible acknowledgment of the weight of evidence about market concentration, properly recognizing that buyers are unlikely to see lower prices from a merger to near-monopoly even if the merged firm obtains substantial cognizable variable cost reductions from the integration?

Efficiencies have at times persuaded the enforcement agencies not to bring a case. Moreover, notwithstanding the "sliding scale" approach of the Merger Guidelines, and the Guidelines statement that "[e]fficiencies almost never justify a merger to monopoly or near-monopoly," *Horizontal Merger Guidelines* § 4, efficiency arguments have occasionally been successful before the agencies in highly-concentrated markets. Indeed, on rare occasions, the agencies have refrained from challenging a merger among the only two firms participating in a market on efficiency grounds (as in some defense industry cases).

But efficiencies have historically had a less friendly reception in the courts, as is suggested by comparing the results in the entry and efficiencies cases. While efficiencies have played a role in successfully defending against merger challenges in some cases, efficiencies have not yet been the sole reason for a successful

er, whether the aggregate economic welfare analysis possibility inherent in these footnotes is adopted as the efficiency section is implemented.

judicial defense to a government merger challenge. In contrast, as we observed in *Waste Management*, defendants have at times been successful in overcoming the government's *prima facie* case with proof that entry would solve the competitive problem. What accounts for these different litigation results?

The answer is probably not to be found in differences in the level of post-merger concentration in the cases. For example, the concentration levels in *Heinz*, where the defendant's rebuttal based on efficiencies failed to overcome the government's *prima facie* case, were not much higher than those found in *Baker Hughes*, where the government's *prima facie* case was successfully rebutted on ease of entry grounds. One explanation relates the difference in the outcomes of the cases to differences in the defenses emphasized by the merging firms. When *Baker Hughes* was decided, proof of ease of entry, the main defense in that case, was a well-established route to rebutting the *prima facie* case based on concentration. In contrast, the merging firms in *Heinz* raised a less established rebuttal, relying primarily on evidence of efficiencies to explain why the merger would not harm competition. Once the appeals court concluded that the district court's acceptance of that defense was unwarranted, it was left with the unrebutted inference of harm to competition arising from the reduction in the number of sellers. Under this interpretation of the decisions, the focus on concentration in *Heinz* is more related to the continuing development of doctrinal standards related to the efficiency defense than to any rethinking of the totality-of-the-circumstances approach to merger analysis set forth in *Baker Hughes*.

It may be appropriate for courts to be more skeptical of an efficiencies defense than an entry defense. As previously noted, the modern trend may be for courts to analyze efficiencies as a defense—that is, to view them as offered to defeat the government's proof of higher prices or other competitive harm rather than as an affirmative defense that would excuse higher prices. This would mean that the defendants must meet a burden of production to raise efficiencies, but that the government would have the burden of persuasion to show that efficiencies do not undermine its showing of harm to competition. In practice, however, regardless of the formal allocation of the burdens of production and persuasion, defendants must typically prove efficiencies because the relevant evidence is more likely under their control. In contrast, the government may more often be able to test entry claims by developing evidence from other sources, such as the experience of other firms considering entry under pre-merger conditions, which may be similar to some extent to entry conditions after the merger. In addition, some suggest that efficiency claims are generally more prospective and more speculative than entry claims, consistent with studies showing that mergers often turn out not to be profitable for the acquiring firm. But others may disagree, highlighting the key role of efficiencies as a motive for merger.

Do factors like these explain why courts appear to make it more difficult for a rebuttal to succeed if based on efficiencies? Should the courts treat entry arguments as a "defense" on which the defendant has a burden of production but plaintiff retains a burden of proof, or treat efficiency arguments as an "affirmative defense" on which defendant bears both burdens? Should efficiencies be treated differently in cases of coordinated as opposed to unilateral competitive effects?

5. FAILING FIRMS

The final step in the Merger Guidelines analysis of horizontal mergers involves consideration of the special status of "failing firms." The Supreme Court created a narrow "failing company" defense to Clayton Act § 7 in

International Shoe Co. v. FTC, 280 U.S. 291 (1930). The Guidelines incorporate failing firms considerations as a defense, and allow the acquisition of a firm notwithstanding possible harm to competition (1) if the firm would be unable to meet its financial obligation in the near future and unable to reorganize successfully; (2) if it has made unsuccessful good-faith efforts to sell its assets to a buyer who would keep its assets in the relevant market and pose a less severe danger to competition than the proposed merger; and (3) if the assets of the failing firm would exit the relevant market absent the merger. *Horizontal Merger Guidelines* § 5.1. The Merger Guidelines also allow an analogous defense, not found in the case law, for a "failing division" of an otherwise healthy firm. *Horizontal Merger Guidelines* § 5.2.

These requirements are construed strictly. *See FTC v. Harbour Group Investments*, 1990–2 TRADE CAS. (CCH) ¶ 69,247 (D.D.C. 1990). For example, a footnote to the Merger Guidelines notes that "[a]ny offer to purchase the assets of the failing firm for a price above the liquidation value of those assets—the highest valued use outside the relevant market * * *—will be regarded a reasonable alternative offer." *Horizontal Merger Guidelines* § 5.1 n.39. This provision suggests why conflict may arise over the requirement that the failing firm seek multiple alternative purchasers. The shareholders can be expected to favor a buyer who will pay a premium over the liquidation value of the assets. Having found such a buyer, the company has little incentive to seek out a less anticompetitive purchaser, who might make a lower offer that the agencies may insist it take instead.

A weakened or "flailing" firm, in financial trouble but not close to bankruptcy, will not satisfy the strict tests for application of the failing firm defense when it seeks to merge with a rival. The merger partners may, however, argue that their transaction is unlikely to harm competition because the acquired firm, as a result of its financial distress, is unlikely to be a significant competitive force in the future absent the merger. This argument is sometimes termed a *General Dynamics* defense. *See United States v. General Dynamics Corp.*, 415 U.S. 486, 506–08 (1974). In 1997, the Federal Trade Commission relied upon a *General Dynamics* argument to conclude that Boeing's acquisition of McDonnell Douglas did not violate Clayton Act § 7.

Sidebar 5–12:
Merger Remedies

When confronted with a merger that poses anticompetitive hazards, a government enforcement agency can pursue one of two remedial paths. It can seek to prohibit the merger outright, or it can negotiate a settlement that permits the transaction to proceed only if the merging parties take measures to resolve the competitive problem. It may be possible to cure a competitive overlap by compelling the parties to divest assets or take other steps to transfer some of the competitive capacity that the merger would have created to a third party.

Merger policy today features substantial reliance on settlements. The adoption of pre-merger notification systems, such as the Hart–Scott–

Rodino Antitrust Improvements Act (see Sidebar 5–3), has played an important role in this development by giving the U.S. government the right to review transactions before they are completed. The mandatory waiting periods of many merger notification mechanisms worldwide create a natural opportunity for negotiation as the government identifies possible problems and brings them to the attention of the merging parties. In a number of instances, the parties are fully aware of a competitive problem and will approach the government with a proposed solution even before filing the required pre-merger notification.

In cases involving anything less than a simple condemnation of the entire proposed merger, the design of merger remedies, whether by settlement or in litigation, can pose a number of challenges. *See generally* Deborah Platt Majoras, *Houston, We Have a Competitive Problem: How Can We Remedy It?* (April 17, 2002), *available at* http://www.usdoj.gov/ atr/public/speeches/11112.htm. One task is to identify the assets to be divested. What collection of human capital, physical facilities, and intellectual property is necessary to put the buyer of divested assets in a position to exert a strong competitive influence in the market? If the merging parties own several plants in the relevant market, which plant or plants should be divested? Are there trademarks, patents, or copyrights that the prospective buyer must obtain in order to operate successfully? If the divestiture does not encompass the right combination of assets, the buyer may not be able to replicate the competitive presence that the seller previously exerted. As you might imagine, the merging parties generally would prefer to satisfy a demand for divestitures by selling off what they believe to be their weakest assets.

A second challenge that arises in the course of negotiated settlements is to determine the timing of the execution of the remedy. Sometimes the government will explain its concerns, and encourage the merging firms to restructure their transaction ("fix-it-first") in order to obviate the need for a court or Federal Trade Commission order. Another approach is for the government simply to obtain the defendant's promise to carry out the required remedy, such as a divestiture, by some time certain in the future. To ensure that such promises are fulfilled, the government might also insist that the merging parties agree to alienate other valued assets—sometimes called "crown jewels"—if the parties fail to meet the deadlines specified in the settlement. A more ironclad way for the government to assure itself that the remedy will be executed properly is to demand that the parties identify and gain the government's approval for the prospective buyer before the settlement is entered. A "buyer-up-front" provision gives the government greater assurance that the divestiture will be carried out in a timely manner, that a suitable purchaser will obtain the assets, and that the package of assets (as evaluated by the prospective buyer) is sufficient to transfer the relevant competitive capability. But such a provision can delay consummation of the transaction— and achievement of the efficiencies from merger—while the parties find, and obtain approval for, a buyer.

A third challenge, determining the capability of the buyer of divested assets, is closely related to the second. The government would prefer a purchaser that is both experienced in the relevant market and will be able to use the assets in a manner that exerts a competitive influence in the market. The merging parties, by contrast, may prefer to divest the assets to a buyer that is likely to be a comparatively ineffective or submissive market participant. The government agencies do not insist that the prospective buyer be the "best" from a competitive standpoint, but they do ask that a prospective purchaser satisfy certain basic standards of capability in order to be confident that the divestiture will solve the competitive problem otherwise created by the merger. In some cases, the merging parties offer to improve the buyer's capability by assisting the buyer after assets are divested—for example, by offering to manage a divested factory until the buyer becomes familiar with the industry. But these and other forms of "continuing entanglements" raise questions about the buyer's incentives and ability to compete effectively in the relevant market. To avoid such entanglements, the government may seek to guarantee commercial viability of the carved-out assets by insisting upon a broader divestiture than might strictly be suggested by focusing on the threatened harm to competition—for example, to include production facilities for key inputs or additional products necessary to preserve economies in joint production and distribution. But broadening the required divestiture may deprive the merging firms of some of the desired efficiency benefits of their transaction.

The actual negotiation of settlement terms can be a contentious process, as each side measures the wisdom of making specific concessions against the risks associated with litigating the government's request for a preliminary injunction in court. A district court's issuance of a preliminary injunction is likely to kill a transaction, as few companies are willing to cope with the uncertainty and delay of seeking vindication before a court of appeals.

In some recent cases, the inadequacy of a settlement proposal has been a central issue in the preliminary injunction action. *See, e.g., United States v. Franklin Elec. Co.*, 130 F. Supp. 2d 1025 (W.D. Wis. 2000). When the Justice Department (but not the FTC) reaches a civil settlement with an antitrust defendant, and asks a court to enter the settlement as a final judgment, the court is obliged, under the Tunney Act, to review whether the settlement is in the public interest. The court must consider a range of issues, but generally defers to the government. *U.S. v. SBC Commc'ns, Inc.*, 489 F. Supp. 2d 1 (D.D.C. 2007).

In the many instances in which the merging parties and the government achieve a settlement, does the chosen remedy ensure that competition is preserved? In the typical settlement, it is difficult for those other than the parties to the negotiations and their rivals to answer this question. But neither the industry participants nor the government has an incentive to depict the settlement as anything other than a successful resolution of the competition policy issues.

A 1999 FTC study examined the efficacy of merger remedies. STAFF OF THE BUREAU OF COMPETITION OF THE FEDERAL TRADE COMMISSION, A STUDY OF THE COMMISSION'S DIVESTITURE PROCESS (1999). Though not attempting to assess the impact of the remedies in a comprehensive manner, the FTC study raised concerns about the ability of settling firms to limit the effectiveness of the relief in protecting post-merger competition by manipulating the settlement process, and led the Commission to insist more frequently upon the use of "crown jewel" and "buyer-up-front" measures, discussed above, in negotiating remedies. Justice Department policy as to merger remedies differs in some respects from the approach of the FTC. For example, the Antitrust Division encourages parties to implement a "fix-it-first" remedy and it disfavors use of "crown jewel" measures. ANTITRUST DIVISION POLICY GUIDE TO MERGER REMEDIES (2004).

D. CONCLUSION

In this chapter, we have seen how the courts and federal enforcement agencies analyze horizontal mergers. Merger analysis today is conducted within a traditional doctrinal framework that relies on a structural presumption of harm from high and increasing market concentration. But as that presumption has eroded over time, consistent with antitrust law's shift to focus on core economic concepts, a broader economic analysis, guided by the government's Horizontal Merger Guidelines, has become the rule in the federal enforcement agencies and the courts. We followed the structure of the Merger Guidelines by examining (1) market definition, the identification of market participants, and the determination of market concentration; (2) competitive effects theories; (3) new competition through supply substitution or entry; (4) efficiencies; and (5) failing firms.

E. PROBLEMS AND EXERCISES

Problem 5–1:
Chic Shampoo

a. *The Facts*

Chic Shampoo, Inc. is considering an acquisition of Stellar Shampoo Corp. Chic and Stellar are two of only six firms that sell shampoo in the U.S.

Each of the six firms in the shampoo industry sells one brand, except that both Chic and Stellar also sell an anti-dandruff variant. (Thus, Chic sells "Chic Regular" and "Chic Dandruff," but each rival other than Stellar sells only a regular shampoo.) Annual sales revenues by brand and firm are indicated in the following table:

Brand	Annual Revenue (millions)
Chic Regular	$1.0
Chic Dandruff	1.0
Stellar Regular	1.0
Stellar Dandruff	1.0
Forest Regular	1.0
Newport Regular	1.0
Plymouth Regular	1.0
Sudbury Regular	3.0
Total (all brands)	$10.0

Shampoo brands differ in their chemical composition, and on many dimensions directly apparent to consumers, like texture, color, smell, and lather. The regular shampoo products all clean hair equally well. Five of the six brands (all but Plymouth) have developed product images and reputations for quality through extensive national television and magazine advertising. Drug stores, supermarkets, and convenience stores will not stock any shampoo that lacks a national reputation. Plymouth differs from the others in that it is distributed through hairdressers. All brands are offered for sale throughout the U.S., with similar market shares in all regions of the country. The leading national producer of soap and detergent, the Sparkling division of Rainbow, a large consumer products company, says it could quickly and easily produce a high quality regular shampoo, but that its existing brand names may not convey an image appropriate for the sale of shampoo. Dandruff shampoo is more difficult to formulate and manufacture than regular shampoo, and only Chic and Stellar have been able to produce a high-quality anti-dandruff product.

According to Chic's CEO, the proposed merger of Chic and Stellar would help Chic in three main ways: by allowing Chic to use Stellar's high speed bottling equipment to lower the unit costs of producing additional units of the Chic product, by giving Chic the ability to obtain more and better shelf space from supermarkets than either company would get on its own, and by allowing Chic to consolidate duplicative management activities.

b. *Problem and Skills Exercise*

Your law firm has been retained to advise Chic on the likely response of the Federal Trade Commission or Antitrust Division of the Justice Department to this proposal. You are preparing to meet with Chic's executives. Draft a brief memorandum, not to exceed five (5) pages, advising your client to the extent possible based on what you know so far, of the likelihood of a government challenge under the Merger Guidelines and relevant case law. Identify any additional information you would like your client to provide you in order to help you with your analysis.

Bonus questions: (1) Assume instead that Sudbury is a dandruff shampoo rather than a regular shampoo. How does your analysis change? (2) Returning to the original facts, suppose that regular shampoo manufacturers could easily formulate a dandruff shampoo (though Sparkling could not), but that successful marketing of a dandruff shampoo would require substantial advertising expenditures. How does your analysis change?

Problem 5–2:
Super Propane

a. *The Facts*

Super Propane ("Super") is one of only five major marketers of propane in the State of Tazland. Propane is a chemical by-product of the extraction of natural gas, and is produced in Canada and some regions of the United States. It is thereafter transported by pipelines and tankers throughout North America, and sold to local or regional marketers, like Super. Super engages in the retailing and wholesaling of propane, as well as the sale of various products that use propane, such as propane heating equipment, cooking equipment, and forklifts.

Super proposes to acquire one of its rivals, GKB Propane ("GKB"). Like Super, GKB retails and wholesales propane in Tazland, but it does not sell any propane-using products. GKB also owns and operates a propane storage facility in Sun City, the capital of Tazland, that is the largest on the Eastern seaboard of the United States. The facility has the added advantage of being located at an access point to one of few supply pipelines that pass through Tazland. With direct pipeline access, GKB avoids the additional costs associated with transporting propane from the pipeline to its storage facility, a cost that its rivals must incur. Obtaining direct pipeline access has become quite difficult for several reasons. First, physical access to the pipeline is limited, and is only available at two or three locations in Tazland. Second, building propane storage facilities requires local zoning and regulatory approvals that are only infrequently granted by local authorities.

In the last decade, two other wholesaler/retailers have succeeded in securing the approvals necessary to construct storage facilities. The approval process took 12–18 months in each case. The actual construction followed and was completed in both instances within twelve months after that. One of those wholesaler/retailers had previously operated solely in the neighboring State of Currland, and had never before sold propane in Tazland.

The combination of GKB's direct access to the pipeline and significant storage capacity permit GKB to alter its inventory substantially, which in turn allows it to "stock up" when prices are most favorable from its suppliers. It can then sell the propane through its retail and wholesale business as needed, frequently at a cost advantage over its rivals. It also permits GKB to bid for long-term supply contracts that are currently beyond Super's reach due to its limited storage capacity and consequent dependence on spot market prices. To bid effectively on long-term contracts, a supplier must have predictable and adequate long-term sources of supply–something GKB has and Super does not. At the present time, however, GKB's storage facility is only operating at about 60% of its design capacity. At full capacity, propane costs could be even lower.

Super and GKB currently account for 35% and 20% respectively of total propane sales in Tazland. Their two principal rivals account for 25% and 10%. Although their combination will mean they will account for 55% of total propane sales in Tazland, Super and GKB contend that it will lower their joint operating costs, lower their joint production costs, allow for more complete utilization of GKB's storage facility, and facilitate long-overdue reductions in their respective work forces. These combined effects, they argue, will better enable them jointly to bid for long-term contracts in Tazland as well as in several neighboring states.

b. *Problem and Skills Exercise*

You are an attorney in the Antitrust Bureau of the Tazland Attorney General's Office. You have been asked to evaluate the proposed merger under the Horizontal Merger Guidelines and applicable case law. Draft a memorandum of no more than five (5) pages advising the Antitrust Bureau Chief as to (1) the best arguments the State of Tazland could make to support its challenge of the proposed transaction; and (2) the likelihood that the challenge will succeed at least at the preliminary injunction stage.

*

Part III

CONDUCT HAVING EXCLUSIONARY EFFECTS

Chapter 6

EXCLUSIONARY CONDUCT BY A SINGLE, DOMINANT FIRM

INTRODUCTION

In creating a national antitrust law in 1890, Congress sought to unravel supplier cartels and discourage producers from imposing unreasonable limits on the commercial freedom of their distributors and retailers. In Chapters 2, 3, and 4 we saw how courts developed doctrines to address collective efforts of firms to restrain trade. An equally important congressional aim in establishing the U.S. antitrust system was to curb the power of individual, dominant corporate enterprises.

The control of unreasonably exclusionary behavior by dominant firms is the subject of this Chapter. The chief means for limiting such conduct in the United States is Section 2 of the Sherman Act, whose basic goal—barring unreasonable efforts by single firms to suppress competition—has been embraced in virtually every competition law subsequently adopted. Section 2's chief modern counterpart is Article 82 of the E.U. Treaty, which forbids the "abuse of a dominant market position."

Statutory Framework

Section 2 of the Sherman Act encompasses three separate offenses: (1) monopolization, (2) attempted monopolization, and (3) conspiracy to monopolize. As formulated by the Supreme Court in *United States v. Grinnell Corp.*, 384 U.S. 563, 570–71, 86 S.Ct. 1698, 1704 (1966):

> The offense of monopoly under § 2 of the Sherman Act has two elements: (1) the possession of monopoly power in the relevant market and (2) the willful acquisition or maintenance of that power as distinguished from growth or development as a consequence of a superior product, business acumen, or historic accident.

As we will see in the remainder of this Chapter, modern judicial decisions continue to employ this basic framework.

The controlling modern formulation of the offense of attempted monopolization appears in *Spectrum Sports, Inc. v. McQuillan*, 506 U.S. 447, 456, 113 S.Ct. 884, 890 (1993), where the Supreme Court said:

* * * [I]t is generally required that to demonstrate attempted monopolization a plaintiff must prove (1) that the defendant has engaged in predatory or anticompetitive conduct with (2) a specific intent to monopolize and (3) a dangerous probability of achieving monopoly power.

The rarely invoked conspiracy to monopolize offense requires concerted action (like Section 1 of the Sherman Act) and specific intent to achieve a monopoly, but the plaintiff need not prove that the defendants have monopoly power. *See American Tobacco Co. v. United States,* 328 U.S. 781, 66 S.Ct. 1125 (1946). In contrast to the U.S. framework, Article 82 of the E.U. Treaty does not distinguish among monopolization, attempt to monopolize, and conspiracy to monopolize. It is directed at "abusive" conduct by "dominant" firms, which potentially sweeps more broadly than Section 2. For most offenses, it has in common the power (dominance) + conduct (abuse) formula that guides U.S. law, especially with respect to monopolization. But a dominant firm can also violate Article 82 through "exploitive" abuses, such as charging high prices, although exploitive cases are increasingly rare. *See* Sidebar 6–5: *Comparative Perspectives: The Treatment of Anticompetitive Single Firm Conduct in the U.S. and E.U.*

In this chapter we focus primarily on the offense of monopolization, but we will also consider attempted monopolization and abuse of dominance. As we shall see, giving operational content to these theories of liability requires a competition policy system to address three basic issues. The first is to define *the status of "monopoly" or "dominance."* Section 2 and Article 82 are concerned with the exercise of substantial market power and ignore the conduct of individual firms that are commercially insignificant. In studying the market power requirement, we will return to a theme we introduced in examining horizontal mergers in Chapter 5: the results in specific cases involving the use of market shares to measure market power depend crucially on how courts define the *relevant market* and evaluate the defendant's importance within that market.

The second basic issue is to define *improper behavior.* Antitrust laws rarely condemn monopoly itself. Making the mere possession of substantial market power illegal would ensnare firms that achieved preeminence through laudable means such as reducing costs and improving product quality. A competition system that punished such success inevitably would dampen the initiative to develop new products or processes that benefit consumers.

Implicit in the analysis of conduct is an evaluation of two factors: the anticompetitive effect of the conduct and its procompetitive rationales. In earlier cases, courts generally did not identify these considerations separately. Recent cases have tended to focus distinctly on each. The plaintiff offers a hypothesis of competitive harm, and the burden of production shifts to the defendant to offer a procompetitive reason for its acts. This trend in analysis highlights the third basic issue in our study of single-firm behavior: *what constitutes a legitimate business justification for conduct asserted to be improper?* The inquiry associated with defining improper behavior and evaluating redeeming justifications is difficult in many cases. Much business behavior is competitively ambiguous, and courts have struggled to develop coherent principles for determining when the anticompetitive features of various practices are so pronounced as to render the behavior improper.

Thesis, Antithesis and Synthesis? Three Perspectives on Exclusion

Antitrust's concern about possible harm to competition from exclusionary conduct has waxed and waned over time. These changes can most readily be appreciated by looking to the views of leading judges and commentators on allegations of exclusion by single firms, not involving horizontal or vertical agreements.

Later in this chapter, we will read Judge Learned Hand's influential 1945 *Alcoa* opinion. Judge Hand displayed deep concern about exclusionary conduct. Only if "exclusion" were interpreted very narrowly, he wrote, "as limited to maneuvers not honestly industrial, but actuated solely by a desire to prevent competition," could Alcoa's conduct in expanding capacity in advance of the growth of demand "be deemed not 'exclusionary.'" Hand refused to entertain such an interpretation, because to do so "would permit just such consolidations as [the Sherman Act] was designed to prevent." Judge Hand thus primarily feared *false acquittals* (sometimes referred to as "false negatives"), the possibility that antitrust law, by failing to find violations in a monopolist's exclusionary conduct, could create a lethargic monopolist with little incentive to cut costs or innovate, although his decision also included some often-quoted language warning of the consequences of *false convictions* (sometimes referred to as "false positives").

In contrast to Judge Hand's vision is Judge Robert H. Bork's in THE ANTITRUST PARADOX. First published in 1978, this volume set forth the Chicago School perspective on antitrust and expressed deep skepticism about exclusion as an antitrust theory, particularly as applied to dominant firm conduct. In the passage below, Bork assessed the possibility that a firm could exclude or foreclose its rivals by refusing to deal with certain suppliers or distributors:

> Where an *efficiency potential* appears in a case involving an individual refusal to deal, and there is *no clear evidence* that the purpose of the refusal was predatory, courts should generally find the refusal lawful, both because of tie-breaker considerations and because predation by an individual refusal to deal will be *very uncommon*.

ROBERT H. BORK, THE ANTITRUST PARADOX 346 (1978) (emphasis added). Note the "music" in this passage. To prove the benefits to competition, a "potential" is sufficient. To prove the harm, "clear evidence" would be required. The anticompetitive outcome will be "very uncommon." Elsewhere in THE ANTITRUST PARADOX, Bork recognizes that firms can impede rivals in ways that harm competition:

> By disturbing optimal distribution patterns one rival can impose costs upon another, that is, force the other to accept higher costs. This may or may not be a serious cost increase, but if it is (and the matter can only be determined empirically), the imposition of costs *may conceivably* be a means of predation. The predator will suffer cost increases, too, and that sets *limits* to the types of cases in which this tactic will be used for predation. There is a further *complication*, moreover, in that the behavior involved will often be capable of creating efficiencies.

Id. at 156 (emphasis added). Note the skepticism resonating in Bork's phrase "may conceivably," and observe how Bork immediately turns from the anti-competitive theory to a limitation and a complication.

In discussing exclusion, therefore, Judge Bork is describing a problem that he thinks is exceedingly rare. THE ANTITRUST PARADOX does identify one such case, the Supreme Court's decision in *Lorain Journal*, which we shall read later in this chapter. Bork was also concerned in the book with the misuse of government processes as a method of exclusion. And two decades later Judge Bork found another anticompetitive example in *United States v. Microsoft Corp.*, 253 F.3d 34 (D.C. Cir. 2001), where he personally represented one of Microsoft's excluded rivals (Netscape).

In sum, Judge Bork's primary concern is the opposite of Judge Hand's. Bork is worried about *false convictions*, the possibility that enforcing antitrust rules against alleged episodes of exclusionary conduct would chill aggressive competition. Bork fears that the primary consequence of opening the doors wide to exclusion allegations may be to keep prices high and discourage innovation, to deny consumers the benefits of efficiencies that may flow from a large firm's scale and scope, and to spur inefficient rivals to misuse the antitrust laws by bringing lawsuits after losing on the merits in the marketplace.

Under the influence of Judge Bork and some of his Chicago School colleagues, as well as a number of other influential commentators, especially the late Phillip E. Areeda, who was associated with the "Harvard School," *see* Chapter 1, *supra*, courts today tend to approach exclusion cases with skepticism. Although we will read some cases in which plaintiffs prevailed, such as *Microsoft* and *Aspen Skiing*, most of the more recent monopolization decisions have been decided in favor of the defendants. One common judicial strategy for throwing out an exclusion case is to conclude that the alleged exclusion was too small to harm competition given the limited scope or duration of the impairment. (An example is *Omega Environmental*, Casebook, Chapter 7, *infra*). As a result, the burden of production never shifts from the plaintiff to the defendant, so courts rarely demand evidence of or evaluate whether the defendant had reasonable business justifications for the otherwise seemingly exclusionary conduct. It is also rare to find a court analyzing whether the structure of the market is conducive to coordination, even absent the excluded rival (although *Brooke Group*, which we will read later in this Chapter, is an example of a case where the Court did so), or analyzing whether the loss of the particular excluded firm would make coordination more likely or more effective (but *JTC Petroleum*, which we read in Chapter 1, is an contrary example). Cost-based tests for predation, a hallmark of the Harvard School, are often advocated by those who claim they minimize false positives and provide guidance to dominant firms with respect to the permissible scope of liability for "predatory" or "exclusionary" conduct. As we will learn, in practice, such cost-based tests have proven to be difficult to satisfy and hence tend to favor plaintiffs. *See, e.g., Brooke Group* (Casebook, Chapter 6, *infra*,); *Cascade Health* (Casebook, Chapter 6, *infra*). For a discussion of the combined effect of Chicago and Harvard skepticism about challenges to dominant firm behavior, see William E. Kovacic, *The Intellectual DNA of Modern U.S. Competition Law for Dominant Firm Conduct: The Chicago/Harvard Double Helix*, 2007 COLUM. BUS. L. REV. 1 (2007).

The most influential contemporary antitrust commentary on exclusionary conduct takes a view between those of Hand and Bork. In 1986, Professors Thomas Krattenmaker and Steven Salop wrote that they:

> * * * do not believe that economic theory or antitrust policy suggests that virtually all exclusion claims are chimerical. Rather, * * * in carefully defined circumstances, certain firms can attain monopoly power by making arrangements with their suppliers that place their competitors at a cost disadvantage. * * * [C]laims of antitrust exclusion should be judged according to whether the challenged practice places rival competitors at a cost disadvantage sufficient to allow the defendant firm to exercise monopoly power by raising its price.

Thomas G. Krattenmaker and Steven C. Salop, *Anticompetitive Exclusion: Raising Rivals' Costs to Achieve Power over Price*, 96 YALE L.J. 209, 213–14 (1986); *see also* Steven C. Salop & David T. Scheffman, *Raising Rivals' Costs*, 73 AM. ECON. REV. 267 (1983) (introducing economic theory). Krattenmaker and Salop recognize the efficiency potential of exclusionary conduct, and thus incorporate cost savings and other efficiencies in their analysis, although they call for such justifications to be proven rigorously rather than assumed or accepted upon a mere showing of plausibility. 96 YALE L.J. at 277–82. This intermediate perspective has been influential at the federal antitrust enforcement agencies, particularly during the William J. Clinton Administration, when the Justice Department and FTC brought high profile cases that included allegations of unlawful exclusion against such firms as Microsoft, Intel, Toys–R–Us, Master Card, and Visa. Most notably, it arguably underlies the unanimous *en banc* opinion of the D.C. Circuit in *Microsoft*, which we will read later in this Chapter. It has also been influential at the European Commission.

But the intermediate perspective has not captured the field. The Chicago and Harvard Schools' skepticism about exclusion cases remains influential. As we will see later in this Chapter, the Supreme Court has recently expressed concern about the chilling effect of monopolization litigation on the legitimate business conduct of dominant firms and the danger that inefficient rivals will misuse the antitrust laws by bringing such cases. It has also extended the use of cost-based standards for defining predation. During the George W. Bush administration, moreover, senior Justice Department officials sounded similar themes in speeches and amicus briefs and brought no monopolization cases (though their counterparts at the FTC brought several).

Exclusionary Conduct and Dominant Firms

First, in this Chapter we examine exclusionary conduct in the context of evaluating the behavior of dominant firms, because most allegations of anticompetitive acts against dominant firms involve exclusion. However, it is also possible to imagine a dominant firm harming competition by colluding with fringe rivals or individually non-dominant firms engaging in collective conduct that excludes. We will examine more of these kinds of exclusionary conduct in Chapter 7.

Legal debates about dominant firm conduct often focus on the capacity of the antitrust system: (1) to develop analytical tests that accurately identify anticompetitive behavior, and (2) to apply the tests sensibly in practice. As discussed in Chapter 1, the Chicago and Harvard Schools tend to resolve these issues differently than the Post–Chicago school. The Chicago and Harvard Schools generally proscribe a narrower range of behavior than the Post–Chicago School, although conceptual differences between the groups about when exclusion is "improper" have diminished somewhat over time. Although there are differences of view between the Chicago and Harvard Schools, as a general matter they both have less confidence than the Post–Chicago School in the capacity of courts and enforcement agencies to accurately distinguish between anticompetitive and procompetitive behavior in practice. Fears about the magnitude of failures in implementation have led the Chicago School to prefer comparatively bright-line rules that err toward nonintervention. The Post–Chicago School is more sanguine about the prospects for accurate implementation and therefore entertains the use of more comprehensive reasonableness standards that create more possibilities for finding liability.

As we shall learn, the debate has practical consequences for the selection of specific standards for judging exclusionary conduct, because those standards can be structured to hinder or facilitate claims of exclusion. For example, one's views about the likely market impact of specific conduct and the skill of courts and enforcement agencies in applying concepts in practice can be cast as presumptions. Observers who conclude that (a) successful efforts by a dominant firm to exclude equally or more efficient rivals are rare, and (b) attempts by courts and enforcement agencies to apply conceptually sound theories are excessively prone to misapplication, may adopt a strong presumption disfavoring intervention. Observers who conclude that (a) successful efforts to exclude by means other than efficiency are common enough to warrant serious attention, and (b) courts and enforcement agencies can make suitably accurate diagnoses and impose appropriate cures, are more likely to favor intervention when potentially harmful conduct is identified. As you learn in this Chapter about the economics of exclusionary conduct, and the legal rules governing the conduct of such firms, you may find it instructive to consider whether legal doctrine is or should be based on either of these presumptions.

In Section A of this Chapter we explore the modern economic framework for understanding how firms may harm competition through exclusionary conduct. Section B turns the clock back to examine the origins and development of the traditional approach to analyzing exclusionary conduct, particularly *Grinnell's* power + exclusionary conduct formula and the pivotal role it assigns to market definition. Section C examines the leading modern court decisions on monopolization. It notes how the traditional dichotomy between power and conduct can be unduly rigid and emphasizes the tension that has emerged between the modern legal rules governing non-price exclusionary conduct and predatory pricing. It also examines some other recurring kinds of conduct that have received considerable attention in the courts and at the enforcement agencies, such as refusals to deal and refusals to license intellectual property rights. Section D looks at the controlling case law on attempt to monopolize. The Chapter concludes with a brief overview of the challenges associated with crafting effective remedies in monopolization cases in Section E and some Problems in Section G.

A. THE ECONOMICS OF EXCLUSION

Our discussion of *JTC Petroleum* in Chapter 1 and the economics of collusion in Chapter 3 illustrate the close relationship between collusion and exclusion. Collusion is threatened by the ability and willingness of rivals to deviate from (cheat on) the coordinated consensus. The economics of collusion revolves around whether and how rivals can be induced to cooperate rather than to compete. This section will show how a similar outcome to what might arise from successful collusion can be achieved if a dominant firm or a group of firms acts to exclude rivals that might otherwise not go along with collusive conduct. That is, the economics of exclusion can be understood simply as pointing out that collusive outcomes can be achieved indirectly, as by denying actual or would-be competitors access to low cost inputs or access to customers. Our window into the economics of exclusion is a leading Supreme Court decision concerning dominant firm conduct, *Lorain Journal*.

1. *LORAIN JOURNAL* CASE STUDY

During the late 1940s, the Justice Department challenged the efforts of the publisher of an Ohio newspaper, The Lorain Journal, to force its advertisers to refrain from placing advertisements with a local radio station with which the publisher competed to sell advertising services. The lawsuit relied upon an attempted monopolization theory to oppose the threatened refusal to deal. In 1951, the Supreme Court sustained the district court's finding that the threatened refusal to deal was improper and violated Section 2 of the Sherman Act. The economic question the case raises is whether the dominant firm harmed competition through actions that hindered the ability of its only rival to sell its services to an important class of customers.

LORAIN JOURNAL CO. v. UNITED STATES

United States Supreme Court, 1951.
342 U.S. 143, 72 S.Ct. 181, 96 L.Ed. 162.

Mr. Justice BURTON delivered the opinion of the Court.

* * *

This is a civil action, instituted by the United States in the District Court for the Northern District of Ohio, against The Lorain Journal Company, an Ohio corporation, publishing, daily except Sunday, in the City of Lorain, Ohio, a newspaper here called the Journal. * * *

The appellant corporation, here called the publisher, has published the Journal in the City of Lorain since before 1932. In that year it, with others, purchased the Times–Herald which was the only competing daily paper published in that city. Later, without success, it sought a license to establish and operate a radio broadcasting station in Lorain.

The court below describes the position of the Journal, since 1933, as 'a commanding and an overpowering one. It has a daily circulation in Lorain of over 13,000 copies and it reaches ninety-nine per cent of the families in the city.' * * * Lorain is an industrial city on Lake Erie with a population of about 52,000 occupying 11,325 dwelling units. The Sunday News, appearing only on Sundays, is the only other newspaper published there. * * *

* * *

From 1933 to 1948 the publisher enjoyed a substantial monopoly in Lorain of the mass dissemination of news and advertising, both of a local and national character. However, in 1948 the Elyria–Lorain Broadcasting Company, a corporation independent of the publisher, was licensed by the Federal Communications Commission to establish and operate in Elyria, Ohio, eight miles south of Lorain, a radio station whose call letters, WEOL, stand for Elyria, Oberlin and Lorain. Since then it has operated its principal studio in Elyria and a branch studio in Lorain. * * *

* * *

Substantially all of the station's income is derived from its broadcasts of advertisements of goods or services. * * *

The court below found that appellants knew that a substantial number of Journal advertisers wished to use the facilities of the radio station as well. For some of them it found that advertising in the Journal was essential for the promotion of their sales in Lorain County. It found that at all times since WEOL commenced broadcasting, appellants had executed a plan conceived to eliminate the threat of competition from the station. Under this plan the publisher refused to accept local advertisements in the Journal from any Lorain County advertiser who advertised or who appellants believed to be about to advertise over WEOL. The court found expressly that the purpose and intent of this procedure was to destroy the broadcasting company.

The court characterized all this as 'bold, relentless, and predatory commercial behavior.' * * * To carry out appellants' plan, the publisher monitored WEOL programs to determine the identity of the station's local Lorain advertisers. Those using the station's facilities had their contracts with the publisher terminated and were able to renew them only after ceasing to advertise through WEOL. The program was effective. Numerous Lorain County merchants testified that, as a result of the publisher's policy, they either ceased or abandoned their plans to advertise over WEOL.

"Having the plan and desire to injure the radio station, no more effective and more direct device to impede the operations and to restrain the commerce of WEOL could be found by the Journal than to cut off its bloodstream of existence—the advertising revenues which control its life or demise." " * * * [T]he very existence of WEOL is imperiled by this attack upon one of its principal sources of business and income."

* * *

The conduct complained of was an attempt to monopolize interstate commerce. It consisted of the publisher's practice of refusing to accept local Lorain advertising from parties using WEOL for local advertising. Because of the Journal's complete daily newspaper monopoly of local advertising in Lorain and its practically indispensable coverage of 99% of the Lorain families, this practice forced numerous advertisers to refrain from using WEOL for local advertising. That result not only reduced the number of customers available to WEOL in the field of local Lorain advertising and strengthened the Journal's monopoly in that field, but more significantly tended to destroy and eliminate WEOL altogether. Attainment of that sought-for elimination would automatically restore to the publisher of the Journal its substantial monopoly in Lorain of the mass dissemination of all news and advertising, interstate and national, as well as local. It would deprive not merely Lorain but Elyria and all surrounding communities of their only nearby radio station.

* * *

The publisher's attempt to regain its monopoly of interstate commerce by forcing advertisers to boycott a competing radio station violated Section 2. The findings and opinion of the trial court describe the conduct of the publisher upon which the Government relies. The surrounding circumstances are important. The most illuminating of these is the substantial monopoly which was enjoyed in Lorain by the publisher from 1933 to 1948, together with a 99% coverage of Lorain families. Those factors made the Journal an indispensable medium of advertising for many Lorain concerns. Accordingly, its publisher's refusals to print Lorain advertising for those using WEOL for like advertising often amounted to an effective prohibition of the use of WEOL for that purpose. Numerous Lorain advertisers wished to supplement their local newspaper advertising with local radio advertising but could not afford to discontinue their newspaper advertising in order to use the radio.

WEOL's greatest potential source of income was local Lorain advertising. Loss of that was a major threat to its existence. The court below found unequivocally that appellants' conduct amounted to an attempt by the publisher to destroy WEOL and, at the same time, to regain the publisher's pre–1948 substantial monopoly over the mass dissemination of all news and advertising.

To establish this violation of Section 2 as charged, it was not necessary to show that success rewarded appellants' attempt to monopolize. The injunctive relief under Section 4 sought to forestall that success. While appellants' attempt to monopolize did succeed insofar as it deprived WEOL of income, WEOL has not yet been eliminated. The injunction may save it. * * *

* * *

Assuming the interstate character of the commerce involved, it seems clear that if all the newspapers in a city, in order to monopolize the dissemination of news and advertising by eliminating a competing radio station, conspired to accept no advertisements from anyone who advertised over that station, they would violate Sections 1 and 2 of the Sherman Act. * * * It is consistent with that result to hold here that a single newspaper, already enjoying a substantial monopoly in its area, violates the 'attempt to monopolize' clause of Section 2 when it uses its monopoly to destroy threatened competition.[1]

---

1. Appellants have sought to justify their conduct on the ground that it was part of the publisher's program for the protection of the Lorain market from outside competition. The publisher claimed to have refused advertising from Elyria or other out-of-town advertisers for the reason that such advertisers might compete with Lorain concerns. The publisher then classified WEOL as the publisher's own competitor from Elyria and asked its Lorain advertisers to refuse to employ WEOL as an advertising medium in competition with the

The publisher claims a right as a private business concern to select its customers and to refuse to accept advertisement from whomever it pleases. We do not dispute that general right. 'But the word 'right' is one of the most deceptive of pitfalls; it is so easy to slip from a qualified meaning in the premise to an unqualified one in the conclusion. Most rights are qualified.' The right claimed by the publisher is neither absolute nor exempt from regulation. Its exercise as a purposeful means of monopolizing interstate commerce is prohibited by the Sherman Act. The operator of the radio station, equally with the publisher of the newspaper, is entitled to the protection of that Act. '*In the absence of any purpose to create or maintain a monopoly*, the act does not restrict the long recognized right of trader or manufacturer engaged in an entirely private business, freely to exercise his own independent discretion as to parties with whom he will deal'. (Emphasis supplied.) United States v. Colgate & Co., 250 U.S. 300, 307, 39 S.Ct. 465, 468.

* * *

———

The Court concluded that the newspaper's conduct violated the antitrust laws because the defendant made it more difficult for the radio station, its only rival, to compete, threatening the radio station's existence, and because the newspaper was unable to provide a persuasive rationale for threatening to withhold cooperation from local advertisers if they placed advertisements with the radio station. Why would these facts imply that competition was harmed rather than simply that one competitor was injured?

Exclusionary tactics come in a wide range of varieties, many of which were separately categorized in traditional antitrust thinking.

- In the actual case, the newspaper unilaterally refused to deal with certain other firms, namely those who also dealt with its rivals. Recall that Judge Bork was skeptical about whether *unilateral refusals to deal* should be viewed as anticompetitive, though he conceded that *Lorain Journal* was properly decided.

But the newspaper could have instead employed other tactics in its competitive battle for advertisers.

- The newspaper could have contracted with its advertisers for exclusivity, as by giving advertisers a lower price in exchange for their commitment not to advertise with any radio station located in the same part of the state. This is called *exclusive dealing*.
- The newspaper could have competed for advertisers by charging less for newspaper advertising or building a new radio station to compete with WEOL. These strategies might have had the effect of drawing radio advertiser dollars away from WEOL, possibly harming WEOL and forcing it to exit the market. As we will see, there is a substantial

Journal. We find no principle of law which required Lorain advertisers thus to boycott an Elyria advertising medium merely because the publisher of a Lorain advertising medium had chosen to boycott some Elyria advertisers who might compete for business in the Lorain market. Nor do we find any principle of law which permitted this publisher to dictate to prospective advertisers that they might advertise either by newspaper or by radio but that they might not use both facilities.

debate as to when, if at all, price cutting or new product development should ever be viewed as harmful to competition.

- The newspaper could have cut price to a low level that the radio station was unable to match, forcing WEOL out of business. As we will see in the case law, this kind of tactic, which has been the subject of substantial attention in antitrust history and substantial debate as to its rationality, is called *predatory pricing* if the price is below the alleged monopolist's costs and other conditions are met.

- If the newspaper had already owned a radio station, it could have offered an attractive package price to advertisers that advertised both in the newspaper and on its affiliated radio station, if their total advertising purchases exceeded a given threshold level. This offer might have shifted advertisers away from using WEOL and toward the affiliated radio station, possibly harming WEOL and forcing it to exit. This tactic involves both bundling of services and loyalty discounts (the discount for exceeding a threshold), and its treatment under antitrust principles has been the subject of recent controversy.

All of these tactics in some sense could exclude the competing radio station, WEOL. Some have greater exclusionary potential than others, and some would likely have stronger legitimate business justifications than others. But each can be understood through a single economic lens, the modern economic framework of raising rivals' costs.

2. THE MODERN ECONOMICS OF EXCLUSION: RAISING RIVALS' COSTS

To understand how competition could be harmed by exclusionary conduct, we turn to the modern economic analysis of exclusion or, using the terminology that Krattenmaker and Salop made famous, the economics of "raising rivals' costs." As that terminology suggests, today the terms "exclusion" and "foreclosure" are employed broadly to include practices beyond complete foreclosure that disadvantage rivals by raising their costs or reducing their access to the market. (Moreover, the exclusionary conduct is thought of as raising "costs" even if it involves reducing rival access to customers or the market. These practices increase costs by making marketing more expensive.) As an economic matter, complete foreclosure is not necessary for exclusionary conduct to confer market power on the remaining firms.

The modern economic literature on exclusionary practices shows how they can harm competition by leading rivals to participate in, or accede to, what might be termed an "involuntary" horizontal cartel. Suppose, for example, that firms A and B would like to collude with firm C, their only rival in a market protected from entry.

Firms A and B cannot do so because C would increase output were A and B to raise price, and prevent the industry price from rising. If A could somehow raise C's marginal costs, or otherwise make it more difficult for C to sell more, then C would be led to do what it would not have done previously: reduce its output and go along with a higher price.

Figure 6–1:

Involuntary Cartel–Restricting Rival Access to Supply

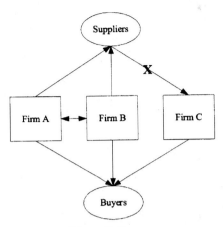

1. Firms A and B are colluding;

2. Firm C either refuses to join Firms A & B, or
Firms A & B are not interested in inviting C to join;

3. Firms A & B secure agreement of their suppliers
to refuse to sell to Firm C, or at least to refuse to
sell to Firm C on equally desirable terms.

    Firm A might be able to accomplish this end by foreclosing C from access to low cost sources of supply or distribution, perhaps through exclusive contracts (or vertical merger) with input suppliers or distributors, or by making it more difficult for firm C to attract customers, perhaps by denying firm C access to complementary products (for example, as through tying).

Figure 6–2:
Involuntary Cartel—Restricting Rival Access to Distribution

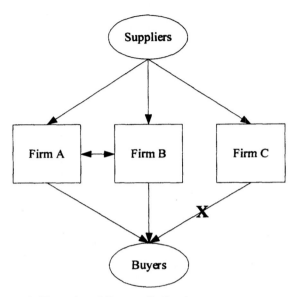

1. Firms A and B are colluding;

2. Firm C either refuses to join Firms A & B, or Firms A & B are not interested in inviting C to join;

3. Firms A & B secure agreement of their customers either to refuse to purchase from Firm C, or at least to refuse to purchase from Firm C on equally desirable terms.

Then, A and B could take advantage of the less aggressive competition from C to exercise market power.

Note that firm C need not be an incumbent producer. It could instead be a firm whose potential entry constrains anticompetitive behavior. By raising its costs, or reducing its access to the market, the remaining firms can reduce output to raise price without fearing new competition. Note also that nothing in the example constrains the firms to three. There may be multiple firms playing the roles of each actor (A, B, or C) in the hypothetical example. Some exclusionary practices, for example, may raise costs for a class of actual or potential rivals in the position of firm C.

For three reasons it is not a foregone conclusion that a raising rivals' costs strategy would work for firm A. First, firm C may have alternative ways to obtain supply or distribution at favorable costs. Suppose, for example, that firm A has paid a key input supplier only to sell to firm A, or, at a minimum, paid the supplier not to sell to firm C (without constraining the supplier's ability to sell to firm B). If firm C can obtain similar inputs at comparable cost and quality from another supplier, then firm A's conduct will not exclude firm C. Alternatively, if firm C can convince the supplier to terminate its exclusivity agreement with firm A, and sell to firm C after all, then firm C will again not be excluded. However, firm A may stack the deck against the latter method of evading firm A's strategy. If firm A's exclusionary contract with the supplier confers market power on firm A, and the market would otherwise be competitive, then firm A may be willing to pay more to the supplier to exclude firm C than the excluded firm would be willing to pay to avoid the foreclosure.

Second, firm B may not go along with A in reducing output once C is taken out of the picture. Firm B instead may choose to "cheat" on what is effectively a cooperative agreement with firm A to raise price. This problem is not necessarily insurmountable. Firm A may be a monopolist—there may be no firm B, as in many of the dominant firm cases highlighted in this Chapter. Firm B may face capacity constraints or other barriers to expansion, or firms A and B may be able to deter deviation in much the way that some voluntary cartels are able to do so (*see* Chapter 3, *supra*). Finally, the strategy of excluding firm C may be unprofitable for firm A if it must bear the full costs of doing so (*e.g*, the payments to suppliers needed to induce them not to deal with firm C), while firm A must share with firm B the benefits of any higher prices that may result. On the other hand, if firm A obtains a large fraction of the producer benefits from higher prices, perhaps because its market share is large, it may find it worthwhile to pay all of the costs, without requiring help from firm B.

Even if the raising rivals' costs strategy disadvantages firm C and reduces competition, it is not necessarily harmful economically on balance, as it may simultaneously confer efficiencies upon firm A. For example, a manufacturer may foreclose rivals from effective distribution by requiring the dealer not to handle the products of rival manufacturers, but the same practice may also lead the manufacturer to increase its promotional effort, reduce dealer free-riding, and result in better service to customers.

Notwithstanding these caveats, it should be clear that exclusionary arrangements with suppliers, distributors, or customers, or even for single-firm refusals to deal, sometimes may harm competition in much the same way that a voluntary cartel does. The main difference is that firm C does not go along with the industry output reduction voluntarily; it is coerced into doing so involuntarily. In this way, the modern analysis of exclusion suggests more of a concern with the anticompetitive dangers than Chicago School adherents might have supposed.

The modern view also suggests greater concern with chilling aggressive competition and denying consumers the benefits of efficiencies than Judge Hand perceived in *Alcoa*. As the involuntary cartel intuition emphasizes, the mere foreclosure of some rivals (or, more generally, raising rivals' costs) is not enough for exclusion to generate harm to competition. It is necessary also to show that the remaining rivals could and would take advantage by reducing output and raising price, and that the market price then would rise. It is also necessary to show that any resulting harm to competition would not be outweighed by any efficiencies resulting from the challenged conduct. For example, if cost saving resulting from the exclusionary conduct would lead the market price to fall on balance, notwithstanding the exclusionary potential for the conduct, competition would be enhanced.

Applying the Raising Rivals' Costs Framework

In applying the raising rivals' costs framework to analyze the cases, it is useful to break down the analysis into three steps. It is worth emphasizing that this is a framework for an economic analysis of the conduct. It could also be the framework for a legal analysis if a reasonableness assessment were employed, but other legal rules may call for various types of truncated analyses or burden-shifting.

Exclusion, or "Raising Rivals' Costs." The first step considers whether a firm in the role of firm C has been excluded. How does the conduct alleged to harm competition in fact disadvantage some rival or rivals, by raising their costs or reducing their access to the market, causing those firms to become less aggressive competitors? This step of the inquiry commonly will focus on whether the excluded firms have practical alternative means of obtaining supply or distribution at favorable costs.

Market Power, or "Power Over Price." Second, if the excluding firm or firms in the role of firm A are able successfully to disadvantage firms in the role of firm C, would allow firm A to obtain or keep market power? One way to address this question is to begin by considering whether a hypothetical cartel composed of all sellers in the roles of firms A, B, and C would find it profitable to charge a price above the competitive level, whether such a hypothetical collusive arrangement is achieved voluntarily or involuntarily. In other words, are firms A, B, and C the only participants in a relevant market? If not, the exclusion of firm C could not possibly confer market power on firm A. Even if the exclusion of sellers in the role of firm C would in principle confer market power on firm A, one must ask whether the exclusionary conduct would be profitable for firm A, taking into account the costs of doing so along with the monopoly profits firm A would reasonably expect to receive, and whether any sellers in the role of firm B would go along with the scheme as opposed to cheating on it.

Efficiency Justifications. The final step identifies any legitimate business justifications for the exclusionary conduct, and asks whether any resulting benefit to competition would outweigh the potential harm to competition demonstrated through the first two steps. If the exclusionary practice confers cost savings on firm A, will firm A have an incentive to lower price that would outweigh any incentive to exercise market power by raising price, for example?

Lorain Journal Revisited

With the raising rivals' costs framework in hand we return to the *Lorain Journal* decision, and see how it may be understood within the modern economic framework for analyzing exclusion. The Lorain Journal newspaper can be represented as a seller in the position of firm A. WEOL, the new radio station, is the excluded firm, in the role of firm C. There are no firms B. The exclusionary practice is the newspaper's unilateral refusal to accept advertisements from any Lorain County advertiser who advertised over WEOL.

Step 1: Raising Rivals' Costs. If advertisers are thought of as a radio station's customers—taking the view that the station uses its programming to create a listening audience, which it then sells to advertisers—then the conduct under review limits WEOL's access to key advertiser customers. As a result, WEOL will find it more difficult to obtain advertising revenues and will become a less effective competitor. According to the Supreme Court, the Lorain Journal's conduct "tended to destroy and eliminate WEOL altogether." *Lorain Journal*, 342 U.S. at 150. There is no suggestion that WEOL had other ways to obtain advertising revenues.

Step 2: Market Power. The Supreme Court found that eliminating WEOL "would automatically restore to the publisher of the Journal its substantial monopoly in Lorain of the mass dissemination of all news and advertising, interstate and national, as well as local." *Id.* A market defined so that Lorain Journal and WEOL are the only rivals for local advertising is implicit in this conclusion. If one of the only two firms in a market protected from entry can exclude the other, it is immediately evident that the first will obtain monopoly power. The conduct at issue appears not to be very costly to the Lorain Journal. There is no suggestion, for example, that many advertisers chose to rely on WEOL exclusively. Thus, Lorain Journal's conduct did not reduce its advertising revenues.

Step 3: Efficiencies. The newspaper's justification for its conduct, dismissed by the court in a footnote, *id.* at n.8, appears to describe its desire to maintain its market power, not any effort to lower costs or otherwise obtain an efficiency. Commentators consistently treat this case as one in which the defendant presented no efficiency justification. *See, e.g.*, R. BORK, THE ANTITRUST PARADOX at 345.

Accordingly, from a modern perspective, the *Lorain Journal* facts, as recounted by the Supreme Court, add up to a solid economic case. The Lorain Journal created an involuntary cartel by excluding its only rival for advertising revenues, thereby protecting its monopoly power. The conduct had no efficiency justification, so it clearly harmed competition on balance. As you read the other cases in this chapter consider whether the exclusionary practice also harms competition according to the modern economic logic of raising rivals' costs, by creating an involuntary cartel.

Now consider the other, hypothetical tactics noted above that a newspaper might have employed to compete with rival radio station. These include exclusive contracts with advertisers, very low prices charged to advertisers, the construction of an affiliated radio station to compete with the rival, and bundling the price of advertising for advertisers that purchase space in the newspaper as well as time on its hypothetical affiliated radio station. Would each of these tactics be likely to foreclose WEOL from access to advertisers (raising that rival's costs)? Would each likely confer market power on the Lorain Journal newspaper? Would any appear to have a plausible efficiency justification?

As you consider the cases discussed in the remainder of this chapter, it will be useful to apply this economic framework to consider whether the conduct they evaluate appears to harm competition. This economic framework could be understood as what a court would do were it to apply an unstructured reasonableness approach to evaluating dominant firm exclusionary conduct.

As you read the decisions, however, you will discover that antitrust rules do not necessarily call for review under an unstructured rule of reason. The rules often incorporate presumptions or screens, much as the rule of reason was structured in analyzing horizontal agreements. In that context, per se rules, quick look rules and the like were defended as giving better guidance to courts and firms seeking to understand how to conduct their affairs within the law, and as reducing the transactions costs of resolving disputes. In the context of exclusionary conduct, some modern structured rules are designed particularly to given firms confidence that certain kinds of procompetitive conduct, particularly aggressive price-cutting, could not be challenged as anticompetitive. You will want to consider whether, in light of the economic framework for exclusion set forth here, the older rules too often discouraged procompetitive conduct, and whether the modern rules solve the problem or go too far in the other direction of allowing anticompetitive exclusionary behavior.

B. TRADITIONAL ANALYSIS OF EXCLUSIONARY CONDUCT

1. *ALCOA* AND THE ORIGINS OF THE POWER + CONDUCT FRAMEWORK

Section 2 of the Sherman Act prohibits *"monopolization,"* not *"monopoly."* Use of the term "monopolization" indicates legislative concern not with the status of monopoly alone, but rather with *how* a firm obtains or protects a commanding commercial position. As noted above in the Chapter Introduction, in *Grinnell* the Supreme Court described the test for monopolization as being comprised of two distinct elements: (1) monopoly power; that was (2) willfully acquired or maintained. The conduct requirement can be seen as an effort to give effect to the language of Section 2. The two part approach has required courts to define what constitutes *monopoly* (or, in the modern language of antitrust economics and law, *substantial market power*) and to specify behavior that constitutes illegal monopolization (today referred to as "predatory" or "exclusionary" conduct). To succeed in a Section 2 claim for monopolization, therefore, the modern judicial test for establishing illegal monopolization requires the plaintiff to prove that the defendant enjoyed monopoly power and that it achieved or maintained its market position through improper means.

The test originated with one of the most controversial Section 2 prosecutions in U.S. antitrust history—the U.S. government's case against the Aluminum Corporation of America—"Alcoa." After its creation in 1888, Alcoa quickly became the nation's leading aluminum producer. The firm grew mainly by virtue of owning patents that dramatically reduced the cost of producing aluminum. But Alcoa also used exclusionary techniques that caught the Justice Department's attention. Making aluminum requires lots of electricity, and Alcoa's contracts with electric power companies forbade them to supply electricity to other aluminum manufacturers. In 1912, Alcoa and the Justice Department signed a consent decree invalidating the restrictive contract provisions and barring Alcoa from enforcing such arrangements with electricity suppliers.

From 1920 until the late 1930s, private and public efforts to enforce the Sherman Act's prohibition against monopolization fell into repose. The Supreme Court's decision in *United States v. U.S. Steel Corp.*, 251 U.S. 417 (1920), suggested that the Court had embraced a permissive view of dominant firm behavior and would intervene to correct only the most flagrant, persistent abuses of monopoly power.

From the onset of the Depression in 1929 until the mid–1930s, antitrust enforcement waned as the United States experimented with central planning and comprehensive regulation of prices and entry to spur recovery. The early New Deal of Franklin Roosevelt's presidency de-emphasized competition, including antitrust enforcement, in favor of planning measures such as the National Industrial Recovery Act to promote economic growth.

In the mid–1930s, Roosevelt heeded advisors who urged greater reliance on competition policy and renewed antitrust enforcement. Particularly under the leadership of Thurman Arnold as the Assistant Attorney General for Antitrust, the government initiated a number of major Section 2 cases. The first and most important was *Alcoa*.

By 1937, Alcoa had become the sole U.S. producer of virgin aluminum ingot. The Justice Department launched a new case, again alleging that the company had used exclusionary practices to perpetuate its monopoly position. Expanded demand for aluminum as a material for building airplanes, automobiles, home appliances, and ships had given Alcoa a position of great commercial prominence. The government alleged that Alcoa wrongly had discouraged entry and expansion by its competitors by adding substantially to its existing productive capacity in order to fulfill new demand. When Alcoa increased capacity, the government argued, its competitors feared they could not attract the minimum critical mass of customers necessary to support efficient operations. Alcoa's capacity additions also were said to reveal its willingness to boost output dramatically (and depress market prices) if its competitors tried to expand their sales by undercutting Alcoa's prices. Alcoa responded that only a perverse reading of Section 2 would bar a firm from adding facilities to supply new demand. The district court exonerated the company, finding that it neither held a monopoly nor behaved wrongfully.

The Supreme Court lacked a quorum to hear the direct appeal of the suit, as several Justices had played a role in the case before joining the Court and were hence recused. Congress passed a special law that made the U.S. Court of Appeals for the Second Circuit the court of last resort and authorized it to hear the case sitting "as the Supreme Court." The Second Circuit's opinion in the case, authored by Judge Learned Hand, thus carries the authority of a Supreme Court precedent. As you shall see, before reaching the question of whether Alcoa acted improperly, the court first sought to determine whether Alcoa had monopoly power.

UNITED STATES v. ALUMINUM CO. OF AMERICA
Circuit Court of Appeals for the Second Circuit, 1945.
148 F.2d 416.

LEARNED HAND, Circuit Judge:

* * *

I.

* * *

* * * [T]he most important question in the case is whether the monopoly in 'Alcoa's' production of 'virgin' ingot, secured by the two patents until 1909, and in part perpetuated between 1909 and 1912 by the unlawful practices, forbidden by the decree of 1912, continued for the ensuing twenty-eight years; and whether, if it did, it was unlawful under § 2 of the Sherman Act. It is undisputed that throughout this period 'Alcoa' continued to be the single producer of 'virgin' ingot in the United States; and the plaintiff argues that this without more was enough to make it an unlawful monopoly. It also takes an alternative position: that in any event during this period 'Alcoa' consistently pursued unlawful exclusionary practices, which made its dominant position certainly unlawful, even though it would not have been, had it been retained only by 'natural growth.' Finally, it asserts that many of these practices were of themselves unlawful, as contracts in restraint of trade under Sec. 1 of the [Sherman] Act. 'Alcoa's' position is that the fact that it alone continued to make 'virgin' ingot in this country did not, and does not, give it a monopoly of the market; that it was always subject to the competition of imported 'virgin' ingot, and of what is called 'secondary' ingot; and that even if it had not been, its monopoly would not have been retained by unlawful means, but would have been the result of a growth which the Act does not forbid, even when it results in a monopoly. We shall first consider the amount and character of this competition; next, how far it established a monopoly; and finally, if it did, whether that monopoly was unlawful under § 2 of the Act.

From 1902 onward until 1928 'Alcoa' was making ingot in Canada through a wholly owned subsidiary; so much of this as it imported into the United States it is proper to include with what it produced here. In the year 1912 the sum of these two items represented nearly ninety-one per cent of the total amount of 'virgin' ingot available for sale in this country. This percentage varied year by year up to and including 1938: in 1913 it was about seventy-two per cent; in 1921 about sixty-eight per cent; in 1922 about seventy-two; with these exceptions it was always over eighty per cent of the total and for the last five years 1934–1938 inclusive it averaged over ninety per cent. The effect of such a proportion of the production upon the market we reserve for the time being, for it will be necessary first to consider the nature and uses of 'secondary' ingot, the name by which the industry knows ingot made from aluminum scrap. This is of two sorts, though for our purposes it is not important to distinguish between them. One of these is the clippings and trimmings of 'sheet' aluminum, when patterns are cut out of it, as a suit is cut from a bolt of cloth. The chemical composition of these is obviously the same as that of the 'sheet' from which they come; and, although they are likely to accumulate dust or other dirt in the factory, this may be removed by well known processes. If a record of the original composition of the 'sheet' has been preserved, this scrap may be remelted into new ingot, and used again for the same purpose. It is true that some of the witnesses—

Arthur V. Davis, the chairman of the board of 'Alcoa' among them—testified that at each remelting aluminum takes up some new oxygen which progressively deteriorates its quality for those uses in which purity is important; but other witnesses thought that it had become commercially feasible to remove this impurity, and the judge made no finding on the subject. Since the plaintiff has the burden of proof, we shall assume that there is no such deterioration. Nevertheless, there is an appreciable 'sales resistance' even to this kind of scrap, and for some uses (airplanes and cables among them), fabricators absolutely insist upon 'virgin': just why is not altogether clear. The other source of scrap is aluminum which has once been fabricated and the article, after being used, is discarded and sent to the junk heap, as for example, cooking utensils, like kettles and pans, and the pistons or crank cases of motorcars. These are made with a substantial alloy and to restore the metal to its original purity costs more than it is worth. However, if the alloy is known both in quality and amount, scrap, when remelted, can be used again for the same purpose as before. In spite of this, as in the case of clippings and trimmings, the industry will ordinarily not accept ingot so salvaged upon the same terms as 'virgin.' There are some seventeen companies which scavenge scrap of all sorts, clean it, remelt it, test it for its composition, make it into ingots and sell it regularly to the trade. There is in all these salvage operations some inevitable waste of actual material; not only does a certain amount of aluminum escape altogether, but in the salvaging process itself some is skimmed off as scum and thrown away. The judge found that the return of fabricated products to the market as 'secondary' varied from five to twenty-five years, depending upon the article; but he did not, and no doubt could not, find how many times the cycle could be repeated before the metal was finally used up.

There are various ways of computing 'Alcoa's' control of the aluminum market—as distinct from its production—depending upon what one regards as competing in that market. The judge figured its share—during the years 1929–1938, inclusive—as only about thirty-three percent; to do so he included 'secondary,' and excluded that part of 'Alcoa's own production which it fabricated and did not therefore sell as ingot. If, on the other hand, 'Alcoa's' total production, fabricated and sold, be included, and balanced against the sum of imported 'virgin' and 'secondary,' its share of the market was in the neighborhood of sixty-four per cent for that period. The percentage we have already mentioned—over ninety—results only if we both include all 'Alcoa's' production and exclude 'secondary'. That percentage is enough to constitute a monopoly; it is doubtful whether sixty or sixty-four percent would be enough; and certainly thirty-three per cent is not. Hence it is necessary to settle what he shall treat as competing in the ingot market. That part of its production which 'Alcoa' itself fabricates, does not of course ever reach the market as ingot; and we recognize that it is only when a restriction of production either inevitably affects prices, or is intended to do so, that it violates § 1 of the Act. However, even though we were to assume that a monopoly is unlawful under Sec. 2 only in case it controls prices, the ingot fabricated by 'Alcoa,' necessarily had a direct effect upon the ingot market. All ingot—with trifling exceptions—is used to fabricate intermediate or end, products; and therefore all intermediate, or end, products which 'Alcoa' fabricates and sell, pro tanto reduce the demand for ingot itself. The situation is the same, though reversed, as in Standard Oil Co. v. United States, 221 U.S. 1, 77, 31 S.Ct. 502, 523, where the court answered the defendant's argument that they had no control over the crude oil by saying that 'as substantial power over the crude product was the inevitable result of the absolute control which existed over the refined product, the monopolization of the one carried with it the power to control the other.' We cannot therefore agree that the computation of the percentage of 'Alcoa's' control over the ingot market should not include the whole of its ingot production.

As to 'secondary,' as we have said, for certain purposes the industry will not accept it at all; but for those for which it will, the difference in price is ordinarily not very great; the judge found that it was between one and two cents a pound, hardly enough margin on which to base a monopoly. Indeed, there are times when all differential disappears, and 'secondary' will actually sell at a higher price: *i.e.*, when there is a supply available which contains just the alloy that a fabricator needs for the article which he proposes to make. Taking the industry as a whole, we can say nothing more definite than that, although 'secondary' does not compete at all in some uses, (whether because of 'sales resistance' only, or because of actual metallurgical inferiority), for most purposes it competes upon a substantial equality with 'virgin.' On these facts the judge found that 'every pound of secondary or scrap aluminum which is sold in commerce displaces a pound of virgin aluminum which otherwise would, or might have been, sold.' We agree: so far as 'secondary' supplies the demand of such fabricators as will accept it, it increases the amount of 'virgin' which must seek sale elsewhere; and it therefore results that the supply of that part of the demand which will accept only 'virgin' becomes greater in proportion as 'secondary' drives away 'virgin' from the demand which will accept 'secondary.' (This is indeed the same argument which we used a moment ago to include in the supply that part of 'virgin' which 'Alcoa' fabricates; it is not apparent to us why the judge did not think it applicable to that item as well.) At any given moment therefore 'secondary' competes with 'virgin' in the ingot market; further, it can, and probably does, set a limit or 'ceiling' beyond which the price of 'virgin' cannot go, for the cost of its production will in the end depend only upon the expense of scavenging and reconditioning. It might seem for this reason that in estimating 'Alcoa's' control over the ingot market, we ought to include the supply of 'secondary,' as the judge did. Indeed, it may be thought a paradox to say that anyone has the monopoly of a market in which at all times he must meet a competition that limits his price. We shall show that it is not.

In the case of a monopoly of any commodity which does not disappear in use and which can be salvaged, the supply seeking sale at any moment will be made up of two components: (1) the part which the putative monopolist can immediately produce and sell; and (2) the part which has been, or can be, reclaimed out of what he has produced and sold in the past. By hypothesis he presently controls the first of these components; the second he has controlled in the past, although he no longer does. During the period when he did control the second, if he was aware of his interest, he was guided, not alone by its effect at that time upon the market, but by his knowledge that some part of it was likely to be reclaimed and seek the future market. That consideration will to some extent always affect his production until he decides to abandon the business, or for some other reason ceases to be concerned with the future market. Thus, in the case at bar 'Alcoa' always knew that the future supply of ingot would be made up in part of what it produced at the time, and, if it was as far-sighted as it proclaims itself, that consideration must have had its share in determining how much to produce. How accurately it could forecast the effect of present production upon the future market is another matter. Experience, no doubt, would help; but it makes no difference that it had to guess; it is enough that it had an inducement to make the best guess it could, and that it would regulate that part of the future supply, so far as it should turn out to have guessed right. The competition of 'secondary' must therefore be disregarded, as soon as we consider the position of 'Alcoa' over a period of years; it was as much within 'Alcoa's' control as was the production of the 'virgin' from which it had been derived. This can be well illustrated by the case of a lawful monopoly: e.g. a patent or a copyright. The monopolist cannot prevent those to whom he sells from reselling at whatever prices they please. Nor can he prevent their reconditioning articles worn by use, unless they in fact make a new article. At any moment his control over the market will therefore be limited by that part of what he has formerly sold, which the price he now charges may bring upon the market, as second hand or reclaimed articles. Yet no one would think of saying that for this reason the patent or the copyright did not confer a monopoly. Again, consider the situation of the owner of the only supply of some raw material like iron ore. Scrap iron is a constant factor in the iron market; it is scavenged, remelted into pig, and sold in competition with newly smelted pig; an owner of the sole supply of ore must always face that competition and it will serve to put a 'ceiling' upon his price, so far as there is enough of it. Nevertheless, no one would say that, even during the period while the pig which he has sold in the past can so return to the market, he does not have a natural monopoly. Finally, if 'Alcoa' is right, precisely the same reasoning ought to lead us to include that part of clippings and trimmings which a fabricator himself saves and remelts—'process scrap'—for that too pro tanto reduces the market for 'virgin.' It can make no difference whether the original buyer reclaims, or a professional scavenger. Yet 'Alcoa' itself does not assert that such 'process scrap' competes; indeed it was at pains to prove that this scrap was not included in its computation of 'secondary.'

We conclude therefore that 'Alcoa's' control over the ingot market must be reckoned at over ninety per cent; that being the proportion which its production bears to imported 'virgin' ingot. If the fraction which it did not supply were the produce of domestic manufacture there could be no doubt that this percentage gave it a monopoly—lawful or unlawful, as the case might be. The producer of so large a proportion of the supply has complete control within certain limits. It is true that, if by raising the price he reduces the amount which can be marketed—as always, or almost always, happens— he may invite the expansion of the small producers who will try to fill the place left open; nevertheless, not only is there an inevitable lag in this, but the large producer is in a strong position to check such competition; and, indeed, if he has retained his old plant and personnel, he can inevitably do so. There are indeed limits to his power; substitutes are available for almost all commodities, and to raise the price enough is to evoke them. Moreover, it is difficult and expensive to keep idle any part of a plant or of personnel; and any drastic contraction of the market will offer increasing temptation to the small producers to expand. But these limitations also exist when a single producer occupies the whole market: even then, his hold will depend upon his moderation in exerting his immediate power.

The case at bar is however different, because, for aught that appears there may well have been a practically unlimited supply of imports as the price of ingot rose. Assuming that there was no agreement between 'Alcoa' and foreign producers not to import, they sold what could bear the handicap of the tariff and the cost of transportation. For the period of eighteen years— 1920–1937—they sold at times a little above 'Alcoa's' prices, at times a little under; but there was substantially no gross difference between what they received and what they would have received, had they sold uniformly at 'Alcoa's' prices. While the record is silent, we may therefore assume—the plaintiff having the burden—that, had 'Alcoa' raised its prices, more ingot would have been imported. Thus there is a distinction between domestic and foreign competition: the first is limited in quantity, and can increase only by an increase in plant and personnel; the second is of producers who, we must assume, produce much more than they import, and whom a rise in price will presumably induce immediately to divert to the American market what they have been selling elsewhere. It is entirely consistent with the evidence that it was the threat of greater foreign imports which kept 'Alcoa's' prices where they were, and prevented it from exploiting its advantage as sole domestic producer; indeed, it is hard to resist the conclusion that potential imports did put a 'ceiling' upon those prices. Nevertheless, within the limits afforded by the tariff and the cost of transportation, 'Alcoa' was free to raise its prices as it chose, since it was free from domestic competition, save as it drew other metals into the market as substitutes. * * *

* * * Having proved that 'Alcoa' had a monopoly of the domestic ingot market, the plaintiff had gone far enough; if it was an excuse, that 'Alcoa' had not abused its power, it lay upon 'Alcoa' to prove that it had not. But the whole issue is irrelevant anyway, for it is no excuse for 'monopolizing' a market that the monopoly has not been used to extract from the consumer more than a 'fair' profit. The [Sherman] Act has wider purposes. Indeed, even though we disregard all but economic considerations, it would by no means follow that such concentration of producing power is to be desired, when it has not been used extortionately. Many people believe that possession of unchallenged economic power deadens initiative, discourages thrift and depresses energy; that immunity from competition is a narcotic, and rivalry is a stimulant, to industrial progress; that the spur of constant stress is necessary to counteract an inevitable disposition to let well enough alone. Such people believe that competitors, versed in the craft as no consumer can be, will be quick to detect opportunities for saving and new shifts in production, and be eager to profit by them. In any event the mere fact that a producer, having command of the domestic market, has not been able to make more than a 'fair' profit, is no evidence that a 'fair' profit could not have been made at lower prices. United States v. Corn Products Refining Co., 234 F. 964, 1014– 15 (S.D.N.Y.1916). True, it might have been thought adequate to condemn only those monopolies which could not show that they had exercised the highest possible ingenuity, had adopted every possible economy, had anticipated every conceivable improvement, stimulated every possible demand. No doubt, that would be one way of dealing with the matter, although it would

imply constant scrutiny and constant supervision, such as courts are unable to provide. Be that as it may, that was not the way that Congress chose; it did not condone 'good trusts' and condemn 'bad' ones; it forbad all. Moreover, in so doing it was not necessarily actuated by economic motives alone. It is possible, because of its indirect social or moral effect, to prefer a system of small producers, each dependent for his success upon his own skill and character, to one in which the great mass of those engaged must accept the direction of a few. These considerations, which we have suggested only as possible purposes of the Act, we think the decisions prove to have been in fact its purposes.

* * *

We have been speaking only of the economic reasons which forbid monopoly; but, as we have already implied, there are others, based upon the belief that great industrial consolidations are inherently undesirable, regardless of their economic results. In the debates in Congress Senator Sherman himself * * * showed that among the purposes of Congress in 1890 was a desire to put an end to great aggregations of capital because of the helplessness of the individual before them. * * * Throughout the history of [the antitrust] statutes it has been constantly assumed that one of their purposes was to perpetuate and preserve, for its own sake and in spite of possible cost, an organization of industry in small units which can effectively compete with each other. We hold that 'Alcoa's' monopoly of ingot was of the kind covered by § 2.

It does not follow because 'Alcoa' had such a monopoly, that it 'monopolized' the ingot market: it may not have achieved monopoly; monopoly may have been thrust upon it. If it had been a combination of existing smelters which united the whole industry and controlled the production of all aluminum ingot, it would certainly have 'monopolized' the market. * * * We may start therefore with the premise that to have combined ninety per cent of the producers of ingot would have been to 'monopolize' the ingot market; and, so far as concerns the public interest, it can make no difference whether an existing competition is put an end to, or whether prospective competition is prevented. The Clayton Act itself speaks in that alternative: 'to injure, destroy, or prevent competition.' § 13(a) 15 U.S.C.A. Nevertheless, it is unquestionably true that from the very outset the courts have at least kept in reserve the possibility that the origin of a monopoly may be critical in determining its legality; and for this they had warrant in some of the congressional debates which accompanied the passage of the Act. This notion has usually been expressed by saying that size does not determine guilt; that there must be some 'exclusion' of competitors; that the growth must be something else than 'natural' or 'normal'; that there must be a 'wrongful intent,' or some other specific intent; or that some 'unduly' coercive means must be used. At times there has been emphasis upon the use of the active verb, 'monopolize,' as the judge noted in the case at bar. What engendered these compunctions is reasonably plain; persons may unwittingly find themselves in possession of a monopoly, automatically so to say: that is, without having intended either to put an end to existing competition, or to prevent competition from arising when none had existed; they may become monopolists by force of accident. Since the Act makes 'monopolizing' a crime, as well as a civil wrong, it would be not only unfair, but presumably contrary to the intent of Congress, to include such instances. A market may, for example, be so limited that it is impossible to produce at all and meet the cost of production except by a plant large enough to supply the whole demand. Or there may be changes in taste or in cost which drive out all but one purveyor. A single producer may be the survivor out of a group of active competitors, merely by virtue of his superior skill, foresight and industry. In such cases a strong argument can be made that, although the result may expose the public to the evils of monopoly, the Act does not mean to condemn the resultant of those very forces which it is its prime object to foster: finis opus coronat ["the end crowns the work" Eds.]. The successful competitor, having been urged to compete, must not be turned upon when he wins. * * * 'Alcoa's' size was 'magnified' to make it a 'monopoly'; indeed, it has never been anything else; and its size, not only offered it an 'opportunity for abuse,' but it 'utilized' its size for 'abuse,' as can easily be shown.

It would completely misconstrue 'Alcoa's' position in 1940 to hold that it was the passive beneficiary of a monopoly, following upon an involuntary elimination of competitors by automatically operative economic forces. Already in 1909, when its last lawful monopoly ended, it sought to strengthen its position by unlawful practices, and these concededly continued until 1912. In that year it had two plants in New York, at which it produced less than 42 million pounds of ingot; in 1934 it had five plants (the original two, enlarged; one in Tennessee; one in North Carolina; one in Washington), and its production had risen to about 327 million pounds, an increase of almost eight-fold. Meanwhile not a pound of ingot had been produced by anyone else in the United States. This increase and this continued and undisturbed control did not fall undesigned into 'Alcoa's' lap; obviously it could not have done so. It could only have resulted, as it did result, from a persistent determination to maintain the control, with which it found itself vested in 1912. There were at least one or two abortive attempts to enter the industry, but 'Alcoa' effectively anticipated and forestalled all competition, and succeeded in holding the field alone. True, it stimulated demand and opened new uses for the metal, but not without making sure that it could supply what it had evoked. There is no dispute as to this; 'Alcoa' avows it as evidence of the skill, energy and initiative with which it has always conducted its business; as a reason why, having won its way by fair means, it should be commended, and not dismembered. We need charge it with no moral derelictions after 1912; we may assume that all it claims for itself is true. The only question is whether it falls within the exception established in favor of those who do not seek, but cannot avoid, the control of a market. It seems to us that that question scarcely survives its statement. It was not inevitable that it should always anticipate increases in the demand for ingot and be prepared to supply them. Nothing compelled it to keep doubling and redoubling its capacity before others entered the field. It insists that it never excluded competitors; but we can think of no more effective exclusion than progressively to embrace each new opportunity as it opened, and to face every newcomer with new capacity already geared into a great organization, having the advantage of experience, trade connections and the elite of personnel. Only in case we interpret 'exclusion' as limited to maneuvres not honestly industrial, but actuated solely by a desire to prevent competition, can such a course, indefatigably pursued, be deemed not 'exclusionary.' So to limit it would in our judgment emasculate the Act; would permit just such consolidations as it was designed to prevent.

* * *

In studying Alcoa's position in the aluminum industry, Judge Hand wrote against a backdrop of Supreme Court decisions that seemed to have set general boundaries for determining when market shares permitted an inference of substantial market power. In the Note that follows, we discuss those cases, as well as Judge Hand's analysis of market power in *Alcoa*.

Note on the Origins of Alcoa's Market Share Benchmarks

Judge Hand's three market share benchmarks have proved to be extraordinarily influential and durable. But where did he get the idea that a 90% market share was certainly sufficient to establish a monopoly, that 60–64% was doubtful, and that 33% was insufficient? The answer likely lies in his synthesis of several earlier Supreme Court cases involving prosecutions under Section 2.

Standard Oil and United States Steel

The most important case in the early history of the U.S. antitrust laws is *Standard Oil Company of New Jersey v. United States*, 221 U.S. 1, 31 S.Ct. 502 (1911). In deliberations leading to passage of the Sherman Act of 1890, Standard Oil and its chief architect, John D. Rockefeller, provided a major target for congressional opprobrium. Following a series of highly critical accounts of Standard's behavior, first in a series of magazine articles and a book by journalist Ida M. Tarbell (*see* IDA M. TARBELL, THE HISTORY OF THE STANDARD OIL COMPANY (1904)), and later in official reports of the Federal Bureau of Corporations, President Theodore Roosevelt directed his attorney general to prepare a case against the petroleum giant.

In 1906, the Justice Department filed a civil action against Standard under Sections 1 and 2 of the Sherman Act. The government charged the company with monopolizing and attempting to monopolize the refining and marketing of petroleum products through various predatory means, including local price-cutting, bribery, obtaining rebates from railroads, and commercial espionage. After a fifteen-month trial, the U.S. district court in St. Louis issued a judgment for the government and ordered that the trust be dissolved.

Standard appealed the decision to the Supreme Court, attacking the trial court's conclusions that it had monopoly power and used improper business tactics. The company also assailed the district court's remedy, arguing that the forced dissolution of the firm into over 30 successor firms would yield economic chaos. On May 11, 1911, the Supreme Court upheld the trial court's finding of illegal monopolization and endorsed the dissolution decree. (You may recall from Chapter 2 that *Standard Oil* marked the modern origin of the "rule of reason" for purposes of Section 1 of the Sherman Act.) The Court's only concession to the defendant was to extend from 30 days to six months the period for executing the mandated divestitures.

In *Standard Oil*, both direct and circumstantial evidence led the Supreme Court to conclude that the defendant had substantial market power. Chief Justice Edward White's majority opinion spent little time defining a relevant market and analyzing the defendant's position in it. The parties agreed that the production of crude oil and the refining, transportation, and marketing of petroleum products constituted the relevant arenas of industrial activity. The Court accepted the government's allegation that Standard had achieved a 90 percent share of commerce in petroleum refining and had sustained its commanding position for well over a decade. The size and durability of the company's market share weighed decisively against its argument that it lacked a monopoly.

The Court did not require the government to show that Standard dominated all phases of the petroleum industry. Control over refining gave Standard power to govern commerce in the upstream (crude oil production) and downstream (marketing) segments. The Court's reliance on circumstantial evidence (Standard's share of activity) to determine the company's status proved influential. Later antitrust cases would treat a durable market share of 90 percent or more as creating a strong presumption of monopoly power.

The conclusion that Standard was a monopolist rested on more than market shares. In discussing Standard's dominance, the Court recited how the company *exercised* its power. The company preyed upon and then acquired competing refiners and secured its grip over refining by purchasing the transportation arteries (pipelines and rail tank cars) that linked refineries to crude oil production areas and to end users of products such as kerosene and gasoline. Here the Court suggested that proof of successful efforts to suppress and assimilate rivals—*direct evidence of the capacity to restrict competition*—could reinforce the inference of monopoly power derived from analyzing market shares. Thus did the Court plant the idea that evidence of a firm's actual success in subduing competitors could demonstrate its market power.

Standard Oil was one of many monopolization cases the Justice Department initiated from 1905 through 1912. The targets of these cases, companies such as Standard, General Electric, DuPont, American Tobacco, International Harvester, and U.S. Steel, had exploited lax enforcement and favorable judicial interpretations to achieve market supremacy by purchasing competitors. In *United States v. E.C. Knight Co.*, 156 U.S. 1, 15 S.Ct. 249 (1895), the Supreme Court had rejected the Justice Department's challenge to a series of acquisitions that gave the defendant control of over 98 percent of the country's sugar refining capacity. It reached this result by concluding that "manufacturing" was not "commerce" under the Sherman Act and therefore left sugar refining outside the statute's reach. The decision helped trigger a massive wave of mergers that ended in 1904, when the Court upheld the government's effort in *Northern Securities Co. v. United States*, 193 U.S. 197, 24 S.Ct. 436 (1904) to undo the combination of the Great Northern and Northern Pacific railroads.

Among its efforts to reverse the effects of the turn-of-the-century merger wave, the Justice Department filed a monopolization case against U.S. Steel in 1911. The complaint in *United States v. United States Steel Corp.*, 251 U.S. 417, 40 S.Ct. 293 (1920), alleged that U.S. Steel had achieved monopoly power through anticompetitive mergers with competitors and requested the dissolution of the company. The trial court found that U.S. Steel had used a series of mergers to achieve market shares of 80 to 95 percent of U.S. production of numerous steel products, proceeded to raise prices dramatically, and realized extraordinary profits. The district court also reported that, from 1907 until 1911, U.S. Steel's president, E.H. Gary, organized regular dinners at which the company and its competitors met to cooperate in setting prices and production limits.

The district court nonetheless exonerated the defendant. Although U.S. Steel had attained market shares of 80 to 95 percent, the trial court emphasized that the company's share had fallen to 40.9 percent by the trial's end in 1917. The sharp decline in U.S. Steel's market share and the steady expansion by its rivals negated a finding of monopoly power. The court also downplayed the "Gary Dinners," noting that the gatherings had ceased before the government began its lawsuit. The Justice Department did not challenge, as a separate Section 1 offense, the participation by U.S. Steel and its rivals in the Gary Dinners. Nor did any competitors testify to decry oppression by the defendant. Instead, they appeared in droves to attest to U.S. Steel's adherence to decent methods of commerce.

By a 4–3 vote, the Supreme Court sustained the trial court's ruling and emphasized the absence of persuasive proof that U.S. Steel held substantial market power. Justice McKenna's majority opinion stated that the decline in U.S. Steel's market share, from 80–95 percent to about 41 percent, belied market preeminence. After all, how could a firm surrender half of its share of the market and still be considered "dominant"?

Beyond the circumstantial evidence (U.S. Steel's declining market share), the Court also pointed to the absence of direct proof of market power. U.S. Steel might have responded to entry and expansion by competitors with the sort of aggressive countermoves employed by Standard Oil. For example, U.S. Steel might have cut prices selectively in markets targeted by entrants or tried to deny competitors access to a vital input, such as iron ore. The Court said the government had introduced no evidence that U.S. Steel had abused its competitors or customers. Indeed, hundreds of U.S. Steel rivals had attested to the firm's propriety. U.S. Steel perhaps tried to persuade its rivals to collude, but the Court said these efforts seemed ineffective and had no impact on market conditions. The Court also dismissed the suggestion of the government's expert, an economist, that the uniformity of industry prices during the period in question probably resulted from actual or tacit collusion. The Court refused to rely on such "speculation" when U.S. Steel had produced so many testimonials from the company's rivals indicating that competition was robust.

The Court arguably misapprehended the significance of the Gary Dinners and the pricing patterns that followed them. The Gary Dinners may have helped develop understandings by which the producers organized their behavior. U.S. Steel may have announced its willingness to tolerate its rivals if they priced at or near the company's relatively high price. If so, it is hardly surprising, or inconsistent with the government's theory, that competitors would heap praise upon U.S. Steel. The defendant may have orchestrated a collusive pricing arrangement that let its rivals expand output gradually and obtain supra-competitive profits in the process. If U.S. Steel helped keep industry-wide prices above competitive levels, the rivals' gratitude was much deserved.

Judge Hand's 90 percent benchmark thus likely came from *Standard Oil*. For his view that 33 percent would be insufficient, he probably used *U.S. Steel* as the guidepost, for the Supreme Court had taken the decline in U.S. Steel's market share to roughly 41 percent as signifying a lack of monopoly power. Reflecting the paucity of case law addressing market shares of 40 to 90 percent, Hand further noted that "it is doubtful whether sixty or sixty-four percent would be enough."

Figure 6–3 summarizes the results in cases that probably helped shape his thinking on this question.

Figure 6–3:
Pre-*Alcoa* Decisions and the Inference of Monopoly Power

Case	Defendant's Market Share	Monopoly Inferred?
Standard Oil (1911)	90%	Yes
American Tobacco (1911)	90%	Yes
International Harvester (1914)	85%	Yes
U.S. Steel (1920)	41%	No
Standard Oil of Indiana (1931)	26%	No
Appalachian Coals (1933)	12, 54, 64, or 74%; (depending on definition of relevant market)	No: (Decision suggests that proper market definition yielded share between 12% and 54% and no more than 64%.)

A Closer Look at Alcoa and Market Definition

The *Alcoa* court ultimately agreed with the government's claim that the defendant's share of sales in a properly defined relevant market was 90 percent, well within the zone of concern that *Standard Oil* had identified in 1911. To reach 90 percent, the court made a number of difficult (and disputed) judgments about the relevant market's contours and Alcoa's share of activity in the market. The court had to decide whether to limit the product market to virgin ingot or combine virgin ingot and "secondary" (recycled) aluminum; to count aluminum that Alcoa produced but consumed itself to make aluminum products for later resale; and to treat foreign suppliers as being able to increase shipments to the United States. if U.S. aluminum prices increased. Figure 6–4 indicates how sensitive the calculation of Alcoa's market share is to the assumptions the court made about the aluminum industry.

Figure 6–4:
Assumptions Underlying Calculation of Alcoa's Market Share

Relevant Market	Alcoa's Activity	Imports	Alcoa's Market Share
Virgin Ingot Only	External/Captive Output	10% only	90%
Virgin/Recycled	External/Captive Output	10% only	64%
Virgin/Recycled	External output only	10% only	33%
Any of Above	Any of Above	Unlimited	Uncertain, but smaller

One can quarrel with a number of the choices Judge Hand and his colleagues made in pegging Alcoa's market share at 90 percent. The record suggests that some purchasers of aluminum ingot (notably, aircraft manufacturers) regarded recycled aluminum as an unacceptable substitute for virgin ingot. Yet it also seems that many purchasers regarded virgin ingot and secondary aluminum as fungible. The court reasonably doubted the substitutability of secondary aluminum for all uses, but excluding all secondary aluminum from the market definition ignored the many customers for whom secondary was a suitable alternative. Alcoa presumably had some ability to adjust current output to account for competition in the secondary market, but it is unclear from the court's discussion how the company could wholly negate the constraining influence of recycling by cutting its new production.

The decision to include all of Alcoa's "captive production"—aluminum that Alcoa produced and transferred to its wholly owned subsidiaries to fabricate aluminum parts and make finished products—also involves difficult judgments. The court reasoned that, if the price of aluminum ingot began to rise, Alcoa would divert its ingot away from its own fabricators and sell the ingot on the open market. Since Alcoa had an established network for selling virgin ingot, shifting output from internal consumption to external sales probably would have required a relatively modest effort. Not all companies might be able to make this switch fluidly. The ability to respond to price increases in the external market would depend on having an external sales network and substantial freedom to renege on commitments made to the firm's internal users of the product and, indirectly, to the customers who purchase the fabricated items that the firm produces.

The treatment of imports is a clearer issue in *Alcoa*. The court correctly noted that existing tariffs and quotas severely constrained the ability of foreign suppliers to respond to aluminum price increases in the United States. In recent times, the reduction of tariff and non-tariff barriers to trade through the World Trade Organization framework and other international agreements has boosted the ability of producers in many product markets to compete for sales worldwide. Today the geographic dimension of relevant markets that once were delimited by high trade barriers has become increasingly global.

Alcoa has exerted a profound, lasting impact on the analysis of monopoly power. The decision has anchored the analysis of market power in the process of defining relevant markets and calculating market shares as a surrogate for market power. *Alcoa* also emphasized—perhaps inordinately—the legal presumptions that flow from particular market share thresholds. Market definition became a high stakes, strategic battle that frequently determined litigation outcomes.

With so much depending on market definition, *Alcoa* also underscored the critical nature of certain industry data. Antitrust specialists need not agree or disagree with *Alcoa*'s market definition and market power analysis to recognize the importance of digging beneath the numbers where market shares are offered as proxies for market power. The exercises of defining a relevant market and attributing shares to individual market participants often rests upon a foundation of debatable assumptions. In many instances, there may be no particularly convincing basis for choosing between alternative hypotheses about which products or geographic locations belong inside the circle that delimits the relevant market. Where the basis for defining the relevant market or attributing market shares is uncertain, one should place less weight upon the resulting market shares as bases for inferring the presence or absence of market power.

Sidebar 6–1:
Durable Goods Monopoly—Three Economic Issues

Alcoa has prompted economists to study several issues raised directly or indirectly by the case. This Sidebar briefly surveys the literature on three of these issues.

Competition From Used or Recycled Products

Judge Learned Hand considered whether competition from sellers of secondary aluminum constrains the pricing of virgin aluminum in the context of market definition. The secondary product is ingot made from aluminum scrap. This is an instance of the more general question of whether recycled or used products should be counted as substitutes for new production.

Judge Hand addressed this question in the context of market definition. He recognized that secondary competes with virgin in ingot market, probably setting a ceiling on the price of virgin aluminum. But Hand also observed that Alcoa knows that some of its virgin production will later return to the market, recycled from scrap. That consideration must affect Alcoa's decision as to present production. "The competition of 'secondary' must therefore be disregarded, as soon as we consider the position of 'Alcoa' over a period of years; it was as much within 'Alcoa's' control as was the production of 'virgin' from which it had been derived." Accordingly, Judge Hand excluded secondary aluminum from the relevant product market. Had he done otherwise, Alcoa's market share would have been calculated as 64% rather than 90%.

In part, the question of whether competition from used or recycled products constrains the potential exercise of market power by producers of new products turns on two familiar considerations. One comes up in market definition: do buyers consider the two products close substitutes? (Perhaps not. Metal produced from scrap could have additional impurities, making them unsuitable for some buyers. Relatedly, many new car buyers probably do not consider used cars close substitutes at current prices, though others likely do.) Another may arise in analyzing the significance of market shares. Can sellers of used or recycled products expand their output cheaply, or are they effectively constrained as to how much they put on the market?

The economics literature spawned by Judge Hand's analysis of the competitive role of secondary aluminum focuses upon an additional consideration that arises in durable goods markets, where the products at issue are not just any substitutes, but are derived from new production in the past. The new issue is whether the secondary product has been recovered from discarded scrap, or whether it was sold as used every time it previously changed hands. The recovery of discarded products is merely an alternative production process using different inputs, over which the producer of new products has no control. But if buyers of new products place value on them when they are used, by selling used goods to other buyers (some of whom may recondition them for sale in competition with new products), then a new product monopolist will recognize (as Hand observed) that it can restrict the supply of used goods in the future by reducing output in the present. Under such circumstances, the presence of a substantial market in used products can constrain the price of new products, but a new product monopolist may be able offset this procompetitive force to a significant degree by reducing new production in anticipation of its future return to the marketplace. *See generally*, Darius W. Gaskins, Alcoa *Revisited: The Welfare Implications of a Secondhand Market*, 7 J. ECON. THEORY 254 (1974); Peter L. Swan, Alcoa: *The Influence of Recycling on Monopoly Power*, 88 J. POL. ECON. 76 (1980), Robert E. Martin, *Monopoly Power and the Recycling of Raw Materials*, 30 J. INDUS. ECON. 405 (1982). *Cf.* Dennis W. Carlton & Robert Gertner, *Market Power and Mergers in Durable–Good Industries*, 32 J. L. & ECON. S203 (1989) (Pt. 2, October) (analyzing additional complications arising when the new product industry has an oligopoly market structure); Carl Shapiro, *Comment on Carlton and Gertner*, 32 J. L. & ECON. S227 (1989) (Pt. 2, October).

These threads were integrated in an empirical study of Alcoa itself by economist Valerie Suslow, using modern empirical methods unavailable at the time the *Alcoa* case was litigated. Suslow finds that Alcoa possessed substantial market power: it recognized that it faced a downward sloping demand curve, and could therefore elevate price by reducing output. In consequence, she finds, Alcoa's markup of price over its marginal cost was equal to about 60% of price during the 1930s. (She does not specifically identify the competitive price, however.) This market power was not significantly undermined by competition with secondary aluminum recovered from scrap, but not primarily because Alcoa restricted virgin aluminum production in order to limit the future supply of the secondary product (Judge Hand's argument). The recycled product did not come onto the market for five to twenty-five years after the virgin aluminum was sold; in a growing market, therefore, secondary aluminum production would always be small relative to virgin aluminum and have little influence on virgin aluminum prices. Rather, competition from secondary aluminum was not a big threat to Alcoa for a more pedestrian reason: mainly because secondary aluminum was only an imperfect substitute to buyers of virgin aluminum. Valerie Y. Suslow, *Estimating Monopoly Behavior With Competitive Recycling: An Application to* Alcoa, 17 RAND J. ECON. 389 (1986).

Can the Monopolist Commit to High Future Prices?

Nobel Prize-winning economist Ronald Coase highlighted the significance of another important issue unique to durable goods markets: time. The buyer of a durable good like a computer or an automobile makes use of her purchase over a period of time. Often, the buyer has the option of purchasing immediately, or waiting a while (while continuing to use her existing car or computer) in the hope that the delay will allow her to purchase the product at a lower price in the future.

A monopolist seller, in turn, must decide how much to produce (and charge) both initially and in the future. It might want to keep output low, and charge a price well in excess of the competitive level. If it charges a high price initially, however, it will end up selling only to those buyers who value the product the most. The seller will then be tempted by another profit opportunity: by cutting price, it can sell even more to customers who didn't purchase initially (when the price was so high) but are nevertheless willing to pay more than seller's cost. In other words, the durable goods monopolist has an incentive to price discriminate over time. Initially, the monopolist would charge a monopoly price, but over time it would maximize profits by gradually lowering price, selling more and more until price falls to the competitive level.

Ronald Coase argued that this strategy would not be successful. Buyers—even those willing to pay a great deal—would recognize that the seller has a powerful incentive to lower price in the future, and would find it worth their while to delay purchases awaiting the price cuts. If so, the monopoly seller would be unable ever to charge a price greater than the competitive level. The durable goods monopolist competes in effect competes with its future self, and, notwithstanding its monopoly, cannot exercise market power! Ronald Coase, *Durability and Monopoly*, 15 J. L. & Econ. 143 (1972). This proposition—that a durable goods monopolist will be unable to exercise market power because rational buyers will balk at paying monopoly prices—is widely known as the "Coase conjecture" (and is a proposition distinct from the same economist's "Coase theorem" at the core of modern law and economics).

An extensive economics literature has identified factors that may preserve some ability for the durable goods monopolist to exercise market power, notwithstanding its Coase conjecture incentive not to raise price. If the durable goods monopolist can commit not to cut price in the future, buyers will not delay their purchases in anticipation of a price reduction, so the monopolist will be able successfully to charge a high price today. Sellers can make such commitments, for example, by limiting capacity (an artist making only so many prints before destroying the plates), or by contracting to pay a penalty if it cuts price in the future (see the discussion of "most favored customer" provisions in Chapter 3, Sidebar 3-6). Adjustment costs that keep sellers from adjusting price quickly might also lessen buyer incentives to wait for prices to fall. In addition, sellers can avoid competing with themselves by leasing rather than selling the durable product, making it impossible for buyers to obtain any advantage from delaying their purchase. Or they can reduce the problem by limiting durability through "planned obsolescence" (as through frequent product upgrades).

Excess Capacity as a Barrier to Entry

Judge Hand argued that Alcoa's policy of expanding capacity in anticipation of demand deterred entry by prospective rivals, and thus insulated Alcoa from competition. This is an example of a class of theories that economists have come to term *"strategic entry deterrence."*

The central idea behind strategic entry deterrence is simple: if firms convince their potential rivals that entry will lead to a competitive marketplace with a low post-entry price, then potential competitors will refrain from entry no matter how high the pre-entry price charged by incumbents. To set up this threat, incumbents must make irreversible investments in instruments of entry deterrence. These might include excess low cost capacity (Judge Hand's suggestion in *Alcoa*), brand proliferation, high advertising, or contract provisions by which sellers agree to match good-faith offers by rivals. These investments are often costly to the monopolist, but the payoff is greater if they guarantee that the monopolist can protect a high price by deterring new competition.

Theories like these are well-established as possibilities in the economics literature. *See generally* Steven C. Salop, *Strategic Entry Deterrence*, 69 AM. ECON. REV. 335 (Papers & Proceedings 1979); Richard J. Gilbert, *Mobility Barriers and the Value of Incumbency*, in 1 HANDBOOK OF INDUSTRIAL ORGANIZATION 475 (Richard Schmalensee & Robert Willig, eds. 1989). A survey of firms suggests that practices such as these are prevalent. Robert H. Smiley, *Empirical Evidence on Strategic Entry Deterrence*, 6 INT'L J. INDUS. ORG. 167 (1988). On the other hand, an empirical study of thirty-eight chemical product industries called into question the specific method of entry deterrence that concerned Judge Hand, finding that incumbent firms in that industry rarely built excess capacity preemptively in an effort to deter entry. Marvin B. Lieberman, *Excess Capacity as a Barrier to Entry: An Empirical Appraisal*, 35 J. INDUS. ECON. 607 (1987).

Judge Hand's opinion in *Alcoa* inspired extensive and continuing discussions among courts and commentators about the reach of Section 2. One focus of debate is Hand's evaluation of antitrust's goals. Hand provided a memorable statement of the reason for curbing monopolies ("Many people believe that possession of unchallenged economic power deadens initiative, discourages thrift and depresses energy. . . .") and supplied an elegant synthesis of the non-economic aims that motivated Congress to adopt the Sherman Act. Yet Hand also recognized the hazards of a rule of law that condemned commercial preeminence without regard to the means of its attainment ("The successful competitor, having been urged to compete, must not be turned upon when he wins."). Judge Hand resolved this dilemma—how to deter monopoly within diminishing incentives to compete—by embracing a vision of antitrust that favored strict limits on dominant firm conduct to promote economic decentralization and to achieve a more egalitarian political and social environment.

Judge Hand condemned Alcoa's strategy of anticipating and responding to new demand for aluminum by expanding its own production capacity on the ground that it preempted entry and expansion by competing aluminum producers. Such conduct, Judge Hand concluded, satisfied the behavioral element of the monopolization offense. Because Judge Hand dismissed other allegations of wrongful acts, this behavior alone supplied the ingredient of bad conduct. Many commentators have assailed Hand's analysis. Should Alcoa have deferred increases in capacity and simply let rivals build new plants and serve all new demand? Was it rational for Alcoa, or any firm, to ignore increases in demand and remain content with its existing productive capabilities? And couldn't failure to expand output have resulted in even higher prices? How, in any event, were business managers to know when the addition of new capacity had gone too far?

The historical context of the case amplifies its significance. Aluminum was used to build all kinds of military hardware, especially aircraft, and became an essential input into the United States' ability to wage war in World War II. Would it have served the interests of the United States in the 1930s if Alcoa, especially after Adolph Hitler's rise to power in Germany in 1933, had built no new plants until 1938, when the Justice Department filed its antitrust case?

In *American Tobacco Co. v. United States*, 328 U.S. 781, 66 S.Ct. 1125 (1946), the first Section 2 case to reach the Supreme Court after *Alcoa*, the Court endorsed Judge Hand's opinion and adopted *Alcoa's* expansive view of when dominant firm conduct is improper. Two years after *American Tobacco*, in *United States v. Griffith*, 334 U.S. 100, 107, 68 S.Ct. 941, 945 (1948), the Court in dicta seemed to approve some of *Alcoa's* fullest implications when it said monopoly power, however acquired, "may itself constitute an evil and stand condemned under § 2 even though it remains unexercised." The *Griffith* Court, however, also condemned the practice of the defendant theater owners of buying film distribution rights for all their movie theaters as a block. Since some of Griffith's theaters had monopoly power and others did not, block purchasing abused the defendant's dominant position by allowing it to gain an advantage in competitive markets. (As we shall see, this latter theory has since been rejected by the Supreme Court. *See Note on the Status of Essential Facilities and Leveraging After Trinko, infra.*)

As blessed by *American Tobacco* and *Griffith*, *Alcoa* revitalized government efforts to enforce the Sherman Act's ban upon monopolization. In a number of cases, the government's theory of liability sought to define, in the tradition of *Alcoa*, broad limits on dominant firm behavior. Litigation involving United Shoe Machinery provides a major illustration. In *United States v. United Shoe Mach. Corp.*, 110 F.Supp. 295 (D. Mass. 1953), *aff'd per curiam*, 347 U.S. 521, 74 S.Ct. 699 (1954), the government challenged the country's largest producer of machines used to produce footwear. United Shoe's share of shoe machinery output was 75 to 85 percent, and the trial court found that the company had monopoly power. In a famous opinion by Judge Charles Wyzanski, the district court went on to condemn United Shoe's policy of leasing (and refusing to sell) its machines and its imposing lease terms that forced its customers to obtain maintenance and service on leased machines from United Shoe only.

At trial, United Shoe strived to show that its success was attributable to superior research and to its skill in meeting customer needs, not to any oppressive behavior. As the following passage indicates, Judge Wyzanski declined to find that the absence of obviously "predatory" conduct could exculpate United Shoe:

> It is only fair to add that the more than 14,000 page record, and the more than 5,000 exhibits, representing the diligent seven year search made by Government counsel aided by this Court's orders giving them full access to United's power does not rest on predatory practices. Probably few monopolies could produce a record so free

from any taint of that kind of wrong-doing. The violation with which United is now charged depends not on moral considerations, but on solely economic considerations. United is denied the right to exercise effective control of the market by business policies that are not the inevitable consequences of its capacities or its natural advantages. That those policies are not immoral is irrelevant.

Defendant seems to suggest that even if its control of the market is not attributable exclusively to its superior performance, its research, and its economies of scale, nonetheless, United's market control should not be held unlawful, because only through the existence of some monopoly power can the thin shoe machinery market support fundamental research of the first order, and achieve maximum economies of production and distribution.

To this defense the shortest answer is that the law does not allow an enterprise that maintains control of a market through practices not economically inevitable, to justify that control because of its supposed social advantage. It is for Congress, not for private interests, to determine whether a monopoly, not compelled by circumstances, is advantageous. And it is for Congress to decide on what conditions, and subject to what regulations, such a monopoly shall conduct its business.

110 F.Supp. at 345. Notwithstanding United Shoe's benign explanations, Judge Wyzanski found that the lease-only and service practices improperly impeded entry by rival shoe machinery producers and discouraged competition from independent service organizations. 110 F.Supp. at 345–46.

Like Judge Hand's analysis of Alcoa's capacity expansion efforts, Judge Wyzanski's evaluation of United Shoe's leasing and service policies—and his suggestion that a dominant firm risks Section 2 liability when it "maintains control of a market through practices not economically inevitable"—have inspired extensive debate. Some observers have argued that the challenged leasing terms may have helped assure the quality of the shoe machinery and enabled United Shoe to provide better services and information to its customers. The service agreements may have supplied an important source of feedback by which United spotted possibilities for improving its existing machines and used its research and development program to implement. Evidence recited by Judge Wyzanski indicated that many customers found United Shoe's leasing and service practices agreeable—an indication, perhaps, that the company's asserted justification was genuine. *Compare* Scott E. Masten & Edward A. Snyder, United States v. United Shoe Machinery Corporation: *On the Merits*, 36 J.L. & Econ. 33 (1993) (emphasizing efficiency grounds for leasing terms) *with* Joseph F. Brodley & Ching-to Albert Ma, *Contract Penalties, Monopolizing Strategies, and Antitrust Policy*, 45 Stan. L. Rev. 1161 (1993) (rejecting efficiency interpretation of *United Shoe's* terms).

Until the mid–1970s, *Alcoa's* expansive concept of improper exclusion influenced antitrust policy and jurisprudence concerning dominant firms. By the end of the 1970s, however, the ascent of Chicago School and other academic perspectives in the antitrust literature and in the courts provided different answers to the Section 2 policy questions framed in Judge Hand's opinion. Decisions in this era reflect increased concern with efficiency, with preserving incentives for dominant firms to compete aggressively, and supplying clear rules by which companies can plan operations to minimize antitrust risk. Two landmarks in this development stand out. The first is *Berkey Photo, Inc. v. Eastman Kodak Co.*, 603 F.2d 263 (2d Cir. 1979). In largely rejecting a private challenge to Kodak's conduct in the amateur film and camera markets, the court of appeals harshly criticized *Alcoa* and called Judge Hand's analysis of the monopolization conduct element a standardless "wishing well" that lent itself to ready manipulation. 603 F.2d at 273.

The second landmark appeared in 1980, as the Federal Trade Commission contributed to the new, efficiency-oriented jurisprudence in resolving its challenge to Du Pont's conduct in the chemical industry. The Commission alleged that Du Pont violated Section 5 of the FTC Act by attempting to monopolize the market for titanium dioxide, a chemical pigment used in making white paint. When the FTC issued its administrative complaint in 1978, Du Pont accounted for 42 percent of titanium dioxide sales. The complaint alleged that the company had acted illegally by announcing new expansions of capacity to capture all anticipated increases in demand—the same kind of conduct condemned as monopolization in *Alcoa*. In prosecuting the case, the FTC staff introduced internal Du Pont documents indicating that the company believed its announcements of new capacity would discourage entry and expansion by its rivals and enable Du Pont to charge supracompetitive prices. An administrative trial absolved the company of liability, and the Commission voted 5–0 to dismiss its complaint.

We now turn to some additional and important foundation developments that have influenced the courts' approach to the question of power. We will return to the related issue of conduct when we look at more contemporary developments in the law of monopolization in Section C, infra.

2. INJECTING ECONOMIC ANALYSIS INTO THE MARKET DEFINITION PROCESS VIA CROSS–ELASTICITY OF DEMAND: THE *CELLOPHANE* DECISION (AND FALLACY)

A competition policy system could take many approaches to defining "monopoly." Modern economics treats *market power* as the ability to charge prices above a competitive level without suffering an immediate and unprofitably substantial loss of sales. By this measure, however, many firms have some market power. An antitrust system that scrutinized all instances of market power would require an immense investment in enforcement resources and would likely deter procompetitive activities. As a concession to administrative necessity and in order to target the most serious market imperfections, antitrust systems ordinarily equate monopoly or dominance with *substantial and durable* market power.

Even with broad agreement on this principle, one must devise practical methods for deciding whether a firm possesses substantial market power. In Chapter 5 we grouped these methods into two categories: *direct* evidence and *circumstantial* evidence. The main direct techniques for identifying substantial market power are to (a) measure the elasticity of demand for the products of the firm believed to possess a monopoly or (b) show that the alleged monopolist actually has used business methods other than superior performance to exclude its rivals from the market.

Problems in using direct evidence to identify monopoly power have elevated the importance of circumstantial proof. For nearly a century, courts have used the defendant's share of sales—its "market share"—as the chief circumstantial measurement tool. *Alcoa* illustrated that to use market shares to measure market power, one first must define a *relevant market*. As we saw in Chapter 5, the relevant market has *product* and *geographic* dimensions. Courts typically determine the product dimension by identifying the array of products that customers regard as acceptable substitutes for the defendant's product. The relevant market's geographic bounds are set by studying the location of suppliers from which a customer might purchase products deemed to be acceptable substitutes for the alleged monopolist's products. After drawing the relevant market's boundaries, the court calculates the defendant's market share by comparing its activity in the relevant product (measured by sales, units, or capacity) to the activity of all firms in the relevant market.

The value of market shares as proxies for measuring market power depends on the soundness of the market definition. Has the court correctly decided which products customers regard as acceptable substitutes for the defendant's products? Has it properly identified, and assigned proper market shares to all suppliers who serve the relevant market? Does a modest market share conclusively establish the lack of substantial market power? Does the presence of a high share invariably prove that defendant is a monopolist? The reliability of the answers given to these questions deeply influences the importance one should credit to market shares.

The Justice Department's success in achieving a finding of liability in *Alcoa* inspired a new wave of efforts following World War II to enforce Section 2 of the Sherman Act. One of the most important of these initiatives was the *Cellophane* case, which we first reviewed in Chapter 5 in connection with merger analysis. In a complaint filed in 1947, the government charged Du Pont with monopolization, attempted monopolization, and conspiracy to monopolize in a market consisting of cellophane. The trial court ruled for Du Pont on all issues, and the government appealed to the Supreme Court.

The pivotal issue was whether Du Pont had monopoly power. The company argued that buyers of cellophane routinely turned to other flexible wrapping materials when Du Pont attempted to raise the price of cellophane. Because cellophane appeared to face many close substitutes, Du Pont contended that the relevant market consisted of many flexible wrapping materials. The case provided the Supreme Court with its own opportunity to explain the methodology courts should use to define markets and calculate market shares. As you review the excerpt from the case reproduced in Chapter 5, consider again the methodology the Court uses to define Du Pont's market share, and the flaws in its analysis. Consider also how and why the analysis of market power and market definition are so integral to both merger and monopolization analysis.

UNITED STATES v. E. I. DU PONT DE NEMOURS & CO.
United States Supreme Court, 1956.
351 U.S. 377, 76 S.Ct. 994, 100 L.Ed. 1264.

[The relevant excerpt can be found in Chapter 5, *supra* at 482. You should also re-read the notes following the case and Sidebar 5–4: The *Cellophane* Fallacy.]

Sidebar 6–2:
The Section 2 Conduct Standard After *Alcoa*— Flirting with No Fault

The issuance of the *Alcoa* decision in 1945 and its validation by the Supreme Court in *American Tobacco* in 1946 galvanized commentators and enforcement officials to consider a renewed campaign to use Section 2 to challenge dominant enterprises. *See* William E. Kovacic, *Failed Expectations: The Troubled Past and Uncertain Future of the Sherman Act as a Tool for Deconcentration*, 74 Iowa L. Rev. 1105, 1118–19, 1133–36 (1989).

From academia came two influential papers in 1947 that made the case for a Section 2 renaissance. Declaring that *Alcoa* and *American Tobacco* "mark the new birth of Section 2," Eugene Rostow of the Yale Law School faculty proposed a new campaign of monopolization cases to deconcentrate American industry and "eliminate the wastes, the non-use of capacity, and the restrictionism of monopolistic industrial organization." Eugene Rostow, *The New Sherman Act: A Positive Instrument of Progress*, 14 U. Chi. L. Rev. 567, 577, 568 (1947). Edward Levi, the Dean of the University of Chicago Law School, said that *Alcoa* and *American Tobacco* raised prospects for "a new interpretation of the Sherman Act" that "can give the act strength *against monopolies as such*, and also against control by three, four, or five corporations acting together." Edward Levi, *The Antitrust Laws and Monopoly*, 14 U. Chi. L. Rev. 153, 183 (1947) (emphasis added). As Rostow and Levi envisioned it, employing Section 2 *against monopolies as such* meant reducing—perhaps eliminating—attention to the means by which monopolies took shape and instead embracing a "no-fault" interpretation of the statute—directly attacking substantial, persistent monopoly power.

From 1947 until the mid–1950s, the Department of Justice pursued an impressive array of cases against dominant firms. The government declined the invitation of Levi and Rostow to press no-fault theories of liability, but federal prosecutors took full advantage of the attenuated conduct requirement that emerged from *Alcoa* and *American Tobacco*. Key subjects of Justice Department monopolization actions included the distribution and exhibition of motion pictures, cellophane, shoe machinery, Pullman sleeping cars, telephone equipment, film processing, and bananas. Despite occasional setbacks such as the loss on liability in *du Pont (Cellophane)*, the government usually prevailed on liability issues. Nonetheless, a widespread perception that the remedial results in these matters had been ineffectual led to renewed calls by blue ribbon commissions and individual commentators for more aggressive measures to attack monopoly power directly and to break dominant firms into smaller successor companies.

Modern consideration of proposals to deconcentrate oligopolies originated in Carl Kaysen's and Donald Turner's Antitrust Policy: An Econom-

IC AND LEGAL ANALYSIS, which appeared in 1959. Viewed as the leading synthesis of antitrust law and economics of its time, the Kaysen–Turner volume declared that "[t]he principal defect of present antitrust law is its inability to cope with market power created by jointly acting oligopolists." Id. at 110. The two scholars called for new legislation to restructure concentrated industries and provided the foundation for similar recommendations by a host of legislative committees, blue ribbon task forces, and individual commentators in the 1960s and 1970s. In general terms, the deconcentration proposals would have broken up oligopolistic industries unless existing concentration resulted solely from lawful patents or unless dissolution would cause the loss of substantial scale economies. The deconcentration enthusiasts also urged that the government bring more Section 2 cases with structural relief as the preferred remedy.

These deconcentration proposals yielded no legislation, but they had a powerful (and unintended) impact on the future direction of antitrust. From 1969 to 1982 the Federal Trade Commission and the Justice Department undertook a new wave of dominant firm exclusionary conduct cases. Such matters did not employ no-fault concepts, but, in the tradition of *Alcoa*, they rested upon relatively broad views of what constitutes improper exclusion. In this period the federal antitrust authorities brought abuse of dominance cases against major firms in the computer, telecommunications, petroleum, food, photocopier, chemical, and tire industries. With rare exceptions, such as the Justice Department's restructuring of AT & T and an FTC consent decree that diminished the market power of Xerox in the copier industry, the government failed to establish liability in these matters.

The deconcentration proposals of the late 1950s and the 1960s had another important effect. They stimulated research and discussion concerning the structuralist assumptions that had guided antitrust policy since *Alcoa*. As the evidence (much of it assembled by Chicago School figures such as Yale Brozen, Harold Demsetz, and Richard Posner) began to mount that broad-based assaults on concentration were neither analytically justified nor costless, serious opposition arose within academia, government agencies, and the business community. A catalyzing event took place in 1974 in what came to be known as the Airlie House Conference. *See* INDUSTRIAL CONCENTRATION: THE NEW LEARNING (Harvey J. Goldschmid et al., eds., 1974) (collecting papers and proceedings at Airlie House Conference). At the Airlie House meeting, critics of structuralism synthesized a developing literature that challenged the economic basis for deconcentration. The results of the conference and related research were widely seen as refuting major elements of structuralist oligopoly theory and discrediting deconcentration. By drawing critical scrutiny to structuralism, the deconcentration proposals indirectly helped inject Chicago School views into the mainstream of antitrust analysis and thus helped foster a broader conservative redirection of antitrust.

C. THE CONTEMPORARY LAW AND ECONOMICS OF MONOPOLIZATION

As we indicated earlier, Section 2 of the Sherman Act does not prohibit the status of monopoly. Monopolization doctrine requires the plaintiff to show that the defendant used improper exclusionary acts to gain or sustain substantial market power. How should the law define what behavior is improper? Developing and selling a superior product—for example, introducing jet aircraft that make propeller-driven airliners obsolete—can drive inferior products and their makers from the market. Such behavior takes sales away from rivals and can "exclude" them, yet the means of exclusion (creating superior products) yields great benefits to society. An undiscriminating ban on all conduct that excludes could encompass virtually any business tactic that increased a firm's sales, no matter how much the practice in question increased consumer well-being by reducing prices or improving product quality. Perhaps the chief analytical challenge in establishing standards of conduct for dominant firms, therefore, is to determine whether specific acts (or certain classes of conduct) that may result in significant exclusion also have competitively redeeming features that might warrant shielding them from liability. Hence conduct that merely excludes must be differentiated from what the law condemns as "exclusionary conduct."

The traditional framework developed in *Alcoa* and other cases such as *Grinnell* suggested that the issue of conduct should be judged in isolation as part of a two stage inquiry. The "power *plus*-conduct" formulation, *i.e.*, considering first whether the defendant has monopoly power, and only then whether it has "willfully acquired or maintained" that power, encouraged this analytical division. Conduct in turn has often been judged based on evidence of its effects on competition. One way to understand the raising rival's cost framework, for example, is to recognize that it examines *conduct* to see if it raises rival's costs; it examines *effects* of that conduct to see if it may confer power over price.

Yet power, conduct, and effects are almost always interrelated: power represents the potential to cause anticompetitive effects through conduct; observed anticompetitive effects evidence the exercise of power through conduct. The traditional power-plus-conduct formula did not readily lend itself to this kind of simultaneous evaluation of power, conduct, and effects. As we observed when we studied the government's challenge of the proposed merger of Staples and Office Depot in Chapter 5, sometimes the same evidence tends to establish both power and effects.

In contrast to the traditional two-step approach, Professor Steven Salop has argued for an integrated, "first principles" approach to analyzing alleged antitrust offenses:

> * * * The first principles approach centers on an examination of the competitive effects of the conduct at issue. This is appropriate because competitive effect is the true core of antitrust. Although market power and market definition have a role in antitrust analysis, their proper roles are as parts of and in reference to the primary evaluation of the alleged anticompetitive conduct and its likely mar-

ket effects. They are not valued for their own sake, but rather for the roles they play in an evaluation of market effects.

Market power and market definition, therefore, should not be analyzed in a vacuum or in a threshold test divorced from the conduct and allegations about its effects. Instead, market power should be measured as the power profitably to raise or maintain price above the competitive benchmark price, which is the price that would prevail in the absence of the alleged anticompetitive restraint. The competitive benchmark may be the current price, the perfectly competitive price, or some other in-between price, depending on the particular allegations of anticompetitive effect being asserted. This integrated approach to antitrust analysis is the first principles approach.

Steven C. Salop, *The First Principles Approach to Antitrust,* Kodak, *and Antitrust at the Millennium,* 68 ANTITRUST L.J. 187, 188–89 (2000).

This "first principles" approach is consistent with the Supreme Court's observation in *Nat'l Soc'y of Prof'l Eng'rs* (see Chapter 2) that the relevant inquiry under Section 1 of the Sherman Act "focuses directly on the challenged restraint's impact on competitive conditions." 435 U.S. at 688. It is also consonant with the observation in *Indiana Federation of Dentists* that "[s]ince the purpose of the inquiries into market definition and market power is to determine whether an arrangement has the potential for genuine adverse effects on competition, 'proof of actual detrimental effects, such as a reduction of output,' can obviate the need for an inquiry into market power, which is but a 'surrogate for detrimental effects.' " *FTC v. Indiana Fed'n of Dentists,* 476 U.S. 447, 460–61 (1986) (Casebook, Chapter 2, *supra*). The Court's observations in these two cases highlight two fundamental insights of the First Principles approach: (1) the central goal of antitrust analysis is to evaluate likely or actual anticompetitive effects; and (2) evaluation of power, conduct, and effects are necessarily interrelated. Assessment of the competitive effects of conduct involves evaluation of the constraints on the firm's exercise of market power. Conduct cannot be assessed without knowing whether the firm can exercise market power. Similarly, market definition and market power cannot be assessed without reference to the conduct and the competitive effects alleged (as we saw with respect to the *Cellophane* fallacy).

In this section of the Chapter, therefore, we have excerpted a variety of the leading cases on monopolization without regard to the traditional, dichotomous framework. As you read the cases, note how the inquires into power, conduct, and effects—even when formally divided—are necessarily interrelated.

1. NON–PRICE EXCLUSIONARY CONDUCT

Lorain Journal involved efforts by an incumbent firm to forestall a competitor's efforts to establish access to customers whose trade was essential to its survival. Other cases have posed the problem of a refusal to deal in the context of the incumbent's efforts to cease or adjust an existing pattern of cooperation with a competitor.

The formative treatment of this issue took shape in the early 1980s when Aspen Skiing Co., the owner of three of the four mountain slopes in Aspen,

Colorado, decided to withdraw from a joint marketing arrangement with Aspen Highlands Skiing Corp., the owner of the fourth slope. The two firms together had for some time offered an all-Aspen ticket that entitled skiers to ski any of the Aspen slopes for a single price. When Aspen Skiing ended the relationship, Aspen Highlands attacked the refusal to continue dealing as illegal monopolization. In one of its most important modern analyses of dominant firm conduct, the Supreme Court unanimously upheld the trial court's finding of liability.

Aspen Skiing's significance, however, is not limited to the narrow context of addressing refusals to deal. As you read the case, note how the Court moves beyond the traditional *Alcoa-Grinnell* formulation of "willful acquisition or maintenance" to more specifically define "exclusionary" conduct. Note too how the Court utilizes a structured framework for evaluating the effects— both pro- and anti-competitive—of allegedly exclusionary conduct. Finally, consider the economic theory behind the Court's conclusion that Aspen Skiing's conduct was properly labeled as "exclusionary."

ASPEN SKIING CO. v. ASPEN HIGHLANDS SKIING CORP.

United States Supreme Court, 1985.
472 U.S. 585, 105 S.Ct. 2847, 86 L.Ed.2d 467.

Justice STEVENS delivered the opinion of the Court:

In a private treble-damages action, the jury found that petitioner Aspen Skiing Company (Ski Co.) had monopolized the market for downhill skiing services in Aspen, Colorado. The question presented is whether that finding is erroneous as a matter of law because it rests on an assumption that a firm with monopoly power has a duty to cooperate with its smaller rivals in a marketing arrangement in order to avoid violating § 2 of the Sherman Act.

* * *

Aspen is a destination ski resort with a reputation for "super powder," "a wide range of runs," and an "active night life," including "some of the best restaurants in North America." Between 1945 and 1960, private investors independently developed three major facilities for downhill skiing: Aspen Mountain (Ajax), Aspen Highlands (Highlands), and Buttermilk. A fourth mountain, Snowmass, opened in 1967.

The development of any major additional facilities is hindered by practical considerations and regulatory obstacles. The identification of appropriate topographical conditions for a new site and substantial financing are both essential. Most of the terrain in the vicinity of Aspen that is suitable for downhill skiing cannot be used for that purpose without the approval of the United States Forest Service. That approval is contingent, in part, on environmental concerns. Moreover, the county government must also approve the project, and in recent years it has followed a policy of limiting growth.

Between 1958 and 1964, three independent companies operated Ajax, Highlands, and Buttermilk. In the early years, each company offered its own day or half-day tickets for use of its mountain. In 1962, however, the three competitors also introduced an interchangeable ticket.[7] The 6–day, all-Aspen ticket provided convenience to the vast majority of skiers who visited the resort for weekly periods, but preferred to remain flexible about what mountain they might ski each day during the visit. It also emphasized the unusual variety in ski mountains available in Aspen.

As initially designed, the all-Aspen ticket program consisted of booklets containing six coupons, each redeemable for a daily lift ticket at Ajax, Highlands, or Buttermilk. * * * The revenues from the sale of the 3–area coupon books were distributed in accordance with the number of coupons collected at each mountain.

In 1964, Buttermilk was purchased by Ski Co., but the interchangeable ticket program continued. In most seasons after it acquired Buttermilk, Ski Co. offered 2–area, 6–or 7–day tickets featuring Ajax and Buttermilk in competition with the 3–area, 6–coupon booklet. Although it sold briskly, the all-Aspen ticket did not sell as well as Ski Co.'s multiarea ticket until Ski Co. opened Snowmass in 1967. Thereafter, the all-Aspen coupon booklet began to outsell Ski Co.'s ticket featuring only its mountains.

In the 1971–1972 season, the coupon booklets were discontinued and an "around the neck" all-Aspen ticket was developed. This refinement on the interchangeable ticket was advantageous to the skier, who no longer found it necessary to visit the ticket window every morning before gaining access to the slopes. Lift operators at Highlands monitored usage of the ticket in the 1971–1972 season by recording the ticket numbers of persons going onto the slopes of that mountain. Highlands officials periodically met with Ski Co. officials to review the figures recorded at Highlands, and to distribute revenues based on that count.

* * *

* * * Highlands' share of the revenues from the ticket was 17.5% in 1973–1974, 18.5% in 1974–1975, 16.8% in 1975–1976, and 13.2% in 1976–1977.[8] During these four seasons, Ski Co. did not offer its own 3–area, multiday ticket in competition with the all-Aspen ticket.[9] By 1977, multiarea tickets accounted for nearly 35% of the total market. Holders of multiarea passes also accounted for additional daily ticket sales to persons skiing with them.

Between 1962 and 1977, Ski Co. and Highlands had independently offered various mixes of 1–day, 3–day, and 6–day passes at their own mountains. In

---

7. Friedl Pfeiffer, one of the developers of Buttermilk, initiated the idea of an all-Aspen ticket at a luncheon with the owner of Highlands and the President of Ski Co. Pfeiffer, a native of Austria, informed his competitors that " '[i]n St. Anton, we have a mountain that has three different lift companies—lifts owned by three different lift companies. . . . We sell a ticket that is interchangeable.' It was good on any of those lifts; and he said, 'I think we should do the same thing here.' " * * *

8. Highlands' share of the total market during those seasons, as measured in skier visits was 15.8% in 1973–1974, 17.1% in 1974–1975, 17.4% in 1975–1976, and 20.5% in 1976–1977.

9. In 1975, the Colorado Attorney General filed a complaint against Ski Co. and Highlands alleging, in part, that the negotiations over the 4–area ticket had provided them with a forum for price fixing in violation of § 1 of the Sherman Act and that they had attempted to monopolize the market for downhill skiing services in Aspen in violation of § 2. In 1977, the case was settled by a consent decree that permitted the parties to continue to offer the 4–area ticket provided that they set their own ticket prices unilaterally before negotiating its terms.

every season except one, however, they had also offered some form of all-Aspen, 6–day ticket, and divided the revenues from those sales on the basis of usage. Nevertheless, for the 1977–1978 season, Ski Co. offered to continue the all-Aspen ticket only if Highlands would accept a 13.2% fixed share of the ticket's revenues.

Although that had been Highlands' share of the ticket revenues in 1976–1977, Highlands contended that that season was an inaccurate measure of its market performance since it had been marked by unfavorable weather and an unusually low number of visiting skiers. Moreover, Highlands wanted to continue to divide revenues on the basis of actual usage, as that method of distribution allowed it to compete for the daily loyalties of the skiers who had purchased the tickets. Fearing that the alternative might be no interchangeable ticket at all, and hoping to persuade Ski Co. to reinstate the usage division of revenues, Highlands eventually accepted a fixed percentage of 15% for the 1977–1978 season. * * *

In the 1970's the management of Ski Co. increasingly expressed their dislike for the all-Aspen ticket. They complained that a coupon method of monitoring usage was administratively cumbersome. They doubted the accuracy of the survey and decried the "appearance, deportment, [and] attitude" of the college students who were conducting it. In addition, Ski Co.'s president had expressed the view that the 4–area ticket was siphoning off revenues that could be recaptured by Ski Co. if the ticket was discontinued. In fact, Ski Co. had reinstated its 3–area, 6–day ticket during the 1977–1978 season, but that ticket had been outsold by the 4–area, 6–day ticket nearly two to one.

In March 1978, the Ski Co. management recommended to the board of directors that the 4–area ticket be discontinued for the 1978–1979 season. The board decided to offer Highlands a 4–area ticket provided that Highlands would agree to receive a 12.5% fixed percentage of the revenue—considerably below Highlands' historical average based on usage. Later in the 1978–1979 season, a member of Ski Co.'s board of directors candidly informed a Highlands official that he had advocated making Highlands "an offer that [it] could not accept."

Finding the proposal unacceptable, Highlands suggested a distribution of the revenues based on usage to be monitored by coupons, electronic counting, or random sample surveys. If Ski Co. was concerned about who was to conduct the survey, Highlands proposed to hire disinterested ticket counters at its own expense—"somebody like Price Waterhouse"—to count or survey usage of the 4–area ticket at Highlands. Ski Co. refused to consider any counterproposals, and Highlands finally rejected the offer of the fixed percentage.

As far as Ski Co. was concerned, the all-Aspen ticket was dead. In its place Ski Co. offered the 3–area, 6–day ticket featuring only its mountains. In an effort to promote this ticket, Ski Co. embarked on a national advertising campaign that strongly implied to people who were unfamiliar with Aspen that Ajax, Buttermilk, and Snowmass were the only ski mountains in the area. For example, Ski Co. had a sign changed in the Aspen Airways waiting room at Stapleton Airport in Denver. The old sign had a picture of the four mountains in Aspen touting "Four Big Mountains" whereas the new sign retained the picture but referred only to three.

Ski Co. took additional actions that made it extremely difficult for Highlands to market its own multiarea package to replace the joint offering. Ski Co. discontinued the 3–day, 3–area pass for the 1978–1979 season, and also refused to sell Highlands any lift tickets, either at the tour operator's discount or at retail. Highlands finally developed an alternative product, the "Adventure Pack," which consisted of a 3–day pass at Highlands and three vouchers, each equal to the price of a daily lift ticket at a Ski Co. mountain. The vouchers were guaranteed by funds on deposit in an Aspen bank, and were redeemed by Aspen merchants at full value. Ski Co., however, refused to accept them.

Later, Highlands redesigned the Adventure Pack to contain American Express Traveler's Checks or money orders instead of vouchers. Ski Co. eventually accepted these negotiable instruments in exchange for daily lift tickets. Despite some strengths of the product, the Adventure Pack met considerable resistance from tour operators and consumers who had grown accustomed to the convenience and flexibility provided by the all-Aspen ticket.

Without a convenient all-Aspen ticket, Highlands basically "becomes a day ski area in a destination resort." Highlands' share of the market for downhill skiing services in Aspen declined steadily after the 4–area ticket based on usage was abolished in 1977: from 20.5% in 1976–1977, to 15.7% in 1977–1978, to 13.1% in 1978–1979, to 12.5% in 1979–1980, to 11% in 1980–1981. Highlands' revenues from associated skiing services like the ski school, ski rentals, amateur racing events, and restaurant facilities declined sharply as well.

II

In 1979, Highlands filed a complaint in the United States District Court for the District of Colorado naming Ski Co. as a defendant. Among various claims, the complaint alleged that Ski Co. had monopolized the market for downhill skiing services at Aspen in violation of § 2 of the Sherman Act, and prayed for treble damages. The case was tried to a jury which rendered a verdict finding Ski Co. guilty of the § 2 violation and calculating Highlands' actual damages at $2.5 million.

In her instructions to the jury, the District Judge explained that the offense of monopolization under § 2 of the Sherman Act has two elements: (1) the possession of monopoly power in a relevant market, and (2) the willful acquisition, maintenance, or use of that power by anticompetitive or exclusionary means or for anticompetitive or exclusionary purposes. Although the first element was vigorously disputed at the trial and in the Court of Appeals, in this Court Ski Co. does not challenge the jury's special verdict finding that it possessed monopoly power.[20] Nor does Ski Co. criticize the trial court's instructions to the jury concerning the second element of the § 2 offense.

On this element, the jury was instructed that it had to consider whether "Aspen Skiing Corporation willfully acquired, maintained, or used that power

---

20. The jury found that the relevant product market was "[d]ownhill skiing at destination ski resorts," that the "Aspen area" was a relevant geographic submarket, and that during the years 1977–1981, Ski Co. possessed monopoly power, defined as the power to control prices in the relevant market or to exclude competitors.

by anti-competitive or exclusionary means or for anti-competitive or exclusionary purposes." The instructions elaborated:

"In considering whether the means or purposes were anti-competitive or exclusionary, you must draw a distinction here between practices which tend to exclude or restrict competition on the one hand and the success of a business which reflects only a superior product, a well-run business, or luck, on the other. The line between legitimately gained monopoly, its proper use and maintenance, and improper conduct has been described in various ways. It has been said that obtaining or maintaining monopoly power cannot represent monopolization if the power was gained and maintained by conduct that was honestly industrial. Or it is said that monopoly power which is thrust upon a firm due to its superior business ability and efficiency does not constitute monopolization.

"For example, a firm that has lawfully acquired a monopoly position is not barred from taking advantage of scale economies by constructing a large and efficient factory. These benefits are a consequence of size and not an exercise of monopoly power. Nor is a corporation which possesses monopoly power under a duty to cooperate with its business rivals. Also a company which possesses monopoly power and which refuses to enter into a joint operating agreement with a competitor or otherwise refuses to deal with a competitor in some manner does not violate Section 2 if valid business reasons exist for that refusal.

"In other words, if there were legitimate business reasons for the refusal, then the defendant, even if he is found to possess monopoly power in a relevant market, has not violated the law. We are concerned with conduct which unnecessarily excludes or handicaps competitors. This is conduct which does not benefit consumers by making a better product or service available—or in other ways—and instead has the effect of impairing competition.

"To sum up, you must determine whether Aspen Skiing Corporation gained, maintained, or used monopoly power in a relevant market by arrangements and policies which rather than being a consequence of a superior product, superior business sense, or historic element, were designed primarily to further any domination of the relevant market or sub-market."

The jury answered a specific interrogatory finding the second element of the offense as defined in these instructions.

Ski Co. filed a motion for judgment notwithstanding the verdict, contending that the evidence was insufficient to support a § 2 violation as a matter of law. In support of that motion, Ski Co. incorporated the arguments that it had advanced in support of its motion for a directed verdict, at which time it had primarily contested the sufficiency of the evidence on the issue of monopoly power. Counsel had, however, in the course of the argument at that time, stated: "Now, we also think, Judge, that there clearly cannot be a requirement of cooperation between competitors."[22] The District Court denied Ski

---

22. Counsel also appears to have argued that Ski Co. was under a legal obligation to refuse to participate in any joint marketing arrangement with Highlands: "Aspen Skiing

Co.'s motion and entered a judgment awarding Highlands treble damages of $7,500,000, costs and attorney's fees.[23]

The Court of Appeals affirmed in all respects. 738 F.2d 1509 (C.A.10 1984). The court advanced two reasons for rejecting Ski Co.'s argument that " 'there was insufficient evidence to present a jury issue of monopolization because, as a matter of law, the conduct at issue was pro-competitive conduct that a monopolist could lawfully engage in.' " First, relying on United States v. Terminal Railroad Assn. of St. Louis, 224 U.S. 383, 32 S.Ct. 507 (1912), the Court of Appeals held that the multiday, multiarea ticket could be characterized as an "essential facility" that Ski Co. had a duty to market jointly with Highlands. 738 F.2d, at 1520–1521. Second, it held that there was sufficient evidence to support a finding that Ski Co.'s intent in refusing to market the 4–area ticket, "considered together with its other conduct," was to create or maintain a monopoly. Id., at 1522.

In its review of the evidence on the question of intent, the Court of Appeals considered the record "as a whole" and concluded that it was not necessary for Highlands to prove that each allegedly anticompetitive act was itself sufficient to demonstrate an abuse of monopoly power. Id., at 1522, n.18.[25] The court noted that by "refusing to cooperate" with Highlands, Ski Co. "became the only business in Aspen that could offer a multi-day multi-mountain skiing experience"; that the refusal to offer a 4–mountain ticket resulted in "skiers' frustration over its unavailability"; that there was apparently no valid business reason for refusing to accept the coupons in Highlands' Adventure Pack; and that after Highlands had modified its Adventure Pack to meet Ski Co.'s objections, Ski Co. had increased its single ticket price to $22 "thereby making it unprofitable . . . to market [the] Adventure Pack." Id., at 1521–1522. In reviewing Ski Co.'s argument that it was entitled to a directed verdict, the Court of Appeals assumed that the jury had resolved all contested questions of fact in Highlands' favor.

III

In this Court, Ski Co. contends that even a firm with monopoly power has no duty to engage in joint marketing with a competitor, that a violation of § 2

Corporation is required to compete. It is required to make independent decisions. It is required to price its own product. It is required to make its own determination of the ticket that it chooses to offer and the tickets that it chooses not to offer."

In this Court, Ski Co. does not question the validity of the joint marketing arrangement under § 1 of the Sherman Act. Thus, we have no occasion to consider the circumstances that might permit such combinations in the skiing industry. See generally National Collegiate Athletic Assn. v. Board of Regents of Univ. of Okla., 468 U.S. 85, 113–115, 104 S.Ct. 2948, 2966–2968 (1984); Broadcast Music, Inc. v. Columbia Broadcasting System, Inc., 441 U.S. 1, 18–23, 99 S.Ct. 1551, 1561–1564 (1979); Continental T.V., Inc. v. GTE Sylvania, Inc., 433 U.S. 36, 51–57, 97 S.Ct. 2549, 2558–2561 (1977).

23. The District Court also entered an injunction requiring the parties to offer jointly a 4–area, 6–out–of–7–day coupon booklet substantially identical to the "Ski the Summit" booklet accepted by Ski Co. at its Breckenridge resort in Summit County, Colorado. The injunction was initially for a 3–year period, but was later extended through the 1984–1985 season by stipulation of the parties. Highlands represents that "it will not seek an extension of the injunction." No question is raised concerning the character of the injunctive relief ordered by the District Court.

25. See Continental Ore Co. v. Union Carbide & Carbon Corp., 370 U.S. 690, 699, 82 S.Ct. 1404, 1410 (1962); Associated Press v. United States, 326 U.S. 1, 14, 65 S.Ct. 1416, 1421 (1945).

cannot be established without evidence of substantial exclusionary conduct, and that none of its activities can be characterized as exclusionary. It also contends that the Court of Appeals incorrectly relied on the "essential facilities" doctrine and that an "anticompetitive intent" does not transform nonexclusionary conduct into monopolization. In response, Highlands submits that, given the evidence in the record, it is not necessary to rely on the "essential facilities" doctrine in order to affirm the judgment.

"The central message of the Sherman Act is that a business entity must find new customers and higher profits through internal expansion—that is, by competing successfully rather than by arranging treaties with its competitors." United States v. Citizens & Southern National Bank, 422 U.S. 86, 116, 95 S.Ct. 2099, 2116 (1975). Ski Co., therefore, is surely correct in submitting that even a firm with monopoly power has no general duty to engage in a joint marketing program with a competitor. Ski Co. is quite wrong, however, in suggesting that the judgment in this case rests on any such proposition of law. For the trial court unambiguously instructed the jury that a firm possessing monopoly power has no duty to cooperate with its business rivals.

The absence of an unqualified duty to cooperate does not mean that every time a firm declines to participate in a particular cooperative venture, that decision may not have evidentiary significance, or that it may not give rise to liability in certain circumstances. The absence of a duty to transact business with another firm is, in some respects, merely the counterpart of the independent businessman's cherished right to select his customers and his associates. The high value that we have placed on the right to refuse to deal with other firms does not mean that the right is unqualified.[27]

In Lorain Journal Co. v. United States, 342 U.S. 143, 72 S.Ct. 181 (1951), we squarely held that this right was not unqualified. Between 1933 and 1948 the publisher of the Lorain Journal, a newspaper, was the only local business disseminating news and advertising in that Ohio town. In 1948, a small radio station was established in a nearby community. In an effort to destroy its small competitor, and thereby regain its "pre–1948 substantial monopoly over the mass dissemination of all news and advertising," the Journal refused to sell advertising to persons that patronized the radio station. Id., at 153, 72 S.Ct., at 186.

In holding that this conduct violated § 2 of the Sherman Act, the Court dispatched the same argument raised by the monopolist here:

> "The publisher claims a right as a private business concern to select its customers and to refuse to accept advertisements from whomever it pleases. We do not dispute that general right. 'But the word "right" is one of the most deceptive of pitfalls; it is so easy to slip from a qualified meaning in the premise to an unqualified one in the conclusion. Most rights are qualified.' ... The right claimed by the publisher is neither absolute nor exempt from regulation. Its exercise as a purposeful means of monopolizing interstate commerce is prohibited by the Sherman Act. The operator of the radio station,

---

27. Under § 1 of the Sherman Act, a business "generally has a right to deal, or refuse to deal, with whomever it likes, as long as it does so independently." Monsanto Co. v. Spray–Rite Service Corp., 465 U.S. 752, 761, 104 S.Ct. 1464, 1469 (1984); United States v. Colgate & Co., 250 U.S. 300, 307, 39 S.Ct. 465, 468 (1919).

equally with the publisher of the newspaper, is entitled to the protection of that Act. 'In the absence of any purpose to create or maintain a monopoly, the act does not restrict the long recognized right of trader or manufacturer engaged in an entirely private business, freely to exercise his own independent discretion as to parties with whom he will deal.' (Emphasis supplied.) United States v. Colgate & Co., 250 U.S. 300, 307. * * *"

The Court approved the entry of an injunction ordering the Journal to print the advertisements of the customers of its small competitor.

In Lorain Journal, the violation of § 2 was an "attempt to monopolize," rather than monopolization, but the question of intent is relevant to both offenses. In the former case it is necessary to prove a "specific intent" to accomplish the forbidden objective—as Judge Hand explained, "an intent which goes beyond the mere intent to do the act." United States v. Aluminum Co. of America, 148 F.2d 416, 432 (C.A.2 1945). In the latter case evidence of intent is merely relevant to the question whether the challenged conduct is fairly characterized as "exclusionary" or "anticompetitive"—to use the words in the trial court's instructions—or "predatory," to use a word that scholars seem to favor. Whichever label is used, there is agreement on the proposition that "no monopolist monopolizes unconscious of what he is doing." As Judge Bork stated more recently: "Improper exclusion (exclusion not the result of superior efficiency) is always deliberately intended."[29]

The qualification on the right of a monopolist to deal with whom he pleases is not so narrow that it encompasses no more than the circumstances of Lorain Journal. In the actual case that we must decide, the monopolist did not merely reject a novel offer to participate in a cooperative venture that had been proposed by a competitor. Rather, the monopolist elected to make an important change in a pattern of distribution that had originated in a competitive market and had persisted for several years. The all-Aspen, 6–day ticket with revenues allocated on the basis of usage was first developed when three independent companies operated three different ski mountains in the Aspen area. It continued to provide a desirable option for skiers when the market was enlarged to include four mountains, and when the character of the market was changed by Ski Co.'s acquisition of monopoly power. Moreover, since the record discloses that interchangeable tickets are used in other multimountain areas which apparently are competitive,[30] it seems appropriate to infer that such tickets satisfy consumer demand in free competitive markets.

29. R. Bork, The Antitrust Paradox 160 (1978) (hereinafter Bork).

30. Ski Co. itself participates in interchangeable ticket programs in at least two other markets. For example, since 1970, Ski Co. has operated the Breckenridge resort in Summit County, Colorado. Breckenridge participates in the "Ski the Summit" 4–area interchangeable coupon booklet which allows the skier to ski at any of the four mountains in the region: Breckenridge, Copper Mountain, Keystone, and Arapahoe Basin. In the 1979–1980 season Keystone and Arapahoe Basin—which are jointly operated—had about 40% of the Summit County market, and the other two ski mountains each had a market share of about 30%. During the relevant period of time, Ski Co. also operated Blackcomb Mountain, northeast of Vancouver, British Columbia, which has an interchangeable ticket arrangement with nearby Whistler Mountain, an independently operated facility. Interchangeable lift tickets apparently are also available in some European skiing areas.

Ski Co.'s decision to terminate the all-Aspen ticket was thus a decision by a monopolist to make an important change in the character of the market.[31] Such a decision is not necessarily anticompetitive, and Ski Co. contends that neither its decision, nor the conduct in which it engaged to implement that decision, can fairly be characterized as exclusionary in this case. It recognizes, however, that as the case is presented to us, we must interpret the entire record in the light most favorable to Highlands and give to it the benefit of all inferences which the evidence fairly supports, even though contrary inferences might reasonably be drawn. Continental Ore Co. v. Union Carbide & Carbon Corp., 370 U.S. 690, 696, 82 S.Ct. 1404, 1409 (1962).

Moreover, we must assume that the jury followed the court's instructions. The jury must, therefore, have drawn a distinction "between practices which tend to exclude or restrict competition on the one hand, and the success of a business which reflects only a superior product, a well-run business, or luck, on the other." Supra, at 2854. Since the jury was unambiguously instructed that Ski Co.'s refusal to deal with Highlands "does not violate Section 2 if valid business reasons exist for that refusal," we must assume that the jury concluded that there were no valid business reasons for the refusal. The question then is whether that conclusion finds support in the record.

IV

The question whether Ski Co.'s conduct may properly be characterized as exclusionary cannot be answered by simply considering its effect on Highlands. In addition, it is relevant to consider its impact on consumers and whether it has impaired competition in an unnecessarily restrictive way.[32] If a firm has been "attempting to exclude rivals on some basis other than efficiency,"[33] it is fair to characterize its behavior as predatory. It is, accordingly, appropriate to examine the effect of the challenged pattern of conduct on consumers, on Ski Co.'s smaller rival, and on Ski Co. itself.

SUPERIOR QUALITY OF THE ALL–ASPEN TICKET

The average Aspen visitor "is a well-educated, relatively affluent, experienced skier who has skied a number of times in the past...." Over 80% of the skiers visiting the resort each year have been there before—40% of these repeat visitors have skied Aspen at least five times. Over the years, they developed a strong demand for the 6–day, all-Aspen ticket in its various refinements. Most experienced skiers quite logically prefer to purchase their tickets at once for the whole period that they will spend at the resort; they can then spend more time on the slopes and enjoying apres-ski amenities and

---

31. "In any business, patterns of distribution develop over time; these may reasonably be thought to be more efficient than alternative patterns of distribution that do not develop. The patterns that do develop and persist we may call the optimal patterns. By disturbing optimal distribution patterns one rival can impose costs upon another, that is, force the other to accept higher costs." Bork 156.

In § 1 cases where this Court has applied the per se approach to invalidity to concerted refusals to deal, "the boycott often cut off access to a supply, facility or market necessary to enable the boycotted firm to compete, ... and frequently the boycotting firms possessed a dominant position in the relevant market." Northwest Wholesale Stationers, Inc. v. Pacific Stationery & Printing Co., 472 U.S. 284, 294, 105 S.Ct. 2613, 2619.

32. "Thus, 'exclusionary' comprehends at the most behavior that not only (1) tends to impair the opportunities of rivals, but also (2) either does not further competition on the merits or does so in an unnecessarily restrictive way." 3 P. Areeda & D. Turner, Antitrust Law 78 (1978).

33. Bork 138.

less time standing in ticket lines. The 4–area attribute of the ticket allowed the skier to purchase his 6–day ticket in advance while reserving the right to decide in his own time and for his own reasons which mountain he would ski on each day. It provided convenience and flexibility, and expanded the vistas and the number of challenging runs available to him during the week's vacation.[34]

While the 3–area, 6–day ticket offered by Ski Co. possessed some of these attributes, the evidence supports a conclusion that consumers were adversely affected by the elimination of the 4–area ticket. In the first place, the actual record of competition between a 3–area ticket and the all-Aspen ticket in the years after 1967 indicated that skiers demonstrably preferred four mountains to three. Highlands' expert marketing witness testified that many of the skiers who come to Aspen want to ski the four mountains, and the abolition of the 4–area pass made it more difficult to satisfy that ambition. A consumer survey undertaken in the 1979–1980 season indicated that 53.7% of the respondents wanted to ski Highlands, but would not; 39.9% said that they would not be skiing at the mountain of their choice because their ticket would not permit it.

Expert testimony and anecdotal evidence supported these statistical measures of consumer preference. A major wholesale tour operator asserted that he would not even consider marketing a 3–area ticket if a 4–area ticket were available.[35] During the 1977–1978 and 1978–1979 seasons, people with Ski Co.'s 3–area ticket came to Highlands "on a very regular basis" and attempted to board the lifts or join the ski school.[36] Highlands officials were left to explain to angry skiers that they could only ski at Highlands or join its ski school by paying for a 1–day lift ticket. Even for the affluent, this was an irritating situation because it left the skier the option of either wasting 1 day of the 6–day, 3–area pass or obtaining a refund which could take all morning and entailed the forfeit of the 6–day discount. An active officer in the Atlanta Ski Club testified that the elimination of the 4–area pass "infuriated" him.

HIGHLANDS' ABILITY TO COMPETE

The adverse impact of Ski Co.'s pattern of conduct on Highlands is not disputed in this Court. Expert testimony described the extent of its pecuniary

34. Highlands' expert marketing witness testified that visitors to the Aspen resort "are looking for a variety of skiing experiences, partly because they are going to be there for a week and they are going to get bored if they ski in one area for very long; and also they come with people of varying skills. They need some variety of slopes so that if they want to go out and ski the difficult areas, their spouses or their buddies who are just starting out skiing can go on the bunny hill or the not-so-difficult slopes." The owner of a condominium management company added: "The guest is coming for a first-class destination ski experience, and part of that, I think, is the expectation of perhaps having available to him the ability to ski all of what is there; i.e., four mountains vs. three mountains. It helps enhance the quality of the vacation experience."

35. "Our philosophy is that ... to offer [Aspen] as a premier ski resort, our clients

should be offered all of the terrain. Therefore, we would never consciously consider offering a three-mountain ticket if there were a four-mountain ticket available."

36. For example, the marketing director of Highlands' ski school reported that one frustrated consumer was a dentist from "the Des Moines area [who] came out with two of his children, and he had been told by our base lift operator that he could not board. He became somewhat irate and she had referred him to my office, which is right there on the ski slopes. He came into my office and started out, 'Well, I want to go skiing here, and I don't understand why I can't.' When we got the situation slowed down and explained that there were two different tickets, well, what came out is irritation occurred because he had intended when he came to Aspen to be able to ski all areas...."

injury. The evidence concerning its attempt to develop a substitute product either by buying Ski Co.'s daily tickets in bulk, or by marketing its own Adventure Pack, demonstrates that it tried to protect itself from the loss of its share of the patrons of the all-Aspen ticket. The development of a new distribution system for providing the experience that skiers had learned to expect in Aspen proved to be prohibitively expensive. As a result, Highlands' share of the relevant market steadily declined after the 4-area ticket was terminated. The size of the damages award also confirms the substantial character of the effect of Ski Co.'s conduct upon Highlands.[38]

SKI CO.'S BUSINESS JUSTIFICATION

Perhaps most significant, however, is the evidence relating to Ski Co. itself, for Ski Co. did not persuade the jury that its conduct was justified by any normal business purpose. Ski Co. was apparently willing to forgo daily ticket sales both to skiers who sought to exchange the coupons contained in Highlands' Adventure Pack, and to those who would have purchased Ski Co. daily lift tickets from Highlands if Highlands had been permitted to purchase them in bulk. The jury may well have concluded that Ski Co. elected to forgo these short-run benefits because it was more interested in reducing competition in the Aspen market over the long run by harming its smaller competitor.

That conclusion is strongly supported by Ski Co.'s failure to offer any efficiency justification whatever for its pattern of conduct.[39] In defending the decision to terminate the jointly offered ticket, Ski Co. claimed that usage could not be properly monitored. The evidence, however, established that Ski Co. itself monitored the use of the 3-area passes based on a count taken by lift operators, and distributed the revenues among its mountains on that basis. Ski Co. contended that coupons were administratively cumbersome, and that the survey takers had been disruptive and their work inaccurate. Coupons, however, were no more burdensome than the credit cards accepted at Ski Co. ticket windows. Moreover, in other markets Ski Co. itself participated in interchangeable lift tickets using coupons. As for the survey, its own manager testified that the problems were much overemphasized by Ski Co. officials, and were mostly resolved as they arose. Ski Co.'s explanation for the rejection of Highlands' offer to hire—at its own expense—a reputable national accounting firm to audit usage of the 4-area tickets at Highlands' mountain, was that there was no way to "control" the audit.

In the end, Ski Co. was pressed to justify its pattern of conduct on a desire to disassociate itself from what it considered the inferior skiing services

---

38. In considering the competitive effect of Ski Co.'s refusal to deal or cooperate with Highlands, it is not irrelevant to note that similar conduct carried out by the concerted action of three independent rivals with a similar share of the market would constitute a per se violation of § 1 of the Sherman Act. See Northwest Wholesale Stationers, Inc. v. Pacific Stationery & Printing Co., 105 S.Ct. 2613, 2619–2620. Cf. Lorain Journal Co. v. United States, 342 U.S. 143, 154, 72 S.Ct. 181, 187 (1951).

39. "The law can usefully attack this form of predation only when there is evidence of specific intent to drive others from the market by means other than superior efficiency and when the predator has overwhelming market size, perhaps 80 or 90 percent. Proof of specific intent to engage in predation may be in the form of statements made by the officers or agents of the company, evidence that the conduct was used threateningly and did not continue when a rival capitulated, or evidence that the conduct was not related to any apparent efficiency. These matters are not so difficult of proof as to render the test overly hard to meet." Bork 157.

offered at Highlands. The all-Aspen ticket based on usage, however, allowed consumers to make their own choice on these matters of quality. Ski Co.'s purported concern for the relative quality of Highlands' product was supported in the record by little more than vague insinuations, and was sharply contested by numerous witnesses. Moreover, Ski Co. admitted that it was willing to associate with what it considered to be inferior products in other markets.

Although Ski Co.'s pattern of conduct may not have been as " 'bold, relentless, and predatory' " as the publisher's actions in Lorain Journal, the record in this case comfortably supports an inference that the monopolist made a deliberate effort to discourage its customers from doing business with its smaller rival. The sale of its 3–area, 6–day ticket, particularly when it was discounted below the daily ticket price, deterred the ticket holders from skiing at Highlands. The refusal to accept the Adventure Pack coupons in exchange for daily tickets was apparently motivated entirely by a decision to avoid providing any benefit to Highlands even though accepting the coupons would have entailed no cost to Ski Co. itself, would have provided it with immediate benefits, and would have satisfied its potential customers. Thus the evidence supports an inference that Ski Co. was not motivated by efficiency concerns and that it was willing to sacrifice short-run benefits and consumer goodwill in exchange for a perceived long-run impact on its smaller rival.

Because we are satisfied that the evidence in the record,[44] construed most favorably in support of Highlands' position, is adequate to support the verdict under the instructions given by the trial court, the judgment of the Court of Appeals is

Affirmed.

Justice WHITE took no part in the decision of this case.

———

Aspen Skiing's holding that a monopolist can violate Section 2 by changing its distribution pattern—and that as a remedy a monopolist can be required to cooperate with its competitors in a joint marketing arrangement—has stimulated extensive debate among commentators and courts. Some have suggested that such a standard raises the risks associated with undertaking legitimate collaboration with a direct rival (e.g., a research and development joint venture), as a lawsuit could accompany the decision later to terminate or otherwise alter such an arrangement. By raising the potential costs of abandoning such relationships, *Aspen* might make it less likely that collaborative arrangements will be formed in the first place.

Some lower courts sought to confine *Aspen Skiing* by depicting its outcome as the product of unusual facts and a frail defense by the monopolist. Aspen Skiing does not seem to have contested the plaintiff's suggestion that

44. Given our conclusion that the evidence amply supports the verdict under the instructions as given by the trial court, we find it unnecessary to consider the possible relevance of the "essential facilities" doctrine, or the somewhat hypothetical question whether no-nexclusionary conduct could ever constitute an abuse of monopoly power if motivated by an anticompetitive purpose. If, as we have assumed, no monopolist monopolizes unconscious of what he is doing, that case is unlikely to arise.

the relevant market consisted of skiing in the Aspen area of Colorado—a market definition that excluded other ski resorts and gave Aspen a market share from which substantial market power easily would be inferred. In *Olympia Equip. Leasing Co. v. Western Union Tel. Co.*, 797 F.2d 370, 379 (7th Cir. 1986), the Seventh Circuit observed that "[i]f [*Aspen*] stands for any principle that goes beyond its unusual facts, it is that a monopolist may be guilty of monopolization if it refuses to cooperate with a competitor in circumstances where some cooperation is indispensable to effective competition." Successful defensive strategies by monopolists have consisted mainly of providing a business justification to excuse the challenged refusal to deal. *See, e.g., Trans Sport, Inc. v. Starter Sportswear, Inc.*, 964 F.2d 186 (2d Cir. 1992) (emphasizing defendant manufacturer's effort to curb free-riding by plaintiff distributor).

In *Verizon Commc'ns Inc. v. Law Offices of Curtis V. Trinko, LLP*, 540 U.S. 398 (2004), the Supreme Court appeared to significantly limit the scope of *Aspen Skiing*, and with it the degree to which the antitrust laws will support a duty to deal, especially with rivals. We will read the case later in this Chapter when we consider refusals to deal in greater depth. In relation to its holding that rivals may have a duty to deal only under limited circumstances, the Court identified *Aspen Skiing* as being "at or near the outer boundary of § 2 liability." But it did not discuss *Aspen Skiing's* definition of exclusionary conduct or its approach to structuring a Section 2 monopolization inquiry and thus appeared to sub silentio reject a call by the defendant and amici to adopt a more restrictive general definition of "exclusionary."

Note that the framework embraced in *Aspen Skiing* called for a consideration of the monopolist's "business justifications," such as efficiencies, which can be related to *Alcoa's* observation that liability should not attach to competitive successes occasioned by skill, foresight, business acumen, or simple luck. In evaluating asserted efficiency rationales, courts will consider whether the record shows that theoretically plausible justifications in fact motivated the defendant's refusal to deal. This approach to the analysis of efficiencies was also evident in *Eastman Kodak Co. v. Image Tech. Servs., Inc.*, 504 U.S. 451 (1992).

In *Kodak* the Court sustained a reversal of summary judgment dismissing claims that Kodak had imposed an illegal tying arrangement and had monopolized and attempted to monopolize. The Court focused on Kodak's policy of selling replacement parts for Kodak photocopiers and micrographic equipment only to buyers of Kodak equipment who used Kodak service or repaired their own machines. Image Technical, an independent service organization (ISO), alleged that Kodak adopted the policy, which was a change from its past conduct, to eliminate ISOs from the continued servicing of Kodak equipment.

The record on appeal stipulated that Kodak lacked market power in the market for sales of original equipment. Based on that lack of market power, Kodak argued that it could not sensibly charge existing, "locked-in" users of Kodak machines supracompetitive prices for parts or service. If it did, it would quickly acquire a reputation for gouging its customers in the aftermarket for parts and services and lose sales to rival new equipment manufacturers. Prospective purchasers would account for the price of parts and services in estimating the life cycle cost of operating Kodak machines, and look for alternatives. Thus, unless it was planning to exit the market for new equipment sales (and did not care if it gained a reputation for opportunism), Kodak said it could not exercise power in a market defined as the supply of parts and service for Kodak equipment.

The Supreme Court began the analysis of the Section 2 claims by observing that Image Technical had "presented evidence that Kodak took exclusionary action to maintain its parts monopoly and used its control over parts to strengthen its monopoly share of the Kodak service market. Liability turns, then, on whether 'valid business reasons' can explain Kodak's actions." 504 U.S. at 483, *citing Aspen Skiing Co.*, 472 U.S. at 605; and *Alcoa*, 148 F.2d at 432. *Kodak* repeated *Aspen Skiing*'s admonition that a monopolist may refuse to deal with rivals "only if there are legitimate competitive reasons for the refusal." *Id.* at 483 n.32. In rejecting Kodak's argument, the Supreme Court said "Kodak's theory does not explain the actual market behavior revealed in the record," pointing to evidence that Kodak in fact had raised service prices for its customers without losing equipment sales. 504 U.S. at 473.

Justice Scalia dissented from the Court majority's ruling, but he endorsed the view that the conduct of a monopolist is to be judged by a more demanding standard than that applied to a firm lacking market power: "Where a defendant maintains substantial monopoly power, his activities are examined through a special lens: Behavior that might otherwise not be of concern to the antitrust laws—or that might be viewed as procompetitive— can take on exclusionary connotations when practiced by a monopolist." 504 U.S. at 488 (Scalia, J., dissenting).

In the Note that follows, we examine the economics of market power in the kind of "aftermarkets" at issue in *Kodak*. As we shall see, as in *Aspen Skiing*, the Supreme Court attached considerable importance to Kodak's refusal to continue to sell parts to ISOs—a departure from its previous policy. Had Kodak never sold parts and service separate from its original equipment (for example, by bundling parts and service together with the copier in structuring the product's warranty), it would have faced no Sherman Act liability. Like the *Aspen Skiing* decision, the Court's opinion in *Image Technical* suggests that dominant firms devote greater care in deciding whether to work with or supply competitors. The decision also places a premium on developing a convincing justification for the termination of a relationship once formed, and upon documenting justifications contemporaneously.

Note on Kodak and the Economics of Market Power in Aftermarkets

Kodak sold copiers in an original equipment market (OEM) in competition with Canon, Xerox, and other rivals. Kodak also sold aftermarket parts and service to its "installed base" of customers, firms that had previously purchased a Kodak copier. Originally, Kodak competed with a number of independent service organizations (ISOs) in providing aftermarket parts and service to its equipment. The ISO plaintiffs alleged that Kodak thereafter sought to exclude them from competing in the aftermarket for parts and service, allowing Kodak to raise prices above competitive levels. In its defense, Kodak argued, among other things, that because the original equipment market for copiers was competitive, then it could not have been profitable for it to exercise market power in the aftermarket. This note examines the economic conditions under which it could have been profitable for Kodak to increase aftermarket prices above the competitive level—*i.e.*, to exercise market power—notwithstanding a competitive original equipment market.*

Assume, as the Court majority supposes, that the typical buyer of Kodak copiers is locked-in to that brand. That is, the buyer can not substitute parts for other copiers or service technicians trained on other copiers, and it can not sell its Kodak copiers in the used market.** Assume further, as the Court also presumes, that the OEM market is competitive and that Kodak obtains a monopoly in the aftermarket.

Finally, suppose for the moment, as Kodak claimed, that most buyers of new equipment are well-informed about the likely cost of aftermarket parts and service at the time they make their original equipment purchase. These customers have a good understanding of the probability that a copier will need service over its lifetime and the likely cost of that service. When choosing between a Kodak copier and a rival brand, these informed customers compare lifecycle costs, which include the costs of aftermarket parts and service. This assumption connects Kodak's OEM sales and its aftermarket prices. If Kodak raises aftermarket prices, it will lose original equipment sales to informed buyers that recognize that their lifecycle costs have risen above the competitive level.

The profitability to Kodak of raising aftermarket prices above the competitive level depends on tallying up all the gains and losses from doing so. Higher aftermarket prices would allow Kodak to earn more on parts and service sold to its "installed base" of customers that had previously purchased a Kodak copier; these customers are locked-in and would not switch to other copiers. But higher aftermarket prices would lower aftermarket sales, as some copier owners would choose not to repair an old copier. And, more importantly, a higher aftermarket price would discourage some new purchasers from choosing the Kodak brand, driving them to products sold by Canon, Xerox or other rivals. The profitability to Kodak of raising aftermarket prices turns on whether the increase in profits earned in supplying parts and service to its installed base exceeds the reduction in profits arising from losses of sales both in the parts and service aftermarket and in the original equipment market.

The dominant effect of higher aftermarket prices could be to increase profits for Kodak if the original equipment market is very important to Kodak relative to the aftermarket. In a declining original equipment market, for example, Kodak might not lose very much even if higher aftermarket prices led most OEM customers to prefer other brands. Then Kodak might have a strong incentive to engage in "installed-base opportunism" by raising aftermarket prices above competitive levels. By contrast, if copier sales are rapidly growing, the market for new equipment would likely be more important to

---

* Aftermarkets are common in durable products like copiers or automobiles. But they also arise in other settings. Suppose that a university decides to require its students to live in dormitories, and that it simultaneously raises the price of room and board. Could the higher price of housing have an anticompetitive motive?

** The analysis would be the same if there were a market for used Kodak copiers, so long as used products sold at a large discount, making it expensive for the buyer to switch copier brands once it adopted Kodak products.

Kodak than aftermarket sales to its installed base, making it less likely that installed base opportunism would be profitable. Accordingly, if Kodak's new copier sales growth had begun to slow, that development might have made it profitable for the company to change its business strategy and raise the price of copier parts and service.

Kodak might also find it profitable to raise aftermarket prices even if original equipment sales are important to it, if the link between higher aftermarket prices and lower original equipment sales is weak. That might happen if, contrary to what Kodak urged the court to assume, many customers are not well-informed. If a substantial fraction of copier buyers are not well-informed, Kodak would not be penalized significantly in the OEM market if it charges a monopoly price for aftermarket services.***

It is possible that most copier buyers would be informed, and, in consequence, would make copier decisions by comparing lifecycle costs across brands. In particular, large firms that purchase many copiers likely have the ability and incentive to work out lifecycle cost projections and use those estimates when making OEM purchase decisions.**** The *Kodak* majority was skeptical of this argument, however, in part because it saw little evidence that Kodak lost OEM sales when it raised the price of service to its installed base. This observation suggested to the Court that a substantial fraction of copier buyers were not well-informed about lifecycle costs, perhaps because the buyers found it too expensive to gather the necessary information. (When you last purchased a new car, did you analyze the lifetime costs of ownership, including future repair costs and gasoline expenditures as well as the original cost of the automobile?) If the typical copier buyer was becoming less informed than in the past—for example, if copiers were increasingly being purchased by small businesses unlikely to engage in lifecycle costing—Kodak could have found it profitable to alter its business strategy by raising aftermarket prices.

For two economic perspectives on Kodak's argument that competition in original equipment markets prevents anticompetitive harm in aftermarkets, see Severin Borenstein, Jeffrey K. MacKie–Mason & Janet S. Netz, *Antitrust Policy in Aftermarkets*, 63 ANTITRUST L. J. 455 (1995) and Carl Shapiro, *Aftermarkets and Consumer Welfare: Making Sense of* Kodak, 63 ANTITRUST L. J. 483 (1995). For an economic argument that Kodak's refusal to deal with the independent service organizations was not installed-base opportunism facilitated by imperfect information, but instead an effort to discriminate in price

---

*** Another way to attenuate the link between OEM sales and aftermarket prices is to suppose that Kodak can identify which OEM customers are well-informed, and that it can discriminate in price in the copier market against those who are not. Then Kodak would profit by raising the price in the aftermarket, and simultaneously lowering prices in the OEM market by a compensating amount, but only to the well-informed customers, diminishing the incentive for well-informed customers to switching to rival copiers. This scheme would allow Kodak to take advantage of the uninformed customers in its installed base without raising lifecycle prices to the well-informed customers.

**** It may be particularly easy for buyers to understand lifecycle costs in markets for other types of durable equipment (but apparently not for copiers), where manufacturers offer buyers long term service contracts at the time of the original equipment purchase. The price of those contracts would inform buyers about the expected lifecycle cost of aftermarket parts and service. It is possible that what economists call a "moral hazard" problem—the concern that firms with service contracts will not take care of their machines, raising the costs of repair—makes it unprofitable for copier manufacturers to offer such contracts.

by charging more to customers that use their copiers the most intensively (and thus would need parts and service more frequently), see Benjamin Klein, *Market Power in Antitrust: Economic Analysis after* Kodak, 3 Sup. Ct. Econ. Rev. 43 (1993). The economics of price discrimination are sketched in Sidebar 7–7.

———

We will return to the consideration of the treatment of refusals to deal as exclusionary conduct in Section C4, *infra*. As noted above, *Aspen Skiing* was also significant for its definition of "exclusionary conduct" and its framework for analyzing power, conduct, and effects. We now return to a focus on those elements of the monopolization offense.

Our next case arose out of the governments' prosecution in the late 1990s of Microsoft Corporation for monopolizing the market for Intel-compatible PC operating systems. The case, which was initiated in May, 1998, and settled by the federal government and some of the states that had joined in the prosecution in November 2002, was one of the most closely watched and debated monopolization cases in history. As you read the excerpt that follows, note how the court of appeals structured its analysis, but also how its inquiries into power, conduct, and effects are intertwined. Note also how the court addresses efficiency justifications. Excerpts from the testimony of the principal economic experts in the case are reproduced in Chapter 8 and may also be reviewed at this time. Those excerpts largely focus on market definition and market power, but again illustrate the interdependencies of power, conduct, and effects.

UNITED STATES v. MICROSOFT CORP.

United States Court of Appeals for the District of Columbia Circuit, 2001.
253 F.3d 34.

Before: EDWARDS, Chief Judge, WILLIAMS, GINSBURG, SENTELLE, RANDOLPH, ROGERS and TATEL, Circuit Judges.

Opinion for the Court filed PER CURIAM.

* * *

II.   MONOPOLIZATION
* * *

A.   *Monopoly Power*

While merely possessing monopoly power is not itself an antitrust violation, it is a necessary element of a monopolization charge. The Supreme Court defines monopoly power as "the power to control prices or exclude competition." *United States v. E.I. du Pont de Nemours & Co.*, 351 U.S. 377, 391, 76 S.Ct. 994, 100 L.Ed. 1264 (1956). More precisely, a firm is a monopolist if it can profitably raise prices substantially above the competitive level. Where evidence indicates that a firm has in fact profitably done so, the existence of monopoly power is clear. *See Rebel Oil Co. v. Atl. Richfield Co.*, 51 F.3d 1421, 1434 (9th Cir.1995); *see also FTC v. Indiana Fed'n of Dentists*, 476 U.S. 447,

460–61, 106 S.Ct. 2009, 90 L.Ed.2d 445 (1986) (using direct proof to show market power in Sherman Act § 1 unreasonable restraint of trade action). Because such direct proof is only rarely available, courts more typically examine market structure in search of circumstantial evidence of monopoly power. Under this structural approach, monopoly power may be inferred from a firm's possession of a dominant share of a relevant market that is protected by entry barriers. "Entry barriers" are factors (such as certain regulatory requirements) that prevent new rivals from timely responding to an increase in price above the competitive level.

The District Court considered these structural factors and concluded that Microsoft possesses monopoly power in a relevant market. Defining the market as Intel-compatible PC operating systems, the District Court found that Microsoft has a greater than 95% share. It also found the company's market position protected by a substantial entry barrier.

Microsoft argues that the District Court incorrectly defined the relevant market. It also claims that there is no barrier to entry in that market. Alternatively, Microsoft argues that because the software industry is uniquely dynamic, direct proof, rather than circumstantial evidence, more appropriately indicates whether it possesses monopoly power. Rejecting each argument, we uphold the District Court's finding of monopoly power in its entirety.

1. Market Structure

a. Market definition

"Because the ability of consumers to turn to other suppliers restrains a firm from raising prices above the competitive level," *Rothery Storage & Van Co. v. Atlas Van Lines, Inc.*, 792 F.2d 210, 218 (D.C.Cir.1986), the relevant market must include all products "reasonably interchangeable by consumers for the same purposes." In this case, the District Court defined the market as "the licensing of all Intel-compatible PC operating systems worldwide," finding that there are "currently no products—and . . . there are not likely to be any in the near future—that a significant percentage of computer users worldwide could substitute for [these operating systems] without incurring substantial costs." Calling this market definition "far too narrow," Microsoft argues that the District Court improperly excluded three types of products: non-Intel compatible operating systems (primarily Apple's Macintosh operating system, Mac OS), operating systems for non-PC devices (such as hand-held computers and portal websites), and "middleware" products, which are not operating systems at all.

We begin with Mac OS. Microsoft's argument that Mac OS should have been included in the relevant market suffers from a flaw that infects many of the company's monopoly power claims: the company fails to challenge the District Court's factual findings, or to argue that these findings do not support the court's conclusions. The District Court found that consumers would not switch from Windows to Mac OS in response to a substantial price increase because of the costs of acquiring the new hardware needed to run Mac OS (an Apple computer and peripherals) and compatible software applications, as well as because of the effort involved in learning the new system and transferring files to its format. The court also found the Apple system less appealing to consumers because it costs considerably more and supports fewer applications. Microsoft responds only by saying: "the district court's market definition is so narrow that it excludes Apple's Mac OS, which has competed with Windows for years, simply because the Mac OS runs on a different microprocessor." This general, conclusory statement falls far short of what is required to challenge findings as clearly erroneous. Microsoft neither points to evidence contradicting the District Court's findings nor alleges that supporting record evidence is insufficient. And since Microsoft does not argue that even if we accept these findings, they do not support the District Court's conclusion, we have no basis for upsetting the court's decision to exclude Mac OS from the relevant market.

Microsoft's challenge to the District Court's exclusion of non-PC based competitors, such as information appliances (handheld devices, etc.) and portal websites that host serverbased software applications, suffers from the same defect: the company fails to challenge the District Court's key factual findings. In particular, the District Court found that because information appliances fall far short of performing all of the functions of a PC, most consumers will buy them only as a supplement to their PCs. The District Court also found that portal websites do not presently host enough applications to induce consumers to switch, nor are they likely to do so in the near future. Again, because Microsoft does not argue that the District Court's findings do not support its conclusion that information appliances and portal websites are outside the relevant market, we adhere to that conclusion.

This brings us to Microsoft's main challenge to the District Court's market definition: the exclusion of middleware. * * *

Operating systems perform many functions, including allocating computer memory and controlling peripherals such as printers and keyboards. Operating systems also function as platforms for software applications. They do this by "exposing"—*i.e.*, making available to software developers—routines or protocols that perform certain widely-used functions. These are known as Application Programming Interfaces, or "APIs." * * * Software developers wishing to include [any] function in an application need not duplicate it in their own code. Instead, they can "call"—*i.e.*, use—the Windows API. Windows contains thousands of APIs, controlling everything from data storage to font display.

Every operating system has different APIs. Accordingly, a developer who writes an application for one operating system and wishes to sell the application to users of another must modify, or "port," the application to the second operating system. This process is both time-consuming and expensive.

"Middleware" refers to software products that expose their own APIs. Because of this, a middleware product written for Windows could take over some or all of Windows's valuable platform functions—that is, developers might begin to rely upon APIs exposed by the middleware for basic routines rather than relying upon the API set included in Windows. If middleware were written for multiple operating systems, its impact could be even greater. The more developers could rely upon APIs exposed by such middleware, the less expensive porting to different operating systems would be. Ultimately, if developers could write applications relying exclusively on APIs exposed by middleware, their applications would run on any operating system on which the middleware was also present. Netscape Navigator and Java–both at issue in this case—are middleware products written for multiple operating systems.

Microsoft argues that, because middleware could usurp the operating system's platform function and might eventually take over other operating system functions (for instance, by controlling peripherals), the District Court erred in excluding Navigator and Java from the relevant market. The District Court found, however, that neither Navigator, Java, nor any other middleware product could now, or would soon, expose enough APIs to serve as a platform for popular applications, much less take over all operating system functions. Again, Microsoft fails to challenge these findings, instead simply asserting middleware's "potential" as a competitor. The test of reasonable interchangeability, however, required the District Court to consider only substitutes that constrain pricing in the reasonably foreseeable future, and only products that can enter the market in a relatively short time can perform this function. Whatever middleware's ultimate potential, the District Court found that consumers could not now abandon their operating systems and switch to middleware in response to a sustained price for Windows above the competitive level. Nor is middleware likely to overtake the operating system as the primary platform for software development any time in the near future.

Alternatively, Microsoft argues that the District Court should not have excluded middleware from the relevant market because the primary focus of the plaintiffs' § 2 charge is on Microsoft's attempts to suppress middleware's threat to its operating system monopoly. According to Microsoft, it is "contradict[ory]," to define the relevant market to exclude the "very competitive threats that gave rise" to the action. The purported contradiction lies between plaintiffs' § 2 theory, under which Microsoft preserved its monopoly against middleware technologies that threatened to become viable substitutes for Windows, and its theory of the relevant market, under which middleware is not presently a viable substitute for Windows. Because middleware's threat is only nascent, however, no contradiction exists. Nothing in § 2 of the Sherman Act limits its prohibition to actions taken against threats that are already well-developed enough to serve as present substitutes. Because market definition is meant to identify products "reasonably interchangeable by consumers," and because middleware is not now interchangeable with Windows, the District Court had good reason for excluding middleware from the relevant market.

b. Market power

Having thus properly defined the relevant market, the District Court found that Windows accounts for a greater than 95% share. The court also found that even if Mac OS were included, Microsoft's share would exceed 80%. Microsoft challenges neither finding, nor does it argue that such a market share is not predominant.

Instead, Microsoft claims that even a predominant market share does not by itself indicate monopoly power. Although the "existence of [monopoly] power ordinarily may be inferred from the predominant share of the market," *Grinnell*, 384 U.S. at 571, we agree with Microsoft that because of the possibility of competition from new entrants, looking to current market share alone can be "misleading." In this case, however, the District Court was not misled. Considering the possibility of new rivals, the court focused not only on Microsoft's present market share, but also on the structural barrier that protects the company's future position. That barrier—the "applications barrier to entry"—stems from two characteristics of the software market: (1) most consumers prefer operating systems for which a large number of applications have already been written; and (2) most developers prefer to write for operating systems that already have a substantial consumer base. This "chicken-and-egg" situation ensures that applications will continue to be written for the already dominant Windows, which in turn ensures that consumers will continue to prefer it over other operating systems.

Challenging the existence of the applications barrier to entry, Microsoft observes that software developers do write applications for other operating systems, pointing out that at its peak IBM's OS/2 supported approximately 2,500 applications. This misses the point. That some developers write applications for other operating systems is not at all inconsistent with the finding that the applications barrier to entry discourages many from writing for these less popular platforms. Indeed, the District Court found that IBM's difficulty in attracting a larger number of software developers to write for its platform seriously impeded OS/2's success.

Microsoft does not dispute that Windows supports many more applications than any other operating system. It argues instead that "[i]t defies common sense" to suggest that an operating system must support as many applications as Windows does (more than 70,000, according to the District Court) to be competitive. Consumers, Microsoft points out, can only use a very small percentage of these applications. As the District Court explained, however, the applications barrier to entry gives consumers reason to prefer the dominant operating system even if they have no need to use all applications written for it:

> The consumer wants an operating system that runs not only types of applications that he knows he will want to use, but also those types in which he might develop an interest later. Also, the consumer knows that if he chooses an operating system with enough demand to support multiple applications in each product category, he will be less likely to find himself straitened later by having to use an application whose features disappoint him. Finally, the average user knows that, generally speaking, applications improve through successive versions. He thus wants an operating system for which successive generations of his favorite applications will be released—promptly at that. The fact that a vastly larger number of applications are written for Windows than for other PC operating systems attracts consumers to Windows, because it reassures them that their interests will be met as long as they use Microsoft's product.

Findings of Fact ¶ 37. Thus, despite the limited success of its rivals, Microsoft benefits from the applications barrier to entry.

* * *

Microsoft next argues that the applications barrier to entry is not an entry barrier at all, but a reflection of Windows' popularity. It is certainly true that Windows may have gained its initial dominance in the operating system market competitively—through superior foresight or quality. But this case is not about Microsoft's initial acquisition of monopoly power. It is about Microsoft's efforts to maintain this position through means other than competition on the merits. Because the applications barrier to entry protects a dominant operating system irrespective of quality, it gives Microsoft power to stave off even superior new rivals. The barrier is thus a characteristic of the operating system market, not of Microsoft's popularity, or, as asserted by a Microsoft witness, the company's efficiency. *See* Direct Testimony of Richard Schmalensee ¶ 115.

Finally, Microsoft argues that the District Court should not have considered the applications barrier to entry because it reflects not a cost borne disproportionately by new entrants, but one borne by all participants in the operating system market. According to Microsoft, it had to make major investments to convince software developers to write for its new operating system, and it continues to "evangelize" the Windows platform today. Whether costs borne by all market participants should be considered entry barriers is the subject of much debate. We need not resolve this issue, however, for even under the more narrow definition it is clear that there are barriers. When Microsoft entered the operating system market with MS–DOS and the first version of Windows, it did not confront a dominant rival operating system with as massive an installed base and as vast an existing array of applications as the Windows operating systems have since enjoyed. Moreover, when Microsoft introduced Windows 95 and 98, it was able to bypass the applications barrier to entry that protected the incumbent Windows by including APIs from the earlier version in the new operating systems. This made porting existing Windows applications to the new version of Windows much less costly than porting them to the operating systems of other entrants who could not freely include APIs from the incumbent Windows with their own.

2. *Direct Proof*

Having sustained the District Court's conclusion that circumstantial evidence proves that Microsoft possesses monopoly power, we turn to Microsoft's alternative argument that it does not behave like a monopolist. Claiming that software competition is uniquely "dynamic," the company suggests a new rule: that monopoly power in the software industry should be proven directly, that is, by examining a company's actual behavior to determine if it reveals the existence of monopoly power. According to Microsoft, not only does no such proof of its power exist, but record evidence demonstrates the absence of monopoly power. The company claims that it invests heavily in research and development, and charges a low price for Windows (a small percentage of the price of an Intel compatible PC system and less than the price of its rivals).

Microsoft's argument fails because, even assuming that the software market is uniquely dynamic in the long term, the District Court correctly applied the structural approach to determine if the company faces competition in the short term. Structural market power analyses are meant to determine whether potential substitutes constrain a firm's ability to raise prices above the competitive level; only threats that are likely to materialize in the relatively near future perform this function to any significant degree. The District Court expressly considered and rejected Microsoft's claims that innovations such as handheld devices and portal websites would soon expand the relevant market beyond Intel-compatible PC operating systems. Because the company does not challenge these findings, we have no reason to believe that prompt substitutes are available. The structural approach, as applied by the District Court, is thus capable of fulfilling its purpose even in a changing market. Microsoft cites no case, nor are we aware of one, requiring direct evidence to show monopoly power in any market. We decline to adopt such a rule now.

Even if we were to require direct proof, moreover, Microsoft's behavior may well be sufficient to show the existence of monopoly power. Certainly, none of the conduct Microsoft points to—its investment in R & D and the relatively low price of Windows—is inconsistent with the possession of such power. The R & D expenditures Microsoft points to are not simply for Windows, but for its entire company, which most likely does not possess a monopoly for all of its products. Moreover, because innovation can increase an already dominant market share and further delay the emergence of competition, even monopolists have reason to invest in R&D. Microsoft's pricing behavior is similarly equivocal. The company claims only that it never charged the short-term profit-maximizing price for Windows. Faced with conflicting expert testimony, the District Court found that it could not accurately determine what this price would be. In any event, the court found, a price lower than the short-term profit-maximizing price is not inconsistent with possession or improper use of monopoly power. Microsoft never claims that it did not charge the long-term monopoly price. Microsoft does argue that the price of Windows is a fraction of the price of an Intel-compatible PC system and lower than that of rival operating systems, but these facts are not inconsistent with the District Court's finding that Microsoft has monopoly power. *See Findings of Fact* ¶ 36 ("Intel-compatible PC operating systems other than Windows [would not] attract[ ] significant demand ... even if Microsoft held its prices substantially above the competitive level.").

More telling, the District Court found that some aspects of Microsoft's behavior are difficult to explain unless Windows is a monopoly product. For instance, according to the District Court, the company set the price of Windows without considering rivals' prices, something a firm without a monopoly would have been unable to do. The District Court also found that Microsoft's pattern of exclusionary conduct could only be rational "if the firm knew that it possessed monopoly power." It is to that conduct that we now turn.

B. *Anticompetitive Conduct*

* * *

* * * [A]fter concluding that Microsoft had monopoly power, the District Court held that Microsoft had violated § 2 by engaging in a variety of exclusionary acts to maintain its monopoly by preventing the effective distribution and use of products that might threaten that monopoly. Specifically, the District Court held Microsoft liable for: (1) the way in which it integrated IE ["Internet Explorer" Internet browser, Eds.] into Windows; (2) its various dealings with Original Equipment Manufacturers ("OEMs"), Internet Access Providers ("IAPs"), Internet Content Providers ("ICPs"), Independent Software Vendors ("ISVs"), and Apple Computer; (3) its efforts to contain and to subvert Java technologies; and (4) its course of conduct as a whole. Upon appeal, Microsoft argues that it did not engage in any exclusionary conduct.

Whether any particular act of a monopolist is exclusionary, rather than merely a form of vigorous competition, can be difficult to discern: the means of illicit exclusion, like the means of legitimate competition, are myriad. The challenge for an antitrust court lies in stating a general rule for distinguishing between exclusionary acts, which reduce social welfare, and competitive acts, which increase it.

From a century of case law on monopolization under § 2, however, several principles do emerge. First, to be condemned as exclusionary, a monopolist's act must have an "anticompetitive effect." That is, it must harm the competitive *process* and thereby harm consumers. In contrast, harm to one or more *competitors* will not suffice. * * *

Second, the plaintiff, on whom the burden of proof of course rests, must demonstrate that the monopolist's conduct indeed has the requisite anticompetitive effect. In a case brought by a private plaintiff, the plaintiff must show that its injury is "of 'the type that the statute was intended to forestall,' "*Brunswick Corp. v. Pueblo Bowl–O–Mat, Inc.*, 429 U.S. 477, 487–88, 97 S.Ct. 690, 50 L.Ed.2d 701 (1977); no less in a case brought by the Government, it must demonstrate that the monopolist's conduct harmed competition, not just a competitor.

Third, if a plaintiff successfully establishes a *prima facie* case under § 2 by demonstrating anticompetitive effect, then the monopolist may proffer a "procompetitive justification" for its conduct. If the monopolist asserts a procompetitive justification—a nonpretextual claim that its conduct is indeed a form of competition on the merits because it involves, for example, greater efficiency or enhanced consumer appeal—then the burden shifts back to the plaintiff to rebut that claim.

Fourth, if the monopolist's procompetitive justification stands unrebutted, then the plaintiff must demonstrate that the anticompetitive harm of the conduct outweighs the procompetitive benefit. In cases arising under § 1 of the Sherman Act, the courts routinely apply a similar balancing approach under the rubric of the "rule of reason." * * *

Finally, in considering whether the monopolist's conduct on balance harms competition and is therefore condemned as exclusionary for purposes of § 2, our focus is upon the effect of that conduct, not upon the intent behind it. Evidence of the intent behind the conduct of a monopolist is relevant only to the extent it helps us understand the likely effect of the monopolist's conduct.

With these principles in mind, we now consider Microsoft's objections to the District Court's holding that Microsoft violated § 2 of the Sherman Act in a variety of ways.

1. *Licenses Issued to Original Equipment Manufacturers*

The District Court condemned a number of provisions in Microsoft's agreements licensing Windows to OEMs, because it found that Microsoft's imposition of those provisions (like many of Microsoft's other actions at issue in this case) serves to reduce usage share of Netscape's browser and, hence, protect Microsoft's operating system monopoly. The reason market share in the browser market affects market power in the operating system market is complex, and warrants some explanation.

Browser usage share is important because * * * a browser (or any middleware product, for that matter) must have a critical mass of users in order to attract software developers to write applications relying upon the APIs ["Application Programming Interfaces," Eds.] it exposes, and away from the APIs exposed by Windows. Applications written to a particular browser's APIs, however, would run on any computer with that browser, regardless of the underlying operating system. If a consumer could have access to the applications he desired—regardless of the operating system he uses—simply by installing a particular browser on his computer, then he would no longer feel compelled to select Windows in order to have access to those applications; he could select an operating system other than Windows based solely upon its quality and price. In other words, the market for operating systems would be competitive.

Therefore, Microsoft's efforts to gain market share in one market (browsers) served to meet the threat to Microsoft's monopoly in another market (operating systems) by keeping rival browsers from gaining the critical mass of users necessary to attract developer attention away from Windows as the platform for software development. * * *

In evaluating the restrictions in Microsoft's agreements licensing Windows to OEMs, we first consider whether plaintiffs have made out a *prima facie* case by demonstrating that the restrictions have an anticompetitive effect. In the next subsection, we conclude that plaintiffs have met this burden as to all the restrictions. We then consider Microsoft's proffered justifications for the restrictions and, for the most part, hold those justifications insufficient.

a. Anticompetitive effect of the license restrictions

The restrictions Microsoft places upon Original Equipment Manufacturers are of particular importance in determining browser usage share because having an OEM pre-install a browser on a computer is one of the two most cost-effective methods by far of distributing browsing software. The District Court found that the restrictions Microsoft imposed in licensing Windows to OEMs prevented many OEMs from distributing browsers other than IE. In particular, the District Court condemned the license provisions prohibiting the OEMs from: (1) removing any desktop icons, folders, or "Start" menu entries; (2) altering the initial boot sequence; and (3) otherwise altering the appearance of the Windows desktop.

The District Court concluded that the first license restriction—the prohibition upon the removal of desktop icons, folders, and Start menu entries—thwarts the distribution of a rival browser by preventing OEMs from removing visible means of user access to IE. The OEMs cannot practically install a second browser in addition to IE, the court found, in part because "[p]re-installing more than one product in a given category ... can significantly increase an OEM's support costs, for the redundancy can lead to confusion among novice users." * * *

Microsoft denies the "consumer confusion" story; it observes that some OEMs do install multiple browsers and that executives from two OEMs that do so denied any knowledge of consumers being confused by multiple icons.

Other testimony, however, supports the District Court's finding that fear of such confusion deters many OEMs from pre-installing multiple browsers. Most telling, in presentations to OEMs, Microsoft itself represented that having only one icon in a particular category would be "less confusing for endusers." Accordingly, we reject Microsoft's argument that we should vacate the District Court's Finding of Fact 159 as it relates to consumer confusion.

As noted above, the OEM channel is one of the two primary channels for distribution of browsers. By preventing OEMs from removing visible means of user access to IE, the license restriction prevents many OEMs from pre-installing a rival browser and, therefore, protects Microsoft's monopoly from the competition that middleware might otherwise present. Therefore, we conclude that the license restriction at issue is anticompetitive. * * *

The second license provision at issue prohibits OEMs from modifying the initial boot sequence—the process that occurs the first time a consumer turns on the computer. Prior to the imposition of that restriction, "among the programs that many OEMs inserted into the boot sequence were Internet sign-up procedures that encouraged users to choose from a list of IAPs assembled by the OEM." *Findings of Fact* ¶ 210. Microsoft's prohibition on any alteration of the boot sequence thus prevents OEMs from using that process to promote the services of IAPs, many of which—at least at the time Microsoft imposed the restriction—used Navigator rather than IE in their internet access software. Microsoft does not deny that the prohibition on modifying the boot sequence has the effect of decreasing competition against IE by preventing OEMs from promoting rivals' browsers. Because this prohibition has a substantial effect in protecting Microsoft's market power, and does so through a means other than competition on the merits, it is anticompetitive. * * *

Finally, Microsoft imposes several additional provisions that, like the prohibition on removal of icons, prevent OEMs from making various alterations to the desktop: Microsoft prohibits OEMs from causing any user interface other than the Windows desktop to launch automatically, from adding icons or folders different in size or shape from those supplied by Microsoft, and from using the "Active Desktop" feature to promote third-party brands. These restrictions impose significant costs upon the OEMs; prior to Microsoft's prohibiting the practice, many OEMs would change the appearance of the desktop in ways they found beneficial.

The dissatisfaction of the OEM customers does not, of course, mean the restrictions are anticompetitive. The anticompetitive effect of the license restrictions is, as Microsoft itself recognizes, that OEMs are not able to promote rival browsers, which keeps developers focused upon the APIs in Windows. This kind of promotion is not a zero-sum game; but for the restrictions in their licenses to use Windows, OEMs could promote multiple IAPs and browsers. By preventing the OEMs from doing so, this type of license restriction, like the first two restrictions, is anticompetitive: Microsoft reduced rival browsers' usage share not by improving its own product but, rather, by preventing OEMs from taking actions that could increase rivals' share of usage.

b. Microsoft's justifications for the license restrictions

Microsoft argues that the license restrictions are legally justified because, in imposing them, Microsoft is simply "exercising its rights as the holder of valid copyrights." Microsoft also argues that the licenses "do not unduly restrict the opportunities of Netscape to distribute Navigator in any event."

Microsoft's primary copyright argument borders upon the frivolous. The company claims an absolute and unfettered right to use its intellectual property as it wishes * * *. That is no more correct than the proposition that use of one's personal property, such as a baseball bat, cannot give rise to tort liability. As the Federal Circuit succinctly stated: "Intellectual property rights do not confer a privilege to violate the antitrust laws." *In re Indep. Serv. Orgs. Antitrust Litig.*, 203 F.3d 1322, 1325 (Fed. Cir. 2000).

Although Microsoft never overtly retreats from its bold and incorrect position on the law, it also makes two arguments to the effect that it is not exercising its copyright in an unreasonable manner, despite the anticompetitive consequences of the license restrictions discussed above. In the first variation upon its unqualified copyright defense, Microsoft cites two cases indicating that a copyright holder may limit a licensee's ability to engage in significant and deleterious alterations of a copyrighted work. The relevance of those two cases for the present one is limited, however, both because those cases involved substantial alterations of a copyrighted work, and because in neither case was there any claim that the copyright holder was, in asserting its rights, violating the antitrust laws.

The only license restriction Microsoft seriously defends as necessary to prevent a "substantial alteration" of its copyrighted work is the prohibition on OEMs automatically launching a substitute user interface upon completion of the boot process. We agree that a shell that automatically prevents the Windows desktop from ever being seen by the user is a drastic alteration of Microsoft's copyrighted work, and outweighs the marginal anticompetitive effect of prohibiting the OEMs from substituting a different interface automatically upon completion of the initial boot process. We therefore hold that this particular restriction is not an exclusionary practice that violates § 2 of the Sherman Act.

In a second variation upon its copyright defense, Microsoft argues that the license restrictions merely prevent OEMs from taking actions that would reduce substantially the value of Microsoft's copyrighted work: that is, Microsoft claims each license restriction in question is necessary to prevent OEMs from so altering Windows as to undermine "the principal value of Windows as a stable and consistent platform that supports a broad range of applications and that is familiar to users." Microsoft, however, never substantiates this claim, and, because an OEM's altering the appearance of the desktop or promoting programs in the boot sequence does not affect the code already in the product, the practice does not self-evidently affect either the "stability" or the "consistency" of the platform. * * * Therefore, we conclude Microsoft has not shown that the OEMs' liberality reduces the value of Windows except in the sense that their promotion of rival browsers undermines Microsoft's monopoly—and that is not a permissible justification for the license restrictions.

Apart from copyright, Microsoft raises one other defense of the OEM license agreements: It argues that, despite the restrictions in the OEM license, Netscape is not completely blocked from distributing its product. That claim is insufficient to shield Microsoft from liability for those restrictions because, although Microsoft did not bar its rivals from all means of distribution, it did bar them from the cost-efficient ones.

* * *

2. *Integration of IE and Windows*

* * *

Technologically binding IE to Windows, the District Court found, both prevented OEMs from pre-installing other browsers and deterred consumers from using them. In particular, having the IE software code as an irremovable part of Windows meant that pre-installing a second browser would "increase an OEM's product testing costs," because an OEM must test and train its support staff to answer calls related to every software product preinstalled on the machine; moreover, pre-installing a browser in addition to IE would to many OEMs be "a questionable use of the scarce and valuable space on a PC's hard drive."

* * * [The District Court] findings of fact in support of that conclusion center upon three specific actions Microsoft took to weld IE to Windows: excluding IE from the "Add/Remove Programs" utility; designing Windows so as in certain circumstances to override the user's choice of a default browser other than IE; and commingling code related to browsing and other code in the same files, so that any attempt to delete the files containing IE would, at the same time, cripple the operating system.

a. Anticompetitive effect of integration

As a general rule, courts are properly very skeptical about claims that competition has been harmed by a dominant firm's product design changes. In a competitive market, firms routinely innovate in the hope of appealing to consumers, sometimes in the process making their products incompatible with those of rivals; the imposition of liability when a monopolist does the same thing will inevitably deter a certain amount of innovation. This is all the more true in a market, such as this one, in which the product itself is rapidly changing. Judicial deference to product innovation, however, does not mean that a monopolist's product design decisions are per se lawful.

The District Court first condemned as anticompetitive Microsoft's decision to exclude IE from the "Add/Remove Programs" utility in Windows 98. Microsoft had included IE in the Add/Remove Programs utility in Windows 95, but when it modified Windows 95 to produce Windows 98, it took IE out of the Add/Remove Programs utility. This change reduces the usage share of rival browsers not by making Microsoft's own browser more attractive to consumers but, rather, by discouraging OEMs from distributing rival products. Because Microsoft's conduct, through something other than competition on the merits, has the effect of significantly reducing usage of rivals' products

and hence protecting its own operating system monopoly, it is anticompetitive
* * *.

Second, the District Court found that Microsoft designed Windows 98 "so
that using Navigator on Windows 98 would have unpleasant consequences for
users" by, in some circumstances, overriding the user's choice of a browser
other than IE as his or her default browser. Plaintiffs argue that this override
harms the competitive process by deterring consumers from using a browser
other than IE even though they might prefer to do so, thereby reducing rival
browsers' usage share and, hence, the ability of rival browsers to draw
developer attention away from the APIs exposed by Windows. Microsoft does
not deny, of course, that overriding the user's preference prevents some
people from using other browsers. Because the override reduces rivals' usage
share and protects Microsoft's monopoly, it too is anticompetitive.

Finally, the District Court condemned Microsoft's decision to bind IE to
Windows 98 "by placing code specific to Web browsing in the same files as
code that provided operating system functions." Putting code supplying
browsing functionality into a file with code supplying operating system
functionality "ensure[s] that the deletion of any file containing browsing-
specific routines would also delete vital operating system routines and thus
cripple Windows...." * * * [P]reventing an OEM from removing IE deters it
from installing a second browser because doing so increases the OEM's
product testing and support costs; by contrast, had OEMs been able to remove
IE, they might have chosen to pre-install Navigator alone.

Microsoft denies, as a factual matter, that it commingled browsing and
non-browsing code, and it maintains the District Court's findings to the
contrary are clearly erroneous. * * *

* * *

In view of the contradictory testimony in the record, some of which
supports the District Court's finding that Microsoft commingled browsing and
non-browsing code, we cannot conclude that the finding was clearly erroneous. Accordingly, we reject Microsoft's argument that we should vacate
Finding of Fact 159 as it relates to the commingling of code, and we conclude
that such commingling has an anticompetitive effect * * *.

b. Microsoft's justifications for integration

Microsoft proffers no justification for two of the three challenged actions
that it took in integrating IE into Windows—excluding IE from the Add/Re-
move Programs utility and commingling browser and operating system code.
Although Microsoft does make some general claims regarding the benefits of
integrating the browser and the operating system, it neither specifies nor
substantiates those claims. Nor does it argue that either excluding IE from
the Add/Remove Programs utility or commingling code achieves any inte-
grative benefit. Plaintiffs plainly made out a *prima facie* case of harm to
competition in the operating system market by demonstrating that Microsoft's actions increased its browser usage share and thus protected its operating system monopoly from a middleware threat and, for its part, Microsoft
failed to meet its burden of showing that its conduct serves a purpose other
than protecting its operating system monopoly. Accordingly, we hold that
Microsoft's exclusion of IE from the Add/Remove Programs utility and its

commingling of browser and operating system code constitute exclusionary conduct, in violation of § 2.

As for the other challenged act that Microsoft took in integrating IE into Windows—causing Windows to override the user's choice of a default browser in certain circumstances—Microsoft argues that it has "valid technical reasons." Specifically, Microsoft claims that it was necessary to design Windows to override the user's preferences when he or she invokes one of "a few" out "of the nearly 30 means of accessing the Internet." * * * The plaintiff bears the burden not only of rebutting a proffered justification but also of demonstrating that the anticompetitive effect of the challenged action outweighs it. In the District Court, plaintiffs appear to have done neither, let alone both; in any event, upon appeal, plaintiffs offer no rebuttal whatsoever. Accordingly, Microsoft may not be held liable for this aspect of its product design.

[The court's discussion of the remaining categories of conduct found to be anticompetitive by the district court—agreements with Internet Service Providers, dealings with Internet Access Providers, Internet Content Providers, Independent Software Vendors and Apple Computer, and conduct affecting Sun Microsystems's Java and Intel—were also largely upheld. Eds.]

* * *

C. Causation

As a final parry, Microsoft urges this court to reverse on the monopoly maintenance claim, because plaintiffs never established a causal link between Microsoft's anticompetitive conduct, in particular its foreclosure of Netscape's and Java's distribution channels, and the maintenance of Microsoft's operating system monopoly. This is the flip side of Microsoft's earlier argument that the District Court should have included middleware in the relevant market. According to Microsoft, the District Court cannot simultaneously find that middleware is not a reasonable substitute and that Microsoft's exclusionary conduct contributed to the maintenance of monopoly power in the operating system market. Microsoft claims that the first finding depended on the court's view that middleware does not pose a serious threat to Windows, while the second finding required the court to find that Navigator and Java would have developed into serious enough cross-platform threats to erode the applications barrier to entry. We disagree.

Microsoft points to no case, and we can find none, standing for the proposition that, as to § 2 liability in an equitable enforcement action, plaintiffs must present direct proof that a defendant's continued monopoly power is precisely attributable to its anticompetitive conduct. * * *

* * * To require that § 2 liability turn on a plaintiff's ability or inability to reconstruct the hypothetical marketplace absent a defendant's anticompetitive conduct would only encourage monopolists to take more and earlier anticompetitive action.

We may infer causation where exclusionary conduct is aimed at producers of nascent competitive technologies as well as when it is aimed at producers of established substitutes. Admittedly, in the former case there is added uncertainty, inasmuch as nascent threats are merely *potential* substitutes. But the underlying proof problem is the same—neither plaintiffs nor the court can confidently reconstruct a product's hypothetical technological development in a world absent the defendant's exclusionary conduct. To some degree, "the defendant is made to suffer the uncertain consequences of its own undesirable conduct." 3 AREEDA & HOVENKAMP, ANTITRUST LAW ¶ 651c, at 78.

Given this rather edentulous test for causation, the question in this case is not whether Java or Navigator would actually have developed into viable platform substitutes, but (1) whether as a general matter the exclusion of nascent threats is the type of conduct that is reasonably capable of contributing significantly to a defendant's continued monopoly power and (2) whether Java and Navigator reasonably constituted nascent threats at the time Microsoft engaged in the anticompetitive conduct at issue. As to the first, suffice it to say that it would be inimical to the purpose of the Sherman Act to allow monopolists free reign to squash nascent, albeit unproven, competitors at will—particularly in industries marked by rapid technological advance and frequent paradigm shifts. As to the second, the District Court made ample findings that both Navigator and Java showed potential as middleware platform threats.

Microsoft's concerns over causation have more purchase in connection with the appropriate remedy issue, i.e., whether the court should impose a structural remedy or merely enjoin the offensive conduct at issue. As we point out later in this opinion, divestiture is a remedy that is imposed only with great caution, in part because its long-term efficacy is rarely certain. Absent some measure of confidence that there has been an actual loss to competition that needs to be restored, wisdom counsels against adopting radical structural relief. * * *

* * *

Note how much of the evidence relied upon by the court in resolving the monopoly power issue in *Microsoft*, and how much of the argument it weighed, originated with the testimony of the economic experts reproduced in Chapter 8. Which of the government's approaches to establishing monopoly power proved persuasive to the courts and why? What particular evidence did the court find persuasive? What legal standard did it use? How did the court integrate economic concepts, legal theory and the evidence to reach its conclusions? And finally, how did the court respond to Microsoft's expert's positions on monopoly power? Why were they rejected? Consider Figure 6–5, which follows, and summarizes the government's positions, Microsoft's and the court of appeals'.

In the final portion of the case excerpt, the D.C. Circuit was unequivocal in its conclusion that the antitrust laws should be able to reach conduct that threatens to forestall or completely impede emerging competitive threats. But how developed and concrete must those threats be? Would the court's conclusion have been altered had Navigator and Java never actually made it to market? In other words, how "nascent" and how "imminent" must the competitive threat be before the plaintiff can satisfy the Sherman Act's threshold requirements of substantiality?

More broadly, what are the permissible boundaries of a dominant firm's responses to new competition? Must it sit back and avoid aggressive responses for fear that it will cross the line of legality? Will the cost in terms of diminished competitive vigor outweigh the value of too strict a standard? Given what we have read about Microsoft's conduct, would you agree with Microsoft's position that its hands were being tied unfairly by the court, impeding Microsoft's own ability to innovate without promoting innovation by its rivals?

What, if any, limitations does the court put on its own analysis of causation? Of what significance is the court's suggestion that somewhat attenuated claims of causation may not defeat liability in a case seeking injunctive relief, but could influence the choice of remedy? How would it affect a private action brought seeking treble damages? We will return to that statement and examine its impact on the remedial portion of the decision later in this chapter.

Figure 6–5:
Proving Microsoft's Market Power

Governments	Microsoft	Court of Appeals
• persistent high share of defined relevant market (double inference)	• no market power in any relevant market ("behavioral" approach)	• persistent high share in properly defined relevant market

• barriers to entry
  • sunk costs
  • scale economies
	• leap-frog competition
	  • innovation
	  • intense competition
		• barriers to entry
		  • applications

• switching costs
  • network effects
  • applications
	• no significant barriers to entry
	  • sunk costs
	  • switching costs
	  • network effects
	  • applications
		• conduct constituting the exercise of market power (single inference) *and* actual anticompetitive effects

• conduct constituting the exercise of market power (single inference) *and* actual anticompetitive effects
  • exclusionary
  • collusive
    • prices
    • profit margins
    • equity value
	• not possible to define a relevant market and calculate market shares
	  • middleware
	  • servers
	  • other OSs	

	• profits and margins normal for software	

	• conduct evidencing vibrant competition
	  • investment in R&D
	  • low price for Windows	

Recall that under the traditional framework, a finding of monopoly power would not have constituted a violation of Section 2 of the Sherman Act by itself. In addition, the plaintiff, in this instance the federal government and 19 states, also had to establish that the monopoly power found was either willfully acquired or willfully maintained. "Willfulness," as we have learned, means by some predatory or exclusionary means. The plaintiffs conceded that Microsoft got to be a monopolist through competitive means; their challenge instead focused on its "maintenance" of that power.

How did the court structure its inquiry into Microsoft's conduct? How did it allocate burdens of production and proof? Consider the following Figure, which summarizes the court's approach.

Figure 6–6:

***Microsoft's* Structured Analysis**

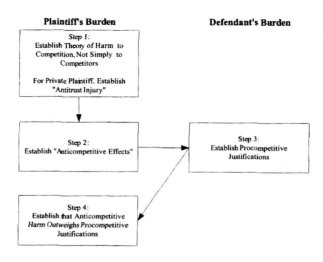

Would the same structure apply whether the case were one under Section 1 or Section 2 of the Sherman Act? How does the court's approach compare to the one we considered at the end of Chapter 2 under the federal government's Collaboration Guidelines? How does it compare to the five-step analysis of the Horizontal Merger Guidelines? To Justice Breyer's suggested approach in his dissent in *California Dental* (Casebook, Chapter 2, *supra*)? To the implicit framework used by the Supreme Court in *Aspen Skiing*?

How distinct were the two traditional elements of power and conduct in the cases we have read? To illustrate the point, consider the excerpts from *Aspen Skiing* and especially *Microsoft*. How distinct was the court's analysis of power and conduct in each case? What role did evidence of actual effects play in assessing both power and conduct? In *Microsoft*, did the court rely upon distinct evidence in each, or did the relevant evidence overlap? If the latter, what could explain such an "overlap"? Are there common concepts at work that cut across and possibly unify the two traditional legal factors under Section 2?

What definition of "exclusionary" did the court of appeals use? How did the inquiry into monopoly power also involve evaluation of conduct, and vice versa? Why is that so? What was the relevance of Microsoft's actual conduct to the monopoly power inquiry? What does it suggest about the continued distinctiveness of the elements of a Section 1 and Section 2 Sherman Act violation when evidence of actual anticompetitive effects is presented?

Consider finally whether there is a downside to "structured" analysis. Does it really reflect an "improvement" over previous, more open ended approaches? If so, how so? Will it tend to be too rigid? Does it generally favor plaintiffs or defendants, which might perpetuate fears of over and under-deterrence and consequent costs of error, *i.e.*, incorrect judgments? Does it really clarify the relevant factors and the relative burdens of proof? Will it reliably include all of the useful evidence, or possibly exclude information that could affect the outcome of particular cases? Does it provide clear guidance to business firms, and if it does not, what costs are associated with complying with antitrust rules that do not?

In the wake of *Aspen Skiing* and *Kodak*, commentators debated whether they could be read to infer harm to competition from the absence of a legitimate business justification for the monopolist's conduct, in the absence affirmative evidence of anticompetitive effects. *Compare* Jonathan B. Baker, *Promoting Innovation Competition Through the* Aspen/Kodak *Rule*, 7 GEO. MASON. L. REV. 495 (1999) (arguing that the cases establish a truncated rule) *with* Timothy J. Muris, *The FTC and the Law of Monopolization*, 67 ANTITRUST L. J. 693 (2000) (arguing that they do not). Does *Microsoft* support either of these two views?

By the time the government actions against Microsoft were initiated in May, 1998 in the United States, the European Commission had begun its own investigation of Microsoft's anticompetitive conduct in Europe. In Section F of this Chapter we will consider the court of appeals' treatment of remedies in the U.S. case. In the Note that follows, we explore the similarities and differences in the conduct challenged and the remedies ordered in the U.S. and E.U. cases against Microsoft.

Note on Microsoft Prosecution in the European Union

In December of 1998, after the U.S. antitrust case against Microsoft was well under-way, Sun Microsystems filed a complaint with the Directorate General for Competition ("DG–Comp") of the European Commission ("EC") in Brussels alleging that Microsoft was refusing to supply it with interoperability information necessary to permit its work group server operating system software to interoperate with Microsoft's dominant PC operating system.* Under EC procedures, receipt of the complaint triggered an initial investigation by the EC. The following February, the Commission expanded the scope of that investigation to include allegations that Microsoft had tied its new media player, Windows Media Player, to Windows, much in the way that the U.S. case was considering allegations that it had tied its Internet browser, Internet Explorer ("IE"), to Windows.

As a consequence of its investigation, which continued for several years, the EC ultimately presented Microsoft with three "Statements of Objections,"** the

---

* This chronology of events is adapted from a more comprehensive detailing of the development of the EC's investigation and prosecution of Microsoft on its website. *See* http://ec.europa.eu/comm/competition/antitrust/cases/microsoft/investigation.html.

rough equivalent in the U.S. of an administrative complaint. Collectively, the three statements alleged that Microsoft had abused its dominant position in the European Union ("E.U.") by failing to supply interoperability information to Sun and others and by tying its Windows Media Player to Windows, which impaired competition for media players. Under EC procedures, Microsoft then had a period of time to respond.

Ultimately rejecting those responses as inadequate, on March 24, 2004 the Commission issued its decision, concluding that Microsoft had in fact violated Article 82. As a remedy, the EC ordered Microsoft: (1) to produce an un-bundled version of Windows that did not include Windows Media Player, in order to permit OEMs and consumers to substitute their own choice of media player, such as those from RealNetworks and Apple; (2) to disclose information sufficient to permit rival producers of work group server operating systems to produce software that would more easily interoperate with Windows client software; and (3) requiring it to pay a record fine of € 497 million. *See* Commission Decision of 24.03.2004, relating to a proceeding under Article 82 of the E.U. Treaty (Case Comp/C–3/37.792 Microsoft), *available at* http://ec.europa.eu/comm/competition/ antitrust/cases/decisions/37792/en.pdf.

The case was appealed to the European Court of First Instance ("CFI") and, in a comprehensive decision that was widely perceived as a very significant victory for the EC, the CFI affirmed the EC's decision in all substantive respects on September 17, 2007. *See* Case T–201/04, *Microsoft v Commission*, Judgment of the Court of First Instance (Grand Chamber) of 17 September 2007, O.J. 2007 C269/45.

The EC's case against Microsoft involved some of the same facts and theories that had been raised in the U.S. Both cases proceeded from the critical assumption that Microsoft had obtained and was seeking to abuse monopoly power in the market for Intel-compatible PC operating systems. Both the U.S. enforcement authorities and courts, as well as the EC and the CFI, readily concluded that Microsoft had durable monopoly power and that it was insulated from competition by significant barriers to entry. Both also readily concluded that Microsoft had undertaken conduct to fortify its monopoly from still developing competitive threats (although they were more fully formed in Europe) and that it lacked any legitimate justification for its actions.

But there were also differences, some that were important. Whereas the U.S.'s case challenged a wide range of Microsoft's conduct as both tying and monopolization, the EC's case was relatively more narrowly drawn. Also, whereas the U.S. case focused on Microsoft's tying of its IE Internet browser to Windows, the EC's case focused on the tying of Windows Media Player to Windows.*** Uniquely, the EC's case challenged Microsoft's refusal to provide information necessary to facilitate interoperability between Windows and work group servers running non-Microsoft operating systems.

More fundamentally, the core of the U.S. case (as it emerged from the court of appeals) proceeded from the theory that Microsoft's conduct, even when directed

---

** These statements were issued on August 1, 2000, August 30, 2001, and August 6, 2003. *Id.*

*** As we shall see later in this Chapter and in Chapter 7, it should be noted that in the U.S. the D.C. Circuit reversed the district court's finding of liability based on Microsoft's tying of IE to Windows, because in the court's view the district court had improperly applied a per se standard. Because the case was settled after remand, the tying claims were never re-tried.

outside of the market for Intel-compatible PC operating systems ("PC OS"), had the effect of maintaining Microsoft's PC OS monopoly and hence constituted unlawful "monopoly maintenance" under Section 2. The court of appeals reversed the district court's judgment that Microsoft had attempted to monopolize a distinct Internet browser "market" because it failed to prove two requirements for a successful claim of attempt to monopolize: (1) the existence of a distinct relevant market for Internet browsers; and (2) that the "market" is protected from competition by substantial entry barriers. *Microsoft Corp.*, 253 F.3d at 80–84. In contrast, the EC's case, based on the "abuse of dominance" provisions in Article 82, was focused more on Microsoft's use of its monopoly power in PC OS to gain a competitive advantage in the markets for work group server operating systems and media players. In the U.S., such claims must satisfy the seemingly more stringent requirements of the offense of attempted monopolization.

Perhaps the most substantial point of difference between the two cases concerned remedy. As we shall learn later in this Chapter, following the remand of the D.C. Circuit's decision that we just reviewed, the U.S. case settled and a consent decree was entered. In contrast to the EC's case, Microsoft was not required to unbundle its Internet browser from Windows. Other, less invasive steps were agreed to that in theory could facilitate greater competition for browsers. Also, no major fines were imposed on Microsoft, although U.S. enforcement agencies lack the same authority that the EC has to impose them. The variation of approach to remedies—the more restrained approach of the U.S. Department of Justice as compared to the seemingly more interventionist approach of the EC—led to vocal criticism from the head of the Antitrust Division.

We will more fully explore the law and economics of tying in Chapter 7, including further consideration of the *Microsoft* cases in the U.S. and the E.U. We will also examine the issues posed by refusals to share information, such as Microsoft's interoperability information, later in this Chapter.

———

2. PREDATORY PRICING

Traditionally, antitrust doctrine provided only murky guidance to dominant firms on pricing practices such as how much they could increase output and how low they could set their prices in response to entry or expansion by a competitor. Antitrust law provides two mechanisms for challenging such "predatory pricing:" Section 2 of the Sherman Act and Section 2(a) of the Clayton Act as amended by the Robinson–Patman Act, which forbids certain forms of price discrimination. In the 1950s and 1960s, cases interpreting these provisions often accepted the idea that a dominant firm could use its "deep pockets" to finance below-cost sales to drive competitors from the market. A number of decisions displayed solicitude for the smaller, vanquished target of the dominant firm's pricing strategy.

Utah Pie Co. v. Continental Baking Co., 386 U.S. 685, 87 S.Ct. 1326 (1967) reflects this traditional view. In *Utah Pie* the Supreme Court used Section 2(a) of the Robinson–Patman Act to condemn the pricing conduct of Continental Baking, a national supplier of baked goods, in entering the Salt Lake City market for frozen dessert pies. The plaintiff, Utah Pie, was a local firm that held two-thirds of the Salt Lake City frozen pie market before Continental appeared on the scene. Continental priced its pies in Salt Lake

City much lower than the company charged in nearby California and in other parts of the country. Utah Pie's share fell to under 50 percent of the market, and it sued Continental for predatory pricing.

The Supreme Court ruled that Utah Pie had produced enough evidence to sustain a jury verdict of unlawful price discrimination. The Court noted that, to support a finding of probable competitive injury, Utah Pie had shown that Continental: (1) charged prices "less than its direct cost plus an allocation for overhead," 386 U.S. at 698, which (2) created a "drastically declining price structure;" and (3) that it did so with anticompetitive intent, which was evident from its "persistent sales below cost and radical price cuts themselves discriminatory." *Id.* at 702 & n.14. The Court's reasoning suggested that a firm might incur liability for setting its prices below its average total costs. Critics called *Utah Pie* a formula for shielding local firms (including those with high market shares) from challenge by external suppliers.

Partly in response to *Utah Pie*, the 1970s and 1980s featured extensive academic literature about the appropriate antitrust standard for predatory pricing. The academic commentary inspired by this literature continues to evolve today. Four schools of thought have emerged:

- The *cost-based school* proposes that courts focus on the relationship between the dominant firm's costs and prices. The most influential cost-based approach, offered by Phillip Areeda and Donald Turner, recommended that courts adopt presumptions that pricing below a firm's average variable costs is illegal and that pricing at or above average variable cost is lawful. *See* Phillip A. Areeda & Donald F. Turner, *Predatory Pricing and Related Practices Under Section 2 of the Sherman Act*, 88 HARV. L. REV. 697 (1975).

- The *recoupment school* suggests that courts first ask whether the market's structural features, such as entry barriers, would permit the dominant incumbent to charge supra-competitive prices after it subdues its rivals. Only if such conditions exist would a court analyze the relationship between the dominant firm's prices and costs. *See, e.g.*, Paul L. Joskow & Alvin K. Klevorick, *A Framework for Analyzing Predatory Pricing*, 89 YALE L.J. 213 (1979).

- The *per se lawful school* urges courts to find no Section 2 liability based on predatory pricing. *See, e.g.*, ROBERT H. BORK, THE ANTITRUST PARADOX 154 (1978). Per se lawful advocates emphasize the rarity of the phenomenon due to the ability of entrants to neutralize the incumbent's predatory pricing tactics and warn that aggressive policing of price cuts would harm consumers by discouraging dominant firms from lowering prices. They also caution that courts too often will condemn benign behavior by mistake (false positives), and are willing to sacrifice the occasional meritorious accusation of predatory pricing for the sake of avoiding policies that would chill desirable price-cutting.

- The *game theoretic school* proposes that courts use a full, fact-specific analysis of the incumbent's response to entry (including evidence of its intent) and market conditions. Game theorists argue that predatory pricing could be a rational strategy and warn that under some circumstances incumbents can exclude equally efficient rivals by setting prices at or above average variable cost. *See, e.g.,* Jean Tirole, The Theory of Industrial Organization 361–88 (1988).

From the mid–1970s through the early 1990s, courts generally accepted the idea that price-cost tests should anchor predatory pricing analysis. Most tribunals in this period treated pricing at or above average variable cost as creating a rebuttable presumption of legality. Many cases endorsed the recoupment school's view that plaintiffs be required to prove that the defendant was likely to recoup its investment in below-cost pricing—for example, by showing that entry into the market was difficult and new challengers would not arise to face the incumbent. No court embraced the per se lawful approach, but the perspective of the per se lawful proponents was very influential and persuade courts to impose tougher evidentiary burdens on predatory pricing plaintiffs. *See, e.g., Matsushita Elec. Indus. Co. v. Zenith Radio Corp.,* 475 U.S. 574, 106 S.Ct. 1348 (1986)(Casebook, Chapter 3, *supra*).

The Supreme Court reformulated its predatory pricing test significantly in 1993. As in *Utah Pie,* the context again was a Robinson–Patman Act primary line price discrimination dispute—this time a complaint pressed by Liggett & Myers (later acquired by Brooke Group) against Brown & Williamson (B & W). Liggett had tried to halt the decline of its cigarette business by offering cheap generic cigarettes in competition with popular brands. Liggett alleged that B & W unlawfully used below-cost sales in the form of rebates to cigarette wholesalers to punish Liggett and force it to raise the price it charged for generics. Liggett's sales of generic cigarettes had eroded B & W's branded sales. B & W had a market share of only 12 percent, but Liggett argued that every dollar B & W spent on below-cost pricing was rewarded with more than a dollar gained by stopping the loss of branded cigarette sales. A jury awarded Liggett nearly $149 million in damages. The trial court set aside the verdict, the Fourth Circuit affirmed, and the Supreme Court agreed that no reasonable jury could have concluded that B & W's conduct was illegal.

BROOKE GROUP LTD. v. BROWN & WILLIAMSON TOBACCO CORP.

United States Supreme Court, 1993.
509 U.S. 209, 113 S.Ct. 2578, 125 L.Ed.2d 168.

Mr. Justice KENNEDY delivered the opinion of the Court:

* * *

I.

In 1980, Liggett pioneered the development of the economy segment of the national cigarette market by introducing a line of "black and white" generic cigarettes. The economy segment of the market, sometimes called the generic segment, is characterized by its bargain prices and comprises a variety of different products: black and whites, which are true generics sold in plain white packages with simple black lettering describing their contents; private label generics, which carry the trade dress of a specific purchaser, usually a retail chain; branded generics, which carry a brand name but which, like black and whites and private label generics, are sold at a deep discount and with little or no advertising; and "Value–25s," packages of 25 cigarettes that are sold to the consumer some 12.5% below the cost of a normal 20–cigarette pack. By 1984, when Brown & Williamson entered the generic segment and set in motion the series of events giving rise to this suit, Liggett's black and whites represented 97% of the generic segment, which in turn accounted for a little more than 4% of domestic cigarette sales. Prior to Liggett's introduction of black and whites in 1980, sales of generic cigarettes amounted to less than 1% of the domestic cigarette market.

* * * Cigarette manufacturing has long been one of America's most concentrated industries, and for decades, production has been dominated by six firms: R.J. Reynolds, Philip Morris, American Brands, Lorillard, and the two litigants involved here, Liggett and Brown & Williamson. R.J. Reynolds and Philip Morris, the two industry leaders, enjoyed respective market shares of about 28% and 40% at the time of trial. Brown & Williamson ran a distant third, its market share never exceeding 12% at any time relevant to this dispute. Liggett's share of the market was even less, from a low of just over 2% in 1980 to a high of just over 5% in 1984.

The cigarette industry also has long been one of America's most profitable, in part because for many years there was no significant price competition among the rival firms. List prices for cigarettes increased in lock-step, twice a year, for a number of years, irrespective of the rate of inflation, changes in the costs of production, or shifts in consumer demand. Substantial evidence suggests that in recent decades, the industry reaped the benefits of prices above a competitive level, though not through unlawful conduct of the type that once characterized the industry.

By 1980, however, broad market trends were working against the industry. Overall demand for cigarettes in the United States was declining, and no immediate prospect of recovery existed. As industry volume shrank, all firms developed substantial excess capacity. This decline in demand, coupled with the effects of nonprice competition, had a severe negative impact on Liggett. Once a major force in the industry, with market shares in excess of 20%, Liggett's market share had declined by 1980 to a little over 2%. With this meager share of the market, Liggett was on the verge of going out of business.

* * *

II.

Liggett contends that Brown & Williamson's discriminatory volume rebates to wholesalers threatened substantial competitive injury by furthering a predatory pricing scheme designed to purge competition from the economy segment of the cigarette market. This type of injury, which harms direct competitors of the discriminating seller, is known as primary-line injury. We last addressed primary-line injury over 25 years ago, in *Utah Pie Co. v. Continental Baking* Co., 386 U.S. 685, 87 S.Ct. 1326 (1967). * * *

Utah Pie has often been interpreted to permit liability for primary-line price discrimination on a mere showing that the defendant intended to harm competition or produced a declining price structure. The case has been criticized on the grounds that such low standards of competitive injury are at odds with the antitrust laws' traditional concern for consumer welfare and price competition. We do not regard the *Utah Pie* case itself as having the full significance attributed to it by its detractors. *Utah Pie* was an early judicial inquiry in this area and did not purport to set forth explicit, general standards for establishing a violation of the Robinson–Patman Act. As the law has been explored since *Utah Pie*, it has become evident that primary-line competitive injury under the Robinson–Patman Act is of the same general character as the injury inflicted by predatory pricing schemes actionable under § 2 of the Sherman Act. * * * There are, to be sure, differences between the two statutes. For example, we interpret § 2 of the Sherman Act to condemn predatory pricing when it poses "a dangerous probability of actual monopolization," whereas the Robinson–Patman Act requires only that there be "a reasonable possibility" of substantial injury to competition before its protections are triggered. But whatever additional flexibility the Robinson–Patman Act standard may imply, the essence of the claim under either statute is the same: A business rival has priced its products in an unfair manner with an object to eliminate or retard competition and thereby gain and exercise control over prices in the relevant market.

Accordingly, whether the claim alleges predatory pricing under § 2 of the Sherman Act or primary-line price discrimination under the Robinson–Patman Act, two prerequisites to recovery remain the same. First, a plaintiff seeking to establish competitive injury resulting from a rival's low prices must prove that the prices complained of are below an appropriate measure of its rival's costs.[1] *See, e.g., Cargill, Inc. v. Monfort of Colorado, Inc.*, 479 U.S. 104, 117, 107 S.Ct. 484, 493 (1986); *Matsushita Elec. Industrial Co. v. Zenith Radio Corp.*, 475 U.S. 574, 585, n. 8, 106 S.Ct. 1348, 1355 (1986) * * *. Although *Cargill* and *Matsushita* reserved as a formal matter the question " 'whether recovery should ever be available ... when the pricing in question is above some measure of incremental cost,' " the reasoning in both opinions suggests that only below-cost prices should suffice, and we have rejected elsewhere the notion that above-cost prices that are below general market levels or the costs of a firm's competitors inflict injury to competition cognizable under the antitrust laws. "Low prices benefit consumers regardless of how those prices are set, and so long as they are above predatory levels, they do not threaten competition.... We have adhered to this principle regardless of the type of antitrust claim involved." As a general rule, the exclusionary effect of prices above a relevant measure of cost either reflects the lower cost structure of the alleged predator, and so represents competition on the merits, or is beyond the practical ability of a judicial tribunal to control without courting intolerable risks of chilling legitimate price-cutting. * * * "To hold that the antitrust laws protect competitors from the loss of profits due to such price competition would, in effect, render illegal any decision by a firm to cut prices in order to increase market share. The antitrust laws require no such perverse result."

---

1. Because the parties in this case agree that the relevant measure of cost is average variable cost, however, we again decline to resolve the conflict among the lower courts over the appropriate measure of cost. *See Car-* *gill, Inc. v. Monfort of Colorado, Inc.*, 479 U.S. 104, 117–118, n. 12, 107 S.Ct. 484, 493, n. 12 (1986); *Matsushita Elec. Industrial Co. v. Zenith Radio Corp.*, 475 U.S. 574, 585, n. 8, 106 S.Ct. 1348, 1355, n. 8 (1986).

Even in an oligopolistic market, when a firm drops its prices to a competitive level to demonstrate to a maverick the unprofitability of straying from the group, it would be illogical to condemn the price cut: The antitrust laws then would be an obstacle to the chain of events most conducive to a breakdown of oligopoly pricing and the onset of competition. Even if the ultimate effect of the cut is to induce or reestablish supracompetitive pricing, discouraging a price cut and forcing firms to maintain supracompetitive prices, thus depriving consumers of the benefits of lower prices in the interim, does not constitute sound antitrust policy.

The second prerequisite to holding a competitor liable under the antitrust laws for charging low prices is a demonstration that the competitor had a reasonable prospect, or, under § 2 of the Sherman Act, a dangerous probability, of recouping its investment in below-cost prices. *See Matsushita*, 475 U.S., at 589, 106 S.Ct., at 1357; *Cargill*, 479 U.S., at 119, n. 15, 107 S.Ct., at 494, n. 15. "For the investment to be rational, the [predator] must have a reasonable expectation of recovering, in the form of later monopoly profits, more than the losses suffered." *Matsushita*, 475 U.S., at 588–589, 106 S.Ct., at 1356–1357. Recoupment is the ultimate object of an unlawful predatory pricing scheme; it is the means by which a predator profits from predation. Without it, predatory pricing produces lower aggregate prices in the market, and consumer welfare is enhanced. Although unsuccessful predatory pricing may encourage some inefficient substitution toward the product being sold at less than its cost, unsuccessful predation is in general a boon to consumers.

That below-cost pricing may impose painful losses on its target is of no moment to the antitrust laws if competition is not injured: It is axiomatic that the antitrust laws were passed for "the protection of competition, not competitors." *Brown Shoe Co. v. United States*, 370 U.S. 294, 320, 82 S.Ct. 1502, 1521 (1962). * * * Even an act of pure malice by one business competitor against another does not, without more, state a claim under the federal antitrust laws; those laws do not create a federal law of unfair competition or "purport to afford remedies for all torts committed by or against persons engaged in interstate commerce."

For recoupment to occur, below-cost pricing must be capable, as a threshold matter, of producing the intended effects on the firm's rivals, whether driving them from the market, or, as was alleged to be the goal here, causing them to raise their prices to supracompetitive levels within a disciplined oligopoly. This requires an understanding of the extent and duration of the alleged predation, the relative financial strength of the predator and its intended victim, and their respective incentives and will. * * * The inquiry is whether, given the aggregate losses caused by the below-cost pricing, the intended target would likely succumb.

If circumstances indicate that below-cost pricing could likely produce its intended effect on the target, there is still the further question whether it would likely injure competition in the relevant market. The plaintiff must demonstrate that there is a likelihood that the predatory scheme alleged would cause a rise in prices above a competitive level that would be sufficient to compensate for the amounts expended on the predation, including the time value of the money invested in it. As we have observed on a prior occasion, "[i]n order to recoup their losses, [predators] must obtain enough market power to set higher than competitive prices, and then must sustain those prices long enough to earn in excess profits what they earlier gave up in below-cost prices." *Matsushita*, 475 U.S., at 590–591, 106 S.Ct., at 1358.

Evidence of below-cost pricing is not alone sufficient to permit an inference of probable recoupment and injury to competition. Determining whether recoupment of predatory losses is likely requires an estimate of the cost of the alleged predation and a close analysis of both the scheme alleged by the plaintiff and the structure and conditions of the relevant market. If market circumstances or deficiencies in proof would bar a reasonable jury from finding that the scheme alleged would likely result in sustained supracompetitive pricing, the plaintiff's case has failed. In certain situations—for example, where the market is highly diffuse and competitive, or where new entry is easy, or the defendant lacks adequate excess capacity to absorb the market shares of his rivals and cannot quickly create or purchase new capacity— summary disposition of the case is appropriate.

These prerequisites to recovery are not easy to establish, but they are not artificial obstacles to recovery; rather, they are essential components of real market injury. As we have said in the Sherman Act context, "predatory pricing schemes are rarely tried, and even more rarely successful," *Matsushita*, 475 U.S., at 589, 106 S.Ct., at 1357, and the costs of an erroneous finding of liability are high. "[T]he mechanism by which a firm engages in predatory pricing—lowering prices—is the same mechanism by which a firm stimulates competition; because 'cutting prices in order to increase business often is the very essence of competition . . . [;] mistaken inferences . . . are especially costly, because they chill the very conduct the antitrust laws are designed to protect.' " *Cargill*, 479 U.S., at 122, n. 17, 107 S.Ct., at 495, n. 17 (quoting Matsushita, 475 U.S., at 594, 106 S.Ct., at 1360). It would be ironic indeed if the standards for predatory pricing liability were so low that antitrust suits themselves became a tool for keeping prices high.

Liggett does not allege that Brown & Williamson sought to drive it from the market but that Brown & Williamson sought to preserve supracompetitive profits on branded cigarettes by pressuring Liggett to raise its generic cigarette prices through a process of tacit collusion with the other cigarette companies. Tacit collusion, sometimes called oligopolistic price coordination or conscious parallelism, describes the process, not in itself unlawful, by which firms in a concentrated market might in effect share monopoly power, setting their prices at a profit-maximizing, supracompetitive level by recognizing their shared economic interests and their interdependence with respect to price and output decisions.

In *Matsushita*, we remarked upon the general implausibility of predatory pricing. *Matsushita* observed that such schemes are even more improbable when they require coordinated action among several firms. *Matsushita* involved an allegation of an express conspiracy to engage in predatory pricing. The Court noted that in addition to the usual difficulties that face a single firm attempting to recoup predatory losses, other problems render a conspiracy "incalculably more difficult to execute." In order to succeed, the conspirators must agree on how to allocate present losses and future gains among the firms involved, and each firm must resist powerful incentives to cheat on whatever agreement is reached.

However unlikely predatory pricing by multiple firms may be when they conspire, it is even less likely when, as here, there is no express coordination. Firms that seek to recoup predatory losses through the conscious parallelism of oligopoly must rely on uncertain and ambiguous signals to achieve concerted action. The signals are subject to misinterpretation and are a blunt and imprecise means of ensuring smooth cooperation, especially in the context of changing or unprecedented market circumstances. This anticompetitive minuet is most difficult to compose and to perform, even for a disciplined oligopoly.

From one standpoint, recoupment through oligopolistic price coordination could be thought more feasible than recoupment through monopoly: In the oligopoly setting, the victim itself has an economic incentive to acquiesce in the scheme. If forced to choose between cutting prices and sustaining losses, maintaining prices and losing market share, or raising prices and enjoying a share of supracompetitive profits, a firm may yield to the last alternative. Yet on the whole, tacit cooperation among oligopolists must be considered the least likely means of recouping predatory losses. In addition to the difficulty of achieving effective tacit coordination and the high likelihood that any attempt to discipline will produce an outbreak of competition, the predator's present losses in a case like this fall on it alone, while the later supracompetitive profits must be shared with every other oligopolist in proportion to its market share, including the intended victim. In this case, for example, Brown & Williamson, with its 11–12% share of the cigarette market, would have had to generate around $9 in supracompetitive profits for each $1 invested in predation; the remaining $8 would belong to its competitors, who had taken no risk.

* * *

To the extent that the Court of Appeals may have held that the interdependent pricing of an oligopoly may never provide a means for achieving recoupment and so may not form the basis of a primary-line injury claim, we disagree. A predatory pricing scheme designed to preserve or create a stable oligopoly, if successful, can injure consumers in the same way, and to the same extent, as one designed to bring about a monopoly. However unlikely that possibility may be as a general matter, when the realities of the market and the record facts indicate that it has occurred and was likely to have succeeded, theory will not stand in the way of liability. *See Eastman Kodak Co. v. Image Technical Services, Inc.,* 504 U.S. 451, 466, 467, 112 S.Ct. 2072 (1992).

* * *

III.

* * *

Liggett's theory of competitive injury through oligopolistic price coordination depends upon a complex chain of cause and effect: Brown & Williamson would enter the generic segment with list prices matching Liggett's but with massive, discriminatory volume rebates directed at Liggett's biggest wholesalers; as a result, the net price of Brown & Williamson's generics would be below its costs; Liggett would suffer losses trying to defend its market share and wholesale customer base by matching Brown & Williamson's rebates; to avoid further losses, Liggett would raise its list prices on generics or acquiesce in price leadership by Brown & Williamson; higher list prices to consumers would shrink the percentage gap in retail price between generic and branded cigarettes; and this narrowing of the gap would make generics less appealing to the consumer, thus slowing the growth of the economy segment and reducing cannibalization of branded sales and their associated supracompetitive profits.

Although Brown & Williamson's entry into the generic segment could be regarded as procompetitive in intent as well as effect, the record contains sufficient evidence from which a reasonable jury could conclude that Brown & Williamson envisioned or intended this anticompetitive course of events. * * * There is also sufficient evidence in the record from which a reasonable jury could conclude that for a period of approximately 18 months, Brown & Williamson's prices on its generic cigarettes were below its costs and that this below-cost pricing imposed losses on Liggett that Liggett was unwilling to sustain, given its corporate parent's effort to locate a buyer for the company. Liggett has failed to demonstrate competitive injury as a matter of law, however, because its proof is flawed in a critical respect: The evidence is inadequate to show that in pursuing this scheme, Brown & Williamson had a reasonable prospect of recovering its losses from below-cost pricing through slowing the growth of generics. * * *

No inference of recoupment is sustainable on this record, because no evidence suggests that Brown & Williamson—whatever its intent in introducing black and whites may have been—was likely to obtain the power to raise the prices for generic cigarettes above a competitive level. Recoupment through supracompetitive pricing in the economy segment of the cigarette market is an indispensable aspect of Liggett's own proffered theory, because a slowing of growth in the economy segment, even if it results from an increase in generic prices, is not itself anticompetitive. Only if those higher prices are a product of nonmarket forces has competition suffered. If prices rise in response to an excess of demand over supply, or segment growth slows as patterns of consumer preference become stable, the market is functioning in a competitive manner. Consumers are not injured from the perspective of the antitrust laws by the price increases; they are in fact causing them. Thus, the linchpin of the predatory scheme alleged by Liggett is Brown & Williamson's ability, with the other oligopolists, to raise prices above a competitive level in the generic segment of the market. Because relying on tacit coordination among oligopolists as a means of recouping losses from predatory pricing is "highly speculative," competent evidence is necessary to allow a reasonable inference that it poses an authentic threat to competition. The evidence in this case is insufficient to demonstrate the danger of Brown & Williamson's alleged scheme.

Based on Liggett's theory of the case and the record it created, there are two means by which one might infer that Brown & Williamson had a reasonable prospect of producing sustained supracompetitive pricing in the generic segment adequate to recoup its predatory losses: first, if generic output or price information indicates that oligopolistic price coordination in fact produced supracompetitive prices in the generic segment; or second, if evidence about the market and Brown & Williamson's conduct indicate that the alleged scheme was likely to have brought about tacit coordination and oligopoly pricing in the generic segment, even if it did not actually do so.

In this case, the price and output data do not support a reasonable inference that Brown & Williamson and the other cigarette companies elevated prices above a competitive level for generic cigarettes. Supracompetitive pricing entails a restriction in output. In the present setting, in which output expanded at a rapid rate following Brown & Williamson's alleged predation, output in the generic segment can only have been restricted in the sense that it expanded at a slower rate than it would have absent Brown & Williamson's intervention. Such a counterfactual proposition is difficult to prove in the best of circumstances; here, the record evidence does not permit a reasonable inference that output would have been greater without Brown & Williamson's entry into the generic segment.

Following Brown & Williamson's entry, the rate at which generic cigarettes were capturing market share did not slow; indeed, the average rate of growth doubled. During the four years from 1980 to 1984 in which Liggett was alone in the generic segment, the segment gained market share at an average rate of 1% of the overall market per year, from 0.4% in 1980 to slightly more than 4% of the cigarette market in 1984. In the next five years, following the alleged predation, the generic segment expanded from 4% to more than 15% of the domestic cigarette market, or greater than 2% per year.

While this evidence tends to show that Brown & Williamson's participation in the economy segment did not restrict output, it is not dispositive. One could speculate, for example, that the rate of segment growth would have tripled, instead of doubled, without Brown & Williamson's alleged predation. But there is no concrete evidence of this. Indeed, the only industry projection in the record estimating what the segment's growth would have been without Brown & Williamson's entry supports the opposite inference. In 1984, Brown & Williamson forecast in an important planning document that the economy segment would account for 10% of the total cigarette market by 1988 if it did not enter the segment. In fact, in 1988, after what Liggett alleges was a sustained and dangerous anticompetitive campaign by Brown & Williamson, the generic segment accounted for over 12% of the total market. Thus the segment's output expanded more robustly than Brown & Williamson had estimated it would had Brown & Williamson never entered.

Brown & Williamson did note in 1985, a year after introducing its black and whites, that its presence within the generic segment "appears to have resulted in ... a slowing in the segment's growth rate." * * * But this statement was made in early 1985, when Liggett itself contends the below-cost pricing was still in effect and before any anticompetitive contraction in output is alleged to have occurred. Whatever it may mean, this statement has little value in evaluating the competitive implications of Brown & Williamson's later conduct, which was alleged to provide the basis for recouping predatory losses.

In arguing that Brown & Williamson was able to exert market power and raise generic prices above a competitive level in the generic category through tacit price coordination with the other cigarette manufacturers, Liggett places its principal reliance on direct evidence of price behavior. This evidence demonstrates that the list prices on all cigarettes, generic and branded alike, rose to a significant degree during the late 1980's. From 1986 to 1989, list prices on both generic and branded cigarettes increased twice a year by similar amounts. Liggett's economic expert testified that these price increases outpaced increases in costs, taxes, and promotional expenditures. The list prices of generics, moreover, rose at a faster rate than the prices of branded cigarettes, thus narrowing the list price differential between branded and generic products. Liggett argues that this would permit a reasonable jury to find that Brown & Williamson succeeded in bringing about oligopolistic price coordination and supracompetitive prices in the generic category sufficient to slow its growth, thereby preserving supracompetitive branded profits and recouping its predatory losses.

A reasonable jury, however, could not have drawn the inferences Liggett proposes. All of Liggett's data are based upon the list prices of various categories of cigarettes. Yet the jury had before it undisputed evidence that during the period in question, list prices were not the actual prices paid by consumers. As the market became unsettled in the mid–1980's, the cigarette companies invested substantial sums in promotional schemes, including coupons, stickers, and giveaways, that reduced the actual cost of cigarettes to consumers below list prices. This promotional activity accelerated as the decade progressed. Many wholesalers also passed portions of their volume rebates on to the consumer, which had the effect of further undermining the significance of the retail list prices. Especially in an oligopoly setting, in which price competition is most likely to take place through less observable and less regulable means than list prices, it would be unreasonable to draw conclusions about the existence of tacit coordination or supracompetitive pricing from data that reflect only list prices.

Even on its own terms, the list price data relied upon by Liggett to demonstrate a narrowing of the price differential between generic and full-priced branded cigarettes could not support the conclusion that supracompetitive pricing had been introduced into the generic segment. Liggett's gap data ignore the effect of "subgeneric" cigarettes, which were priced at discounts of 50% or more from the list prices of normal branded cigarettes. Liggett itself, while supposedly under the sway of oligopoly power, pioneered this development in 1988 with the introduction of its "Pyramid" brand. * * * By the time of trial, five of the six major manufacturers offered a cigarette in this category at a discount from the full list price of at least 50%. Thus, the price difference between the highest priced branded cigarette and the lowest price cigarettes in the economy segment, instead of narrowing over the course of the period of alleged predation as Liggett would argue, grew to a substantial extent. * * *

It may be that a reasonable jury could conclude that the cumulative discounts attributable to subgenerics and the various consumer promotions did not cancel out the full effect of the increases in list prices, and that actual prices to the consumer did indeed rise, but rising prices do not themselves permit an inference of a collusive market dynamic. Even in a concentrated market, the occurrence of a price increase does not in itself permit a rational inference of conscious parallelism or supracompetitive pricing. Where, as here, output is expanding at the same time prices are increasing, rising prices are equally consistent with growing product demand. Under these conditions, a jury may not infer competitive injury from price and output data absent some evidence that tends to prove that output was restricted or prices were above a competitive level.

Quite apart from the absence of any evidence of that sort, an inference of supracompetitive pricing would be particularly anomalous in this case, as the very party alleged to have been coerced into pricing through oligopolistic coordination denied that such coordination existed: Liggett's own officers and directors consistently denied that they or other firms in the industry priced their cigarettes through tacit collusion or reaped supracompetitive profits. Liggett seeks to explain away this testimony by arguing that its officers and directors are businesspeople who do not ascribe the same meaning to words like "competitive" and "collusion" that an economist would. This explanation is entitled to little, if any, weight. * * *

Not only does the evidence fail to show actual supracompetitive pricing in the generic segment, it also does not demonstrate its likelihood. At the time Brown & Williamson entered the generic segment, the cigarette industry as a whole faced declining demand and possessed substantial excess capacity. These circumstances tend to break down patterns of oligopoly pricing and produce price competition. The only means by which Brown & Williamson is alleged to have established oligopoly pricing in the face of these unusual competitive pressures is through tacit price coordination with the other cigarette firms.

Yet the situation facing the cigarette companies in the 1980's would have made such tacit coordination unmanageable. Tacit coordination is facilitated by a stable market environment, fungible products, and a small number of variables upon which the firms seeking to coordinate their pricing may focus. Uncertainty is an oligopoly's greatest enemy. By 1984, however, the cigarette market was in an obvious state of flux. The introduction of generic cigarettes in 1980 represented the first serious price competition in the cigarette market since the 1930's. This development was bound to unsettle previous expectations and patterns of market conduct and to reduce the cigarette firms' ability to predict each other's behavior.

The larger number of product types and pricing variables also decreased the probability of effective parallel pricing. When Brown & Williamson entered the economy segment in 1984, the segment included Value–25s, black and whites, and branded generics. With respect to each product, the net price in the market was determined not only by list prices, but also by a wide variety of discounts and promotions to consumers and by rebates to wholesalers. In order to coordinate in an effective manner and eliminate price competition, the cigarette companies would have been required, without communicating, to establish parallel practices with respect to each of these variables, many of which, like consumer stickers or coupons, were difficult to monitor. Liggett has not even alleged parallel behavior with respect to these other variables, and the inherent limitations of tacit collusion suggest that such multivariable coordination is improbable.

In addition, R.J. Reynolds had incentives that, in some respects, ran counter to those of the other cigarette companies. It is implausible that without a shared interest in retarding the growth of the economy segment, Brown & Williamson and its fellow oligopolists could have engaged in parallel pricing and raised generic prices above a competitive level. * * *

Even if all the cigarette companies were willing to participate in a scheme to restrain the growth of the generic segment, they would not have been able to coordinate their actions and raise prices above a competitive level unless they understood that Brown & Williamson's entry into the segment was not a genuine effort to compete with Liggett. If even one other firm misinterpreted Brown & Williamson's entry as an effort to expand share, a chain reaction of competitive responses would almost certainly have resulted, and oligopoly discipline would have broken down, perhaps irretrievably. * * *

Liggett argues that the means by which Brown & Williamson signaled its anticompetitive intent to its rivals was through its pricing structure. According to Liggett, maintaining existing list prices while offering substantial rebates to wholesalers was a signal to the other cigarette firms that Brown & Williamson did not intend to attract additional smokers to the generic segment by its entry. But a reasonable jury could not conclude that this pricing structure eliminated or rendered insignificant the risk that the other firms might misunderstand Brown & Williamson's entry as a competitive move. The likelihood that Brown & Williamson's rivals would have regarded its pricing structure as an important signal is low, given that Liggett itself, the purported target of the predation, was already using similar rebates, as was R.J. Reynolds * * *. And despite extensive discovery of the corporate records of R.J. Reynolds and Philip Morris, no documents appeared that indicated any awareness of Brown & Williamson's supposed signal by its principal rivals. Without effective signaling, it is difficult to see how the alleged predation could have had a reasonable chance of success through oligopoly pricing.

Finally, although some of Brown & Williamson's corporate planning documents speak of a desire to slow the growth of the segment, no objective evidence of its conduct permits a reasonable inference that it had any real prospect of doing so through anticompetitive means. It is undisputed that when Brown & Williamson introduced its generic cigarettes, it offered them to a thousand wholesalers who had never before purchased generic cigarettes. The inevitable effect of this marketing effort was to expand the segment, as the new wholesalers recruited retail outlets to carry generic cigarettes. Even with respect to wholesalers already carrying generics, Brown & Williamson's unprecedented volume rebates had a similar expansionary effect. Unlike many branded cigarettes, generics came with no sales guarantee to the wholesaler; any unsold stock represented pure loss to the wholesaler. By providing substantial incentives for wholesalers to place large orders, Brown & Williamson created strong pressure for them to sell more generic cigarettes. In addition, * * * many wholesalers passed portions of the rebates about which Liggett complains on to consumers, thus dropping the retail price of generics and further stimulating demand. Brown & Williamson provided a further, direct stimulus, through some $10 million it spent during the period of alleged predation placing discount stickers on its generic cartons to reduce prices to the ultimate consumer. In light of these uncontested facts about Brown & Williamson's conduct, it is not reasonable to conclude that Brown & Williamson threatened in a serious way to restrict output, raise prices above a competitive level, and artificially slow the growth of the economy segment of the national cigarette market.

* * *

IV.

We understand that the chain of reasoning by which we have concluded that Brown & Williamson is entitled to judgment as a matter of law is demanding. But a reasonable jury is presumed to know and understand the law, the facts of the case, and the realities of the market. We hold that the evidence cannot support a finding that Brown & Williamson's alleged scheme was likely to result in oligopolistic price coordination and sustained supracompetitive pricing in the generic segment of the national cigarette market. Without this, Brown & Williamson had no reasonable prospect of recouping its predatory losses and could not inflict the injury to competition the antitrust laws prohibit. The judgment of the Court of Appeals is *affirmed*.

[The dissenting opinion of Justices Stevens, White, and Blackmun is omitted. Eds.]

––––––––

Under *Brooke Group*, a plaintiff alleging predatory pricing under Section 2 of the Sherman Act or Section 2(a) of the Robinson–Patman Act must satisfy a formidable two-part test. It must show that the defendant set its prices below an "appropriate measure" of its costs and enjoyed a "dangerous probability" of recouping its investment in below-cost sales once the episode of predation had ended. In *Brooke Group*, although Liggett established that Brown & Williamson had priced below its average variable cost, the Court concluded that it was entitled to judgment as a matter of law on the question of recoupment.

Together, *Matsushita* and *Brooke Group* have proven to be formidable hurdles to the successful prosecution of predatory pricing cases. Since *Matsushita* was decided in 1986, no plaintiff, including the Department of Justice, has succeeded in satisfying the two prong "below cost + recoupment" standard. What might explain the paucity of successful challenges to predatory pricing during that time? One explanation is that, as critics of predatory pricing urged, the practice is rarely successful and hence rarely tried. Another explanation could be that *Brooke Group* established a standard that, even if economically sound in theory, is too demanding as an evidentiary matter. As is discussed in Sidebar 6–3, which follows, some commentators have argued that it might also mean that the theory is not entirely sound as a matter of economics, or is simply not complete.

First note that the Court in *Brooke Group* did not specify a measure of cost that should be used in predatory pricing costs, although most lower costs have assumed it should be average variable cost. Determining whether a dominant firm's prices are "below cost," however, has proven to be a challenging task. *See, e.g., United States v. AMR Corp.*, 335 F.3d 1109 (10th Cir. 2003) (affirming summary judgment for American Airlines and rejecting all four tests of cost proffered by the Department of Justice). For an arguably more receptive view of predatory pricing claims, see *Spirit Airlines, Inc. v. Northwest Airlines, Inc.*, 431 F.3d 917, 945 (6th Cir. 2005) (reversing district court's award of summary judgment to the defendant airline and remanding for trial, concluding that the jury, not the court, should referee what one expert witness termed an "intellectual disagreement" over the appropriate measure of average variable costs).

Second, the Court's emphasis on recoupment continues to raise questions for the analysis of predatory pricing in the typical monopolization case, where the plaintiff must prove that the defendant has substantial market power. It is unclear, for example, whether *Brooke Group* meant to suggest that the recoupment test imposes an element of proof above and beyond the plaintiff's showing that the defendant has monopoly power. A well-reasoned finding that a defendant has monopoly power ought to rest partly on the conclusion that entry barriers are high and that rivals cannot readily enter the market and compete away the defendant's monopoly profits. In consequence, a finding of durable monopoly power could suggest that recoupment is likely and would obviate the need for a separate recoupment inquiry. *See, e.g., Multistate Legal Studies, Inc. v. Harcourt Brace Jovanovich Legal and Professional Publications, Inc.*, 63 F.3d 1540 (10th Cir. 1995) (plaintiff created a triable issue of fact concerning recoupment by offering sufficient evidence that entry into the market was difficult). Perhaps the Court anticipated circumstances where a firm that already has monopoly power invests in predation to maintain such power, rather than to gain it in the first place. In such a case, one might ask whether the anticipated returns from predation (preserving the flow of monopoly profits) was likely to exceed the investment in predation. If not, then the low price might not be considered exclusionary.

A third issue concerns intent evidence. Suppose that the plaintiff uncovers documents from the defendant's files suggesting the defendant's belief that it is succeeding in recouping its investment in predatory pricing. Imagine that the plaintiff obtains an annual strategic plan prepared for the defendant's Board of Directors in which the defendant's top officials describe how a below-cost pricing scheme actually yielded net benefits in the form of higher profits or other gains to the company. *Brooke Group* does not say whether the fact finder should accept such a document at face value as proving the dangerous probability—indeed, the certainty—of recoupment. Liggett believed that it had provided exactly such evidence of B & W's awareness of the success of its strategy, yet the Supreme Court majority discounted such evidence as being inconsistent with observable behavior in the market.

Finally, as is probably apparent from *Brooke Group* and these notes, predatory pricing as a theory of monopolization has engendered a great deal of legal and economic controversy. In *Brooke Group* and *Matsushita* and *Cargill*, which preceded it, the Supreme Court appeared to embrace the notion that to be predatory a price must be "below cost." But can an above cost price ever be predatory? These four issues are explored at greater length in Sidebar 6–3, which follows a Note on the Supreme Court's extension of *Brooke Group's* analytical framework in *Weyerhaeuser*.

Note on Weyerhaeuser and Predatory Overbuying

In *Weyerhaeuser Co. v. Ross–Simmons Hardwood Lumber Co.*, ___ U.S. ___, 127 S.Ct. 1069 (2007), the Supreme Court applied *Brooke Group* to decide a case alleging predatory bidding. The case involved two firms with hardwood lumber mills that processed red alder logs in the Pacific Northwest. Weyerhaeuser bought 65% of the logs in the region. Ross–Simmons, a rival to Weyerhaeuser, lost money and exited the market as the price of its key input, alder sawlogs, rose, and the price for its output, finished hardwood lumber, fell.

Ross–Simmons filed an antitrust complaint charging Weyerhaeuser with monopolization. In particular, Ross–Simons alleged that Weyerhaeuser had engaged in predatory bidding in order to exercise monopsony power. Its theory was that Weyerhaeuser bid up the price of logs to exceed the competitive level, presumably by overbuying, in order to force Ross–Simmons to exit. Ross–Simmons claimed that Weyerhaeuser would eventually recoup the short term losses from paying a higher than competitive price for logs by restricting its purchases of logs, forcing log prices below the competitive level. A jury returned a verdict in favor of Ross–Simmons, and the Ninth Circuit affirmed. The Supreme Court vacated that judgment on the ground that the lower courts should have applied *Brooke Group* to evaluate the claim. In particular, the Court held that to prevail on a predatory bidding claim, the plaintiff must prove an analogue to the price-cost test employed for predatory pricing—namely that "the alleged predatory bidding led to below-cost pricing of the predator's outputs"—and plaintiff must prove that recoupment is likely. *Id. at* 1078.

The application of the below-cost pricing test to Ross–Simmons' allegations in this case is subtle. The problem is that predatory bidding could raise the price of logs in a localized region without leading to an increase in the price of finished wood. The price of finished wood would not rise because Weyerhaeuser sells the latter product in a national market in competition with firms that purchase logs elsewhere, where the price of logs did not change. Even if the price of finished wood does not change, and no other firms are charging prices below cost for finished wood, Weyerhaeuser could nevertheless be charging below *its* marginal cost of producing finished wood during the predatory bidding stage, satisfying the below-cost pricing test. Weyerhaeuser's marginal cost would rise because it bid up the price it pays for logs. Note that this test may not work if Weyerhaeuser exercises market power in the finished wood market, raising its price for finished wood above the competitive level. Under such circumstances, it is possible for Weyerhaeuser to engage in predatory bidding, and increase the price it pays for logs, without raising its marginal cost above the price it receives for finished wood.

The Court applied *Brooke Group* to predatory bidding because it saw the practice as analogous to predatory pricing, the conduct at issue in *Brooke Group*. As in *Brooke Group*, the Court was concerned with the possibility that if it adopted a test that was easier for plaintiffs to satisfy, it would chill procompetitive conduct, such as the acquisition of logs by an efficient sawmill seeking to expand. Although it recognized that the short-run benefit of predatory buying goes to log suppliers, and not necessarily to consumers, *id.* at 1077 n.4, it did not view that observation as sufficient reason to limit *Brooke Group* to predatory pricing. It is noteworthy, moreover, that the Court extended *Brooke Group* without considering the recent academic commentary noted by some appeals courts that highlights settings in which price predation could be a rational business strategy. For a further discussion of the issues posed by buyer market power, including anticompetitive overbuying, see Symposium, *Buyer Power and Antitrust*, 72 ANTITRUST L.J. 505 (2005).

Sidebar 6–3:
The Economic Debate About Predatory
Pricing: A Short History*

Predatory pricing is a common feature of popular accounts of monopolization, and was widely considered a serious problem during the early decades of the 20th Century. The "academic model of the classic predator," widely accepted before the 1960s, "was a firm of such unequal size and financial strength that a drastic cut of price in some small part of its territory, sustained with monopoly profits earned elsewhere, could eliminate a smaller competitor, leaving the predator to raise its prices and recoup its losses in that market." Terry Calvani & James M. Lynch, *Predatory Pricing Under the Robinson–Patman and Sherman Acts: An Introduction*, 51 Antitrust L.J. 375, 376 (1982). In business folklore, the "paradigm case" was *Standard Oil*, (discussed in Chapter 2, *supra*). Predatory pricing also is a concern under the abuse of dominance principles of other antitrust jurisdictions, and has even been the object of enforcement guidelines. *See, e.g.*, Competition Bureau of Canada, *Predatory Pricing Enforcement Guidelines* (1992) (*available at* http://www.competitionbureau.gc.ca/epic/site/cb-bc.nsf/en/01746e.html).

In this Sidebar, we expand upon the brief introduction to the various approaches to predatory pricing outlined at the beginning of this section of the Chapter, just before *Brooke Group*. To do so, we explore some of the considerable body of literature directed at evaluating the profitability, and hence the likelihood, of predatory pricing as an exclusionary strategy.

The Chicago School Challenge

The traditional view of predatory pricing was challenged by Chicago School commentators. John McGee exhaustively reviewed the trial record in *Standard Oil*, and found no evidence of price predation. John S. McGee, *Predatory Price Cutting: The* Standard Oil *(N.J.) Case* 1 J. L. & Econ. 137 (1958). More generally, Chicago-oriented commentators argued, below-cost pricing was irrational, because the predator could not reasonably expect to recoup its initial losses from doing so.** *See, e.g.*, Robert H. Bork, The Antitrust Paradox 144–55 (1978). *But cf.* Richard A. Posner, Antitrust Law 208–10 (2d ed.2001) (recognizing that predatory pricing in one market could be profitable if it deters entry or competition in other markets).

Recoupment appears implausible, in the Chicago view, because the profits expected to follow the exit of the prey must substantially exceed the certain losses that come from below-cost pricing, given both the time value of money and the risk that the future profits will not be achieved.

---

* Some of the material in this Sidebar was adapted from Jonathan B. Baker, *Predatory Pricing After* Brooke Group: *An Economic Approach*, 62 Antitrust L.J. 585 (1994).

** As noted in the introductory material to this Chapter, Chicago School commentators have, however, been somewhat less hostile to the possibility of non-price predation (discussing the views of Robert H. Bork). Indeed, *Standard Oil* is today understood as exemplifying this anticompetitive possibility by Chicago-oriented commentators. Elizabeth Granitz & Benjamin Klein, *Monopolization by "Raising Rivals' Costs": The* Standard Oil *Case*, 39 J. L. & Econ. 1 (1996). As the title of Granitz and Klein's article suggests, the idea of non-price predation has been generalized in the "raising rivals' costs" framework for analyzing exclusionary conduct.

Future profits are uncertain for two reasons. The predator's low price may not induce its rival or rivals to exit, acquiesce to a takeover, or compete less aggressively. Moreover, even if the victims do exit, the predatory pricing scheme will not have been worthwhile unless the later monopoly price is high enough for long enough to generate profits that would more than offset the initial losses. Yet the predator cannot be sure that outcome will occur. Before recoupment is complete, the predator's product may become obsolete or otherwise undesirable to buyers, or the subsequent monopoly price may induce new entry. For example, if the prey is forced to exit from the market, the purchaser of its assets may be a plausible candidate for new entry. Or, a large customer, fearing that successful predation may lead to an increase in the price of a product it buys, could sign a long-term contract with a new entrant or the prey, at a price above the predatory price, in order to preserve future competition. In other words, there may be events beyond the control of the predator, including counter-strategies by the prey, that will ultimately undermine the scheme, which makes it all the more risky to undertake. *See, e.g.,* Frank H. Easterbrook, *Predatory Strategies and Counterstrategies*, 48 U. CHI. L. REV. 263 (1981).

The Areeda–Turner Test

If the Chicago School is correct to view predatory pricing as implausible, aggressive antitrust enforcement against low prices, for fear that they are predatory, may do more harm than good. Under such circumstances, antitrust enforcement is more likely to chill robust competition than to prevent harmful monopolization. Mainstream antitrust commentators responded to this criticism by developing cost-based tests for distinguishing between predatory pricing, which could harm competition, and robust competition, which should be permitted. The most influential test was proposed by Professors Areeda and Turner from the Harvard School in 1975. Phillip Areeda & Donald F. Turner, *Predatory Pricing and Related Practices Under Section 2 of the Sherman Act*, 88 HARV. L. REV. 697 (1975). *See also* James D. Hurwitz & William E. Kovacic, *Judicial Analysis of Predation: The Emerging Trends*, 35 VAND. L.REV. 63 (1982) (describing the range of tests proposed for identifying predatory pricing); Joseph F. Brodley, et al., *Predatory Pricing: Strategic Theory and Legal Policy*, 88 GEO. L. J. 2239, 2250–62 (2000)(describing evolution of legal standards)("*Strategic Theory*").

Areeda and Turner reasoned that a profit-maximizing firm not attempting to drive out its rivals is unlikely to set price below its own marginal cost—the incremental cost of making and selling the last unit of output—as doing so would require the seller to sacrifice short run profits. But they did not propose prohibiting prices set below a firm's marginal cost, as marginal cost is too difficult to infer from accounting records. Areeda and Turner saw average variable cost as a reasonable surrogate for marginal cost, and one that is practical to determine using historical accounting records. Accordingly, Areeda and Turner proposed that allegations of price predation be tested by comparing the monopolist's price with its average variable cost. Prices above that level would be presumed lawful, and prices below that level would be presumed unlawful.

Even this test was too harsh on price-cutters for many Chicago School commentators. Under the Chicago view, which takes predatory pricing to be irrational and, therefore, implausible, episodes in which price appears to be less than marginal cost or average variable cost almost always reflect errors in the measurement of cost or competition, not price predation.*** For example, it is frequently difficult to determine cost while the alleged predator is making substantial investments in acquiring physical capital, research and development, or developing a brand reputation (as through advertising). If accountants record such investments as expenses in the period they are made, revenues may fall short of accounting expenses during that period, so average revenue (price) will be less than some measure of cost. Such expenditures are not an appropriate basis for an antitrust violation, even if accounting practice suggests that price is less than cost during the investment period, unless the investments themselves harm competition. Similarly, a competitive firm's investments might include investments in market share, undertaken through temporary or permanent price reductions. Again, this practice would not necessarily be an appropriate basis for an antitrust violation. Some hypothetical examples suggested by business settings found in the case law illustrate this point:

- Competing spark plug manufacturers might sell their product to automobile manufacturers for incorporation into new vehicles at a price below marginal or average variable cost, in order to attract buyers of replacement spark plugs. Such a strategy might be effective if many replacement buyers will stick with the original brand even when charged a price above marginal cost.

- Competing photocopier manufacturers might price copiers below cost in order to attract buyers who can later be charged above-cost prices for dedicated replacement parts, and service.

- Competing firms producing both cameras and film might set camera prices below cost in order to sell more film at high price-cost margins.

- Competing sellers of some types of computer software might price their product below cost when high switching costs impede migration of the installed base to rival software, in order to increase the number of customers to whom they can later sell high-margin product upgrades.

- Competing computer manufacturers might price a new product below its initial variable cost, in order to generate the scale economies and cost reductions from learning-by-doing that would justify the low price.

In all these cases, the reduction of price below cost may reflect a procompetitive investment in future competition, not price predation.

Although the Areeda–Turner standard for testing predatory pricing won influence in the courts, Chicago commentators were concerned that it swept in too much procompetitive conduct, and would in consequence chill procompetitive price-cutting. In response to this criticism, the Supreme Court has required that a plaintiff alleging predatory pricing by a

*** Here, as elsewhere in the analysis of predation, Richard Posner is an exception, accepting the practical possibility of price predation, at least as a method of maintaining (as opposed to obtaining) a monopoly. Richard A. Posner, Antitrust Law 207–23 (2d ed. 2001).

monopolist prove more than that the price was below an appropriate measure of cost (although it has never endorsed any particular measure). In a series of decisions including *Matsushita* (Casebook, Chapter 3, *supra*) and *Brooke Group*, the Court made clear that a predatory pricing plaintiff must also demonstrate that the predator had a reasonable prospect of recouping the costs of predation through the later exercise of market power. Kenneth G. Elzinga & David E. Mills, *Trumping the Areeda–Turner Test: The Recoupment Standard in* Brooke Group, 62 ANTITRUST L.J. 559 (1994).

If Chicago School commentators are correct in their view that price predation is almost invariably irrational because recoupment is almost always implausible, then this additional element of the predatory pricing offense provides a nearly insurmountable hurdle for plaintiffs to overcome, and properly so. Indeed, after *Brooke Group*, it is easier to make the case that the legal standard for proof of monopolization through price predation has chilled predatory pricing complaints than to make the case that the law chills aggressive price-cutting.

Post–Chicago Antitrust Commentary

Beginning in the late 1970s and early 1980s, economists developed new theories that challenged the Chicago School view that price predation was irrational as a business strategy. These theories took on directly the claim that recoupment is almost never plausible. *See generally* Paul Milgrom & John Roberts, *New Theories of Predatory Pricing*, in INDUSTRIAL STRUCTURE IN THE NEW INDUSTRIAL ECONOMICS 112–37 (Giacomo Bonanno & Dario Brandolini, eds. 1990); Jansuz Ordover & Garth Saloner, *Predation, Monopolization, and Antitrust*, in 1 HANDBOOK OF INDUSTRIAL ORGANIZATION 537–96 (Richard Schmalensee & Robert Willig, eds. 1989); Brodley, et al., *Strategic Theory, supra.*

One contemporary recoupment theory,[****] in which predation occurs in one market while recoupment occurs rapidly and profitably in many others, is suggested by the following hypothetical example. Suppose a chain store faces local non-chain rivals in each of a large number of towns. The chain cuts price drastically in a few towns. When the chain's rivals in those towns either exit or begin to compete less aggressively with the chain, the price war ends, and high prices are restored. In addition, the chain store's rivals in all the other towns, in which the chain did not cut prices, also respond by avoiding aggressive competition with the chain. As a result, prices also increase in the towns in which predation did not occur.

In the example, the firm developed a reputation as a predator by reducing price in a small number of markets ("reputation effect" predation). In effect, it engaged in selective predation. The rivals in the markets in which predation occurred may have ended up crippled or destroyed. But rivals competing against the predator in markets in which predation did not occur were not injured directly. They never experienced a price war—but they were intimidated by the threat of a price war into engaging in less aggressive behavior than they would otherwise have found most profitable.

[****] Although this theory was new in terms of formal economic modeling, it had been antic-ipated by Richard Posner. RICHARD A. POSNER, ANTITRUST LAW 186 (1976).

In other modern theories, the predator succeeds (1) by convincing investors or lenders no longer to support the prey ("deep pocket" or "financial market" predation); (2) by convincing a prospective entrant that the predator's costs are too low to make entry profitable (predation through "cost-signaling"); or (3) by convincing a prospective entrant that it's product will not be attractive to buyers ("test market" predation). *See generally* Brodley, et al., *Strategic Theory, supra*; Douglas G. Baird, Robert H. Gertner & Randal C. Picker, Game Theory and the Law 180–86 (1994).

Concerns that these modern theories of price predation can pose substantial problems of evidence and proof have been addressed by law professor Joseph Brodley and his economist co-authors, Patrick Bolton and Michael H. Riordan. Their article seeks to develop administrable methods of discriminating between predatory and competitive pricing, informed by post-Chicago developments in economics and by examples taken from the economic literature and the case law. Brodley, et al., *Strategic Theory, supra. See also* Joseph F. Brodley, et al., *Predatory Pricing: Response to Critique and Further Elaboration*, 89 Geo. L.J. 2495 (2001).

For example, in the modern economic theories, the successful predator's price cuts need not necessarily go below any particular measure of cost in order for it to discourage the prey from aggressive competition.***** Brodley, Bolton and Riordan would nevertheless effectively require a plaintiff to demonstrate that the predator has lowered price below a measure of the predator's incremental costs. Brodley, et al., *Strategic Theory*, 88 Geo. L. J. at 2271–74. They also suggest ways of demonstrating that a monopolist or coordinating oligopoly has engaged in each of four predatory strategies, and that recoupment is likely.

These modern economic theories of predatory pricing have as yet had little influence in the courts. Brodley, et al., *Strategic Theory*, 88 Geo. L.J. at 2258–60. *But see Spirit Airlines, Inc. v. Northwest Airlines, Inc.*, 431 F.3d 917 (6th Cir. 2005). *Cf. Advo, Inc. v. Philadelphia Newspapers, Inc.*, 51 F.3d 1191, 1196 n.4 (3d Cir. 1995) (modern reputational effect theory "makes economic sense," but was not supported on the facts). Moreover, Chicago-oriented commentators question whether the new theories can be practically applied, and whether the competitive problems they identify are sufficiently common as to make increased antitrust enforcement worthwhile in light of the costs of chilling aggressive price competition. Brodley, et al., *Strategic Theory, supra. See also* Adriaan ten Kate & Gunnar Niels, *On the Rationality of Predatory Pricing: The Debate Between Chicago and Post–Chicago*, 47 Antitrust Bull. 1 (2002) (ques-

***** *Cf.* Aaron S. Edlin, *Stopping Above–Cost Predatory Pricing*, 111 Yale L.J. 941 (2002) (a (natural) monopolist with a cost advantage over its potential rivals can deter entry notwithstanding its high pre-entry price; predatory incumbent responses arise in response to mistakes by entrants, who may not realize that the incumbent's costs are so low or that market demand is low). For a reply, see Einer Elhauge, *Why Above–Cost Price Cuts to Drive Out Entrants are not Predatory—and the Implications for Defining Costs and Market Power*, 112 Yale L. J. 681 (2003). In part, the debate between Edlin and Elhauge turns on whether antitrust should primarily be concerned with consumer welfare or aggregate economic welfare (see *Note on Efficiencies and Consumer Welfare*, Casebook, Chapter 5, *supra*). If antitrust law condemns above-cost price reductions that exclude entrants, Elhauge emphasizes, it risks encouraging entry by high-cost producers, and thus a loss of production efficiency. In contrast, Edlin emphasizes that even high-cost entry can lower consumer prices, especially when the incumbent is exercising market power.

tioning practical applicability of modern predatory pricing theories); RICHARD A. POSNER, ANTITRUST LAW 221 (2d ed. 2001) (the conditions required for one modern theory to apply are "too exacting to make it an answer to the claim that predatory pricing can be a rational strategy for a monopolist"). Accordingly, the influence of the post-Chicago perspective on price predation, which is more sympathetic to the possibility than the Chicago School view, remains to be seen.

3. INTEGRATING THE TREATMENT OF NON–PRICE EXCLUSIONARY CONDUCT AND PREDATORY PRICING: THE CHALLENGES OF ASSESSING BUNDLED REBATES AND OTHER MIXED CONDUCT

Introduction:
LePage's and the Tension Between the
Standards for Evaluating Price Predation
and Non–Price Exclusionary Conduct

As we have seen in this Chapter, the modern law of monopolization has developed along two lines. Today's law of predatory pricing is shaped largely by the Supreme Court's decisions in *Matsushita*, which we read in Chapter 3, *and Brooke Group*. In these two cases, the Supreme Court developed a two part test for predatory pricing. To be actionable under the antitrust laws, such pricing must be (1) below some appropriate measure of cost, and (2) it must be probable that the alleged predator will be able to recoup its losses through the later exercise of market power. This paradigm assumes that successful predatory pricing is a two step process. In stage one, the "short run," the predator lowers its price below cost, sacrificing all profit and incurring losses, in order to exclude or discipline its rivals. In stage two, the "long run," the predator, having vanquished or humbled its rivals, will be in a position to exercise market power and hence "recoup" its short run losses.

Non-price exclusionary conduct, on the other hand, has been defined by *Aspen*, *Kodak*, and to some degree the Supreme Court's decision in *Verizon* (Casebook, Section C4, *infra*). Recall that the standard for judging non-price exclusionary conduct took shape in *Aspen*, where the Court reasoned:

> The question whether Ski Co.'s conduct may properly be characterized as exclusionary cannot be answered by simply considering its effect on Highlands. In addition, it is relevant to consider its impact on consumers and whether it has impaired competition in an unnecessarily restrictive way.[32] If a firm has been "attempting to exclude rivals on some basis other than efficiency,"[33] it is fair to characterize its behavior as predatory. It is, accordingly, appropriate to examine the effect of the challenged pattern of conduct on consumers, on Ski Co.'s smaller rival, and on Ski Co. itself.

---

32. "Thus 'exclusionary' comprehends at the most behavior that not only (1) tends to impair the opportunities of rivals, but also (2) either does not further competition on the merits or does so in an unnecessarily restrictive way." 3 P. Areeda & D. Turner, Antitrust Law 78 (1978).

33. Bork [The Antitrust Paradox] 138.

From the first quoted sentence, it seems clear that in the Court's view "exclusion" is not the same as "exclusionary." Competition on the merits and exclusionary conduct alike will produce winners and losers. So to judge whether conduct that excludes is exclusionary, the majority directs us to consider the impact of the conduct on consumers, the targeted rival, and on the alleged predator. Inherent in this approach is a framework that involves shifting burdens of production: the plaintiff demonstrates exclusion or impairment of rivals and consequent actual or likely impact on consumers (injury to competition). The defendant must then come forward with "business justifications." The approach is suggestive of a kind of "balancing," as we have seen discussed under Section 1 of the Sherman Act, at least when the defendant can meet its burden of production by presenting evidence of legitimate purposes. But in practice, resolving such cases may turn more on the relative strength of the evidence of effects and justifications rather than some dollar-for-dollar balancing of consumer and producer surplus.

The standards for judging price predation and non-price exclusionary conduct, therefore, are today in tension. The price predation standard, which focuses on measures of cost and theories of recoupment, has proven to be very difficult to satisfy, and it singularly focuses on the impact of the strategy on the alleged predator. In contrast, the standard for proving non-price exclusionary conduct has led to some significant plaintiff's victories, and focuses on an assessment of consumer welfare in addition to producer welfare. The choice of standard, therefore, can make a difference in the outcome of specific cases. Can they nevertheless be reconciled?

The seeming disparity between these two sets of standards appeared to be headed for possible resolution by the Supreme Court in *LePage's Inc. v. 3M Company*, 324 F.3d 141 (3d Cir. 2003), *cert. denied*, 542 U.S. 953 (2004). *LePage's* involved a Section 2 Sherman Act challenge by a manufacturer of private label transparent tape against the dominant manufacturer (3M makes "Scotch" brand tape). The case focused in large part on the legality of 3M's "bundled rebate" program, pursuant to which it offered very substantial discounts to its transparent tape customers who also purchased its other product lines. Relying in part on the *Aspen Skiing* framework, LePage's secured a multi-million dollar verdict in the district court arguing that 3M's bundled rebates had the effect of excluding it from the market for transparent tape, and ultimately resulted in higher prices to consumers after it was forced to exit the market. 3M failed to persuade the district court that it had any procompetitive justification for the strategy.

3M's defense was instead constructed on the law of predatory pricing. It urged the Third Circuit to reject LePage's' reliance on *Aspen* and *Kodak* in favor of application of *Brooke Group* and *Matsushita*. Because its bundled rebates allegedly remained "above cost," it reasoned that no Section 2 liability should follow. The Third Circuit concluded that no predatory pricing claim had been alleged, and that the mere fact that a pricing strategy was at issue did not automatically convert the case into one of predatory pricing, although the panel's reasoning on the point is sparse and has been criticized. LePage's, therefore, was not required to prove that 3M priced below cost in some way or that it was in a position to recoup losses.

The case garnered a great deal of attention in the antitrust and business community, and a number of amicus briefs were filed with the Court both for and against the petition for a writ of certiorari. Perhaps the most influential brief, however, was that of the Solicitor General, filed at the Court's invitation. While pointing out what it viewed as deficiencies in the reasoning of the Third Circuit, the government nevertheless concluded that Supreme Court review was not warranted. It emphasized two factors overall: (1) the absence of any conflict in the circuits concerning the competitive consequences of bundled rebates, and (2) the prematurity of the challenge—there was as yet no clear consensus among courts and commentators as to the utility of bundled rebates and the appropriate test to be used in judging their legality.

Yet as to the latter point, the government argued that bundled rebates are distinguishable from predatory pricing, and hence should not be evaluated, as 3M had urged, under the standards of *Brooke Group*, which have been justified based on fears of false positives, loss of immediate consumer benefits, predictability for defendants, and administrability for courts. Indeed, it argued, although "bundled rebates are widespread and are likely, in many cases, to be pro-competitive ... the bundling of rebates (as distinct from the price reductions that may result) is not necessarily procompetitive." The brief continues:

> Unlike a low but above-cost price on a single product, a bundled rebate or discount can—under certain theoretical assumptions— exclude an equally efficient competitor, if the competitor competes with respect to but one component of the bundle and cannot profitably match the discount aggregated over the other products, even if the post-discount prices for both the bundle as a whole and each of its components are above cost.

Similarly, some commentators have argued that loyalty discounts, which typically provide larger discounts for customers that commit to purchase ascending percentages of their needs from the supplier, cannot be viewed as presumptively procompetitive, as is the case with simple lowering of prices. Although loyalty discounts may initially result in lower prices to some customers, they may actually lead to higher prices for others, especially those who do not qualify for (or decline to accept) the discounts, when compared to prices that were available before the program was implemented. Hence, and in contrast with a reduction in price, the net consumer welfare consequences of the practice (before accounting for any competitive consequences of their potential exclusionary effect on rivals) can be difficult to determine, and as with bundled rebates, are not therefore *necessarily* procompetitive.

The Supreme Court ultimately denied 3M's petition for certiorari, but debate raged on among enforcers and commentators in the United States and Europe.

On April 2, 2007, the Antitrust Modernization Commission, which was created by Congress in 2002 to undertake a wide-ranging study of U.S. antitrust laws, issued its final report. The report recommended a three part test for evaluating bundled rebates:

> To prove a violation of Section 2 [based on bundled discounts or rebates], a plaintiff should be required to show each one of the following elements (as well as other elements of a Section 2 claim):

(1) after allocating all discounts and rebates attributable to the entire bundle of products to the competitive product, the defendant sold the competitive product below its incremental cost for the competitive product; (2) the defendant is likely to recoup these short term losses; and (3) the bundled discount or rebate program has had or is likely to have an adverse effect on competition.

See http://www.amc.gov/report_recommendation/toc.htm. Would adoption of the AMC's proposed test effectively overrule *LePage's*? Would it require use of *Brooke Group* in cases of bundled rebates? Is it consistent with the government's position before the Supreme Court in *LePage's*?

In our next case, the U.S. Court of Appeals for the Ninth Circuit sought to answer some of these questions when it considered another example of a bundled rebate. Having been recently reversed by the Supreme Court for its failure to use a cost-based standard in *Weyerhaeuser*, the court proceeded cautiously. Indeed, in an unusual move, after oral argument had already been conducted in the case, the court issued an order calling for amici to brief the questions whether bundled rebates should be judged by a "below cost" standard, and, if so, what the appropriate measure of costs should be. *Cascade Health Solutions v. PeaceHealth*, 479 F.3d 726 (9th Cir. 2007). As you read the following excerpt from the court's decision on the merits, note how it took into account not only *Brooke Group*, but the AMC proposal and a variety of other sources.

CASCADE HEALTH SOLUTIONS v. PEACEHEALTH

United States Court of Appeals for the Ninth Circuit, 2008.
515 F.3d 883.

Before: RONALD M. GOULD, RICHARD A. PAEZ and JOHNNIE B. RAWLINSON, Circuit Judges.

GOULD, Circuit Judge:

* * *

McKenzie and PeaceHealth are the only two providers of hospital care in Lane County, Oregon. The jury found and, for the purposes of this appeal, the parties do not dispute, that the relevant market in this case is the market for primary and secondary acute care hospital services in Lane County. Primary and secondary acute care hospital services are common medical services like setting a broken bone and performing a tonsillectomy. Some hospitals also provide what the parties call "tertiary care," which includes more complex services like invasive cardiovascular surgery and intensive neonatal care.

In Lane County, PeaceHealth operates three hospitals while McKenzie operates one. McKenzie's sole endeavor is McKenzie–Willamette Hospital, a 114–bed hospital that offers primary and secondary acute care in Springfield, Oregon. McKenzie does not provide tertiary care. In the time period leading up to and including this litigation, McKenzie had been suffering financial losses, and, as a result, merged with Triad Hospitals, Inc.[1] so that it could add tertiary services to its menu of care.

---

1. As a result of the merger, McKenzie's name changed to Cascade Health Solutions. For the purposes of this opinion, we, like the parties, continue to refer to Cascade Health Solutions as McKenzie.

* * * In Lane County, PeaceHealth has a 90% market share of tertiary neonatal services, a 93% market share of tertiary cardiovascular services, and a roughly 75% market share of primary and secondary care services.

* * * [T]here appear to be three major participants in the market for hospital services: hospitals, insurers, and patients. Hospitals, like those operated by PeaceHealth and McKenzie, provide services to patients and sell services to insurers. Insurers are usually commercial health insurance companies that seek to buy medical services from hospitals on the best terms possible. The insurers in turn sell insurance services to patients and employers. Patients buy health insurance from insurers (often through their employers) and sometimes buy services from hospitals.

In the transaction between a hospital that sells care services and an insurer that buys care services, the price agreed upon is often referred to as a "reimbursement rate." For example, in a hospital-insurer contract, the agreed upon price might be "a 90% reimbursement rate." A 90% reimbursement rate price means that, when the insurer must purchase services from the hospital, the insurer gets a 10% discount off the hospital's regular price, also called the charge master or list price. It follows that hospitals prefer high reimbursement rates and insurers prefer low reimbursement rates, as each group pursues its own economic interest.

* * * On McKenzie's monopolization and attempted monopolization claims, McKenzie's primary theory was that PeaceHealth engaged in anticompetitive conduct by offering insurers "bundled" or "package" discounts. McKenzie asserted that PeaceHealth offered insurers discounts of 35% to 40% on tertiary services if the insurers made PeaceHealth their sole preferred provider for *all* services-primary, secondary, and tertiary. McKenzie introduced evidence of a few specific instances of PeaceHealth's bundled discounting practices.

For example, in 2001, PeaceHealth was the only preferred provider of hospital care under the preferred provider plan ("PPP") of Regence BlueCross BlueShield of Oregon ("Regence").[2] At that time, Regence was paying PeaceHealth a 76% reimbursement rate for all of PeaceHealth's medical services, including primary, secondary, and tertiary services. Around that time, pursuant to McKenzie's request, Regence considered adding McKenzie to the PPP as a preferred provider of primary and secondary services. When Regence's contract with PeaceHealth came up for its annual renewal, Regence solicited two proposals from PeaceHealth. Under one proposal, PeaceHealth would remain the only preferred provider. Under the other proposal, McKenzie would be added as a preferred provider. PeaceHealth offered an 85% reimbursement rate for all services if it remained Regence's sole preferred provider of primary, secondary, and tertiary services, and a 90% reimbursement rate if McKenzie was added as a preferred provider of primary and secondary services. Regence thereafter declined to include McKenzie as a preferred provider.

---

2. In a preferred provider plan, health care providers contract with an insurer to provide health care to the insurer's customers. The insurer's customers pay much higher prices if they obtain services from providers other than those with whom their insurer has contracted.

That same year, McKenzie sought and received admission as a preferred provider of primary and secondary services under the preferred plan offered by Providence Health Plan ("Providence"). Until then, PeaceHealth was the only preferred provider of primary, secondary, and tertiary services in the Providence preferred plan. Upon McKenzie's admission as a preferred provider, PeaceHealth increased its reimbursement rate with Providence from 90% to 93%. The evidence showed that insurers who made PeaceHealth their exclusive preferred provider across all services, thus purchasing from PeaceHealth a full complement of primary, secondary, and tertiary services, paid lower reimbursement rates than insurers who purchased tertiary services from PeaceHealth, but at least some primary and secondary services from McKenzie.

* * *

We address initially the attempted monopolization claim. Section 2 of the Sherman Act makes it illegal to "attempt to monopolize ... any part of the trade or commerce among the several States, or with foreign nations."15 U.S.C. § 2. "[T]o demonstrate attempted monopolization a plaintiff must prove (1) that the defendant has engaged in predatory or anticompetitive conduct with (2) a specific intent to monopolize and (3) a dangerous probability of achieving monopoly power." *Spectrum Sports, Inc. v. McQuillan,* 506 U.S. 447, 456, 113 S.Ct. 884, 122 L.Ed.2d 247 (1993) * * * .

PeaceHealth's appeal centers on the first element of the *Spectrum Sports* test, the conduct element. Anticompetitive conduct is behavior that tends to impair the opportunities of rivals and either does not further competition on the merits or does so in an unnecessarily restrictive way. *Aspen Skiing Co. v. Aspen Highlands Skiing Corp.,* 472 U.S. 585, 605 n. 32, 105 S.Ct. 2847, 86 L.Ed.2d 467 (1985). PeaceHealth contends that we should vacate the jury's verdict because the district court incorrectly instructed the jury about when bundled discounting can amount to anticompetitive conduct. This leads us to consider at some length the phenomena of bundles and bundled discounts.

1

Bundling is the practice of offering, for a single price, two or more goods or services that could be sold separately. A bundled discount occurs when a firm sells a bundle of goods or services for a lower price than the seller charges for the goods or services purchased individually. As discussed above, PeaceHealth offered bundled discounts to Regence and other insurers in this case. Specifically, PeaceHealth offered insurers discounts if the insurers made PeaceHealth their exclusive preferred provider for primary, secondary, and tertiary care.

Bundled discounts are pervasive, and examples abound. Season tickets, fast food value meals, all-in-one home theater systems-all are bundled discounts. Like individual consumers, institutional purchasers seek and obtain bundled discounts, too. The varied and pervasive nature of bundled discounts illustrates that such discounts transcend market boundaries. On the one hand, the world's largest corporations offer bundled discounts as their product lines expand with the convergence of industries. On the other hand, a street-corner vendor with a food cart—a merchant with limited capital— might offer a discount to a customer who buys a drink and potato chips to complement a hot dog. The fact that such diverse sellers offer bundled discounts shows that such discounts are a fundamental option for both buyers and sellers.[5]

Bundled discounts generally benefit buyers because the discounts allow the buyer to get more for less.[6] Bundling can also result in savings to the seller because it usually costs a firm less to sell multiple products to one customer at the same time than it does to sell the products individually.

Not surprisingly, the Supreme Court has instructed that, because of the benefits that flow to consumers from discounted prices, price cutting is a practice the antitrust laws aim to promote. *See Matsushita Elec. Indus. Co. v. Zenith Radio Corp.*, 475 U.S. 574, 594, 106 S.Ct. 1348, 89 L.Ed.2d 538 (1986) ("[C]utting prices in order to increase business often is the very essence of competition."). Consistent with that principle, we should not be too quick to condemn price-reducing bundled discounts as anticompetitive, lest we end up with a rule that discourages legitimate price competition.

However, it is possible, at least in theory, for a firm to use a bundled discount to exclude an equally or more efficient competitor and thereby reduce consumer welfare in the long run. For example, a competitor who sells only a single product in the bundle (and who produces that single product at a lower cost than the defendant) might not be able to match profitably the price created by the multi-product bundled discount. This is true even if the post-discount prices for both the entire bundle and each product in the bundle are above the seller's cost. [One district court opinion on bundled discounts] * * * provides an example of such a situation:

> Assume for the sake of simplicity that the case involved the sale of two hair products, shampoo and conditioner, the latter made only by A and the former by both A and B. Assume as well that both must be used to wash one's hair. Assume further that A's average variable cost for conditioner is $2.50, that its average variable cost for shampoo is $1.50, and that B's average variable cost for shampoo is $1.25. B therefore is the more efficient producer of shampoo. Finally, assume that A prices conditioner and shampoo at $5 and $3, respectively, if bought separately but at $3 and $2.25 if bought as part of a package. Absent the package pricing, A's price for both products is $8. B therefore must price its shampoo at or below $3 in order to compete effectively with A, given that the customer will be paying A

---

5. That bundled discounts are a common feature of our current economic system is relevant to our analysis of allegedly anticompetitive conduct under § 2 of the Sherman Act. The Supreme Court, in assessing the *stare decisis* effect of its prior precedents under § 1 of the Sherman Act, recently noted that "[f]rom the beginning the Court has treated the Sherman Act as a common-law statute," and that "[j]ust as the common law adapts to modern understanding and greater experience, so too does the Sherman Act's prohibition on 'restraint[s] of trade' evolve to meet the dynamics of present economic conditions." *Leegin Creative Leather Prods., Inc. v. PSKS, Inc.*, ___ U.S. ___, 127 S.Ct. 2705, 2720, 168 L.Ed.2d 623 (2007) (third alteration in original). The

frequency with which we see bundled discounts in varied contexts does not insulate such discounts from antitrust review, but it heightens the need to ensure that the rule adopted does not expose inventive and legitimate forms of price competition to an overbroad liability standard.

6. The Supreme Court has recognized the principle that package pricing is usually procompetitive, noting that "[b]uyers often find package sales attractive; a seller's decision to offer such packages can merely be an attempt to compete effectively-conduct that is entirely consistent with the Sherman Act." *Jefferson Parish Hosp. Dist. No. 2 v. Hyde*, 466 U.S. 2, 12, 104 S.Ct. 1551, 80 L.Ed.2d 2 (1984).

$5 for conditioner irrespective of which shampoo supplier it chooses. With the package pricing, the customer can purchase both products from A for $5.25, a price above the sum of A's average variable cost for both products. In order for B to compete, however, it must persuade the customer to buy B's shampoo while purchasing its conditioner from A for $5. In order to do that, B cannot charge more than $0.25 for shampoo, as the customer otherwise will find A's package cheaper than buying conditioner from A and shampoo from B. On these assumptions, A would force B out of the shampoo market, notwithstanding that B is the more efficient producer of shampoo, without pricing either of A's products below average variable cost.

It is worth reiterating that, as the example above shows, a bundled discounter can exclude rivals who do not sell as great a number of product lines without pricing its products below its cost to produce them. Thus, a bundled discounter can achieve exclusion without sacrificing any short-run profits.

In this case, McKenzie asserts it could provide primary and secondary services at a lower cost than PeaceHealth. Thus, the principal anticompetitive danger of the bundled discounts offered by PeaceHealth is that the discounts could freeze McKenzie out of the market for primary and secondary services because McKenzie, like seller B in * * * [the above example], does not provide the same array of services as PeaceHealth and therefore could possibly not be able to match the discount PeaceHealth offers insurers.

From our discussion above, it is evident that bundled discounts, while potentially procompetitive by offering bargains to consumers, can also pose the threat of anticompetitive impact by excluding less diversified but more efficient producers. These considerations put into focus this problem: How are we to discern where antitrust law draws the line between bundled discounts that are procompetitive and part of the normal rough-and-tumble of our competitive economy and bundled discounts, offered by firms holding or on the verge of gaining monopoly power in the relevant market, that harm competition and are thus proscribed by § 2 of the Sherman Act?

2

In this case, the district court based its jury instruction regarding the anticompetitive effect of bundled discounting on the Third Circuit's en banc decision in *LePage's Inc. v. 3M*, 324 F.3d 141 (3d Cir. 2003) (en banc). In that case, the plaintiff, LePage's, was the market leader in sales of "private label" (*i.e.*, store brand) transparent tape. As LePage's market share fell and its profitability declined, it brought suit asserting that 3M, who manufactured Scotch tape, some private label tape, and many other products that LePage's did not produce (like healthcare products and retail automotive products), leveraged its monopoly over Scotch brand tape to monopolize the private label tape market. Specifically, LePage's alleged that 3M's multi-tiered bundled rebate structure was anticompetitive. The bundled rebate structure offered progressively higher rebates when customers increased purchases across 3M's different product lines-discounts LePage's could not offer because it did not sell the same diverse array of products as 3M. A jury found that 3M's conduct violated § 2 of the Sherman Act and 3M appealed.

The primary issue before the Third Circuit was whether 3M unlawfully maintained its monopoly power through the bundled discount program. 3M argued that its bundled rebate structure was legal as a matter of law because it never priced below cost. 3M relied heavily on the United States Supreme Court's decision in *Brooke Group Ltd. v. Brown & Williamson Tobacco Corp.,* 509 U.S. 209, 113 S.Ct. 2578, 125 L.Ed.2d 168 (1993). In *Brooke Group,* a primary-line price discrimination case brought under the Robinson–Patman Act, the Supreme Court held that, in a single product predatory pricing case, a plaintiff must prove (1) that its rival's low prices were below an appropriate measure of its rival's costs and (2) that its rival "had a reasonable prospect, or, under § 2 of the Sherman Act, a dangerous probability, of recouping its investment in below-cost prices." In *LePage's,* the Third Circuit, in a 7–3 en banc decision, refused to apply *Brooke Group*'s below-cost pricing requirement to bundled discounting.

The Third Circuit first distinguished *Brooke Group* by noting that the defendant in that case was an oligopolist while 3M was a monopolist. The court reasoned that while *Brooke Group*'s requirement of below-cost pricing with a probability of recoupment is appropriate when the defendant is an oligopolist who still faces competition when it tries to recoup the losses it suffered during the predation period, below-cost pricing and a probability of recoupment should not be required when the defendant is a monopolist whose behavior will be unconstrained by the market after it eliminates its lone rival. The court in *LePage's* also noted that the plaintiff in *Brooke Group* simply challenged the defendant's pricing practices, not bundling accomplished through discounting. The court reasoned that *Brooke Group* did not require below-cost pricing for *any* pricing practice to be deemed exclusionary.

The court noted that "[t]he principal anticompetitive effect of bundled rebates as offered by 3M is that when offered by a monopolist they may foreclose portions of the market to a potential competitor who does not manufacture an equally diverse group of products and who therefore cannot make a comparable offer." The Third Circuit concluded that the jury could reasonably have found that 3M used its monopoly in transparent tape along with its extensive catalog of other products to exclude LePage's from the market and that 3M did not present any adequate business justification for its bundled discounting program. The court thus affirmed the jury verdict in LePage's favor, even though LePage's economist testified that LePage's was not as efficient a tape producer as 3M.

In this case, the district court used *LePage's* to formulate its jury instruction. Specifically, the district court instructed the jury that

> plaintiff ... contends that defendant has bundled price discounts for its primary, secondary, and tertiary acute care products and that doing so is anticompetitive. Bundled pricing occurs when price discounts are offered for purchasing an entire line of services exclusively from one supplier. Bundled price discounts may be anti-competitive if they are offered by a monopolist and substantially foreclose portions of the market to a competitor who does not provide an equally diverse group of services and who therefore cannot make a comparable offer.

As 3M did in *LePage's*, PeaceHealth argues that the jury instruction incorrectly stated the law because it allowed the jury to find that a defendant with monopoly power (or, in the case of an attempted monopolization claim, a dangerous probability of achieving monopoly power) engaged in exclusionary conduct by simply offering a bundled discount that its competitor could not match. The instruction did not require the jury to consider whether the defendant priced below cost. *LePage's*, PeaceHealth asserts, was wrongly decided because it allows the jury to conclude, from the structure of the market alone, that a competitor has been anticompetitively excluded from the market. We generally review jury instructions for abuse of discretion, but we review de novo whether jury instructions correctly stated the law.

As the bipartisan Antitrust Modernization Commission ("AMC")[10] recently noted, the fundamental problem with the *LePage's* standard is that it does not consider whether the bundled discounts constitute competition on the merits, but simply concludes that all bundled discounts offered by a monopolist are anticompetitive with respect to its competitors who do not manufacture an equally diverse product line. Anti-trust Modernization Comm'n, *Report and Recommendations* 97 (2007) [hereinafter AMC Report]. The *LePage's* standard, the AMC noted, asks the jury to consider whether the plaintiff has been excluded from the market, but does not require the jury to consider whether the plaintiff was at least as efficient of a producer as the defendant. Thus, the *LePage's* standard could protect a less efficient competitor at the expense of consumer welfare. * * *

The AMC also lamented that *LePage's* "offers no clear standards by which firms can assess whether their bundled rebates are likely to pass antitrust muster." The Commission noted that efficiencies, and not schemes to acquire or maintain monopoly power, likely explain the use of bundled discounts because many firms without market power offer them. The AMC thus proposed a three-part test that it believed would protect pro-competitive bundled discounts from antitrust scrutiny. The AMC proposed that:

> Courts should adopt a three-part test to determine whether bundled discounts or rebates violate Section 2 of the Sherman Act. To prove a violation of Section 2, a plaintiff should be required to show each one of the following elements (as well as other elements of a Section 2 claim): (1) after allocating all discounts and rebates attributable to the entire bundle of products to the competitive product, the defendant sold the competitive product below its incremental cost for the competitive product; (2) the defendant is likely to recoup these short-term losses; and (3) the bundled discount or rebate program has had or is likely to have an adverse effect on competition.

The AMC reasoned that the first element would (1) subject bundled discounts to antitrust scrutiny only if they could exclude a hypothetical equally efficient competitor and (2) provide sufficient clarity for businesses to determine whether their bundled discounting practices run afoul of § 2. The AMC concluded that the three-part test would, as a whole, bring the law on bundled discounting in line with the Supreme Court's reasoning in *Brooke Group*.

---

10. Congress created the AMC in the Antitrust Modernization Commission Act of 2002, Pub.L. No. 107–273, § § 11051–60, 116 Stat. 1758, 1856–59. * * *

3

We must decide whether we should follow *LePage's* or whether we should part ways with the Third Circuit by adopting a cost-based standard to apply in bundled discounting cases.

Observers have commented that, in some respects, bundled discounts are similar to both predatory pricing and tying. As the Supreme Court explained in *Brooke Group,* a plaintiff in a single product predatory pricing case must establish that the defendant priced below cost and that there was a probability the defendant could recoup the losses it suffered during the predation period. In a normal tying case, however, while a plaintiff must prove that it was "coerced" into buying the tied products from the defendant, a plaintiff does not need to prove that the defendant priced the products below cost, and therefore the plaintiff also does not need to prove any recoupment of losses.

However, "[o]ne difference between traditional tying by contract and tying via package discounts is that the traditional tying contract typically forces the buyer to accept both products, as well as the cost savings." Conversely, "the package discount gives the buyer the choice of accepting the cost savings by purchasing the package, or foregoing the savings by purchasing the products separately." The package discount thus does not constrain the buyer's choice as much as the traditional tie. For that reason, the late-Professor Areeda and Professor Hovenkamp suggest that "[a] variation of the requirement that prices be 'below cost' is essential for the plaintiff to establish one particular element of unlawful bundled discounting—namely, that there was actually 'tying'—that is, that the purchaser was actually 'coerced' (in this case, by lower prices) into taking the tied-up package."

In addition, the Supreme Court has forcefully suggested that we should not condemn prices that are above some measure of incremental cost. In *Brooke Group,* the Court held that "a plaintiff seeking to establish competitive injury resulting from a rival's low prices must prove that the prices complained of are below an appropriate measure of its rival's costs." In the course of rejecting the plaintiff's argument that a predatory pricing plaintiff need not prove below-cost pricing, the Court wrote that it has "rejected ... the notion that above-cost prices that are below general market levels or the costs of a firm's competitors inflict injury to competition cognizable under the antitrust laws." The Court went on to emphasize that "[l]ow prices benefit consumers regardless of how those prices are set, and so long as they are above predatory levels, they do not threaten competition." The Court also noted the broad application of the principle that only below-cost prices are anticompetitive, stating that "[w]e have adhered to this principle regardless of the type of antitrust claim involved." "As a general rule," the Court concluded, "the exclusionary effect of prices above a relevant measure of cost either reflects the lower cost structure of the alleged predator, and so represents competition on the merits, or is beyond the practical ability of a judicial tribunal to control without courting intolerable risks of chilling legitimate price-cutting."

The Court recently reemphasized these principles in *Weyerhaeuser Co. v. Ross–Simmons Hardwood Lumber Co.,* ___ U.S. ___, 127 S.Ct. 1069, 1078, 166 L.Ed.2d 911 (2007), a case in which the Court held that *Brooke Group's* below-cost pricing requirement applies in cases in which the plaintiff alleges that the defendant engaged in predatory bidding—the practice of bidding up input costs to drive rivals out of business. Specifically, the Court held that a predatory bidding "plaintiff must prove that the alleged predatory bidding led to below-cost pricing of the predator's outputs. That is, the predator's bidding on the [input] side must have caused the cost of the relevant output to rise above the revenues generated in the sale of those outputs."*Weyerhaeuser,*127 S.Ct. at 1078.

Of course, in neither *Brooke Group* nor *Weyerhaeuser* did the Court go so far as to hold that in every case in which a plaintiff challenges low prices as exclusionary conduct the plaintiff must prove that those prices were below cost. But the Court's opinions strongly suggest that, in the normal case, above-cost pricing will not be considered exclusionary conduct for antitrust purposes, and the Court's reasoning poses a strong caution against condemning bundled discounts that result in prices above a relevant measure of costs.

The Supreme Court's long and consistent adherence to the principle that the antitrust laws protect the process of competition, and not the pursuits of any particular competitor, reinforce our conclusion of caution concerning bundled discounts that result in prices above an appropriate measure of costs. The Court voiced this principle most notably in *Brunswick Corp. v. Pueblo Bowl–O–Mat,* 429 U.S. 477, 97 S.Ct. 690, 50 L.Ed.2d 701 (1977). * * *

* * *

One of the challenges of interpreting and enforcing the amorphous prohibitions of § § 1 and 2 of the Sherman Act is ensuring that the antitrust laws do not punish economic behavior that benefits consumers and will not cause long-run injury to the competitive process. A bundled discount, however else it might be viewed, is a price discount on a collection of goods. The Supreme Court has undoubtedly shown a solicitude for price competition. In *Weyerhaeuser,* Justice Thomas, writing for the Court, reminded us that, in *Brooke Group,* the Court had cautioned that "the costs of erroneous findings of predatory-pricing liability were quite high because [t]he mechanism by which a firm engages in predatory pricing—lowering prices—is the same mechanism by which a firm stimulates competition, and therefore, mistaken findings of liability would chill the very conduct the antitrust laws are designed to protect."

Given the endemic nature of bundled discounts in many spheres of normal economic activity, we decline to endorse the Third Circuit's definition of when bundled discounts constitute the exclusionary conduct proscribed by § 2 of the Sherman Act. Instead, we think the course safer for consumers and our competitive economy to hold that bundled discounts may not be considered exclusionary conduct within the meaning of § 2 of the Sherman Act unless the discounts resemble the behavior that the Supreme Court in *Brooke Group* identified as predatory.[12] Accordingly, we hold that the exclusionary conduct element of a claim arising under § 2 of the Sherman Act cannot be

---

12. McKenzie contends that *Brooke Group* is not persuasive in this case because *Brooke Group* dealt with liability for primary-line price discrimination in violation of § 2(a) of the Robinson–Patman Act, whereas this case arises under § 2 of the Sherman Act. However, the Court made clear in *Brooke Group* that, whether a predatory pricing claim arises under § 2(a) of the Robinson–Patman Act or § 2 of the Sherman Act, the concerns are essentially the same * * *.

satisfied by reference to bundled discounts unless the discounts result in prices that are below an appropriate measure of the defendant's costs.[13]

4

The next question we must address is how we define the appropriate measure of the defendant's costs in bundled discounting cases and how we determine whether discounted prices fall below that mark. Defining the appropriate measure of costs in a bundled discounting case is more complex than in a single product case. In a single product case, we may simply ask whether the defendant has priced its product below its incremental cost of producing that product because a rival that produces the same product as efficiently as the defendant should be able to match any price at or above the defendant's cost. However, as we discussed above, a defendant offering a bundled discount, without pricing below cost either the individual products in the bundle or the bundle as a whole, can, in some cases, exclude a rival who produces one of the products in the bundle equally or more efficiently than the defendant. Thus, simply asking whether the defendant's prices are below its incremental costs might fail to alert us to bundled discounts that threaten the exclusion of equally efficient rivals. Nonetheless, we are mindful that, in single product pricing cases, the Supreme Court has not adopted rules condemning prices above a seller's incremental costs. With these considerations in mind, we assess the rules the parties and amici propose for us to use in bundled discounting cases to determine the appropriate measure of a defendant's costs and whether a defendant has priced below that level.

PeaceHealth and some amici urge us to adopt a rule they term the "aggregate discount" rule. This rule condemns bundled discounts as anticompetitive only in the narrow cases in which the discounted price of the entire bundle does not exceed the bundling firm's incremental cost to produce the entire bundle. PeaceHealth and amici argue that support for such a rule can be found in the Supreme Court's single product predation cases—*Brooke Group* and *Weyerhaeuser*.

We are not persuaded that those cases require us to adopt an aggregate discount rule in multi-product discounting cases. As we discussed above, bundled discounts present one potential threat to consumer welfare that single product discounts do not: A competitor who produces fewer products than the defendant but produces the competitive product at or below the defendant's cost to produce that product may nevertheless be excluded from the market because the competitor cannot match the discount the defendant offers over its numerous product lines. This possibility exists even when the defendant's prices are above cost for each individual product and for the bundle as a whole. Under a discount aggregation rule, anticompetitive bundled discounting schemes that harm competition may too easily escape liability.

Additionally, as commentators have pointed out, *Brooke Group*'s safe harbor for above-cost discounting in the single product discount context is not based on a theory that above-cost pricing strategies can never be anticompeti-

---

13. Of course, even if the exclusionary conduct element is satisfied by bundled discounts at price levels that yield a conclusion of below-cost sales, under the appropriate measure, there cannot be Sherman Act § 2 liability for attempted monopolization unless the other elements of a specific intent to monopolize and dangerous probability of success are satisfied.

tive, but rather on a cost-benefit rejection of a more nuanced rule. That is, the safe harbor rests on the premise that "any consumer benefit created by a rule that permits inquiry into above-cost, single-product discounts, but allows judicial condemnation of those deemed legitimately exclusionary, would likely be outweighed by the consumer harm occasioned by overdeterring nonexclusionary discounts." So, in adopting an appropriate cost-based test for bundled discounting cases, we should not adopt an aggregate discount rule without inquiring whether a rule exists that is more likely to identify anticompetitive bundled discounting practices while at the same time resulting in little harm to competition.

The first potential alternative cost-based standard we consider derives from the district court's opinion in *Ortho* [*Ortho Diagnostic Sys., Inc. v. Abbott Labs., Inc.*, 920 F.Supp. 455 (S.D.N.Y.1996)]. This standard deems a bundled discount exclusionary if the plaintiff can show that it was an equally efficient producer of the competitive product, but the defendant's bundled discount made it impossible for the plaintiff to continue to produce profitably the competitive product. * * * Under this standard, above-cost prices are not per se legal. Instead, this standard treats below-cost prices as simply one beacon for identifying discounts that create the risk of excluding firms that are as efficient as the defendant—the unique anticompetitive risk posed by bundled discounts. Under *Ortho*'s standard, an above-cost discount can still be anticompetitive if a plaintiff proves it is as efficient a producer as the defendant, but is excluded because the defendant sells in more product markets than the plaintiff and can "spread the total discount over all those product lines and . . . force competitors to provide the entire dollar amount of the discount on a smaller collection of products." As compared to the discount aggregation rule, *Ortho*'s approach does a better job of identifying bundled discounts that threaten harm to competition.

However, one downside of *Ortho*'s standard is that it does not provide adequate guidance to sellers who wish to offer procompetitive bundled discounts because the standard looks to the costs of the actual plaintiff. A potential defendant who is considering offering a bundled discount will likely not have access to information about its competitors' costs, thus making it hard for that potential discounter, under the *Ortho* standard, to determine whether the discount it wishes to offer complies with the antitrust laws. Also, the *Ortho* standard, which asks whether the actual plaintiff is as efficient a producer as the defendant, could require multiple suits to determine the legality of a single bundled discount. While it might turn out that the plaintiff in one particular case is not as efficient a producer of the competitive product as the defendant, another rival might be. This second rival would have to bring another suit under the *Ortho* approach. We decline to adopt a rule that might encourage more antitrust litigation than is reasonably necessary to ferret out anticompetitive practices. Accordingly, we do not adopt *Ortho*'s approach, which we believe would be unduly cumbersome for sellers to assess and thus might chill procompetitive bundled discounting.

Instead, as our cost-based rule, we adopt what amici refer to as a "discount attribution" standard.[14] Under this standard, the full amount of the

---

14. In the academic literature, this standard is sometimes referred to as a "discount allocation" or "discount reallocation" standard.

discounts given by the defendant on the bundle are allocated to the competitive product or products. If the resulting price of the competitive product or products is below the defendant's incremental cost to produce them, the trier of fact may find that the bundled discount is exclusionary for the purpose of § 2. This standard makes the defendant's bundled discounts legal unless the discounts have the potential to exclude a *hypothetical* equally efficient producer of the competitive product.[15]

In their leading treatise on antitrust law, Professors Areeda and Hovenkamp support an approach that focuses on whether a bundled discount excludes a hypothetical equally efficient rival. Rejecting *Ortho*'s "actual plaintiff" standard, they explain:

> [W]e would not require a showing that the actual plaintiff be equally efficient. The relevant question is not necessarily whether a particular plaintiff was equally efficient, but whether the challenged bundling practices would have excluded an equally efficient rival, without reasonable justification. This rule is preferable on grounds of both administrability and principle. On the first, proving whether a hypothetical equally efficient rival is excluded by a multiproduct discount is typically quite manageable. By contrast, proof that the plaintiff is equally efficient can be quite difficult, particularly in cases where the defendant produces a larger product line than the plaintiff and there are joint costs.
>
> A requirement that the bundling practice be sufficiently severe so as to exclude an equally efficient single-product rival, and without an adequate business justification, seems to strike about the right balance between permitting aggressive pricing while prohibiting conduct that can only be characterized as anticompetitive. Requiring the defendant's pricing policies to protect the trade of higher cost rivals is overly solicitous of small firms and denies customers the benefits of the defendant's lower costs. Further, if the practice will exclude an equally efficient rival, then it will exclude whether or not the rival is equally efficient in fact.

---

15. A variation of the example from *Ortho* illustrates how the discount attribution standard condemns discounts that could not be matched by an equally or more efficient producer of the competitive product. Recall that the example involves A, a firm that makes both shampoo and conditioner. A's incremental cost of shampoo is $1.50 and A's incremental cost of conditioner is $2.50. A prices shampoo at $3 and conditioner at $5, if purchased separately. However, if purchased as a bundle, A prices shampoo at $2.25 and conditioner at $3. Purchased separately from A, the total price of one unit of shampoo and one unit of conditioner is $8. However, with the bundled discount, a customer can purchase both products from A for $5.25, a discount of $2.75 off the separate prices, but at a price that is still above A's variable cost of producing the bundle. Applying the discount attribution rule to the example, we subtract the entire discount on the package of products, $2.75, from the separate per unit price of the competitive product, shampoo, $3. The resulting effective price of shampoo is thus $0.25, meaning that, if a customer must purchase conditioner from A at the separate price of $5, a rival who produces only shampoo must sell the shampoo for $0.25 to make customers indifferent between A's bundle and the separate purchase of conditioner from A and shampoo from the hypothetical rival. A's pricing scheme thus has the effect of excluding any potential rival who would produce only shampoo, and would produce it at an incremental cost above $0.25. However, as we noted above, A's incremental cost of producing shampoo is $1.50. Thus, A's pricing practices exclude potential competitors that could produce shampoo more efficiently than A (*i.e.*, at an incremental cost of less than $1.50). A's discount could thus be considered exclusionary under our rule, supporting Sherman Act § 2 liability if the other elements were proved.

Judge Posner's work on antitrust law also supports an approach that asks whether a bundled discount excludes a hypothetical equally efficient rival, stating that the acts of a monopolist should be deemed exclusionary if "the challenged practice is likely in the circumstances to exclude from the defendant's market an equally or more efficient competitor."

Areeda and Hovenkamp also support using a discount attribution approach to determine if a bundled discount is exclusionary. They state:

> To see whether a package price is "exclusionary" ... one simply attributes the entire discount on all products in the package to the product for which exclusion is claimed. If the resulting price is less than the defendant's cost, then the package discount is exclusionary as against a rival who makes only one of the two goods in the package.

The discount attribution standard has also been used by two of the district courts in the small number of published opinions dealing with allegedly exclusionary bundled discounts. The discount attribution standard is also the standard endorsed by the AMC.

The discount attribution standard provides clear guidance for sellers that engage in bundled discounting practices. A seller can easily ascertain its own prices and costs of production and calculate whether its discounting practices run afoul of the rule we have outlined. Unlike under the *Ortho* standard, under the discount attribution standard a bundled discounter need not fret over and predict or determine its rivals' cost structure.

We are aware that liability under the discount attribution standard has the potential to sweep more broadly than under the aggregate discount rule or the *Ortho* standard. However, there is limited judicial experience with bundled discounts, and academic inquiry into the competitive effects of bundled discounts is only beginning. By comparison, the Supreme Court's decision in *Brooke Group* (prefaced by the Court's discussion of predatory pricing in *Matsushita*) marked the culmination of nearly twenty years of scholarly and judicial analysis of the feasibility and competitive effects of single product predatory pricing schemes. The cost-based standard we adopt will allow courts the experience they need to divine the prevalence and competitive effects of bundled discounts and will allow these difficult issues to further percolate in the lower courts. * * * Pending further judicial and academic inquiry into the prevalence of anticompetitive bundled discounts, we think it preferable to allow plaintiffs to challenge bundled discounts if those plaintiffs can prove a defendant's bundled discounts would have excluded an equally efficient competitor.

* * *

5

The next issue before us is the appropriate measure of incremental costs in a bundled discounting case. In single product predatory pricing cases, the appropriate measure of incremental costs is an open question in this circuit. The Supreme Court has likewise refused to decide the matter.

As our cases and the relevant academic literature thoroughly discuss, firms face both fixed costs—costs that a firm must bear regardless of the amount of output—and variable costs—costs that change with the amount of output. The sum of fixed and variable costs is a firm's total cost. Marginal cost is the increase to total cost that occurs as a result of producing one additional unit of output. Average cost is the sum of fixed costs and total variable costs, divided by the amount of output. In their oft-cited 1975 law review article, Professors Areeda and Turner concluded that the optimal measure of a firm's cost in a predatory pricing case is marginal cost—the cost to produce one additional unit and the price that would obtain in the market under conditions of perfect competition. *See* Phillip Areeda & Donald F. Turner, *Predatory Pricing and Related Practices Under Section 2 of the Sherman Act,* 88 Harv. L.Rev. 697, 712, 716 (1975). However, Professors Areeda and Turner also recognized that "[t]he incremental cost of making and selling the last unit cannot readily be inferred from conventional business accounts, which typically go no further than showing observed average variable cost." *Id.* at 716. Thus, the professors adopted average variable cost as a surrogate for marginal cost. *Id.* A number of circuits have adopted the Areeda–Turner formulation and concluded that prices below average variable cost can indicate predation.

Likewise, "we have approved the use of marginal or average variable cost statistics in proving predation." We have also held that a plaintiff can establish a prima facie case of predatory pricing by proving that the defendant's prices were below average variable cost. We see no reason to depart from these principles in the bundled discounting context, and we hold that the appropriate measure of costs for our cost-based standard is average variable cost.

6

In summary, we hold the following: To prove that a bundled discount was exclusionary or predatory for the purposes of a monopolization or attempted monopolization claim under § 2 of the Sherman Act, the plaintiff must establish that, after allocating the discount given by the defendant on the entire bundle of products to the competitive product or products, the defendant sold the competitive product or products below its average variable cost of producing them. The district court's jury instruction on the attempted monopolization claim, which built on the holding of *LePage's* that we have rejected, thus contained an error of law.[21]

* * *

21. As we noted above, the AMC's proposed standard in bundled discounting cases, in addition to requiring below-cost pricing, also contains two further proposed elements.

The second element proposed by the AMC is that there is a dangerous probability that the defendant will recoup its investment in the bundled discounting program. This requirement, adopted from *Brooke Group,* is imported from the single product predatory pricing context, but we think imported incorrectly. We do not believe that the recoupment requirement from single product cases translates to multiproduct discounting cases. Single-product pred-

atory pricing, unlike bundling, necessarily involves a loss for the defendant. For a period of time, the defendant must sell below its cost, with the intent to eliminate its competitors so that, when its competition is eliminated, the defendant can charge supracompetitive prices, recouping its losses and potentially more. By contrast, as discussed above, exclusionary bundling does not necessarily involve any loss of profits for the bundled discounter. As the example from *Ortho* illustrates, a bundled discounter can exclude its rivals who do not sell as many product lines even when the bundle as a whole, and the individual products within it, are priced above the discounter's incremental

* * * We vacate the judgment entered in McKenzie's favor and remand for further proceedings consistent with our opinion.

* * *

───────

LePage's and *Cascade Health* appear at first glance to be in conflict, at least with respect to the propriety of using some kind of cost-based standard to identify exclusionary bundled rebates. What explains that conflict? Why was the Third Circuit in *LePage's* opposed to embracing a cost-based standard? What reasons did the Ninth Circuit provide in *Cascade Health* for embracing one? On the other hand, can it be argued that both circuits have rejected a strict application of *Brooke Group* to bundled rebates? *LePage's* concluded that *Brooke Group* was not relevant at all. *Cascade Health* cited it to support use of a cost-based test, but it declined PeaceHealth's invitation to apply it literally through adoption of an "aggregate discount rule" in favor of a "discount attribution" standard. It also declined to impose a recoupment requirement. What was the court's reasoning on each point? How did it in effect distinguish *Brooke Group* even as it drew some guidance from it?

What role did the AMC Report play in the Ninth Circuit's ultimate decision? Whereas the court adopted the first step of the AMC test—a discount attribution test—it specifically rejected the two remaining parts of the proposed AMC test. What reasons did it provide for doing so? Note that the court declined to mandate evidence of recoupment in bundled rebate cases. Why? Did that rejection mean it also was distinguishing portions of *Brooke Group* and agreeing in part with the Third Circuit that rigid application of *Brooke Group's* two-part test to bundled rebates would be under-deterrent? Could its rationale support the rejection of *Brooke Group* in other circumstances?

Cascade Health challenged PeaceHealth's bundled rebates under Section 2 of the Sherman Act, but it also challenged PeaceHealth's decision to bundle primary, secondary, and tertiary care services together as a tying arrangement under Section 1 of the Sherman Act. As we will learn in Chapter 7, tying has a long history under Section 1 and has been treated as per se unlawful when, in addition to other requirements, the seller has market power in the tying product (here primary and secondary care services). When market power

cost to produce them. The trier of fact can identify cases that present this possibility for anticompetitive exclusion by applying the discount attribution standard outlined above. Under that standard, the ultimate question is whether the bundled discount would exclude an equally efficient rival. But because discounts on all products in the bundle have been allocated to the competitive product in issue, a conclusion of below-cost sales under the discount attribution standard may occur in some cases even where there is not an actual loss because the bundle is sold at a price exceeding incremental cost. In such a case, we do not think it is analytically helpful to think in terms of recoupment of a loss that did not occur.

The third element proposed by the AMC is that "the bundled discount or rebate program has had or is likely to have an adverse effect on competition." We view this final element as redundant because it is no different than the general requirement of "antitrust injury" that a plaintiff must prove in any private antitrust action. For these reasons, while adopting the AMC's proposal to require below-cost sales to prove exclusionary conduct, we do not adopt the element of recoupment, which we think may be inapplicable in some cases, and we do not adopt the element of "adverse effect on competition" as we think that is superfluous in light of the general and pre-existing requirement of antitrust injury under *Brunswick*.

is present, the reasoning goes, the conditional sale of the tying product in connection with the tied product (here tertiary care services) "coerces" the purchaser to accept a deal that it might otherwise have rejected on the merits.

The district court granted PeaceHealth's motion for summary judgment on the tying claims, concluding that there was insufficient evidence of coercion. Cascade Health cross-appealed. The Ninth Circuit reversed and remanded the tying claim for additional factual development:

> * * * [W]hen all justifiable factual inferences are drawn in McKenzie's favor, there is no doubt that PeaceHealth's practice of giving a larger discount to insurers who dealt with it as an exclusive preferred provider may have coerced some insurers to purchase primary and secondary services from PeaceHealth rather than from McKenzie. We conclude that, as a whole, the evidence shows genuine factual disputes about whether PeaceHealth forced insurers either as an implied condition of dealing or as a matter of economic imperative through its bundled discounting, to take its primary and secondary services if the insurers wanted tertiary services.

515 F.3d at 914. In support of this conclusion, the court reasoned, in part:

> Finally, the Supreme Court has condemned tying arrangements when the seller has the market power to force a purchaser to do something that he would not do in a competitive market. *Jefferson Parish,* 466 U.S. at 17, 104 S.Ct. 1551. PeaceHealth was the only provider of tertiary services in the relevant geographic market. The substantial market power PeaceHealth possessed as a result of being the exclusive provider of tertiary services in Lane County creates a possibility that PeaceHealth was able to force unwanted purchases of primary and secondary services. In light of the evidence adduced by McKenzie at summary judgment, whether PeaceHealth in fact used its market power to effectively coerce purchases of primary and secondary services is a question that can be answered only through further factual development. The need for further factual development renders summary judgment on McKenzie's tying claim inappropriate. Because a trier of fact might reasonably determine McKenzie established a claim of illegal tying based on the evidence in the record, we vacate the district court's order granting summary judgment to PeaceHealth and remand for further proceedings.

Id. at 915–16. What might explain the court's seeming receptivity to Cascade Health's tying claim, but its rejection of its claim under Section 2, which targeted not the mere fact of the bundle, but the bundled rebate? How are the two claims related? In a footnote, the Ninth Circuit provided the following additional guidance to the district court on remand:

> If, on remand, McKenzie stakes its tying claim not on a theory that PeaceHealth explicitly (*e.g.*, by contract) or implicitly coerced insurers to purchase primary and secondary services from PeaceHealth as a condition to obtaining tertiary services, but on a theory that PeaceHealth's bundled discounts effectively left insurers with no rational economic choice other than purchasing tertiary services from PeaceHealth, such a claim might raise the question of whether, to establish the coercion element of a tying claim through a bundled

discount, McKenzie must prove that PeaceHealth priced below a relevant measure of its costs. Some commentators would require a plaintiff alleging that a bundled discount amounts to an illegal tie to prove below-cost prices. It is unclear whether the AMC intended its three-part test to apply when a plaintiff alleging an illegal tying arrangement asserts that the defendant's pricing practices coerced unwanted purchases of the tied product. *See* AMC Report, *supra,* at 114 n. 157 ("The recommended three-part test is proposed here for challenges to bundled *pricing* practices, and its purpose, as the text explains, is to avoid deterring procompetitive price reductions. The Commission is not recommending application of this test outside the bundled pricing context, for example in tying or exclusive dealing cases. The Commission did not undertake to study tying and exclusive dealing issues more generally."). The parties have not briefed this issue to us, and the parties did not raise the issue before the district court. We therefore leave it to the district court, if necessary, to decide the issue in the first instance on remand.

Id. at 916 n.27. We will return to the question whether exclusionary pricing conduct should be treated differently than non-price exclusionary conduct, like tying and exclusive dealing, in Chapter 7.

Sidebar 6–4:
Should There Be A Unitary Standard for Judging Exclusionary Conduct?*

Introduction

The very general standards of *Alcoa* ("skill, foresight, luck or business acumen") and *Grinnell* ("willful acquisition or maintenance") can be of limited use in differentiating aggressive, but legitimate competitive strategies from those deserving condemnation under Section 2. Other tests and standards, especially those in *Aspen Skiing* ("non-efficiency based competition" that "unnecessarily excludes") and *Brooke Group* (below cost pricing plus a dangerous probability of recoupment) developed to help divine that line with greater economic sophistication and reliability.

Cascade Health illustrates, however, how the differing approaches of *Aspen Skiing* and *Brooke Group* have themselves generated some tension and uncertainty in the law of monopolization. As noted earlier in this Chapter, no plaintiff, public or private has prevailed in a case controlled by *Brooke Group*. In contrast, in the few recent cases in which plaintiffs have prevailed under Section 2, cases like *LePage's* and *Microsoft*, the courts relied on *Aspen Skiing*. The choice of standard clearly can affect the outcome of monopolization challenges. In litigation, that almost guarantees that plaintiffs and defendants will battle over the characterization of their claim: is it price predation subject to *Brooke Group* (and therefore likely to fail) or non-price exclusionary conduct controlled by

---

* Portions of this Sidebar are adapted from Andrew I. Gavil, *Exclusionary Distribution Strategies by Dominant Firms: Striking a Bet-* *ter Balance,* 72 ANTITRUST L.J. 3 (2004). *See also Symposium—Identifying Exclusionary Conduct Under Section 2,* 73 ANTITRUST L.J. 311 (2006).

Aspen Skiing (and therefore at least possibly a basis for success for the plaintiff)? As was evident in both *LePage's* and *Cascade Health*, dominant firm defendants see in *Brooke Group* a deferential standard that provides them with significant discretion to structure their primary competitive conduct free from any serious threat of antitrust liability. Plaintiffs see an insurmountable burden that will in effect immunize competitively harmful exclusionary conduct from judicial review. Does this necessarily suggest a need for reform?

As was true of the long-running debates over the propriety of per se vs. rule of reason treatment for various kinds of conduct (recall Chapters 2 and 4), the current tension between *Aspen Skiing* and *Brooke Group* can be understood on two levels. For litigants, the choice of standard is a dispassionate strategic calculation that can lead to victory or defeat. For the antitrust system, the choice of standard is about striking the optimal balance between incidence of false positives on the one hand and incidence of false negatives and increased processing costs on the other. Standards that demand greater economic certainty can reduce the incidence of false positives, but they almost invariably do so by increasing processing costs and possibly the incidence of false negatives, as some of the demanded information proves to be unavailable or too costly to secure.

Cascade Health is again illustrative of the challenge. The defendants successfully argued that the jury instructions used at trial did not sufficiently differentiate between efficient and inefficient bundled rebates. As a consequence, those instructions would lead to greater false positives—efficient bundled rebates could be condemned or simply never implemented for fear of antitrust liability exposure. The solution—partially embraced by the Ninth Circuit—was to elevate the burden of proof, but not necessarily to the level commanded by *Brooke Group* or the Antitrust Modernization Commission. The Ninth Circuit can be understood as trying to strike an optimal balance between an undemanding standard that might produce false positives and an overly demanding one that might be costly to administer and produce false negatives. The end result was a test that was more favorable to defendants than *Aspen Skiing* and *LePage's*, but better for plaintiffs than *Brooke Group*.

Which approach under Section 2 can minimize error costs—both false positives and false negatives—as well as direct costs? Perhaps multiple standards are preferable to a unitary standard, precisely because they are flexible, which allows for some fine-tuning for categories of conduct that are more or less likely to be pernicious. *See, e.g.,* Mark S. Popofsky, *Defining Exclusionary Conduct: Section 2, the Rule of Reason, and the Unifying Principle Underlying Antitrust Rules*, 73 ANTITRUST L.J. 435 (2006) (rejecting one-size fits all standard in favor of a unitary principle that guides all standards—the rule of reason). Perhaps, for example, simple price predation warrants a unique and elevated standard of proof, because the likely incidence and consequences of false positives is especially great when price reducing strategies are challenged. On the other hand, *LePage's* and *Cascade Health* certainly suggest that continued use of multiple standards under Section 2 will place a premium on "characterization" and hence lead to increased and arguably pointless litigation. Would it be better to have a unitary standard for judging all instances of exclusionary conduct? If so, what should that standard be, and what role, if any, can *Aspen Skiing* and *Brooke Group* play in fashioning its content? Is there a unitary standard that would not only reduce direct costs, making it preferential to a regime of multiple standards, but also minimize both kinds of error costs?

The Standards Wars

This Sidebar examines a continuing debate among enforcers and commentators about the propriety of using a unitary standard for all claims of exclusionary conduct. Such a standard could supercede the traditional formulations from *Alcoa* and *Grinnell* and resolve the current tension between *Aspen Skiing* and *Brooke Group*. The five tests themselves fall into two classes, one inspired by *Brooke Group* and the other by *Aspen Skiing* and the D.C. Circuit's decision in *Microsoft*.

A.   *Inspired by Brooke Group*

The Profit Sacrifice and No Economic Sense Tests

The *Matsushita-Brooke Group* standard for predatory pricing is rooted in scholarship that focused on the significance of evidence of "profit sacrifice." Whereas in predatory pricing cases all profits are sacrificed, some have suggested more recently that evidence of the sacrifice of some, but not all profits, could provide an equally valuable guide to defining all exclusionary conduct. This approach could elevate the basic framework of *Brooke Group* to the status of a unitary standard.

Under one proposal, the test would ask first, whether the challenged conduct "is profitable to the defendant in light of its incremental costs and incremental benefits," and second, "whether the conduct enabled the defendant to gain additional market power or a dangerous probability thereof." *See, e.g,* A. Douglas Melamed, *Exclusive Dealing Agreements and Other Exclusionary Conduct—Are There Unifying Principles?*, 73 Antitrust L.J. 375, 389–403 (2006) ("Unifying Principles"). Conduct that is costly to a firm in the short run may be difficult to justify as "efficient." Melamed suggests a number of benefits of the test that can be directly associated with minimizing false positives and direct costs. The test finds some support in references by the Supreme Court to the significance of evidence of profit sacrifice in *Aspen Skiing*, 472 U.S. 585, 608, 610–11; and *Verizon Commnc's Inc. v. Law Offices of Curtis V. Trinko*, 540 U.S. 398, 409 (2004) (Casebook, Section C4, *infra*).

Like all of the proposed tests to be discussed, however, the profit sacrifice test also has been the subject of criticism. First, to the degree it is a variation of *Brooke Group*, it is subject to the same question of whether it is difficult to satisfy and hence tends to under-deter anticompetitive conduct. Second, measuring "profit" can be very difficult, because it must be assessed relative to the profits available from some specific, alternative business strategy. Third, the sacrifice test is procedurally objectionable, because it shifts the burden of pleading and production from the defendant to the plaintiff on issues likely to turn on evidence solely within the hands of the defendant.

Most significantly, the sacrifice test is objectionable because it ignores low or no cost predation strategies, including strategies that confer market power by raising rivals's costs. It also redirects the Section 2 inquiry away from a focused inquiry into competitive effects and uses profit sacrifice as a surrogate for effects. Consider, for example, whether there were practices analyzed in *Microsoft* that were condemned as exclusionary by the D.C. Circuit, but which likely involved little if any sacrifice of profit for Microsoft, yet produced anticompetitive effect. *See also Note on Cheap Exclusion, infra* at 717. For a more comprehensive presentation of these objections, see Steven C. Salop, *Exclusionary Conduct, Effect on Consumers, and the Flawed Profit–Sacrifice Standard*, 73 ANTITRUST L.J. 311 (2006) ("Flawed Profit–Sacrifice Standard"). For a further defense and response to objections, see Melamed, *Unifying Principles*, 73 ANTITRUST L.J. at 393–403.

The profit sacrifice test is related to the "no economic sense" test ("NES"). The NES test asks: would the monopolist have undertaken the conduct but for its anticompetitive effects? Put another way, it asks whether there was any legitimate business reason for the conduct. Like profit sacrifice, it would be all-encompassing, as advocated by some, and could cover all conduct by dominant firms that exclude. It might also be used in a more limited way, applying for example only to certain categories of conduct, such as refusals to deal. For a defense of the NES test, see Gregory J. Werden, *Identifying Exclusionary Conduct Under Section 2: The "No Economic Sense" Test*, 73 ANTITRUST L.J. 413 (2006) ("No Economic Sense"). *See also id.* at 422–25 (distinguishing NES from profit sacrifice and arguing that profit sacrifice "is neither necessary nor sufficient for conduct to be exclusionary").

The NES test has not been expressly embraced by any court and has been subjected to some of the same criticisms as the profit sacrifice test. It focuses exclusively on the incentives of the dominant firm, largely ignoring the effects of its conduct on rivals or consumers. It also has been criticized as largely a surrogate for the alleged predator's intent. *See* Salop, *Flawed Profit–Sacrifice Standard, supra*. The NES test also seems to provide a monopolist with a complete defense to conduct that excludes, so long as it can point to some efficiency gains. It is seemingly indifferent to the amount of those gains (provided they are sufficient to justify the conduct in some sense) and the degree to which the challenged conduct also may have resulted in significant anticompetitive effects. Even if the overwhelmingly predominant effect of the conduct is to facilitate the exercise of market power, the conduct could be immunized from challenge.

The "Equally Efficient Rival" Test

The "equally efficient rival" test is associated with the work of Judge Richard A. Posner, who proposed a two-step framework for analyzing exclusionary conduct. The first step asks whether the conduct, if undertaken by a monopolist, could exclude "an equally or more efficient competitor." If the answer is "yes," the monopolist could rebut a presumption that the conduct is exclusionary by proving that "although it is a monopolist and the challenged practice is exclusionary, the practice is, on balance, efficient." RICHARD A. POSNER, ANTITRUST LAW 18–21 (2d ed. 2001). His approach rules out Section 2 challenges by unsuccessful rivals, some of whom may be inclined to blame the dominant firm's practices for their competitive failure. In essence, it presumes that their complaints are unlikely to prove worthy of judicial consideration.

Although no court has embraced Posner's standard as proposed, some have included considerations about rival efficiency in their tests. Recall that *Cascade Health*, for example, cited Judge Posner's work with approval, and justified its choice of cost allocation standard in part because it would only prohibit bundled rebates that would exclude an equally efficient rival. *Cascade Health*, 502 F.3d at 916 ("This standard makes the defendant's bundled discounts legal unless the discounts have the potential to exclude a hypothetical equally efficient producer of the competitive product.")

Posner's approach can be questioned on a number of grounds: (1) it implicitly presumes that the exclusion of a *less* efficient rival will be harmless;** (2) it initially redirects the inquiry away from a focus on the efficiency of the challenged practice; *cf.* Einer Elhauge, *Defining Better Monopolization Standards*, 56 Stan. L. Rev. 253 (2003) (arguing for standard that distinguishes between conduct that improves monopolist's own efficiency, which would be permitted, and conduct that impairs rivals' efficiency and results in market-wide anticompetitive effects, which would be prohibited); and (3) determining whether a hypothetical competitor is "equally efficient" can be difficult. *See* Salop, *Flawed Profit–Sacrifice Standard*, *supra* at 328–29 (critique of equally efficient rival standard).

B. *Inspired by Aspen Skiing and Microsoft*

Recall that there were two important features to the approach developed by the Supreme Court in *Aspen Skiing*. It defined "exclusionary" as excluding a rival "on some basis other than efficiency" or "in an unnecessarily restrictive way." Casebook, *supra* at 632. It also structured its analysis around inquiries into the effect of the challenged conduct on rivals, consumers, and the dominant firm, itself, which included an inquiry into any legitimate business justifications for the conduct. Similarly, the D.C. Circuit in *Microsoft* established a structured analysis that looked first to the conduct's anticompetitive effects (effects on rivals and consumers) and then to the dominant firm's legitimate justifications for its conduct. Casebook, *supra* at 647.

The profit sacrifice, NES, and less efficient rival tests are quite different in design and likely effect. They involve truncated tests, which focus on what proponents perceive as more economically sound criteria for judging exclusionary conduct. They can be understood as alternatives to the kind of structured, fact-intensive analysis contemplated by *Aspen Skiing* and *Microsoft*, as was *Brooke Group*. The goal of each is to provide economically defensible standards that minimize false positives and direct costs. It is unclear that they do so, however, and they may significantly increase the incidence and consequences of false negatives.

Two other approaches have been proposed, however, that are much closer in design and operation to *Aspen Skiing* and *Microsoft*, although each also has some unique features and goals. These tests proceed with a

---

** Even a less efficient rival can stimulate competition and lower prices in a market where a dominant firm is charging monopoly prices. For example, assume that a dominant firm with costs of $5 is currently selling a product for $10. A less efficient entrant with costs of $6 could easily prompt a significant decrease in price if it charged $7.50. *Cf.* Aaron S. Edlin, *Stopping Above–Cost Predatory Pricing*, 111 Yale L.J. 941, 945 (2002). The elimination of such a rival could be especially costly for competition if it was on the path to improved efficiency, as with a firm that is striving to reach scale economies.

greater degree of concern about false negatives than do the *Brooke Group*-styled tests.

The Disproportionality Standard

The "disproportionality" test, which has been attributed to Professor Herbert Hovenkamp, would limit the definition of exclusionary conduct to actions that:

> (1) are reasonably capable of creating, enlarging, or prolonging monopoly power by impairing the opportunities of rivals; and

> (2) that either (2a) do not benefit consumers at all, or (2b) are unnecessary for the particular consumer benefits that the acts produce, or (2c) produce harms disproportionate to the resulting benefits.

3 Phillip Areeda & Herbert Hovenkamp, Antitrust Law ¶ 651a, at 72 (2d ed. 2002). In the first instance, Hovenkamp's test focuses on monopoly power and anticompetitive effects—two filters that guard against false positives. The test then moves on to perform a triage on conduct, dividing it into three categories worth condemning, albeit with varying levels of inquiry: (1) conduct with no legitimate justification (an easy case for condemnation); (2) conduct that may have some efficiency benefits, but is unnecessary to achieve those benefits (another case for condemnation along the lines established in ancillary restraint analysis); and (3) conduct that causes competitive harm that is "disproportionate" to any efficiency benefits (likely to be the most elaborate of the required analyses).

Hovenkamp's framework draws from a number of areas of antitrust law, such as the "quick look" and ancillary restraints approaches under Section 1 and merger analysis. Like those other areas, it acknowledges the possibility that conduct that excludes can lead to both inefficiencies and efficiencies, and that those effects will need to be evaluated. The "disproportionality" qualification can be understood as a concession to the concerns expressed in *Brooke Group* and in the *Brooke Group*-derived tests discussed above. It gives additional weight to producer surplus and is an effort to control for imperfect evidence and imperfect decisionmaking in order to reduce false positives. It tries to safeguard the dominant firm's incentives to innovate and pursue efficiency-based competitive strategies by ensuring that close cases will go to the defendant.

The Consumer Welfare Effect Standard

Professor Steven C. Salop advocates a more express focus on consumer welfare and an un-weighted reasonableness standard. His approach would evaluate harm to consumer surplus as well as gain in producer surplus, but cases would not turn on the net effect on aggregate welfare. *See Note on Efficiencies and Consumer Welfare, supra* at 571. Instead, Salop explains that "[t]his consumer welfare analysis is more geared towards comparing the magnitudes of various effects to predict the likely overall impact on *consumers.*" Salop, *Flawed Profit–Sacrifice Standard, supra* at 331–32 (emphasis original).

Salop's "consumer welfare effect" standard is thus centered on the anticompetitive effects of allegedly exclusionary conduct, "on the net impact [of the conduct] on consumer welfare, that is, market price and output." Salop, *Flawed Profit–Sacrifice Standard*, *supra* at 329. It provides:

> * * * [O]ne would conclude that exclusionary conduct violates the antitrust laws if it reduces competition without creating a sufficient improvement in performance to fully offset these potential adverse effect[s] on prices and thereby prevent consumer harm. Such conduct could be labeled "unreasonably exclusionary."

Id. at 330. Salop analogizes his approach not only to Section 1 of the Sherman Act, but to merger analysis under Horizontal Merger Guidelines and refers to it as a "competitive effects-based antitrust standard" that as in other areas of antitrust law "essentially would compare the beneficial and harmful competitive aspects of the alleged exclusionary conduct in order to determine the overall impact on consumers." *Id.* Distinguishing his proposal from others, he explains:

> * * * [T]his test focuses on the effect of the conduct on the market, that is, consumers and the competitive process. In contrast, the other standards—profit sacrifice, no economic sense, equally efficient competitor—are focused instead on the impact of the conduct on the alleged miscreant. This is the key reason why the other standards are flawed.

Id. at 331.

The disproportionality and consumer welfare effects tests are more consistent with how courts have approached monopolization claims other than predatory pricing and are general enough to accommodate many kinds of situations. The primary criticisms that have been directed at them, lodged most vocally by advocates of the NES and profit sacrifice tests, is that they provide less guidance to dominant firms, are less likely to produce consistent results, and are costly to implement because they are so fact-intensive. For critics, that adds up to a substantial risk of false positives. Some critics have especially decried Professor Salop's advocacy of a consumer welfare effects standard and of any kind of "balancing" of harms and benefits as unworkable, although that arguably misreads Professor Salop's proposal. For a sampling of the criticisms, see Melamed, *Unifying Principles*, *supra* at 379–83; Werden, *No Economic Sense*, *supra* at 428–32. For a response to these criticisms, see Salop, *Flawed Profit–Sacrifice Standard*, *supra* at 330–33.

Conclusion

As you can now see, the question whether there is a unitary standard that should cover all types of exclusionary conduct has produced a lively debate. Which if any of the cases we have read in this Chapter turned on the choice of standard? Would they have been decided differently if one of the above standards had been adopted? Would the plaintiffs have prevailed in *Lorain Journal*, *Aspen Skiing*, *Microsoft*, or *LePage's* if one of the *Brooke Group*-inspired tests had applied? Would defendants have still won *Brooke Group* if one of the *Aspen Skiing/Microsoft*-inspired tests had applied? As you read the remainder of the cases in this Chapter, consider these same questions.

One way to understand the various tests is in terms of the assumptions the various proponents bring to the table about how likely dominant firms are to pursue exclusionary strategies and how competent the antitrust system is to evaluate them. Recall from our consideration of predatory pricing, that the two part test of *Brooke Group* grew out of strong skepticism that predatory pricing could be a profitable strategy and hence that it was likely to occur. It also reflected a skepticism that courts (especially juries) could successfully differentiate between truly predatory pricing and aggressive, competitive pricing. The result was a standard that places a "thumb on the scale" in favor of defendants by imposing an arguably demanding burden of proof on plaintiffs asserting exclusionary conduct claims. Avoiding false positives and their predicted consequences was the predominant motivation.

Proponents of the profit sacrifice, NES, and perhaps to a lesser extent the equally efficient rival standards, share this same kind of skepticism about the likely merits of exclusion claims and of the antitrust system's ability to evaluate them accurately. Once these presumptions are in place, fears of false positives take hold. These standards can be understood, therefore, as efforts similarly to place a thumb on the scale in favor of dominant firms.

Proponents of alternate standards, such as the disproportionality and consumer welfare effect frameworks, are less sanguine about the motivations of dominant firms, more persuaded that profitable exclusionary strategies exist, and at least a little more confident that the courts can, if properly guided, get exclusion cases "right." They are also concerned that the extension of demanding standards into areas where the threat of false positives is perhaps less pronounced than it was in the case of predatory pricing, and where the potential harm of false negatives is by comparison more pronounced, could lead to significant under-deterrence. These commentators are more comfortable with employing a reasonableness framework to identify anticompetitive conduct, perhaps structured in the form of burden-shifting on the model of the emerging framework for evaluating agreements under Section 1 of the Sherman Act. Like the Merger Guidelines, their approach is more demanding of dominant firms and requires them to make a significant showing that their strategy will in fact produce efficiencies likely to dissipate any anticompetitive effects.

4. UNILATERAL REFUSALS TO DEAL AS EXCLUSIONARY CONDUCT

Since the earliest days of monopolization cases under Section 2 of the Sherman Act, the courts have been required to judge the legality of refusals by dominant firms to deal with their rivals, customers, or suppliers. For the most part, courts have declined to require monopolists to cooperate with another business entity. This general policy took shape in *United States v. Colgate & Co.*, 250 U.S. 300, 39 S.Ct. 465 (1919), where the Supreme Court provided a much-quoted statement about the extent of a firm's freedom to choose its commercial partners:

> In the absence of any purpose to create or maintain a monopoly, the [Sherman] act does not restrict the long recognized right of trader or manufacturer engaged in an entirely private business, freely to exercise his independent discretion as to parties with whom he will deal.

Id. at 307. The question of whether a firm has lost the immunity of *Colgate* by seeking to "create or maintain a monopoly" has inspired countless antitrust disputes.

Refusal to deal cases have arisen in three different fact patterns, although there are variations. The first includes cases in which a dominant firm threatens to cease cooperation with a customer or supplier that is considering forming a relationship with the dominant firm's competitors. *Lorain Journal*, which we considered at the beginning of this chapter, is an example. The second consists of challenges to a dominant firm's attempt to withdraw from an existing contractual relationship or to impose new terms on an existing relationship. *Aspen Skiing* and *Kodak*, are examples of this pattern. The third concerns the refusal of a dominant firm to provide access to a facility— sometimes called an "essential facility"—that a rival requires in order to compete with the dominant firm. One well-known instance of this pattern was *MCI Commc'ns Corp. v. American Tel. & Tel. Co.*, 708 F.2d 1081 (7th Cir. 1983).

In each of these cases, the plaintiff typically is seeking injunctive relief from the court, ordering the dominant firm to deal. Courts, commentators and parties, therefore, often pose the issue in such cases as whether a court should impose a "duty to deal" on dominant firms. Such duty to deal issues can arise, however, regardless of whether the allegedly exclusionary conduct is a refusal to deal. Imposed dealing also has been ordered as a remedy for other kinds of exclusionary conduct. Recall, for example, that although a refusal to deal was not one of the kinds of conduct challenged in the U.S. case against Microsoft, it was the basis for a portion of the European Commission's case. Yet both the Commission and the U.S. Justice Department deemed forced dealing—sharing of communications protocols by Microsoft to facilitate inter-operability between Microsoft's Windows and other software—as an appropriate remedy. *See Note on the Microsoft Prosecution in the European Union*, *supra*.

In our next case, the Supreme Court appeared to significantly limit the scope of *Aspen Skiing*, and with it the degree to which the antitrust laws will support a duty to deal, especially with rivals. As you read the case, however, consider how broadly the decision itself should be interpreted. For example, how significant to the Court's rationale is the regulatory context in which the case arose? Would the Court support an antitrust driven "duty to assist rivals" absent that context? In other contexts? As a remedy for other kinds of exclusionary conduct?

VERIZON COMMUNICATIONS INC. v. LAW OFFICES OF CURTIS V. TRINKO, LLP

United States Supreme Court, 2004.
540 U.S. 398, 124 S.Ct. 872, 157 L.Ed.2d 823.

Justice SCALIA delivered the opinion of the Court.

The Telecommunications Act of 1996 imposes certain duties upon incumbent local telephone companies in order to facilitate market entry by competitors, and establishes a complex regime for monitoring and enforcement. In this case we consider whether a complaint alleging breach of the incumbent's duty under the 1996 Act to share its network with competitors states a claim under § 2 of the Sherman Act.

I

Petitioner Verizon Communications Inc. is the incumbent local exchange carrier (LEC) serving New York State. Before the 1996 Act, Verizon, like other incumbent LECs, enjoyed an exclusive franchise within its local service area. The 1996 Act sought to "uproo[t]" the incumbent LECs' monopoly and to introduce competition in its place. Central to the scheme of the Act is the incumbent LEC's obligation to share its network with competitors, including provision of access to individual elements of the network on an "unbundled" basis. New entrants, so-called competitive LECs, resell these unbundled network elements (UNEs), recombined with each other or with elements belonging to the LECs.

Verizon, like other incumbent LECs, has taken two significant steps within the Act's framework in the direction of increased competition. First, Verizon has signed interconnection agreements with rivals such as AT & T, as it is obliged to do [under the Act]. * * *

Second, Verizon has taken advantage of the opportunity provided by the 1996 Act for incumbent LECs to enter the long-distance market (from which they had long been excluded). That required Verizon to satisfy, among other things, a 14–item checklist of statutory requirements, which includes compliance with the Act's network-sharing duties. * * *

Part of Verizon's UNE obligation is the provision of access to operations support systems (OSS), a set of systems used by incumbent LECs to provide services to customers and ensure quality. Verizon's interconnection agreement and long-distance authorization each specified the mechanics by which its OSS obligation would be met. As relevant here, a competitive LEC sends orders for service through an electronic interface with Verizon's ordering system, and as Verizon completes certain steps in filling the order, it sends confirmation back through the same interface. Without OSS access a rival cannot fill its customers' orders.

In late 1999, competitive LECs complained to regulators that many orders were going unfilled, in violation of Verizon's obligation to provide access to OSS functions. The PSC [New York's Public Service Commission] and FCC [Federal Communications Commission] opened parallel investigations, which led to a series of orders by the PSC and a consent decree with the FCC. Under the FCC consent decree, Verizon undertook to make a "voluntary contribution" to the U.S. Treasury in the amount of $3 million; under the PSC orders, Verizon incurred liability to the competitive LECs in the amount of $10 million. Under the consent decree and orders, Verizon was subjected to new performance measurements and new reporting requirements to the FCC and PSC, with additional penalties for continued noncompliance. In June 2000, the FCC terminated the consent decree. The next month the PSC relieved Verizon of the heightened reporting requirement.

Respondent Law Offices of Curtis V. Trinko, LLP, a New York City law firm, was a local telephone service customer of AT & T. The day after Verizon entered its consent decree with the FCC, respondent filed a complaint in the District Court for the Southern District of New York, on behalf of itself and a class of similarly situated customers. The complaint, as later amended, alleged that Verizon had filled rivals' orders on a discriminatory basis as part of an anticompetitive scheme to discourage customers from becoming or remaining customers of competitive LECs, thus impeding the competitive LECs' ability to enter and compete in the market for local telephone service. * * * The complaint sought damages and injunctive relief for violation of § 2 of the Sherman Act pursuant to the remedy provisions of §§ 4 and 16 of the Clayton Act. * * *

The District Court dismissed the complaint in its entirety. As to the antitrust portion, it concluded that respondent's allegations of deficient assistance to rivals failed to satisfy the requirements of § 2. The Court of Appeals for the Second Circuit reinstated the complaint in part, including the antitrust claim. We granted certiorari, limited to the question whether the Court of Appeals erred in reversing the District Court's dismissal of respondent's antitrust claims.

II

To decide this case, we must first determine what effect (if any) the 1996 Act has upon the application of traditional antitrust principles. The Act imposes a large number of duties upon incumbent LECs—above and beyond those basic responsibilities it imposes upon all carriers. * * *

That Congress created these duties, however, does not automatically lead to the conclusion that they can be enforced by means of an antitrust claim. Indeed, a detailed regulatory scheme such as that created by the 1996 Act ordinarily raises the question whether the regulated entities are not shielded from antitrust scrutiny altogether by the doctrine of implied immunity. * * *

Congress, however, precluded that interpretation. Section 601(b)(1) of the 1996 Act is an antitrust-specific saving clause providing that "nothing in this Act or the amendments made by this Act shall be construed to modify, impair, or supersede the applicability of any of the antitrust laws." This bars a finding of implied immunity. As the FCC has put the point, the saving clause preserves those "claims that satisfy established antitrust standards."

But just as the 1996 Act preserves claims that satisfy existing antitrust standards, it does not create new claims that go beyond existing antitrust standards; that would be equally inconsistent with the saving clause's mandate that nothing in the Act "modify, impair, or supersede the applicability" of the antitrust laws. We turn, then, to whether the activity of which respondent complains violates pre-existing antitrust standards.

III

The complaint alleges that Verizon denied interconnection services to rivals in order to limit entry. If that allegation states an antitrust claim at all, it does so under § 2 of the Sherman Act, which declares that a firm shall not "monopolize" or "attempt to monopolize." It is settled law that this offense requires, in addition to the possession of monopoly power in the relevant market, "the willful acquisition or maintenance of that power as distinguished from growth or development as a consequence of a superior product, business acumen, or historic accident." *United States v. Grinnell Corp.,* 384 U.S. 563, 570–71, 86 S. Ct. 1698, 16 L.Ed.2d 778 (1966). The mere possession of monopoly power, and the concomitant charging of monopoly prices, is not only not unlawful; it is an important element of the free-market system. The opportunity to charge monopoly prices—at least for a short period—is what attracts "business acumen" in the first place; it induces risk taking that produces innovation and economic growth. To safeguard the incentive to innovate, the possession of monopoly power will not be found unlawful unless it is accompanied by an element of anticompetitive *conduct*.

Firms may acquire monopoly power by establishing an infrastructure that renders them uniquely suited to serve their customers. Compelling such firms to share the source of their advantage is in some tension with the underlying purpose of antitrust law, since it may lessen the incentive for the monopolist, the rival, or both to invest in those economically beneficial facilities. Enforced sharing also requires antitrust courts to act as central planners, identifying the proper price, quantity, and other terms of dealing—a role for which they are ill-suited. Moreover, compelling negotiation between competitors may facilitate the supreme evil of antitrust: collusion. Thus, as a general matter, the Sherman Act "does not restrict the long recognized right of [a] trader or manufacturer engaged in an entirely private business, freely to exercise his own independent discretion as to parties with whom he will deal." *United States v. Colgate & Co.,* 250 U.S. 300, 307, 39 S.Ct. 465, 63 L.Ed. 992 (1919).

However, "[t]he high value that we have placed on the right to refuse to deal with other firms does not mean that the right is unqualified." *Aspen Skiing Co. v. Aspen Highlands Skiing Corp.,* 472 U.S. 585, 601, 105 S.Ct. 2847, 86 L.Ed.2d 467 (1985). Under certain circumstances, a refusal to cooperate with rivals can constitute anticompetitive conduct and violate § 2. We have been very cautious in recognizing such exceptions, because of the uncertain virtue of forced sharing and the difficulty of identifying and remedying anticompetitive conduct by a single firm. The question before us today is whether the allegations of respondent's complaint fit within existing exceptions or provide a basis, under traditional antitrust principles, for recognizing a new one.

The leading case for § 2 liability based on refusal to cooperate with a rival, and the case upon which respondent understandably places greatest reliance, is *Aspen Skiing.* * * * We upheld a jury verdict for the plaintiff, reasoning that "[t]he jury may well have concluded that [the defendant] elected to forgo these short-run benefits because it was more interested in reducing competition ... over the long run by harming its smaller competitor."

Aspen Skiing is at or near the outer boundary of § 2 liability. The Court there found significance in the defendant's decision to cease participation in a cooperative venture. The unilateral termination of a voluntary (*and thus presumably profitable*) course of dealing suggested a willingness to forsake short-term profits to achieve an anticompetitive end. Similarly, the defendant's unwillingness to renew the ticket *even if compensated at retail price* revealed a distinctly anticompetitive bent.

The refusal to deal alleged in the present case does not fit within the limited exception recognized in *Aspen Skiing.* The complaint does not allege that Verizon voluntarily engaged in a course of dealing with its rivals, or would ever have done so absent statutory compulsion. Here, therefore, the defendant's prior conduct sheds no light upon the motivation of its refusal to deal—upon whether its regulatory lapses were prompted not by competitive zeal but by anticompetitive malice. The contrast between the cases is heightened by the difference in pricing behavior. In *Aspen Skiing*, the defendant turned down a proposal to sell at its own retail price, suggesting a calculation that its future monopoly retail price would be higher. Verizon's reluctance to interconnect at the cost-based rate of compensation available tells us nothing about dreams of monopoly.

The specific nature of what the 1996 Act compels makes this case different from *Aspen Skiing* in a more fundamental way. In *Aspen Skiing*, what the defendant refused to provide to its competitor was a product that it already sold at retail—to oversimplify slightly, lift tickets representing a bundle of services to skiers. Similarly, in *Otter Tail Power Co. v. United States*, 410 U.S. 366, 93 S.Ct. 1022, 35 L.Ed.2d 359 (1973), another case relied upon by respondent, the defendant was already in the business of providing a service to certain customers (power transmission over its network), and refused to provide the same service to certain other customers. In the present case, by contrast, the services allegedly withheld are not otherwise marketed or available to the public. The sharing obligation imposed by the 1996 Act created "something brand new"—"the wholesale market for leasing network elements." The unbundled elements offered pursuant to [the Act] exist only deep within the bowels of Verizon; they are brought out on compulsion of the 1996 Act and offered not to consumers but to rivals, and at considerable expense and effort. New systems must be designed and implemented simply to make that access possible—indeed, it is the failure of one of those systems that prompted the present complaint.[3]

We conclude that Verizon's alleged insufficient assistance in the provision of service to rivals is not a recognized antitrust claim under this Court's existing refusal-to-deal precedents. This conclusion would be unchanged even if we considered to be established law the "essential facilities" doctrine crafted by some lower courts, under which the Court of Appeals concluded respondent's allegations might state a claim. We have never recognized such a doctrine, and we find no need either to recognize it or to repudiate it here. It suffices for present purposes to note that the indispensable requirement for invoking the doctrine is the unavailability of access to the "essential facilities"; where access exists, the doctrine serves no purpose. * * * Respondent believes that the existence of sharing duties under the 1996 Act supports its case. We think the opposite: The 1996 Act's extensive provision for access makes it unnecessary to impose a judicial doctrine of forced access. To the extent respondent's "essential facilities" argument is distinct from its general § 2 argument, we reject it.

IV

Finally, we do not believe that traditional antitrust principles justify adding the present case to the few existing exceptions from the proposition

---

3. Respondent also relies upon *United States v. Terminal Railroad Assn. of St. Louis*, 224 U.S. 383, 32 S.Ct. 507, 56 L.Ed. 810 (1912), and *Associated Press v. United States*, 326 U.S. 1, 65 S.Ct. 1416, 89 L.Ed. 2013 (1945). These cases involved concerted action, which presents greater anticompetitive concerns and is amenable to a remedy that does not require judicial estimation of free-market forces: simply requiring that the outsider be granted nondiscriminatory admission to the club.

that there is no duty to aid competitors. Antitrust analysis must always be attuned to the particular structure and circumstances of the industry at issue. Part of that attention to economic context is an awareness of the significance of regulation. * * * "[A]ntitrust analysis must sensitively recognize and reflect the distinctive economic and legal setting of the regulated industry to which it applies." *Concord v. Boston Edison Co.*, 915 F.2d 17, 22 (C.A. 1 1990)(Breyer, C.J.)(internal quotation marks omitted).

One factor of particular importance is the existence of a regulatory structure designed to deter and remedy anticompetitive harm. Where such a structure exists, the additional benefit to competition provided by antitrust enforcement will tend to be small, and it will be less plausible that the antitrust laws contemplate such additional scrutiny. Where, by contrast, "[t]here is nothing built into the regulatory scheme which performs the antitrust function," *Silver v. New York Stock Exchange*, 373 U.S. 341, 358, 83 S.Ct. 1246, 10 L.Ed.2d 389 *(1963)*, the benefits of antitrust are worth its sometimes considerable disadvantages. Just as regulatory context may in other cases serve as a basis for implied immunity, it may also be a consideration in deciding whether to recognize an expansion of the contours of § 2.

The regulatory framework that exists in this case demonstrates how, in certain circumstances, "regulation significantly diminishes the likelihood of major antitrust harm." *Concord v. Boston Edison Co., supra*, at 25. Consider, for example, the statutory restrictions upon Verizon's entry into the potentially lucrative market for long-distance service. To be allowed to enter the long-distance market in the first place, an incumbent LEC must be on good behavior in its local market. Authorization by the FCC requires state-by-state satisfaction of [the Act's] competitive checklist, which as we have noted includes the nondiscriminatory provision of access to UNEs. * * *

* * *

The regulatory response to the OSS failure complained of in respondent's suit provides a vivid example of how the regulatory regime operates. When several competitive LECs complained about deficiencies in Verizon's servicing of orders, the FCC and PSC responded. The FCC soon concluded that Verizon was in breach of its sharing duties, imposed a substantial fine, and set up sophisticated measurements to gauge remediation, with weekly reporting requirements and specific penalties for failure. * * *

Against the slight benefits of antitrust intervention here, we must weigh a realistic assessment of its costs. Under the best of circumstances, applying the requirements of § 2 "can be difficult" because "the means of illicit exclusion, like the means of legitimate competition, are myriad." Mistaken inferences and the resulting false condemnations "are especially costly, because they chill the very conduct the antitrust laws are designed to protect." *Matsushita Elec. Industrial Co. v. Zenith Radio Corp.*, 475 U.S. 574, 594, 106 S.Ct. 1348, 89 L.Ed.2d 358 (1986). The cost of false positives counsels against an undue expansion of § 2 liability. One false-positive risk is that an incumbent LEC's failure to provide a service with sufficient alacrity might have nothing to do with exclusion. Allegations of violations of [1996 Act] duties are difficult for antitrust courts to evaluate, not only because they are highly technical, but also because they are likely to be extremely numerous, given the incessant, complex, and constantly changing interaction of competitive and incumbent LECs implementing the sharing and interconnection obligations. *Amici* States have filed a brief asserting that competitive LECs are threatened with "death by a thousand cuts,"—the identification of which would surely be a daunting task for a generalist antitrust court. Judicial oversight under the Sherman Act would seem destined to distort investment and lead to a new layer of interminable litigation, atop the variety of litigation routes already available to and actively pursued by competitive LECs.

Even if the problem of false positives did not exist, conduct consisting of anticompetitive violations of [the 1996 Act] may be, as we have concluded with respect to above-cost predatory pricing schemes, "beyond the practical ability of a judicial tribunal to control." *Brooke Group Ltd. v. Brown & Williamson Tobacco Corp.*, 509 U.S. 209, 223, 113 S.Ct. 2578, 125 L.Ed.2d 168 (1993). Effective remediation of violations of regulatory sharing requirements will ordinarily require continuing supervision of a highly detailed decree. We think that Professor Areeda got it exactly right: "No court should impose a duty to deal that it cannot explain or adequately and reasonably supervise. The problem should be deemed irremedia[ble] by antitrust law when compulsory access requires the court to assume the day-to-day controls characteristic of a regulatory agency." * * * An antitrust court is unlikely to be an effective day-to-day enforcer of these detailed sharing obligations.[4]

The 1996 Act is in an important respect much more ambitious than the antitrust laws. It attempts *"to eliminate the monopolies* enjoyed by the inheritors of AT & T's local franchises." Section 2 of the Sherman Act, by contrast, seeks merely to prevent *unlawful monopolization*. It would be a serious mistake to conflate the two goals. The Sherman Act is indeed the "Magna Carta of free enterprise," but it does not give judges *carte blanche* to insist that a monopolist alter its way of doing business whenever some other approach might yield greater competition. We conclude that respondent's complaint fails to state a claim under the Sherman Act.[5]

* * *

Justice STEVENS, with whom Justice SOUTER and Justice THOMAS join, concurring in the judgment [omitted].

———

Trinko attracted a great deal of attention even before it was decided, and the Supreme Court's decision triggered a great deal of discussion in the antitrust community. The long term significance of the Supreme Court's decision in *Trinko* is still difficult to predict. On the one hand, it addresses a very narrow legal question in a very unique fact setting: courts should be reluctant to utilize the antitrust laws to scrutinize purely unilateral refusals

---

4. The Court of Appeals also thought that respondent's complaint might state a claim under a "monopoly leveraging" theory * * *. We disagree. To the extent the Court of Appeals dispensed with a requirement that there be a "dangerous probability of success" in monopolizing a second market, it erred, *Spectrum Sports, Inc. v. McQuillan*, 506 U.S. 447, 459, 113 S. Ct. 884, 122 L.Ed.2d 247 (1993). In any event, leveraging presupposes anticompetitive conduct, which in this case could only be the refusal-to-deal claim we have rejected.

5. Our disposition makes it unnecessary to consider petitioner's alternative contention that respondent lacks antitrust standing.

to assist rivals by firms in industries subject to extensive, competition-focused regulation that includes specific mechanisms to require dealings with rivals by incumbent monopolists. Indeed, there is already evidence in the lower courts that this narrow view of the case is taking hold. *See, e.g., Covad Commcn's Co. v. Bell Atl. Corp.*, 398 F.3d 666 (D.C. Cir. 2005) (*Trinko* does not affect a claim by a rival that the dominant firm refused to deal with the rival's customers); *Nobody v. Clear Channel Commc'ns, Inc.*, 311 F. Supp. 2d 1048, 1112–14 (D. Colo. 2004) (reading *Trinko* narrowly). *But see MetroNet Services Corp. v. Qwest Corp.*, 383 F.3d 1124 (9th Cir. 2004).

However, the language and rationale of *Trinko* are far more sweeping. For example, the Court constructed its ultimately dismissive view of Trinko's complaint by articulating some key assumptions about antitrust law and the limits of antitrust enforcement: (1) "forced" sharing tramples on the dominant firm's "right" to be free to choose its trading partners, and erodes its incentive to innovate; (2) the presence of an elaborate regulatory scheme directed at competition obviates the need for private antitrust enforcement; and (3) antitrust rules must be crafted to minimize the threat of false positives, the danger of which is amplified by the institutional limitations of courts. These are hardly self-evident assertions, and each is subject to debate. Moreover, the case was appealed based on Verizon's motion to dismiss for failure to state a claim under Federal Rule of Civil Procedure 12(b)(6), so there is no record upon which the Court's detailed discussion rests. For a more detailed discussion, see Andrew I. Gavil, *Exclusionary Distribution Strategies by Dominant Firms: Striking a Better Balance*, 72 ANTITRUST L.J. 3 (2004).

On the other hand, was the Court justified in its reluctance to use antitrust law to impose upon dominant firms a duty to deal with their rivals? What reasons does it cite for that reluctance? Are those reasons persuasive? In all cases? Did you find the Court's distinction of *Aspen Skiing* persuasive? What did the Court mean when it suggested that *Aspen* lies "at or near the outer boundary of § 2 liability"? Do *Aspen Skiing* and *Kodak* provide an viable, alternative framework for evaluating refusals to deal?

Finally, what are the decision's implications for other areas of federal government regulation that involve conduct that might also fall within the scope of the antitrust laws? *Trinko*'s skepticism about the value of antitrust enforcement, especially through private, civil treble damage actions, and its expressed preference for government regulation, quickly resurfaced when the Supreme Court endorsed implied antitrust immunity in a case that presented some parallel questions of whether private rights of action under the antitrust laws should be permitted against conduct already the subject of regulation by the Securities and Exchange Commission. *See Credit Suisse Sec. (USA) LLC v. Billing*, ___ U.S. ___, 127 S.Ct. 2383 (2007).

Trinko also affected two other traditional theories of antitrust liability: the "essential facilities" doctrine, which had been thought to constitute one basis for judicially mandated dealing, and "monopoly leveraging," which involves the alleged use of monopoly power to obtain a competitive advantage in an adjacent or complementary product market. The Note that follows examines the status of these two possibilities for liability under Section 2 after *Trinko*.

Note on the Status of Essential Facilities
and Leveraging after Trinko

Essential Facilities

In the final paragraph of Part III of its opinion, *Trinko* holds that the "essential facilities" doctrine, sometimes also referred to as the "bottleneck" doctrine, would not alter its conclusion that the antitrust laws did not impose a duty to deal with rivals on Verizon, given that the Telecommunications Act already did so. The Court also asserted that the doctrine was a creature of lower courts, and that the Supreme Court "never recognized such a doctrine." It concluded that there was "no need either to recognize it or to repudiate it here," however, and concluded: "[i]t suffices for present purposes to note that the indispensable requirement for invoking the doctrine is the unavailability of access to the 'essential facilities'; where access exists, the doctrine serves no purpose." 540 U.S. at 410–11.

Prior to *Trinko*, it was widely believed that the Court had in fact long endorsed the essential facilities doctrine, albeit in very limited circumstances. *See* Robert Pitofsky, et al., *The Essential Facilities Doctrine Under U.S. Antitrust Law*, 70 ANTITRUST L.J. 443 (2002) ("The essential facilities doctrine has a long and respected history as part of U.S. antitrust law."). The doctrine was associated with a line of Supreme Court decisions beginning with *United States v. Terminal Railroad Assn.*, 224 U.S. 383, 32 S.Ct. 507, 56 L.Ed. 810 (1912), and continuing through later decisions such as *Associated Press v. United States*, 326 U.S. 1, 65 S.Ct. 1416, 89 L.Ed. 2013 (1945), *United States v. Griffith*, 334 U.S. 100, 68 S.Ct. 941 (1948), and *Otter Tail Power Co. v. United States*, 410 U.S. 366, 93 S.Ct. 1022, 35 L.Ed.2d 359 (1973). It was generally viewed as a narrow exception to the general principle repeated in both *Aspen Skiing* and *Trinko*, that the antitrust laws in general do not impose upon a monopolist any duty to deal with its rivals. Essential facilities claims thus have been rare and are evenly more rarely successful. *See, e.g., Blue Cross & Blue Shield United of Wisconsin v. Marshfield Clinic*, 65 F.3d 1406 (7th Cir. 1995); *Alaska Airlines, Inc. v. United Airlines, Inc.*, 948 F.2d 536 (9th Cir. 1991).

As noted at the outset of our discussion of refusals to deal, the essential facilities doctrine was never really distinct from the general law of refusals to deal. It functioned more like a specialized application of the law concerning such refusals, triggered by a monopolist's control over some physical plant, access to which was necessary if there was to be any meaningful competition at all. Under one widely-cited articulation, the essential facility doctrine requires the plaintiff to prove (1) control of an essential facility by a monopolist, (2) the inability of a competitor reasonably to duplicate the essential facility, (3) the denial of use of the facility to a competitor, and (4) the feasibility of providing access to the facility. *MCI Commc'ns Corp. v. American Tel. & Tel. Co.*, 708 F.2d 1081, 1132–33 (7th Cir.1983). The influence of this formulation on the law of concerted refusals to deal is evident in *Northwest Wholesale Stationers, Inc. v. Pacific Stationery and Printing Co.*, 472 U.S. 284, 294 (1985) (noting that per se unlawful concerted refusals to deal typically involve efforts to disadvantage competitors by " 'either directly denying or persuading or coercing suppliers or customers to deny relationships the competitors need in the competitive struggle' ").

Trinko's skepticism about the essential facilities doctrine reflects the influence of an important critique of the doctrine by the late Professor Phillip Areeda, which was cited by the Court in *Trinko*. *See* Phillip Areeda, Essential Facilities: *An Epithet in Need of Limiting Principles*, 58 ANTITRUST L.J. 841 (1989) ("Essential Facilities"). Areeda suggested, for example, that the Supreme Court had never actually used the phrase "essential facility" and had not expressly endorsed its use. He also reasoned that many of the Supreme Court cases often cited to support the doctrine involved concerted action, not unilateral action, and thus raised more substantial competitive concerns not present in truly unilateral cases.

Perhaps most importantly, Areeda argued that court-imposed duties to deal undermine incentives to innovate. For the monopolist, fear that it will be ordered to share the fruits of its work with its rivals may inhibit it from undertaking research and development in the first place; the incentives of the rival might also be undermined if instead of relying on its own skill, it seeks to free ride on the monopolists' efforts with the help of court intervention. Areeda also articulated one last powerful point: imposing a duty to deal may be especially difficult to administer and may require continuing supervision by the courts. *See Trinko*, 540 U.S. at 415 ("An antitrust court is unlikely to be an effective day-to-day enforcer of these detailed sharing obligations.") This is especially true in cases where the monopolist has never offered access to the specific "facility" to anyone, in which case the court would have to determine and then periodically evaluate prices and terms of sale. *Trinko* referred to almost all of these points either expressly or implicitly in its brief discussion of the essential facilities doctrine. *Id.* at 410 n.3 & 410–11. For an additional critique and suggestions for limiting principles, see Abbott B. Lipsky, Jr. & J. Gregory Sidak, *Essential Facilities*, 51 STAN. L. REV. 1187 (1999).

Trinko surely narrowed the circumstances under which courts may impose a duty on a monopolist to deal. Moreover, some commentators have read its discussion of the essential facilities doctrine to signal the doctrine's formal demise, or at least to signal its inapplicability in the context of a regulated industry that involves provisions for access. Even Professor Areeda, however, acknowledged that the doctrine could play a useful role in antitrust, provided it is narrowly tailored. *See* Areeda, *Essential Facilities*, *supra* at 852. In fact, Areeda appeared to approve of the result in *MCI*. *Id.* at 845 n.21 ("*MCI* * * *, which rests on the essential facilities notion, is probably correct.") In addition, some commentators recently have tried to address the challenge of providing a methodology for determining the prices and conditions under which a vertically integrated monopolist could be required to deal with an unintegrated rival in its output market. *See* Steven C. Salop, *Proposed Legal Rule for Unilateral Refusals to Deal, available at* http:// www.usdoj.gov/atr/public/hearings/single_firm/docs/218654.htm. It remains to be seen, therefore, whether under appropriate and limited circumstances, the Court would approve the imposition of a duty to deal on a monopolist whose control of a facility effectively barred all competition.

Monopoly Leveraging

Prior to *Trinko*, there was some case law supporting the idea that a monopolist can violate Section 2 when it "leverages" its monopoly power in one market to gain a competitive advantage in a second, adjacent or complementary market, where it competes but does not also have a monopoly position. Such claims were raised in *Berkey* as well as *Microsoft*.

In the final portion of its opinion, *Trinko* also rejected the plaintiff's claim that Verizon could be found liable under Section 2 based on a theory of "monopoly leveraging." Referencing its standards for claims of attempt to monopolize, the Court held: "[t]o the extent the Court of Appeals dispensed with a requirement that there be a 'dangerous probability of success' in monopolizing a second market, it erred, *Spectrum Sports, Inc. v. McQuillan*, 506 U.S. 447, 459, 113 S.Ct. 884, 122 L.Ed.2d 247 (1993). In any event, leveraging presupposes anticompetitive conduct, which in this case could only be the refusal-to-deal claim we have rejected." *Trinko*, 540 U.S. at 415 n.4.

Although as noted above there is some possibility that the essential facilities doctrine survived *Trinko* under the right circumstances, this holding is unequivocal: there is no distinct monopoly leveraging doctrine apart from attempt to monopolize. We will revisit the offense of attempt to monopolize later in this Chapter when we read *Spectrum Sports*. Comparative perspectives on refusals to deal, particularly those involving intellectual property, are discussed in Sidebar 6–6, *infra*; with respect to monopoly leveraging, see *Note on the Prosecution of Microsoft in the European Union, supra*.

Note on "Cheap Exclusion"

Exclusionary conduct cases may be the most contested area in antitrust. Disputes extend, for example, over the standards for identifying exclusionary or predatory conduct ("bad acts") in monopolization cases; whether unilateral refusals to deal should ever be the basis for antitrust liability, particularly when the dominant firm's conduct involves goods protected by intellectual property; whether new product introductions should ever be the basis for antitrust liability; and over the standards for identifying exclusionary group boycotts—all issues discussed in this Chapter. Those favoring antitrust intervention in these areas often emphasize that anticompetitive exclusion can be as harmful as anticompetitive collusion. Those skeptical of such intervention point out that much conduct that appears exclusionary in fact promotes competition, that it can be difficult to tell whether the anticompetitive harm outweighs the procompetitive benefit, and that antitrust intervention in this area risks chilling legitimate and beneficial firm conduct.

In 2005, several members of the senior antitrust enforcement staff at the Federal Trade Commission attempted to describe the enforcement priorities supported by the case law to develop a consensus norm around the idea of "cheap exclusion." *See generally* Susan A. Creighton, et al., *Cheap Exclusion*, 72 ANTI-TRUST L.J. 975 (2005). Under this view, anticompetitive exclusion is most likely to occur, and most clearly anticompetitive, if it is "cheap" in two senses: inexpensive for the excluding firms to undertake, and undertaken without a legitimate business justification.

Examples of cheap exclusion may include abuse of governmental processes, such as obtaining a patent by fraud; abuse of voluntary standard setting agreements to exclude rivals; or product redesign to create incompatibility for rivals with no benefit for buyers. The idea of cheap exclusion sharply distinguishes predatory pricing, which is both expensive for the predator (as it must initially make sales below cost) and beneficial to buyers (who purchase at a low price). Exclusive dealing lies in between. Under some circumstances it could be both an inexpensive strategy to implement and confer little benefit on buyers, and in consequence represent a good target for antitrust intervention.

How well does the idea of "cheap exclusion" rationalize the exclusionary conduct cases? Does it tend to describe those that are the most convincing examples of anticompetitive conduct, and not those that are less convincing? Was any of the conduct in *Microsoft* an example of cheap exclusion?

The authors also argued that a focus on cheap exclusion was warranted from the point of view of allocating scarce government enforcement resources:

> * * * In the efficient allocation of always-scarce enforcement resources, exclusionary conduct that is likely to be common (relative to other forms of exclusion), and lacks any legitimate competitive benefit, makes an attractive target. Put differently, when fishing, the best place to fish is where the fish are plentiful, and the things you catch are likely to be fish.

Id. at 978. In this passage, can the "cheap" in "cheap exclusion" also be read as referring to the cost of prosecuting such cases? Based on what you have seen so far of antitrust, and particularly of Section 2, does the theory of cheap exclusion represent a realistic assessment of the relative costs of bringing antitrust suits? Is it true that cases in which firms undertake conduct that excludes inexpensively (as opposed to the more costly kinds of conduct, such as predatory pricing) and for which they offer no legitimate business justification, will be easy to bring? Recall that under the framework set out in *Microsoft*, a defendant does not have to meet a burden of production with regard to its legitimate business justifications until the government has first offered evidence that the defendant is a monopolist and that its conduct resulted in a significant anticompetitive effect. If the plaintiff, private or public, must still prove monopoly power and anticompetitive effect, will cheap exclusion cases necessarily be relatively more simple to bring?

Perhaps then, these government enforcers were trying to lay the intellectual foundation for a simpler brand of antitrust, where obviously anticompetitive conduct is more easy to reach and condemn. We have seen examples of this effort in cases such as *Polygram* (Casebook, Chapter 2, *supra*). If so, perhaps inherent in the idea of cheap exclusion is a confession that the cost of bringing more complex cases involving more ambiguous conduct has become increasingly prohibitive, even for the government, and that the antitrust laws are in need of a correction of sorts that makes it easier to skewer the bad fish.

Sidebar 6–5:
Comparative Perspectives:
The Treatment of Anticompetitive Single Firm
Conduct in the U.S. and E.U.

As we have discussed at various points in this Chapter, Article 82 of the Treaty or Rome, which prohibits "abuse of a dominant position," is a counterpart to Section 2 of the Sherman Act, which prohibits monopolization, attempt to monopolize, and conspiracies to monopolize. Although the two provisions share some common core concepts, they also have some important differences and as a general matter, Article 82 sweeps more broadly than Section 2. This Sidebar examines some of those similarities and differences, as well as efforts to encourage the U.S. and the E.U. to move toward more uniform policies on anticompetitive conduct by single firms.

Monopoly vs. Dominant Firm Status

Although it is common today for antitrust lawyers and economists to use "monopolist" and "dominant firm" interchangeably, the two terms are potentially distinct. As we have already seen, to be subject to Section

2's prohibition of monopolization, a firm must possess "monopoly power." Similarly, as we shall see later in the Chapter, for the offense of attempt to monopolize it is necessary to demonstrate a "dangerous probability" of achieving monopoly status. Traditionally, such power was demonstrated through market definition and market share calculations. Recall that Hand's market share benchmarks in *Alcoa* established a U.S. guideline for monopolization that required something more than roughly a 70% share of a relevant market. Attempt cases typically require market shares of at least 50%. Although courts are increasingly turning to direct evidence of power as a complement or substitute for market share evidence, these market share thresholds remain very influential in the cases, as was evident in *Microsoft*. Their influence also means that the reach of Section 2 is limited.

In contrast, Article 82's concept of "dominance" can be triggered at significantly lower market share thresholds. The European Court of Justice has long recognized that "very large shares are in themselves, and save in exceptional circumstances, evidence of the existence of a dominant position." *See* Case 85/76, *Hoffmann-La Roche & Co. AG v Comm'n*, [1979] ECR 461, at ¶ 41. Interpreting *Hoffmann-La Roche* and other later decisions of the European Court of Justice, a recent study of the standards for proving abuse of dominance in the E.U., prepared by the staff of the Directorate General for Competition of the European Commission ("DG Comp"), concluded that a firm's possession of a 50% share would be sufficient to establish dominance, "provided that rivals hold a much smaller share of the market." *See* European Commission, *DG Competition discussion paper on the application of Article 82 of the Treaty to exclusionary abuses*, ¶ 31 (Dec. 2005), *available at* http://www. ec.europa.eu/comm/competition/antitrust/others/discpaper2005.pdf ("Article 82 Discussion Paper"). The Article 82 Discussion Paper also states that "dominance is more likely to be found in the market share range of 40% to 50% than below 40%, although [firms] * * * with market shares below 40% could be considered to be in a dominant position." *Id*. Firms with less than a 25% share, however, are not likely to qualify as "dominant." *Id*.

Other jurisdictions utilizing the "abuse of dominance" standard similarly have permitted dominance findings with shares as low as 35%. *See* Brian A. Facey & Dany H. Assaf, *Monopolization and Abuse of Dominance in Canada, the United States and the European Union: A Survey*, 70 ANTITRUST L.J. 513 (2002). *But see* Paul Crampton, *"Abuse" of "Dominance" in Canada: Building on the International Experience*, 73 ANTITRUST L.J. 803 (2006) (arguing for a minimum 50% share threshold). And some jurisdictions recognize the possibility of "joint dominance," a concept of shared power that is outside the scope of Section 2 in the U.S.

Although both the U.S. and the E.U. thus use a conceptually similar market power threshold test for addressing unilateral conduct, "dominance" is potentially more inclusive a test than "monopoly power," which is used somewhat uniquely in the U.S.

Monopolization vs. Abuse

Similarities and differences also arise in the scope of conduct that can fall within the reach of each jurisdiction's approach. For most offenses, Section 2 and Article 82 share the power (monopoly or dominance) + conduct (exclusionary or abusive) formula that guides U.S. law, especially with respect to monopolization. But a dominant firm can also violate Article 82 through "exploitive" abuses, such as charging high prices. By virtue of the terms of Section 2 of the Sherman Act and long-standing judicial interpretation, there is no equivalent prohibition under U.S. law. DG Comp has not used its excessive pricing authority expansively, but the E.U. member states have shown a greater willingness to apply this measure under their own national competition laws. A second and potentially very significant difference concerns the proof requirements of an offense. The bare terms of Article 82 seem to permit a finding of abuse even absent a showing of actual or likely anticompetitive effects.

As a consequence of these differences, the European Court of First Instance (CFI) and the European Court of Justice have tended to create a wider zone of liability for dominant firms under Article 82 than the decisions of the U.S. courts under Section 2 of the Sherman Act. At the margin, U.S. courts have tended to say that courts and enforcement agencies commit greater errors by intervening too much rather than too little, especially in cases of single-firm conduct. (Recall Sidebar 1–4, *Economics and the Development of Legal Rules*.) This perspective does not appear in E.U. jurisprudence or in speeches by E.U. enforcement officials.

In their holdings and in their attitude, modern U.S. Supreme Court decisions in cases such as *Brooke Group* and *Trinko* have demonstrated greater skepticism about claims of anticompetitive single firm conduct than judicial decisions in the E.U. *See, e.g.*, Case T–340/03, *France Telecom SA v. Commission*, [2007] E.C.R. ___; Case T–203/01, *Manufacture Francaise des Pneumatiques Michelin v. Commission*, [2003] E.C.R. II–4071.("*Michelin II*"); and Case T–219/99, *British Airways PLC v. Commission*, [2003] E.C.R. II–5917. And as we discussed in the *Note on Microsoft Prosecution in the European Union, supra*, and will discuss *infra* in Sidebar 6–6, which concerns unilateral refusals to deal, E.U. decisions in Case C–418/01, *IMS Health GmbH v. NDC Health GmbH*, [2004] E.C.R. I–5039, and *Microsoft* evidence a greater inclination to condemn refusals to deal than these modern U.S. rulings. For example, unlike *Brooke Group* and *Weyerhaeuser*, the *France Telecom* decision rejects the need to apply a recoupment test to resolve allegations of exclusionary pricing. And *Michelin II* was far more receptive to complaints about the exclusionary effects of rebate schemes than U.S. cases like *Cascade Health*.

A major question for the two jurisdictions is whether an effects-oriented standard will become the common core of analysis in single firm conduct matters. The Article 82 Discussion Paper and speeches by E.U. officials indicate receptivity to greater express reliance on an effects test and to reduced emphasis on the category-based assessment sometimes evident in cases such as *British Airways*. Even if there were broad E.U./U.S. agreement in concept on the value of an effects test, however, there might still remain differences in application. Outcomes often will hinge upon the quantum and quality of evidence that an agency or court demands before it is willing to find actual anticompetitive effects or to infer likely adverse effects.

Managing Diversity and Promoting Convergence

Why should antitrust policy-makers be concerned about differences in antitrust institutions, statutes, and judicial interpretations across jurisdictions, especially the U.S. and the E.U.?

First, by operating the two largest, most well-funded, most-experienced, and most developed competition policy systems in the world, the E.U. and the U.S. deeply influence both other nations adopting competition policies and all of the multinational and regional competition policy networks. The ability of the still-emerging global competition policy system to manage diversity and convergence, therefore, will depend in large part on the ability of the U.S. and the E.U. to do so.

In addition, at least two practical, economic costs of leaving such differences unaddressed are apparent.

First, there is increasing interdependence among the major competition policy enforcement regimes, especially the E.U. and U.S. In many areas of regulatory policy, the jurisdiction with the most intervention-minded policy has power to set a global standard. For matters such as abuse of dominance or mergers, multinational enterprises that operate in the E.U. and the U.S. likely will conform their behavior to the practice of the most restrictive major jurisdiction with competition laws in order to reduce the risk and attendant costs of being investigated and potentially prosecuted for an infringement.

Second, even when the E.U. and U.S. apply the same substantive standards and ordinarily reach the same assessment of the same commercial practice, differences in the procedures for investigations and agency decision-making can impose significant costs on affected enterprises. In the case of merger reviews, these costs include the time and out-of-pocket expense of learning and complying with varied filing requirements and accounting for differences in the timing of government reviews. Where it is possible to achieve simpler, more common procedures, the E.U. and U.S. agencies can reduce the cost of executing routine transactions.

On the other hand, there are also costs to imposing uniformity across jurisdictions with regard to substantive principles, analytical approaches, and implementation techniques. Indeed, some degree of difference is not only inevitable but healthy. Complete homogeneity across individual systems—harmonization of doctrine and process—would limit experimentation and diversity of approaches. The history of competition policy includes innovations pioneered in some jurisdictions that were later followed by others. The U.S. Horizontal Merger Guidelines (discussed in Chapter 5), and the U.S.'s Leniency Policies (discussed in Chapter 3) are examples. Insistence on uniformity across systems, or a requirement that innovations within individual jurisdictions proceed only after a broad consensus among the global community of competition authorities has been achieved, would stymie these and other valuable measures.

To address these costs of divergence, a former Chairman of the FTC proposed creating mechanisms to promote adoption of competition policy norms that are superior in the sense that they (a) promote the accurate diagnosis of the actual or likely competitive significance of observed behavior, and (b) promote the design of government intervention (by initiating a case, by performing a study, or by acting as an advocate before other public institutions) that corrects the problem at issue. *See* Timothy J. Muris, *Competition Agencies in a Market–Based Global Economy* (Brussels, July 23, 2002), *available at* http://www.ftc.gov/speeches/ muris/020723brussels.shtm, and Timothy J. Muris, *Merger Enforcement in a World of Multiple Arbiters* (Washington, D.C., Dec. 21, 2001), *available at* http://www.ftc.gov/speeches/muris/brookings.pdf. Perceiving the proper role of E.U. and U.S. competition agency officials to be the continuing pursuit of *better* practices can focus attention on the need for the continuing reassessment and improvement of competition policy doctrine and institutions. One possible example of an effort to implement the core ideas of these proposals more broadly is the Unilateral Conduct Working Group, created in May 2006 by the International Competition Network, a virtual organization of most of the world's antitrust enforcers. The stated goals of the Working Group are "to promote greater convergence and sound enforcement of laws governing unilateral conduct." *See* http://www.internationalcompetitionnetwork.org/index.php/en/ working-groups/unilateral-conduct.

It is possible that these costs will recede over time even without such efforts, however, as a result of the global success of the E.U. model. By far, most of the 80 or so jurisdictions that have adopted new competition laws in the past 30 years have civil law systems. Their competition systems usually rely on an administrative enforcement model that resembles the E.U. regime. By comparison, few civil law countries have established competition systems that use the adversarial prosecution model employed in the U.S. Because the E.U.'s institutional platform is more compatible with the institutional arrangements in most civil law countries, many transition economies have been inclined to look first to E.U. models in designing and implementing their competition systems. This has been especially true of nations seeking membership in the E.U. This condition means that E.U. norms, more than U.S. norms, tend to be more readily absorbed into the newer competition policy regimes.

Conclusion

This brief examination of the similarities and differences in the E.U. and U.S. approaches to dominant firm conduct illustrates many of the broader challenges facing the still emerging global competition system. The ability of the U.S., E.U., and other jurisdictions to respond to those challenges will have profound consequences for the continued evolution of competition policy throughout the world.

5. REFUSALS TO LICENSE INTELLECTUAL PROPERTY RIGHTS

Recall from earlier in this Chapter, that in the early 1990s *Kodak* faced a significant challenge from a group of "Independent Service Organizations" ("ISOs"), who provided replacement parts and repair services for Kodak photocopying machines. After the Supreme Court decided that summary judgment for Kodak was unwarranted, it remanded the case for a trial, at which the ISOs prevailed. On appeal from its loss at trial, Kodak continued to assert its intellectual property rights ("IPRs") as a defense for its refusal to deal with the ISOs, arguing that the district court erred when it failed to properly instruct the jury as to the legal import of its patented parts and copyrighted software. More specifically, it argued that the presence of such IPRs affects the analysis of a refusal to deal when it takes the form of a refusal to license intellectual property.

In *Image Tech. Servs., Inc. v. Eastman Kodak, Co.*, 125 F.3d 1195 (9th Cir. 1997), the Ninth Circuit agreed, viewing Kodak's assertion of IPRs as a "presumptively legitimate business justification." *Id.* at 1219. But it nevertheless affirmed the district court's finding of liability against Kodak, concluding that the district court's failure to so instruct the jury was harmless error because Kodak's defense based on IPRs was pretext. In support of this conclusion, the Ninth Circuit observed that although Kodak held 220 patents covering 65 parts for its high volume photocopiers and micrographics equipment, its refusal to deal involved thousands of unpatented parts that were covered in its complete refusal to deal. *Id.* Moreover, it concluded that evidence of Kodak's subjective intent in refusing to deal with the ISOs also supported the view that its defense based on IP rights was pretext. *Id.* ("Evidence regarding the state of mind of Kodak employees may show pretext, when such evidence suggests that the proffered business justification played no part in the decision to act.").

Kodak triggered a still robust controversy about the appropriate treatment of refusals to license intellectual property as a basis for antitrust liability, in part because the decision included arguably contradictory themes. The court observed that "[c]ase law * * * supports the right of a patent or copyright holder to refuse to sell or license protected work," *id.* at 1215, and that "patent and copyright holders may refuse to sell or license protected work." *Id.* It also concluded that there was "no reported case in which a court has imposed antitrust liability for a unilateral refusal to sell or license a patent or copyright" and that "[c]ourts do not generally view a monopolist's unilateral refusal to license a patent as "exclusionary conduct." *Id.* at 1216. As already noted above, it concluded, therefore, that IPRs provide a "presumptively legitimate business justification" for a refusal to license. *Id.* at 1219.

Yet the court also held that "neither patent nor copyright holders are immune from antitrust liability." *Id.* at 1215. In the court's view, "the presumption of legitimacy can be rebutted by evidence that the monopolist acquired the protection of the intellectual property laws in an unlawful manner. The presumption may also be rebutted by evidence of pretext." *Id.* at 1219. And, also as already noted, subjective evidence could be used to establish pretext.

Despite its mixed messages, critics viewed *Kodak* as an assault on IPRs. In their view, it leaned too strongly in favor of antitrust rights and against IPRs, which, they feared, could undermine the incentives for dominant firms to innovate. They also complained of the unreliability of evidence of subjective intent and of the remedial problems associated with a court imposed system of compulsory IP licensing.

Two years after the *Kodak* remand, the Federal Circuit, which exercises exclusive jurisdiction over the appeals of patent and copyright disputes, took issue with *Kodak* in a high profile case involving Intel Corporation, the largest manufacturer of high performance computer microprocessors in the world. See *Intergraph Corp. v. Intel Corp.*, 195 F.3d 1346 (Fed. Cir.1999). *See also In The Matter of Intel Corp.*, Dkt. No. 9288, Decision and Order, *available at* http://www.ftc.gov/os/1999/08/intel.do.htm (FTC 1999) (a related case that was settled by the FTC and Intel). *Intergraph* can be seen as favoring IPRs, in contrast to *Kodak*, which was widely perceived as favoring antitrust.

Shortly after the Federal Circuit's decision in *Intergraph*, the court again found itself at the center of a controversy that pitted intellectual property rights against antitrust law. Like Kodak, it pitted ISOs against a well-known equipment supplier, Xerox. Matching the principles set forth in *Intergraph* against those articulated in the various opinions in *Kodak*, the court again appeared to reject antitrust as an effective means of policing exercises of intellectual property rights.

CSU, L.L.C. v. XEROX CORP.

United States Court of Appeals for the Federal Circuit, 2000.
203 F.3d 1322.

Before MAYER, Chief Judge, ARCHER, Senior Circuit Judge, and PLAGER, Circuit Judge.

MAYER, Chief Judge.

CSU, L.L.C. appeals the judgment of the United States District Court for the District of Kansas, dismissing on summary judgment CSU's claims that Xerox's refusal to sell patented parts and copyrighted manuals and to license copyrighted software violate the antitrust laws. Because we agree with the district court that CSU has not raised a genuine issue as to any material fact and that Xerox is entitled to judgment as a matter of law, we affirm.

BACKGROUND

Xerox manufactures, sells, and services high-volume copiers. Beginning in 1984, it established a policy of not selling parts unique to its series 10 copiers to independent service organizations ("ISOs"), including CSU, unless they were also end-users of the copiers. In 1987, the policy was expanded to include all new products as well as existing series 9 copiers. Enforcement of this policy was tightened in 1989, and Xerox cut off CSU's direct purchase of restricted parts. Xerox also implemented an "on-site end-user verification" procedure to confirm that the parts ordered by certain ISOs or their customers were actually for their end-user use. Initially this procedure applied to only the six most successful ISOs, which included CSU.

To maintain its existing business of servicing Xerox equipment, CSU used parts cannibalized from used Xerox equipment, parts obtained from other ISOs, and parts purchased through a limited number of its customers. For approximately one year, CSU also obtained parts from Rank Xerox, a majority-owned European affiliate of Xerox, until Xerox forced Rank Xerox to stop selling parts to CSU and other ISOs. In 1994, Xerox settled an antitrust lawsuit with a class of ISOs by which it agreed to suspend its restrictive parts policy for six and one-half years and to license its diagnostic software for four and one-half years. CSU opted out of that settlement and filed this suit alleging that Xerox violated the Sherman Act by setting the prices on its patented parts much higher for ISOs than for end-users to force ISOs to raise their prices. This would eliminate ISOs in general and CSU in particular as competitors in the relevant service markets for high speed copiers and printers.

Xerox counterclaimed for patent and copyright infringement and contested CSU's antitrust claims as relying on injury solely caused by Xerox's lawful refusal to sell or license patented parts and copyrighted software. Xerox also claimed that CSU could not assert a patent or copyright misuse defense to Xerox's infringement counterclaims based on Xerox's refusal to deal.

The district court granted summary judgment to Xerox dismissing CSU's antitrust claims and holding that if a patent or copyright is lawfully acquired, the patent or copyright holder's unilateral refusal to sell or license its patented invention or copyrighted expression is not unlawful exclusionary conduct under the antitrust laws, even if the refusal to deal impacts competition in more than one market. The court also held, in both the patent and copyright contexts, that the right holder's intent in refusing to deal and any other alleged exclusionary acts committed by the right holder are irrelevant to antitrust law. This appeal followed.

DISCUSSION

* * *

As a general proposition, when reviewing a district court's judgment involving federal antitrust law, we are guided by the law of the regional circuit in which that district court sits, in this case the Tenth Circuit. We apply our own law, not regional circuit law, to resolve issues that clearly involve our exclusive jurisdiction. * * * The district court's grant of summary judgment as to CSU's antitrust claims arising from Xerox's refusal to sell its patented parts is therefore reviewed as a matter of Federal Circuit law, while consideration of the antitrust claim based on Xerox's refusal to sell or license its copyrighted manuals and software is under Tenth Circuit law.

A.

Intellectual property rights do not confer a privilege to violate the antitrust laws. *See Intergraph Corp. v. Intel Corp.*, 195 F.3d 1346, 1362, 52 USPQ2d 1641, 1652 (Fed.Cir.1999). "But it is also correct that the antitrust laws do not negate the patentee's right to exclude others from patent property." *Id.* (citation omitted). "The commercial advantage gained by new technology and its statutory protection by patent do not convert the possessor thereof into a prohibited monopolist." "The patent right must be 'coupled with violations of § 2', and the elements of violation of 15 U.S.C. § 2 must be met." * * *

A patent alone does not demonstrate market power. The United States Department of Justice and Federal Trade Commission have issued guidance that, even where it exists, such "market power does not 'impose on the intellectual property owner an obligation to license the use of that property to others.'" *Intergraph*, 195 F.3d at 1362, 52 USPQ2d at 1652 (citing United States Department of Justice and Federal Trade Comm'n Antitrust Guidelines for the Licensing of Intellectual Property 4 (1995)).* There is "no reported case in which a court ha[s] imposed antitrust liability for a unilateral refusal to sell or license a patent...." *Id.* The patentee's right to exclude is further supported by section 271(d) of the Patent Act which states, in pertinent part, that "[n]o patent owner otherwise entitled to relief ... shall be denied relief or deemed guilty of misuse or *illegal extension of the patent right* by reason of his having ... (4) refused to license or use any rights to the patent ..." 35 U.S.C. § 271(d) (1999) (emphasis added).

* * *

To support its argument that Xerox illegally sought to leverage its presumably legitimate dominance in the equipment and parts market into dominance in the service market, CSU relies on a footnote in *Eastman Kodak Co. v. Image Technical Services, Inc.*, 504 U.S. 451, 480 n. 29, 112 S.Ct. 2072, 2089 n. 29, 119 L.Ed.2d 265 (1992), that "[t]he Court has held many times that power gained through some natural and legal advantage such as a patent, ... can give rise to liability if 'a seller exploits his dominant position in one market to expand his empire into the next.' " Notably, *Kodak* was a tying case when it came before the Supreme Court, and no patents had been asserted in defense of the antitrust claims against Kodak. Conversely, there are no claims in this case of illegally tying the sale of Xerox's patented parts to unpatented products. Therefore, the issue was not resolved by the *Kodak* language cited by CSU. Properly viewed within the framework of a tying case, the footnote can be interpreted as restating the undisputed premise that the patent holder cannot use his statutory right to refuse to sell patented parts to gain a monopoly in a market *beyond the scope of the patent.* * * *

The cited language from *Kodak* does nothing to limit the right of the patentee to refuse to sell or license in markets within the scope of the statutory patent grant. In fact, we have expressly held that, absent exceptional circumstances, a patent may confer the right to exclude competition altogether in more than one antitrust market. * * *

CSU further relies on the Ninth Circuit's holding on remand in *Image Technical Services* that " 'while exclusionary conduct can include a monopolist's unilateral refusal to license a [patent] or to sell its patented ... work, a monopolist's 'desire to exclude others from its [protected] work is a presumptively valid business justification for any immediate harm to consumers.' " 125 F.3d at 1218, 44 USPQ2d at 1081 (citing *Data General Corp. v. Grumman Sys. Support Corp.*, 36 F.3d 1147, 1187, 32 USPQ2d 1385, 1417 (1st Cir. 1994)). By that case, the Ninth Circuit adopted a rebuttable presumption that the exercise of the statutory right to exclude provides a valid business justification for consumer harm, but then excused as harmless the district court's error in failing to give any instruction on the effect of intellectual property rights on the application of the antitrust laws. It concluded that the jury must have rejected the presumptively valid business justification as pretextual. This logic requires an evaluation of the patentee's subjective motivation for refusing to sell or license its patented products for pretext. We decline to follow *Image Technical Services.*

---

* [This proposition has now been endorsed by the Supreme Court. *See Illinois Tool Works*   *Inc. v. Independent Ink, Inc.*, 547 U.S. 28 (2006). Eds.]

We have held that "if a [patent infringement] suit is not objectively baseless, an antitrust defendant's subjective motivation is immaterial." We see no more reason to inquire into the subjective motivation of Xerox in refusing to sell or license its patented works than we found in evaluating the subjective motivation of a patentee in bringing suit to enforce that same right. In the absence of any indication of illegal tying, fraud in the Patent and Trademark Office, or sham litigation, the patent holder may enforce the statutory right to exclude others from making, using, or selling the claimed invention free from liability under the antitrust laws. We therefore will not inquire into his subjective motivation for exerting his statutory rights, even though his refusal to sell or license his patented invention may have an anticompetitive effect, so long as that anticompetitive effect is not illegally extended beyond the statutory patent grant. It is the infringement defendant and not the patentee that bears the burden to show that one of these exceptional situations exists and, in the absence of such proof, we will not inquire into the patentee's motivations for asserting his statutory right to exclude. Even in cases where the infringement defendant has met this burden, which CSU has not, he must then also prove the elements of the Sherman Act violation.

We answer the threshold question of whether Xerox's refusal to sell its patented parts exceeds the scope of the patent grant in the negative.[2] Therefore, our inquiry is at an end. Xerox was under no obligation to sell or license its patented parts and did not violate the antitrust laws by refusing to do so.

B.

The Copyright Act expressly grants a copyright owner the exclusive right to distribute the protected work by "transfer of ownership, or by rental, lease, or lending." 17 U.S.C. § 106(3) (1996). "[T]he owner of the copyright, if [it] pleases, may refrain from vending or licensing and content [itself] with simply exercising the right to exclude others from using [its] property."

The Supreme Court has made clear that the property right granted by copyright law cannot be used with impunity to extend power in the marketplace beyond what Congress intended. *See United States v. Loew's, Inc.*, 371 U.S. 38, 47–48, 83 S.Ct. 97, 103–04, 9 L.Ed.2d 11 (1962) (block booking of copyrighted motion pictures is illegal tying in violation of Sherman Act). The Court has not, however, directly addressed the antitrust implications of a unilateral refusal to sell or license copyrighted expression.

* * *

Perhaps the most extensive analysis of the effect of a unilateral refusal to license copyrighted expression was conducted by the First Circuit in *Data General Corp. v. Grumman Systems Support Corp.*, 36 F.3d 1147, 32 USPQ2d 1385. There, the court noted that the limited copyright monopoly is based on Congress' empirical assumption that the right to "exclude others from using their works creates a system of incentives that promotes consumer welfare in the long term by encouraging investment in the creation of desirable artistic

---

2. Having concluded that Xerox's actions fell within the statutory patent grant, we need not separately consider CSU's allegations of patent misuse and they are rejected.

and functional works of expression... .We cannot require antitrust defendants to prove and reprove the merits of this legislative assumption in every case where a refusal to license a copyrighted work comes under attack." The court went on to establish as a legal standard that "while exclusionary conduct can include a monopolist's unilateral refusal to license a copyright, an author's desire to exclude others from use of its copyrighted work is a presumptively valid business justification for any immediate harm to consumers." The burden to overcome this presumption was firmly placed on the antitrust plaintiff. The court gave no weight to evidence showing knowledge that developing a proprietary position would help to maintain a monopoly in the service market in the face of contrary evidence of the defendant's desire to develop state-of-the-art diagnostic software to enhance its service and consumer benefit.

As discussed above, the Ninth Circuit adopted a modified version of this *Data General* standard. Both courts agreed that the presumption could be rebutted by evidence that "the monopolist acquired the protection of the intellectual property laws in an unlawful manner." *Image Technical Servs.*, 125 F.3d at 1219, 44 USPQ2d at 1082 (citing *Data General*, 36 F.3d at 1188, 32 USPQ2d at 1418). The Ninth Circuit, however, extended the possible means of rebutting the presumption to include evidence that the defense and exploitation of the copyright grant was merely a pretextual business justification to mask anticompetitive conduct. The hazards of this approach are evident in both the path taken and the outcome reached. The jury in that case was instructed to examine each proffered business justification for pretext, and no weight was given to the intellectual property rights in the instructions. This permitted the jury to second guess the subjective motivation of the copyright holder in asserting its statutory rights to exclude under the copyright laws without properly weighing the presumption of legitimacy in asserting its rights under the copyright laws. While concluding that the failure to weigh the intellectual property rights was an abuse of discretion, the Ninth Circuit nevertheless held the error harmless because it thought the jury must have rejected the presumptive validity of asserting the copyrights as pretextual. This is in reality a significant departure from the First Circuit's central premise that rebutting the presumption would be an uphill battle and would only be appropriate in those rare cases in which imposing antitrust liability is unlikely to frustrate the objectives of the Copyright Act.

We believe the First Circuit's approach is more consistent with both the antitrust and the copyright laws and is the standard that would most likely be followed by the Tenth Circuit in considering the effect of Xerox's unilateral right to refuse to license or sell copyrighted manuals and diagnostic software on liability under the antitrust laws. We therefore reject CSU's invitation to examine Xerox's subjective motivation in asserting its right to exclude under the copyright laws for pretext, in the absence of any evidence that the copyrights were obtained by unlawful means or were used to gain monopoly power beyond the statutory copyright granted by Congress. In the absence of such definitive rebuttal evidence, Xerox's refusal to sell or license its copyrighted works was squarely within the rights granted by Congress to the copyright holder and did not constitute a violation of the antitrust laws.

* * *

What explains the different outcomes in *Kodak* and *Xerox*? Do they agree on the general rule that IPRs can provide a presumptively legitimate defense to a refusal to deal? If so, what "exceptions" did each court recognize? Are there any differences? Did the Ninth and Federal Circuits merely disagree about the propriety of considering "pretext" as a defense? About using pretext as a defense when it is invoked based on subjective evidence? Is it true, as *Xerox* appears to assume, that the Ninth Circuit relied solely on subjective evidence in rejecting Kodak's purported business justification? Do the two decisions evidence a more fundamental disagreement about the relative balance to be struck between antitrust laws and intellectual property laws?

Debate about the relative merits of *Kodak* and *Xerox* have continued and in some quarters have become quite heated. The question of whether and under what conditions antitrust liability can be based on a dominant firm's unilateral refusal to license has also spread to the European Union. In the Sidebar that follows, we explore some of these contemporary developments.

Sidebar 6–6:
The Continuing Controversy Over Antitrust Liability for Unilateral Refusals to License Intellectual Property Rights

Reactions to Kodak, Intergraph, and Xerox

Kodak, *Intergraph* and *Xerox* garnered a great deal of attention. In responding directly and critically to *Kodak*, and in appearing to favor the protection of intellectual property rights over principles of competition under the antitrust laws, *Intergraph* and *Xerox* arguably sought to diminish the role antitrust could play in policing exclusionary conduct effectuated through the exercise of intellectual property rights. The decisions also appeared to signal an institutional shift in responsibility away from federal antitrust enforcement agencies and into the hands of the Federal Circuit. The Federal Circuit might now have a major role to play in striking the balance between antitrust and intellectual property. *See Symposium: The Federal Circuit and Antitrust*, 69 ANTITRUST L.J. 627 (2002).*

Intergraph and *Xerox* also sounded alarms with those who cautioned of the danger of permitting intellectual property rights too readily to

---

* It is arguable that today the Federal Circuit would not have jurisdiction to hear a case like *Xerox*. In *Holmes Group, Inc. v. Vornado Air Circulation Systems, Inc.*, 535 U.S. 826, 122 S.Ct. 1889 (2002), the Supreme Court held that the Federal Circuit's appellate jurisdiction is limited to cases initiated under the patent laws and does not include patent counterclaims filed in response to non-patent claims. Recall that CSU initiated its antitrust claims against Xerox and Xerox responded with a patent infringement counterclaim, which at that time provided the basis for an appeal to the Federal Circuit. In light of *Vornado*, the case could no longer be appealed to the Federal Circuit and would instead go to the Tenth Circuit, where the complaint was originally filed. Might *Vornado* prompt a race to the courthouse by patent holders who anticipate antitrust claims and wish to insure that their appeals, if any, will be heard by the Federal Circuit?

trump antitrust policies, especially because IPRs are so prevalent in high-technology industries. A former chair of the Federal Trade Commission argued, for example, that "[b]eyond the matter of result, the court [in *Xerox*] reached its decision in sweeping language that exalts patent and copyright rights over other considerations and throws into doubt the validity of previous lines of authority that attempted to strike a balance between intellectual property and antitrust." Robert Pitofsky, *Challenges of the New Economy: Issues at the Intersection Of Antitrust And Intellectual Property*, 68 ANTITRUST L.J. 913, 920 (2001) ("*Challenges of the New Economy*").** Pitofsky also viewed *Xerox's* three exceptions for fraud, sham litigation, and efforts to extend the patent as through tying as "extremely narrow limits on a virtually unfettered right of a patent holder to refuse to deal in order to achieve an anticompetitive objective." *Id*. at 921. Pitofsky continued:

> More important than the *Xerox* result itself, questions arise as to what the Federal Circuit's approach portends—*i.e.*, an approach that seems to exalt protection of intellectual property rights—with respect to continuing validity in the Federal Circuit of the long-standing balance between antitrust and intellectual property. Let me be clear that I have no quarrel with the fundamental rule that a patent holder has no obligation to license or sell in the first instance. A patent holder is not under any general obligation to create competition against itself within the scope of its patent. But what will the rules be when the patent holder conditions the availability of its patented products or inventions on terms that affect competition? The *Xerox* opinion could be read to say that the invocation of intellectual property rights settles the matter, except in the three narrow situations described in the opinion, regardless of the effect of the refusal to deal on competition or the importance of the refusal to deal to protect incentives to innovate. That should not be the way these issues are addressed.

Id. at 921–22. For a response to Pitofsky that defends *Xerox* and challenges his reading of the case as "overly expansive," see R. Hewitt Pate, *Refusals to Deal and Intellectual Property Rights*, 10 GEO. MASON L. REV. 429, 431 & n.10 (2002).

The doctrinal and economic issues raised by *Kodak*, *Intergraph* and *Xerox* continue to garner serious attention in the antitrust community both in the U.S. and in Europe. Despite that attention, however, they are far from resolved and have illuminated some fairly fundamental points of difference among antitrust commentators and enforcers.***

** Pitofsky cited two other explications of this traditional balance. *See* Willard K. Tom & Joshua A. Newberg, *Antitrust and Intellectual Property: From Separate Spheres to Unified Field*, 66 ANTITRUST L.J. 167, 173–75 (1998); and Louis Kaplow, *The Patent Antitrust Intersection: A Reappraisal*, 97 HARV. L. REV. 1815 (1984).

*** The literature is extensive. For a sampling, see Joseph P. Bauer, *Refusals to Deal with Competitors by Owners of Patents and Copyrights: Reflections on the* Image Technical *and* Xerox *Decisions*, 55 DEPAUL L. REV. 1211 (2006); Michael A. Carrier, *Refusals to License Intellectual Property after* Trinko, 55 DEPAUL L. REV. 1191 (2006); Herbert Hovenkamp, et al., *Unilateral Refusals to License*, 2 J. COMP. L. & ECON. 1 (2006); A. Douglas Melamed & Ali M. Stoeppelwerth, *The CSU Case: Facts, Formalism and the Intersection of Antitrust and Intellectual Property Law*, 10 GEO. MASON L. REV. 407 (2002).

The 2007 FTC/DOJ IP Report

Following extensive hearings, the FTC and the Department of Justice issued a joint report in April 2007 on the interface of antitrust and intellectual property rights. *See* ANTITRUST ENFORCEMENT AND INTELLECTUAL PROPERTY RIGHTS: PROMOTING INNOVATION AND COMPETITION (Apr. 2007), *available at* http://www.usdoj.gov/atr/public/hearings/ip/222655.htm (*"IP Report"*). Chapter 1 of the Report addresses unilateral refusals to license patents and is focused largely on *Kodak* and *Xerox*, summarizing the various arguments that have been raised in support of and in opposition to the perceived approaches set forth in the two cases. *Xerox* generally appeared to garner greater support than *Kodak* among those invited to testify and by the agencies, themselves. However, although *Kodak* had few true defenders, some of the most potent criticisms of Xerox were not fully aired, particularly the degree to which it appears to be indifferent to the potential anticompetitive effects of any specific refusal to deal, an issue posed by former Chairman Pitofsky in his 2001 article.

It is also arguable that both cases have been read somewhat extremely. The Report appeared to acknowledge that *Kodak* has been caricatured as a decision hostile to unilateral refusals to deal.**** *Xerox* quickly became a standard-barer for those with strident views of the value of IPRs, which may reflect a more general political ideology that seeks to protect all kinds of property rights from what is perceived as government regulation. The D.C. Circuit cited *Xerox* in *United States v. Microsoft Corp.*, 253 F.3d 34 (D.C. Cir. 2001), however, in aid of its conclusion that Microsoft's invocation of IPRs in the context of a broader range of anticompetitive conduct "border[ed] upon the frivolous":

> The company claims an absolute and unfettered right to use its intellectual property as it wishes: "[I]f intellectual property rights have been lawfully acquired," it says, then "their subsequent exercise cannot give rise to antitrust liability." That is no more correct than the proposition that use of one's personal property, such as a baseball bat, cannot give rise to tort liability. As the Federal Circuit succinctly stated: "Intellectual property rights do not confer a privilege to violate the antitrust laws." *In re Indep. Serv. Orgs. Antitrust Litig.*, 203 F.3d 1322, 1325 (Fed. Cir. 2000).

Id. at 63. Perhaps the two cases can more readily be reconciled than was evident in the testimony before the agencies. It is also possible that neither *Kodak* nor *Xerox* provide an optimal framework for resolving the tensions that arise in considering refusals to license, and hence that a framework remains to be defined.

After summarizing the arguments for and against *Kodak* and *Xerox*, the Report identifies four policy issues that relate to the question wheth-

---

**** The Report correctly observes that *Kodak* can be distinguished from the typical refusal to license case in part on the ground that Kodak's refusal to sell encompassed far more non-patented than patented products. *See IP Report*, at 30 & n.109. It appears to imply that the differences between *Kodak* and *Xerox* perhaps have been exaggerated. *See also* Bruce Abramson, *Intellectual Property and the Al-* *leged Collapsing of Aftermarkets*, 38 RUTGERS L.J. 399, 429 (2007) ("Under an objectively neutral reading, both courts recognized the room for tension between an otherwise legitimate exertion of IP rights and anticompetitive effects in a single-supplier aftermarket, and both concluded that the resolution lies in fact-specific analyses.").

er antitrust liability should attach to a refusal to license: (1) Should antitrust law accord special treatment to patents, or is conventional antitrust analysis sufficiently sensitive to the issues raised by patents? (2) Should a patent holder be presumed to possess market power? (3) Is compulsory licensing a workable remedy for a unilateral refusal to license patents? (4) And would prohibiting unilateral refusals to license have a significant ill effect on incentives to invest in innovation?

In addressing these issues, largely by summarizing the testimony of the various speakers who testified at the government's hearings, the Report goes on to consider the two critical economic issues in the debate: (1) the likely impact of a regime of compulsory licensing on incentives to innovate; and (2) whether and under what circumstances refusals to license can produce significant anticompetitive effects.

The Report appears to emphasize arguments voiced by proponents of *Xerox*, who frequently assert that a regime of compulsory licensing would diminish the value of IPRs and hence inhibit innovation. The discussion of potential adverse effects is arguably deficient in important respects. It is devoted largely to summarizing testimony offered to demonstrate procompetitive justifications for refusals to license and almost wholly ignores more substantial examples of anticompetitive uses drawn from the commentary and case law. *See, e.g.*, Pitofsky, *Challenges of the New Economy*, 68 ANTITRUST L.J. at 922–23 (discussing specific examples of refusals to license that might raise significant anticompetitive concerns).

The Report then concludes on an awkward and indeterminate note: "The Agencies * * * conclude that antitrust liability for mere unilateral, unconditional refusals to license patents will not play a meaningful part in the interface between patent rights and antitrust protections." The Report's penultimate conclusion—likely the product of compromise between the two federal agencies*****—thus fails to take a firm position in favor of *Kodak* or *Xerox*, although it is strongly suggestive of a very limited view of the role of antitrust laws in policing refusals to deal. It also invites additional questions: When is a refusal to license wholly "unilateral"? When is it "conditional," and why should conditionality, however it is defined, tip the implicit balance from IPRs to antitrust, which presumably would in any case be guided by a concern for significant anticompetitive effects?****** These issues will likely produce additional debate and ultimately will have to be resolved in future cases in the U.S.

Treatment in the European Union: Evolving Standards

The antitrust treatment of unilateral refusals to license IPRs has not been a uniquely American phenomenon. Quite to the contrary, the issues

***** The suggestion that the two federal agencies may have differing views on the appropriate treatment of refusals to license is supported by the actions of the agencies in the years immediately preceding the Report. Whereas the FTC has been more active in initiating enforcement actions against holders of IPRs, officials in leadership positions at the DOJ have been aggressively promoting defer-

ence to IPRs to promote innovation, a position that is far more consonant with *Xerox* and a very limited role for antitrust.

****** For a further discussion of the IP Report's distinction between conditional and unconditional refusals to license, see Willard K. Tom, *The DOJ/FTC Report on Antitrust Enforcement and Intellectual Property Rights*, AN-TITRUST, Summer 2007, at 35, 37.

have also proven to be something of a preoccupation for antitrust enforcers in other jurisdictions.

The standards for evaluating the competitive consequences of unilateral refusals to license were developed in the E.U. primarily in two decisions of the European Court of Justice ("ECJ"), *Volvo v. Veng,* Case 238/87, [1988] ECR 6211 and *RTE and ITP v. Commission,* Case C–241/91P, [1995] ECR I 743 (*"Magill"*). These decisions established the broad principal that unilateral refusals to license will only be deemed anticompetitive, and a violation of Article 82 of the Treaty as an "abuse of dominant position," under "exceptional circumstances." Much of the commentary and decisional law, therefore, has focused on defining these "exceptional" circumstances, a debate that has become the focal point of European efforts to strike a balance between the protections accorded IP rights and the interests of competition laws.

The European Court of Justice again explored refusals to license as a basis for violation of Art. 82 in Case C–418/01, *IMS Health GmbH & Co. OHG* v. *NDC Health GmbH & Co. KG,* [2004] ECR I5039, a private action in which the German national court referred the case to the ECJ under European procedures seeking a clarification of "exceptional circumstances."

The Court of Justice reaffirmed its general view that a refusal to license cannot alone constitute an abuse of dominant position under Article 86, except under "exceptional circumstances." To establish such circumstances, it held, three conditions must be met:

(1) the undertaking which requested the license must intend to offer new products or services not offered by the owner of the copyright and for which there is potential consumer demand;

(2) the refusal cannot be justified by objective considerations, and

(3) the refusal is such as to reserve to the undertaking which owns the copyright the relevant market, by eliminating all competition on that market.

In December 2005, the Directorate General for Competition of the European Commission released a staff discussion paper on application of Article 82 to exclusionary conduct. *See DG Competition Discussion Paper on the Application of Article 82 of the Treaty to Exclusionary Abuses* (Dec. 2005) ("Discussion Paper"), *available at* http://ec.europa.eu/comm/competition/antitrust/art82/discpaper2005.pdf Section 9.2.2.6 of the *Discussion Paper* specifically addresses refusals to license. While locating them in the general context of all refusals to deal, it also makes some specific observations regarding the treatment of refusals to license IPRs. Drawing on *Volvo, Magill,* and *IMS Health,* the *Discussion Paper* states:

238. There is no general obligation for the IPR holder to license the IPR, not even where the holder acquires a dominant position in the technology or product market. The very aim of the exclusive right is to prevent third parties from applying the IPR to produce and distribute products without the consent of the holder of the rights. This protection would be eroded if the holder of a successful IPR would be required to grant a license to competitors from the moment the IPR or the product incorporat-

ing the IPR becomes dominant in the market. Imposing on the holder of the rights the obligation to grant to third parties a license for the supply of products incorporating the IPR, even in return for a reasonable royalty, would lead to the holder being deprived of the substance of the exclusive right.

239.   The refusal to license an * * * [IPR] therefore does not in itself constitute an abuse [of dominant position within the meaning of Article 82]. Only under exceptional circumstances can the refusal to license be considered an abuse. * * *

Discussion Paper, § 9.2.2.6, ¶¶57 238–39 (footnotes omitted). To define "exceptional circumstances," the *Discussion Paper* incorporates by reference five conditions identified as necessary prerequisites to all actionable refusals to deal:

1.   The behavior can be properly characterized as a refusal to supply;

2.   The refusing undertaking is dominant;

3.   The input is indispensable;

4.   The refusal is likely to have a negative effect on competition; and

5.   The refusal is not objectively justified.

Id. § 9.2.2. The *Discussion Paper* notes, however, that in the context of IPRs, the five conditions would not be sufficient. In addition:

> * * * [T]he refusal to grant a licence [must also prevent] * * * the development of the market for which the licence in an indispensable input, to the detriment of consumers. This may only be the case if the undertaking which requests the license does not intend to limit itself essentially to duplicating the goods or services already offered on this market by the owner of the IPR, but intends to produce new goods or services not offered by the owner of the right and for which there is a potential consumer demand.

Id. § 9.2.2.6, ¶ 239 (footnote omitted). In a final paragraph, the *Discussion Paper* also takes the position that "A refusal to license an IPR protected technology which is indispensable as a basis for follow-on innovation by competitors may be abusive even if the license is not sought to directly incorporate the technology in clearly identifiable new goods and services" on the theory that the refusal to license "should not impair consumers' ability to benefit from innovation brought about by the dominant undertaking's competitors." *Id*. ¶ 240.

How does the *Discussion Paper's* stated approach compare to the test set out in *IMS Health*? To the approach taken in *Kodak* and *Xerox*? DG–Comp has been evaluating comments received in 2006 on the *Discussion Paper*, and this framework may not be the final word on its approach to refusals to license.

Most recently, the Court of First Instance ("CFI") considered the application of *Magill* and *IMS Health* in Microsoft's appeal of the European Commission's 2004 finding that it had abused its dominant position in part by refusing to license. *See* Case T–201/04, *Microsoft v. Commission*, Judgment of the Court of First Instance (Grand Chamber) of 17 September 2007, O.J. 2007 C269/45. Recall from the *Note on the*

Prosecution of Microsoft in the E.U., Casebook, *supra*, that one of the two principal grounds for the Commission's challenge to Microsoft's behavior concerned its refusal to license certain communication protocols, which would have permitted greater interoperability between work group servers running non-Microsoft operating systems and Windows client PC operating systems, facilitating increased competition between Microsoft and its rivals in the market for work group server operating systems. In response to Microsoft's assertion that its refusal to deal was not subject to objection under Article 82 because of its IPRs, the Commission argued in the alternative that (1) it did not have to satisfy the "exceptional circumstances" called for by *Magill* and *IMS Health*, because Microsoft was only asserting trade secrets and it had used them in connection with other objectionable conduct; (2) the specific exceptional circumstances set forth in those cases were suggestive, and did not limit the CFI's discretion to consider other relevant and exceptional circumstances, and finally (3) in any event, the standards of *Magill* and *IMS Health*, if applied, had been satisfied. *Id.*, ¶¶ 107, 112; 302–04.

After canvassing the various relevant cases and arguments of the parties, the CFI provided this synthesis of the applicable principles:

> 331.   It follows from the case-law cited above that the refusal by an undertaking holding a dominant position to license a third party to use a product covered by an intellectual property right cannot in itself constitute an abuse of a dominant position within the meaning of Article 82 E.C. It is only in exceptional circumstances that the exercise of the exclusive right by the owner of the intellectual property right may give rise to such an abuse.

> 332.   It also follows from that case-law that the following circumstances, in particular, must be considered to be exceptional:

> — in the first place, the refusal relates to a product or service indispensable to the exercise of a particular activity on a neighbouring market;

> — in the second place, the refusal is of such a kind as to exclude any effective competition on that neighbouring market;

> — in the third place, the refusal prevents the appearance of a new product for which there is potential consumer demand.

> 333.   Once it is established that such circumstances are present, the refusal by the holder of a dominant position to grant a licence may infringe Article 82 E.C. unless the refusal is objectively justified.

Id., ¶¶ 331–33. After a lengthy analysis of the record and the arguments of the parties, the CFI concluded that the Commission had satisfied the exceptional circumstances test of *Magill* and *IMS Health*, and that Microsoft's arguments to the contrary were "wholly unfounded." *Id.*, ¶ 712. Moreover, it concluded that "Microsoft, which bore the initial burden of proof * * *, did not sufficiently establish that if it were required to disclose the interoperability information that [it] would have a significant negative impact on its incentives to innovate." *Id.*, ¶ 697. Hence, along with other points discussed, Microsoft's refusal to license could not be "objectively justified."

How does the CFI's framework compare to other approaches we have reviewed? Is it consistent with the framework set forth in the *Discussion Paper*? Is it closer in specifics and/or intentions to *Kodak* or *Xerox*? And finally, how does it compare to the kinds of general standards for refusals to deal that we have seen in cases like *Trinko* and in the *Note on the Status of Essential Facilities and Leveraging after Trinko*?

For another comparative perspective, see Competition Bureau of Canada, *Intellectual Property Enforcement Guidelines* § 4.2.2 (2000) (discussing treatment of refusals to license intellectual property), *available at* http://strategis.ic.gc.ca/pics/ct/ipege.pdf.

Conclusion

Every authority to consider the question explored in this Sidebar—whether a refusal to license patents or copyrights can provide the basis for antitrust liability—has concurred that if the answer is ever "yes," it will be in limited circumstances. There is widespread consensus that IPRs promote innovation and that the right to exclude others from using the IP is fundamental to the idea of IPRs.

All authorities also appear to agree that there can be limited exceptions to this general principal. The differences surface in the degree to which the law should recognize those exceptions, the specific conditions that justify them, and their likely consequences for both competition and the incentives to innovate. How those questions are resolved can have very significant implications for the legal standards used to judge refusals to deal, specifically whether they will be weighted in favor of IPRs or antitrust enforcement. The critical policy question is how can intellectual property law's desire to promote competition by rewarding innovation and the antitrust law's concern that competition can sometimes suffer at the hand of intellectual property owners be harmonized.

We will examine additional types of potentially exclusionary conduct involving intellectual property rights in Chapter 10.

6. PRODUCT DESIGN AND DEVELOPMENT DECISIONS

A number of Sherman Act monopolization cases have involved claims that a dominant firm made product design decisions that deliberately sought to exclude competitors by means other than technical superiority. In most of these cases, the plaintiff produces products that are complementary to or components used to make the dominant firm's product. In such cases, the dominant firm desires to provide the complementary product or input by itself and has designed its principal product in a manner that the plaintiff believes artificially precludes compatibility with the plaintiff's product.

Courts in monopolization cases have given dominant firms relatively broad freedom to design and introduce their products as they wish. One of the formative cases in this area is *Berkey Photo, Inc. v. Eastman Kodak Co.*, 603 F.2d 263 (2d Cir. 1979), which we introduced briefly above in this Chapter. In *Berkey*, the Second Circuit analyzed Kodak's conduct in designing new varieties of amateur film and cameras. Conceded to hold a monopoly in the film market, Kodak introduced a new type of amateur film and made it available in a configuration compatible only with one of Kodak's cameras. The plaintiff was Berkey Photo, which produced its own line of cameras and offered photograph finishing services in competition with Kodak. Berkey alleged that Kodak, by reason of its monopoly power in the film industry, had an obligation under Section 2 to give competing camera makers and photograph finishers advance notice of its new film designs.

In responding to Berkey, Kodak probably felt the ambivalence that grips many firms as they watch other companies develop goods that complement their own products. On the one hand, firms typically see the development of complementary goods as a benefit, because the emergence of such goods can increase the attractiveness of (and demand for) the original product. At the same time, the producer of the original good would like to obtain some of the revenues generated by sales of the complementary products. The producer is likely to view the creation of complements as, in some sense, the result of its own labors and will desire to receive some of the gains. The original producer also may realize that the creator of complements may be best positioned to challenge the producer in the market for the original product itself.

At trial, the jury found that Kodak's conduct was unreasonably exclusionary and awarded Berkey treble damages, costs, and attorneys fees totaling nearly $100 million. The Second Circuit absolved Kodak of Section 2 liability and vacated all but $1 million of the damage award. In refusing to require Kodak to provide Berkey advance notice of its product design choices, the court said that "any firm, even a monopolist, may generally bring its products to market whenever and however it chooses," without regard to the impact on its rivals. 603 F.2d at 286. The court emphasized that requiring pre-disclosure by a dominant firm, by enabling its rivals to free-ride on its research and development activities, would reduce the incumbent's incentive to innovate:

> Kodak did not have a duty to predisclose information about the 110 camera system to competing camera manufacturers. * * * [A] firm may normally keep its innovations secret from its rivals as long as it wishes, forcing them to catch up on the strength of their own efforts after the new product is introduced. It is the possibility of success in the marketplace, attributable to superior performance, that provides the incentives on which the proper functioning of our competitive economy rests. If a firm that has engaged in the risks and expenses of research and development were required in all circumstances to share with its rivals the benefits of those endeavors, this incentive would very likely be vitiated.

603 F.2d at 281. The court also noted the severe administrative difficulty of "discerning workable guidelines" for courts and companies to follow in deciding when pre-disclosure was required.

Subsequent appellate decisions have adopted a similarly permissive philosophy. In the late 1970s and early 1980s, IBM defeated many challenges from companies that produced tape drives or disk drives that were compatible with IBM's mainframe computers. Some plaintiffs alleged that IBM deliberately reconfigured its mainframe computers to impair compatibility with the their products and ensure that IBM alone would be the supplier of "peripheral devices" that operated with its mainframe computers. Courts typically rejected these claims where IBM provided evidence that its design choice in some way improved the quality of its machines, even though one aim of the design choice was to frustrate compatibility. *See, e.g., Memorex Corp. v. IBM Corp.*, 636 F.2d 1188 (9th Cir. 1980). In another category of cases, plaintiffs unsuccessfully insisted that IBM had a duty to reveal new interface designs in advance of their introduction. In *California Computer Products, Inc. v. IBM Corp.*, 613 F.2d 727, 744 (9th Cir. 1979), the Ninth Circuit explained that IBM "need not have provided its rivals with disk products to examine and copy nor have constricted its product development so as to facilitate the sales of rival products."

Although courts have accorded dominant firms extensive latitude in making product design choices, they also have indicated that such freedom has limits. In *Berkey*, the Second Circuit explained that "[i]f a monopolist's products gain acceptance in the market, * * * it is of no importance that a judge or jury may later regard them as inferior, so long as that success was not based on any form of coercion." 603 F.2d at 287. The court of appeals also found that Berkey might have been entitled to recover for Kodak's refusal to package its new film in formats compatible to Berkey's designs, if Berkey had shown that it suffered damages as a result. The Second Circuit concluded that Berkey had presented no evidence of such harm. *Id.* at 290. Several cases have said that deliberate efforts to create incompatibility with a rival's products without achieving any improvement in quality or reduction in cost could be illegal. *See Transamerica Computer Co. v. IBM Corp.*, 698 F.2d 1377, 1383 (9th Cir. 1983); *Northeastern Telephone Co. v. AT & T Co.*, 651 F.2d 76, 94–96 (2d Cir. 1981).

One of the most notable proceedings to yield restrictions upon a dominant firm's innovation-related activities is *In re Xerox Corp.*, 86 F.T.C. 364 (1975). Here the FTC alleged that Xerox had violated Section 5 of the FTC Act by maintaining a non-competitive market structure in the market for plain-paper photocopiers. With a market share of over 90 percent in plain-paper copiers, Xerox was alleged to have (a) built a "patent thicket" around the company's pathbreaking dry paper copier technology and (b) aggressively pursued patent infringement claims against any company that drew near to the thicket with its own copier design. The parties reached a settlement by which Xerox, among other requirements, agreed to make any three patents in its intellectual property portfolio available to competitors without charge. The settlement spurred new entry into the photocopier industry and dramatically reduced the market share of Xerox. For a thought-provoking analysis of the long-term impact of the case, see Willard K. Tom, *The 1975 Xerox Consent Decree: Ancient Artifacts and Current Tensions*, 68 ANTITRUST L.J. 967 (2001).

Sidebar 6–7:
Berkey Photo and the Ethical Dilemmas
of Antitrust Litigation

In the field of civil litigation, antitrust monopolization cases often involve some of the highest stakes. In some instances such as *Standard Oil v. United States* and *United States v. Microsoft*, the issue is the defendant's future existence, as the government sometimes seeks divestiture as the central remedy. In private treble damage actions, a defendant's exposure can run into the hundreds of millions of dollars. In the *Berkey* case, for example, the plaintiff not only sought treble damages of nearly $100 million but also requested broad injunctive relief, including a requirement that Kodak pre-disclose its film designs. Since that time, private plaintiffs have brought cases seeking over $1 billion.

The often large consequences of success or failure place immense pressure on the attorneys who represent the parties, and the imperative to succeed can create temptations to cut ethical corners. As the *Berkey* episode demonstrates, succumbing to that pressure can ruin an otherwise distinguished career.*

In *Berkey* and in many other antitrust cases, documents and experts play crucial roles. Through discovery, the plaintiff hunts for the candid documents that betray the defendant's awareness of its dominance or reveal its anticompetitive aims. The defendant seeks internal records acknowledging that poor business judgment, rather than any improper acts of the defendant, caused the plaintiff's demise. Each side typically retains an economist to give expert testimony on the issues. The experts prepare reports and notes which themselves can be the subject of a discovery request.

Soon after Berkey filed its antitrust lawsuit in January 1973, Eastman Kodak retained the law firm of Donovan, Leisure, Newton & Irvine to defend it. Donovan Leisure had a storied history of acting for companies in high profile antitrust disputes. Among other noteworthy representations, Donovan Leisure had appeared for the defendants in *Appalachian Coals* and *Socony Vacuum*, two cases we saw in Chapter 2. In *Berkey*, Donovan Leisure retained a prominent economist, Merton Peck of Yale University, to testify about the economic issues in the case and entrusted his preparation to one of the law firm's most respected partners, Mahlon Perkins, Jr.

As directed by Perkins, Professor Peck reviewed a large body of internal Kodak records and drafted reports of his views on the case for the Donovan Leisure litigation team. Peck routinely collected his handwritten notes and reports and periodically shipped them to Perkins, who would be the custodian for Peck's materials and who ultimately would help Peck prepare his trial testimony. As is common in antitrust pre-trial discovery practice, Berkey's lawyers sought to take Peck's deposition and demanded that Donovan Leisure produce all reports and notes that Peck had prepared, as well as any documents the economist had relied upon to formulate his opinions.**

In March 1977, Berkey took Peck's deposition, which Perkins defended. Berkey's outside counsel, Alvin Stein, asked Peck if he had prepared notes or reports in connection with his work for Kodak. Peck replied that he had done so and had sent the materials to Perkins. Stein recalled receiving no such documents, and he asked Perkins why Donovan Leisure had not produced Peck's papers and reports. For reasons the Donovan

---

* This Sidebar draws heavily on James Stewart's superb account of the *Berkey* litigation. *See* JAMES B. STEWART, THE PARTNERS 327–65 (1983).

** Today testifying experts are required to prepare and disclose reports detailing their opinions and the bases therefore. The duty to disclose includes "the data or other information considered by the witness in forming" the opinions. *See* FED. R. CIV. P. 26(a)(2)(B)(ii).

Leisure partner could never explain, Perkins replied that the documents had been destroyed. This was a falsehood. At that moment, the documents sat in boxes in Perkins's office. As the case progressed Perkins would place the documents in a suitcase and remove them to his apartment.

Stein was disbelieving. He insisted that Perkins explain the disappearance of the materials. After several days, Perkins told a new story. He had destroyed the original documents, but he also had retained copies. He would use the copies to satisfy Stein's request. Stein found this explanation equally incredible and asked the federal judge handling the case, Marvin Frankel, to compel Donovan Leisure to explain its treatment of Peck's notes and reports. At Frankel's direction, Perkins prepared a sworn affidavit reciting that he had destroyed the originals but had preserved copies.

The trial took place before a jury from July 1977 through January 1978. During the trial, Stein pressed Peck to testify about his preparation of notes and reports for Donovan Leisure. Peck mentioned one document that Stein had never seen. This aroused Stein's suspicions that Donovan Leisure had continued to refuse compliance with his discovery request, and he again asked Judge Frankel to press his opponents to explain the omissions. Visibly upset by the apparent irregularities, Frankel instructed Donovan Leisure to submit another sworn affidavit describing their handling of the Peck documents. Deciding that he could not submit another false affidavit, Perkins informed his partners about his deceit. Soon afterwards, Perkins and the leadership of the Donovan Leisure litigation team met with Stein and Judge Frankel in the judge's chambers and disclosed the deliberate withholding of discovery materials. The Donovan Leisure partners also performed the painful task of informing their client of Perkins's misconduct.

On January 22, 1978, after deliberating for nine days, the jury returned a verdict of guilty on the monopolization claims. Judge Frankel rejected Kodak's subsequent motion for judgment notwithstanding the verdict, and his opinion castigated Donovan Leisure for the firm's ethical lapse. Kodak dismissed Donovan Leisure and retained Sullivan & Cromwell to handle the appeal. As recounted earlier in this Chapter, Kodak gained nearly total vindication before the Second Circuit, whose opinion on Section 2 issues marked an important turning point in the modern development of exclusionary conduct jurisprudence.

In the Fall of 1978, Mahlon Perkins, Jr. appeared in federal district court, pleaded guilty to a misdemeanor for contempt of court, and later served a 30 day prison sentence. The Perkins episode has powerful lessons for those who aspire to the practice of antitrust law. Antitrust attorneys, especially lawyers who are junior in their careers, spend much of their time handling documents. Seeing a document that may be, or clearly is, adverse to a client's interests sometimes can induce an immediate wish to make the document and the "problem" disappear. Smart lawyers often prove to be very good at explaining away seemingly grim documents. Notice how Kodak ultimately prevailed in the *Berkey* appeal, regardless of how troublesome Merton Peck's notes and draft reports might have seemed to Mahlon Perkins before the trial began. The Perkins matter shows that the greatest dangers arise when a lawyer seeks to destroy records that are responsive to legitimate discovery requests. When such misconduct is exposed, there is little escape from prosecution or sanctions for contempt, perjury, or obstruction of justice.

At some point in most legal careers, a day comes when the ethical choice is starkly presented. One option is to play by the rules, produce the document, and use your wits to diminish its importance. It might also appear that an alternative is to suppress the document and hope no one notices. Sometimes tremendous pressure from clients, peers, or supervisors may make the second option alluring. If you are pressed to explain your decision to take the first path, a suitable answer might be: "Have you every heard about the *Berkey* case and Mahlon Perkins?"

Although decisions since *Berkey* have continued to provide dominant firms with wide discretion in making product design decisions free from serious concerns about antitrust liability, there have also been instances that illustrate how a dominant firm can use a variety of strategies to impede or forestall competition from new and innovative products.

Berkey and other cases suggested standards for judging whether and when a dominant firm's investment in new products might be scrutinized as an instrument of strategic entry deterrence. Antitrust's fundamental task here is to find ways to differentiate and challenge those research and development ("R & D") and marketing strategies involving new products that deter competition by rivals without producing benefits to buyers, and it is a tough assignment. One reason it is difficult is that firms will often not know how their R & D efforts will work out. Thus, both the buyer benefits and the rival deterrent effects of R & D must be assessed from an *ex ante* perspective, focusing on what would be reasonable to expect at the time of innovation—a question related to, but not identical with, asking whether the R & D actually benefitted buyers or harmed competitors.

One approach to this task was suggested by *Berkey*, which explained that Kodak's introduction of a new film format and simultaneous withdrawal of an old format, forcing photographers to buy photofinishing from Kodak rather than Berkey, could have supplied the "bad act" necessary to support a charge of monopolization—but only if the new format had not been better or cheaper than the old. *Berkey Photo*, 603 F.2d at 287 n.39. *See* Jonathan B. Baker, *Product Differentiation Through Space and Time: Some Antitrust Policy Issues*, 42 ANTITRUST BULL. 177, 190–96 (1997).

The use of product design strategies targeted at impeding competition from new and innovative products also was at the heart of the 1998 prosecution of Microsoft for monopolization, which we studied earlier in this chapter. Recall from the excerpt reproduced earlier in this chapter that Microsoft utilized a combination of design strategies and licensing restrictions to impair the ability of rival middleware, especially Internet browsers, to find its way onto the Windows desktop. OEMs were contractually restricted from removing any desktop icons, folders, or "Start" menu entries, and otherwise altering the appearance of the Windows desktop. Also, as we learned earlier in this Chapter, Microsoft's exclusion of IE from the Add/Remove Programs utility and its commingling of browser and operating system code was deemed by the court to constitute exclusionary conduct.

To remedy this conduct, the Consent Decree negotiated between Microsoft and the government mandates certain changes in Microsoft's contractual policies and requires it to disclose certain information to facilitate the interoperability of rival middleware with Windows. Does it also explicitly or implicitly mandate design changes?

IN THE UNITED STATES DISTRICT COURT
FOR THE DISTRICT OF COLUMBIA

UNITED STATES OF AMERICA, Plaintiff, v. MICROSOFT CORPORATION, Defendant.	Civil Action No. 98–1232 (CKK) *Filed:* September 7, 2006

MODIFIED FINAL JUDGMENT

Originally Entered November 12, 2002; Modified *September 7,* 2006

* * *

C.   Microsoft shall not restrict by agreement any OEM licensee from exercising any of the following options or alternatives:

1.   Installing, and displaying icons, shortcuts, or menu entries for, any Non–Microsoft Middleware or any product or service (including but not limited to IAP products or services) that distributes, uses, promotes, or supports any Non–Microsoft Middleware, on the desktop or Start menu, or anywhere else in a Windows Operating System Product where a list of icons, shortcuts, or menu entries for applications are generally displayed, except that Microsoft may restrict an OEM from displaying icons, shortcuts and menu entries for any product in any list of such icons, shortcuts, or menu entries specified in the Windows documentation as being limited to products that provide particular types of functionality, provided that the restrictions are non-discriminatory with respect to non-Microsoft and Microsoft products.

2.   Distributing or promoting Non–Microsoft Middleware by installing and displaying on the desktop shortcuts of any size or shape so long as such shortcuts do not impair the functionality of the user interface.

3.   Launching automatically, at the conclusion of the initial boot sequence or subsequent boot sequences, or upon connections to or disconnections from the Internet, any Non–Microsoft Middleware if a Microsoft Middleware Product that provides similar functionality would otherwise be launched automatically at that time, provided that any such Non–Microsoft Middleware displays on the desktop no user interface or a user interface of similar size and shape to the user

interface displayed by the corresponding Microsoft Middleware Product.

4. Offering users the option of launching other Operating Systems from the Basic Input/Output System or a non-Microsoft boot-loader or similar program that launches prior to the start of the Windows Operating System Product.

5. Presenting in the initial boot sequence its own IAP offer provided that the OEM complies with reasonable technical specifications established by Microsoft, including a requirement that the end user be returned to the initial boot sequence upon the conclusion of any such offer.

6. Exercising any of the options provided in Section III.H of this Final Judgment.

D. Starting at the earlier of the release of Service Pack 1 for Windows XP or 12 months after the submission of this Final Judgment to the Court, Microsoft shall disclose to ISVs, IHVs, IAPs, ICPs, and OEMs, for the sole purpose of interoperating with a Windows Operating System Product, via the Microsoft Developer Network ("MSDN") or similar mechanisms, the APIs and related Documentation that are used by Microsoft Middleware to interoperate with a Windows Operating System Product. For purposes of this Section III.D, the term APIs means the interfaces, including any associated callback interfaces, that Microsoft Middleware running on a Windows Operating System Product uses to call upon that Windows Operating System Product in order to obtain any services from that Windows Operating System Product. In the case of a new major version of Microsoft Middleware, the disclosures required by this Section III.D shall occur no later than the last major beta test release of that Microsoft Middleware. In the case of a new version of a Windows Operating System Product, the obligations imposed by this Section III.D shall occur in a Timely Manner.

E. Starting nine months after the submission of this proposed Final Judgment to the Court, Microsoft shall make available for use by third parties, for the sole purpose of interoperating or communicating with a Windows Operating System Product, on reasonable and non-discriminatory terms (consistent with Section III.I), any Communications Protocol that is, on or after the date this Final Judgment is submitted to the Court, (i) implemented in a Windows Operating System Product installed on a client computer, and (ii) used to interoperate, or communicate, natively (*i.e.*, without the addition of software code to the client operating system product) with a Microsoft server operating system product.

* * *

H. Starting at the earlier of the release of Service Pack 1 for Windows XP or 12 months after the submission of this Final Judgment to the Court, Microsoft shall:

1. Allow end users (via a mechanism readily accessible from the desktop or Start menu such as an Add/Remove icon) and OEMs (via standard preinstallation kits) to enable or remove access to each Microsoft Middleware Product or Non–Microsoft Middleware Product by (a)

displaying or removing icons, shortcuts, or menu entries on the desktop or Start menu, or anywhere else in a Windows Operating System Product where a list of icons, shortcuts, or menu entries for applications are generally displayed, except that Microsoft may restrict the display of icons, shortcuts, or menu entries for any product in any list of such icons, shortcuts, or menu entries specified in the Windows documentation as being limited to products that provide particular types of functionality, provided that the restrictions are non-discriminatory with respect to non-Microsoft and Microsoft products; and (b) enabling or disabling automatic invocations pursuant to Section III.C.3 of this Final Judgment that are used to launch Non–Microsoft Middleware Products or Microsoft Middleware Products. The mechanism shall offer the end user a separate and unbiased choice with respect to enabling or removing access (as described in this subsection III.H.1) and altering default invocations (as described in the following subsection III.H.2) with regard to each such Microsoft Middleware Product or Non–Microsoft Middleware Product and may offer the end-user a separate and unbiased choice of enabling or removing access and altering default configurations as to all Microsoft Middleware Products as a group or all Non–Microsoft Middleware Products as a group.

2.   Allow end users (via an unbiased mechanism readily available from the desktop or Start menu), OEMs (via standard OEM preinstallation kits), and Non–Microsoft Middleware Products (via a mechanism which may, at Microsoft's option, require confirmation from the end user in an unbiased manner) to designate a Non–Microsoft Middleware Product to be invoked in place of that Microsoft Middleware Product (or vice versa) in any case where the Windows Operating System Product would otherwise launch the Microsoft Middleware Product in a separate Top–Level Window and display either (i) all of the user interface elements or (ii) the Trademark of the Microsoft Middleware Product.

Notwithstanding the foregoing Section III.H.2, the Windows Operating System Product may invoke a Microsoft Middleware Product in any instance in which:

(a)   that Microsoft Middleware Product would be invoked solely for use in interoperating with a server maintained by Microsoft (outside the context of general Web browsing), or

(b)   that designated Non–Microsoft Middleware Product fails to implement a reasonable technical requirement (*e.g.*, a requirement to be able to host a particular ActiveX control) that is necessary for valid technical reasons to supply the end user with functionality consistent with a Windows Operating System Product, provided that the technical reasons are described in a reasonably prompt manner to any ISV that requests them.

3.   Ensure that a Windows Operating System Product does not (a) automatically alter an OEM's configuration of icons, shortcuts or menu entries installed or displayed by the OEM pursuant to Section III.C of this Final Judgment without first seeking confirmation from

the user and (b) seek such confirmation from the end user for an automatic (as opposed to user-initiated) alteration of the OEM's configuration until 14 days after the initial boot up of a new Personal Computer. Any such automatic alteration and confirmation shall be unbiased with respect to Microsoft Middleware Products and Non–Microsoft Middleware. Microsoft shall not alter the manner in which a Windows Operating System Product automatically alters an OEM's configuration of icons, shortcuts or menu entries other than in a new version of a Windows Operating System Product.

* * *

Although the Final Consent Decree clearly appears to mandate design changes as a remedy for Microsoft's anticompetitive conduct, the leadership of the U.S. Department of Justice quickly lashed out at other antitrust enforcement jurisdictions, especially the European Commission and the Korean Fair Trade Commission, when they sought to impose additional restrictions on Microsoft's design autonomy. Why might the Antitrust Division have been concerned about other enforcers imposing more demanding restrictions than those included in the U.S. Consent Decree? Why might those other enforcers be inclined to do so? Why might antitrust enforcement agencies generally need to be especially sensitive to the implications of antitrust remedies that impose conditions or restrictions on a dominant firm's design autonomy? For a further discussion of these issues, see Harry First & Andrew I. Gavil, *Re-Framing Windows: The Durable Meaning of the* Microsoft *Antitrust Litigation*, 2006 UTAH L. REV. 641.

Note on Business Torts and the Antitrust Laws

Some critics of the use of the antitrust laws to police exclusionary conduct have suggested that antitrust is unnecessary given that much exclusionary conduct can be challenged by the victim as a business tort. For example, if one firm destroys its rival's in-store product displays, that conduct could be tort. If it also satisfies the elements of an antitrust offense, and in particular if it leads to harm to competition, the same conduct could also form the basis for an antitrust complaint. Under this view, the main effect of introducing antitrust liability is to elevate damages in such cases from single to treble, leading private plaintiffs to bring too many frivolous lawsuits. More generally, the Supreme Court has referred derisively to "private state tort suits masquerading as antitrust actions" in the hope of securing treble damages. *Copperweld Corp. v. Independence Tube Corp.*, 467 U.S. 752, 777 (1984). One way to understand the potent slogan repeated so often by the Court, that the antitrust laws "protect competition not competitors" is as an expression of this difference. Tort laws protect competitors; the antitrust laws protect competition.

Consider the following response from four F.T.C. officials:

> [W]hile claims of tortious conduct are frequently heard, the elements of actual monopolization under Section 2 (where the conduct is usually unilateral) are considerably more difficult to establish. The antitrust plaintiff must prove that the alleged predator has acquired monopoly

power and that the effect of the conduct is anticompetitive exclusion, not simply the imposition of costs on a competitor. That a competitor has been harmed can justify a tort suit by that competitor, if the other relevant elements of the tort are established, but to show an antitrust violation one must prove harm to competition. But the point remains that when all the elements of monopolization, including injury to competition, are present, tortious conduct—rarely, if ever, an efficiency-enhancing form of "competition on the merits"—can be a cheap form of exclusion.

Susan A. Creighton, et al., *Cheap Exclusion*, 72 Antitrust L.J. 975, 990 (2005) (footnotes omitted). Would consumers be better off if the conduct viewed as a basis for a Section 2 violation in *Alcoa, Lorain Journal, Aspen Skiing, Brooke Group,* or *Microsoft* (most plaintiff victories) could not be reached under the antitrust laws, but could only be challenged under tort law? Can it be persuasively argued that public enforcement of antitrust, even with respect to tortious behavior, can add value, in part because where the conduct is not only tortious (harm to competitor) but also anticompetitive (harm to competition), a single competitor may not necessarily suffer the same harm consumers suffer and therefore its incentives to pursue the matter may be inadequate to protect the public interest?

7. PATTERN OR PRACTICE: PREPARING A "MONOPOLY BROTH"

Part of the urgency to develop a new framework for analyzing monopolization claims stems from cases in which the dominant firm is said to have used a variety of improper tactics to exclude rivals. The case prosecuted by the Justice Department and the state governments against Microsoft illustrates the point. The government plaintiffs alleged that Microsoft had used a multi-faceted strategy to suppress competition from other actual or potential producers of software. As no single business tactic would forestall competition, the company was said to have used a variety of means—including exclusive dealing, tying, and threats to punish firms engaged in new product development—to extinguish "middleware" threats to the Windows operating system. The government plaintiffs argued that the courts should not examine each element of Microsoft's conduct in insolation, but instead should consider the "pattern or practice" of alleged misconduct.

The legal foundation for the "pattern or practice" concept (sometimes called the "monopoly broth" theory by commentators and courts) first appeared in *Continental Ore Co. v. Union Carbide & Carbon Corp.*, 370 U.S. 690, 82 S.Ct. 1404 (1962). In *Continental Ore*, the Supreme Court confronted allegations that the defendants had violated Sections 1 and 2 of the Sherman Act through a broad collection of improper acts. The Supreme Court wrote that "plaintiffs should be given the full benefit of their proof without tightly compartmentalizing the various factual components and wiping the slate clean after scrutiny of each. * * * [T]he duty of the jury was to look at the whole picture and not merely at the individual figures in it." 370 U.S. at 699.

Continental Ore creates an important possibility for plaintiffs alleging unlawful exclusion. Assume that the plaintiff alleges that the defendant engaged in wrongful acts A, B, and C. Suppose further that none of the acts, examined individually, provides the requisite element of improper conduct to support a finding of monopolization liability. *Continental Ore* appears to teach that the court should examine the entire pattern of the defendant's behavior and can assemble the subcritical elements of behavior—A and B and C—into a critical mass of improper conduct that might be called ABC.

Applying the pattern or practice theory poses the challenging task of defining what quantum of individual acts suffices to create the critical mass of illegality. Suppose, again, that the plaintiff accuses the defendant of improper acts A, B, and C. The plaintiff argues that even if A, B, and C do not individually support a finding of illegality, the combination of ABC does. If the defendant shows there is no basis for allegation A, does the combination of B and C supply the necessary pattern of illegality? A court might find it difficult to provide operational criteria that give business managers a clear sense of when a collection of aggressive tactics will be considered an illegal pattern or practice. The result could be a very general form of guidance that an aggregation of tactics could constitute, at some undefined point, an improper course of conduct.

The *Microsoft* case might have provided an occasion for the D.C. Circuit to examine the pattern or practice concept—the district court expressly relied upon Continental Ore to conclude that Microsoft was separately liable under Section 2 for its "general course of conduct." But the court of appeals declined to address the issue,"because the District Court did not point to any series of acts, each of which harms competition only slightly but the cumulative effect of which is significant enough to form an independent basis for liability." United States v. Microsoft Corp., 253 F.3d 34, 78 (D.C. Cir. 2001). This conclusion, however, did not significantly alter the outcome of the case, which largely rested upon findings that a number of the defendant's practices individually supported a finding of monopolization liability.

D. THE OFFENSE OF ATTEMPT TO MONOPOLIZE

Section 2 of the Sherman Act proscribes attempts to monopolize as well as monopolization and conspiracies to monopolize. The attempt offense can be prosecuted as a felony, but few cases have explored this avenue of enforcement. Justice Holmes provided an early formative statement on attempts to monopolize in *Swift & Co. v. United States*, 196 U.S. 375, 25 S.Ct. 276 (1905). Drawing closely on the criminal law analogue, he concluded that attempted monopolization consisted of conduct that closely approaches but does not quite attain completed monopolization, plus a wrongful intent to monopolize. Thus conduct amounts to an attempt to monopolize if there is a "specific intent" to monopolize and a "dangerous probability" that, if unchecked, such conduct will ripen into monopolization. Beyond these formulas lurk difficult questions: what kinds of evidence will be relevant to an inquiry into "specific intent"? How much market power must a defendant have before there is a "dangerous probability" that its conduct threatens to achieve monopoly? What kind of conduct will support an accusation of "attempt to monopolize" if it is normal in the competitive process for firms to strive to secure a competitive advantage over their rivals?

For most of the 20th century, the Supreme Court shed little light on these issues, and lower court decisions reflected considerable disarray. As the offense of monopolization expanded—especially in *Alcoa*—the role of attempt to monopolize became uncertain. As with monopolization, efforts to develop a legal test for attempt displayed tension between prohibiting undesirable business conduct that is likely to result in monopoly and avoiding the suppression of desirable rivalry. Since many business practices support both inferences, actions to punish attempts require close scrutiny of the market context and justifications for the defendant's conduct. In 1993, the Supreme Court provided an important clarification of the attempt offense in *Spectrum Sports, Inc. v. McQuillan*, our next case.

SPECTRUM SPORTS, INC. v. MCQUILLAN

Supreme Court of the United States, 1993.
506 U.S. 447, 113 S.Ct. 884, 122 L.Ed.2d 247.

Justice WHITE delivered the opinion of the Court.

Section 2 of the Sherman Act makes it an offense for any person to "monopolize, or attempt to monopolize, or combine or conspire with any other person or persons, to monopolize any part of the trade or commerce among the several States...." The jury in this case returned a verdict finding that petitioners had monopolized, attempted to monopolize, and/or conspired to monopolize. The District Court entered a judgment ruling that petitioners had violated § 2, and the Court of Appeals affirmed on the ground that petitioners had attempted to monopolize. The issue we have before us is whether the District Court and the Court of Appeals correctly defined the elements of that offense.

I

Sorbothane is a patented elastic polymer whose shock-absorbing characteristics make it useful in a variety of medical, athletic, and equestrian products. BTR, Inc. (BTR), owns the patent rights to sorbothane, and its wholly owned subsidiaries manufacture the product in the United States and Britain. Hamilton–Kent Manufacturing Company (Hamilton–Kent) and Sorbothane, Inc. (S.I.), were at all relevant times owned by BTR. S.I. was formed in 1982 to take over Hamilton–Kent's sorbothane business. Respondents Shirley and Larry McQuillan, doing business as Sorboturf Enterprises, were regional distributors of sorbothane products from 1981 to 1983. Petitioner Spectrum Sports, Inc. (Spectrum), was also a distributor of sorbothane products. Petitioner Kenneth B. Leighton, Jr., is a co-owner of Spectrum. Kenneth Leighton, Jr., is the son of Kenneth Leighton, Sr., the president of Hamilton–Kent and S.I. at all relevant times.

In 1980, respondents Shirley and Larry McQuillan signed a letter of intent with Hamilton–Kent, which then owned all manufacturing and distribution rights to sorbothane. The letter of intent granted the McQuillans exclusive rights to purchase sorbothane for use in equestrian products. Respondents were designing a horseshoe pad using sorbothane.

In 1981, Hamilton–Kent decided to establish five regional distributorships for sorbothane. Respondents were selected to be distributors of all sorbothane products, including medical products and shoe inserts, in the Southwest. Spectrum was selected as distributor for another region.

In January 1982, Hamilton–Kent shifted responsibility for selling medical products from five regional distributors to a single national distributor. In April 1982, Hamilton–Kent told respondents that it wanted them to relinquish their athletic shoe distributorship as a condition for retaining the right to develop and distribute equestrian products. As of May 1982, BTR had moved the sorbothane business from Hamilton–Kent to S.I. In May, the marketing manager of S.I. again made clear that respondents had to sell their athletic distributorship to keep their equestrian distribution rights. At a meeting scheduled to discuss the sale of respondents' athletic distributorship to petitioner Leighton, Jr., Leighton, Jr., informed Shirley McQuillan that if she did not come to agreement with him she would be " 'looking for work.' " Respondents refused to sell and continued to distribute athletic shoe inserts.

In the fall of 1982, Leighton, Sr., informed respondents that another concern had been appointed as the national equestrian distributor, and that they were "no longer involved in equestrian products." In January 1983, S.I. began marketing through a national distributor a sorbothane horseshoe pad allegedly indistinguishable from the one designed by respondents. In August 1983, S.I. informed respondents that it would no longer accept their orders. Spectrum thereupon became national distributor of sorbothane athletic shoe inserts. Respondents sought to obtain sorbothane from the BTR's British subsidiary, but were informed by that subsidiary that it would not sell sorbothane in the United States. Respondents' business failed.

Respondents sued petitioners seeking damages for alleged violations of §§ 1 and 2 of the Sherman Act * * *.

The case was tried to a jury * * *. All of the defendants were found to have violated § 2 by, in the words of the verdict sheet, "monopolizing, attempting to monopolize, and/or conspiring to monopolize." * * * The jury awarded $1,743,000 in compensatory damages on each of the violations found to have occurred. This amount was trebled under § 4 of the Clayton Act. The District Court also awarded nearly $1 million in attorney's fees and denied motions for judgment notwithstanding the verdict and for a new trial.

The Court of Appeals for the Ninth Circuit affirmed the judgment in an unpublished opinion. The court expressly ruled that the trial court had properly instructed the jury on the Sherman Act claims and found that the evidence supported the liability verdicts as well as the damages awards on these claims. * * * On the § 2 issue that petitioners present here, the Court of Appeals, noting that the jury had found that petitioners had violated § 2 without specifying whether they had monopolized, attempted to monopolize, or conspired to monopolize, held that the verdict would stand if the evidence supported any one of the three possible violations of § 2. The court went on to conclude that a case of attempted monopolization had been established.[4] The

---

4. The District Court's jury instructions were transcribed as follows:

"In order to win on the claim of attempted monopoly, the Plaintiff must prove each of the following elements by a preponderance of the evidence: first, that the Defendants had a specific intent to achieve monopoly power in the relevant market; second, that the Defendants engaged in exclusionary or restric-

tive conduct in furtherance of its specific intent; third, that there was a dangerous probability that Defendants could sooner or later achieve [their] goal of monopoly power in the relevant market; fourth, that the Defendants' conduct occurred in or affected interstate commerce; and, fifth, that the Plaintiff was injured in the business or property

court rejected petitioners' argument that attempted monopolization had not been established because respondents had failed to prove that petitioners had a specific intent to monopolize a relevant market. The court also held that in order to show that respondents' attempt to monopolize was likely to succeed it was not necessary to present evidence of the relevant market or of the defendants' market power. In so doing, the Ninth Circuit relied on *Lessig v. Tidewater Oil Co.,* 327 F.2d 459 (CA9), cert. denied, 377 U.S. 993, 84 S.Ct. 1920 (1964), and its progeny. The Court of Appeals noted that these cases, in dealing with attempt to monopolize claims, had ruled that "if evidence of unfair or predatory conduct is presented, it may satisfy both the specific intent and dangerous probability elements of the offense, without any proof of relevant market or the defendant's marketpower *[sic]*." If, however, there is insufficient evidence of unfair or predatory conduct, there must be a showing of "relevant market or the defendant's marketpower *[sic]*." The court went on to find:

> "There is sufficient evidence from which the jury could conclude that the S.I. Group and Spectrum Group engaged in unfair or predatory conduct and thus inferred that they had the specific intent and the dangerous probability of success and, therefore, McQuillan did not have to prove relevant market or the defendant's marketing power."

The decision below, and the *Lessig* line of decisions on which it relies, conflicts with holdings of courts in other Circuits. Every other Court of Appeals has indicated that proving an attempt to monopolize requires proof of a dangerous probability of monopolization of a relevant market. We granted certiorari * * * to resolve this conflict among the Circuits. We reverse.

II

While § 1 of the Sherman Act forbids contracts or conspiracies in restraint of trade or commerce, § 2 addresses the actions of single firms that monopolize or attempt to monopolize, as well as conspiracies and combinations to monopolize. Section 2 does not define the elements of the offense of attempted monopolization. Nor is there much guidance to be had in the scant legislative history of that provision, which was added late in the legislative process. See 1 E. Kintner, Legislative History of the Federal Antitrust Laws and Related Statutes 23–25 (1978); 3 P. Areeda & D. Turner, Antitrust Law ¶ 617, pp. 39–41 (1978). * * *

This Court first addressed the meaning of attempt to monopolize under § 2 in *Swift & Co. v. United States,* 196 U.S. 375, 25 S.Ct. 276 (1905). The Court's opinion, written by Justice Holmes, contained the following passage:

> "Where acts are not sufficient in themselves to produce a result which the law seeks to prevent—for instance, the monopoly—but require further acts in addition to the mere forces of nature to bring that result to pass, an intent to bring it to pass is necessary in order to produce a dangerous probability that it will happen. * * * But

by the Defendants' exclusionary or restrictive conduct.

"If the Plaintiff has shown that the Defendant engaged in predatory conduct, you may infer from that evidence the specific intent and the dangerous probability element of the offense without any proof of the relevant market or the Defendants' marketing *[sic]* power." * * *

when that intent and the consequent dangerous probability exist, this statute, like many others and like the common law in some cases, directs itself against that dangerous probability as well as against the completed result." *Id.,* at 396, 25 S.Ct., at 279.

The Court went on to explain, however, that not every act done with intent to produce an unlawful result constitutes an attempt. "It is a question of proximity and degree." *Id.,* at 402, 25 S.Ct., at 281. *Swift* thus indicated that intent is necessary, but alone is not sufficient, to establish the dangerous probability of success that is the object of § 2's prohibition of attempts.

The Court's decisions since *Swift* have reflected the view that the plaintiff charging attempted monopolization must prove a dangerous probability of actual monopolization, which has generally required a definition of the relevant market and examination of market power. * * *

* * * [T]his Court reaffirmed in *Copperweld Corp. v. Independence Tube Corp.,* 467 U.S. 752, 104 S.Ct. 2731 (1984), that "Congress authorized Sherman Act scrutiny of single firms only when they pose a danger of monopolization. Judging unilateral conduct in this manner reduces the risk that the antitrust laws will dampen the competitive zeal of a single aggressive entrepreneur." *Id.,* at 768, 104 S.Ct., at 2740. Thus, the conduct of a single firm, governed by § 2, "is unlawful only when it threatens actual monopolization." *Id.,* at 767, 104 S.Ct., at 2739.

The Courts of Appeals other than the Ninth Circuit have followed this approach. Consistent with our cases, it is generally required that to demonstrate attempted monopolization a plaintiff must prove (1) that the defendant has engaged in predatory or anticompetitive conduct with (2) a specific intent to monopolize and (3) a dangerous probability of achieving monopoly power. See 3 Areeda & Turner, *supra,* ¶ 820, at 312. In order to determine whether there is a dangerous probability of monopolization, courts have found it necessary to consider the relevant market and the defendant's ability to lessen or destroy competition in that market.

Notwithstanding the array of authority contrary to *Lessig,* the Court of Appeals in this case reaffirmed its prior holdings; indeed, it did not mention either this Court's decisions discussed above or the many decisions of other Courts of Appeals reaching contrary results. Respondents urge us to affirm the decision below. We are not at all inclined, however, to embrace *Lessig*'s interpretation of § 2, for there is little, if any, support for it in the statute or the case law, and the notion that proof of unfair or predatory conduct alone is sufficient to make out the offense of attempted monopolization is contrary to the purpose and policy of the Sherman Act.

* * *

* * * The purpose of the [Sherman] Act is not to protect businesses from the working of the market; it is to protect the public from the failure of the market. The law directs itself not against conduct which is competitive, even severely so, but against conduct which unfairly tends to destroy competition itself. It does so not out of solicitude for private concerns but out of concern for the public interest. *See, e.g., Brunswick Corp. v. Pueblo Bowl–O–Mat, Inc.,* 429 U.S. 477, 488, 97 S.Ct. 690, 697 (1977); *Cargill, Inc. v. Monfort of Colorado, Inc.,* 479 U.S. 104, 116–117, 107 S.Ct. 484, 492–493 (1986); *Brown*

Shoe Co. v. United States, 370 U.S. 294, 320, 82 S.Ct. 1502, 1521 (1962). Thus, this Court and other courts have been careful to avoid constructions of § 2 which might chill competition, rather than foster it. It is sometimes difficult to distinguish robust competition from conduct with long-term anticompetitive effects; moreover, single-firm activity is unlike concerted activity covered by § 1, which "inherently is fraught with anticompetitive risk." *Copperweld,* 467 U.S., at 767–769, 104 S.Ct., at 2739–2740. For these reasons, § 2 makes the conduct of a single firm unlawful only when it actually monopolizes or dangerously threatens to do so. *Id.,* at 767, 104 S.Ct., at 2739. The concern that § 2 might be applied so as to further anticompetitive ends is plainly not met by inquiring only whether the defendant has engaged in "unfair" or "predatory" tactics. Such conduct may be sufficient to prove the necessary intent to monopolize, which is something more than an intent to compete vigorously, but demonstrating the dangerous probability of monopolization in an attempt case also requires inquiry into the relevant product and geographic market and the defendant's economic power in that market.

III

We hold that petitioners may not be liable for attempted monopolization under § 2 of the Sherman Act absent proof of a dangerous probability that they would monopolize a particular market and specific intent to monopolize. In this case, the trial instructions allowed the jury to infer specific intent and dangerous probability of success from the defendants' predatory conduct, without any proof of the relevant market or of a realistic probability that the defendants could achieve monopoly power in that market. In this respect, the instructions misconstrued § 2, as did the Court of Appeals in affirming the judgment of the District Court. Since the affirmance of the § 2 judgment against petitioners rested solely on the legally erroneous conclusion that petitioners had attempted to monopolize in violation of § 2 and since the jury's verdict did not negate the possibility that the § 2 verdict rested on the attempt to monopolize ground alone, the judgment of the Court of Appeals is reversed, * * * and the case is remanded for further proceedings consistent with this opinion.

Summarizing the elements of the attempt offense, the Court in *Spectrum Sports* said the plaintiff must prove that (1) the defendant has engaged in predatory or anticompetitive conduct with (2) a specific intent to monopolize and (3) a dangerous probability of achieving monopoly power. Repudiating the view of the Ninth Circuit's earlier *Lessig* decision that a dangerous probability of success could be inferred from proof of predatory conduct alone, the Court held that satisfying the dangerous probability element required an assessment of the defendant's market power.

A finding that the defendant possessed a dangerous probability of success can occur at market share thresholds well below those needed to establish actual monopolization. Although results in individual cases vary, courts generally have presumed that market shares below 50 percent do not show the requisite dangerous probability of attaining a monopoly. As with monopolization cases, courts in attempt disputes adjust the inferences to be drawn from market shares depending on the height of entry barriers.

E. REMEDIES

*Note on the Success of Conduct Remedies in Monopolization Cases**

Though frequently imposed, conduct remedies do not enjoy a favorable reputation in the antitrust literature, particularly in the case of dominant firm behavior. One often-voiced criticism, particularly in older commentary, is that conduct remedies do little to unravel existing accumulations of market power and provide feeble alternatives to structure solutions, such as divestiture, that directly dismantle positions of dominance. This critique reflects the strong influence of the structuralist school of antitrust, which posits market structure as the key determinant of competitive vigor and tends to equate concentrated markets with a lack of competition. In the view of structrualists, conduct remedies that have not reduced the defendant's market share dramatically—below 50 percent, to use a rough rule of thumb—have failed their essential purpose.

Experience with the *United States v. United Shoe Mach. Corp.*, 110 F.Supp. 295 (D. Mass. 1953), *aff'd per curiam*, 347 U.S. 521, 74 S.Ct. 699 (1954) litigation sometimes is offered to illustrate this point. In a monopolization case concluded in the early 1950s, the DOJ prevailed on the issue of liability but failed to persuade the court to order divestiture. Emphasizing that the defendant owned a single facility, the court forbad the continuation of United's lease-only policy and required United to unbundle service from the supply of its machines. United's market share fell to the low 60s until 1968, when the Supreme Court granted the government's request for divestiture. The failure to grant divestiture in the original 1950s proceeding is offered as an example of the weakness of conduct remedies and the relative superiority of divestiture.

Criticism of the remedial history of the *United Shoe Machinery* litigation may rest on questionable assumptions derived from structuralist economic models that enjoyed widespread acceptance in the 1950s and 1960s. One point for reconsideration is whether a fall from roughly 85 percent to 60 percent constitutes a remedial failure. The Supreme Court's 1968 opinion treats United's market share as the sole index of remedial effectiveness. Such an approach ignores other data—such as industry patterns of entry, profitability, and innovation—that might provide a more reliable measure of the remedy's impact.

A second basic concern with conduct remedies is that they can entail extensive judicial supervision and continuing intervention to interpret remedial commands and see that they are obeyed. This possibility is perhaps most evident where the court seeks to force an incumbent dominant firm to grant access to a valuable commercial asset. For example, in *Otter Tail Power Co. v. United States*, 410 U.S. 366 (1973), the Supreme Court ordered an integrated electric utility to "wheel" bulk power over its long distance transmission lines to municipally-owned distribution systems. If a court decides to mandate access to a key asset, it must be prepared to specify the price and quality terms on which the defendant must provide access. In setting appropriate access charges, courts may find themselves enmeshed in ratemaking exercises for which they are institutionally ill-suited. Similarly, the consent decree in AT & T, which was entered in 1982, required continuing oversight by the federal district court until the enactment of the Telecommunications Act of 1996.

* This Note is adapted from William E. Kovacic, *Failed Expectations: The Troubled Past and Uncertain Future of the Sherman Act as a*   *Tool of Deconcentration*, 74 Iowa L. Rev. 1105 (1989).

Perhaps the most dramatic form of judicial intervention in civil cases is the entry of an order that requires the defendant to be restructured into two or more entities or to divest substantial assets to another purchaser. Divestiture orders offer the possibility of swiftly dissipating the defendant's market power by introducing new competitors into the market. In some instances, the divestiture remedy may involve a single instance of judicial intervention and avoid the need to exercise continuing oversight responsibilities associated with some controls on conduct.

Divestiture orders are most common, and the least controversial, in merger challenges, and it is easy to see why. Recall from Chapter 5 that when a court concludes that a merger will be anticompetitive, it enjoins the merger, *i.e.*, it prohibits the combining of the firms or assets at issue. When it reaches such a conclusion after a merger or acquisition has already been consummated, it will typically seek to undo the effort through divestiture. Although it can sometimes be difficult to "unscramble the eggs," *i.e.*, disentangle assets that have already been commingled, the mere fact that the assets once existed separately provides the court with at least some guidance as to how to achieve the divestiture with minimal damage to the efficient operation of the firms.

Similarly, divestiture has been a common and generally accepted remedy for Section 2 monopolization cases, where the monopolist became dominant at least in part through acquisitions, even though the acquisitions themselves were not independent violations. Again, it is easy to see why. When a monopolist acquired its dominant position at least in part through the acquisition of rivals, a remedy for abusing that position might include dismantling its monopoly. As in the case of illegal mergers, the fact that its constituent parts once existed independently, provides the court with valuable guidance in approaching the divestiture process.

Nevertheless, divestiture remains a drastic and rarely employed remedy outside of these narrow circumstances. It is almost unheard of in Section 1 cases, and remains controversial in Section 2 cases—especially when the dominant firm achieved its dominance through internal growth as opposed to acquisitions. Courts in civil cases, especially abuse of dominance matters, have tended to regard divestiture as a riskier form of intervention than conduct controls. The perceptions of risk are most acute where a restructuring might destroy valuable efficiencies. Courts also might fear that a divestiture will reduce employment and impose significant losses on investors. Because courts tend to see divestiture as entailing greater risks, plaintiffs are well-advised to devote additional effort to demonstrating that a divestiture plan will produce substantial net competitive benefits without substantial adverse affects.

Divestiture measures also can be difficult to administer. In the most simple type of divestiture, a court can order existing organizational units within the firm to be spun off as separate entities. Such a move ordinarily will require some difficult judgments about how to allocate personnel and assets that serve the company as a whole, but there generally will be no need to sever existing design or production teams, and perhaps no need to separate physical facilities. In the harder case, the firm's operations are carried out in fully integrated teams. If a restructuring program is to be carried out, the court will have to decide how personnel who serve in the unitary teams will be allocated to the new enterprise, and how equipment and physical facilities will be divided.

Divestitures must also meet financial market tests for practicality and value. Whereas divestiture of assets may be appealing as an economic matter, the assets must have value in the market sufficient to attract buyers at reasonable prices.

For example, it may be difficult to sell off assets deemed to be over-priced or lacking in value. Older physical facilities may be economically inefficient, out of date and unattractive to purchasers. Finding purchasers for assets ordered to be divested, therefore, may not always be a simple matter, and courts often turn to Special Masters to oversee divestiture orders over some specified period of time.

If the plaintiff proposes a structural solution, how should the court determine whether structural relief is appropriate? In 2001 the court of appeals decision in *United States v. Microsoft Corp.* devoted extensive attention to the duties of the trial judge in such instances. As we saw earlier in this Chapter, the D.C. Circuit affirmed much of the trial court's ruling that Microsoft had violated Section 2 of the Sherman Act by using improper means to preserve monopoly power in the software sector. In addition to extensive conduct remedies, the district court had endorsed the government's proposal that Microsoft—a unitary firm that had achieved its dominance through internal growth—be broken into two. The court of appeals reversed and remanded.

UNITED STATES v. MICROSOFT CORP.

United States Court of Appeals for the District of Columbia, 2001.
253 F.3d 34.

PER CURIAM:

* * *

V. Trial Proceedings and Remedy

* * * We conclude * * * that the District Court's remedies decree must be vacated for three independent reasons: (1) the court failed to hold a remedies-specific evidentiary hearing when there were disputed facts; (2) the court failed to provide adequate reasons for its decreed remedies; and (3) this Court has revised the scope of Microsoft's liability and it is impossible to determine to what extent that should affect the remedies provisions.

A. *Factual Background*

On April 3, 2000, the District Court concluded the liability phase of the proceedings by the filing of its Conclusions of Law holding that Microsoft had violated §§ 1 and 2 of the Sherman Act. The court and the parties then began discussions of the procedures to be followed in the imposition of remedies. Initially, the District Court signaled that it would enter relief only after conducting a new round of proceedings. In its Conclusions of Law, the court stated that it would issue a remedies order "following proceedings to be established by further Order of the Court." And, when during a post-trial conference, Microsoft's counsel asked whether the court "contemplate[d] further proceedings," the judge replied, "Yes. Yes. I assume that there would be further proceedings." The District Court further speculated that those proceedings might "replicate the procedure at trial with testimony in written form subject to crossexamination."

On April 28, 2000, plaintiffs submitted their proposed final judgment, accompanied by six new supporting affidavits and several exhibits. In addition to a series of temporary conduct restrictions, plaintiffs proposed that Microsoft be split into two independent corporations, with one continuing Microsoft's operating systems business and the other undertaking the balance of

Microsoft's operations. Microsoft filed a "summary response" on May 10, contending both that the proposed decree was too severe and that it would be impossible to resolve certain remedies-specific factual disputes "on a highly expedited basis." Another May 10 submission argued that if the District Court considered imposing plaintiffs' proposed remedy, "then substantial discovery, adequate time for preparation and a full trial on relief will be required." * * *

After the District Court revealed during a May 24 hearing that it was prepared to enter a decree without conducting "any further process," Microsoft renewed its argument that the underlying factual disputes between the parties necessitated a remedies-specific evidentiary hearing. In two separate offers of proof, Microsoft offered to produce a number of pieces of evidence. * * *

[Here the court summarized Microsoft's offers of proof concerning the likely adverse effects of the plaintiffs' proposed remedies. Microsoft had offered testimony by several economic experts, an investment bank, and Microsoft executives, including the company's chairman, Bill Gates. Eds.]

Over Microsoft's objections, the District Court proceeded to consider the merits of the remedy and on June 7, 2000 entered its final judgment. The court explained that it would not conduct "extended proceedings on the form a remedy should take," because it doubted that an evidentiary hearing would "give any significantly greater assurance that it will be able to identify what might be generally regarded as an optimum remedy." The bulk of Microsoft's proffered facts were simply conjectures about future events, and "[i]n its experience the Court has found testimonial predictions of future events generally less reliable even than testimony as to historical fact, and cross-examination to be of little use in enhancing or detracting from their accuracy." Nor was the court swayed by Microsoft's "profession of surprise" at the possibility of structural relief. "From the inception of this case Microsoft knew, from well-established Supreme Court precedents dating from the beginning of the last century, that a mandated divestiture was a possibility, if not a probability, in the event of an adverse result at trial."

The substance of the District Court's remedies order is nearly identical to plaintiffs' proposal. The decree's centerpiece is the requirement that Microsoft submit a proposed plan of divestiture, with the company to be split into an "Operating Systems Business," or "OpsCo," and an "Applications Business," or "AppsCo." OpsCo would receive all of Microsoft's operating systems, such as Windows 98 and Windows 2000, while AppsCo would receive the remainder of Microsoft's businesses, including IE [Internet Explorer Internet browser] and Office [Microsoft Office]. The District Court identified four reasons for its "reluctant[ ]" conclusion that "a structural remedy has become imperative." First, Microsoft "does not yet concede that any of its business practices violated the Sherman Act." Second, the company consequently "continues to do business as it has in the past." Third, Microsoft "has proved untrustworthy in the past." And fourth, the Government, whose officials "are by reason of office obliged and expected to consider—and to act in—the public interest," won the case, "and for that reason alone have some entitlement to a remedy of their choice."

* * *

[The court of appeals concluded that the trial court's efforts to accelerate the conduct of the case on the merits by limiting the number of witnesses for each side did not constitute error. Eds.]

C. Failure to Hold an Evidentiary Hearing

* * * It is a cardinal principle of our system of justice that factual disputes must be heard in open court and resolved through trial-like evidentiary proceedings. Any other course would be contrary "to the spirit which imbues our judicial tribunals prohibiting decision without hearing." A party has the right to judicial resolution of disputed facts not just as to the liability phase, but also as to appropriate relief. Normally, an evidentiary hearing is required before an injunction may be granted." Other than a temporary restraining order, no injunctive relief may be entered without a hearing. *See generally* Fed. R. Civ. P. 65. A hearing on the merits—*i.e.*, a trial on liability—does not substitute for a relief-specific evidentiary hearing unless the matter of relief was part of the trial on liability, or unless there are no disputed factual issues regarding the matter of relief.

This rule is no less applicable in antitrust cases. The Supreme Court "has recognized that a 'full exploration of facts is usually necessary in order (for the District Court) properly to draw (an antitrust) decree' so as 'to prevent future violations and eradicate existing evils.' " *United States v. Ward Baking Co.*, 376 U.S. 327, 330–31, 84 S.Ct. 763 (1964). Hence a remedies decree must be vacated whenever there is "a bona fide disagreement concerning substantive items of relief which could be resolved only by trial." *Id.* at 334, 84 S.Ct. 763 * * *

Despite plaintiffs' protestations, there can be no serious doubt that the parties disputed a number of facts during the remedies phase. In two separate offers of proof, Microsoft identified 23 witnesses who, had they been permitted to testify, would have challenged a wide range of plaintiffs' factual representations, including the feasibility of dividing Microsoft, the likely impact on consumers, and the effect of divestiture on shareholders. To take but two examples, where plaintiffs' economists testified that splitting Microsoft in two would be socially beneficial, the company offered to prove that the proposed remedy would "cause substantial social harm by raising software prices, lowering rates of innovation and disrupting the evolution of Windows as a software development platform." And where plaintiffs' investment banking experts proposed that divestiture might actually increase shareholder value, Microsoft proffered evidence that structural relief "would inevitably result in a significant loss of shareholder value," a loss that could reach "tens—possibly hundreds—of billions of dollars."

Indeed, the District Court itself appears to have conceded the existence of acute factual disagreements between Microsoft and plaintiffs. The court acknowledged that the parties were "sharply divided" and held "divergent opinions" on the likely results of its remedies decree. The reason the court declined to conduct an evidentiary hearing was not because of the absence of disputed facts, but because it believed that those disputes could be resolved only through "actual experience," not further proceedings. But a prediction about future events is not, as a prediction, any less a factual issue. Indeed, the Supreme Court has acknowledged that drafting an antitrust decree by necessity "involves predictions and assumptions concerning future economic and business events." *Ford Motor Co. v. United States*, 405 U.S. 562, 578, 92 S.Ct. 1142 (1972). Trial courts are not excused from their obligation to resolve such matters through evidentiary hearings simply because they consider the bedrock procedures of our justice system to be "of little use."

* * *

Plaintiffs further argue—and the District Court held—that no evidentiary hearing was necessary given that Microsoft long had been on notice that structural relief was a distinct possibility. It is difficult to see why this matters. Whether Microsoft had advance notice that dissolution was in the works is immaterial to whether the District Court violated the company's procedural rights by ordering it without an evidentiary hearing. To be sure, "claimed surprise at the district court's decision to consider permanent injunctive relief does not, alone, merit reversal." But in this case, Microsoft's professed surprise does not stand "alone." There is something more: the company's basic procedural right to have disputed facts resolved through an evidentiary hearing.

* * *

D. Failure to Provide an Adequate Explanation

We vacate the District Court's remedies decree for the additional reason that the court has failed to provide an adequate explanation for the relief it ordered. The Supreme Court has explained that a remedies decree in an antitrust case must seek to "unfetter a market from anticompetitive conduct," *Ford Motor Co.*, 405 U.S. at 577, 92 S.Ct. 1142, to "terminate the illegal monopoly, deny to the defendant the fruits of its statutory violation, and ensure that there remain no practices likely to result in monopolization in the future," *United States v. United Shoe Mach. Corp.*, 391 U.S. 244, 250, 88 S.Ct. 1496 (1968); *see also United States v. Grinnell Corp.*, 384 U.S. 563, 577, 86 S.Ct. 1698 (1966).

The District Court has not explained how its remedies decree would accomplish those objectives. Indeed, the court devoted a mere four paragraphs of its order to explaining its reasons for the remedy. They are: (1) Microsoft "does not yet concede that any of its business practices violated the Sherman Act"; (2) Microsoft "continues to do business as it has in the past"; (3) Microsoft "has proved untrustworthy in the past"; and (4) the Government, whose officials "are by reason of office obliged and expected to consider—and to act in—the public interest," won the case, "and for that reason alone have some entitlement to a remedy of their choice." Nowhere did the District Court discuss the objectives the Supreme Court deems relevant.

* * *

F. On Remand

As a general matter, a district court is afforded broad discretion to enter that relief it calculates will best remedy the conduct it has found to be unlawful. This is no less true in antitrust cases. *See, e.g.,* Ford Motor Co., *405 U.S. at 573, 92 S.Ct. 1142 ("The District Court is clothed with 'large discretion' to fit the decree to the special needs of the individual case.");* Md. & Va. Milk Producers Ass'n, Inc. v. United States, *362 U.S. 458, 473, 80 S.Ct. 847 (1960) ("The formulation of decrees is largely left to the discretion of the trial court....."). And divestiture is a common form of relief in successful antitrust prosecutions: it is indeed "the most important of antitrust remedies."* See, e.g., United States v. E.I. du Pont de Nemours & Co., 366 U.S. 316, 331, 81 S.Ct. 1243 (1961).

On remand, the District Court must reconsider whether the use of the structural remedy of divestiture is appropriate with respect to Microsoft, which argues that it is a unitary company. By and large, cases upon which plaintiffs rely in arguing for the split of Microsoft have involved the dissolution of entities formed by mergers and acquisitions. On the contrary, the Supreme Court has clarified that divestiture "has traditionally been the remedy for Sherman Act violations whose heart is intercorporate *combination and control," du Pont*, 366 U.S. at 329, 81 S.Ct. 1243 (emphasis added), and that "[c]omplete divestiture is particularly appropriate where asset or stock *acquisitions* violate the antitrust laws," *Ford Motor Co.*, 405 U.S. at 573, 92 S.Ct. 1142 (emphasis added).

One apparent reason why courts have not ordered the dissolution of unitary companies is logistical difficulty. As the court explained in *United States v. ALCOA*, 91 F.Supp. 333, 416 (S.D.N.Y.1950), a "corporation, designed to operate effectively as a single entity, cannot readily be dismembered of parts of its various operations without a marked loss of efficiency." A corporation that has expanded by acquiring its competitors often has preexisting internal lines of division along which it may more easily be split than a corporation that has expanded from natural growth. Although time and corporate modifications and developments may eventually fade those lines, at least the identifiable entities preexisted to create a template for such division as the court might later decree. With reference to those corporations that are not acquired by merger and acquisition, Judge Wyzanski accurately opined in *United Shoe*:

> United conducts all machine manufacture at one plant in Beverly, with one set of jigs and tools, one foundry, one laboratory for machinery problems, one managerial staff, and one labor force. It takes no Solomon to see that this organism cannot be cut into three equal and viable parts.

United States v. United Shoe Machinery Corp., 110 F.Supp. 295, 348 (D.Mass. 1953).

Depending upon the evidence, the District Court may find in a remedies proceeding that it would be no easier to split Microsoft in two than United Shoe in three. Microsoft's Offer of Proof in response to the court's denial of an evidentiary hearing included proffered testimony from its President and CEO Steve Ballmer that the company "is, and always has been, a unified company without free-standing business units. Microsoft is not the result of mergers or acquisitions." Microsoft further offered evidence that it is "not organized along product lines," but rather is housed in a single corporate headquarters and that it has

> only one sales and marketing organization which is responsible for selling all of the company's products, one basic research organization,

one product support organization, one operations department, one information technology department, one facilities department, one purchasing department, one human resources department, one finance department, one legal department and one public relations department.

If indeed Microsoft is a unitary company, division might very well require Microsoft to reproduce each of these departments in each new entity rather than simply allocate the differing departments among them.

In devising an appropriate remedy, the District Court also should consider whether plaintiffs have established a sufficient causal connection between Microsoft's anticompetitive conduct and its dominant position in the OS market. "Mere existence of an exclusionary act does not itself justify full feasible relief against the monopolist to create maximum competition." Rather, structural relief, which is "designed to eliminate the monopoly altogether ... require[s] a clearer indication of a *significant causal connection* between the conduct and creation or maintenance of the market power." Absent such causation, the antitrust defendant's unlawful behavior should be remedied by "an injunction against continuation of that conduct."

* * * [W]e have found a causal connection between Microsoft's exclusionary conduct and its continuing position in the operating systems market only through inference. Indeed, the District Court expressly did not adopt the position that Microsoft would have lost its position in the OS market but for its anticompetitive behavior. *Findings of Fact* § 411 ("There is insufficient evidence to find that, absent Microsoft's actions, Navigator and Java already would have ignited genuine competition in the market for Intel-compatible PC operating systems."). If the court on remand is unconvinced of the causal connection between Microsoft's exclusionary conduct and the company's position in the OS market, it may well conclude that divestiture is not an appropriate remedy.

While we do not undertake to dictate to the District Court the precise form that relief should take on remand, we note again that it should be tailored to fit the wrong creating the occasion for the remedy.

* * *

How should a court decide the scope of equitable remedies once an antitrust violation has been found? What should the scope of those remedies be? In *Microsoft*, the district court had ordered a combination of "behavioral" or "conduct" remedies, as well as "structural" remedies. What might lead a court to select one or the other, or, as the *Microsoft* district court did, both? Why did the court of appeals conclude that an evidentiary hearing is required before an order of divestiture can be entered? Would the same reasoning require a hearing before *any* equitable remedy is entered?

Recall from our earlier readings on *Microsoft* in this Chapter that before reaching its decision to remand the question of remedy, the D.C. Circuit affirmed in part, reversed in part, and remanded in part the district court's conclusion that Microsoft had violated Sections 1 and 2 of the Sherman Act.

On remand the Antitrust Division, under leadership that had changed due to the presidential election of 2000, quickly announced that it would neither pursue any of the remanded claims of liability, nor seek a break up of Microsoft. Thereafter, it and 9 of the remaining 18 litigating states reached a settlement with Microsoft that involved a variety of conduct remedies, which would be imposed for five years. But nine other states rejected the settlement as inadequate and asked the district court to proceed with the remand, urging broader conduct remedies.

Faced with an unprecedented situation, the district court divided the proceedings into two "tracks." Track 1 focused on the required procedures for federal court approval of a government negotiated consent decree under the Tunney Act, 15 U.S.C. § 16(e). Track 2 proceeded to trial on the remanded question of remedy, in which the nine non-settling states sought to augment the agreement reached with Microsoft by the Department of Justice and joined in by the nine settling states. The district court ultimately approved the settlement of the case in the Tunney Act proceeding, and ordered little in the way of additional relief in the remedy trial pursued in the end solely by the State of Massachusetts. The D.C. Circuit affirmed in almost all respects. On the merits it affirmed, finding no abuse of discretion by the district court, instead praising its handling of the complex two track proceedings. *See Massachusetts v. Microsoft Corp.*, 373 F.3d 1199 (D.C. Cir. 2004). For further discussion of the Tunney Act, see Sidebar 9–6, *infra*.

What challenges confronted the district court in working on two "tracks"? How might it be possible to enter a remedial decree pursuant to a settlement, yet to also order additional remedial steps in a second and independent judicial proceeding?

F. CONCLUSION

Jurisprudence concerning dominant firm behavior reflects a fundamental dilemma in economics and law about the design of policies governing large business enterprises. Judge Learned Hand displayed that ambivalence memorably in *Alcoa*. Hand warned that "unchallenged economic power deadens initiative, discourages thrift and depresses energy," yet he also cautioned that the "[s]uccessful competitor, having been urged to compete, must not be turned upon when he wins." How is a competition policy system to discourage overreaching by dominant enterprises without promoting passivity as a way of commercial life?

Efforts to resolve the dilemma have proceeded on two basic fronts. The first is to refine tools used to identify conditions of genuine dominance. Aided in large measure by analytical advances in the U.S. merger guidelines that we studied in Chapter 5, antitrust agencies and courts have improved their capacity to measure market power accurately and directly. There still remain, however, difficult measurement problems in industries undergoing rapid technological change or other forms of dynamism.

The second frontier of activity involves the definition of unreasonable exclusion. *Alcoa* defined improper conduct expansively and reflected an implicit assumption that aggressive intervention to police dominant firms was appropriate because firms rarely gained or sustained dominance through superior performance. By the late 1970s and early 1980s, courts and enforcement agencies in varying degrees had begun to heed the cautions of critics about (1) possible justifications for acts previously deemed to constitute improper means of exclusion; (2) the role of superior performance in yielding dominance; and (3) the capacity of judges and antitrust officials to correctly diagnose competitive maladies and impose useful cures. Through the 1980s and 1990s, debate surfaced in which some commentators, operating within an efficiency framework, have suggested new possibilities for intervention and sought to develop analytical tools that courts and enforcement bodies can administer successfully.

The modern ferment in analysis has inspired the search for a new framework for analyzing claims of dominant firm exclusion. The pursuit of a new framework reflects dissatisfaction with formalistic, traditional methodologies that, by placing specific methods of exclusion in discrete categories, can sometimes divert attention from questions that should supply the foundation for evaluating all allegations of dominant firm misconduct. Our discussion of these issues, and of the ongoing evolution of a modern analytical framework for evaluating claims of exclusion, continues in Chapter 7.

G. PROBLEMS AND EXERCISES
Problem 6–1:
Amerinet

a. *The Facts*

Amerinet is the largest Internet service provider ("ISP") in the United States. Amerinet is the leading provider of "Jiffy Messaging" ("JM") services, which permit individuals to send and receive electronic messages in real time with other members of their "crony lists." Amerinet is pursuing a series of business initiatives (part of the company's "Amerinet Anywhere" strategy) that would permit wireless access to Amerinet's services through a portable, handheld device that has voice and JM capabilities. Amerinet calls the new handheld device and related services by the name of "AmeriPhone." To carry out its plans, Amerinet intends to use the following approaches.

(a) Amerinet intends to contract with the most popular mobile telephone manufacturers to supply the hardware for the AmeriPhone. The manufacturers will be required to agree that they will not produce or sell a similar device to any competitor of Amerinet.

(b) Amerinet will sell its AmeriPhone and related services through independent distributors. Amerinet will require all of its distributors to agree that the AmeriPhone service can be sold only to customers of Amerinet's basic Internet access service. Amerinet plans to configure its wireless Internet service so that it only works with the branded Amerinet handset.

(c) To encourage retail sales of the AmeriPhone service, Amerinet wants to initiate a nationwide marketing campaign for the service. The campaign would feature a highly promoted, uniform, low monthly price. Amerinet wants this price to be available to customers at all of its retail outlets, including its independent distributors.

b. *Problem and Skills Exercise*

You are an Assistant General Counsel at Amerinet. You have been asked to advise Amerinet about the possible antitrust consequences of proceeding with these business strategies. Draft a memorandum of no more than five (5) pages evaluating the legality of the proposed strategies based on the cases we have studied. Identify for Amerinet any additional information you might need to know about the market to evaluate its proposals.

Problem 6–2:
Mountain Air

a. *The Facts*

Mountain Air and Icarus Air have 85% and 5%, respectively, of a properly defined relevant market consisting of passenger airline traffic through Denver, Colorado. Icarus is a small, low-cost airline, and it recently emerged from a bankruptcy reorganization after one of its planes crashed with a large loss of life.

Last winter Icarus offered discounted fares to induce vacationers to fly Icarus to Denver. Mountain swiftly matched these fares. Icarus believes Mountain's discounted fares fail to recover Mountain's short-run average variable costs. Icarus had identified witnesses who will testify that a Mountain official told a large travel agency: "We'll give seats away to melt Icarus's revenues, and then raise fares later once Icarus has fallen to earth." If Icarus quits Denver, the City of Denver (which owns Denver's airport) will insist that Icarus's gates and other airport assets be sold to an airline other than Mountain.

Before its bankruptcy, Icarus formed a code-sharing arrangement with Mountain by which the two firms jointly served routes west of Denver that Mountain did not serve but Icarus did. After Icarus emerged from bankruptcy, Mountain ended the agreement and began serving the routes by itself. Mountain has gotten complaints from customers who say Icarus provided better service. Mountain has told the public that it fears harm to its reputation by working with an airline that had a recent crash. Mountain's internal marketing studies (a) predict lucrative profits from taking over Icarus's routes, (b) conclude that customers view Icarus as being at least as safe as Mountain, and (c) say Icarus "needs code-sharing with Mountain to sustain operations in Denver."

In the past, when Mountain has perceived that a low-cost entrant such as Icarus might offer service on routes served by Mountain, Mountain has publicly announced that it has future plans to greatly increase its own service on the routes that the entrant is thinking of serving. Mountain's internal marketing studies indicate that Mountain believes such announcements discourage entrants from initiating service. Mountain sometimes adds the capacity and service that its advance announcements promise, but sometimes it withdraws its promise if it appears that the entrant is not going to enter the market after all.

b. *Problem and Skills Exercise*

You are a private attorney and have been retained by Mountain to evaluate its possible antitrust vulnerability for these practices in the United States. Mountain also would like your views about whether the same strategies it has used in the United States would be acceptable in the European Union. Prepare a brief memorandum of no more than five (5) pages advising Mountain on each of the questions it has posed.

Chapter 7

CONCERTED CONDUCT HAVING
EXCLUSIONARY EFFECTS

INTRODUCTION

Chapter 6 introduced the treatment of conduct having exclusionary anticompetitive effects. As we learned, single firms may undertake a variety of "exclusionary" strategies to obtain or maintain market power. We also learned that a central challenge for antitrust law and economics in this area is to differentiate between aggressive, but legitimate conduct that may exclude rivals on the merits, and truly "predatory" or "exclusionary" conduct, which alone warrants condemnation.

Although some exclusionary strategies are "unilateral," such as predatory pricing and some refusals to deal, others require the willing or unwilling participation of additional firms. When rival firms are involved, the strategies will be "horizontal;" when suppliers or customers are involved, they will be "vertical." Chapter 6 focused largely on unilateral exclusionary conduct, whereas this chapter looks at concerted conduct, both horizontal and vertical, that excludes. Although the courts and enforcers have sometimes treated these two forms of exclusionary conduct differently, we will see that the economic theory of exclusion is largely the same in all cases of allegedly exclusionary conduct, regardless of form.

When exclusionary strategies are undertaken by dominant or would-be dominant firms, they are typically addressed under Section 2 of the Sherman Act—the principal focus of Chapter 6. But as we first noted in Chapters 2 and 4, concerted exclusionary conduct, whether "horizontal" or "vertical," may raise antitrust issues under Section 1 of the Sherman Act or Section 3 of the Clayton Act, regardless of whether the alleged predator is a dominant firm. Examples include group boycotts having exclusionary effects, which we briefly discussed in Chapter 2, as well as interbrand vertical restraints such as exclusive dealing and tying, which we first noted in Chapter 4.

In this Chapter, we seek to expand our understanding of the law and economics of exclusionary conduct. What forms can it take? What effects can it have? One of the characteristics of exclusionary conduct that was evident in Chapter 6 is that its immediate impact is on rivals of the predator. Customers or consumers may not be affected at all, at first, or be affected only indirectly.

How does that complicate the evaluation of conduct alleged to be exclusionary? Might not all aggressively competitive conduct "injure" rivals to some extent? Should antitrust law only be concerned with exclusionary conduct when it appears substantial enough to diminish competition and result in collusive effects? Why?

On another level, we will observe how the attitudes of commentators, courts, and antitrust enforcement agencies toward exclusionary conduct have developed over time, moving from per se levels of scrutiny in some instances, to less skepticism and greater acceptance. What explains these trends? Traditional case law looked upon exclusion very harshly, but in the face of significant criticism from Chicago School supporters and judges, support for harsh treatment of exclusionary conduct waned. What was the nature of that criticism? How is it evident in the cases? Why was it persuasive in whole or part? After a time, Post–Chicago commentators responded to the Chicago School critique, arguing that enforcers and courts should take concerns about exclusion more seriously than had been suggested by Chicagoans. One of the enduring contributions of the Post–Chicago School of antitrust may be its advocacy of increased scrutiny of exclusionary strategies, and its development of the economic tools to undertake that scrutiny. What is the basis for the Post–Chicago view that exclusion should be taken seriously? What are the economic requirements of a plausible case of exclusion from its point of view?

As you read the Chapter, consider the various questions just posed. Also consider what the conduct described in this Chapter has in common with the conduct studied in Chapter 6. How is it alike? When might it be different? Should it matter that exclusionary conduct is undertaken by a single firm or more than one firm? Should "market power" play a role in the analysis? If so, how?

A. EXCLUSIONARY GROUP BOYCOTTS

Chapter 2's discussion of boycotts focused on those having collusive effects and culminated with our examination of the Supreme Court's decision in *Superior Court Trial Lawyers* ("*SCTLA*"). *SCTLA* was controversial owing in large part to the political and constitutional context of the lawyers's actions. Nevertheless, it aptly illustrates how a boycott can be used by competing firms as a method of implementing an agreement to fix prices. The "boycott" label in those circumstances serves simply as a description of the means utilized to implement an agreement on price: "we will not sell to you unless you agree to pay the price we have collectively agreed upon." Arguably, the label adds nothing to the analysis of competitive effect. Viewed as such, a collusive group boycott is indistinguishable from any price fixing agreement and is deserving therefore of per se treatment, especially when there is evidence that it achieved its desired result, *i.e.*, higher prices.

Here we turn our attention to group boycotts having exclusionary effects. The modern exclusionary boycott is more complex to evaluate than the collusive boycott for two reasons: (I) its effects are less obvious, and (ii) its potentially legitimate justifications are more varied. Before looking at the more contemporary treatment of such cases, we will explore some of the traditional cases.

1. FOUNDATION CASES: FROM *EASTERN STATES* TO *KLOR'S*

Exclusionary group boycotts have a long history under U.S. antitrust laws. In *Eastern States Retail Lumber Dealers' Ass'n v. United States*, 234 U.S. 600 (1914), the Supreme Court affirmed a decree enjoining a group of retail lumber dealers from collectively refusing to purchase supplies from wholesalers engaged in the practice of "dual distributing," *i.e.*, selling lumber at both wholesale and retail. The boycott, which was organized under the auspices of the retailers's trade association, was designed to coerce dual distributors into exiting the retail end of the business, where their vertical integration into wholesaling promised them a decided cost advantage. The boycott took the form of a "blacklist," which identified dual distributors. The list was circulated to association members and customers, who in turn agreed not to purchase supplies from the listed firms. With reference to *Standard Oil's* "rule of reason," the Court condemned the boycott:

> A retail dealer has the unquestioned right to stop dealing with a wholesaler for reasons sufficient to himself, and may do so because he thinks such dealer is acting unfairly in trying to undermine his trade. * * *

> [But] [w]hen the retailer goes beyond his personal right, and, conspiring and combining with others of like purpose, seeks to obstruct the free course of * * * commerce and to unduly suppress competition by placing obnoxious wholesaler dealers under the coercive influence of a condemnatory report circulated among others, or possible customers of the offenders, he exceeds his lawful rights. * * *

Id. at 614.

Was the boycott in *Eastern States* collusive or exclusionary? Emphasizing the probability that the retail dealers were parties to a price fixing cartel, Judge Posner appears to suggest that the essential anticompetitive character of the refusal to deal in *Eastern States* was its tendency to produce collusive effects. *See, e.g., JTC Petroleum Co. v. Piasa Motor Fuels, Inc.*, 190 F.3d.775, 778 (7th Cir. 1999) (Casebook, Chapter 1, *supra*). But Justice Scalia appears to characterize the conduct in *Eastern States* as exclusionary. It was targeted at and intended to disadvantage wholesalers that were also retail rivals of association members. In contrast to *JTC*, there was no allegation of any ongoing cartel among the boycotting association members. As such, its "success," *i.e.*, its anticompetitive effect, depended upon the ability of the colluding firms to either coerce their rivals into abandoning dual distribution or to exclude them effectively. *See Hartford Fire Ins. Co. v. California*, 509 U.S. 764, 803 (1993) (viewing *Eastern States* as a conditional boycott). Which interpretation of *Eastern States* is more compelling? Does it matter from the point of view of antitrust analysis? Might it affect the analysis of *antitrust injury* for purposes of a private civil action initiated by an excluded firm?

The Court similarly condemned a boycott in *Fashion Originators' Guild of America v. FTC*, 312 U.S. 457 (1941) ("FOGA"), making clear that group boycotts would be condemned regardless of their direct relationship to price fixing. In doing so, it ruled inadmissible the Guild's defenses—that the agreement at issue had not "fixed or regulated prices, parcelled out or limited production, or brought about a deterioration in quality." *Id.* at 466. This brought the Court much closer in *FOGA* than in *Eastern States* to condemning boycotts as per se violations of the Sherman Act.

FOGA involved a boycott organized by designers and manufacturers of women's garments, primarily "high fashion" dresses, that was organized through their trade association, the Fashion Originators' Guild of America. The members objected to the sale by some of their retailing customers, such as department stores, of "pirated" designs, which were sold by lower cost manufacturers, who allegedly copied the designs of Guild members and sold them for less, having avoided the design costs. The members of FOGA agreed that they would boycott retailers that also sold such "pirated designs." More than 12,000 retailers signed agreements to "cooperate" with the boycott, and the record disclosed that more than half did so because they felt "constrained by threats that Guild members would not sell to retailers who failed to yield to their demands." According to the Court, "In 1936, [the 176 members of the Guild] sold in the United States more than 38% of all women's garments wholesaling at $6.75 and up, and more than 60% of those at $10.75 and above." *Id.* at 462.

But the Guild's conduct went beyond mere boycott. The Court observed that it also (1) prohibited its members from participating in retail advertising; (2) regulated the discount they may allow; (3) prohibited their selling at retail; (4) cooperated with local guilds in regulating days upon which special sales were held; (5) prohibited its members from selling women's garments to persons who conduct businesses in residences, residential quarters, hotels or apartment houses; and (6) denied the benefits of membership to retailers who participate with dress manufacturers in promoting fashion shows unless the merchandise used is actually purchased and delivered. *Id.* at 463. According to the Court, collectively, the boycott and these other acts had actual anticompetitive effects:

> * * * [A]mong the many respects in which the Guild's plan runs contrary to the policy of the Sherman Act are these: it narrows the outlets to which garment and textile manufacturers can sell and the sources from which retailers can buy; subjects all retailers and manufacturers who decline to comply with the Guild's program to an organized boycott; takes away the freedom of action of members by requiring each to reveal to the Guild the intimate details of their individual affairs; and has both as its necessary tendency and as its purpose and effect the direct suppression of competition from the sale of unregistered textiles and copied designs. * * *

Id. at 465. The Court specifically rejected the defendants' plea that no violation could be found absent a finding that the Guild "fixed or regulated prices, parcelled out or limited production, or brought about a deterioration in quality," declaring that "action falling into these three categories does not exhaust the types of conduct banned by the Sherman and Clayton Acts." *Id.* at 466. It also rejected FOGA's defense that its actions were "reasonable," justified by its desire to protect against design pirates, affirming the Commission's decision to exclude most of the defendants' justification-related evidence. *Id*. at 467–68. For another example of the Court's treatment of concerted group boycotts, see *Associated Press v. United States*, 326 U.S. 1, 12 (1945) (by-laws of cooperative news gathering agency that precluded members from sharing gathered news with non-members unreasonably restrained trade "on their face," citing *FOGA* and *Socony–Vacuum Oil*).

Per se treatment of all group boycotts did not become fully cemented in antitrust law, however, until the Court's 1959 decision in *Klor's v. Broadway–Hale Stores, Inc.*, 359 U.S. 207 (1959). Klor's operated a retail radio, television, and appliance store. It claimed that its rival Broadway–Hale, which operated a chain of department stores (one of which was next door to Klor's), conspired with ten leading national manufacturers and some of their distributors to refuse to deal with Klor's, or to deal with it only on less favorable terms than Broadway–Hale. Klor's maintained that this boycott violated Sections 1 and 2 of the Sherman Act. *Id*. at 208–09.

As the Court detailed, the defendants did not contest the main of Klor's' allegations. Yet they sought summary judgment on the ground that "there were hundreds of other household appliance retailers, some within a few blocks of Klor's who sold many competing brands of appliances, including those the defendants refused to sell to Klor's," in essence arguing that even if the allegations were true, the boycott could have no effect on competition. *Id*. at 209–10. The District Court agreed and dismissed the complaint, characterizing it as a " 'purely private quarrel' between Klor's and Broadway–Hale, which did not amount to a 'public wrong proscribed by the [Sherman] Act.' " *Id*. at 209–10. The Supreme Court reversed, firmly locating "group boycotts" in the "per se" category of cases:

> Group boycotts, or concerted refusals by traders to deal with other traders, have long been held to be in the forbidden category. They have not been saved by allegations that they were reasonable in the specific circumstances, nor by a failure to show that they "fixed or regulated prices, parcelled out or limited production, or brought about a deterioration in quality." Even when they operated to lower prices or temporarily to stimulate competition they were banned.
> * * *
> Plainly the allegations of this complaint disclose such a boycott. This is not a case of a single trader refusing to deal with another nor even of a manufacturer and a dealer agreeing to an exclusive distributorship. Alleged in this complaint is a wide combination consisting of manufacturers, distributors and a retailer. This combination takes from Klor's its freedom to buy appliances in an open competitive market and drives it out of business as a dealer in the defendants' products. It deprives the manufacturers and distributors of their freedom to sell to Klor's at the same prices and conditions made available to Broadway–Hale and in some instances forbids them from selling to it on any terms whatsoever. * * * It clearly has, by its "nature" and "character," a "monopolistic tendency." As such it is not to be tolerated merely because the victim is just one merchant whose business is so small that his destruction makes little difference to the economy. Monopoly can as surely thrive by the elimination of such small businessmen, one at a time, as it can by driving them out

in large groups. In recognition of this fact the Sherman Act has consistently been read to forbid all contracts and combinations "which 'tend to create a monopoly,'" whether "the tendency is a creeping one" or "one that proceeds at full gallop."

Id. at 212–14 (footnotes omitted).

Did *Klor's* involve a collusive or an exclusionary group boycott? Can you tell from the evidence relied upon by the Court? Was the case really *horizontal*, focused on the competitive relationship between Klor's and Broadway–Hale, or was it *vertical*, more likely focused on the relationships between the major appliance manufacturers and Klor's? Recall that in *FOGA*, the boycotting manufacturers constituted a very substantial share of the market for women's dresses, making their threat of boycott a credible weapon against individual retailers. Is the same true in *Klor's*? Is it likely that Broadway–Hale was in a position to coerce such well known appliance manufacturers as General Electric and RCA not to sell to Klor's? If not, what might explain their decision to discontinue sales to Klor's?

One explanation long entertained by commentators is that Klor's was a discounter who was free riding on the promotional efforts of Broadway–Hale. As we discussed in Chapter 4, free riders can undermine a manufacturer's ability to attract aggressive and service-oriented retailers. Assume, for example, that Broadway–Hale engaged in a great deal of promotional activities, had well-trained sales people, and maintained attractive showrooms. Obviously, that level of service is costly, but may increase sales overall for the retailer as well as the manufacturers. If Klor's simply placed a sign in its window that said "Buy It Here for Less," and undertook none of the efforts that Broadway–Hale did, it might have been able to divert enough customers from Broadway–Hale to make its efforts uneconomical. Customers would learn all they needed to know about the product from Broadway–Hale, then buy from Klor's. If as a consequence Broadway–Hale gave up on its efforts, sales overall might actually decrease, hurting the manufacturers' efforts to increase output. Viewing the arrangement as "horizontal," and invoking the per se rule might not allow for such a justification. For a more convincing example of a dealer cartel soliciting its supplier to refuse to deal with discounters, see *United States v. General Motors Corp.*, 384 U.S. 127 (1966) (unlawful for associations of automobile dealers to agree with manufacturer to refuse to deal with discounting dealers).

There is no suggestion in *Klor's*, however, that this scenario in fact was the case. We are left, therefore, with something of a puzzle: why did the manufacturers go along with Broadway–Hale's request to boycott Klor's? The defendants offered no apparent justification, relying instead on the argument that Klor's' elimination could not affect competition given the many other retailers in the area. One commentator has suggested, therefore, that the outcome might be justified because the boycott did not yield any identifiable efficiencies and took from consumers a retailer that they apparently liked. *See* Robert H. Bork, THE ANTITRUST PARADOX 332 (1978). On the other hand, as we learned in Chapter 4, today the law generally provides manufacturers with greater autonomy in structuring their dealer relations, and specifically allows them to refuse to sell to free riding retailers. Hence in *NYNEX Corp. v. Discon, Inc.*, 525 U.S. 128 (1998) (Casebook, *supra* Chapter 4), it seemed clear that from the Supreme Court's perspective, the continued vitality of *Klor's* depends upon its status as a "horizontal," collusive effects case, which seems to require some stretching of its facts.

2. CONTEMPORARY ANALYSIS OF EXCLUSIONARY GROUP BOYCOTTS

Eastern States, *FOGA*, and *Klor's* established that group boycotts, also known as "concerted refusals to deal," were per se unlawful. But collectively, those decisions did not provide a coherent framework for differentiating collusive boycotts, which perhaps are more obviously deserving of harsh treatment, from boycotts that exclude, but which in some fashion could be subject to legitimate justifications. As we now move on to the more modern cases, recall the material we read at the outset of Chapter 6 on the economics of exclusion. How might exclusionary group boycotts fit into that framework? Are they objectionable because they can raise rivals costs and confer power over price on the boycotting firms? Are there examples of "naked" exclusionary boycotts that are objectionable because they lack any legitimate business justification?

Consider the *Northwest Wholesale Stationers* case, which follows. The Court, as you shall see, seeks to maintain the applicability of a per se rule to exclusionary "boycotts." But note the conditions it places on its use. What are those conditions? What is the economic rationale behind them? Would imposing the same conditions on boycotts having collusive effects make sense? How do the conditions distinguish the analysis of boycotts having exclusionary effects from boycotts having collusive ones? Finally, consider how the Court tries to situate its discussion of boycotts relative to the foundation cases we discussed above.

NORTHWEST WHOLESALE STATIONERS, INC. v. PACIFIC STATIONERY & PRINTING CO.

Supreme Court of the United States, 1985.
472 U.S. 284, 105 S.Ct. 2613, 86 L.Ed.2d 202.

Justice BRENNAN delivered the opinion of the Court.

This case requires that we decide whether a *per se* violation of § 1 of the Sherman Act occurs when a cooperative buying agency comprising various retailers expels a member without providing any procedural means for challenging the expulsion. The case also raises broader questions as to when *per se* antitrust analysis is appropriately applied to joint activity that is susceptible of being characterized as a concerted refusal to deal.

I

Because the District Court ruled on cross-motions for summary judgment after only limited discovery, this case comes to us on a sparse record. Certain background facts are undisputed. Petitioner Northwest Wholesale Stationers is a purchasing cooperative made up of approximately 100 office supply retailers in the Pacific Northwest States. The cooperative acts as the primary wholesaler for the retailers. Retailers that are not members of the cooperative can purchase wholesale supplies from Northwest at the same price as members. At the end of each year, however, Northwest distributes its profits to members in the form of a percentage rebate on purchases. Members therefore effectively purchase supplies at a price significantly lower than do nonmembers.[1] Northwest also provides certain warehousing facilities. The cooperative arrangement thus permits the participating retailers to achieve economies of scale in purchasing and warehousing that would otherwise be unavailable to them. In fiscal 1978 Northwest had $5.8 million in sales.

Respondent Pacific Stationery & Printing Co. sells office supplies at both the retail and wholesale levels. Its total sales in fiscal 1978 were approximately $7.6 million; the record does not indicate what percentage of revenue is attributable to retail and what percentage is attributable to wholesale. Pacific became a member of Northwest in 1958. In 1974 Northwest amended its bylaws to prohibit members from engaging in both retail and wholesale operations. A grandfather clause preserved Pacific's membership rights. In 1977 ownership of a controlling share of the stock of Pacific changed hands, and the new owners did not officially bring this change to the attention of the directors of Northwest. This failure to notify apparently violated another of Northwest's bylaws.

In 1978 the membership of Northwest voted to expel Pacific. Most factual matters relevant to the expulsion are in dispute. No explanation for the expulsion was advanced at the time, and Pacific was given neither notice, a hearing, nor any other opportunity to challenge the decision. Pacific argues that the expulsion resulted from Pacific's decision to maintain a wholesale operation. Northwest contends that the expulsion resulted from Pacific's failure to notify the cooperative members of the change in stock ownership. * * *

Pacific brought suit in 1980 in the United States District Court * * * alleging a violation of § 1 of the Sherman Act. The gravamen of the action was that Northwest's expulsion of Pacific from the cooperative without procedural protections was a group boycott that limited Pacific's ability to compete and should be considered *per se* violative of § 1. On cross-motions for summary judgment the District Court rejected application of the *per se* rule and held instead that rule-of-reason analysis should govern the case. Finding no anticompetitive effect on the basis of the record as presented, the court granted summary judgment for Northwest.

The Court of Appeals for the Ninth Circuit reversed, holding "that the uncontroverted facts of this case support a finding of *per se* liability." The court reasoned that the cooperative's expulsion of Pacific was an anticompetitive concerted refusal to deal with Pacific on equal footing, which would be a *per se* violation of § 1 in the absence of any specific legislative mandate for self-regulation sanctioning the expulsion. The court noted that § 4 of the Robinson–Patman Act, 15 U.S.C. § 13b, specifically approves the price discrimination occasioned by such expulsion and concluded that § 4 therefore provided a mandate for self-regulation. Such a legislative mandate, according

---

1. Although this patronage rebate policy is a form of price discrimination, § 4 of the Robinson–Patman Act specifically sanctions such activity by cooperatives:

"Nothing in this Act shall prevent a cooperative association from returning to its mem-

bers, producers, or consumers the whole, or any part of, the net earnings or surplus resulting from its trading operations, in proportion to their purchases or sales from, to, or through the association." 49 Stat. 1528, 15 U.S.C. § 13b. * * *

to the court, would ordinarily result in evaluation of the challenged practice under the rule of reason. But, drawing on *Silver v. New York Stock Exchange*, 373 U.S. 341, 348–349 (1963), the court decided that rule-of-reason analysis was appropriate only on the condition that the cooperative had provided procedural safeguards sufficient to prevent arbitrary expulsion and to furnish a basis for judicial review. Because Northwest had not provided any procedural safeguards, the court held that the expulsion of Pacific was not shielded by Robinson–Patman immunity and therefore constituted a *per se* group boycott in violation of § 1 of the Sherman Act.

* * *

II

The decision of the cooperative members to expel Pacific was certainly a restraint of trade in the sense that every commercial agreement restrains trade. Whether this action violates § 1 of the Sherman Act depends on whether it is adjudged an *unreasonable* restraint. Rule-of-reason analysis guides the inquiry, unless the challenged action falls into the category of "agreements or practices which because of their pernicious effect on competition and lack of any redeeming virtue are conclusively presumed to be unreasonable and therefore illegal without elaborate inquiry as to the precise harm they have caused or the business excuse for their use."

This *per se* approach permits categorical judgments with respect to certain business practices that have proved to be predominantly anticompetitive. Courts can thereby avoid the "significant costs" in "business certainty and litigation efficiency" that a full-fledged rule-of-reason inquiry entails. The decision to apply the *per se* rule turns on "whether the practice facially appears to be one that would always or almost always tend to restrict competition and decrease output ... or instead one designed to 'increase economic efficiency and render markets more, rather than less, competitive.'"

This Court has long held that certain concerted refusals to deal or group boycotts are so likely to restrict competition without any offsetting efficiency gains that they should be condemned as *per se* violations of § 1 of the Sherman Act. The question presented in this case is whether Northwest's decision to expel Pacific should fall within this category of activity that is conclusively presumed to be anticompetitive. * * *

The Court of Appeals drew from *Silver v. New York Stock Exchange*, 373 U.S. 341 (1963), a broad rule that the conduct of a cooperative venture-including a concerted refusal to deal-undertaken pursuant to a legislative mandate for self-regulation is immune from *per se* scrutiny and subject to rule-of-reason analysis only if adequate procedural safeguards accompany self-regulation. We disagree and conclude that the approach of the Court in *Silver* has no proper application to the present controversy.

* * *

Finding exchange self-regulation—including the power to expel members and limit dealings with nonmembers—to be an essential policy of the Securities Exchange Act, the Court held [in *Silver*] that the Sherman Act should be construed as having been partially repealed to permit the type of exchange activity at issue. But the interpretive maxim disfavoring repeals by implication led the Court to narrow permissible self-policing to situations in which adequate procedural safeguards had been provided. * * *

Thus it was the specific need to accommodate the important national policy of promoting effective exchange self-regulation, tempered by the principle that the Sherman Act should be narrowed only to the extent necessary to effectuate that policy, that dictated the result in *Silver*.

* * *

* * * [T]here can be no argument that § 4 of the Robinson–Patman Act should be viewed as a broad mandate for industry self-regulation. No need exists, therefore, to narrow the Sherman Act in order to accommodate any competing congressional policy requiring discretionary self-policing. * * * [T]he absence of procedural safeguards can in no sense determine the antitrust analysis. If the challenged concerted activity of Northwest's members would amount to a *per se* violation of § 1 of the Sherman Act, no amount of procedural protection would save it. If the challenged action would not amount to a violation of § 1, no lack of procedural protections would convert it into a *per se* violation because the antitrust laws do not themselves impose on joint ventures a requirement of process.

This case therefore turns not on the lack of procedural protections but on whether the decision to expel Pacific is properly viewed as a group boycott or concerted refusal to deal mandating *per se* invalidation. "Group boycotts" are often listed among the classes of economic activity that merit *per se* invalidation under § 1. Exactly what types of activity fall within the forbidden category is, however, far from certain. * * * Some care is therefore necessary in defining the category of concerted refusals to deal that mandate *per se* condemnation.

Cases to which this Court has applied the *per se* approach have generally involved joint efforts by a firm or firms to disadvantage competitors by "either directly denying or persuading or coercing suppliers or customers to deny relationships the competitors need in the competitive struggle." In these cases, the boycott often cut off access to a supply, facility, or market necessary to enable the boycotted firm to compete, and frequently the boycotting firms possessed a dominant position in the relevant market. In addition, the practices were generally not justified by plausible arguments that they were intended to enhance overall efficiency and make markets more competitive. Under such circumstances the likelihood of anticompetitive effects is clear and the possibility of countervailing procompetitive effects is remote.

Although a concerted refusal to deal need not necessarily possess all of these traits to merit *per se* treatment, not every cooperative activity involving a restraint or exclusion will share with the *per se* forbidden boycotts the likelihood of predominantly anticompetitive consequences. * * *

Wholesale purchasing cooperatives such as Northwest are not a form of concerted activity characteristically likely to result in predominantly anticompetitive effects. Rather, such cooperative arrangements would seem to be "designed to increase economic efficiency and render markets more, rather than less, competitive." The arrangement permits the participating retailers to achieve economies of scale in both the purchase and warehousing of wholesale supplies, and also ensures ready access to a stock of goods that might otherwise be unavailable on short notice. The cost savings and order-filling guarantees enable smaller retailers to reduce prices and maintain their retail stock so as to compete more effectively with larger retailers.

Pacific, of course, does not object to the existence of the cooperative arrangement, but rather raises an antitrust challenge to Northwest's decision to bar Pacific from continued membership.[6] It is therefore the action of expulsion that must be evaluated to determine whether *per se* treatment is appropriate. The act of expulsion from a wholesale cooperative does not necessarily imply anticompetitive animus and thereby raise a probability of anticompetitive effect. Wholesale purchasing cooperatives must establish and enforce reasonable rules in order to function effectively. Disclosure rules, such as the one on which Northwest relies, may well provide the cooperative with a needed means for monitoring the creditworthiness of its members.[7] Nor would the expulsion characteristically be likely to result in predominantly anticompetitive effects, at least in the type of situation this case presents. Unless the cooperative possesses market power or exclusive access to an element essential to effective competition, the conclusion that expulsion is virtually always likely to have an anticompetitive effect is not warranted. Absent such a showing with respect to a cooperative buying arrangement, courts should apply a rule-of-reason analysis. At no time has Pacific made a threshold showing that these structural characteristics are present in this case.[8]

* * * A plaintiff seeking application of the *per se* rule must present a threshold case that the challenged activity falls into a category likely to have predominantly anticompetitive effects. The mere allegation of a concerted refusal to deal does not suffice because not all concerted refusals to deal are predominantly anticompetitive. When the plaintiff challenges expulsion from a joint buying cooperative, some showing must be made that the cooperative possesses market power or unique access to a business element necessary for effective competition. Focusing on the argument that the lack of procedural safeguards required *per se* liability, Pacific did not allege any such facts. Because the Court of Appeals applied an erroneous *per se* analysis in this case, the court never evaluated the District Court's rule-of-reason analysis rejecting Pacific's claim. A remand is therefore appropriate for the limited purpose of permitting appellate review of that determination.

6. Because Pacific has not been wholly excluded from access to Northwest's wholesale operations, there is perhaps some question whether the challenged activity is properly characterized as a concerted refusal to deal. To be precise, Northwest's activity is a concerted refusal to deal with Pacific on substantially equal terms. Such activity might justify *per se* invalidation if it placed a competing firm at a severe competitive disadvantage.

7. Pacific argues, however, that this justification for expulsion was a pretext because the members of Northwest were fully aware of the change in ownership despite lack of formal notice. According to Pacific, Northwest's motive in the expulsion was to place Pacific at a competitive disadvantage to retaliate for Pacific's decision to engage in an independent wholesale operation. Such a motive might be more troubling. If Northwest's action were not substantially related to the efficiency-enhancing or procompetitive purposes that otherwise justify the cooperative's practices, an inference of anticompetitive animus might be appropriate. But such an argument is appropriately evaluated under the rule-of-reason analysis.

8. Given the state of this record it is difficult to understand how the Court of Appeals could have concluded that Pacific "loses the ability to use Northwest's superior warehousing and expedited order-filling facilities, as well as any competitive advantages that may flow simply from being known in the industry as a member of an established cooperative." The District Court had specifically found no anticompetitive effect.

III

"The *per se* rule is a valid and useful tool of antitrust policy and enforcement." It does not denigrate the *per se* approach to suggest care in application. In this case, the Court of Appeals failed to exercise the requisite care and applied *per se* analysis inappropriately.

* * *

———

Note how the framework set forth in *Northwest Wholesale Stationers* appears to create a "quasi" or "qualified" per se rule for exclusionary group boycotts: the per se rule can only be invoked if certain conditions are first satisfied. The framework is summarized in Figure 7–1:

Figure 7–1:
Framework for Analyzing Exclusionary Group Boycotts Under *Northwest Wholesale Stationers*

"Cases to which this Court has applied the *per se* approach have generally involved joint efforts by a firm or firms to disadvantage competitors by . . ."

Three Steps/Requirements:

- cutting off access to a supply, facility, or market necessary to enable the boycotted firm to compete (*Exclusionary Conduct*)
- frequently the boycotting firms possessed a dominant position in the relevant market (*Market Power*)
- no plausible arguments that the boycott enhanced overall efficiency (*No Procompetitive Justification*)

Does the Court require that all three elements be satisfied to condemn an exclusionary group boycott under this rule or does the decision leave open the possibility that a violation could be found if some, but not all, of these factors are present?

Why did the Court in *Northwest Wholesale Stationers* suggest such a seemingly *qualified* per se rule? Is a "qualified" rule really a true per se rule at all? How does it differ from the rule of reason approach? What is missing? Can it even fairly be labeled as a per se rule, or does it more resemble an abbreviated, more highly structured form of the rule of reason? If the latter, how does it relate to the Supreme Court's "quick look" approach, which we explored in Chapter 2? How does it mesh with the foundation group boycott cases, such as *Eastern States*, *FOGA* and *Klor's*? How does *Northwest Wholesale Stationers* framework compare to the approach of the D.C. Circuit in *Microsoft*, which we studied in Chapter 6? *See* Figure 6–6, *supra*.

Consider as well the economic rationale for differentiating the treatment of group boycotts having exclusionary effects from those having collusive effects, like *Superior Court Trial Lawyers*. What justifies treating them differently? Why might group boycotts having collusive effects be more deserving of per se condemnation than those having exclusionary effects? Are there possible justifications more likely to be associated with the latter? Why should that make a difference? What is different that specifically explains the *particular* qualifying factors cited by the Court in *Northwest Wholesale Stationers*? Are they tailored to identifying exclusionary boycotts likely to produce unacceptable levels of anti-competitive effects? How might you analyze them in relation to minimizing the incidence of false positives?

Finally, review Figure 2–3 (Collusive Group Boycotts) and especially Figure 2–4 (Exclusionary Group Boycotts). Which of the three scenarios portrayed in Figure 2–4 is reflected in *Northwest Wholesale Stationers*? Would the framework set forth in *Northwest Wholesale Stationers* work equally well for all three? Should it? For a case that appears to distinguish and limit the scope of *Northwest Wholesale Stationers*, see *Craftsman Limousine, Inc. v. Ford Motor Co.*, 363 F.3d 761 (8th Cir. 2004).

Note on Toys "R" Us and the Continued Vitality of the Northwest Wholesale Stationers Framework

In Chapter 8, we will examine the Seventh Circuit's analysis of exclusion in *Toys "R" Us, Inc. v. FTC*, 221 F.3d 928 (7th Cir. 2000), which applied the framework set forth in *Northwest Wholesale Stationers* to conclude that the toy retailer, Toys "R" Us ("TRU"), had engaged in an unlawful group boycott. According to the FTC, in response to the emergence of discounting warehouse clubs as a serious source of competition for toy sales, TRU, which nationally accounted for more than 20 percent of all retail toy sales, successfully solicited agreements from toy manufacturers that accounted for 40 percent of U.S. toy sales to limit the supply of select toys to the clubs. The alleged purpose of the boycott was to make it more difficult for consumers to comparison shop, thereby insulating TRU from price competition from the clubs. The Commission also had found that, as a consequence, TRU was able to maintain its profit margins.

When we review this case, we will note that while the boycott was exclusionary, there was also evidence that it facilitated the exercise of market power by TRU. In the notes following *Interstate Circuit*, we also saw in Chapter 3 that the court of appeals viewed the conspiracy among the manufacturers that was organized by TRU as "horizontal." Why might these two factors have been important to the Court for purposes of applying *Northwest Wholesale Stationers*?

————————

In our next case, the Second Circuit faced allegations that the two largest credit card networks, Visa and MasterCard, prohibited their member banks from dealing with rival issuers of credit cards. Note how in analyzing the facts of the case, the court articulates a framework for evaluating exclusionary restraints undertaken in connection with the operation of an otherwise legitimate joint venture. How does that framework compare to the approach outlined by the Court in *Northwest Wholesaler Stationers*? Is it similar to the framework adopted by the D.C. Circuit in *Polygram*, (Casebook, Chapter 2, *supra*)? If so, does it suggest that it may be possible to articulate a common framework for evaluating both collusive and exclusionary conduct, at least in the context of joint ventures? How would such a framework account for the differing economic issues that arise in collusive vs. exclusionary effects cases?

UNITED STATES v. VISA U.S.A., INC.

United States Court of Appeals for the Second Circuit, 2003.
344 F.3d 229.

Before: OAKES, LEVAL, and CABRANES, Circuit Judges.

LEVAL, Circuit Judge.

* * * The U.S. Department of Justice ("DOJ") brought this civil enforcement action challenging the organizational structure of two of the nation's four major payment card systems. The complaint charged that MasterCard and Visa U.S.A., which are organized as joint ventures owned by their member banking institutions, conspired to restrain trade in two ways: (1) By enacting rules permitting a member-owner of one to function as a director of the other (an arrangement the government described as "dual governance") (Count I); and (2) by enacting and enforcing "exclusionary rules," which prohibit their member banks from issuing American Express ("Amex") or Discover cards (Count II).

After a 34–day trial, the court, in a commendably comprehensive and careful opinion, ruled in the defendants' favor as to dual governance (Count I). As to Count II, however, the court held that Visa U.S.A. and MasterCard violated * * * [Section 1 of the Sherman] Act by enforcing their respective versions of the exclusionary rule, barring their member banks from issuing Amex or Discover cards. * * *

* * *

For the reasons set forth below, we affirm the judgment.

BACKGROUND

I. Description of the General Purpose Payment Card Industry

A. The Structure of the Visa and MasterCard Networks

Visa U.S.A. and MasterCard are two of the United States's four major network systems in the payment card industry, the other two being Amex and Discover.[2] Visa U.S.A. and MasterCard are organized as open joint ventures, owned by the numerous banking institutions that are members of the networks. * * * MasterCard is owned by its approximately 20,000 member banks; Visa U.S.A. is owned by its approximately 14,000 member banks. Because MasterCard allows its member banks to issue Visa cards, and Visa U.S.A. likewise allows its members to issue MasterCard cards, many of Visa U.S.A.'s 14,000 members are also members of the MasterCard network. * * *

The member banks of the MasterCard and Visa U.S.A. card networks may function either as "issuers" or "acquirers" or both. A member bank serving as an "issuer" issues cards to cardholders; it serves as the liaison between the network and the individual cardholder. A member bank serving as an "acquirer" acquires the card-paid transactions of a merchant; a particular acquiring bank acts as liaison between the network and those merchants accepting the network's payment cards with whom it has contracted.

When a consumer uses a Visa card or a MasterCard card to pay for goods or services, the accepting merchant relays the transaction information to the acquiring bank with whom it has contracted. The acquirer processes and

---

2. The four major systems each issue credit and charge cards. A *charge card* requires that the balance be paid in full at the end of every billing cycle. A *credit card* allows customers to pay only a portion of the monthly balance, charging interest on the unpaid balance.

packages that information and transmits it to the network (Visa U.S.A. or MasterCard). The network then relays the transaction information to the cardholder's issuing bank, which approves the transaction if the cardholder has a sufficient credit line. Approval is sent by the issuer to the acquirer, which relays it to the merchant.

Payment requests are sent by the merchant to the acquirer, which forwards the requests to the issuer. The issuer then pays the acquiring bank the amount requested, less what is called an "interchange fee"—typically 1.4%. The acquirer retains an additional fee—approximately .6%. Thus, the issuing bank and the acquirer withhold an aggregate of approximately 2% of the amount of the transaction from the merchant. This is known as the "merchant discount." For a $100 sale, the merchant typically will receive $98, the issuing bank retaining $1.40, while the acquiring bank retains 60 cents.

Both MasterCard and Visa are *open* joint ventures, meaning that there is no limit to the number of banks that may become members, either as issuers or as acquirers. Any member may serve as both an issuer and as an acquirer. Members agree to abide by their association's by-laws and other regulations.

A member of either the Visa U.S.A. or MasterCard network may also be a member of the other network. Thus a bank that is a member of Visa U.S.A.'s network and issues Visa cards may also be a member of the MasterCard network and issue MasterCard cards. On the other hand, both MasterCard and Visa U.S.A. have promulgated rules that prohibit their members from issuing American Express or Discover cards. Those rules—Visa's by-law 2.10(e) and MasterCard's Competitive Programs Policy ("CPP")[3]—are the focus of this action, and were held by the district court to violate the Sherman Act.

B. The Structure of the American Express and Discover Networks

American Express and Discover, the other two major card systems in the United States, are quite differently organized. They are not joint venture membership associations. Rather, each is a vertically integrated entity, acting for profit, which combines issuing, acquiring, and network functions. (The parties and the District Court occasionally refer to this structure as a "closed loop.") Amex and Discover deal directly with consumers (by issuing cards), and with merchants (by acquiring and processing transactions). When a consumer makes a purchase with an American Express card, for example, the merchant contacts Amex directly, and if the customer has sufficient credit available, Amex approves the sale. Amex then pays the merchant directly, retaining a percentage—usually 2.73%. (Discover is organized similarly to Amex. Its merchant discount is usually 1.5%.)

---

3. Visa U.S.A.'s by-law 2.10(e), passed in 1991, states,

> The membership of any Member shall automatically terminate in the event it, or its parent, subsidiary or affiliate, issues, directly or indirectly, Discover Cards, or American Express Cards, or any other card deemed competitive by the Board of Directors. E–2897; SPA 97.

MasterCard's CPP, passed in 1996, provides that

> With the exception of participation in Visa, which is essentially owned by the same member entities, and several pre-existing programs to the extent individual members participate ... members of MasterCard may not participate either as issuers or acquirers in competitive general purpose card programs. E–2265; SPA 101.

Since at least 1995, American Express has sought to change its structure by soliciting banks to issue American Express cards. This effort has been successful outside of the continental United States and abroad, where banks such as Puerto Rico's Banco Popular have begun issuing Amex-branded cards. In the continental United States, in contrast, Amex has been unsuccessful in its attempt to solicit outside issuers. Because of Visa U.S.A.'s and Master-Card's exclusionary rules, any bank that undertook to issue Amex-branded cards would be forced to give up issuing both Visa and MasterCard cards—a move no U.S. bank has been willing to make.

* * *

II. COMPETITION IN THE GENERAL PURPOSE PAYMENT CARD INDUSTRY

Competition in the payment card industry takes place at the "network" level, as well as at the "issuing" and "acquiring" levels. At the network level, the four brands compete with one another to establish brand loyalty in favor of the Visa, MasterCard, Amex, or Discover card. At the issuing level, approximately twenty thousand banks that issue Visa and MasterCard cards to customers compete with one another and with Amex and Discover. Unlike the network services market, which has only four major participants, approximately 20,000 entities compete for customers in the issuing market, and no single participant is dominant. American Express is the largest single card issuer in the United States, as measured by transaction volume. By the same measure, Discover is the fifth largest issuer. The other large issuers are member banks in the Visa and MasterCard networks.

III. THE CHALLENGED REGULATIONS

* * *

DISCUSSION

* * *

For the government to prevail in a rule of reason case under Section 1, the district court concluded, and the parties do not argue otherwise, that the following must be shown: As an initial matter, the government must demonstrate that the defendant conspirators have "market power" in a particular market for goods or services.[4] Next, the government must demonstrate that within the relevant market, the defendants' actions have had substantial adverse effects on competition, such as increases in price, or decreases in output or quality. Once that initial burden is met, the burden of production shifts to the defendants, who must provide a procompetitive justification for the challenged restraint. If the defendants do so, the government must prove either that the challenged restraint is not reasonably necessary to achieve the

---

4. Some authorities suggest that the market power requirement is unnecessary. *See, e.g., FTC v. Indiana Fed'n of Dentists,* 476 U.S. 447, 460, 106 S.Ct. 2009, 90 L.Ed.2d 445 (1986); * * * *NCAA v. Bd. of Regents,* 468 U.S. 85, 110 n. 42, 104 S.Ct. 2948, 82 L.Ed.2d 70 (similar). * * * Whether market power is a necessary element is of no moment here; the district court found that the defendants had market power in the relevant markets, and as indicated below, we see no reason to question that finding.

defendants' procompetitive justifications, or that those objectives may be achieved in a manner less restrictive of free competition.

* * *

I. RELEVANT MARKETS AND MARKET POWER

The district court determined, and we agree, that this case involves two interrelated, but separate, product markets: (1) what the court called the general purpose card market, consisting of the market for charge cards and credit cards, and (2) the network services market for general purpose cards.

A distinct product market comprises products that are considered by consumers to be "reasonabl[y] interchangeab[le]" with what the defendant sells. *Eastman Kodak Co. v. Image Tech. Servs., Inc.,* 504 U.S. 451, 482, 112 S. Ct. 2072, 119 L.Ed.2d 265 (1992); *United States v. E.I. du Pont de Nemours & Co.,* 351 U.S. 377, 404, 76 S.Ct. 994, 100 L.Ed. 1264 (1956). After hearing substantial expert testimony, the district court found as a matter of fact that other forms of payment—such as cash, checks, debit cards, and proprietary cards (*e.g.,* the Sears or Macy's cards)—are not considered by most consumers to be reasonable substitutes for general purpose credit or charge cards. As the government's expert witness explained, based on empirical analysis of consumer preferences, if prices for general purpose payment cards were to rise significantly, cardholders would likely pay the increased fees, rather than abandon their cards in favor of other forms of payment. Thus, general purpose payment cards constitute a distinct market, separate from the market for such other payment alternatives. We find no reason to doubt the court's conclusion.

Further, we agree with the district court that the four payment card networks compete with one another in a market for "network services." General purpose card networks * * * "provide the infrastructure and mechanisms through which general purpose card transactions are conducted, including the authorization, settlement, and clearance of transactions." Whereas in the market for general purpose *cards,* the issuers are the sellers, and cardholders are the buyers, in the market for general purpose card *network services,* the four networks themselves are the sellers, and the issuers of cards and merchants are the buyers. Issuing banks purchase network services from MasterCard and/or Visa U.S.A., and those two brands compete with Amex and Discover for the banks' business. Networks also compete for merchants, because the price merchants pay for acceptance of payment cards (the merchant discount) is affected by the size of the interchange fee, which is set by the network.

The district court found, on the basis of expert testimony, that there are no products reasonably interchangeable, in the eyes of issuers or merchants, with the network services provided by the four major brands. This was a reasonable finding: (1) Network-level costs are so high that banks and merchants cannot provide these services for themselves, and (2) issuance and acceptance of credit and charge cards is so profitable (and network service fees so negligible in comparison) that even a large increase in network fees would not provide a rational financial incentive to abandon the business of issuing or accepting payment cards.

We agree with the district court's finding that Visa U.S.A. and Master-Card, jointly and separately, have power within the market for network services. Market power has been defined by the Supreme Court to mean the "power to control prices or exclude competition." *du Pont,* 351 U.S. at 391, 76 S.Ct. 994. *NCAA,* at 109 n. 38, 104 S.Ct. 2948. Such power may be proven through evidence of specific conduct undertaken by the defendant that indicates he has the power to affect price or exclude competition. Alternatively, market power may be presumed if the defendant controls a large enough share of the relevant market. [The district court judge] * * * based her finding of market power first on the fact that merchants testified that they could not refuse to accept payment by Visa or MasterCard, even if faced with significant price increases, because of customer preference. Indeed, despite recent increases in both networks' interchange fees, no merchant had discontinued acceptance of their cards. In addition, the court inferred market power from the defendants' large shares of a highly concentrated market: In 1999, Visa U.S.A. members accounted for approximately 47% of the dollar volume of credit and charge card transactions, while MasterCard members accounted for approximately 26%. (American Express accounted for 20%; Discover, for 6%.)

The evidence relied on by the district court was sufficient to sustain a finding of market power. In addition, Amex, despite repeated recent attempts, has been unable to persuade any issuing banks in the continental United States to utilize its network services because the exclusivity rule would require such issuing banks to give up membership in the Visa and MasterCard consortiums, and banks are unwilling to do so. In short, Visa U.S.A. and MasterCard have demonstrated their power in the network services market by effectively precluding their largest competitor from successfully soliciting any bank as a customer for its network services and brand.

II. HARMS TO COMPETITION

* * * The district court found that Visa U.S.A. and MasterCard's exclusionary rules harm competition by "reducing overall card output and available card features," as well as by decreasing network services output and stunting price competition. We cannot say that these conclusions were erroneous.

The most persuasive evidence of harm to competition is the total exclusion of American Express and Discover from a segment of the market for network services. As noted, there are only four major payment card network providers in the United States. While competition among (and within) these networks is robust at the issuing level (where 20,000 separate issuers compete to provide products to consumers), at the network level (where four major networks seek to sell their technical, infrastructure, and financial services to issuer banks) competition has been seriously damaged by the defendants' exclusionary rules. * * * The district court cited evidence that three major U.S. issuer banks—Banco Popular, Advanta, and Bank One—would have contracted with American Express to issue Amex cards in the United States but for the exclusionary rules. In addition, Banco Popular has contracted with Amex to issue its cards in Puerto Rico, where no exclusionary rules apply.

As a result, then, of the challenged policies, only two rival networks are effectively able to compete for the business of issuer banks. Testimony at trial revealed that Visa U.S.A. and MasterCard "pay millions of dollars in incentive payments in the form of discounts from the price for network services to selected issuing banks to compete for their business and [that] the banks play Visa and MasterCard against [each] other to obtain lower net prices and higher value for card network services." With only two viable competitors, however, such price and product competition is necessarily limited. Trial testimony strongly indicated that price competition and innovation in services would be enhanced if four competitors, rather than only two, were able to compete in this manner for issuing banks. Indeed, the district court found, based on testimony from Visa U.S.A. and MasterCard executives, that both defendants would "respond to ... greater network competition by offering new and better products and services." * * *

In foreign countries, where Visa International rather than Visa U.S.A. operates the Visa network, and no exclusionary rule applies, Amex has succeeded in convincing banks that issue Visa cards also to issue Amex cards. This has caused Visa International to "proactively strengthen" its product offerings to member banks abroad. In addition, an internal Visa International memorandum cautions that Visa U.S.A. would have to compete more vigorously for market share if Amex were permitted to partner with its member banks: "To date, AmEx has been precluded from partnering with U.S. banks, although that situation could change. Since bank partners could significantly increase [Amex's] acceptance and cards, Visa needs to monitor the situation and counter with competitive products that meet banks['] needs."

The district court also found that product innovation and output has been stunted by the challenged policies. By excluding Amex and Discover from the market for outside card issuers, Visa U.S.A. and MasterCard effectively deny consumers access to products that could be offered only by a network in partnership with individual banks. Such products include cards that are able to link "to transaction accounts, to asset management accounts, to sale of mortgages or other financial products that [banks] offer [ ]."

We find no error in the district court's finding that competition has been harmed by the defendants' exclusionary rules.

III.   THE DEFENDANTS' ARGUMENTS
* * *

A. *Harms to Competition*

First, the defendants argue that the district court erred by mistaking harm to a *competitor* for harm to *competition*. They cite the familiar formula that the "antitrust laws protect competition, not competitors." Visa U.S.A. contends, for example, that "[t]he decision and remedy in this case will not benefit consumer welfare. Instead, virtually the sole beneficiary will be AmEx which hopes to gain not by offering lower prices or better products but largely by undermining its major brand competitors."

Defendants contend the exclusionary rules are akin to "exclusive distributorship" arrangements, which we have held are "presumptively legal." We find this argument unpersuasive.

Defendants are certainly correct that the proper inquiry is whether there has been an "*actual* adverse effect on competition as a whole in the relevant market." We have held that competition is not adversely affected if, despite an exclusive dealership arrangement, "competitors can reach the ultimate consumer of the product by employing existing or potential alternative channels of distribution."

The defendants argue that the harms identified by the district court as stemming from their exclusionary rules—that the types of cards that consumers can get from their banks are limited and [that] banks are prevented from combining their particular issuing skills with the AmEx brand—are not harms to Amex's ability to compete as a network (or Discover's), but rather harms to its distributive capacity, in much the same way Pepsi–Cola's distributive capacity might be limited by an exclusive arrangement between Coca–Cola and its truckers. For an exclusive dealership arrangement to cause a harm to competition (and overcome the presumption of legality), it must prevent competitors from getting their products to consumers at all. There is no question, the defendants argue, that Amex and Discover can get their products to consumers, as evidenced by the fact that they are respectively the largest and fifth largest issuers of payment cards in the United States.

The analogy to an exclusive arrangement between Coca–Cola and its truckers is not persuasive. The basic flaw in the analogy is that it depicts Visa U.S.A. (or MasterCard) as a single entity (like Coca–Cola) demanding a restrictive provision in its contract with a supplier of services to it. Visa U.S.A. and MasterCard, however, are not single entities; they are consortiums of competitors. * * * These competitors have agreed to abide by a restrictive exclusivity provision to the effect that in order to share the benefits of their association by having the right to issue Visa or MasterCard cards, they must agree not to compete by issuing cards of Amex or Discover. The restrictive provision is a horizontal restraint adopted by 20,000 competitors.

* * * Each has agreed not to compete with the others in a manner which the consortium considers harmful to its combined interests. Far from being "presumptively legal," such arrangements are exemplars of the type of anticompetitive behavior prohibited by the Sherman Act.

In the market for *network services,* where the four networks are sellers and issuing banks and merchants are buyers, the exclusionary rules enforced by Visa U.S.A. and MasterCard have absolutely prevented Amex and Discover from selling their products at all.

Without doubt the exclusionary rules in question harm competitors. The fact that they harm competitors does not, however, mean that they do not also harm competition. We find no fault with the district court's finding that the exclusion of Amex and Discover from the ability to market their cards and programs to banks has harmed competition in the market for network services, and that Visa U.S.A. and MasterCard would be impelled to design and market their products more competitively if the banks to which they sell their services were free to purchase network services from Amex and Discover. Nor do we fault the district court's determination that certain types of products combining unique features of cards offered by Amex and Discover with the advantages of linkage to cardholders' bank accounts would likely become available. The district court was justified in finding harm to competition.

B. Procompetitive Justifications

* * * The defendants assert that the principal benefit of the exclusionary rules is to promote "cohesion" within the MasterCard and Visa U.S.A. networks, so that those networks may compete effectively in the marketplace. Thus, the defendants argue, the exclusionary rules are ancillary to legitimate, procompetitive business strategies. * * *

The district court found no evidence to suggest that allowing member banks to issue cards of rival networks would endanger cohesion in a manner adverse to the competitive process. MasterCard members have long been permitted to issue Visa cards, and vice versa, without such consequences. Moreover, as the district court noted, there is no evidence that the defendants' network cohesion has been harmed overseas, where, in the absence of exclusionary rules, Amex has contracted with Visa and MasterCard member banks to issue Amex-branded payment cards.

In sum, the defendants have failed to show that the anticompetitive effects of their exclusionary rules are outweighed by procompetitive benefits.

* * *

———

The analysis of exclusionary conduct in *Visa* raises a number of interesting questions. First, note that the court does not use the word "boycott" at all to describe the challenged conduct, nor does it refer to any of the classic boycott cases, such as *Eastern States*, *FOGA*, or *Klor's*. Neither does it mention *Northwest Wholesale Stationers*. But could the exclusionary rule adopted by Visa and MasterCard literally have been described as a "boycott" of firms like American Express and Discover? If so, why did the court steer clear of all suggestion that it was viewing the conduct as a boycott, subject to any of these cases?

One answer may lie in the analytical framework the court sets out in Section III of its opinion. How similar or different is it from the framework advocated in *Northwest Wholesale Stationers*? How similar is it to framework developed in the government's *Guidelines for Collaborations Among Competitors* (2000), which is discussed in Sidebar 2–5? Does the court's framework draw attention to similarities in the analysis of conduct having collusive and exclusionary effects? Note the role of market power in both *Northwest Wholesale Stationers* and *Visa*, as well as evidence of both anticompetitive effects and business justifications, all of which have been increasingly important to the cases we have seen in Chapters 2, 4, 5, and 6. Is it fair to say that the framework can be the same for collusive and exclusionary effects cases, although the economic analysis of competitive effects and justifications differs? Would applying the label "boycott" and invoking the older cases have added anything to this analysis?

In Section II of the Discussion, what "harms to competition" does the court associate with the exclusionary rule? As we did with the court's finding of market power, consider here what evidence the court cites in support of that conclusion. Is the evidence cited related to exclusionary effects? Collusive effects? Both? Why does the court deem it significant that competition was different outside of the United States, where the exclusionary rule did not apply? If the exclusionary rule made economic sense to Visa U.S.A. and MasterCard in the United States, why do you suppose Visa Int'l and Master-Card did not implement the exclusionary rule outside of the United States? Finally, what arguments did the defendants offer to justify the exclusionary rule? Why did the court reject them?

The competitive analysis of conduct in the credit card industry is complicated by the fact that it involves "two-sided" markets. Sidebar 7–1 discusses the economic issues associated with such markets.

Sidebar 7–1:
The Economics of Two–Sided Markets With Network Effects

Payment systems are an example of what economists term "two-sided" markets with network effects.* They are an intermediary (or product "platform") in which there are two types of end users, each of whom finds the platform more desirable if the platform does well in attracting the other type of end user. "Network effects" arise when the value of a product to a buyer depends on the number of other users. Communications systems are an example: a telephone is more valuable the more numbers you can call. Software can also exhibit network effects: its value may be higher the more other users there are, with whom compatible files can be exchanged. When network effects are strong, there is often a tendency for one product to dominate the market. Network effects are discussed more fully in Sidebar 10–1.

Payment systems like the Visa, Master Card, American Express, and Discover networks are two-sided platforms with network effects. Payment systems simultaneously attempt to attract cardholders to use their card, and merchants to accept it. In addition, merchants are more likely to accept a payment system's card the greater its number of cardholders, and cardholders are more likely to obtain a card the greater the number of merchants that accept it.

Newspapers and magazines are also two-sided platforms with network effects. These publications earn revenue by selling advertising space to advertisers and subscriptions to consumers who read the publications. The advertisers value the publication because it provides access to consumers, and the consumers may value the ads directly (because they value advertising information) or indirectly (because they value the content that the ads make possible). Other examples might include shopping malls, which attract retailers and shoppers, securities exchanges, which attract buyers and sellers, and computer operating systems, which attract both computer users and developers of applications software.

In many industries served by two-sided platforms, such as payment systems, the end users often employ multiple platforms, notwithstanding

---

* In this context, the term "market" is used in a general way, not necessarily in the way the term is used in antitrust analysis. Accord- ingly, some authors writing about antitrust issues prefer the term "two-sided platforms."

the way network effects often lead one product or service to dominate. Many consumers have cards from more than one network in their wallets, and most merchants accept more than one type of card. But card brands are differentiated to some extent, and not all merchants accept all cards.

Two-sided platforms have multiple ways of charging for their services. A payment system may charge cardholders an annual fee and charge merchants a specified percentage of each transaction (the "merchant discount").** Some newspapers and magazines are free and earn all their revenue from advertising, whereas others charge fees to both advertisers and subscribers. Some have a great deal of advertising and a low subscription price, while others earn most of their revenue from subscriptions. A shopping mall may charge retailers a rent based on their sales volume and may make implicit payments to shoppers by offering them free parking and other services.

Several forces affect the platform's pricing decisions. A platform will want to keep the price to one group of end users (*e.g.*, the cardholders, as opposed to the merchants) relatively low, or even to subsidize those users, if that group of end users is more highly responsive to price or if attracting more of that group of end users would make a relatively larger difference in attracting the other group of end users (*e.g.*, the merchants). The result may be that the price to one group of end users is high relative to the marginal cost of serving those end users, while the price to the other group of end users is low relative to the marginal cost of serving them (or even below that marginal cost).

This pricing pattern—a high price cost margin on some services, perhaps even accompanied by below-cost pricing on others—would not necessarily reflect the exercise of market power if there is adequate competition among platforms. Magazines may provide an example. In that situation, the platform as a whole, taking into account the revenues it receives from both groups of users, would not earn supracompetitive profits. However, if competition is more limited, so the platforms are able to exercise market power, then the prices for one or both services would be greater than those that would obtain under competition. One would expect the price to rise more on the side of the market where end user demand is less responsive to price, and where demand by those end users is more highly sensitive to the loss of the other group of end users.

To apply this framework to payment systems pricing, suppose that cardholders are more price-sensitive than merchants, and that merchants care more about whether the payment systems platform attracts cardholders than the reverse. Then fees to cardholders would be low (or even negative, for example if the platform pays cardholders to sign up through rewards programs) and merchant discounts high. This would be true whether there is competition among payment systems or whether there is a payment systems monopoly. A payment systems monopolist also most likely would look more to higher merchant discounts in order to exercise market power, and look relatively less to increasing cardholder fees.

** As was explained in *Visa*, the merchant discount is the sum of the "interchange fee" charged by Master Card or Visa plus a small fee paid to the bank that processes transactions for the merchant.

How does the idea of two-sided platforms with network effects help in understanding the payment card industry and the *Visa* litigation? First, should a court be cautious about inferring market power solely from a high merchant discount? Trends in interchange fees and merchant discounts are interpreted from a two-sided platform perspective by economists who worked for Visa in Benjamin Klein, et al., *Competition in Two–Sided Markets: The Antitrust Economics of Payment Card Interchange Fees*, 73 ANTITRUST L.J. 571 (2006).

Second, in the *Visa* case, the court defines a market for network services, where the four networks are sellers and issuing banks and merchants are buyers. Is doing so consistent with the market definition approach of the Merger Guidelines? Is it appropriate to consider demand substitution from one group of buyers (merchants) in defining markets while ignoring the other group of buyers (cardholders)? Is there a sensible way to consider both while defining markets, or would it be better only to consider one side at a time while defining the market, and then account for the interaction between the two sides of the platform in evaluating anticompetitive effects and efficiencies? For a discussion of how the Justice Department analyzes market definition in payment systems cases, see Renata B. Hesse & Joshua H. Soven, *Defining Relevant Product Markets in Electronic Payment Network Antitrust Cases*, 73 ANTITRUST L.J. 709 (2006).

Third, the appeals court in *Visa* affirmed the district court's conclusion that the Visa and Master Card networks (including member banks) collectively exercised market power, raising what they charge merchants or cardholders (or both) above the competitive level, by impairing the ability of American Express or Discover to compete. How do the concepts of two-sided platforms and network effects illuminate the analysis of that competitive effects question?

For further discussion of the economic issues raised by two-sided platforms, see Jean–Charles Rochet & Jean Tirole, *Two-Sided Markets: A Progress Report*, 37 RAND J. ECON. 645 (2006); Mark Armstrong, *Competition in Two–Sided Markets*, 37 RAND J. ECON. 667 (2006). For a discussion of various antitrust issues that two-sided platforms may raise, see David Evans & Richard Schmalensee, *The Industrial Organization of Markets with Two–Sided Platforms*, 3 COMPETITION POL'Y INT'L 151 (2007); Janusz Ordover, *Comments on Evans & Schmalensee's "The Industrial Organization of Markets with Two–Sided Platforms,"* 3 COMPETITION POL'Y INT'L 181 (2007).

B. INTERBRAND VERTICAL RESTRICTIONS

INTRODUCTION

As we discussed at the outset of Chapter 4, vertical restraints traditionally have been categorized into two principal groups—"intrabrand" and "interbrand." Recall from Chapter 4 that intrabrand restraints only affect competition for the same brand of product or service, whereas interbrand restraints affect competition between different brands, *i.e.*, among "rivals."

As was illustrated in Figure 4–3, interbrand restraints arise in the context of distribution strategies and often take the form of "exclusive dealing" and "tying" arrangements, although there are other variations. In exclusive dealing arrangements, a supplier and its customer, typically a retail dealer, agree that the dealer will buy exclusively from the supplier. Similarly, "output" or "requirements" contracts can make such supply arrangements effectively exclusive. Under an output contract, a buyer agrees to purchase all of a supplier's output of a specified good or service. Conversely, under a requirements contract a buyer agrees to purchase all of its requirements for a certain product or service from a specified seller. In the output context the seller is effectively precluded from supplying other buyers; in the requirements context, the buyer is effectively precluded from buying from other sellers. Because the typical exclusive dealing arrangement limits the dealer's discretion to buy from rival suppliers, by implication it also limits those suppliers's access to the dealer.

As we shall see, however, although exclusive dealing, output, and requirements contracts all involve exclusion to some degree, they also can have many pro-competitive justifications and are very common. For example, in the franchise context, one would not expect to find Exxon Mobil gasoline at an Shell station, or a McDonald's "Big Mac" at Burger King. These are examples of the effects of exclusive dealing agreements between the franchisors and the franchisees. Yet the use of exclusive dealing arrangements in these contexts clearly does not preclude vibrant competition among and between competing exclusive franchisees, and there are a variety of justifications for them.

Tying is not always easily defined. In theory, it simply describes an arrangement whereby a supplier conditions the sale of one product, the "tying" product, on the purchaser's agreement to purchase another, usually complementary product, the "tied" product. As with exclusive dealing, tying affects both the purchaser and rivals of the supplier. The purchaser is neither free to decline to purchase the tied product, nor able to purchase the tied product from other suppliers. Other suppliers are precluded from serving the needs of the dealer for the tied product. *See* Figure 4–3, *supra*.

Recall that a principal justification for permitting intrabrand restraints is their ability to enhance interbrand competition, which, according to the Supreme Court, "is the primary concern of antitrust law." *Sylvania*, 433 U.S. at 52, n.19 (Casebook, Chapter 4, *supra*). In *Leegin*, (Casebook, Chapter 4, *supra*), the Court further explained that intrabrand restraints only pose a significant anticompetitive risk when: (1) they are being used to facilitate a dealer or manufacturer cartel; or (2) when the dealer or manufacturer has market power and the intrabrand restraint is being used to implement an exclusionary strategy. *See* Figure 4–2, *supra*.

Interbrand restraints also can promote interbrand competition, but in contrast to intrabrand restraints, by definition every interbrand restraint limits some interbrand competition. They can be suspect because of their potential for *collusive or exclusionary* anticompetitive effects. Consumers might experience the collusive effects of interbrand restraints, for example, in the form of higher prices or reduced choice with respect to a tied product. Rivals, on the other hand, might be the most immediate targets of a tying arrangement and would experience its exclusionary effects, which in turn might result in collusive effects for consumers if the exclusion is substantial enough and other conditions are present. Similarly, every tying arrangement precludes some degree of competition in the tied product or service. So one might expect that the law would treat interbrand vertical restraints more harshly than intrabrand ones, or at least with some greater degree of scrutiny.

Over time, however, economists and courts have increasingly endorsed the idea that vertical interbrand restraints can be pro-competitive and promote legitimate competitive strategies. The challenge is to develop a legal and economic framework for distinguishing reasonably exclusionary restraints from unreasonably exclusionary ones—those whose exclusionary effects are so significant, or which are so lacking in business justifications, that they warrant prohibition under the antitrust laws. As a consequence, the analysis of interbrand restraints has grown increasingly similar to that used to evaluate other exclusionary arrangements, such as exclusion by a dominant firm (Chapter 6) and exclusionary group boycotts, which we studied earlier in this Chapter.

The study of vertical interbrand restraints is complicated by two other factors: one economic and the other legal. First, even more so than was true in the case of intrabrand vertical restraints, the economic analysis of interbrand restraints can be complex. Some of that complexity has flowed from efforts to apply the "tying" label, and the per se rule that accompanies it, to integrated products, *i.e.*, products that are sold as a single package (like an automobile or computer), but which can be seen literally as a bundle of "separate" products (*e.g.*, tires, radios, engines or hardware and software). Additional issues have arisen from the sale of intellectual property, such as patents, copyrights and even trademarks, with non-intellectual property.

Second, and again somewhat similarly to the history of intrabrand restraints, the law of interbrand restraints has been characterized by intense academic and legal debate for years, and some very distinct and still evolving legal rules. For example, although exclusive dealing has always been examined under some version of a reasonableness test, tying has for a long time been labeled "per se" unlawful. But, as you will see, the current status of the per se rule is at best uncertain, in part due to years of criticism. Many commentators even believe that it is just a matter of time before the Supreme Court formally abandons the per se rule for tying, except perhaps in rare and extreme circumstances. As we will learn later in this Chapter in the *Microsoft* litigation, the D.C. Circuit simply refused to apply it to "technological tying," the integration of seemingly separable software programs, such as Internet browsers, media players, and security software, into a single computer operating system, on the ground that it was ill-suited to the analysis of platform software.

Finally, although tying and exclusive dealing can be evaluated under Section 1 of the Sherman Act as "contracts in restraint of trade," they also can be the focus of allegations of exclusionary conduct by a single firm under Section 2 of the Sherman Act, and are most specifically addressed under Section 3 of the Clayton Act. We will consider the role of Section 3 of the Clayton Act later in this Chapter. We have already examined dominant firm exclusionary conduct in Chapter 6.

These factors—complex economic analysis, the presence of some history of per se treatment, and the applicability of multiple statutory prohibitions—all make for a complicated picture.

1. TYING AND THE "LEVERAGING" PROBLEM

Tying has a long and distinct history of treatment under the antitrust laws that pre-dates even the adoption of the Clayton Act in 1914, Section 3 of which includes a specific prohibition of tying and exclusive dealing agreements that "substantially lessen competition" or "tend to monopoly." The provision was adopted in part in response to *Henry v. A.B. Dick Co.*, 224 U.S. 1 (1912) and the then still pending *United States v. United Shoe Mach. Co.*, 247 U.S. 32 (1918). *See International Business Mach. Corp. v. United States*, 298 U.S. 131, 137–38 (1936) (discussing the origins of the Clayton Act's prohibition of tying).

Three early cases provided the foundation for the later treatment of tying as per se unlawful—*United Shoe Mach. Corp. v. United States*, 258 U.S. 451 (1922), *Int'l Business Mach. Corp. v. United States*, 298 U.S. 131 (1936) ("*IBM*"), and *Int'l Salt Co. v. United States*, 332 U.S. 392 (1947). *United Shoe* and *IBM* both arose under Section 3 of the Clayton Act, whereas *International Salt* was brought under both Section 3 of the Clayton Act and Section 1 of the Sherman Act. All three cases involved allegations that the defendants had conditioned the leasing of one product on the purchaser's agreement to buy, or in the case of *United Shoe* lease, another, unwanted product; in all three cases the defendants asserted that the tying arrangement was protected by patent rights in the tying product; and in all three cases the Supreme Court condemned the practice as unlawful.

Typical of the Court's reasoning is the following excerpt from *IBM*. There the Court condemned IBM's lease agreements, which conditioned the leasing of its mechanical tabulation machines on the lessee's agreement to use only IBM punch cards in the machines. The Court found the lease provision to be a clear violation of Section 3:

> Despite the plain language of section 3, making unlawful the tying clause when it tends to create a monopoly, appellant insists that it does not forbid tying clauses whose purpose and effect are to protect the good will of the lessor in the leased machines, even though monopoly ensues. In support of this contention appellant places great emphasis on the admitted fact that it is essential to the successful performance of the leased machines that the cards used in them conform, with relatively minute tolerances, to specifications as to size, thickness, and freedom from defects which would affect adversely the electrical circuits indispensable to the proper operation of the machines. The point is stressed that failure, even though occasional, to conform to these requirements, causes inaccuracies in the functioning of the machine, serious in their consequences and difficult to trace to their source, with consequent injury to the reputation of the machines and the good will of the lessors. There is no contention that others than appellant cannot meet these requirements. It affirmatively appears, by stipulation, that others are capable of manufacturing cards suitable for use in appellant's machines,

and that paper required for that purpose may be obtained from the manufacturers who supply appellant. * * * The suggestion that without the tying clause an adequate supply of cards would not be forthcoming from competitive sources is not supported by the evidence. * * *

Appellant is not prevented from proclaiming the virtues of its own cards or warning against the danger of using, in its machines, cards which do not conform to the necessary specifications, or even from making its leases conditional upon the use of cards which conform to them. For aught that appears such measures would protect its good will, without the creation of monopoly or resort to the suppression of competition.

The Clayton Act names no exception to its prohibition of monopolistic tying clauses. Even if we are free to make an exception to its unambiguous command, we can perceive no tenable basis for an exception in favor of a condition whose substantial benefit to the lessor is the elimination of business competition and the creation of monopoly, rather than the protection of its good will, and where it does not appear that the latter can not be achieved by methods which do not tend to monopoly and are not otherwise unlawful.

298 U.S. at 138–40 (citations omitted). *IBM* illustrates the earliest and most rudimentary features of the "tying" arrangement: (1) the presence of two products, one desired, the other not; (2) a degree of "forcing," in the sense that the purchaser has no choice but to take the second product to get the first; and (3) a legal inference that the effects of such forcing can be "monopolistic." Note too, however, that IBM's proffered justifications, that tying was necessary to guarantee the proper functioning of the machines and to maintain its good will, were not rejected outright as might be expected with a true per se rule, but were rejected because unsupported by the evidence.

A decade later, the Court explicitly extended the per se idea to tying in *International Salt*, where the defendant required lessees of its patented salt dispensing machines also to acquire all of their salt needs from the lessor:

The appellant's patents confer a limited monopoly of the invention they reward. From them appellant derives a right to restrain others from making, vending or using the patented machines. But the patents confer no right to restrain use of, or trade in, unpatented salt. By contracting to close this market for salt against competition, International has engaged in a restraint of trade for which its patents afford no immunity from the anti-trust laws.

Appellant contends, however, that summary judgment was unauthorized because it precluded trial of alleged issues of fact as to whether the restraint was unreasonable within the Sherman Act or substantially lessened competition or tended to create a monopoly in salt within the Clayton Act. We think the admitted facts left no genuine issue. Not only is price-fixing unreasonable, *per se*, United States v. Socony–Vacuum Oil Co., 310 U.S. 150; United States v. Trenton Potteries Co., 273 U.S. 392, but also it is unreasonable, *per se*, to foreclose competitors from any substantial market. Fashion Originators' Guild of America v. Federal Trade Commission, 312 U.S.

457. The volume of business affected by these contracts cannot be said to be insignificant or insubstantial and the tendency of the arrangement to accomplishment of monopoly seems obvious. Under the law, agreements are forbidden which "tend to create a monopoly," and it is immaterial that the tendency is a creeping one rather than one that proceeds at full gallop; nor does the law await arrival at the goal before condemning the direction of the movement.

332 U.S. at 395–96. Do you find persuasive the Court's suggestion that patent rights afford some degree of monopoly power? We will examine that question in greater depth in our next case, *Jefferson Parish Hosp. Dist. No. 2 v. Hyde* and in the notes that follow.

International Salt sought to distinguish its leases from those struck down in *IBM* on a number of grounds. First, it argued in vain that its lease provisions were reasonable because they permitted lessees to purchase "salt of equal grade" from any competitor if it were offered at a price lower than its own. Although the Court observed that the provision afforded "a measure of protection to the lessee," it concluded that its effect was nevertheless unreasonable. International Salt retained its "priority on the business at equal prices," and competitors could only hope to divert salt sales if they undercut International Salt's prices. *Id*. at 397. Moreover, like IBM, International Salt argued that the tying arrangement was necessary to assure "satisfactory functioning and low maintenance costs" for its dispensing machines. *Id*. As in *IBM*, the Court responded by accepting the proposition that "a lessor may impose on a lessee reasonable restrictions designed in good faith to minimize maintenance burdens and to assure satisfactory operation," but it found International Salt's restrictions to be far broader than necessary to accomplish that goal. *Id*.

Taken together, *United Shoe, IBM,* and *International Salt* laid the foundation for the definition of tying and its harsh treatment under federal antitrust laws. Tying entered its second principal phase of development, however, with a series of cases from *Times-Picayune Pub. Co. v. United States,* 345 U.S. 594 (1953) to the Supreme Court's decision in *United States Steel Corp. v. Fortner Enters., Inc.,* 429 U.S. 610 (1977) ("*Fortner II*"), the last significant tying case to be decided by the Court until we enter the modern period with *Jefferson Parish* (1984), our next case. These cases progressively refined the definition of tying, and the conditions under which it could be condemned under the per se rule, until a four part test emerged:

- there must be *two distinct products* or services;
- there must be a *conditioned sale, i.e.,* the tying product must be available only on the condition that the second, tied product also be purchased;
- the seller must have "*appreciable economic power*" in the tying product, such that "forcing" is likely, *i.e.,* it appears that the second product would either not be purchased at all, or would not be purchased from the seller of the tying product, but for the seller's market power; and
- the arrangement must affect a "*substantial volume of commerce* in the tied market."

Fortner Enters., Inc. v. United States Steel Corp., 394 U.S. 495, 503 (1969) (*"Fortner I"*). *See also Northern Pac. Ry. Co. v. United States*, 356 U.S. 1, 5–6 (1958); *United States v. Loew's, Inc.*, 371 U.S. 38 (1962); *Fortner II*, 429 U.S. at 613–16. A great deal of case law developed over the years addressing each of the four requirements.

As you read the next case, *Jefferson Parish*, consider carefully how the Court approaches and interprets each of the elements of a traditional tying offense. What test does the Court employ to define the "two product" requirement? When is a sale "conditional," *i.e.*, really a tie-in? What does the Court mean by "economic power"? How much "economic power" is needed to justify invocation of the per se rule? Is "economic power" the same as "market power"? Is there any role in this framework to argue that the tie-in is efficient in some way? Does the Court's approach as a whole appear to be consistent with any per se rule we have seen? Consider, too, the concurring Justices' arguments for abandoning the per se rubric altogether, and the majority's response.

Finally, you should also recall and consider *Northwest Wholesale Stationers*, which we read at the beginning of this Chapter. Even though traditionally *Jefferson Parish* and *Northwest Wholesale Stationers* would be categorized as distinct, one dealing with tying, the other with group boycotts, consider whether there are any similarities in the Court's approach in the two cases, particularly with regard to the application of the per se rule. What explains this similarity, if any?

JEFFERSON PARISH HOSPITAL DISTRICT. NO. 2 v. HYDE
Supreme Court of the United States, 1984.
466 U.S. 2, 104 S.Ct. 1551, 80 L.Ed.2d 2.

Justice STEVENS delivered the opinion of the Court.

At issue in this case is the validity of an exclusive contract between a hospital and a firm of anesthesiologists. We must decide whether the contract gives rise to a *per se* violation of § 1 of the Sherman Act because every patient undergoing surgery at the hospital must use the services of one firm of anesthesiologists, and, if not, whether the contract is nevertheless illegal because it unreasonably restrains competition among anesthesiologists.

In July 1977, respondent Edwin G. Hyde, a board certified anesthesiologist, applied for admission to the medical staff of East Jefferson Hospital. The credentials committee and the medical staff executive committee recommended approval, but the hospital board denied the application because the hospital was a party to a contract providing that all anesthesiological services required by the hospital's patients would be performed by Roux & Associates. * * * Respondent then commenced this action seeking a declaratory judgment that the contract is unlawful and an injunction ordering petitioners to appoint him to the hospital staff. After trial, the District Court denied relief, finding that the anticompetitive consequences of the Roux contract were minimal and outweighed by benefits in the form of improved patient care. The Court of Appeals reversed because it was persuaded that the contract was illegal "*per se.*" We granted certiorari and now reverse.

I

In February 1971, shortly before East Jefferson Hospital opened, it entered into an "Anesthesiology Agreement" with Roux & Associates ("Roux"). * * * The contract provided that any anesthesiologist designated by Roux would be admitted to the hospital's medical staff. The hospital agreed to provide the space, equipment, maintenance, and other supporting services necessary to operate the anesthesiology department. It also agreed to purchase all necessary drugs and other supplies. All nursing personnel required by the anesthesia department were to be supplied by the hospital, but Roux had the right to approve their selection and retention.[3] The hospital agreed to "restrict the use of its anesthesia department to Roux & Associates and [that] no other persons, parties or entities shall perform such services within the Hospital for the ter[m] of this contract."[4]

The 1971 contract provided for a one-year term automatically renewable for successive one-year periods unless either party elected to terminate. In 1976, a second written contract was executed containing most of the provisions of the 1971 agreement. Its term was five years and the clause excluding other anesthesiologists from the hospital was deleted; the hospital nevertheless continued to regard itself as committed to a closed anesthesiology department. Only Roux was permitted to practice anesthesiology at the hospital. * * *

The exclusive contract had an impact on two different segments of the economy: consumers of medical services, and providers of anesthesiological services. Any consumer of medical services who elects to have an operation performed at East Jefferson Hospital may not employ any anesthesiologist not associated with Roux. No anesthesiologists except those employed by Roux may practice at East Jefferson.

There are at least 20 hospitals in the New Orleans metropolitan area and about 70 per cent of the patients living in Jefferson Parish go to hospitals other than East Jefferson. Because it regarded the entire New Orleans metropolitan area as the relevant geographic market in which hospitals compete, this evidence convinced the District Court that East Jefferson does not possess any significant "market power"; therefore it concluded that petitioners could not use the Roux contract to anticompetitive ends. The same evidence led the Court of Appeals to draw a different conclusion. Noting that 30 percent of the residents of the Parish go to East Jefferson Hospital, and that in fact "patients tend to choose hospitals by location rather than price or quality," the Court of Appeals concluded that the relevant geographic market was the East Bank of Jefferson Parish. The conclusion that East Jefferson Hospital possessed market power in that area was buttressed by the facts that the prevalence of health insurance eliminates a patient's incentive to compare

---

3. The contract required all of the physicians employed by Roux to confine their practice of anesthesiology to East Jefferson.

4. Originally Roux agreed to provide at least two full time anesthesiologists acceptable to the hospital's credentials committee. Roux agreed to furnish additional anesthesiologists as necessary. The contract also provided that Roux would designate one of its qualified anes-

thesiologists to serve as the head of the hospital's department of anesthesia.

The fees for anesthesiological services are billed separately to the patients by the hospital. They cover the hospital's costs and the professional services provided by Roux. After a deduction of eight percent to provide a reserve for uncollectible accounts, the fees are divided equally between Roux and the hospital.

costs, that the patient is not sufficiently informed to compare quality, and that family convenience tends to magnify the importance of location.[8]

The Court of Appeals held that the case involves a "tying arrangement" because the "users of the hospital's operating rooms (the tying product) are also compelled to purchase the hospital's chosen anesthesia service (the tied product)." Having defined the relevant geographic market for the tying product as the East Bank of Jefferson Parish, the court held that the hospital possessed "sufficient market power in the tying market to coerce purchasers of the tied product." Since the purchase of the tied product constituted a "not insubstantial amount of interstate commerce," under the Court of Appeals' reading of our decision in *Northern Pacific R. Co. v. United States*, 356 U.S. 1 (1957) the tying arrangement was therefore illegal *"per se."*

II

Certain types of contractual arrangements are deemed unreasonable as a matter of law. The character of the restraint produced by such an arrangement is considered a sufficient basis for presuming unreasonableness without the necessity of any analysis of the market context in which the arrangement may be found. A price fixing agreement between competitors is the classic example of such an arrangement. It is far too late in the history of our antitrust jurisprudence to question the proposition that certain tying arrangements pose an unacceptable risk of stifling competition and therefore are unreasonable *"per se."* The rule was first enunciated in *International Salt Co. v. United States*, 332 U.S. 392 (1947) and has been endorsed by this Court many times since. The rule also reflects congressional policies underlying the antitrust laws. In enacting § 3 of the Clayton Act Congress expressed great concern about the anticompetitive character of tying arrangements. While this case does not arise under the Clayton Act, the congressional finding made therein concerning the competitive consequences of tying is illuminating, and must be respected.

It is clear, however, that every refusal to sell two products separately cannot be said to restrain competition. If each of the products may be purchased separately in a competitive market, one seller's decision to sell the two in a single package imposes no unreasonable restraint on either market, particularly if competing suppliers are free to sell either the entire package or its several parts. * * * Buyers often find package sales attractive; a seller's decision to offer such packages can merely be an attempt to compete effectively—conduct that is entirely consistent with the Sherman Act.

Our cases have concluded that the essential characteristic of an invalid tying arrangement lies in the seller's exploitation of its control over the tying product to force the buyer into the purchase of a tied product that the buyer

---

8. While the Court of Appeals did discuss the impact of the contract upon patients, it did not discuss its impact upon anesthesiologists. The District Court had referred to evidence that in the entire State of Louisiana there are 156 anesthesiologists and 345 hospitals with operating rooms. The record does not tell us how many of the hospitals in the New Orleans metropolitan area have "open" anesthesiology departments and how many have closed de-partments. Respondent, for example, practices with two other anesthesiologists at a hospital which has an open department; he previously practiced for several years in a different New Orleans hospital and, prior to that, had practiced in Florida. The record does not tell us whether there is a shortage or a surplus of anesthesiologists in any part of the country, or whether they are thriving or starving.

either did not want at all, or might have preferred to purchase elsewhere on different terms. When such "forcing" is present, competition on the merits in the market for the tied item is restrained and the Sherman Act is violated. * * *

Accordingly, we have condemned tying arrangements when the seller has some special ability—usually called "market power"—to force a purchaser to do something that he would not do in a competitive market. * * *[20] When "forcing" occurs, our cases have found the tying arrangement to be unlawful.

Thus, the law draws a distinction between the exploitation of market power by merely enhancing the price of the tying product, on the one hand, and by attempting to impose restraints on competition in the market for a tied product, on the other. When the seller's power is just used to maximize its return in the tying product market, where presumably its product enjoys some justifiable advantage over its competitors, the competitive ideal of the Sherman Act is not necessarily compromised. But if that power is used to impair competition on the merits in another market, a potentially inferior product may be insulated from competitive pressures. This impairment could either harm existing competitors or create barriers to entry of new competitors in the market for the tied product and can increase the social costs of market power by facilitating price discrimination, thereby increasing monopoly profits over what they would be absent the tie.[23] And from the standpoint of the consumer—whose interests the statute was especially intended to serve—the freedom to select the best bargain in the second market is impaired by his need to purchase the tying product, and perhaps by an inability to evaluate the true cost of either product when they are available only as a package.[24] In sum, to permit restraint of competition on the merits through tying arrangements would be * * * to condone "the existence of power that a free market would not tolerate."

Per se condemnation—condemnation without inquiry into actual market conditions—is only appropriate if the existence of forcing is probable.[25] Thus, application of the *per se* rule focuses on the probability of anticompetitive consequences. Of course, as a threshold matter there must be a substantial potential for impact on competition in order to justify *per se* condemnation. If only a single purchaser were "forced" with respect to the purchase of a tied item, the resultant impact on competition would not be sufficient to warrant the concern of antitrust law. * * * Similarly, when a purchaser is "forced" to buy a product he would not have otherwise bought even from another seller in

---

20. This type of market power has sometimes been referred to as "leverage." Professors Areeda and Turner provide a definition that suits present purposes. " 'Leverage' is loosely defined here as a supplier's ability to induce his customer for one product to buy a second product from him that would not otherwise be purchased solely on the merit of that second product." V. P. Areeda & D. Turner, Antitrust Law ¶ 1134a, at 202 (1980).

23. Sales of the tied item can be used to measure demand for the tying item; purchasers with greater needs for the tied item make larger purchases and in effect must pay a higher price to obtain the tying item.

24. Especially where market imperfections exist, purchasers may not be fully sensitive to the price or quality implications of a tying arrangement, and hence it may impede competition on the merits.

25. The rationale for *per se* rules in part is to avoid a burdensome inquiry into actual market conditions in situations where the likelihood of anticompetitive conduct is so great as to render unjustified the costs of determining whether the particular case at bar involves anticompetitive conduct.

the tied product market, there can be no adverse impact on competition because no portion of the market which would otherwise have been available to other sellers has been foreclosed.

Once this threshold is surmounted, *per se* prohibition is appropriate if anticompetitive forcing is likely. For example, if the government has granted the seller a patent or similar monopoly over a product, it is fair to presume that the inability to buy the product elsewhere gives the seller market power. Any effort to enlarge the scope of the patent monopoly by using the market power it confers to restrain competition in the market for a second product will undermine competition on the merits in that second market. Thus, the sale or lease of a patented item on condition that the buyer make all his purchases of a separate tied product from the patentee is unlawful.

The same strict rule is appropriate in other situations in which the existence of market power is probable. When the seller's share of the market is high, or when the seller offers a unique product that competitors are not able to offer, the Court has held that the likelihood that market power exists and is being used to restrain competition in a separate market is sufficient to make *per se* condemnation appropriate. * * * When, however, the seller does not have either the degree or the kind of market power that enables him to force customers to purchase a second, unwanted product in order to obtain the tying product, an antitrust violation can be established only by evidence of an unreasonable restraint on competition in the relevant market.

In sum, any inquiry into the validity of a tying arrangement must focus on the market or markets in which the two products are sold, for that is where the anticompetitive forcing has its impact. Thus, in this case our analysis of the tying issue must focus on the hospital's sale of services to its patients, rather than its contractual arrangements with the providers of anesthesiological services. In making that analysis, we must consider whether petitioners are selling two separate products that may be tied together, and, if so, whether they have used their market power to force their patients to accept the tying arrangement.

III

The hospital has provided its patients with a package that includes the range of facilities and services required for a variety of surgical operations.[27] At East Jefferson Hospital the package includes the services of the anesthesiologist.[28] Petitioners argue that the package does not involve a tying arrangement at all—that they are merely providing a functionally integrated package of services. * * *

Our cases indicate, however, that the answer to the question whether one or two products are involved turns not on the functional relation between

27. The physical facilities include the operating room, the recovery room, and the hospital room where the patient stays before and after the operation. The services include those provided by staff physicians, such as radiologists or pathologists, and interns, nurses, dietitians, pharmacists and laboratory technicians.

28. It is essential to differentiate between the Roux contract and the legality of the contract between the hospital and its patients.

The Roux contract is nothing more than an arrangement whereby Roux supplies all of the hospital's needs for anesthesiological services. That contract raises only an exclusive dealing question. The issue here is whether the hospital's insistence that its patients purchase anesthesiological services from Roux creates a tying arrangement.

them, but rather on the character of the demand for the two items.[30] * * * [A] tying arrangement cannot exist unless two separate product markets have been linked.

The requirement that two distinguishable product markets be involved follows from the underlying rationale of the rule against tying. The definitional question depends on whether the arrangement may have the type of competitive consequences addressed by the rule. The answer to the question whether petitioners have utilized a tying arrangement must be based on whether there is a possibility that the economic effect of the arrangement is that condemned by the rule against tying—that petitioners have foreclosed competition on the merits in a product market distinct from the market for the tying item.[34] Thus, in this case no tying arrangement can exist unless there is a sufficient demand for the purchase of anesthesiological services separate from hospital services to identify a distinct product market in which it is efficient to offer anesthesiological services separately from hospital services.

Unquestionably, the anesthesiological component of the package offered by the hospital could be provided separately and could be selected either by the individual patient or by one of the patient's doctors if the hospital did not insist on including anesthesiological services in the package it offers to its customers. As a matter of actual practice, anesthesiological services are billed separately from the hospital services petitioners provide. There was ample and uncontroverted testimony that patients or surgeons often request specific anesthesiologists to come to a hospital and provide anesthesia, and that the choice of an individual anesthesiologist separate from the choice of a hospital is particularly frequent in respondent's specialty, obstetric anesthesiology. * * * The record amply supports the conclusion that consumers differentiate between anesthesiological services and the other hospital services provided by petitioners.[39]

30. The fact that anesthesiological services are functionally linked to the other services provided by the hospital is not in itself sufficient to remove the Roux contract from the realm of tying arrangements. We have often found arrangements involving functionally linked products at least one of which is useless without the other to be prohibited tying devices. In fact, in some situations the functional link between the two items may enable the seller to maximize its monopoly return on the tying item as a means of charging a higher rent or purchase price to a larger user of the tying item. See n. 23, *supra*.

34. Of course, the Sherman Act does not prohibit "tying," it prohibits "contract[s] . . . in restraint of trade." Thus, in a sense the question whether this case involves "tying" is beside the point. The legality of petitioners' conduct depends on its competitive consequences, not whether it can be labeled "tying." If the competitive consequences of this arrangement are not those to which the *per se* rule is addressed, then it should not be condemned irrespective of its label.

39. One of the most frequently cited statements on this subject was made by Judge Van

Dusen in *United States v. Jerrold Electronics Corp.*, 187 F.Supp. 545 (E.D.Pa.1960), aff'd, 365 U.S. 567, 81 S.Ct. 755, 5 L.Ed.2d 806 (1961) (*per curiam*). * * *

"There are several facts presented in this record which tend to show that a community television system cannot properly be characterized as a single product. Others who entered the community antenna field offered all the equipment necessary for a complete system, but none of them sold their gear exclusively as a single package as did Jerrold. The record also establishes that the number of pieces in each system varied considerably so that hardly any two versions of the alleged product were the same. Furthermore, the customer was charged for each item of equipment and not a lump sum for total payment. Finally, while Jerrold had cable and antennas to sell which were manufactured by other concerns, it required that the electronic equipment in the system be bought from it." 187 F.Supp., at 559.

The record here shows that other hospitals often permit anesthesiological services to be

Thus, the hospital's requirement that its patients obtain necessary anesthesiological services from Roux combined the purchase of two distinguishable services in a single transaction. Nevertheless, the fact that this case involves a required purchase of two services that would otherwise be purchased separately does not make the Roux contract illegal. * * * Only if patients are forced to purchase Roux's services as a result of the hospital's market power would the arrangement have anticompetitive consequences. If no forcing is present, patients are free to enter a competing hospital and to use another anesthesiologist instead of Roux. The fact that petitioners' patients are required to purchase two separate items is only the beginning of the appropriate inquiry.[42]

IV

The question remains whether this arrangement involves the use of market power to force patients to buy services they would not otherwise purchase. Respondent's only basis for invoking the *per se* rule against tying and thereby avoiding analysis of actual market conditions is by relying on the preference of persons residing in Jefferson Parish to go to East Jefferson, the closest hospital. A preference of this kind, however, is not necessarily probative of significant market power.

Seventy per cent of the patients residing in Jefferson Parish enter hospitals other than East Jefferson. Thus East Jefferson's "dominance" over persons residing in Jefferson Parish is far from overwhelming.[43] The fact that a substantial majority of the parish's residents elect not to enter East Jefferson means that the geographic data does not establish the kind of dominant market position that obviates the need for further inquiry into actual competitive conditions. The Court of Appeals acknowledged as much; it

purchased separately, that anesthesiologists are not fungible in that the services provided by each are not precisely the same, that anesthesiological services are billed separately, and that the hospital required purchases from Roux even though other anesthesiologists were available and Roux had no objection to their receiving staff privileges at East Jefferson. Therefore, the *Jerrold* analysis indicates that there was a tying arrangement here. *Jerrold* also indicates that tying may be permissible when necessary to enable a new business to break into the market. See *id.*, at 555–558. Assuming this defense exists, and assuming it justified the 1971 Roux contract in order to give Roux an incentive to go to work at a new hospital with an uncertain future, that justification is inapplicable to the 1976 contract, since by then Roux was willing to continue to service the hospital without a tying arrangement.

42. Petitioners argue and the District Court found that the exclusive contract had what it characterized as procompetitive justifications in that an exclusive contract ensures 24–hour anesthesiology coverage, enables flexible scheduling, and facilitates work routine, professional standards and maintenance of equipment. The Court of Appeals held these

findings to be clearly erroneous since the exclusive contract was not necessary to achieve these ends. * * * In the past, we have refused to tolerate manifestly anticompetitive conduct simply because the health care industry is involved. * * * We have also uniformly rejected similar "goodwill" defenses for tying arrangements, finding that the use of contractual quality specifications are generally sufficient to protect quality without the use of a tying arrangement. Since the District Court made no finding as to why contractual quality specifications would not protect the hospital, there is no basis for departing from our prior cases here.

43. In fact its position in this market is not dissimilar from the market share at issue in *Times–Picayune*, which the Court found insufficient as a basis for inferring market power. See 345 U.S., at 611–613, 73 S.Ct., at 881–883. Moreover, in other antitrust contexts this Court has found that market shares comparable to that present here do not create an unacceptable likelihood of anticompetitive conduct. See *United States v. Connecticut National Bank*, 418 U.S. 656, 94 S.Ct. 2788, 41 L.Ed.2d 1016 (1974); *United States v. du Pont & Co.*, 351 U.S. 377, 76 S.Ct. 994, 100 L.Ed. 1264 (1956).

recognized that East Jefferson's market share alone was insufficient as a basis to infer market power, and buttressed its conclusion by relying on "market imperfections" that permit petitioners to charge noncompetitive prices for hospital services: the prevalence of third party payment for health care costs reduces price competition, and a lack of adequate information renders consumers unable to evaluate the quality of the medical care provided by competing hospitals. While these factors may generate "market power" in some abstract sense,[46] they do not generate the kind of market power that justifies condemnation of tying.

Tying arrangements need only be condemned if they restrain competition on the merits by forcing purchases that would not otherwise be made. A lack of price or quality competition does not create this type of forcing. If consumers lack price consciousness, that fact will not force them to take an anesthesiologist whose services they do not want—their indifference to price will have no impact on their willingness or ability to go to another hospital where they can utilize the services of the anesthesiologist of their choice. Similarly, if consumers cannot evaluate the quality of anesthesiological services, it follows that they are indifferent between certified anesthesiologists even in the absence of a tying arrangement-such an arrangement cannot be said to have foreclosed a choice that would have otherwise been made "on the merits."

Thus, neither of the "market imperfections" relied upon by the Court of Appeals forces consumers to take anesthesiological services they would not select in the absence of a tie. It is safe to assume that every patient undergoing a surgical operation needs the services of an anesthesiologist; at least this record contains no evidence that the hospital "forced" any such services on unwilling patients.[47] The record therefore does not provide a basis for applying the *per se* rule against tying to this arrangement.

V

In order to prevail in the absence of *per se* liability, respondent has the burden of proving that the Roux contract violated the Sherman Act because it unreasonably restrained competition. That burden necessarily involves an

---

46. As an economic matter, market power exists whenever prices can be raised above the levels that would be charged in a competitive market.

47. Nor is there an indication in the record that petitioner's practices have increased the social costs of its market power. Since patients' anesthesiological needs are fixed by medical judgment, respondent does not argue that the tying arrangement facilitates price discrimination. Where variable-quantity purchasing is unavailable as a means to enable price discrimination, commentators have seen less justification for condemning tying. While tying arrangements like the one at issue here are unlikely to be used to facilitate price discrimination, they could have the similar effect of enabling hospitals "to evade price control in the tying product through clandestine transfer of the profit to the tied product...." Insurance companies are the principal source of price restraint in the hospital industry; they place some limitations on the ability of hospitals to exploit their market power. Through this arrangement, petitioners may be able to evade that restraint by obtaining a portion of the anesthesiologists' fees and therefore realize a greater return than they could in the absence of the arrangement. This could also have an adverse effect on the anesthesiology market since it is possible that only less able anesthesiologists would be willing to give up part of their fees in return for the security of an exclusive contract. However, there are no findings of either the District Court or the Court of Appeals which indicate that this type of exploitation of market power has occurred here. * * * Moreover, there is nothing in the record which details whether this arrangement has enhanced the value of East Jefferson's market power or harmed quality competition in the anesthesiology market.

inquiry into the actual effect of the exclusive contract on competition among anesthesiologists. This competition takes place in a market that has not been defined. The market is not necessarily the same as the market in which hospitals compete in offering services to patients; it may encompass competition among anesthesiologists for exclusive contracts such as the Roux contract and might be statewide or merely local.[48] There is, however, insufficient evidence in this record to provide a basis for finding that the Roux contract, as it actually operates in the market, has unreasonably restrained competition. The record sheds little light on how this arrangement affected consumer demand for separate arrangements with a specific anesthesiologist.[49] * * *

In sum, all that the record establishes is that the choice of anesthesiologists at East Jefferson has been limited to one of the four doctors who are associated with Roux and therefore have staff privileges.[51] Even if Roux did not have an exclusive contract, the range of alternatives open to the patient would be severely limited by the nature of the transaction and the hospital's unquestioned right to exercise some control over the identity and the number of doctors to whom it accords staff privileges. If respondent is admitted to the staff of East Jefferson, the range of choice will be enlarged from four to five doctors, but the most significant restraints on the patient's freedom to select a specific anesthesiologist will nevertheless remain.[52] Without a showing of actual adverse effect on competition, respondent cannot make out a case under the antitrust laws, and no such showing has been made.

* * *

[The Concurring Opinion of Mr. Justice BRENNAN, with who Mr. Justice MARSHALL joined, has been omitted. Eds.]

* * *

Justice O'CONNOR, with whom the Chief Justice, Justice POWELL, and Justice REHNQUIST join, concurring in the judgment.

48. While there was some rather impressionistic testimony that the prevalence of exclusive contracts tended to discourage young doctors from entering the market, the evidence was equivocal and neither the District Court nor the Court of Appeals made any findings concerning the contract's effect on entry barriers. * * * It is possible that under some circumstances an exclusive contract could raise entry barriers since anesthesiologists could not compete for the contract without raising the capital necessary to run a hospital-wide operation.* * *

49. While it is true that purchasers may not be fully sensitive to the price or quality implications of a tying arrangement, so that competition may be impeded, this depends on an empirical demonstration concerning the effect of the arrangement on price or quality, and the record reveals little if anything about the effect of this arrangement on the market for anesthesiological services.

51. The effect of the contract has, of course, been to remove the East Jefferson Hospital from the market open to Roux's competitors. Like any exclusive requirements contract, this contract could be unlawful if it foreclosed so much of the market from penetration by Roux's competitors as to unreasonably restrain competition in the affected market, the market for anesthesiological services. However, respondent has not attempted to make this showing.

52. The record simply tells us little if anything about the effect of this arrangement on price or quality of anesthesiological services. As to price, the arrangement did not lead to an increase in the price charged to the patient. As to quality, the record indicates little more than that there have never been any complaints about the quality of Roux's services, and no contention that his services are in any respect inferior to those of respondent. Moreover, the self interest of the hospital, as well as the ethical and professional norms under which it operates, presumably protect the quality of anesthesiological services.

* * * I concur in the Court's decision * * * but write separately to explain why I believe the Hospital–Roux contract, whether treated as effecting a tie between services provided to patients, or as an exclusive dealing arrangement between the Hospital and certain anesthesiologists, is properly analyzed under the Rule of Reason.

I

Tying is a form of marketing in which a seller insists on selling two distinct products or services as a package. * * * In this case the allegation is that East Jefferson Hospital has unlawfully tied the sale of general hospital services and operating room facilities (the tying service) to the sale of anesthesiologists' services (the tied services). The Court has on occasion applied a *per se* rule of illegality in actions alleging tying in violation of § 1 of the Sherman Act.

Under the usual logic of the *per se* rule, a restraint on trade that rarely serves any purposes other than to restrain competition is illegal without proof of market power or anti-competitive effect. In deciding whether an economic restraint should be declared illegal *per se*, "[t]he probability that anticompetitive consequences will result from a practice and the severity of those consequences [is] balanced against its pro-competitive consequences. Cases that do not fit the generalization may arise, but a *per se* rule reflects the judgment that such cases are not sufficiently common or important to justify the time and expense necessary to identify them." Only when there is very little loss to society from banning a restraint altogether is an inquiry into its costs in the individual case considered to be unnecessary.

Some of our earlier cases did indeed declare that tying arrangements serve "hardly any purpose beyond the suppression of competition." However, this declaration was not taken literally even by the cases that purported to rely upon it. In practice, a tie has been illegal only if the seller is shown to have "sufficient economic power with respect to the tying product to appreciably restrain free competition in the market for the tied product...." Without "control or dominance over the tying product," the seller could not use the tying product as "an effectual weapon to pressure buyers into taking the tied item," so that any restraint of trade would be "insignificant." The Court has never been willing to say of tying arrangements, as it has of price-fixing, division of markets and other agreements subject to *per se* analysis, that they are always illegal, without proof of market power or anticompetitive effect.

The *"per se"* doctrine in tying cases has thus always required an elaborate inquiry into the economic effects of the tying arrangement.[1] As a result, tying doctrine incurs the costs of a rule of reason approach without achieving its benefits: the doctrine calls for the extensive and time-consuming economic analysis characteristic of the rule of reason, but then may be interpreted to prohibit arrangements that economic analysis would show to be

---

1. This inquiry has been required in analyzing both the prima facie case and affirmative defenses. Most notably, *United States v. Jerrold Electronics Corp.*, 187 F. Supp. 545, 559–560 (E.D. Pa.1960), aff'd *per curiam*, 365 U.S. 567, 81 S.Ct. 755, 5 L.Ed.2d 806 (1961), upheld a requirement that buyers of television systems purchase the complete system, as well as installation and repair service, on the grounds that the tie assured that the systems would operate and thereby protected the seller's business reputation.

beneficial. Moreover, the *per se* label in the tying context has generated more confusion than coherent law because it appears to invite lower courts to omit the analysis of economic circumstances of the tie that has always been an necessary element of tying analysis.

The time has therefore come to abandon the *"per se"* label and refocus the inquiry on the adverse economic effects, and the potential economic benefits, that the tie may have. The law of tie-ins will thus be brought into accord with the law applicable to all other allegedly anticompetitive economic arrangements, except those few horizontal or quasi-horizontal restraints that can be said to have no economic justification whatsoever.[2] This change will rationalize rather than abandon tie-in doctrine as it is already applied.

II

Our prior opinions indicate that the purpose of tying law has been to identify and control those tie-ins that have a demonstrable exclusionary impact in the tied product market, or that abet the harmful exercise of market power that the seller possesses in the tying product market. Under the rule of reason tying arrangements should be disapproved only in such instances.

Market power in the *tying* product may be acquired legitimately (*e.g.*, through the grant of a patent) or illegitimately (*e.g.*, as a result of unlawful monopolization). In either event, exploitation of consumers in the market for the tying product is a possibility that exists and that may be regulated under § 2 of the Sherman Act without reference to any tying arrangements that the seller may have developed. The existence of a tied product normally does not increase the profit that the seller with market power can extract from sales of the *tying* product. A seller with a monopoly on flour, for example, cannot increase the profit it can extract from flour consumers simply by forcing them to buy sugar along with their flour. Counterintuitive though that assertion may seem, it is easily demonstrated and widely accepted. *See, e.g.*, R. Bork, The Antitrust Paradox 372–374 (1978); P. Areeda, Antitrust Analysis 735 (3d ed. 1981).

Tying may be economically harmful primarily in the rare cases where power in the market for the tying product is used to create *additional* market power in the market for the tied product.[4] The antitrust law is properly concerned with tying when, for example, the flour monopolist threatens to use its market power to acquire additional power in the sugar market, perhaps by

---

2. Tying law is particularly anomalous in this respect because arrangements largely indistinguishable from tie-ins are generally analyzed under the rule of reason. For example, the *"per se"* analysis of tie-ins subjects restrictions on a franchisee's freedom to purchase supplies to a more searching scrutiny than restrictions on his freedom to sell his products. And exclusive contracts, that, like tie-ins, require the buyer to purchase a product from one seller, are subject only to the rule of reason.

4. Tying might be undesirable in two other instances, but the Hospital–Roux arrangement involves neither one.

In a regulated industry a firm with market power may be unable to extract a supercompetitive profit because it lacks control over the prices it charges for regulated products or services. Tying may then be used to extract that profit from sale of the unregulated, tied products or services.

Tying may also help the seller engage in price discrimination by "metering" the buyer's use of the tying product. Price discrimination may be independently unlawful. Price discrimination may, however, *decrease* rather than increase the economic costs of a seller's market power. * * *

driving out competing sellers of sugar, or by making it more difficult for new sellers to enter the sugar market. But such extension of market power is unlikely, or poses no threat of economic harm, unless the two markets in question and the nature of the two products tied satisfy three threshold criteria.

First, the seller must have power in the tying product market.[6] Absent such power tying cannot conceivably have any adverse impact in the tied-product market, and can be only procompetitive in the tying product market.[7] * * *

Second, there must be a substantial threat that the tying seller will acquire market power in the tied-product market. No such threat exists if the tied-product market is occupied by many stable sellers who are not likely to be driven out by the tying, or if entry barriers in the tied product market are low. * * * If, on the other hand, the tying arrangement is likely to erect significant barriers to entry into the tied-product market, the tie remains suspect.

Third, there must be a coherent economic basis for treating the tying and tied products as distinct. All but the simplest products can be broken down into two or more components that are "tied together" in the final sale. Unless it is to be illegal to sell cars with engines or cameras with lenses, this analysis must be guided by some limiting principle. For products to be treated as distinct, the tied product must, at a minimum, be one that some consumers might wish to purchase separately *without also purchasing the tying product.*[8] When the tied product has no use other than in conjunction with the tying product, a seller of the tying product can acquire no *additional* market power by selling the two products together. * * *

Even when the tied product does have a use separate from the tying product, it makes little sense to label a package as two products without also considering the economic justifications for the sale of the package as a unit. When the economic advantages of joint packaging are substantial the package is not appropriately viewed as two products, and that should be the end of the tying inquiry. * * *[10]

These three conditions—market power in the tying product, a substantial threat of market power in the tied product, and a coherent economic basis for

---

6. The Court has failed in the past to define how much market power is necessary, but in the context of this case it is inappropriate to attempt to resolve that question.* * *

7. A common misconception has been that a patent or copyright, a high market share, or a unique product that competitors are not able to offer suffices to demonstrate market power. While each of these three factors might help to give market power to a seller, it is also possible that a seller in these situations will have no market power: for example, a patent holder has no market power in any relevant sense if there are close substitutes for the patented product. Similarly, a high market share indicates market power only if the market is properly defined to include all reasonable substitutes for the product.* * *

8. Whether the tying product is one that consumers might wish to purchase without the tied product should be irrelevant. Once it is conceded that the seller has market power over the tying product it follows that the seller can sell the tying product on noncompetitive terms. The injury to consumers does not depend on whether the seller chooses to charge a supercompetitive price, or charges a competitive price but insists that consumers also buy a product that they do not want.

10. The examination of the economic advantages of tying may properly be conducted as part of the rule-of-reason analysis, rather than at the threshold of the tying inquiry. * * *

treating the products as distinct—are only threshold requirements. Under the rule of reason a tie-in may prove acceptable even when all three are met. Tie-ins may entail economic benefits as well as economic harms, and if the threshold requirements are met these benefits should enter the rule-of-reason balance.

> "Tie-ins ... may facilitate new entry into fields where established sellers have wedded their customers to them by ties of habit and custom. * * * They may permit clandestine price cutting in products which otherwise would have no price competition at all because of fear of retaliation from the few other producers dealing in the market. They may protect the reputation of the tying product if failure to use the tied product in conjunction with it may cause it to misfunction. * * * And, if the tied and tying products are functionally related, they may reduce costs through economies of joint production and distribution." *Fortner I*, 394 U.S., at 514 n. 9, 89 S.Ct., at 1264 n. 9 (Justice WHITE, dissenting).

The ultimate decision whether a tie-in is illegal under the antitrust laws should depend upon the demonstrated economic effects of the challenged agreement. It may, for example, be entirely innocuous that the seller exploits its control over the tying-product to "force" the buyer to purchase the tied product. For when the seller exerts market power only in the tying product market, it makes no difference to him or his customers whether he exploits that power by raising the price of the tying product or by "forcing" customers to buy a tied product. On the other hand, tying may make the provision of packages of goods and services more efficient. A tie-in should be condemned only when its anticompetitive impact outweighs its contribution to efficiency.

III

Application of these criteria to the case at hand is straightforward.

Although the issue is in doubt, we may assume that the hospital does have market power in the provision of hospital services in its area. * * *

Second, in light of the hospital's presumed market power, we may also assume that there is a substantial threat that East Jefferson will acquire market power over the provision of anesthesiological services in its market. By tying the sale of anesthesia to the sale of other hospital services the hospital can drive out other sellers of those services who might otherwise operate in the local market. * * *

But the third threshold condition for giving closer scrutiny to a tying arrangement is not satisfied here: there is no sound economic reason for treating surgery and anesthesia as separate services. Patients are interested in purchasing anesthesia only in conjunction with hospital services, so the hospital can acquire no *additional* market power by selling the two services together. Accordingly, the link between the hospital's services and anesthesia administered by Roux will affect neither the amount of anesthesia provided nor the combined price of anesthesia and surgery for those who choose to become the hospital's patients. In these circumstances, anesthesia and surgical services should probably not be characterized as distinct products for tying purposes.

Even if they are, the tying should not be considered a violation of § 1 of the Sherman Act because tying here cannot increase the seller's already absolute power over the volume of production of the tied product, which is an inevitable consequence of the fact that very few patients will choose to undergo surgery without receiving anesthesia. The hospital-Roux contract therefore has little potential to harm the patients. On the other side of the balance, * * * the tie-in conferred significant benefits upon the hospital and the patients that it served.

The tie-in improves patient care and permits more efficient hospital operation in a number of ways. From the viewpoint of hospital management, the tie-in ensures 24 hour anesthesiology coverage, aids in standardization of procedures and efficient use of equipment, facilitates flexible scheduling of operations, and permits the hospital more effectively to monitor the quality of anesthesiological services. Further, the tying arrangement is advantageous to patients because * * * the closed anesthesiology department places upon the hospital, rather than the individual patient, responsibility to select the physician who is to provide anesthesiological services. The hospital also assumes the responsibility that the anesthesiologist will be available, will be acceptable to the surgeon, and will provide suitable care to the patient. * * * Such an arrangement, which has little anticompetitive effect and achieves substantial benefits in the provision of care to patients, is hardly one that the antitrust law should condemn.[13] * * *

* * *

[The concurring Justices's discussion of exclusive dealing is reproduced *infra*, at 828. Eds.]

————

A critical issue in *Jefferson Parish* was the analysis of the "two product" requirement dictated by previous Supreme Court tying decisions. Why was the two product requirement adopted in those cases? What function does it serve in the analysis of tying? What specific test did the majority embrace for satisfying the two product requirement? Did you find the majority's conclusion persuasive that surgery and anesthesia are two distinct services? What was the concurring Justices' view? What did they mean when they asserted that "there is no sound economic reason for treating surgery and anesthesia as separate services?" For a later discussion of the two market issue by the Supreme Court, see *Eastman Kodak Co. v. Image Tech. Servs., Inc.*, 504 U.S. 451, 462–63 (1992) (concluding that defendant was not entitled to summary judgment on question whether parts and service constituted two products for purposes of tying).

How persuasive a case do the concurring Justices in *Jefferson Parish* make for abandoning the per se rule against tying? Given the majority's rejection of the plaintiff's claim owing to Jefferson Parish Hospital's 30% market share, how truly "per se" is the so called per se rule for tying? We will return to the arguments of the concurring judgments shortly, but first, in

13. The Court of Appeals disregarded the benefits of the tie because it found that there were less restrictive means of achieving them. In the absence of an adequate basis to expect any harm to competition from the tie-in, this objection is simply irrelevant.

Sidebar 7–2, we more closely examine the Court's decision-making process in the case, with the aid of the papers of Justice Thurgood Marshall.

Both the *Jefferson Parish* majority and dissent appeared to agree that tying cannot be anticompetitive absent market power in the tying product. But what degree of market power should be necessary, and how should it be established? Should it be inferred from market shares calculated in a relevant market? Recall that the district court viewed the entire New Orleans metropolitan area as the relevant geographic market, but the court of appeals viewed it solely as the East Bank of Jefferson Parish. Did the Supreme Court agree with the district court or the court of appeals? Why? How did it affect the Court's analysis of market power?

Traditionally, the courts presumed that a patent conferred market power. If the tying product was patented, therefore, tying was frequently condemned. *See, e.g, United States v. Loew's, Inc.*, 371 U.S. 38 (1962). Note that the majority and the concurrence differ as to the propriety of this assumption. Citing *Loew's* and several other previous decisions of the Court, Justice Stevens writes: "if the government has granted the seller a patent or similar monopoly over a product, it is fair to presume that the inability to buy the product elsewhere gives the seller market power." *Jefferson Parish*, 466 U.S. at 16. In contrast, Justice O'Connor terms this presumption a "common misperception." *Id.* at 37 n.7 (O'Connor, J., concurring). In her view, "a patent holder has no market power in any relevant sense if there are close substitutes for the patented product." *Id.* Who has the better argument? Does a patent necessarily convey some degree of market power? If so, will it always be sufficient to threaten competition for the tied product? The Supreme Court has since endorsed Justice O'Connor's view, rejecting the notion that market power can be presumed in a tying case when the tying product is patented. *See Illinois Tool Works Inc. v. Independent Ink, Inc.*, 547 U.S. 28 (2006).

Justice O'Connor clearly doubted whether the Roux contract should even be treated as a tying arrangement. As we shall see, *infra*, she preferred to analyze it as exclusive dealing. What difference would this characterization make? Would it eliminate any concern about application of the per se rule?

Sidebar 7–2:
The Per Se Rule, The Rule of Reason, and Tying— A View From the Marshall Papers

Justice Thurgood Marshall's papers reveal that the Supreme Court's deliberations leading to the issuance of the *Jefferson Parish* decision featured a robust debate over the desirability of maintaining a per se rule against tying arrangements.* Justice Sandra Day O'Connor corresponded extensively with Justice John Paul Stevens, who eventually wrote for the majority in the case. Justice O'Connor unsuccessfully urged Justice Stevens to abandon the per se standard of earlier Supreme Court tying decisions in favor of a new rule of reason analytical framework. In a

---

* This Sidebar is adapted from William E. Kovacic, *Antitrust Decision Making and the Supreme Court: Perspectives from the Thur-* *good Marshall Papers*, 42 ANTITRUST BULL. 93, 97–99 (1997).

memorandum dated February 27, 1984, O'Connor summarized her proposed standard:

> I must emphasize that I would not apply a "per se" approach in any circumstances. If that does not come through in my draft, I will offer appropriate changes. I have tried to make clear that the three conditions I describe are merely threshold conditions, necessary, but not sufficient, to establish harmful economic effects from the tie. It is only when the three conditions are met that a further inquiry into economic impacts is required under the Rule of Reason. My "different label," in other words, is intended to go with a different mode of analysis. The purpose of the threshold conditions is to avoid the lengthy and cumbersome processes of a trial if it is unnecessary.

Several of O'Connor's colleagues also wrote letters stating their opposition to the continued application of a per se rule to tying. In a letter dated December 28, 1983, Justice Lewis Powell gave Justice Stevens his reactions to an initial draft of the *Jefferson Parish* opinion:

> As you know, I have thought—both when practicing law and since coming to the Court—that the *per se* rule has been unwisely expanded. At least for me, the rule of reason—enabling judgments to be made on the basis of economic effects—is a far more sensible application of the Sherman Act in our free enterprise system. I therefore would be reluctant to join much of your opinion.

In the same vein, in a January 4, 1984 letter to Justice Stevens, then Associate Justice William Rehnquist said "I think this case offers an opportunity to cut back on the broad sweep of the *per se* prohibition against tying, and I am reluctant to join an opinion which passes up that opportunity, to say nothing of one which may broaden its sweep."

Justice Stevens considered but rejected these recommendations, often emphasizing (as his majority opinion ultimately did) fidelity to past Supreme Court decisions that had used the per se nomenclature for tying. Justice O'Connor offered her views in a concurring opinion that called for replacing the per se analytical framework with a structured rule of reason approach. As you see in the reproduction of *Jefferson Parish* above, her reasonableness standard attracted the votes of Chief Justice Warren Burger and Justices Powell and Rehnquist.

Justice Stevens is the only member of the *Jefferson Parish* majority who remains on the Court today and none of the concurring justices remain. Stevens also joined the majority opinion written by Justice Blackmun in the Court's last consideration of tying, *Eastman Kodak Co. v. Image Tech. Servs., Inc.,* 504 U.S. 451, 461–62, 112 S.Ct. 2072, 119 L.Ed.2d 265 (1992). Also joining the *Kodak* majority opinion were Chief Justice Rehnquist and Justices White, Kennedy, and Souter. Justice Scalia wrote a dissent, which was joined by Justices O'Connor and Thomas. One wonders whether the Court, if faced with a tying case in the future, will feel as strongly as Justice Stevens did about standing by the label the Court has applied to tying in the past, especially given its willingness to abandon the per se rule in other, equally long-standing contexts, such as resale price maintenance. *See Leegin* (Casebook, *supra*, Chapter 4).

Justice O'Connor's concurring opinion in *Jefferson Parish* drew on long-standing criticisms of the per se rule against tying. As a practice, literal tying is ubiquitous, and economists have developed many models to explain how it can be pro-competitive. There are also some accepted theories of how it can be anticompetitive, but as was true in the area of resale price maintenance, it has been argued that the presence of both possibilities counsels against use of even a qualified per se rule. In the Sidebar that follows, we examine more particularly the economics of tying, and the controversy that has surrounded its association with the per se rule.

Sidebar 7–3:
The Economics of Tying

As the foregoing material reveals, tying was for a long time treated very simply and harshly under both the Clayton and Sherman Acts. A fundamental economic assumption of that harsh treatment was that a firm engaged in tying was trying to expand or "leverage" its monopoly from one product market, the tying product market, to another market, that of the tied product. In the Court's view, this injured buyers of the tied products and excluded rivals in the sale of the tied product.

In this Sidebar, we discuss how these traditional assumptions were questioned over time and have eroded as a consequence, leaving tying doctrine in a somewhat uncertain state.

The Chicago School Critique

The assumption that tying is almost always anticompetitive came under pointed attack from Chicago School proponents in the late 1950s. *See* Ward S. Bowman, Jr., *Tying Arrangements and the Leverage Problem*, 67 YALE L.J. 19 (1957). Bowman responded in two ways. First, he argued that tying could have pro-competitive uses. He also asserted that the "leverage" idea was largely implausible absent an independent reason to believe that the seller could monopolize the tied product market. If the seller were in fact a monopolist of the tying product, it could maximize its profits by charging the monopolist's price for the tying product, and "tying" could add nothing to that profit. Some explanation other than "leverage" would have to be found. This became known as the "single monopoly profit" theory.

Bowman's critique of tying doctrine has not gone entirely unchallenged, *See*, *e.g.*, Louis Kaplow, *Extension of Monopoly Power Through Leverage*, 85 COLUM. L. REV. 515 (1985), but it has over time had a lasting impact on the economic analysis of tying. It also has eroded support for use of any version of a per se rule, and later commentators, not limited to the Chicago School, who agreed with and built upon his views were cited with approval by the concurring Justices in *Jefferson Parish*. 466 U.S. at 36 (O'Connor, J., concurring), *citing* ROBERT H. BORK, THE ANTITRUST PARADOX 372–74 (1978); PHILLIP AREEDA, ANTITRUST ANALYSIS 735 (3d ed. 1981).

Many tying or bundling examples involve product complements. These are goods that buyers use together, like a computer and a printer, or a printer and ink.* The single monopoly profit issue is raised by any type of exclusivity in the sale of product complements, not simply tying and not simply manufacturer-dealer relationships. (Vertically related sellers produce complements in a special sense: the buyer purchases both the product and distribution services.) The economics of exclusion, and the limitations of the "single monopoly profit" theory, are discussed more extensively below in connection with vertical mergers.

Pro and Anti–Competitive Uses of Tying

As we have already observed, courts traditionally have condemned tying arrangements on the theory that they can harm competition by having collusive or exclusionary effects, and they did so by invoking variants of the per se rule. Although a slim majority of the Supreme Court still clung to the per se rule in *Jefferson Parish*, it is more widely accepted today that tying may have an unusually wide range of economic explanations, some anticompetitive, some procompetitive, and one (price discrimination) with ambiguous economic consequences. As a consequence, its status as a "per se violation" remains unstable, and some have seriously questioned how often tying is likely to lead to anticompetitive effects at all.

Anticompetitive Effects of Tying. Because purchasers from the tying seller must buy both the tying and the tied product, even though they might have preferred to buy only the tying product, or to have purchased the tied product from another supplier, courts concluded that tying can lead to collusive anticompetitive effects. Having to purchase a second, unwanted product is the economic equivalent of being charged a higher price. Likewise, having to forego choice also may be viewed as a collusive effect. These theories of anticompetitive harm, however, were the focus of the Chicago School critique of tying—how could such "forcing" actually benefit the seller of the tying and tied products? If it was in a position to "force," why not simply charge a higher price for the tying product? In raising these questions, the Chicago School "single monopoly profit" theory cast doubt on the validity of the collusive effects view of tying, and invited debate about other possible explanations for the selling firm's use of tying. *See Jefferson Parish Hosp. Dist. No. 2 v. Hyde*, 466 U.S. 2, 36, 104 S.Ct. 1551, 1570–71 (1984) (O'Connor, J., concurring) (observing that any anticompetitive explanation must overcome the single monopoly profit theory).

The "single monopoly profit" critique of the collusive effects theory of tying, however, does not necessarily address the possibility that tying can harm competition as a method of *exclusion* (or, more generally, raising rival's costs), which protects or confers market power. A hypothetical example involving tying illustrates how a monopolist might be able to achieve additional market power through tying.** Suppose that a small

---

* More technically, if the price of a product increases, buyers will purchase less of it, more of its demand substitutes, and less of its demand complements.

** The example is adapted from Dennis W. Carlton & Michael Waldman, *The Strategic Use of Tying to Preserve and Create Market Power in Evolving Industries*, 33 RAND J. ECON. 194 (2002), where it is attributed to Robert Gertner.

resort island has a single hotel. Guests and local residents can eat at the hotel restaurant or at independent local restaurants. If the hotel requires guests to eat at the hotel (bundling or tying the hotel room with its restaurant), then the independent restaurants will lose patronage. If the independent restaurants fail, that will give the hotel dining room the ability to charge a monopoly price to the local residents, even though they do not stay at the hotel.

A key feature of this example is that the tied product (restaurant meals) can be used by buyers who do not use the tying product (hotel rooms). This permits the monopolist of the tying product to exercise market power with a new group of customers, even if the tying product's customers use the tied product in fixed proportions (one night's stay and three restaurant meals).***

In Chapter 6, we examined excerpts from the government's monopolization case against Microsoft. The case also included a claim that Microsoft violated Section 1 of the Sherman Act when it tied its Internet Explorer browser to the Windows operating system, excluding Netscape's competing browser. That claim can be understood in this framework. (We will see how the court resolved the tying claims in our next case excerpt, which follows this Sidebar.) The possibility that computer users could one day employ Netscape's browser (along with Sun's Java programming language) to run applications programs on all computer operating systems (not just Windows) means that in the future, a new group of browser users could arise that would use an Internet browser while sidestepping Microsoft's operating systems monopoly. By tying its own browser to Windows, Microsoft could exclude Netscape from the current market (in which Windows has a monopoly) and, in consequence, from the nascent future market, in which other operating systems would compete with Windows using the browser as a platform on which to run applications programs.**** *See generally* Dennis W. Carlton & Michael Waldman, *The Strategic Use of Tying to Preserve and Create Market Power in Evolving Industries*, 33 RAND J. Econ. 194, 209–12 (2002). For a broader survey of procompetitive and anticompetitive uses of tying, see Dennis W. Carlton & Michael Waldman, *Theories of Tying and Implications for Antitrust* (July 2005) (*available at* http://ssrn.com/abstract= 809304).

Much of the case law has focused on the possible exclusionary harm of tying. By effectively cutting off rival suppliers of the tied product from some or all of their potential customers, tying can reduce competition in the *market for the tied product*. The firm engaged in tying might thereby obtain or maintain power over price with respect to the tied product, as in the resort example. Note, however, that in the Microsoft example, the government successfully argued that tying might also be a method of perpetuating a dominant position in the *market for the tying product*. By

---

*** The possibility of anticompetitive exclusion in markets in which products are used in variable proportions is explored in *Note on the Single Monopoly Profit Theory, infra* at 861.

**** Another possibility, not raised in the case, by which tying the browser to Windows could increase Microsoft's market power would arise if browsers can be used in computers without Windows does not have a monopoly, for example, if browsers can also be used with cell phones that do not run on the Windows operating system. Then it might be possible for Microsoft to exclude Netscape from both markets by excluding it from selling browsers to personal computer users.

tying Internet Explorer, its Internet browser, to its dominant Windows operating system, Microsoft snuffed out the possibility that competing browsers could evolve from being merely Internet browsers into an alternative operating system to Windows. Even though the court of appeals reversed the government's claim that Microsoft attempted to monopolize the alleged browser market, and reversed and remanded the specific tying claim for a variety of reasons we will examine shortly, as we learned in Chapter 6, it affirmed the district court's conclusion that the tying arrangement constituted unjustified exclusionary conduct for purposes of the government's Section 2 Sherman Act monopolization claim. *United States v. Microsoft Corp.*, 253 F.3d 34 (D.C. Cir. 2001).

Tying also may harm competition if it is used as a method of *evading rate regulation. See, e.g., Jefferson Parish*, 466 U.S. at 36 n.4 (O'Connor, J., concurring). A regulated firm that sells both a regulated and an unregulated product can effectively raise the price of the regulated good by tying its sale to that of an unregulated product and charging a high price for the unregulated good (and thus for the bundle). In the usual situation of public utility regulation, we assume that the unregulated firm would charge too high a price by reducing output too much. Regulation then expands output by forcing down the price. If so, evading regulation would lead to an allocative efficiency loss.*****

Procompetitive Uses of Tying. Tying also can promote competition in a number of ways. For example, through tying, a seller can make sure that its product is used with other products that do not degrade the first good's performance. This practice could allow the seller to protect its reputation through *assuring product quality*. This argument was asserted, but seemingly unsupported by the evidence, even in very early cases, such as *IBM* and *International Salt*, but has on occasion proven effective. *See, e.g., Dehydrating Process Co. v. A.O. Smith Corp.*, 292 F.2d 653 (1st Cir.1961). Also, *compare Mozart Co. v. Mercedes–Benz of North America, Inc.*, 833 F.2d 1342,1348–51 (9th Cir. 1987) (accepting "quality control defense" to tying), *with Metrix Warehouse, Inc. v. Daimler–Benz Aktiengesellschaft*, 828 F.2d 1033, 1040–42 (4th Cir. 1987) (rejecting the same defense in connection with the same parties and practices).

Tying also may reduce production or distribution costs when sellers experience *economies of joint production, distribution, and marketing*. Related buyer-side economies sometimes arise in the *development of a new industry*, when it is expensive for buyers to learn how to integrate components. *See, e.g., United States v. Jerrold Elecs. Corp.*, 187 F.Supp. 545 (E.D. Pa. 1960), *aff'd per curiam*, 365 U.S. 567 (1961). Tying can also promote the sale of a system of related products by *preventing excessive markups by the seller of complementary goods*. This procompetitive benefit is closely related to the possible benefit of vertical integration in avoiding double marginalization (transferring inputs at marginal cost). *See Note on Eliminating Double Marginalization, infra.* Tying may also undermine a seller cartel by *facilitating secret price-cutting*.

Ambiguous Competitive Effects—Price Discrimination. Tying can be a means of *price discrimination*, where the term is used here in its economic sense of charging different markups over marginal cost to

---

***** On the other hand, if the regulated price were set at an inefficiently low level, evasion of regulation through tying or otherwise could reduce an allocative efficiency loss.

different customers. If the marginal cost of producing and selling the good to those customers is identical, then price discrimination would occur when those customers are charged different prices. Buyers willing to pay more without cutting back markedly on their purchases are charged a higher markup than buyers unwilling to do so. For price discrimination to be successful, the seller must be able to *sort buyers* into different groups based on their willingness to pay, and *prevent arbitrage*, that is, prevent those buyers able to purchase the product at a low price from reselling it to those forced by the seller to purchase at a higher price.

For example, tying can create price discrimination through *metering*. *See, e.g., Jefferson Parish*, 466 U.S. at 15 n.23, 19 n.30. *See also id.* at 36 n.4 (O'Connor, J., Concurring). Some commentators have suggested that Xerox adopted such a policy in the early days of the photocopier, when copiers required special paper. At that time, Xerox leased its copier machines at a low rental and charged a price for copier paper well in excess of the marginal cost of that paper, arguably tying the two products together by forcing copier users to purchase paper at a high price through Xerox. This policy could be understood as metering. Intensive copier users were likely willing to pay more for a copier than more casual users; if so, Xerox was effectively able to extract a higher price for the copier from intensive users by requiring those buyers to purchase the high volumes of paper they required at a substantial premium relative to the cost of paper.****** A more contemporary example might involve the pricing of printers and toner cartridges. We will revisit the economics of price discrimination in greater detail in Sidebar 7–8.

Figure 7–2:

Summary of Potential Pro- and Anti-competitive Effects of Tying

Anticompetitive Effects of Tying	Pro-Competitive Effects of Tying
• raise prices to consumers or limit their choices (collusive effects) • exclude or impair rival by raising costs, leading to higher consumer prices (exclusionary effects) • evade rate regulation • facilitate price discrimination (as through metering)	• assure product quality • achieve economies through joint production, distribution or marketing • undermine seller cartel by facilitating secret price-cutting • prevent excessive mark-ups by the seller of complementary goods or services • avoid double marginalization • facilitate price discrimination (as through metering)

Conclusion

In this Sidebar we have canvassed some of the most prevalent arguments for and against maintaining a per se rule against ty-

---

****** If the buyer is risk-averse and unsure whether its business will succeed, while the seller is risk neutral, metering could also be a pro-competitive method of allocating risk between the parties.

ing.******* In doing so, we also examined the variety of pro-and anticompetitive uses of tying arrangements. As should be evident, the issue is complex, both legally and economically. On the other hand, the trend has been fairly consistent in recent years, pointing towards greater tolerance for tying arrangements. That trend will likely continue, given the variety of economic justifications for tying arrangements, and the precarious status of the per se rule.

In Chapter 6, we studied portions of the D.C. Circuit's opinion in the government's case against Microsoft. Our earlier excerpt did not include the court's discussion of one of the most challenging issues in the case, the district court's finding that Microsoft had violated Section 1 of the Sherman Act by unlawfully tying Internet Explorer, its Internet browser, to its Windows operating system. *United States v. Microsoft Corp.*, 87 F. Supp. 2d 30 (D.D.C. 2000). Microsoft successfully challenged that finding in the court of appeals.

As you read the excerpt below, consider everything we have read so far about tying, including the discussion in Sidebar 7–3. What was the government and district court's anticompetitive theory with regard to Microsoft's tying? Did the court of appeals reject that theory, or just the district court's use of the per se rule? What were Microsoft's responses and proffered justifications? On what basis did the D.C. Circuit conclude that the per se rule should not be applied? In doing so, how did it account for the majority's decision in *Jefferson Parish*?

UNITED STATES v. MICROSOFT CORP.

United States Court of Appeals for the District of Columbia Circuit, 2001.
253 F.3d 34.

PER CURIAM

* * *

IV. TYING

* * * The District Court concluded that Microsoft's contractual and technological bundling of the IE [Internet Explorer] web browser (the "tied" product) with its Windows operating system ("OS") (the "tying" product) resulted in a tying arrangement that was per se unlawful. We hold that the rule of reason, rather than per se analysis, should govern the legality of tying arrangements involving platform software products. The Supreme Court has warned that " '[i]t is only after considerable experience with certain business relationships that courts classify them as *per se* violations....' " *Broad. Music, Inc. v. CBS*, 441 U.S. 1, 9, 99 S.Ct. 1551, 60 L.Ed.2d 1 (1979) (quoting *United States v. Topco Assocs.*, 405 U.S. 596, 607–08, 92 S.Ct. 1126, 31 L.Ed.2d 515 (1972)). While every "business relationship" will in some sense have unique features, some represent entire, novel categories of dealings. As we shall explain, the arrangement before us is an example of the latter, offering the first up-close look at the technological integration of added

---

******* For an interesting discussion of consumer protection issues raised by tying, see Richard Craswell, *Tying Requirements in Com-* *petitive Markets: The Consumer Protection Issues*, 62 B.U. L. REV. 661 (1982).

functionality into software that serves as a platform for third-party applications. There being no close parallel in prior antitrust cases, simplistic application of per se tying rules carries a serious risk of harm. Accordingly, we vacate the District Court's finding of a per se tying violation and remand the case. Plaintiffs may on remand pursue their tying claim under the rule of reason.

The facts underlying the tying allegation substantially overlap with those set forth in Section II.B in connection with the § 2 monopoly maintenance claim. The key District Court findings are that (1) Microsoft required licensees of Windows 95 and 98 also to license IE as a bundle at a single price; (2) Microsoft refused to allow OEMs to uninstall or remove IE from the Windows desktop; (3) Microsoft designed Windows 98 in a way that withheld from consumers the ability to remove IE by use of the Add/Remove Programs utility; and (4) Microsoft designed Windows 98 to override the user's choice of default web browser in certain circumstances. The court found that these acts constituted a per se tying violation. * * *

There are four elements to a per se tying violation: (1) the tying and tied goods are two separate products; (2) the defendant has market power in the tying product market; (3) the defendant affords consumers no choice but to purchase the tied product from it; and (4) the tying arrangement forecloses a substantial volume of commerce. *See Eastman Kodak Co. v. Image Tech. Servs., Inc.,* 504 U.S. 451, 461–62, 112 S.Ct. 2072, 119 L.Ed.2d 265 (1992); *Jefferson Parish Hosp. Dist. No. 2 v. Hyde,* 466 U.S. 2, 12–18, 104 S.Ct. 1551, 80 L.Ed.2d 2 (1984).

Microsoft does not dispute that it bound Windows and IE in the four ways the District Court cited. Instead it argues that Windows (the tying good) and IE browsers (the tied good) are not "separate products," and that it did not substantially foreclose competing browsers from the tied product market. (Microsoft also contends that it does not have monopoly power in the tying product market, but * * * we uphold the District Court's finding to the contrary.)

We first address the separate-products inquiry, a source of much argument between the parties and of confusion in the cases. Our purpose is to highlight the poor fit between the separate-products test and the facts of this case. We then offer further reasons for carving an exception to the per se rule when the tying product is platform software. * * *

A. Separate–Products Inquiry Under the Per Se Test

The requirement that a practice involve two separate products before being condemned as an illegal tie started as a purely linguistic requirement: unless products are separate, one cannot be "tied" to the other. Indeed, the nature of the products involved in early tying cases * * * led courts either to disregard the separate-products question, or to discuss it only in passing. * * *

The first case to give content to the separate-products test was *Jefferson Parish*. That case addressed a tying arrangement in which a hospital conditioned surgical care at its facility on the purchase of anesthesiological services from an affiliated medical group. The facts were a challenge for casual separate-products analysis because the tied service—anesthesia—was neither intuitively distinct from nor intuitively contained within the tying service—

surgical care. A further complication was that, soon after the Court enunciated the per se rule for tying liability in *International Salt Co.* and *Northern Pacific Railway Co.*, new economic research began to cast doubt on the assumption, voiced by the Court when it established the rule, that " 'tying agreements serve hardly any purpose beyond the suppression of competition.' "

The *Jefferson Parish* Court resolved the matter in two steps. First, it clarified that "the answer to the question whether one or two products are involved" does not turn "on the functional relation between them...." In other words, the mere fact that two items are complements, that "one ... is useless without the other," does not make them a single "product" for purposes of tying law. Second, reasoning that the "definitional question [whether two distinguishable products are involved] depends on whether the arrangement may have the type of competitive consequences addressed by the rule [against tying]," the Court decreed that "no tying arrangement can exist unless there is a sufficient *demand* for the purchase of anesthesiological services separate from hospital services to identify a distinct product market in which it is *efficient* to offer anesthesiological services separately from hospital service."

The Court proceeded to examine direct and indirect evidence of consumer demand for the tied product separate from the tying product. Direct evidence addresses the question whether, when given a choice, consumers purchase the tied good from the tying good maker, or from other firms. * * * Indirect evidence includes the behavior of firms without market power in the tying good market, presumably on the notion that (competitive) supply follows demand. If competitive firms always bundle the tying and tied goods, then they are a single product. Here the Court noted that only 27% of anesthesiologists in markets other than the defendant's had financial relationships with hospitals, and that, unlike radiologists and pathologists, anesthesiologists were not usually employed by hospitals, *i.e.*, bundled with hospital services. With both direct and indirect evidence concurring, the Court determined that hospital surgery and anesthesiological services were distinct goods.

To understand the logic behind the Court's consumer demand test, consider first the postulated harms from tying. The core concern is that tying prevents goods from competing directly for consumer choice on their merits, *i.e.*, being selected as a result of "buyers' independent judgment." With a tie, a buyer's "freedom to select the best bargain in the second market [could be] impaired by his need to purchase the tying product, and perhaps by an inability to evaluate the true cost of either product...." Direct competition on the merits of the tied product is foreclosed when the tying product either is sold only in a bundle with the tied product or, though offered separately, is sold at a bundled price, so that the buyer pays the same price whether he takes the tied product or not. In both cases, a consumer buying the tying product becomes entitled to the tied product; he will therefore likely be unwilling to buy a competitor's version of the tied product even if, making his own price/quality assessment, that is what he would prefer.

But not all ties are bad. Bundling obviously saves distribution and consumer transaction costs. This is likely to be true, to take some examples from the computer industry, with the integration of math co-processors and memory into microprocessor chips and the inclusion of spell checkers in word processors. Bundling can also capitalize on certain economies of scope. A possible example is the "shared" library files that perform OS and browser functions with the very same lines of code and thus may save drive space from the clutter of redundant routines and memory when consumers use both the OS and browser simultaneously. Indeed, if there were no efficiencies from a tie (including economizing on consumer transaction costs such as the time and effort involved in choice), we would expect distinct consumer demand for each individual component of every good. In a competitive market with zero transaction costs, the computers on which this opinion was written would only be sold piecemeal—keyboard, monitor, mouse, central processing unit, disk drive, and memory all sold in separate transactions and likely by different manufacturers.

Recognizing the potential benefits from tying, the Court in *Jefferson Parish* forged a separate-products test that, like those of market power and substantial foreclosure, attempts to screen out false positives under per se analysis. The consumer demand test is a rough proxy for whether a tying arrangement may, on balance, be welfare-enhancing, and unsuited to per se condemnation. In the abstract, of course, there is always direct separate demand for products: assuming choice is available at zero cost, consumers will prefer it to no choice. Only when the efficiencies from bundling are dominated by the benefits to choice for enough consumers, however, will we actually observe consumers making independent purchases. In other words, perceptible separate demand is inversely proportional to net efficiencies. On the supply side, firms without market power will bundle two goods only when the cost savings from joint sale outweigh the value consumers place on separate choice. So bundling by all competitive firms implies strong net efficiencies. If a court finds either that there is no noticeable separate demand for the tied product or, there being no convincing direct evidence of separate demand, that the entire "competitive fringe" engages in the same behavior as the defendant, then the tying and tied products should be declared one product and per se liability should be rejected.

Before concluding our exegesis of *Jefferson Parish*'s separate-products test, we should clarify two things. First, *Jefferson Parish* does not endorse a direct inquiry into the efficiencies of a bundle. Rather, it proposes easy-to-administer proxies for net efficiency. In describing the separate-products test we discuss efficiencies only to explain the rationale behind the consumer demand inquiry. To allow the separate-products test to become a detailed inquiry into possible welfare consequences would turn a screening test into the very process it is expected to render unnecessary.

Second, the separate-products test is not a one-sided inquiry into the cost savings from a bundle. Although *Jefferson Parish* acknowledged that prior lower court cases looked at cost-savings to decide separate products, the Court conspicuously did not adopt that approach in its disposition of the tying arrangement before it. Instead it chose proxies that balance costs savings against reduction in consumer choice.

With this background, we now turn to the separate products inquiry before us. The District Court found that many consumers, if given the option, would choose their browser separately from the OS. Turning to industry custom, the court found that, although all major OS vendors bundled browsers with their OSs, these companies either sold versions without a browser, or allowed OEMs or end-users either not to install the bundled browser or in any event to "uninstall" it. The court did not discuss the record evidence as to whether OS vendors other than Microsoft sold at a bundled price, with no discount for a browserless OS, perhaps because the record evidence on the issue was in conflict.

Microsoft does not dispute that many consumers demand alternative browsers. But on industry custom Microsoft contends that no other firm requires non-removal because no other firm has invested the resources to integrate web browsing as deeply into its OS as Microsoft has. (We here use the term "integrate" in the rather simple sense of converting individual goods into components of a single physical object (*e.g*, a computer as it leaves the OEM, or a disk or sets of disks), without any normative implication that such integration is desirable or achieves special advantages.) Microsoft contends not only that its integration of IE into Windows is innovative and beneficial but also that it requires non-removal of IE. In our discussion of monopoly maintenance we find that these claims fail the efficiency balancing applicable in that context. But the separate-products analysis is supposed to perform its function as a proxy *without* embarking on any direct analysis of efficiency. Accordingly, Microsoft's implicit argument—that in this case looking to a competitive fringe is inadequate to evaluate fully its potentially innovative technological integration, that such a comparison is between apples and oranges—poses a legitimate objection to the operation of *Jefferson Parish*'s separate-products test for the per se rule.

In fact there is merit to Microsoft's broader argument that *Jefferson Parish*'s consumer demand test would "chill innovation to the detriment of consumers by preventing firms from integrating into their products new functionality previously provided by standalone products—and hence, by definition, subject to separate consumer demand." The per se rule's direct consumer demand and indirect industry custom inquiries are, as a general matter, backward-looking and therefore systematically poor proxies for overall efficiency in the presence of new and innovative integration. The direct consumer demand test focuses on historic consumer behavior, likely before integration, and the indirect industry custom test looks at firms that, unlike the defendant, may not have integrated the tying and tied goods. Both tests compare incomparables—the defendant's decision to bundle in the presence of integration, on the one hand, and consumer and competitor calculations in its absence, on the other. If integration has efficiency benefits, these may be ignored by the *Jefferson Parish* proxies. Because one cannot be sure beneficial integration will be protected by the other elements of the per se rule, simple application of that rule's separate-products test may make consumers worse off.

In light of the monopoly maintenance section, obviously, we do not find that Microsoft's integration is welfare-enhancing or that it should be absolved of tying liability. Rather, we heed Microsoft's warning that the separate-products element of the per se rule may not give newly integrated products a fair shake.

B. Per Se Analysis Inappropriate for this Case.

We now address directly the larger question as we see it: whether standard per se analysis should be applied "off the shelf" to evaluate the defendant's tying arrangement, one which involves software that serves as a platform for third-party applications. There is no doubt that "[i]t is far too late in the history of our antitrust jurisprudence to question the proposition that *certain* tying arrangements pose an unacceptable risk of stifling competition and therefore are unreasonable '*per se.*'" *Jefferson Parish,* 466 U.S. at 9, 104 S.Ct. 1551 (emphasis added). But there are strong reasons to doubt that the integration of additional software functionality into an OS falls among these arrangements. Applying per se analysis to such an amalgamation creates undue risks of error and of deterring welfare-enhancing innovation.

* * *

In none of these [previous Supreme Court tying] cases was the tied good physically and technologically integrated with the tying good. Nor did the defendants ever argue that their tie improved the value of the tying product to users *and* to makers of complementary goods. In those cases where the defendant claimed that use of the tied good made the tying good more valuable to users, the Court ruled that the same result could be achieved via quality standards for substitutes of the tied good. Here Microsoft argues that IE and Windows are an integrated physical product and that the bundling of IE APIs* with Windows makes the latter a better applications platform for third-party software. It is unclear how the benefits from IE APIs could be achieved by quality standards for different browser manufacturers. We do not pass judgment on Microsoft's claims regarding the benefits from integration of its APIs. We merely note that these and other novel, purported efficiencies suggest that judicial "experience" provides little basis for believing that, "because of their pernicious effect on competition and lack of *any* redeeming virtue," a software firm's decisions to sell multiple functionalities as a package should be "conclusively presumed to be unreasonable and therefore illegal without elaborate inquiry as to the precise harm they have caused or the business excuse for their use."

* * *

While the paucity of cases examining software bundling suggests a high risk that per se analysis may produce inaccurate results, the nature of the platform software market affirmatively suggests that per se rules might stunt valuable innovation. We have in mind two reasons.

First, as we explained in the previous section, the separate-products test is a poor proxy for net efficiency from newly integrated products. Under per se analysis the first firm to merge previously distinct functionalities (*e.g,* the inclusion of starter motors in automobiles) or to eliminate entirely the need for a second function (*e.g,* the invention of the stain-resistant carpet) risks being condemned as having tied two separate products because at the moment of integration there will appear to be a robust "distinct" market for the tied product. Rule of reason analysis, however, affords the first mover an opportu-

---

* ["API" stands for "Application Programming Interface," and is explained by the court in the excerpt from its opinion that appears in Chapter 6. Eds.]

nity to demonstrate that an efficiency gain from its "tie" adequately offsets any distortion of consumer choice.

The failure of the separate-products test to screen out certain cases of productive integration is particularly troubling in platform software markets such as that in which the defendant competes. Not only is integration common in such markets, but it is common among firms without market power. We have already reviewed evidence that nearly all competitive OS vendors also bundle browsers. Moreover, plaintiffs do not dispute that OS vendors can and do incorporate basic internet plumbing and other useful functionality into their OSs. Firms without market power have no incentive to package different pieces of software together unless there are efficiency gains from doing so. The ubiquity of bundling in competitive platform software markets should give courts reason to pause before condemning such behavior in less competitive markets.

Second, because of the pervasively innovative character of platform software markets, tying in such markets may produce efficiencies that courts have not previously encountered and thus the Supreme Court had not factored into the per se rule as originally conceived. For example, the bundling of a browser with OSs enables an independent software developer to count on the presence of the browser's APIs, if any, on consumers' machines and thus to omit them from its own package. It is true that software developers can bundle the browser APIs they need with their own products, but that may force consumers to pay twice for the same API if it is bundled with two different software programs. It is also true that OEMs can include APIs with the computers they sell, but diffusion of uniform APIs by that route may be inferior. * * * [O]ur qualms about redefining the boundaries of a defendant's product and the possibility of consumer gains from simplifying the work of applications developers makes us question any hard and fast approach to tying in OS software markets.

There may also be a number of efficiencies that, although very real, have been ignored in the calculations underlying the adoption of a per se rule for tying. We fear that these efficiencies are common in technologically dynamic markets where product development is especially unlikely to follow an easily foreseen linear pattern. * * *

These arguments all point to one conclusion: we cannot comfortably say that bundling in platform software markets has so little "redeeming virtue," and that there would be so "very little loss to society" from its ban, that "an inquiry into its costs in the individual case [can be] considered [ ] unnecessary." *Jefferson Parish,* 466 U.S. at 33–34, 104 S.Ct. 1551 (O'Connor, J., concurring). We do not have enough empirical evidence regarding the effect of Microsoft's practice on the amount of consumer surplus created or consumer choice foreclosed by the integration of added functionality into platform software to exercise sensible judgment regarding that entire class of behavior. (For some issues we have no data.) * * * We remand the case for evaluation of Microsoft's tying arrangements under the rule of reason. That rule more freely permits consideration of the benefits of bundling in software markets, particularly those for OSs, and a balancing of these benefits against the costs to consumers whose ability to make direct price/quality tradeoffs in the tied market may have been impaired.

Our judgment regarding the comparative merits of the per se rule and the rule of reason is confined to the tying arrangement before us, where the tying product is software whose major purpose is to serve as a platform for third-party applications and the tied product is complementary software functionality. While our reasoning may at times appear to have broader force, we do not have the confidence to speak to facts outside the record, which contains scant discussion of software integration generally. Microsoft's primary justification for bundling IE APIs is that their inclusion with Windows increases the value of third-party software (and Windows) to consumers. Because this claim applies with distinct force when the tying product is *platform* software, we have no present basis for finding the per se rule inapplicable to software markets generally. Nor should we be interpreted as setting a precedent for switching to the rule of reason every time a court identifies an efficiency justification for a tying arrangement. Our reading of the record suggests merely that integration of new functionality into platform software is a common practice and that wooden application of per se rules in this litigation may cast a cloud over platform innovation in the market for PCs, network computers and information appliances.

* * *

———

The D.C. Circuit's treatment of tying in *Microsoft* is noteworthy in a number of ways. First, the court appears to carve out an exception to the per se rule against tying for "platform software." Whereas the district court viewed itself as bound to apply the per se rule, 87 F. Supp. 2d at 51 ("To the extent that the Supreme Court has spoken authoritatively on these issues * * * this Court is bound to follow its guidance and is not at liberty to extrapolate a new rule governing the tying of software products."), the court of appeals concluded that it was not. Why? How persuasive are its arguments for doing so? What role does its perception of possible efficiencies play in that conclusion? How can its willingness to entertain Microsoft's assertions of efficiencies be squared with the court's conclusion elsewhere in its opinion that Microsoft's election to bundle IE and Windows had an anticompetitive effect and *no* justifications? Moreover, is the court's insistence that the exception be limited to "platform software" persuasive? Is it likely that others will cite the case to support further erosion of the per se rule, such as it is?

Second, do you agree with the court's interpretation and application of *Jefferson Parish's* "two product" test? What did the court of appeals mean when it said that test was fashioned to "screen out false positives under per se analysis"? The court reasoned: "The consumer demand test is a rough proxy for whether a tying arrangement may, on balance, be welfare-enhancing, and unsuited to per se condemnation." Do you agree? How could the consumer demand test accomplish this goal?

In a portion of the opinion not excerpted here, the court provided some specific guidelines for the district court to follow when the case resumed in district court. On remand, however, the federal government and the states concluded that they would not pursue the tying claim. Why might they have reached that decision?

2. EXCLUSIVE DEALING: THE BASIS AND LIMITS OF FORECLOSURE ANALYSIS

The categorization of an exclusionary vertical interbrand restraint as "tying" often is a matter of perspective, and the perspective can have an important impact on the analysis of its effects. The law of tying, as we saw in *Jefferson Parish*, can be read to emphasize the effects of the restraint on consumers: those who purchase the tying product are "forced" to also purchase the tied product. So the anticompetitive effect of tying on consumers can be *collusive*, taking the form of diminished choice or higher prices, since being coerced into buying an unwanted product or service is essentially the same as paying more than you otherwise would have.

But as we learned in Sidebar 7–3, tying also can be viewed as *exclusionary* from the perspective of rival suppliers of the tied product, whose potential customers dwindle in number if the tying arrangement is successful. From their perspective, the tying arrangement is indistinguishable from an "exclusive dealing" arrangement, because for all intents and purposes, its customers, actual or potential, must agree to buy exclusively from the dominant firm engaged in tying. So tying arrangements can be viewed as "exclusive dealing" and so it was in *Jefferson Parish*. The excerpt below from the concurring opinion of Justice O'Connor in *Jefferson Parish* illustrates the point. But while all tying agreements can be viewed in some sense as exclusive dealing agreements, not all exclusive dealing arrangements can be fairly characterized as "tying."

Should the distinction be legally significant? Historically, it has been, even though both tying and exclusive dealing were addressed together in Section 3 of the Clayton Act. (Casebook, Appendix A, *infra*). Before we begin our consideration of the cases, therefore, it is important to note that additional legal fact, which distinguishes the treatment of interbrand restraints from intrabrand ones.

Sidebar 7–4:
Section 3 of the Clayton Act and the Role of "Incipiency"

In 1914, almost a quarter century after the passage of the Sherman Act, Congress passed the second of the U.S.'s principal antitrust statutes, the Clayton Act. As a general matter, the Clayton Act was designed to augment and thereby strengthen the Sherman Act, primarily by more particularly identifying and prohibiting certain categories of conduct— *e.g.*, price discrimination (Section 2), vertical exclusionary practices such as tying and exclusive dealing (Section 3) and mergers (Section 7). In other ways, however, it is more narrow. For example, Sections 2 (price discrimination) and 3 (exclusive dealing and tying), exclude "services" and are limited in scope to sales of goods. (That limitation explains why *Jefferson Parish* was solely a Section 1 Sherman Act case.) The Clayton Act also contains the modern remedial provisions of the federal antitrust laws, authorizing suits by injured persons or firms (Section 4) and both the United States (Section 4A) and the various States (Section 4C), which are discussed at length in Chapter 9.

The Clayton Act goes beyond the Sherman Act in two significant ways. First and most significantly, it uses an "incipiency" standard: conduct is prohibited if its effects "may" tend to be anticompetitive. This incipiency standard can be interpreted in two ways—as a simple issue of timing or as an adjustment to the substantive standard used to prove an offense.

As a simple matter of timing, the incipiency standard can be interpreted as authorizing challenges to certain categories of conduct before they result in actual anticompetitive effects. Such challenges would be based on the prediction that the conduct, if it proceeds, "may" lead to substantial anticompetitive effects. This timing theory of incipiency proceeds on the assumption that it is far easier to enjoin certain kinds of suspect conduct before they cause anticompetitive effects than it is to remedy those effects once they have occurred. Our consideration of mergers in Chapter 5 exemplifies this concept of "incipiency"—mergers can be challenged under Section 7 of the Clayton Act before they are consummated. Without this incipiency provision with respect to mergers, challenge would have to await evidence that the combined firms are actually acting to lessen competition after the merger is completed, or that their combination violated the provisions of Sections 1 and 2 of the Sherman Act, as some of the pre-Clayton act cases held. *See, e.g., Northern Securities Co. v. United States*, 193 U.S. 197 (1904). Under such circumstances, the principal remedy for an anticompetitive merger would be divestiture of assets that have already been commingled and perhaps reorganized—a potentially difficult task.

A second way to implement the "may" language of incipiency alters the substantive legal standard for establishing a violation. For example, recall that in Chapter 5 we discussed the impact of antitrust's "structural" period of merger analysis. During that period it was common for the Supreme Court to cite "trends towards concentration" in an industry as a basis for condemning a merger. Note the rationale: the merger is not unlawful because it will itself lead to higher prices, but because it may in the future lead to higher prices due to the "trend." As we learned in Chapter 5, this approach, which reflected incipiency in the substantive standards for analyzing mergers, has been all but abandoned in the merger context. As we shall see as this Chapter unfolds, serious discussion of such an approach to proving violations of Section 3 also has vanished. In effect, the courts have merged the standards of Section 3 with the rule of reason standard of Section 1 of the Sherman Act. A substantive incipiency standard remains critical today solely as a feature of the analysis of secondary line price discrimination. With respect to other aspects of the Clayton Act, only the timing interpretation of incipiency remains vital.

Even the limited timing interpretation, however, has injected some difficult issues into the antitrust debate. As we will examine in Chapter 9, there is an inherent tension between the remedial provisions of the Clayton Act, particularly Section 4, and its substantive offenses. Section 4 authorizes private parties injured by antitrust violations to sue for treble damages. Demonstrating such injury and damages in connection with Sherman Act offenses, which demand proof of past conduct and demonstrable anticompetitive effects, is reasonably straightforward. But how can a party seeking to invoke the incipiency standards of the Clayton Act demonstrate either concrete "injury" or quantifiable damages?

A solution may be found in Section 16 of the Act, which authorizes suits for injunctive relief against any "threatened loss or damage." Like Section 4, it also authorizes the recovery of attorneys fees by a prevailing plaintiff. Hence, suits to enjoin conduct that "threatens injury" would appear to be a better fit for any incipiency-based challenge.

The Clayton Act also used a different formulation of "restraint of trade"—"substantial lessening of competition," which is used in lieu of "restraint of trade" throughout the Clayton Act. In the material that follows we will examine the scope of the Clayton Act, as well as the degree to which these two features alter the nature of the effects inquiry. As noted above, however, over time, "substantial lessening of competition" and "restraint of trade" have become largely indistinguishable.

Finally, the Clayton Act substituted particularity for the Sherman Act's generality. For example, Section 2 of the Clayton Act specifically addresses price discrimination; Section 7 focuses on mergers and acquisitions—and Section 3, which concerns us here, focuses on interbrand vertical restraints, such as tying and exclusive dealing.

Despite their common prohibition under Section 3, in contrast to tying, exclusive dealing arrangements have never been classified as per se unlawful. Quite to the contrary, their economic utility has long been recognized. Nevertheless, some hostility to exclusive dealing was evident in the early cases, manifested in the form of relatively minimal requirements for proving the requisite anticompetitive effect. Two such cases are particularly worth noting before we look at the more contemporary authorities.

Note on Standard Stations and Tampa Electric

In *Standard Oil Co. v. United States*, 337 U.S. 293 (1949) ("*Standard Stations*"), the government challenged exclusive supply contracts between Standard's wholly owned subsidiary, Standard Stations, and its independent dealers, who sold automotive gasoline and accessories. The challenge was brought under Section 1 of the Sherman Act, as well as Section 3 of the Clayton Act, and sought to enjoin Standard from enforcing those contracts, which prohibited independent gasoline retailers from selling any brand of gasoline other than Standard.

According to the Court, Standard was the largest seller of automotive petroleum products in what was described as "the Western area," comprising Arizona, California, Idaho, Nevada, Oregon, Utah and Washington, and accounted for 23% of all gasoline sales to consumers in that area. Retail service-station sales by Standard's six leading competitors accounted for 42.5% of the total taxable gallonage. The remaining retail sales were divided among more than seventy small companies. Of the total amount of gasoline sold in the Western area, 6.8% was sold through Standard's company-owned stations, and 6.7% was sold to independent dealers subject to the exclusive contracts. It was also "undisputed that Standard's major competitors employ[ed] similar exclusive dealing arrangements" and that only 1.6% of retail outlets in the Western area were "split-pump" stations that sold gasoline from more than one supplier. Exclusive dealing agreements thus could be understood as a feature of competition, coexisting with a competitive market in which suppliers went head to head through company-owned stations and directly vied to "sign up" exclusive dealers.

By a 5–4 margin, the Court condemned the exclusive agreements and enjoined their enforcement. First, however, it distinguished them from tying, recognizing their potential economic utility to buyers and sellers. Note how the following excerpt illustrate's both the Court's traditional hostility to tying and its recognition of economic justifications for exclusive dealing:

In favor of confining the standard laid down by the *International Salt* case to tying agreements, important economic differences may be noted. Tying agreements serve hardly any purpose beyond the suppression of competition. The justification most often advanced in their defense—the protection of the good will of the manufacturer of the tying device—fails in the usual situation because specification of the type and quality of the product to be used in connection with the tying device is protection enough. If the manufacturer's brand of the tied product is in fact superior to that of competitors, the buyer will presumably choose it anyway. The only situation, indeed, in which the protection of good will may necessitate the use of tying clauses is where specifications for a substitute would be so detailed that they could not practicably be supplied. In the usual case only the prospect of reducing competition would persuade a seller to adopt such a contract and only his control of the supply of the tying device, whether conferred by patent monopoly or otherwise obtained, could induce a buyer to enter one. The existence of market control of the tying device, therefore, affords a strong foundation for the presumption that it has been or probably will be used to limit competition in the tied product also.

Requirements contracts, on the other hand, may well be of economic advantage to buyers as well as to sellers, and thus indirectly of advantage to the consuming public. In the case of the buyer, they may assure supply, afford protection against rises in price, enable long-term planning on the basis of known costs, and obviate the expense and risk of storage in the quantity necessary for a commodity having a fluctuating demand. From the seller's point of view, requirements contracts may make possible the substantial reduction of selling expenses, give protection against price fluctuations, and—of particular advantage to a newcomer to the field to whom it is important to know what capital expenditures are justified—offer the possibility of a predictable market. They may be useful, moreover, to a seller trying to establish a foothold against the counterattacks of entrenched competitors. Since these advantages of requirements contracts may often be sufficient to account for their use, the coverage by such contracts of a substantial amount of business affords a weaker basis for the inference that competition may be lessened than would similar coverage by tying clauses, especially where use of the latter is combined with market control of the tying device.

337 U.S. at 305–07.

The Court nevertheless condemned the challenged agreements. It did so based on its conclusion that evidence of the procompetitive justifications was lacking and on its view of the Clayton Act's broad sweep. Interpreting the legislative history of the Act, the Court reasoned that evidence of general injury to competition of the sort expected under a rule of reason analysis under Section 1 of the Sherman Act was not also required to establish a violation of Section 3. Instead, all that was necessary to satisfy Section 3 was "proof that competition has been foreclosed in a substantial share of the line of commerce affected." *Id.* at 314. The Court concluded that the 6.7% foreclosure that resulted from Standard's contracts met this standard of "substantiality." *Id.*

A little more than a decade later, the Court appeared to change course in its interpretation of exclusive dealing in *Tampa Elec. Co. v. Nashville Coal Co.*, 365 U.S. 320 (1961). *Tampa* tested the legality under the Clayton Act of a 20 year requirements agreement entered into between Tampa, a Florida electric utility, and Nashville, a coal supplier. The agreement was reached before Tampa began construction of two new coal-fired power plants. After the plants were completed, but before any coal had actually been delivered under the contract, Nashville notified Tampa that it would not honor the agreement because in its view it was void and unenforceable under the Clayton Act. Tampa initiated the declaratory judgment action, alleging that between the time the contract was concluded and the completion of the plants, the price of coal rose unexpectedly. Nashville sought to relieve itself of the contract's obligations to sell coal to Tampa at what had become unfavorable prices.

The case turned in large part on a debate about the definition of the relevant geographic market for purposes of assessing the impact of the agreements. That debate was resolved when the Supreme Court defined the market more broadly, as was urged by the supplier, and found that it "foreclosed" less than 1% of coal supplies in the defined Southeast region. Distinguishing but not overruling *Standard Stations*, the Court appeared to enhance the burden of proving the requisite anticompetitive effect, describing its approach in terms akin to a rule of reason analysis under Section 1:

> * * * [T]he competition foreclosed by the contract must be found to constitute a substantial share of the relevant market. That is to say, the opportunities for other traders to enter into or remain in that market must be significantly limited as was pointed out in *Standard Oil Co. v. United States, supra.* There the impact of the requirements contracts was studied in the setting of the large number of gasoline stations—5,937 or 16% of the retail outlets in the relevant market—and the large number of contracts, over 8,000, together with the great volume of products involved. This combination dictated a finding that "Standard's use of the contracts (created) just such a potential clog on competition as it was the purpose of § 3 to remove" where, as there, the affected proportion of retail sales was substantial. 337 U.S. at 314. * * *

> To determine substantiality in a given case, it is necessary to weigh the probable effect of the contract on the relevant area of effective competition, taking into account the relative strength of the parties, the proportionate volume of commerce involved in relation to the total volume of commerce in the relevant market area, and the probable immediate and future effects which pre-emption of that share of the market might have on effective competition therein. It follows that a mere showing that the contract itself involves a substantial number of dollars is ordinarily of little consequence.

365 U.S. at 328–29.

Some commentary has argued that *Standard Stations* utilized a "quantitative substantiality" test inspired by the Supreme Court's narrow reading of the Clayton Act's legislative history, whereas *Tampa* employs a "qualitative substantiality" test more akin to the rule of reason. *See* ABA SECTION OF ANTITRUST LAW,

ANTITRUST LAW DEVELOPMENTS 212–13 (6th ed. 2007). Yet, *Tampa*, itself, attempts to distinguish *Standard Stations* factually, arguing simply that the "less than 1%" foreclosure in *Tampa* was insufficiently substantial. That would appear to be an equally mechanical "quantitative" test. More importantly, perhaps, *Tampa's* arguably generous reading of *Standard Stations* appears to sidestep the facts, noted above, that the retail gasoline business was vigorously competitive, and that exclusive dealing agreements were prevalent, suggesting that they had been selected as part of competitive, not anticompetitive, strategies. The final paragraph of the quoted excerpt, however, undeniably resonates with a rule of reason type analysis.

Five years after *Tampa*, the Supreme Court arguably returned to greater scrutiny of even very low levels of market foreclosure. In *FTC v. Brown Shoe Co.*, 384 U.S. 316 (1966), the Court upheld an FTC decision under Section 5 of the FTC Act, (Appendix A, *infra*), objecting to exclusive dealing contracts by a shoe manufacturer that accounted for less than 1% of national shoe sales. As we shall see, the foreclosure levels that concerned the Court in *Standard Stations* and *Brown Shoe* would raise little or no concern under contemporary standards. Our task is to explain why, and to understand the methodology that informs the modern analysis of exclusive dealing.

––––––––––

We now turn again to *Jefferson Parish*, after which we will consider a modern exemplar of exclusive dealing analysis in *Omega Environmental*. As you read *Jefferson Parish*, contrast it with the excerpts you have just read from *Standard Stations* and *Tampa*, and when you read *Omega*, compare it with the *Jefferson Parish* concurrence. What differences do you see in the analytical approach laid out in each case? Would *Omega Environmental's* approach also work for tying arrangements? Why do you think tying has been subjected to a greater degree of scrutiny than exclusive dealing? Should it continue to be?

In each case you should also consider the nature and purpose of the distribution strategy that is under examination. Why might Jefferson Parish Hospital have entered into an exclusive supply contract with a group of anesthesiologists? Why might the anesthesiologists have agreed to the contract? What alternative strategies might the hospital have pursued?

Finally, recall from the beginning of Chapter 6 the modern economics of exclusion. Is "foreclosure" analysis consistent with the economic framework discussed there?

JEFFERSON PARISH HOSPITAL DISTRICT NO. 2 v. HYDE

Supreme Court of the United States, 1984.
466 U.S. 2, 104 S.Ct. 1551, 80 L.Ed.2d 2.

[The facts of the case are reproduced *supra*, at 794 Eds.]

Justice O'CONNOR, with whom the Chief Justice, Justice POWELL, and Justice REHNQUIST join, concurring in the judgment.

* * *

IV

Whether or not the hospital-Roux contract is characterized as a tie between distinct products, the contract unquestionably does constitute exclusive dealing. Exclusive-dealing arrangements are independently subject to scrutiny under § 1 of the Sherman Act, and are also analyzed under the rule of reason.*

The hospital-Roux arrangement could conceivably have an adverse effect on horizontal competition among anesthesiologists, or among hospitals. Dr. Hyde * * * may have grounds to complain that the exclusive contract stifles horizontal competition and therefore has an adverse, albeit indirect, impact on consumer welfare even if it is not a tie.

Exclusive-dealing arrangements may, in some circumstances, create or extend market power of a supplier or the purchaser party to the exclusive-dealing arrangement, and may thus restrain horizontal competition. Exclusive dealing can have adverse economic consequences by allowing one supplier of goods or services unreasonably to deprive other suppliers of a market for their goods, or by allowing one buyer of goods unreasonably to deprive other buyers of a needed source of supply. In determining whether an exclusive-dealing contract is unreasonable, the proper focus is on the structure of the market for the products or services in question—the number of sellers and buyers in the market, the volume of their business, and the ease with which buyers and sellers can redirect their purchases or sales to others. Exclusive dealing is an unreasonable restraint on trade only when a significant fraction of buyers or sellers are frozen out of a market by the exclusive deal. When the sellers of services are numerous and mobile, and the number of buyers is large, exclusive-dealing arrangements of narrow scope pose no threat of adverse economic consequences. To the contrary, they may be substantially procompetitive by ensuring stable markets and encouraging long term, mutually advantageous business relationships.

At issue here is an exclusive dealing arrangement between a firm of four anesthesiologists and one relatively small hospital. There is no suggestion that East Jefferson Hospital is likely to create a "bottleneck" in the availability of anesthesiologists that might deprive other hospitals of access to needed anesthesiological services, or that the Roux associates have unreasonably narrowed the range of choices available to other anesthesiologists in search of a hospital or patients that will buy their services. * * * Even without engaging in a detailed analysis of the size of the relevant markets we may readily conclude that there is no likelihood that the exclusive dealing arrangement challenged here will either unreasonably enhance the hospital's market position relative to other hospitals, or unreasonably permit Roux to acquire power relative to other anesthesiologists. Accordingly, this exclusive-dealing arrangement must be sustained under the rule of reason.

* * *

---

* As noted in Sidebar 7–4, because only services were involved, Section 3 of the Clayton Act was inapplicable. Eds.

According to the *Jefferson Parish* concurrence, under what circumstances could an exclusive dealing arrangement be anticompetitive? What factors would have to be evaluated in order to reach that conclusion? What factors would tend to mitigate any such effects? Why did the concurring Justices conclude that the facts in *Jefferson Parish* did not present an anticompetitive example of exclusive dealing?

As we turn to *Omega Environmental*, note the court's reading of *Tampa* and *Jefferson Parish*. Do you agree with the Ninth Circuit's reading of the cases? How does it handle the overlapping provisions of Section 1 of the Sherman Act and Section 3 of the Clayton Act? Do you agree with its reasoning? Its conclusions? What specific factors does the court consider relevant in determining whether the arrangements in question were anticompetitive? What function the exclusive dealing agreements played for the parties, and any alternatives they might have pursued? Finally, what evidence do you see if the more modern economic analysis, as opposed to the more traditional "foreclosure" approach?

OMEGA ENVIRONMENTAL, INC. v. GILBARCO, INC.

United States Court of Appeals for the Ninth Circuit, 1997.
127 F.3d 1157.

Before: WRIGHT, PREGERSON and THOMPSON, Circuit Judges.

EUGENE A. WRIGHT, Circuit Judge.

In this complex antitrust case we must decide, among other issues, whether the district court erred in submitting to the jury the plaintiffs' Clayton Act § 3 exclusive dealing and other state law claims.

I

Background

Manufacturers of petroleum dispensing equipment[1] sell their products, both directly and through authorized distributors, to the owners of retail gasoline outlets, including major oil companies, independent business persons ("jobbers"), national and regional convenience store chains, and independent regional oil companies. Five manufacturers—Gilbarco, Dresser Wayne, Tokheim, Schlumberger, and Bennett—currently compete for these sales in the United States.

Larger customers, such as the major oil companies and national convenience store chains, generally purchase their dispensers directly from the manufacturers through annually negotiated contracts. Major oil companies often negotiate prices for their affiliated jobbers, but the jobbers are not required to purchase their dispensers from their major oil company's principal supplier. Smaller customers typically purchase their dispensers from the approximately 500 authorized dispenser distributors. Although these distributors can and do sell the dispensing equipment of each manufacturer, each is the authorized dispenser distributor of only one manufacturer.

---

1. "Petroleum dispensing equipment" includes dozens of products, from the canopies that protect motorists from the rain, to the vapor recovery systems that capture escaping fumes. Only the retail dispensers are here at issue.

Dispenser manufacturers compete for sales at major oil companies and industry trade shows and during the annual negotiations of their contracts with the major oil companies. Customers purchasing either directly or through authorized distributors typically seek competitive bids before making their purchases. It is undisputed that competition among distributors is intense.

Defendant Gilbarco, Inc. is the market leader in product innovation and improvement, and its products are widely recognized as among the best in the industry. It also leads in sales, capturing roughly 55% of the domestic market for dispensers in 1995. Approximately one-third of its dispenser sales are made directly to end users while the remaining two-thirds are through authorized distributors. These percentages vary greatly among dispenser manufacturers. * * *

Gilbarco has some 120 authorized distributors operating under its standard form "Domestic Distributor Agreement." The agreements have an initial term of one year and are thereafter expressly terminable by either party, without cause and without penalty, on 60 days notice.

Plaintiff Omega Environmental, Inc. was organized in 1991. It introduced no manufacturing capacity to the industry, but instead proposed to develop a national service and distribution network by purchasing existing concerns. This network would provide "one-stop shopping" to consumers of petroleum dispensers and related equipment. Each Omega distributor would offer multiple product lines, and the network would engage in consolidated purchasing from manufacturers. To that end, Omega targeted for acquisition a number of existing distributors and servicers, including two authorized Gilbarco distributors, plaintiffs ATS–Omega ("ATS") and Kelley–Omega ("Kelley").

In December 1993, in response to Omega's introduction of a distribution strategy at odds with its own, Gilbarco had internal meetings and met separately with its Distributor Advisory Council and Omega representatives. In February 1994, Gilbarco notified each of its authorized distributors that it intended to "continue to do business with service station equipment distributors who [s]ell only the Gilbarco line of retail dispensers." Accordingly, it notified Kelley, acquired by Omega in 1993, that its distributorship agreement would not be renewed. In April 1994, one month after Omega purchased ATS, Gilbarco gave ATS 60 days notice that it was terminating their agreement. This suit followed.

* * *

III

ANALYSIS

* * *

The main antitrust objection to exclusive dealing is its tendency to "foreclose" existing competitors or new entrants[4] from competition in the covered portion of the relevant market during the term of the agreement.

---

4. Plaintiffs cast their argument in terms of "entry barriers," while Gilbarco discusses "foreclosure from the relevant market." Aside from the status of the allegedly affected competitors, *i.e.*, incumbent firms or new entrants, we perceive little meaningful difference.

There are, however, well-recognized economic benefits to exclusive dealing arrangements, including the enhancement of interbrand competition. And, as then-Judge Breyer noted, in the analogous context of requirements contracts, "virtually *every* contract to buy 'forecloses' or 'excludes' alternative sellers from *some* portion of the market, namely the portion consisting of what was bought." *Barry Wright Corp. v. ITT Grinnell Corp.*, 724 F.2d 227, 236 (1st Cir.1983). We thus analyze challenges to exclusive dealing arrangements under the antitrust rule of reason. * * * [S]*ee Tampa Electric Co. v. Nashville Coal Co.*, 365 U.S. 320, 327 (1961). Only those arrangements whose "probable" effect is to "foreclose competition in a substantial share of the line of commerce affected" violate Section 3. *Tampa Elec.*, 365 U.S. at 327.

The parties agree that the plaintiffs have correctly defined the relevant market as the "the sale of retail gasoline dispensers from manufacturers in the United States." Plaintiffs contend, however, that Gilbarco's policy forecloses from competition 24% of the available *distributors*. The focus on this subset of the relevant market is misplaced:

> The foreclosure effect, if any, depends on the market share involved. The relevant market for this purpose includes the full range of selling opportunities reasonably open to rivals, namely, all the product and geographic sales they may readily compete for, using easily convertible plants and marketing organizations.

2A Phillip E. Areeda *et al.*, *Antitrust Law* ¶ 570b1 at 278 (1995). * * *

The foreclosed market, in purely quantitative terms, is more accurately described as the percentage of Gilbarco's total market share sold through its authorized distributors. Seventy percent of Gilbarco's total dispenser sales are through distributors, and it captured 55% of the total market in 1995. Construing this evidence in the plaintiffs' favor, the jury could reasonably have concluded that Gilbarco's policy foreclosed roughly 38% of the relevant market for sales [70% of 55% Eds.]. Although 38% appears significant, we conclude that it "considerably overstates the size of the foreclosure and its likely anticompetitive effect for several reasons."

First, exclusive dealing arrangements imposed on distributors rather than end-users are generally less cause for anticompetitive concern. If competitors can reach the ultimate consumers of the product by employing existing or potential alternative channels of distribution, it is unclear whether such restrictions foreclose from competition *any* part of the relevant market.

The record contains undisputed evidence that direct sales to end-users are an alternative channel of distribution in this market. Gilbarco, Dresser Wayne, Tokheim, Schlumberger and Bennett respectively make 30%, 73%, 35%, 15%, and 15% of their sales without the aid of distributors. The plaintiffs' own expert testified that these direct purchases fall within the relevant market.

The record also contains undisputed evidence of potential alternative sources of distribution. Existing companies, such as the service contractors that regularly sell and service petroleum dispensing equipment, can and do become authorized dispenser distributors. ATS, for example, was an ASC before becoming an authorized Gilbarco distributor, and neither it nor Kelley had been distributors prior to becoming Gilbarco distributors. Their own experiences refute their theory.

Contrary to plaintiffs' contention, these alternatives are relevant to assessing market foreclosure. These alternatives eliminate substantially any foreclosure effect Gilbarco's policy might have. Omega nonetheless complains that they are inadequate substitutes for the existing distributors: "[A]lmost all [of] the 500 existing distributors—who have proven finances, abilities and customer relationships—are restricted by exclusive dealing." The short answer is that the antitrust laws were not designed to equip the plaintiffs' hypothetical competitor with Gilbarco's legitimate competitive advantage. Competitors are free to sell directly, to develop alternative distributors, or to compete for the services of the existing distributors. Antitrust laws require no more.

Second, the short duration and easy terminability of these agreements negate substantially their potential to foreclose competition. Because *all* of Gilbarco's distributors are available within one year, and *most* (90% according to the plaintiffs) are available on 60 days notice, a competing manufacturer need only offer a better product or a better deal to acquire their services.

Plaintiffs' expert opined that no distributor would abandon the Gilbarco line for an untested product with no reputation. We agree with the unremarkable proposition that a competitor with a proven product and strong reputation is likely to enjoy success in the marketplace, but reject the notion that this is anticompetitive. It is the essence of competition.

Nor did plaintiffs produce credible evidence to support their contention that Gilbarco's policy actually deterred entry into this market. The actual entry and expansion of Schlumberger in 1991, through the purchase of a small dispenser manufacturer, Southwest, demonstrate the contrary. The record shows that Schlumberger has built a substantial distribution network since it entered the market. * * *

Our discussion of the mitigating effect of the contracts' short duration and easy terminability also disposes of plaintiffs' contention that the agreements harm competition by facilitating tacit price coordination among dispenser manufacturers. They argue, essentially, that exclusive dealing limits the ability of distributors to extract lower prices from manufacturers by forcing the manufacturers to bid against each other. If the policy facilitates collusion by limiting the distributors' ability to obtain better prices, it does so in most cases for no more than 60 days.

Nor are we persuaded that a jury could reasonably infer probable injury to competition even in this highly concentrated market where the undisputed evidence shows increasing output, decreasing prices, and significantly fluctuating market shares among the major manufacturers.

We conclude that, even construed in the light most favorable to Omega, the evidence presented did not support the jury's verdict. The district court erred by denying Gilbarco's motion for judgment as a matter of law on the Clayton Act claim.

* * *

Judge Pregerson dissented from the court's conclusion that the district court erred in denying Gilbarco's motion for judgment as a matter of law on the Clayton Act § 3 claim. First, he argued that *Tampa* and *Jefferson Parish* require examination of four critical factors: "(1) the dominance of the seller; (2) the existence of an industry-wide practice of exclusive dealing; (3) the proportion of affected commerce in comparison to the entire market; and (4) the probable effect immediately and in the future of the exclusive dealing, including effects on the ability of the consumer to change products." 127 F.3d at 1170. In his view the majority "shortchanged" the required analysis by adopting a blanket presumption that restrictions on distributors should be treated more leniently from end-users, and that short contract length and easy terminability mitigate any potential anti-competitive effects of exclusive dealing. *Id.* at 1170–71. Do you agree with these criticisms of the majority? What was its rationale for these two assumptions? How were they supported?

Here is an excerpt from the remainder of Judge Pregerson's dissenting opinion:

PREGERSON, Circuit Judge, dissenting.

* * *

A fair reading of the extensive trial record shows more than substantial evidence to support each element of a Clayton Act § 3 claim.

Omega presented evidence to establish the following:

- Gilbarco dominates the retail petroleum dispenser market.

- The number of established distributors of retail petroleum dispensers in the United States is limited to five hundred.

- Gilbarco uses exclusive dealing arrangements to prevent its distributors from carrying any competing brands of retail petroleum dispensers.

- Gilbarco's use of exclusive dealing arrangements forecloses 38% of the total retail petroleum dispenser market.

- Gilbarco's use of exclusive dealing arrangements creates entry barriers for new manufacturers of retail petroleum dispensers.

- Gilbarco's use of exclusive dealing arrangements inflates the prices at which existing manufacturers sell retail petroleum dispensers to their distributors.

These facts constitute substantial evidence in support of the jury's verdict finding Gilbarco liable for violating § 3 of the Clayton Act.

I. BACKGROUND

A. *The United States Market for Retail Petroleum Dispensers*

A few firms manufacture the vast majority of the retail petroleum fuel dispensers sold in the United States. These firms are Gilbarco, Dresser–

Wayne, Tokheim, and Schlumberger. Gilbarco has 55% of the market, Dresser–Wayne has 18%, Tokheim has 16.1%, and Schlumberger has 7.7%. Omega's expert * * * testified that the retail petroleum dispenser industry is an oligopoly dominated by Gilbarco, with Dresser–Wayne and Tokheim being the other two significant manufacturers. In the past, several manufacturers of retail petroleum dispensers attempted and failed to enter the retail petroleum dispenser market in the United States because they could not obtain or create distributors.

* * *

Gilbarco prohibits its distributors from carrying more than one brand of retail petroleum dispenser. Dresser–Wayne and Tokheim also have a policy of allowing their distributors to carry only one brand of retail petroleum dispenser. Gilbarco's standard contract with its distributors has an initial term of one year and is terminable on sixty days notice.

B. Omega's Entry

* * *

Important in [Omega's] * * * one-stop shopping idea was recruiting distributors who could install the petroleum dispensers and service them over a long period of time. To this end, Omega contacted existing distributors of retail petroleum dispensers. One such distributor joined the Omega network because he believed he could purchase parts from Omega "at a very small markup cost ... as opposed to paying fifteen or twenty percent markup."

Gilbarco distributors who only carried one line of retail petroleum dispenser became worried about the possible effects of Omega's proposed venture on their businesses. One Gilbarco distributor testified at trial that he did not want to face competition from Omega as a company that could offer more than one line of equipment, charge cheaper prices, and be the "Walmart" of the industry. This distributor was concerned that Omega distributors would gain sales at his expense by offering more choices to customers and "play[ing] one ... manufacturer [of retail petroleum dispensers] off against another to get lower prices."

A second Gilbarco distributor wrote a letter to Gilbarco stating the following: "I feel that a Gilbarco distributor purchased by Omega should be cancelled immediately. I repeat: They are very dangerous."

C. Retaliation Against Omega

On December 7, 1993, representatives of Omega met with representatives of Gilbarco. In the December meeting, Omega disclosed that it planned to issue catalogs and "provide one-stop shopping for customers."

Gilbarco reacted negatively to the prospect of interbrand price competition for retail petroleum dispensers. Gilbarco's sales manager for North America testified that he feared that Omega might become a large enough distributor to insist upon volume discounts. Gilbarco also did not want Omega to publish throughout the marketplace the lower prices that Gilbarco was able to offer to major oil companies.

At a Gilbarco Distributor Advisory Council ("DAC")[3] meeting held on December 15, 1993, Gilbarco representatives expressed their concerns about Omega. Distributors at the Gilbarco DAC meeting stated that it would be difficult to compete against Omega. These distributors asked Gilbarco to cancel any distributorship that became a part of Omega.

Gilbarco reminded distributors of its exclusive dealing policy in a February 8, 1994, memorandum stating:

> [I]t is [Gilbarco's] general intention to continue to do business with service station equipment distributors who:
>
> — Sell only the Gilbarco line of retail dispensers;
>
> — Are not owned by competing companies; and
>
> — Sell in an export market only with the agreement of the local Gilbarco distributor.

* * *

III.   SUBSTANTIAL EVIDENCE OF CLAYTON ACT § 3 VIOLATION

A.   *First Two Tampa Factors: Defining the Line of Commerce and Area of Competition*

In this case, the first two *Tampa* factors—the line of commerce and area of competition—consist of the sale of retail gasoline dispensers in the United States *to small independent buyers who purchase retail petroleum dispensers from distributors*. The majority incorrectly defines the line of commerce and area of competition as the sale of *all* retail petroleum dispensers from manufacturers. To understand why the relevant market does not include *all* sales of retail petroleum dispensers, it is important to understand the retail petroleum dispenser market.

The sale of retail petroleum dispensers to end-users occurs in two ways: (1) direct sales from manufacturers of petroleum dispensers to major oil companies and large convenience store chains; and (2) sales from distributors of petroleum dispensers to independent gasoline station owners, regional petroleum marketers, and small oil companies ("small independent buyers").

Major oil companies purchase retail petroleum dispensers from more than one manufacturer. The major oil companies want to have more than one supplier to ensure an alternate source of petroleum dispensing products. Gilbarco gives some major oil companies discounts on retail petroleum dispensers.

Small independent buyers, in contrast, purchase retail petroleum dispensers from a single distributor and develop long-term relationships with that distributor. The key reason for the small independent buyers to stay with a particular distributor is that they want a single reliable source of service and products. * * *

As a result of the small independent buyers' reliance on particular distributors, small independent buyers normally do not change distributors.

---

3. Gilbarco communicates to its distributors through its DAC. The other major manu-facturers of retail petroleum dispensers also use DACs.

For example, the customer base of one Gilbarco distributor has not changed significantly in the last forty years.

This evidence shows that the sale of retail petroleum dispensers to small independent buyers is an entirely different market from the sale of retail petroleum dispensers to major oil companies. Unlike major oil companies, small independent buyers have strong reasons to buy from a single distributor. Nor is there any evidence in the record to suggest that small independent buyers have the option of purchasing retail petroleum dispensers directly from manufacturers such as Gilbarco. Gilbarco's own reluctance to allow discounts and dissemination of price information to small independent buyers—though discounts and price dissemination were common for major oil companies—shows that Gilbarco itself sought to maintain two distinct markets. By failing to recognize the substantial evidence in the record showing this bifurcation in the retail petroleum dispenser market, the majority incorrectly defines the line of commerce and area of competition.

B.   Third Tampa Factor: Substantial Foreclosure

1.   Dominance of Gilbarco

In the present case, the parties do not dispute that Gilbarco dominates the retail petroleum industry with a fifty-five percent market share. The three major manufacturers of retail petroleum dispensers in the United States—Gilbarco, Dresser–Wayne, and Tokheim—have almost ninety percent of the market. * * *

2.   Industry–Wide Practice of Exclusive Dealing

The parties do not dispute that Gilbarco, Dresser–Wayne, and Tokheim use exclusive dealing arrangements in the retail petroleum dispenser market by prohibiting their distributors from selling competing brands of retail petroleum dispensers. Because Gilbarco, Dresser–Wayne, and Tokheim control almost ninety percent of the United States market, their common use of exclusive dealing arrangements constitutes an industry-wide practice.

3.   Proportion of Affected Commerce in Comparison to Entire Market

The proportion of the market for retail petroleum dispensers affected by Gilbarco's exclusive dealing policies is significant. The majority recognizes that Gilbarco's exclusive dealing to distributors affected thirty-eight percent of all retail petroleum dispensers sold in the United States. If we look to the relevant market—the sale of retail petroleum dispensers to small independent buyers—the percentage is even higher. A market foreclosure of thirty-eight percent or more is enough to make a § 3 Clayton Act violation a possibility.

4.   Probable Effect of the Exclusive Dealing

The majority accords considerable weight to its determination that Omega failed to prove that Gilbarco's exclusive dealing arrangements *actually* deterred entry into the market for retail petroleum dispensers. Although an inquiry into actual effect is necessary, *Tampa* makes clear that a Clayton Act § 3 claim only requires proof of the *"probable* effect of the contract on the relevant area of effective competition." There is no requirement that *actual* deterrence be proved.

The majority states that the jury could not reasonably infer probable injury to competition "where the undisputed evidence shows increasing output, decreasing prices, and significantly fluctuating market shares among the major manufacturers." The majority's reasoning is not persuasive. Even assuming that the evidence at trial showed increasing output, the jury reasonably could have inferred probable injury to competition due to the substantial evidence of price distortion and entry barriers created by Gilbarco's exclusive dealing arrangements.

a. Price Distortion

Omega presented evidence to show that Gilbarco's exclusive dealing arrangements prevented the prices of retail petroleum dispensers from falling as much as they would have without the exclusive dealing arrangements. The exclusive dealing arrangements for retail petroleum dispensers allowed manufacturers of retail petroleum dispensers to avoid intense price competition among themselves. Moreover, despite some decrease in prices, the prices of retail petroleum dispensers did not change much over time suggesting price stagnation.

[Plaintiff's expert] * * * testified that under certain circumstances, exclusive dealing may have pro-competitive effects, *e.g.,* preventing free-riding and focusing a distributor's attention on a particular product. [He] * * * concluded, however, that the exclusive dealing arrangements in the retail petroleum dispenser industry have no such pro-competitive effects.

b. Entry Barriers

Omega also presented substantial evidence that Gilbarco's exclusive dealing arrangements caused actual as well as probable injury by shutting out potential competitors. * * *

* * *

* * * [T]he only effective means of selling retail petroleum distributors to small independent buyers is through an existing distributor. There are only five hundred established distributors of retail petroleum dispensers in the United States. New entrants into the retail petroleum dispenser market need to gain access to this closed group of five hundred established distributors in order to sell to small independent buyers.

In order to gain access to this group of five hundred distributors, a new entrant theoretically has two options: (1) have existing distributors carry the new entrant's brand in addition to the brand of retail petroleum dispenser they already carry or (2) have distributors switch from their old brand of retail petroleum dispenser to the new entrant's brand. For the reasons stated below, neither of these options is a practical possibility.

i) Carrying More Than One Brand

Exclusive dealing eliminates the possibility of distributors carrying more than a single brand of retail petroleum dispenser. * * *

ii) Switching Brands

It is also difficult for existing distributors to switch brands. Although a Gilbarco distributor has the contractual right to terminate his exclusive dealing arrangement with Gilbarco on sixty days notice and switch to a new manufacturer, this contractual right means little.* * *

* * * [T]he short term and easy terminability provisions of the exclusive dealing arrangements are irrelevant. No distributor would ever terminate voluntarily for fear of losing its customers and ultimately its business.

* * *

* * * Omega presented substantial evidence at trial that Gilbarco's exclusive dealing arrangements prevented distributors from carrying more than one brand of retail petroleum dispenser or from switching brands. Thus, Gilbarco's exclusive dealing arrangements had the anticompetitive effect of preventing movement of distributors between manufacturers.

In summary, Omega presented substantial evidence showing that (1) the line of commerce is retail petroleum dispensers; (2) the relevant market is the sale of retail petroleum dispensers to small independent buyers; (3) Gilbarco dominated the relevant market; (4) exclusive dealing is widely practiced in the relevant market; (5) the proportion of the relevant market affected by Gilbarco's exclusive dealing arrangements is very significant; and (6) Gilbarco's use of exclusive dealing arrangements in the relevant market causes serious anticompetitive effects by keeping the price of retail petroleum dispensers artificially high and creating entry barriers to the relevant market for new entrants.

Looking at the totality of the circumstances as we are required to do under *Tampa*, [and] *Jefferson Parish* * * *, I believe that the record contains substantial evidence to support the jury's conclusion that Gilbarco's use of exclusive dealing arrangements tends to suppress competition in the relevant market and therefore violates the Rule of Reason.

* * *

Do you agree with the majority or the dissent in *Omega Environmental*? Why? Which of the majority's conclusions does the dissent take issue with? Is the split in the panel driven by the judges' differing views of the law, the facts, or the economics of exclusive dealing? What was the dissent's economic theory of harm? The dissent concludes that Gilbarco's use of exclusive dealing agreements could raise barriers to entry for manufacturers of retail petroleum dispensers and that the result was increased prices. Did the dissenting judge think that the exclusive dealing raised the distribution costs of rival manufacturers and thus allowed Gilbarco to exercise some power over price? Did he think the agreements facilitated better tacit coordination among the manufacturers?

How relevant should evidence of actual anticompetitive effect be in exclusive dealing cases, as opposed to evidence of "foreclosure"? Is substantial foreclosure a sufficient basis for inferring anticompetitive effects, such as higher prices? Would the incipiency standard of Section 3 of the Clayton Act justify making such an inference? Should the absence of any evidence of actual anticompetitive effects be sufficient to defeat such an inference drawn from some percentage of foreclosure? What evidence is cited in the opinions on this point and to what end?

One point that divided the majority and the dissent concerns the legal significance of the duration and ease of termination of the exclusive contracts. Who makes the better point here?

Judge Richard A. Posner of the Seventh Circuit U.S. Court of Appeals took the position in his 1976 monograph that exclusive dealing agreements that are of short duration or that readily can be canceled cannot have any significant exclusionary effect. RICHARD A. POSNER, ANTITRUST LAW: AN ECONOMIC PERSPECTIVE 201–02 (1976) ("Whether . . . [an exclusive dealing] contract will have any exclusionary effect depends on its duration."). After his appointment to the bench, he later wrote that position into the law of exclusive dealing in *Roland Mach. Co. v. Dresser Indus., Inc.*, 749 F.2d 380, 394 (7th Cir. 1984), which the majority cited and relied upon in *Omega Environmental*, 127 F.3d at 1163. *See also Thompson Everett, Inc. v. National Cable Advertising, L.P.*, 57 F.3d 1317, 1326 (4th Cir. 1995)(holding exclusive dealing agreements of a one year duration to be presumptively lawful); *U.S. Healthcare, Inc. v. Healthsource, Inc.*, 986 F.2d 589, 596 (1st Cir. 1993) (where exclusive dealing contracts could be terminated on 30 days' notice, any constraint on competition was minimal).

Professor Herbert Hovenkamp would qualify the simple short duration exception, however, by also requiring that there be no apparent impediments to switching. 11 HERBERT HOVENKAMP, ANTITRUST LAW ¶ 1821d3, at 185 (2d ed. 2005)("[E]ven a high foreclosure percentage will not exclude competition if the period covered by the exclusive dealing arrangement is short *and* there are no other impediments to switching.") (emphasis original). Others, too, have questioned the assumption that short duration exclusive dealing contracts are presumptively contestable and cannot injure competition, especially if as a result of the exclusive dealing the manufacturer is more likely to gain market power and perhaps share supracompetitive profits with the distributor in return for its agreement to abide by exclusivity. Should it matter if the costs to distributors of switching suppliers is significant? Which is the more persuasive position, and why? The *Dentsply* case, discussed in the following Note, rejected the short duration exception.

Note on the Treatment of Exclusive Dealing in Microsoft and Dentsply

One of the arguable surprises in the *Microsoft* litigation was the district court's decision to dismiss the government's stand-alone exclusive dealing claims and the court of appeals' curious reaction to the government's decision not to appeal that ruling. In addition to the monopolization and tying claims, which we have discussed in Chapter 6 and earlier in this Chapter, the government alleged that Microsoft had entered into exclusive dealing agreements with personal computer ("PC") manufacturers and Internet access providers ("IAPs"), pursuant to which they became committed to the use of Internet Explorer to the exclusion of any other Internet browser, most particularly the then popular Netscape Navigator. As we have already discussed, the government's larger theory was that Microsoft's actions *in toto* derailed potential future threats to its PC operating system monopoly.

It was undisputed that despite being effectively cut off from PC manufacturers and IAPs, Netscape was still able to distribute its browser directly to customers via download from its Internet web site (although access at the time was predominantly by slower dial-up telephone lines) or through retail computer outlets. The government argued, however, that Microsoft had secured a decided competitive advantage by effectively excluding Netscape from the *best*, *i.e.*, most cost-effective, channels for distributing browser software. Many consumers, whose PCs or IAP-supplied software included Internet Explorer, simply would not undertake the additional transaction costs in terms of time, money, and effort to obtain a second browser in the aftermarket or via Internet download. Hence, Microsoft's conduct imposed costs on Netscape, which was forced to start "giving away" its browser software, and proved to be an effective exclusionary strategy—Netscape's market share steadily and substantially declined after Microsoft initiated these practices. Netscape's decline, in the government's view, significantly diminished the possibility that its Internet browser could ever evolve into a competitive alternative to Windows. Microsoft responded that even though Netscape's market share fell, its total sales, and the number of customers using Netscape's Navigator product, both expanded, suggesting no exclusion. It also contended that Netscape's decline was a consequence of the inferiority of its product, not any actions of Microsoft.

Although the district court ruled in favor of the government on its monopolization claim under Section 2 of the Sherman Act and its tying claim under Section 1, it rejected a stand alone challenge to exclusive dealing. First, the district court observed that "[w]here courts have found that the agreements in question failed to foreclose absolutely outlets that together accounted for a substantial percentage of the total distribution of the relevant products, they have consistently declined to assign liability." *United States v. Microsoft Corp.*, 87 F. Supp. 2d 30, 52 (D.D.C. 2000). Citing *Omega Environmental*, the court further observed that "[o]ther courts in similar contexts have declined to find liability where alternative channels of distribution are available to the competitor, even if those channels are not as efficient or reliable as the channels foreclosed by the defendant." *Id.* at 54.

Was the Microsoft district court's conclusion consistent with *Tampa* and *Jefferson Parish*? Is its reading of *Omega Environmental* reasonable? Should it be necessary for a plaintiff challenging exclusive dealing to demonstrate that there are *no* alternative means of distribution? Should it matter to the analysis of exclusive dealing whether selling through any particular channel of distribution is significantly more cost-effective than any other channel? Why might a firm use exclusive dealing in order to preclude its rival from having access to the "best" channel of distribution? How might such exclusive dealing benefit a seller in a way that reflects injury to competition? What kinds of business justifications might it offer in defense?

On appeal, Microsoft sought to use its victory on the exclusive dealing claim to attack the district court's judgment on the monopolization and tying claims. Microsoft argued that, because the standards for evaluating exclusion under Sections 1 and 2 of the Sherman Act are the same, its victory on the government's Section 1 exclusive dealing claim should have precluded any finding that its exclusive dealing agreements were "exclusionary" for purposes of the government's Section 2 claim.

In rejecting Microsoft's position, the court of appeals appeared to cast doubt on the district court's reading of *Omega Environmental* and the other exclusive dealing cases it had relied upon: "The District Court appears to have based its holding with respect to § 1 upon a 'total exclusion test' rather than the 40% standard drawn from the caselaw. Even assuming the holding is correct, however, we nonetheless reject Microsoft's contention." *United States v. Microsoft Corp.*, 253 F.3d 34, 70 (D.C. Cir. 2001). Citing *Tampa Electric* and other authorities, the D.C. Circuit concluded that the evidence was sufficient to support the district court's findings that Microsoft's exclusive dealing agreements had harmed competition, and that it had failed to establish any procompetitive justifications for their use. *Id.* at 70–71. But was Microsoft right? Is it possible to reconcile the district court's seemingly inconsistent conclusions with respect to the legality of Microsoft's exclusive dealing under Sections 1 and 2? Should the district court have found either no violation under Section 1 and 2, or, given its conclusion that Microsoft's exclusive dealing was exclusionary, that Microsoft's exclusive dealing constituted an independent Section 1 violation?

In *United States v. Dentsply, Int'l, Inc.*, 399 F.3d 181 (3d Cir. 2005), the Third Circuit held that exclusive supply contracts between a dominant manufacturer of prefabricated artificial teeth and its dealers violated Section 2 of the Sherman Act. Dentsply's market share (75–80%), evidence that it actually excluded its rivals from having access to dealers, and its ability to set prices without serious regard for the prices of its rivals, all suggested that it indeed possessed the requisite monopoly power. *Id.* at 187–91. The court also found the use of exclusive dealing under the circumstances to be exclusionary. In its view, "[t]he test is not total foreclosure, but whether the challenged practices bar a substantial number of rivals or severely restrict the market's ambit." *Id.* at 191. Because Dentsply's exclusive dealing agreements "help keep sales of competing teeth below the critical level necessary for any rival to pose a real threat to Dentsply's market share," they had the requisite anticompetitive effect. *Id.* Critical to the court's reasoning was its rejection of the district court's attribution of great competitive significance to the presence of alternate channels of distribution, especially direct sales. Such alternatives simply were not economically equivalent to dealers, and barring rivals from dealers impaired Dentsply's rivals and created barriers to entry. *Id.* at 191–96.

Notably, the Third Circuit found that Dentsply's rivals were foreclosed from access to dealers even though Dentsply's associations with those dealers were "essentially terminable at will." *Id.* at 185. "Although its rivals could theoretically convince a dealer to buy their products and drop Dentsply's line, that has not occurred." *Id.* at 189. The appeals court concluded that the dealers "acceded to heavy economic pressure" in sticking with Dentsply. *Id.* at 196. Finally, shifting the burden to Dentsply, the Third Circuit found a lack of evidence that Dentsply's exclusive dealing produced significant efficiencies. *Id.* at 196–97.

Compare the approach of the Third Circuit in *Dentsply* to the approach of the Ninth Circuit in *Omega Environmental*, where the plaintiff similarly but unsuccessfully claimed that distributors were a superior channel of distribution compared to the alternatives, such as direct sales. Can the two cases be reconciled? Is it enough that Dentsply's market share was roughly twice that of Gilbarco? Do *Omega Environmental* and *Dentsply* involve the application of different economic approaches to the analysis of exclusionary exclusive dealing, or were the facts in each case simply distinguishable?

Some commentators and government officials have referred to *Dentsply* as an example of the use of "naked" exclusionary contracts. This is an allusion to an economics literature explaining why all the dealers of a product might agree to work exclusively with one manufacturer, even though doing so would allow the dominant manufacturer to obtain market power to the disadvantage of all the dealers. Each dealer would decide to accept exclusivity with the dominant supplier if each dealer expects the other dealers to work exclusively with that firm. Under such circumstances, no individual dealer would believe that shifting business to a rival manufacturer would do much to help the rival succeed, so the dealers have little to lose by accepting an exclusive arrangement with the monopolist. *See* Eric B. Rasmussen, et al., *Naked Exclusion*, 81 AM. ECON. REV.1137 (1991); Ilya R. Segal & Michael D. Whinston, *Naked Exclusion: Comment*, 90 AM. ECON. REV. 296 (2000). How well does this theory explain the decision in *Dentsply*? Does *Dentsply* convincingly refute the argument for a short duration exception? Would *Omega Environmental* have come out differently had it been decided after *Dentsply*?

How do *Omega Environmental* and *Dentsply* compare to *Microsoft*? How would the exclusive dealing claim in *Microsoft* have been decided under the approach of the Ninth Circuit in *Omega Environmental*? The Third Circuit in *Dentsply*?

The complaint in *Dentsply* alleged violations of Sections 1 and 2 of the Sherman Act, as well as Section 3 of the Clayton Act, and the district court found for the defendant on all of the government's theories. The Antitrust Division thereafter decided to base its appeal solely on Section 2. Why would the government elect to do so? Is Section 2 a stricter standard than either Section 1 of the Sherman Act or Section 3 of the Clayton Act? Should there be much doubt that if the government could prevail under Section 2 it also should have been able to prevail under the other statutes?

Finally, consider the economic theory of harm in *Dentsply*. Although the Third Circuit did not expressly rely on the literature of raising rivals' costs, its analysis is arguably consistent with it. Distribution through dealers was optimal for manufacturers, yet Dentsply's policies tended to foreclose that optimal channel to its rivals, which in turn precluded them from realizing scale economies and other efficiencies. "Foreclosure," alone, was not the source of competitive injury, however. Shunting those rivals to alternate, less effective channels of distribution imposed costs on them and appeared to facilitate Dentsply's maintenance of monopoly power. Was that also the case in *Gilbarco*, at least in the dissent's view? Was it also the case in *Microsoft*? Is it necessary to have a monopolistic market share to achieve that result? If so, is there much chance of prevailing on an exclusive dealing claim under any antitrust statute absent monopoly power?

In the next Sidebar, we explore these issues and the continuing and lively debate about the economic and legal analysis of exclusive dealing.

Sidebar 7–5:
Assessing the Contemporary Law and Economics of Exclusive Dealing

Introduction

As we have seen, exclusive dealing was never accorded the same harsh treatment as tying. Largely, this is because the efficient uses of exclusive dealing arrangements have long been acknowledged, *See, e.g.*, *Standard Stations*, 337 U.S. at 306–07 (discussing potential competitive benefits of exclusive dealing arrangements), and are now widely accepted. These include, prevention of interbrand free-riding, providing an alternative to more costly vertical integration by sellers, facilitating expansion or entry by a new firm, and improving the efficacy of intrabrand restraints. *See, e.g.*, 11 HERBERT HOVENKAMP, ANTITRUST LAW ¶ ¶ 1810–14 (2d ed. 2005) (discussing various economic benefits of exclusive dealing).

Most of these advantages are associated with the seller, but there are also pro-competitive reasons that dealers might seek to enter exclusive dealing arrangements with their suppliers. Dealers who seek exclusivity are unlikely to be motivated by a desire to limit their supply options, but could be seeking better pricing, a reliable and uninterrupted stream of supply, better quality and product uniformity, or other cost-related efficiencies. *See* Richard M. Steuer, *Customer–Instigated Exclusive Dealing*, 68 ANTITRUST L.J. 239 (2000).

Figure 7–3:

Summary of Potential Effects of Exclusive Dealing

Potential Anticompetitive Effects of Exclusive Dealing	Potential Justifications for Exclusive Dealing
• exclude or impair access of rivals to most cost-effective distribution channels (downstream dealers), or most cost-effective input sources (upstream suppliers), leading to: 　○ higher prices 　○ reduced consumer choice In addition, cost of vertical integration could be forced on rivals and/or potential entrants (two-level entry).	• reduce transaction costs • secure dealer loyalty • prevent interbrand free riding • competition for exclusive contracts And in the case of output and requirements variants: • protect buyers and sellers from price fluctuations • ensure long term supply/customer stability • ensure consistent operation at efficient scale

Note the similarity between some of these justifications for exclusive dealing, and the justifications we discussed in Chapter 4 in connection with *Sylvania*. (*See* Figure 4–4, *supra*). For example, recall that the prevention of intrabrand free riding was a recognized procompetitive justification for the use of vertical intrabrand restraints such as territorial, location, and customer restrictions, as well as resale price maintenance. Similarly, the prevention of interbrand free riding is a recognized justification for permitting exclusive dealing. *See, e.g.*, Howard Marvel, *Exclusive Dealing*, 25 J.L. & ECON. 1 (1982). The incentive for a manufacturer to undertake substantial promotional efforts, such as advertising, would be dissipated if those efforts succeeded in attracting a customer only to have it "switch brands" at the dealer level. For a further elaboration of how exclusive dealing can be used to redress interbrand free-riding, see Benjamin Klein & Andres V. Lerner, *The Expanded Economics of Free–Riding: How Exclusive Dealing Prevents Free Riding and Creates Undivided Loyalty*, 74 ANTITRUST L.J. 473 (2007).

Recall as well from Chapter 4, that intrabrand restraints can be used to induce retailers to carry and promote the product of a particular manufacturer. Again, exclusive dealing can be justified on the same grounds—by limiting a dealer to the sale of a single brand, the supplier can enhance the dealer's incentive to promote the supplier's product. It is commonplace, therefore, for exclusive distributing and exclusive dealing to go hand in hand: to provide sufficient incentives for the dealer to carry only the supplier's product, the supplier may need to agree not to appoint any other competing dealer within a specified territory. By insulating the dealer from intrabrand competition, the supplier can secure the dealer's commitment to focus its marketing energies on interbrand competition. Protecting quality and reputation may also justify either intrabrand or interbrand restraints.

The typical franchise agreement provides an example. As an inducement to franchisees, franchisors often grant exclusive territories that insulate franchisees from intrabrand competition. This is designed to secure the franchisee's best efforts to promote the franchisor's product or service, and perhaps to alleviate any intrabrand free riding problems. A franchisor also typically prohibits its franchisees from selling the goods of the franchisors' competitors. Hence, it is unusual to find multiple McDonald's restaurants located very close to each other in the same neighborhood and we wouldn't expect to find Burger King food for sale at a McDonald's. This combination of restraints on intra-and interbrand competition might enhance the incentives for the franchisees to promote the franchisor's product and prevents interbrand free riding. Exclusive dealing in the franchise context might also be prompted by the franchisee's interest in securing lower prices, uniform quality and a stable source of supply. And it might protect the franchisor's reputation by making sure that the products sold under its name all satisfy its quality standards

Finally, exclusive dealing may reflect competition *for* distribution (often termed "competition for exclusives"). Suppliers may be willing to pay dealers in order to secure their services exclusively as part of a competitive, not an anticompetitive strategy. *See* Benjamin Klein, *Exclusive Dealing as Competition for Distribution "On the Merits,"* 12 GEO. MASON L. REV. 119 (2003) (arguing that even if such payments raise the costs of distribution for rivals, competition among dealers will mean they get passed on to consumers and that competition for exclusives may reflect their perceived desirability from the point of view of greater efficiency in promotion and distribution).

In recognition of these various justifications, today exclusive dealing is less likely to be deemed unlawful than in the past. But the courts have not yet completed their evolution from traditional to modern economic approaches for evaluating exclusive dealing arrangements. This Sidebar examines some of the most influential of these approaches.

Traditional Foundations: Foreclosure Analysis and the Role of Inference

From *Standard Stations* and *Tampa Electric* on to *Jefferson Parish* the focal point of exclusive dealing analysis largely remained "foreclosure." Although the nature of the inquiry broadened and the degree of foreclosure prerequisite to a finding of violation grew significantly from the single digits of *Standard Stations* to the "more than 30%" of *Jefferson Parish*, courts consistently have relied upon inference to establish the requisite competitive injury. From significant foreclosure, the courts *infer* the requisite harm to competition. Evidence of restricted output and higher prices typically have not been required. As the concurring opinion in *Jefferson Parish* asserted:

> In determining whether an exclusive-dealing contract is unreasonable, the proper focus is on the structure of the market for the products or services in question—the number of sellers and buyers in the market, the volume of their business, and the ease with which buyers and sellers can redirect their purchases or sales to others. Exclusive dealing is an unreasonable restraint on trade only when a significant fraction of buyers or sellers are frozen out of a market by the exclusive deal.

466 U.S. at 45 (O'Connor, J., concurring). *See also* 11 HOVENKAMP, ¶ 1821c, at 176 ("When the numbers are large enough to be threatening, they establish the inference of prima facie illegality, thus shifting the burden to the defendant to show that exclusive dealing is justified under the circumstances.").

This approach is analogous to the *Philadelphia National Bank* presumption and the Horizontal Merger Guidelines' reliance on the Herfindahl–Hershman Index of concentration, which we explored in Chapter 5 (Mergers). In both instances, courts and agencies draw an inference of likely anticompetitive effects from varying degrees of market concentration. As Justice O'Connor reasoned in her *Jefferson Parish* concurrence, in the context of exclusive dealing, the higher the degree of foreclosure, the more reliable the inference that competition will be substantially impaired by exclusive dealing.

Chicago, Post–Chicago, and Other Modern Approaches to Analyzing Exclusionary Conduct

The traditional framework for analyzing exclusive dealing has been criticized by both Chicago and Post–Chicago School commentators, as well as others. First, both Chicago and Post–Chicago commentators have argued that evidence of "foreclosure" is an unreliable basis for inferring anticompetitive effects. In addition, they have agreed that the potential efficiencies of exclusive dealing are significant, and that they must be evaluated carefully. They disagree, however, about the overall likelihood that exclusive dealing can nevertheless facilitate the creation or exercise of market power.

Chicago School. Commentators generally associated with the Chicago School have not necessarily been of one mind when it comes to exclusionary conduct. For example, noting that both exclusive dealing and vertical mergers are but two forms of vertical integration that create efficiencies, Robert Bork labeled as "fallacious" the notion that either could create any restriction of output. ROBERT H. BORK, THE ANTITRUST PARADOX 303 (1978). "Increased efficiency," he argued, "cannot be classified as improperly exclusionary, and there is every reason to believe that exclusive dealing and requirements contracts have no purpose other than the creation of efficiency." *Id.* at 309. Moreover, Chicago School oriented commentators have frequently appealed to the "single monopoly profit" theory in analyzing exclusionary conduct—the idea that anticompetitive explanations for exclusionary conduct are implausible because such actions cannot enhance the monopoly power already available to a monopolist—discussed previously in Sidebar 7–3 in connection with tying and more fully below in connection with vertical mergers. In the context of exclusionary conduct that denies a rival access to a key input, the argument would run that a monopoly supplier of an input already earns its monopoly profit, so cannot be acting to harm competition by excluding a downstream rival from the input.

But specifically distancing himself from Bork on this issue, Judge Richard Posner has consistently spurned the position that anticompetitive exclusion is "virtually impossible." "Although documented cases of genuinely exclusionary practices are rare, they do exist, and economic theory points to conditions occasionally encountered in which they are a rational profit-maximizing tactic." RICHARD A. POSNER, ANTITRUST LAW 194 (2d ed. 2001). As was discussed in Sidebar 6–4, Posner would focus on whether a monopolist's conduct excludes "an equally or more efficient competitor." *Id.* at 194–95.

Post-Chicago School. In an influential article published in 1986, the Post–Chicago critique of both traditional caselaw and the Chicago School's skeptical view of exclusion took shape. *See* Thomas G. Krattenmaker & Steven C. Salop, *Anti-Competitive Exclusion: Raising Rivals' Costs to Achieve Power Over Price*, 96 YALE L.J. 209, 231–34 (1986) (discussing "Discredited Foreclosure Theory"). In Krattenmaker and Salop's view, the determination whether a vertical exclusionary practice is anticompetitive should turn not on "foreclosure," in and of itself, but on the practice's tendency to raise rivals's costs, which in turn may facilitate the exercise of power over price in the supply market. Recall that we discussed the theory of raising rivals's costs at the beginning of Chapter 6. They thus concluded that "[f]oreclosure theory may still be correct, but not for the reasons originally advanced." *Id.* at 234.

To illustrate, they offer four examples of anti-competitive exclusionary practices that demonstrate the link between cost-raising strategies and exclusion. *See id.* at 234–42. While recognizing the well-known efficiency justifications for exclusive dealing in both input and output markets, they also argue that exclusive rights contracts like exclusive dealing and tying can be anticompetitive when they impose costs on rivals not incurred by the excluding firm. By imposing such costs on its rivals, the predator can obtain some degree of power over price—of market power.

For example, recall the anticompetitive theories at work in *Omega Environmental*, *Microsoft*, and *Dentsply*. Suppose that a supplier can distribute its product through either of two alternate channels, but one is decidedly more effective and less costly. By securing exclusive contracts with distributors in the more cost-effective channel, the supplier can force its rivals to rely on the more costly distribution channel. By doing so the predator "raises its rival's costs." Such a strategy might result in the rival's exit from the market, or it may remain, but be forced to raise its prices in light of its higher costs. In either case, the predator thus will have obtained "power over price"—enjoying lower costs, it can raise prices and increase its profits.

Recall that in *Omega Environmental* the court focused on calculating the percentage of total distribution foreclosed by exclusive dealing—in that instance 38%. In part because more than 60% of distribution took place through direct sales by the manufacturers to end-users, the court concluded that the agreements had no significant anticompetitive effect. What if, as the dissent argued, sales through distributors were in fact more cost effective than direct sales, especially for a new entrant who lacked the sales force and know-how, to succeed in direct sales? A raising rival's costs analysis would have asked whether the independent distributors subject to the exclusive dealing agreements represented a more cost-effective manner of distribution than direct sales. If the answer was yes, there might have been a basis for considering whether the agreements conveyed power over price by raising the costs of distribution for rivals precluded from gaining access to the independent distributors. Hence, the importance in the dissent's discussion of "switching costs." Even though the contracts were terminable on short notice, switching costs might prevent distributors from abandoning Gilbarco in favor of alternate suppliers. To induce those distributors to switch suppliers, new entrants would have to neutralize those costs, probably by incurring them themselves, so even with short termination provisions, the exclusive contracts could raise the cost of entry. A similar analysis was urged by the government in *Microsoft*.

Competition for exclusivity would not necessarily prevent harm to competition under this analysis, for several reasons. First, if the dominant firm has recently signed long-term contracts for exclusivity with many or most distributors, it may not be practical for a rival or new entrant to obtain adequate distribution. Second, the dominant firm may be willing to pay more for exclusivity than would its rivals, funding those payments with a share of its monopoly profits. Third, distributors may be unwilling to sign up with a rival manufacturer, and instead would accept the exclusivity agreement offered by the dominant supplier, because they fear that few other distributors will do so and that in consequence, the rival manufacturer will not be able to achieve sufficient scale of operations to succeed in the marketplace. The distributors may reason that it is better to stick with the dominant firm than risk getting stuck selling only the products of an unsuccessful or even failing manufacturer. (This kind of dynamic, in which, expectations that other distributors will sign exclusive agreements with the dominant supplier keep dealers from switching even in the absence of direct switching costs, was noted above in the discussion of "naked exclusion" in connection with *Dentsply*.)

Krattenmaker and Salop, and other Post–Chicago commentators, thus conclude that the focus of the competitive inquiry in exclusive dealing and other cases of allegedly exclusionary conduct should be its impact on rivals' costs and on its potential to facilitate the exercise of market power: when exclusive dealing can impose costs on a rival, it can convey power over price. They drop reliance on inferences of harm from foreclosure, therefore, in favor of proof of harm to competition. *See, e.g.*, Krattenmaker & Salop, 96 YALE L.J. at 236–38 (discussing "real foreclosure" of inputs occasioned by the contractual arrangements and conduct of rivals and their tendency to impose increased costs on rivals).

What of the "single monopoly profit" critique, which we discussed in Sidebar 7–3? Post–Chicago commentators emphasize that it does not invariably hold, for example, if the related products—the upstream and downstream products (when exclusion operates through foreclosure of access to a key input) or the tying and tied products—are used in *variable proportions* in production of the final product or in consumption by buyers, rather than in *fixed proportions*. We will further discuss the importance of variable proportions and the single monopoly profit theory later in this Chapter in connection with vertical mergers in the *Note on the "Single Monopoly Profit Theory"*.

Modernizing the Foreclosure Framework in the Courts

Although raising rivals' costs has had some significant influence, courts such as the Ninth Circuit in *Omega Environmental* have not framed their analysis in those terms. In addition, some commentators have argued that it can be difficult to differentiate conduct that raises rivals' costs from normal competitive conduct. Courts largely have continued to utilize the basic foreclosure framework set forth in *Standard Stations* and *Tampa Electric*. In doing so, however, they progressively have imposed greater burdens of proof on plaintiffs challenging exclusive dealing. *See, e.g., Omega Environmental*, 127 F.3d at 1162–63 (assuming plaintiff has the burden to define a relevant market and evaluating use of relevant market in assessing foreclosure); *MCM Partners, Inc. v. Andrews–Bartlett & Assocs. Inc.*, 62 F.3d 967, 976 (7th Cir. 1995) (holding that plaintiff in an exclusive dealing case must allege relevant market in order to facilitate evaluation of whether trade was substantially lessened). This was also true in both *Microsoft* and *Dentsply*. In another interesting decision, a plaintiff argued based on cases like *NCAA* (Casebook, Chapter 2, *supra,*) that evidence of actual competitive effects should obviate the need to prove a relevant market for purposes of its challenge to the defendant's exclusivity incentives program. But the Seventh Circuit disagreed, holding that in vertical cases, plaintiffs also are required to prove at least the "rough contours" of a relevant market and substantial market shares. *Republic Tobacco Co. v. North Atl. Trading Co.*, 381 F.3d 717 (7th Cir. 2004).

On the other hand, courts do not routinely inquire directly into either the supplier's market power or the anticompetitive effects in such cases. Instead, consistent with the traditional approach, they commonly *infer* anticompetitive effect from the share of the relevant market foreclosed by the contract challenged. In contrast with past cases, however, they are more inclined to permit defendants to rebut that inference by establishing any of a variety of recognized pro-competitive justifications for the challenged practices, or by demonstrating that no substantial lessening of competition is likely due to the short duration of the exclusive dealing agreement, or to other factors. *See, e.g., Omega Environmental*, 127 F.3d at 1163–64 (citing "undisputed evidence of potential alternative sources of distribution," "short duration and easy terminability of these agreements," evidence of actual and significant entry, and evidence of increasing output, lower prices and fluctuating market shares all as factors militating against inference of probable injury to competition); *Barr Labs., Inc. v. Abbott Labs.*, 978 F.2d 98, 111 (3d Cir. 1992) (citing minimal increase in defendant's market share, minimal increase in market concentration, evidence of ease of entry and legitimate business justifications as sufficient to rebut case based on 15% foreclosure). One court of appeals has likened this contemporary approach to the rule of reason:

To condemn [exclusive dealing arrangements] after *Tampa* requires a detailed depiction of circumstances and the most careful weighing of alleged dangers and potential benefits, which is to say the normal treatment afforded by the rule of reason.

U.S. Healthcare, Inc. v. Healthsource, Inc., 986 F.2d 589, 595 (1st Cir. 1993). *See also* POSNER, ANTITRUST LAW, *supra*, at 264 & n.6 (noting that rule of reason approach now applies regardless of the specific antitrust statute used to challenge exclusive dealing).

The relevant inquiry, however, has not been limited to the supply foreclosed by the specific contract challenged. Historically, the courts also have considered more broadly the percentage of supply in a relevant market that is rendered unavailable by virtue of similar arrangements between all relevant suppliers and their dealers. *See, e.g., Tampa Elec. Co. v. Nashville Coal Co.*, 365 U.S. 320, 333 (1961); *Standard Oil Co. v. United States*, 337 U.S. 293, 314 (1949); *Omega Environmental*, 127 F.3d at 1162–63 & n.5. The more widespread the practice, it is asserted, the greater the practical effect of the foreclosure and the potential harm to competition. *See* 11 HOVENKAMP, ¶ 1821c, at 177 ("When exclusive dealing is used to facilitate collusion, the percentage foreclosure by any single firm might be less, but then the relevant question becomes the aggregate foreclosure imposed by the upstream firms in the collusive group."). But Hovenkamp and others also have questioned the significance of the widespread use of exclusive dealing, arguing that in a market characterized by robust competition it may merely evidence industry recognition that the arrangements promise significant pro-competitive virtues. *Id.* ¶ 1821e, at 188–89.

Some courts focus on evidence of actual anticompetitive effects. *See, e.g., Western Parcel Express v. United Parcel Serv. of Am., Inc.*, 190 F.3d 974, 975–77 (9th Cir. 1999) (rejecting challenge to exclusive dealing agreements absent evidence that they created substantial barriers to entry, and concluding that defendant "does not have nor will have the ability to exclude competition in the relevant market"); *Omega Environmental*, 127 F.3d at 1164 ("Nor did plaintiffs produce credible evidence to support their contention that Gilbarco's policy actually deterred entry into this market."); *U.S. Healthcare*, 986 F.2d at 597 (noting "permanent tension" that "prevails between the 'no sparrow shall fall' concept of antitrust * * * and the ascendant view that antitrust protects 'competition, not competitors.' "); *Roland Mach. Co. v. Dresser Indus.*, 749 F.2d 380, 394 (7th Cir. 1984) (plaintiff in exclusive dealing challenge must prove actual exclusion and "that the probable (not certain) effect of the exclusion will be to raise prices above (and therefore reduce output below) the competitive level, or otherwise injure competition"). As other commentators have observed, in doing so, the courts pay little attention to any arguable distinctions between the Sherman Act and Clayton Act's requirements.

Conclusion

One possible interpretation of these various developments is that the analysis of exclusivity is becoming increasingly indistinguishable from the analysis of other forms of exclusionary conduct. Driven by the importance of core economic concepts, the analysis of exclusion today is more likely to turn on a structured rule of reason analysis, such as what we saw developed for other exclusionary conduct earlier in this Chapter in *Visa*, in which likely anticompetitive exclusion, market power, and efficiency play critical roles. In doing so, it is also likely to incorporate in some way the raising rival's costs inquiry, even if its analysis is not formally framed in those terms. With a structured approach, the burden of production shifts to the defendant in the presence of evidence that its exclusionary contracts raised rivals's costs, impaired entry, or otherwise significantly impeded important rivals. Condemnation could follow a that point in the absence of a plausible efficiency justification and evidence to support it. On the other hand, a structured approach may also mean a defendant can seek summary judgment if it obviously lacks market power and hence the ability to affect competition. If the case cannot be resolved through these forms of truncated analysis, a full reasonableness analysis would be undertaken. That analysis would require the plaintiff to demonstrate that the harm to its rival led or would reasonably be expected to lead to higher prices or other anticompetitive effects, taking into account both anticompetitive effects and pro-competitive efficiencies. Less uncertain than the particulars of the still developing framework are its implications: as was true of vertical intrabrand non-price restraints like those permitted in *Sylvania* and *Leegin*, today it is rare for a court to strike down exclusivity.

C. VERTICAL MERGERS

In Chapter 5 we examined horizontal mergers. As we explained, when horizontal mergers raise competitive concerns, those concerns typically involve the threat of *collusive* effects—either the post-merger ability of the merged firms to raise price unilaterally, or the post-merger ability of the merged firms to coordinate their pricing or other competitive conduct with their remaining rivals.

Here we address *vertical* mergers—mergers that involve firms at different levels of a chain of production or distribution. They are addressed here because in contrast to horizontal mergers, vertical mergers raise competitive concerns primarily when they threaten *exclusionary* anticompetitive effects. As we shall see, therefore, the analysis of vertical mergers proceeds much like the analysis of other exclusionary conduct.

Antitrust law's approach to the analysis of vertical mergers has evolved over time in parallel to the way horizontal merger law has developed, but with even less input from the courts. As with horizontal merger analysis, a Supreme Court decision from antitrust's structural era remains formally controlling precedent, but is no longer closely tied to enforcement agency practice or the likely decisions of the courts today.

1. VERTICAL MERGER ANALYSIS BEFORE 1980

We will begin by reading an excerpt from the Supreme Court's decision in that case, *Brown Shoe*, which we reviewed in Chapter 5 in connection with horizontal merger analysis and the "submarket" approach to market definition. Consistent with those earlier excerpts, which questioned relatively small reductions in horizontal competition, the Court here highlights a competitive concern that arises from small amounts of foreclosure by contemporary standards: "Brown's avowed policy of forcing its own shoes upon its retail subsidiaries" meant that other shoe manufacturers were denied access to Kinney retail outlets, which accounted for only 1.2% of shoes sold. As you read it, note too the similarity between the Court's analytical approach to vertical integration by merger, and the approach it took to analyzing vertical integration by contract—*i.e.*, exclusive dealing in the cases we previously examined.

BROWN SHOE CO. v. UNITED STATES

Supreme Court of the United States, 1962.
370 U.S. 294, 82 S.Ct. 1502, 8 L.Ed.2d 510.

[The Court's analysis of the legislative history of the Clayton Act and its analysis of the horizontal aspects of the merger were highlighted in an excerpt from this decision set forth in Chapter 5. An introductory note to the earlier excerpt sketches the facts, some of which are repeated here.

Brown was the fourth largest shoe manufacturer in the country, accounting for about 4% of total domestic production and 6% of wholesale shoes sold nationally. It was also the nation's third largest shoe retailer, controlling 1,230 retail shoe outlets. Of these, 470 were company owned and operated, and the rest were mainly independently-owned stores operating under the Brown franchise program. Most retail shoe stores were independent of any manufacturer: the 1230 retail shoe outlets controlled by Brown accounted for only 20% of the firm's approximately 6000 retail customers.

Kinney was primarily in the retail business, though it also was the twelfth largest domestic shoe manufacturer, with about a 0.5% share. It was the country's eighth largest retailer, with over 350 retail outlets, accounting for 1.2% of shoes sold (and 2% of children's shoes sold). Kinney-manufactured products accounted for about one-fifth of the company's retail sales. Brown was the largest outside supplier of the shoes sold in Kinney's retail outlets, supplying nearly 8% of those products. Eds.]

* * *

IV.

THE VERTICAL ASPECTS OF THE MERGER

Economic arrangements between companies standing in a supplier-customer relationship are characterized as 'vertical.' The primary vice of a vertical merger or other arrangement tying a customer to a supplier is that, by foreclosing the competitors of either party from a segment of the market otherwise open to them, the arrangement may act as a 'clog on competition,' which 'deprive(s) * * * rivals of a fair opportunity to compete.'[40] Every extended vertical arrangement by its very nature, for at least a time, denies to

---

40. In addition, a vertical merger may disrupt and injure competition when those independent customers of the supplier who are in competition with the merging customer, are forced either to stop handling the supplier's lines, thereby jeopardizing the goodwill they have developed, or to retain the supplier's lines, thereby forcing them into competition with their own supplier.

competitors of the supplier the opportunity to compete for part or all of the trade of the customer-party to the vertical arrangement. However, the Clayton Act does not render unlawful all such vertical arrangements, but forbids only those whose effect 'may be substantially to lessen competition, or to tend to create a monopoly' 'in any line of commerce in any section of the country.' * * *

* * *

The Probable Effect of the Merger.

* * *

Since the diminution of the vigor of competition which may stem from a vertical arrangement results primarily from a foreclosure of a share of the market otherwise open to competitors, an important consideration in determining whether the effect of a vertical arrangement 'may be substantially to lessen competition, or to tend to create a monopoly' is the size of the share of the market foreclosed. However, this factor will seldom be determinative. If the share of the market foreclosed is so large that it approaches monopoly proportions, the Clayton Act will, of course, have been violated. * * * On the other hand, foreclosure of a *de minimis* share of the market will not tend 'substantially to lessen competition.'

Between these extremes, in cases such as the one before us, in which the foreclosure is neither of monopoly nor *de minimis* proportions, the percentage of the market foreclosed by the vertical arrangement cannot itself be decisive. In such cases, it becomes necessary to undertake an examination of various economic and historical factors in order to determine whether the arrangement under review is of the type Congress sought to proscribe.

A most important such factor to examine is the very nature and purpose of the arrangement. Congress not only indicated that 'the tests of illegality (under § 7) are intended to be similar to those which the courts have applied in interpreting the same language as used in other sections of the Clayton Act,' but also chose for § 7 language virtually identical to that of § 3 of the Clayton Act, which had been interpreted by this Court to require an examination of the interdependence of the market share foreclosed by, and the economic purpose of, the vertical arrangement. Thus, for example, if a particular vertical arrangement, considered under § 3, appears to be a limited term exclusive-dealing contract, the market foreclosure must generally be significantly greater than if the arrangement is a tying contract before the arrangement will be held to have violated the Act. The reason for this is readily discernible. The usual tying contract forces the customer to take a product or brand he does not necessarily want in order to secure one which he does desire. Because such an arrangement is inherently anticompetitive, we have held that its use by an established company is likely 'substantially to lessen competition' although only a relatively small amount of commerce is affected. Thus, unless the tying device is employed by a small company in an attempt to break into a market, the use of a tying device can rarely be harmonized with the strictures of the antitrust laws, which are intended primarily to preserve and stimulate competition. On the other hand, requirement contracts are frequently negotiated at the behest of the customer who has chosen the particular supplier and his product upon the basis of competitive merit. Of course, the fact that requirement contracts are not inherently anticompetitive will not save a particular agreement if, in fact, it is likely 'substantially to lessen competition, or to tend to create a monopoly.' Yet a requirement contract may escape censure if only a small share of the market is involved, if the purpose of the agreement is to insure to the customer a sufficient supply of a commodity vital to the customer's trade or to insure to the supplier a market for his output and if there is no trend toward concentration in the industry. Similar considerations are pertinent to a judgment under § 7 of the Act.

* * *

* * * In 1955, the date of this merger, Brown was the fourth largest manufacturer in the shoe industry. * * * Not only was Brown one of the leading manufacturers of men's, women's, and children's shoes, but Kinney, with over 350 retail outlets, owned and operated the largest independent chain of family shoe stores in the Nation. Thus, in this industry, no merger between a manufacturer and an independent retailer could involve a larger potential market foreclosure. Moreover, it is apparent both from past behavior of Brown and from the testimony of Brown's President, that Brown would use its ownership of Kinney to force Brown shoes into Kinney stores. Thus, in operation this vertical arrangement would be quite analogous to one involving a tying clause.[55]

* * *

The existence of a trend toward vertical integration, which the District Court found, is well substantiated by the record. Moreover, the court found a tendency of the acquiring manufacturers to become increasingly important sources of supply for their acquired outlets. The necessary corollary of these trends is the foreclosure of independent manufacturers from markets otherwise open to them. And because these trends are not the product of accident but are rather the result of deliberate policies of Brown and other leading shoe manufacturers, account must be taken of these facts in order to predict the probable future consequences of this merger. It is against this background of continuing concentration that the present merger must be viewed.

Brown argues, however, that the shoe industry is at present composed of a large number of manufacturers and retailers, and that the industry is dynamically competitive. But remaining vigor cannot immunize a merger if the trend in that industry is toward oligopoly. It is the probable effect of the merger upon the future as well as the present which the Clayton Act commands the courts and the Commission to examine.

Moreover, as we have remarked above, not only must we consider the probable effects of the merger upon the economics of the particular markets affected but also we must consider its probable effects upon the economic way of life sought to be preserved by Congress. Congress was desirous of preventing the formation of further oligopolies with their attendant adverse effects

---

55. Moreover, ownership integration is a   contract integration.
more permanent and irreversible tie than is

upon local control of industry and upon small business. Where an industry was composed of numerous independent units, Congress appeared anxious to preserve this structure. * * *

The District Court's findings, and the record facts * * * convince us that the shoe industry is being subjected to just such a cumulative series of vertical mergers which, if left unchecked, will be likely 'substantially to lessen competition.'

We reach this conclusion because the trend toward vertical integration in the shoe industry, when combined with Brown's avowed policy of forcing its own shoes upon its retail subsidiaries, may foreclose competition from a substantial share of the markets for men's, women's, and children's shoes, without producing any countervailing competitive, economic, or social advantages.

————

In analyzing this vertical merger, *Brown Shoe* examined more than the extent of the market foreclosed to rivals; it also considered the purpose of the acquisition and whether there was a trend toward vertical integration in the industry. But foreclosure is termed a vertical merger's "primary vice" and, not surprisingly, the percentage of the market foreclosed to rivals became the central issue for analyzing vertical mergers in the wake of this decision. Throughout antitrust's structural era, in parallel with antitrust's concern about small increases in horizontal concentration, vertical mergers were barred when they denied rivals access to small parts of the market, particularly in concentrated markets. Note how this parallels the early exclusive dealing cases, especially *Standard Stations*.

In *Brown Shoe*, the Court appears concerned primarily with the prospect that "Brown would use its ownership of Kinney to force Brown shoes into Kinney stores" thereby "foreclos[ing] competition from a substantial share of the markets for men's, women's, and children's shoes." 370 U.S. at 334. The foreclosed rivals would appear to be other shoe manufacturers, who would be denied access to Kinney's retail outlets. As with vertical exclusion cases generally, a vertical merger can in principle harm competition by denying horizontal rivals access either to upstream inputs or as in this case, downstream customers. The same merger can do both: the Court could have chosen also to analyze the transaction as harming *Kinney*'s rivals by foreclosing them from access to a key input, namely Brown's shoes.

The note at the start of the case indicates, however, that Kinney sold only 1.2% of all shoes (and 2% of children's shoes). If rival shoe manufacturers are kept from retail outlets accounting for no more than 2% of the market, is it likely that the price of shoes will rise? Does it matter to the analysis that the shoe industry was relatively unconcentrated by modern standards? If higher prices are not the problem, what problem is the Supreme Court trying to solve by upholding the government's challenge to this shoe industry merger?

Finally, consider how the case might have been decided if instead of acquiring Kinney, Brown Shoe had entered into an exclusive dealing agreement with it. Would the Court's analysis have been different? Its conclusion? *See FTC v. Brown Shoe Co.*, 384 U.S. 316 (1966).

Note on Ford Motor Co. v. United States (Autolite)

The Supreme Court reaffirmed *Brown Shoe*'s concern with the anticompetitive potential of vertical mergers foreclosing rivals from small portions of a market toward the end of antitrust's structural era in its only other (and still most recent) substantive vertical merger decision, *Ford Motor Co. v. United States*, 405 U.S. 562 (1972) (*Autolite*). However, the upstream and downstream markets in *Autolite* were substantially more concentrated than their counterparts in *Brown Shoe*.

In *Autolite*, the Court upheld a district court's decision prohibiting Ford's acquisition of a leading manufacturer of original equipment spark plugs that "marked 'the foreclosure of Ford as a purchaser of about ten per cent of total [spark plug] industry output." *Id.* at 568. The upstream (spark plug) and downstream (automobile) markets were both concentrated: "Prior to the acquisition * * * there were only two major independent producers and only two significant purchasers of original equipment spark plugs." *Id.* at 570. In addition, as Justice Stewart emphasized in a concurring opinion, the transaction "eliminated one of the only two independent producers with a sufficient share of the aftermarket [replacement spark plugs] to give it a chance to compete effectively without an OE [original equipment] tie," and thus "had the probable effect of indefinitely postponing the day when existing market forces" could undermine the oligopoly market structure. *Id.* at 581 (Stewart, J., concurring). The Court also followed *Philadelphia National Bank* in refusing to consider the defense "that the acquisition had some beneficial effect" in making the merged firm a more effective competitor with automobile and spark plug manufacturers. *Id.* at 569.

The lower courts took their lead from the Supreme Court in *Brown Shoe* and *Autolite*, and upheld challenges to vertical mergers excluding rivals from small portions of a market. An instructive and not atypical example comes from a 1975 decision by the Federal Trade Commission, later affirmed by the Ninth Circuit, challenging two vertical acquisitions in the cement industry. The acquiring firm was Ash Grove, a manufacturer of portland cement accounting for 13% to 18% of total annual sales of portland in the Kansas City area. The acquired firms were downstream buyers of portland: two ready-mix cement producers.

One of the acquired firms, Fordyce, produced 14% of the local output, purchased 10% of the cement shipped into Kansas City, and was the largest independent ready-mix manufacturer in town. (The two larger firms had already been acquired by other portland manufacturers.) The other, Lee, was the seventh largest Kansas city ready-mixer. Lee accounted for 4.3% of ready-mix market sales and purchased 3.1% of all shipments of portland cement into the market area. The challenge to the smaller of these acquisitions was too much for a dissenting Commissioner, but even he had no problem with the small foreclosure percentages presented by the larger acquisition, thus suggesting how lines were drawn during antitrust's structural era:

> One can hardly deny that, if each of the 4 largest cement firms doing business in a given city is allowed to buy a customer holding 10 percent of the local concrete market, other cement producers are going to be foreclosed from at least 40 percent of the total business in

town and hence that one of the major arteries feeding into the competitive life-line of that particular market might well suffer some significant amount of clogging. Those are the kinds of numbers that can leave the competition gasping for breath.

My Brethren lose their grip on the realities of the competitive arena, however, when they let their justifiable concern with the probable effects of such a substantial merger [the acquisition of Fordyce] spill over onto * * * Ash Grove's acquisition of a small ready mixer [Lee]. * * *

* * * To be sure, this market is already concentrated and the law is reasonably intended to deal not just with the kind of monopolization that leaps upon us in great bounds but the kind that enters in small increments and sneaks in on little cat feet in the middle of the night. But 3.1 percent of a market?

In re Ash Grove Cement Co., 85 F.T.C. 1123, 1154 (1975) (dissenting statement of Commissioner Thompson), *aff'd sub nom., Ash Grove Cement Co. v. FTC*, 577 F.2d 1368 (9th Cir. 1978).

Sidebar 7–6:
Vertical Integration and Transaction Cost Economics

Suppliers and their customers may take many different approaches to structuring their distribution systems. A firm might decide, for example, to acquire all or many of its inputs from various suppliers, act largely as an "assembler" of those inputs, and sell its assembled and finished product either directly or through a network of independent wholesalers and/or retail dealers. A personal computer manufacturer, for example, might elect to purchase processors, hard drives, modems, and flat panel displays from various suppliers, rather than manufacture them itself. It then would assemble those various inputs into a finished product—a PC—which it would in turn sell through direct sales or through dealers.

In the alternative, a firm might elect to *vertically integrate* backwards or forwards. With *backward integration*, a firm will decide to assume responsibility for producing one of its inputs. An automobile manufacturer, for example, might decide to produce its own tires rather than purchase them from independent tire manufacturers, or a PC manufacturer might decide to produce some of its own circuit boards. *Forward integration* might involve a movement down the distribution chain, such as when an automobile manufacturer or gasoline producer decides to own and operate its own retail dealership, or, in our PC example, when a company decides to sell directly to consumers through Internet sites and catalogue sales, rather than by using independent retail dealers.

Vertical integration can be accomplished in a number of ways. The automobile manufacturer in our example might decide to expand into tire manufacturing by building its own facility. In the alternative, it might acquire an existing tire manufacturer. Finally, it might vertically integrate with a tire manufacturer by entering into an exclusive dealing, output or requirements contract that binds the two links in the distribution chain more closely together. What factors might motivate firms to choose a particular strategy?

Whether or not a firm integrates vertically by owning and operating assets in two or more stages of production or levels of distribution usually depends on relative operating costs or efficiencies. If internal integration is more cost-effective, the firm will tend to integrate and operate at both the manufacturing and retailing levels; on the other hand, the firm will operate at only one level and will not expand vertically if utilizing unaffiliated suppliers and dealers is less costly. *See* OLIVER E. WILLIAMSON, *Transaction Cost Economics*, *in* 1 HANDBOOK OF INDUSTRIAL ORGANIZATION 136, 150–59 (Richard Schmalensee & Robert D. Willig, Eds., 1989). Vertical integration in this view usually results from the firm's effort to achieve efficiencies—*i.e.*, lower costs—not available to it with other market arrangements such as contracts.

Similar transactional savings frequently are sought by firms that integrate vertically on a less formal basis—that is, through contracts. A firm may seek a stable supply or output by arranging a long-term exclusive dealing agreement or by requiring that dealers buying its product for resale concentrate sales and advertising efforts within assigned territories. On the other hand, such restraints may merely mask efforts by manufacturers or dealers to fix prices horizontally, as can be the case with resale price maintenance. Or the producer may attempt to extract a monopoly price at retail because it cannot do so at the manufacturing point.

Vertical contractual restraints and vertical integration by ownership thus may often be substitutes for one another. In organizing production and distribution, the firm must decide which activities it can best conduct internally and which functions are best contracted out to separate business entities. In recognition of their common economic justifications and limited anticompetitive potential, these approaches arguably should be treated consistently under the antitrust laws to permit firms to choose the mix of strategies that minimizes transaction costs. As Michael Katz observes, however, modern antitrust doctrine falls short of this goal:

> * * * [T]here is one particularly striking incongruity in U.S. antitrust policy. Integrated firms are allowed to implement almost any contract internally. Thus, antitrust laws that restrict independent firms' writing of arm's length contracts may have the effect of encouraging vertical integration even in cases in which this form of business organization is not the most efficient one. For this reason, a public policy that prevents pernicious vertical practices by unintegrated firms may actually be worse than a policy that allows these practices. * * *

MICHAEL KATZ, *Vertical Contractual Relations*, *in* 1 HANDBOOK OF INDUSTRIAL ORGANIZATION 715 (Richard Schmalensee & Robert D. Willig, Eds., 1989).

How similar or different is the courts' treatment of vertical integration through merger and vertical integration by contract based on what you have learned so far? Would you agree with Katz's conclusion that by being more restrictive the law of exclusive dealing might have inadvertently been encouraging inefficient levels of vertical integration? Could the converse be true, *i.e.*, could a hostile attitude towards vertical mergers encourage inefficient levels of exclusive contracting? Why might it be important to ensure, as Katz suggests, that antitrust doctrine remains "neutral," *i.e.*, that it creates neither incentives nor disincentives for firms choose one distribution strategy over another?

2. VERTICAL MERGER ANALYSIS SINCE 1980

Chicago school commentators proffered two main criticisms of the structural era's case law. First, as was discussed above in Sidebar 7–5, they emphasized that foreclosure of rivals does not necessarily harm competition. After all, all vertical agreements foreclose someone. As Judge Bork explained in analyzing "the series of vertical mergers that spurred the Federal Trade Commission to intervene in the cement industry," "[f]oreclosure may occasionally be a threat to individual firms. It is never a threat to competition." ROBERT H. BORK, THE ANTITRUST PARADOX 244 (1978) (citing cases prior to *Ash Grove*). This criticism called into question whether small amounts of foreclosure could harm competition. Under such circumstances, it may be plausible that the foreclosed rivals could merely find other supply or distribution relationships, at little or no cost penalty. Judge Bork made this point while ridiculing another vertical merger government case: If "eager suppliers and hungry customers" find themselves "unable to find each other, forever foreclosed and left to languish," then the F.T.C. "could have cured this aspect of the situation by throwing an industry social mixer." *Id.* at 232.

Second, Chicago School critics emphasized that vertical integration was often procompetitive, for much the same reasons that other vertical practices could often be efficient. With specific reference to *Autolite*, Judge Bork asserted that "The structure of an industry * * * will be whatever is most efficient for [that industry] * * *. The decision to make oneself or buy from others is always made on the basis of the difference in cost and effectiveness, criteria the law should permit the manufacturer to apply without interference." ROBERT H. BORK, THE ANTITRUST PARADOX 236 (1978).

Although there have been few opportunities for the Supreme Court to revisit vertical merger analysis, as is true in the area of horizontal mergers, it is likely that today's Supreme Court would take these criticisms seriously and would not still agree with its older decisions in *Brown Shoe* and *Autolite*. They would more likely look to the different attitudes and approaches to analysis that have been developed in government enforcement guidelines, to which we turn in our next Note.

Note on the Federal Vertical Merger Guidelines—1982, 1984

This powerful criticism of prior vertical merger enforcement set the stage for a retrenchment by the federal enforcement agencies and courts during the 1980s. The 1982 Merger Guidelines, amended in 1984, reframed vertical merger analysis around the question of whether such transactions would harm horizontal competition in either upstream or downstream markets. The section on "Horizontal Effects from Non–Horizontal Mergers" in the 1984 Merger Guidelines (§ 4) remains in force as a statement of Justice Department enforcement policy.*

The 1984 Guidelines set forth three theories by which a vertical merger could harm competition. The first, commonly described as raising "two-level entry" barriers, requires extensive integration between the upstream and downstream markets, such that a new entrant to one level also must enter the other level simultaneously. Under such circumstances, the Guidelines indicate, additional vertical integration may increase the difficulty of simultaneous entry. This could harm competition either upstream or downstream, if market concentration and other characteristics at one market level suggest that the increased difficulty of entry is likely to affect market performance. 1984 Merger Guidelines § 4.21.

Figure 7–4:

Two Level Entry

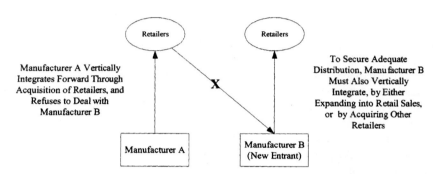

The second theory is that vertical integration could facilitate horizontal collusion. 1984 Merger Guidelines § 4.22. For example, the Guidelines suggest that the acquisition of retailers by manufacturers may make it easier for the manufacturers to detect cheating, facilitating manufacturer-level coordination. Or the vertical merger may facilitate collusion by eliminating a particularly disruptive buyer, who is sufficiently important to sellers as to be in a position to induce seller cheating.

Finally, the 1984 Guidelines explain that a vertical merger can be used by monopoly public utilities subject to rate regulation as a tool for evading that regulation. 1984 Merger Guidelines § 4.23. Integration may allow the merged firm to shift costs from unregulated to regulated activities undetected by the regulatory agency. The result might be higher prices for the regulated service (which is permitted by the regulator to pass through costs) and, perhaps also, distorted competition in the unregulated market (where the merged firm's activities would now effectively be subsidized).

---

* The 1992 and 1997 merger guidelines revisions were limited to horizontal mergers.

Figure 7–5:
Theories of Anticompetitive Exclusion Through Vertical Merger

Exclusion/Foreclosure	**Facilitate Coordination**	**Exercise of Pre-existing Market Power**
• Input foreclosure • Customer foreclosure • Impose requirement of two-level entry on potential rivals	• Elimination of disruptive buyer • Information exchange (misuse of confidential information)	• Evasion of Regulation • Facilitation of price discrimination

---

The 1984 Merger Guidelines also were more sympathetic to the efficiency defense in vertical merger analysis than in analyzing horizontal mergers:

> An extensive pattern of vertical integration may constitute evidence that substantial economies are afforded by vertical integration. Therefore, the Department will give relatively more weight to expected efficiencies in determining whether to challenge a vertical merger than in determining whether to challenge a horizontal merger.

1984 Merger Guidelines § 4.24.

How closely do these guidelines for the exercise of prosecutorial discretion comport with Supreme Court vertical merger decisions like *Brown Shoe* and *Autolite*? Can either case be interpreted as examples of any of these three theories of anticompetitive vertical integration, or are the 1984 Guidelines better understood as rooted in an economic approach to antitrust divorced from the social and political goals that animated antitrust enforcement in antitrust's pre-Chicago structural era?

Note on the "Single Monopoly Profit" Theory

If a firm has obtained a monopoly in one market, can it profit by extending its monopoly to another market? What if it also monopolizes the market for a key input or the market for downstream distribution? What if it also monopolizes the market for a demand complement (like a computer operating system monopolist extending its monopoly to word processing software)?

It is sometimes suggested that a pre-existing monopolist could not have an anticompetitive motive to acquire any of its input suppliers or its distributors. Under this view there is only a "single monopoly profit" and a firm cannot make more money by trying to "extend" its monopoly to a second market. *See, e.g., G.K.A. Beverage Corp. v. Honickman*, 55 F.3d 762, 767 (2d Cir. 1995) ("a vertically structured monopoly can take only one monopoly profit"); *Jefferson Parish Hosp. Dist. No. 2 v. Hyde*, 466 U.S. 2, 36–37, 104 S.Ct. 1551, 1570–71 (1984) (O'Connor, J., concurring) ("A seller with a monopoly on flour...cannot increase the profit it can extract from flour consumers simply by forcing them to buy sugar along with their flour," though it may be possible for the flour monopolist "to use its market power to acquire additional power in the sugar market, perhaps by driving out competing sellers of sugar..."); *Town of Concord v. Boston Edison Co.*, 915 F.2d 17, 23, 32 (1st Cir. 1990) (Breyer, C.J.) ("the extension of monopoly power from one to two levels does not *necessarily*, nor in an *obvious* way, give a firm added power to raise prices"). If the single monopoly profit theory is correct, a monopolist would not have an anticompetitive motive to contract with suppliers or distributors for exclusivity (achieving de facto vertical integration by contract) or to bundle or tie the sale of a product it monopolizes with the sale of a complementary product it sells in a competitive market.

Yet it has long been recognized, even by commentators associated with the Chicago School, who have advocated reliance on the single monopoly profit theory and who are typically skeptical of antitrust intervention in exclusionary conduct cases involving vertical mergers, vertical agreements, or tying, that the single monopoly profit theory is not invariably correct. *See, e.g.,* Ward S. Bowman, Jr., *Tying Arrangements and the Leverage Problem*, 67 YALE L.J. 19 (1957); RICHARD A. POSNER, ANTITRUST LAW 224–29 (2d ed. 2001). Indeed, in discussing vertical mergers, Robert Bork observed that cases in which a key assumption underlying the single monopoly profit theory does not hold "are quite common," ROBERT H. BORK, THE ANTITRUST PARADOX 229 (1978), though he nevertheless recommended caution in vertical merger enforcement, in part to permit firms to achieve efficiencies. *Id.* at 230. Post–Chicago commentators instead emphasize that the single monopoly profit theory is based on assumptions that are not "realistic," and conclude that it should not be credited as a basis for presuming that vertical mergers or related exclusionary conduct are pro-competitive. *See* Michael H. Riordan & Steven C. Salop, *Evaluating Vertical Mergers: A Post–Chicago Approach*, 63 ANTITRUST L.J. 513, 516–19 (1995). The following hypothetical example, based on the discussion in the Riordan & Salop article, illustrates some of the circumstances under which the single monopoly profit theory does and does not apply.

Suppose that refrigerators are produced in a competitive industry. The cooling system is the most costly part of refrigerator manufacturing, mainly because the key coolant chemical, Freezon, is expensive. A standard-size refrigerator can be manufactured at a cost (including a competitive profit) of $100 plus the cost of the Freezon. The standard refrigerator uses four pounds of Freezon. In other words, in this example Freezon is used in *fixed proportions* with other inputs into manufacturing a standard-size refrigerator: for every one refrigerator produced, the manufacturer will need four pounds of Freezon.

Chempont is the monopoly producer of Freezon. Chempont can produce Freezon for $10 per pound. If Chempont were to sell Freezon at cost, then refrigerator manufacturers would pay $40 for Freezon, produce standard-size refrigerators for $140, and sell the refrigerators at the competitive price of $140.

But Chempont knows that the monopoly price of a standard-size refrigerator is $300.* In consequence it would want to price Freezon at $50 per pound. At this price, it will cost the refrigerator manufacturers $300 to manufacture a standard-size refrigerator ($100 in manufacturing costs plus $200 for coolant). The competitive manufacturing industry then will be led to sell refrigerators for $300, the monopoly price. But the refrigerator makers do not capture the monopoly profits. Chempont does. Chempont earns $160 in monopoly profits for each refrigerator sold (the $200 price it charges for coolant less its $40 coolant manufacturing cost), while no refrigerator manufacturer earns more than a competitive return.

Chillaire is the leading manufacturer of kitchen refrigerators. If Chempont were to acquire Chillaire and refuse to sell Freezon to any rival refrigerator manufacturer, it could obtain a refrigerator monopoly in addition to its coolant chemical monopoly. But doing so would *not* allow Chempont to increase its profits. The merged firm would continue to sell refrigerators at the monopoly price of $300, and would continue to earn $160 in monopoly profits on each refrigerator

---

* The monopoly price depends on the extent to which refrigerator buyers will reduce their purchases as the price rises and on the cost of producing refrigerators. That price is assumed to be $300 in this example.

sold. Similarly, if instead of a merger, Chempont were to make an exclusive distribution contract with one refrigerator manufacturer, such as Chillaire, that made that firm the only refrigerator manufacturer that can use Freezon (and thus made Chillaire the only refrigerator manufacturer able to produce), that contract for exclusivity would not increase Chempont's profits. In this example, there is indeed only one monopoly profit.

To construct an example in which the single monopoly profit theory does not apply, begin by supposing that before Freezon was invented, refrigerator manufacturers used a different chemical, Iceon, as a coolant. Iceon is produced in a competitive market, at a price equal to its manufacturing cost of $10 per pound. When Iceon is used in refrigerator cooling systems, it takes 21 pounds of Iceon to manufacture a standard-size refrigerator for a per-refrigerator cost of $210. The invention of Freezon made Iceon-cooled refrigerators uneconomic: even when Chempont charges a monopoly price for Freezon, a Freezon-based refrigerator sells for $300, while an Iceon-based refrigerator would have to sell for $310 ($100 in manufacturing costs plus $210 for the coolant).

Now suppose that a clever engineer discovers that a mixture of Freezon and Iceon also works well as a refrigerator coolant. Suppose that this process is not patentable and the knowledge quickly spreads throughout the industry. Refrigerator manufacturers switch from using four pounds of Freezon to using a combination of one pound of Freezon and ten pounds of Iceon. With Freezon selling at $50 per pound,** the new approach reduces coolant costs to $150 and lowers the price of a refrigerator from $300 to $250, which benefits consumers.*** Chempont continues to exercise market power in Freezon, but its monopoly profits are less than before. Now it earns profits of only $40 ($50 in revenue less $10 in costs for the one pound of Freezon sold per refrigerator).

The refrigerator maker now has a choice between using Freezon alone or a Freezon/Iceon mix.**** From its perspective, Freezon and Iceon are substitutes: the manufacturer can reduce its need for Freezon as a coolant by increasing its use of Iceon. For this reason, the manufacturers of Iceon are rivals to Chempont in selling coolant chemicals to refrigerator manufacturers. These assumptions mean that Freezon is now used in *variable proportions* in the manufacture of refrigerators, not *fixed proportions*. Some manufacturers might choose to use four pounds of Freezon per refrigerator, whereas others might elect to use just one pound, combining it with Iceon.

** To avoid complicating the example, assume that Chempont would not find it profitable to respond by altering the price of Freezon. For example, suppose that over time Chempont has developed a large second market for Freezon, using it to make household air conditioners. Also assume that Iceon cannot be used for air conditioners. Suppose further that the air conditioning market has grown to become much more important to Chempont than the refrigerator market and that Chempont cannot discriminate in price among users (cannot charge a different price to refrigerator manufacturers than it does to air conditioner manufacturers). Then it is plausible that developments in the refrigerator market would not alter Chempont's view that the most profitable price for Freezon is $50 per pound.

*** Note that this benefit to consumers, and the resulting reduction in the allocative efficiency loss of monopoly, comes at a social cost in the form of a production inefficiency. The social cost of producing one pound of Freezon and ten pounds of Iceon is $110, while the social cost of producing four pounds of Freezon is only $40.

**** Again to keep the example simple, assume that only one Freezon/Iceon mix is possible. Often in other contexts, variable proportion production technologies will permit many more combinations, much as salad dressing can be made with various combinations of oil and vinegar.

Figure 7–6:

Comparing Costs: Freezon vs. Iceon vs. Freezon–Iceon Mix

	Freezon Only	**Iceon Only**	**Freezon-Iceon Mix**
Refrigerator Costs	$100	$100	$100
Coolant Costs	$200	$210	$150
Totals	$300	$310	$250

With this market structure, Chempont can increase its monopoly profits by merging with Chillaire and refusing to sell Freezon to any other refrigerator producer, or, equivalently, by contracting with Chillaire to make it the exclusive buyer of Freezon.***** Without access to Freezon, rival refrigerator manufacturers cannot produce refrigerators for less than $310 (the unit cost when using Iceon alone), and so will exit the market even when Chillaire charges the monopoly price of $300. The merged firm will return to the original production technology of employing four pounds of Freezon as the coolant.****** Put differently, Freezon uses the vertical merger to exclude Iceon from the coolant input market, which permits it to return the refrigerator price to the monopoly level and allows it to increase its profits. The vertical merger can also be understood as raising entry barriers into the refrigerator industry, relative to the situation where Chempont faced more open competition from Iceon.

In the example, there was only a single monopoly profit when the monopolist's product was used in fixed proportions. In that case, a vertical merger or vertical agreement would not allow the upstream monopolist to increase its market power. The reason was simple: when the inputs were used in fixed proportions, they did not have substitutes, so there was no way to increase the exercise of market power by excluding rivals. But the single monopoly profit argument did not apply when the product was used in variable proportions. Then it was possible for the input monopolist to increase its profits through vertical integration or vertical contracting by preventing downstream firms from substituting some other input. By excluding firms selling the substitute input, the input monopolist could increase its monopoly profits.

There can be more than a single monopoly profit even if the upstream product is used by purchasers in fixed proportions. This can happen if the product has current or potential substitutes and the vertical arrangement operates to reduce the rivalry from those substitutes.******* For example, suppose that the other refrigerator makers exit the market. Then the vertical

---

***** From the perspective of refrigerator consumers, the vertical merger also can be understood as bundling or tying the sale of Freezon to the sale of Chillare refrigerator bodies. As this observation suggests, tying can have similar exclusionary effects as exclusive dealing contracts or vertical integration.

****** The merged firm's coolant cost falls to $40, generating a production efficiency, rela- tive to the situation where refrigerator makers were using Iceon as well as Freezeon.

******* The upstream product is used in fixed proportions with other inputs, but it is not essential, because some other product could be used instead in combination with the other inputs.

merger could raise entry barriers into the coolant chemical industry by forcing a new entrant to engage in more difficult "two level" entry: it must do more than simply invent a new coolant chemical; it must also enter the refrigerator manufacturing business. (For other examples illustrating the failure of the single monopoly profit theory to hold even when the product is used in fixed proportions, see the *Note on Intrabrand Competition and the "Single Monopoly Profit" Theory*, Casebook, *supra* Chapter 4, and Sidebar 7–3 on the economics of tying.)

There are other ways the single monopoly profit theory would not hold, even if the upstream product is used in fixed proportions. If vertical integration would permit Chempont to discriminate in price, or to evade coolant chemical price regulation, for example, it may again be possible for Chempont to increase its monopoly profits. (Economic price discrimination can be anticompetitive or procompetitive, as discussed in Sidebar 7–8, *infra*.) Moreover, if Chempont is not initially a monopolist, there are more possibilities for vertical agreements to harm competition—not surprisingly, as it would no longer be appropriate to view Chempont's conduct through the lens of single *monopoly* product theory.

As was true in the area of horizontal mergers, the lower courts were quick to follow the lead of the enforcement agencies and recede from the prior judicial hostility to vertical mergers. By 1989, a district court could write: "vertical integration is not an unlawful or even suspect category under the antitrust laws." *Reazin v. Blue Cross and Blue Shield of Kan., Inc.*, 663 F.Supp. 1360, 1489 (D. Kan. 1987), *aff'd*, 899 F.2d 951 (10th Cir. 1990). The *O'Neill v. Coca–Cola* case excerpt that follows illustrates how far the judicial analysis of vertical mergers moved in the dozen years that followed the F.T.C.'s decision in *Ash Grove*. Notice also how that movement toward a focus on the question of whether competition was harmed in any narrow economic sense was facilitated by the introduction of a robust inquiry into "antitrust injury," which we first explored in Chapter 1.

O'NEILL v. COCA–COLA CO.

United States District Court for the Northern District of Illinois, 1987.

669 F.Supp. 217.

BUA, District Judge.

Before this court are the motions of defendants, The Coca–Cola Company, Inc. and PepsiCo, Inc., to dismiss plaintiff Dixie O'Neill's claims for declaratory and injunctive relief for alleged antitrust injury she, and the class she seeks to represent, will suffer from alleged antitrust violations resulting from defendants' vertical acquisitions of certain bottling facilities. * * * For the reasons stated herein, both defendants' motions are granted and plaintiff's claims are dismissed in their entirety.

* * *

II. Facts

A. Acquisitions of Bottling Concerns

Coca–Cola and PepsiCo dominate the highly concentrated United States soft drink industry with 37.4% and 28.9% respective national market shares of all carbonated soft drink products. Coca–Cola and PepsiCo produce syrups and concentrates which are sold to bottlers who add carbonated water, bottle, and sell the resulting carbonated soft drinks. Coca–Cola and PepsiCo both grant exclusive territorial marketing areas to their respective trademark licensee bottlers and prohibit them from distributing competing flavors of other companies.

On May 30, 1986, PepsiCo announced its purchase of MEI Corporation ("MEI"), the third largest independent bottler of PepsiCo carbonated soft drink products. * * * [Also in 1986, Coca–Cola acquired the soft drink bottling assets of BCI Holding Corporation ("Beatrice") and JTL Corporation ("JTL"), and merged them. Later that year, Coke transferred all its bottling operations to its Coca–Cola Enterprises ("CCE") subsidiary, and sold 51% of CCE stock to the public (while continuing to hold the remaining 49%).—Eds.]

* * *

B. Transshipment Restrictions

PepsiCo grants each of its licensed bottlers an exclusive territory in which to produce and market PepsiCo products. To protect the exclusivity of these territories, PepsiCo forbids its bottlers to supply retailers who buy or sell outside their territories, buy from or sell to other retailers within their territories, or facilitate transshipment by selling to intermediaries. PepsiCo enforces this policy by firing, boycotting, or otherwise punishing those who violate the noted prohibitions.

III. Discussion

O'Neill brings this action individually as a purchaser of Coca–Cola and PepsiCo carbonated soft drink products, and as a representative of a class of all purchasers of Coca–Cola and PepsiCo carbonated soft drinks, pursuant to Rule 23 of the Federal Rules of Civil Procedure. O'Neill's complaint sets forth two claims. In Count I, O'Neill complains that defendants, with their respective acquisitions of JTL, Beatrice, and MEI bottlers, have violated the antitrust laws. Specifically, O'Neill alleges that these acquisitions effectively reduce competition in the soft drink industry, thereby increasing prices for herself and all consumers of Coca–Cola and PepsiCo soft drinks. O'Neill asserts that PepsiCo's acquisition of MEI provides PepsiCo with ownership of bottlers that produce approximately 33% of all PepsiCo brand carbonated soft drinks in the United States. O'Neill similarly asserts that Coca–Cola's retention of the largest single interest in CCE stock permits it to control, through CCE, ownership of bottlers that produce approximately 31% of all Coca–Cola brand carbonated soft drinks in the United States.

* * *

B. Standing to Assert Claims Under Count I

O'Neill, as a consumer, alleges higher prices as her antitrust injury resulting from Coca–Cola's and PepsiCo's vertical acquisitions. Higher prices, as well as lower output, are "the principal vices proscribed by the antitrust laws." Although higher prices are specifically recognized as an antitrust injury, the question in this case is whether the alleged antitrust violation proximately threatens plaintiff with such an injury.

* * *

O'Neill argues that PepsiCo's and Coca–Cola's acquisitions of MEI, JTL, and Beatrice will have the following anticompetitive effects: increasing barriers to entry and mobility in the carbonated soft drink market; reducing or eliminating existing suppliers, customers, distributors and retailers of all three bottlers; increasing interdependent pricing practices between PepsiCo and Coca–Cola; reducing or eliminating preexisting competition between defendants and the bottlers; and increasing concentration of distribution channels and the industry in general. O'Neill claims that the vertical acquisitions violate antitrust laws and that these mergers, producing the aforementioned results, will increase the price of PepsiCo and Coca–Cola soft drink products, thereby causing her to suffer pocketbook injury.

O'Neill does not specifically allege how higher prices will result from these alleged consequences of the vertical acquisitions. Nor does O'Neill show that higher prices are likely to result from the vertical acquisitions. Indeed, O'Neill burdens this court to provide the causal links between what she alleges to be the consequences of the vertical acquisitions and how those consequences result in higher prices.

Accepting O'Neill's allegations of the consequences of vertical acquisitions to be true, higher prices could theoretically result from either of two ways. The reduced competition between the bottlers and manufacturers may allow for an increase in prices by the manufacturer who now owns and controls the bottler's operation and resale prices to the wholesaler. If the wholesaler faces a higher purchasing price from the manufacturer/bottler, the wholesaler could theoretically pass any additional costs on to the retailer who may in turn pass on the increase in price to the consumer. Alternatively, or additionally, O'Neill implies that the vertical acquisitions will increase the potential for interdependent pricing practices between PepsiCo and Coca–Cola. Presumably, O'Neill wishes the court to infer that such potential for interdependent pricing will result in price-fixing, yielding higher prices for the consumer. However, as the following discussion details, O'Neill fails to show that either of these paths to higher consumer prices are probable or proximately threaten her with antitrust injury.

If O'Neill seeks to show higher prices resulting from the elimination or reduction of any preexisting competition between the manufacturer and bottler, her approach fails in two manners. First, O'Neill is unable to show any indication that such elimination of any preexisting competition between bottlers and manufacturers will have any perceivable effect on price. It is not any more self-evident that the elimination of such competition will result in higher prices as opposed to lower prices. For example, the vertical acquisitions may just as likely lead to economies in scale that could reduce prices to consumers as they could theoretically lead to increased prices from manufacturers who now control the bottlers' resale price to wholesalers. O'Neill offers no proof that the elimination of competition will more likely lead to the detrimental consequence of higher prices as opposed to the beneficial consequence of lower prices.

Second, even if this court were to assume that higher prices would naturally result from the elimination of any preexisting competition between the manufacturers and the bottlers, O'Neill does not show that she purchases any of the products of either defendant in any of the areas serviced by the JTL, Beatrice, or MEI acquisitions. Even if this court were to assume that higher prices threatened a consumer serviced by these bottlers and that higher prices were proximately related to the vertical acquisitions, absent evidence that she resides in an area serviced by or regularly purchases from retailers receiving carbonated beverages from these bottlers, O'Neill cannot be considered to suffer any injury.

* * *

* * * O'Neill's implied claim that vertical acquisitions will result in interdependent pricing that will yield higher consumer prices is fatally speculative. O'Neill offers no indication that vertical acquisitions have any rational nexus to the potential for interdependent pricing practices between the defendants. Again, even if this court were to assume true that interdependent pricing was a natural consequence of such vertical acquisitions, O'Neill does not claim she purchases products from any of the retailers serviced by the acquired bottlers. What Coca–Cola and PepsiCo acquire within their respective vertical chains of production, distribution, and sales has no self-evident, logical relationship to how they may behave outside of their individual vertical chains toward each other and ultimately toward the consumer. Acquiring independent bottlers may have serious ramifications for other independent bottlers who do business with these defendants within their respective vertical markets. It does not, however, dictate how PepsiCo and Coca–Cola will behave toward each other or whether such acquisitions are more likely to lead to collusive pricing as opposed to predatory pricing. Pure speculation, or vaguely defined links are not sufficient to establish a chain of causation that demonstrates a threat of antitrust injury. Mere opinion or conclusory statements of what may happen when three bottlers are purchased by two dominant concentrate manufacturers are not sufficient to establish price-fixing as a threatened antitrust injury.

* * * Because O'Neill fails to assert any logical connection between vertical acquisitions and how they ultimately affect the regional or national pricing policies of PepsiCo and Coca–Cola, O'Neill is unable to establish that she is proximately threatened by an antitrust injury. As such, O'Neill is without standing and defendants' motions to dismiss Count I of the amended complaint are granted.

––––––

What fraction of which markets was foreclosed to whom by the acquisition of soft drink bottlers by the leading manufacturers of soft drink concentrate (Coke and Pepsi)? Should the court have allowed the plaintiff to obtain discovery on any of the following theories by which the merger could have harmed competition?

(1) *Input foreclosure*: Coke and Pepsi could use the vertical acquisitions of bottlers to cut off or limit the access of rival soft drink concentrate manufacturers (perhaps Cadbury Schweppes) from access to the best (most efficient) bottlers. Or, even if the unaffiliated bottlers are not more efficient than the ones that Coke and Pepsi acquired, the unaffiliated bottlers might recognize that they no longer need fear competition from those affiliated with Coke and Pepsi when rival soft drink manufacturers are looking for bottlers, and, consequently, charge higher prices for bottling services. Either way, the merger would raise distribution costs for those rivals and create "two-level" entry barriers for potential entrants at the concentrate manufacturing level, thereby reducing the competition that Coke and Pepsi face and allowing Coke and Pepsi to raise the price of soft drinks sold at retail.

(2) *Customer foreclosure*: The vertical mergers could lead Coke and Pepsi to shift their bottling business from those independent bottlers they previously employed to bottlers affiliated with Coke and Pepsi. The unaffiliated bottlers could, in consequence, have higher costs (because they operate at lower scale) or even exit from the market, thereby raising the bottling and distribution costs facing fringe soft drink concentrate manufacturers. This would reduce the competition that Coke and Pepsi face, allowing them to raise the price of soft drinks sold at retail.

(3) *Facilitate collusion through the elimination of a disruptive buyer*: Coke and Pepsi could acquire bottlers that were instrumental in preventing them from successful tacit collusion in the sale of concentrate to bottlers. The result could be higher concentrate prices to bottlers.

(4) *Facilitate collusion through information exchange*: The vertical mergers could give Coke and Pepsi access to sensitive competitive information about each other obtained by buyers in the normal course of business (such as planned introduction of new products or reduced soft drink concentrate prices), thereby making it easier for the two to reach consensus on terms of coordination or to detect and police cheating. The result could be tacit collusion among soft drink concentration manufacturers.

On the other hand, how could vertical integration in this industry benefit competition? Are efficiency explanations for the vertical mergers more plausible than anticompetitive ones? Will the mergers reduce concentrate distribution costs, and make Coke and Pepsi lower cost competitors, by (1) allowing the bottlers to achieve greater economies of scale? (2) assuring the manufacturers that they will have more reliable bottlers? (3) better aligning the incentives of the manufacturer and bottler, eliminating bottler free riding in promotion? (4) eliminating "double marginalization?"

Note on Eliminating Double Marginalization

One of the potential efficiency benefits of vertical integration is that it can eliminate double marginalization (or successive markups). To see why, suppose an upstream firm, say a television manufacturer, has a (marginal) cost of 70 and transfers its product to retailers at a wholesale price of 100. Suppose the retailers have (marginal) distribution costs of their own of 10, so their total cost is 110. With a cost of 110, the retailers' profit-maximizing decision is to add a further markup of 30 to generate a retail price of 140.

What would happen to the retail price if the upstream producer and downstream distributor merged? The merged firm no longer has to set a wholesale price. In selecting its retail price, it would recognize that its costs are 80 (70 in manufacturing plus 10 in retailing), which is less than the cost of 110 that the stand-alone retailer faced. With a lower cost than the stand-alone retailer, the merged firm has an incentive to lower price below what the stand-alone retailer charged, say to 105, and in consequence to expand output. Doing so simultaneously benefits consumers and increases the merged firm's profits. Both are possible because buyers and the seller share in the efficiency gains that come from reducing the allocative efficiency loss. Although the merged firm continues to price in excess of the social cost of production and distribution, here 80, the retail price has fallen closer to the social cost, generating efficiencies that sellers and buyers can share.

It is possible that the firms could reach the same outcome through vertical contract, short of merger. The agreement would require the manufacturer to set a wholesale price of 70, its cost, leading the retailer to lower the price to consumers to the same lower level that the vertically integrated firm would charge. To make this deal profitable for the manufacturer, the retailer would need to pay the manufacturer a fixed sum (one that does not vary with the amount sold, and hence would not affect the retailer's marginal cost). The fixed sum would need to equal the lost manufacturer profits resulting from lowering the wholesale price plus a share of the increased profits that accrue from increasing output. This kind of contract is called a "two-part tariff" because the manufacturer and retailer negotiate both a (lower) wholesale price and a fixed "franchise fee." But it may be impractical for the manufacturer and retailer to negotiate such a complex contract, particularly when consumer demand is not stable or the retailers compete.

The efficiency benefits of eliminating double marginalization can appear in contexts beyond the manufacturer/retailer relationship, whenever complementary products are sold at separate markups. For example, if hotels buy lift tickets from a nearby ski resort and sell ski packages, and both the lodging and the lift tickets are sold above cost, a similar inefficiency results that could be eliminated by merger or contract.

Sidebar 7–7:
The Influence of Post–Chicago
Exclusionary Effects Theories
on Vertical Merger Enforcement Trends
in the U.S. and E.U.

During the 1990s, the federal enforcement agencies demonstrated a renewed interest in vertical merger analysis. In part, this reflected the influence of modern thinking about exclusionary conduct under the "raising rivals' costs" framework we have discussed at the beginning of Chapter 6. As a methodology for vertical merger analysis, raising rivals costs can be understood as a more general description of the concern with two-level entry set forth in the 1984 Merger Guidelines. This new framework for analyzing vertical mergers was developed by Michael Riordan and Steven Salop. *See* Michael H. Riordan & Steven C. Salop, *Evaluating Vertical Mergers: A Post–Chicago Approach*, 63 ANTITRUST L.J. 513, 520–22 (1995). As with former Judge Robert Bork, Riordan & Salop undertake an economic analysis of vertical mergers, unconcerned with other goals that might have been important to the Supreme Court in 1972. *Compare* ROBERT H. BORK, THE ANTITRUST PARADOX 225–45 (1978).

The federal enforcement agencies questioned a small but significant number of vertical mergers during the 1990s—small in absolute number or relative to the number of horizontal mergers subject to equally close scrutiny, but significant and more than had generated enforcement attention during the previous decade. For example, the Justice Department's complaint against Lockheed Martin's acquisition of Northrop Grumman—which was abandoned by the parties after the government announced its challenge—was a vertical merger case. Lockheed Martin produced platforms for fighter aircraft and integrated the electronics systems for various military projects including ships, submarines and satellites. Northrop produced a number of electronic subsystems such as radar and sonar that were inputs into Lockheed's stage of production. Similarly, the FTC's investigation of Time Warner's acquisition of Turner Broadcasting did not just focus on the horizontal aspect of the deal arising out of the combination of the cable programming assets of the firms (Time Warner owned HBO; Turner owned CNN, Turner Classic Movies, and the WTBS cable superstation). The consent settlement also addressed vertical issues that arose because Time Warner operated cable systems covering 17 percent of cable households, which meant it was both a programming provider and a cable service provider. Few vertical merger challenges have been brought by the federal agencies in recent years.

In 2007, the European Commission also adopted Guidelines for non-horizontal mergers. *See Guidelines on the Assessment of Non–Horizontal Mergers Under the Council Regulation on the Control of Concentrations Between Undertakings, available at* http://ec.europa.eu/comm/competition/mergers/legislation/nonhorizontalguidelines.pdf. The Guidelines recognize that vertical mergers and mergers involving complementary products often are procompetitive because they can provide substantial scope for efficiencies, including better coordination of product design and the organization of the production process and incentives for lower prices. This incentive for lower prices can arise because an integrated firm can capture a higher fraction of the benefits of a price decrease than either unintegrated firm could have captured before the merger, an effect that is often referred to as the internalization of double-mark-ups or "double-marginalization".

The European Guidelines take a modern "post-Chicago" approach to the concept of foreclosure, distinguishing between input and customer foreclosure. They also recognize that for foreclosure to lead to consumer harm, it is not necessary that the rivals exit the market. The relevant benchmark instead is whether the merger would lead to higher prices for consumers.

Input foreclosure arises where the merger is likely to raise the costs of downstream rivals by restricting their access to an important input. The merged entity may do so by restricting access to the products that it otherwise would supply to its unaffiliated downstream rivals, thereby raising their costs. For example, when the input market is oligopolistic, and competition is imperfect, a decision of the merged firm to restrict access to its inputs reduces the competitive pressure exercised on remaining input suppliers, which may allow them to raise the input price they charge to nonintegrated downstream competitors.* Rivals' higher input costs may give the merged firm the ability and incentive to profitably increase its price to consumers.

Customer foreclosure arises where the firm forecloses upstream rivals by restricting their access to a sufficient customer base, as by integrating with an important customer in the downstream market. If actual or potential rivals in the upstream market (the input market) lose access to a sufficient customer base, their ability or incentive to compete may be reduced. This in turn may raise downstream rivals' costs by making it harder for them to obtain input supplies at similar prices as absent the merger, which may allow the merged entity profitably to establish higher prices in the downstream market.

The European Guidelines also assess the potential for vertical mergers to *facilitate tacit or express coordination* in oligopoly markets by eliminating a maverick competitor, by increasing the degree of symmetry among competitors, by increasing the ability to detect deviations and more effectively punishing companies that deviate from the coordinated outcome, and by eliminating disruptive buyers that significantly tempt such deviations.

It remains to be seen how the tension between the seemingly more interventionist approach to vertical mergers by the European Commission and the less interventionist approach of the 1984 vertical merger guidelines in the U.S. will be resolved over time.

Although the principal focus of agency and judicial scrutiny has remained and is very likely to remain on horizontal mergers, it appears that vertical mergers that raise significant concerns will continue to arise, as well, particularly in industries facing significant competitive pressures to vertically integrate. Like horizontal mergers, however, vertical mergers will be analyzed primarily with reference to government guidelines, more recent lower court

* In essence, input foreclosure by the merged entity may expose its downstream rivals to non-vertically integrated suppliers with increased market power.

decisions, and economic commentary, as the influence of Supreme Court decisions from the structural era continues to wane.

D. SECONDARY LINE PRICE DISCRIMINATION AND THE CHALLENGE OF *MORTON SALT*

Introduction: The Robinson Patman Act—An Overview

Section 2 of the Clayton Act, as originally signed into law in 1914, included a prohibition of "price discrimination," where the effect "may be substantially to lessen competition or tend to create a monopoly in any line of commerce." Price discrimination, literally the charging of different prices to at least two different customers, was viewed at the time as a serious weapon of the trusts, who were wielding it to discipline and destroy their rivals. By selectively reducing prices, often to predatory or "below cost" levels, the trust could impede entry by would-be rivals or drive existing rivals from the market. Price discriminations used in this fashion were characterized as "primary line"—its competitive effects occurred at the same functional level of the market, *i.e.*, rivals of the discriminating seller.

But price discrimination might also arise in the context of competitive struggles between two competing purchasers from a common supplier. In that context, one of the purchasers might seek favorable treatment from the supplier in the form of better pricing, conditions of sale or allowances not made available to its rival, a fellow purchaser. In these instances, the price discrimination was categorized as "secondary line." Although the discrimination originated with an upstream seller, as in the case of primary line discrimination, its effects were felt at the "secondary" or dealer level, one step removed. The discrimination would not injure one of the discriminator's rivals, but instead the "disfavored purchaser," a rival of the favored purchaser and customer of the discriminating seller.

Two issues arose under the original language of Section 2 of the Clayton Act. First, courts and commentators questioned whether it condemned both primary and secondary line price discrimination, or was limited in scope to just primary line injury. The question was answered in *George Van Camp & Sons Co. v. American Can Co.*, 278 U.S. 245 (1929), where the Supreme Court held that the Act covered both types of injury. The second issue concerned the nature and extent of the competitive effects required to make out a violation of Section 2 of the Clayton Act. From 1914 to 1936 the provision was consistently read as limiting the Act to discriminations that resulted in *generalized competitive injury*.

In 1936, in the wake of the Great Depression, the law of price discrimination underwent a major revision in the form of the Robinson–Patman Act, which amended Section 2 of the Clayton Act. (Casebook, Appendix A, *infra*.). Concerned about the rapid growth of large chain stores, particularly their emergence in the grocery retailing business, and their impact on smaller, "mom-and-pop" grocery stores, Congress acted to strengthen the provisions of the original Clayton Act, particularly as it applied to secondary line injury occasioned by the presence of "power buyers." Many in the Congress firmly believed that such power buyers, like large supermarket chains, were systematically extracting favorable terms from their suppliers, which in turn facilitated their ascendance over equally efficient, but disfavored smaller-scale merchants.

To strengthen the Clayton Act's prohibition of price discrimination, Congress added a conjunctive, alternative standard of injury to the "substantially to lessen competition or tend to create a monopoly" formula of the original Section 2. As amended, the prohibition also condemned price discrimination where the effect may be "to injure, destroy, or prevent *competition with any person* who either grants or knowingly receives the benefit of such discrimination, *or with customers of either of them*...." 15 U.S.C. § 13(a) (emphasis added). Although not expressly limited, this amended competitive effects language of the Robinson–Patman Act was quite clearly incorporated to enhance the Clayton Act's prohibition of secondary line price discrimination so it might more effectively outlaw successful efforts by powerful buyers to secure price concessions to the detriment of their smaller rivals. As the Supreme Court later held in *FTC v. Morton Salt Co.*, 334 U.S. 37 (1948), this "new provision * * * was intended to justify a finding of injury to competition by a showing of 'injury to a competitor victimized by the discrimination.'" *Id.* at 49. Evidence of generalized competitive injury, such as higher prices, lower output or other manifestations of anticompetitive effects, was no longer required of secondary line claimants.

It is important to note, too, that Section 2 of the Clayton Act goes beyond simple price discrimination by a seller. Section 2(f) of the Act makes it unlawful to knowingly solicit and receive a price discrimination that violates Section 2(a)—the flip side of offering one. Potentially less obvious forms of price discrimination are also addressed. Section 2(c) prohibits the granting of phantom brokerage allowances, and has been invoked even in cases of commercial bribery. Sections 2(d) and (e) extend the prohibitions of Section 2(a) to discriminatory promotional allowances and services, which can mask price discriminations, and require that such allowances and services be made available to all customers on "proportionately equal terms." Implementing these standards has proved to be a long-standing challenge. *See FTC v. Fred Meyer, Inc.*, 390 U.S. 341 (1968); *see also* FTC GUIDES FOR ADVERTISING ALLOWANCES AND OTHER MERCHANDISING PAYMENTS AND SERVICES, 16 C.F.R. § 240 (Aug. 17, 1990) ("*Fred Meyer* Guides"). Significantly, neither Section 2(d) nor 2(e) contain any competitive injury language such as that found in Section 2(a), making them potentially sweeping in scope.

Also significant are the Act's two affirmative defenses. The "cost justification" defense contained in Section 2(a) permits the seller to lower its price to a customer in recognition of efficiencies, *i.e.*, lower costs it incurs in selling to that customer, but is not available as a defense to a Section 2(d) or (e) violation. The "meeting competition" defense of Section 2(b) allows a seller to lower its prices selectively if necessary to meet (not beat) the price of one of its rivals, and can be used to defend alleged violations of Sections 2(a), as well as 2(d) and (e). *See generally Falls City Indus., Inc. v. Vanco Beverage, Inc.*, 460 U.S. 428 (1983). There are also some "non-statutory" defenses that have been recognized by the courts over the years, such as the defense for "functional discounts." *See Texaco Inc. v. Hasbrouck*, 496 U.S. 543 (1990).

A complete discussion of the law and economics of price discrimination is beyond the scope of this Casebook. For more comprehensive treatments of the history and development of the considerable body of law on price discrimination, see RICHARD A. POSNER, THE ROBINSON PATMAN ACT: FEDERAL REGULATION OF PRICE DIFFERENCES (1976); FREDERICK ROWE, PRICE DISCRIMINATION UNDER THE ROBINSON-PATMAN ACT (1962); HARRY L. SHNIDERMAN & BINGHAM B. LEVERICH, PRICE DISCRIMINATION IN PERSPECTIVE (2d ed. 1987). For a more contemporary guide to the cases, see 1 THEODORE L. BANKS, DISTRIBUTION LAW: ANTITRUST PRINCIPLES AND PRACTICE § 3 (2d ed. 2003).

In Chapter 6, in *Brooke Group* we considered the treatment of *primary line price discrimination*, which is analyzed today largely as an instance of unilateral, predatory conduct, akin to "predatory pricing." In this section, we address *secondary line price discrimination* as an additional example of exclusionary vertical agreements. In particular, we will examine the controversy that has surrounded the Act's diminished injury standard as interpreted in *Morton Salt*—a very live controversy that is evident in the most recent cases and enforcement actions of the Federal Trade Commission.

Before doing so, however, we revisit and expand upon the economics of price discrimination, explored earlier in the context of our consideration of tying in Sidebar 7–3.

Sidebar 7–8:
The Economics of Price Discrimination

Price discrimination in the economic sense is ubiquitous in the economy. It is particularly prevalent in industries where producers face high fixed costs and low marginal costs, so long as the seller has a way of sorting customers based on their willingness to pay for the product. For example, the marginal cost to a movie theater of filling any seat in its auditorium is probably very small if some seats would otherwise go empty, as the major costs—facility construction, film rental, on-site staff, food for resale—do not appear to vary with the number of seats filled. With marginal cost near zero, the business would probably not be profitable were the theater to set price equal to marginal cost; the industry would likely not survive unless the theaters charged some price in excess of marginal cost.

But the theaters can do even better if they can sort their patrons into a price-insensitive group (relatively inelastic demand, *e.g.*, those who come to the movie theater on weekend evenings) and a price-sensitive group (relatively elastic demand, *e.g.*, those willing to come at other times), and charge a higher price to the first group. Moreover, such price discrimination is not necessarily inconsistent with competition, where competition in this context is understood as free entry. The high price charged to the price-insensitive group would then be limited by the threat of new competition, and the firm as a whole would not earn more than competitive profits. *See In re Brand Name Prescription Drugs Antitrust Litig.*, 288 F.3d 1028 (7th Cir. 2002) (Posner, J.) (sellers of prescription drugs may charge different prices to different customers or different customer groups without exercising monopoly power).

Price discrimination and related practices like producing products in multiple versions—all ways of selling a product at different prices to different consumers according to how much they are willing to pay for it—are a particularly natural way to recover the high fixed costs of information and information technology. *See generally* CARL SHAPIRO & HAL R. VARIAN, INFORMATION RULES: A STRATEGIC GUIDE TO THE NETWORK ECONOMY 19–81 (1999) (chapters on pricing information and versioning information). As with price discrimination generally, the licensing of intellectual property at a price above its marginal cost (often zero) is not necessarily inconsistent with competition, and thus does not necessarily reflect the exercise of market power. *See* Chapter 10, *infra*.

Price discrimination can be harmful or beneficial to buyers. *See, e.g.*, *Jefferson Parish*, 466 U.S. at 36 n.4 (O'Connor, J., concurring). It is harmful if it permits the seller to raise price to a group of buyers; it is beneficial if it encourages the seller to serve a previously unserved group of buyers. To see why either possibility could occur, consider the following hypothetical example.

Eastern is the only airline flying between Washington, D.C. and Boston. It is thus a monopolist. There are two kinds of passengers, business and leisure. All business passengers are identical, and would be willing to pay $200 for a one way ticket. All leisure passengers are identical, and would be willing to pay $100 for a one way ticket. All costs are fixed (none vary with the number of passengers): the plane costs $1000 per flight to operate regardless of the number of passengers who fly. (The numbers in the example are wildly unrealistic; they have been chosen to make the math simple!)

First, it is possible that price discrimination would benefit buyers by making a product available to a group of buyers who otherwise would be unserved. To see why, assume that the typical flight carries 10 business passengers and 5 leisure passengers. The carrier compares the following two alternatives—no price discrimination and price discrimination—and selects the alternative that leads to the highest profit.

If price discrimination were prohibited, the airline could charge only one price. What price would it select? The best price must either be $100 (in which case Eastern will serve both business and leisure passengers) or $200 (in which case it will serve only business passengers). Eastern evaluates these alternatives by comparing the resulting profit. If the price is $100, 15 passengers will fly (both groups). Eastern will receive revenues of $1500 and earn a profit of $500. If the price is instead $200, 10 fly (only business passengers). Eastern will receive revenues of $2000 and earn a profit of $1000. Comparing these alternatives, Eastern would pick a price of $200 if it is limited to one price (*i.e.*, prevented from discriminating in price). Leisure travelers would not fly; only business travelers would be served.

With price discrimination, Eastern can do better, and so may some customers. Suppose that the airline offers two types of tickets: restricted tickets (*e.g.*, with advance purchase requirements and limited refundability) and unrestricted. Business travelers will only purchase unrestricted tickets (assuming the price is no more than $200). Leisure travelers will purchase either restricted or unrestricted, and choose the type with the lowest price (assuming the price is no more than $100).

Eastern's best strategy now is to sell unrestricted tickets for $200 and restricted tickets for $100. The 10 business travelers will buy $200 (unrestricted) tickets, generating $2000 in revenue. The 5 leisure travelers will buy $100 (restricted) tickets, generating $500 more revenue. Eastern's total revenue now is $2500, and it earns a profit of $1500. In this example, permitting price discrimination may induce Eastern to serve the leisure customers, who previously would have gone unserved, without charging more to its business customers.

But price discrimination need not necessarily benefit Eastern's buyers. It may instead allow the seller to charge more to a group of buyers lacking attractive alternatives (and thus facing inelastic demand). To see why, assume (contrary to what was previously supposed) that the typical flight carries 5 business passengers and 10 leisure passengers.

If the airline can charge only one price, what price would be best under these assumptions? As before, the best price must either be $100 (in which case Eastern will serve both business and leisure passengers) or $200 (in which case it will serve only business passengers). If the price is $100, 15 passengers will fly (both groups). Eastern will receive revenues of $1500 and earn a profit of $500. If the price is instead $200, 5 fly (only business passengers). Eastern will receive revenues of $1000 and earn a profit of $0. Comparing these alternatives, Eastern would pick a price of $100 if it is limited to one price (prevented from discriminating in price). Both leisure travelers and business travelers would be served.

To understand the consequences of price discrimination, suppose instead, as before, that the airline offers two types of tickets, restricted and unrestricted. Eastern's best strategy now is again to sell unrestricted tickets for $200 and restricted tickets for $100. The 5 business travelers will buy $200 (unrestricted) tickets, generating $1000 in revenue. The 10 leisure travelers will buy $100 (restricted) tickets, generating $1000 more revenue. Eastern's total revenue now is $2000, and it earns a profit of $1000. In this second example, price discrimination induces Eastern to sort out the business travelers and charge them a higher price, while still serving the leisure travelers.

In this simple example, price discrimination has distributional consequences—it transfers wealth from business travelers to the airline—but does not create an allocative efficiency loss, because all fifteen passengers fly regardless of Eastern's pricing policy. This special feature of the example need not hold in general, in which case output would be reduced. Suppose, for example, that when the airline set a price of $100 for all seats, some of the five leisure passengers were spouses or other companions, who decided to join a business traveler at the last minute. When Eastern decides to discriminate in price, these leisure passengers would no longer buy tickets—they are too late to purchase restricted tickets and unwilling to pay the high price for unrestricted seats. Price discrimination would remain profitable for Eastern, but now some passengers who would previously have purchased tickets are no longer served (output is reduced), generating an efficiency loss.

The sports and entertainment industries are increasingly shifting from setting a single price to discriminating in price, for example by charging higher prices for the most popular concerts or games. Is this change in business practice likely pro-competitive or anticompetitive?

> As we shall now see, these economic explanations have little to do with the arcane law of price discrimination—a fact that has been central to long-standing criticisms of U.S. price discrimination laws.

The Supreme Court's first opportunity to interpret the impact of the Robinson–Patman amendments on secondary line price discrimination came in *FTC v. Morton Salt Co.*, 334 U.S. 37 (1948). *Morton Salt* involved a challenge to the quantity discount practices of the leading manufacturer of table salt. In the FTC's view, those discounts, which were only offered to Morton Salt's larger customers, illustrated the kind of secondary line injury the Robinson–Patman Act was designed to redress.

One of the critical issues in the case concerned the competitive effects standard applicable in a secondary line injury case. Morton Salt argued unsuccessfully that in order to prevail, the FTC was required to demonstrate generalized injury to competition. The Court unequivocally rejected this view, relying on the Act's incipiency "may" language, and the Robinson–Patman Act's very specific legislative history:

> The statute requires no more than that the effect of the prohibited price discriminations "may be substantially to lessen competition * * * or to injure, destroy, or prevent competition." After a careful consideration of this provision of the Robinson–Patman Act, we have said that "the statute does not require that the discriminations must in fact have harmed competition, but only that there is a reasonable possibility that they 'may' have such an effect." *Corn Products Co. v. Federal Trade Comm'n*, 324 U.S. 726, 742. Here the Commission found what would appear to be obvious, that the competitive opportunities of certain merchants were injured when they had to pay respondent substantially more for their goods than their competitors had to pay. The findings are adequate.

> * * *

> Furthermore, in enacting the Robinson–Patman Act, Congress was especially concerned with protecting small businesses which were unable to buy in quantities, such as the merchants here who purchased in less-than-carload lots. To this end it undertook to strengthen this very phase of the old Clayton Act. The committee reports on the Robinson–Patman Act emphasized a belief that § 2 of the Clayton Act had "been too restrictive, in requiring a showing of general injury to competitive conditions...." *The new provision, here controlling, was intended to justify a finding of injury to competition by a showing of "injury to the competitor victimized by the discrimination."*

334 U.S. at 46–47, 49 (footnotes omitted; emphasis added).

The final, italicized phrase became critical: injury to generalized competition could be inferred from injury to a single disfavored purchaser. But all the Court required in order to establish injury to a competitor was evidence of a difference in price over time. Combined, these two inferences became known as the *"Morton Salt inference"*—from a persistent difference in price over time one could infer injury to a competitor, and from injury to a competitor, one could further infer injury to competition. The Court stated the modern formulation in *Vanco Beverage*: "injury to competition is established prima facie by proof of a substantial price discrimination between competing purchasers over time." *Falls City Indus., Inc. v. Vanco Beverage, Inc.*, 460 U.S. 428, 435 (1983).

Morton Salt's minimal standard of proof, coupled with more recent cases in the primary line area that mandate more substantial evidence of injury to competition, have led to continuing controversy. In fact, no U.S. antitrust statute has been subjected to as much harsh criticism and repeated calls for reform or repeal as the Robinson–Patman Act. For one of the classic Chicago School criticisms of the statute, see Edward H. Levi, *The Robinson–Patman Act—Is It in the Public Interest?*, 1 ABA ANTITRUST SECTION 60 (1952); *see also* RICHARD A. POSNER, THE ROBINSON–PATMAN ACT: FEDERAL REGULATION OF PRICE DIFFERENCES (1976). In April 2007, the Antitrust Modernization Commission called for its repeal in its final Report. *See* Antitrust Modernization Commission, *Report and Recommendations* 312 (Apr. 2007), *available at* http://www.amc.gov/report_recommendation/toc.htm.

Since the Supreme Court's 1992 decision in *Brooke Group*, defendants in secondary line price discrimination cases have argued that like *Brooke Group*, which harmonized the law of primary line price discrimination with the law of predatory pricing by applying the same standard of competitive harm, courts should harmonize secondary line injury with more contemporary notions of competitive harm. All of the courts of appeals to face that specific argument have rejected it, however, in light of the unambiguous language and history of the Robinson–Patman Act's injury requirement for secondary line cases, as it was interpreted in *Morton Salt*. *See, e.g., Chroma Lighting v. GTE Prods. Corp.*, 111 F.3d 653 (9th Cir. 1997). *But see Boise Cascade Corp. v. FTC*, 837 F.2d 1127, 1144 (D.C. Cir.1988) (imposing higher competitive injury standard before *Brooke Group*). For a further discussion of these cases and a proposal for harmonizing *Morton Salt* with more contemporary notions of competitive injury, see Andrew I. Gavil, *Secondary Line Price Discrimination and the Fate of* Morton Salt: *To Save it Let it Go*, 48 EMORY L.J. 1057 (1999).

The tension between *Morton Salt* and *Brooke Group* has still not been resolved, but in our next case, the Supreme Court came as close as it has ever come to suggesting that a more substantial competitive injury standard should be implied in secondary line price discrimination cases. Attend carefully to the Court's invocation of both cases.

VOLVO TRUCKS NORTH AMERICA, INC. v. REEDER–SIMCO GMC, INC.

Supreme Court of the United States, 2006.
546 U.S. 164, 126 S.Ct. 860, 163 L.Ed.2d 663.

GINSBURG, J., delivered the opinion of the Court, in which ROBERTS, C. J., and O'CONNOR, SCALIA, KENNEDY, SOUTER, and BREYER, JJ., joined. STEVENS, J., filed a dissenting opinion, in which THOMAS, J., joined.

Justice GINSBURG delivered the opinion of the Court.

* * *

I

Volvo manufactures heavy-duty trucks. Reeder sells new and used trucks, including heavy-duty trucks. * * * Reeder generally sold Volvo's trucks through a competitive bidding process. In this process, the retail customer describes its specific product requirements and invites bids from several dealers it selects. The customer's "decision to request a bid from a particular dealer or to allow a particular dealer to bid is controlled by such factors as an existing relationship, geography, reputation, and cold calling or other marketing strategies initiated by individual dealers."

Once a Volvo dealer receives the customer's specifications, it turns to Volvo and requests a discount or "concession" off the wholesale price (set at 80% of the published retail price). It is common practice in the industry for manufacturers to offer customer-specific discounts to their dealers. Volvo decides on a case-by-case basis whether to offer a discount and, if so, what the discount rate will be, taking account of such factors as industry-wide demand and whether the retail customer has, historically, purchased a different brand of trucks. The dealer then uses the discount offered by Volvo in preparing its bid; it purchases trucks from Volvo only if and when the retail customer accepts its bid.

Reeder was one of many Volvo dealers, each assigned by Volvo to a geographic territory. Reeder's territory encompassed ten counties in Arkansas and two in Oklahoma ... Although nothing prohibits a Volvo dealer from bidding outside its territory, Reeder rarely bid against another Volvo dealer. In the atypical event that the same retail customer solicited a bid from more than one Volvo dealer, Volvo's stated policy was to provide the same price concession to each dealer competing head to head for the same sale.

In 1997, Volvo announced a program it called "Volvo Vision," in which the company addressed problems it faced in the market for heavy trucks, among them, the company's assessment that it had too many dealers. Volvo projected enlarging the size of its dealers' markets and reducing the number of dealers from 146 to 75. Coincidentally, Reeder learned that Volvo had given another dealer a price concession greater than the concessions Reeder typically received, and "Reeder came to suspect it was one of the dealers Volvo sought to eliminate." Reeder filed suit against Volvo in February 2000, alleging losses attributable to Volvo's violation of the Arkansas Franchise Practices Act and the Robinson–Patman Act.

* * *

II

Section 2, "when originally enacted as part of the Clayton Act in 1914, was born of a desire by Congress to curb the use by financially powerful corporations of localized price-cutting tactics which had gravely impaired the competitive position of other sellers." *FTC v. Anheuser–Busch, Inc.,* 363 U.S. 536, 543, and n. 6, 80 S.Ct. 1267, 4 L.Ed.2d 1385 (1960). Augmenting that provision in 1936 with the Robinson–Patman Act, Congress sought to target the perceived harm to competition occasioned by powerful buyers, rather than sellers; specifically, Congress responded to the advent of large chainstores, enterprises with the clout to obtain lower prices for goods than smaller buyers could demand. * * *

Pursuant to § 4 of the Clayton Act, a private plaintiff may recover threefold for actual injury sustained as a result of a violation of the Robinson–Patman Act. See 15 U.S.C. § 15(a); *J. Truett Payne Co. v. Chrysler Motors Corp.,* 451 U.S. 557, 562, 101 S.Ct. 1923, 68 L.Ed.2d 442 (1981).

Mindful of the purposes of the Act and of the antitrust laws generally, we have explained that Robinson–Patman does not "ban all price differences charged to different purchasers of commodities of like grade and quality," *Brooke Group Ltd. v. Brown & Williamson Tobacco Corp.,* 509 U.S. 209, 220, 113 S.Ct. 2578, 125 L.Ed.2d 168 (1993); rather, the Act proscribes "price discrimination only to the extent that it threatens to injure competition," Our decisions describe three categories of competitive injury that may give rise to a Robinson–Patman Act claim: primary-line, secondary-line, and tertiary-line. Primary-line cases entail conduct—most conspicuously, predatory pricing— that injures competition at the level of the discriminating seller and its direct competitors. Secondary-line cases, of which this is one, involve price discrimination that injures competition among the discriminating seller's customers (here, Volvo's dealerships); cases in this category typically refer to "favored" and "disfavored" purchasers. Tertiary-line cases involve injury to competition at the level of the purchaser's customers.

To establish the secondary-line injury of which it complains, Reeder had to show that (1) the relevant Volvo truck sales were made in interstate commerce; (2) the trucks were of "like grade and quality"; (3) Volvo "discriminate[d] in price between" Reeder and another purchaser of Volvo trucks; and (4) "the effect of such discrimination may be . . . to injure, destroy, or prevent competition" to the advantage of a favored purchaser, *i.e.,* one who "receive[d] the benefit of such discrimination." 15 U.S.C. § 13(a). It is undisputed that Reeder has satisfied the first and second requirements. Volvo and the United States, as *amicus curiae,* maintain that Reeder cannot satisfy the third and fourth requirements, because Reeder has not identified any differentially-priced transaction in which it was both a "purchaser" under the Act and "in actual competition" with a favored purchaser for the same customer.

A hallmark of the requisite competitive injury, our decisions indicate, is the diversion of sales or profits from a disfavored purchaser to a favored purchaser. *FTC v. Sun Oil Co.,* 371 U.S. 505, 518–519, 83 S.Ct. 358, 9 L.Ed.2d 466 (1963) (evidence showed patronage shifted from disfavored dealers to favored dealers); *Falls City Industries, Inc. v. Vanco Beverage, Inc.,* 460 U.S. 428, 437–438, and n. 8, 103 S.Ct. 1282, 75 L.Ed.2d 174 (1983) (complaint "supported by direct evidence of diverted sales"). We have also recognized that a permissible inference of competitive injury may arise from evidence that a favored competitor received a significant price reduction over a substantial period of time. See *FTC v. Morton Salt Co.,* 334 U.S. 37, 49–51, 68 S.Ct. 822, 92 L.Ed. 1196 (1948); *Falls City Industries,* 460 U.S., at 435, 103 S.Ct. 1282. Absent actual competition with a favored Volvo dealer, however, Reeder cannot establish the competitive injury required under the Act.

III

The evidence Reeder offered at trial falls into three categories: (1) comparisons of concessions Reeder received for four successful bids against *non-Volvo* dealers, with larger concessions other successful Volvo dealers received for *different sales* on which Reeder did not bid (purchase-to-purchase comparisons); (2) comparisons of concessions offered to Reeder in connection with several unsuccessful bids against *non-Volvo* dealers, with greater concessions accorded other Volvo dealers who competed successfully for *different sales* on which Reeder did not bid (offer-to-purchase comparisons); and (3) evidence of two occasions on which Reeder bid against another Volvo dealer (head-to-head comparisons). The Court of Appeals concluded that Reeder demonstrated competitive injury under the Act because Reeder competed with favored purchasers "at the same functional level ... and within the same geographic market." As we see it, however, selective comparisons of the kind Reeder presented do not show the injury to competition targeted by the Robinson–Patman Act.

A

Both the purchase-to-purchase and the offer-to-purchase comparisons fall short, for in none of the discrete instances on which Reeder relied did Reeder compete with beneficiaries of the alleged discrimination *for the same customer*. Nor did Reeder even attempt to show that the compared dealers were consistently favored vis-à-vis Reeder. Reeder simply paired occasions on which it competed with *non-Volvo* dealers for a sale to Customer A with instances in which other Volvo dealers competed with *non-Volvo* dealers for a sale to Customer B. The compared incidents were tied to no systematic study and were separated in time by as many as seven months.

We decline to permit an inference of competitive injury from evidence of such a mix-and-match, manipulable quality. No similar risk of manipulation occurs in cases kin to the chain-store paradigm. Here, there is no discrete "favored" dealer comparable to a chain store or a large independent department store-at least, Reeder's evidence is insufficient to support an inference of such a dealer or set of dealers. For all we know, Reeder, on occasion, might have gotten a better deal vis-à-vis one or more of the dealers in its comparisons.

* * *

B

Reeder did offer evidence of two instances in which it competed head to head with another Volvo dealer. When multiple dealers bid for the business of the *same* customer, only one dealer will win the business and thereafter purchase the supplier's product to fulfill its contractual commitment. Because Robinson–Patman "prohibits only discrimination 'between different *purchasers*,'" Volvo and the United States argue, the Act does not reach markets characterized by competitive bidding and special-order sales, as opposed to sales from inventory. We need not decide that question today. Assuming the Act applies to the head-to-head transactions, Reeder did not establish that it was *disfavored* vis-à-vis other Volvo dealers in the rare instances in which they competed for the same sale-let alone that the alleged discrimination was substantial. See 1 ABA Section of Antitrust Law, Antitrust Law Developments 478–479 (5th ed. 2002) ("No inference of injury to competition is permitted when the discrimination is not substantial."(collecting cases)).

Reeder's evidence showed loss of only one sale to another Volvo dealer, a sale of 12 trucks that would have generated $30,000 in gross profits for Reeder. Per its policy, Volvo initially offered Reeder and the other dealer the same concession. Volvo ultimately granted a larger concession to the other dealer, but only after it had won the bid. In the only other instance of head-to-head competition Reeder identified, Volvo increased Reeder's initial 17% discount to 18.9%, to match the discount offered to the other competing Volvo dealer; neither dealer won the bid. In short, if price discrimination between two purchasers existed at all, it was not of such magnitude as to affect substantially competition between Reeder and the "favored" Volvo dealer.

IV

Interbrand competition, our opinions affirm, is the "primary concern of antitrust law." *Continental T. V., Inc. v. GTE Sylvania, Inc.,* 433 U.S. 36, 51–52, n. 19, 97 S.Ct. 2549, 53 L.Ed.2d 568 (1977). The Robinson–Patman Act signals no large departure from that main concern. Even if the Act's text could be construed in the manner urged by Reeder and embraced by the Court of Appeals, we would resist interpretation geared more to the protection of existing *competitors* than to the stimulation of *competition*.[4] In the case before us, there is no evidence that any favored purchaser possesses market power, the allegedly favored purchasers are dealers with little resemblance to large independent department stores or chain operations, and the supplier's selective price discounting fosters competition among suppliers of different brands. See *id.,* at 51–52, 97 S.Ct. 2549 (observing that the market impact of a vertical practice, such as a change in a supplier's distribution system, may be a "simultaneous reduction of intrabrand competition and stimulation of interbrand competition"). By declining to extend Robinson–Patman's governance to such cases, we continue to construe the Act "consistently with broader policies of the antitrust laws." *Brooke Group,* 509 U.S., at 220, 113 S.Ct. 2578 (quoting *Great Atlantic & Pacific Tea Co. v. FTC,* 440 U.S. 69, 80, n. 13, 99 S.Ct. 925, 59 L.Ed.2d 153 (1979)); see *Automatic Canteen Co. of America v. FTC,* 346 U.S. 61, 63, 73 S.Ct. 1017, 97 L.Ed. 1454 (1953) (cautioning against Robinson–Patman constructions that "extend beyond the prohibitions of the Act and, in doing so, help give rise to a price uniformity and rigidity in open conflict with the purposes of other antitrust legislation").

* * *

For the reasons stated, the judgment of the Court of Appeals for the Eighth Circuit is reversed, and the case is remanded for further proceedings consistent with this opinion.

It is so ordered.

———

Volvo Trucks is an illuminating study in the nuances of antitrust decision-making at the Supreme Court. As it once was with other, older and

---

4. The dissent assails Volvo's decision to reduce the number of its dealers. But Robinson–Patman does not bar a manufacturer from restructuring its distribution networks to improve the efficiency of its operations. If Volvo did not honor its obligations to Reeder as its franchisee, "[a]ny remedy . . . lies in state laws addressing unfair competition and the rights of franchisees, not in the Robinson–Patman Act." Brief for United States as *Amicus Curiae* 28.

criticized antitrust precedent, the Court is formally respectful of *Morton Salt*, acknowledging its holding and its long history. Yet the Court's narrow reading of the Robinson–Patman Act as it applied to bidding situations was hardly compelled. *Volvo Trucks* can fairly be read therefore, as grudgingly acknowledging the lenient competitive injury standard of the Robinson–Patman Act, but limiting the scope of its application.

The final section of its opinion, however, may have signaled a more radical departure from *Morton Salt*. There the Court stated that the Robinson–Patman Act signals no large departure from antitrust law's primary concern, interbrand competition. Drawing from precedent under the Sherman Act, especially *Brooke Group* and *Sylvania*, two of the pillars of modern antitrust analysis at the Court, it further cautioned that it would resist any interpretation of the Act geared more to the protection of existing competitors than to the stimulation of competition. It observed that in the instant case there was no evidence that any favored purchaser possesses market power. Moreover, it appeared that the supplier's selective price discounting fosters competition among suppliers of different brands. By declining to extend the Robinson–Patman Act to such cases, the Court reasoned, it aims to construe the Act consistently with the pro-competitive polices of other antitrust laws. 546 U.S. at 180–81.

Dissenting, Justice Stevens, joined by Justice Thomas, argued that the Court's reading of the Act ignored decades of precedent—including *Morton Salt*—as well as the plain language of the statute. *Id.* at 873–76. Concluding, Stevens openly concedes that the Act may not make economic sense, yet he also argues that it is inappropriate for the Court to ignore its language and history simply because it may disagree with the Act's policy. *Id.* (Stevens, J., dissenting).

The decision, therefore, can be viewed both narrowly and broadly. Narrowly, the case holds that competitive bidding generally falls outside of the reach of the Robinson–Patman Act because it never involves two competing sales—just one. As the dissent points out, this was not a necessary reading of the Act. However, it is perhaps a reasonable one. More broadly, the decision seems intended to signal that a clear majority of the Court is willing to stretch the Act's language—and discount its origins and legislative history—in order to harmonize it with other antitrust laws, *i.e.*, to read it far more narrowly in order to dissipate its arguably unique purposes and potentially *anti*-competitive application. It remains to be seen how far the Court is willing to push its desire to harmonize the Robinson–Patman Act with other antitrust laws and whether it would do so in a more traditional secondary line case.

Note on the FTC's Diminishing Enforcement of the Robinson Patman Act and the Consent Order in In re McCormick & Co. (2000)

As a consequence of persistent doubts about the wisdom and efficacy of the Robinson–Patman Act, particularly as it concerns secondary line price discrimination, enforcement of its provisions has evolved largely into a private affair. Whereas private treble damage actions by disfavored purchasers continue to be filed, the FTC has largely exited from the field of enforcement.

In the 1960s the FTC filed a minimum of ten Robinson–Patman Act cases per year and in some years issued substantially more. In 1966, for example, the

Commission issued 73 Robinson–Patman complaints, with most being consent orders involving small clothing manufacturers. But in the early 1970s the average number of FTC complaints fell to four per year, and by the late 1970s had dropped to an average of two per year. In the complete decade of the 1980s the FTC initiated a total of only five Robinson Patman matters, including but a single new case from 1982 through 1989. The FTC issued no Robinson Patman complaints in the 1990s and has issued a single case—*McCormick*—since January 1, 2000.

FTC price discrimination investigations and actions, therefore, tend to attract a great deal of attention and commentary. Such was the case when the FTC divided 3–2 over the entry of a consent judgment in *In re McCormick & Co.* entered in April, 2000, where the Commission majority found that spice giant McCormick's sales of spices at favorable prices to selected grocery store chains violated the Robinson–Patman Act.[1]

The Complaint in the matter accused McCormick, the dominant manufacturer of spices and seasonings, of granting aggregate discounts to some of its supermarket customers through a variety of means, including up-front cash payments "similar to slotting allowances," free goods, off-invoice discounts, cash rebates and performance funds. In addition, it was accused of requiring its supermarket customers to allocate up to 90% of their spice shelf spice to McCormick products. The consent decree prohibited these practices for a period of 20 years, while preserving McCormick's access to the two Robinson–Patman affirmative defenses, meeting competition, and cost justification.

The core controversy in the action, however, concerned the continued vitality of the "*Morton Salt* inference." In their statements in *McCormick*,[2] the majority and dissent both sought to qualify and thereby limit the *Morton Salt* inference, but in quite different ways. The majority appeared to rely on a market power screen, maintaining that the case for use of the *Morton Salt* inference "is strengthened" by the combination of the discriminating seller's market power and its concurrent use of exclusivity with its customers:

> In examining McCormick's discounts, the Commission did not simply apply the *Morton Salt* presumption in finding injury to competition, but examined other factors, including the market power of McCormick and the fact that discounts to favored chains were conditioned on an agreement to devote all or a substantial portion of shelf space to the McCormick line of products.

What theory of injury might have animated the majority to focus on these two factors—market power, and the shelf space commitments? Would those factors implicate primary line injury to McCormick's spice manufacturing rivals or secondary line injury to "disfavored purchasers"? Could it implicate both?

In the dissent's view the case presented a case of primary, not secondary line price discrimination. McCormick's conduct was a threat, if at all, only to its spice manufacturing competitors:

> We question whether the facts in this case support the application of the *Morton Salt* inference. The Robinson–Patman Act was primarily intended to prevent price discrimination in favor of large buyers at the expense of

---

1. *In the Matter of McCormick & Co., Inc.,* No. C–3939, 2000 WL 521741 (F.T.C. Apr. 27, 2000).

2. The Dissenting Statement of Commissioners Orson Swindle and Thomas B. Leary, and the Statement of Chairman Robert Pitofsky and Commissioners Sheila F. Anthony and Mozelle W. Thompson responding to the dissenters appears at 2000 WL 521741 (F.T.C. Apr. 27, 2000).

small buyers. When a small buyer pays more than a large buyer for an item in an industry with low profit margins and keen competition, the *Morton Salt* inference may make sense. In such circumstances, it is reasonable to infer that the purchasing power of the large buyer will cause the price discrimination to be repeated across many items, with consequent competitive injury to the small buyer.

The complaint does not allege that the favored grocery stores were larger than the disfavored grocery stores or that they purchased more spices from McCormick. Since the favored stores here were not necessarily purchasing larger quantities of spices than the disfavored stores, it is unlikely that McCormick granted lower prices to the favored grocery stores because of their buying power. In fact, the most plausible explanation for the lower prices granted in the five instances alleged in the complaint is that they were the almost fortuitous and incidental result of McCormick's responses during its price war with [its principal rival] * * *. If the favored stores were not accorded lower spice prices because of their buying power, there is little reason to believe that the favored stores generally would receive lower prices from the suppliers of the thousands of products sold in the typical grocery store. It follows that it is unlikely that the ability of the disfavored grocery stores to compete with favored stores would be harmed—the underlying rationale for use of the *Morton Salt* inference.

McCormick's alleged market power as a supplier and its alleged discriminatory prices may have harmed the ability of [McCormick's rivals] * * * to compete with McCormick. But this does not make it any more plausible that McCormick's alleged discriminatory prices harmed the ability of the disfavored grocery stores to compete with the favored grocery stores.

Do you agree with the dissenting Commissioners' challenge to the majority's theory of the case? Was it a primary line case "masquerading" as a secondary line one? The majority responded as follows:

Our colleagues suggest that this is a primary-line case (*i.e.*, injury at the producer level) masquerading as a secondary line (injury at the retailer level) enforcement action. But that kind of distinction between primary-line and secondary-line anti-competitive effects is unduly rigid and mechanical—particularly in light of the facts of this matter. It is true that part of the injury at the secondary level occurred because McCormick's behavior injured its only full-line competitor. But that is just one part of the secondary-line case. The fact remains that favored chain store buyers received from a dominant seller substantially better discounts than disfavored buyers, and they were injured, and competition at the secondary line was injured, as a result. Moreover, with [its principal rival] * * * out of the picture as an aggressive competitor, chain stores and other retailers at the secondary level will be denied benefits of future competition.

Who in your view has the best of the arguments in *McCormick*, the majority or the dissent? Perhaps only one thing is certain—neither camp was comfortable relying on the *Morton Salt* inference absent conditionalities that were connected to some theory of *injury to competition*. For the majority, secondary line price discrimination was more likely to result in injury to competition because of *seller* market power. For the dissent, secondary line price discrimination was unlikely to result in injury to competition absent proof of *buyer* market power. Which approach makes more sense given what you've learned in this Chapter about the law, and the economics, of price discrimination? Do the opinions in McCormick and the Supreme Court's decision in *Volvo Trucks* point the way toward a future consensus that will involve a more limited price discrimination prohibition than intended by the Robinson–Patman Act and its drafters in 1936?

E.   CONCLUSION

In this Chapter we have explored four principal kinds of conduct that can lead to exclusionary anticompetitive effects: (1) exclusionary group boycotts; (2) tying; (3) exclusive dealing; and (4) vertical mergers. Note how under the influence of commentators, lower courts, and enforcement agencies the analysis of each has evolved significantly, and in a common direction. Today, to make out a significant case of anticompetitive exclusion, a plaintiff can no longer hope to rely simply on inferences drawn from small percentages of "foreclosure," nor can it readily invoke per se rules. Instead, the economic analysis of the effects of foreclosure on rivals' costs and market prices will be central to the inquiry.

F.   PROBLEMS AND EXERCISES
Problem 7–1:
Printing Products Corporation

a.   *The Facts*

You have been retained as antitrust counsel by Printing Products Corp. ("PPC"), a U.S. manufacturer of computer printers, facsimile machines, and photocopying equipment, to advise it in connection with a distribution strategy it plans to implement in connection with its new line of combination printer/copier/facsimile machines.

At one time, PPC was a dominant player in the market for photocopying machines, and later expanded its operations into printers and ultimately facsimile machines. It also competes in the sale of combination machines, which are popular with more cost-conscious purchasers, such as small businesses and individuals. These devices combine the capabilities of printers, copiers, and facsimile machines into a single machine, generally at a much lower cost to the purchaser than two or three separate machines. The profitability of sales of combination machines, however, is very limited. Given the intense competition PPC faces from several other domestic and foreign brands, the machines themselves are sold at prices very close to their costs.

Like dedicated machines, each combination machine is sold with one installed toner cartridge, which permits the actual printing. The ink supply in those toner cartridges is finite, and once it has been exhausted the cartridge must be replaced. Replacement cartridges must be of the design specified for each particular model of machine, and can cost as much as 25% of the price of the machine, itself. PPC, of course, sells replacement cartridges. It also has a recycling program, whereby used cartridges can be returned to PPC for refurbishing and reloading. They are thereafter sold along side new replacement cartridges as a slightly less expensive alternative. As a general rule, sales of recycled and replacement cartridges are very profitable for PPC and others.

In recent years, several firms have begun to compete with PPC and the other manufacturers in the sale of replacement and recycled cartridges. Typically, like the machine manufacturers, these firms do not fabricate cartridges themselves, but purchase them from cartridge manufacturers, often the vary same suppliers used by the machine manufacturers, and offer free shipping to consumers willing to return empty cartridges for recycling.

PPC has designed a new toner cartridge to accompany its latest combination machine model. More ink efficient and less costly to produce, the new cartridge will be produced for PPC by Machine Cartridge Corp. ("MCC"), a manufacturer of original equipment and replacement cartridges. In connection with the planned introduction of the new machine and cartridge, PPC has asked for your advice on the legality under the federal antitrust laws of the following distribution strategies.

First, PPC is currently negotiating a contract with MCC, pursuant to which MCC would supply all of PPC's requirements of new, recycled, and replacement cartridges for the next three years. In addition, the contract would prohibit MCC from selling recycled or replacement cartridges for the new machines to any other manufacturer or cartridge supplier for the duration of the contract. The contract cannot be cancelled in its first year. It can be cancelled thereafter by either party, but only for "good cause shown" and only with six (6) months prior written notice.

Second, PPC proposes that the three year warranty to customers of the new PPC combination model include the following provision:

> **C.   VOIDING OF WARRANTY**. If, at any time during the warranty period, customer uses a toner cartridge other than an unmodified new, replacement or recycled cartridge purchased from PPC, or if it uses a copy cartridge that has been modified in any way from its original configuration, THIS WARRANTY SHALL BE VOID.

b.   *Problem and Skills Exercise*

You have been asked to draft an advice letter analyzing the antitrust issues involved in connection with each aspect of PPC's proposed distribution strategy and evaluating the antitrust risks, if any, that may arise if they are implemented. In preparation for drafting that letter, you are to meet with PPC's Vice President for Sales and Marketing, Catherine Fenteen, in order to gather more information about the proposal. Draft ten (10) interview questions you will ask her with respect to the strategy.

Problem 7–2:
Printing Products—Machine Cartridge Merger

a.   *The Facts*

Assume the same facts as in Problem 7–1, but now PPC has come to you with an alternate distribution strategy. In lieu of its contractual relationship with MMC, it proposes to acquire MMC and thereafter commit its facilities to manufacturing toner cartridges exclusively for PPC. Assume that PPC has substantial operations in Europe, as well, and that MMC is based in Germany and produces 35% of the toner cartridges sold through all manufacturers in the member countries of the European Union.

b. Problem and Skills Exercise

Draft a brief memorandum of no more than five (5) pages analyzing the issues involved in PPC's proposed acquisition, taking into account the Non–Horizontal Merger provisions of the 1984 Guidelines, the EC's Guidelines for Non–Horizontal Mergers, and any applicable caselaw we have studied.

Problem 7–3:
"Buy the Best for Less at Best's" [1]

a. The Facts

Most retailing activity in the Springfield City area is concentrated in four large suburban shopping malls and in its downtown business district. Area residents generally shop at multiple malls and some go downtown, too. The Springfield City area is served by two major department store chains, Woodies and Jelleff's. Each of these chains has a "flagship" store downtown. Woodies also has stores at two of the four major malls and Jelleff's has stores at the other two major malls. Each of the four malls has different owners. Major malls commonly have department stores as "anchor" tenants, which help to draw customers to the mall. It is common for the contract between a large shopping mall and a major department store anchor tenant to give the department store reduced rent and the right to veto other potential tenants. Woodies and Jelleff's negotiated such provisions at each of the malls. Veto rights are rarely exercised in practice because of the fear that desirable customers would simply shop at other, competing malls that would rent to the vetoed stores.

Best's is a large and very popular children's clothing store in downtown Springfield. Best's has only one store, but it is something of an institution in Springfield. It sells name-brand merchandise in a no-frills setting at a steep discount, as much as 25–30% below manufacturers' suggested retail prices. Best's merchandise is not sorted carefully by size; it does not keep all the styles and sizes in stock; its employees do not provide much assistance to customers; and it often has long lines at check outs. The department stores are full-line, full-service stores, and generally charge full prices, although Woodies and Jelleff's have seasonal sales and offer some discounts at their flagship stores downtown. Last year, Woodies accounted for 40% of children's clothing sold in the Springfield area; Jelleff's had a 35% share; Best's had 5%; and the various other mall stores and mail order/catalogue/Internet sales sources collectively had the remaining 20%.

Best's has been purchased by investors who see expansion opportunities in the discount no-frills children's clothing business. Best's new CEO, Harold Heft, was quoted saying, "Soon Springfield consumers will find us in the major shopping malls." However, none of the four major shopping malls

---

1. This Problem was developed by Professors Steven C. Salop and Jonathan B. Baker.

would rent retail space to Best's. Each mall manager gave basically the same story: "We'd like to have you, but our anchor department store tenant has vetoed your request." Heft also has discovered that Woodies complained about Best's prices to several of his biggest suppliers of name-brand children's merchandise, though none have cut-off Best's. Heft recently attended a meeting of the Springfield Chamber of Commerce. Woodies' CEO, Roy Chalk, told Heft, "If you'll stop your deep discounting, we'll let you into the two malls where we have locations and we'll also withdraw our complaints with your suppliers. I talked to Jelleff's and I think they'll do the same."

b. Problem and Skills Exercise

You have been retained to advise Best's. Howard Heft has asked you whether Best's could obtain mall space in Springfield by bringing an action under the federal antitrust laws. Draft a memorandum of 3–5 pages answering his question, including specific and detailed analysis to support your advice. You may assume that Heft has reported correctly on his conversations and that you will be able to prove so in court. You may also assume that "the Springfield City area" is a relevant geographic market and that "children's clothing" is a relevant product market.

Part IV

CONSTRUCTING THE MODERN
ANTITRUST CASE

Chapter 8

INTEGRATING CORE CONCEPTS WITH MORE STRUCTURED ANTITRUST ANALYSIS

INTRODUCTION

As we have noted since Chapter 1, a principal thesis of this Casebook is that the economic concepts developed in the previous chapters, especially those developed in Chapter 5 on mergers and acquisitions, have become the core concepts for much of modern antitrust law. In contrast to the legal categories that predominated in antitrust analysis in the U.S. for nearly its first full century, these concepts—anticompetitive effects (and its surrogate, "market power"), entry, and efficiency—are becoming increasingly critical to the resolution of antitrust issues regardless of the legal categorization of the case.

Although we believe there is abundant evidence that the continued influence of the traditional legal categories is waning, courts, commentators and enforcement agencies have been slow to articulate a unitary framework for a concept-driven law of antitrust. It is still common, therefore, to find courts, litigators, and enforcement authorities simultaneously referring both to the traditional categories and to the modern concepts.

Nevertheless, as this Chapter explores, those concepts have expanded from their origins in the law of mergers, and in some cases the law of monopolization, to virtually every sort of antitrust offense. Although there are exceptions, which we will refer to as we proceed, a full appreciation for the ascendance of concepts over categories is a critical first step in mastering contemporary antitrust analysis. What should already be evident is that the concepts are becoming increasingly outcome-determinative in antitrust cases and that the traditional legal pigeon holes are becoming less useful. Indeed, there is a wide range of transactions and conduct for which the traditional framework now provides insufficient guidance.

One concrete manifestation of that sea change is the increased incidence of cross-fertilization in the cases. Whereas traditional case law decisions tended to rely narrowly on authority sharing a common legal category, today it is far more common for courts to view concept-based authorities as interchangeable across those categories. A Section 1 Sherman Act case today, for example, will more readily cite Section 2 Sherman Act and Section 7 Clayton Act authorities on such common elements as market definition, market power, and entry, rather than be confined solely to other Section 1 cases. We will see many examples of such cross-fertilization in this Chapter.

The change is also evident in the emergence of a common analytical framework that is likely to guide the evaluation of virtually every contemporary antitrust case. The components of that framework include:

- a cognizable theory of anticompetitive effects, most typically collusive or exclusionary effects, and, in the case of private civil actions, a linkage between those effects and the plaintiff (*i.e.*, "antitrust injury");

- evidence of actual or predicted anticompetitive effects, presumed (per se offenses), direct, or circumstantial;

- an evaluation of conditions of entry, which is typically integrated with the inquiry into effects; and

- an evaluation of business justifications, especially efficiencies.

Through this framework, antitrust continues to serve as a laboratory for integrating law and economic concepts. With Chapters 2–7 as prelude, this Chapter seeks to illustrate how that framework now pervades contemporary antitrust law and practice.

A. ESTABLISHING A COGNIZABLE THEORY OF ANTICOMPETITIVE EFFECTS

1. ANTITRUST INJURY: REVISITING THE *BRUNSWICK* FORMULATION

The year 1977 was something of a watershed for antitrust law. As we discussed in Chapter 4 in connection with *Sylvania*, over more than half a century the Supreme Court had come to rely very heavily on per se rules across much of antitrust law. Although per se rules had the advantage of simplicity, widespread commentary argued that they were being over-utilized and in many instances deterred legitimate, pro-competitive conduct. In *Sylvania*, the Court demonstrated that it had heard that call for reform and it was prepared to alter the course of antitrust. Although *Sylvania's* most immediate effect was on the treatment of vertical, non-price intra-brand restraints, it had broader ramifications for virtually all of antitrust. By demonstrating the Court's willingness to utilize economic principles more freely, and to consider more fully the welfare effects of efficiency promoting conduct, it paved the way for later cases like *Broadcast Music* (1979) and others. Although similar changes of direction were already evident in the lower courts, in many ways, modern antitrust law can be dated from the 1976 term of the Court.

Earlier in that term, before *Sylvania*, the Court in *Brunswick* faced an issue that at the time may have seemed less obviously profound: can a competitor challenge the acquisition of its principal rival by an even larger rival for whom the acquisition is a means of entering the market? As we saw in Chapter 1, to answer that question, the Court had to ask two others: (1) what makes acquisitions and mergers anticompetitive? and (2) who can be harmed by them? By focusing on these two questions, the Court in *Brunswick* sparked an era of more critical analysis of the core purposes of specific antitrust prohibitions. That analysis begins with an evaluation of their potential anticompetitive effects. As we observed in Chapter 1, the Court answered them by instructing courts to limit suits to those parties suffering "antitrust injury." The principal excerpt from *Brunswick* is presented in Chapter 1 and should be reviewed at this point. Recall that the Court held:

> * * * [T]hat the plaintiffs to recover treble damages on account of § 7 violations, they must prove more than injury causally linked to an illegal presence in the market. Plaintiffs must prove *antitrust* injury, which is to say injury of the type the antitrust laws were intended to prevent and that flows from that which makes defendants' acts unlawful. The injury should reflect the anticompetitive effect either of the violation or of anticompetitive acts made possible by the violation. It should, in short, be "the type of loss that the claimed violations . . . would be likely to cause."

Brunswick Corp. v. Pueblo Bowl–O–Mat, Inc., 429 U.S. 477, 489 (1977) (emphasis original). In our next Note, we examine how the application of "antitrust injury" is integrated with the inquiry into the nature of the antitrust effects associated with specific conduct: collusive or exclusionary.

Distinguishing Collusive and Exclusionary Antitrust Injury: Note on Brunswick and Monfort

What according to the Court in *Brunswick* is the essential "anticompetitive" characteristic of a merger? Note that there was no hint of any exclusionary conduct by Brunswick directed at Pueblo. Instead, Brunswick's conduct consisted of acquiring some of Pueblo's local rivals, who otherwise were likely to go out of business. What then was the essence of Pueblo's complaint about the acquisition? It asked for the "damages" it would suffer from facing new competition from Brunswick, as compared to the profits it would have earned if its local rivals had closed, ceding the market to Pueblo.

But such damages were in fact a consequence of *increased*, not decreased competition. Pueblo was implicitly arguing that but for Brunswick's acquisition of its local rivals, the rivals would have shut their doors, and Pueblo would have thereafter enjoyed some degree of market power. Increased competition from its larger, perhaps more efficient rival, Brunswick, eroded Pueblo's hoped for increased profitability. Asking for the difference between its pre-entry and post-entry profits was tantamount, therefore, to asking the Court to protect its hoped for market power—hence the Court's response that to do so would be "inimical" to the purposes of the antitrust laws.

What would make an acquisition or merger "anticompetitive"? Recall from Chapter 5, that for Brunswick's acquisitions to have been anticompetitive, they would have had to *decrease* competition, allowing for the prediction that the acquisition would lead to collusive effects (most likely higher prices)—either unilateral or coordinated. But how could an existing rival suffer damages from such higher prices? Quite to the contrary, it would appear that rivals of firms engaging in anticompetitive mergers almost surely would benefit from higher prices themselves. The apparent message of *Brunswick*, therefore, could be that rivals *never* suffer antitrust injury from conduct that results in collusive effects—

be it price fixing, divisions of markets, horizontal mergers or *Sylvania* type vertical restraints. Who does suffer from the collusive effects? Primarily buyers— downstream firms or consumers that have to pay the higher prices. So under this interpretation of *Brunswick*, only those who actually suffer from collusive anti- competitive effects of conduct that violates the antitrust laws are permitted to seek treble damages under Section 4 of the Clayton Act.

Rivals, however, often are among the most direct targets of *exclusionary* conduct, and should stand in better stead to allege antitrust injury from exclusion. In *Cargill, Inc. v. Monfort of Colorado, Inc.*, 479 U.S. 104, 107 S.Ct. 484 (1986), this very argument was made in support of a challenge to the merger of two of Monfort's principal rivals. Two factors distinguished *Monfort* from *Brunswick*. First, it was brought under Section 16 of the Clayton Act, 15 U.S.C. § 26, solely for injunctive relief—no damages were sought. In contrast to Section 4, which requires actual injury, Section 16 authorizes antitrust actions for injunctive relief against "threatened loss or damage by a violation of the antitrust laws." Second, Monfort's complaint ultimately was interpreted by the lower courts as alleging that the merged firms would engage in predatory pricing—a form of dominant firm exclusionary conduct that we studied in Chapter 6.

Despite these differences, the Supreme Court extended *Brunswick*, finding that Monfort had not alleged any cognizable antitrust injury. While noting that Section 16 did in fact extend to "threatened" injury, and was therefore not as narrow as Section 4, the Court held that even threatened injury must, as was the case in *Brunswick*, be "injury of the type the antitrust laws were designed to prevent." 479 U.S. at 112. The threatened injury redressable under Section 16, therefore, must be of a type cognizable under Section 4 if the injury were to come to fruition. *Id.* at 113.

The second issue proved more complex, owing to Monfort's general assertions that the merger would "impair its ability to compete." The Court interpreted the allegations as meaning one of two things, both connected to an anticipated intensification of price competition post-merger. Either that invigorated competi- tion was a consequence of the merged firms' increased efficiency (lower, yet *above* cost pricing), or a consequence of their predatory pricing (lower, but *below*-cost pricing). If the former, Monfort had not alleged antitrust injury, because losses attributable to lower prices occasioned by the efficiencies associated with a merger are pro-, not anti-competitive consequences of a merger. As in *Brunswick*, any such "losses" would not constitute cognizable "antitrust injury." *Id.* at 114–17.

The Court further reasoned, however, that "[i]n contrast to price cutting aimed simply at increasing market share, predatory pricing has as its aim the elimination of competition. Predatory pricing is thus a practice 'inimical to the purposes of [the antitrust] laws,' *Brunswick*, 429 U.S., at 488, 97 S.Ct., at 697, and one capable of inflicting antitrust injury." *Id.* at 118. This route also proved to be unavailable to Monfort, however, on the facts of the record. It never squarely alleged that after the merger the merged firms would engage in true predatory pricing. In any event, the Court noted, the facts found in the district court below did not appear to support such a claim. *Id.* at 119 & n.15.

Monfort thus supports several propositions concerning antitrust injury. First, whether a private action seeks damages under Section 4 of the Clayton Act, or injunctive relief under Section 16, the plaintiff must allege antitrust injury. Second, the decision appears to reenforce the implicit message of *Brunswick*— competitors cannot suffer antitrust injury as a consequence of the collusive effects of their rivals' conduct. Finally, it also suggests rather strongly that antitrust injury *will* lie for a rival targeted by exclusionary conduct—Monfort simply failed to allege such conduct clearly and with evidentiary support. *See General Lease-ways, Inc. v. Nat'l Truck Leasing Ass'n*, 744 F.2d 588, 597 (7th Cir.1984)(it would "advance ... objectives of the antitrust laws" to permit plaintiff to seek an injunction preventing its expulsion from an association of its rivals, who allegedly had formed a cartel and sought to exclude plaintiff for attempting to disrupt it). And what of consumers? It would appear that, as in the case of collusive effects, they too should be able to establish antitrust injury from exclusionary conduct, because of its ultimate effect of reducing competition and raising prices. *See, e.g., Blue Shield of Virginia v. McCready*, 457 U.S. 465 (1982)(*Brunswick* satisfied by consumer in exclusionary group boycott case).

Nevertheless, in a curious concurring opinion in *Trinko* (Casebook, *supra* Chapter 6), Justice Stevens, joined by Justices Souter and Thomas, maintained that Trinko—a customer of AT & T, the rival whose competitive efforts were impaired by Verizon—lacked standing to sue Verizon for the diminished service it had received from AT & T as a consequence of Verizon's actions. Justice Stevens argued that Trinko's injuries were too remote, relying heavily on two other Supreme Court decisions interpreting the scope of Section 4 of the Clayton Act, *Associated Gen'l Contractors*, Casebook, *infra* Chapter 9, and, by allusion, *Illinois Brick*, Casebook, *infra* Chapter 9. He also reasoned that recovery by Trinko could lead to speculative and duplicative damage recoveries. *See Verizon Commc'ns, Inc. v. Trinko*, 540 U.S. 398, 416–18 (2004) (Stevens, J., concurring).

It is difficult to reconcile Justice Stevens' view with the logic of *Brunswick* and *Monfort*, however. Exclusionary strategies can cause two distinct types of antitrust injury, injury to rivals and injury to consumers. Rivals may suffer the most immediate harm—their ability to compete is impaired or destroyed. But consumers pay the ultimate price of exclusion in the form of diminished competition. For their exclusionary injury, rivals typically seek lost profits, or, if they have been entirely driven from the market, "going concern value." *See* Casebook, *infra* Chapter 9F3b. The essential characteristic of these damages, however, is their common focus on the exclusionary strategy's effect on its targeted rival or rivals. Rivals, however, act only as an early trip wire for harm to consumers. Consumers will seek to recover for the overcharge, or other value of diminished competition that the exclusion of rivals facilitated. But for that exclusion, they typically argue, prices would have been lower, or quality and choice higher. Rival and consumer injury and damages thus involve different types of harm and even different types of evidence. What they share is common causation: they are both efforts to quantify the competitive injuries that flow from the dominant firm's exclusionary conduct. Compensating the injured does not involve any "duplicative" damages. For a more comprehensive critique of Justice Stevens' concurring opinion on similar grounds, see Roger D. Blair & Christine A. Piette, *Antitrust Injury and Standing in Foreclosure Cases*, 31 J. Corp. L. 401 (2006).

Antitrust injury is but one aspect of a broader set of restrictions the Court has placed on private recoveries under the Clayton Act. We will examine some of the other restrictions in Chapter 9, in connection with the Court's decisions on standing, *e.g., Associated General Contractors* (Casebook, Chapter 9, *infra*) and indirect purchasers, *e.g., Illinois Brick* (Casebook, Chapter 9, *infra*) and will revisit some of the issues raised by *Monfort* in Sidebar 8–1. As was evident in Justice Stevens' concurring opinion in *Trinko*, it can be difficult at times to integrate these various restrictions into a cohesive, doctrinal whole.

2. THE EXPANSION AND MODERN
DEMANDS OF *BRUNSWICK*

Brunswick had a very substantial and immediate impact on antitrust law. The Supreme Court quickly extended it from mergers to secondary-line injury under the Robinson–Patman Act in *J. Truett Payne Co. v. Chrysler Motors Corp.*, 451 U.S. 557, 101 S.Ct. 1923 (1981), and to Sherman Act Section 1 offenses in *Blue Shield of Virginia v. McCready*, 457 U.S. 465 (1982) (*Brunswick* satisfied by consumer-plaintiff in exclusionary group boycott case) and *Atlantic Richfield Co. v. USA Petroleum Co.*, 495 U.S. 328, 110 S.Ct. 1884 (1990) (maximum resale price maintenance). In all of these instances, the Court used "antitrust injury" to probe and better define the anticompetitive consequences of conduct alleged to have violated some antitrust law. And in each case the consequence was a narrowing of the scope of prohibited conduct. In essence, the Court was demanding that every private plaintiff provide a clear articulation of both a theory of anticompetitive effects and allegations of personal injury directly tied to those effects. As it had declared in *Brunswick*, the plaintiff's injury "should reflect the anticompetitive effect either of the violation or of anticompetitive acts made possible by the violation. It should, in short, be 'the type of loss that the claimed violations * * * would be likely to cause.' " 429 U.S. at 479.

The analysis of antitrust injury is now a staple of private litigation under the antitrust laws—and many cases are dismissed on the ground that the plaintiff has failed to satisfy *Brunswick*. In reading our next case, note how the court begins by defining the potential anticompetitive effect of the conduct challenged in the abstract, and then moving on to consideration of the relationship of the particular plaintiffs to those effects.

BIG BEAR LODGING ASSOCIATION
v. SNOW SUMMIT, INC.

United States Court of Appeals for the Ninth Circuit, 1999.
182 F.3d 1096.

Before HUG, Chief Judge, BROWNING and NOONAN, Circuit Judges.
JAMES R. BROWNING, Circuit Judge.

* * *

I

* * *

Plaintiffs provide lodging accommodations and lodging referral services in the Big Bear Valley recreational area in the San Bernardino mountains of Southern California. For years, the two ski resorts in the area, Snow Summit, Inc., and Bear Mountain, Inc., offered bulk discounts on ski lift tickets to lodges and tourist businesses, including several Plaintiffs. By virtue of these discounts, Plaintiffs were able to offer "ski packages," combinations of lodging and lift tickets, at attractive prices. Sales of such "ski packages" constituted a substantial portion of the business done by some Plaintiffs.

In about January 1994, Richard Kun, president of Snow Summit, helped form the Defendant Big Bear Lake Resort Association. Kun asked the City of

Big Bear Lake to refrain from enacting a tax on Snow Summit or Bear Mountain in exchange for the Resort Association's commitment to collect funds from the lodges and ski resorts in Big Bear Valley and to use said funds to promote Big Bear Valley. He also asked the city to reduce its transient occupancy tax on local lodges from eight to six percent. The Resort Association eventually entered into an agreement with the Big Bear Chamber of Commerce, providing that the organizations would grant reciprocal memberships to each other at no cost, and that inquiries for lodging received by the Chamber of Commerce would be referred to the Resort Association.

Kun advised Plaintiff Robert Pool that Snow Summit would continue to sell discount lift tickets to Pool and Plaintiff Sleepy Forest Resorts only if Pool joined the Resort Association. Plaintiffs Pool, Sleepy Forest, Mark Twain Hannah, and members of the Big Bear Lodging Association joined the Resort Association. Because their businesses were located within the city of Big Bear Lake, Plaintiff lodges paid 2.5% of their lodging accommodation income as dues to the Association. Lodges located outside the city were charged only 0.5% of their income as dues.

Since its formation, the Resort Association has engaged in activities discriminatory to certain members, including some Plaintiffs. The Resort Association favored friends of directors of the Association by providing them with choice lodging referrals and preferential advertising, and removed advertisements purchased by Pool and Sleepy Forest from magazines the Resort Association mailed to potential customers. In the fall of 1995, Pool and Sleepy Forest quit the Resort Association because of these discriminatory practices. In October 1995, Kun advised Pool that, unless Pool and Sleepy Forest rejoined the Resort Association, neither Snow Summit nor Bear Mountain would sell them discount lift tickets nor would they honor any tickets purchased by them. Moreover, he said Snow Summit would no longer supply discount lift tickets to Sleepy Forest. Snow Summit and Bear Mountain agreed that they would refuse to sell discount lift tickets to non-members of the Resort Association. Kun advised Resort Association members that they were prohibited from selling, trading or conveying Snow Summit discount lift tickets to Pool or Sleepy Forest.

In 1996, the Resort Association adopted rules prohibiting members from belonging to other local referral services in which non-members participated, and from referring any business to non-members. * * *

* * *

Resort Association members also engaged in a price-fixing conspiracy, agreeing on uniform rates and charges for lodge accommodations, ski packages and resort services; publishing and disseminating advertising materials reflecting the agreed-upon rates; communicating for the purpose of implementing this conspiracy; and charging and collecting the agreed-upon rates.

Plaintiffs assert the Defendants' alleged conduct violated sections 1 and 2 of the Sherman Act and California's Cartwright Act, and breached Plaintiffs' subscription agreements with the Resort Association. The district court dismissed Plaintiffs' complaint without leave to amend, stating only: "This is not an antitrust case, period." * * *

II

* * *

To have standing to bring an antitrust case, a plaintiff must demonstrate that the harm the plaintiff has suffered or might suffer from the practice is an "antitrust injury," that is, an "injury of the type the antitrust laws were intended to prevent and that flows from that which makes defendants' acts unlawful." *Atlantic Richfield Co. v. USA Petroleum Co.*, 495 U.S. 328, 334, 110 S.Ct. 1884, 109 L.Ed.2d 333 (1990) * * *. The injury must be "attributable to an anti-competitive aspect of the practice under scrutiny." *Id.*

1. Price Fixing

Plaintiffs sufficiently allege a conspiracy to fix prices of lodging accommodations, lift tickets, and ski packages, a *per se* antitrust violation. Plaintiffs, however, have failed to allege antitrust injury resulting from all aspects of the alleged price-fixing conspiracy.

Certain Plaintiffs have alleged antitrust injury resulting from the alleged price-fixing of lift tickets. Pool, Sleepy Forest, and Plaintiff Lodging Association purchase lift tickets and thus suffer injury due to the presumably inflated price[3] of those tickets.[4] The remaining Plaintiffs should be granted leave to amend to allege, if they are able to do so, that they too purchase resort services at prices fixed by Defendants or were otherwise injured by Defendants' price-fixing.

Plaintiffs have not alleged antitrust injury resulting from the price-fixing of ski packages and lodging accommodations. They are competitors to, rather than customers of, Defendants in the sale of these services. Thus, Plaintiffs stand to benefit from the fact that prices for those services are inflated. Competitors, however, may have standing to challenge practices used to enforce a price-fixing conspiracy. Plaintiffs have alleged injuries resulting from their exclusion from the Resort Association, but have not alleged that these injuries resulted from the price-fixing conspiracy. * * * Plaintiffs should be granted leave to amend to allege, if they are able to do so, injury resulting from practices used to enforce the alleged price-fixing conspiracy.

* * *

2. Agreement by Snow Summit and Bear Mountain to Sell Discount Lift Tickets on Fixed Terms

Plaintiffs allege that the ski resorts agreed to sell discount lift tickets to lodge operators only if they joined the Resort Association. An agreement among competitors "for the purpose of coercing more favorable terms of trade from third parties than they could obtain through the normal play of competitive forces" violates antitrust law. * * * Plaintiffs allege that the condition that lodges must belong to the Resort Association is a "more favorable term of trade" for the ski resorts, because it permits the resorts to shift the costs of

---

3. Because price-fixing is a *per se* antitrust violation, price inflation is presumed. * * *

4. Defendants argue that Plaintiffs have standing to bring an antitrust action only if they compete with Defendants. This is incorrect. Consumers have standing to challenge antitrust violations that cause them injury. Indeed, purchasers are preferred antitrust plaintiffs in price-fixing cases. *See* 2 Phillip E. Areeda & Herbert Hovenkamp, Antitrust Law § 370 (1995).

promoting tourism in the region from themselves (imposed through a threat-ened city tax) to the broader tourism business community (imposed through Resort Association dues).

Pool, Sleepy Forest and Plaintiff Lodging Association purchased lift tickets for resale and thus allege sufficient antitrust injury to challenge this agreement. As to these Plaintiffs, we reverse the district court's dismissal of the claim that the ski resorts have unlawfully conspired to sell discount lift tickets only to Resort Association members in violation of Sherman Act § 1 and the Cartwright Act.* The court should grant the remaining Plaintiffs leave to amend the complaint to allege antitrust injury with respect to this claim, if they can do so.

3. Group Boycott

Plaintiffs have alleged a group boycott by the Resort Association and its members against non-members. Resort Association rules allegedly bar mem-bers from belonging to any other referral associations, and from forwarding lodging referrals to non-members. The ski resorts also allegedly refuse to sell discount lift tickets to non-members and at least Snow Summit allegedly informed Resort Association members that they cannot resell discount lift tickets to certain non-members. Thus, the boycott restricts non-members' access to customers (by blocking referrals) and supplies (by withholding discount ski lift tickets) that may be necessary for effective competition. *Cf. Northwest Wholesale Stationers, Inc. v. Pacific Stationery and Printing Co.,* 472 U.S. 284, 294, 105 S.Ct. 2613, 86 L.Ed.2d 202 (1985) * * *. Plaintiffs are all non-members of the Resort Association and thus suffer an antitrust injury as the direct targets of the boycott.[6]

We reverse the district court's dismissal of Plaintiffs' claim that Defen-dants participated in a group boycott in violation of Sherman Act § 1 and the Cartwright Act.

* * *

---

* [The Cartwright Act is California's state antitrust statute. Eds.]

6. Plaintiff referral associations that allege a loss of membership due to the RA's policies may establish standing in their own right and otherwise may be able to establish standing to sue on behalf of their members.

Figure 8–1:
The Big Bear Conspiracy

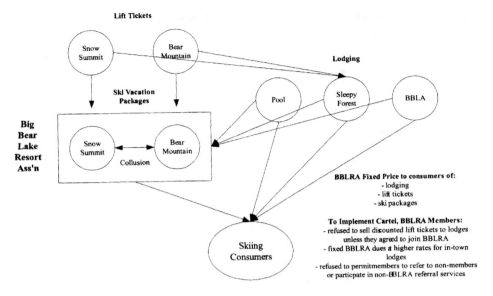

Which aspects of BBLRA's conduct involved collusive effects? Exclusionary? How did the Ninth Circuit use *Brunswick's* concept of antitrust injury to identify those effects? How did it relate those effects to the plaintiffs?

As we observed in Chapter 1 in connection with our first look at *Brunswick*, application of its concept of "antitrust injury" throughout antitrust has led to more discerning analysis of the anticompetitive effects associated with the specific conduct being challenged. As a consequence, two questions have become threshold ones for every private antitrust case: (1) how might the challenged conduct be "anticompetitive"? and (2) who will suffer the consequences of any anticompetitive effects that flow from the conduct?

Brunswick's influence also has spread in a second significant way. Even though its antitrust injury requirement emerged solely as an interpretation of Section 4 of the Clayton Act—the private right of action—the mandate that private parties articulate a viable theory of anticompetitive effects, *i.e.*, that they allege and prove injury to competition, not just to competitors, has spilled over to influence the public enforcement side of antitrust, as well. As the United States Court of Appeals for the District of Columbia Circuit observed in *Microsoft*:

> * * * [T]he plaintiff, on whom the burden of proof of course rests, must demonstrate that the monopolist's conduct indeed has the requisite anticompetitive effect. In a case brought by a private plaintiff, the plaintiff must show that its injury is "of 'the type that the statute was intended to forestall,' " [citing *Brunswick*]; *no less in a case brought by the Government, it must demonstrate that the monopolist's conduct harmed competition, not just a competitor.*

United States v. Microsoft Corp., 253 F.3d 34, 58–59 (D.C. Cir. 2001)(emphasis added). Although the substantive antitrust standards arguably require such a showing, *Brunswick* has heightened the attention courts now routinely direct at the plaintiff's allegations of competitive harm in all antitrust cases.

In addition, the FTC and the Antitrust Division of the Department of Justice have self-imposed such requirements in their own enforcement Guidelines. This is especially apparent in the 1992 revisions to the *Horizontal Merger Guidelines*, which greatly expanded upon the agencies' competitive effects analysis. It is also true of the 2000 *Collaboration Guidelines*, which were discussed in Chapter 2.

Hence, "antitrust injury" has had a profound and far-ranging impact on antitrust analysis and enforcement, as we now explore in greater depth in Sidebar 8–1.

Sidebar 8–1:
The Political Economy of Antitrust Injury

Brunswick could be interpreted as a reaction to the broad sweep of antitrust prohibitions as they stood in 1977, a counterbalance of sorts to curtail the flow of poorly conceived antitrust cases triggered by the twin attractions of lenient burdens of proof for antitrust liability and treble damages. This Sidebar explores how it came to serve that function, and inquires whether today there are instances in which *Brunswick* may tend to overcompensate for the harshness of past doctrines that have long since been abandoned.

Today there is probably a consensus that the expansion of antitrust injury has for the most part been laudatory because it demanded a more focused, threshold inquiry into the theory of anticompetitive effects behind each case. By demanding of private plaintiffs both a clearly articulated anticompetitive theory and a link between themselves and the competitive injury they allege, *Brunswick* and its progeny probably have improved the quality of antitrust analysis and discouraged a variety of less than meritorious antitrust cases from being brought. *See generally* Jonathan M. Jacobson & Tracy Greer, *Twenty-One Years of Antitrust Injury: Down the Alley With* Brunswick v. Pueblo Bowl–O–Mat, 66 ANTITRUST L.J. 273 (1998). *Brunswick's* concept of antitrust injury accomplished this end by exerting an economically driven doctrinal pressure on virtually all antitrust prohibitions. It demanded that each be justified by a defensible, economically grounded theory of anticompetitive effects. *See generally* William H. Page, *The Chicago School and the Evolution of Antitrust: Characterization, Antitrust Injury, and Evidentiary Sufficiency*, 75 VA. L. REV. 1221 (1989).

One example of this phenomenon is the now abandoned per se prohibition of maximum resale price maintenance. In *Atlantic Richfield Co. v. USA Petroleum Co.*, 495 U.S. 328, 334, 110 S.Ct. 1884, 109 L.Ed.2d 333 (1990), the Supreme Court utilized a *Brunswick* style analysis to expose its arguably non-economic underpinnings. Seven years later, in *State Oil Co. v. Khan*, 522 U.S. 3 (1997) (discussed in Chapter 4, *supra*), the Court built upon *Atlantic Richfield* to justify its decision to abandon the per se rule entirely.

But the courts' application of "antitrust injury" has not been without controversy. First, the easily satisfied standards of proof to which *Brunswick* appeared to respond have largely been abandoned since it was decided in 1977. To the extent those now superceded lenient standards constituted part of the justification for *Brunswick's* expansion, therefore, it is fair to ask whether aggressive application of the antitrust injury standard is still warranted. Perhaps with the more rigorous standards of proof that prevail today, *Brunswick's* role as a check on over-deterrence is no longer needed.

This possibility has lead some critics to argue that zealous application of *Brunswick* today may result in distortions of antitrust doctrine and the creation of unnecessarily restrictive standing rules. Those rules can be difficult to satisfy, which in turn may lead to instances of *under-*deterrence. *See, e.g.,* Joseph P. Bauer, *The Stealth Assault on Antitrust Enforcement: Raising the Barriers for Antitrust Injury and Standing*, 62 U. Pitt. L. Rev. 437 (2001); Roger D. Blair & Jeffrey L. Harrison, *Rethinking Antitrust Injury*, 42 Vand. L. Rev. 1539 (1989). In this view, antitrust injury has something of a "shoot the messenger" character. Without first examining the substantiality of the allegations of violation, courts appear eager to examine the nature of the plaintiff, first. Doing so, of course, is motivated by a concern that, even with more substantial burdens of proof, the lure of treble damages and attorneys fees will prove to be too powerful even for plaintiffs with relatively weak antitrust claims. Weeding them out sooner rather than later benefits antitrust enforcement as a whole. But in doing so based on an expansive reading of antitrust injury, *Brunswick* may leave no likely or similarly motivated plaintiffs to pursue possibly valid allegations of antitrust violations.

Second, courts applying the antitrust injury doctrine appear to assume that all of antitrust is concerned with but a single genre of "antitrust injury"—"injury to competition, not competitors." This is cited as the as if it were the only kind of "injury the antitrust laws were intended to prevent." That may not be a fair characterization of antitrust law. The now discarded per se rule against minimum resale price maintenance, for example, traditionally was motivated at least in part by concerns for dealer autonomy. In cases like *Pace Elecs., Inc. v. Canon Computer Sys., Inc.*, 213 F.3d 118 (3d Cir. 2000) (Casebook, Chapter 4, *supra*), courts accepted that dealers terminated for refusing to adhere to such schemes may therefore suffer injury *of the type the prohibition of minimum RPM* was intended to prevent. Similarly, notwithstanding the Court's decision in *J. Truett Payne*, the courts have long acknowledged that the prohibition of secondary line price discrimination under the Robinson–Patman Act was motivated in large part by concerns for individual dealers, on the theory that their elimination represents an incipient threat to "competition." Again, the theory is that individual competitors can serve as an early trip wire for the protection of competition, which perhaps justifies a more expansive definition of "antitrust injury."

Ironically, the "competition, not competitors" formula relied upon so heavily in *Brunswick* was drawn from the Supreme Court's *Brown Shoe* decision, which came to symbolize protection of *competitors* over the cause of competition generally, not the reverse as one might assume from its use in *Brunswick. See Brown Shoe Co. v. United States*, 370 U.S. 294, 320 (1962) (Casebook, Chapter 5, *supra*.) Indeed, the phrase "competition, not competitors" is used twice in *Brown Shoe*, and in the later context it is clear that the Court did not intend by the turn of phrase to forsake the fate of individual competitors. To the contrary, the unmistakable message is that as goes the fate of competitors, so goes competition. *Id*. at 344. In short, to the extent an economic approach to antitrust has not fully occupied the field, sweeping away all non-economic goals, there may be more than one kind of "injury the antitrust laws were designed to prevent." Arguably, the courts have not fully adapted *Brunswick* to account for all of antitrust's diversity.

Third, challenges based on the asserted absence of antitrust injury frequently are launched in the form of either a motion to dismiss or for summary judgment very early in the litigation. As we will see as this Chapter progresses, the evidence necessary to support an allegation of market wide competitive injury can be very difficult to assemble. Does a definition of antitrust injury that demands such evidence as a threshold matter—before any discovery is permitted in the case—unduly burden private plaintiffs?

Consider too the import such a requirement may have on the private enforcement of per se prohibitions. By affixing the per se label to some categories of conduct, antitrust law presumes that such conduct will result in unreasonable anticompetitive effects. Yet by their nature, antitrust injury-based challenges demand allegations and evidence of actual anticompetitive effects—"injury of the type the antitrust laws was intended to prevent." Used in this arguably expansive way, antitrust injury could effectuate a conversion of a per se offense into a rule of reason offense, at least at the pleading stage, creating something of a discordant model in which a reasonability standard is used to judge the allegations of injury, but a per se standard is used to assess liability. This could be so even in those cases where the courts are unwilling to challenge the per se rule for liability. If per se rules are to retain their vitality, however, how can antitrust injury warrant a conclusion in such cases that particular plaintiffs have not suffered injury of the kind the antitrust laws were intended to prevent? Would that in effect erode the efficacy of the per se rule? If so, can antitrust injury serve as a back door of sorts for eliminating per se rules, or at least for rendering them less potent?

In this context, consider *Big Bear*, which involved allegedly per se violations. Should all would-be plaintiffs have standing to challenge per se violations? By rejecting some of the claims posed on antitrust injury grounds, the Ninth Circuit's holding in *Big Bear* seems to suggest the answer is "no." Must a private party pursuing a per se theory still demonstrate that there was "injury to competition" and that it suffered the kind of injury predicted by the per se rule? Under the language quoted above from the D.C. Circuit's *Microsoft* decision, should the government be required to satisfy the antitrust injury requirement when it pursues a per se case?

B. ANTICOMPETITIVE EFFECTS AND MARKET POWER

INTRODUCTION

Once the various traditional Sherman and Clayton Act offenses are arrayed side-by-side, as in Figure 8–2, it is apparent that two criteria are a part of almost all contemporary antitrust offenses: (1) *conduct* that falls within one of the statutory categories; and (2) actual or potential collusive or exclusionary *effects* that can be attributed to the conduct. Not all offenses require a showing of actual effects, however. Actual and probable effects are often inferred from circumstantial evidence, such as high market shares, particularly in monopolization and merger litigation.

Figure 8–2:
Elements of Antitrust Offenses Compared

Sherman § 1	Sherman § 2	Clayton § 3	Clayton § 7
(1) concerted action	(1) unilateral action	(1) conditioned sale	(1) merger or acquisition
(2) unreasonable restraint of trade	(2) monopoly power	(2) substantial lessening of competition	(2) substantial lessening of competition
	(3) "willfully acquired or maintained," *i.e.*, anticompetitive, exclusionary conduct		

It is also apparent that different institutional approaches to evaluating conduct and effects can arise, and may affect the analysis. For example, how a particular case proceeds may depend in the first instance on whether it is being evaluated by an enforcement agency or a court. Courts are bound by rules of evidence and procedure, and must take into account burdens of production and proof. The ultimate goal of the process is to determine whether the party bearing the burden of proof has produced sufficient evidence from which a reasonable jury could find for it.

Somewhat in contrast, agencies operate with greater discretion. They can consider a broader range of evidence and may not strictly allocate burdens to the parties in exercising that discretion. For example, in an effort to dissuade the government from challenging a merger, the merging firms may be inclined to volunteer their best arguments and evidence of efficiencies, even though in the context of litigation they might delay doing so until after the plaintiff has completed its case-in-chief in recognition of established burdens of production and proof.

For most antitrust cases, therefore, the critical questions become: (1) how can we identify anticompetitive conduct; and (2) how can we determine whether the actual or probable effect of the conduct is significantly anticompetitive? Earlier chapters explored the many kinds of conduct that can give rise to anticompetitive effects as they have traditionally been grouped. This section focuses more specifically on how anticompetitive effects are proven today in proceedings before agencies and courts—regardless of the specific offense charged. Before moving ahead to consider those issues, however, we need to review again what we mean by "collusive" and "exclusionary" effects, an issue we first visited in Chapter 1, and which we explore from a different perspective in Sidebar 8–2.

Sidebar 8–2:
Collusive vs. Exclusionary Effects: Are There Two Kinds of Market Power?

As a general matter, there is consensus today that no firm or firms can successfully raise price or divide markets—*i.e.*, cause collusive anticompetitive effects—without market power. In fact, the courts often refer to claims based on evidence of actual collusive anticompetitive effects as cases involving the "exercise of market power." And the principal anticompetitive effect of exclusionary conduct is to confer some measure of power over price. Yet, there are some important, older precedents that appeared to suggest that collusive and exclusionary effects evidence analytically distinct forms of market power, and some modern commentary that appears to agree.

Our discussion of the contemporary "raising rivals' costs" approach to exclusionary effects analysis at the beginning of Chapter 6 emphasizes the commonalities between collusive and exclusionary effects, by depicting the latter as the creation of an "involuntary cartel." One advantage of this perspective is that it ties both types of effects to the economic concept of market power, and thus highlights that mere exclusion (without a likely effect on price or other dimension of competition) is not sufficient to demonstrate harm to competition.

Some might suggest that this approach downplays the significance of exclusion as a distinct method of obtaining market power. That problem is avoided by an alternative perspective on collusive and exclusionary effects analysis, advanced by Thomas Krattenmaker and Steven Salop, the legal commentators most responsible for restoring concern for exclusionary effects to the antitrust agenda after the rise of the Chicago School, and Professor Robert Lande. *See* Thomas G. Krattenmaker, Robert H. Lande & Steven C. Salop, *Monopoly Power and Market Power in Antitrust Law*, 76 GEO. L.J. 241 (1987).

To examine the question, these commentators focus on the often cited definition of monopoly power (market power) in the *Cellophane* case as "the power to control prices *or* exclude competition," *United States v. E.I. du Pont de Nemours & Co.*, 351 U.S. 377, 391 (1956)(emphasis added). Attending to the Court's use of the disjunctive "or," they separate the two segments of *Cellophane's* definition in order to give each a distinctive role. They accept that "the core concept of market power or monopoly power is a firm's ability to increase profits and harm consumers by charging prices above competitive levels." Krattenmaker, Lande &

Salop, 76 GEO. L.J. at 249. But they emphasize that this could happen in two ways, consistent with the two parts of the Court's definition in *Cellophane*.

Krattenmaker, Lande, and Salop term the power to control price profitably by restraining one's own output "classical" or "Stiglerian" market power. The latter term, which honors economist George Stigler, is chosen to recognize the focus of Chicago School antitrust analysis on this possibility. *Cf.* William M. Landes & Richard A. Posner, *Market Power in Antitrust Cases*, 94 HARV. L. REV. 937, 977 (1981) (influential Chicago-oriented analysis of market power that downplays the power to exclude competition in discussing the *Cellophane* formulation).

Krattenmaker, Lande, and Salop highlight that the *Cellophane* definition also recognizes a second route by which market power could be achieved. If a firm or group of firms raises price above the competitive level (or prevents price from falling to the competitive level) by raising rivals' costs and thereby causing them to restrain their output, the resulting power is termed "exclusionary" or "Bainian" market power. The latter term recognizes the contribution of a pioneering pre-Chicago industrial organization economist, Joe S. Bain, to the analysis of exclusion.

If there are in fact two forms of market power, Bainian and Stiglerian, is one any more important than the other for antitrust purposes? Krattenmaker, Lande, and Salop suggest that Bainian market power may be more fundamental:

> Those who believe that antitrust is on strongest ground in prohibiting hard core price fixing among competitors probably would focus on Stiglerian power. However, as Stigler himself and others have emphasized, successful price fixing of significant duration depends on the existence of constraints on new entry. In this sense, exclusion, either natural or as the result of deliberate, credible conduct, is the key underpinning to the exercise of market power. Thus, Bainian power may be considered more fundamental.

Krattenmaker, Lande & Salop, 76 GEO. L.J. at 249 n.47.

Do you agree that Stiglerian (classical) and Bainian (exclusionary) market power are distinct? If they are, do you agree that Bainian market power is more fundamental? Are Stiglerian and Bainian market power just two sides of a single coin—two ways of looking at the same kind of anticompetitive effect? Is the debate one of academic concern only, or does it have genuine significance for how antitrust offenses are defined and proved? Consider these questions in the material that follows on how anticompetitive effects are proven in contemporary antitrust litigation.

1. ESTABLISHING AN ANTITRUST VIOLATION THROUGH EVIDENCE OF ACTUAL ANTICOMPETITIVE EFFECTS

Once a *theory of anticompetitive injury* is identified through successful application of *Brunswick*, the stage is set for what is often the make or break phase of the modern antitrust case—*proof of anticompetitive effects*. As we will see in the remainder of this section of the Chapter, anticompetitive effects can be demonstrated directly or inferred. In both instances, "market power" is at the heart of the inquiry. First, we examine an increasingly significant method for establishing anticompetitive effects—evidence of actual anticompetitive effect, *i.e.*, effects that result from the actual exercise of market power.

Recall from Chapter 2, that with noteworthy consistency in cases beginning with *NCAA v. Bd. of Regents of the Univ. of Okla.*, 468 U.S. 85 (1984) and *FTC v. Indiana Fed'n of Dentists*, 476 U.S. 447 (1986) ("*IFD*"), the Supreme Court has emphasized that evidence of actual anticompetitive effects in the form of reduced output, higher prices or diminished quality, obviates the need for an inquiry into market power as evidenced by market shares or some other measure. Taken together, *NCAA* and *IFD* marked a significant watershed with respect to the standards for proving anticompetitive effects. By focusing on the value of evidence of demonstrable anticompetitive effects, both cases implicitly assume that market power is a prerequisite to the proof of a rule of reason offense—without it significant anticompetitive effects are unlikely. But the Court in both cases also acknowledged that market power can be established either through evidence of actual anticompetitive effects, or via inference drawn from direct or circumstantial evidence of market power.

The Supreme Court's emphasis on actual effects evidence in *NCAA* and *IFD* could have more than one interpretation, with implications for when a defendant can proffer evidence of low market share to rebut a plaintiff's evidence of actual anticompetitive effects. First, the Court could be declaring that, as a matter of law, direct evidence is superior to circumstantial evidence. This legal rule could be described in evidentiary terms, as follows: *a plaintiff's proffer of evidence of actual anticompetitive effect shifts the burden of production to the defendant, creating a presumption of violation, which cannot be rebutted by circumstantial evidence of the lack of market power, in the form of low market share, alone. See Note on the Development of the "Quick Look,"* Chapter 2, *supra*. But this interpretation risks inaccurate judgments when the direct evidence of effects is weak and the evidence of low market share is persuasive.

Second, the Court could be insisting that not just any direct evidence of anticompetitive effect will do; only *strong* direct evidence of *significant* anticompetitive effects will preclude a defendant from offering a rebuttal based on low market share alone. But would this rule be administrable? How "strong" is strong enough? How "significant" is significant enough? Can this second approach actually be harmonized with the first? Could the majority opinion in *California Dental* (Casebook, Chapter 2, *supra*) be interpreted as an attempt to do so?

Third, the Court may not have shifted burdens at all, but merely have concluded on the facts in those two cases, albeit on a less than comprehensive examination, that the direct evidence outweighed the circumstantial evidence. But if so, won't litigants still have to make an extensive (and possibly expensive) marshaling of both direct and circumstantial evidence in every case? Again, might *California Dental* be viewed as illustrating this dilemma? Did the FTC undertake an extensive marshaling of the evidence of anticompetitive effects there? Did the majority and dissent agree in their assessment of its efforts?

Regardless of interpretation, other important questions about the emerging evidentiary framework for proving anticompetitive effects also remain open, including whether a plaintiff should be required to proffer actual anticompetitive effects evidence in addition to market share, and whether a defendant can rebut a claim of anticompetitive effects based on evidence of high market shares with evidence of the absence of actual anticompetitive effects.

Figure 8–3:
Contemporary Methods for Proving Anticompetitive Effects

- direct evidence of actual anticompetitive effects, *i.e.*, the exercise of market power, *e.g.*:
  - reduced output/higher prices
  - diminished quality or service
  - diminished innovation
  - diminished buyer choice
  - actual exclusion of rivals
- circumstantial proof of anticompetitive effects (actual or predicted), inferred from market power, *e.g.*:
  - high market share in a properly defined relevant market
  - direct measures of market power (*e.g.*, demand elasticities)

This evidentiary framework is emerging with greater clarity in the courts of appeals. In fact, although both *NCAA* and *IFD* arose under Section 1 of the Sherman Act, we will shortly see that the lower courts are applying this approach under both Section 1 and Section 2. The cases that follow, the Sixth Circuit's decision in *Re/Max Int'l, Inc. v. Realty One, Inc.*, 173 F.3d 995 (6th Cir. 1999), and the Seventh Circuit's decision in *Toys "R" Us, Inc. v. FTC*, 221 F.3d 928 (7th Cir. 2000), are representative examples of this trend.

RE/MAX INTERNATIONAL v. REALTY ONE, INC.
United States Court of Appeals for the Sixth Circuit, 1999.
173 F.3d 995.

Before RYAN and BATCHELDER, Circuit Judges; CAMPBELL District Judge.

RYAN, Circuit Judge.

* * *

I. BACKGROUND
* * *

At the heart of the disagreement between the parties to this lawsuit are disputes about (1) who is economically dominant and (2) who employs the best formula for compensating real-estate sales agents for their services. Because it is conducive to more easily understanding the nature of the two-pronged dispute between the parties, we begin by addressing the second aspect first— who employs the more efficient formula for compensating sales agents.

* * * [O]rdinarily, a real-estate agent who lists a house for sale agrees to represent the homeowner/seller, doing so for a fixed fee, called a "commission," that is a percentage of the selling price. If another real-estate agent, working for a different broker, brings a purchaser to the deal, the two agents usually split the commission 50/50. * * * Then, ordinarily, although there can be different arrangements, each sales agent must split his or her 3–1/2% Commission 50/50 with the broker with which he is affiliated. * * * But Re/Max agencies, throughout the Re/Max nationwide franchise system, compensate their sales agents very differently.

Under its system, Re/Max requires that its franchisees adopt the "Re/Max 100% Concept" which allows real-estate sales agents to receive 95% to 100% of their share of sales commissions, instead of the traditional practice of splitting commissions 50/50 with the salesperson's broker/employer. * * * In return, Re/Max agents pay the broker/employer a flat monthly fee for desk space, telephone services, secretarial support, and the like. Re/Max contends that the 100% Concept attracts more experienced, more knowledgeable—and this is important—more efficient agents. Indeed, Re/Max recruits and hires only experienced agents, on the theory that novices could not survive without a guaranteed minimum income if commissions were not immediately forthcoming—and ordinarily they are not—when inexperienced agents are "in training" and learning the business.

* * *

Re/Max contends that defendants Realty One, Inc. and Smythe Cramer Company have dominance in the northeast Ohio real-estate markets and have used that dominance to defeat Re/Max's attempt to introduce its unique and, it claims, more-efficient sales-agent compensation system. Re/Max argues that the defendants control the northeast Ohio markets in two ways: (1) by obtaining the listings for a large majority of homes for sale and (2) by attracting and employing the large majority of experienced real-estate agents. There is nothing, of course, illegal in that. What is illegal, according to Re/Max, is the means it claims the defendants have employed to perpetuate that dominance—the defendants' so-called "adverse splits" policy * * *. According to Re/Max, the real and intended effect of this policy is that the defendants essentially refuse to sell homes to customers brought to them by Re/Max agents. In consequence, Re/Max argues, it cannot attract experienced agents for its sales force, because, given Realty One's policy of boycotting purchasers produced by Re/Max, experienced agents would not make enough money working for Re/Max. Without experienced agents, Re/Max argues, it is prevented from entering the northeast Ohio real-estate market.

* * *

1.   The Plaintiffs' Claims

* * *

* * * Re/Max claims, *inter alia*, that it is the means the defendants have chosen to dominate the relevant market for hiring real-estate sales agents—their "adverse splits" policy—which violates state and federal antitrust laws. * * * Although * * * the standard practice in the industry is that commis-

sions are split equally when one brokerage brings the seller and another brokerage brings the buyer to a transaction, in 1987 Realty One and Smythe Cramer began notifying Re/Max brokerages that the split would be 70/30 or 75/25, in favor of the defendants, whenever a Re/Max agent was on the other side of the table from a Realty One or Smythe Cramer agent. It is undisputed that the policy was designed to deter defections of sales agents from the defendants' employment to the plaintiffs'.

* * *

In simplified terms, then, the plaintiffs' claim is that the defendants control the market for knowledgeable and experienced sales agents who have developed an expertise in certain communities in northeast Ohio, and, through the unfair adverse-splits policy, have prevented Re/Max from recruiting those agents, thereby depriving Re/Max franchises of the information and expertise they need to effectively serve buyers and sellers of homes. Instead of competing with Re/Max in the experienced-agent market by raising the compensation of their own experienced agents, as Re/Max has, the defendants have tried to drive Re/Max out of northeast Ohio by imposing the adverse splits, which do not allow Re/Max agents, and thus Re/Max franchises, to do business profitably. * * *

* * *

III. DISCUSSION
* * *

* * * Although the district court correctly concluded that Re/Max failed to define the relevant geographic markets, the court erroneously rejected evidence tending to show that the defendants had the ability to exclude competition. For instance, Re/Max presented evidence showing that the adverse-splits policy has prevented new Re/Max franchises from forming and may have driven several franchises out of business. Additionally, there is evidence that adopting adverse splits without market power is economically irrational, and that doing so has failed elsewhere. Because these factors raise genuine issues of material fact, summary judgment against Re/Max on the § 2 monopolization claims was inappropriate.

The offense of monopolization under § 2 has two elements: "(1) the possession of monopoly power in the relevant market and (2) the willful acquisition or maintenance of that power as distinguished from growth or development as a consequence of a superior product, business acumen, or historic accident." *United States v. Grinnell Corp.*, 384 U.S. 563, 570–71, 86 S.Ct. 1698, 16 L.Ed.2d 778 (1966).

There are two ways to establish the first element, that is, that the defendant holds monopoly power. The first is by presenting direct evidence "showing the exercise of actual control over prices or the actual exclusion of competitors." The second is by presenting circumstantial evidence of monopoly power by showing a high market share within a defined market. In recent years, parties and courts have increasingly moved toward utilizing the circumstantial method as a "shortcut." However, this does not undercut the continued viability of the first avenue of establishing monopoly power. For the reasons below, we find that although the plaintiffs failed to define the relevant market with precision and therefore failed to establish the defendants' monopoly power through circumstantial evidence, there does exist a genuine issue of material fact as to whether the plaintiffs' evidence shows direct evidence of a monopoly, that is, actual control over prices or actual exclusion of competitors. * * *

* * *

* * * Re/Max argues that it need not define the relevant geographic markets for § 2 purposes if it can show the defendants have actually succeeded in setting prices or excluding competition. The plaintiffs point to evidence that sales commissions are higher and less negotiable in northeast Ohio than elsewhere in the U.S.; that Realty One has admitted being able to charge high rates in the western Cleveland suburbs because of its market dominance there; and that both defendants have been successful in imposing adverse commission splits which would be economically impossible to do without monopoly power.

We agree that an antitrust plaintiff is not required to rely on indirect evidence of a defendant's monopoly power, such as high market share within a defined market, when there is direct evidence that the defendant has actually set prices or excluded competition. This court recognized such a rule in *Byars v. Bluff City News Co.*, 609 F.2d 843, 850 (6th Cir.1979) * * *.

* * * If the evidence that the retailers received less service at greater cost was credited by the district court, it "lends strong support to plaintiff's contention that [the defendant] possesses monopoly power." *Id.* at 853 n. 26. As we stated: "[T]he simplest way of showing monopoly power is to marshal evidence showing the exercise of actual control over prices or the actual exclusion of competitors." *Id.* at 850.

This view has been adopted, at least implicitly, in four sister circuits: the First, Eighth, Ninth, and Tenth. As the Eighth Circuit has stated:

> * * * "proof of actual detrimental effects, such as a reduction of output," can obviate the need for an inquiry into market power, which is but a "surrogate for detrimental effects." [*Flegel v. Christian Hosp.*, 4 F.3d 682, 688 (8th Cir.1993)] (*quoting* [*FTC v. Indiana Fed'n of Dentists*, 476 U.S. 447, 461, 106 S.Ct. 2009 (1986)]).

Other circuits also look to evidence of actual detrimental effects in the absence of market definition and market share, but require unambiguous evidence that a defendant can control prices or exclude competition. On the other hand, the Fifth Circuit has rejected a plaintiff's claim in light of the defendant's low market share even though there was evidence of control over prices.

The Supreme Court has noted on at least two occasions that direct evidence of monopoly power will support an antitrust claim. See *Eastman Kodak Co. v. Image Technical Servs., Inc.*, 504 U.S. 451, 477, 112 S.Ct. 2072, 119 L.Ed.2d 265 (1992); *Indiana Fed'n*, 476 U.S. at 460–61, 106 S.Ct. 2009. In *Eastman Kodak*, * * * [b]ecause evidence existed that Kodak had increased prices and excluded competition in the market for the secondary product, it bore the "substantial burden" of proving that it did not, in fact, possess monopoly power. *Id.* at 469, 112 S.Ct. 2072. Similarly, the *Indiana Federation* Court rejected defendant Federation's contention that the lack of proof regarding the relevant market required summary judgment in its favor. 476 U.S. at 460, 106 S.Ct. 2009. Instead, the Court looked to evidence that the Federation had actually defeated insurance companies' requests to view insureds' x-rays in holding that detailed market analysis was not required. *Id.* at 461, 106 S.Ct. 2009. * * * The defendants contend that these cases are inapposite because they do not discuss § 2. However, we see no reason to believe that monopoly power in the § 1 context is any different from the § 2 monopoly power the plaintiffs allege here.

Similarly, there is sufficient evidence in this case to permit a jury to conclude that markets for real-estate brokerage services are relatively localized, even if they are larger than those the plaintiffs posit, and that there have been actual, sustained adverse effects on competition in those areas where one defendant or both predominate. Therefore, the plaintiffs have sustained their burden at this stage of proceedings despite the lack of reasonable and detailed market analysis.

Of course, the defendants also challenge the plaintiffs' factual claim that the defendants have actually exercised monopoly control. First, the defendants reject both the basis and the relevance of the conclusion that northeast Ohio sales commission rates are higher than in other comparable metropolitan areas. As for the basis, defendants argue that: (a) the study in question reviewed data for 1991 only, when the relevant time period here is 1987 to 1995; (b) there is no evidence that the rates charged by the defendants are not economically justified; (c) there is no evidence that commission rates are high in individual markets, as opposed to the whole northeast Ohio region; (d) there is no evidence that either of the defendants charges a lower rate in those areas where Re/Max admits neither defendant has a monopoly; and (e) Re/Max agents usually charge the same rates as the defendants' agents. As for the relevance of the challenged conclusion, the defendants argue that even if a defendant's rates are higher than the norm, this does not demonstrate that a defendant has the power to set them, as opposed to being able to charge more for better service.

Second, the defendants deny that their ability to impose adverse commission splits demonstrates monopoly power. They argue that many Re/Max franchises have opened after the imposition of adverse splits, thus showing that the splits policy cannot exclude competition. Neither, they claim, does the policy have any effect on consumers, in light of the fact that the splits are aimed against agents and in the absence of evidence that rates paid by clients have risen since the policy was adopted. Interestingly, Realty One indicates that it has not excluded competition because the adverse-splits policy was *unsuccessful* in preventing agents from defecting to Re/Max.

We agree, for the reasons stated by the defendants, that Re/Max's argument regarding the 1991 survey may be rejected out of hand. But, the plaintiffs' other argument—that the defendants' ability to impose adverse splits demonstrates their monopoly power—is considerably more plausible. Obviously, if a monopolist successfully uses its power to prevent competition from ever entering the marketplace, the losing competitor's antitrust claim should not be dismissed simply because the monopolist's prices remained constant, because the plaintiff cannot show it was ever established in the market, or because the plaintiff was able to survive for a period before being forced to terminate operations. In any of these situations, consumers would be harmed if the new competitor offered better service at the same price as the monopolist, but was defeated because of the monopolist's refusal to deal. * * * [I]f the evidence, viewed in the light most favorable to Re/Max, clearly demonstrates the defendants' ability to exclude Re/Max from the marketplace, summary judgment should not have been entered for the defendants.

* * *

————

What was the theory of anticompetitive effects behind Re/Max's complaint, collusive or exclusionary? If its complaint stopped at allegations of higher real estate sales commissions, could it have satisfied *Brunswick*? If its theory of injury is linked instead to the exclusionary effects of Realty One's "adverse splits policy," why is the court still addressing commission rates? What is the relevance of this evidence of actual *collusive* effects to Re/Max's case?

Next we examine the Federal Trade Commission's case against toy retailer Toys R Us ("TRU"), which we first discussed in Chapter 3 following *Interstate Circuit*. The case involved a mix of vertical and horizontal behavior with both exclusionary and collusive effects. TRU, the nation's leading toy retailer, solicited agreements from its principal toy suppliers that favored it at the expense of competing warehouse and discount sellers. As was the case in *Interstate Circuit*, the FTC found (and the Seventh Circuit affirmed) that TRU also functioned as the hub of a conspiracy among the manufacturers. Compliance with TRU's demands would not have made economic sense, according to the FTC, absent knowledge that the other principal manufacturers would also be joining in.

The government relied in large part on evidence of the actual effects of TRU's conduct, both collusive and exclusionary. The anticompetitive effects of the conduct appeared exclusionary from the perspective of TRU's warehouse rivals, whose costs were raised and whose ability to compete with TRU was impaired. But from the point of view of consumers, the conduct had collusive effects—by directly impairing comparative shopping, consumer search costs were increased, consumer choice was impaired, and the price of toys was effectively increased.

As you read the following excerpt from the case, consider which of these effects persuaded the Seventh Circuit that a violation had occurred. Put another way—at its core, is *Toys R Us* built on evidence of actual collusive or actual exclusionary effects? Both? Does it matter to the analysis? What guidance can be gleaned from the last paragraph, excerpted from the court's opinion?

Consider as well the similarities in the analytical framework used by the Sixth Circuit in *Re/Max* and the Seventh Circuit in *Toys R Us*. What role does evidence of actual anticompetitive effects play? How substantial must the effects be? How does it interact with circumstantial evidence in the form of small market share? How does the court respond to arguments by the defendant that the actual effects evidence should be discounted in light of the purportedly low market shares of the defendants?

TOYS "R" US, INC. v. FEDERAL TRADE COMMISSION
United States Court of Appeals for the Seventh Circuit, 2000.
221 F.3d 928.

Before COFFEY, KANNE, and DIANE P. WOOD, Circuit Judges.

DIANE P. WOOD, Circuit Judge.

[The facts of the case are discussed in Chapter 3, immediately following *Interstate Circuit* and can be reviewed at this time. Eds.]

* * *

II

On appeal, TRU makes [the argument that] * * * whether the restrictions were vertical or horizontal, they were not unlawful because TRU has no market power, and thus the conduct can have no significant anticompetitive effect * * *.

B. *Degree of TRU's Market Power*

* * *

TRU seems to think that anticompetitive effects in a market cannot be shown unless the plaintiff, or here the Commission, first proves that it has a large market share. This, however, has things backwards. As we have explained elsewhere, the share a firm has in a properly defined relevant market is only a way of estimating market power, which is the ultimate consideration. The Supreme Court has made it clear that there are two ways of proving market power. One is through direct evidence of anticompetitive effects. See *FTC v. Indiana Fed'n of Dentists*, 476 U.S. 447, 460–61, 106 S.Ct. 2009, 90 L.Ed.2d 445 (1986) * * *. The other, more conventional way, is by proving relevant product and geographic markets and by showing that the defendant's share exceeds whatever threshold is important for the practice in the case.

The Commission found here that, however TRU's market power as a toy retailer was measured, it was clear that its boycott was having an effect in the market. It was remarkably successful in causing the 10 major toy manufacturers to reduce output of toys to the warehouse clubs, and that reduction in output protected TRU from having to lower its prices to meet the clubs' price levels. Price competition from conventional discounters like Wal–Mart and K–Mart, in contrast, imposed no such constraint on it, or so the Commission found. In addition, the Commission showed that the affected manufacturers accounted for some 40% of the traditional toy market, and that TRU had 20% of the national wholesale market and up to 49% of some local wholesale markets. Taking steps to prevent a price collapse through coordination of action among competitors has been illegal at least since *United States v. Socony–Vacuum Oil Co.*, 310 U.S. 150, 60 S.Ct. 811, 84 L.Ed. 1129 (1940).

Proof that this is what TRU was doing is sufficient proof of actual anticompetitive effects that no more elaborate market analysis was necessary.

* * *

———

As we first noted in Chapters 6 and 7, some of antitrust's most celebrated early cases were based on allegations of exclusionary conduct. But as we also observed, the standards for proving unlawful exclusion have become progressively more demanding over time. That in part was a consequence of intense Chicago School criticism of the likelihood that exclusionary conduct would succeed and the efficacy of government intervention to stop it. Arguing that exclusionary conduct rarely was a profit-maximizing strategy, and was, therefore, rarely the most probable explanation for observed, aggressive competitive behavior, and that judicial remedies in such cases tended to do more harm than good, the Chicago School attacked traditional antitrust theories such as predatory pricing and tying with increased success. Support for harsh rules directed at exclusionary conduct waned over time.

As a consequence, exclusionary effects cases all but vanished from the federal government's enforcement agenda by the 1980s, and this trend continued into the early 1990s. Successful private actions, too, became increasingly rare. Exclusionary conduct cases frequently faced skeptical courts and a focused effort by the government as an amicus to enhance the burdens of proof associated with allegations of exclusionary conduct. Such efforts bore significant fruit in *Jefferson Parish* (tying), *Matsushita* (predatory pricing), *Brooke Group* (predatory pricing), and *Trinko* (refusals to deal), all of which demonstrably raised the bar for plaintiffs alleging exclusionary conduct.

During the 1990s, the Clinton-era federal enforcement agencies returned to the exclusionary conduct arena, influenced in large part by Post–Chicago economic theories. In many respects, these government efforts tried to build on the successes of private plaintiffs in two path-breaking, and rare, plaintiffs victories in *Aspen Skiing Co.* (1985) and *Kodak* (1992). Significant exclusionary conduct cases were initiated against *Microsoft, Intel, American Airlines, Visa,* and *Dentsply.* Those cases, taken together, appeared to stand for the proposition that, absent a legitimate business justification, some kinds of exclusionary conduct by a monopolist could be enough to establish a Section 2 violation. The government succeeded in obtaining some kind of relief, either through a court judgment or settlement, in four of the five cases, and was unsuccessful only in *American Airlines*, a predatory pricing case.

The revival of interest in exclusion cases also was aided by the Supreme Court's favorable treatment of evidence of actual anticompetitive effects, which we discussed in Chapter 2 and immediately prior to *Re/Max*. Even though *NCAA* and *IFD* were collusive effects cases, the framework they spawned for distinguishing evidence of actual effects from inferential evidence has arguably carried over to exclusionary effects cases. That trend included the Supreme Court's *Kodak* decision, noted in *Re/Max*, in which the Court concluded that it was "clearly reasonable to infer that Kodak has market power to raise prices *and drive out competition* * * * since respondents offer direct evidence that Kodak did so." 504 U.S. at 477 (emphasis added). Recall, too, that *Re/Max* held: "There are two ways to establish the first element [of a claim of monopolization], that is, that the defendant holds monopoly power. The first is by presenting direct evidence 'showing the exercise of actual control over prices or the *actual exclusion of competitors*.' The second is by presenting circumstantial evidence of monopoly power by showing a high market share within a defined market."

As we noted prior to our reading of *Re/Max*, *NCAA*, and *IFD* were both Section 1 Sherman Act cases. In both cases the fact of agreement was conceded. Thus the only issue was whether the conduct resulted in an unreasonable restraint of trade. In contrast, *Kodak*, and *Re/Max* raised both Section 1 and Section 2 claims. Recall from Chapter 6 that traditionally, the first element of a claim for monopolization is "monopoly power." Hence, in the excerpts just quoted, these courts linked the significance of the actual effects evidence to a finding of monopoly power. When the finding of monopoly power is based on evidence of actual anticompetitive effects, however, what remains to be considered in order to establish a violation of Section 2? If agreement is involved, would the same evidence also necessarily satisfy Section 1 under *NCAA* and *IFD*? Might evidence of actual anticompetitive effects provide a unitary framework for analyzing Section 1 and Section 2 cases? Sidebar 8–3 considers these questions in greater depth.

Finally, note how the plaintiffs' victories in both *Re/Max* and *Toys* were constructed primarily on evidence of actual effects, collusive and exclusionary. Would they have been as successful if the evidence had been less compelling? What role, if any, did circumstantial evidence play? Which party raised it and how? Consider the following possibilities:

- What if there is evidence in a case of actual exclusion, but not of subsequent collusive effects? Should evidence of actual exclusion, like evidence of actual collusive effects, be treated as "cutting to the chase," in all cases, and deemed generally sufficient to support a presumption of violation?

- What if a rival establishes evidence of collusive effects, but none of actual exclusion? Could Re/Max, for example, have satisfied *Brunswick's* requirement of antitrust injury under such circumstances?

- Would *Re/Max* and/or *Toys R Us* have been decided the same way if the plaintiffs had combined evidence of actual anticompetitive effects with inferential evidence of market power? For example, could Re/Max have demonstrated its actual exclusion, and then sought to infer Realty One's market power through market share evidence? Did it in fact try to do so?

- What role did circumstantial evidence of market power play in each case, and which party raised it? How was it received and analyzed by each court?

- Why in both cases did the defendants fail in their efforts to rebut the evidence of actual effects? What were their respective defenses? Were they the same? Should they have succeeded?

- And finally—can there be any defense to a case built on evidence of actual anticompetitive effects? We will revisit that question later in this Chapter.

Sidebar 8–3:
Actual Anticompetitive Effects, Market Power,
and the Diminishing Vitality of the
Copperweld "Gap"*

In Chapter 3 we discussed *Copperweld Corp. v. Independence Tube Corp.*, 467 U.S. 752 (1984). Although *Copperweld's* narrow holding concerned the capacity of a parent corporation and its wholly owned subsidiary to "conspire" for purposes of the Sherman Act, recall that it also incorporated a broader vision of the Sherman Act as a law with a "gap" in its coverage. This conclusion followed from the Court's assumption that "[c]oncerted activity subject to § 1 is judged more sternly than unilateral activity under § 2." 467 U.S. at 768. "More sternly" meant under a lesser burden of proof than that applied to offenses under Section 2. That elevated scrutiny is expressed in the form of disparate standards for proving anticompetitive effect: whereas Section 1 violations can be established through evidence of a mere "unreasonable restraint of trade," Section 2 scrutinizes unilateral conduct "only when ... [it] pose[s] a danger of monopolization." *Id.*

This dichotomy, the Court reasoned, reflected Congress's views that "[c]oncerted activity inherently is fraught with anticompetitive risk," whereas "[j]udging unilateral conduct" under an elevated standard "reduces the risk that the antitrust laws will dampen the competitive zeal of a single aggressive entrepreneur." *Id.* at 768–69. Hence, a "gap" in the Sherman Act's coverage—unreasonable restraints of trade perpetrated by a single "economic entity," such as a parent and its wholly owned subsidiary, lie beyond the reach of Section 1, yet fall short of the "monopolization" or "attempt to monopolize" offenses of Section 2.

As a matter of proof, however, what differentiates the anticompetitive effects of a Section 1 violation from a Section 2 violation?

The most tangible method for demonstrating this difference at the time *Copperweld* was decided was market shares. In Chapters 5 and 6 we saw that market share data long has been a staple of merger law under Section 7 of the Clayton Act and monopolization law under Section 2 of the Sherman Act. Market power, however, began to make its way into Section 1 analysis only a few years before *Copperweld* in the wake of the Court's 1977 *Sylvania* decision. "Market power" became more important as reliance on the per se rule diminished.

The theory behind reliance on market share evidence as a measure of market power is intuitively straight-forward: a firm's ability to raise price and reduce output successfully depends on likely demand and supply responses to changes in price. On the supply side, attempts to raise price and restrict output can be successful in the long term only if the remaining actual or potential capacity in the relevant market is insufficient to offset the diminished output of the firm raising price. Where new output is available, supply will quickly increase and prices will return to the prior level. The attempt to raise price likely will fail. Because a high

---

** This Sidebar is adapted from Andrew I. Gavil, Copperweld *2000: The Vanishing Gap* *Between Sections 1 and 2 of the Sherman Act*, 68 ANTITRUST L.J. 87 (2000).

market share may suggest the absence of alternate industry capacity, it arguably permits the court to draw an inference that it is more probable than not that a firm can profitably raise price. As we have observed in this Chapter, in evidentiary terms, *market shares constitute circumstantial evidence of market power*, and market power provides circumstantial evidence of the capacity to cause anticompetitive effects. Of course, as we first noted in Chapter 5 (mergers) and will explore more fully later in this Chapter, any inference of anticompetitive effects that is drawn from evidence of high market shares can be rebutted with evidence that tends to undermine the assumption that supply responses will not be adequate. Evidence of *conditions of entry* and *efficiency* thus become crucial.

In the years since *Copperweld*, the Supreme Court has continued to assume that "market power" and "monopoly power" are distinct, and that the latter connotes "something more" than the former: "Monopoly power under § 2 requires, of course, something greater than market power under § 1." *Eastman Kodak Co. v. Image Technical Servs., Inc.*, 504 U.S. 451, 481 (1992). But "monopoly power" has been defined traditionally as "the power to control prices or exclude competition." *United States v. E.I. du Pont de Nemours & Co.*, 351 U.S. 377, 391 (1956). In *NCAA*, the Court defined "market power" as "the ability to raise prices above those that would be charged in a competitive market." *NCAA*, 468 U.S. at 109 n.38.

The easiest way to visualize this supposed difference between *market* power and *monopoly* power is in a divergence in market shares: mid-range market shares like 40–60% might be sufficient to infer "market power," whereas higher shares, perhaps over 70%, would be necessary to infer "monopoly power." This is what the *Copperweld* Court presumably had in mind when it declared that there was a "gap" between Section 1 and Section 2 offenses. Indeed, without it, one can hardly construct the *Copperweld* gap—that gap, comprised of unreasonable restraints of trade perpetrated by single firms that fall short of monopoly, is a creature of reliance on circumstantial market share evidence. But can the gap be maintained in cases that rely on evidence of actual competitive effects?

After *NCAA* and *IFD*, it would appear that evidence of the actual ability to restrict output, raise price, or otherwise determine product characteristics normally shaped by competition, establishes market power, at least in a Section 1 case, and it may do so more reliably than market share evidence. We observed this contemporary evidentiary framework at work in both *Re/Max* and *Toys R Us*, both of which relied upon evidence of actual anticompetitive effects. But recall that *Re/Max* was also a Section 2 case. To establish the monopoly power element of their Section 2 monopolization claim, the plaintiffs there sought to import the evidentiary principles of *NCAA* and *IFD*, as well as *Kodak*, into Section 2. In lieu of defining relevant markets and calculating market shares, they instead relied upon direct evidence of higher prices and actual exclusion of competitors.

As we read in the excerpt from *Re/Max*, the Sixth Circuit rejected the defendants' contention that a claim of monopolization *must* rise or fall solely on circumstantial evidence in the form of very high market shares: "[A]n antitrust plaintiff is not required to rely on indirect evidence of a defendant's monopoly power, such as high market share within a defined market, when there is direct evidence that the defendant has actually set prices or excluded competition." *Re/Max*, 173 F.3d at 1018. The court found support for this view in the decisions of four other circuit courts of appeal, as well as the Supreme Court's decisions in *IFD*, *NCAA*, and *Kodak*. *See also Broadcom Corp. v. Qualcomm Inc.*, 501 F.3d 297, 307 n.3 (3d Cir. 2007) ("direct proof of monopoly power does not require a definition of the relevant market"); *PepsiCo, Inc. v. Coca–Cola Co.*, 315 F.3d 101, 107–08 (2d Cir. 2002) ("a relevant market definition is not a necessary component of a monopolization claim" where there is direct evidence of monopoly power); *Conwood Co., L.P. v. U.S. Tobacco Co.*, 290 F.3d 768, 783 n.2 (6th Cir.2002) (monopoly power "may be proven directly by evidence of the control of prices or the exclusion of competition, or it may be inferred from one firm's large percentage share of the relevant market").

In dismissing the import of market shares in the face of evidence of the actual exercise of market power, the court had to confront an unanswered question from *Copperweld*: in terms of proof, what distinguishes a Section 1 from a Section 2 violation when *direct evidence* is relied upon to demonstrate anticompetitive effect? Consistent with *Copperweld*'s vision of the Sherman Act, the defendant argued that reliance on Section 1 cases like *NCAA* and *IFD* in connection with an allegation of monopolization would be misplaced. Surely, as the Court assumed in *Copperweld*, and maintained in *Kodak*, proof of "monopoly power" for purposes of Section 2 requires something more than proof of "market power" for purposes of Section 1.

But the Sixth Circuit rejected any such formalistic distinction, instead embracing the more modern trend in the cases that equates monopoly and market power when they are established through evidence of actual anticompetitive effects: "[W]e see no reason to believe that monopoly power in the § 1 context is any different from the § 2 monopoly power the plaintiffs allege here." *Re/Max*, 173 F.3d at 1019. In doing so, the court arguably followed the views of contemporary antitrust commentators and economists, who increasingly have disavowed any clear dividing line between market and monopoly power. *See, e.g.*, Thomas G. Krattenmaker, et al., *Monopoly Power and Market Power in Antitrust Law*, 76 Geo. L. J. 241, 247 (1987) ("Economists use both 'market power' and 'monopoly power' to refer to the power of a single firm or group of firms to price profitably above marginal cost. * * * We believe that antitrust law should dispense with the idea that market power and monopoly power are different concepts."). Although these commentators readily acknowledge that market power will always be a matter of degree, none suggest that there is a meaningful, objective market share threshold for distinguishing "monopoly power" from ordinary "market power" when the evidence of market power is measured directly. *But see* Dennis W. Carlton & Jeffrey M. Perloff, Modern Industrial Organization 93 (4th ed. 2005) (noting that although monopoly power and market power typically are used interchangeably, "[o]ne might usefully distinguish between the terms by using *monopoly power* to describe a firm that makes a profit if it sets its price optimally above its marginal cost, and *market power* to describe a firm that earns only the competitive profit when it sets its price optimally above its marginal cost."); Gregory J. Werden, *Demand Elasticities in Antitrust Analysis*, 66

ANTITRUST L.J. 363, 372–73 (1998) (suggesting that market power could be viewed with reference to short-run marginal cost, whereas monopoly power might be measured with respect to long-run marginal cost).

If commentators and courts such as the Sixth Circuit in *Re/Max* are correct in their position that market power and monopoly power cannot be distinguished as an economic matter, should evidence of actual anti-competitive effects establish market power for purposes of a Section 1 rule of reason case as well as monopoly power for a Section 2 case? If so, there would no longer appear to be any meaningful distinction between the burden of proof faced by plaintiffs in Section 1 or Section 2 cases when they rely on evidence of actual anticompetitive effects. *Copper-weld*'s theory of the gap, therefore, could only be maintained in cases based solely on circumstantial evidence, where maintenance of a gap might be an accommodation for the uncertainties associated with defining relevant markets and calculating market shares.

The trend towards crediting evidence of actual anticompetitive effect for purposes of both market power and the ultimate question of anticompetitive consequences has continue in the courts, see *United States v. Visa U.S.A., Inc.*, 344 F.3d 229 (2d Cir. 2003) (discussed in Chapter 7, *supra*) and before the Federal Trade Commission. *See, e.g., In the Matter of Polygram Holding, Inc.*, Dkt. No. 9298, at 20–21 & n.26 (FTC July, 28, 2003), *available at* http://www.ftc.gov/os/2003/07/polygramopinion.pdf, *aff'd on other grounds, Polygram Holdings, Inc. v. FTC*, 416 F.3d 29 (D.C. Cir. 2005).

One court, however, has limited reliance on direct evidence, particularly in the context of claims of vertical, exclusionary conduct. In *Republic Tobacco Co. v. N. Atl. Trading Co.*, 381 F.3d 717 (7th Cir. 2004), the Seventh Circuit rejected the plaintiff's argument that it need not establish a relevant market because it had presented direct evidence of actual anticompetitive effects, *i.e.*, actual exclusion and higher retail prices. To reach that result, the Seventh Circuit read the relevant cases—*FTC v. Indiana Fed'n of Dentists*, 476 U.S. 447 (1986) and *Toys "R" Us, Inc. v. FTC*, 221 F.3d 928 (7th Cir. 2000)—narrowly, arguing that evidence of actual anticompetitive effects can suffice to meet an antitrust plaintiff's burden of production solely in horizontal cases. In vertical cases, plaintiffs also are required to prove at least the "rough contours" of a relevant market and substantial market shares. The court also appeared to denigrate the value of actual effects evidence, characterizing it as a "relaxed" evidentiary standard compared to market share evidence, and implying that reliance on direct evidence in the "wrong" context could lead to false positives and hence over-deterrence. Is evidence of actual anticompetitive effects, such as higher market prices and reduced output, necessarily easier to develop than circumstantial evidence? For a critical analysis of *Republic Tobacco*, arguing that the court's formalistic distinction between vertical and horizontal cases led it to bypass a valuable opportunity to clarify the standards for defining and proving direct evidence, see Andrew I. Gavil, *On the Utility of "Direct Evidence of Anticompetitive Effects": A Comment on the Seventh Circuit's* Republic Tobacco *Decision*, ANTITRUST, Spring 2005, at 59.

Note on Actual Anticompetitive Effects
Affecting Non–Price Competition

Although price and output have emerged as the principal measures of a competitive market—and therefore of anticompetitive effects—there are other indicia of healthy competition. Here we examine conduct that affects non-price competition, primarily product quality and variety. In Chapter 10 we will also examine conduct that inhibits innovation.

In *National Soc'y of Prof'l Eng'rs v. United States*, 435 U.S. 679 (1978) the Supreme Court observed:

> The Sherman Act reflects a legislative judgment that ultimately competition will produce not only lower prices, but also better goods and services. "The heart of our national economic policy long has been faith in the value of competition." The assumption that competition is the best method of allocating resources in a free market recognizes that all elements of a bargain—quality, service, safety, and durability—and not just the immediate cost, are favorably affected by the free opportunity to select among alternative offers.

435 U.S. at 695. The message is implicit that efforts to suppress or impair product services, quality, safety, or durability are proper bases for antitrust scrutiny. Adequate quantity and competitive pricing are not the only two dimensions of competition.

In re Detroit Auto Dealers Ass'n, 955 F.2d 457 (6th Cir. 1992), illustrates how such broader concerns about the purposes and benefits of competition can be addressed under the antitrust laws. Detroit Auto dealers involved an FTC challenge to an agreement among rival auto dealers to limit their hours of operation. The FTC had concluded that show room hours were a form of output and a dimension of competition. As the court described, the FTC: " * * * found that a car dealer was 'a provider of sales and support services,' and that its 'output' is not measured in terms of units sold." *Id.* at 470. The court also reviewed the FTC's conclusions with respect to the Association's proffered justifications:

> The Commission concluded in note 22 that the "efficiency justifications" presented by the dealers "(1) lower dealer overhead costs, (2) the ability to attract higher-quality sales personnel, and (3) the prevention of unionization" were not "plausible." Although conceding that "dealer overhead may have been reduced," the Commission concluded that "unit costs did not decrease," based on its prior conclusion that there was a reduction in "output," that is, showroom hours of operation. * * * The Commission found, moreover, that preventing unionization could not be "legitimate" justification for competitive purposes because of a "national policy favoring the association of employees to bargain in good faith with employers over wages, hours and working conditions." We are not sure such a policy, if it exists, precludes this purported justification, but we have agreed with the Commission that the dealers' agreement does not come within the nonstatutory exemption, and that acts designed to impede union organization may be antithetical to a national labor policy.

Id. at 471. Although the court took issue with some of the FTC's reasoning, it ultimately concluded:

> While we do not agree in all respects with the Commission's rationale, we find some legal basis and support for its conclusions in an area

that is murky and unclear. Limitation of hours has been held to be an anticompetitive restraint although relief in that case was limited and the damages to users or customers was found to be "entirely speculative." We do not equate limitation of hours to price-fixing, but we do not find error in the Commission's conclusion that hours of operation in this business is a means of competition, and that such limitation may be an unreasonable restraint of trade.[15]

Id. at 472.

What is the "anti-competitive effect" alleged is *Detroit Auto Dealers*? Should the conduct at issue—a coordinated restriction of show room hours—be categorized as conduct having collusive or conduct having exclusionary effects? What was the value to the defendants of the restriction? The impact on consumers? Why were the Association's proffered justifications rejected?

In a series of articles, commentators Neil W. Averitt and Robert H. Lande have argued that "consumer choice" is "the ultimate goal of antitrust," citing *Detroit Auto Dealers* as a prime example of how concern for restrictions on "consumer sovereignty" is a central feature of antitrust and consumer protection law. *See, e.g.,* Neil W. Averitt & Robert H. Lande, *Consumer Sovereignty: A Unified Theory of Antitrust and Consumer Protection Law*, 65 ANTITRUST L.J. 713 (1997); Robert H. Lande, *Consumer Choice as the Ultimate Goal of Antitrust*, 62 U. PITT. L. REV. 503 (2001). Would you agree? To what degree is the court's rationale in *Detroit Auto Dealers* driven by concern for consumer choice and sovereignty?

Are there other dimensions of competition which, like hours of operation, arguably benefit consumers and warrant protection? Might there be instances in which an agreement to lessen such conduct could be justified? What if the auto dealers had agreed to limit their hours of operation for security reasons, arguing that it is more difficult to guarantee the safety of their customers late at night? What if they had agreed to limit the provision of "loaner" cars during service visits only to customers who purchased their vehicles at the dealership?

Sidebar 8–4:
The Role of Information as Non–Price Competition

As *Nat'l Soc'y of Prof'l Eng'rs* and *Detroit Auto Dealers* suggest, there are dimensions of competition other than price and quantity that may warrant protection under the antitrust laws. Firms frequently compete, for example, with respect to the quality of their products, the quantity and quality of their services, product variety, hours of operation, and many other factors that might influence consumer spending choices. In this Sidebar, we explore some of the concerns that can arise with respect to one particular dimension of non-price competition—"information."

"Information" can be a critical determinant of competition. As we first noted in Chapter 1, access to information about products and prices

---

15. Neither do we necessarily agree that "the parties' focus on retail prices misses the point in this case." Under a Rule of Reason analysis effect on prices, output and market forces in a competitive market of a particular practice is frequently relevant and may be determinative. The special factors noted in this case support the Commission's conclusion on restraint of trade despite lack of evidence of increased prices.

is necessary to the proper functioning of markets. Without it, buyers and sellers of products and services can be deceived, or may simply make uninformed decisions. Suppression of information, or the conveyance of inaccurate information, can be manipulated to achieve collusive or exclusionary effects.

For the most part, information problems are addressed by consumer protection and other laws, such as prohibitions of false and deceptive advertising. But suppression or restraints of information can have a serious enough impact on competition to raise antitrust concerns. Cases like *Nat'l Soc'y of Prof'l Eng'rs* (suppression of price information through ban on competitive bidding), *Indiana Federation of Dentists* (ban on supply of x-rays to insurers), and *California Dental Ass'n* (disclosure requirements for professional advertising), all concerned efforts by competitors to in some way limit the supply of information in ways that were challenged as anticompetitive. By increasing the cost to consumers of acquiring information about competing products, a firm can impede their ability to choose desirable products and to switch from undesirable to desirable ones. This in turn may enhance a firm's ability to exercise market power.

Two other examples of information related antitrust theories can be found in *Toys R Us*, discussed *supra*, and the government's 1998 prosecution of *Microsoft*, which we discussed in Chapters 6 and 7.

In *Toys R Us*, the FTC alleged that TRU sought the agreement of its toy manufacturing suppliers that they would either not sell certain toys to its warehouse competitors or that they would not sell toys packaged in the same way as they were packaged for TRU. These restrictions can be viewed as an effort by TRU to impose higher information and search costs on consumers. As a consequence of the differential packaging, consumers were less able to comparison shop based on price and product features, which may have facilitated TRU's exercise of market power.

Whereas *Toys R Us* involved efforts to protect and extend market power by increasing consumer search costs, the *Microsoft* litigation included claims that deception had been used as a component of a broader scheme to monopolize. It therefore illustrates the relatively rare instance where deception can rise to the level of being an antitrust violation. In Chapter 10, we will also examine how deception might be used to lessen competition through manipulation of the standard setting process. *See Abuse of Standard Setting: Note on Rambus Litigation*, *infra*, Chapter 10.

Recall that Microsoft was found to have undertaken efforts to impede competition for its Windows operating system from Netscape's "Navigator" Internet browser and Sun Microsystems' "Java," a set of technologies developed to facilitate cross-platform programming. Java was not an operating system itself, but "middleware," software designed to operate on top of any existing operating system, but which in turn could provide a platform itself for other kinds of software. In contrast to Microsoft Windows, however, Java was neutral with respect to its underlying operating system—by design, it could run on any platform. Hence, programs written for Java would work with any underlying operating system that also ran Java, not just Windows.

The court found that Microsoft viewed Java's ability to work cross-platform as a threat to the dominance of its Windows operating system.

To the extent programmers accepted Sun's call to develop programs for Java, those programs would work cross-platform. Software developers and eventually PC manufacturers and consumers would become less dependent on Windows, which ran on more than 90% of personal computers.

To respond to that threat, Microsoft feigned a desire to cooperate with Sun in the development and promotion of Java. Under license from Sun, it proceeded to develop for Windows its own version of the Java compiler, known as the "Java Virtual Machine" ("JVM"), which translates code into instructions to the underlying operating system. The court of appeals found nothing objectionable from an antitrust viewpoint in Microsoft's development of a Windows JVM. Indeed, the evidence demonstrated that the Windows JVM made Java-based programs run faster on Windows-based desktop PCs. But the court also found that Microsoft had designed its JVM to be Windows specific—*i.e.*, programs written for the Windows JVM with the development tools provided by Microsoft would not be platform neutral—*a fact that Microsoft did not share with the developers*—and which was wholly inconsistent with Sun's goal of maintaining platform neutrality for Java:

> * * * As a result, * * * developers who relied upon Microsoft's public commitment to cooperate with Sun and who used Microsoft's tools to develop what Microsoft led them to believe were cross-platform applications ended up producing applications that would run only on the Windows operating system.

> * * * Microsoft documents confirm that Microsoft intended to deceive Java developers, and predicted that the effect of its actions would be to generate Windows-dependent Java applications that their developers believed would be cross-platform; these documents also indicate that Microsoft's ultimate objective was to thwart Java's threat to Microsoft's monopoly in a market for operating systems. * * *

> Microsoft's conduct related to its Java developer tools served to protect its monopoly of the operating system in a manner not attributable either to the superiority of the operating system or to the acumen of its makers, and therefore was anticompetitive. Unsurprisingly, Microsoft offers no procompetitive explanation for its campaign to deceive developers. Accordingly, we conclude this conduct is exclusionary, in violation of § 2 of the Sherman Act.

Microsoft Corp., 253 F.3d at 76–77. *See also Caribbean Broad. Sys., Ltd. v. Cable & Wireless PLC*, 148 F.3d 1080 (D.C.Cir.1998)(allegations that predator used fraudulent misrepresentations as part of attempt to monopolize were adequate to state an antitrust claim).

Collectively, these cases demonstrate how information relating to price, product features and quality, can be suppressed, manipulated or altered to achieve anticompetitive results, some collusive and others exclusionary. Note how they have arisen under both Section 1 and Section 2 of the Sherman Act, and that under Section 1 they have been variously resolved under the per se rule, the "quick look," and the rule of reason. What distinguished cases decided under each of these approaches? Why should *Nat'l Soc'y of Prof'l Eng'rs* be closer to a per se case, and

> *Indiana Federation of Dentists* a quick look? What made *Detroit Auto Dealer's* appropriate for treatment under the rule of reason? How can courts determine which legal framework is best in each such case? How significant should the role of price be?

2. WHEN CIRCUMSTANTIAL EVIDENCE OF MARKET POWER JUSTIFIES THE INFERENCE OF ANTICOMPETITIVE EFFECTS

Evidence of the actual exercise of market power is not always available. In Section 1 and Section 2 Sherman Act cases, anticompetitive effects often are either presumed—as in the per se offenses of Section 1—or inferred from evidence of market power, typically high market shares. In many other antitrust offenses, challenge is authorized before the full effects of conduct are felt, *e.g.*, attempt to monopolize, and all of the incipiency offenses under the Clayton Act. Merger challenges, for example, are almost always inferential/circumstantial cases because they are most often brought prospectively.

The field of mergers has laid the foundation for two general methods for inferring anticompetitive effects from evidence of market power. In the first, direct evidence of market power is used to infer anticompetitive effects. Thus, where price/cost ratios, direct measures of demand elasticities, or econometric analysis of prices supports the assertion that a firm or firms possess market power, the inference of anticompetitive effects can be made, provided it is linked to conduct that cannot be justified in some way on legitimate grounds. We describe this approach as the *"single inference"* method: from direct evidence of market power, anticompetitive effects are inferred. The evidence of market power is direct, but the conclusion as to anticompetitive effects is the product of inference: "market power," as opposed to evidence of actual price increases or the exclusion of rivals, justifies the presumption that illegitimate conduct will have anticompetitive consequences. It shifts a burden of production to the defending party.

In the second methodology, neither evidence of actual anticompetitive effects, nor direct evidence of market power is available. In such circumstances, market power can be inferred from market share calculations, which in turn are derived after a relevant market is defined. In a sense, this method involves a *"double inference:"* from evidence of high market shares, market power is inferred, and from evidence of market power, anticompetitive harm is inferred.

In merger analysis, the *Philadelphia Nat'l Bank* presumption, which we studied in Chapter 5, is an example of the "double inference" method—from high market shares, market power is inferred, and from market power, anticompetitive effects—unilateral or coordinated—are predicted. (*See* Sidebar 5–6, *supra*). Similarly, in our study of Sherman Act Section 2, we saw that monopoly power, which traditionally meant high market shares, was a necessary ingredient of a Section 2 monopolization violation. Linked with evidence of exclusionary conduct, monopoly power permits the inference of "monopolization," which can be interpreted as a kind of anticompetitive effect. Figure 8–4 summarizes these various approaches.

Figure 8–4:
Single and Double Inference Methodologies Compared

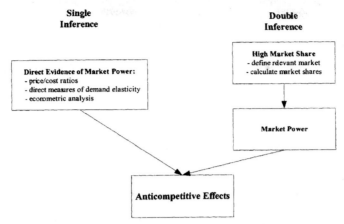

Before proceeding to a consideration of the cases, it is worthwhile to reflect on the challenges inherent in making these two inferential approaches operable. First, in both instances, there can be important conditions and assumptions necessary to justify drawing an inference of market power from direct or circumstantial evidence. Absent those preconditions, the inferences may not be warranted. Persistently high profits, for example, remains controversial as a yardstick of market power. Moreover, drawing the inference under some conditions may be affirmatively misleading, and could result in condemnation of conduct that is not very likely to have any significant anticompetitive effect. Similarly, controversy persists over the reliability of inferences of market power drawn from high market shares.

Second, although the theoretical bases for the single and double inferences may be relatively clear and compelling, invoking them in the context of litigation or agency negotiations requires a step beyond theory. What form will the necessary evidence take? How often will it be available and at what cost? Who will have the burden of producing it? The next Sidebar looks more closely at these sorts of issues as they pertain to the use of single inference evidence of anticompetitive effects. You might also want to review Sidebar 5–6 at this time, which addressed the issues that arise in connection with use of double inference evidence, typically high market shares. Note how taken together both Sidebars sound a cautionary note, and commend a more critical reading of the materials that follow when inferences provide the foundation for the plaintiff's case.

Sidebar 8–5:
The "Single Inference" Method for Inferring Anticompetitive Effects

The single inference method of inferring anticompetitive effect relies on direct evidence of market power and infers anticompetitive effect from that evidence. Although the evidence of market power is direct, the evidence as to anticompetitive effect is circumstantial—it requires an inference drawn from the direct proof of market power. At least three types of direct evidence of market power have been discussed in the case law and the economic literature:

- price and conduct comparisons across markets and over time;
- direct measures of the structure of demand; and
- accounting estimates of margins and profits.

Price and Conduct Comparisons Across Markets and Over Time

Often the most persuasive evidence of market power comes from direct comparisons of prices between the markets in question and comparable markets thought to perform competitively. These might be based upon different regions of the country, or a "before and after" comparison with the same market at an earlier time, for example. When a competitive benchmark is available, this type of comparison constitutes a "natural experiment" that can identify the presence or absence of market power.

The examples discussed in detail below illustrate the power of direct evidence on pricing for demonstrating market power. Two factors are critical in making such comparisons persuasive. The first is whether the benchmark market is likely to perform competitively, or at least more competitively than the market under review, if the anticompetitive theory is correct, so that the comparison between them provides a natural experiment. In a before-and-after comparison, for example, the benchmark would be the period before the conduct under review has occurred, and the comparison would ask whether price is higher in the period after the conduct took place. In a comparison across markets, the benchmark market might be relatively unconcentrated, and the comparison would ask whether prices are higher in more concentrated markets. The second factor is whether differences in price between the benchmark market and the market under review could have explanations other than market power, most importantly differences in cost. More generally, the observed differences in price must be greater than can be accounted for by differences in cost or other factors. Another innocent explanation that might apply in some cases is that the observed differences in price merely reflect price discrimination in competitive markets.

1. Traditional Models: American Tobacco and Addyston Pipe

One example of direct evidence of market power, from which anticompetitive effect can be inferred, comes from a mid–20th century conspiracy to monopolize case against the tobacco industry. The Supreme Court upheld a jury verdict finding that the leading tobacco firms had conspired to fix prices in the sale of cigarettes and exclude undesired competition. In part, this conclusion was based on evidence that cigarette prices rose during a period (the Great Depression) when the costs of tobacco leaf were unusually low and manufacturing costs had been declining. *American Tobacco Co. v. United States*, 328 U.S. 781, 805 (1946). "No economic justification for this raise was demonstrated," according to the Court. Thus, the "record of price changes is circumstantial evidence of the existence of a conspiracy and of a power and intent to exclude competition coming from cheaper grade cigarettes." *Id.* at 804–05.

Another example of direct evidence of market power based on pricing comes from *Addyston Pipe.* Our discussion of this decision in Chapter 2 focused on its elaboration of rule of reason doctrine. The underlying facts can be quickly sketched. The defendants were six manufacturers of cast iron pipe, who commonly participated in procurement auctions run by local gas and water utilities. Instead of competing against each other when customers put out pipe orders for bid, the firms reached an agreement to divide up a number of markets in the southern and central part of the country, city-by-city, for two years. "The record is full of instances * * * in which, after the successful bidder had been fixed by the 'auction pool,' or had been fixed by the arrangement as to 'reserve' cities, the other defendants put in bids at the public letting as high as the selected bidder requested, in order to give the appearance of active competition between the defendants." *Addyston Pipe*, 85 F. at 275. Territory more than 500 miles from the firms' foundries was called "free" territory, as opposed to "pay" territory, where the reserved cities were located. In free territory, the firms were allowed to bid any price.

The evidence concerning price variation across cities provided a direct basis for inferring that the firms exercised market power. Prices were higher in the reserved cities than the free cities, even though costs appeared to be lower in reserved cities, demonstrating directly that the firms had exercised market power. 85 F. at 277. This outcome was particularly hard to rationalize as derived innocently, from differences in the cost of serving the various locations, because shipping costs were substantial, typically on the order of 10% to 25% of price.* This was far from the only evidence from which anticompetitive effect was inferred in *Addyston Pipe*—indeed, the agreement in that case would today likely be held illegal *per se*, as an agreement among rivals concerning price that lacked any business justification, without regard to the presence or absence of evidence of injury to competition. The case nevertheless provides a useful example of the "single inference" method.

2. *Modern Econometric Tools: Staples*

A modern example comes from the *Staples* merger case, which we studied in Chapter 5. According to George Cary, the then Senior Deputy Director of the FTC's Bureau of Competition and the FTC's lead counsel when the preliminary injunction hearing was held, the FTC had a "one-fact case." The key fact was what the trial court called the "compelling" pricing evidence. *Staples*, 970 F.Supp. at 1076. That evidence showed that Staples charged significantly higher prices—at least 5 percent and as much as 13 percent higher—in geographic markets (cities) where it had no office superstore competition than in markets where it competed with the two other superstore chains, notwithstanding the presence of a wide range of non-superstore retailers of office supplies in single superstore

---

* According to the appellate court, the defendants also claimed that "the prices at a city like St. Louis, in which the specifications were detailed and precise, were higher because pipe had to be made especially for the job, and they could not use stock on hand." 85 F. at 278. In theory, this possibility could have provided a cost-related explanation for high prices in the reserved cities, and thus undermined the direct evidence of market power. But it was apparently not a major focus of the litigation.

markets. *Id.* at 1075–76. The direct evidence on pricing was not limited to comparisons of prices across markets. The court also relied on before and after comparisons, finding that Staples changed price zones to lower prices when faced with the entry of another superstore, but not for other retailers. *Id.* at 1077–78.

The direct evidence on pricing was a key basis for concluding that a hypothetical office superstore monopolist could profitably raise price, and thus provided a basis for defining a product market limited to "consumable office supplies sold through office superstores." Within this market, the proposed merger would have been a merger to monopoly in many metropolitan area geographic markets, and it increased concentration substantially in many other markets where a third superstore chain would remain as a competitor. In this way, direct evidence on *market power*—the likely market power of superstores acting collectively—provided circumstantial evidence of *anticompetitive effect*, making *Staples* a single inference case. Alternatively, if the decision is understood as using the pricing evidence to define the product market, to infer market power from high concentration (often merger to monopoly) in the various geographic markets, and to infer anticompetitive effects from market power, it is a double inference case.

But the district court also recognized that the pricing evidence provided *direct evidence of anticompetitive effect*. The FTC showed that prices were higher when Staples was the only superstore chain in the market, relative to prices when Staples competed with Office Depot, its merger partner, and no other superstore chain. The FTC also showed that prices were higher when Staples competed head to head with Office Max, the third major superstore chain. The lowest prices were consistently evident only when Staples, Office Depot, and Office Max were all competing. *See generally* Jonathan B. Baker, *Econometric Analysis in FTC v. Staples,* 18 J. PUB. POL. & MARKETING 11 (1999) ("*Econometric Analysis*"). According to the court:

> * * * [D]irect evidence shows that by eliminating Staples' most significant, and in many markets only, rival, this merger would allow Staples to increase prices or otherwise maintain prices at an anticompetitive level. The merger would eliminate head-to-head competition between the two lowest cost and lowest priced firms in the superstore market.

Staples, 970 F.Supp. at 1082–83 (footnote omitted). To the extent the court relied on direct evidence of anticompetitive effect, it was not engaging in either a single inference or a double inference method of inferring anticompetitive effects from market power. Thus, in *Staples,* the pricing evidence lent support to *both* proof of likely anticompetitive effects, and single or double inference proof of market power from which anticompetitive effects could be inferred. These alternative methods of proving anticompetitive effect, therefore, were aligned, which made the evidence especially compelling.**

** It is worth noting that a court may find it valuable or necessary to define a market even when it does not employ the double inference method of proving harm to competition. Market definition allows for the identification of market participants, which a court may need to know in order to determine, for example, whether demand elasticities are properly estimated (without omitting the influence of a key rival) or to identify the maverick whose incen-

The merging firms' response to the pricing evidence in *Staples* is instructive as to the significance and probative value of direct evidence of market power. The firms made two primary, though unsuccessful, arguments. First, they contended that superstores were constrained by competition from a wide range of non-superstore retailers of office supplies. They argued that if the product market were defined properly, to encompass the sale of consumable office supplies by all sellers, not just office superstores, the resulting low market shares for the merging firms—a combined share of only 5.5% nationwide—would properly reflect the low potential for anticompetitive effect from the proposed acquisition. In short, the parties argued that the *double inference* method of inferring anticompetitive effect should be preferred to the *single inference* method proposed by the F.T.C. and adopted by the court. They asked the court to prefer circumstantial evidence of anticompetitive effect based on market shares and a disputed market definition to circumstantial evidence of anticompetitive effect based on direct evidence of market power from pricing comparisons across markets and over time.

Second, the merging firms contended that the F.T.C. had made the wrong inference from the pricing data because it failed to control for differences in cost across cities. In particular, the parties insisted that Staples' prices were high in single superstore markets and other markets where Office Depot did not compete because, on average, costs other than those the F.T.C could observe and control for statistically, perhaps resulting from local zoning provisions or congestion, were high in those markets. They asserted that these higher costs simultaneously led Staples to raise the price higher than what it charged elsewhere and independently discouraged Office Depot from entering. If so, inferring market power from pricing differences was unwarranted.

This critique led to an argument about the proper competitive benchmark. The parties were essentially arguing that cities with multiple superstore chains were not a good benchmark for identifying the competitive price because they were also lower marginal cost locations. They preferred before and after comparisons within the same market, on the ground that these comparisons would be less subject to unobservable cost variation. The F.T.C. was less troubled by cross-market comparisons because the merging firms' concern about unobservable zoning or congestion costs had negligible support in the parties documents. The F.T.C. also presented statistical evidence showing that before-and-after studies gave a similar prediction as cross-market studies as to the likely increase in price from the merger. *See generally* Baker, *Econometric Analysis*, *supra*. This statistical evidence was consistent with before and after documentary evidence demonstrating that Staples placed cities in a lower-priced "price zone" following the entry of superstore rivals into those markets, but did not alter price zones in response to the entry of other retailers. The court relied heavily on that documentary evidence in finding for the FTC.

3. *Modern Econometric Tools: Bid–Rigging*

Market power has also been demonstrated through direct comparisons of pricing, both before-and-after comparisons and cross-market

tives may be relevant to analysis of coordinated competitive effects.

comparisons, in other settings. One approach that has been used to distinguish bid rigging, a form of price-fixing, from competitive bidding in formal auctions compares the behavior of the firms under investigation to the behavior of a class of firms that are assumed *not* to be involved in bid rigging. The methodology requires that the firms bid in multiple auctions, as for different road building contracts, school milk procurements, forest timber sales, oil drilling tracts, etc. The analyst looks at the way the competitive firms alter their bids in response to variation in the characteristics across auctions, and infers that the firms under investigation are conspiring rather than bidding competitively—that they are making phantom bids that feign competition, as with the firms in *Addyston Pipe*—if they do not alter their bids across auctions in similar ways. *See, e.g.,* Patrick Bajari & Garrett Summers, *Detecting Collusion in Procurement Auctions: Select Survey of Recent Research*, 70 ANTITRUST L. J. 143 (2002); J. Douglas Zona & Robert H. Porter, *Detection of Bid Rigging in Procurement Auctions*, 101 J. POL. ECON. 518 (1993); J. Douglas Zona & Robert H. Porter, *Ohio Milk Markets: An Analysis of Bidding*, 30 RAND J. ECON. 263 (1999).

Before-and-after price comparisons are also widely employed in price-fixing cases—comparing prices before the alleged conspiracy period to prices during the time the conspiracy was said to operate. They are mainly used in this setting to assess buyer damages, though they may also provide evidence of liability. Statistical methodologies are commonly employed to control for other factors, such as cost, that could provide alternative explanations for the observed price increases. *See generally* Jonathan B. Baker & Daniel L. Rubinfeld, *Empirical Methods in Antitrust Litigation: Review and Critique*, 1 AM. J. L. & ECON. 386, 392–98 (1999)(*"Empirical Methods"*).

4. *Price Discrimination*

Economic price discrimination—charging different prices for the same product to different customers—also can provide direct evidence of market power based on pricing. *See* GEORGE STIGLER, THE ORGANIZATION OF INDUSTRY 14 (1968) (describing "the absence of systematic price discrimination" as evidence of competition). *But cf.* Symposium: *Competitive Price Discrimination*, 70 ANTITRUST L.J. 593 (2003) (debating whether price discrimination should be deemed to reflect market power when entry is easy and anticompetitive effects are absent). When firms discriminate in price, they charge a higher price to those customers willing to pay more, or to a group of buyers with relatively inelastic demand. (The economics of price discrimination are discussed in more detail in Sidebar 7–8, *supra.*) Evidence of price discrimination can arise through a comparison of the price charged different customers or in different markets for similar products. Or it can come from before and after comparisons of pricing in the same market, when market demand is thought to vary in elasticity over time.

To be probative of market power, such comparisons must involve similar products, or otherwise control for product differences likely to affect the price. This issue would arise in determining the extent of a price increase resulting from price discrimination by airlines, for example. When business passengers pay more for a ticket on the same aircraft than leisure passengers, who buy their tickets weeks in advance, the two groups of travelers are buying a somewhat different product. The business traveler is purchasing more than a seat on the aircraft; she is also acquiring the ability to decide whether or not to fly at the last minute.

Before terming the price difference economic price discrimination, and treating it as direct evidence of market power, one must first ask whether the higher last-minute price reflects price discrimination against a group of buyers with inelastic demand, or whether it instead reflects the added cost to the airline of holding the seat open until the last minute, where it might not be filled. Of course, both factors might prove to be important. *Cf. Blue Cross & Blue Shield United of Wisconsin v. Marshfield Clinic*, 65 F.3d 1406, 1412 (7th Cir.1995) (questioning inference of market power from high prices on the ground that the higher priced product was higher quality). Price comparisons over time similarly require controlling for cost differences over time before they are used to identify market power. *See generally* Jonathan B. Baker & Timothy F. Bresnahan, *Empirical Methods of Identifying and Measuring Market Power*, 61 ANTITRUST L.J. 3 (1992).

Price discrimination is quite common, particularly in high-tech markets and other industries with low marginal costs and high fixed costs (like airlines). This observation may suggest that market power is common, in the sense that the firms have some ability to raise price by reducing output, but it does not necessarily mean that anticompetitive effects are common in those industries. As discussed in Chapter 7, price discrimination may occur in free entry markets, where the prospect of entry prevents the firms from charging prices in excess of competitive levels. *See generally*, Symposium: *Competitive Price Discrimination*, 70 ANTITRUST L.J. 593 (2003). In such situations, moreover, price discrimination may be efficient, allowing sellers to make their product available to buyers who would not otherwise be served.

The possibility of competitive price discrimination could arise when firms that sell multiple products or at multiple locations charge higher margins of price over marginal cost in some geographic markets or product markets than in others. Higher margins would be expected in those markets where demand is relatively less responsive to price (less elastic).*** But prices are not too high on average; this is a competitive benchmark that looks at prices in all markets simultaneously, not in markets individually. To explain differences in prices between markets by competitive price discrimination rather than market power, the defendant firm or firms must show that the price-cost margins in the low margin markets, if applied in all markets, would be insufficient to allow an efficient firm to cover its fixed costs. In addition, the defendant must show that prices are kept at competitive levels on average by the threat of entry, by demonstrating that entry of a new multi-market seller, able to hold down profits of incumbents to competitive levels, would be easy.****

*** In principle, competitive price discrimination could also arise if price margins over marginal cost vary cyclically, rising during periods when demand grows less responsive to price (less elastic), as might occur during economic booms.

**** Absent free entry, the interaction among incumbent firms may be insufficient to allow the firms to charge prices above marginal cost while capping those prices on average—that is, without also leading the firms to charge higher than competitive prices on average. In general, therefore, circumstantial evidence that the market has a competitive structure (low concentration) will not be as convincing as evidence of free entry as a

These observations about price discrimination highlight a broader proposition that should be noted in connection with the use of direct measures of market power to infer anticompetitive effect: the inference of anticompetitive effect from direct evidence of market power is merely an *inference*. Evidence of entry conditions and efficiencies can be used to rebut that inference, as will be discussed later in this Chapter.

5. *Conduct*

As we are observing in this Chapter, courts increasingly have found evidence of actual anticompetitive effects sufficient to shift the burden of production from a plaintiff to a defendant in a range of antitrust cases. In each such instance, however, the effect followed from certain *conduct*. Evidence of conduct that produces an actual output reduction, including a reduction in non-price dimensions of competition such as product variety and innovation, would constitute proof of market power, and so allow the inference of anticompetitive effect. After all, a firm or group of firms that raise price by reducing industry output are almost by definition *exercising market power*. See NCAA v. Bd. of Regents of Univ. of Oklahoma, 468 U.S. 85, 104–05 n.29 (1984) ("The evidence establishes the fact that the networks are * * * paying * * * large fees because the NCAA agrees to limit production.").

Direct Measures of the Structure of Demand (Buyer Substitution)

The power to raise price by reducing output is closely related to the responsiveness of buyers to higher prices—that is to the *elasticity of buyer demand*. *See* Casebook, *supra* Chapter 1. Moreover, observations on the historical response of buyers to price changes can permit economic experts to learn about demand elasticities, as has previously been discussed in connection with market definition under the Merger Guidelines.

Similar issues arise in proving a dominant firm's market power under Sherman Act § 2. Landes and Posner, in their influential article on market power, pointed out that if direct evidence of elasticities is available, they can be used "to measure the firm's market power directly," in which case "no market share criterion of market power is either necessary or appropriate." William M. Landes & Richard A. Posner, *Market Power in Antitrust Cases*, 94 Harv. L. Rev. 937, 953 (1981) (showing how the elasticity of demand facing a dominant firm can be inferred from knowledge of the market elasticity of demand, firm market share, and the elasticity of supply of the competitive fringe).

One common use of direct evidence of prospective market power involves the analysis of mergers among sellers of differentiated products. Here, prospective market power may be inferred from evidence that the products of the merging firms are close substitutes for buyers. In general, evidence about buyer substitution for this purpose is similar to the type of evidence about buyer substitution analyzed for market definition purposes under the Merger Guidelines. Some of that evidence may be direct, including buyer surveys or systematic (econometric) analyses of

means of demonstrating competitive price discrimination in rebuttal to direct evidence of market power based upon price differences across markets. Defendants making this re- buttal argument would thus be more likely to focus on entry conditions than market structure.

historical buyer responses to price increases.***** For surveys and critical discussion of the latter methods, which are increasingly important in merger practice before the federal antitrust agencies, see Baker & Rubinfeld, *Empirical Methods*, 1 AM. J. L. & ECON. at 392–98; Jonathan B. Baker, *Contemporary Empirical Merger Analysis*, 5 GEO. MASON L. REV. 347 (1997) ("*Empirical Merger Analysis*").

Accounting Estimates of Margins and Profits

At one time, accounting estimates of firm profit rates were thought to provide strong direct evidence of market power, and thus circumstantial evidence of anticompetitive effect. During the 1970s, according to Professor Elzinga, antitrust came close to adopting accounting rates of return as "a primary device for unmasking monopoly." Kenneth G. Elzinga, *Unmasking Monopoly, in* ECONOMICS AND ANTITRUST POLICY 18 (Robert J. Larner & James W. Meehan, Jr., Eds., 1989).

This initiative foundered for several reasons. First, high profit rates, even if measured successfully, do not necessarily derive from the exercise of market power. They may be related to success in lowering costs or other efficiencies, such as superior product design or superior distribution, and may be consistent with competitive returns in an industry in which firms must make substantial, but risky investments. As the literature on finance explains, high average returns on investment may be required to induce investors to accept high risks. Elzinga makes the point with an example:

> If ten wildcatters drill for oil and nine strike out instead of striking oil, the rate of return earned by the one successful driller provides no information for diagnosing the presence of monopoly rents for that firm. The risk-adjusted rate of return on invested funds for the entire set of wildcatters could be modest (or normal) even if the rate of return on invested funds for the fortunate driller was substantial.

Id. at 20. Conversely, if a monopolist is not forced by competition to keep costs low, but takes its reward for monopoly in the form of what economist J.R. Hicks termed "a quiet life," its inefficient methods of production may lead it to earn low, not high, profits.

Second, accounting measures of profitability may deviate substantially from the relevant economic concepts. The way accountants spread costs over time and adjust asset values for depreciation means, according to two influential commentators, that "there is no way in which one can look at accounting rates of return and infer anything about relative economic profitability or, a fortiori, about the presence or absence of monopoly profits." Franklin M. Fisher & John J. McGowan, *On the*

***** As with market definition, other evidence as to the structure of demand will be indirect, based on the views and actions taken by sellers, who have an economic interest in understanding buyer substitution patterns. Such evidence may appear in marketing documents of the merging firms or testimony of their marketing executives that shows whether the firms track and respond to the prices of each other's products, for example. Reliance on this evidence to infer buyer substitution patterns, and thus to infer anticompetitive effect, would constitute a double inference, but a different double inference from the most common double inference in antitrust practice, a reliance on market shares to infer market power and thus anticompetitive effect.

Misuse of Accounting Rates of Return to Infer Monopoly Profits, 73 Am. Econ. Rev. 82, 90 (1983).

These problems loom so large that antitrust today does not rely heavily on profitability measures in making inferences about market power. Judge Posner summarized the current consensus view this way:

> * * * [I]t is always treacherous to try to infer monopoly power from a high rate of return. * * * [N]ot only do measured rates of return reflect accounting conventions more than they do real profits (or losses), as an economist would understand these terms, but there is not even a good economic theory that associates monopoly power with a high rate of return. Firms compete to become and to remain monopolists, and the process of competition erodes their profits. Conversely, competitive firms may be highly profitable merely by virtue of having low costs as a result of superior efficiency, yet not sufficiently lower costs than all other competitors to enable the firm to take over its market and become a monopolist.

Blue Cross & Blue Shield United of Wisconsin v. Marshfield Clinic, 65 F.3d 1406, 1412 (1995) (citations omitted).

Finally, the relationship between price and marginal cost, termed price-cost margins, has also been proposed as a form of direct evidence of market power. Economists often report price-cost margins in terms of the Lerner Index, defined as the difference between price and marginal cost, expressed as a ratio of price. If price equals marginal cost, the Lerner Index equals zero. As marginal cost becomes a very small fraction of price, the Lerner Index approaches one. In one case cited by Professor Elzinga, for example, an economist testified that "a Lerner Index so close to its theoretical maximum of 1.0 makes the inference of market power indisputable." Kenneth G. Elzinga, *Unmasking Monopoly*, *supra* at 18.

One problem with relying on the Lerner Index as evidence of market power involves difficulties measuring marginal cost. Average variable cost is a common proxy, but, for reasons set forth in our earlier discussion of price-cost comparisons employed to detect predatory pricing, the proxy may not capture marginal cost well. *See* Casebook, Chapter 6, *supra*. *See also* Baker, *Contemporary Empirical Merger Analysis*, 5 Geo. Mason L. Rev. at 358 ("an estimator of marginal cost that excludes all promotional expenditures on the ground that they are predetermined in the very short run may systematically understate the incremental cost related to the intermediate-term pricing decision most relevant to merger analysis.").

Putting aside problems with measuring marginal cost, interpreting high price-cost margins as evidence of market power raises issues similar to those involved in inferring market power from price comparisons across markets and over time, and those involved in inferring market power from high profits. For example, to interpret the Lerner Index as a gauge of market power, it is necessary to assume that the competitive price would be equal to marginal cost. But, as discussed above in connection with price discrimination, that may not be a good assumption for industries with high fixed cost and low marginal costs—the very industries in which the Lerner Index would be very high. Competitive benchmarks derived from before-and-after comparisons and cross-market "natural experiments" are more likely to be convincing.

Price-cost margins have been the subject of renewed attention at the antitrust enforcement agencies in recent years because they are used to calibrate demand elasticities, for market definition and for simulating the price rise under the unilateral theory of competitive effect for mergers among sellers of differentiated products. *See generally* Gregory J. Werden, *Demand Elasticities in Antitrust Analysis*, 66 ANTITRUST L. J. 363 (1998); Gregory J. Werden & Luke M. Froeb, *Unilateral Competitive Effects of Horizontal Mergers, in* HANDBOOK OF ANTITRUST ECONOMICS (Paolo Buccirossi, ed. 2008).

Conclusion

Methods of inferring anticompetitive effect from direct evidence of market power often appear more complex than the double inference approach of inferring anticompetitive effect from market shares, which provide indirect evidence on market power. Direct evidence of market power also may not be available, may be very costly to develop, and when it is available it may not be strongly probative. But the single inference approach to assessing anticompetitive effect is increasingly important in antitrust practice, on its own or in conjunction with market share evidence, because it offers the possibility of greater precision in identifying and measuring market power.

What are the relative advantages and disadvantages of relying on: (1) evidence of actual anticompetitive effects; (2) direct evidence of market power as a basis for inferring anticompetitive effects, or (3) circumstantial evidence of market power as a basis for inferring anticompetitive effects? What kind of evidence will a party need to establish each? What kind of witnesses and documents?

Of course, it is frequently the case that a party will offer evidence it asserts satisfies some or all of the three tests—evidence of actual anticompetitive effects, and both single and double inference evidence of market power. Which approaches are used in the following excerpt from the Second Circuit's decision in *Tops Markets*? As you read the case, note how *Tops Markets* also reenforces the framework discussed earlier in this Chapter in *Re/Max* and *Toys* with respect to the role of evidence of actual anticompetitive effects. Also, consider whether any of the issues posed in Sidebar 8–5 appear either explicitly or implicitly in the court's opinion.

TOPS MARKETS, INC. v. QUALITY MARKETS, INC.
United States Court of Appeals for the Second Circuit, 1998.
142 F.3d 90.

Before: FEINBERG, CARDAMONE, and WALKER, Circuit Judges.

CARDAMONE, Circuit Judge:

* * *

The corporate parties to this action include: plaintiff Tops Markets, * * * operating 53 supermarkets and 87 convenience stores in western New York; defendant Penn Traffic Company (Penn), which owns and operates 267 supermarkets and 15 discount department stores throughout New York, Pennsylvania, Ohio and West Virginia; defendant Quality Markets (Quality), a New York corporation that is a division of Penn and competes with Tops by operating supermarkets in western New York and western Pennsylvania; and defendant Sunrise Properties (Sunrise), a * * * wholly-owned subsidiary of Penn that owns and develops commercial real estate for Penn and its divisions. * * * The remaining party is defendant James V. Paige, Jr., a Jamestown, New York, real estate developer.

For purposes of reviewing the grant of summary judgment in this antitrust appeal, the relevant geographical market is that to which the parties stipulated: an area in the southeastern portion of Chautauqua County, New York, extending approximately seven to ten miles in all directions from the city of Jamestown. The area includes 17 municipalities and is populated by approximately 75,000 people. The parties also stipulated that the relevant product market consists of the retail sale by "supermarkets" of predominantly food items, together with general household merchandise. A "supermarket" is defined as a retail store with at least 7,500 square feet of retail space that sells a full range of perishable and non-perishable food items and general household merchandise.

The Jamestown market recently has undergone dramatic changes. In 1992 Quality owned five of the nine supermarkets in the geographical market. Of the remaining four supermarkets, "Bells" and "Super Duper" each owned and operated two. In January 1993 Quality acquired and within one year closed both "Bells" stores. In April 1995 it purchased both "Super Duper" stores and immediately shut them both as well. In May 1995 Wegmans, a Quality competitor, successfully opened a large 100,000 square foot supermarket in the Jamestown market area.

Tops owned a supermarket in the Jamestown market until 1984 when it voluntarily terminated operations there. Seven years later, in 1991, it resolved to re-enter the Jamestown market and commissioned studies to evaluate the feasibility and profitability of numerous potential sites for a new store location. These studies determined certain property located on Washington Street in Jamestown was the most suitable spot for a supermarket. The Washington Street site consisted of several parcels of land, four of which were owned by defendant Paige.

Paige agreed to sell his four parcels to Tops. * * * The contract also called for Paige to obtain options to purchase the remaining parcels he did not own at the Washington Street site, giving him until March 15, 1992 to comply with this requirement. The contract specified that if Paige failed to acquire these additional parcels, Tops could elect unilaterally to terminate the agreement.

When Quality discovered Tops' intention to re-enter the Jamestown market at the Washington Street site, it expressed an interest in acquiring two of Paige's Washington site parcels. Paige and Sunrise subsequently entered into a "Back–Up" agreement * * * under which Sunrise would acquire * * * non-contiguous parcels lacking any frontage on Washington Street. The contract of sale was made expressly contingent upon the termination of Paige's prior contract with Tops.

Sunrise and Paige restructured their contract * * * to grant Sunrise the option to purchase the same two parcels * * *. [When Paige notified Sunrise that his contract with Tops had terminated], Sunrise * * * exercised its option and did acquire title to the two Washington Street parcels * * *. This lawsuit followed.

Plaintiff eventually acquired the entire Washington Street site when the Jamestown Urban Renewal Agency, exercising its power of eminent domain, condemned the property and later sold it to Tops. Tops opened a superstore at the site on April 19, 1997.

* * *

* * * [B]efore a factfinder may consider the harms and benefits of the challenged behavior, a plaintiff initially must show that "the challenged action had an *actual* adverse effect on competition as a whole in the relevant market; to prove it has been harmed as an individual competitor will not suffice." This requirement ensures that otherwise routine disputes between business competitors do not escalate to the status of an antitrust action. * * * [A] plaintiff may succeed only when the loss he asserts derives from activities that have a "competition-*reducing*" effect. *Atlantic Richfield Co. v. USA Petroleum Co.*, 495 U.S. 328, 342–44, 110 S.Ct. 1884, 1893–95, 109 L.Ed.2d 333 (1990) (emphasis in original).

The district court found that Tops failed to produce evidence to sustain this initial burden, despite having two independent means by which to satisfy the adverse-effect requirement. On the one hand, it could have shown an actual adverse effect on competition, such as reduced output. *See F.T.C. v. Indiana Fed'n of Dentists*, 476 U.S. 447, 460–61, 106 S.Ct. 2009, 2018–19, 90 L.Ed.2d 445 (1986). Alternatively, if it failed to make such a showing, it could have demonstrated "adverse effect" indirectly by establishing that Quality had sufficient market power to cause an adverse effect on competition. Market power is but a "surrogate for detrimental effects." *Indiana Fed'n of Dentists*, 476 U.S. at 461, 106 S.Ct. at 2019 (quoting 7 Phillip E. Areeda, *Antitrust Law* § 1511, at 429 (1986)).

Plaintiff failed to demonstrate an actual detrimental effect on competition. It relied almost entirely on the affidavit of Robert F. Kennedy (the Kennedy Affidavit), which discussed Quality's high market share and the competitive advantages that could have resulted in *potentially* higher prices, but significantly did not allege that prices were *actually* higher in the Jamestown market. The Kennedy Affidavit further failed to provide sufficient proof that Tops' exclusion from the market had, in fact, resulted in any decrease in the quality of service to Jamestown area shoppers.

Nor did Tops allege that other supermarkets were excluded from the market. The only clear effect of defendants' alleged conspiracy was to bar plaintiff from opening a store at the Washington Street site. But, the fact that Tops may have been prevented from competing in the Jamestown market does not alone prove an adverse effect on competition as a whole. For even if plaintiff were hindered from competing, nothing changed in the relevant product market from the consumer's perspective.

Tops' showing of Quality's market power was also insufficient to satisfy its burden of demonstrating an adverse effect on the market as a whole. The

Kennedy Affidavit asserted that, at all relevant times, Quality's share of the total sales of food items and general household merchandise in the Jamestown area market exceeded 72 percent. Plaintiff asks us to infer that this high market share equates to market power.

Even assuming this market share data implies that Quality possessed market power, Tops still would fail to satisfy its burden under the adverse-effect requirement. Market power, while necessary to show adverse effect indirectly, alone is insufficient. A plaintiff seeking to use market power as a proxy for adverse effect must show market power, plus some other ground for believing that the challenged behavior could harm competition in the market, such as the inherent anticompetitive nature of the defendant's behavior or the structure of the interbrand market.

Yet, plaintiff provided no evidence other than market share to prove that defendants' action had an adverse effect on competition. The Kennedy Affidavit does not cure this deficiency. It declares that the nature of the interbrand market is such that supermarkets compete for geographic location, seeking a site with close proximity to high concentrations of people, convenience, accessibility, visibility and space. But Quality's purchase of the Washington Street site was not shown either directly or indirectly to have any adverse effect on competition. While Tops may not have readily acquired the location it preferred, Quality's one-time purchase of the site did not foreclose other prospective supermarket competitors from entering the market in desirable locations. We find particularly significant Wegmans' subsequent acquisition of land and construction of a 100,000 square foot store on a different site, which demonstrates the absence of geographic barriers preventing competitors from entering the Jamestown area. Within one year after opening, Wegmans captured approximately 26 percent of the Jamestown market.

Hence, despite Quality's presumed market power, Tops still failed to show any adverse effect on competition as a whole. As such, Judge Elfvin properly dismissed its § 1 Sherman Act claim.

* * *

At this point we have explored three possible approaches to establishing anticompetitive effects:

- evidence of actual anticompetitive effects;
- circumstantial evidence of anticompetitive effects based on the "single inference" method, *i.e.*, direct measures of market power; and
- circumstantial evidence of anticompetitive effects based on the "double inference" method, *i.e.*, inferring market power from high market shares, and anticompetitive effects from market power.

See Figure 8–4, *supra*. Which of these methods did the plaintiff seek to utilize in *Tops Markets*? Why was the effort unsuccessful? What was the perceived relationship between evidence of actual anticompetitive effects and market power?

What was the defendant's strategy in attacking the plaintiff's evidence? What evidence, if any, could the plaintiff have offered to survive the defendant's motion for summary judgment? What was the significance of the entry and apparent success of another grocer, Wegmans? We will revisit that question when we return to *Tops Markets* later in this Chapter.

Finally, what did the court mean when it said "Market power, while necessary to show adverse effect indirectly, alone is insufficient"? Was it rejecting use of the double inference as a method of establishing unreasonable restraint of trade for purposes of a Section 1 Sherman Act offense? Qualifying it?

C.   CASE STUDY: PROVING ANTICOMPETITIVE EFFECTS BEFORE AGENCIES AND COURTS IN THE *MICROSOFT* PROSECUTION

How as a practical matter will parties go about meeting these various standards for proving anticompetitive effects in litigation or before government enforcement agencies? To explore that question further, we now turn to the 1998 monopolization prosecution of Microsoft, which was initiated by the Justice Department and a group of states. We have mentioned various aspects of the case in previous Chapters, particularly Chapters 6 and 7. Here we will focus on one particular, yet critical issue in the case, monopoly power, which we will examine through excerpts from the actual expert testimony admitted in the case, as well as the decision of the court of appeals.

The government relied on two economists: Frederick R. Warren–Boulton was a principal with an economic consulting firm, a former professor, and a former chief economist at the Antitrust Division of the Department of Justice; Franklin M. Fisher was a professor of economics at MIT. He was also the chief economic witness for IBM in the government's 1970s prosecution of the company under Section 2 of the Sherman Act, which was voluntarily dismissed by the government in 1982. Microsoft's principal economic witness was Richard L. Schmalensee, a professor of Economics and Management and then Dean of MIT's Sloan School of Management.

Unique in *Microsoft* was *how* the expert testimony was introduced. First, in contrast to the confidentiality that often shrouds all or part of the expert reports, and sometimes the testimony, in private antitrust litigation, public access to the *Microsoft* expert testimony was unencumbered. As a consequence, we can examine unredacted excerpts from the actual testimony introduced at trial. Second, you will notice that the excerpted testimony is not in "question and answer" format. To avoid what could easily have become a very protracted bench trial, the court required that virtually all direct testimony be submitted in advance, and in writing. As a consequence, the witnesses prepared detailed narratives in contrast to the more typical "question and answer" format of trial; trial time focused largely on cross-examination. For these two reasons—the public nature of the testimony and its narrative form—we have a unique and readily accessible opportunity to review how each of the party's economists proposed to establish that Microsoft did or did not possess monopoly power.

As you read through the testimony, consider how each economist used the various methods we have studied to address the market power question. Do they rely on evidence of actual adverse competitive effects or circumstantial evidence in the form of market power? If the latter, what kind of evidence of market power did they offer? "Direct" measures of Microsoft's market power? If so, what specific evidence did they cite to support their assertions? Or did they define relevant markets, calculate market shares, and analyze whether inferences of market power could be justified? What other factors did they address that influenced their opinions on market power? What kinds of evidence do they each rely upon?

In judging these excerpts, keep in mind that we have provided only brief excerpts from the prepared, direct testimony. That testimony went on for hundreds of pages, and, in addition, there was considerable cross examination of all of the experts at trial. Only a snapshot of their testimony is presented here, limited to the question of proving Microsoft's monopoly power.

UNITED STATES v. MICROSOFT CORP.
United States District Court for the District of Columbia, 2000.
Civil Action Nos. 98–1232–33.

Direct Testimony of Frederick R. Warren–Boulton (For the Government)*

* * *

II. INTRODUCTION

5. Based on my analysis of Microsoft's conduct and its competitive effects, I have drawn the following three basic conclusions:

6. First, Microsoft has monopoly power in a relevant market. Using the basic methodology for defining markets supplied by the 1992 *Horizontal Merger Guidelines*—an accepted approach for delineating antitrust markets in Sherman Act cases—I conclude that operating systems compatible with Intel x86/Pentium architecture personal computers (PCs) comprise a relevant market.

7. The evidence also demonstrates that Microsoft possesses monopoly power in that market. Microsoft for several years has enjoyed, and is projected for several years to retain, a market share in excess of 90%. This market share is protected by substantial barriers to entry. Operating system markets exhibit "network effects." The greater the number of users a particular operating system enjoys, the more likely it is that software developers will write applications for that operating system. This, in turn, makes the operating system still more attractive to users and, as a consequence, makes software developers more likely to develop applications for that operating system, and, given scarce resources, less likely to develop applications for alternative operating systems. The end result is that in such markets, the very network effects that drive users toward the dominant firm make displacing that firm difficult.

* * *

---

* [Available at http://www.usdoj.gov/atr/ cases/f2000/2079.htm. The cross examination is   available beginning at 1998 WL 803824 (D.D.C. TRANS). Eds.]

IV. Microsoft Has Monopoly Power in the PC Operating System Market

17. The starting point for an antitrust analysis of Microsoft's actions is the question: Does Microsoft have monopoly power in a properly defined relevant market? In answering this question, it is important to keep in mind that the purpose of defining markets in this case is to determine whether Microsoft's conduct has the potential to harm consumer or social welfare. If Microsoft lacks monopoly power in any relevant market, any profit-maximizing unilateral conduct is unlikely significantly to harm consumer welfare.

18. My assessment of whether Microsoft possesses monopoly power proceeds in the following steps. First, I will define the relevant market. I begin by setting out certain relevant industry facts and defining some terms for the purpose of the ensuing discussion. I then briefly summarize the principles of market definition I believe are appropriate here. Next, I apply those principles to the facts, and explain how they lead me to the conclusion that PC operating systems are an antitrust market. Second, having defined the market, I then assess Microsoft's power within it. I show that Microsoft possesses monopoly power in the PC operating system market, and that this power, in large measure, is secured by barriers to entry created by the large number of applications available exclusively for Microsoft operating systems.

19. I then explain how non-Microsoft browsers, both by themselves and in conjunction with Java cross-platform technologies, threaten that monopoly. I will show that browsers and Java threaten to eliminate the most significant of the entry barriers that shields Microsoft's monopoly from effective competition and, therefore, that Microsoft stands to gain significantly from eliminating the browser threat.

A. *PC Operating Systems Comprise a Relevant Antitrust Market*

* * *

2. *Principles of Market Definition*

26. The first step in ascertaining whether a firm possesses monopoly power is to define the market. For this task, I draw upon the principles for defining markets set forth in the 1992 *Horizontal Merger Guidelines*, promulgated jointly by the U.S. Department of Justice and the Federal Trade Commission. The *Guidelines* supply a well-accepted method for delineating markets and are commonly relied upon by both economists and courts to define relevant antitrust markets.

* * *

29. There is an important distinction I should mention about applying the *Guidelines* to this case. As I have explained, the *Guidelines* inquire as to the profitability to a hypothetical monopolist of raising price. In a merger case, the prices used as the starting point in the analysis are prevailing or existing prices. This is because, in a merger case, the concern is not so much whether the merging firms presently are exercising market power, but rather whether the merger will *increase* the market power of the merging firms.

30. In contrast, in a monopolization case such as this, the question is whether the firm in question already possesses monopoly power. In such circumstances, the appropriate benchmark is not the prevailing price but

rather the competitive price; and the question is whether a hypothetical monopolist of the candidate market could profitably charge a price in excess of *the competitive* level. Because the prevailing price might be a monopoly price, it is not meaningful to ask whether a hypothetical monopolist could profitably increase the price above the prevailing price; even a monopolist cannot charge greater than a monopoly price without having its conduct constrained sufficiently to make that price increase unprofitable. Using the competitive price thus yields a proper market definition in the circumstances of this case.

31. In applying the hypothetical monopolist test to possible markets (that is, determining whether such a firm could profitably impose a "small but significant and nontransitory" price increase over the competitive price), an economist ideally would like to have reliable and precise estimates of what is known as the "own price elasticity" (considered over the relevant price range) for the product or group of products that comprise the possible market.[13] The own price elasticity, together with the marginal cost, essentially tells an economist when the imposition of a particular price increase will be profitable.

32. Such data, however, are often not available—either to economists or to antitrust tribunals. It is thus appropriate to rely, as the *Guidelines* explain, on "all relevant evidence"[15] in applying the hypothetical monopolist test. This includes, but is not limited to, the perceptions of market participants and the characteristics of the industry in question.

3. PC Operating Systems Comprise a Relevant Market

33. Applying the hypothetical monopolist test, it is my opinion that PC operating systems comprise a relevant antitrust market. I reach this conclusion based on two distinct types of evidence. First, the characteristics of the product in question, and the demand for it, readily support the conclusion that operating systems designed for other (non-PC) hardware platforms would not constrain, and have not constrained, the ability of a monopolist of PC operating systems to exercise monopoly power. Second, evidence from OEMs [Original Equipment Manufacturers—Eds.], the major direct purchasers of PC operating systems, confirms that even a large increase in the current price of the dominant PC operating system, Windows, would not result in significant switching by them or their consumers to other PC operating systems, let alone to operating systems designed for other processors.

34. As an initial matter, it is important to observe that consumers do not demand operating systems simply for the sake of having an operating system. Rather, consumers demand computers, for which an operating system is one (albeit a key) component. In economic terms, this means that demand for an operating system is a *derived* demand: demand for an operating system is derived from demand for a computer system. Moreover, an operating system is essential on every PC and consumers generally demand only one operating system per personal computer.

35. A consequence of these facts—that operating systems are demanded in fixed proportions and that demand for operating systems derives from

---

13. More precisely, the price elasticity for a product (or group of products) is the percentage reduction in unit sales for the product that would result from a one percent increase in the price of that product, holding all else constant.

15. Guidelines § 1.11.

consumer demand for PCs—is that consumers faced with an increase in the price of PC operating systems can effectively substitute away from PC-compatible operating systems only by substituting away from PCs. Such substitution, however, would impose significant costs on end users and on PC-manufacturers.

36. Both end users contemplating switching to alternatives to PCs and new users considering such alternatives would face significant costs or disadvantages. End users purchase computers, not for the operating system itself, but rather to run applications; and applications are typically designed for a particular operating system. Because the PC platform is dominant, other platforms (and, as discussed below, non-Microsoft operating systems that also run on the PC platform) typically have far fewer applications available. Thus, both new end users and users considering switching to another platform would face the disadvantage of a smaller portfolio of available applications. Switchers would also need to expend time and money learning how to use a computer designed for a different processor. And both switchers and new users would have to bear costs resulting from any incompatibility or impaired compatibility between their computer and PCs used by colleagues or others with whom the users may wish to communicate or share files.

37. Because there is generally one operating system on a PC, the increase in the price of the PC that would result from a given percent increase in the price of the operating system would be at most the increase in the price of the operating system times the share of the operating system cost in the price of a PC. But the operating system for PCs accounts for only a small share of the price of the PC—on average about 2.5%—and at most 10% for very inexpensive PCs. Thus, even a 10% increase in the price of the OS would result at most in a 1% increase in the price of even inexpensive PCs. Given the cost to users of switching to another platform, such a small increase in the price of the PC platform would not be expected to result in a large reduction in the demand for PCs, and thus for PC operating systems. In economic terms, the price elasticity of derived demand for PC operating systems must be very low for at least a significant price range above the competitive price for PC operating systems, leading me to conclude that PC operating systems are a separate market.

38. The large costs that PC manufacturers and end users would incur in substituting away from the PC platform reinforces this conclusion. OEMs make a significant investment in developing the machines they sell; to substitute to another hardware platform (one not based on the Intel-chip), such as the "PowerPC" chip, would require incurring significant costs.

39. The testimony of, and documents authored by, OEM executives further supports this conclusion. These executives explain that, if confronted with a 10% increase in their Windows license, they would not switch to operating system products for other hardware platforms. To the contrary, they make clear that preloading Microsoft's Windows operating system is commercially necessary.

40. OEM executives also explain that Intel-compatible operating system products that are designed, not for personal computers, but rather to operate "servers" are not viable substitutes for a desktop operating systems. [sic] Server operating systems are generally more expensive yet do not provide the

features consumers demand when they purchase PC operating systems. Therefore, the existence of server operating systems would not constrain the ability of a monopolist of operating systems for PCs to exercise monopoly power. Accordingly, I conclude that operating systems for Intel-compatible personal computers comprise a relevant product market.

* * *

B. Microsoft Possesses Monopoly Power in the PC Operating System Market

42. Once the market is properly defined, the next step is to determine whether Microsoft possesses monopoly power within it. Monopoly power is the ability of a firm profitably to raise market price above the competitive level for an extended period of time or to exclude competition.

43. There are four reasons why I believe that Microsoft possesses monopoly power in the PC operating systems market. First, Microsoft's share of this market has been at a very high level since at least the early 1990s and is expected to remain high. Second, barriers to effective entry into the PC operating system market are high, and other PC operating systems cannot easily increase their shares of that market because the huge stock of applications written for Windows 95/98 will not run on those systems. Third, Microsoft has engaged in conduct that would not be effective or profitable if it did not have monopoly power. Fourth, the pattern of OS prices, Microsoft's margins, and the market value of Microsoft equity are themselves consistent with Microsoft possessing monopoly power.

1. Microsoft has an Overwhelming Share of the PC Operating System Market

44. The first step in determining whether a firm has monopoly power is usually to determine the level and stability of its share of the relevant market. According to Microsoft's figures, 80.8% out of the estimated 209.2 million PCs shipped worldwide since July of 1995 include a Microsoft operating system. During this period, naked PCs, *e.g.*, PCs shipped without any operating system at all, accounted for 31.5 million units, or 15% of the total PCs shipped. In other words, of the PCs shipped with an operating system, Microsoft's share was 95.1%.

45. This high market share has been remarkably stable. * * * Microsoft's share of PCs shipped with an operating system has been above 90% since at least the early 1990s and this dominance is forecast through at least 2001.

2. Barriers to Entering the PC Operating System Market are High

46. Microsoft's high market share has been protected by high—indeed formidable—barriers both to the entry of new PC operating systems and to the ability of rival PC operating systems to acquire market share, even in response to prices above competitive levels. First, as I will explain, PC operating systems are characterized by scale economies and sunk costs that make the cost of entry high. Second, switching operating systems would impose significant costs on users; this tends to "lock" users into Microsoft operating systems. Third, operating systems exhibit network effects, a consequence of which is greatly to increase the costs of, and reduce the probability of, a successful challenge to Microsoft's market dominance.

47. First, operating systems in particular, and software in general, are characterized by economies of scale. The bulk of the costs are development costs—the costs that must be expended to create the software, irrespective of how many copies ultimately are sold. These costs include, for example, writing, testing and debugging program code. The cost of producing and marketing individual copies of the product ("the marginal costs") are, by comparison, quite small.

48. The costs of developing an operating system to compete with Microsoft's Windows operating system would be immense. For instance, IBM, a company that is very experienced in developing competitive software, was reported to have spent a staggering amount on the OS/2 project through 1996. Moreover, these costs are what in economic terms are called "sunk" because only a small portion of either initial fixed development costs and any subsequent negative cash flow could be recovered if the entrant were to exit the market. Moreover, competition between two suppliers, each with very high fixed costs and very low marginal costs, would likely result in a decrease in prices, further reducing the profitability of entry to the would-be entrant. Entry into head-to-head operating system competition with Microsoft thus would be time consuming, risky, and costly; profiting from such entry would be at best very uncertain and long in coming.

49. A second barrier both to entry and to expansion by an existing competitor is that users tend to become "locked in" to a particular operating systems. As discussed above, users are reluctant to switch from Windows to another operating system, even another PC operating system, because to do so requires them to replace application software, to convert files, and to learn how to operate the new software. Often, switching operating systems also means replacing or modifying hardware. Businesses can face even greater switching costs, as they must integrate PCs using the new operating systems and application software within their PC networks and train their employees to use the new software. Accordingly, both personal and corporate consumers are extremely reluctant to change PC operating systems. The software "lock-in" phenomenon creates a barrier to entry for new PC operating systems to the extent that consumers' estimate of the switching costs is large relative to the perceived incremental value of the new operating system.

* * *

51. A third entry barrier is created by the well-understood fact that operating systems are characterized by "network effects." Network effects occur when the value of an item to a user increases as the total number of users increases. Examples of products subject to network effects include fax machines and both local and long distance telephone networks. A fax machine is not particularly valuable until a large number of other people have fax machines that use the same standards and protocols. Similarly, the more users within a given region that a local phone network serves, the more valuable that network is to each user.

52. Operating systems are subject to network effects because, among other things, the value of an operating system product is largely dependent on the number of applications available for it. Today, applications written for one

vendor's operating system product generally will not work on another vendor's operating system. * * *

53. As an operating system gains popularity, the incentive to develop software for that operating system increases because the larger number of users for the operating system product implies a greater potential market for software developers. The development of yet more applications for that operating system, in turn, increases the value of the operating system to end users who, as explained, purchase operating systems in significant part based upon the quality and variety of applications available for it. * * *

54. This phenomenon—known in economics as "positive feedback"— creates what is best termed the "applications barrier to entry." Simply put, an operating system product can rise to dominate the market, and once that dominance is achieved maintain it, because of both the large number of complementary software applications available for it and the flow of new applications that are written to it. This too is well-recognized by Microsoft. * * *

* * *

56. It is clear that the applications barrier to entry sustains Microsoft's dominance, critically contributes to its monopoly power, and helps explain why other Intel-compatible operating systems, such as OS/2 and Linux, have persistently small market shares. * * * [B]ecause of economies to scale, the marginal costs of producing additional copies of these operating systems is very low. Thus, one might expect that, if Microsoft attempted to exercise monopoly power, vendors of these operating systems would flood the market with their product and constrain Microsoft's behavior. This, however, has not occurred. No rival has succeeded in mounting a sustained effective threat to Microsoft's market dominance.

57. One reason for the lack of success is that alternative operating systems lack the installed base of applications that Microsoft's PC operating system products enjoy. To offer a product that a significant number of consumers wish to have installed on their PCs, vendors of these operating systems would have to create, or induce others to create, an extensive set of compatible software applications. This would be not merely expensive, but also very risky because it would involve significant sunk costs, as explained above.

* * *

3. Microsoft's Monopoly Power is Evidenced by its Use

60. Microsoft has engaged in conduct that it could not profitably pursue unless it possessed monopoly power. For instance, when one OEM removed the IE [Internet Explorer browser—Eds.] icon from the Windows 95 desktop, Microsoft responded by threatening to terminate that OEMs' Windows 95 license. The OEM capitulated to Microsoft's demands. It is plain it did so because, as OEMs universally explain, a Windows license is essential to remaining competitive in the OEM market. This capitulation is itself evidence of Microsoft's monopoly power.

4. *Microsoft's Monopoly Power is Reflected in its Prices, in its Margins, and in the Market Value of Its Equity*

61. * * * An internal Microsoft document acknowledges that it has increased its operating system product "prices over the last ten years [while] other components' prices [for PC computers] have come down and continue to come down. This is particularly true of CPU prices."

62. Microsoft's monopoly power in operating systems has translated into extraordinarily high net profit margins that have been increasing over time.[38] Even more telling is Microsoft's extraordinarily high market capitalization. With a price/earnings ratio more than double the S & P 500 average, the financial markets are signaling very optimistic investor expectations regarding Microsoft's future growth in earnings.

63. My analysis thus far has shown that Microsoft possesses monopoly power in the desktop operating system market. Although the barriers to entry and to the growth of other PC operating systems that protect Microsoft's monopoly power are formidable, they are not impenetrable. There is no reason to believe that the market, if left to function properly, will not in time generate alternatives to Microsoft's operating system that will be sufficiently superior to overcome the entry barrier advantage that Microsoft enjoys.

64. Microsoft, however, has interfered with these market forces. As I explain below, Microsoft has engaged in a course of conduct with the apparent purpose, and evident effect, of reinforcing its monopoly power in the PC operating system market.

* * *

———

Direct Testimony of Franklin M. Fisher (For the Government)*

* * *

III. THE ECONOMICS OF COMPETITION AND MONOPOLY

* * *

A. How Does One Identify Monopoly Power?

32. * * * [T]he hallmark of monopoly power is the absence or ineffectiveness of competitive constraints on price, output, product decisions, and quality. The issue of monopoly power is conventionally addressed by defining "the relevant market" and assessing shares in that market. A large share of a properly defined market is an indication of a firm's ability successfully to raise price. Because its purpose is the identification of monopoly power, if it exists, the "relevant market" should include all those products that reasonably serve

---

38. * * * Among the Fortune 500 largest U.S. corporations, Microsoft ranks 137th in revenue, 165th in assets, 15th in profits, 7th in growth of earnings per share, 3rd in profits as percentage of assets, 2nd in market value, and 1st in profits as a percentage of revenues. *Fortune* (Apr. 27, 1998).

* [Available at http://www.usdoj.gov/atr/cases/f213400/213457.htm. The cross examination is available beginning at 1999 WL 3397 (D.D.C. TRANS). Eds.]

to constrain the behavior of the alleged monopolist. Such constraints arise from three sources: substitution by consumers to other products (demand substitutability), substitution by producers to other products (supply substitutability), and entry of new productive capacity. As market power is a matter of degree, so too is the extent to which each of these factors imposes a constraint.

* * *

38. Having defined an appropriate market, one then goes on to consider market share and the ability of firms not in the market to enter, in the event of an attempt by the alleged monopolist to earn supra-normal profits through an exercise of power. As noted above, a key distinguishing feature of monopoly power is its durability. If the attempt by a firm to earn supra-normal profits by pricing above competitive levels would be rapidly frustrated by entry, that firm does not possess monopoly power.

39. Economists generally refer to factors that would prevent entry in the face of supra-normal profits as "barriers to entry." (Such factors also limit expansion of existing firms. I use the term "barriers to entry" to refer both to limits on entry of new firms and to limits on the expansion of existing firms.) Where there are significant barriers to entry, monopoly power can be present. Where there are no barriers or barriers are low, monopoly power cannot exist.

B. What Is the Role of Network Effects?

40. The barriers to entry in the present case include two phenomena known respectively as economies of scale and network effects.

41. An economy of scale is a phenomenon in which the average cost of production falls as more units of a product are produced. The software business exhibits substantial economies of scale, because most of the costs of software production come in the creation of the software and are independent of the number of copies that are produced.

42. A network effect is a phenomenon in which the attractiveness of a product to customers increases with the use of that product by others. This means, for example, that the fact that many applications are written for a given operating system and cannot easily run on the other operating systems will make that operating system more attractive to users—a network effect. (This may be reinforced by other network effects related to the operating system and applications—the desirability of using a common word-processing system, for example.)

43. Where network effects are present, a firm that gains a large share of the market, whether through innovation, marketing skill, historical accident, or any other means, may thereby gain monopoly power. This is because it will prove increasingly difficult for other firms to persuade customers to buy their products in the presence of a product that is widely used. The firm with a large share may then be able to charge high prices or slow down innovation without having its business bid away.

44. Such a circumstance can occur "naturally" in the sense that if network effects are sufficiently strong, a firm may acquire monopoly power without engaging in anti-competitive conduct. However, the fact that the successful firm has acquired monopoly power with a "natural" barrier to

entry does not justify its taking anti-competitive acts to extend that power to another market or, in particular, its engaging in anti-competitive acts that serve to buttress and protect its power in the original market.

45.   In the absence of anti-competitive conduct, market forces and developments can erode monopoly power based solely on network effects. This is in fact why Microsoft felt it necessary to take the actions discussed below with respect to Java and internet browsers.

* * *

IV.   ECONOMIC ANALYSIS OF MICROSOFT'S ACTIONS

A.   Market Power

1.   Personal Computer Operating Systems

62.   Microsoft possesses monopoly power in the market for operating systems for Intel-compatible desktop personal computers. There are no reasonable substitutes for Microsoft's Windows operating systems for Intel-compatible desktop PCs. Operating systems for non-Intel-based computers are not a reasonable substitute for Microsoft's Windows operating system.

63.   As numerous representatives from personal computer OEMs have testified, OEMs do not believe they have any alternative to the acquisition and installation of Microsoft's Windows operating system. * * * [Here Dr. Fisher quoted various excerpts from the deposition testimony and documentary evidence in the case record. Eds.]

64.   Microsoft's share of personal computer operating systems is very high and has remained stable over time. Microsoft's worldwide share of shipments of Intel-based operating systems has been approximately 90 percent or more in recent years. Even if operating systems for non-Intel-based computers are included in the market definition, Microsoft's share is still very high and stable.

65.   Microsoft's high market share is an indication that it possesses monopoly power. The analysis of barriers to entry confirms that monopoly power exists.

66.   Operating systems are characterized by network effects, and all software is characterized by economies of scale. Users want the operating system that will permit them to run all the applications programs they want to use; developers tend to write applications for the most popular operating system; and applications software written for a specific operating system cannot run on a different operating system without extensive and costly modifications or add-ons. (Operating systems provide application programming interfaces (APIs) through which applications interact with the operating system and through the operating system with the computer hardware. Applications developers must write their programs to interact with a particular operating system's APIs. The time and expense of then "porting" the application to a different operating system can be substantial. An API set to which applications may be written is often referred to in the industry as a "platform.")

67.   There are other network effects as well. For example, the presence of a common interface may enable firms to avoid training costs when

personnel are moved within the firm or new personnel are hired from outside. This gives firms an incentive to have the same user interface throughout its own computers and the same interface that is widely used by other firms. Other network effects include the ease of exchanging files and the opportunity to learn from others. * * *

68. As discussed above, there is nothing inherently anti-competitive about network effects. However, to the extent that anti-competitive conduct by Microsoft exists, network effects increase the risk that such conduct will further entrench Microsoft's monopoly.

69. The existence of network effects also implies that the effect of anti-competitive contracts or conduct will not be dissipated merely by terminating the anti-competitive contracts or stopping the anti-competitive conduct.

70. As the result of economies of scale and network effects, Microsoft's high market share leads to more applications being written for its operating system, which reinforces and increases Microsoft's market share, which in turn leads to still more applications being written for Windows than for other operating systems, and so on. This in turn supports the conclusion, also supported by Microsoft's internal documents and other evidence, that this share is not likely to be eroded by new entry as long as the applications programming barrier to entry remains strong.

71. There is abundant document and deposition testimony on the importance of network effects, scale economies, and the applications programming barrier to entry. * * * [Here, again, Dr. Fisher quoted various excerpts from the deposition testimony and documentary evidence on record in the case. Eds.]

72. Microsoft does not appear to consider other operating systems vendors as a material constraint on its pricing of the Windows operating system. * * *

* * *

74. Microsoft argues that it faces competition from its own installed base (*i.e.*, the copies of earlier versions of its operating system already in the hands of users). (Richard Schmalensee 9/4/98 Expert Report pp. 6–7.) Even if that were true because of the absence of other competition, it does not follow that whatever constraint its own installed base poses is sufficient to prevent Microsoft from having monopoly power; indeed, the contrary is the case.

75. New operating systems are principally acquired in connection with the purchase of new computers and only secondarily in connection with upgrades. At best, Microsoft's installed-base argument relates to its pricing of upgrades. It does not apply to the more important channel of new computers.

76. New computers are bought largely to take advantage of developments in hardware or software. The fact that a given user has an old operating system will not do much to keep that user from changing computers when hardware or software advances, and a new computer is required to use those advances.

77. Moreover, Microsoft has taken action to ensure that installed-base competition is minimal.* * * Microsoft's licenses preclude customers from transferring their licenses to use Windows separately from their PCs; the

ability to so transfer licenses would be a necessary condition for the development of a secondary market for such licenses that would permit OEMs to acquire such licenses as an alternative to licensing the use of Microsoft's newest version of its operating system. Microsoft's contracts with OEMs also generally prohibit them from shipping PCs to consumers with earlier versions of Microsoft's operating system once a new version is released.

78. Despite all the evidence set out above, Microsoft denies that it has monopoly power. Professor Schmalensee's expert report uses a well-known formula for profit-maximizing pricing and concludes that it shows that Microsoft does not have monopoly power. The proper conclusion from Schmalensee's argument cannot be that Microsoft lacks monopoly power. If any conclusion can be drawn, it would be that Microsoft is not maximizing its short-run profits.

* * *

Direct Testimony of Richard L. Schmalensee (For Microsoft)*

I. Introduction

* * *

2. Microsoft does not have monopoly power in the PC operating system market alleged by Plaintiffs—or in any relevant antitrust market in which *Windows* is licensed. Microsoft cannot and has not excluded entry by others. It has maintained its leadership in providing operating systems for Intel-compatible computers through its superior foresight, skill, and efficiency. Microsoft cannot control prices except in the trivial sense in which every owner of intellectual property, from book authors to chip designers, can do so. Current and future competition from numerous sources has constrained Microsoft from charging a monopoly price for *Windows*.

* * *

II. Competition in the Microcomputer Software Industry Is Intense

29. This section describes competition in the microcomputer software industry.[2] In Part A, I show that there are no significant barriers to entering the microcomputer software industry or entering particular software categories within this industry. In Part B, I describe the intense rivalry that has characterized most major microcomputer software categories in the last two decades. In particular, I show that category leaders frequently have been displaced. In Part C, I explain the consequence of this form of competition for the prices charged and the profits realized by microcomputer software firms. I demonstrate that high prices and margins are a characteristic of this industry

---

* [The cross-examination is available beginning at 1999 WL 12849 (D.D.C. TRANS). Eds.]

2. My focus here is on software written for computers that use microprocessors (including computers based on the Intel x86 chips, the Apple Macintosh and Power PCs, network computers, hand-held computers such as the *PalmPilot*, and workstations from Sun and others). Where I use sales statistics from market research firms, I specify more precisely which elements are included.

and provide no evidence of monopoly power—high profits and margins accrue to all successful software producers.

30.   Before I turn to these sections, I will explain how competition in the microcomputer software industry is very different from that typically found in manufacturing industries. It is not well described by standard economics textbook models of competition. Much of the economic analysis presented by Plaintiffs in this matter is misguided because it relies on chalk-board theories that are inconsistent with how competition actually works in this industry, the historical record of competition, and the experience of industry participants.

31.   Dr. Warren–Boulton, for example, testified that the price of *Windows* is higher than the competitive price and concludes from this observation that Microsoft exercises monopoly power. However, he was unable to specify the competitive price for *Windows*, and he gave the following Alice-in-Wonderland response to one of several attempts to get him to say what the competitive price is (Transcript, November 19, 1998, A.M. session, p. 40):

Q.   Do you know what the competitive price of *Windows 98* is?

A.   Significantly below whatever it is.

32.   It is impossible to infer anything about the exercise of monopoly power from the price of software products because their prices always exceed the "competitive" level ordinarily defined by economists. Textbook models say that the competitive price should equal the marginal cost of production. That is roughly **zero** for software because it costs almost nothing to reproduce and distribute software once it has been created. Yet software companies would not develop new products if they could only charge the textbook "competitive" price (unless there is an ancillary source of revenue, as may be the case for Web-browsing software and a few other software categories that generate substantial complementary revenues). When it comes to determining the competitive price for software, standard economic approaches like those apparently relied upon by Dr. Warren–Boulton simply do not provide an explanatory framework for this industry.

33.   Competition in the software industry is based on sequential races for the leadership of categories such as word processing, spreadsheets, personal financial software, games, operating systems, and utilities—not to mention currently unknown categories from which the next generation of "killer applications" will emerge. Many firms enter the race to lead or create a category. A firm can win the race for a category by virtue of being first to market with an innovative product desired by consumers, or by offering a product that consumers consider substantially better than existing products. That winning firm obtains a large share of sales in its category as a result of product superiority and scale economies. It charges prices that reflect the value to consumers of the intellectual property it has created, and it enjoys the profits that arise from its success and risk taking. However, its prices are constrained by the risk of being displaced, which also forces it to continue to innovate.

34.   Consumers that already have the leader's product do not switch to obtain trivial improvements. But the existence of some switching costs does not mean that consumers are "locked-in" to a particular alternative. Rather,

they stay with the current leader until a product comes along that is sufficiently superior to warrant abandoning their investments in the leader. If the pace of innovation were slow and there were thus no realistic prospect of a desirable alternative coming along, perhaps it would be meaningful to talk about consumers being "locked in." But the history and reality of the microcomputer software industry are that superior alternatives come often. There are many examples of wholesale abandonment of category leaders' software products.[3]

35. The history of innovation in the software industry shows that breakthroughs can occur very quickly and are often made possible by hardware innovations. Category leadership is often transitory despite the operation of so-called "network effects" and the investment in particular software made by users. Leaders are regularly displaced and, over time, there is a sequence of winners. As with most other creative enterprises, software firms vary from those that have had one-time "hits" to those that have hits time and time again.

36. Dr. Warren–Boulton and Professor Fisher ignore this lesson of history. They infer that Microsoft has a monopoly in part because it has had a high share of the operating-system category for a number of years. In fact, Microsoft has won several races to provide the best operating-system software between 1981, when it first introduced *MS-DOS*, and 1995 when it introduced *Windows 95*. As was noted by numerous industry observers at the time, Microsoft faced serious competition for leadership—as it does today—in each of these races. It succeeded through superior foresight, efficiency, and innovation that enabled it to bring better products to consumers. Inferring that Microsoft has a monopoly because it has won several races in a row is like concluding that the Boston Celtics had a monopoly in professional basketball when they won the NBA championship eight straight seasons (1959–66). They have not won two seasons in a row since then.

37. Microsoft is one of the most successful microcomputer software firms. It is now the leader in several software categories. Yet, through actions and words, Microsoft demonstrates that it is not living the "quiet life" of a traditional monopolist. Rather, like other firms in this industry, it is in a constant struggle for competitive survival. That struggle—the race to win and the victor's perpetual fear of being displaced—is the source of competitive vitality in the microcomputer software industry.

A. No Significant Entry Barriers

38. There are no barriers in the microcomputer software industry that prevent existing firms, or individuals or small start-up ventures, from entering the races for category leadership or from winning those races. Competitors cannot win by introducing a trivial advance over existing leaders. But it is not efficient for firms that produce trivial advances to win, because that would require asking consumers to scrap investments in their current software for minimal gain. Recognizing this fact, firms try to win by "leapfrogging" the existing leader with substantial improvements. (Entry and success in micro-

---

3. Moreover, categories die with some regularity. Advances in some software categories make other categories irrelevant, and technical change in computer hardware both makes some categories obsolete and continually creates new categories.

computer software operating systems appears harder than for most microcomputer software categories, but it is nevertheless eminently feasible, as I discuss in the next section.)

39.   Hundreds of firms have the assets necessary to compete effectively. At least 12,000 firms are actively competing in the microcomputer software industry. More than 2,000 firms have entered the microcomputer software industry since 1991. More than 190 IPOs ["Initial Public Offerings"—Eds.] for microcomputer software or Internet-related software companies have taken place since January 1997.

[Dean Schmalansee next discussed four factors in support of his contention that there were no significant entry barriers in the "microcomputer software industry:" (1) abundant supplies of both software programmers and financial capital; (2) technological advances in hardware that create new opportunities for software developers and innovations in software; (3) ready availability of consumer information on new and improved products; and (4) readily available and low cost means of new software product distribution, including downloading from the Internet. Eds.]

* * *

53.   Of course, it is not as if anyone with a bright idea and some programming experience can become the next Marc Andreessen [a co-founder of Netscape—Eds.]. There are "barriers" to entering the software industry just as there are "barriers" to entering the economics profession, fast-food franchises, and the automobile industry. People who are not trained in economics tend to think of barriers as obstacles that entrants face—for example, scraping together the money to start a business and developing a reputation with customers—and "high" barriers as obstacles that are large in some absolute sense.

54.   Economists, however, apply a more rigorous approach and consider a cost or obstacle to be a barrier to entry if and only if it can prevent a more efficient entrant (more efficient in the sense of having a better product or a lower cost of production) from competing effectively with (and perhaps displacing) a less efficient incumbent.[21] That refined definition confines the use of the pejorative term "barrier" to those instances in which the barrier prevents an entrant from making consumers better off. Although there is no generally accepted definition of what is a "high" barrier to entry, I would define "high" as a barrier that is large relative to the expected gains from entry.

55.   Three factors **could** discourage entry or make it harder for entrants to succeed: sunk costs, switching costs, and network effects. Each of these factors could be a barrier to entry, and perhaps even a "high" barrier to entry, in the colloquial sense of those terms: they are obstacles that may require more money to overcome than most of us have in the bank. **None** of these factors, however, is a barrier to entry in the sense in which economists

---

21. In his paper, "Diagnosing Monopoly," Professor Fisher has noted, "A barrier to entry exists when entry would be socially beneficial but is somehow prevented." (in Fisher, Frank lin M., *Industrial Organization, Economics, and the Law*, The Massachusetts Institute of Technology: Cambridge, MA, 1991, p. 22).
* * *

use the term because none prevents a more efficient entrant from getting into the microcomputer software business.

[Here, Dean Schmalansee discussed (1) sunk costs; (2) switching costs; and (3) network effects. First, he maintained that "[t]he sunk costs required to enter the microcomputer software industry do not appear substantial compared with other industries." Schmalansee Direct Testimony, ¶ 57. Second, he testified that switching costs occasioned by the need to learn new products and convert old files to new formats do not "necessarily represent any economic inefficiency. More importantly, switching costs seem low in microcomputer software. History has shown that when faced with a superior alternative, software users switch and do so in droves." Schmalansee Direct Testimony, ¶ 59. Finally, he asserted that network effects "are a double-edged sword. * * * Although network effects may inhibit switching away from the leader in a category, they also make it hard for the leader to retain significant volume once consumers start switching toward an attractive challenger." Schmalansee Direct Testimony, ¶ 61. Eds.]

* * *

III. Microsoft Has Faced and Continues to Face Competition from Other Platforms

92.   This section shows that Microsoft does not have "monopoly power" over operating systems, as economists define that term. * * *

* * *

98.   Professor Fisher and Dr. Warren–Boulton ignore those aspects of the software industry that facilitate entry. [Discussed by Dean Schmalansee in ¶ ¶ 53–61, *supra*. Eds.] Instead, they focus almost exclusively on what they refer to as the "applications barrier to entry." (Fisher ¶¶ 65–71, Warren–Boulton ¶ 54) Getting ISVs ["Independent Software Vendors"—Eds.] to write applications for a software platform does not constitute a "high barrier to entry" into the software platform category. It is a challenge faced by anyone—incumbent or new entrant—in developing a new operating system.

[Here Dean Schmalensee argued that all purveyors of successful software platforms must persuade ISVs to write applications for their platforms, and that there was no evidence in his view of an "applications barrier to entry," asserting that "[f]rom a practical standpoint, the evidence speaks clearly that applications software emerges quickly for promising software platforms." ¶ 107. Eds.]

* * *

115.   * * * [W]hen economists use the phrase "barrier to entry" we do not just mean that "entry is hard." By that definition, there are barriers to entry in all industries and pursuits in life. For assessing competition, economists define an entry barrier as a cost or obstacle that deters more efficient entry.

116.   The stock of applications for a software platform does not constitute an economic "barrier to entry" in this rigorous sense. The mere fact that a new software platform does not have a pre-existing stock of applications

does not mean that consumers would be better off if this entrant succeeded, or that consumers are worse off because they have applications available to them for the incumbent software platform. For entry to be efficient, the software platform entrant has to convince consumers and ISVs to write applications for its platform and reduce the cost to consumers of switching from their existing applications. The fact that a software platform entrant does not have a pre-existing stock of applications also does not mean the entrant faces higher costs than the incumbent. Successful software platform providers, like Microsoft, have spent and continue to spend significant resources to persuade ISVs to write new and improved applications for their constantly evolving platforms. They did not find a pre-existing stock of applications awaiting their entry either.

* * *

135. Far from living the quiet life of a monopolist immune from entry, Microsoft perceives itself as being in a constant competitive struggle to maintain its leadership in operating systems. And, indeed, it faces competition today from rivals big and small, as it has since it first released *MS-DOS*. * * *

136. Microsoft faces competition from existing operating systems that run on Intel-compatible hardware. These include IBM's *OS/2*, Be's *BeOS*, Sun Microsystems's *Solaris*, and the nonproprietary *Linux* (although there are commercial distributors of *Linux* from Caldera and Red Hat). Microsoft also faces competition from operating systems running on other hardware, such as the Macintosh. Increases in sales of the Macintosh reduce the sales of Intel-compatible computers and therefore the sales of *Windows*. Of course, as in any business, the known competition is the easiest to contend with. Of far greater concern to Microsoft is the competition from new and emerging technologies, some of which are currently visible and others of which certainly are not. This array of known, emerging, and wholly unknown competitors places enormous pressure on Microsoft to price competitively and innovate aggressively.

* * *

160. These competitive pressures on *Windows* show just how porous the so-called entry barriers into the operating system category are. Competitors range from a 22–year old college student in Finland who wrote a competing operating system while studying for a degree in computer science to IBM, a company that has a current stock-market value of $158 billion and has 2,500 programmers working on Java-related projects. In between, the competitors range from Red Hat and Caldera at the small end, to Sun Microsystems and 3Com at the high end. These firms—and other individual programmers and companies that we do not know about yet—are investing their time and energy, as well as millions of dollars, into displacing *Windows*. This activity provides strong evidence against assertions by Professor Fisher and Dr. Warren–Boulton that entry barriers are high: rational, profit-seeking firms simply do not make large investments in attempt to pursue the impossible. The investments by these firms show that whatever entry barriers may exist, many credible firms and individuals believe them to be surmountable.

* * *

161. It is the constant threat that its competitors will provide a more appealing software platform for ISVs and consumers that makes Microsoft constantly strive to improve *Windows* and to keep *Windows* prices low. Regardless of whether one thinks that Microsoft faces great, moderate, or little competition for its operating system, Microsoft behaves as if it faces * * * intense dynamic competition * * *.

162. First, Microsoft charges far less for *Windows* than it would if it did not face dynamic competition for the software platform category and had the kind of monopoly power that Professor Fisher and Dr. Warren–Boulton ascribe to it. Second, Microsoft engages in intense efforts to innovate and stay ahead of potential rivals. Although it is true, as Dr. Warren–Boulton has testified during cross-examination, that "there is not an economic theory that tells you that a monopolist will not innovate," Microsoft's relentless innovation is far more consistent with the behavior of a firm engaged in leapfrog competition with rivals than with the behavior of a secure monopolist. Third, Microsoft's quality-adjusted prices have fallen dramatically over time. This pattern is consistent with what I would expect under dynamic competition.

* * *

177. There are two commonly used methods for assessing monopoly power in antitrust analysis. The structural approach relies on information concerning the relative sizes of market participants. In particular, it attempts to infer the existence (or lack thereof) of monopoly power by ascertaining the geographic and product boundaries for the market and then calculating the shares of the firms within those boundaries. The structural approach is useful in merger analysis because it provides the enforcement agencies with a screening test to determine if particular mergers may have anticompetitive consequences, something that is not knowable in advance but must be inferred from the structure of the market following the merger. Mergers that result in substantial increases in concentration within relevant antitrust markets are, and I believe should be, subjected to closer scrutiny.* * * The structural approach can also be useful, at least as a starting point, in antitrust analyses when there are clearly defined market boundaries.

178. The behavioral approach relies on direct evidence concerning how the firms that are under scrutiny behave. Rather than attempting to devise sharp boundaries, the behavioral approach focuses on identifying the constraints that, in fact, do or do not limit the ability of firms to raise prices or deter entry. It also examines the pricing, innovation, output, and other behavior of a firm to see whether and to what extent the firm exhibits the behavior economists would expect of firms with monopoly power.

179. The behavioral approach is especially useful when market boundaries are blurred, and the decision to include or exclude competitors from the analysis arbitrarily determines the outcome of the structural investigation. I believe that the behavioral approach is appropriate in many antitrust inquiries, particularly when market boundaries are difficult to draw and thus controversial. The behavioral approach is less prone to error than the structural approach because it allows the economist, and the ultimate decisionmaker, to weigh all of the relevant evidence on market constraints (rather than

inferring what behavior is likely to be based on examining market structure).
* * *

180. The behavioral approach is especially desirable in the microcomputer software industry. Because software code can be shortened, or expanded, or divided in chunks across software products in many different ways, market boundaries are extremely fuzzy. I will show this in more detail in the next section. Many applications packages have absorbed other applications packages—*e.g.*, word processing absorbed spell-checking and grammar-checking programs, spreadsheets absorbed equation solvers, operating systems absorbed many utilities and Internet communication protocols. Every software category leader is threatened from many directions—from new entrants into the category, from absorption into other software categories, and from niche players who may overtake the leader. Entry possibilities are numerous and multifaceted. And entry barriers, as I showed in this section and the previous one, are relatively low. Competition from the existing installed base and from piracy further makes market boundaries hard to draw.

181. * * * *Windows* has a high share of sales of software platforms for Intel-compatible computers. In the next week, consumers could not find an alternative software platform that performs as well as *Windows*. OEMs would be hard pressed to give new computer users an operating system that they would like as much as *Windows*. Yet, despite what would appear to be an ironclad monopoly, the evidence based on real-world observations is that Microsoft does not **behave** like a firm with monopoly power.

182. The reason is that Microsoft is constrained by the past, present, and future. The past constrains Microsoft because it has to convince users of older versions of its software platform to upgrade and ISVs to write applications that will make the newer version more valuable to these past licensees. The present constrains Microsoft because higher prices induce piracy and cause at least some consumers to choose alternative software platforms. Most importantly, though, the future constrains Microsoft because if it slips today, it raises the odds that one of the known or unknown firms that are constantly challenging its leadership position in software platforms will break out of the pack and make Microsoft one of the many "has beens" in this young industry.

* * *

185. The relevant analysis should not be based on the approach described in the *1992 Merger Guidelines* and relied upon by Dr. Warren–Boulton. The issue at this stage of the analysis is not whether Microsoft could raise the price by 5 percent for a nontransitory period of time—the question asked by the *Merger Guidelines* for the purpose of evaluating the competitive effects of a merger. The issue is whether Microsoft could recoup its allegedly substantial investments over a long period of time. To answer that question, it is necessary to examine long-run competition and therefore long-run entry and other supply responses. Therefore, the relevant antitrust market should consist of productive capacity that could be deployed over the relevant period of time. Professor Fisher and Dr. Warren–Boulton claim that Microsoft made predatory investments that it expected to recoup in the future as a result of disabling Netscape. The relevant time period for antitrust analysis thus

consists of the long run over which Microsoft would have expected to recoup its predatory investments under Plaintiffs' theory.

186. In the long-run, Microsoft faces actual or potential competition from (1) Netscape; (2) other software firms such as Oracle, Caldera, Red Hat, and Novell; (3) Sun; and (4) other hardware/software firms such as IBM, Apple and 3Com. Moreover, these competitors often form alliances as AOL, Netscape, and Sun recently announced. Much of Microsoft's future competition is unknown. It was not known in 1994 that Netscape, Java and *Linux* would become competitive threats to Microsoft. It is not known today who will become competitive threats to Microsoft in 2002. Perhaps interest in the *BeOS* will explode; perhaps a scaled-up *Palm OS* will enchant developers of desktop applications; or perhaps a student just admitted to MIT will develop a killer operating system.

187. Under the theory of the case presented by Professor Fisher and Dr. Warren–Boulton, the relevant antitrust market for considering whether Microsoft has long-run monopoly power should include Sun, Netscape, and other similar firms that pose a threat to Microsoft. In particular, * * * Netscape and Sun are competing with *Windows* by producing middleware. Middleware is an economic substitute for *Windows*. It was recognized by Microsoft as a substitute, and it is recognized by Professor Fisher and Dr. Warren–Boulton as a competitive threat because it is a substitute. These and other actual and prospective middleware entrants should be included in the relevant antitrust market. Professor Fisher and Dr. Warren–Boulton have adopted an illogical and inconsistent approach to market definition by failing to include middleware and other potential entrants, while simultaneously labeling them threats to *Windows*.

188. I do not believe that it is possible to measure Microsoft's economic power over price or entry by calculating shares of this or any other relevant market. Market share figures are not helpful in an industry like software in which entry is possible from many known and unknown sources—and in which any successful competitor has the ability to supply all of the market without building factories or purchasing expensive capital equipment. However, the market share approach adopted by Professor Fisher and Dr. Warren–Boulton, if applied to a relevant antitrust market that properly includes potential entrants, would show that Microsoft does not have a large enough market share to exercise long-run monopoly power. Microsoft has a 9 percent share of total U.S. software revenues and a 10 percent share of total software revenues worldwide. Only about 0.1 percent of the world's professional developers work for Microsoft. Although I do not believe that either of these figures provides a meaningful estimate of "market share," they do demonstrate that Microsoft does not exercise any control over the productive capacity needed to compete for the operating system category.

* * *

189. Professor Fisher and Dr. Warren–Boulton have erroneously concluded that Microsoft has monopoly power because they assume away the many constraints on Microsoft's behavior and ignore the past and the future. They rely heavily on market share data that provide little information about monopoly power in the microcomputer software industry. And they focus

almost exclusively on immediate constraints and therefore ignore the dynamics of competition in this industry.

* * *

191.   Dr. Warren–Boulton (¶ 7) has testified that the "first and foremost" evidence that Microsoft has monopoly power is that it has more than a 90 percent share of his "relevant market," operating systems for Intel-compatible computers. "High" market shares in dynamically competitive markets—especially those involving intellectual capital—provide no evidence that the incumbent has monopoly power. Successful software firms obtain high shares because of product quality, scale economies and network effects (which are greater in operating systems than in other categories). They cannot maintain those shares unless they continue to win the races for category leadership. * * *

192.   Microsoft and other successful software firms have to price low and innovate to maintain their leads. I agree with Professor Fisher's conclusion that

> ***It is a mistake to believe that a large market share is equivalent to monopoly.*** When such a share can only be maintained by reducing prices toward (but not beyond) costs or introducing better products, monopoly power is absent and competition is doing its job.[155] (emphasis added)

The stability of Microsoft's market share reflects the fact that it has maintained its leadership of the operating system category through superior foresight, ingenuity and efficiency. Professor Fisher and Dr. Warren–Boulton have not argued or shown otherwise.

193.   Dr. Warren–Boulton's second basis for concluding that Microsoft has monopoly power is that it charges prices that exceed the "competitive level". *All successful software firms charge prices that exceed marginal cost, which is the normal definition used by economists of the competitive price.* As I discussed in the previous section, it is impossible to infer anything whatsoever about monopoly power from the fact that software prices are higher than the usual competitive benchmark. Microsoft, like all successful software firms and owners of copyrighted works, charges more than this so-called competitive level. And, like many firms, it does not charge the same price to every customer.[156]

194.   Dr. Warren–Boulton (¶ 39) also relies on the testimony of computer manufacturers who specialized in selling Intel-compatible computers, who say they do not have an alternative to *Windows*. But, as I have noted, this testimony merely confirms that ***in the short run***, given the products currently on the market, Microsoft has the most popular operating system for the Intel-compatible computers those OEMs are producing. This testimony says nothing about what could happen in even a few years.

---

155. Fisher, Franklin M.; McGowan, John J.; and Greenwood, Joen E., *Folded, Spindled, and Mutilated*, MIT Press: Cambridge, MA, 1983, p. 275.

156. Charging different customers different prices—what economists call price discrimination—is common.

195. The fourth observation on which Dr. Warren–Boulton relies is the claim that Microsoft's prices for the operating system have not declined as rapidly as the price of PC hardware components. This involves the comparison of products that have different production processes, technologies, costs of materials, and changes in quality. It is like comparing the salaries of university professors with the cost of textbooks—just because they are complementary products does not mean that their prices should track each other. Dr. Warren–Boulton's comparison is specious and meaningless. As I indicated above, the quality-adjusted prices of Microsoft's operating systems have declined tremendously over time.

196. Dr. Warren–Boulton has also testified (¶ 62 and Transcript of Trial Proceedings, November 19, 1998, A.M. session, pp. 26–27) that the fact that Microsoft has a "high" net margin on sales (revenue less costs) provides evidence that it has monopoly power over the operating system. That conclusion is wrong. ***All successful software packages have high profit margins.*** The fact that Microsoft, as a company, has a high margin reflects the fact that it has many successful software packages. It has created what the public wants and regards as valuable. Dr. Warren–Boulton offers no evidence that Microsoft's margins reflect any more than its return from successful innovation and operating what is generally regarded as a highly efficient company (which is to be commended, not condemned). * * *

197. Moreover, there is a lengthy literature in economics that explains the numerous reasons why the accounting rates of return relied upon by Dr. Warren–Boulton do not provide reliable indicators or monopoly power. As Professor Fisher has noted,

> Is it then true that one can look at a firm's profit rate and conclude very simply that there is monopoly power if it is high and an absence of such power if it is low? The answer is no.[160]

> ... the problems involved are so large as to make ***any*** inference from accounting rates of return as to the presence of economic profits, and a fortiori monopoly profits, totally impossible in practice.[161] (emphasis in the original)

198. Finally, Dr. Warren–Boulton has testified that two facts inform him that Microsoft will continue to have monopoly power in the operating system. The fact that Microsoft—as a company—has a high profit margin and the fact that Microsoft—again as a company—has a high "price-earnings ratio". The price-earnings ratio is the ratio of the stock price to the earnings per share. The price-earnings ratio for Microsoft's stock reflects the market's expectation that Microsoft's earnings will grow. But Microsoft's earnings will grow because the overall market for microcomputer software and Internet-related services will grow, and because Microsoft has a number of business ventures under way that will further contribute to its growth in earnings. There is no way to determine from the price-earnings ratio whether earnings from the *Windows* operating system will grow, or whether they will grow as fast as the overall market for microcomputer software. There is no basis in

---

160. Fisher, Frank, "Diagnosing Monopoly," *Southern Economic Journal*, v. 45 n.4, April, 1979.

161. Fisher, Franklin M.; McGowan, John J.; and Greenwood, Joen E., *Folded, Spindled, and Mutilated*, MIT Press: Cambridge, MA, 1983, p. 219.

economics for inferring anything whatsoever about monopoly power from the price-earnings ratio for a company.

199.　Dr. Warren–Boulton has relied on the *1992 Merger Guidelines* to assess whether Microsoft has monopoly power. * * * Those guidelines are helpful for evaluating the probable economic effects of mergers. They are not helpful in evaluating whether a firm has monopoly power over copyrighted works in an industry that is subject to high rates of technological innovation and leapfrog competition.

200.　Dr. Warren–Boulton's inappropriate use of the *Merger Guidelines* leads him to reach conclusions that are logically wrong. He testified (¶ 37) that Microsoft faces an extremely inelastic demand for the PC operating system. He also cites the testimony of OEM executives who claim that they would not switch operating systems if Microsoft increased its license fees by 10 percent. The only logical inference from these observations is that Microsoft could increase its profits under his analysis by raising its prices.

* * *

202.　Microsoft does not raise price even though it apparently could for a very simple reason that Professor Fisher and Dr. Warren–Boulton have assumed away—competition exists. Microsoft faces long-run competition from its installed base, pirated copies of its operating system, existing vendors of operating systems, and a long list of potential entrants. Neither Professor Fisher nor Dr. Warren–Boulton have explained—and, indeed, cannot explain—why Microsoft does not raise its prices and earn the billions of dollars that would be available to it under the theories advanced by Plaintiffs.

* * *

———

Which technique or techniques for establishing market power were evident in the excerpted testimony of the three economists? Did they rely on evidence of actual anticompetitive effects? Single inference evidence of market power? Double inference evidence of market power? What evidence did the economists themselves cite in support of their respective positions? What was the nature of the criticism that each side's expert leveled at the other? Did they disagree about the underlying facts? Economic theory? The application of economic theory to the facts presented?

Ultimately, the district court sided almost entirely with the government on the question of Microsoft's monopoly power, and the court of appeals affirmed that conclusion "in its entirety." Here as an excerpt of the discussion of market power from the court of appeals' decision.

UNITED STATES v. MICROSOFT CORP.

United States Court of Appeals for the District of Columbia Circuit, 2001.
253 F.3d 34.

[The relevant excerpt from the court of appeals' decision is reproduced in Chapter 6, *supra*, at 640. Eds.]

Note how much of the evidence relied upon by the court in resolving the monopoly power issue in *Microsoft*, and how much of the argument it weighed, originated with the testimony of the economic experts. Which of the government's approaches to establishing monopoly power proved persuasive to the courts and why? What particular evidence did the court find persuasive? How did the expert's address conditions of entry? What legal standard did it use? How did the court integrate economic concepts, legal theory, and the evidence to reach its conclusions? And finally, how did the court respond to Microsoft's expert's positions on monopoly power? Why were they rejected? Consider Figure 6–5, which follows the main excerpt from the court's opinion in Chapter 6, and summarizes the government's positions, Microsoft's, and the court of appeals'.

Recall from Chapter 6 that a finding of monopoly power would not have constituted a violation of Section 2 of the Sherman Act by itself. In addition, the plaintiff, in this instance the federal government and 19 states, also had to establish that the monopoly power found was either willfully acquired or willfully maintained. "Willfulness," as we learned in Chapter 6, means by some predatory or exclusionary means. The plaintiffs conceded that Microsoft got to be a monopolist through competitive means; their challenge instead focused on its "maintenance" of that power. Note as was evident in the expert's testimony, as well as in the court's analysis of monopoly power, the inquiry into monopoly power can often involve evaluation of conduct. Why is that so? What is the relevance of conduct to the monopoly power inquiry? Does it have anything to do with what we learned earlier in this Chapter about the role of evidence of actual anticompetitive effects? What does it suggest about the continued distinctiveness of the elements of a Section 1 and Section 2 Sherman Act violation?

D. THE ROLE OF INTENT IN ANTITRUST ANALYSIS

It might seem logical to assume that "intent" also would be a factor, if not a required element, of many antitrust offenses. After all, if the point of antitrust analysis frequently is to distinguish between "hard competition" and "predation," subjective intent would appear to be relevant to the inquiry. Defendants could be expected to offer exculpatory evidence of their "good," *i.e.*, competitive, intentions, whereas prosecutors and plaintiffs alike would try to focus attention on evidence suggesting a desire to injure consumers or vanquish rivals.

But evidence of intent can at once be both revealing and unreliable. Documents and testimony referring colorfully to a defendant's seeming intent to "drive out the competition" or "crush" its rivals, may be commonplace in the files of many a firm. Consider for example, the following deposition colloquy, reported in *Blair Foods, Inc. v. Ranchers Cotton Oil*, 610 F.2d 665 (9th Cir.1980), a case alleging attempt to monopolize under Section 2, as well as conspiracy claims under Section 1:

Q. There was no doubt in your mind that Blair [the plaintiff] was a part of the business scene?

A. He (sic) was making himself a part of it at that time.

Q. Did you have any objection to that?

A. I would like to see all of my competitors bow out of business.

Q. You would?

A. Yes.

Q. You would like the entire Northern California area for yourself?

A. The whole world, yes. Wouldn't that be nice?

Q. Have you always felt that way?

[The Questioning Attorney]: Let the record show the witness is laughing at this. Counsel is taking it up as a serious matter.

The Witness: You ask a silly question, you get a silly answer.

Id. at 667 n.1.

Critics of reliance on these sorts of statements point out that they could be as consistent with hard competition as with predation, and by themselves reveal little about the nature of the conduct undertaken and its consequences, especially in cases of alleged exclusionary conduct. *See, e.g.,* Frank H. Easterbrook, *On Identifying Exclusionary Conduct*, 61 NOTRE DAME L. REV. 972 (1986). The same statements could be found in the files of a firm that realized the goal of vanquishing its rival through efficiencies and innovation and one that did so through true predation. Antitrust standards that too readily rely on this sort of evidence, therefore, easily could dampen legitimately aggressive competitive spirits for fear of antitrust exposure.

On the other hand, to completely discount evidence of intent might be to ignore relevant and probative evidence with respect to the effects of conduct and possible justifications for it. In fact, evidence of intent may be most useful when it explains and illuminates the utility and efficacy of specific conduct. In such circumstances, internal documents describing the goals of particular conduct may well facilitate the investigation of its impact. This might be especially true where collusive effects are at issue. Evidence discussing intended effects on prices, for example, may not exhibit the inherent ambiguity of aggressive talk of injuring rivals. Some kind of "balance" therefore may be needed between the two extreme positions. *See generally* Marina Lao, *Reclaiming a Role for Intent Evidence in Monopolization Analysis*, 54 AM. U. L. REV. 151 (2004).

"Intent," therefore, has played varying roles in antitrust. But those roles vary with the civil or criminal nature of the alleged violation, and with the particular offense alleged under Section 1 or 2 of the Sherman Act.

Intent and Criminal Antitrust. Owing in large part to its origins as a "white collar" criminal statute, the Sherman Act has been read to incorporate the traditional requirement of the criminal law of "intent" or "mens rea." Hence the Supreme Court, relying on that tradition, has held that

> * * * [A]n effect on prices, without more, will not support a criminal conviction under the Sherman Act. * * * Rather, we hold that a defendant's state of mind or intent is an element of a criminal antitrust offense which must be established by evidence and inferences drawn therefrom and cannot be taken from the trier of fact

through reliance on a legal presumption of wrongful intent from proof of an effect on prices.

United States v. U.S. Gypsum Co., 438 U.S. 422, 435 (1978). The Court concluded that it was "unwilling to construe the Sherman Act as mandating a regime of strict-liability criminal offenses." *Id.* at 436. Having concluded that intent was an element of a criminal Section 1 Sherman Act violation, the Court endorsed use of the traditional criminal law's "bifurcated" concept— intent could be established *either* by (1) purpose to bring about an anticompetitive result *or* (2) knowledge of the probable consequences of the conduct— *both* were not required. *Id.* at 444–45 & n.21. The Court reasoned:

> The business behavior which is likely to give rise to criminal antitrust charges is conscious behavior normally undertaken only after a full consideration of the desired results and a weighing of the costs, benefits, and risks. A requirement of proof not only of this knowledge of likely effects, but also of a conscious desire to bring them to fruition or to violate the law would seem, particularly in such a context, both unnecessarily cumulative and unduly burdensome. *Where carefully planned and calculated conduct is being scrutinized in the context of a criminal prosecution, the perpetrator's knowledge of the anticipated consequences is a sufficient predicate for a finding of criminal intent.*

Id. at 445–46 (emphasis added).

Gypsum involved an alleged agreement to fix prices, which was largely evidenced by an exchange of price information by gypsum board producers. In defense of their actions, the producers asserted that the price information exchanges were undertaken for purposes of complying with the Robinson– Patman Act and were therefore exempt from Sherman Act scrutiny. Although this defense was ultimately rejected, its incorporation in the case meant it was not presented as a true "per se" price fixing indictment—a defense was considered and rejected.

Today, criminal prosecutions under Section 1 of the Sherman Act are almost exclusively reserved for per se offenses, such as price fixing, bid-rigging and division of markets. *See* ANTITRUST DIVISION MANUAL § IIIC5 ("Standards for Determining Whether to Proceed by Civil or Criminal Investigation"); Donald I. Baker, *To Indict or Not To Indict: Prosecutorial Discretion in Sherman Act Enforcement*, 63 CORNELL L. REV. 405 (1978). But does *Gypsum's* formulation of an intent requirement make sense for a per se offense? Would it make more sense for a rule of reason offense? How likely is it that the government would criminally prosecute a rule of reason offense? Can you see any problems that would arise in doing so? *See, e.g., United States v. Brown*, 936 F.2d 1042, 1045–46 (9th Cir.1991) (*Gypsum* intent requirement inapplicable to per se case).

Intent in Civil Antitrust Cases. As we learned in Chapter 6, Section 2 of the Sherman Act prohibits three distinct offenses: monopolization, attempt to monopolize and conspiracy to monopolize. Here again we see the influence of the traditional criminal law approach to addressing matters of intent.

"Monopolization," constituting the *completed* offense, has consistently been interpreted as a "general intent" offense, *i.e.*, "no intent is relevant except that which is relevant to any liability, criminal or civil: *i.e.*, an intent to bring about the forbidden act." *United States v. Aluminum Co. of Am.*, 148 F.2d 416, 432 (2d Cir.1945). Noting that "the question of intent is relevant" to both the offense of attempt to monopolize and monopolization, the Supreme Court elaborated on *Alcoa* in *Aspen Skiing*:

> In the former case [attempt to monopolize] it is necessary to prove a "specific intent" to accomplish the forbidden objective—as Judge Hand explained, "an intent which goes beyond the mere intent to do the act." United States v. Aluminum Co. Of America, 148 F.2d 416, 432 (C.A.2 1945). In the latter case [monopolization] evidence of intent is merely relevant to the question whether the challenged conduct is fairly characterized as "exclusionary" or "anticompetitive * * * or "predatory" * * *. Whichever label is used, there is agreement on the proposition that "no monopolist monopolizes unconscious of what he is doing."

Aspen Skiing, 472 U.S. at 602 (quoting *Alcoa*). To the extent general intent is a formal requirement, therefore, it is readily inferred from the fact that the defendant has engaged in a predatory or exclusionary act constituting monopolization.

As *Aspen Skiing* also points out, however, in contrast, the offense of attempt to monopolize requires a showing of "specific intent." As we learned in Chapter 6, Justice Holmes is largely responsible for reading "specific intent" into the offense of attempted monopolization. *See Spectrum Sports, Inc. v. McQuillan*, 506 U.S. 447, 454–55 (1993) (discussing *Swift & Co. v. United States*, 196 U.S. 375, 396 (1905)). *Swift* was influenced by the common law origins of the Sherman Act and its status as a criminal statute. Given Justice Holmes' status as a scholar of the common law, it is not surprising that these facts would add up to a specific intent requirement—attempt crimes at common law were generally associated with "specific intent." *See also* Casebook, Chapter 3, *supra*, at 342 (discussing "invitations to collude" and role of intent under Section 5 of the FTC Act in *Stone Container*). Courts typically demand evidence of specific intent as well in cases alleging conspiracy to monopolize.

Sorting out the role of intent in civil Section 1 cases, however, has proved to be more of a challenge. You may recall from Chapter 2, that the Supreme Court's *Chicago Bd. of Trade* decision set forth the earliest and most significant definition of the rule of reason. The oft quoted language from *Chicago Bd. of Trade*, which invited evaluation of the history, purpose and effect of restraints of trade as part of the rule of reason inquiry, incorporated a role for purpose and intent:

> The history of the restraint, the evil believed to exist, the reason for adopting the particular remedy, *the purpose or end sought to be attained*, are all relevant facts. This is not because a good intention will save an otherwise objectionable regulation or the reverse, but because knowledge of intent may help the court to interpret facts and to predict consequences.

246 U.S. at 238 (emphasis added).

Over time, this portion of *Chicago Bd. of Trade* has spawned several rules of thumb regarding intent in Sherman 1 cases: (1) good intentions are not a defense to a Sherman Act violation—*i.e.*, when an agreement is established and there is evidence that the agreement unreasonably restrained trade, good intentions should be given no weight; (2) conversely, bad intentions alone cannot make a violation out of conduct that does *not* unreasonably restrain trade; but (3) evidence of intent remains relevant to the extent it makes an inference of anticompetitive effects more or less probable. To illustrate these rules, consider the following excerpt from the remand in *California Dental Ass'n*, a Supreme Court decision we studied in Chapter 2. Note how the Ninth Circuit appears to incorporate all of the rules of thumb outlined above.

CALIFORNIA DENTAL ASSOCIATION v. FTC
United States Court of Appeals for the Ninth Circuit, 2000.
224 F.3d 942.

Before: CHOY, and HALL, Circuit Judges, and REAL, District Judge.

CYNTHIA HOLCOMB HALL, Circuit Judge:

After affirming our prior judgment in part and reversing in part, the United States Supreme Court remanded this case for a determination of whether the California Dental Association's advertising restrictions are anti-competitive under rule-of-reason analysis. Having closely examined the record under the rule of reason, we conclude that the Federal Trade Commission failed to prove that the restrictions are anticompetitive. We therefore vacate and remand with instruction that the Commission dismiss its case against the Association.

* * *

[To review the facts in the case, see the excerpts from the Supreme Court's opinion, Casebook, *supra*, at 187. Eds.]

II.

* * *

Intent to Restrain Competition

Our prior opinion held that the CDA constituted an agreement among its members. We did not dwell on the issue of intent, however, observing that "whatever its motivation, the point of the advertising policy was clearly to limit the types of advertising in which dentists could engage." We then observed that good "motives will not validate an otherwise anticompetitive practice," citing NCAA v. Board of Regents, 468 U.S. 85, 101 n. 23, 104 S.Ct. 2948, 82 L.Ed.2d 70 (1984). This truncated discussion of intent reflects the well-established pattern of the Supreme Court to examine intent only in those close cases where the plaintiff falls short of proving that the defendant's actions were anticompetitive. Even then, "an admitted intention to limit competition will not make illegal conduct that we know to be pro-competitive or otherwise immune from antitrust control." 7 Phillip E. Areeda, Antitrust Law § 1506 (1986). And, while "smoking gun" evidence of an intent to restrain competition remains relevant to the court's task of discerning the competitive consequences of a defendant's actions, "ambiguous indications of intent do not help us 'predict [the] consequences [of a defendant's acts]' "and are therefore of no value to a court analyzing a restraint under the rule of reason, where the court's ultimate role is to determine the net effects of those acts. *Id.* Under such circumstances, we apply the rule of reason without engaging in the relatively fruitless inquiry into a defendant's intent.

* * *

We do see substantial evidence that the CDA intended to restrict certain types of advertising, but in light of the CDA's plausibly procompetitive justifications for the restrictions, such intent has no bearing on the question of whether those restrictions are in fact likely to prove anticompetitive or procompetitive. And the record reveals no unambiguous evidence that the CDA intended to restrain trade, so further analysis of CDA's intent becomes superfluous. Under such circumstances, intent "drops out" of our rule-of-reason inquiry, just as it did in our prior opinion, and the case hinges on the actual economic consequences of the CDA's restrictions.

* * *

———

Based on the Ninth Circuit's approach, when would evidence of intent be relevant under the rule of reason? What kinds of intent evidence might be relevant? How can intent make a finding of anticompetitive effect more or less likely? Should exculpatory be as relevant as inculpatory evidence of intent? If so, is there a way to avoid creating an incentive for firms to routinely paper their files with manufactured "good intent" evidence? Should the answers to these questions vary depending upon whether the case is based on collusive or exclusionary effects? On whether the case is brought under Section 1, as were *Chicago Bd. of Trade* and *California Dental*, or as a monopolization case under Section 2?

Consider the following statement from the monopolization analysis in *United States v. Microsoft Corp.*:

> * * * [I]n considering whether the monopolist's conduct on balance harms competition and is therefore condemned as exclusionary for purposes of § 2, our focus is on the effect of that conduct, not upon the intent behind it. Evidence of the intent behind the conduct of a monopolist is relevant only to the extent it helps us understand the likely effect of the monopolist's conduct. [*citing* both *Chicago Bd. of Trade* (a Section 1 rule of reason case) and *Aspen Skiing Co.* (a Section 2 monopolization case)]

253 F.3d. at 59. Is the D.C. Circuit's approach consistent with the Ninth Circuit's in *California Dental*? Should it be? The *Microsoft* litigation has renewed debate about the role of intent in monopolization cases. *Contrast* Steven C. Salop & R. Craig Romaine, *Preserving Monopoly: Economic Analysis, Legal Standards, and Microsoft*, 7 GEO. MASON L. REV. 617, 652 (1999) (no need for separate intent requirement in monopolization cases where firm engages in exclusionary conduct with insufficient offsetting efficiencies) *with* Ronald A. Cass & Keith Hylton, *Antitrust Intent*, 74 S. CAL. L. REV. 657 (2001)

(advocating limited use of objective specific intent requirement in monopolization cases, even where evidence of anticompetitive effect is present).

California Dental and *Microsoft*, however, appear to reflect the general rule—whether for purposes of monopolization under Section 2, or restraint of trade under Section 1, evidence of intent may aid the judgment of effects, but intent without effects will not suffice. Why would that be so? How might very specific evidence of intent tied to particular conduct illuminate its actual or likely effects? Are there no possible instances of unambiguous, anticompetitive intent evidence that might aid antitrust analysis in such cases? What would be lost if very strong evidence of anticompetitive intentions was deemed sufficient to support a finding of violation, even in the absence of evidence that the defendant was able to realize its goals? Would legitimate conduct be deterred?

E. THE EXPANDING ROLE OF CONDITIONS OF ENTRY

Our most extensive previous exploration of entry was in Chapter 5, where we saw that the Horizontal Merger Guidelines, and contemporary merger analysis more generally, assign a great deal of significance to conditions of entry. Uncommitted entry directly affects the identity of firms included in the relevant market for purposes of calculating market shares and committed entry can deter or counteract what would otherwise be the adverse competitive effects of merger.

But even before we studied mergers, in Chapter 2 we saw that conditions of entry have been deemed relevant to the proof of anticompetitive effects under Sections 1 and 2 of the Sherman Act. *See, e.g., Antitrust Guidelines for Collaborations Among Competitors,* § 3.35 (2000) (adapting standards from Merger Guidelines to context of Competitor Collaborations). They also proved significant in the application of Clayton Act Section 3, as we saw in Chapter 7.

As with market power, accommodating the economic significance of entry poses a significant challenge. How can its multi-faceted role be transposed into operative legal standards? Also as with market power, there is a dichotomy between reliance on evidence of conditions of entry in the form of actual past entry, expansion and exit, and circumstantial evidence of conditions of entry as reflected in the structure of a market. Lack of clarity as to the content of the "reasonableness" and "substantial lessening of competition" standards also have generated lack of clarity and consequent uncertainty about the use of entry evidence. And there may also be some underlying disagreement among economists as to what constitutes a "barrier to entry," as we observed in the *Microsoft* expert testimony and explore further in Sidebar 8–6.

As a consequence, there is a lack of precision and consistency in how entry is used in antitrust cases. The central question is: "When can entry solve the competitive problems posed by certain conduct?" In answering that question, however, others may arise, including:

> (1) What do we mean economically and legally by "ease of entry" or "barriers to entry"?

(2) Why are conditions of entry significant and when? Must entry fully eliminate anticompetitive effects, or will it be sufficient that it alleviates or significantly mitigates those effects? In short, how significant and how certain must the impact of entry be before it is deemed legally sufficient to counteract anticompetitive effects?

(3) Will conditions of entry matter regardless of whether the case is built on evidence of actual anticompetitive effects as opposed to inferences drawn from market shares? Should the possibility of future entry ever be sufficient to counteract evidence of present, actual anticompetitive effects? Must it be "probable"?

(4) Who bears the burden of producing evidence as to conditions of entry? How much evidence (and of what kind) must a party produce in order to "win" the entry point? What sort of evidence bears directly or inferentially on entry and why? Are there distinctions between "committed" and "uncommitted" entry that are significant for purposes of antitrust analysis?

In Chapter 5 we focused our attention on the role entry plays in mergers in *Waste Management* and *Baker Hughes*. Recall that under the Merger Guidelines, entry must be *"timely, likely, and sufficient"* before it can be credited. *Horizontal Merger Guidelines*, § 3.0. In this Chapter we look beyond mergers and find that the significance of entry now bears on almost all antitrust analysis. Consider the approach of the Guidelines and the questions just posed as we now turn to the non-merger cases.

REBEL OIL CO. v. ATLANTIC RICHFIELD CO.
United States Court of Appeals for the Ninth Circuit, 1995.
51 F.3d 1421.

Before: POOLE, BEEZER and KLEINFELD, Circuit Judges.

BEEZER, Circuit Judge:

This case presents three antitrust claims arising from the defendant's conduct in the retail gasoline market in Las Vegas, Nevada. The plaintiffs contend that the defendant engaged in predatory pricing between 1985 and 1989, selling self-serve, cash-only gasoline below marginal cost. The plaintiffs claim that the alleged predatory pricing was an attempt by the defendant to monopolize the market, in violation of Sherman Act § 2. The plaintiffs also claim that the predatory pricing scheme involved a conspiracy to restrain trade, in violation of Sherman Act § 1, and primary-line price discrimination, in violation of Clayton Act § 2, as amended by the Robinson–Patman Act, 15 U.S.C. § 13(a).

The district court granted summary judgment in favor of the defendant on all three antitrust claims, concluding that the defendant did not possess enough power in the market to allow the predatory scheme to succeed, and therefore that the plaintiffs had not suffered any injury cognizable under the antitrust laws. * * * We affirm in part and reverse and remand in part.

* * *

II

* * * A mere showing of substantial or even dominant market share alone cannot establish market power sufficient to carry out a predatory

scheme. The plaintiff must show that new rivals are barred from entering the market and show that existing competitors lack the capacity to expand their output to challenge the predator's high price.

Entry barriers are "additional long-run costs that were not incurred by incumbent firms but must be incurred by new entrants," or "factors in the market that deter entry while permitting incumbent firms to earn monopoly returns." The main sources of entry barriers are: (1) legal license requirements; (2) control of an essential or superior resource; (3) entrenched buyer preferences for established brands; (4) capital market evaluations imposing higher capital costs on new entrants; and, in some situations, (5) economies of scale. In evaluating entry barriers, we focus on their ability to constrain not "those already in the market, but ... those who would enter but are prevented from doing so." *United States v. Syufy Enter.*, 903 F.2d 659, 672 n. 21 (9th Cir.1990).

To justify a finding that a defendant has the power to control prices, entry barriers must be significant—they must be capable of constraining the normal operation of the market to the extent that the problem is unlikely to be self-correcting. Barriers to entry are insignificant when natural market forces will likely cure the problem. In such cases, judicial intervention into the market is unwarranted. * * *

Rebel introduced affidavits from experts stating that potential new competitors in the Las Vegas market face high barriers to entry, the most significant being a legal license. Since July 1, 1987, Nevada law has barred major oil refiners from entering the market and directly operating gasoline stations. The law contains a "grandfather" provision that permitted existing company-operated stations to remain. At the time, ARCO owned 15 stations in Las Vegas, far more than any other major oil company. Because major oil refiners, which includes all Los Angeles refiners, are barred from entering, Rebel contended that only independent "chain" marketers or individual entrepreneurs are candidates to enter the Las Vegas retail gasoline market. Rebel claims that neither is capable of effectively competing with ARCO.

Rebel's experts contend that the unique nature and structure of the gasoline market in Las Vegas is a barrier to independent "chain" marketers who would seek to enter the market. Rebel argues there is no year-round independent source of wholesale gasoline in Las Vegas, demonstrated by the fact that 95 percent of the gasoline sold in Las Vegas arrives via the Cal–Nev pipeline. The Cal–Nev pipeline requires a minimum shipment of 420,000 gallons. Rebel's experts contend that because costs and quality maintenance limit storage of any shipment to one month, a new entrant must have the capacity to sell 420,000 gallons a month, which would require the acquisition of 10 to 15 retail outlets.

Apart from the large capital investment associated with opening and operating 10 to 15 stations, Rebel contends that both independent "chain" marketers and individual entrepreneurs would have trouble ensuring a reliable wholesale supply of gasoline at a competitive price, for two reasons. First, wholesale sellers will simply note market conditions and raise their wholesale prices, seizing the excess profits that are made available if ARCO raises its prices. Rebel's expert contends that historical data indicates that wholesale sellers have behaved in this manner. Second, since 1989, regulations in Clark

County, Nevada, have required the use of oxygenated gasoline during six months each year. ARCO uses ethanol as an oxygenate, which is 3 cents per gallon cheaper than Methyl Tertiary Butyl Ether (MTBE), the oxygenate used by every other wholesale supplier. Rebel claims this is a significant cost disadvantage to new entrants. Rebel also introduced affidavits indicating that high capital costs of $7.5 to $15 million, the unavailability of loan capital, and the "chilling" effect of ARCO's prior predatory behavior discouraged potential new competitors in the market.

Assertions in expert affidavits do not automatically create a genuine issue of material fact. * * * [W]e are obligated to look at the record to determine whether, in light of any undisputed facts, the inferences to be drawn from the expert's affidavits are reasonable.

It is undisputed that seven independent marketers, operating a total of 17 stations, entered the Las Vegas market between 1983 and 1990, not counting attempted entrants who failed in their first year of operation. Most of the new rivals entered before 1988. Only two rivals entered after 1988, operating one station apiece.

Undisputed evidence of entry between 1983 and 1990, the alleged predation period, might contradict an inference that ARCO engaged in predatory pricing during that period, as a firm is unlikely to enter a market when a rival is selling products below cost. But it does not necessarily contradict the threat of market power, which is the issue in this appeal. The crux of Rebel's argument is that ARCO obtained or has come close to obtaining market power since the enactment of the Divorcement Law and the oxygenate regulations in 1987 and 1988, respectively. We know of no authority that would require, as proof of market power, evidence of entry barriers throughout the period of predation. Indeed, predatory claims, including Rebel's, suggest that market power is not gained until after years of below-cost pricing, during which competitors exit the market and the defendant's market share increases. To determine whether Rebel's claim of entry barriers is reasonable, we must consider those entries occurring *after* 1988, when the alleged barriers were in place and when ARCO allegedly obtained the power to charge supracompetitive prices.

The fact that entry has occurred does not necessarily preclude the existence of "significant" entry barriers. If the output or capacity of the new entrant is insufficient to take significant business away from the predator, they are unlikely to represent a challenge to the predator's market power. *See* * * * Department of Justice Merger Guidelines § 3.0 (1992) (entry must be "timely, likely, and sufficient in magnitude, character and scope to deter or counteract the [anti]competitive effects of concern"). Barriers may still be "significant" if the market is unable to correct itself despite the entry of small rivals. This is the position taken by Rebel's expert. He claims the new entry after 1988 was *de minimis* because the new rivals were "all small independent dealers with insignificant volumes, whose operations do not contradict the existence of barriers to entry in the Las Vegas market."

* * *

* * * The conclusion of Rebel's expert that "significant" entry barriers were erected by the Nevada Divorcement Law and the oxygenate regulations

is not contradicted or rendered unreasonable by the fact that two small rivals entered the market after the enactment of these laws. ARCO operates or supplies 53 "ARCO"-branded gas stations. A juror could reasonably conclude that two gasoline stations would have insufficient capacity to offset supracompetitive pricing by a would-be monopolist. Rebel's evidence on entry barriers is sufficient to create a genuine issue of material fact, but this does not end our inquiry.

Market power cannot be inferred solely from the existence of entry barriers and a dominant market share. The ability to control output and prices—the essence of market power—depends largely on the ability of existing firms to quickly increase their own output in response to a contraction by the defendant. Competitors may not be able to increase output if there are barriers to expansion. One such barrier is lack of excess capacity. Excess capacity is the capacity of the rivals in a market to produce more than the market demands at a competitive price. If existing competitors are producing at full capacity, they may lack the ability to quickly expand supply and counteract a predator's supracompetitive pricing. On the other hand, if rivals have idle plants and can quickly respond to any predator's attempt to raise prices above competitive levels, the predator will suffer an immediate loss of market share to competitors. In that instance, the predator does not have market power.

Excess capacity is a technical concept that is difficult to measure without an analysis of a firm's costs. Instead, evidence of past output expansion may be used as a surrogate. If there is undisputed evidence indicating that competitors have expanded output in the recent past, or have the ability to expand output in the future, summary disposition may be appropriate. Prior expansion by competitors would suggest that the defendant during that expansion lacked the market power to control marketwide output in the first place. If a firm has not obtained that power and is not reasonably close to obtaining it, "it matters little that high barriers to entry exist to help that firm maintain a monopoly power it could never achieve."

On this point, Rebel's claim of attempted monopolization falters. It is undisputed that in 1988 and 1989 two firms, Texaco and Southland, expanded their operations in Las Vegas by acquiring the assets of exiting or bankrupt rivals. Texaco acquired 14 gasoline stations from the Exxon Corporation and turned the stations into dealerships. Another 21 former "Circle K" outlets became Texaco dealerships while "Circle K" was in bankruptcy, and another 5 "Jet" stations became Texaco dealerships. In addition, the Southland Corporation added 32 more stores to its chain of "7–11" stores by acquiring the assets of "Stop N Go" markets in Las Vegas.

Rebel argues that these acquisitions do not prove "expansion" occurred, because the acquisitions involved gasoline stations already in the market. The upshot of Rebel's argument apparently is that because there is no increase in stations, Texaco and Southland dealers have no ability to increase *marketwide* output than they did before the acquisition. Rebel's argument ignores an important fact: gasoline stations do not produce gasoline. Stations are merely retail distribution outlets. Gasoline is produced in Los Angeles refineries, then shipped to Las Vegas via the Cal–Nev pipeline. Competitors do not have to build more gas stations to satisfy customers' wants. They can simply purchase and transport more gasoline via the pipeline. This means that, where sufficient competing retail outlets exist, a would-be monopolist must control marketwide output at the *wholesale* supply level in order to pose any threat of monopolizing the *retail* market. In essence, Rebel must show that ARCO had monopoly power, or was dangerously close to achieving it, at the wholesale supply level.

As the expansion by Texaco and Southland suggests, the wholesale gasoline supply in Las Vegas is highly elastic, which does not support an inference that ARCO controls the supply of wholesale gasoline. * * * The expansion suggests that if ARCO attempted to curtail the total volume of gasoline sold to Las Vegas motorists, existing competitors could easily offset that action by delivering more gasoline. The expansion contradicts Rebel's position that ARCO is reasonably close to controlling the gasoline supply and retail gasoline prices.

* * *

* * * Rebel failed to establish a genuine issue of material fact on market power to support its attempted monopolization claim. Although there is a genuine issue regarding market share and entry barriers, there appears to be no genuine issue regarding the ability of ARCO's existing competitors to increase their output. The undisputed record indicates that the gasoline supply in Las Vegas is highly elastic and that competitors could increase their output if ARCO raised prices. Consequently, Rebel failed to produce sufficient evidence to support a finding that ARCO is dangerously close to obtaining the power to monopolize the market. Rebel's failure to make a sufficient showing of market power demonstrates that ARCO's alleged predatory pricing has not threatened consumer welfare in a manner cognizable under § 2 of the Sherman Act. For this reason, Rebel cannot obtain damages, because any injury from ARCO's alleged below-cost pricing is not antitrust injury under Sherman Act § 2.

* * *

How did the Ninth Circuit in *Rebel Oil* integrate entry into the existing legal framework for analyzing a claim of monopolization? How did the court use the Horizontal Merger Guidelines to explain the relevance of entry to Section 2 Sherman Act analysis? Would the rationale for its incorporation into monopolization also support its inclusion as a relevant factor under a rule of reason analysis under Section 1 of the Sherman Act?

How did the court define "entry"? What did it mean by its use of "entry barriers"? Recall again the testimony of the *Microsoft* economists—was the Ninth Circuit's definition of "entry barriers" here more consistent with the approach of any of the experts? How do these "barriers" to entry affect the analysis of the competitive effects of the defendant's conduct? What kind of evidence of conditions of entry did it consider? How did it weight that evidence? What was the ultimate import, if any, of the court's analysis of entry?

Note on Allocating the Burden of Production With Respect to Entry

The Ninth Circuit revisited the question of entry shortly after *Rebel Oil* in *Image Technical Servs., Inc. v. Eastman Kodak Co.*, 125 F.3d 1195 (9th Cir.1997), on remand from the Supreme Court. Again integrating entry as a factor relevant to the monopoly power requirement of a claim of monopolization, the court reasoned that "[b]arriers to entry 'must be capable of constraining the normal operation of the market to the extent that the problem is unlikely to be self-correcting.'" 125 F.3d at 1208—quoting *Rebel Oil*, which in turn was relying on one of the Ninth Circuit's most significant treatments of entry in the merger context, *United States v. Syufy Enters.*, 903 F.2d 659, 663 (9th Cir.1990).

Kodak implicitly argued that it was the *plaintiffs's* burden to prove there were meaningful entry barriers. Without directly questioning that allocation of burdens, the Ninth Circuit rejected Kodak's position as inconsistent with the record evidence:

> Kodak has 220 patents and controls its designs and tools, brand name power and manufacturing capability. Kodak controls original equipment manufacturers through various contract arrangements. Kodak has consistently maintained a high share of the service market. These factors together with the economies of scale, support a finding of high barriers to entry by new manufacturers and to increased output by established suppliers.

125 F.3d at 1208. With respect to burdens, the court then noted that Kodak "fail[ed] to rebut this evidence." *Id.* The court concluded that "[a]lthough some new entry was possible, the record reflects substantial evidence of entry barriers sufficient to prevent Kodak's monopoly from self-correcting." *Id.*

Note that, as in *Rebel Oil*, the court ties the entry inquiry directly to competitive effects. The relevant question is thus not the abstract—"Is entry easy?"—rather it is "Is entry easy enough to solve the competitive problem here?" This focus is analogous to the Horizontal Merger Guidelines' requirement that entry be "sufficient" to solve the competitive problem. Entry, therefore, will be a fact-specific inquiry tied to the competitive problem under investigation.

It is also worth noting that the court appeared to view entry as relevant to the burdens of production of both parties. Yet, it appeared to allocate the initial burden of producing evidence of difficult entry to the *plaintiff*, who had to make an initial showing that entry was relatively difficult in order to support its claim of monopoly power. Both *Rebel Oil* and *Kodak* thus hold that the plaintiff must initially come forward with entry evidence as an element of its proof of monopoly power when it elects to do so by circumstantial evidence. According to the Ninth Circuit, the plaintiff must "(1) define the relevant market, (2) show that the defendant owns a dominant share of that market, and (3) *show that there are significant barriers to entry and show that existing competitors lack the capacity to increase their output in the short run.*" *Kodak*, 125 F.3d at 1202 (*quoting, Rebel Oil*, 51 F.3d at 1434) (emphasis added). Kodak was faulted not for failing to prove that entry was easy, therefore, but for failing "to rebut" the plaintiff's evidence that entry would not serve as an antidote to Kodak's monopoly power. *See also Broadcom Corp. v. Qualcomm Inc.*, 501 F.3d 297, 307 (3d Cir. 2007) ("To support an inference of monopoly power, a plaintiff typically must plead and prove that a firm has a dominant share in a relevant market, and that significant 'entry barriers' protect that market."); *Western Parcel Express v. United Parcel Serv. of*

Am., 190 F.3d 974, 976 (9th Cir.1999) (plaintiff "failed to present evidence that there were barriers to expansion in the relevant market").

Like the Merger Guidelines, therefore, the Ninth Circuit ties the entry inquiry directly to competitive effects. But it may be at odds with the Guidelines with respect to allocating burdens of production.

As we noted in Chapter 5, the Merger Guidelines disavow any interest in specifying burdens of proof. *Horizontal Merger Guidelines*, § 0.1 ("[T]he Guidelines do not attempt to assign the burden of proof, or the burden of coming forward with evidence, on any particular issue."). Yet on the question of entry, the overall analytical structure of the Guidelines to some extent arguably implies that entry—at least committed entry—is considered only after an initial evaluation of market concentration and competitive effects suggests that a merger is likely to present a competitive problem.

Recall also from Chapter 5 that the Merger Guidelines distinguish between "uncommitted" and "committed" entry. Uncommitted entrants are included in the relevant market for purposes of calculating market shares and HHIs and thus form part of the evaluation of market concentration. Committed entrants are not evaluated until later in the Guidelines, after market definition, market concentration, and competitive effects have been evaluated and suggest a competitive problem. The Guidelines's standard at that stage of analysis—that committed entry be "timely, likely, and sufficient"—thus analytically appears to be associated with *rebutting* a case of effects already established, or a hypothetical one.

Although the Guidelines were designed solely as a Guide to the exercise of prosecutorial discretion, we observed in Chapter 5 that they have very much been integrated into the judicial analysis of mergers. When they made the transition to the courts, therefore, it is not surprising that entry was viewed as a "defense." For example, *Waste Management* addresses entry as a "rebuttal" factor, designed to respond to the government's showing of concentration. Following *Philadelphia Nat'l Bank* and *General Dynamics*, the court discusses entry as a factor tending to undermine the presumption of anticompetitive effects associated with increased concentration. This was also true in *Baker Hughes*, which treated entry as part of its "rebuttal" analysis.

As a practical matter, the actual treatment of entry evidence by government enforcement agencies may be more varied. Entry probably does not receive very much attention in mergers that fall within the Guidelines's safe harbors. But when the FTC or Antitrust Division conclude that a Second Request is warranted as part of a merger investigation, entry evidence is likely to be included in the subjects to be pursued. Similarly, when the government proceeds to court to challenge a merger, it likely will offer whatever evidence it has available that entry will not be sufficient to solve the competitive problems posed by the merger. But the court will likely continue to apply some form of the *Philadelphia Nat'l Bank* presumption, which almost necessarily renders entry a "rebuttal" factor— and the government, like any plaintiff, may not be *required* to address entry as part of its case-in-chief.

Entry also is addressed in the *Antitrust Guidelines for Collaborations Among Competitors* (2000). These Guidelines apply to all manner of collaborations, which typically are subject to analysis under Section 1 of the Sherman Act. As do the Horizontal Merger Guidelines, the Collaboration Guidelines declare that they "neither describe how the Agencies litigate cases nor assign burdens of proof or production." *Collaboration Guidelines*, § 1.1, n.3. But also as with the Horizontal Merger Guidelines, the Collaboration Guidelines consider committed entry only after there is some evidence that a given collaboration will likely produce anticompetitive effects, suggesting that entry is a "rebuttal" factor. And the Guidelines embrace the same three part test of "timely, likely, and sufficient" that is the cornerstone of the Merger Guidelines's approach to entry: "Where the nature of the agreement and market share and concentration data suggest a likelihood of anticompetitive harm * * * the Agencies inquire whether entry would be timely, likely, and sufficient in magnitude, character and scope to deter or counteract the anticompetitive harm of concern." *Collaboration Guidelines*, § 3.35. Indeed, if entry meets this three part standard, the Guidelines declare that "the relevant agreement ordinarily requires no further analysis." *Id.*

The Collaboration Guidelines also make some specific adaptations to entry analysis in order to satisfy the specific demands of the collaboration context. These adaptations flow from features of the typical collaboration that may distinguish it from the typical merger in ways that alter the entry calculus. Mentioned differences include:

- collaborations may have a more limited scope than mergers, restricting only certain business activities of the collaborating firms;

- collaboration agreements typically are limited in duration, in contrast to the permanence of mergers;

- some entrants may be participants in the agreement, which may restrict or totally eliminate the chance that they will enter independently, and increase the cost of entry for non-participating firms.

How might each of these factors affect the analysis of entry? Will they make entry analysis easier or more complex as a general matter than in the merger context? Does each factor make it more or less probable that entry will be sufficient to solve any competitive problem? Do they suggest that entry should be evaluated differently in Section 1 Sherman Act cases as compared to Section 7 Clayton Act mergers? From Section 2 Sherman Act monopolization claims, such as those in *Rebel Oil* and *Kodak*?

Beyond questioning whether the burden of producing evidence of entry may be different under Sections 1 and 2 of the Sherman Act and Section 7 of the Clayton Act, some additional questions loom. Can such differences be justified analytically? On what basis? Are the examples provided in the Collaboration Guidelines persuasive? Comprehensive? Which party, if any, is likely to be in the better position to assemble evidence of entry? Who, analytically, *should* have to?

———

We first examined our next case, *Tops Markets*, earlier in this Chapter in connection with proving anticompetitive effect. The portion excerpted there was limited to the court's consideration of the plaintiff's Section 1 Sherman Act claim. Produced here is an excerpt from the court's subsequent treatment and rejection of the plaintiff's Section 2 claim. Note the critical role that entry plays in that conclusion, and note, too, how the court allocates the burden of production on the parties with respect to entry.

TOPS MARKETS, INC. v. QUALITY MARKETS, INC.
United States Court of Appeals for the Second Circuit, 1998.
142 F.3d 90.

Before: FEINBERG, CARDAMONE, and WALKER, Circuit Judges.

CARDAMONE, Circuit Judge:

[The facts of the case and its treatment of the plaintiff's Sherman Act Section 1 claims are reproduced *supra*, at 937. Eds.]

* * *

II THE SHERMAN ACT, § 2
* * *

The district court granted summary judgment in favor of defendants regarding Tops' claim for completed monopolization. It held, as a matter of law, without even addressing the issue of defendants' conduct, that Quality lacked the requisite monopoly power. We must therefore carefully consider whether the relevant evidence created an issue of fact for the jury regarding monopoly power.

Monopoly power, also referred to as market power, is "the power to control prices or exclude competition." *United States v. E.I. du Pont de Nemours & Co.*, 351 U.S. 377, 391, 76 S.Ct. 994, 1005, 100 L.Ed. 1264 (1956). It may be proven directly by evidence of the control of prices or the exclusion of competition, or it may be inferred from one firm's large percentage share of the relevant market. Tops sought to prove Quality's monopoly power by proffering evidence on both points.

With respect to direct evidence, plaintiff produced the Kennedy Affidavit, which explained Quality's potential ability to control prices in the following terms:

> Currently, consumers in general must choose between Wegmans and a Quality store which will almost always be closer to their homes than Wegmans' Ellicott facility. Those Jamestown area residents living in outlying areas will most likely find it less convenient and impracticable (especially for purchases of perishable goods) to shop at Wegmans. This scenario would certainly endow Quality with the power to raise prices and limit both selections of grocery items and services *unless the competitive structure of the industry were to change*, i.e., *unless another competitor were to open a centrally located store which would give the majority of consumers a meaningful choice as to where to fill their weekly grocery list.*

Kennedy's conclusion expressly assumes, without offering any support, that no other competitors would enter the market were Quality to raise its prices. This proposition suggesting Quality's purported monopoly power is too speculative to create an issue of fact for the jury. It neither demonstrates Quality's present ability to raise prices, nor evidences the exclusion of competition from the Jamestown market area.

Tops next presented evidence of Quality's high market share in the Jamestown market to establish indirectly Quality's monopoly power. While market share is not the functional equivalent of monopoly power, it nevertheless is highly relevant to the determination of monopoly power. A court may infer monopoly power from a high market share. *See [United States v.]*

Grinnell, 384 U.S. [563 (1966)] at 571, 86 S.Ct. at 1704 ("The existence of [monopoly] power ordinarily may be inferred from the predominant share of the market."); *Broadway Delivery Corp. v. United Parcel Serv. of America, Inc.*, 651 F.2d 122, 129 (2d Cir.1981) ("[T]he higher a market share, the stronger is the inference of monopoly power."); *cf. United States v. Philadelphia Nat'l Bank*, 374 U.S. 321, 363, 83 S.Ct. 1715, 1741–42, 10 L.Ed.2d 915 (1963) (explaining that where a merger results in one firm controlling a high percentage of the relevant market, it is inherently likely to lessen competition substantially).

A court will draw an inference of monopoly power only after full consideration of the relationship between market share and other relevant market characteristics. These characteristics include the "strength of the competition, the probable development of the industry, the barriers to entry, the nature of the anticompetitive conduct and the elasticity of consumer demand."

In the case at hand, Tops presented evidence that Quality's share of the total sales of food items and general household merchandise by Jamestown area supermarkets always exceeded 72 percent. At the time Quality contracted with Paige in 1992 to purchase the Washington Street property, Quality's market share stood at roughly 73 percent. After its acquisition and closing of the "Bells" and "Super Duper" stores and the opening of the Wegmans store, Quality's share steadied at 74 percent in 1995.

Tops asks us to infer Quality's monopoly power from these statistics. We have held that a market share of over 70 percent is usually "strong evidence" of monopoly power. Nonetheless, such evidence does not conclusively establish Quality's monopoly power.

At this juncture, either plaintiff or defendants may introduce evidence regarding these other market factors to determine whether Quality possessed monopoly power. *See* 2A Phillip E. Areeda & Herbert Hovenkamp, *Antitrust Law,* § 532a, at 161 (1995) ("[T]he courts generally allow the defendant to rebut inferences of market power by showing easy entry conditions."). The Quality defendants point to several facts in the record suggesting there are no barriers to entry, and Tops failed to produce any further evidence to rebut this assertion. Tops alleges that site availability in the Jamestown market was extremely limited, but offers no proof demonstrating what geographic barriers inhibit a competitor's ability to enter that market. Instead, the record suggests that undeveloped land on which to locate a supermarket has been available at all relevant times throughout the market area. As already noted, Wegmans, a major competitor of Quality, opened a 100,000 square foot store at a different site in 1995 and quickly gained a respectable share of the market. Even Tops' own contemporaneous market studies indicate that Quality did not have such a strong market position as to enable it to exclude competitors. According to these studies, competitors, like Tops and Wegmans, could readily enter the Jamestown market at any number of available sites and successfully compete for supermarket sales.

We agree with Judge Elfvin's conclusion that as a matter of law, despite evidence of Quality's high market share, consideration of other relevant factors does not support a conclusion that Quality did, in fact, possess monopoly power. We cannot be blinded by market share figures and ignore marketplace realities, such as the relative ease of competitive entry. Had

Wegmans not gained such a high market share within such a short period, we might recognize at least a *genuine* issue of material fact as to monopoly power, in light of Quality's over—70 percent market share. Wegmans' successful entry, however, itself refutes any inference of the existence of monopoly power that might be drawn from Quality's market share. If Quality were to raise its prices above their competitive level, new competitors could and would enter the market and, by undercutting those prices, quickly erode Quality's market share.

On this record we can draw no reasonable inference other than that Quality lacks monopoly power. Despite its high market share, no other evidence—such as barriers to entry, the elasticity of demand, or the nature of defendant's conduct—supports the conclusion that Quality can control prices or exclude competition and in fact, Wegmans' quick garnishment of such high market share dispositively refutes such a conclusion. Thus, absent a showing of Quality's monopoly power, Tops' claim for completed monopolization was properly dismissed.

* * *

————

Is there any evidence in *Tops* that the court applied the "timely, likely and sufficient" standard outlined in the Horizontal Merger and Collaboration Guidelines? Did the court offer any evidentiary support for its critical conclusion that "If Quality were to raise its prices above their competitive level, new competitors could and would enter the market and, by undercutting those prices, quickly erode Quality's market share"? Wasn't that what the plaintiff was in fact trying to do, but was precluded from doing by Quality's conduct?

Consider *Rebel Oil* and *Tops Markets* together. What definition of "entry barriers" did each court use? Was it the same? If not, did the difference in definition affect the court's evaluation of entry? *Tops Markets*, you will recall, was also brought as a Section 1 case. Should the court's analysis of entry with respect to the Section 2 claim have relevance as well to the Section 1 analysis? If so, how?

Recall, as well, the central role that entry conditions played in the *Microsoft* case, where the analysis of entry was considered to be an integral aspect of the evaluation of Microsoft's monopoly power. Again, consider how the economists defined "entry barrier" in that case. How was entry treated in terms of the parties' respective burden of production? Did the government economists presume that monopoly power could not be shown without demonstrating that entry was difficult? Did Microsoft's economist undertake to "rebut" the government's showing of difficult entry? What did the Court of Appeals conclude? Sidebar 8–6, which follows, more fully examines the proof problems that can arise in connection with inquiries regarding conditions of entry.

Sidebar 8–6:
Defining and Proving Entry Conditions

Economists have long recognized that an attempt to exercise market power could be defeated or deterred by new supply entering the market. But antitrust law largely ignored this possibility until the mid–1970s, when two appeals courts rejected monopolization allegations by defining broad product markets to account for the possibility of supply substitution. *See Telex Corp. v. IBM Corp.,* 510 F.2d 894 (10th Cir.1975); *Twin City Sportservice, Inc. v. Charles O. Finley & Co.,* 512 F.2d 1264 (9th Cir.1975). When the courts began to take seriously the possibility that entry, or just the potential for entry, could prevent even so-called monopolists from exercising market power, they looked to the economic literature on entry for guidance. This Sidebar describes an economic debate over the appropriate definition of "entry barriers," looks at how the courts have reacted to that debate, and discusses types of evidence commonly relied upon in litigation for identifying and drawing conclusions about conditions of entry.

Economic Debates

The economic analysis of new competition before the mid–1970s was dominated by the contrasting views of two pioneering industrial organization economists, Joe S. Bain and George Stigler, on defining "barriers to entry." *See generally* Janusz A. Ordover & Daniel M. Wall, *Proving Entry Barriers: A Practical Guide to the Economics of New Entry,* ANTITRUST, Winter 1988, at 12 ("Proving Entry Barriers"); Gregory J. Werden, *Network Effects and Conditions of Entry: Lessons from the* Microsoft *Case,* 69 ANTITRUST L.J. 87, 97–100 (2001) (reviewing the economic literature on "barriers to entry"). Bain was interested in the effect of market structure on firm conduct and industry performance. He emphasized the way a range of structural factors created entry barriers, preventing new competition even when incumbents' prices exceeded competitive levels (which might be expected to attract entry). Bain's list of important entry barriers included absolute cost advantages of incumbents, product differentiation, and economies of scale (lower costs attributable to increases in output and sales). JOE S. BAIN, BARRIERS TO NEW COMPETITION (1956).

Stigler, too, was interested in the determinants of market concentration. But his approach to the question could be read as resisting the interventionist implications of Bain's analysis of entry barriers. Some of Stigler's fire was directed at the claim that high capital requirements could prevent new competition when incumbents were exercising market power. GEORGE STIGLER, THE ORGANIZATION OF INDUSTRY 113–22 (1968). He questioned the once common appeal to "imperfections-in-the-capital-market" by asking whether even large capital requirements would stand in the way of a firm seeking to finance a reasonable entry plan, given the wide range of well-funded participants in financial and credit markets.*

---

* Many modern commentators follow Stigler's lead in suggesting that capital markets generally work well enough so as to permit entrants to obtain financing for plausible entry plans without penalty relative to financing costs borne by incumbents. But others ques-

CONSTRUCTING THE MODERN ANTITRUST CASE

In analyzing entry, as elsewhere in Chicago School critiques of structural era antitrust, Stigler suggested that many practices previously thought harmful to competition in fact reflected healthy competition. He defined entry barriers as the *additional long-run costs that must be incurred by an entrant relative to the long-run costs faced by incumbent firms*. GEORGE STIGLER, THE ORGANIZATION OF INDUSTRY 67–70 (1968). This definition might include the possibility, of great concern to Chicago School antitrust commentators, that entry would be prevented by regulation, patents, tariffs or other government action. But if incumbents obtained an advantage over entrants by being first to make expenditures that entrants would need to replicate in order to compete, or if the market could not support multiple firms at the scale needed to achieve low costs, those advantages should merely be seen as an appropriate reward that competition provides to the incumbent, who had the foresight or luck to enter first.

Stigler's definition of entry barriers thus excluded multiple factors that Bain had suggested might inhibit new competition when incumbent firms were charging prices above the competitive level. Scale economies would not count when entrants could, in principle, achieve comparably low costs through internal growth. Product differentiation also would not count, unless the costs of advertising, product design or other means of achieving differentiation were higher for a new firm than for an incumbent firm. Accordingly, Stigler's perspective on entry barriers suggested more permissive antitrust standards than did Bain's.

Can the dispute between the economic experts in the *Microsoft* litigation—between Warren–Boulton and Fisher on the government side and Schmalensee on the defense side—be understood as an argument about whether to apply a Bainian or Stiglerian definition of entry barriers? *See* Werden, 69 ANTITRUST L.J. at 100 (concluding that Schmalensee adopted what is essentially Stigler's definition to reject the applications barrier to entry as a matter of definition).

During the 1970s, economists began to look at entry deterrence in strategic terms. *See generally* Steven C. Salop, *Strategic Entry Deterrence*, 69 AM. ECON. REV. 335 (1979) (Papers and Proceedings issue, May, 1979); Richard J. Gilbert, *Mobility Barriers and the Value of Incumbency*, *in* 1 HANDBOOK OF INDUSTRIAL ORGANIZATION 475 (Richard Schmalensee & Robert D. Willig, eds., 1989). This work focused on the significance of "sunk" costs, that is expenditures by entrants that could not be recouped in the event the firm were later to exit. If the fixed costs of entry are not sunk, and entrants have variable costs comparable to those of incumbents, the market is "contestable" and performs competitively regardless of market concentration among incumbent sellers. WILLIAM J. BAUMOL, ET AL., CONTEST-

---

tion whether financial markets invariably work this well, citing adverse selection and moral hazard problems endemic to capital markets that may limit the availability of capital and thus make it difficult for worthy firms to convince lenders of the promise of their entry plans. *See, e.g.,* Joseph E. Stiglitz & Andrew Weiss, *Credit Rationing in Markets with Imperfect Information*, 71 AM. ECON. REV. 912 (1983). Capital market imperfections could, for example, make predatory pricing a viable strat-egy. Patrick Bolton, et al., *Predatory Pricing: Strategic Theory and Legal Policy*, 88 GEO. L. J. 2239, 2285–99 (2000). It is possible that discrimination by race and gender could create imperfections in capital markets, limiting the ability of some borrowers to obtain financing for promising projects. *Cf.* Ian Ayers, *Fair Driving: Gender and Race Discrimination in Retail Car Negotiations*, 104 HARV. L. REV. 817 (1991) (discussing possible discrimination in automobile retailing).

ABLE MARKETS AND THE THEORY OF INDUSTRY STRUCTURE (1982). But if entry requires sunk expenditures (irreversible investments), and incumbents would be expected to react quickly to cut price in response to entry, entry may be deterred even if the pre-entry price exceeds competitive levels. This may occur because the prospective entrant, recognizing the prospect of post-entry competition, will not expect to earn a contribution margin (revenues less variable costs) adequate to cover its own sunk costs.

The strategic approach to understanding entry conditions offered industrial organization economists a way to transcend the old debate between Bain and Stigler. It explained that high fixed expenditures by entrants could, under some circumstances, deter entry, even if the expenditures merely mimicked costs previously borne by incumbents. That might occur if fixed expenditures would also be sunk. The categories of fixed expenditures highlighted by Bain—including the product design and advertising expenditures that often underlie product differentiation, and the up front costs of developing a large production facility—often are irreversible to a significant extent. That is, much of the brand reputation and product development costs may not be transferrable to another product if entry does not succeed. The plant and equipment used to produce a new product may have no other use, and would merely be sold as scrap in the event of exit. If so, the presence of these fixed (and sunk) expenditures may deter entry, as Bain supposed. But if the same fixed expenditures would not be sunk, entry would not be deterred, as those following Stigler suggested. The economic logic of strategic entry deterrence underlies the analysis of the "likelihood" of entry in the Horizontal Merger Guidelines.

Entry in the Courts

The courts have followed the economists in disputing whether Bain or Stigler's definition of entry barriers should be preferred. In a merger case decided in 1985, the Federal Trade Commission formally adopted Stigler's definition, but nonetheless effectively accepted Bain's approach. Although the term "barrier to entry" was defined in terms of long run cost disadvantages of an entrant relative to incumbents, the FTC went on to agree with Bain by identifying an entry "impediment" as any condition that necessarily delays entry, allowing market power to be exercised in the interim. *In re Echlin Mfg. Co.*, 105 F.T.C. 479, 485–86 (1985).

Some circuit courts appear to follow Bain in focusing on the marketplace consequences of market structure rather than upon a comparison of entrant costs with incumbent costs. *See, e.g., Rebel Oil Co. v. Atlantic Richfield Co.*, 51 F.3d 1421, 1440 (9th Cir.1995) (recognizing that entry, even if easy for some firms, may be insufficient to solve a competitive problem arising from monopolization "if the market is unable to correct itself despite the entry of small rivals"); *Colorado Interstate Gas v. Natural Gas Pipeline*, 885 F.2d 683, 695 n. 21 (10th Cir.1989). But the Third Circuit has appeared sympathetic to a Stiglerian perspective by rejecting high capital requirements and the need for sellers to develop a reputation for delivering a quality good or service as entry barriers. *Advo, Inc. v. Philadelphia Newspapers, Inc.*, 51 F.3d 1191, 1200–02 (3d Cir. 1995). The Stigler–Bain debate also arose in *Microsoft*. Inquiring whether "costs borne by all market participants should be considered entry barriers"—effectively, the choice between Bain and Stigler—the D.C.

Circuit nevertheless side-stepped the issue, noting that although the question was "the subject of much debate," it "need not resolve" it in order to find entry barriers into the operating system market monopolized by Microsoft. *United States v. Microsoft Corp.*, 253 F.3d 34, 56 (D.C. Cir. 2001).

The courts have largely not addressed the modern economic argument that sunk investments could discourage entry. Although that argument was rejected in *United States v. Syufy Enters.*, 903 F.2d 659 (9th Cir.1990), it was arguably misunderstood. Jonathan B. Baker, *The Problem with* Baker Hughes *and* Syufy: *On the Role of Entry in Merger Analysis*, 65 ANTITRUST L.J. 353, 369–70 (1997).

Entry Evidence

What evidence should count in favor or against the proposition that entry, or its threat, would prevent the exercise of market power? Entry has not been the subject of as much analysis in the courts outside the merger setting as it has been under Clayton Act § 7. One important potential difference is that the alleged competitive harm from a merger is typically evaluated prospectively—the question is whether entry in the future will solve a potential competitive problem. In contrast, the alleged competitive harm from Sherman Act violations, such as monopolization, is more often evaluated retrospectively—here the question is whether entry (or its threat) in fact prevented the alleged harm from occurring. Entry evidence thus cannot be assessed in a vacuum (as "barriers" with "height" analyzed in the abstract); entry conditions are relevant only to the extent that new competition would cure the competitive problem at issue, so entry evidence must be analyzed with reference to the allegations before the court.

Some courts that find for defendants in monopolization cases have inferred that entry is easy based upon evidence that firms have actually entered the market with seemingly little difficulty. *See, e.g., Tops Markets, Inc. v. Quality Markets, Inc.*, 142 F.3d 90, 99 (2d Cir.1998). Such evidence must be analyzed with care to ensure that it is probative. For example, before accepting such evidence in a case where the alleged harm is retrospective and defendants claim entry cured the problem, a court could look at, among other things, the price effects of entry and the success or difficulties entrants faced in capturing business. Where the alleged harm would be prospective, a court could reasonably ask whether entrants today can employ the same approaches as were successful in the past, whether they could do so as cheaply as did their predecessors, and whether entrants today could reasonably expect to receive as high a price as did their predecessors (who may have entered when there was less post-entry competition or when the market was larger).

Two commentators have explained that evidence of past entry may be "double-edged," consistent with either low entry barriers in the past or the past exercise of market power. Ordover & Wall, *Proving Entry Barriers, supra* at 13 (if the market has experienced "a reasonable amount" of entry and exit in response to market signals like price fluctuations or changes in cost, then "the plausible inference can usually be made that conditions of entry and exit do not unduly favor incumbent firms over potential entrants," but entry under such conditions "does not necessarily prove the absence of barriers" because the market may not be behaving competitively, "thus creating opportunities for entrants that should not be there"). Similarly, the absence of past entry could be consistent either with a competitive market or entry barriers. *Id.* at 13–14.

Particularly when the alleged harm is prospective, courts have analyzed the likely entry plan, perhaps modeling that plan on recent examples of successful and unsuccessful entry. They may then evaluate whether the inputs that an entrant must assemble to succeed can be obtained quickly and easily. *See, e.g., Advo, Inc. v. Philadelphia Newspapers, Inc.,* 51 F.3d 1191, 1200–02 (3d Cir.1995) (recoupment of losses from below-cost pricing unlikely because entry would prevent price increases). By contrast, if even the best-situated potential entrants could not surmount the difficulties of doing so rapidly, entry may be found insufficient to solve the competitive problem. *See, e.g., United States v. Microsoft Corp.,* 253 F.3d 34, 56 (D.C. Cir. 2001); *United States v. United Tote, Inc.,* 768 F.Supp. 1064 (D. Del. 1991) (entry would not prevent harm from merger). Even if such inputs can be assembled easily, a court could reasonably go on to ask whether, considering additional factors such as the size of the market and the likely extent of post-entry competition, entry would be profitable, and thus likely to counteract or deter the exercise of market power. Ordover & Wall, *Proving Entry Barriers, supra* at 14. By framing the question this way, the courts would focus on whether entry *would* be likely to solve the competitive problem, not merely on whether new competition *could* in theory do so, in harmony to the way committed entry is analyzed under the Merger and Collaboration Guidelines.

F. REBUTTING THE CONTEMPORARY AN-TITRUST CASE: THE ROLE OF BUSINESS JUSTIFICATIONS AND EFFICIENCIES

INTRODUCTION

"Business justifications," including "efficiencies," in various forms, have been important factors in antitrust analysis for almost all of its history. The great trusts argued that their size and conduct were the mere consequence of economies of scale and cost advantages. And parties to horizontal mergers urged for many years before the Horizontal Merger Guidelines embraced the subject more squarely that mergers were driven by a desire to lower costs, not to attain monopoly power. *Alcoa's* recognition that a monopoly achieved through "skill, foresight and business acumen" was also a tacit recognition that efficiencies should be a defense to inferences of anticompetitive effects drawn from other factors, a recognition made more formal in *Aspen Skiing* when the Supreme Court squarely considered the "business justifications" offered by Aspen Skiing Company for its exclusionary conduct.

Business justifications generally divide into the economic and non-economic, with efficiency, broadly conceived, accounting for the bulk of the economic claims. As was true with entry, therefore, we begin with some very fundamental questions:

- What do we mean by "efficiencies"? Are they always cost-reducing? Output-enhancing? Are there other, non-cost and output related kinds of efficiencies?

- How can efficiencies be proved in the non-merger context, where actual effects and efficiencies, not mere predictions, are likely to be at issue? What are the sources of evidence of efficiencies?

- Why should efficiencies or other business explanations for seemingly anticompetitive conduct "justify" that conduct? How can their effects be "balanced" against evidence of anticompetitive effect? Will the nature of the evidence of anticompetitive effect affect the process, *i.e.*, will more or different kinds of evidence of efficiency be demanded in cases based on evidence of actual anticompetitive effects? In other words, how much efficiency should counterbalance how much (and what kind) of anticompetitive effect?

- What business justifications, economic and non-economic, have the courts recognized as valid? Under what circumstances? For what purposes?

- Which party will bear the burden of producing evidence of efficiency? The burden of persuasion?

- Finally, which statutory or non-statutory defenses obviate the need for inquiry into other sorts of justifications for potentially anticompetitive conduct?

1. DEFINING AND INCORPORATING EFFICIENCIES INTO NON–MERGER ANTITRUST ANALYSIS: THE FOUNDATION CASES

We begin our more in depth examination of the role of efficiencies in non-merger analysis with two cases we have already studied—*Sylvania* and *Broadcast Music*. Few cases have had as much impact on the courts' willingness to embrace economic concepts of efficiency and incorporate them more systematically into antitrust analysis. The submersion of the rule of reason in the years preceding *Sylvania* undoubtedly forestalled serious consideration of "efficiencies," but since that time the courts have readily accepted the notion that conduct that ostensibly appears to restrain trade may instead have the effect of preventing free riding, lowering transaction costs, and facilitating other output-promoting transactions. The utility of such conduct has been recognized since *Addyston Pipe* and has been acknowledged by the Supreme Court in its recent decisions involving joint ventures and vertical restraints

. .

Through *Sylvania* and *Broadcast Music*, the Court opened wide the door to consideration of methods of improving productive and allocative efficiency as a part of the antitrust equation. Although we examined these cases at greater length in Chapters 2 and 4, we revisit them here with excerpts limited to the Court's discussion of efficiencies in each.

Note in each instance how the court equates increased output with efficiency. Why would the two go hand in hand? Why should we presume that arrangements that increase output are likely to be "efficient"? Recall that in

NCAA, evidence of *reduced* output was synonymous with anticompetitive effects. Why might output effects provide such a surrogate for distinguishing pro from anti-competitive conduct? In that connection, recall our discussion of the Coffee Shop in Chapter 1—how did the Coffee hypothetical approach these issues?

Also consider the nature and degree of evidence cited in each case by the Court. As we learned in Chapter 5, the typical inquiry into anticompetitive effects and efficiencies associated with mergers is based on prediction, because it proceeds before the transaction has been consummated. But the typical Section 1 or Section 2 case will be based on some actual market effects. How does that affect the efficiency inquiry? What sources of evidence will the parties look to in assessing efficiencies? And what quantity and quality of efficiency evidence should be demanded? Should it depend upon the strength of the evidence of anticompetitive effect?

CONTINENTAL T. V., INC. v. GTE SYLVANIA INC.

Supreme Court of the United States, 1977.
433 U.S. 36, 97 S.Ct. 2549, 53 L.Ed.2d 568.

Mr. Justice POWELL delivered the opinion of the Court.

* * *

III

[The relevant portion of the decision is reproduced in Chapter 4, *supra*, at 359–65. Eds.]

* * *

———

Sylvania, as we learned in Chapter 4, was an important watershed decision in several ways. Initially, its impact was greatest in the area it most narrowly addressed—vertical, intrabrand, non-price restraints. In jettisoning the per se rule of *Arnold, Schwinn*, *Sylvania* ignited a major renaissance in the use of distribution restraints. Since it was decided, there have been very few instances of such agreements that have been condemned under the Sherman Act. (*See* Sidebar 4–1, *supra*).

But what was the *efficiency* rationale of *Sylvania*? Why is "free-riding" a "market imperfection"? Will that always be the case? How does a supplier's decision to eliminate intrabrand free riding enhance the "efficiency" of its distribution system? Will it always be so? Before entertaining the argument that vertical restraints can help to eliminate free riding, should a court require evidence that the particular product involved in fact has a service component? That the supplier had some reason to believe that free riding is in fact a problem? If a plaintiff-dealer, offers evidence that the vertical restraint had a negative impact on intrabrand competition, such as higher prices, should the supplier have to demonstrate that the vertical restraints in fact eliminated free riding and led to greater overall output? Finally, what if there are is no contemporaneous evidence to support the assertion that a competition-restraining practice was adopted to alleviate free-riding? What if all promotional services are paid for by the manufacturer, so dealers cannot be the victims of any free-riding? With respect to these last two questions, see *Toys R Us*, 221 F.3d at 937–38.

Consider the seemingly conflicting goals outlined in footnote 24 of the *Sylvania* Court's opinion and the accompanying text. "Free-riding" may be destructive for the manufacturer if it undermines the dealer's incentive to provide services that in turn may increase demand for the manufacturer's product. Yet the provision of services typically involves some costs, which may translate into higher prices, and as the Court notes in footnote 24, to increase sales, a manufacturer facing interbrand competition has an interest in minimizing its costs of distribution. How can a manufacturer intent on increasing demand for its product best strike the balance between the increased costs (and prices) associated with demand-promoting dealer services and the potential for diminished demand from higher prices? Should a dealer be able to invoke the antitrust laws if the manufacturer strikes the balance incorrectly, *i.e.*, costs, and prices increase, but demand does not? What if a dealer terminated as a "free-rider" can establish that it provided all of the services demanded by a manufacturer, but that it did so more efficiently than its rival dealers, who consequently could not meet its lower prices and hence demanded its termination by the manufacturer? Shouldn't the manufacturer have the necessary incentive to adjust to such situations on its own, *i.e.*, without antitrust intervention? If the dealer's allegations were true, would you expect the manufacturer to praise rather than terminate the efficient dealer?

Broadcast Music, which we turn to next, provided substantial evidence that *Sylvania* had significance far beyond the law of intrabrand vertical restraints. It signaled a new mode of antitrust analysis in the Supreme Court that was driven by economic concepts, not formal legal categories, and was far more receptive to concerns about efficient business practices. Recall that the case involved the creation of the blanket license by members of BMI and ASCAP and had as profound an impact on competitor collaborations as *Sylvania* had on dealer relations.

BROADCAST MUSIC, INC. v. COLUMBIA BROADCASTING SYSTEM, INC.

Supreme Court of the United States, 1979.
441 U.S. 1, 99 S.Ct. 1551, 60 L.Ed.2d 1.

Mr. Justice WHITE delivered the opinion of the Court.

* * *

C

* * *

[The relevant portion of the decision is reproduced in Chapter 2, *supra*, at 107–14. Eds.]

* * *

———

What explains the defendants' victories in *Sylvania* and *Broadcast Music*? Did the plaintiffs fail to meet their initial burden of production as to anticompetitive effects? Did the defendants successfully rebut a presumption? Or did the plaintiffs fail to meet their burden of persuasion, once the defendants had rebutted an initial showing of anticompetitive effects through evidence of efficiencies?

What definition of "efficiency" did the Supreme Court appear to use in *Sylvania* and *BMI*? Is it clear in both cases that consumer prices would be lower? That output in the relevant markets would expand? Why, in other words, did the Court conclude in both instances that the defendants' interests were aligned with those of consumers?

As we have noted several times, *Sylvania* and *Broadcast Music* had a profound impact on antitrust analysis. After the two decisions, courts proved far more receptive to procompetitive justifications, especially when evidence of significant anticompetitive effects was unimpressive or lacking. But "efficiency" could mean many things in different contexts and may mask important value judgments about the goals of antitrust laws. And the presumption that manufacturers' and consumers' interests often align was far from non-controversial.

Note on Defining and Incorporating Efficiencies Into Non–Merger Antitrust Analysis: The Role of Expanding Output And Lower Costs

Sylvania and *Broadcast Music* focused antitrust on the analysis of efficiency to a greater degree than it had in the past. But what makes conduct "efficient" and why should that defeat or excuse a demonstration that it also may lead to anticompetitive effects?

Recall that in Chapter 1, we discussed how markets are valued for their ability to produce three distinct, but often interrelated, kinds of efficiencies: (1) allocative efficiency; (2) production efficiency; and (3) consumption efficiency. The first, allocative efficiency, refers to how a society allocates its resources generally. The second, production efficiency, typically focuses on individual firms, and asks whether they are producing their goods or services at the lowest cost. Consumption efficiency looks at buyers and asks whether the buyers that value specific products and services the most are getting them. Should courts treat different kinds of efficiencies differently for purposes of assessing the defendants' efforts to rebut evidence that specific conduct is anticompetitive? Are allocative, production, and consumption efficiencies equally important to antitrust?

Conduct that promotes output often is equated by the courts with "allocative efficiency." But *Broadcast Music* seemed to focus more on the relationship of cost-reduction to efficiency—"production efficiency." The virtue of the blanket license was its ability to reduce transaction costs. But wasn't the true virtue of lowering transaction costs the increased availability of copyrighted compositions, *i.e.*, increased output? Will conduct that reduces the costs of product development, production or distribution always lead to increased output? In either event, what is the rationale behind equating output with efficiency? And which kinds of efficiencies are at stake: allocative, production, or consumption?

We might also inquire whether buyers are ultimate beneficiaries of the purported efficiency. In other words, are the lower costs being passed on, in whole or part, in the form of lower prices? Should that matter to the antitrust analysis? Will output increase if the lower costs are not passed on? And finally, if our goal is to establish an operative analytical framework that can be used in various kinds of antitrust cases, we might ask: are output enhancement and/or cost reduction *surrogates for efficiency*, just as market power appears to act as a surrogate for anticompetitive effects? Or are they, like reduced output and higher prices, evidence of actual, albeit *pro*, competitive effects? If surrogates, how reliable are they as bases for inferring increased competition?

Increases in output might not always be pro-competitive. For example, in the possibly rare case of truly predatory pricing, output would increase, at least in the short-term. But it would ultimately decrease in the long-term if the predation scheme was successful and the predator eventually reduced output and raised price to recoup its losses. Increased output might also not be pro-competitive if it is achieved through quality or choice reduction. As a general matter, therefore, output increases are procompetitive only when four conditions are present:

- the output increase is market-wide;*
- there has not been an offsetting reduction in the quality of the product or service;
- there has not been an offsetting diminution of product variety; and
- it is a long-run, not a short-run increase.

If these conditions are met, and the use of output-enhancement and/or cost reduction is justifiable as a measure of competitive effect, how much weight should such evidence be given? Should it rebut a presumption that the conduct is anticompetitive? Should it matter if the plaintiff shifted its burden by reliance on evidence of actual effects or circumstantial evidence? Is it possible to have both evidence of actual anticompetitive effects, such as higher prices and lower output, *and* evidence of actual pro-competitive effects, such as lower costs? How could a plaintiff respond? Moreover, just as with anticompetitive effect, should even the slightest evidence of increased output be sufficient to justify a presumption of efficiency?

Conversely, what role should evidence of reduced output play? As we noted in *NCAA*, reduced output perhaps is the very definition of a collusive anticompetitive effect. If so, should evidence of reduced output create a presumption of anti-competitiveness? Rebuttable? Irrebuttable? What if conduct reduces costs *and* output? Is that likely?

We have already seen several different approaches to answering some of these questions. We now turn to the various government Guidelines's treatment of these questions in greater depth.

2. THE DEFINITION AND TREATMENT OF EFFICIENCIES UNDER GOVERNMENT GUIDELINES**

The 1997 amendments to the Horizontal Merger Guidelines provided the most complete statement concerning the role of efficiencies ever to come from

---

* An increase in market share alone, without an increase in market-wide output, would not suffice.

** The discussion here builds on the *Note on Efficiencies and Consumer Welfare*, *supra* Chapter 5, which should be reviewed at this time.

the federal enforcement agencies. As we learned in Chapter 5 in connection with our study of the Guidelines, as well as *Staples*, those Guidelines adopted a three part test for defining "cognizable efficiencies." To qualify as cognizable, efficiencies have to be (1) merger-specific, (2) verifiable, and (3) not arising from an anticompetitive reduction in output or service.

The Merger Guidelines were later used as the template for the Collaboration Guidelines, issued in 2000, which also require that efficiencies be verifiable in order to be "cognizable." *Collaboration Guidelines*, § 3.36(a). In effect, the Collaboration Guidelines also require that the efficiencies be "collaboration specific," but they do so by reference to the availability of less restrictive alternative means of achieving the efficiencies. "Cognizable efficiencies" are thus limited to those efficiencies "for which the relevant agreement is reasonably necessary." *Collaboration Guidelines*, § 3.36(b). To qualify as "reasonably necessary," the Guidelines ask whether the participants "could have achieved or could achieve similar efficiencies by practical, significantly less restrictive means." If not, the restrictive features of the collaboration may not be viewed as reasonably necessary to secure the efficiencies. Note how this approach is very much derivative of the ancillary restraint model we reviewed in Chapter in connection with *Addyston Pipe*. Finally, the Collaboration Guidelines require that verified efficiencies "do not arise from anticompetitive reductions in output or service" and indicate that "[c]ognizable efficiencies are assessed net of costs produced by the competitor collaboration or incurred in achieving those efficiencies." *Collaboration Guidelines*, § 3.36. This requirement too is drawn from the Merger Guidelines.

But how do the various Guidelines define "efficiency," and why do they require merger-specificity and verifiability?

Defining "Efficiency. Perhaps surprisingly, neither the Merger Guidelines nor the Collaboration Guidelines ever actually define "efficiency." In place of a definition, they offer some examples of efficiencies—most of which are tied directly to cost reductions. For example, the Merger Guidelines assert that "mergers have the potential to generate significant efficiencies by permitting a better utilization of existing assets, *enabling the combined firm to achieve lower costs* in producing a given quantity and quality than either firm could have achieved without the proposed transaction." *Horizontal Merger Guidelines*, § 4 (emphasis added). They continue:

> Efficiencies generated through merger can enhance the merged firm's ability and incentive to compete, which may result in lower prices, improved quality, enhanced service, or new products. * * * In a coordinated interaction context * * *, marginal cost reductions may make coordination less likely or effective by enhancing the incentive of a maverick to lower price or by creating a new maverick firm. In a unilateral effects context * * *, marginal cost reductions may reduce the merged firm's incentive to elevate prices. * * *

Id.

Similarly, the Collaboration Guidelines discuss how cooperation among competitors can "enable participants to offer goods or services that are cheaper, more valuable to consumers, or brought to market faster than would be possible absent the collaboration." *Collaboration Guidelines*, § 2.1. They continue:

Efficiency gains from competitor collaborations often stem from combinations of different capabilities or resources. For example, one participant may have special technical expertise that usefully complements another participant's manufacturing process, allowing the latter participant to lower its production cost or improve the quality of its product. In other instances, a collaboration may facilitate the attainment of scale or scope economies beyond the reach of any single participant. For example, two firms may be able to combine their research or marketing activities to lower their cost of bringing their products to market, or reduce the time needed to develop and begin commercial sales of new products. Consumers may benefit from these collaborations as the participants are able to lower prices, improve quality, or bring new products to market faster.

Id.

The government Guidelines thus focus significantly on a "lower cost" definition of efficiencies, identifying a number of possible, pro-competitive consequences that could result from conduct that lowers the product development, production, or marketing costs of the merging or collaborating firms. But the Guidelines also recognize that other "efficiencies" may result that may not derive exclusively from cost savings, such as the development of new products.

Figure 8–5:
Competitive Benefits of Efficiencies Related to Lower Costs

Direct Competitive Benefits	**Indirect Benefits**
• lower prices • improve quality • enhance service • new products • reduce product development time • greater innovation	• diminish incentive to coordinate with rivals • reduce incentive to raise prices

What do the Guidelines mean, however, by "cost"? Is it limited to out-of-pocket payments? Does it include fixed and variable costs? Does "cost" mean capital costs? Does it include labor costs? Opportunity costs? Presumably, a merger that reduces any of these kinds of costs can improve the "efficiency" of the merged firm. In addition, will all of the cost savings mentioned in the Guidelines necessarily lead to higher output? Is it possible that a merger could produce efficiencies *and* anticompetitive effects? We'll return to that question shortly.

Crediting Efficiencies in the Face of Anticompetitive Harm—the Role of Verification and Relatedness. Once a party comes forward with evidence of efficiencies, both the Merger Guidelines and the Collaboration Guidelines demand that they be "verifiable." As we also have seen, the Merger Guidelines demand that the efficiencies be "merger specific," whereas the Collaboration Guidelines require that efficiencies be "reasonably necessary" to achieve the beneficial aspects of the collaboration. What is the rationale behind these requirements and why do they qualify claims of efficiency? Do they largely serve similar functions? The Merger Guidelines maintain:

Efficiencies are difficult to verify and quantify, in part because much of the information relating to efficiencies is uniquely in the possession of the merging firms. Moreover, efficiencies projected reasonably and in good faith by the merging firms may not be realized. Therefore, the merging firms must substantiate efficiency claims so that the Agency can verify by reasonable means the likelihood and magnitude of each asserted efficiency, how and when each would be achieved (and any costs of doing so), how each would enhance the merged firm's ability and incentive to compete, and why each would be merger-specific. Efficiency claims will not be considered if they are vague or speculative or otherwise cannot be verified by reasonable means.

Horizontal Merger Guidelines, § 4. An almost identical paragraph appears in Section 3.36(a) of the Collaboration Guidelines. The Merger Guidelines also provide some examples of efficiencies that are more or less likely to be verifiable.

Figure 8–6:

Contrasting Efficiencies More or Less Likely to be Deemed Cognizable Under the Merger Guidelines

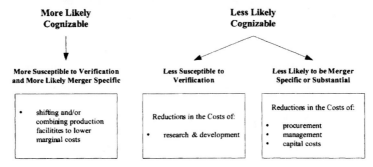

Why do the Guidelines at once tout the benefits of efficiencies and express some skepticism about parties' ability to verify them? Is the same skepticism warranted with respect to entry? What would distinguish evidence of entry from evidence of efficiencies in a way that would suggest that verification will not be as difficult a task?

Finally, how much and what kind of efficiency should be sufficient enough to offset how much and what kind of anticompetitive effect? Must the efficiency and anticompetitive effect be specifically quantifiable? If so, would it be sufficient that the absolute amount of efficiency is greater than the amount of anticompetitive harm? Or would the efficiency need to be causally connected to the harm, so it is likely to keep it from occurring? Can the efficiency be largely theoretical? Although it may be easy to resolve issues in lopsided cases—lots of harm and only little in the way of efficiencies, or conversely, lots of efficiencies and little in the way of harm—closer cases will present greater challenges. Indeed, the assessment of how much harm and how much efficiency will result from certain conduct often may be dependent upon the quality of the evidence, and may even require credibility assessments typically of the sort left to the fact-finder, including juries.

Contrast, for example, the treatment of efficiencies in three cases we have studied: *Staples*, *Sylvania*, and *Broadcast Music*. How would you characterize the treatment of efficiencies in each? Which involved relatively stronger evidence of efficiencies? Of anticompetitive effects? What form did the evidence of efficiencies and anticompetitive effects respectively take? How did the strength of the evidence on each side affect the courts' analysis? The Collaboration Guidelines offer the following counsel:

> The Agencies' comparison of cognizable efficiencies and anticompetitive harms is necessarily an approximate judgment. In assessing the overall competitive effect of an agreement, the Agencies consider the magnitude and likelihood of both the anticompetitive harms and cognizable efficiencies from the relevant agreement. The likelihood and magnitude of anticompetitive harms in a particular case may be insignificant compared to the expected cognizable efficiencies, or vice versa. *As the expected anticompetitive harm of the agreement increases, the Agencies require evidence establishing a greater level of expected cognizable efficiencies in order to avoid the conclusion that the agreement will have an anticompetitive effect overall.* When the anticompetitive harm of the agreement is likely to be particularly large, extraordinarily great cognizable efficiencies would be necessary to prevent the agreement from having an anticompetitive effect overall.

Collaboration Guidelines, § 3.37 (emphasis added). Note the "sliding scale" approach suggested in the language emphasized here. How would such a sliding scale work? What factors might cause the scale to tilt in favor of efficiencies or harm? Could such a scale be used effectively in an administrative or judicial setting, or is its utility limited to the agency setting? Was it used implicitly or explicitly in *Staples* or any of our other cases?

3. THE CHALLENGES OF PROVING EFFICIENCIES AND BUSINESS JUSTIFICATIONS

As we discussed earlier in the Chapter, both the Collaboration and Merger Guidelines require that efficiency claims be "verifiable." Speculative, unsubstantiated, or uncertain claims of efficiency generally will be deemed insufficient to refute evidence of anticompetitive effects, whether actual or inferential.

The Guidelines' expressed concern for overstated or unjustifiable claims of efficiencies mirrors similar concerns expressed by the courts. After-the-fact rationalizations, as well as pretextual or theoretical justifications for anticompetitive conduct that are not grounded in and supported by the actual evidence, therefore, have been rejected. As you read the next two prominent examples of such treatment, also keep in mind some of our previous examples of judicial treatment, such as *Sylvania, Broadcast Music, Staples, Heinz,* and *Microsoft.* Are the cases consistent in their treatment of justifications? Are the outcomes reasonably predictable? Are there common elements that generally have led the courts to accept or reject justifications for allegedly anticompetitive conduct?

ASPEN SKIING CO. v. ASPEN HIGHLANDS SKIING CORP.

Supreme Court of the United States, 1985.
472 U.S. 585, 105 S.Ct. 2847, 86 L.Ed.2d 467.

Justice STEVENS delivered the opinion of the Court.

* * *

IV

[The relevant portion of the decision is reproduced in Chapter 6, *supra*, at 624–35. Eds.]

* * *

EASTMAN KODAK CO. v. IMAGE TECHNICAL SERVICES, INC.

Supreme Court of the United States, 1992.
504 U.S. 451, 112 S.Ct. 2072, 119 L.Ed.2d 265.

[The case is discussed following *Aspen Skiing* in Chapter 6, *supra* at 636. Recall that Kodak was accused by independent service organizations ("ISOs") of changing its policy of selling replacement parts to ISOs and trying to monopolize the service aftermarket for its photocopiers. The Supreme Court was evaluating whether it was improper to grant summary judgment to Kodak. Eds.]

* * *

III

* * *

* * * Kodak contends that it has three valid business justifications for its actions: "(1) to promote interbrand equipment competition by allowing Kodak to stress the quality of its service; (2) to improve asset management by reducing Kodak's inventory costs; and (3) to prevent ISOs from free-riding on Kodak's capital investment in equipment, parts and service." Factual questions exist, however, about the validity and sufficiency of each claimed justification, making summary judgment inappropriate.

Kodak first asserts that by preventing customers from using ISO's, "it [can] best maintain high quality service for its sophisticated equipment" and avoid being "blamed for an equipment malfunction, even if the problem is the result of improper diagnosis, maintenance or repair by an ISO." Respondents have offered evidence that ISO's provide quality service and are preferred by some Kodak equipment owners. This is sufficient to raise a genuine issue of fact. See International Business Machines Corp. v. United States, 298 U.S. at 139–140 (rejecting IBM's claim that it had to control the cards used in its machines to avoid "injury to the reputation of the machines and the good will of" IBM in the absence of proof that other companies could not make quality cards); International Salt Co. v. United States, 332 U.S. 392, 397–398, 92 L. Ed. 20, 68 S. Ct. 12 (1947) (rejecting International Salt's claim that it had to control the supply of salt to protect its leased machines in the absence of proof that competitors could not supply salt of equal quality).

Moreover, there are other reasons to question Kodak's proffered motive of commitment to quality service; its quality justification appears inconsistent with its thesis that consumers are knowledgeable enough to lifecycle price, and its self-service policy. Kodak claims the exclusive-service contract is warranted because customers would otherwise blame Kodak equipment for breakdowns resulting from inferior ISO service. Thus, Kodak simultaneously claims that its customers are sophisticated enough to make complex and subtle lifecycle-pricing decisions, and yet too obtuse to distinguish which breakdowns are due to bad equipment and which are due to bad service. Kodak has failed to offer any reason why informational sophistication should be present in one circumstance and absent in the other. In addition, because self-service customers are just as likely as others to blame Kodak equipment for breakdowns resulting from (their own) inferior service, Kodak's willingness to allow self-service casts doubt on its quality claim. In sum, we agree with the Court of Appeals that respondents "have presented evidence from which a reasonable trier of fact could conclude that Kodak's first reason is pretextual."

There is also a triable issue of fact on Kodak's second justification—controlling inventory costs. As respondents argue, Kodak's actions appear inconsistent with any need to control inventory costs. Presumably, the inventory of parts needed to repair Kodak machines turns only on breakdown rates, and those rates should be the same whether Kodak or ISO's perform the repair. More importantly, the justification fails to explain respondents' evidence that Kodak forced OEM's, equipment owners, and parts brokers not to sell parts to ISO's, actions that would have no effect on Kodak's inventory costs.

Nor does Kodak's final justification entitle it to summary judgment on respondents' § 2 claim. Kodak claims that its policies prevent ISO's from "exploit[ing] the investment Kodak has made in product development, manufacturing and equipment sales in order to take away Kodak's service revenues." Kodak does not dispute that respondents invest substantially in the service market, with training of repair workers and investment in parts inventory. Instead, according to Kodak, the ISO's are free-riding because they have failed to enter the equipment and parts markets. This understanding of free-riding has no support in our case law.[33] To the contrary, as the Court of Appeals noted, one of the evils proscribed by the antitrust laws is the creation of entry barriers to potential competitors by requiring them to enter two

---

33. Kodak claims that both Continental T. V. and Monsanto support its free-rider argument. Neither is applicable. In both Continental T. V., 433 U.S. at 55, and Monsanto, 465 U.S. at 762–763, the Court accepted free-riding as a justification because without restrictions a manufacturer would not be able to induce competent and aggressive retailers to make the kind of investment of capital and labor necessary to distribute the product. In Continental T. V. the relevant market level was retail sale of televisions and in Monsanto retail sales of herbicides. Some retailers were investing in those markets; others were not, relying, instead, on the investment of the other retailers. To be applicable to this case, the ISO's would have to be relying on Kodak's investment in the service market; that, however, is not Kodak's argument.

markets simultaneously. Jefferson Parish, 466 U.S. at 14; Fortner, 394 U.S. at 509.

None of Kodak's asserted business justifications, then, are sufficient to prove that Kodak is "entitled to a judgment as a matter of law" on respondents' § 2 claim. Fed. Rule Civ. Proc. 56(c).

* * *

———

What explains the Court's rejection of the justifications proffered in *Aspen Skiing* and *Kodak*? Were the efficiencies and justifications in either case unverified? Were they too insubstantial in comparison to the evidence of anticompetitive effects? Were there theoretical problems with the defendants presentation of their alleged efficiencies? Note that *Aspen Skiing* had been tried and came to the Court with a complete trial record, whereas *Kodak* was being decided at the summary judgment stage. How might that difference have affected the Court's approach to treating each defendant's justifications? Were Kodak's defenses rejected for different reasons than Aspen Skiing Co.'s? Were Kodak's defenses being rejected as a matter of law or merely as a basis for granting summary judgment?

Following remand from the Supreme Court, *Kodak* went to trial and resulted in a verdict in favor of the plaintiffs. Pursuant to that verdict, the district court entered an injunction and a judgment for $71.8 million in treble damages. Although some of the damage verdict was reversed, the court of appeals affirmed the finding of liability in all respects. With respect to Kodak's continuing assertion that its actions were justified, the court held:

> The ISOs' evidence suffices to support the jury's rejection of Kodak's business justifications, as the record reflects evidence of pretext. The ISOs presented evidence that: (1) Kodak adopted its parts policy only after an ISO won a contract with the State of California; (2) Kodak allowed its own customers to service their machines; (3) Kodak customers could distinguish breakdowns due to poor service from breakdowns due to parts; and (4) many customers preferred ISO service.

Image Tech. Svcs., Inc. v. Eastman Kodak Co., 125 F.3d 1195, 1213–14 (9th Cir.1997). How did each of these particular kinds of evidence tend to demonstrate "pretext"?

Sidebar 8–7:
The Crucial Role of Expert Testimony in Contemporary Antitrust Analysis*

Driven in large part by antitrust's movement towards greater reliance on economic concepts, expert economic analysis has become a staple

---

* This Sidebar is adapted in part from Andrew I. Gavil, *Defining Reliable Forensic Economics in the Post–Daubert/Kumho Tire Era: Case Studies from Antitrust*, 57 WASH. & LEE L. REV. 831 (2000). *See also* Andrew I. Gavil, *Competition Policy, Economics, and Economists: Are We Expecting Too Much?*, in 2005

of antitrust litigation and is a typical component of advocacy before federal and state antitrust enforcement agencies. The role of experts is also manifest in the size of the economic staffs at the DOJ and FTC, and their influence is evident in the various agency Guidelines and policy statements. In addition, due to technological advances, the cost of complex econometric and statistical analysis has fallen considerably, and the supply of economic consulting firms, groups and individual economists specializing in antitrust issues has grown significantly. From negotiations with a federal, state or foreign antitrust enforcement agency for the approval of a merger, to litigating before the courts, therefore, antitrust lawyers commonly work in tandem today with antitrust economists.

Increased reliance on experts, however, has not proceeded without controversy and some tension. As we observed in *Microsoft*, opposing experts often can take seemingly irreconcilable positions. If one expert's opinion can be discredited or eliminated, the party she represents often will find itself on the losing end of a negotiation with the government, or litigation. Discrediting the opinion of the opponent's expert, therefore, has become an integral part of many a testifying expert's role. But polarized expert testimony can diminish the perception that experts are capable of rendering unbiased opinions and ultimately undermine support for reliance on the experts in the first place. *See, e.g.,* Richard A. Posner, *An Economic Approach to the Law of Evidence*, 51 STAN. L. REV. 1477, 1540 (1999) (discussing ideological divisions among antitrust economists). It can also complicate rather than facilitate the institutional task of the decision-maker, be it an agency official or a federal judge.

Expert Testimony and the Federal Courts

Traditionally, conflicts between economists in antitrust cases were resolved through party challenges to the *evidentiary sufficiency* of the expert's testimony. Such challenges were initiated through motions for summary judgment or for judgment as a matter of law. *See, e.g., Matsushita Elec. Indus. Co. v. Zenith Radio Corp.*, 475 U.S. 574 (1986); *Eastman Kodak Co. v. Image Tech. Servs., Inc.*, 504 U.S. 451 (1992); *Brooke Group Ltd. v. Brown & Williamson Tobacco Corp.*, 509 U.S. 209 (1993).

Today, this "battle of the experts" is governed in federal court by provisions of both the Federal Rules of Civil Procedure and the Federal Rules of Evidence. Rule 26(a)(2)(A) of the Federal Rules of Civil Procedure, requires an early, mandatory disclosure of the identity of expert witnesses that may testify at trial pursuant to Rules 702, 703, and 705 of the Federal Rules of Evidence. Rule 26(a)(2)(B) further imposes an enhanced disclosure expectation with respect to the basis, content, and scope of the expert's expected testimony, all of which must be supplied in a written report to facilitate further discovery and trial preparation. These disclosure requirements tend to highlight the role of the expert promptly and invite examination of her anticipated testimony.

FORDHAM CORP. L. INST. 575 (B. Hawk, ed. 2006); Andrew I. Gavil, *After* Daubert: *Discerning the Increasingly Fine Line Between the Admissibil-* *ity and Sufficiency of Expert Testimony in Antitrust Litigation*, 65 ANTITRUST L.J. 663 (1997).

Although as noted above, the traditional approach to this process of examination focused on *evidentiary sufficiency*, since 1993 courts have increasingly entertained challenges to expert testimony as matters of *evidentiary admissibility* under the Federal Rules of Evidence. Owing to *Daubert v. Merrell Dow Pharms.*, 509 U.S. 579 (1993), *General Elec. Co. v. Joiner*, 522 U.S. 136 (1997) and *Kumho Tire Co. v. Carmichael*, 526 U.S. 137 (1999), federal courts must undertake a multi-factored inquiry into the "relevance" and "reliability" of expert testimony under Rule 702 of the Federal Rules of Evidence, which was amended in 2000 to reflect the directives of *Daubert* and its progeny. Figure 8–7 summarizes these factors. Often, such "admissibility" decisions also serve as a prelude to a sufficiency determination: if the expert's testimony is excluded on admissibility grounds, the opposing party will move for summary judgment arguing that the remaining lay testimony is insufficient to warrant a trial.

Figure 8–7:
Original *Daubert* Factors

- whether the methodology can be and has been tested;

- whether the methodology has been subjected to peer review and publication;

- the known or potential rate of error of a particular methodology;

- the existence and maintenance of standards controlling the methodology's operation; and

- the "general acceptance" of the methodology in the relevant scientific community.

Daubert and Antitrust

Increasingly, the lower courts have been applying these principles to antitrust cases. Frequent targets of "*Daubert* motions" are experts testifying on (1) conspiracy, *See, e.g., City of Tuscaloosa v. Harcros Chemicals, Inc.*, 158 F.3d 548 (11th Cir.1998), (2) market power, *see, e.g., Concord Boat Corp. v. Brunswick Corp.*, 207 F.3d 1039 (8th Cir.2000), and (3) damages and remedies, *See, e.g., Conwood v. U.S. Tobacco Co.*, 290 F.3d 768 (6th Cir.2002). *Daubert*-type motions also have arisen in the context of class action certification under Rule 23 of the Federal Rules of Civil Procedure. *See, e.g., In re Visa Check/MasterMoney Antitrust Litigation*, 280 F.3d 124 (2d Cir.2001). Consistent with the Court's view in *Kumho Tire* that *Daubert* applies to all expert testimony, but that its list of factors must be adapted to the needs of particular expert testimony, the persistent challenge in these cases has been to identify the *criteria of reliability* for evaluating expert *economic* testimony.

SMS Sys. Maint. Svcs., Inc. v. Digital Equip. Corp., 188 F.3d 11 (1st Cir. 1999), *cert. denied*, 528 U.S. 1188 (2000) is illustrative. In an attempt to replicate the success of the plaintiff independent service organizations ("ISOs") in *Eastman Kodak Co. v. Image Technical Servs., Inc.*, the plaintiffs in *SMS* challenged Digital Equipment Corporation's ("DEC") alleged implementation of a mandatory extended warranty program. The plaintiffs, ISOs who had previously been engaged in the servicing of DEC computers and equipment, alleged that this change in policy constituted monopolization of a relevant market defined as "the services aftermarket for DEC computers." *SMS Systems*, 188 F.3d at 13.

As we have learned, "monopoly power" is a required element of a claim of monopolization under Section 2 of the Sherman Act. SMS sought to establish DEC's monopoly power through both direct and circumstantial evidence, relying primarily on the testimony of an economist. To support his opinion that DEC possessed monopoly power, the expert testified that DEC had "a much greater share of the services market than it should enjoy, given low customer satisfaction." Characterizing the import of his testimony, the court observed: "If DEC did not have monopoly power, this argument runs, it would not have been able to keep its large share of the aftermarket in spite of rampant dissatisfaction." *Id.* at 25.

The court took issue, however, with the expert's data collection, especially as it related to his critical conclusion that DEC customer satisfaction was low. Observing that he "did not conduct a customer satisfaction survey," but rather relied on "his interpretation of certain internal DEC documents," the court asserted that "[e]xpert opinions * * * are no better than the data and methodology that undergird them." It labeled the expert's conclusions "highly suspect," because they depended upon sources cited in his report that he "neither attaches nor discusses." *Id.* Relying in part on *Kumho Tire's* assertion that the courts must " 'make certain that an expert * * * employs in the courtroom the same level of intellectual rigor that characterizes the practice of an expert in the relevant field,' " the court maintained that "an expert must vouchsafe the reliability of the data on which he relies and explain how the cumulation of that data was consistent with standards of the expert's profession." *Id.* It then concluded:

> Not only did [the expert] fail to discuss in his report the nature of the data and its meaning, but he failed to explain whether the information-gathering technique used in the DEC documents was valid, whether the data was sufficiently representative to permit him to draw any relevant conclusions, and whether the sampling methodology used to compile these documents corresponded to methods that might be considered legitimate in his discipline. Expert testimony that offers only a bare conclusion is insufficient to prove the expert's point.

Id.

SMS Systems provides some useful insights into the standards to be applied in evaluating expert economic testimony in antitrust cases. Its assertion that the expert must employ in the courtroom "the same level of intellectual rigor that characterizes the practice of an expert in the relevant field," can be viewed as one criteria of reliability for expert testimony. The court also calls attention to the importance of examining the reliability of the data that underscores the expert opinion, particularly demanding that the underlying data be available for examination by the fact finder and the parties, and that the methods used in gathering the data be demonstrably reliable. *Cf.* Jonathan B. Baker, *Econometric Analysis in* FTC v. Staples, 18 J. Pub. Pol'y & Mktg. 11, 18–19 (1999) (discussing importance of access to expert's underlying data in evaluating reliability of regression analysis). The expert also must have some methodology for insuring that data collected from internal corporate documents is "sufficiently representative" to justify drawing any conclusions therefrom, and her "sampling methodology" must correspond to "methods that might be considered legitimate" in the relevant discipline.

Other "criteria of reliability" also have surfaced. First, with respect to regression analysis, often used to support conspiracy claims and damage projections, the exclusion of a significant independent variable that affects the outcome of the analysis may warrant exclusion of the expert's testimony. This was apparent in *Blomkest* (discussed in Chapter 3), *Concord Boat*, 207 F.3d at 1056–57; and *Blue Dane Simmental Corp. v. Am. Simmental Ass'n*, 178 F.3d 1035, 1039–41 (8th Cir.1999). *See also* Daniel L. Rubinfeld, *Reference Guide on Multiple Regression, in* REFERENCE MANUAL ON SCIENTIFIC EVIDENCE 179, 188 (2d ed. 2000) (discussing criteria for evaluating reliability of regression analysis).

Variations of the "significant variable" idea have surfaced in other cases. In *Concord Boat*, for example, the expert's testimony as to the defendant's alleged market power, as well as the alleged impact of its action on the plaintiffs, its competitive rivals, failed to take into account the plaintiff's own market blunders. It therefore did not reflect the "reality of the market place," and provided no basis for distinguishing the effects of lawful, as opposed to allegedly unlawful, acts of the defendant. *Concord Boat* suggests, therefore, that as a general matter unjustified omission of factors that could affect the outcome of the expert's testimony could warrant its exclusion.

Concord Boat also maintained that the expert's application of a methodology to the facts of a case must demonstrate "fit,"which is arguably required under revised Rule 702. But "fit" also can be viewed as a criteria of reliability for the methodology itself. "Fit" may ask: "Is the methodology employed by the expert being used for the purposes for which it was designed?" If not, the testimony might be excluded. This also was illustrated in *Concord Boat*, when the plaintiff's economist sought to estimate damages attributable to the defendant's conduct based on a methodology designed for other purposes. *See, e.g., Concord Boat*, 207 F.3d at 1046–47, 1055–56.

The Role of Economists as Law Clerks and Court–Appointed Experts

One factor yet to fully evolve, but with important potential implications for how *Daubert* inquiries are to be conducted, is the use of court appointed expert witnesses. Specifically encouraged by Justice Breyer in his concurring opinion in *Joiner*, 522 U.S. at 149–50 (Breyer, J., concurring), and authorized by Federal Rule of Evidence 706, court-appointed expert witnesses may play an increasingly significant role in antitrust litigation as a response to *Daubert*. Such experts can aid the court in conducting *Daubert* hearings and in evaluating the reliability of expert testimony supplied by the parties. They can also provide an independent source of economic expertise to evaluate the evidence. *See, e.g., New York v. Kraft General Foods, Inc.*, 926 F.Supp. 321, 351–52 (S.D.N.Y. 1995) (merger challenge rejected in part on authority of court appointed economist Dr. Alfred Kahn); *In re Auction Houses Antitrust Litigation*, 2000 WL 1840030 (S.D.N.Y. 2000) (economist appointed to aid in valuation of proposed settlement). In seeking to encourage more private antitrust enforcement in Europe, the European Commission also has endorsed the use of court-appointed experts in antitrust cases, although its has recommended that they be used in lieu of party-retained experts. Echoing Judge Posner's criticisms, the EC argued that adversarial experts are generally unhelpful. It also expressed concern that use of party-retained experts can drive up the costs of antitrust litigation. *See* Green Paper on Damages Actions for Breach of the EC Antitrust Rules (Dec. 2005), *available at* http://eur-lex.europa.eu/LexUriServ/site/en/com/2005/com 2005_0672en01.pdf.

Reliance on court appointed experts, however, presents some challenges, as well. As one commentator has pointed out, if differences in the testimony of antitrust economists reflect a lack of consensus on basic principles, it may prove difficult to identify a non-partisan court-appointed expert. Posner, *An Economic Approach to the Law of Evidence*, 51 STAN. L. REV. at 1540. Moreover, a district court judge may by virtue of having selected an expert be inclined to adopt her recommendations without serious challenge. Moreover, although court-appointed experts may provide a valuable complement to party-retained experts, they are unlikely to prove to be adequate substitutes. *See* Andrew I. Gavil, *The Challenges of Economic Proof in a Decentralized and Privatized European Competition Policy System: Lessons from the American Experience*, 4 J. COMPETITION L. & ECON. 177 (2008). *See generally* ABA Section of Antitrust Law, *Final Report of Economic Evidence Task Force* (2006), *available at* http://www.abanet.org/antitrust/at-reports/01–c-ii.pdf.

Justice Breyer also reminds us that judicial law clerks with economic expertise can serve as an important source of economic expertise for the court, and cites the example of economist Carl Kaysen's role as a law clerk in *United Shoe Machinery* (discussed in Chapter 6, *supra*). *Joiner*, 522 U.S. at 149 (*citing* Carl Kaysen, *In Memoriam: Charles E. Wyzanski, Jr.*, 100 HARV. L. REV. 713, 713–15 (1987)). We also examined the influential role that law clerks can play in connection with the Supreme Court's *Maricopa* and *Sylvania* decisions.

Conclusion

Because antitrust law is very likely to remain dependent upon evolving trends in economics, *Daubert* in all probability will prove to be a critical vehicle for navigating its future development. In place of motions to dismiss and summary judgment, ideological and methodological conflicts based on economics may present themselves more frequently, and be resolved, in the context of *Daubert* admissibility hearings. But *Daubert* has yet to spawn a clear, cost-effective method of testing expert economic opinions in antitrust cases. Whether *Daubert* can improve antitrust decision-making, therefore, remains to be seen.

4. LEGALLY NON–COGNIZABLE BUSINESS JUSTIFICATIONS

You may recall from Chapter 2, that the conduct of the defendants in some of the earliest cases under the Sherman Act tested the meaning of "reasonableness." In both *Joint Traffic Association* and *Trans-Missouri Freight* the defendants, who conceded they had fixed prices, argued in their defense that the prices fixed were "reasonable." In both instances the Supreme Court rejected the defenses as unacceptable in principle. The defendants in *Trenton Potteries* tried the same approach after the Court had decided *Standard Oil* and *Chicago Board of Trade*, but were similarly rebuffed.

With the revival of the rule of reason in the late 1970s came renewed attempts to offer justifications for conduct that in some ways were the analytical equivalent of asserting that the prices set were reasonable. These efforts were most evident in the context of challenges to the anticompetitive conduct of some professions. Recall, for example, that in *Nat'l Soc'y of Prof'l Eng'rs* (discussed in Chapter 2) the government challenged one of the Society's canons of ethics that banned competitive bidding. The Society defended the canon on the grounds that it tended to protect public safety—competitive bidding would lead to lower prices, which in turn would result in shoddy design and construction. This argument, of course, implied that competition among engineers was undesirable and likely to harm consumers. The Supreme Court rejected the argument in no uncertain terms:

> The early cases * * * foreclose the argument that because of the special characteristics of a particular industry, monopolistic arrangements will better promote trade and commerce than competition. [citing *Trans-Missouri Freight* and *Joint Traffic Association*]. That kind of argument is properly addressed to Congress and may justify an exemptions from the statute for specific industries, but it is not permitted by the Rule of Reason.

435 U.S. at 689–90.

In the case excerpt from *Maricopa* that follows, consider carefully the defense offered by the Society, and the Court's response to it. How did *Nat'l Soc'y of Prof'l Eng'rs* influence the Court's reasoning? Do you agree with the Court? You might also want to review at this time the discussion of Chapter 1 of the possible goals of antitrust laws.

ARIZONA v. MARICOPA COUNTY MEDICAL SOCIETY

Supreme Court of the United States, 1982.
457 U.S. 332, 102 S.Ct. 2466, 73 L.Ed.2d 48.

Justice STEVENS delivered the opinion of the Court.

[The facts and a more extensive excerpt from the decision are reproduced in Chapter 2, *supra*, at 116-21. Eds.]

* * *

III

* * *

The respondents' principal argument is that the per se rule is inapplicable because their agreements are alleged to have procompetitive justifications. The argument indicates a misunderstanding of the per se concept. The anticompetitive potential inherent in all price-fixing agreements justifies their facial invalidation even if procompetitive justifications are offered for some.[23] Those claims of enhanced competition are so unlikely to prove significant in any particular case that we adhere to the rule of law that is justified in its general application. Even when the respondents are given every benefit of the doubt, the limited record in this case is not inconsistent with the presumption that the respondents' agreements will not significantly enhance competition.

The respondents contend that their fee schedules are procompetitive because they make it possible to provide consumers of health care with a uniquely desirable form of insurance coverage that could not otherwise exist. The features of the foundation-endorsed insurance plans that they stress are a choice of doctors, complete insurance coverage, and lower premiums. The first two characteristics, however, are hardly unique to these plans. Since only about 70% of the doctors in the relevant market are members of either foundation, the guarantee of complete coverage only applies when an insured chooses a physician in that 70%. If he elects to go to a nonfoundation doctor, he may be required to pay a portion of the doctor's fee. It is fair to presume, however, that at least 70% of the doctors in other markets charge no more than the "usual, customary, and reasonable" fee that typical insurers are willing to reimburse in full. Thus, in Maricopa and Pima Counties as well as in most parts of the country, if an insured asks his doctor if the insurance coverage is complete, presumably in about 70% of the cases the doctor will say "Yes" and in about 30% of the cases he will say "No."

It is true that a binding assurance of complete insurance coverage—as well as most of the respondents' potential for lower insurance premiums[25]— can be obtained only if the insurer and the doctor agree in advance on the maximum fee that the doctor will accept as full payment for a particular service. Even if a fee schedule is therefore desirable, it is not necessary that the doctors do the price fixing. * * * [I]nsurers are capable not only of fixing maximum reimbursable prices but also of obtaining binding agreements with providers guaranteeing the insured full reimbursement of a participating provider's fee. In light of these examples, it is not surprising that nothing in the record even arguably supports the conclusion that this type of insurance program could not function if the fee schedules were set in a different way.

The most that can be said for having doctors fix the maximum prices is that doctors may be able to do it more efficiently than insurers. The validity of that assumption is far from obvious,[28] but in any event there is no reason to

23. "Whatever economic justification particular price-fixing agreements may be thought to have, the law does not permit an inquiry into their reasonableness. They are all banned because of their actual or potential threat to the central nervous system of the economy." *United States v. Socony–Vacuum Oil Co.*, 310 U.S. 150, 226, n. 59, 60 S.Ct. 811, 844, n. 59, 84 L.Ed. 1129 (1940).

25. We do not perceive the respondents' claim of procompetitive justification for their fee schedules to rest on the premise that the fee schedules actually reduce medical fees and accordingly reduce insurance premiums, thereby enhancing competition in the health insurance industry. Such an argument would merely restate the long-rejected position that fixed prices are reasonable if they are lower than free competition would yield. It is arguable, however, that the existence of a fee schedule, whether fixed by the doctors or by the insurers, makes it easier—and to that extent less expensive—for insurers to calculate the risks that they underwrite and to arrive at the appropriate reimbursement on insured claims.

28. In order to create an insurance plan under which the doctor would agree to accept as full payment a fee prescribed in a fixed schedule, someone must canvass the doctors to determine what maximum prices would be high enough to attract sufficient numbers of individual doctors to sign up but low enough to

believe that any savings that might accrue from this arrangement would be sufficiently great to affect the competitiveness of these kinds of insurance plans. It is entirely possible that the potential or actual power of the foundations to dictate the terms of such insurance plans may more than offset the theoretical efficiencies upon which the respondents' defense ultimately rests.[29]

* * *

IV

Having declined the respondents' invitation to cut back on the per se rule against price fixing, we are left with the respondents' argument that their fee schedules involve price fixing in only a literal sense. For this argument, the respondents rely upon *Broadcast Music, Inc. v. Columbia Broadcasting System, Inc.*, 441 U.S. 1, 99 S.Ct. 1551, 60 L.Ed.2d 1 (1979).

* * *

This case is fundamentally different. Each of the foundations is composed of individual practitioners who compete with one another for patients. Neither the foundations nor the doctors sell insurance, and they derive no profits from the sale of health insurance policies. The members of the foundations sell medical services. Their combination in the form of the foundation does not permit them to sell any different product.[33] Their combination has merely permitted them to sell their services to certain customers at fixed prices and arguably to affect the prevailing market price of medical care.

The foundations are not analogous to partnerships or other joint arrangements in which persons who would otherwise be competitors pool their capital and share the risks of loss as well as the opportunities for profit. In such joint ventures, the partnership is regarded as a single firm competing with other sellers in the market. The agreement under attack is an agreement among hundreds of competing doctors concerning the price at which each will offer his own services to a substantial number of consumers. It is true that some are surgeons, some anesthesiologists, and some psychiatrists, but the doctors do not sell a package of three kinds of services. If a clinic offered complete

make the insurance plan competitive. In this case that canvassing function is performed by the foundation; the foundation then deals with the insurer. It would seem that an insurer could simply bypass the foundation by performing the canvassing function and dealing with the doctors itself. Under the foundation plan, each doctor must look at the maximum-fee schedule fixed by his competitors and vote for or against approval of the plan (and, if the plan is approved by majority vote, he must continue or revoke his foundation membership). A similar, if to some extent more protracted, process would occur if it were each insurer that offered the maximum-fee schedule to each doctor.

29. In this case it appears that the fees are set by a group with substantial power in the market for medical services, and that there is

competition among insurance companies in the sale of medical insurance. Under these circumstances the insurance companies are not likely to have significantly greater bargaining power against a monopoly of doctors than would individual consumers of medical services.

33. It may be true that by becoming a member of the foundation the individual practitioner obtains a competitive advantage in the market for medical services that he could not unilaterally obtain. That competitive advantage is the ability to attract as customers people who value both the guarantee of full health coverage and a choice of doctors. But, as we have indicated, the setting of the price by doctors is not a "necessary consequence" of an arrangement with an insurer in which the doctor agrees not to charge certain insured customers more than a fixed price.

medical coverage for a flat fee, the cooperating doctors would have the type of partnership arrangement in which a price-fixing agreement among the doctors would be perfectly proper. But the fee agreements disclosed by the record in this case are among independent competing entrepreneurs. They fit squarely into the horizontal price-fixing mold.

* * *

Justice POWELL, with whom THE CHIEF JUSTICE and Justice REHN-QUIST join, dissenting.

* * *

IV

The Court acknowledges that the per se ban against price fixing is not to be invoked every time potential competitors literally fix prices. One also would have expected it to acknowledge that per se characterization is inappropriate if the challenged agreement or plan achieves for the public procompetitive benefits that otherwise are not attainable. The Court does not do this. And neither does it provide alternative criteria by which the per se characterization is to be determined. It is content simply to brand this type of plan as "price fixing" and describe the agreement in Broadcast Music—which also literally involved the fixing of—as "fundamentally different."

In fact, however, the two agreements are similar in important respects. Each involved competitors and resulted in cooperative pricing.[9] Each arrangement also was prompted by the need for better service to the consumers.[10] And each arrangement apparently makes possible a new product by reaping otherwise unattainable efficiencies.[11] The Court's effort to distinguish Broadcast Music thus is unconvincing.[12]

* * *

9. In this case the physicians in effect vote on foundation maximum-fee schedules. In Broadcast Music, the copyright owners aggregated their copyrights into a group package, sold rights to the package at a group price, and distributed the proceeds among themselves according to an agreed-upon formula.

10. In this case, the foundations' maximum-fee schedules attempt to rectify the inflationary consequence of patients' indifference to the size of physicians' bills and insurers' commitment to reimburse whatever "usual, customary, and reasonable" charges physicians may submit. In Broadcast Music, the market defect inhered in the fact that "those who performed copyrighted music for profit were so numerous and widespread, and most performances so fleeting, that as a practical matter it was impossible for the many individual copyright owners to negotiate with and license the users and to detect unauthorized uses."

11. In this case, the record before us indicates that insurers—those best situated to decide and best motivated to inspire trust in their judgment—believe that the foundations are the most efficient providers of the maximum-fee scheduling service. In Broadcast Music, we found that the blanket copyright clearinghouse system "reduce[d] costs absolutely...."

12. The Court states that in Broadcast Music "there was little competition among individual composers for their separate compositions." This is an irrational ground for distinction. Competition could have existed, but did not because of the cooperative agreement. That competition yet persists among physicians is not a sensible reason to invalidate their agreement while refusing similarly to condemn the Broadcast Music agreements that were completely effective in eliminating competition. The Court also offers as a distinction that the foundations do not permit the creation of "any different product." But the foundations provide a "different product" to precisely the same extent as did Broadcast Music's clearinghouses. The clearinghouses provided only what copyright holders offered as individual sellers—the rights to use individual compositions. The clearinghouses were

What accounts for the division in the Court in *Maricopa*? Is it a matter of how efficiencies are defined? Of how they are proved? Is a debate over the scope of cognizable defenses to antitrust claims? For a further discussion of how consideration of efficiencies should be integrated into antitrust analysis, see *Polygram Holdings* (discussed in Chapter 2).

5. THE LIMITED ROLE OF STATUTORY EXEMPTIONS

Do you think that competition should be mandated for all industries under the federal antitrust laws? Note that the Court in *Maricopa* instructs the defendants to redirect their arguments to Congress. Why? Under what circumstances should Congress relieve the firms in an industry of the mandate to compete?

Although a comprehensive treatment is beyond the scope of this Casebook, note that Congressionally created, industry-wide exemptions exist for certain labor union activities, 29 U.S.C. §§ 105 (Norris–LaGuardia Act), the business of insurance, 15 U.S.C. §§ 1011–13 (McCarran–Ferguson Act), for certain agricultural cooperatives, 7 U.S.C. §§ 291–92 (Capper–Volstead Act), for certain newspaper joint ventures, 15 U.S.C. §§ 1801–04 (Newspaper Preservation Act) and for medical peer review proceedings that meet certain guidelines, 42 U.S.C. §§ 11101, 11111–15 (Health Care Quality Improvements Act). There are also long-standing non-statutory exemptions for labor, *Brown v. Pro Football*, 518 U.S. 231 (1996), and baseball. *See Fed'l Baseball Club of Baltimore, Inc. v. Nat'l League of Prof. Baseball Clubs*, 259 U.S. 200 (1922); *Flood v. Kuhn*, 407 U.S. 258 (1972). For additional discussions of exemptions under U.S. antitrust law, see ABA SECTION OF ANTITRUST LAW, ANTITRUST LAW DEVELOPMENTS 1305–1500 (6th ed. 2007); ANTITRUST MODERNIZATION COMMISSION, FINAL REPORT AND RECOMMENDATIONS 333–78 (2007), *available at* http://www.amc.gov/report_recommendation/chapter4.pdf.

Figure 8–8:

Major U.S. Antitrust Exemptions*

Statutory Exemptions from the Antitrust Laws

Agricultural Marketing Agreement Act, 7 U.S.C. §§ 608b–608c

able to obtain these same rights more efficiently, however, because they eliminated the need to engage in individual bargaining with each individual copyright owner.

In the same manner, the foundations set up an innovative means to deliver a basic service—insured medical care from a wide range of physicians of one's choice—in a more economical manner. The foundations' maximum-fee schedules replace the weak cost containment incentives in typical "usual, customary, and reasonable" insurance agreements with a stronger cost control mechanism: an absolute ceiling on maximum fees that can be charged.

The conduct of the insurers in this case indicates that they believe that the foundation plan as it presently exists is the most efficient means of developing and administering such schedules. At this stage in the litigation, therefore, we must agree that the foundation plan permits the more economical delivery of the basic insurance service—"to some extent, a different product."

* Source: ANTITRUST MODERNIZATION COMMISSION, REPORT AND RECOMMENDATIONS, at 378 (2007), *available at* http://www.amc.gov/report_recommendation/toc.htm.

Anti–Hog–Cholera Serum and Hog–Cholera Virus Act, 7 U.S.C. § 852

Capper–Volstead Act, 7 U.S.C. §§ 291–92

Charitable Donation Antitrust Immunity Act, 15 U.S.C. §§ 37–37a

Defense Production Act exemption, 50 U.S.C. app. § 2158

Export Trading Company Act, 15 U.S.C. §§ 4001–21

Fishermen's Collective Marketing Act, 15 U.S.C. §§ 521–22

Health Care Quality Improvement Act, 42 U.S.C. §§ 11101–52

Labor exemptions (statutory and non-statutory), 15 U.S.C. § 17; 29 U.S.C. §§ 52, 101–15,151–69; (and common law)

Local Government Antitrust Act, 15 U.S.C. §§ 34–36

Medical resident matching program exemption, 15 U.S.C. § 37b

National Cooperative Research and Production Act, 15 U.S.C. §§ 4301–06

Need–Based Educational Aid Act, 15 U.S.C. § 1 note

Newspaper Preservation Act, 15 U.S.C. §§ 1801–04

Non-profit agricultural cooperatives exemption, 15 U.S.C. § 17

Small Business Act exemption, 15 U.S.C. §§ 638(d), 640

Soft Drink Interbrand Competition Act, 15 U.S.C. §§ 3501–03

Sports Broadcasting Act, 15 U.S.C. §§ 1291–95

Standard Setting Development Organization Advancement Act, 15 U.S.C. §§ 4301–05, 4301 note

Webb–Pomerene Export Act, 15 U.S.C. §§ 61–66

Statutory Exemptions Created as Part of a Regulatory Regime

Air transportation exemption, 49 U.S.C. §§ 41308–09, 42111

McCarran–Ferguson Act, 15 U.S.C. §§ 1011–15

Motor transportation exemption, 49 U.S.C. §§ 13703, 14302–03

Natural Gas Policy Act exemption, 15 U.S.C. § 3364(e)

Railroad transportation exemption, 49 U.S.C. §§ 10706, 11321(a)

Shipping Act, 46 U.S.C. app. §§ 1701–19

Judicially Created Exemptions

Baseball exemption

Filed-rate/*Keogh* doctrine

Noerr-Pennington Immunity

State Action Doctrine

Various implied immunities created in specific regulatory settings

––––––––––

Would you support legislative exemptions for any industries? Why might some industries seek exemptions? Why might some succeed in getting them?

In the U.S., only Congress can create exemptions to the antitrust laws. In contrast, Article 81(3) of the E.U. Treaty authorizes the European Commission to create firm and industry specific exemptions, and exempt specific agreements or categories of agreements that might otherwise violate Article 81(1), provided they contribute to "improving the production or distribution of goods" or promote "technical or economic progress." *See* Article 81(3) of the Treaty of Rome (Appendix A). Since 1962, the EC often has invoked these provisions, which can be read as permitting exemptions based on goals other than economic efficiency, such as promoting more general economic progress. What are the advantages and disadvantages of such a process? Would you favor such an approach over the U.S., which leaves such decisions solely to Congress?

G. STRUCTURING THE ANALYSIS OF ANTI-COMPETITIVE EFFECTS, EFFICIENCIES, AND BUSINESS JUSTIFICATIONS

We have now seen how the modern antitrust case is assembled. It can usefully be viewed as a series of elements, as is depicted in Figure 8–9. Recall from the introductory material in this Chapter, that these elements have increasingly become common to many antitrust offenses. As you reflect on them, consider how they might fit into a model of decision-making for adversarial litigation, which includes allocating burdens of production and proof. What would a plaintiff need to show to meet its burden of production (and defeat a motion for summary judgment)? If it was able to meet that burden of production, and the defendant was unable to respond with evidence of cognizable efficiencies, could these elements provide the basis for a truncated analysis? Would they also permit a truncated analysis that terminates weak cases when a plaintiff is unable to allege or meet a burden of production as to certain elements? If both the plaintiff and the defendant satisfy their respective burdens of production, what will the plaintiff need to demonstrate in order to meet its ultimate burden of proof and prevail?

Figure 8–9:
The Elements of Modern Antitrust Analysis

(1) Theory of Anticompetitive Harm (Collusive or Exclusionary Effects)

(2) Conduct that Falls Within One of Statutory Prohibitions Caused or is Likely to Cause that Harm

(3) Actual or Predicted Anticompetitive Effects
- presumed (per se)
- actual
- inferred (through single or double inference)

(4) Conditions of Entry (to establish power or rebut prediction of effects)
- Stiglerian
- Strategic Entry Deterrence

(5) Cognizable Business Justifications, Especially Efficiency
- permissible vs. impermissible justifications
- allocative, production, consumption efficiencies

The influence of the Horizontal Merger Guidelines on antitrust analysis should now be quite apparent. Note how the concepts developed in the Guidelines—inferential methods for predicting anticompetitive effects, entry, and efficiency—have become core concepts for much of antitrust analysis, regardless of the specific legal pigeon hole of an alleged offense. What remains is to revisit a question we first encountered near the end of Chapter 2: can these concepts be organized to produce a structured approach to antitrust analysis that can serve agencies and courts, alike?

As should be evident at this point in our study, the integration of anticompetitive effects, entry, business justifications and efficiency has not proceeded smoothly. Courts, whether proceeding under Section 1 or Section 2, have not frequently been attentive to the importance of specifying the factors they view as most relevant, the burdens of production and proof allocated to the parties, and how cases should be resolved where there is evidence of both anticompetitive effect and business justification.

In Chapter 2 we first examined the collective impact of cases like *NCAA*, *Indian Fed'n of Dentists*, and *California Dental* on efforts by the federal enforcement agencies to synthesize a structured approach for analyzing competitor collaborations in the 2000 Guidelines for Competitor Collaborations. We also saw how the FTC and the D.C. Circuit tried to structure the analysis in *Polygram Holdings. Aspen Skiing Co.*, *Microsoft*, and *Visa* brought the law of monopolization closer to a structured approach. Each example of a structured analysis evaluated anticompetitive effect and business justifications, while looking for ways to truncate the inquiry when it could be justified.

Consider now five models of structured antitrust analysis that we have studied. From Section 1 analysis, the *Collaboration Guidelines* and *Polygram Holdings*. From Section 2, *Microsoft* and *Visa*. And from Section 7 of the Clayton Act, the *Horizontal Merger Guidelines*. Consider how each one addresses concerns about structuring the analysis of allegedly anticompetitive conduct. Consider, too, how each effort appears to be concept-driven. Are the same concepts focal to each? How important are variations among the various statutory schemes we have studied? Do they seem to be fading in importance as the courts and agencies, guided by common, core economic concepts, seek to articulate a framework, complete with shifting burdens, that draws freely on precedent from Sherman Act Section 1, as well as merger law under Clayton Act Section 7. In a real sense, these various approaches to structuring the analysis can be viewed as efforts to synthesize much of what we have examined thus far in our study of antitrust law. Consider carefully the extent to which each succeeds.

Consider finally whether there are down-sides to a "structured" analysis based on the elements discussed in Figure 8–9. Is it an improvement over previous, more open-ended approaches, such as the rule of reason in *Chicago Bd. of Trade* and the "willful acquisition or maintenance" model of *Alcoa* and *Grinnell*? If so, how so? Will it tend to be too rigid? Does it generally favor plaintiffs or defendants? Does it help to minimize error costs, both false positives and false negatives? What is its impact on direct costs of resolving antitrust cases? Does it really clarify the relevant factors and the relative burdens of production and proof? Will it reliably include all of the useful evidence, or possibly exclude information that could affect the outcome of particular cases? Does it provide clear guidance to business firms, and if it does not, what costs are associated with complying with antitrust rules that do not?

H. CONCLUSION

This Chapter has focused on the component parts of the contemporary antitrust case. As we indicated at the outset, the influence of merger and monopolization analysis runs throughout the material. Common concepts now form the essential core of virtually all antitrust cases. It is difficult to imagine a successful antitrust prosecution without a theory of anticompetitive effects, and a method for establishing those anticompetitive effects through evidence.

Common responses have also emerged in the concepts of entry and efficiency. But are these "steps" in the analysis truly distinct? Do they involve an easily discernible and shiftable burden of production? Often it appeared that the evidence that established anticompetitive effects and the evidence that defeated it were not really distinct. Indeed, often the defendants' responses were deeply integrated into the inquiry into effects and market power. Might that be one explanation why it has been difficult for courts to come upon a "structured" analysis?

I. PROBLEMS AND EXERCISES

To explore the questions posed in this Chapter further, we now turn to three problems that present different combinations of evidence of effects and efficiencies. All of the problems are based on the Ready-to-Eat ("RTE") cereal hypothetical first developed in Chapter 6.

The Facts:
A Hypothetical Breakfast Cereal Industry

Many Americans start their day with a bowl of ready-to-eat ("RTE") cereal. Indeed, RTE cereal has been a staple of the breakfast table for over a century and includes a number of varieties of rice, corn, oats, and wheat-based products. Although in the real RTE cereal industry each manufacturer produces many varieties of RTE cereals under multiple brand names (over 200 by one account), we will assume for purposes of this fact pattern that each producer sells one brand. Assume that total U.S. sales of RTE cereals in the most recent year for which statistics are available totaled just over $5 billion.

Of course, the breakfast consumer also faces many other choices, such as egg products, and traditional favorites like waffles, pancakes, and french toast. There are also a variety of wheat and oat based cereals that can be served hot, such as SmoothyWheat and Oat–T–Meal. These hot cereals often come in both "instant" and "quick cook" versions. Some can be prepared simply by adding hot water, others must be cooked conventionally on a stove, and yet others can be prepared in minutes in a microwave oven. Although RTE cereals and hot cereals generally cost about the same per box, their price differs significantly when viewed per serving. For example, a typical 24 oz box of RTE cereal and a typical 16 oz box of instant Oat–T–Meal both cost about

$3.50 in a supermarket. But the RTE contains 25 servings, whereas the instant Oat–T–Meal contains about 10. Thus, the per serving cost is approximately $.14 for RTE cereals, but $.35 for instant Oat–T–Meal. Assume that total U.S. sales of all hot cereals in the most recent year for which statistics are available totaled $500 million. As noted below, with the exception of Oat Cereal Co., which makes Oaties, a popular RTE cereal, as well as Oat–T–Meal, RTE cereals and hot cereals are for the most part produced by different firms.

In the last several decades, there has been a great deal of consolidation in the RTE cereal industry. Whereas in 1975 there were more than a dozen producers, today there remain only five that account for 95% of the sales of RTE cereals in the United States: (1) Crunchy Cereal Co. ("CrunchCo"); (2) Fruity Cereal Co. ("FruitCo"); (3) Oat Cereal Co. ("OatCo"); (4) Flaky–Nut Cereal Co. ("Flaky–NutCo"); and (5) Natural–Wholesome Cereal Co. ("Natural–Wholesome").

Initially, there was little difference in the cereal offerings of each producer. Three of the earliest varieties of RTE cereals were corn flakes, oat circles, and crispy toasted rice. As consumer tastes became more variegated and manufacturing processes matured, the various producers began to differentiate their products based on a number of characteristics. These characteristics can include type of grain, degree of sweetness, physical form, additional ingredients such as fruits and nuts, and perceived purity and healthfulness, which can manifest itself in the form of added vitamins or "organic" ingredients. Each of the principal players in our hypothetical market has sought to use these various characteristics to differentiate its product. Indeed, each has spent years and considerable resources to develop, produce and advertise their respective "flagship brands" of cereals. Hence CrunchCo. is associated with "Crunchies," FruitCo with "Fruities," OatCo with "Oaties," Flaky–NutCo. with "Nutties," and Natural—Wholesome with organic, whole grain cereals ("Earthies"). Table 1 below summarizes each firm's current share of the total dollar volume of RTE cereals sold in the United States:

Table 1

CrunchCo. ("Crunchies")	35%
FruitCo. ("Fruities")	15%
OatCo. ("Oaties")	20%
Flaky–NutCo. ("Nutties")	15%
Natural–Wholesome ("Earthies")	10%
Others	5%

Industry output averages around 85% of capacity, with the exception of CrunchCo., the industry leader, which is operating at only 65% of capacity.

CrunchCo, FruitCo, OatCo and Flaky–NutCo all have had very stable market shares and relatively stable pricing for quite some time. Indeed, although many smaller firms, often with niche products, have entered the RTE business over the years, few survived for more than a year or two. Most of those that have survived and prospered to any degree have been acquired by one of the "Big Four." One exception is Natural–Wholesome, which is itself the product of a merger between the Natural and Wholesome cereals companies. As a general matter, the industry's structure may be due to the economics of RTE cereal production. Costs of production diminish considerably with very large scale production. Nevertheless, there is frequent and vigorous competition in the form of product variation, promotion and advertising, even among the Big Four.

CrunchCo. is one of the oldest RTE manufacturers in the United States and has been continuously producing RTE cereals since the late nineteenth century. It also has a substantial foreign sales division, and sells almost one quarter of its production outside of the United States. It is also the second largest producer of RTE cereals in the world. To insure the quality and stability of its supply of grains, CrunchCo produces almost 75% of its own needs of corn, wheat, and rice on farms in the United States and abroad. The remainder of its needs are purchased from independent farming concerns, typically under long-term exclusive supply contracts. Although CrunchCo has experienced a great deal of internal growth and expansion, it also has acquired at least a half-dozen other producers of RTE cereals, in part in an effort to diversify its cereal line. Most recently, it acquired the Organic Cereal Co., maker of Healthy Harold's, an "all natural" mix of granola, fruit, and grains. The cereal is currently manufactured and sold solely in the Pacific Northwest and is very popular in grocery stores and supermarkets that cater to customers seeking natural, healthy, and organic foods.

For most of its half century in the cereal business, FruitCo. has produced "Fruities," which is promoted under its "Chock Full 'O Fruit" trademark. Although FruitCo. does not produce its own grains, its involvement in fruit growing predates its status as an RTE cereal producer. It thus owns and operates very substantial fruit farms in the southern and western United States, where it grows raisins, apples, and dates. It only uses about half of its annual fruit production for RTE cereal products, and sells the other half to national fruit distributors and to fruit canners throughout the country. It produces no RTE cereals outside of the United States, but it exports roughly 10% of its annual production of RTE cereals, primarily to Canada and Europe.

OatCo. is the leading producer of RTE cereals in Canada, where it is based. As was already mentioned, OatCo. also produces Oat–T–Meal, the most popular brand of instant and quick cook hot oatmeal in the world. It also manufactures private label oat cereals for a variety of national grocery chains, and through its Organic Oats Division, it supplies a certified organic version of Oaties to several natural food manufacturers.

Flaky–NutCo. is one of the largest manufacturers of nuts in the world. It owns and operates production facilities in Asia, the Pacific, and South America. It is the youngest of the Big Four, having begun cereal production just a decade ago through its acquisition of the former Flaky Cereal Co, maker of Flakies. At the time Flaky was acquired by NutCo, it accounted for roughly 5% of U.S. sales of RTE cereals. As noted above, since being acquired by NutCo. and being repositioned under the brand name "Nutties," the combined Flaky–NutCo. has garnered roughly 15% of U.S. RTE cereal sales.

Natural–Wholesome rounds out the RTE cereal industry. In contrast to the Big Four, however, Natural Wholesome produces only certified organic, whole grain natural RTE cereals. These products are made to satisfy the strict regulatory requirements in effect in certain Western States. In order to qualify for certification under these schemes, Natural–Wholesome must only use certified organic ingredients, and its production facilities must meet specific standards. The certification process is so particular, that it can take up to thirty-six months for a firm seeking certification to complete all of the necessary applications and inspections and receive its certification. And as a general matter, certified natural, organic RTE cereal costs about 10% more on average per box than comparable RTE cereals. Nevertheless, certified organic RTE cereal sales have been growing at an average pace of 20% per year, whereas non-certified RTE cereal sales in the United States are growing at only 3% per year.

There are relatively few certified RTE cereal manufacturers that distribute regionally or nationally. Indeed, most tend to be local, selling in a single state or in a multi-state region. Natural Wholesome is the largest of the certified RTE cereal manufacturers. Its annual sales account for approximately 50% of organically certified RTE cereal sales in the U.S. Organic Cereal Co., the maker of Healthy Harold's, produces about 15% of the total.

Natural–Wholesome's cereals for the most part are distributed through different distribution channels than are typical RTE cereals. Whereas most RTE cereals are sold though national grocery wholesalers, or directly to large national supermarket chains, Natural–Wholesome's cereals are sold through regional distributors that cater to natural and organic food groceries and supermarkets. Due to increased competition between traditional and organic supermarkets, however, large traditional supermarket chains have been experimenting with "organic/natural food" aisles, and have recently begun to purchase Natural–Wholesome's cereals directly.

Organic Cereal Co. used to distribute its products exclusively through natural and organic wholesalers, but since being acquired by CrunchCo., it is marketed and sold through both channels of distribution. Typically, though, traditional supermarkets demand up front payments from new suppliers in exchange for access to shelf space. These allowances serve to compensate the supermarket for the risk it takes in providing some if its limited shelf space to a new and unknown product or brand name. As a subsidiary of CrunchCo., the leading producer of non-organic RTE cereals, Organic Cereal has frequently obtained shelf space without having to make these up front payments.

Problem 8–1:
Crunchies–Fruities Strategic Alliance

CrunchCo. and FruitCo. propose to enter into a strategic alliance to expand their joint capacity to produce certified organic RTE cereals. As is indicated in the Fact Pattern, CrunchCo. entered the business through its acquisition of Organic Cereal Co., and currently sells certified organic RTE cereals only in the Pacific Northwest. FruitCo. currently does not produce any certified organic RTE cereals, but roughly 25% of its fruit production is certified organic.

The Alliance, reflected in a lengthy written agreement between the parties, would have an initial term of five (5) years, during which CrunchCo. and FruitCo. will undertake some joint product research and development, and joint marketing. One goal is to expand production at Crunchies' newly acquired Organic Cereal Co.'s plants in California and the Pacific Northwest, which are currently operating at only 60% of capacity. Another goal is to expand the distribution of Organic Cereal's products from the Pacific Northwest to the entire country.

Through the Alliance, CrunchCo. hopes to benefit from FruitCo.'s capacity to produce organically certified fruits, as well as its expertise in incorporating fruits into RTE cereals. Moreover, several of FruitCo.'s fruit processing facilities are located proximate to the Organic Cereal plants now owned by CrunchCo., so the cost of transporting the fruits to the plants will be minimal. Finally, because all organic foods are distributed nationally to natural and organic markets through the same network of suppliers, FruitCo., as a long-time producer of organic fruits, already has established relationships with organic food suppliers. Those relationships will be put to use in marketing the products of the Alliance on a nationwide basis.

For its part, FruitCo. does not currently own any organic cereal production facilities. It sees the Alliance, therefore, as the most effective means of expanding its product line into the booming business of organic RTE cereals.

The Alliance specifically calls for the expansion of the Healthy Harold's line to include several kinds of "Fruity Harold's" cereals, that will include organic fruits grown and supplied by FruitCo. Under the Alliance agreement, FruitCo. has agreed that, for the full term of the agreement, it shall not produce any certified organic RTE cereals on its own or in conjunction with any other firm. The Alliance agreement also provides that FruitCo. will be (1) the exclusive supplier of organic fruits for Fruity Harold's, (2) the exclusive distributor of all Fruity Harold's RTE cereals produced by the Alliance, and (3) the non-exclusive distributor of non-fruity Healthy Harold's cereals. CrunchCo. and FruitCo. have further agreed to appoint a three person Management Committee of CrunchCo. and FruitCo. executives to oversee the business of the Alliance and to make decisions regarding the output and pricing of Fruity Harold's cereals.

You are an attorney for CrunchCo., which has asked you to prepare a memorandum evaluating the legality of the proposed Alliance under federal antitrust laws, as well as under the FTC/DOJ Guidelines for Collaborations Among Competitors. Draft the Memorandum.

Problem 8–2:
Crunchies–Natural–Wholesome Acquisition

For purposes of this problem only, assume that instead of pursuing any alliance with FruitCo., CrunchCo. has decided to acquire Natural–Wholesome. Acquiring Natural–Wholesome will give CrunchCo. prompt access to nationwide distribution, which will in turn allow it to more fully utilize its currently unused plant capacity for certified organic RTE cereals.

You have been asked by CrunchCo. to prepare a memorandum (1) evaluating the legality of the proposed merger under applicable case law, and (2) assessing the likelihood that it might be challenged under the FTC/DOJ Horizontal Merger Guidelines. Draft the Memorandum.

Problem 8–3:
FrunchCo. as a Dominant Firm

Assume for purposes of this question only, that CrunchCo. and FruitCo. are but a single firm, "FrunchCo.", and that FrunchCo. accounts for the sale of 50% of all U.S. sales of RTE cereals (35% + 15%). Assume as well for purposes of this problem that FrunchCo. produces and sells Healthy Harold's, as well as Fruity Harold's, and that together they account for 25% of the total of organically certified RTE cereal sales in the United States, but 78% of organic RTE cereal sales in the Pacific Northwest.

FrunchCo. recently approached its largest direct-buying supermarket chain customer, Delicios, and, for the first time, proposed to it a revised "FrunchCo. Sales Contract." Under the Agreement, which has a term of one (1) year, the supermarket chain would agree to sell FrunchCo. RTE cereals exclusively. The Agreement also includes the following provisions:

- Customer agrees to utilize its best efforts to promote and sell the full line of FrunchCo. Cereals, including all varieties of Crunchies, Fruities, Frunchies, Healthy Harold's and Fruity Harold's;

- Customer may also elect to participate in the FrunchCo. Preferred Organic Cereal Buyer's Program, pursuant to which, FrunchCo. will grant Customer a 5% discount (in addition to all normal promotions) if it purchases all of its requirements of certified organic RTE cereal products from FrunchCo.

Citing its agreement with FrunchCo., Delicios informs Natural–Wholesome that it will no longer purchase any of its certified organic RTE cereals. Shortly thereafter, Natural–Wholesome filed suit against FrunchCo. charging it with violations of Section 2 of the Sherman Act.

As a part of its mandatory expert disclosures under Rule 26(a)(2) of the Federal Rules of Civil Procedure, Natural–Wholesome identified Dr. Susan Hammond as its proposed expert economist. According to the disclosure, Hammond will testify at trial (I) that Organic RTE cereals constitute a relevant product market; (ii) that FrunchCo. possesses monopoly power in that market; and (iii) that FrunchCo. has engaged in exclusionary conduct.

You have been retained by FrunchCo. to defend against Natural–Wholesome's suit. With mandatory initial disclosures completed, you have begun to prepare (1) FrunchCo.'s first set of interrogatories to Natural–Wholesome; and (2) an outline of questions for your upcoming deposition of Dr. Hammond. Draft the following:

(1) five to ten interrogatories directed to the plaintiff, Natural–Wholesome; and

(2) five to ten questions you will ask Dr. Hammond at her deposition.

Chapter 9

IMPLEMENTING COMPETITION POLICY RULES: THE STRUCTURE OF ANTITRUST ENFORCEMENT

In previous chapters we have examined how competition law draws the line between lawful and unlawful behavior, *i.e.*, on the *substance* of antitrust rules. The impact of competition laws, however, derives not solely from the content of their substantive commands, but also from the effectiveness of the institutions entrusted with *implementing* them, which occupies our attention in this Chapter.

A. DESIGNING AND IMPLEMENTING AN ANTITRUST ENFORCEMENT SYSTEM

Assume that a nation has already decided which conduct its competition laws should forbid. Now its lawmakers must determine how to execute the law's prohibitions. Implementing a competition law encompasses a number of steps by which its substantive commands can be applied to specific conduct. In this section we describe those steps, which involve consideration of both the functions and operation of an antitrust enforcement system. Each step often involves complex and challenging policy decisions. This section concludes by briefly reviewing the framework of the world's competition law enforcement systems.

1. A TAXONOMY OF IMPLEMENTATION FUNCTIONS

The process of implementing a competition law's substantive commands can usefully be divided into five sets of factors that are in many respects interdependent:

Defining the Scope of the Law's Application: The Question of Jurisdiction. To understand the importance of defining a law's jurisdiction, imagine a hypothetical world featuring a single government that applies a uniform set of competition policy rules to all entities, public and private. In Chapter 1, we saw that today's global environment is far more complex than such a hypothetical world. Approximately 100 countries now have competition laws, and some permit their political subdivisions (*e.g.*, state governments) to enforce national competition laws. In most countries, economic activity is carried out through a mix of public and private bodies. The mix varies from nation to nation, but many countries rely at least partly on state-owned enterprises to supply goods and services.

The multiplicity of competition authorities across nations and within nations and the mixed public/private nature of most economic systems require the development of jurisdictional principles to answer four questions:

- First, what is the scope of a nation's antitrust jurisdiction over conduct occurring within its borders? In the United States, this question is answered by reference to the commerce clause of the Constitution, and by asking whether in regulating competition Congress intended to go to the full extent of its commerce clause powers.

- Second, what is the *extraterritorial* reach of a nation's competition law, *i.e.*, does it apply to conduct occurring beyond its borders?

- Third, how do national competition laws apply in a *federal* system, which delineates separate roles for the national government and political subdivisions, such as states, counties and municipalities?

- Fourth, do national antitrust commands apply to the *acts of public officials or state-owned enterprises* when such entities restrict competition?

As we shall see, answering these questions in an international setting, indeed, answering them in the context of a setting such as the United States, where concerns about federalism and state sovereign immunity are acute, can pose seemingly intractable challenges.

Investigating and Detecting Violations. A necessary first step in enforcing any law is to identify apparent violations. Means must be provided to investigate and examine the conduct of firms and individuals suspected of violating the antitrust law. These means can involve: (1) required disclosures and notifications; and/or (2) authority to gather information, such as testimony and documentation, that may tend to indicate departures from substantive commands.

A prominent example of a required disclosure is pre-merger notification, a tool used in many competition law systems to uncover competitively questionable mergers and acquisitions prior to consummation. (*See* Sidebar 5–4). More broadly, whether undertaken by public or private parties, means of gathering information must be provided. Those means can be informal, such as gathering publicly available information and conducting voluntary interviews, or formal, as with various court enforceable discovery techniques. In the case of public enforcement authorities, formal discovery might include the power to secure testimony or documents, either through civil means, such as Civil Investigative Demands ("CIDs"), *see* 15 U.S.C. §§ 1311–14 (authorizing DOJ to issue CIDs); 15 U.S.C. § 46 (authorizing FTC to investigate suspected antitrust violations), or through grand jury subpoenas. *See* 18 U.S.C. §§ 6001–05. In federal court litigation, these means include pre-filing informal investigation and post-filing formal disclosures and discovery, such as is provided in Rules 26–37 of the Federal Rules of Civil Procedure.

Prosecution Authority: Rights of Action. By itself, the mere provision of means to collect information about apparent violations may influence the behavior of individuals and companies and even deter some violations. The true impact of an antitrust command, however, depends on whether the law creates effective instrumentalities for filing charges, presenting evidence before an adjudicatory tribunal, and pursuing remedies. Once it is determined that a violation has occurred or is likely to occur, means must be provided to enforce the law. Typically, those means take the form of "rights of action," criminal or civil, which can be vested in one or more actors, such as government enforcement authorities or private parties.

Virtually all competition law systems provide some kind of public right of action for threatened or completed antitrust violations. *See, e.g.,* 15 U.S.C. § 4 (authorizing United States attorneys to institute proceedings to prevent and restrain antitrust violations); 15 U.S.C. § 15a (authorizing United States to sue for damages to its own business or property by reason of an antitrust violation); 15 U.S.C. § 15c (authorizing State attorneys general to sue on behalf of their citizens as parens patriae); and 15 U.S.C. § 45 (authorizing the FTC to prohibit and prevent unfair methods of competition and unfair or deceptive trade practices). Fewer jurisdictions provide a "private" right of action, which has been a central feature of U.S. antitrust law since the Sherman Act was adopted in 1890. The United States is among the few jurisdictions that provide a private right of action that includes the right to recover treble damages, attorneys fees, and costs for violations of the provisions of the Sherman and Clayton Acts. 15 U.S.C. § 15. *See also* 15 U.S.C. § 26 (authorizing suits for injunctive relief against threatened loss or injury). By contrast, the provisions of the Federal Trade Commission Act can only be enforced by the FTC.

Adjudication Authority: The Role of Administrative Agencies and Courts. For a right of action to have value, a competition enforcement system must also create means for deciding whether a private plaintiff's or public prosecutor's claims of misconduct are valid. Adjudication ordinarily encompasses the distinct functions of hearing evidence, deciding guilt or innocence, and imposing sanctions for violations. Rights of action, therefore, typically are exercised before some kind of decision-making body, such as an administrative agency or court, which has been given jurisdiction over the law and the parties sufficient to permit determinations as to both liability and remedies. Frequently, the scope of the right of action, and the scope of jurisdiction to resolve disputes, are defined by statute.

In the United States, jurisdiction to adjudicate claimed violations of the federal antitrust laws is vested in the federal district courts, 15 U.S.C. § 4 (providing United States district courts with jurisdiction to prevent and restrain antitrust violations). This jurisdiction has traditionally been interpreted to be exclusive, meaning that federal antitrust cases, both public and private, can only be decided by federal, not state, courts. *See, e.g., Gen. Inv. Co. v. Lake Shore & Mich. Rwy. Co.,* 260 U.S. 261 (1922) (reading Section 16 of the Clayton Act, 15 U.S.C. § 26, as providing exclusively federal jurisdiction). In addition to subject matter jurisdiction, courts must have proper venue and authority over the parties. *See, e.g.,* 15 U.S.C. § 5 (authorizing broad scope of authority to join additional parties); 15 U.S.C. § 7 (defining "person" for purposes of Sherman Act); and 15 U.S.C. § 22 (authorizing broad scope of venue and nationwide service of process).

Sanctions and Remedies. A person's or firm's willingness to obey a legal command may depend in part on its perception of how effectively the legal system detects and punishes violations. Designing and implementing an effective competition policy system, therefore, also demands attention to the purposes and means of detecting, sanctioning, and remedying violations. Purposes can include deterrence, compensation, and punishment. Sanctions and remedies can be monetary (*e.g.*, fines, penalties, damages, costs and fees), injunctive (*e.g.*, cease and desist, affirmative or negative conduct decrees, or divestiture), and, in the case of criminal violations, prison or forfeiture.

Figure 9–1:

Five Factors Influencing Competition Policy System Design

- The Scope of the Law's Application: The Question of Jurisdiction
- The Power to Investigate and Detect Violations
- Prosecution Authority: Rights of Action
- Adjudication Authority: The Role of Administrative Agencies and Courts
- Sanctions and Remedies

Two examples illustrate the interdependence of these five factors. The first involves the decision to make antitrust offenses crimes. Imposing criminal liability on antitrust violators may affect each variable of the implementation equation. A country that treats antitrust misconduct as a serious crime may use more aggressive measures to detect violations. In the food additives and vitamins cartel cases in Chapter 1, we saw how government prosecutors used investigative tools (*e.g.*, wire taps and electronic surveillance) ordinarily used to gather evidence against drug lords and other dangerous criminals. In addition, because most countries deem the prosecution of crimes to be a function of the executive branch of government, creating criminal liability for antitrust offenses usually will entail giving a prosecutorial role to an executive body (in the United States, the Department of Justice). Moreover, because criminal liability can deprive violators of their personal freedom and create an enduring social stigma, the constitutions of nations that treat antitrust violations as crimes may impose higher evidentiary standards and procedural safeguards for the adjudication of criminal charges. In the United States, for example, the criminalization of antitrust violations under the Sherman Act can implicate the provisions of the Fourth, Fifth, Sixth, and Eighth Amendments to the Constitution.

A second example showing how the elements of implementation interact involves remedies. As noted above, remedies can serve various purposes, including: (1) *deterrence*; (2) *compensation*, and (3) *punishment* or retribution. The importance of each aim varies among legal systems, but deterrence is often a preeminent goal, especially for public enforcement officials. By increasing the violator's costs of behaving improperly, the remedial scheme seeks to discourage affected parties from breaking rules in the first place. Deciding how to punish misconduct requires a country to assess how often violations will be detected, prosecuted, and condemned. To achieve effective deterrence, a nation might raise the level of fines or civil damages—perhaps imposing damages equal to a multiple of actual harm—if it believes illegal conduct is rarely detected or seldom prosecuted successfully.

We can think of the interrelationship of these five design and implementation factors by considering how a firm might decide whether to comply with a competition law's substantive rules. It might use the following checklist:

- Does the law apply to my behavior (the *jurisdictional* issue)?
- If I violate the law, who will notice it (the *detection* issue)?
- If my misconduct is detected, will I be prosecuted (the *prosecution* issue)?
- If I am prosecuted, will I be judged to have broken the law (the *adjudication* issue)?
- If I am deemed guilty, how will I be punished (the *sanctions* issue)?

To sum up, one's willingness to obey the law may depend upon predictions about (a) the likelihood that misdeeds will be detected and prosecuted, and (b) the severity of sanctions likely to be imposed for violations.

2. FACTORS SHAPING INSTITUTIONAL DESIGN CHOICES

As a country evaluates each factor of the implementation process, several larger considerations define the set of possible enforcement solutions. Two key factors stand out. The first involves deciding the degree to which the nation should centralize competition enforcement authority within its borders. The second factor concerns the operation of the laws of other nations. Both factors are considered below.

a. *Distributing Competition Policy Power: The National Level*

In creating a competition policy system, a nation must decide which public entity or entities will enforce the competition law. We can begin by considering a simple model of an organization that centralizes these functions. One means to this end would be to vest all implementation functions in a single arm of the national government. By this approach, *government investigators* would:

- undertake efforts to detect the misconduct (relying on investigations, audits and inspections); and
- use document requests, seizures of property (such as computer records or other physical evidence) and interviews to gather evidence that proves the violation.

A *government prosecutor* would then:

- initiate and litigate charges against the violator;
- conduct pretrial discovery to further support the claim; and
- settle or prosecute the claim before a public court.

A *public court* or *administrative tribunal* would then:

- consider and rule upon pretrial motions;
- conduct a trial (hearing evidence and the arguments of counsel);

- decide guilt or innocence; and

- determine and implement/execute the remedy.

Appeals, perhaps to some *appellate judicial body* might then follow before the matter is concluded.

A second aspect of centralization involves minimizing the number of government bodies that perform implementation functions. For example, a single national competition policy body could investigate and prosecute violations, and a single system of national courts could adjudicate alleged infractions. This simplified mechanism would vest no independent competition policy authority in national agencies responsible for regulating specific sectors, such as telecommunications or transportation. In such a unitary, national system, it is possible that the government of a political subdivision below the national level (*e.g.*, a state) might adopt a competition law of its own and create enforcement bodies that address "local" matters, purely or largely affecting that subdivision alone. Oversight authority for conduct that significantly affects national commerce would reside solely in the national competition agency and in the national courts.

Of course, a nation need not embrace this level of centralization. Policies that distribute competition policy more broadly are possible. In Chapter 1 we explored some of the costs and benefits of decentralizing prosecutorial authority. Among other advantages, decentralization can be an antidote to the failure—due to neglect, capture, change of enforcement priorities, or limited resources—of any single prosecutorial agent to enforce the law. Perhaps the main cost of decentralization is the possibility that the formulation of national competition policy will become fragmented in ways that inhibit the development of coherent antitrust rules. This in return generates costs for enforcers and firms, who may also suffer from lack of clear guidance.

Finally, one decentralization technique is to give private parties authority to perform certain functions. Many law enforcement systems, including competition laws, engage private parties to perform at least some of the implementation functions identified above—to act as "private attorneys general." Governments often provide inducements for private individuals or companies to detect or reveal violations and to help gather evidence of misconduct. Some antitrust laws, including the U.S. system, allow private parties to file and litigate charges against alleged violators if they are injured by the conduct.

Even if the law reserves key implementation functions solely or largely to public institutions, however, a country still could give multiple public bodies authority to perform those functions. A country might select two or more national authorities to enforce the laws and might recognize the role of state governments and their political subdivisions to enforce the national laws or to implement state competition policy commands with substantial spillovers to other states. A country also might create alternative paths for adjudicating competition policy disputes. Rather than channel the adjudication of matters solely through national courts of general jurisdiction, for example, the United States vests some antitrust investigative and adjudicatory functions in a specialized administrative tribunal (the Federal Trade Commission), which was created by statute in 1914.

b.   Distributing Competition Policy Authority: International Relations

The institutional design options presented above for a single nation have important international counterparts. The existence of numerous national competition policy regimes today raises questions about the reach of each national law. With increasing frequency, commercial transactions cross national borders. The operation of national competition systems in more and more countries, therefore, has led to overlapping claims of jurisdiction over conduct that may implicate competition law concerns in more than one nation at a time. This jurisdictional overlap has created tensions that have inspired countries to develop principles for delimiting the application of their national systems and for resolving conflicts that might arise when a single merger or other business practice implicates the laws of two or more countries. Possibilities for addressing the interrelationship of individual national systems include purely voluntary cooperation, bilateral agreements, regional arrangements that coordinate policymaking in a limited geographic region, global mechanisms, or some combination of these measures.

3.   THE COMPETITION POLICY IMPLEMENTATION STATUS QUO

As suggested above, one way to think about antitrust implementation issues is to imagine a simple model and add complications. In the simplest model, the world would consist of a single antitrust jurisdiction with no subdivision of enforcement authority to regions or states within that jurisdiction. The competition law would apply universally to all economic actors, public or private. A single public authority would enforce the law in a unitary court system.

The competition policy status quo today is far more elaborate. Figure 9–2 indicates how the U.S. competition policy system decentralizes the decision to prosecute and uses a wide array of remedies to ensure compliance with substantive antitrust rules:

Figure 9–2:
The Distribution of U.S. Competition Law Enforcement Authority

Entity	Responsibilities
DOJ	Enforces Sherman and Clayton Acts and has exclusive criminal authority; can obtain civil injunctions and can obtain civil damages (trebled) when the federal government is injured in its capacity as a purchaser.
FTC	Enforces FTC Act (which incorporates antitrust authority under Sherman Act), and independently the Clayton Act. Also has authority to address consumer protection issues. Can obtain equitable remedies, including restitution, and seek injunctions in court. Can order firms to cease and desist unlawful conduct and fine them for noncompliance.

Entity	Responsibilities
States	Enforce Sherman and Clayton Acts as well as state antitrust laws; can obtain injunctions and treble damages under federal and state statutes; enforce criminal provisions of state statutes. Can sue as parens patriae on behalf of its citizens.
Private Parties	Enforce Sherman and Clayton Acts and can obtain treble damages and injunctions; prevailing plaintiffs also are entitled to attorneys fees and costs.

Other U.S. government agencies also exercise competition policy authority in special cases. Sectoral regulators such as the Federal Communications Commission and the Federal Energy Regulatory Commission have power to analyze the competitive effects of mergers and impose remedies on service providers under broad "public interest" standards contained in their organic statutes.

The global picture features a wide array of competition policy systems, which combine various features of U.S. and EU models. Nearly 100 jurisdiction have adopted some form of competition policy system, most of which bar cartels and single firm activity, although they tend to embrace the potentially more expansive "abuse of dominance" formula of the EU to the constrained "monopolization" approach of the U.S. Many also preclude at least some categories of vertical relationships and most seek to regulate mergers to some degree, albeit with widely variable pre-merger notification procedures.

Few nations, however, have considered empowering multiple enforcement agencies. And only a minority of jurisdictions have adopted criminal enforcement and private rights of action, two core elements of the U.S. system. The hesitance to approach antitrust violations as criminal offenses, however, may be waning, due in large part to the spectacularly successful U.S. prosecution of the food additive and vitamins cartels we saw in Chapter 1. As we will learn in Sidebar 9–2, at least some of these variations may dissolve over time in light of continuing efforts by individual nations and multinational bodies to consider whether there are certain "best practices" that warrant universal adoption. Similarly, there has been increased interest in Europe in recent years in encouraging private enforcement of antitrust laws, although not with treble damages and U.S.-styled discovery or class actions. *See* Chapter 9E, *infra*.

We now turn to a more in-depth consideration of some of the specific design choices that have been made in the United States.

B. DEFINING THE BOUNDARIES OF NATIONAL JURISDICTION

As noted earlier in this Chapter, the U.S. federal antitrust statutes are grounded in the constitutional power of Congress to regulate interstate or foreign trade or commerce. The Sherman Act governs conduct "in restraint of trade or commerce among the several States, or with foreign nations" and reaches restraints that are "in" interstate commerce *or* that have a substantial "effect" on such commerce. 15 U.S.C. §§ 1–2. *See Mandeville Island Farms, Inc. v. Am. Crystal Sugar Co.*, 334 U.S. 219 (1948). In general, the Sherman Act has been read as co-extensive with the scope of the federal commerce power, although as we shall see, more recently some defendants have sought to narrow its jurisdictional reach.

The Clayton Act as it currently is constituted, has a narrower jurisdictional scope and applies only to persons operating "in" interstate commerce. *See Gulf Oil Corp. v. Copp Paving, Inc.*, 419 U.S. 186 (1974). This "in commerce" requirement has been interpreted as requiring more than a mere effect on commerce, but actual movement of commerce across state lines, and it constrains the reach of Section 2 of the Clayton Act, as amended by the Robinson–Patman Act (price discrimination) and Section 3 of the Clayton Act (exclusionary vertical agreements).

An important exception is the Clayton Act's antimerger provision (Section 7, 15 U.S.C. § 18). In response to *United States v. Am. Bldg. Maint. Indus.*, 422 U.S. 271 (1975), which read Section 7's jurisdictional reach narrowly to keep it consistent with the provisions of Sections 2 and 3 of the Act, Congress amended Section 7 in 1980 to permit jurisdiction over persons "engaged in commerce *or in any activity affecting commerce*." (emphasis added) The amendment was designed to and has had the effect of making antitrust jurisdiction over mergers and acquisitions co-extensive with the reach of the Sherman Act under its more lenient "effects" test. Similarly, to alter a narrow reading of the FTC's jurisdiction in *FTC v. Bunte Bros.*, 312 U.S. 349 (1941), Section 5 the FTC Act was amended in 1975 to authorize jurisdiction over unfair methods of competition or deceptive acts or practices "in or affecting commerce." 15 U.S.C. § 45(a)(2). Since that time, the FTC's jurisdiction under Section 5 resembles that of the Sherman Act.

1. INTERSTATE COMMERCE REQUIREMENT

The Sherman Act's interstate commerce requirement is easily satisfied today. Plaintiffs can establish this jurisdictional element by showing that the challenged conduct: (a) directly interfered with the flow of goods in commerce (the "in commerce" test), or (b) substantially affected interstate commerce (the "effect on commerce" test). As the following case demonstrates, the Sherman Act's "effect on commerce" test can reach a wide range of seemingly local behavior, but defining that reach has generated significant disagreement within the Court.

SUMMIT HEALTH, LTD. v. PINHAS
Supreme Court of the United States, 1991.
500 U.S. 322, 111 S.Ct. 1842, 114 L.Ed.2d 366

Mr. Justice STEVENS delivered the opinion of the Court.

The question presented is whether the interstate commerce requirement of antitrust jurisdiction is satisfied by allegations that petitioners conspired to exclude respondent, a duly licensed and practicing physician and surgeon, from the market for ophthalmological services in Los Angeles because he refused to follow an unnecessarily costly surgical procedure.

In 1987, respondent Dr. Simon J. Pinhas filed a complaint in District Court alleging that petitioners Summit Health, Ltd. (Summit), Midway Hospital Medical Center (Midway), its medical staff, and others had entered into a conspiracy to drive him out of business "so that other ophthalmologists and eye physicians [including four of the petitioners] will have a greater share of the eye care and ophthalmic surgery in Los Angeles." Among his allegations was a claim that the conspiracy violated § 1 of the Sherman Act. The District Court granted defendants' (now petitioners') motion to dismiss the First Amended Complaint (complaint) without leave to amend, but the United States Court of Appeals for the Ninth Circuit reinstated the antitrust claim. We granted certiorari to consider petitioners' contention that the complaint fails to satisfy the jurisdictional requirements of the Sherman Act, as interpreted in *McLain v. Real Estate Bd. of New Orleans, Inc.*, 444 U.S. 232, 100 S.Ct. 502 (1980), because it does not describe a factual nexus between the alleged boycott and interstate commerce.

* * *

II

Congress enacted the Sherman Act in 1890. During the past century, as the dimensions and complexity of our economy have grown, the federal power over commerce, and the concomitant coverage of the Sherman Act, have experienced similar expansion. * * *

We therefore begin by noting certain propositions that are undisputed in this case. Petitioner Summit, the parent of Midway as well as of several other general hospitals, is unquestionably engaged in interstate commerce. Moreover, although Midway's primary activity is the provision of health care services in a local market, it also engages in interstate commerce. A conspiracy to prevent Midway from expanding would be covered by the Sherman Act, even though any actual impact on interstate commerce would be " 'indirect' " and " 'fortuitous.' " *Hospital Building Co. v. Rex Hospital Trustees*, 425 U.S. 738, 744, 96 S.Ct. 1848, 1852 (1976). No specific purpose to restrain interstate commerce is required. *Id.*, at 745, 96 S.Ct., at 1852. As a "matter of practical economics," *ibid.*, the effect of such a conspiracy on the hospital's "purchases of out-of-state medicines and supplies as well as its revenues from out-of-state insurance companies," *id.*, at 744, 96 S.Ct., at 1852, would establish the necessary interstate nexus.

This case does not involve the full range of activities conducted at a general hospital. Rather, this case involves the provision of ophthalmological services. It seems clear, however, that these services are regularly performed for out-of-state patients and generate revenues from out-of-state sources; their importance as part of the entire operation of the hospital is evident from the allegations of the complaint. A conspiracy to eliminate the entire ophthalmological department of the hospital, like a conspiracy to destroy the hospital itself, would unquestionably affect interstate commerce. Petitioners contend, however, that a boycott of a single surgeon has no such obvious effect because the complaint does not deny the existence of an adequate supply of other surgeons to perform all of the services that respondent's current and future patients may ever require. Petitioners argue that respondent's complaint is insufficient because there is no factual nexus between the restraint on this one surgeon's practice and interstate commerce.

There are two flaws in petitioners' argument. First, because the essence of any violation of § 1 is the illegal agreement itself—rather than the overt acts performed in furtherance of it—proper analysis focuses, not upon actual consequences, but rather upon the potential harm that would ensue if the conspiracy were successful. * * * Thus, respondent need not allege, or prove, an actual effect on interstate commerce to support federal jurisdiction.

Second, if the conspiracy alleged in the complaint is successful, " 'as a matter of practical economics' " there will be a reduction in the provision of ophthalmological services in the Los Angeles market. *McLain,* 444 U.S., at 246, 100 S.Ct., at 511 (quoting *Hospital Building Co. v. Rex Hospital Trustees,* 425 U.S., at 745, 96 S.Ct., at 1852). In cases involving horizontal agreements to fix prices or allocate territories within a single State, we have based jurisdiction on a general conclusion that the defendants' agreement "almost surely" had a marketwide impact and therefore an effect on interstate commerce, *Burke v. Ford,* 389 U.S. 320, 322, 88 S.Ct. 443, 444 (1967) (*per curiam*), or that the agreement "necessarily affect[ed]" the volume of residential sales and therefore the demand for financing and title insurance provided by out-of-state concerns. *McLain,* 444 U.S., at 246, 100 S.Ct., at 511. In the latter case, we explained:

> "To establish the jurisdictional element of a Sherman Act violation it would be sufficient for petitioners to demonstrate a substantial effect on interstate commerce generated by respondents' brokerage activity. Petitioners need not make the more particularized showing of an effect on interstate commerce caused by the alleged conspiracy to fix commission rates, or by those other aspects of respondents' activity that are alleged to be unlawful." *Id.,* at 242–243, 100 S.Ct., at 509.

Although plaintiffs in *McLain* were consumers of the conspirators' real estate brokerage services, and plaintiff in this case is a competing surgeon whose complaint identifies only himself as the victim of the alleged boycott, the same analysis applies. For if a violation of the Sherman Act occurred, the case is necessarily more significant than the fate of "just one merchant whose business is so small that his destruction makes little difference to the economy." *Klor's, Inc. v. Broadway–Hale Stores, Inc.,* 359 U.S. 207, 213, 79 S.Ct. 705, 710 (1959) (footnote omitted). The case involves an alleged restraint on the practice of ophthalmological services. The restraint was accomplished by an alleged misuse of a congressionally regulated peer review process, which respondent characterizes as the gateway that controls access to the market for his services. The gateway was closed to respondent, both at Midway and at other hospitals, because petitioners insisted upon adhering to an unnecessarily costly procedure. The competitive significance of respondent's exclusion from the market must be measured, not just by a particularized evaluation of his own practice, but rather, by a general evaluation of the impact of the restraint on other participants and potential participants in the market from which he has been excluded.

We have no doubt concerning the power of Congress to regulate a peer review process controlling access to the market for ophthalmological surgery in Los Angeles. Thus, respondent's claim that members of the peer review committee conspired with others to abuse that process and thereby deny respondent access to the market for ophthalmological services provided by general hospitals in Los Angeles has a sufficient nexus with interstate commerce to support federal jurisdiction.

The judgment of the Court of Appeals is affirmed.

[Dissenting opinion by Justice SCALIA, with whom Justice O'CONNOR, Justice KENNEDY, and Justice SOUTER join, omitted. Eds.]

––––––––

The *Summit* majority emphasized that if the alleged conspiracy succeeded, the plaintiff's exclusion would have curtailed ophthalmology services in Los Angeles, which attracted out-of-state patients and generated revenues from out-of-state sources. In response, the *Summit* dissenting justices argued that the majority's rationale left few matters outside the Sherman Act's reach. Justice Scalia's dissent observed: "Federal courts are an attractive forum, and the treble damages of the Clayton Act an attractive remedy. We have today made them available for routine business torts, needlessly destroying a sensible statutory allocation of federal-state responsibility and contributing to the trivialization of the federal courts." The modest residuum of commerce that remains purely intrastate after *Summit* ordinarily is subject to scrutiny under state antitrust laws.

Perhaps the biggest surprise in *Summit Health* was that the defendant's argument for a more circumspect view of Sherman Act jurisdiction garnered the votes of four of the Justices, which may suggest that support within the Court for continuing the expansive reading of the Sherman Act's jurisdiction that has endured since *Mandeville Island Farms* may be waning. What is the point of difference between the majority and dissent? One explanation may lie in their differing views of the relevant "jurisdictional nexus"—the relationship between the challenged conduct and interstate commerce. Should the "nexus" issue be answered through reference to the general activities of the defendants, or solely through reference to the anticompetitive consequences of the unlawful conduct? Which approach did the majority use? Would use of a different approach have resulted in a different outcome? *See generally* Andrew I. Gavil, *Reconstructing the Jurisdictional Foundation of Antitrust Federalism*, 61 GEO. WASH. L. REV. 657 (1993) (discussing *Summit Health*).

More broadly, what are Justice Scalia's concerns, reflected in his assertion that federal courts are "an attractive forum," that treble damages is "an attractive remedy," and that federal courts should not be available for the prosecution of "routine business torts"? Is he concerned that broad jurisdictional principles invite the filing of anemic antitrust claims and increase the chance of false positives? Does a similar concern underlie the Supreme Court's more recent opinions in *Trinko* (Chapter 6) and *Twombly* (Chapter 3)?

2. FOREIGN JURISDICTIONAL BARRIERS

With increasing frequency, antitrust disputes involve the extraterritorial reach of the U.S. antitrust statutes. The Sherman Act applies to conduct that restrains trade or commerce "among the several States, or with foreign nations." Cases interpreting this limitation generally have concluded that the antitrust laws ordinarily do not apply to conduct by U.S. companies or foreign firms outside the United States, when such conduct neither affects consumers or markets in the United States nor restricts export opportunities for U.S. firms.

The current state of extraterritorial jurisdiction, however, developed over the course of much of the twentieth century. In its first consideration of the issue in *American Banana Co. v. United Fruit Co.*, 213 U.S. 347 (1909), the Supreme Court embraced a very narrow, territorial view of the Sherman Act's jurisdiction over foreign conduct: "[T]he general and almost universal rule is that the character of an act as lawful or unlawful must be determined wholly by the law of the country where the act was done." *Id.* at 356. In so holding, the Court, consistent with the contemporary views of the limits of subject matter and personal jurisdiction, did not admit of the possibility that conduct outside U.S. borders that causes ill effects within its borders could give rise to jurisdiction.

With the expansion of international commerce and the erosion of territorial notions of jurisdiction domestically, *cf. International Shoe Co. v. Washington*, 326 U.S. 310 (1945) (adopting "minimum contacts" test for personal jurisdiction), the courts began to move away from the doctrine of *American Banana*. In what became the most significant symbol of that movement, the now familiar "effects doctrine" emerged in *United States v. Aluminum Co. of Am.*, 148 F.2d 416 (2d Cir.1945)("Alcoa"). Rejecting the rule of territoriality that controlled in *American Banana*, *Alcoa* instead held that foreign conduct having effects on U.S. import commerce indeed fell within the reach of the Sherman Act: "any state may impose liabilities, even upon persons not within its allegiance, for conduct outside its borders that has consequences within its borders which the state reprehends." *Id.* at 443. *See also* U.S. Dep't of Justice and Federal Trade Comm'n, *Antitrust Enforcement Guidelines for International Operations* § 3.1 (1995) (endorsing effects doctrine).

As we shall see in *Hartford Fire*, *Alcoa's* "effects doctrine" is now more generally accepted. But for a time it triggered a great deal of controversy internationally. Some of that controversy stemmed from foreign reactions to the substance of U.S. antitrust commands, especially the notion that Sherman Act violations might be prosecuted criminally. Foreign authorities also reacted with hostility to the liberal scope of U.S. discovery, the availability of class actions, the prospect of large scale treble damages, and the notion that recovery of attorneys fees could be limited to prevailing plaintiffs. As we shall see immediately below in connection with *Hartford Fire*, these tensions led to calls for the recognition by U.S. courts of principles of "comity" to moderate the impact of U.S. antitrust jurisdiction over extraterritorial conduct. Today, however, the effects doctrine is more widely recognized and has been endorsed by the EU. *See, e.g.*, Cases 89/85, *A. Ahlstrom Osakeyhtio v. Commission*, 1988 E.C.R. 5193 ("*Wood Pulp*").

After decades of heightening controversy over the operation of *Alcoa's* effects test, Congress acted in 1982 to codify U.S. antitrust jurisdictional principles in the Foreign Trade Antitrust Improvements Act of 1982 ("FTAIA"), 15 U.S.C. § 6a. The FTAIA excluded from the jurisdiction of the U.S. antitrust laws conduct "involving trade or commerce (other than import trade or import commerce) with foreign nations unless (1) such conduct has a direct, substantial and reasonably foreseeable effect (A) on [domestic or import commerce], or (B) on export trade or export commerce * * * of a person engaged in such commerce in the United States." 15 U.S.C. § 6a. Claimants who base jurisdiction on subclause (B) must show that the conduct involves "injury to export business in the United States." As we shall see in the three cases that follow, however, the full meaning of the FTAIA's convoluted language remains a source of some uncertainty in the courts. The language and the legislative history of the Act strongly suggest that it was intended to promote U.S. exports by precluding the exercise of U.S. jurisdiction over U.S. firms engaged in foreign commerce when the only injured parties are foreign firms or consumers. But other significant issues of interpretation have arisen.

a. Comity

Several judge-made doctrines limit the application of the U.S. antitrust statutes to transnational business activity. Since the mid–1970s, American courts sometimes have used the doctrine of *comity* in determining whether to apply the antitrust laws extraterritorially where doing so might damage relations between the United States and foreign governments. Where the law of the defendant's home country conflicts with the U.S. antitrust laws, courts will balance foreign interests against U.S. interests in deciding whether to exercise jurisdiction. *See, e.g., Timberlane Lumber Co. v. Bank of America*, 549 F.2d 597 (9th Cir.1976).

In *Hartford Fire Ins. Co. v. California*, 509 U.S. 764, 113 S.Ct. 2891 (1993), the Supreme Court considered whether principles of international comity should preclude the exercise of jurisdiction over British reinsurance companies who were alleged to have conspired with American insurance companies to limit certain forms of insurance coverage. It also considered the relationship between the "substantial effects" doctrine of *Alcoa* and the "direct, substantial and reasonably foreseeable effects" standard of the FTAIA.

HARTFORD FIRE INSURANCE CO. v. CALIFORNIA

Supreme Court of the United States, 1993.
509 U.S. 764, 113 S.Ct. 2891, 125 L.Ed.2d 612.

SOUTER, J., announced the judgment of the Court and delivered the opinion for a unanimous Court with respect to Parts I and II–A, the opinion of the Court with respect to Parts III and IV, in which REHNQUIST, C.J., and WHITE, BLACKMUN, and STEVENS, JJ., joined, and an opinion concurring in the judgment with respect to Part II–B, in which WHITE, BLACKMUN, and STEVENS, JJ., joined. SCALIA, J., delivered the opinion of the Court with respect to Part I, in which REHNQUIST, C.J., and O'CONNOR, KENNEDY, and THOMAS, JJ., joined, and a dissenting opinion with respect to Part II, in which O'CONNOR, KENNEDY, and THOMAS, JJ., joined.

The Sherman Act makes every contract, combination, or conspiracy in unreasonable restraint of interstate or foreign commerce illegal. These consolidated cases present questions about the application of that Act to the insurance industry, both here and abroad. The plaintiffs (respondents here) allege that both domestic and foreign defendants (petitioners here) violated the Sherman Act by engaging in various conspiracies to affect the American insurance market. A group of domestic defendants argues that the McCarran–Ferguson Act, 59 Stat. 33, as amended, 15 U.S.C. § 1011 *et seq.,* precludes application of the Sherman Act to the conduct alleged; a group of foreign defendants argues that the principle of international comity requires the District Court to refrain from exercising jurisdiction over certain claims against it. We hold that most of the domestic defendants' alleged conduct is not immunized from antitrust liability by the McCarran–Ferguson Act, and that, even assuming it applies, the principle of international comity does not preclude District Court jurisdiction over the foreign conduct alleged.

I

The two petitions before us stem from consolidated litigation comprising the complaints of 19 States and many private plaintiffs alleging that the defendants, members of the insurance industry, conspired in violation of § 1 of the Sherman Act to restrict the terms of coverage of commercial general liability (CGL) insurance available in the United States. Because the cases come to us on motions to dismiss, we take the allegations of the complaints as true.

According to the complaints, the object of the conspiracies was to force certain primary insurers (insurers who sell insurance directly to consumers) to change the terms of their standard CGL insurance policies to conform with the policies the defendant insurers wanted to sell. The defendants wanted four changes.

First, CGL insurance has traditionally been sold in the United States on an "occurrence" basis, through a policy obligating the insurer "to pay or defend claims, whenever made, resulting from an accident or 'injurious exposure to conditions' that occurred during the [specific time] period the policy was in effect." In place of this traditional "occurrence" trigger of coverage, the defendants wanted a "claims-made" trigger, obligating the insurer to pay or defend only those claims made during the policy period. Such a policy has the distinct advantage for the insurer that when the policy period ends without a claim having been made, the insurer can be certain that the policy will not expose it to any further liability. Second, the defendants wanted the "claims-made" policy to have a "retroactive date" provision, which would further restrict coverage to claims based on incidents that occurred after a certain date. Such a provision eliminates the risk that an insurer, by issuing a claims-made policy, would assume liability arising from incidents that occurred before the policy's effective date, but remained undiscovered or caused no immediate harm. Third, CGL insurance has traditionally covered "sudden and accidental" pollution; the defendants wanted to eliminate that coverage. Finally, CGL insurance has traditionally provided that the insurer would bear the legal costs of defending covered claims against the insured without regard to the policy's stated limits of coverage; the defendants wanted legal defense costs to be counted against the stated limits (providing a "legal defense cost cap").

To understand how the defendants are alleged to have pressured the targeted primary insurers to make these changes, one must be aware of two important features of the insurance industry. First, most primary insurers rely on certain outside support services for the type of insurance coverage they wish to sell. Defendant Insurance Services Office, Inc. (ISO), an association of approximately 1,400 domestic property and casualty insurers (including the primary insurer defendants, Hartford Fire Insurance Company, Allstate Insurance Company, CIGNA Corporation, and Aetna Casualty and Surety Company), is the almost exclusive source of support services in this country for CGL insurance. ISO develops standard policy forms and files or lodges them with each State's insurance regulators; most CGL insurance written in the United States is written on these forms. All of the "traditional" features of CGL insurance relevant to this litigation were embodied in the ISO standard CGL insurance form that had been in use since 1973 (1973 ISO CGL form). For each of its standard policy forms, ISO also supplies actuarial and rating information: it collects, aggregates, interprets, and distributes data on the premiums charged, claims filed and paid, and defense costs expended with respect to each form, and on the basis of this data it predicts future loss trends and calculates advisory premium rates. Most ISO members cannot afford to continue to use a form if ISO withdraws these support services.

Second, primary insurers themselves usually purchase insurance to cover a portion of the risk they assume from the consumer. This so-called "reinsurance" may serve at least two purposes, protecting the primary insurer from catastrophic loss, and allowing the primary insurer to sell more insurance than its own financial capacity might otherwise permit. Thus, "[t]he availability of reinsurance affects the ability and willingness of primary insurers to provide insurance to their customers." Insurers who sell reinsurance themselves often purchase insurance to cover part of the risk they assume from the primary insurer; such "retrocessional reinsurance" does for reinsurers what reinsurance does for primary insurers. Many of the defendants here are reinsurers or reinsurance brokers, or play some other specialized role in the reinsurance business; defendant Reinsurance Association of America (RAA) is a trade association of domestic reinsurers.

The prehistory of events claimed to give rise to liability starts in 1977, when ISO began the process of revising its 1973 CGL form. For the first time, it proposed two CGL forms (1984 ISO CGL forms), one the traditional "occurrence" type, the other "with a new 'claims-made' trigger." The "claims-made" form did not have a retroactive date provision, however, and both 1984 forms covered " 'sudden and accidental' pollution" damage and provided for unlimited coverage of legal defense costs by the insurer. Within the ISO, defendant Hartford Fire Insurance Company objected to the proposed 1984 forms; it desired elimination of the "occurrence" form, a retroactive date provision on the "claims-made" form, elimination of sudden and accidental pollution coverage, and a legal defense cost cap. Defendant Allstate Insurance Company also expressed its desire for a retroactive date provision on the "claims-made" form. Majorities in the relevant ISO committees, however, supported the proposed 1984 CGL forms and rejected the changes proposed by Hartford and Allstate. In December 1983, the ISO Board of Directors approved the proposed 1984 forms, and ISO filed or lodged the forms with state regulators in March 1984.

Dissatisfied with this state of affairs, the defendants began to take other steps to force a change in the terms of coverage of CGL insurance generally available, steps that, the plaintiffs allege, implemented a series of conspiracies in violation of § 1 of the Sherman Act. * * *

* * *

II

* * *

[The Court concluded that the McCarran–Ferguson Act did not confer antitrust immunity upon the insurance-related activities at issue in the plaintiffs' claims. Eds.]

III

* * * [W]e take up the question * * * whether certain claims against the London reinsurers should have been dismissed as improper applications of the Sherman Act to foreign conduct. The Fifth Claim for Relief in the California Complaint alleges a violation of § 1 of the Sherman Act by certain London reinsurers who conspired to coerce primary insurers in the United States to offer CGL coverage on a claims-made basis, thereby making "occurrence CGL coverage * * * unavailable in the State of California for many risks." The Sixth Claim for Relief in the California Complaint alleges that the London reinsurers violated § 1 by a conspiracy to limit coverage of pollution risks in North America, thereby rendering "pollution liability coverage * * * almost entirely unavailable for the vast majority of casualty insurance purchasers in the State of California." The Eighth Claim for Relief in the California Complaint alleges a further § 1 violation by the London reinsurers who, along with domestic retrocessional reinsurers, conspired to limit coverage of seepage, pollution, and property contamination risks in North America, thereby eliminating such coverage in the State of California.

At the outset, we note that the District Court undoubtedly had jurisdiction of these Sherman Act claims, as the London reinsurers apparently concede. * * * Although the proposition was perhaps not always free from doubt, [citing *American Banana*], it is well established by now that the Sherman Act applies to foreign conduct that was meant to produce and did in fact produce some substantial effect in the United States [citing *Alcoa*, *Matsushita* and other authorities]. Such is the conduct alleged here: that the London reinsurers engaged in unlawful conspiracies to affect the market for insurance in the United States and that their conduct in fact produced substantial effect.[1]

According to the London reinsurers, the District Court should have declined to exercise such jurisdiction under the principle of international comity. The Court of Appeals agreed that courts should look to that principle

---

1. Under § 402 of the Foreign Trade Antitrust Improvements Act of 1982 (FTAIA), the Sherman Act does not apply to conduct involving foreign trade or commerce, other than import trade or import commerce, unless "such conduct has a direct, substantial, and reasonably foreseeable effect" on domestic or import commerce. The FTAIA was intended to exempt from the Sherman Act export transactions that did not injure the United States economy, and it is unclear how it might apply to the conduct alleged here. Also unclear is whether the Act's "direct, substantial, and reasonably foreseeable effect" standard amends existing law or merely codifies it. We need not address these questions here. Assuming that the FTAIA's standard affects this litigation, and assuming further that that standard differs from the prior law, the conduct alleged plainly meets its requirements.

in deciding whether to exercise jurisdiction under the Sherman Act. This availed the London reinsurers nothing, however. To be sure, the Court of Appeals believed that "application of [American] antitrust laws to the London reinsurance market 'would lead to significant conflict with English law and policy,'" and that "[s]uch a conflict, unless outweighed by other factors, would by itself be reason to decline exercise of jurisdiction." But other factors, in the court's view, including the London reinsurers' express purpose to affect United States commerce and the substantial nature of the effect produced, outweighed the supposed conflict and required the exercise of jurisdiction in this litigation.

When it enacted the FTAIA, Congress expressed no view on the question whether a court with Sherman Act jurisdiction should ever decline to exercise such jurisdiction on grounds of international comity. See H.R. Rep. No. 97–686, p. 13 (1982) ("If a court determines that the requirements for subject matter jurisdiction are met, [the FTAIA] would have no effect on the court['s] ability to employ notions of comity * * * or otherwise to take account of the international character of the transaction") (citing *Timberlane [Timberlane Lumber Co. v. Bank of America, N.T. & S.A.,* 549 F.2d 597 (1976). Eds.]). We need not decide that question here, however, for even assuming that in a proper case a court may decline to exercise Sherman Act jurisdiction over foreign conduct (or, as Justice SCALIA would put it, may conclude by the employment of comity analysis in the first instance that there is no jurisdiction), international comity would not counsel against exercising jurisdiction in the circumstances alleged here.

The only substantial question in this litigation is whether "there is in fact a true conflict between domestic and foreign law." The London reinsurers contend that applying the Act to their conduct would conflict significantly with British law, and the British Government, appearing before us as *amicus curiae,* concurs. They assert that Parliament has established a comprehensive regulatory regime over the London reinsurance market and that the conduct alleged here was perfectly consistent with British law and policy. But this is not to state a conflict. "[T]he fact that conduct is lawful in the state in which it took place will not, of itself, bar application of the United States antitrust laws," even where the foreign state has a strong policy to permit or encourage such conduct. Restatement (Third) Foreign Relations Law § 415, Comment *j.* No conflict exists, for these purposes, "where a person subject to regulation by two states can comply with the laws of both." Restatement (Third) Foreign Relations Law § 403, Comment *e.* Since the London reinsurers do not argue that British law requires them to act in some fashion prohibited by the law of the United States * * * or claim that their compliance with the laws of both countries is otherwise impossible, we see no conflict with British law. See Restatement (Third) Foreign Relations Law § 403, Comment *e,* § 415, Comment *j.* We have no need in this litigation to address other considerations that might inform a decision to refrain from the exercise of jurisdiction on grounds of international comity.

* * *

Although the Court notes that in adopting the FTAIA Congress expressed no view about whether an American court should decline to exercise Sherman Act jurisdiction on comity grounds, *Hartford* said American courts should consider doing so only where American law and foreign law truly *conflict*. The British reinsurance firms argued that such a conflict existed because their activities were legal under British law. Stating that "[n]o conflict exists 'where a person subject to regulation by two states can comply with the laws of both,'" the Court ruled that a conflict would exist only if the British law compelled the behavior in question. Without a conflict, there was "no need to address other considerations that might inform a decision to refrain from the exercise of jurisdiction on grounds of international comity." What is the impact of this approach on the role of comity?

As early as the late 1950s, noted commentator Kingman Brewster, Jr. advocated a greater role for comity in the form of a "jurisdictional rule of reason" that could serve as an antidote to the unbridled assertion by U.S. courts of effects-based antitrust jurisdiction. *See* KINGMAN BREWSTER, JR., ANTI-TRUST AND AMERICAN BUSINESS ABROAD 446 (1958). One commentator has observed, however, that Brewster, and later courts such as the Ninth Circuit in *Timberlane*, were responding in part to the perceived hostility of foreign nations unaccustomed to and unaccepting of U.S. antitrust laws. Today antitrust laws—and the effects doctrine—are more widely accepted, and national antitrust prosecutors are more sensitive to the international ramifications of their enforcement decisions. These and other factors suggest that *Hartford Fire's* decision to limit the role of comity may in part be a function of changing times, in which more energy has been turned to convergence and harmonization than comity. *See* Spencer Weber Waller, *The Twilight of Comity*, 38 COLUM. J. TRANSNAT'L L. 563 (2000). *See also* Eleanor Fox, *National Law, Global Markets, and* Hartford: *Eyes Wide Shut*, 68 ANTITRUST L.J. 73 (2000) (arguing that *Hartford Fire*, the U.S. Guidelines for International Operations, and the relevant EU authorities all suffer from an insufficiently global perspective).

On the other hand, *Hartford* may also reflect a competing line of thought, more basic and traditional: that once a court determines that Congress has granted it jurisdiction to entertain an antitrust controversy, it lacks the authority to decline to exercise that jurisdiction on grounds of "comity." *See, e.g., Laker Airways Ltd. v. Sabena, Belgian World Airlines*, 731 F.2d 909 (D.C. Cir. 1984):

> [B]oth institutional limitations on the judicial process and Constitutional restrictions on the exercise of judicial power make it unacceptable for the Judiciary to seize the political initiative and determine that legitimate application of American laws must evaporate when challenged by a foreign jurisdiction.

731 F.2d at 954. *See generally* Michael Sennett & Andrew I. Gavil, *Antitrust Jurisdiction, Extraterritorial Conduct and Interest–Balancing*, 19 INT'L LAW. 1185 (1985) (discussing conflict between *Timberlane* and *Laker Airways*). By focusing on "conflict" as a prerequisite to any discussion of comity, *Hartford Fire* left this more structural question for another day. Arguably, by acting through FTAIA to define more specifically U.S. court jurisdiction over extra-territorial conduct, and by doing so without directing courts to moderate their

exercise of the jurisdiction granted through the discretionary exercise of comity analysis, Congress has implicitly rejected such a role for courts.

b. The Substantial Effects Test: Sorting out the Relationship Between Hartford Fire and the FTAIA

As we learned in the previous section, under *McLain* and *Summit Health*, the jurisdictional threshold for domestic antitrust violations is relatively minimal—all that need be alleged is that the challenged conduct *affected* interstate commerce. Although cases like *Alcoa* were perceived as expanding U.S. antitrust jurisdiction through the effects doctrine, they imposed a more elevated jurisdictional standard on foreign conduct than did the domestic cases like *McLain*. As *Hartford Fire* formulated the standard, in order to assert U.S. antitrust jurisdiction over foreign conduct, that conduct must "produce some substantial effect in the United States." Other lower courts argued that general effects on domestic commerce alone would not suffice— the illegal conduct itself had to produce substantial domestic *anticompetitive* effects. *See Nat'l Bank of Canada v. Interbank Card Ass'n*, 666 F.2d 6, 8 (2d Cir. 1981). FTAIA selected yet a different formulation, but as the Court in *Hartford Fire* observed, it was not clear whether FTAIA simply codified prior case law or sought to change it. *Hartford Fire*, 509 U.S. at 796 n.23.

The international vitamin cartel, first discussed early in Chapter 1, led to a significant number of private class actions, including actions brought on behalf of foreign plaintiffs allegedly injured by the cartel's price-fixing activities. In one of those cases, the Supreme Court appeared to resolve a conflict in the circuits that had developed regarding the ability of foreign plaintiffs to sue in U.S. courts under the Sherman Act for injuries suffered abroad. In doing so, it provided additional guidance on the interpretation of FTAIA.

F. HOFFMANN–LA ROCHE LTD. v. EMPAGRAN S.A.
Supreme Court of the United States, 2004.
542 U.S. 155.

Justice BREYER delivered the opinion of the Court.

* * *

We here focus upon anticompetitive price-fixing activity that is in significant part foreign, that causes some domestic antitrust injury, and that independently causes separate foreign injury. We ask two questions about the price-fixing conduct and the foreign injury that it causes. First, does that conduct fall within the FTAIA's general rule excluding the Sherman Act's application? That is to say, does the price-fixing activity constitute "conduct involving trade or commerce ... with foreign nations"? We conclude that it does.

Second, we ask whether the conduct nonetheless falls within a domestic-injury exception to the general rule, an exception that applies (and makes the Sherman Act nonetheless applicable) where the conduct (1) has a "direct, substantial, and reasonably foreseeable effect" on domestic commerce, and (2) "such effect gives rise to a [Sherman Act] claim." §§ 6a(1)(A), (2). We conclude that the exception does not apply where the plaintiff's claim rests solely on the independent foreign harm.

* * *

I

The plaintiffs in this case originally filed a class-action suit on behalf of foreign and domestic purchasers of vitamins under, *inter alia,* § 1 of the Sherman Act and §§ 4 and 16 of the Clayton Act. The complaint alleged that petitioners, foreign and domestic vitamin manufacturers and distributors, had engaged in a price-fixing conspiracy, raising the price of vitamin products to customers in the United States and to customers in foreign countries.

As relevant here, petitioners moved to dismiss the suit as to the *foreign* purchasers (the respondents here), five foreign vitamin distributors located in Ukraine, Australia, Ecuador, and Panama, each of which bought vitamins from petitioners for delivery outside the United States. * * * Respondents have never asserted that they purchased any vitamins in the United States or in transactions in United States commerce, and the question presented assumes that the relevant "transactions occurr[ed] entirely outside U.S. commerce." The District Court dismissed their claims. It applied the FTAIA and found none of the exceptions applicable. Thereafter, the *domestic* purchasers transferred their claims to another pending suit and did not take part in the subsequent appeal.

A divided panel of the Court of Appeals reversed. The panel concluded that the FTAIA's general exclusionary rule applied to the case, but that its domestic-injury exception also applied. It basically read the plaintiffs' complaint to allege that the vitamin manufacturers' price-fixing conspiracy (1) had "a direct, substantial, and reasonably foreseeable effect" on ordinary domestic trade or commerce, *i.e.,* the conspiracy brought about higher domestic vitamin prices, and (2) "such effect" gave "rise to a [Sherman Act] claim," *i.e.,* an injured *domestic* customer could have brought a Sherman Act suit. Those allegations, the court held, are sufficient to meet the exception's requirements.

The court assumed that the foreign effect, *i.e.,* higher prices in Ukraine, Panama, Australia, and Ecuador, was independent of the domestic effect, *i.e.,* higher domestic prices. But it concluded that, in light of the FTAIA's text, legislative history, and the policy goal of deterring harmful price-fixing activity, this lack of connection does not matter. * * *

We granted certiorari to resolve a split among the Courts of Appeals about the exception's application. Compare *Den Norske Stats Oljeselskap As v. HeereMac Vof,* 241 F.3d 420, 427 (C.A.5 2001) (exception does not apply where foreign injury independent of domestic harm), with *Kruman v. Christie's Int'l PLC,* 284 F.3d 384, 400 (C.A.2 2002) (exception does apply even where foreign injury independent) * * *.

II

The FTAIA seeks to make clear to American exporters (and to firms doing business abroad) that the Sherman Act does not prevent them from entering into business arrangements (say, joint-selling arrangements), however anticompetitive, as long as those arrangements adversely affect only foreign markets. See H.R.Rep. No. 97–686, pp. 1–3, 9–10 (1982), U.S.Code Cong. & Admin.News 1982, 2487, 2487–2488, 2494–2495 (hereinafter House Report). It does so by removing from the Sherman Act's reach, (1) export activities and (2) other commercial activities taking place abroad, *unless* those activities adversely affect domestic commerce, imports to the United States, or exporting activities of one engaged in such activities within the United States.

* * *

[The FTAIA's] * * * technical language initially lays down a general rule placing *all* (non-import) activity involving foreign commerce outside the Sherman Act's reach. It then brings such conduct back within the Sherman Act's reach *provided that* the conduct *both* (1) sufficiently affects American commerce, *i.e.*, it has a "direct, substantial, and reasonably foreseeable effect" on American domestic, import, or (certain) export commerce, *and* (2) has an effect of a kind that antitrust law considers harmful, *i.e.*, the "effect" must "giv[e] rise to a [Sherman Act] claim."

We ask here how this language applies to price-fixing activity that is in significant part foreign, that has the requisite domestic effect, and that also has independent foreign effects giving rise to the plaintiff's claim.

III

Respondents make a threshold argument. They say that the transactions here at issue fall outside the FTAIA because the FTAIA's general exclusionary rule applies only to conduct involving exports. The rule says that the Sherman Act "shall not apply to conduct involving trade or commerce (other than import trade or import commerce) *with* foreign nations." § 6a (emphasis added). The word "with" means *between* the United States and foreign nations. And, they contend, commerce between the United States and foreign nations that is not import commerce must consist of export commerce—a kind of commerce irrelevant to the case at hand.

The difficulty with respondents' argument is that the FTAIA originated in a bill that initially referred only to "export trade or export commerce." But the House Judiciary Committee subsequently changed that language to "trade or commerce (other than import trade or import commerce)." And it did so deliberately to include commerce that did not involve American exports but which was wholly foreign. * * *

For those who find legislative history useful, the House Report's account should end the matter. Others, by considering carefully the amendment itself and the lack of any other plausible purpose, may reach the same conclusion, namely that the FTAIA's general rule applies where the anticompetitive conduct at issue is foreign.

IV

We turn now to the basic question presented, that of the exception's application. Because the underlying antitrust action is complex, potentially raising questions not directly at issue here, we reemphasize that we base our decision upon the following: The price-fixing conduct significantly and adversely affects both customers outside the United States and customers within the United States, but the adverse foreign effect is independent of any adverse domestic effect. In these circumstances, we find that the FTAIA exception does not apply (and thus the Sherman Act does not apply) for two main reasons.

First, this Court ordinarily construes ambiguous statutes to avoid unreasonable interference with the sovereign authority of other nations. This rule of construction reflects principles of customary international law—law that (we must assume) Congress ordinarily seeks to follow.

This rule of statutory construction cautions courts to assume that legislators take account of the legitimate sovereign interests of other nations when they write American laws. It thereby helps the potentially conflicting laws of different nations work together in harmony—a harmony particularly needed in today's highly interdependent commercial world.

No one denies that America's antitrust laws, when applied to foreign conduct, can interfere with a foreign nation's ability independently to regulate its own commercial affairs. But our courts have long held that application of our antitrust laws to foreign anticompetitive conduct is nonetheless reasonable, and hence consistent with principles of prescriptive comity, insofar as they reflect a legislative effort to redress *domestic* antitrust injury that foreign anticompetitive conduct has caused.

But why is it reasonable to apply those laws to foreign conduct *insofar as that conduct causes independent foreign harm and that foreign harm alone gives rise to the plaintiff's claim?* Like the former case, application of those laws creates a serious risk of interference with a foreign nation's ability independently to regulate its own commercial affairs. But, unlike the former case, the justification for that interference seems insubstantial. Why should American law supplant, for example, Canada's or Great Britain's or Japan's own determination about how best to protect Canadian or British or Japanese customers from anticompetitive conduct engaged in significant part by Canadian or British or Japanese or other foreign companies?

We recognize that principles of comity provide Congress greater leeway when it seeks to control through legislation the actions of *American* companies, and some of the anticompetitive price-fixing conduct alleged here took place in *America.* But the higher foreign prices of which the foreign plaintiffs here complain are not the consequence of any domestic anticompetitive conduct *that Congress sought to forbid,* for Congress did not seek to forbid any such conduct insofar as it is here relevant, *i.e.,* insofar as it is intertwined with foreign conduct that causes independent foreign harm. Rather Congress sought to *release* domestic (and foreign) anticompetitive conduct from Sherman Act constraints when that conduct causes foreign harm. Congress, of course, did make an exception where that conduct also causes domestic harm. But any independent domestic harm the foreign conduct causes here has, by definition, little or nothing to do with the matter.

We thus repeat the basic question: Why is it reasonable to apply this law to conduct that is significantly foreign *insofar as that conduct causes independent foreign harm and that foreign harm alone gives rise to the plaintiff's claim?* We can find no good answer to the question.

The Areeda and Hovenkamp treatise notes that under the Court of Appeals' interpretation of the statute

> "a Malaysian customer could . . . maintain an action under United States law in a United States court against its own Malaysian supplier, another cartel member, simply by noting that unnamed

third parties injured [in the United States] by the American [cartel member's] conduct would also have a cause of action. Effectively, the United States courts would provide worldwide subject matter jurisdiction to any foreign suitor wishing to sue its own local supplier, but unhappy with its own sovereign's provisions for private antitrust enforcement, provided that a different plaintiff had a cause of action against a different firm for injuries that were within U.S. [other-than-import] commerce. It does not seem excessively rigid to infer that Congress would not have intended that result." P. Areeda & H. Hovenkamp, Antitrust Law ¶ 273, pp. 51–52 (Supp.2003).

We agree with the comment. We can find no convincing justification for the extension of the Sherman Act's scope that it describes.

Respondents reply that many nations have adopted antitrust laws similar to our own, to the point where the practical likelihood of interference with the relevant interests of other nations is minimal. Leaving price fixing to the side, however, this Court has found to the contrary. [citing *Hartford Fire*.]

Regardless, even where nations agree about primary conduct, say price fixing, they disagree dramatically about appropriate remedies. The application, for example, of American private treble-damages remedies to anticompetitive conduct taking place abroad has generated considerable controversy. And several foreign nations have filed briefs here arguing that to apply our remedies would unjustifiably permit their citizens to bypass their own less generous remedial schemes, thereby upsetting a balance of competing considerations that their own domestic antitrust laws embody.

These briefs add that a decision permitting independently injured foreign plaintiffs to pursue private treble-damages remedies would undermine foreign nations' own antitrust enforcement policies by diminishing foreign firms' incentive to cooperate with antitrust authorities in return for prosecutorial amnesty.

Respondents alternatively argue that comity does not demand an interpretation of the FTAIA that would exclude independent foreign injury cases *across the board*. Rather, courts can take (and sometimes have taken) account of comity considerations case by case, abstaining where comity considerations so dictate.

In our view, however, this approach is too complex to prove workable. The Sherman Act covers many different kinds of anticompetitive agreements. Courts would have to examine how foreign law, compared with American law, treats not only price fixing but also, say, information-sharing agreements, patent-licensing price conditions, territorial product resale limitations, and various forms of joint venture, in respect to both primary conduct and remedy. The legally and economically technical nature of that enterprise means lengthier proceedings, appeals, and more proceedings—to the point where procedural costs and delays could themselves threaten interference with a foreign nation's ability to maintain the integrity of its own antitrust enforcement system. Even in this relatively simple price-fixing case, for example, competing briefs tell us (1) that potential treble-damage liability would help enforce widespread anti-price-fixing norms (through added deterrence) and (2) the opposite, namely that such liability would hinder antitrust enforcement (by reducing incentives to enter amnesty programs). How could a court seriously interested in resolving so empirical a matter—a matter potentially related to impact on foreign interests—do so simply and expeditiously?

We conclude that principles of prescriptive comity counsel against the Court of Appeals' interpretation of the FTAIA. Where foreign anticompetitive conduct plays a significant role and where foreign injury is independent of domestic effects, Congress might have hoped that America's antitrust laws, so fundamental a component of our own economic system, would commend themselves to other nations as well. But, if America's antitrust policies could not win their own way in the international marketplace for such ideas, Congress, we must assume, would not have tried to impose them, in an act of legal imperialism, through legislative fiat.

Second, the FTAIA's language and history suggest that Congress designed the FTAIA to clarify, perhaps to limit, but not *to expand* in any significant way, the Sherman Act's scope as applied to foreign commerce. And we have found no significant indication that at the time Congress wrote this statute courts would have thought the Sherman Act applicable in these circumstances.

[Here the Court first noted that "the Solicitor General and petitioners tell us that they have found no case in which any court applied the Sherman Act to redress foreign injury in such circumstances," and then discussed and distinguished six cases cited by respondents in reply. First, the Court deemed it significant that the U.S. government was the plaintiff in three of the cited decisions—previous opinions of the Supreme Court—noting that "A Government plaintiff, unlike a private plaintiff, must seek to obtain the relief necessary to protect the public from further anticompetitive conduct and to redress anticompetitive harm. And a Government plaintiff has legal authority broad enough to allow it to carry out this mission." In such cases, the government obtained relief that "might have helped to protect those injured abroad." But, according to the Court, that "tells us little or nothing about whether this Court would have awarded similar relief at the request of private plaintiffs." Moreover, the Court argued, "[n]either did the Court focus explicitly in its opinions on a claim that the remedies sought to cure only independently caused foreign harm. Thus the three cases tell us even less about whether this Court then thought that foreign private plaintiffs could have obtained foreign relief based solely upon such independently caused foreign injury."

The Court distinguished the other three cases cited—all lower court cases—on the grounds that they either involved mixed domestic and foreign harm, and not solely "independent" foreign harm, or simply did not squarely address the issue of jurisdiction over solely foreign harm. The Court concluded, therefore, that "no pre–1982 case provides significant authority for application of the Sherman Act in the circumstances we here assume." Eds.]

Taken together, these two sets of considerations, the one derived from comity and the other reflecting history, convince us that Congress would not have intended the FTAIA's exception to bring independently caused foreign injury within the Sherman Act's reach.

V

Respondents point to several considerations that point the other way. For one thing, the FTAIA's language speaks in terms of the Sherman Act's *applicability* to certain kinds of *conduct*. The FTAIA says that the Sherman Act applies to foreign "conduct" with a certain kind of harmful domestic effect. Why isn't that the end of the matter? How can the Sherman Act both *apply to the conduct* when one person sues but *not apply to the same conduct* when another person sues? The question of who can or cannot sue is a matter for other statutes (namely, the Clayton Act) to determine.

Moreover, the exception says that it applies if the conduct's domestic effect gives rise to "*a* claim," not to "*the plaintiff's* claim" or "*the* claim *at issue.*" The alleged conduct here did have domestic effects, and those effects were harmful enough to give rise to "*a*" claim. Respondents concede that this claim is not their own claim; it is someone else's claim. But, linguistically speaking, they say, that is beside the point. Nor did Congress place the relevant words "gives rise to a claim" in the FTAIA to suggest any geographical limitation; rather it did so for a here neutral reason, namely, in order to make clear that the domestic effect must be an *adverse* (as opposed to a beneficial) effect.

Despite their linguistic logic, these arguments are not convincing. Linguistically speaking, a statute can apply and not apply to the same conduct, depending upon other circumstances; and those other circumstances may include the nature of the lawsuit (or of the related underlying harm). It also makes linguistic sense to read the words "a claim" as if they refer to the "plaintiff's claim" or "the claim at issue."

At most, respondents' linguistic arguments might show that respondents' reading is the more natural reading of the statutory language. But those arguments do not show that we *must* accept that reading. And that is the critical point. The considerations previously mentioned—those of comity and history—make clear that the respondents' reading is not consistent with the FTAIA's basic intent. If the statute's language reasonably permits an interpretation consistent with that intent, we should adopt it. And, for the reasons stated, we believe that the statute's language permits the reading that we give it.

Finally, respondents point to policy considerations that we have previously discussed, namely, that application of the Sherman Act in present circumstances will (through increased deterrence) help protect Americans against foreign-caused anticompetitive injury. As we have explained, however, the plaintiffs and supporting enforcement-agency *amici* have made important experience-backed arguments (based upon amnesty-seeking incentives) to the contrary. We cannot say whether, on balance, respondents' side of this empirically based argument or the enforcement agencies' side is correct. But we can say that the answer to the dispute is neither clear enough, nor of such likely empirical significance, that it could overcome the considerations we have previously discussed and change our conclusion.

* * *

VI

We have assumed that the anticompetitive conduct here independently caused foreign injury; that is, the conduct's domestic effects did not help to bring about that foreign injury. Respondents argue, in the alternative, that the foreign injury was not independent. Rather, they say, the anticompetitive conduct's domestic effects were linked to that foreign harm. Respondents contend that, because vitamins are fungible and readily transportable, without an adverse domestic effect (*i.e.*, higher prices in the United States), the sellers could not have maintained their international price-fixing arrangement and respondents would not have suffered their foreign injury. They add that this "but for" condition is sufficient to bring the price-fixing conduct within the scope of the FTAIA's exception.

The Court of Appeals, however, did not address this argument, and, for that reason, neither shall we. Respondents remain free to ask the Court of Appeals to consider the claim. The Court of Appeals may determine whether respondents properly preserved the argument, and, if so, it may consider it and decide the related claim.

For these reasons, the judgment of the Court of Appeals is vacated, and the case is remanded for further proceedings consistent with this opinion.

It is so ordered.

Justice O'CONNOR took no part in the consideration or decision of this case.

Justice SCALIA, with whom Justice THOMAS joins, concurring in the judgment.

I concur in the judgment of the Court because the language of the statute is readily susceptible of the interpretation the Court provides and because only that interpretation is consistent with the principle that statutes should be read in accord with the customary deference to the application of foreign countries' laws within their own territories.

————

As a consequence of *Empagran*, it is now settled that foreign plaintiffs may not sue in U.S. courts under the Sherman Act for foreign injuries from international cartels—provided those injuries are "independent" of any domestic U.S. harms caused by the cartel. But what does the Court mean by "independent" foreign effect? Given the possibility of arbitrage, can a worldwide cartel ever be maintained absent the agreement of sellers in other geographic areas? In other words, don't higher prices in the United States always make possible higher prices abroad, and vice versa, *i.e.*, aren't the effects of a cartel necessarily *interdependent*? The plaintiffs, of course, made that very argument to the Court. Was the Court simply begging the real question of the case, therefore, by remanding the case to the court of appeals? What argument could the plaintiffs make on remand? How could the defendants respond? If the lower courts find that the foreign effects of the international vitamin cartel were indeed intertwined with domestic U.S. effects, might *Empagran* prove to be a very narrow precedent?

On remand, the D.C. Circuit resolved that issue, again concluding that the federal courts were without jurisdiction under the FTAIA to hear the foreign plaintiffs' claims. *Empagran S.A. v. F. Hoffmann–LaRoche, Ltd.*, 417 F.3d 1267 (D.C. Cir. 2005). While conceding that "[t]he appellants paint a plausible scenario under which maintaining super-competitive prices in the

United States might well have been a 'but-for' cause of the appellants' foreign injury," the court nevertheless concluded that the FTAIA requires "a direct causal relationship, that is, proximate causation." In its view, the "but for" scenario did not satisfy that standard. *See also In re Monosodium Glutamate Antitrust Litigation*, 477 F.3d 535 (8th Cir. 2007) (following *Empagran*).

Congress clearly intended, of course, to place some limitations on U.S. antitrust jurisdiction over wholly foreign conduct. In the late 1970s and early 1980s, when the FTAIA was adopted, Congress concluded in response to arguments from the private sector that the threat of U.S. Sherman Act liability was inhibiting U.S. exporters from engaging in cooperative activities that would promote U.S. exports. The FTAIA, which included the Export Trading Company Act, was arguably designed, therefore, to promote exports by providing something of a safe harbor for exporters. Congress did not have international cartels in mind when it enacted FTAIA and the Export Trading Company Act. In light of these facts, was there an alternative interpretation of the FTAIA that was available to the Court in *Empagran*?

What is the relationship, if any, between the foreign conduct issues being posed in cases like *Hartford Fire* and *Empagran* and the split in the Supreme Court in *Summit Health*? What are the policy implications, in terms of effective enforcement, compensation, and deterrence, of restrictive jurisdictional rules?

Why would foreign plaintiffs pursue antitrust claims in U.S. courts when so many nations have their own competition laws? A variety of factors may be at work.

First, relatively few foreign antitrust laws grant private rights of action, and nations that allow private suits typically permit recovery for actual damages only, not treble damages. Also, when attorneys fee shifting exists overseas, it is usually symmetric: although a prevailing plaintiff may recover fees as under U.S. law, a prevailing defendant also will have the right to recover fees—*i.e.*, the loser pays the winner's attorneys fees regardless of who is the plaintiff and the defendant. As we have seen, Section 4 of the Clayton Act allows only a prevailing plaintiff to recover treble damages, attorneys fees and costs of suit. 15 U.S.C. § 15.

Other less obvious factors may also be at work. U.S. federal courts in most cases have more liberal pleading standards, and authorize far more extensive discovery than do their foreign counterpart jurisdictions. The Federal Rules of Civil Procedure also provide for the use of class actions, a device not commonly available in other jurisdictions. The combination of class actions, treble damages, discovery, and attorneys fees can facilitate very substantial potential recoveries. Indeed, the possibility of such recoveries has spawned an active class action bar in the United States, the availability of which may itself may be a factor that facilitates the initiation of U.S. antitrust claims by foreign plaintiffs.

The greater attractiveness of the U.S. private enforcement system has led foreign firms to sue in the United States for damages suffered offshore due to illegal behavior that occurs, at least in part, within the United States. When should the U.S. courts avail themselves to foreign claimants—and perhaps allow recovery by large classes of foreign companies and individuals? What policy reasons might be urged in favor of and against permitting such suits to proceed? Would liberal recourse by foreign parties to the U.S. courts raise the potential cost to defendants of participation in hard core cartels and help deter misconduct?

c. Act of State Doctrine

A second limit on extraterritoriality is the act of state doctrine, which bars U.S. courts from considering the validity of sovereign acts by foreign governments where such acts occur in the foreign state. In most cases, the act of state doctrine is invoked by a private party defendant who argues that injuries asserted to arise from misconduct in a foreign jurisdiction resulted from intervention by a foreign government. In *W.S. Kirkpatrick & Co. v. Environmental Tectonics Corp.*, 493 U.S. 400, 110 S.Ct. 701 (1990), the Supreme Court refused to ban the application of the Robinson–Patman Act to the alleged payment of bribes to government officials in Nigeria to obtain a government contract. The Court ruled that act of state issues "only arise when a court must decide—that is, when the outcome of the case turns upon—the effect of official action by a foreign sovereign." The doctrine allows the U.S. antitrust laws to be applied if judicial inquiry "involves only the 'motivation' for, rather than the 'validity' of, a foreign sovereign act." Here the act of state doctrine did not apply because the plaintiff did not contest the validity of the contract issued by the Nigerian Government, but only questioned the motive (a possible bribe) for the agreement.

d. Foreign Sovereign Immunity

A further jurisdictional limitation involves the potential antitrust liability of foreign governments for their own sovereign acts. The Foreign Sovereign Immunities Act, 28 U.S.C. § 1602, immunizes foreign governments from suits challenging the acts of the sovereign. Such immunity may be lost when the sovereign's acts are purely "commercial" in nature. *See Alfred Dunhill of London v. Republic of Cuba*, 425 U.S. 682 (1976). Courts also will not impose antitrust liability on private parties for conduct that otherwise would constitute an antitrust violation, if it was a consequence of compulsion by a foreign government. *See Interamerican Ref. Corp. v. Texaco Maracaibo, Inc.*, 307 F.Supp. 1291, 1297–98 (D. Del.1970).

Sidebar 9–1:
Suing OPEC*

Suing either the Organization of Petroleum Exporting Countries ("OPEC") or its member nations offers a useful way to think about the myriad special defenses and immunities that potentially apply in the foreign commerce area when sovereign nations participate in anticompetitive activity. While there are older decisions rejecting suit against OPEC on two different grounds, a close examination of more recent developments suggests that OPEC's conduct may some day be judged on the merits.

---

* This Sidebar was prepared by Professor Spencer Weber Waller and is adapted from Spencer Weber Waller, *Suing OPEC*, 64 U. PITT. L. REV. 105 (2002) and JAMES R. ATWOOD, KINGMAN BREWSTER, & SPENCER WEBER WALLER, ANTITRUST AND AMERICAN BUSINESS ABROAD (3d ed. 1997 & supp.).

Foreign Sovereign Immunity

The Foreign Sovereign Immunities Act ("FSIA"), 28 U.S.C. § 1602 et seq., bars all suits against foreign states and their instrumentalities unless one of the Act's exceptions apply. For antitrust purposes, the most important exception is for "commercial activities." Foreign states are not immune from a suit:

> in which the action is based upon a commercial activity carried on in the United States by the foreign state; or upon an act performed in the United States in connection with a commercial activity of the foreign state elsewhere; or upon an act outside the territory of the United States in connection with a commercial activity of the foreign state elsewhere and that act causes a direct effect in the United States. * * *

28 U.S.C. § 1605(a)(2). There is also the additional key sentence: "The commercial character of an activity shall be determined by reference to the nature of the course of conduct or particular transaction or act, rather than by reference to its purpose." 28 U.S.C. § 1603(d).

The legislative history of these provisions suggests that state conduct normally performed by private persons should be regarded as commercial, even where the object of the activity is to fulfill a governmental purpose. For example, contracting to buy provisions for the armed services or to repair an embassy building are to be treated as commercial, since private parties normally negotiate and sign contracts. On the other hand, if the activity is normally done only by governments—such as imposing a tariff or issuing export licenses—immunity is available even if there are important business or commercial motivations behind the government action.

Characterizing the conduct of the OPEC nations is difficult. A district court in the late 1970s undertook its own study of OPEC's price-setting efforts and concluded that they were accomplished through (1) taxation of private companies, (2) production controls administered by "conservation" laws, and (3) direct price quotations on government-owned oil. The first two functions were deemed clearly governmental in nature. The third, while commercial at first blush, was merely a different "medium" by which the OPEC governments were performing sovereign acts. The court noted considerable acceptance within the United Nations, and indeed by the United States, of the sovereign right of states to exercise control over the extraction and exploitation of their natural resources. Thus:

> The control over a nation's natural resources stems from the nature of sovereignty. By necessity and by traditional recognition, each nation is its own master in respect to its physical attributes. The defendants' control over their oil resources is an especially sovereign function because oil, as their primary, if not sole, revenue-producing resource, is crucial to the welfare of their nations' peoples.

International Ass'n of Machinists v. Organization of Petroleum Exporting Countries, 477 F.Supp. 553, 568 (C.D. Cal.1979), *aff'd on other grounds*, 649 F.2d 1354 (9th Cir. 1981), *cert. denied*, 454 U.S. 1163 (1982)("*OPEC*").

The district court's analysis of sovereign immunity was understandable—but arguably wrong, even in 1979 under the "nature not purpose" standard for the commercial activity exception of the FSIA. It is more likely in error today.

The first *OPEC* decision came at the high water mark of state involvement in natural resources markets. Since that time, most nations have privatized key aspects of their extractive industries, making it more clear that the activities of the OPEC nations are the kinds of activities customarily engaged in by private firms, and hence not immune under the FSIA. On appeal, the Ninth Circuit admitted this flaw in the district court's opinion, but found a way around it to nonetheless avoid adjudicating the merits of the case. While questioning the district court's sovereign immunity analysis, the court of appeals affirmed the dismissal of the first *OPEC* decision on act of state grounds.**

Act of State

The Supreme Court subsequently clarified the scope of the act of state doctrine in *W.S. Kirkpatrick & Co. v. Environmental Tectonics Corp., Int'l*, 493 U.S. 400 (1990), a unanimous decision authored by Justice Scalia. At issue in *Kirkpatrick* was whether the act of state doctrine barred a United States court from entertaining a cause of action that did not rest upon the asserted invalidity of an official act of a foreign sovereign, but required imputing to foreign officials an unlawful motivation in the performance of such an official act.

Environmental Tectonics was an unsuccessful bidder on a military procurement contract awarded by the Republic of Nigeria. The successful bidder, Kirkpatrick & Co., had made arrangements with a Nigerian citizen, whereby the citizen would endeavor to secure the contract for Kirkpatrick. The Nigerian citizen and Kirkpatrick agreed that, in the event the contract was awarded to Kirkpatrick, Kirkpatrick would pay two Panamanian entities controlled by the Nigerian citizen a "commission" equal to 20 per cent of the contract price, which would, in turn, be given as a bribe to officials of the Nigerian government. Nigerian law prohibited both the payment and the receipt of bribes in connection with the award of government contracts.

The Supreme Court held that the act of state doctrine was inapplicable because nothing in the case required the Court to declare invalid the official act of a foreign sovereign. Under *Kirkpatrick*, act of state issues only arise when the outcome of the case turns upon the effect of official action by a foreign sovereign. *Kirkpatrick* thus overruled a line of lower court cases which had applied the act of state doctrine to dismiss claims that called for examination of the *motives* of a foreign government in taking action. The Court noted that, in every case in which the Supreme Court has held the act of state doctrine applicable, the relief sought or the defense interposed would have required a United States court to declare invalid the official act of a foreign sovereign performed in its own territory.

** On a related issue, in *Prewitt Enters. v. OPEC*, 353 F.3d 916 (11th Cir. 2003), the Eleventh Circuit held that OPEC as an organization could not be validly served with process because of an agreement between OPEC and the Austrian Government granting it immunity from service of process. The Eleventh Circuit noted, however, that in its view OPEC would not qualify for immunity under the FSIA as a result of its commercial activities.

Because the legality of the Nigerian contract itself was not a question before the Court in *Kirkpatrick*, there was no occasion to apply the act of state doctrine at all. The Court emphasized, however, that the doctrine does not establish an exception to the court's power to decide cases and controversies properly presented to it merely because judicial review in a United States court might embarrass a foreign government. It merely requires that, in the process of deciding such cases, the acts of foreign sovereigns within their own jurisdictions shall be deemed valid. *Kirkpatrick* thus further weakened the key portion of the original *OPEC* Ninth Circuit decision, which sought to justify the application of the act of state doctrine based on the potential for embarrassing the executive branch by drawing an analogy to the domestic political question doctrine.

Foreign Sovereign Compulsion

The OPEC defendants would not be able to take advantage of another frequently discussed, but seldom litigated, special defense in international antitrust litigation. The foreign sovereign compulsion defense may provide a safe harbor for a private defendant who has been compelled to engage in conduct which violates United States antitrust law. While the contours and exceptions of the defense are hotly debated, the defense has only been successful once, and has been otherwise rejected because the court determined that the defendants had acted pursuant to the advice, encouragement, or prodding of a foreign government, but had not been subject to outright compulsion. *See* Spencer Weber Waller, *Redefining the Foreign Compulsion Defense: The Japanese Automobile Restraints and Beyond*, 14 Law & Pol'y Int'l Bus. 747 (1982). Whatever comfort this defense may provide to private firms acting under the directions of a state, therefore, it has no application in the OPEC context, where the behavior of the foreign governments themselves are at issue.

Comity

The OPEC defendants undoubtedly also would raise issues of comity. Whether comity provides a separate basis for dismissing such a suit depends on the reading of *Hartford Fire Ins. Co. v. California*, 509 U.S. 764 (1993)(Casebook, Chapter 9, *supra*). Recall that in *Hartford* the Court, by a 5–4 vote, appeared to limit comity to those few situations akin to foreign compulsion where the foreign law required a violation of the Sherman Act. In the event of such a "true conflict," the Court appeared willing to permit the balancing of United States and foreign interests to determine whether jurisdiction should be exercised or declined. Thus, the Court seems to have both transformed foreign compulsion into a balancing test rather than a complete defense and virtually eliminated another potential defense for OPEC nations in future litigation.

Conclusion

A case against OPEC is thus a perfect exercise to analyze the various special defenses and immunities in foreign commerce antitrust cases and to contemplate whether such a suit would be successful and whether even a "successful" antitrust suit against OPEC (by the federal agencies, state attorneys general, or private parties) would be in the interests of the United States.

If an antitrust violation was found, what would constitute an effective remedy in light of the remedial goals of deterrence, compensation, and punishment? What practical hurdles might lie in its path? Could a U.S. court effectively enjoin OPEC? How would it enforce its orders against OPEC member countries and their officials? Could private parties, perhaps organized into a class, establish their injury and accurately prove their damages? Could they collect those damages? Who would be the "best" plaintiff—the federal government? a group of states? a private class action? And finally, consider the institutional ramifications for the U.S. antitrust enforcement system if a violation was established, but no effective remedy was possible. Does that prospect help to explain the development of doctrines like act of state and foreign sovereign compulsion?

e.　*International Tensions*

Efforts to apply the U.S. antitrust laws to foreign firms occasionally have created tensions between the United States and other countries. Four points of friction stand out. The first arises from the distinctive U.S. scheme of civil remedies. A number of foreign governments have reacted warily to efforts by U.S. plaintiffs to obtain treble damages from foreign firms and to obtain expansive discovery overseas. Some nations have adopted laws that restrict discovery within their borders, limit the enforcement of U.S. judgments, or entitle firms that sue in the country's courts to "claw-back" from the plaintiff two-thirds of any treble damage judgment paid in the U.S.

The second deals with efforts to apply antitrust laws extraterritorially to dismantle foreign impediments to trade. American policymakers have complained that foreign firms—sometimes with the encouragement of their governments—collude to impede American exporters from selling abroad. In 1992 the Justice Department announced that it would enforce U.S. antitrust laws against "conduct occurring overseas that restrains United States exports, whether or not there is direct harm to U.S. consumers." U.S. Department of Justice, *Statement of Enforcement Policy Regarding Anticompetitive Conduct that Restricts U.S. Exports, reprinted in* 62 ANTITRUST & TRADE REG. REP. (BNA) 483 (Apr. 9, 1992). The 1992 policy statement reversed the position the DOJ had taken in its 1988 Antitrust Enforcement Guidelines for International Operations, which said the Department would not challenge foreign cartels unless there was direct competitive harm to U.S. consumers. While such policies are seldom tested in court, their validity (and application) are debated. For example, a foreign cartel to raise prices abroad might increase opportunities for U.S. exporters. On the other hand, a boycott refusing to deal with U.S. exporters could injure them. And foreign nations that collude to impede U.S. exporters might simply be responding with countervailing power to the longstanding U.S. policy of allowing domestic export cartels, which as we discuss in the next paragraph, are exempt from the U.S. antitrust laws.

A third source of dispute arises from policies that give rival firms antitrust dispensations for export-related collaboration. The Export Trading Company Act of 1982 (ETCA) allows U.S. exporters to obtain a Certificate of Review from the Secretary of Commerce that immunizes export-related cooperation which neither substantially reduces competition in the U.S. nor substantially restrains exports by a U.S. competitor. 15 U.S.C. §§ 4001–21. The Certificate shields the holder from all criminal and treble damage liability under the U.S. antitrust laws for conduct described in the Certificate while the Certificate is in effect. The ETCA's standards basically codify requirements established by the Webb–Pomerene Export Trade Act of 1918, which also confers limited antitrust immunity for the joint marketing activities of export associations. 15 U.S.C. §§ 61–65. Unlike the Webb–Pomerene Act, the ETCA applies to the export of services, including the licensing of intellectual property rights. Some foreign countries—especially developing countries— regard export cartel exemptions suspiciously as instruments that permit wealthier economies to exploit poorer nations. American firms operating under the ECTA thus still may face prosecution by the growing number of foreign countries that have adopted competition laws with anti-cartel measures.

The fourth point of friction stems from dissimilarities in national substantive antitrust rules and analytical approaches. The U.S. and EU have on rare occasion openly disagreed about the actual or likely anticompetitive effects of conduct and hence reached different conclusions about whether it violated competition laws. Differences also have surfaced in selecting the appropriate remedy for agreed upon violations. This was true both in the case of the General Electric–Honeywell merger in 2001 and in the prosecution of Microsoft in Europe and Korea. In the *Microsoft* cases, U.S. officials were publicly critical of the EC decision in 2004 and the decision of the Korea Fair Trade Commission in 2005. The tensions triggered by this sort of divergence are explored in Sidebar 9–2.

Sidebar 9–2:
Paths to International Convergence

As we first noted in Chapter 1, concerns about the costs associated with the proliferation of competition policy systems have inspired considerable discussion about approaches for promoting acceptance of common procedural and substantive norms. *See International Competition Policy Advisory Committee to the Attorney General and Assistant Attorney General for Antitrust*, FINAL REPORT Appendix 1–C (2000) ("ICPAC Report"), *available at* http://www.usdoj.gov/atr/icpac/finalreport.htm. The perceived urgency to promote competition policy convergence increased in 2001 following the European Union's decision to block General Electric's acquisition of Honeywell. In that instance, the U.S. Department of Justice had approved the transaction with relatively minor modifications, and the EU's intervention triggered a sharp exchange of words between top officials at the DOJ and the Competition Directorate.

Modern efforts to reconcile disparate legal regimes, including competition policy systems, have two basic elements. The first is *establishing an intellectual consensus* about what constitutes superior norms. The ingredients of consensus-building often include the identification of possible substantive and procedural standards, experimentation by one or more jurisdictions, and debate—for example, in conferences or in professional journals—about the conceptual merits and practical results of specific approaches. The second element of convergence is a *process of acceptance* by which individual jurisdictions embrace common procedural or substantive norms.

The process of acceptance can proceed in at least two ways. One method is for two or more jurisdictions to adopt common approaches voluntarily and unilaterally. This method sometimes is called *soft convergence*. Without the benefit of a treaty or other formal agreement, different countries might choose to emulate procedures or substantive rules that the experience of another jurisdiction has proven to be successful. The 1982 U.S. Department of Justice Merger Guidelines provide an example. As amended in 1984 by the DOJ and reissued jointly with the FTC with modifications in 1992 and 1997, the Merger Guidelines have influenced many jurisdictions (including the European Union) in formulating their own merger control regimes. The analytical quality of and practical experience with the U.S. Guidelines, rather than any binding international agreement, have motivated their emulation by jurisdictions outside the United States. A second path of acceptance, sometimes called *hard convergence*, is a formal agreement by which nations commit themselves to abide by common principles. Soft and hard convergence are not mutually exclusive techniques, as progress through soft convergence sometimes serves as a precursor to formulating binding agreements on international norms.

Modern initiatives concerning competition policy convergence generally seek to encourage the formulation of an intellectual consensus and to facilitate acceptance of superior norms either by a voluntary process of opting-in or through participation in binding international agreements. Convergence-related activities have taken essentially three paths.

Bilateral agreements. Bilateral agreements usually commit the participants to cooperate in executing enforcement initiatives, to take measures to avoid or manage disputes, and to develop collaborative working groups to address issues of common substantive and procedural interest. The United States has established bilateral accords with Australia (1982), Brazil (1999), Canada (1984, superseded by a new agreement in 1995), the European Commission (1991, supplemented in 1998), Germany (1976), Israel (1999), and Japan (1999). In 1994, Congress passed the International Antitrust Enforcement Assistance Act (IAEAA), 15 U.S.C. §§ 6200–12, which authorized the U.S. to enter into Antitrust Mutual Assistance Agreements ("AMAAs") with foreign antitrust enforcement agencies, which facilitate the exchange of confidential information with foreign governments. Owing to some of IAEAA's requirements, however, foreign jurisdictions have been reluctant to enter into formal AMAAs, however, and since the law's passage, the United States has entered into only one such agreement—with Australia.

Regional Agreements. A number of regional organizations have created competition policy initiatives that directly or indirectly promise to promote convergence. Some arrangements, such as the Asia–Pacific Economic Cooperation and Mercosur, have focused mainly on consensus-building by holding regular conferences and workshops on competition policy. Other agreements contain rudimentary competition policy commitments (such as the North American Free Trade Agreement) or, in the case of the Andean Pact and the Caribbean Community, create a system of binding competition policy commands and a common mechanism for enforcement involving cross-border matters within the region. Other regional undertakings—such as the Free Trade Agreement of the Americas and the Common Market of Eastern and Southern Africa—are engaged in negotiations to establish binding regional standards for the establishment of national competition policy systems.

Global Networks. Several institutions with broad international representation have established programs to facilitate the identification and adoption of best practices in competition policy. Two of the oldest institutions are the Organization for Economic Cooperation and Development (OECD) and the United Nations Conference on Trade and Development (UNCTAD). The OECD operates a Competition Law and Policy Committee that meets four times annually and whose secretariat has produced a number of studies and recommendations concerning international competition policy. The OECD's membership consists mainly of developed market economies, but the organization in 2001 began a Global Competition Forum to engage transition economies in discussions about competition policy. UNCTAD's chief constituency has consisted of developing nations, and its programs have focused chiefly on providing technical assistance and other policy guidance to countries with new competition policy regimes.

Both OECD and UNCTAD have served to encourage the development of an intellectual consensus and to facilitate soft convergence by offering models of procedure and substantive rules that nations might emulate unilaterally. The framework for broad international hard convergence began to emerge in 1996 when the World Trade Organization (WTO) announced the formation of a Trade and Competition Policy Working Group. The WTO initiative may foreshadow development of binding principles that would be applied and enforced through the WTO's existing apparatus of trade dispute institutions. In 2001, the WTO's ministerial meeting in Doha, Qatar announced that the Working Group would focus on gaining acceptance for general principles concerning transparency, non-discriminatory treatment, and capacity building.

A number of countries saw limits to the ability of the OECD, UNCTAD, or WTO to serve as platforms for achieving international competition policy convergence. OECD's membership, emphasizing well-established industrialized states, might be ill-suited to promote broad agreement among older and newer market economies. UNCTAD's focus on emerging markets could slight the interests and experience of older competition regimes, and some feared that WTO's trade-related orientation would unduly subordinate competition policy concerns.

These and other impulses stimulated the formation in 2001 of the International Competition Network (ICN). Membership in the ICN is limited to nations with competition policy systems. Through 2007, nearly 100 countries had joined the network, including a significant number of emerging market economies. ICN has established working groups on cartels, competition policy implementation, merger control, and unilateral conduct, with the aim of identifying best practices for adoption of its members and promoting soft convergence. ICN intends to work extensively with the private sector, academic groups, and other non-government organizations to formulate policy proposals. For additional information, see http://www.internationalcompetitionnetwork.org/. *See also* William E. Kovacic, *Extraterritoriality, Institutions, and Convergence in International Competition Policy*, 97 AM. SOC'Y OF INT'L L. PROC. 309 (2003).

C. AN OVERVIEW OF THE AMERICAN SYSTEM FOR PROSECUTING AND ADJUDICATING ANTITRUST VIOLATIONS

1. NATIONAL PROSECUTORS: THE DEPARTMENT OF JUSTICE AND THE FEDERAL TRADE COMMISSION

In the United States, two major federal government agencies—the Justice Department's Antitrust Division and the Federal Trade Commission—share enforcement responsibility for the Nation's antitrust laws. The Justice Department enforces the Sherman and Clayton Acts. The Antitrust Division is headed by an Assistant Attorney General, who is nominated by the President and confirmed by the Senate. The Department exercises its enforcement authority through civil and criminal actions. The DOJ brings all of its lawsuits in the federal courts. When it files civil suits, the Department can obtain equitable relief (*e.g.*, an injunction forbidding specific conduct) or collect treble damages when it sues on behalf of the United States as a purchaser of goods and services. Section 4B of the Clayton Act creates a four-year statute of limitations from the time the claim for relief "accrues." No statute of limitations governs suits for injunctive relief, and (unlike private parties) neither the Justice Department nor the FTC are constrained by the equitable doctrine of laches.

The Justice Department alone can prosecute federal antitrust crimes. DOJ usually seeks criminal sanctions when direct rivals covertly engage in naked output restraints and realize the likely anticompetitive effects of their conduct. The Department must commence its criminal antitrust suits within five years of the offense, 18 U.S.C. § 3282. Where an illegal conspiracy is continuing in nature, the limitations period begins to run only from the "last act" in furtherance of the conspiracy. Nearly all DOJ criminal suits have consisted of Sherman Act Section 1 cases against hard core horizontal restraints such as price-fixing, bid-rigging, and market division schemes. Since the 1980s the Department often has pursued multi-count indictments that charge defendants with Sherman Act violations and other offenses concerning conduct providing the basis for antitrust prosecution. Commonly alleged collateral offenses include conspiracy to defraud the government, mail fraud, wire fraud, and making false statements to government officials.

The FTC shares responsibility with the Justice Department for civil enforcement of the Clayton Act, but also enforces various consumer protection laws. The FTC is headed by five commissioners appointed by the President and confirmed by the Senate. Commissioners serve seven-year terms, and no more than three commissioners may belong to the same political party. Antitrust cases are developed by the agency's Bureau of Competition, with assistance from the Bureau of Economics. There is also a Bureau of Consumer

Protection. The FTC exercises its enforcement authority through administrative adjudication and uses Section 13(b) of the FTC Act to file civil suits in federal district court for injunctive relief to preserve the status quo pending the conclusion of an administrative proceeding. To avoid redundant investigations and prosecutions, the FTC and Justice Department use a "clearance" procedure to notify each other before commencing investigations and to decide which agency will handle specific matters.

The FTC alone may enforce Section 5 of the FTC Act and its prohibition of unfair methods of competition. Courts have interpreted Section 5 as enabling the FTC to prosecute conduct that violates the letter of the antitrust statutes (including the Sherman Act) and to proscribe behavior that contradicts their spirit. The FTC's remedial authority is limited to issuing equitable decrees such as cease and desist orders and restitution. The FTC's history, operations, and programs are the subject of an extensive set of papers collected in *Federal Trade Commission 90th Anniversary Symposium*, 72 ANTITRUST L.J. 745 (2005).

The FTC and the Justice Department use policymaking tools other than litigation. As we saw in Chapters 1 and 5, both agencies influence counseling and adjudication by promulgating enforcement guidelines such as the Justice Department/FTC Horizontal Merger Guidelines. Each agency also gives business officials guidance about the antitrust consequences of proposed conduct. The Antitrust Division issues "business review letters," 28 C.F.R. § 50.6, and the FTC issues "advisory opinions," 16 C.F.R. § 1.1. These procedures can be time-consuming and do not preclude subsequent changes in the government's enforcement posture. Both agencies also advise other government bodies such as regulatory commissions and legislative committees about the competitive effects of existing or proposed regulations and statutes.

Sidebar 9–3:
Detecting Antitrust Violations: The Role
of Information Gathering

No system of antitrust rules can succeed unless prosecutors can obtain information that illuminates the purpose and effect of specific business practices and identifies possible violations of the law. Antitrust prosecutors tend to rely on six basic sources of information to identify and prove violations of the law.

Publicly available information. In market economies, business actors voluntarily disclose substantial information about themselves to the public. To attract investors and employees, companies frequently reveal their business plans, including product development strategies and intentions to acquire or spin-off assets. A wide range of company outsiders— business journalists, securities analysts, and debt ratings services—press company managers to provide information about the firm's operations. Many countries have adopted securities laws that compel firms to disclose a wide range of information to the investing public about events or trends that promise to have a material impact on firm performance. These public sources of information frequently supply antitrust prosecutors with data needed to develop an investigation plan and perform research tasks (such as identifying industry participants and calculating market shares) central to analyzing possible violations.

Voluntary disclosures of information to antitrust prosecutors. Antitrust officials obtain substantial amounts of valuable data from industry insiders. A disaffected employee may provide information about her employer that identifies a price-fixing cartel. Individual consumers may submit complaints about suspicious sales practices to an enforcement agency. Firms sometimes provide complaints, in conversations or in "white papers," to enforcement agencies concerning business phenomena, such as a merger involving a company's suppliers or competitors. The volume of information obtained through voluntary disclosures depends partly on the enforcement agency's success in publicizing its interest in receiving information about potential antitrust violations and its willingness, at least in some circumstances, to preserve the confidentiality of its sources.

Civil compulsory process. Antitrust agencies rely heavily upon legally enforceable demands that individuals or institutions provide testimony or written information in civil cases. Compulsory civil process is crucial, for example, in forcing the defendant in a monopolization case to provide business records that reveal its assessment of its own market power and shed light on the legitimacy of justifications asserted for challenged conduct. Compulsory civil process also may be necessary to induce reluctant third parties, often including firms that have continuing business relationships with the target, to supply information. In the United States, the DOJ and the FTC routinely use civil investigative demands (essentially, subpoenas) to collect documents and compel individuals to provide testimony. Once a complaint is filed, private plaintiffs also may use compulsory discovery techniques (depositions, interrogatories, and document requests) to build the factual foundation for antitrust cases. Some jurisdictions, such as the European Union, that enforce their laws only through civil sanctions allow the competition authority to conduct surprise inspections of business offices, sometimes referred to as "dawn raids." In recent years, the U.S. and the Competition Directorate of the EC have coordinated joint efforts to exercise their respective authority to gather information on potential antitrust law violations that affect both jurisdictions.

Criminal compulsory process and covert surveillance. To collect information concerning possible antitrust crimes such as horizontal price-fixing, the DOJ empanels grand juries that issue subpoenas to compel the appearance of witnesses and the presentation of documents. In cooperation with the Federal Bureau of Investigation, the DOJ also may obtain warrants to search business offices and the homes of employees suspected of participating in criminal antitrust conspiracies; use wire taps to monitor telephone conversations; secretly photograph and videotape suspected cartel meetings; and enlist informants to wear tape recorders to monitor conversations involving cartel members. The United States and other countries that use criminal investigative techniques typically subject their application to strict control by a judicial officer who is independent of the prosecutor.

Rewards for information. In the early 1990s, the DOJ broadened the availability of immunity from criminal prosecution for companies that disclose their participation in illegal cartel activities. The DOJ leniency program, described in Sidebar 3–4 *supra*, provides complete criminal immunity for the first violator to reveal the scheme, so long as the informing party has not orchestrated the illegal arrangement. In recent years, some governments have begun considering whether to provide bounties to individuals who provide information that facilitates the successful prosecution of hard core antitrust violations.

Data from other government agencies. Antitrust agencies often use information routinely collected and maintained by other government bodies. A major example involves government procurement authorities, which frequently are targets of bid-rigging schemes. Competition policy agencies in many countries have created close working relationships with government purchasing units to identify suspicious bidding patterns and to cooperate in prosecuting violators.

2.   STATE PROSECUTORS: STATE ATTORNEYS GENERAL AND THE MULTISTATE ANTITRUST TASK FORCE OF THE NATIONAL ASSOCIATION OF ATTORNEYS GENERAL

The Sherman Act was not America's first antitrust experiment. At least 26 states had adopted constitutional or statutory "antimonopoly" measures by 1890. *See* David Millon, *The First Antitrust Statute*, 29 Washburn L.J. 141 (1990) (reporting that 12 states had adopted general antitrust statutes prior to enactment of the Sherman Act). From 1890 until 1920, the states used their antitrust statutes to achieve significant victories. Measured by the number of cases filed and the amount of fines recovered, state enforcement rivaled the Justice Department's early accomplishments in applying the Sherman Act. *See, e.g.,* James May, *Antitrust Practice and Procedure in the Formative Era: The Constitutional and Conceptual Reach of State Antitrust Law, 1880–1918,* 135 U. Pa. L. Rev. 495, 497–507 (1987).

For the half-century following the end of World War I, state antitrust enforcement lapsed. Resource constraints, doubts about the constitutional reach of the state statutes, and the emergence of sustained federal enforcement stifled state antitrust activity. But the seeds of a major revival were planted in the 1970s, as over 20 states enacted new antitrust statutes, and federal grants enabled the states to create new, or expand existing, antitrust offices. Through the 1970s, the states prosecuted local horizontal output restraints and filed federal antitrust suits on behalf of state and local bodies who had been victimized by bid-rigging. Until that time, however, the idea that states might play a major part in merger enforcement was alien to state authorities.

State enforcement today proceeds along two paths. One is to apply state antitrust and related laws. Many states have "baby FTC Acts," which mirror Section 5 of the FTC Act and authorize state challenges to unfair and deceptive trade practices. Most states also have antitrust statutes that contain close analogues to Sections 1 and 2 of the Sherman Act, and the courts of many states rely on federal antitrust jurisprudence to construe these provisions. Over twenty states also have enacted antimerger provisions. *See* Antitrust Law Section, ABA, State Antitrust Practice and Statutes (3d ed. 2004).

But some state courts have declined to interpret provisions similar to Section 1 of the Sherman Act to serve as merger control measures akin to Section 7 of the Clayton Act. *See State ex rel. Van de Kamp v. Texaco, Inc.*, 46 Cal.3d 1147, 252 Cal.Rptr. 221, 762 P.2d 385, 1988–2 Trade Cas. (CCH) ¶ 68,288 (Cal. 1988). State statutes usually allow the state attorney general to file civil or criminal suits and permit private suits for damages and injunctions.

The second path for state enforcement is to file federal antitrust suits. Like any private person injured or threatened with injury by reason of antitrust violations, states and their political subdivisions may sue under Sections 4 and 16 of the Clayton Act to obtain damages and injunctive relief, respectively. *See Chattanooga Foundry & Pipe Works v. City of Atlanta*, 203 U.S. 390 (1906) (states and subdivisions like municipalities are "persons" for purposes of private right of action). However, in *Hawaii v. Standard Oil of California*, 405 U.S. 251 (1972), the Supreme Court concluded that Section 4 of the Clayton Act did not entitle states to sue in their sovereign capacity as *parens patriae* to recover damages for injury to their economies.

Congress tried to overcome this restriction through the Hart–Scott–Rodino Antitrust Improvements Act of 1976, which added Sections 4C through 4H to the Clayton Act. These provisions enabled states to seek treble damages as *parens patriae* for injuries to natural persons within their borders and sought to provide an alternative to class actions where many individuals each had suffered relatively small monetary harm. The Supreme Court severely limited the effect of this reform in *Illinois Brick Co. v. Illinois*, 431 U.S. 720 (1977), however, which we examine later in this Chapter. *Illinois Brick* held that states could not invoke the *parens patriae* mechanism to sue on behalf of consumers who were not "direct purchasers" of the product affected by anticompetitive conduct. *Illinois Brick*'s impact has been attenuated significantly by state statutes (called *"Illinois Brick* repealers") that allow indirect purchasers in state antitrust cases to recover damages as a matter of state law. In *California v. ARC America Corp.*, 490 U.S. 93 (1989), the Supreme Court ruled that the federal antitrust laws do not preempt such state statutes which allow recovery by indirect purchasers.

States face fewer curbs when they seek injunctions under Section 16 of the Clayton Act. In *California v. American Stores Co.*, 495 U.S. 271 (1990), the Supreme Court reversed the Ninth Circuit's conclusion that Section 16 of the Clayton Act did not authorize states to obtain injunctive relief as *parens patriae* for actual or threatened harm to their economy.

American Stores involved a challenge by the State of California under Section 7 of the Clayton Act to the merger of two competing supermarket chains. The FTC had already reviewed the transaction and reached an agreement with American requiring certain divestitures, but California deemed the settlement inadequate to preserve competition in 62 California cities. The specific issue before the Court was whether California had the right to seek divestiture pursuant to Section 16 for a violation of Section 7 of the Clayton Act. Based on its interpretation of the relevant statutes, as well as the legislative history, the Court concluded that indeed California could seek divestiture, reasoning that:

> Section 16, construed to authorize a private divestiture remedy when appropriate in light of equitable principles, fits well in a statutory

scheme that favors private enforcement, subjects mergers to searching scrutiny, and regards divestiture as the remedy best suited to redress the ills of an anticompetitive merger.

495 U.S. at 284.

As noted above, before the State of California had begun its suit, the merging parties had agreed to an FTC consent order forcing divestiture of some retail outlets. When the state proceeded successfully with its own action seeking additional divestitures it became evident to the U.S. antitrust community that state governments had become partners of the DOJ and FTC in public enforcement of the Clayton Act's antimerger provision. By elevating the states' role in the public enforcement arena, *American Stores* also may have helped lay the foundation for the more active role that the state governments have played in nonmerger matters, including the *Microsoft* monopolization case, which was initiated in 1998.

But *American Stores* creates possibilities for inconsistency in public enforcement of Section 7. State efforts since 1990 to enforce Section 7 sometimes have diverged from Justice Department and FTC case selection preferences. To some degree, state officials have displayed greater skepticism toward mergers than their federal counterparts. Some state merger prosecutions have relied upon policy considerations, such as protecting existing levels of employment, that the federal agencies do not entertain. *See, e.g., Pennsylvania v. Russell Stover Candies Co.,* 1993–1 Trade Cas. (CCH) ¶ 70,224 (E.D. Pa. 1993); *Connecticut v. Newell Co.,* 1992–2 Trade Cas. (CCH) ¶ 70,008 (D. Conn.1992). Indeed, in response to their perception that the federal Merger Guidelines, adopted in 1982 during the Reagan Administration, were unduly lenient, the National Association of Attorneys General ("NAAG") adopted its own, alternate set of Guidelines in the late 1980s. Revised in 1993, those Guidelines remain influential for States contemplating merger enforcement.

What are the costs and benefits of maintaining an antitrust enforcement system with multiple enforcers? What particular costs and benefits are associated with having two federal enforcement agencies? With having both federal and state public enforcement agencies? *Contrast* Richard A. Posner, *Antitrust in the New Economy,* 68 ANTITRUST L.J. 925, 940–42 (2001) (arguing that states should be stripped of their authority to enforce federal antitrust laws), *with* Harry First, *Delivering Remedies: The Role of the States in Antitrust Enforcement,* 69 GEO. WASH. L. REV. 1004 (2001) (responding to Judge Posner).

3. ADJUDICATION: THE ROLE OF THE COURTS

The federal antitrust system gives federal judges—and particularly Supreme Court justices—considerable discretion to interpret the antitrust laws and regulations. Judges exercise this discretion in three principal ways. First, they play a pivotal role in defining liability standards. Antitrust liability standards have changed over time, often in response to new economic learning and to shifting views about antitrust's goals. The adoption of price-cost relationships and recoupment tests to evaluate predatory pricing claims (*see* Chapter 6, *supra*) and the movement from per se condemnation to rule of reason treatment for vertical restraints (*see* Chapter 4, *supra*) are two noteworthy examples of judicial modifications of liability rules.

Second, judges have defined which "persons" qualify to press claims for relief under the Clayton Act. As we will see in Section F below, the requirements that the plaintiff establish injury to her business or property, antitrust injury, standing, and directness are largely the products of judicial construction.

Third, judges define procedural and evidentiary requirements that plaintiffs must satisfy to establish liability. The non-interventionist leaning of Supreme Court antitrust jurisprudence since *Sylvania* sometimes has taken the form of elevated burdens of pleading (*e.g., Twombly*), more ready access to summary judgment (*e.g., Matsushita*), and more formidable burdens of proof. Throughout the Casebook we have seen many examples of how the courts, especially the Supreme Court, have become increasingly demanding of antitrust plaintiffs, public and private. Establishing violations today under the rule of reason, for monopolization, and for anticompetitive mergers can be difficult as a consequence.

Judges do not consider issues of standing/injury, substantive liability standards, evidentiary requirements, and remedies in isolation. These considerations are closely interrelated, as the court can adjust its treatment of any single factor to offset the perceived inadequacies of another factor. Judges can neutralize expansive per se liability rules, for example, by imposing antitrust injury requirements that effectively preclude damage recoveries by private plaintiffs or by defining evidentiary standards in ways that ensure that violations of nominally draconian conduct standards rarely will be proven.

D. ANTITRUST ENFORCEMENT UNDER THE U.S. CONSTITUTIONAL SCHEME: ANTITRUST FEDERALISM AND ANTITRUST'S RELATIONSHIP WITH THE FIRST AMENDMENT

As we observed in Chapter 1, antitrust is only one of many forms of government intervention in the economy. "Competition policy," broadly conceived, can be implemented by more than one federal entity, and in the U.S.'s federal system, state and local public entities, as well. Whereas some such regulatory measure may seek to cure market failures, others may reflect successful efforts by private interests to enlist the state in restricting output or otherwise reducing competition.

This poses a dilemma for competition policy. First, firms know that government controls can encumber rivals more effectively than private trade restraints. Manipulating the machinery of government—for example, by filing baseless patent infringement lawsuits, by lobbying for public adoption of exclusionary standards, or otherwise engaging in conduct that may impose significant costs on rivals as a consequence of subsequent government action—can impede entry and hinder competition. And it may do so with less risk of incurring the kind of costs associated with exclusionary strategies such as below-cost pricing. Compared to private output restriction agreements, which may be difficult to reach and enforce, government bodies have superior tools for reaching consensus in the form of legislation, policing violations of that legislation, and punishing deviations, even through criminal sanctions.

Moreover, First Amendment guarantees of free speech and petitioning contemplate few limits on the ability of citizens or firms to urge public officials to adopt favored policies, including measures that may favor some rivals over others and reduce competition. These protections may encourage private firms to seek public assistance in achieving anticompetitive goals, safe in the knowledge that in the asking they will retain constitutionally conferred immunity from prosecution.

Finally, the backdrop of federalism preserves a substantial economic policymaking role to state governments—at least for activities occurring largely within their own boundaries, and sovereign immunity under the Eleventh Amendment may insulate states from suits under federal law by injured persons.

In this Section we will examine the principles adopted by the courts to manage these conflicts between federal antitrust laws and competition-suppressing government regulation. Their task in doing so has been to reconcile conflicting approaches for organizing the economy. These principles have emerged mainly in the context of antitrust litigation that attacks:

- anticompetitive action undertaken by states and their subdivisions (*e.g.*, counties, municipalities);

- anticompetitive action undertaken by private parties acting with the apparent approval of a public entity, typically pursuant to a publicly adopted regulatory scheme; and

- private efforts to elicit anticompetitive government regulation or intervention.

1. FEDERAL REGULATION

Antitrust exemptions that result from federal intervention in the market arise in two basic ways—by express directive or by implication. Express directives can take two basic forms. First, Congress may expressly declare that the antitrust laws do not apply to a particular industry or set of industry practices. *See* Figure 8–8, *supra* (listing principal federal statutory exemptions). In other instances, Congress has expressly committed the task of evaluating competition in an industry to just one federal antitrust enforcer. For example, common carriers are outside the jurisdiction of the FTC Act but are subject to antitrust oversight by the DOJ.

In a second (and small) set of cases, immunity arises by implication. Where Congress creates a pervasive regulatory scheme, courts sometimes have implied antitrust immunity for the activity of regulated firms if application of the antitrust laws would disrupt the operation of the regulatory plan. In *Credit Suisse Securities (USA) LLC v. Billing*, ___ U.S. ___, 127 S.Ct. 2383 (2007), the Court ruled that there was a "plain repugnancy" between the plaintiffs' antitrust claims and federal securities laws, and that permitting private antitrust suits directed at conduct also regulated by federal securities laws would be "clearly incompatible" with the federal regulatory scheme, which already prohibited the practices. *Credit Suisse* built upon the Court's earlier decision in *Verizon Commc'ns, Inc. v. Trinko*, 540 U.S. 398 (2004). In *Trinko*, the fact that a dominant firm's duty to deal with rivals was the subject of federal regulation under the 1996 Telecommunications Act persuaded the Court to establish narrow rules of antitrust liability for refusals to deal.

Regulatory complexity alone does not establish immunity. The Supreme Court has warned that "[r]epeals of the antitrust laws by implication from a regulatory statute are strongly disfavored, and have only been found in cases of plain repugnancy between the antitrust and regulatory provisions." *United States v. Philadelphia Nat'l Bank*, 374 U.S. 321, 350–51 (1963); *see also National Gerimedical Hosp. & Gerontology Ctr. v. Blue Cross*, 452 U.S. 378, 389–90 (1981). *Cf. Ricci v. Chicago Mercantile Exchange*, 409 U.S. 289 (1973) (even if immunity is not warranted, agency may have primary jurisdiction over competition matters).

The Court also has held that the power to exempt conduct from antitrust attack resides with Congress—not individual federal officials. *See Otter Tail Power Co. v. United States*, 410 U.S. 366 (1973). Moreover, firms usually cannot avoid antitrust liability by arguing that federal officials endorsed conduct that otherwise violated the antitrust laws unless the federal officials had actual authority to immunize the behavior. Recall that in *Socony Vacuum Oil* in Chapter 2 that the Supreme Court refused to entertain the defendants' argument that Department of Interior officials privately had encouraged them to engage in the concerted action at issue. *Compare Office of Personnel Mgmt. v. Richmond*, 496 U.S. 414 (1990) (officials lacking actual authority cannot bind the government). Nevertheless, one can imagine that a defendant's reasonable, good faith reliance on the approval of a federal official might weigh against a finding of criminal intent in an antitrust case or could count in favor of applying a rule of reason (rather than a per se test) in a civil action.

Private plaintiffs sometimes have argued that cooperation between agencies of the federal government or combinations by federal officials and private actors constituted antitrust violations. But courts consistently have refused to apply the antitrust statutes to the acts of federal agencies or individual federal officials acting within their official capacity. *See Rex Sys., Inc. v. Holiday*, 814 F.2d 994 (4th Cir.1987) (military procurement decisions immune).

The presence of federal regulation also can limit the remedies available in an antitrust case. The Supreme Court has held, for example, that treble damages are unavailable for private shippers who challenge, on antitrust grounds, the reasonableness of rates submitted to and approved by the ICC. *See Keogh v. Chicago & N.W. Ry.*, 260 U.S. 156 (1922). Despite some misgivings, the Supreme Court has endorsed the vitality of the "filed rate" doctrine, stating that *Keogh* does not create general antitrust immunity, but only bars the recovery of treble damages in actions involving ICC-approved rates. *See Square D Co. v. Niagara Frontier Tariff Bureau*, 476 U.S. 409 (1986).

Nevertheless, the "filed rate doctrine" has been expanded by some courts beyond its original ICC context outside of the antitrust area. *See, e.g., Montana–Dakota Util. Co. v. Northwestern Pub. Serv. Co.*, 341 U.S. 246, 71 S.Ct. 692, 95 L.Ed. 912 (1951) (electric utility rates approved by the Federal Power Commission challenged as fraudulent); and *Wegoland Ltd. v. NYNEX Corp.*, 27 F.3d 17 (2d Cir.1994) (RICO–based challenge to utility rates that had been approved by the FCC). It has also been extended to various types of state regulation. *See id.* at 20. But there is an apparent split among courts on whether it should apply in the face of allegations that the filed rate was set pursuant to improper conduct, such as fraud or conspiracy. For a general discussion of the current reach of the filed rate doctrine, see *Blaylock v. First Am. Title Ins. Co.,* 504 F.Supp.2d 1091, 1100–01 (W.D.Wash.2007) (collecting and discussing cases).

Finally, extensive federal regulation that fails to provide immunity nonetheless can give rise to a "regulatory justification defense" to antitrust liability. *See Phonetele, Inc. v. AT & T Co.,* 664 F.2d 716 (9th Cir. 1981) ("[i]f a defendant can establish that, at the time the various anticompetitive acts alleged here were taken, it had a reasonable basis to conclude that its actions were necessitated by concrete factual imperatives recognized as legitimate by the regulatory authority, then its actions did not violate the antitrust laws.") Other tribunals have relied on extensive government rate regulation to reject antitrust claims against public utilities. *See Town of Concord v. Boston Edison Co.,* 915 F.2d 17 (1st Cir. 1990) (Breyer, C.J.). These decisions are important, because the deregulation of industries once subject to complete regulation of rates, service, and entry (*e.g.,* airlines and telecommunications) has increased the number of antitrust disputes that arise where antitrust and other federal regulatory regimes intersect.

2. STATE REGULATION

State governments can limit competition by adopting legislation that sets prices, limits output, or restricts entry into a market. At first glance, such measures might appear to encroach upon the pro-competition policy of the national antitrust laws. How are the interests of national economic integration and state sovereignty to be reconciled? The Supreme Court first tackled this question in the early 1940s following years of economic turmoil brought about by the Great Depression in which the respective roles of competition and regulation dominated debates about economic policy.

PARKER v. BROWN

Supreme Court of the United States, 1943.
317 U.S. 341, 63 S.Ct. 307, 87 L.Ed. 315.

Mr. Chief Justice STONE delivered the opinion of the Court.

The questions for our consideration are whether the marketing program adopted for the 1940 raisin crop under the California Agricultural Prorate Act is rendered invalid (1) by the Sherman Act, or (2) by the Agricultural Marketing Agreement Act of 1937, * * * or (3) by the Commerce Clause of the Constitution.

Appellee, a producer and packer of raisins in California, brought this suit in the district court to enjoin appellants * * * from enforcing, as to appellee, a program for marketing the 1940 crop of raisins produced in 'Raisin Proration Zone No. 1'. After a trial upon oral testimony, a stipulation of facts and certain exhibits, the district court held that the 1940 raisin marketing program was an illegal interference with and undue burden upon interstate commerce and gave judgment for appellee granting the injunction prayed for. * * *

As appears from the evidence and from the findings of the district court, almost all the raisins consumed in the United States, and nearly one-half of the world crop, are produced in Raisin Proration Zone No. 1. Between 90 and 95 per cent of the raisins grown in California are ultimately shipped in interstate or foreign commerce.

* * *

The California Agricultural Prorate Act authorizes the establishment, through action of state officials, of programs for the marketing of agricultural commodities produced in the state, so as to restrict competition among the growers and maintain prices in the distribution of their commodities to packers. The declared purpose of the Act is to 'conserve the agricultural wealth of the State' and to 'prevent economic waste in the marketing of agricultural crops' of the state. It authorizes, § 3, the creation of an Agricultural Prorate Advisory Commission * * *.

Upon the petition of ten producers for the establishment of a prorate marketing plan for any commodity within a defined production zone, § 8, and after a public hearing, § 9, and after making prescribed economic findings, § 10, showing that the institution of a program for the proposed zone will prevent agricultural waste and conserve agricultural wealth of the state without permitting unreasonable profits to producers, the Commission is authorized to grant the petition. The Director, with the approval of the commission, is then required to select a program committee * * *.

The program committee is required, § 15, to formulate a proration marketing program for the commodity produced in the zone, which the Commission is authorized to approve after a public hearing and a finding that 'the program is reasonably calculated to carry out the objectives of this act.' * * *

* * *

The seasonal proration marketing program for raisins, with which we are now concerned, became effective on September 7, 1940. This provided that the program committee should classify raisins as 'standard', 'substandard', and 'inferior' * * *. The committee is required to establish receiving stations within the zone to which every producer must deliver all raisins which he desires to market. The raisins are graded at these stations. All inferior raisins are to be placed in the 'inferior raisin pool', to be disposed of by the committee 'only for assured by-product and other diversion purposes'. All substandard raisins, and at least 20 per cent of the total standard and substandard raisins produced, must be placed in a 'surplus pool'. Raisins in this pool may also be disposed of only for 'assured by-product and other diversion purposes', except that under certain circumstances the program committee may transfer standard raisins from the surplus pool to the stabilization pool. Fifty per cent of the crop must be placed in a 'stabilization pool'.

Under the program the producer is permitted to sell the remaining 30 per cent of his standard raisins, denominated 'free tonnage', through ordinary commercial channels, subject to the requirement that he obtain a 'secondary certificate' authorizing such marketing and pay a certificate fee of $2.50 for each ton covered by the certificate. Certification is stated to be a device for controlling 'the time and volume of movement' of free tonnage into such ordinary commercial channels. Raisins in the stabilization pool are to be disposed of by the committee 'in such manner as to obtain stability in the market and to dispose of such raisins', but no raisins, * * * can be sold by the committee at less than the prevailing market price for raisins of the same variety and grade on the date of sale. * * *

* * *

Validity of the Prorate Program under the Sherman Act

* * * We may assume for present purposes that the California prorate program would violate the Sherman Act if it were organized and made effective solely by virtue of a contract, combination or conspiracy of private persons, individual or corporate. We may assume also, without deciding, that Congress could, in the exercise of its commerce power, prohibit a state from maintaining a stabilization program like the present because of its effect on interstate commerce. * * *

But it is plain that the prorate program here was never intended to operate by force of individual agreement or combination. It derived its authority and its efficacy from the legislative command of the state and was not intended to operate or become effective without that command. We find nothing in the language of the Sherman Act or in its history which suggests that its purpose was to restrain a state or its officers or agents from activities directed by its legislature. In a dual system of government in which, under the Constitution, the states are sovereign, save only as Congress may constitutionally subtract from their authority, an unexpressed purpose to nullify a state's control over its officers and agents is not lightly to be attributed to Congress.

The Sherman Act makes no mention of the state as such, and gives no hint that it was intended to restrain state action or official action directed by a state. The Act is applicable to 'persons' including corporations, § 7, and it authorizes suits under it by persons and corporations. § 15. A state may maintain a suit for damages under it, but the United States may not— conclusions derived not from the literal meaning of the words 'person' and 'corporation' but from the purpose, the subject matter, the context and the legislative history of the statute.

There is no suggestion of a purpose to restrain state action in the Act's legislative history. The sponsor of the bill which was ultimately enacted as the Sherman Act declared that it prevented only 'business combinations'. That its purpose was to suppress combinations to restrain competition and attempts to monopolize by individuals and corporations, abundantly appears from its legislative history.

True, a state does not give immunity to those who violate the Sherman Act by authorizing them to violate it, or by declaring that their action is lawful; and we have no question of the state or its municipality becoming a participant in a private agreement or combination by others for restraint of trade. Here the state command to the Commission and to the program committee of the California Prorate Act is not rendered unlawful by the Sherman Act since, in view of the latter's words and history, it must be taken to be a prohibition of individual and not state action. It is the state which has created the machinery for establishing the prorate program. Although the organization of a prorate zone is proposed by producers, and a prorate program, approved by the Commission, must also be approved by referendum of producers, it is the state, acting through the Commission, which adopts the program and which enforces it with penal sanctions, in the execution of a governmental policy. The prerequisite approval of the program upon referendum by a prescribed number of producers is not the imposition by them of their will upon the minority by force of agreement or combination which the Sherman Act prohibits. The state itself exercises its legislative authority in making the regulation and in prescribing the conditions of its application. The required vote on the referendum is one of these conditions.

The state in adopting and enforcing the prorate program made no contract or agreement and entered into no conspiracy in restraint of trade or to establish monopoly but, as sovereign, imposed the restraint as an act of government which the Sherman Act did not undertake to prohibit.

* * *

———

What are *Parker's* implications for national competition policy? Notice the impact of the regulatory regime at issue in *Parker*. California raisin growers produced virtually all the raisins that were consumed in the United States. Though characterized by the Supreme Court as a matter of state concern, the proration system governed the price of raisins sold throughout the country. By refusing to allow antitrust oversight to interfere with the state's output restrictions, the Supreme Court in effect permitted California— the growers' state—to determine the nationwide price of raisins, noting however, that Congress could legislate otherwise. Why might Congress want to do so? Could it, as *Parker* appeared to assume?

As we shall discuss below in the *Note on Seminole Tribe, Sovereign Immunity and the Continued Vitality of the Parker Framework*, *Parker* was grounded in principles of federalism. More formally, it rested on the assumptions that neither the language nor the legislative history of the Sherman Act suggested any intention on the part of Congress that its provisions should apply to states. As we shall see, if Congress today were inclined to expand the reach of the Sherman Act to reach states, effectively overruling *Parker*, it would face significant obstacles, at least with respect to private actions for damages, owing to the development since *Parker* of a more robust sovereign immunity doctrine under the Eleventh Amendment.

Elaboration of *Parker* was confined to the lower courts until 1975, when *Goldfarb v. Virginia State Bar*, 421 U.S. 773, 95 S.Ct. 2004 (1975) signaled the Court's willingness to narrow *Parker's* broad scope. In *Goldfarb* the Court declined to apply *Parker* to minimum fee schedules set by a county bar association and enforcement of the schedules in disciplinary proceedings conducted by the state bar. The Court termed this conduct "essentially a private anticompetitive activity," as neither Virginia's laws nor the rules of its Supreme Court required the minimum fees. However, in *Bates v. State Bar of Arizona*, 433 U.S. 350, 97 S.Ct. 2691, 53 L.Ed.2d 810 (1977), the Court again declared that the legislative actions of the state—in that case the state Supreme Court's prohibition of attorney advertising—were actions of "the state" that were exempt from the coverage of the Sherman Act. *See also Hoover v. Ronwin*, 466 U.S. 558, 104 S.Ct. 1989, 80 L.Ed.2d 590 (1984).

Parker and these later cases established that the legislative acts of the state (including those of a state Supreme Court acting in a legislative capacity) are acts of the sovereign that are exempt from the reach of the Sherman Act. But they also recognized that states can implement their policies indirectly in many different ways, as through commissions, boards, and other instrumentalities, and that the justification for the *Parker* exemption might become attenuated as the challenged conduct becomes increasingly removed from the state. Tension developed around a key issue: to what extent, if any, should the acts of these kinds of bodies be deemed acts of "the state" for purposes of extending the *Parker* exemption? The Court provided the current framework for answering that question in the following case.

CALIFORNIA RETAIL LIQUOR DEALERS ASS'N v. MIDCAL ALUMINUM, INC.

Supreme Court of the United States, 1980.
445 U.S. 97, 100 S.Ct. 937, 63 L.Ed.2d 233.

Mr. Justice POWELL delivered the opinion of the Court.

In a state-court action, respondent Midcal Aluminum, Inc., a wine distributor, presented a successful antitrust challenge to California's resale price maintenance and price posting statutes for the wholesale wine trade. The issue in this case is whether those state laws are shielded from the Sherman Act by either the "state action" doctrine of *Parker v. Brown*, 317 U.S. 341, 63 S.Ct. 307 (1943), or § 2 of the Twenty-first Amendment.

I

Under § 24866(b) of the California Business and Professions Code, all wine producers, wholesalers, and rectifiers must file fair trade contracts or price schedules with the State. If a wine producer has not set prices through a fair trade contract, wholesalers must post a resale price schedule for that producer's brands. § 24866(a). No state-licensed wine merchant may sell wine to a retailer at other than the price set "either in an effective price schedule or in an effective fair trade contract...." § 24862 (West Supp.1980).

The State is divided into three trading areas for administration of the wine pricing program. A single fair trade contract or schedule for each brand sets the terms for all wholesale transactions in that brand within a given trading area. Similarly, state regulations provide that the wine prices posted by a single wholesaler within a trading area bind all wholesalers in that area. A licensee selling below the established prices faces fines, license suspension, or outright license revocation. Cal.Bus. & Prof.Code Ann. § 24880 (West Supp.1980).[2] The State has no direct control over wine prices, and it does not review the reasonableness of the prices set by wine dealers.

---

2. Licensees that sell wine below the prices specified in fair trade contracts or schedules   also may be subject to private damages suits for unfair competition. § 24752 (West 1964).

Midcal Aluminum, Inc., is a wholesale distributor of wine in southern California. In July 1978, the Department of Alcoholic Beverage Control charged Midcal with selling 27 cases of wine for less than the prices set by the effective price schedule of the E. & J. Gallo Winery. The Department also alleged that Midcal sold wines for which no fair trade contract or schedule had been filed. Midcal stipulated that the allegations were true and that the State could fine it or suspend its license for those transgressions. Midcal then filed a writ of mandate in the California Court of Appeal for the Third Appellate District asking for an injunction against the State's wine pricing system.

The Court of Appeal ruled that the wine pricing scheme restrains trade in violation of the Sherman Act * * *.

* * *

* * * An appeal was brought by the California Retail Liquor Dealers Association, an intervenor. The California Supreme Court declined to hear the case, and the Dealers Association sought certiorari from this Court. We granted the writ, and now affirm the decision of the state court.

II

The threshold question is whether California's plan for wine pricing violates the Sherman Act. This Court has ruled consistently that resale price maintenance illegally restrains trade. In *Dr. Miles Medical Co. v. John D. Park & Sons Co.*, 220 U.S. 373, 407, 31 S.Ct. 376, 384 (1911), the Court observed that such arrangements are "designed to maintain prices . . . , and to prevent competition among those who trade in [competing goods]." * * *

California's system for wine pricing plainly constitutes resale price maintenance in violation of the Sherman Act. The wine producer holds the power to prevent price competition by dictating the prices charged by wholesalers. As Mr. Justice Hughes pointed out in *Dr. Miles*, such vertical control destroys horizontal competition as effectively as if wholesalers "formed a combination and endeavored to establish the same restrictions . . . by agreement with each other." 220 U.S., at 408, 31 S.Ct., at 384. Moreover, there can be no claim that the California program is simply intrastate regulation beyond the reach of the Sherman Act.

Thus, we must consider whether the State's involvement in the price-setting program is sufficient to establish antitrust immunity under *Parker v. Brown*, 317 U.S. 341, 63 S.Ct. 307 (1943). That immunity for state regulatory programs is grounded in our federal structure. "In a dual system of government in which, under the Constitution, the states are sovereign, save only as Congress may constitutionally subtract from their authority, an unexpressed purpose to nullify a state's control over its officers and agents is not lightly to be attributed to Congress." *Id.*, at 351, 63 S.Ct., at 313. In *Parker v. Brown*, this Court found in the Sherman Act no purpose to nullify state powers. Because the Act is directed against "individual and not state action," the Court concluded that state regulatory programs could not violate it. *Id.*, at 352, 63 S.Ct., at 314.

[The Court here discussed its decisions in *Goldfarb v. Virginia State Bar*, 421 U.S. 773, 95 S.Ct. 2004 (1975), *Cantor v. Detroit Edison Co.*, 428 U.S. 579, 96 S.Ct. 3110 (1976), *Bates v. State Bar of Arizona*, 433 U.S. 350, 97 S.Ct.

2691 (1977), and *New Motor Vehicle Bd. of Cal. v. Orrin W. Fox Co.*, 439 U.S. 96, 99 S.Ct. 403 (1978). Eds.]

* * *

These decisions establish two standards for antitrust immunity under *Parker v. Brown.* First, the challenged restraint must be "one clearly articulated and affirmatively expressed as state policy"; second, the policy must be "actively supervised" by the State itself. *City of Lafayette v. Louisiana Power & Light Co.*, 435 U.S. 389, 410, 98 S.Ct. 1123, 1135 (1978)(opinion of Brennan, J.). The California system for wine pricing satisfies the first standard. The legislative policy is forthrightly stated and clear in its purpose to permit resale price maintenance. The program, however, does not meet the second requirement for *Parker* immunity. The State simply authorizes price setting and enforces the prices established by private parties. The State neither establishes prices nor reviews the reasonableness of the price schedules; nor does it regulate the terms of fair trade contracts. The State does not monitor market conditions or engage in any "pointed reexamination" of the program.[9] The national policy in favor of competition cannot be thwarted by casting such a gauzy cloak of state involvement over what is essentially a private price-fixing arrangement. As *Parker* teaches, "a state does not give immunity to those who violate the Sherman Act by authorizing them to violate it, or by declaring that their action is lawful...." 317 U.S., at 351, 63 S.Ct., at 314.

* * *

The first prong of *Midcal's* two-pronged test for application of the state action doctrine to the acts of private parties—the "clear articulation" requirement—asks whether the state has clearly chosen to displace competition. In *Southern Motor Carriers Rate Conference, Inc. v. United States*, 471 U.S. 48 (1985), the Supreme Court ruled that "a state policy that expressly *permits,* but does not compel, anticompetitive behavior may be 'clearly articulated' within the meaning of *Midcal.*" Thus, it is enough that the state policy merely authorizes (but does not command) departures from competition. What is the rationale behind the clear articulation requirement? Does it help to guard against undue encroachment by state conduct on national competition policy? If so, how does it perform that function? What is the likely impact of *Southern Motor Carriers* on its ability to realize its goals?

Midcal's second prong—"active state supervision"—seeks to ensure that *Parker* "will shelter only the particular anticompetitive acts of private parties that, in the judgment of the State, actually further state regulatory policies." Absent such supervision, the courts have declined to apply the state action doctrine. In *Patrick v. Burget*, 486 U.S. 94 (1988), for example, the Court found that Oregon had exercised insufficient oversight of a peer review

---

9. The California program contrasts with the approach of those States that completely control the distribution of liquor within their boundaries. Such comprehensive regulation would be immune from the Sherman Act under *Parker v. Brown*, since the State would "displace unfettered business freedom" with its own power.

mechanism by which physicians determined whether to grant a rival doctor hospital privileges. For state oversight to constitute active supervision, state officials must "have and exercise power to review particular anticompetitive acts of private parties and disapprove those that fail to accord with state policy." Such scrutiny serves to ensure that states do not simply repeal fundamental elements of national competition policy without installing alternative, operational public oversight machinery. *See also 324 Liquor Corp. v. Duffy*, 479 U.S. 335 (1987) (state action doctrine inapplicable to state liquor pricing regulations absent state supervision).

The Supreme Court revisited the active supervision issue in *FTC v. Ticor Title Ins. Co.*, 504 U.S. 621 (1992), where it again withheld application of the state action doctrine, in that case from title insurance companies that jointly set fees for title searches and examinations through rate bureaus subject to state regulation. The defendants' proposed rates took effect unless state regulators exercised a "negative option" to veto the rates. The Supreme Court said that the active supervision test requires an inquiry into "whether the State has exercised sufficient independent judgment and control so that the details of the rates or prices have been established as a product of deliberate state intervention, not simply by agreement among private parties." Several features of the regulatory oversight process belied the existence of adequate "independent judgment and control." In two states, the regulators examined rate filings for "mathematical accuracy" alone or left filings "unchecked altogether." In other states, the regulators failed to press private rate bureaus to comply with requests for information.

Ticor sought to define when nominal state oversight might fall short of active supervision. The Court said an "infrequent lapse of state supervision" might not preclude application of the state action doctrine; oversight tools such as "sampling techniques or a specified rate of return" might provide the requisite "comprehensive supervision without complete control." Moreover, the Court said *Ticor* "should be read in light of the gravity of the antitrust offense [horizontal price-fixing], the involvement of private actors throughout, and the clear absence of state supervision." Despite these attempts at limitation, *Ticor* may pose difficult challenges for firms attempting to predict the effect of state oversight.

The "active supervision" issue continues to be litigated. In a unanimous opinion, the FTC affirmed an ALJ's conclusion that a state action defense did not attach to the joint rate filing activities of a group of household goods movers. In the Commission's view, Kentucky's actions had "fallen far short" of satisfying *Midcal's* standard for "active supervision." *See In the Matter of Kentucky Household Goods Carriers Ass'n, Inc.*, Dkt. No. 9309 (Jun. 21, 2005), *available at* http://www.ftc.gov/os/adjpro/d9309/050622opinionof thecommission.pdf.

Two additional issues have arisen in connection with defining the scope of the state action doctrine. First, whether *Parker* extends to the political subdivisions of the state, and second, whether there is a "conspiracy exception" to *Parker, i.e.*, whether misconduct by government officials, such as colluding with private parties to the detriment of competition, falls outside the scope of *Parker's* protection.

Both issues were addressed in *City of Columbia v. Omni Outdoor Advertising, Inc.*, 499 U.S. 365, 111 S.Ct. 1344, 113 L.Ed.2d 382 (1991). As a general matter, the Court observed, *Parker* does not apply directly to local governments, citing *Town of Hallie v. Eau Claire*, 471 U.S. 34, 38, 105 S.Ct. 1713, 1716 (1985); *Community Commc'ns Co. v. Boulder*, 455 U.S. 40, 50–51, 102 S.Ct. 835, 840–841 (1982); and *Lafayette v. Louisiana Power & Light Co.*, 435 U.S. 389, 412–413, 98 S.Ct. 1123, 1136–1137 (1978) (plurality opinion). The state action doctrine may be available, however, when a municipality's restriction of competition is an authorized implementation of state policy. We will discuss the issues related to municipal liability in the next section of the Chapter.

City of Columbia involved a challenge by an outdoor advertising company to the city's decisions on the placement of billboards, which, it argued, had favored its rivals. State statutes authorized municipalities to adopt zoning and land use regulations affecting construction within their boundaries, including the placement of billboards. The first issue was whether the fact that state law clearly authorized regulation of billboards was enough to invoke the state action doctrine, as the defendants argued. The Court concluded "such an expansive interpretation of the *Parker*-defense authorization requirement would have unacceptable consequences." 499 U.S. at 371. In the Court's view, "in order to prevent *Parker* from undermining the very interests of federalism it is designed to protect, it is necessary to adopt a concept of authority broader than what is applied to determine the legality of the municipality's action under state law. * * * " *Id.* at 372. However, it also concluded that "here no more is needed to establish, for *Parker* purposes, the city's authority to regulate than its unquestioned zoning power over the size, location, and spacing of billboards." *Id.*

Authority to regulate alone, however, is insufficient to trigger *Parker*. According to the Court, the *"Parker* defense also requires authority to suppress competition—more specifically, 'clear articulation of a state policy to authorize anticompetitive conduct' by the municipality in connection with its regulation." *Id.*, *quoting Town of Hallie*, 471 U.S., at 40, 105 S. Ct., at 1717 (internal quotation omitted). To satisfy that requirement, however, it is not necessary that the statute delegating authority to the municipality "explicitly permits the displacement of competition. It is enough, we have held, if suppression of competition is the 'foreseeable result' of what the statute authorizes." *Id.* at 372–73. The Court concluded that this condition was "amply met here." *Id.* at 373. *But see Southern Motor Carriers Rate Conference, Inc. v. United States*, 471 U.S. 48 (1985) (no mention of "foreseeable result" standard).

The Court also resolved a second issue: whether there was a "conspiracy exception" to *Parker*:

> There is no such conspiracy exception. The rationale of *Parker* was that, in light of our national commitment to federalism, the general language of the Sherman Act should not be interpreted to prohibit anticompetitive actions by the States in their governmental capacities as sovereign regulators. * * * The impracticality of such a principle is evident if, for purposes of the exception, "conspiracy" means nothing more than an agreement to impose the regulation in

question. Since it is both inevitable and desirable that public officials often agree to do what one or another group of private citizens urges upon them, such an exception would virtually swallow up the *Parker* rule * * *.

Id. at 374–75.

City of Columbia also hinted at a third possible exception to *Parker* that would permit the antitrust laws to apply to a municipality when it acts as a "market participant" rather than as a regulator. *Id.* at 379. This passing reference has not been clarified by the Supreme Court and, although it has been discussed in some lower court decisions, has not coalesced into a firm exception to *Parker*. *See generally* ABA ANTITRUST SECTION, ANTITRUST LAW DEVELOPMENTS 1282–83 (6th ed. 2007). *See also* ANTITRUST MODERNIZATION COMMISSION, FINAL REPORT AND RECOMMENDATIONS 375–77 (2007) (endorsing market participant exception), *available at* http://www.amc.gov/report_recommendation/chapter4.pdf.

On September 23, 2003, the State Action Task Force at the Federal Trade Commission, which had been established in the summer of 2001, issued a comprehensive Staff Report urging clarifications of the State Action Doctrine. The Report identifies a variety of ways in which the Task Force believes the State Action doctrine is being read too broadly to the detriment of competition, and urges that it be constrained, particularly through refinement of the definition of "the State," and interpretation of both "clear articulation" and "active supervision." *See* FTC, Office of Policy Planning, *Report of the State Action Task Force* (Sept. 2003), *available at* http://www.ftc.gov/os/2003/09/stateactionreport.pdf.

Note on Seminole Tribe, Sovereign Immunity and the Continued Vitality of the Parker Framework

As we have seen, *Parker* spawned a long line of cases, which, over time, have sought to establish a line between permissible and impermissible state action under the Sherman Act. The Court has consistently adhered, however, to the basic premise of *Parker*: that *state* action is outside the purview of the Sherman Act. The more difficult immunity issues have arisen in the context of anticompetitive conduct undertaken by subdivisions of the state, or by private parties purporting to act pursuant to state regulatory schemes.

It is questionable, however, whether the Supreme Court will continue to analyze purely state action immunity in the same way. Recall that in *Parker* the Supreme Court's decision to recognize state action immunity rested on two observations about the Sherman Act: (1) that nothing in its *language* suggested coverage of state action; and (2) that similarly, nothing in its *legislative history* indicated a Congressional intent to authorize application of the Sherman Act to state conduct. The Court assumed, however, that "Congress could, in the exercise of its commerce power, prohibit a state from maintaining a stabilization program like the present because of its effect on interstate commerce." Immunity, therefore, was granted as a matter of statutory interpretation, not constitutional infirmity. Indeed, in observing that the commerce power was adequate to reach the anticompetitive activities of states, the Court left the impression that Congress could, if it wanted to, alter the statute to extend to anticompetitive state action. But who could enforce such an expanded Sherman Act? The Court had no occasion to evaluate the implications of Congress' authorizing public versus private rights of action for a broader Sherman Act.

Any implication that Congress could not only expand coverage of the Act to reach state action, but that it also could permit private suits to challenge state action, appears to be at odds with *Seminole Tribe of Florida v. Florida*, 517 U.S. 44 (1996), in which the Court by a 5–4 vote held that the commerce clause does not provide Congress with authority to abrogate the states' Eleventh Amendment sovereign immunity. Subsequent decisions of the Court have further entrenched that view, and the same five-justice majority now maintains that sovereign immunity is a feature of the Constitution as a whole, not simply a function of the Eleventh Amendment. *See Federal Maritime Comm'n v. South Carolina State Ports Auth.*, 535 U.S. 743, 122 S.Ct. 1864 (2002). It is arguable, therefore, that the question whether a private party can sue a state for alleged violations of the Sherman Act would today have to take account of both *Parker* and *Seminole Tribe. See generally* Susan Beth Farmer, *Balancing State Sovereignty and Competition: An Analysis of the Impact of* Seminole Tribe *on the Antitrust State Action Immunity Doctrine*, 42 VILL. L. REV. 111 (1997).

Seminole Tribe adopted a two-part test for assessing a private party's right to sue a state for damages. The test asks: (1) has Congress expressed an unequivocal intention to abrogate the State's sovereign immunity?; and (2) if it has, has it done so pursuant to a valid exercise of constitutional power? 517 U.S. at 44. This framework would appear to supercede *Parker*, at least with respect to private plaintiffs, even though the answers to the questions it poses can still be found there. According to the Court in *Parker*, the answer to the first question would be an unequivocal "no"—there is no evidence in either the language or legislative history of the Sherman Act that Congress intended for the Act to cover the anticompetitive conduct of states, whether the allegation is pursued by public or private plaintiffs. Hence, there is no evidence of an intention to abrogate sovereign immunity.

Even if Congress were to seek to alter that scheme—as *Parker* assumed it could—the second hurdle erected by *Seminole Tribe* could not be surmounted, at least with respect to private suits for damages. *Parker* acknowledges, as have other cases, that the Sherman Act was adopted pursuant to the commerce clause, and *Seminole Tribe* clearly holds that the commerce clause is an insufficient source of authority to abrogate state sovereign immunity. Hence, Congress's authority to alter state action immunity as it developed under *Parker* probably has been limited by *Seminole Tribe. See* Jean Wegman Burns, *Embracing both Faces of Antitrust Federalism: Parker and ARC America Corp.*, 68 ANTITRUST L.J. 29 (2000).

There are, however, two important exceptions to the rule of *Seminole Tribe*. First, it does not preclude the long recognized right of private parties to vindicate their federal rights by seeking *prospective injunctive relief* against state officials. *See Ex Parte Young*, 209 U.S. 123 (1908). Second, it does not limit Congress's power to authorize suits by the *federal government* against states for violations of federal law. It is here, however, that *Parker* may continue to play a vital role. To the extent the Eleventh Amendment may not bar either private suits against the states for injunctive relief or public suits against the states for damages, *Parker* may, due to its holding that the Sherman Act does not reach state action (assuming that the requirements for establishing state action, currently set forth under the *Midcal* tests, are satisfied).

The courts are still in the process of trying to synthesize and integrate these three complex lines of cases—Parker, *Seminole Tribe*, and *Ex Parte Young*. *See, e.g., TFWS, Inc. v. Schaefer*, 242 F.3d 198 (4th Cir. 2001); *Neo Gen Screening, Inc. v. New England Newborn Screening Program*, 187 F.3d 24 (1st Cir. 1999). It appears likely, however, that *Parker's* role has been fundamentally altered. One set of possible post-*Seminole Tribe* rules might be:

- any suit under the Sherman Act initiated by a private party against a state and seeking damages would be barred—under the analysis required in *Seminole Tribe*, not *Parker*—although *Parker would* provide the answers to *Seminole's* two part test;

- any suit under the Sherman Act initiated by a private party against a state seeking prospective injunctive relief also would be barred—but under the analysis of *Parker* (*i.e., Ex Parte Young* would be irrelevant);

- any suit by the federal government against a state for damages or injunctive relief would continue to be barred—not by *Seminole Tribe* or *Young*, but by *Parker*; and

- if Congress deemed it appropriate to amend the Sherman Act to prohibit the anticompetitive acts of states, it could do so under the authority of *Parker*; however, establishing permissible rights to relief to enforce such an expanded Sherman Act would have to be carefully delineated under *Seminole Tribe* and *Young*, as follows: (1) Congress could grant the federal government a right to relief against the states for damages and/or injunctive relief, but (2) *private parties* could only be authorized to seek prospective injunctive relief as permitted by *Young*.

Even if these rules were to come to fruition, important unanswered questions remain. Paramount among them is whether the concepts of sovereign immunity established by *Parker* and *Seminole Tribe* are co-extensive. For example, if *Parker* immunity reaches deeper into the subdivisions of state government than does *Seminole Tribe*, *Parker* will retain a relatively more vital role in assessing immunity. Under such circumstances, even when immunity is found unavailable under *Seminole Tribe* as a constitutional matter, it might still be urged under *Parker*. On the other hand, if the scope of *Seminole Tribe's* immunity is read more broadly than *Parker's*, *Parker's* role will further diminish.

A second and related question concerns the continued role of the *Midcal* active state supervision test. As Professor Beth Farmer has recognized, *Midcal's* analysis is an attempt to balance the competition policy concerns of the Sherman Act with the sovereign immunity concerns recognized in *Parker*. Requiring "active state supervision" of private conduct is one way to insure that the balance is being properly struck. But it is possible to posit a reading of *Seminole Tribe* so broad that *Midcal's* analysis would be unnecessary. With significantly greater deference to sovereign immunity might come diminished judicial authority to balance competition policy concerns and far broader antitrust immunity, even for essentially private, anticompetitive schemes. If *Seminole Tribe* were to be read that broadly, therefore, the incentive for private firms to secure anticompetitive state action surely would increase.

The courts have been struggling with many of these issues. For example, at various times, the Court itself has referred to *Parker* as an "immunity" and as a "defense." In *South Carolina State Bd. of Dentistry v. FTC*, 455 F.3d 436 (4th Cir. 2006), the Fourth Circuit recently held that the FTC's refusal to apply *Parker* in a pending administrative proceeding was not a collateral order subject to immediate review. In so holding, the court argued that *Parker* and Eleventh Amendment immunity are not co-extensive, and hence *Parker* does not provide "immunity from suit," just a "defense to liability." What is the significance of viewing *Parker* as an "immunity," like sovereign immunity, as opposed to a "defense" to an otherwise potentially valid antitrust claim? Are the interests protected by immunities and defenses the same? Do they procedurally operate in the same way?

3. INTERVENTION BY MUNICIPAL AND OTHER LOCAL AUTHORITIES

As was noted in *City of Columbia v. Omni Outdoor Advertising, Inc.*, 499 U.S. 365, 111 S.Ct. 1344, 113 L.Ed.2d 382 (1991), discussed following *Midcal*, *supra*, under the current state of the law the decisions of political subdivisions such as cities, counties, and townships are not entitled to the same antitrust immunity as the decisions of the state itself. *City of Lafayette v. Louisiana Power & Light Co.*, 435 U.S. 389 (1978). State action immunity based on the acts of a political subdivision exists only if the subdivision acts pursuant to a mandate from the state itself. *See Hertz Corp. v. City of New York*, 1 F.3d 121 (2d Cir.1993) (exercise of city's home-rule authority deemed not to immunize city law that barred rental car firms from imposing certain fees).

In *Town of Hallie v. City of Eau Claire*, 471 U.S. 34 (1985), discussed in *City of Columbia*, the Supreme Court considered how the *Midcal* test applies to anticompetitive conduct by political subdivisions. *Hallie* involved a city's refusal to provide sewage treatment services to neighboring unincorporated townships unless landowners in those areas agreed to have their properties annexed. *Midcal's* clear articulation standard was met if "it was clear that anticompetitive effects logically would result from this broad authority to regulate." *Id*. at 42. The defendant city's behavior was "a foreseeable result of empowering the City to refuse to serve unannexed areas." *Id*. As you saw in the discussion of *City of Columbia*, the Supreme Court concluded that the challenged zoning regulation satisfied *Hallie's* "foreseeable result" test because "[t]he very purpose of zoning regulation is to displace unfettered business freedom in a manner that regularly has the effect of preventing normal acts of competition." 499 U.S. at 373.

Hallie also held that states need not supervise their subdivisions' exercise of authority for state action immunity to apply: "Once it is clear that state authorization exists, there is no need to require the State to supervise actively the municipality's execution of what is a properly delegated function." *Town of Hallie*, 471 U.S. at 47. In a footnote, the Court also suggested without deciding that the same would be true if the actor is a state agency other than a municipality, but it distinguished cases brought against private parties:

> In cases in which the actor is a state agency, it is likely that active state supervision would also not be required, although we do not here decide that issue. Where state or municipal regulation by a private party is involved, however, active state supervision must be shown, even where a clearly articulated state policy exists.

Id. at 46 n.10. *See also Benton, Benton & Benton v. Louisiana Pub. Facilities Auth.*, 897 F.2d 198 (5th Cir.1990) (relying on footnote 10 to conclude that

Hallie obviates the need for states to actively supervise state agencies to create immunity).

The application of the antitrust laws to local governments in *Lafayette* and cases such as *Community Commc's, Co., Inc. v. City of Boulder*, 455 U.S. 40 (1982), which held that Colorado's home rule statute did not immunize the City of Boulder from antitrust liability for its regulation of cable television, raised fears that cities might be exposed to the risk of treble damage liability. Through the Local Government Antitrust Act of 1984 "LGAA", 15 U.S.C. §§ 34–36, Congress responded, barring antitrust damage suits against local governments and against private parties acting under their direction. The LGAA permits suits for equitable relief under Section 16 of the Clayton Act and allows the recovery of attorneys fees for plaintiffs who substantially prevail in such suits.

4. PREEMPTION

State regulation must withstand scrutiny under the Supremacy Clause of the Constitution, which preempts state laws that are inconsistent with federal legislation. The preemption inquiry in antitrust cases has focused on whether state regulation clashes so substantially with the federal antitrust statutes that the two regimes cannot coexist. Preemption occurs only in cases of acute conflict and is a weak check on state regulation that displaces competition.

In *Rice v. Norman Williams Co.*, 458 U.S. 654 (1982), the Supreme Court refused to enjoin enforcement of a California statute that allowed liquor importers to buy liquor outside California only if the liquor was consigned to a licensed importer. The Court held that preemption would occur only if the statute "necessarily constitutes a violation of the antitrust laws in all cases, or if it places irresistible pressure on a private party to violate the antitrust laws in order to comply with the [state] statute." The Court indicated that a facial inconsistency would exist only if conduct compelled by the state law is illegal per se—a condition found lacking in *Rice. See also Fisher v. City of Berkeley*, 475 U.S. 260 (1986) (municipal rent control ordinance held not to be facially preempted by Section 1 of the Sherman Act; ordinance did not necessarily violate Section 1 "in all cases," mainly because the city unilaterally imposed the rent control ordinance and the concerted action needed under Section 1 was lacking). Significant preemption arguments have been made to attack the "master settlement agreement" reached between a number of states and the tobacco industry, with mixed results. *Contrast Sanders v. Brown*, 504 F.3d 903 (9th Cir. 2007) (state statutes implementing "master settlement agreement" with tobacco industry were not preempted by federal antitrust laws) *with Freedom Holdings, Inc. v. Spitzer*, 357 F.3d 205 (2d Cir. 2004) (reaching opposite conclusion).

Sidebar 9–4:
Revisiting Immunities Based on Government Intervention—U.S. and Comparative Perspectives*

As can be seen from the cases and materials presented above, government action can have a substantial impact on competition. *See* JEAN-JACQUES LAFFONT & JEAN TIROLE, A THEORY OF INCENTIVES IN PROCUREMENT AND REGULATION 538–57 (1993); DANIEL F. SPULBER, REGULATION AND MARKETS 21–109 (1989); W. KIP VISCUSI, ET AL., ECONOMICS OF REGULATION AND ANTITRUST 295–329 (1992). In some instances, government dispensations from competition serve to correct market failures. *See* MICHAEL A. CREW & PAUL R. KLEINDORFER, THE ECONOMICS OF PUBLIC UTILITY REGULATION 3–30 (1986) (describing rationale for public intervention to regulate natural monopolies). Whereas in many others regulation that restricts business rivalry by limiting entry into the market, authorizing producers to cooperate in setting prices or other terms of commerce, or granting exclusive privileges to selected entrepreneurs may enable an individual firm or group of firms to gain monopoly rents. *See* Paul L. Joskow & Nancy L. Rose, *The Effects of Economic Regulation, in* II HANDBOOK OF INDUSTRIAL ORGANIZATION 1451, 1469–72 (Richard Schmalensee & Robert Willig eds., 1989). For the most part, government-imposed restraints on competition often are more powerful and effective than private restraints, owing to the government's ability to enforce its will by using the machinery of the state to punish transgressors with civil sanctions or criminal penalties. As the scope of government measures to restrict competition grows, the vitality of a market system can suffer significantly.

For these and other reasons, transition economies—those nations in the process of converting from a high degree of state control to a more market-driven economy—often are encouraged to empower their competition policy authorities to engage in "competition advocacy" or enforcement functions to curb state efforts to suppress competition. *See* WORLD BANK & ORGANIZATION FOR ECONOMIC COOPERATION AND DEVELOPMENT, A FRAMEWORK FOR THE DESIGN AND IMPLEMENTATION OF COMPETITION LAW AND POLICY 93–100 (1999); Craig W. Conrath & Barry T. Freeman, *A Response to "The Effectiveness of Proposed Antitrust Programs for Developing Countries,"* 19 N.C. J. INT'L L. & COM. 233, 243–35 (1994). Many transition economies have taken this advice to heart, perhaps out of their own keen awareness of the dangers of government intervention born from decades of intrusive central economic controls. *See* William E. Kovacic, *Antitrust and Competition Policy in Transition Economies: A Preliminary Assessment,* 2000 FORDHAM CORP. L. INST. 513, 525–26 (B. Hawk, ed. 2000).

Competition authorities in transition economies have developed a variety of tools for restricting the role of the state, including (1) subjecting state-owned enterprises to the same competition policy commands that govern private enterprises, and (2) permitting competition authorities to veto government action that restricts competition, unless such restrictions have been expressly approved by the national legislature. *See*

---

* Parts of this Sidebar are adapted from William E. Kovacic, *Lessons of Competition Policy* *Reform in Transition Economies for U.S. Antitrust Policy*, 74 ST. JOHN'S L. REV. 361 (2000).

Ben Slay, *Industrial De-monopolization and Competition Policy in Poland, in* DE-MONOPOLIZATION AND COMPETITION POLICY IN POST-COMMUNIST ECONOMIES 123, 143 (Ben Slay ed., 1996); William E. Kovacic & Ben Slay, *Perilous Beginnings: The Establishment of Antimonopoly and Consumer Protection Programs in the Republic of Georgia*, 43 ANTITRUST BULL. 15, 39 (1998).

Even as Western consultants counsel transition economies to resist government intervention to suppress business rivalry, however, the United States tolerates large-scale government incursions into the economy that appear to be inconsistent with the pro-competition goals of the federal antitrust laws. At the federal level, for example, Congress continues to embrace measures, in areas such as agriculture, that encourage or mandate cooperation by producers to restrict output and raise prices. *See generally* ABA SECTION OF ANTITRUST LAW, ANTITRUST LAW DEVELOPMENTS 1306–10 (6th ed. 2007). And as we have seen in this Chapter, by displacing the operation of the federal antitrust laws, the judicially-created state action doctrine creates incentives for producer groups to elicit government intervention at the state and local level to forestall competition. *See* John Shepard Wiley, *A Capture Theory of Antitrust Federalism*, 99 HARV. L. REV. 713, 714–15 (1986).

One might accept state measures to suppress rivalry that inflicts harm solely or chiefly on the citizens of the jurisdiction adopting the measures. But in such circumstances, at least in theory, the state's voters have electoral tools to change the policies. The modern state action doctrine is not so discriminating, for it confers immunity without accounting for whether the intervention of one state imposes significant, adverse economic spillovers on the citizens of other states—a fact that was evident in *Parker*, itself, which allowed California raisin growers to in effect set nation-wide raisin prices. *See* Robert P. Inman & Daniel L. Rubinfeld, *Making Sense of the Antitrust State–Action Doctrine: Balancing Political Participation and Economic Efficiency in Regulatory Federalism*, 75 TEX. L. REV. 1203 (1997).

On the other hand, a number of American commentators have suggested that state action immunity can be viewed as a source of desirable experimentation in economic regulation by state governments. *See* Jean Wegman Burns, *Embracing Both Faces of Antitrust Federalism: Parker and ARC America Corp.*, 68 ANTITRUST L.J. 29, 44 (2000). State antitrust officials devote comparatively few resources to opposing measures by state instrumentalities that restrict competition. The acceptance of intervention by state governments also finds support in Supreme Court jurisprudence that applies the commerce clause as a relatively weak limit on state economic regulation and suggests that congressional efforts to abolish or circumscribe the state action doctrine might constitute impermissible infringements of state sovereignty. *See* Inman & Rubinfeld, *supra*, at 1272–73 & n.228; Burns, *supra*, at 38.

Competition-suppressing government intervention at the national or regional levels arguably is more inimical to economic growth in transition economies than in mature Western market countries. The United States is a prosperous nation and has more margin for error in pursuing policies that allow producers to reallocate, rather than pressing them to expand, society's total wealth. Yet regulatory limits on entry by new entrepreneurs or expansion by existing firms also can impose important social costs even in a wealthy country by raising prices and retarding innovation.

Heeding the message conveyed to transition economies would induce American antitrust institutions to devote more energy to resisting government policies at all levels that suppress competition. At the national level, this might entail greater efforts to publicize the harmful effects of federal programs that curb rivalry. One might even consider adopting the practice of the European Union competition regime, embodied in Article 86, to subject government efforts to limit competition to close scrutiny.

At the state level, if the existing dimensions of state action immunity are politically or constitutionally immutable, state antitrust bureaus might assume more responsibility for opposing measures by state governments and their political subdivisions to restrict competition. This would require some reorientation of state antitrust priorities that moves at least some resources now dedicated to pursuing matters treated by federal enforcement agencies toward efforts to oppose state legislative or regulatory encroachments on the competitive process. The urgency for state antitrust officials to undertake a robust advocacy role becomes all the more important if the Supreme Court remains indifferent to state measures that restrict competition and impede the functioning of a national economic union by imposing serious adverse spillovers upon other jurisdictions.

5. PETITIONING

Antitrust challenges to anticompetitive government action often include claims directed at private parties who have succeeded in soliciting government action that reduces competition. Although the government entity may be immune from antitrust liability by virtue of the state action doctrine or some other exemption, such claims pose a distinct question: should that immunity extend to the private parties that have actively sought the anticompetitive state action? The actions of such parties frequently are challenged as monopolization or attempts to monopolize under Section 2 of the Sherman Act.

The analysis of efforts to secure anticompetitive state action is complicated by the First Amendment, which provides in part that "Congress shall make no law * * * abridging * * * the right of the people * * * to petition the Government for a redress of grievances." U.S. Const., amend. I. Such petitioning may include lobbying officers of the legislative or executive branches, initiating lawsuits, and lobbying administrative agencies. Guided mainly by concerns for the protection of First Amendment rights, the Supreme Court has limited the application of the Sherman Act to these kinds of petitioning activities, regardless of their anticompetitive intentions or effects. Regulating abuses of those processes instead falls to other laws designed to safeguard the integrity of the policymaking process. Thus, criminal laws seek to stop bribery. And other anti-corruption, lobbying, and campaign finance laws—along with public discussion and publicity—serve to insure that official actions reflect the public interest.

The contours of Sherman Act immunity took shape in three Supreme Court decisions issued in the 1960s and early 1970s. In *Eastern R.R. Presidents Conference v. Noerr Motor Freight, Inc.*, 365 U.S. 127 (1961), the Court immunized joint efforts by 24 railroads and an association of railroad presidents to obtain legislative and executive action unfavorable to competing trucking firms. The Court emphasized that condemning the railroads' lobbying campaign "would impute to the Sherman Act a purpose to regulate, not business activity, but political activity, a purpose which would have no basis whatever in the legislative history of that Act." A finding of Sherman Act liability also "would raise important constitutional questions" concerning the right to petition under the First Amendment. *Noerr* immunity was later extended to efforts to solicit anticompetitive actions from administrative agencies, *United Mine Workers v. Pennington*, 381 U.S. 657 (1965), and to the initiation of litigation. *California Motor Transp. Co. v. Trucking Unlimited*, 404 U.S. 508 (1972). The resulting principles are collectively referred to as "the *Noerr-Pennington* Doctrine."

Noerr cautioned, however, that immunity might be withheld when petitioning activity "ostensibly directed toward influencing governmental action, is a mere sham to cover * * * an attempt to interfere directly" with a rival's business relationships. 365 U.S. at 144. That admonition took on greater significance after *California Motor Transport*, where the Court ruled that the First Amendment does not protect sham conduct. In so holding, the Court suggested that the Sherman Act can reach misrepresentation or other unethical conduct directed at subverting judicial processes, such as the initiation of baseless lawsuits designed to injure rivals. It reasoned that, in contrast to legislative, executive and administrative processes, the courts are less able to protect themselves from being used for anticompetitive purposes. Moreover, it noted that judicial process involves competing constitutional values, especially due process. The sham exception, therefore, requires courts to weigh the value of the plaintiff's First Amendment rights against the potential fifth amendment due process interests of the defendant. With understatement, the Court said the boundary between legitimate petitioning and sham behavior might prove to be "a difficult line to discern and draw."

Subsequent cases have focused on (1) defining the appropriate targets of petitioning activity, and (2) describing the contours of the sham exception.

For example, in *Allied Tube & Conduit Corp. v. Indian Head, Inc.*, 486 U.S. 492 (1988), the Supreme Court refused to immunize private efforts to influence the standard-setting activities of a private trade association. The Court added, however, that *Noerr* immunity might apply if the defendants' conduct, though directed at a private body, was mainly "political" rather than "commercial." In *FTC v. Superior Court Trial Lawyers' Ass'n*, (Casebook, Chapter 2, *supra*), the Court withheld petitioning immunity from attorneys who collectively refused to represent indigent criminal defendants unless the District of Columbia government raised the fees for such work. In so holding, the Court emphasized that the higher fees ultimately secured were the product of private restraint—the attorneys' collusive group boycott—not simple lobbying for government action, which would have been eligible for *Noerr-Pennington* protection.

Refining the definition of the sham exception in *City of Columbia*, discussed *supra* in connection with the scope of *Parker* immunity, the Supreme Court conferred state action protection on a zoning measure and immunized under *Noerr* the defendant's efforts to persuade the city to adopt the ordinance. In rejecting the plaintiff's assertion that the defendant's petitioning efforts fell within the "sham exception" to *Noerr*, the Court defined sham conduct as involving "activities [that] are 'not genuinely aimed at procuring favorable government action.'" *City of Columbia*, 499 U.S. at 380. Although the *Omni* defendant clearly wished to exclude the plaintiff, "it sought to do so not through the very process of lobbying, or of causing the city council to consider zoning measures, but rather through the ultimate *product* of that lobbying and consideration, viz., the zoning ordinances." *Id.* at 381 (emphasis original). In drawing this distinction between the petitioning efforts themselves and the ultimate ends sought, the Court limited the sham exception to "a context in which the conspirators' participation in the governmental process was itself claimed to be a 'sham,' employed as a means of imposing cost and delay." *Id.* at 381–82.

When should a firm's initiation of proceedings before a court or administrative tribunal be deemed a "sham," such that it will be deprived of *Noerr-Pennington* immunity? The following case provides the Supreme Court's latest word on this issue and on the general contours of petitioning immunity.

PROFESSIONAL REAL ESTATE INVESTORS, INC. v. COLUMBIA PICTURES INDUSTRIES, INC.

Supreme Court of the United States, 1993.
508 U.S. 49, 113 S.Ct. 1920, 123 L.Ed.2d 611.

Justice THOMAS delivered the opinion of the Court.

This case requires us to define the "sham" exception to the doctrine of antitrust immunity first identified in *Eastern Railroad Presidents Conference v. Noerr Motor Freight, Inc.*, 365 U.S. 127, 81 S.Ct. 523 (1961), as that doctrine applies in the litigation context. Under the sham exception, activity "ostensibly directed toward influencing governmental action" does not qualify for *Noerr* immunity if it "is a mere sham to cover . . . an attempt to interfere directly with the business relationships of a competitor." *Id.*, at 144, 81 S.Ct., at 533. We hold that litigation cannot be deprived of immunity as a sham unless the litigation is objectively baseless. * * *

I

Petitioners Professional Real Estate Investors, Inc., and Kenneth F. Irwin (collectively, PRE) operated La Mancha Private Club and Villas, a resort hotel in Palm Springs, California. Having installed videodisc players in the resort's hotel rooms and assembled a library of more than 200 motion picture titles, PRE rented videodiscs to guests for in-room viewing. PRE also sought to develop a market for the sale of videodisc players to other hotels wishing to offer in-room viewing of prerecorded material. Respondents, Columbia Pictures Industries, Inc., and seven other major motion picture studios (collectively, Columbia), held copyrights to the motion pictures recorded on the videodiscs that PRE purchased. Columbia also licensed the transmission of copyrighted motion pictures to hotel rooms through a wired cable system called Spectradyne. PRE therefore competed with Columbia not only for the viewing market at La Mancha but also for the broader market for in-room entertainment services in hotels.

In 1983, Columbia sued PRE for alleged copyright infringement through the rental of videodiscs for viewing in hotel rooms. PRE counterclaimed, charging Columbia with violations of §§ 1 and 2 of the Sherman Act * * *. In particular, PRE alleged that Columbia's copyright action was a mere sham that cloaked underlying acts of monopolization and conspiracy to restrain trade.

* * *

II

PRE contends that "the Ninth Circuit erred in holding that an antitrust plaintiff must, as a threshold prerequisite ... , establish that a sham lawsuit is baseless as a matter of law." It invites us to adopt an approach under which either "indifference to ... outcome," or failure to prove that a petition for redress of grievances "would ... have been brought but for [a] predatory motive," would expose a defendant to antitrust liability under the sham exception. We decline PRE's invitation.

* * *

Our original formulation of antitrust petitioning immunity required that unprotected activity lack objective reasonableness. *Noerr* rejected the contention that an attempt "to influence the passage and enforcement of laws" might lose immunity merely because the lobbyists' "sole purpose ... was to destroy [their] competitors." 365 U.S., at 138, 81 S.Ct., at 530. Nor were we persuaded by a showing that a publicity campaign "was intended to and did in fact injure [competitors] in their relationships with the public and with their customers," since such "direct injury" was merely "an incidental effect of the ... campaign to influence governmental action." *Id.*, at 143, 81 S.Ct., at 532. We reasoned that "[t]he right of the people to inform their representatives in government of their desires with respect to the passage or enforcement of laws cannot properly be made to depend upon their intent in doing so." *Id.*, at 139, 81 S.Ct., at 530. In short, "*Noerr* shields from the Sherman Act a concerted effort to influence public officials regardless of intent or purpose." *Pennington*, 381 U.S., at 670, 85 S.Ct., at 1593.

Nothing in *California Motor Transport* [*Co. v. Trucking Unlimited*, 404 U.S. 508, 92 S.Ct. 609 (1972)], retreated from these principles. Indeed, we recognized that recourse to agencies and courts should not be condemned as sham until a reviewing court has "discern[ed] and draw[n]" the "difficult line" separating objectively reasonable claims from "a pattern of baseless, repetitive claims ... which leads the factfinder to conclude that the administrative and judicial processes have been abused." 404 U.S., at 513, 92 S.Ct., at 613. Our recognition of a sham in that case signifies that the institution of legal proceedings "without probable cause" will give rise to a sham if such activity effectively "bar[s] ... competitors from meaningful access to adjudicatory tribunals and so ... usurp[s] th[e] decisionmaking process." *Id.*, at 512, 92 S.Ct., at 612.

Since *California Motor Transport*, we have consistently assumed that the sham exception contains an indispensable objective component. We have described a sham as "evidenced by repetitive lawsuits carrying the hallmark of *insubstantial* claims." We regard as sham "private action that is not genuinely aimed at procuring favorable government action," as opposed to "a valid effort to influence government action." And we have explicitly observed that a successful "effort to influence governmental action . . . certainly cannot be characterized as a sham." Whether applying *Noerr* as an antitrust doctrine or invoking it in other contexts, we have repeatedly reaffirmed that evidence of anticompetitive intent or purpose alone cannot transform otherwise legitimate activity into a sham.

* * *

In sum, fidelity to precedent compels us to reject a purely subjective definition of "sham." The sham exception so construed would undermine, if not vitiate, *Noerr*. And despite whatever "superficial certainty" it might provide, a subjective standard would utterly fail to supply "real 'intelligible guidance.' "

III

We now outline a two-part definition of "sham" litigation. First, the lawsuit must be objectively baseless in the sense that no reasonable litigant could realistically expect success on the merits. If an objective litigant could conclude that the suit is reasonably calculated to elicit a favorable outcome, the suit is immunized under *Noerr*, and an antitrust claim premised on the sham exception must fail.[5] Only if challenged litigation is objectively meritless may a court examine the litigant's subjective motivation. Under this second part of our definition of sham, the court should focus on whether the baseless lawsuit conceals "an attempt to interfere directly with the business relationships of a competitor," through the "use [of] the governmental *process*—as opposed to the *outcome* of that process—as an anticompetitive weapon." This two-tiered process requires the plaintiff to disprove the challenged lawsuit's *legal* viability before the court will entertain evidence of the suit's *economic* viability. Of course, even a plaintiff who defeats the defendant's claim to *Noerr* immunity by demonstrating both the objective and the subjective components of a sham must still prove a substantive antitrust violation. Proof of a sham merely deprives the defendant of immunity; it does not relieve the plaintiff of the obligation to establish all other elements of his claim.

Some of the apparent confusion over the meaning of "sham" may stem from our use of the word "genuine" to denote the opposite of "sham." The word "genuine" has both objective and subjective connotations. On one hand, "genuine" means "actually having the reputed or apparent qualities or character." "Genuine" in this sense governs Federal Rule of Civil Procedure 56, under which a "genuine issue" is one "that properly can be resolved only

---

5. A winning lawsuit is by definition a reasonable effort at petitioning for redress and therefore not a sham. On the other hand, when the antitrust defendant has lost the underlying litigation, a court must "resist the understandable temptation to engage in *post hoc* reasoning by concluding" that an ultimately unsuccessful "action must have been unreasonable or without foundation." The court must remember that "[e]ven when the law or the facts appear questionable or unfavorable at the outset, a party may have an entirely reasonable ground for bringing suit."

by a finder of fact because [it] may *reasonably* be resolved in favor of either party." On the other hand, "genuine" also means "sincerely and honestly felt or experienced." To be sham, therefore, litigation must fail to be "genuine" in both senses of the word.[6]

IV

We conclude that the Court of Appeals properly affirmed summary judgment for Columbia on PRE's antitrust counterclaim. Under the objective prong of the sham exception, the Court of Appeals correctly held that sham litigation must constitute the pursuit of claims so baseless that no reasonable litigant could realistically expect to secure favorable relief.

The existence of probable cause to institute legal proceedings precludes a finding that an antitrust defendant has engaged in sham litigation. The notion of probable cause, as understood and applied in the common law tort of wrongful civil proceedings, requires the plaintiff to prove that the defendant lacked probable cause to institute an unsuccessful civil lawsuit and that the defendant pressed the action for an improper, malicious purpose. Probable cause to institute civil proceedings requires no more than a "reasonabl[e] belie[f] that there is a chance that [a] claim may be held valid upon adjudication." Because the absence of probable cause is an essential element of the tort, the existence of probable cause is an absolute defense. Just as evidence of anticompetitive intent cannot affect the objective prong of *Noerr*'s sham exception, a showing of malice alone will neither entitle the wrongful civil proceedings plaintiff to prevail nor permit the factfinder to infer the absence of probable cause. When a court has found that an antitrust defendant claiming *Noerr* immunity had probable cause to sue, that finding compels the conclusion that a reasonable litigant in the defendant's position could realistically expect success on the merits of the challenged lawsuit. Under our decision today, therefore, a proper probable cause determination irrefutably demonstrates that an antitrust plaintiff has not proved the objective prong of the sham exception and that the defendant is accordingly entitled to *Noerr* immunity.

* * *

[Concurring Opinion of Mr. Justice SOUTER, omitted. Eds.]

Justice STEVENS, with whom Justice O'CONNOR joins, concurring in the judgment.

While I agree with the Court's disposition of this case and with its holding that "an objectively reasonable effort to litigate cannot be sham regardless of subjective intent," I write separately to disassociate myself from some of the unnecessarily broad dicta in the Court's opinion. Specifically, I disagree with the Court's equation of "objectively baseless" with the answer to the question whether any "reasonable litigant could realistically expect

---

6. In surveying the "forms of illegal and reprehensible practice which may corrupt the administrative or judicial processes and which may result in antitrust violations," we have noted that "unethical conduct in the setting of the adjudicatory process often results in sanctions" and that "[m]isrepresentations, con- doned in the political arena, are not immunized when used in the adjudicatory process." We need not decide here whether and, if so, to what extent *Noerr* permits the imposition of antitrust liability for a litigant's fraud or other misrepresentations.

success on the merits." There might well be lawsuits that fit the latter definition but can be shown to be objectively *unreasonable,* and thus shams. It might not be objectively reasonable to bring a lawsuit just because some form of success on the merits—no matter how insignificant—could be expected. With that possibility in mind, the Court should avoid an unnecessarily broad holding that it might regret when confronted with a more complicated case.

* * *

———

One can ask at least two questions about how future litigants will be able to satisfy the demanding conditions that the *PRE* majority imposes on those who seek to limit *Noerr* immunity by invoking the sham exception. First, what volume of "objectively baseless" activity constitutes sham behavior? For example, in the context of patent infringement litigation, could the initiation of a single baseless infringement suit by a dominant incumbent firm supply the element of improper conduct that establishes illegal monopolization? The bare terms of *PRE* do not seem to demand the barrage of filings featured in *California Motor Transport.* Second, by what evidentiary means should the court decide whether a suit is objectively baseless? Do attorney-client communications, which may be shielded by privilege, inevitably become the focal point of attempts by plaintiffs to determine the defendant's expectation of success in suing? To be a "sham," must a complaint violate the provisions of Rule 11 of the Federal Rules of Civil Procedure, which requires that allegations be well-grounded in law and fact based on an inquiry reasonable under the circumstances?

As noted above, the FTC has focused a great deal of attention on the contours of the State Action doctrine, evaluating whether it has been too permissive to the detriment of competition. Similarly, it studied the application of the *Noerr-Pennington* doctrine, pursuing several enforcement actions directed at anticompetitive petitioning activities. *See* FTC, Office of Policy Planning, *Enforcement Perspectives on the Noerr–Pennington Doctrine* (Oct. 2006), *available at* http://www.ftc.gov/reports/P013518enfperspectNoerr-Penn ingtondoctrine.pdf.

E. PRIVATE RIGHTS OF ACTION

Section 4 of the Clayton Act authorizes private parties injured by an antitrust violation to sue for treble damages. 15 U.S.C. § 15. Section 16 also authorizes suits for injunctions against "threatened loss or damage" to remedy actual or imminent federal antitrust violations. 15 U.S.C. § 26. Successful private plaintiffs are also entitled to recover reasonable attorneys' fees and costs. Section 4A authorizes very limited recovery of pre-judgment interest. 15 U.S.C. § 15A, and post judgment interest is available as in non-antitrust cases. 28 U.S.C. § 1961.

Section 4B of the Clayton Act creates a four-year statute of limitations for private antitrust actions. The limitations period generally runs from the time the plaintiff suffers injury. *Zenith Radio Corp. v. Hazeltine Research, Inc.*, 401 U.S. 321, 338–39 (1971). If the plaintiff alleges concerted anticompetitive behavior, a new claim may arise from subsequent acts in furtherance of a challenged conspiracy.

Section 5(I) of the Clayton Act provides that the statute of limitations for private suits may be suspended while certain federal government antitrust suits are pending and for one year thereafter. This suspension facilitates the operation of Section 5(a), whereby private plaintiffs may use judgments or decrees entered against a defendant in a government antitrust suit as "prima facie evidence against such defendant * * * as to all matters respecting which said judgment or decree would be an estoppel as between the parties." This form of statutory preclusion is distinct from common law claim and issue preclusion, which may also be available. *See, e.g., Parklane Hosiery Co. v. Shore,* 439 U.S. 322 (1979).

The effective scope of Section 5 preclusion, however, may be limited. For example, in *In re Microsoft Corp. Antitrust Litig.,* 355 F.3d 322 (4th Cir. 2004), the Fourth Circuit reversed the district court's order of preclusion in a private case brought by Sun Microsystems following the conclusion of the government's prosecution of Microsoft. The issue was how courts should interpret the "critical and necessary" requirement for collateral estoppel. The Fourth Circuit rejected as too broad the district court's interpretation of "critical and necessary" facts as facts "supportive of" the district court's conclusions, favoring "essential":

> Because a fact that is "supportive of" a judgment may be consistent with it but not necessary or essential to it, the term "supportive of" is a broader term than "critical and necessary." The term "supportive of" sweeps so broadly that it might lead to inclusion of all facts that may have been "relevant" to the prior judgment. Such a broad application of offensive collateral estoppel risks the very unfairness about which the Supreme Court was concerned in *Parklane,* and we conclude therefore that it is inappropriate.

Id. at 327.

Treble damages and attorneys fees have made private enforcement an important antitrust enforcement tool. Although government enforcement actions are influential in setting policy priorities, typically there are far more private than public actions filed each year in the federal courts. These cases can be initiated in the absence of any government interest or prosecution, or, owing to the preclusion provisions of the Clayton Act, they may constitute "follow-on" or complementary private actions that follow on the heels of federal investigations or prosecutions. According to government figures, in the five year period from 2001–2006 an average of 47 civil and criminal antitrust cases were filed each year by the U.S. Department of Justice. For its fiscal years 2002–2006, the Bureau of Competition at the FTC reported an annual average of 29 civil enforcement matters initiated, which includes administrative complaints and accepted consent decrees, as well as actions filed in federal court. During roughly the same period, 829 civil antitrust cases (public and private) were filed in the federal courts. That figure is roughly half of the number of civil antitrust cases that were being filed in the 1970s, although today's cases tend to be larger and more complex.

This decrease in case filings was no doubt in part a reflection of Supreme Court imposed restrictions on the private treble damage remedy, such as

Brunswick, which we first studied in Chapter 1, and *Illinois Brick* and *Associated General Contractors*, which we will study shortly, as well as enhanced burdens of proof. Nevertheless, as we have seen throughout the Casebook, private cases have been and remain the source of important doctrinal developments that have been crucial to the evolution of antitrust law.

Antitrust is one of several federal statutory regimes that give private parties the power to prosecute. The wisdom of using private rights of action to supplement government enforcement is a matter of extensive scholarly debate. Four basic arguments support enforcement by "private attorneys general." First, private enforcement promotes deterrence, because it enlists the help of parties closest to information about violations. For example, a commercial buyer of raw materials may best be able to detect suspicious, cartelistic bidding by suppliers. Second, private suits provide a means for compensation of the victims of antitrust violations, something that public enforcement actions may not be able to do or will only partially do. Third, they afford a safeguard against lax public enforcement that results from neglect, limited resources, or corruption. Fourth, a private right of action can increase overall levels of enforcement without expanding public enforcement bureaus.

For many of these reasons, as part of its efforts to modernize its antitrust system, the European Commission is now openly encouraging the expansion of private rights of action at the member state level, while at the same time venturing to avoid what are viewed as the excesses of the U.S. antitrust system. The Commission has stated that its goal is to promote a "culture of competition" in Europe, not a "culture of litigation." *See* Green Paper on damages actions for breach of the EC antitrust rules, *available at* http://eur-lex.europa.eu/LexUriServ/LexUriServ.do?uri=COM:2005:0672:FIN:EN:PDF. The Green Paper was accompanied by a more extensive Commission Staff Working Paper. *See* Commission Staff Working Paper, Annex to the Green Paper on damages actions for breach of the EC antitrust rules (hereafter "Staff Paper"), *available at* http://ec.europa.eu/comm/competition/antitrust/actionsdamages/sp_en.pdf.

Despite their potential benefits, private enforcement schemes (including private antitrust enforcement) also can have adverse consequences. Private enforcement can generate questionable claims, and can enable firms to use the courts to impede efficient behavior by their rivals. Although private enforcement reduces the need to enlarge public enforcement bodies, private suits can consume substantial social resources in the form of costs incurred to prosecute and defend such cases.

Perhaps recognizing these adverse possibilities, courts have established limits on the ability of private plaintiffs to obtain relief under the Clayton Act. One group of restrictions, treated immediately below, narrows the set of plaintiffs who may challenge antitrust violations. These devices screen claims according to the type of injury alleged (requirements that the plaintiff suffer harm to her business or property and allege antitrust injury) and the plaintiff's proximity to the source of harm (limits on standing and recovery by indirect purchasers). A second group of restrictions increases the evidentiary burden that plaintiffs must satisfy to establish liability. The evidentiary limits apply to public and private antitrust plaintiffs, alike, and are addressed below in connection with the role of the federal courts in the antitrust system.

1. INJURY TO BUSINESS OR PROPERTY

To obtain damages under Section 4 of the Clayton Act, 15 U.S.C. § 15, the plaintiff must show that the defendant's conduct harmed its "business or property." The term "business" broadly encompasses "commercial interests or enterprises." See *Hawaii v. Standard Oil Co.*, 405 U.S. 251, 264 (1972). "Property" includes any legally-protected property interest. In an important recognition of the centrality of consumer harm to antitrust enforcement, in *Reiter v. Sonotone*, 442 U.S. 330, 339 (1979), the Supreme Court held that consumers who pay more for goods acquired for personal use are injured in their "property" under Section 4.

2. ANTITRUST INJURY

As we have observed in Chapters 1 and 8, the Supreme Court's 1977 *Brunswick* decision established the requirement that the private plaintiff in a treble damage action show that its injury resulted from the anticompetitive effects of the defendant's conduct. As we have discussed, this "antitrust injury" requirement has helped to rationalize antitrust private actions by requiring courts to consider carefully the economic basis for alleged violations and injuries of the antitrust laws. When antitrust proof standards were more lax, it provided courts with a mechanism to mitigate the impact of liability standards perceived as excessively harsh, or of the automatic trebling of damages, or both. As such, it has been a screen that helps to diminish the likely incidence of false positives. On the other hand, antitrust injury has been criticized, because especially in the hands of over-zealous judges, it creates an unjustified obstacle to the resolution of some potentially legitimate antitrust claims. By placing artificial limits on who may sue, it creates the possibility of under-deterrence and false negatives.

3. DIRECT PURCHASERS

The same term as *Brunswick*, the Supreme Court expressed concern about the ability of courts to identify damages flowing from the defendant's conduct and to apportion them to differently situated victims. This concern relates to a distinct requirement that considers the plaintiff's proximity to the defendant in the distribution chain through which the defendants goods or services reach end users. The Court relied on the concept of directness first articulated in the late 1960s and reaffirmed in 1977 in the case presented below.

ILLINOIS BRICK CO. v. ILLINOIS
Supreme Court of the United States, 1977.
431 U.S. 720, 97 S.Ct. 2061, 52 L.Ed.2d 707.

Mr. Justice WHITE delivered the opinion of the Court.

Hanover Shoe, Inc. v. United Shoe Machinery Corp., 392 U.S. 481, 88 S.Ct. 2224 (1968), involved an antitrust treble-damages action brought under

§ 4 of the Clayton Act against a manufacturer of shoe machinery by one of its customers, a manufacturer of shoes. In defense, the shoe machinery manufacturer sought to show that the plaintiff had not been injured in its business as required by § 4 because it had passed on the claimed illegal overcharge to those who bought shoes from it. Under the defendant's theory, the illegal overcharge was absorbed by the plaintiff's customers indirect purchasers of the defendant's shoe machinery who were the persons actually injured by the antitrust violation.

In Hanover Shoe this Court rejected as a matter of law this defense that indirect rather than direct purchasers were the parties injured by the antitrust violation. The Court held that except in certain limited circumstances,[2] a direct purchaser suing for treble damages under § 4 of the Clayton Act is injured within the meaning of § 4 by the full amount of the overcharge paid by it and that the antitrust defendant is not permitted to introduce evidence that indirect purchasers were in fact injured by the illegal overcharge. The first reason for the Court's rejection of this offer of proof was an unwillingness to complicate treble-damages actions with attempts to trace the effects of the overcharge on the purchaser's prices, sales, costs, and profits, and of showing that these variables would have behaved differently without the overcharge. A second reason for barring the pass-on defense was the Court's concern that unless direct purchasers were allowed to sue for the portion of the overcharge arguably passed on to indirect purchasers, antitrust violators "would retain the fruits of their illegality" because indirect purchasers "would have only a tiny stake in the lawsuit" and hence little incentive to sue.

In this case we once again confront the question whether the overcharged direct purchaser should be deemed for purposes of § 4 to have suffered the full injury from the overcharge; but the issue is presented in the context of a suit in which the plaintiff, an indirect purchaser, seeks to show its injury by establishing pass-on by the direct purchaser and in which the antitrust defendants rely on Hanover Shoe's rejection of the pass-on theory. Having decided that in general a pass-on theory may not be used defensively by an antitrust violator against a direct purchaser plaintiff, we must now decide whether that theory may be used offensively by an indirect purchaser plaintiff against an alleged violator.

I

Petitioners manufacture and distribute concrete block in the Greater Chicago area. They sell the block primarily to masonry contractors, who submit bids to general contractors for the masonry portions of construction projects. The general contractors in turn submit bids for these projects to customers such as the respondents in this case, the State of Illinois and 700 local governmental entities in the Greater Chicago area* * *. Respondents are thus indirect purchasers of concrete block, which passes through two separate levels in the chain of distribution before reaching respondents. * * *

---

2. The Court cited, as an example of when a pass-on defense might be permitted, the situation where "an overcharged buyer has a pre- existing 'cost-plus' contract, thus making it easy to prove that he has not been damaged...." 392 U.S., at 494, 88 S.Ct., at 2232.

Respondent State of Illinois, on behalf of itself and respondent local governmental entities, brought this antitrust treble-damages action under § 4 of the Clayton Act, alleging that petitioners had engaged in a combination and conspiracy to fix the prices of concrete block in violation of § 1 of the Sherman Act. * * * The only way in which the antitrust violation alleged could have injured respondents is if all or part of the overcharge was passed on by the masonry and general contractors to respondents, rather than being absorbed at the first two levels of distribution.

* * *

We granted certiorari, to resolve a conflict among the Courts of Appeals on the question whether the offensive use of pass-on authorized by the decision below is consistent with Hanover Shoe's restrictions on the defensive use of pass-on. We hold that it is not, and we reverse. We reach this result in two steps. First, we conclude that whatever rule is to be adopted regarding pass-on in antitrust damages actions, it must apply equally to plaintiffs and defendants. Because Hanover Shoe would bar petitioners from using respondents' pass-on theory as a defense to a treble-damages suit by the direct purchasers (the masonry contractors), we are faced with the choice of overruling (or narrowly limiting) Hanover Shoe or of applying it to bar respondents' attempt to use this pass-on theory offensively. Second, we decline to abandon the construction given § 4 in Hanover Shoe that the overcharged direct purchaser, and not others in the chain of manufacture or distribution, is the party "injured in his business or property" within the meaning of the section in the absence of a convincing demonstration that the Court was wrong in Hanover Shoe to think that the effectiveness of the antitrust treble-damages action would be substantially reduced by adopting a rule that any party in the chain may sue to recover the fraction of the overcharge allegedly absorbed by it.

II

* * *

First, allowing offensive but not defensive use of pass-on would create a serious risk of multiple liability for defendants. Even though an indirect purchaser had already recovered for all or part of an overcharge passed on to it, the direct purchaser would still recover automatically the full amount of the overcharge that the indirect purchaser had shown to be passed on; similarly, following an automatic recovery of the full overcharge by the direct purchaser, the indirect purchaser could sue to recover the same amount. * * * [W]e are unwilling to "open the door to duplicative recoveries" under § 4.[11]

---

11. In recognition of the need to avoid duplicative recoveries, courts adopting the view that pass-on theories should not be equally available to plaintiffs and defendants have agreed that defendants should be allowed to assert a pass-on defense against a direct purchaser if an indirect purchaser is also attempting to recover on a pass-on theory in the same lawsuit. Various procedural devices, such as the Multidistrict Litigation Act, 28 U.S.C. § 1407, and statutory interpleader, 28 U.S.C. § 1335, are relied upon to bring indirect and direct purchasers together in one action in order to apportion damages among them and thereby reduce the risk of duplicative recovery. These procedural devices cannot protect against multiple liability where the direct purchasers have already recovered by obtaining a judgment or by settling, as is more likely (and as occurred here); acknowledging that the risk of multiple recoveries is inevitably increased by

Second, the reasoning of Hanover Shoe cannot justify unequal treatment of plaintiffs and defendants with respect to the permissibility of pass-on arguments. The principal basis for the decision in Hanover Shoe was the Court's perception of the uncertainties and difficulties in analyzing price and out-put decisions "in the real economic world rather than an economist's hypothetical model," and of the costs to the judicial system and the efficient enforcement of the antitrust laws of attempting to reconstruct those decisions in the courtroom. This perception that the attempt to trace the complex economic adjustments to a change in the cost of a particular factor of production would greatly complicate and reduce the effectiveness of already protracted treble-damages proceedings applies with no less force to the assertion of pass-on theories by plaintiffs than it does to the assertion by defendants. * * *

It is argued, however, that Hanover Shoe rests on a policy of ensuring that a treble-damages plaintiff is available to deprive antitrust violators of "the fruits of their illegality," a policy that would be furthered by allowing plaintiffs but not defendants to use pass-on theories. We do not read the Court's concern in Hanover Shoe for the effectiveness of the treble-damages remedy as countenancing unequal application of the Court's pass-on rule. Rather, we understand Hanover Shoe as resting on the judgment that the antitrust laws will be more effectively enforced by concentrating the full recovery for the overcharge in the direct purchasers rather than by allowing every plaintiff potentially affected by the overcharge to sue only for the amount it could show was absorbed by it.

We thus decline to construe § 4 to permit offensive use of a pass-on theory against an alleged violator that could not use the same theory as a defense in an action by direct purchasers. In this case, respondents seek to demonstrate that masonry contractors, who incorporated petitioners' block into walls and other masonry structures, passed on the alleged overcharge on the block to general contractors, who incorporated the masonry structures into entire buildings, and that the general contractors in turn passed on the overcharge to respondents in the bids submitted for those buildings. We think it clear that under a fair reading of Hanover Shoe petitioners would be barred from asserting this theory in a suit by the masonry contractors.

* * *

We are left, then, with two alternatives: either we must overrule Hanover Shoe (or at least narrowly confine it to its facts), or we must preclude respondents from seeking to recover on their pass-on theory. We choose the latter course.

III

* * *

allowing offensive but not defensive use of pass-on, proponents of this approach ultimately fall back on the argument that it is better for the defendant to pay sixfold or more damages than for an injured party to go uncompensated. We do not find this risk acceptable. Moreover, even if ways could be found to bring all potential plaintiffs together in one huge action, the complexity thereby introduced into treble-damages proceedings argues strongly for retaining the Hanover Shoe rule.

Permitting the use of pass-on theories under § 4 essentially would transform treble-damages actions into massive efforts to apportion the recovery among all potential plaintiffs that could have absorbed part of the overcharge from direct purchasers to middlemen to ultimate consumers. However appealing this attempt to allocate the overcharge might seem in theory, it would add whole new dimensions of complexity to treble-damages suits and seriously undermine their effectiveness.

As we have indicated, potential plaintiffs at each level in the distribution chain are in a position to assert conflicting claims to a common fund the amount of the alleged overcharge by contending that the entire overcharge was absorbed at that particular level in the chain. A treble-damages action brought by one of these potential plaintiffs (or one class of potential plaintiffs) to recover the overcharge implicates all three of the interests that have traditionally been thought to support compulsory joinder of absent and potentially adverse claimants * * *.

* * *

It is unlikely, of course, that all potential plaintiffs could or would be joined. Some may not wish to assert claims to the overcharge; others may be unmanageable as a class; and still others may be beyond the personal jurisdiction of the court. We can assume that ordinarily the action would still proceed, the absent parties not being deemed "indispensable" under Fed. Rule Civ. Proc. 19(b). But allowing indirect purchasers to recover using pass-on theories, even under the optimistic assumption that joinder of potential plaintiffs will deal satisfactorily with problems of multiple litigation and liability, would transform treble-damages actions into massive multiparty litigations involving many levels of distribution and including large classes of ultimate consumers remote from the defendant. In treble-damages actions by ultimate consumers, the overcharge would have to be apportioned among the relevant wholesalers, retailers, and other middlemen, whose representatives presumably should be joined. And in suits by direct purchasers or middlemen, the interests of ultimate consumers are similarly implicated.

There is thus a strong possibility that indirect purchasers remote from the defendant would be parties to virtually every treble-damages action (apart from those brought against defendants at the retail level). * * * We are no more inclined than we were in Hanover Shoe to ignore the burdens that such an attempt would impose on the effective enforcement of the antitrust laws.

Under an array of simplifying assumptions, economic theory provides a precise formula for calculating how the overcharge is distributed between the overcharged party (passer) and its customers (passees). If the market for the passer's product is perfectly competitive; if the overcharge is imposed equally on all of the passer's competitors; and if the passer maximizes its profits, then the ratio of the shares of the overcharge borne by passee and passer will equal the ratio of the elasticities of supply and demand in the market for the passer's product. Even if these assumptions are accepted, there remains a serious problem of measuring the relevant elasticities—the percentage change in the quantities of the passer's product demanded and supplied in response to a one percent change in price. In view of the difficulties that have been encountered, even in informal adversary proceedings, with the statistical techniques used to estimate these concepts, it is unrealistic to think that elasticity studies introduced by expert witnesses will resolve the pass-on issue. * * *

More important, as the Hanover Shoe Court observed, "in the real economic world rather than an economist's hypothetical model," the latter's drastic simplifications generally must be abandoned. Overcharged direct purchasers often sell in imperfectly competitive markets. They often compete with other sellers that have not been subject to the overcharge; and their pricing policies often cannot be explained solely by the convenient assumption of profit maximization. As we concluded in Hanover Shoe, attention to "sound laws of economics" can only heighten the awareness of the difficulties and uncertainties involved in determining how the relevant market variables would have behaved had there been no overcharge.

* * *

We think the longstanding policy of encouraging vigorous private enforcement of the antitrust laws, supports our adherence to the Hanover Shoe rule, under which direct purchasers are not only spared the burden of litigating the intricacies of pass-on but also are permitted to recover the full amount of the overcharge. We recognize that direct purchasers sometimes may refrain from bringing a treble-damages suit for fear of disrupting relations with their suppliers. But on balance, and until there are clear directions from Congress to the contrary, we conclude that the legislative purpose in creating a group of " 'private attorneys general' " to enforce the antitrust laws under § 4, is better served by holding direct purchasers to be injured to the full extent of the overcharge paid by them than by attempting to apportion the overcharge among all that may have absorbed a part of it.

It is true that, in elevating direct purchasers to a preferred position as private attorneys general, the Hanover Shoe rule denies recovery to those indirect purchasers who may have been actually injured by antitrust violations. Of course, as Mr. Justice BRENNAN points out in dissent, "from the deterrence standpoint, it is irrelevant to whom damages are paid, so long as some one redresses the violation. But § 4 has another purpose in addition to deterring violators and depriving them of "the fruits of their illegality," it is also designed to compensate victims of antitrust violations for their injuries. Hanover Shoe does further the goal of compensation to the extent that the direct purchaser absorbs at least some and often most of the overcharge. In view of the considerations supporting the Hanover Shoe rule, we are unwilling to carry the compensation principle to its logical extreme by attempting to allocate damages among all "those within the defendant's chain of distribution," especially because we question the extent to which such an attempt would make individual victims whole for actual injuries suffered rather than simply depleting the overall recovery in litigation over pass-on issues. Many of the indirect purchasers barred from asserting pass-on claims under the Hanover Shoe rule have such a small stake in the lawsuit that even if they were to recover as part of a class, only a small fraction would be likely to come forward to collect their damages. And given the difficulty of ascertaining the amount absorbed by any particular indirect purchaser, there is little basis for believing that the amount of the recovery would reflect the actual injury suffered.

For the reasons stated, the judgment is reversed, and the case is remanded for further proceedings consistent with this opinion.

So ordered.

[Dissenting opinions of Mr. Justice BRENNAN, with whom Mr. Justice MARSHALL and Mr. Justice BLACKMUN join, omitted. Eds.]

———

For almost thirty years after it was decided, little was known about the internal process at the Supreme Court that produced the *Illinois Brick* decision. With the release of the papers of several Supreme Court justices who participated in the deliberations of *Illinois Brick*, new light has been shed on that process. One notable discovery is that the Court initially voted to uphold indirect purchaser rights, but that after additional internal debate several justices changed their votes to produce the result you have just read. For a more comprehensive discussion of the Supreme Court debates in *Illinois Brick*, see Andrew I. Gavil, *Antitrust Remedy Wars Episode I:* Illinois Brick *from Inside the Supreme Court*, 79 ST. JOHN'S L. REV. 553 (2005). Sidebar 9–5 further examines the rationale and consequence of Illinois Brick, as well as the generation of controversy it triggered.

Sidebar 9–5:
The Aftermath of *Illinois Brick*: *ARC America* and the Emergence of Multi–Jurisdictional Antitrust Litigation*

Illinois Brick ruled that the Clayton Act generally does not permit damage suits for illegal overcharges when the plaintiff does not buy the product directly from one of the violators. In so holding, it established a strong presumption that the Clayton Act's remedial goals are best advanced by allowing direct purchasers to recover all overcharges. The Court feared that permitting indirect purchasers to sue would create intolerable administrative difficulties as courts sought to trace the amount and locus of harm throughout the distribution chain and to apportion damages to each claimant. Uncertainty about the amount of overcharge owing to each plaintiff might "reduce the incentive to sue," and the complexity of tracing and apportionment could lead to duplicative recoveries, thus over-deterring various business practices. As a consequence, indirect purchasers typically have failed in their attempts to recover damages under Section 4 by arguing that the direct purchasers "passed on" the overcharges to them.

Nevertheless, the *Hanover Shoe–Illinois Brick* presumption is not absolute. The Supreme Court indicated that indirect purchasers might be allowed to recover: (1) where fixed quantity, pre-existing cost-plus contracts enable the direct purchaser to pass on overcharges while being

* Portions of this Sidebar are adapted from Andrew I. Gavil, *Federal Judicial Power and the Challenges of Multi–Jurisdictional Direct and Indirect Purchaser Antitrust Litigation*, 69 GEO. WASH. L. REV. 860 (2001).

"insulated from any decrease in its sales * * * because its customer is committed to buying a fixed quantity regardless of price"; or (2) where the customer owns or controls the direct purchaser. A third exception has been recognized when the direct purchaser is a party to the conspiracy. However, these exceptions have proven extremely difficult to establish in practice. *See, e.g., Kansas v. UtiliCorp United, Inc.,* 497 U.S. 199 (1990).

As a general matter, therefore, *Illinois Brick* bars indirect purchasers from pursuing private treble damage antitrust actions in the federal courts to recover overcharges from members of cartels or monopolists. The right of action in such circumstances is limited to the parties who first purchased from the defendant. For example, if a group of tire manufacturers entered into a cartel to fix the price of original equipment tires sold on automobiles, only the automobile manufacturers, who purchased the price-fixed tires, would be allowed to sue for damages. Retail auto dealers, or consumers, for that matter, would not. They would be "indirect purchasers."

Of course, consumers are frequently "indirect purchasers," so *Illinois Brick* was perceived by some to be in conflict with the avowed pro-consumer purposes of the Sherman and Clayton Acts, most particularly the private right of action. As a consequence, in the years immediately following *Illinois Brick*, a number of states responded to it by adopting "*Illinois Brick* repealers." These statutes purported to remove the bar of *Illinois Brick* for purposes of state antitrust law. These repealers were challenged on preemption grounds, but ultimately approved by the Supreme Court in 1989 in *California v. ARC America Corp.,* 490 U.S. 93 (1989), which saw no conflict in the co-existence of differing state and federal rights of action.

Since that time, an impressive divide has opened between the scope of federal and state antitrust remedies. Even as indirect purchasers have been barred from seeking antitrust remedies in federal court, they have been welcomed in the courts of many states. Ironically, state remedies, which were once viewed as so inadequate as to require federal antitrust legislation, are now preferred, particularly for consumer class actions on behalf of indirect purchasers, who would be barred from federal court by *Illinois Brick*.

The movement to compensate for *Illinois Brick* by expanding state antitrust rights of action, combined with a spate of highly visible federal price-fixing and monopolization prosecutions in the 1990s, combined to amplify that divide. Owing in large part to the preclusive provisions of Section 5(a) of the Clayton Act, successful government prosecutions have been followed by the institution of sometimes scores of private treble damage actions. In the past, such cases would almost invariably have been filed exclusively in federal courts. Even if they were initiated in multiple federal venues, or within the same venue, such cases could later be transferred under 28 U.S.C. §§ 1404 and 1406, and/or consolidated pursuant to Rule 42 of the Federal Rules of Civil Procedure. Another alternative was transfer and consolidation under the authority of the Judicial Panel on Multi–District Litigation, 28 U.S.C. § 1407.

Today, however, such follow-on cases are far more likely to be initiated in both federal and state courts—and the direct/indirect purchaser issue is often the divining rod that leads plaintiffs to one or the other. Direct purchaser actions more often are filed in federal courts; state courts are the repository of indirect purchaser actions. Traditionally, efforts to remove state court indirect purchaser actions under 28 U.S.C. § 1441 were met with significant resistance. By definition, indirect purchaser actions do not present any "federal question" because they are barred in federal court due to *Illinois Brick*. And for many years, the Supreme Court limited diversity class actions, and hence diversity removal, to actions where each and every member of the class meets the minimum jurisdictional amount in controversy, currently $75,000. *See Zahn v. International Paper Co.*, 414 U.S. 291 (1973). Two developments have significantly eroded these previous impairments to removal of state antitrust law indirect purchaser cases: (1) In *Exxon Mobil Corp. v. Allapattah Servs., Inc.*, 545 U.S. 546 (2005), the Supreme Court held that *Zahn* had been effectively overruled by the Supplemental Jurisdiction statute, 28 U.S.C. § 1367; and (2) the Class Action Fairness Act of 2004, codified at 28 U.S.C. § 1332(d), expanded removal authority in certain types of large class actions filed in state courts. Taken together, these two developments have increased the possibilities for removal, transfer, and consolidation, at least for pre-trial purposes, of state indirect purchaser actions. But they were not a complete fix for the challenge of multi-forum, multi-jurisdictional direct and indirect purchaser actions arising out of the same conduct.

Multi-*district* litigation, therefore, has become more multi-*jurisdictional*, and the procedural means for capturing the efficiencies to be gained through coordination are far less certain. *See, e.g., In re Microsoft Corp. Antitrust Litig.*, 127 F. Supp.2d 702 (D. Md.2001). Achieving procedural efficiency is left to informal efforts by courts and counsel, not formal means of transfer, consolidation, and coordination. Ironically, this remedial divergence comes at a time when in most other ways, state and federal antitrust laws have converged around common concepts and common standards for liability. Many states today, either by statute or judicial decree, require their courts to follow federal precedent in interpreting and applying their state antitrust laws. Convergence of substantive antitrust liability standards at the state and federal levels thus is becoming an increasing reality for American antitrust, and it increases the likelihood that coordination of state and federal antitrust litigation— particularly on common questions of liability—could yield significant economies. Yet those economies go unrealized as debate continues about the wisdom of the multi-jurisdictional antitrust model.

Critics of the current state of affairs argue that it over-deters anticompetitive conduct and unnecessarily tasks both state and federal courts. Echoing some of the concerns embraced by the Court in *Illinois Brick*, they argue that concurrent prosecution by direct and indirect purchasers of civil actions in state and federal courts substantially increases the likelihood of duplicative and multiple damages. The inadequacy of removal also means that defendants can find themselves responding to multiple class actions in different states, as well as different federal courts. And even when the federal cases can be combined for pre-trial purposes under Section 1407 MDL procedures, current law requires remand for trial. *See Lexecon Inc. v. Milberg Weiss Bershad Hynes & Lerach*, 523 U.S. 26 (1998).

Supporters of remedial diversity respond, however, that such cases are rare and generally involve fairly egregious conduct, such as price fixing. Paralleling the policy arguments we saw urged in connection with interpretation of FTAIA, they assert that the threat of multi-jurisdictional litigation may add significantly to the deterrent value of the private right of action. They also point to various examples of successful informal efforts to coordinate cases by parties and courts. Finally, citing the Supreme Court's rationale in *ARC America*, they point out that the co-existence of direct and indirect purchaser litigation is simply a function of the federal nature of U.S. government, and that no conflict can arise from the mere fact that the federal government and the states have defined the scope of their antitrust remedial rights differently.

After a generation of debate, a consensus may finally be emerging to address the kinds of problems that have arisen as a consequence of the multi-forum, multi-jurisdiction litigation produced by *Illinois Brick* and *ARC America*. In its final report, issued April 2, 2007, the Antitrust Modernization Commission recommended that *Illinois Brick* be legislatively overruled as part of a general reform package that would concentrate related direct and indirect purchaser litigation in the federal courts. *See* http://www.amc.gov/report_recommendation/toc.htm.

4. STANDING

Five years after *Brunswick* and *Illinois Brick*, the Court imposed additional restrictions on the rights of plaintiffs to sue in federal court for antitrust violations. "Standing" focuses on the plaintiff's proximity to the alleged harm. In *Blue Shield of Virginia v. McCready*, 457 U.S. 465 (1982), the Supreme Court held that Section 4 of the Clayton Act gave standing to a health insurance policyholder (McCready) to sue her insurance company for allegedly conspiring with physicians to refuse to deal with a psychologist whose services the plaintiff wanted the insurer to reimburse. The Court observed that "Congress did not intend to allow every person tangentially affected by an antitrust violation" to maintain a treble damage action. To determine standing, it is necessary to examine "the physical and economic nexus between the alleged violation and the harm to the plaintiff." 457 U.S. at 478. The Court rejected the defendants' argument that, because the concerted refusal to deal targeted the psychologists, McCready's injury was "too 'fortuitous' 'incidental' ... and 'remote'" to confer standing. Instead, McCready fell "within the area of the economy ... endangered by the breakdown of competitive conditions, resulting from Blue Shield's selective refusal to reimburse." The Court tightened standing requirements the next year in the case that follows.

ASSOCIATED GENERAL CONTRACTORS OF CALIFORNIA INC. v. CALIFORNIA STATE COUNCIL OF CARPENTERS

United States Supreme Court, 1983.
459 U.S. 519, 103 S.Ct. 897, 74 L.Ed.2d 723.

Justice STEVENS delivered the opinion of the Court.

This case arises out of a dispute between parties to a multiemployer collective bargaining agreement. The plaintiff unions allege that, in violation of the antitrust laws, the multiemployer association and its members coerced certain third parties, as well as some of the association's members, to enter into business relationships with nonunion firms. This coercion, according to the complaint, adversely affected the trade of certain unionized firms and thereby restrained the business activities of the unions. The question presented is whether the complaint sufficiently alleges that the unions have been "injured in [their] business or property by reason of anything forbidden in the antitrust laws" and may therefore recover treble damages under § 4 of the Clayton Act. 15 U.S.C. § 15. Unlike the majority of the Court of Appeals for the Ninth Circuit, we agree with the District Court's conclusion that the complaint is insufficient.

* * *

II

* * *

The Union's antitrust claims arise from alleged restraints caused by defendants in the market for construction contracting and subcontracting.[14] The complaint alleges that defendants "coerced" two classes of persons: (1) landowners and others who let construction contracts, *i.e.*, the defendants' customers and potential customers; and (2) general contractors, *i.e.*, defendants' competitors and defendants themselves. Coercion against the members of both classes was designed to induce them to give some of their business— but not necessarily all of it—to nonunion firms.[16] Although the pleading does not allege that the coercive conduct increased the aggregate share of nonunion firms in the market, it does allege that defendants' activities weakened and restrained the trade "of certain contractors." Thus, particular victims of coercion may have diverted particular contracts to nonunion firms and thereby caused certain unionized subcontractors to lose some business.

We think the Court of Appeals properly assumed that such coercion might violate the antitrust laws. An agreement to restrain trade may be unlawful even though it does not entirely exclude its victims from the market. Coercive activity that prevents its victims from making free choices between market alternatives is inherently destructive of competitive conditions and may be condemned even without proof of its actual market effect.[18]

Even though coercion directed by defendants at third parties in order to restrain the trade of "certain" contractors and subcontractors may have been

14. There is no allegation of wrongful conduct directed at nonunion subcontracting firms. * * * The amended complaint also does not allege any restraint on competition in the market for labor union services. * * *

16. There is no allegation that any person subjected to coercion was required to deal exclusively with nonunion firms.

18. Although we do not know what kind of coercion defendants allegedly employed, we as-

sume for purposes of decision that it had a predatory "nature or character," *Klors, Inc. v. Broadway–Hale Stores, Inc.*, 359 U.S. 207, 211, 79 S.Ct. 705, 709, 3 L.Ed.2d 741 (1959), and that it would "cripple the freedom of traders and thereby restrain their ability to sell in accordance with their own judgment." *Kiefer-Stewart Co. v. Seagram & Sons*, 340 U.S. 211, 213, 71 S.Ct. 259, 260, 95 L.Ed. 219 (1951).

unlawful, it does not, of course, necessarily follow that still another party—the Union—is a person injured by reason of a violation of the antitrust laws within the meaning of § 4 of the Clayton Act.

III

We first consider the language in the controlling statute. The class of persons who may maintain a private damage action under the antitrust laws is broadly defined in § 4 of the Clayton Act. 15 U.S.C. § 15. That section provides:

> "Any person who shall be injured in his business or property by reason of anything forbidden in the antitrust laws may sue therefor in any district court of the United States in the district in which the defendant resides or is found or has an agent, without respect to the amount in controversy, and shall recover threefold the damages by him sustained, and the cost of suit, including a reasonable attorney's fee."

A literal reading of the statute is broad enough to encompass every harm that can be attributed directly or indirectly to the consequences of an antitrust violation. Some of our prior cases have paraphrased the statute in an equally expansive way. But before we hold that the statute is as broad as its words suggest, we must consider whether Congress intended such an open-ended meaning.

The critical statutory language was originally enacted in 1890 as § 7 of the Sherman Act. The legislative history of the section shows that Congress was primarily interested in creating an effective remedy for consumers who were forced to pay excessive prices by the giant trusts and combinations that dominated certain interstate markets.[20] That history supports a broad construction of this remedial provision. A proper interpretation of the section cannot, however, ignore the larger context in which the entire statute was debated.

* * *

Just as the substantive content of the Sherman Act draws meaning from its common-law antecedents, so must we consider the contemporary legal context in which Congress acted when we try to ascertain the intended scope of the private remedy created by § 7.

In 1890, notwithstanding general language in many state constitutions providing in substance that "every wrong shall have a remedy," a number of judge-made rules circumscribed the availability of damages recoveries in both tort and contract litigation—doctrines such as foreseeability and proximate cause, directness of injury, certainty of damages, and privity of contract. Although particular common-law limitations were not debated in Congress, the frequent references to common-law principles imply that Congress simply

---

20. The original proposal, which merely allowed recovery of the amount of actual enhancement in price, was successively amended to authorize double damages and then treble-damages recoveries, in order to provide otherwise remediless small consumers with an adequate incentive to bring suit. The same purpose was served by the special venue provisions, the provision for the recovery of attorneys' fees, and the elimination of any requirement that the amount in controversy exceed the jurisdictional threshold applicable in other federal litigation. * * *

assumed that antitrust damages litigation would be subject to constraints comparable to well-accepted common-law rules applied in comparable litigation.[28]

* * *

As this Court has observed, the lower federal courts have been "virtually unanimous in concluding that Congress did not intend the antitrust laws to provide a remedy in damages for all injuries that might conceivably be traced to an antitrust violation." Hawaii v. Standard Oil Co., 405 U.S. 251, 263 n. 14, 92 S.Ct. 885, 891 n. 14 (1972). Just last Term we stated:

> "An antitrust violation may be expected to cause ripples of harm to flow through the Nation's economy; but 'despite the broad wording of § 4 there is a point beyond which the wrongdoer should not be held liable.' Id., [Illinois Brick Co. v. Illinois, 431 U.S. 720] at 760 [97 S.Ct. 2061 at 2082] (BRENNAN, J., dissenting) [citing Illinois Brick v. Illinois, 431 U.S. 720, 97 S.Ct. 2061 (1977)]. It is reasonable to assume that Congress did not intend to allow every person tangentially affected by an antitrust violation to maintain an action to recover threefold damages for the injury to his business or property." Blue Shield of Virginia, Inc. v. McCready, 457 U.S. 465, 476–77, 102 S.Ct. 2540, 2547 (1982).

It is plain, therefore, that the question whether the Union may recover for the injury it allegedly suffered by reason of the defendants' coercion against certain third parties cannot be answered simply by reference to the broad language of § 4. Instead, as was required in common-law damages litigation in 1890, the question requires us to evaluate the plaintiff's harm, the alleged wrongdoing by the defendants, and the relationship between them.[31]

IV

There is a similarity between the struggle of common-law judges to articulate a precise definition of the concept of "proximate cause," and the struggle of federal judges to articulate a precise test to determine whether a party injured by an antitrust violation may recover treble damages.[33] It is common ground that the judicial remedy cannot encompass every conceivable harm that can be traced to alleged wrongdoing. In both situations the infinite

---

28. The common law, of course, is an evolving body of law. We do not mean to intimate that the limitations on damages recoveries found in common-law actions in 1890 were intended to serve permanently as limits on Sherman Act recoveries. But legislators familiar with these limits could hardly have intended the language of § 7 to be taken literally.

31. The label "antitrust standing" has traditionally been applied to some of the elements of this inquiry. As commentators have observed, the focus of the doctrine of "antitrust standing" is somewhat different from that of standing as a constitutional doctrine. Harm to the antitrust plaintiff is sufficient to satisfy the constitutional standing requirement of injury in fact, but the court must make a further determination whether the plaintiff is a proper party to bring a private antitrust action.

33. Some courts have focused on the directness of the injury. Others have applied the requirement that the plaintiff must be in the "target area" of the antitrust conspiracy, that is, the area of the economy which is endangered by a breakdown of competitive conditions in a particular industry. Another court of appeals has asked whether the injury is "arguably within the zone of interests protected by the antitrust laws." As a number of commentators have observed, these labels may lead to contradictory and inconsistent results. In our view, courts should analyze each situation in light of the factors set forth in the text infra.

variety of claims that may arise make it virtually impossible to announce a black-letter rule that will dictate the result in every case. Instead, previously decided cases identify factors that circumscribe and guide the exercise of judgment in deciding whether the law affords a remedy in specific circumstances.

The factors that favor judicial recognition of the Union's antitrust claim are easily stated. The complaint does allege a causal connection between an antitrust violation and harm to the Union and further alleges that the defendants intended to cause that harm. As we have indicated, however, the mere fact that the claim is literally encompassed by the Clayton Act does not end the inquiry. We are also satisfied that an allegation of improper motive, although it may support a plaintiff's damages claim under § 4, is not a panacea that will enable any complaint to withstand a motion to dismiss. * * *

A number of other factors may be controlling. In this case it is appropriate to focus on the nature of the plaintiff's alleged injury. As the legislative history shows, the Sherman Act was enacted to assure customers the benefits of price competition, and our prior cases have emphasized the central interest in protecting the economic freedom of participants in the relevant market. Last Term in *Blue Shield of Virginia v. McCready, supra,* we identified the relevance of this central policy to a determination of the plaintiff's right to maintain an action under § 4. McCready alleged that she was a consumer of psychotherapeutic services and that she had been injured by the defendants' conspiracy to restrain competition in the market for such services. The Court stressed the fact that "McCready's injury was of a type that Congress sought to redress in providing a private remedy for violations of the antitrust laws." [C]*iting Brunswick Corp. v. Pueblo Bowl–O–Mat, Inc.,* 429 U.S. 477, 487–489, 97 S.Ct. 690, 697, 50 L.Ed.2d 701 (1977). After noting that her injury "was inextricably intertwined with the injury the conspirators sought to inflict on psychologists and the psychotherapy market," the Court concluded that such an injury "falls squarely within the area of congressional concern."

In this case, however, the Union was neither a consumer nor a competitor in the market in which trade was restrained.[40] It is not clear whether the Union's interests would be served or disserved by enhanced competition in the market. As a general matter, a union's primary goal is to enhance the earnings and improve the working conditions of its membership; that goal is not necessarily served, and indeed may actually be harmed, by uninhibited competition among employers striving to reduce costs in order to obtain a competitive advantage over their rivals. At common law—as well as in the early days of administration of the federal antitrust laws—the collective activities of labor unions were regarded as a form of conspiracy in restraint of trade. Federal policy has since developed not only a broad labor exemption from the antitrust laws, but also a separate body of labor law specifically designed to protect and encourage the organizational and representational activities of labor unions. Set against this background, a union, in its capacity as bargaining representative, will frequently not be part of the class the

---

40. Moreover, it has not even alleged any marketwide restraint of trade. The allegedly unlawful conduct involves predatory behavior directed at "certain" parties, rather than a claim that output has been curtailed or prices enhanced throughout an entire competitive market.

Sherman Act was designed to protect, especially in disputes with employers with whom it bargains. In each case its alleged injury must be analyzed to determine whether it is of the type that the antitrust statute was intended to forestall. In this case, particularly in light of the longstanding collective bargaining relationship between the parties, the Union's labor-market interests seem to predominate, and the *Brunswick* test is not satisfied.

An additional factor is the directness or indirectness of the asserted injury. In this case, the chain of causation between the Union's injury and the alleged restraint in the market for construction subcontracts contains several somewhat vaguely defined links. According to the complaint, defendants applied coercion against certain landowners and other contracting parties in order to cause them to divert business from certain union contractors to nonunion contractors. As a result, the Union's complaint alleges, the Union suffered unspecified injuries in its "business activities." It is obvious that any such injuries were only an indirect result of whatever harm may have been suffered by "certain" construction contractors and subcontractors.

If either these firms, or the immediate victims of coercion by defendants, have been injured by an antitrust violation, their injuries would be direct and, as we held in *McCready, supra,* they would have a right to maintain their own treble damages actions against the defendants. An action on their behalf would encounter none of the conceptual difficulties that encumber the Union's claim.[47] The existence of an identifiable class of persons whose self-interest would normally motivate them to vindicate the public interest in antitrust enforcement diminishes the justification for allowing a more remote party such as the Union to perform the office of a private attorney general. Denying the Union a remedy on the basis of its allegations in this case is not likely to leave a significant antitrust violation undetected or unremedied.

Partly because it is indirect, and partly because the alleged effects on the Union may have been produced by independent factors, the Union's damages claim is also highly speculative. There is, for example, no allegation that any collective bargaining agreement was terminated as a result of the coercion, no allegation that the aggregate share of the contracting market controlled by union firms has diminished, no allegation that the number of employed union members has declined, and no allegation that the Union's revenues in the form of dues or initiation fees have decreased. Moreover, although coercion against certain firms is alleged, there is no assertion that any such firm was prevented from doing business with any union firms or that any firm or group of firms was subjected to a complete boycott. Other than the alleged injuries flowing from breaches of the collective bargaining agreements—injuries that would be remediable under other laws—nothing but speculation informs the Union's claim of injury by reason of the alleged unlawful coercion. Yet, as we have recently reiterated, it is appropriate for § 4 purposes "to consider whether a claim rests at bottom on some abstract conception or speculative measure of harm." *Blue Shield of Virginia v. McCready, supra.*

The indirectness of the alleged injury also implicates the strong interest, identified in our prior cases, in keeping the scope of complex antitrust trials within judicially manageable limits. These cases have stressed the importance

---

47. Indeed, if there is substance to the Union's claim, it is difficult to understand why these direct victims of the conspiracy have not asserted any claim in their own right. * * *

of avoiding either the risk of duplicate recoveries on the one hand, or the danger of complex apportionment of damages on the other. [Citing *Hanover Shoe, Inc. v. United Shoe Machinery Corp.*, 392 U.S. 481, 88 S.Ct. 2224, 20 L.Ed.2d 1231 (1968), and *Illinois Brick Co. v. Illinois*, 431 U.S. 720, 97 S.Ct. 2061, 52 L.Ed.2d 707 (1977).] * * *

The same concerns should guide us in determining whether the Union is a proper plaintiff under § 4 of the Clayton Act. As the Court wrote in *Illinois Brick,* massive and complex damages litigation not only burdens the courts, but also undermines the effectiveness of treble-damages suits. In this case, if the Union's complaint asserts a claim for damages under § 4, the District Court would face problems of identifying damages and apportioning them among directly victimized contractors and subcontractors and indirectly affected employees and union entities. It would be necessary to determine to what extent the coerced firms diverted business away from union subcontractors, and then to what extent those subcontractors absorbed the damage to their businesses or passed it on to employees by reducing the workforce or cutting hours or wages. In turn it would be necessary to ascertain the extent to which the affected employees absorbed their losses and continued to pay union dues.

We conclude, therefore, that the Union's allegations of consequential harm resulting from a violation of the antitrust laws, although buttressed by an allegation of intent to harm the Union, are insufficient as a matter of law. Other relevant factors—the nature of the Union's injury, the tenuous and speculative character of the relationship between the alleged antitrust violation and the Union's alleged injury, the potential for duplicative recovery or complex apportionment of damages, and the existence of more direct victims of the alleged conspiracy—weigh heavily against judicial enforcement of the Union's antitrust claim. Accordingly, we hold that, based on the allegations of this complaint, the District Court was correct in concluding that the Union is not a person injured by reason of a violation of the antitrust laws within the meaning of § 4 of the Clayton Act. The judgment of the Court of Appeals is reversed.

It is so ordered.

[The Dissenting opinion of Mr. Justice Marshall has been omitted. Eds.]

————

Associated General directed lower courts to analyze standing in light of five factors:

- the causal connection between the antitrust violation and injury to the plaintiff, and whether the injury was intended;

- the nature of the injury, including whether the plaintiff is a consumer or competitor in the relevant market;

- the directness of the injury and whether claimed damages are too speculative;

- the potential for duplicative recovery and whether apportioning damages would be too complex; and

- the existence of more direct victims.

Are these factors distinct from the "antitrust injury" requirements of *Brunswick*? From the concerns expressed in *Illinois Brick* about indirect purchasers? Are they related? Do they overlap in any significant way? Should they be viewed as independent screens, *i.e.*, a direct purchaser might still be barred under *Associated General* if the causal connection between its harm and the challenged conduct is attenuated? What effects will screening private plaintiffs under *Brunswick* and *Associated General* have on the incidence of private antitrust litigation? Finally, consider the policy arguments for and against the tests for statutory standing set forth in *Brunswick* and *Associated General*. Do you find the case for developing distinct standing requirements for antitrust persuasive? How often are these requirements likely to prove determinative?

5. DEFENSES BASED ON *IN PARI DELICTO* AND UNCLEAN HANDS

Although the Supreme Court has embraced a variety of limitations on the scope of the private right of action, it has rejected for the most part efforts to defend antitrust cases on the ground that the plaintiff either (1) was a participant in the challenged conduct ("in pari delicto"—meaning "of equal fault"); or (2) was otherwise an antitrust scofflaw, itself ("unclean hands").

In *Kiefer–Stewart Co. v. Joseph E. Seagram & Sons, Inc.*, 340 U.S. 211, 214 (1951) (unclean hands) and *Perma Life Mufflers, Inc. v. International Parts Corp.*, 392 U.S. 134, 138–39 (1968) (*in pari delicto*), the Court refused to endorse blanket defenses based on either unclean hands or *in pari delicto*, respectively. In *Perma Life* the Court concluded: "[t]here is nothing in the language of the antitrust acts which indicates that Congress wanted to make the common-law *in pari delicto* doctrine a defense to treble damage actions." *Id.* at 138. Referring more broadly to both the unclean hands defense raised in *Kiefer-Stewart*, and the *in pari delicto* defense urged in *Perma Life*, the Court reasoned:

> * * * [T]he purposes of the antitrust laws are best served by insuring that the private action will be an ever-present threat to deter anyone contemplating business behavior in violation of the antitrust laws. The plaintiff who reaps the reward of treble damages may be no less morally reprehensible than the defendant, but the law encourages his suit to further the overriding public policy in favor of competition. A more fastidious regard for the relative moral worth of the parties would only result in seriously undermining the usefulness of the private action as a bulwark of antitrust enforcement. And permitting the plaintiff to recover a windfall gain does not encourage continued violations by those in his position since they remain fully subject to civil and criminal penalties for their own illegal conduct.

Id. at 139. Some exceptions, first hinted at in *Perma Life*, have emerged, however, and under very limited circumstances these sorts of defenses can be significant. *See generally* ABA SECTION OF ANTITRUST LAW, ANTITRUST LAW DEVELOPMENTS 876–80 (6th ed. 2007).

F. REMEDIES FOR ANTITRUST VIOLATIONS

In this chapter we have looked at the array of remedies that competition policy systems use to correct the harm from antitrust violations and to deter future misconduct. Below we take a closer look at several key elements of the competition policy remedial scheme, including the application of criminal penalties for certain antitrust violations, the role of injunctive relief, including divestiture, and finally treble damages.

1. CRIMINAL SANCTIONS

Criminal sanctions for antitrust violations have increased substantially since 1970 as a consequence of both changes in the relevant legal provisions as well as experience with global cartels such as those we studied in Chapter 1. Today, the Sherman Act sets a maximum fine of $100 million for corporate defendants. Individuals may be punished by fines of up to $1 million and by jail sentences as long as ten years. 15 U.S.C. §§ 1–2. Under 18 U.S.C. § 3571(d), fines may also be "not more than the greater of twice the gross gain or twice the gross loss, unless imposition of a fine under this subsection would unduly complicate or prolong the sentencing process." In addition, in 2006, Congress added antitrust offenses to the list of crimes that can be investigated using court-ordered wiretaps, enhancing the Antitrust Division's investigatory authority. 18 U.S.C. § 2516.

Criminal antitrust sentencing also is addressed by the federal Sentencing Guidelines promulgated by the U.S. Sentencing Commission. *See* U.S. SEN-TENCING GUIDELINES MANUAL § 2R1.1 (2007). Under the Guidelines, which are not binding, judges have been are more likely to impose substantial fines and prison terms upon entities or individuals convicted of bid-rigging, price-fixing, and market allocation schemes. General controversy over the constitutionality of judicial procedures under the Guidelines has injected some uncertainty into this area for antitrust, as well. Nevertheless, according to the Department of Justice criminal fines and jail time for criminal antitrust offenders has risen and defendants today are more likely to receive jail time and more likely to receive longer sentences than ever before.

Figure 9–3 summarizes the amount of criminal fines imposed under U.S. antitrust law by decade since the adoption of the Sherman Act in 1890.

Figure 9–3:
Criminal Antitrust Fines Imposed in U.S. by Decade

Decade	Total Fines Recovered*
1890s	0
1900s	220,000
1910s	546,000
1920s	1,560,000
1930s	1,025,000
1940s	8,110,000
1950s	5,504,000
1960s	14,000,000
1970s	48,497,000

Decade	Total Fines Recovered*
1980s	120,000,000
1990s	1,801,000,000
2000s	2,405,000,000 (through FY 2007)

* **Note**: Fines are presented in current U.S. dollars and are not adjusted for inflation. Fine amounts are rounded to the nearest 1000 dollars.

Data Sources: Richard A. Posner, *A Statistical Study of Antitrust Enforcement*, 13 J.L. & Econ. 365 (1970); Joseph C. Gallo, et al. *Criminal Penalties Under the Sherman Act: A Study of Law and Economics*, 16 Res. L. & Econ. 25 (1994); Gary R. Spratling, *Are the Recent Titanic Fines in Antitrust Cases Just the Tip of the Iceberg?* (Mar.6, 1998), *available at* http://www.usdoj.gov/atr/public/speeches/212581.htm; Joel I. Klein, *The War Against International Cartels: Lessons from the Battlefront* (Oct. 14, 1999), *available at* http://www.usdoj.gov/atr/public/speeches/3747.htm; Scott D. Hammond, *Recent Developments, Trends, and Milestones In The Antitrust Division's Criminal Enforcement Program* (Nov. 16, 2007), *available at* http://www.usdoj.gov/atr/public/speeches/227740.htm; U.S. Dep't of Justice, Antitrust Division, Workload Statistics, FY 1998—2007, *available at* http://www.usdoj.gov/atr/public/workstats.htm.

The following example reveals how the Department of Justice proposed to set the sanction for several key participants in the Vitamins, Inc. cartel, which we introduced in Chapter 1. Reprinted below is the sentencing statement that the DOJ entered to settle criminal charges against the conspiracy's ringleader, Hoffmann–La Roche, and Kuno Sommer, the executive who orchestrated the cartel. To date, the $500 million fine imposed on Hoffman–La Roche remains the largest criminal antitrust fine ever imposed in the U.S.

UNITED STATES v. F. HOFFMANN–LA ROCHE LTD.

United States District Court, N.D. Texas.
May 1999.

Sentencing Statement for the United States

Had this case gone to trial, the United States would have presented evidence to establish the following facts:

* * *

From at least January 1990 until February 1999, Roche, and other worldwide manufacturers of vitamins engaged in an illegal conspiracy, the primary purpose of which was to fix, increase, and maintain the prices and allocate the volume of certain vitamins sold in the United States and worldwide. Initially, this conspiracy focused on vitamins A and E and it quickly evolved into an extremely well organized operation. Throughout the world, on a country and regional level, Roche and other conspirator companies tasked their lower level employees and managers to forward pricing and market share information to higher level management. On a quarterly basis, regional and world marketing managers from the conspirator companies would meet to exchange pricing and sales information in order to have an accurate picture of the overall global demand and price for the vitamins. Once a year, the global marketing directors for each of the conspirator companies, in concert with the various product managers for the companies, would conduct a "budget" meeting. During this meeting, the overall global sales volume for the vitamins would be determined for the current year, and based on agreed-upon projected growth rates, the global sales volume for the coming year would be determined. Next, each company would be allocated a percentage of this projected global market demand as its "budget target" for the following year which it would then implement on a regional or country basis. Finally, vitamin pricing would be reviewed and, if price increases were needed to either account for currency discrepancies or to raise profit levels, new pricing would be agreed upon, to include the timing of the price increases and designation of which company would lead the price increase.

To implement the budgeted amounts of vitamins A and E in the United States, Roche and another coconspirator found it necessary to allocate between themselves various vitamin premix accounts in the U.S. To do this, representatives from the two companies would meet on a quarterly basis to review bid requests that were sent out by the major food and animal feed premix customers in the country. Meeting in private homes to avoid detection, these representatives would determine which customer would "belong" to Roche and which customer would "belong" to the other conspirator company. The representatives would then determine what the winning bid price would be for each company, fill out the bids to either "win" or "lose" the bid, and then mail the bids back to the customers.

Over time, the scope of the conspiracy was adjusted, usually with Roche as the instigator of activity, to either include or exclude additional vitamins and vitamin manufacturers involved in the conspiracy. Over the course of the conspiracy vitamins A, B2 (riboflavin), B5 (Calpan), C, Beta Carotene, and various vitamin premixes were all subject to collusive and illegal agreements and sold to a wide array of customers in America, many with household names such as General Mills, Kelloggs, Coca–Cola, Tyson Foods, and Proctor and Gamble.

Roche and its coconspirators were very concerned with maintaining the secrecy of their cartel activity. It was expressly understood by conspiracy meeting participants that documents were to be kept to a minimum and destroyed after each meeting. Internally, Roche personnel were continually instructed to destroy all documents that might be evidence of illegal agreements with competitors. In those instances where it was necessary to generate spreadsheets to show each conspirator's current market share, companies were never listed by name; instead they were allocated a code number that was used on the spreadsheet to conceal their true identities.

Throughout the course of the conspiracy, Roche sold to U.S. customers over 3.2 billion dollars of vitamins and vitamin premixes that were the subject of and affected by this illegal cartel activity.

WITH RESPECT TO SENTENCING:

The jointly recommended criminal fine of 500 million dollars is an appropriate punishment for Roche in this case. If the court accepts the joint sentencing recommendation, Roche will pay the largest criminal fine ever imposed, not only for an antitrust offense, but the largest fine ever imposed for any criminal offense. From an antitrust perspective, a 500 million dollar fine is 365 million dollars more that the previous record antitrust fine. Overall, a 500 million dollar fine is 140 million dollars more than any criminal fine ever imposed in DOJ history. In this respect, a 500 million dollar fine recognizes the seriousness of the offense, the role played by Roche in the offense, the impact of the offense on American consumers, the fact that Roche is a repeat offender, and the attempts by Roche to obstruct the Antitrust Division's investigation in this matter. Because the obstructive efforts of Roche are relevant for sentencing, let me take a moment to detail these activities.

Roche's quest to maintain the secrecy of its collusive activities led it to actions which obstructed the Government's investigative efforts. Dr. Kuno Sommer, Roche's Worldwide Marketing Director, was interviewed by Department of Justice, Antitrust Division attorneys on March 12, 1997 in connection with a plea agreement reached between the United States and Roche concerning criminal antitrust violations committed by Roche in the sale and production of citric acid. Prior to his interview, Sommer was advised by Antitrust Division enforcement officials that he would also be asked questions about possible criminal antitrust violations concerning other food and animal feed additives, particularly vitamins.

From 1994 to 1997, Dr. Kuno Sommer was the key executive at Roche responsible for the day-to-day supervision and administration of the vitamins cartel. He was not only the senior executive to whom Roche regional managers and global product managers reported, but he was also the senior point of contact between Roche and other conspirator companies.

In order to conceal from Antitrust investigators the existence of collusive agreements and activities between Roche and its vitamin manufacturing competitors, Sommer met separately with at least two other high level Roche executives. At the end of those meetings, it was understood by these individuals that if Sommer was asked about Roche's participation in a vitamins cartel, Sommer would lie and deny that such a cartel existed. At subsequent preparation meetings between Sommer and one or more of the individuals, Sommer's "cover story" denying any cartel activity affecting vitamins was rehearsed. When, on March 12, 1997, Antitrust Division enforcement officials ultimately questioned Sommer about the existence of a vitamins cartel, Sommer lied by stating that there was no conspiracy among the world's leading vitamins manufacturers, including Roche; that he had never participated in meetings, conversations, or agreements to fix, increase, and maintain prices, or allocate sales volumes of, or customers for, certain vitamins with any representative of any other manufacturer of vitamins; and that he was not aware of any meetings or conversations among other representatives of Roche and any other vitamin manufacturer relating to any agreements of conspiracy to fix, increase, or maintain prices, or allocate sales volumes and customers in the vitamin industry.

Sommer's efforts to cover up the conspiracy were successful in delaying and obstructing the Division's vitamins investigation. With renewed confidence in the secrecy of the cartel's activity, Roche and its high level executives continued to participate in the vitamins cartel even while a court was taking Roche's citric acid plea, and even while Roche was cooperating in the citric acid investigation as required by its plea agreement.

Given these circumstances, it is clear that a fine of this magnitude is particularly necessary as a means to deter future international cartel activity. As Roche's conduct has demonstrated, significantly lesser fines are not of sufficient deterrent value to curtail large-scale international collusion. It is important to note that the vitamins cartel was in full swing in October of 1996 when Archer Daniels Midland was assessed a 100 million dollar fine for its role in two international cartels in the food and feed additives industry. Despite this enormous fine, Roche and its coconspirators did not miss a beat in continuing to fix prices and allocate global market share for the vitamins industry.

Of equal importance with the need to properly punish the offender, a 500 million dollar fine, when compared to the possible exposure Roche faces under the Federal Sentencing Guidelines, properly recognizes and rewards the exemplary cooperation Roche has provided to the Antitrust Division. Beginning on March 2, 1999, Roche, through counsel, informed Antitrust Division attorneys that it had colluded with competitors on at least some vitamins and that it was in the process of determining the full extent of Roche's involvement in the illegal activity. From that moment on, the speed, nature, and spirit of Roche's cooperation was unprecedented and a model of what full cooperation should be.

Within a matter of weeks, Roche made available in the United States over a half dozen current and former foreign-based employees that were intimately involved in the day-to-day operations of Roche's conspiracy activities. These witnesses gave candid, complete, and detailed information concerning their participation in the charged conspiracy and that of other companies and individuals involved. This information concerning other corporate and individual coconspirators significantly enhanced the quantity and quality of evidence respecting those coconspirators and has increased the likelihood of expeditious, successful prosecutions of such corporations and individuals. These witnesses also brought forward documents that had not been destroyed during the course of the conspiracy which clearly detailed the extent of information sharing and global market allocation that occurred during the course of the conspiracy. Additionally, these witnesses have provided valuable information concerning a collusive agreement between Roche and other coconspirators on another nonvitamin product which will likely lead to additional prosecutions involving the product.

Roche, through counsel, also informed some of its corporate coconspirators that it was cooperating with the Antitrust Division in this investigation. Consequently, some of these corporate coconspirators have initiated discussions with Division prosecutors to resolve their criminal liability for vitamin price fixing and market allocation conduct. Without this assistance, such corporate coconspirators would likely not be at the negotiating table at this time and the Division's investigation would not be progressing as significantly as it is in terms of additional prospective prosecutions.

The information provided by Roche, through its current and former employees, increased our knowledge of the conspiracy. Roche has committed to, and we fully anticipate and expect that Roche will continue to provide valuable information and assistance as the investigation of criminal cartel activity in the vitamins industry continues, including grand jury appearances and possible testimony at any eventual trial involving such violations. Given all of these circumstances, a 500 million dollar fine not only recognizes the extraordinary cooperation that Roche has and will continue to provide, given the potential liability Roche faces in terms of its Guidelines fine range, such a significant departure from the Guidelines fine range offers a clear incentive to future defendants to provide quick and complete cooperation.

————

The sentencing statement for Roche and Sommer reveals several factors at work. The conspirators fully understood that U.S. antitrust law deemed their conduct to be criminal. In carrying out their scheme, the violators focused on whether they would be apprehended and prosecuted, and how they might be punished. "Vitamins, Inc." exercised caution to hold its meetings and orchestrate most of its affairs outside the United States—expecting, perhaps, that the cartel could exploit gaps in the capacity of the U.S. laws to reach their offshore arrangements and to obtain jurisdiction over culpable individuals. The cartel also strove to conceal the arrangement and avoid detection. The extraordinary size of the fine imposed on HLR—$500 million, the largest criminal fine obtained by DOJ in any matter—reflected a desire to deter similar misconduct by other firms.

Recall, too from our discussion of the *ADM* in Chapter 1 ("Lysine"), that in addition to fines, individuals who commit criminal violations the Sherman Act can be punished with prison sentences. What factors might lead the Justice Department to seek prison time for violators? What factors might lead a court to impose prison time, and how much time is appropriate for individuals who playing leading roles in orchestrating the conspiracy? At this point, you may want to review the excerpt from the Seventh Circuit's decision in *ADM* to enhance the prison sentences of the "ring-leaders" of the Lysine cartel, which we read in Chapter 1. *See also United States v. A. Alfred Taubman*, 297 F.3d 161 (2d Cir.2002) (affirming criminal conviction of individual in price fixing case).

2. CIVIL REMEDIES

Civil remedies for antitrust law violations generally take two basic forms: the chastening effect on the defendant of the lawsuit itself and judicially-imposed remedies. Remedies fall into one of two categories: (1) equitable relief, such as injunctions or divestiture orders, and (2) damages. After briefly considering the role that the mere threat of litigation can play, we turn to judicial treatment of equitable relief and damages.

a. *Lawsuits as Remedies*

The mere filing and prosecution of an antitrust case sometimes alters the defendant's conduct. Prosecuting a group of conspirators under Section 1, or a dominant firm under Section 2, for example, can have two effects. The first is what might be called the *inhibition* effect. The lawsuit itself can give consumers and/or rivals breathing room by inhibiting the defendant from engaging in aggressive commercial moves. Under scrutiny from the court, the prosecutor, and the press, the dominant firm, for example, might hesitate to employ aggressive tactics that strengthen its position in the relevant market or extend its preeminence into another market. The firms' internal business decisions may be subject to more exacting review by in-house and external legal advisors, instilling greater caution throughout the firm.

For a dominant firm, a diminished ability to make swift, decisive commercial adjustments can be significant in highly dynamic industries, where even slight hesitation can be punished by a dramatic loss in sales. Emboldened competitors may perceive how the lawsuit's inhibition effect robs the defendant of some adroitness and may try more aggressive measures with confidence that the defendant will not strike back as forcefully or ruthlessly as it has in the past. The opportunity created by the pendency of the case may help fringe firms to expand operations or allow entrants to gain competitive footholds. Similarly, the pendency of a suit against an alleged cartel might encourage members of the cartel to cheat, and others to compete more aggressively, particularly on price, with less concern that the cartel will be able to execute any effective punishment under the watchful eyes of courts or investigators.

A second lawsuit-generated remedial consequence is the *distraction* effect. To fully respond to a lawsuit, an antitrust defendant must devote a formidable amount of the time of its own employees to support the preparation and presentation of the defense. This distraction has tremendous, under-appreciated costs to the company. The diversion of firm personnel to support the case, as well as the time employees spend in casual conversation or mental speculation about the status of the case, may silently bleed the company's creative resources and blur its competitive vision. Every minute that firm's employees spend in assisting with the case is a minute that will not be devoted to developing new products, improving existing services, or seeking new sales. Where the lawsuit and proposed remedies strike at the heart of what the company believes to be indispensable elements of its culture and strategy, a spare-no-cost defense usually results. The firm's employees may come to believe that their chief goal is to vanquish the government plaintiff rather than surpassing competitors.

Experience with abuse of dominance cases indicates the importance of the inhibition and distraction effects. DOJ's case against IBM for monopolizing the mainframe computer sector provides an important illustration. The IBM case is routinely depicted as a singular example of prosecutorial failure. From the filing of the case on the last day of Lyndon Johnson's presidency in January 1969, until the dismissal of the matter at DOJ's request in 1982, the IBM case consumed vast resources of the government and IBM, alike. The government's case triggered the filing of over 40 private treble damage lawsuits. As it did with DOJ, IBM crushed nearly all of the private plaintiffs—but arguably at a great price in terms of its standing in the very markets that were the subject of the suit. Along with the private lawsuits, the DOJ case caused IBM to elevate the role of lawyers in shaping commercial strategy and led the firm to pull its competitive punches. To help IBM repel its antitrust adversaries, the firm's employees spent countless hours in tasks having nothing to do with designing new products and increasing sales. Once thought to be invincible, an inhibited and distracted IBM failed to grasp the significance of new industry developments, such as the ascent of the personal computer, that propelled an upstart software firm named Microsoft to the fore and opened opportunities for other hardware manufacturers.

Consider how these "remedial" effects of antitrust suits might be considered laudatory or as a basis for criticism of the antitrust system. The difference depends in part on whether the allegations turn out in fact to be well-founded. If they are, the distraction effect of antitrust lawsuits can add to deterrence. Antitrust suits have been faulted, however, for causing all the same distraction effects in weak or meritless antitrust claims. In those instances, the lawsuits themselves can have ironically anti-competitive consequences on the performance of a firm or industry. The difference also depends on precisely what form the inhibition or distraction takes—that is, whether the conduct the firm does not undertake would have been beneficial or harmful.

b. Judicially–Imposed Remedies

Although litigation effects are not insignificant, the principal measure of any successful antitrust prosecution is the remedy secured by the plaintiffs. Courts in civil antitrust cases enjoy broad discretion to terminate unlawful conduct, impose measures to correct improper accumulations of market power, and to diminish the defendant's capacity to suppress rivalry in the future. As we have learned, although the Sherman Act treats antitrust offenses as crimes, few contemporary cases alleging misconduct other than hard core collusion have resulted in criminal charges. For purposes of modern policy, therefore, the central issue for the court is what collection of civil remedies will correct the effects of improper conduct and reinvigorate competition in the future.

Perhaps surprisingly, the challenges of remedying antitrust violations have proved to be formidable and remain a frequent topic of controversy. Courts can bifurcate the trial of liability and remedies, addressing the remedy phase only after liability has been found. These follow-on hearings can be substantial trials in themselves, and frequently require the courts to evaluate competing expert testimony. As you read the cases and materials that follow, assemble a list of issues that might influence a district judge's final remedy decision.

i. Controls on Conduct

The most common remedy in civil prosecutions is termination of the unlawful conduct. But simply terminating the conduct would do little to compensate, punish or deter. As a consequence, the typical equitable remedy also includes restrictions on the conduct of the defendants intended to both prevent the conduct from re-occurring and to restore competitive conditions that may have been altered by the conduct. In a Section 2 prosecution, for example, conduct-related controls often take the form of an injunction prohibiting the specific behavior that the trial established to be improper, but may also involve divestiture, or some other kind of "structural" relief designed to deconcentrate the market.

Our next case excerpt is taken from a case we have already studied—*Nat'l Soc'y of Prof. Eng'rs*. Recall from Chapter 2 that the Society's code of ethics banned competitive bidding by its members. The Supreme Court concluded that such a ban was a violation of the Sherman Act. It then reviewed the district court's remedial order, which went well beyond simply enjoining the ban.

NATIONAL SOCIETY OF PROFESSIONAL ENGINEERS v. UNITED STATES

Supreme Court of the United States, 1978.
435 U.S. 679, 98 S.Ct. 1355, 55 L.Ed.2d 637.

Mr. Justice STEVENS delivered the opinion of the Court.

[For the facts and liability discussion, *see* Casebook, *supra*, at 159-63. Eds.]

* * *

III

The judgment entered by the District Court, as modified by the Court of Appeals, prohibits the Society from adopting any official opinion, policy statement, or guideline stating or implying that competitive bidding is unethical. Petitioner argues that this judgment abridges its First Amendment rights. We find no merit in this contention.

Having found the Society guilty of a violation of the Sherman Act, the District Court was empowered to fashion appropriate restraints on the Society's future activities both to avoid a recurrence of the violation and to eliminate its consequences. *See, e.g., International Salt Co.* v. *United States*, 332 U.S. 392, 400–401; *United States v. Glaxo Group, Ltd.*, 410 U.S. 52, 64. While the resulting order may curtail the exercise of liberties that the Society might otherwise enjoy, that is a necessary and, in cases such as this, unavoidable consequence of the violation. Just as an injunction against price fixing abridges the freedom of businessmen to talk to one another about prices, so too the injunction in this case must restrict the Society's range of expression on the ethics of competitive bidding.[26] The First Amendment does not "make it ... impossible ever to enforce laws against agreements in restraint of trade...." In fashioning a remedy, the District Court may, of course, consider the fact that its injunction may impinge upon rights that would otherwise be constitutionally protected, but those protections do not prevent it from remedying the antitrust violations.

The standard against which the order must be judged is whether the relief represents a reasonable method of eliminating the *consequences* of the illegal conduct. We agree with the Court of Appeals that the injunction, as modified, meets this standard. While it goes beyond a simple proscription against the precise conduct previously pursued, that is entirely appropriate.

"The District Court is not obliged to assume, contrary to common experience, that a violator of the antitrust laws will relinquish the fruits of his violation more completely than the court requires him to do. And advantages already in hand may be held by methods more subtle and informed, and more difficult to prove, than those which, in the first place, win a market. When the purpose to restrain trade

---

26. Thus, in *Goldfarb*, although the bar association believed that its fee schedule accurately reflected ethical price levels, it was nonetheless enjoined "from adopting, publishing, or distributing any future schedules of minimum or suggested fees." *Goldfarb v. Virginia State Bar*, 355 F. Supp. 491, 495–496 (E.D. Va.1973). *See also United States v. National Assn. of Real Estate Boards*, 339 U.S. 485.

appears from a clear violation of law, it is not necessary that all of the untraveled roads to that end be left open and that only the worn one be closed." *International Salt Co., supra*, at 400.

The Society apparently fears that the District Court's injunction, if broadly read, will block legitimate paths of expression on all ethical matters relating to bidding. But the answer to these fears is, as the Court held in *International Salt*, that the burden is upon the proved transgressor "to bring any proper claims for relief to the court's attention." *Ibid*. In this case, the Court of Appeals specifically stated that "[if] the Society wishes to adopt some other ethical guideline more closely confined to the legitimate objective of preventing deceptively low bids, it may move the district court for modification of the decree." 181 U. S. App. D. C., at 46, 555 F.2d, at 983. This is, we believe, a proper approach, adequately protecting the Society's interests. We therefore reject petitioner's attack on the District Court's order.

* * *

———

Nat'l Soc'y of Prof. Eng'rs. leaves little doubt that a district court has discretion to go beyond simply prohibiting the illegal conduct. Why? What does the Court mean when it asks whether the remedy chosen by the district court is a "reasonable method of eliminating the *consequences* of the illegal conduct"? What factors might a court want to consider in making that judgment? Consider the following list of possibilities:

- the scope and duration of the violation;

- the defendant's past history of anticompetitive acts;

- the anticompetitive effects of the conduct that constituted a violation, *i.e.*, were they collusive, exclusionary, or both?;

- the victims of the violation, *i.e.*, were they rivals, consumers or both?;

- the expected benefits to competition of the proposed remedy;

- the expected costs of adopting and implementing the remedy;

- the practicality of the remedy, *i.e.*, how feasible is it?;

- the duration of the remedy; and

- the likely efficacy of the enforcement procedures proposed for implementing the remedy.

Note how most of these factors will be matters of degree. It is not surprising, therefore, that the Court's approach leaves the district court considerable discretion. Evaluating and balancing these factors may turn on factors such as the credibility of witnesses that are uniquely within the purview of the district court. As the following note explores, the courts's success in imposing such remedies has been and continues to be the subject of much debate.

Note on the Success of Conduct Remedies in Monopolization Cases*

Though frequently imposed, conduct remedies do not enjoy a favorable reputation in the antitrust literature, particularly in the case of dominant firm behavior. One often-voiced criticism, particularly in older commentary, is that conduct remedies do little to unravel existing accumulations of market power and provide feeble alternatives to structure solutions, such as divestiture, that directly dismantle positions of dominance. This critique reflects the strong influence of the structuralist school of antitrust, which posits market structure as the key determinant of competitive vigor and tends to equate concentrated markets with a lack of competition. In the view of structuralists, conduct remedies that have not reduced the defendant's market share dramatically—below 50 percent, to use a rough rule of thumb—have failed their essential purpose.

Experience with the *United Shoe Machinery* litigation sometimes is offered to illustrate this point. In a monopolization case concluded in the early 1950s, the DOJ prevailed on the issue of liability but failed to persuade the court to order divestiture. *United States v. United Shoe Mach. Corp.*, 110 F.Supp. 295 (D. Mass. 1953), *aff'd per curiam*, 347 U.S. 521, 74 S.Ct. 699 (1954). Emphasizing that the defendant owned a single facility, the court forbad the continuation of United's lease-only policy and required United to unbundle service from the supply of its machines. United's market share fell to the low 60s until 1968, when the Supreme Court granted the government's request for divestiture. *United States v. United Shoe Mach. Corp.*, 391 U.S. 244, 88 S.Ct. 1496, 20 L.Ed.2d 562 (1968). The failure to grant divestiture in the original 1950s proceeding is offered as an example of the weakness of conduct remedies and the relative superiority of divestiture.

Criticism of the remedial history of the United Shoe Machinery litigation may rest on questionable assumptions derived from structuralist economic models that enjoyed widespread acceptance in the 1950s and 1960s. One point for reconsideration is whether a fall from roughly 85 percent to 60 percent constitutes a remedial failure. The Supreme Court's 1968 opinion treats United's market share as the sole index of remedial effectiveness. Such an approach ignores other data—such as industry patterns of entry, profitability, and innovation—that might provide a more reliable measure of the remedy's impact.

A second basic concern with conduct remedies is that they can entail extensive judicial supervision and continuing intervention to interpret remedial commands and see that they are obeyed. This possibility is perhaps most evident where the remedy involves a judicially-imposed duty to deal with rivals. For example, in *Otter Tail Power Co. v. United States*, 410 U.S. 366 (1973), the Supreme Court ordered an integrated electric utility to "wheel" bulk power over its long distance transmission lines to municipally-owned distribution systems. If a court decides to mandate access to a key asset, it must be prepared to specify the price and quality terms on which the defendant must provide access. In setting appropriate access charges, courts may find themselves enmeshed in ratemaking exercises for which they are institutionally ill-suited. Similarly, the consent decree in AT & T, which was entered in 1982, required continuing oversight by the federal district court until the enactment of the Telecommunications Act of 1996.

ii. Divestiture

Perhaps the most dramatic form of judicial intervention in civil cases is the entry of an order that requires the defendant to be restructured into two

---

* This Note is adapted from William E. Kovacic, *Failed Expectations: The Troubled Past and Uncertain Future of the Sherman Act as a* *Tool of Deconcentration*, 74 Iowa L. Rev. 1105 (1989).

or more entities or to divest substantial assets to another purchaser. Divestiture orders offer the possibility of swiftly dissipating the defendant's market power by introducing new competitors into the market. In some instances, the divestiture remedy may involve a single instance of judicial intervention and avoid the need to exercise continuing oversight responsibilities associated with some controls on conduct.

Divestiture orders are most common, and the least controversial, in merger challenges, and it is easy to see why. Recall from Chapter 5 that when a court concludes that a merger will be anticompetitive, it enjoins the merger, *i.e.*, it prohibits the combining of the firms or assets at issue. When it reaches such a conclusion after a merger or acquisition has already been consummated, it will typically seek to undo the effort through divestiture. Although it can sometimes be difficult to "unscramble the eggs," *i.e.*, disentangle assets that have already been commingled, the mere fact that the assets once existed separately provides the court with at least some guidance as to how to achieve the divestiture with minimal damage to the efficient operation of the firms.

Similarly, divestiture has been a common and generally accepted remedy for Section 2 monopolization cases, particularly *where the monopolist became dominant at least in part through acquisitions*, even though the acquisitions themselves were not independent violations at the time they were made. Again, it is easy to see why. When a monopolist acquired its dominant position at least in part through the acquisition of rivals, a remedy for abusing that position might include dismantling its monopoly. As in the case of illegal mergers, the fact that its constituent parts once existed independently, provides the court with valuable guidance in approaching the divestiture process. Divestiture also has the benefit of making unnecessary ongoing judicial supervision of the relief; once it is accomplished, the firms and the court move on.

Nevertheless, divestiture remains a drastic and rarely employed remedy outside of these narrow circumstances. It is almost unheard of in Section 1 cases, and remains controversial in Section 2 cases—especially when the dominant firm achieved its dominance through internal growth as opposed to acquisitions. Courts in civil cases, especially abuse of dominance matters, have tended to regard divestiture as a riskier form of intervention than conduct controls. The perceptions of risk are most acute where a restructuring might destroy valuable efficiencies. Courts also might fear that a divestiture will reduce employment and impose significant losses on investors. Because courts tend to see divestiture as entailing greater risks, plaintiffs are well advised to devote additional effort to demonstrating that a divestiture plan will produce substantial net competitive benefits without substantial adverse affects.

Divestiture measures also can be difficult to administer. In the most simple type of divestiture, a court can order existing organizational units within the firm to be spun off as separate entities. Such a move ordinarily will require some difficult judgments about how to allocate personnel and assets that serve the company as a whole, but there generally will be no need to sever existing design or production teams, and perhaps no need to separate physical facilities. In the harder case, the firm's operations are carried out in fully integrated teams. If a restructuring program is to be carried out, the court will have to decide how personnel who serve in the unitary teams will be allocated to the new enterprise (assuming they decide for themselves to remain), and how equipment and physical facilities will be divided.

Divestitures must also meet financial market tests for practicality and value. Whereas divestiture of assets may be appealing as an economic matter, the assets must have value in the market sufficient to attract buyers at reasonable prices. For example, it may be difficult to sell off assets deemed to be over-priced or lacking in value. Older physical facilities may be economically inefficient, out of date, and unattractive to purchasers. Finding purchasers for assets ordered to be divested, therefore, may not always be a simple matter, and courts often turn to Special Masters to oversee divestiture orders over some specified period of time.

If the plaintiff proposes a structural solution, how should the court determine whether structural relief is appropriate? In 2001 the court of appeals decision in *United States v. Microsoft Corp.* devoted extensive attention to the duties of the trial judge in such instances. As we saw in Chapter 6, the D.C. Circuit affirmed the trial court's ruling that Microsoft had violated Section 2 of the Sherman Act by using exclusionary means to preserve monopoly power in the software sector. In addition to extensive conduct remedies, the district court had endorsed the government's proposal that Microsoft—a unitary firm that had achieved its dominance through internal growth—be broken into two. The court of appeals reversed and remanded.

UNITED STATES v. MICROSOFT CORP.
United States Court of Appeals for the District of Columbia, 2001.
253 F.3d 34.

PER CURIAM:

* * *

V. TRIAL PROCEEDINGS AND REMEDY

* * * We conclude * * * that the District Court's remedies decree must be vacated for three independent reasons: (1) the court failed to hold a remedies-specific evidentiary hearing when there were disputed facts; (2) the court failed to provide adequate reasons for its decreed remedies; and (3) this Court has revised the scope of Microsoft's liability and it is impossible to determine to what extent that should affect the remedies provisions.

A. *Factual Background*

On April 3, 2000, the District Court concluded the liability phase of the proceedings by the filing of its Conclusions of Law holding that Microsoft had violated §§ 1 and 2 of the Sherman Act. The court and the parties then began discussions of the procedures to be followed in the imposition of remedies. Initially, the District Court signaled that it would enter relief only after conducting a new round of proceedings. In its Conclusions of Law, the court stated that it would issue a remedies order "following proceedings to be established by further Order of the Court." And, when during a post-trial conference, Microsoft's counsel asked whether the court "contemplate[d] further proceedings," the judge replied, "Yes. Yes. I assume that there would be further proceedings." The District Court further speculated that those proceedings might "replicate the procedure at trial with testimony in written form subject to cross-examination."

On April 28, 2000, plaintiffs submitted their proposed final judgment, accompanied by six new supporting affidavits and several exhibits. In addition to a series of temporary conduct restrictions, plaintiffs proposed that Microsoft be split into two independent corporations, with one continuing Microsoft's operating systems business and the other undertaking the balance of Microsoft's operations. Microsoft filed a "summary response" on May 10, contending both that the proposed decree was too severe and that it would be impossible to resolve certain remedies-specific factual disputes "on a highly expedited basis." Another May 10 submission argued that if the District Court considered imposing plaintiffs' proposed remedy, "then substantial discovery, adequate time for preparation and a full trial on relief will be required." * * *

After the District Court revealed during a May 24 hearing that it was prepared to enter a decree without conducting "any further process," Microsoft renewed its argument that the underlying factual disputes between the parties necessitated a remedies-specific evidentiary hearing. In two separate offers of proof, Microsoft offered to produce a number of pieces of evidence. * * *

[Here the court summarized Microsoft's offers of proof concerning the likely adverse effects of the plaintiffs' proposed remedies. Microsoft had offered testimony by several economic experts, an investment bank, and Microsoft executives, including the company's chairman, Bill Gates. Eds.]

Over Microsoft's objections, the District Court proceeded to consider the merits of the remedy and on June 7, 2000 entered its final judgment. The court explained that it would not conduct "extended proceedings on the form a remedy should take," because it doubted that an evidentiary hearing would "give any significantly greater assurance that it will be able to identify what might be generally regarded as an optimum remedy." The bulk of Microsoft's proffered facts were simply conjectures about future events, and "[i]n its experience the Court has found testimonial predictions of future events generally less reliable even than testimony as to historical fact, and cross-examination to be of little use in enhancing or detracting from their accuracy." Nor was the court swayed by Microsoft's "profession of surprise" at the possibility of structural relief. "From the inception of this case Microsoft knew, from well-established Supreme Court precedents dating from the beginning of the last century, that a mandated divestiture was a possibility, if not a probability, in the event of an adverse result at trial."

The substance of the District Court's remedies order is nearly identical to plaintiffs' proposal. The decree's centerpiece is the requirement that Microsoft submit a proposed plan of divestiture, with the company to be split into an "Operating Systems Business," or "OpsCo," and an "Applications Business," or "AppsCo." OpsCo would receive all of Microsoft's operating systems, such as Windows 98 and Windows 2000, while AppsCo would receive the remainder of Microsoft's businesses, including IE [Internet Explorer Internet browser] and Office [Microsoft Office]. The District Court identified four reasons for its "reluctant[ ]" conclusion that "a structural remedy has become imperative." First, Microsoft "does not yet concede that any of its business practices violated the Sherman Act." Second, the company consequently "continues to do business as it has in the past." Third, Microsoft "has proved untrustworthy in the past." And fourth, the Government, whose officials "are by reason of office obliged and expected to consider—and to act in—the public interest," won the case, "and for that reason alone have some entitlement to a remedy of their choice."

* * *

[The court of appeals concluded that the trial court's efforts to accelerate the conduct of the case on the merits by limiting the number of witnesses for each side did not constitute error. Eds.]

C. Failure to Hold an Evidentiary Hearing

* * * It is a cardinal principle of our system of justice that factual disputes must be heard in open court and resolved through trial-like evidentiary proceedings. Any other course would be contrary "to the spirit which imbues our judicial tribunals prohibiting decision without hearing."

A party has the right to judicial resolution of disputed facts not just as to the liability phase, but also as to appropriate relief. "Normally, an evidentiary hearing is required before an injunction may be granted." Other than a temporary restraining order, no injunctive relief may be entered without a hearing. *See generally* Fed. R. Civ. P. 65. A hearing on the merits—*i.e.*, a trial on liability—does not substitute for a relief-specific evidentiary hearing unless the matter of relief was part of the trial on liability, or unless there are no disputed factual issues regarding the matter of relief.

This rule is no less applicable in antitrust cases. The Supreme Court "has recognized that a 'full exploration of facts is usually necessary in order (for the District Court) properly to draw (an antitrust) decree' so as 'to prevent future violations and eradicate existing evils.' " United States v. Ward Baking Co., 376 U.S. 327, 330–31, 84 S.Ct. 763 (1964). Hence a remedies decree must be vacated whenever there is "a bona fide disagreement concerning substantive items of relief which could be resolved only by trial." Id. at 334, 84 S.Ct. 763. * * *

Despite plaintiffs' protestations, there can be no serious doubt that the parties disputed a number of facts during the remedies phase. In two separate offers of proof, Microsoft identified 23 witnesses who, had they been permitted to testify, would have challenged a wide range of plaintiffs' factual representations, including the feasibility of dividing Microsoft, the likely impact on consumers, and the effect of divestiture on shareholders. To take but two examples, where plaintiffs' economists testified that splitting Microsoft in two would be socially beneficial, the company offered to prove that the proposed remedy would "cause substantial social harm by raising software prices, lowering rates of innovation and disrupting the evolution of Windows as a software development platform." And where plaintiffs' investment banking experts proposed that divestiture might actually increase shareholder value, Microsoft proffered evidence that structural relief "would inevitably result in a significant loss of shareholder value," a loss that could reach "tens—possibly hundreds—of billions of dollars."

Indeed, the District Court itself appears to have conceded the existence of acute factual disagreements between Microsoft and plaintiffs. The court acknowledged that the parties were "sharply divided" and held "divergent opinions" on the likely results of its remedies decree. The reason the court declined to conduct an evidentiary hearing was not because of the absence of disputed facts, but because it believed that those disputes could be resolved only through "actual experience," not further proceedings. But a prediction about future events is not, as a prediction, any less a factual issue. Indeed, the Supreme Court has acknowledged that drafting an antitrust decree by necessity "involves predictions and assumptions concerning future economic and business events." Ford Motor Co. v. United States, 405 U.S. 562, 578, 92 S.Ct. 1142 (1972). Trial courts are not excused from their obligation to resolve such matters through evidentiary hearings simply because they consider the bedrock procedures of our justice system to be "of little use."

* * *

Plaintiffs further argue—and the District Court held—that no evidentiary hearing was necessary given that Microsoft long had been on notice that structural relief was a distinct possibility. It is difficult to see why this matters. Whether Microsoft had advance notice that dissolution was in the works is immaterial to whether the District Court violated the company's procedural rights by ordering it without an evidentiary hearing. To be sure, "claimed surprise at the district court's decision to consider permanent injunctive relief does not, alone, merit reversal." But in this case, Microsoft's professed surprise does not stand "alone." There is something more: the company's basic procedural right to have disputed facts resolved through an evidentiary hearing.

* * *

D. Failure to Provide an Adequate Explanation

We vacate the District Court's remedies decree for the additional reason that the court has failed to provide an adequate explanation for the relief it ordered. The Supreme Court has explained that a remedies decree in an antitrust case must seek to "unfetter a market from anticompetitive conduct," Ford Motor Co., 405 U.S. at 577, 92 S.Ct. 1142, to "terminate the illegal monopoly, deny to the defendant the fruits of its statutory violation, and ensure that there remain no practices likely to result in monopolization in the future," United States v. United Shoe Mach. Corp., 391 U.S. 244, 250, 88 S.Ct. 1496 (1968); *see also* United States v. Grinnell Corp., 384 U.S. 563, 577, 86 S.Ct. 1698 (1966).

The District Court has not explained how its remedies decree would accomplish those objectives. Indeed, the court devoted a mere four paragraphs of its order to explaining its reasons for the remedy. They are: (1) Microsoft "does not yet concede that any of its business practices violated the Sherman Act"; (2) Microsoft "continues to do business as it has in the past"; (3) Microsoft "has proved untrustworthy in the past"; and (4) the Government, whose officials "are by reason of office obliged and expected to consider—and to act in—the public interest," won the case, "and for that reason alone have some entitlement to a remedy of their choice." Nowhere did the District Court discuss the objectives the Supreme Court deems relevant.

* * *

F. On Remand

As a general matter, a district court is afforded broad discretion to enter that relief it calculates will best remedy the conduct it has found to be unlawful. This is no less true in antitrust cases. *See, e.g.,* Ford Motor Co., 405 U.S. at 573, 92 S.Ct. 1142 ("The District Court is clothed with 'large discretion' to fit the decree to the special needs of the individual case."); Md. & Va. Milk Producers Ass'n, Inc. v. United States, 362 U.S. 458, 473, 80 S.Ct. 847 (1960) ("The formulation of decrees is largely left to the discretion of the trial court...."). And divestiture is a common form of relief in successful antitrust prosecutions: it is indeed "the most important of antitrust remedies." *See, e.g.,* United States v. E.I. du Pont de Nemours & Co., 366 U.S. 316, 331, 81 S.Ct. 1243 (1961).

On remand, the District Court must reconsider whether the use of the structural remedy of divestiture is appropriate with respect to Microsoft, which argues that it is a unitary company. By and large, cases upon which plaintiffs rely in arguing for the split of Microsoft have involved the dissolution of entities formed by mergers and acquisitions. On the contrary, the Supreme Court has clarified that divestiture "has traditionally been the remedy for Sherman Act violations whose heart is intercorporate *combination and control*," du Pont, 366 U.S. at 329, 81 S.Ct. 1243 (emphasis added), and that "[c]omplete divestiture is particularly appropriate where asset or stock *acquisitions* violate the antitrust laws," Ford Motor Co., 405 U.S. at 573, 92 S.Ct. 1142 (emphasis added).

One apparent reason why courts have not ordered the dissolution of unitary companies is logistical difficulty. As the court explained in United States v. ALCOA, 91 F.Supp. 333, 416 (S.D.N.Y.1950), a "corporation, designed to operate effectively as a single entity, cannot readily be dismembered of parts of its various operations without a marked loss of efficiency." A corporation that has expanded by acquiring its competitors often has preexisting internal lines of division along which it may more easily be split than a corporation that has expanded from natural growth. Although time and corporate modifications and developments may eventually fade those lines, at least the identifiable entities preexisted to create a template for such division as the court might later decree. With reference to those corporations that are not acquired by merger and acquisition, Judge Wyzanski accurately opined in *United Shoe*:

> United conducts all machine manufacture at one plant in Beverly, with one set of jigs and tools, one foundry, one laboratory for machinery problems, one managerial staff, and one labor force. It takes no Solomon to see that this organism cannot be cut into three equal and viable parts.

United States v. United Shoe Machinery Corp., 110 F.Supp. 295, 348 (D. Mass.1953).

Depending upon the evidence, the District Court may find in a remedies proceeding that it would be no easier to split Microsoft in two than United Shoe in three. Microsoft's Offer of Proof in response to the court's denial of an evidentiary hearing included proffered testimony from its President and CEO Steve Ballmer that the company "is, and always has been, a unified company without free-standing business units. Microsoft is not the result of mergers or acquisitions." Microsoft further offered evidence that it is "not organized along product lines," but rather is housed in a single corporate headquarters and that it has

> only one sales and marketing organization which is responsible for selling all of the company's products, one basic research organization, one product support organization, one operations department, one information technology department, one facilities department, one purchasing department, one human resources department, one finance department, one legal department and one public relations department.

If indeed Microsoft is a unitary company, division might very well require Microsoft to reproduce each of these departments in each new entity rather than simply allocate the differing departments among them.

In devising an appropriate remedy, the District Court also should consider whether plaintiffs have established a sufficient causal connection between Microsoft's anticompetitive conduct and its dominant position in the OS market. "Mere existence of an exclusionary act does not itself justify full feasible relief against the monopolist to create maximum competition." Rather, structural relief, which is "designed to eliminate the monopoly altogether ... require[s] a clearer indication of a *significant causal connection* between the conduct and creation or maintenance of the market power." Absent such causation, the antitrust defendant's unlawful behavior should be remedied by "an injunction against continuation of that conduct."

* * * [W]e have found a causal connection between Microsoft's exclusionary conduct and its continuing position in the operating systems market only through inference. Indeed, the District Court expressly did not adopt the position that Microsoft would have lost its position in the OS market but for its anticompetitive behavior. *Findings of Fact* § 411 ("There is insufficient evidence to find that, absent Microsoft's actions, Navigator and Java already would have ignited genuine competition in the market for Intel-compatible PC operating systems."). If the court on remand is unconvinced of the causal connection between Microsoft's exclusionary conduct and the company's position in the OS market, it may well conclude that divestiture is not an appropriate remedy.

While we do not undertake to dictate to the District Court the precise form that relief should take on remand, we note again that it should be tailored to fit the wrong creating the occasion for the remedy.

* * *

How should a court decide the scope of equitable remedies once an antitrust violation has been found? What should the scope of those remedies be? In *Microsoft*, the district court had ordered a combination of "behavioral" or "conduct" remedies, as well as "structural" remedies. What might lead a court to select one or the other, or, as the *Microsoft* court did, both? Why did the Court of Appeals conclude that an evidentiary hearing is required before an order of divestiture can be entered? Would the same reasoning require a hearing before *any* equitable remedy is entered?

Recall from Chapters 6 and 7, that before reaching its decision to remand the question of remedy, the D.C. Circuit affirmed in part, reversed in part, and remanded in part the district court's conclusion that Microsoft had violated Sections 1 and 2 of the Sherman Act. On remand the Antitrust Division, under leadership that had changed due to the Presidential election of 2000, quickly announced that it would neither pursue any of the remanded claims of liability, nor seek a break up of Microsoft. Thereafter, it and nine of the remaining 18 litigating states reached a settlement with Microsoft that involved a variety of conduct remedies, which would be imposed for five years. But the nine other states rejected the settlement as inadequate and asked the district court to proceed with the remand, urging broader conduct remedies.

Faced with an unprecedented situation, the district court divided the proceedings into two "tracks." Track 1 focused on the settlement, which as we will see in the next Sidebar required the court's approval. Track 2 proceeded to trial on the remanded question of remedy, in which the nine non-settling states sought to augment the agreement reached with Microsoft by the Department of Justice and joined in by the nine settling states. What challenges confronted the district court in working on two "tracks"? How might it be possible to enter a remedial decree pursuant to a settlement, yet to also order additional remedial steps in a second and independent judicial proceeding?

The district court ultimately approved the settlement of the case in the Tunney Act proceeding, and ordered little in the way of additional relief in the remedy trial pursued in the end solely by the State of Massachusetts. It also refused to grant intervention in the Tunney Act proceeding to two trade associations that sought to intervene solely for purposes of appealing the district court's approval of the settlement. The D.C. Circuit affirmed in almost all respects, reversing only the denial of intervention. On the merits it found no abuse of discretion by the district court, instead it praised its handling of the complex two track proceedings. *See Massachusetts v. Microsoft Corp.*, 373 F.3d 1199 (D.C. Cir. 2004).

In the following Sidebar, we further examine the court's role in approving federal settlements under the Tunney Act.

Sidebar 9–6:
Federal Settlements, the Tunney Act
and Statutory Preclusion
Under Section 5 of the Clayton Act

The Justice Department and the FTC rely extensively on consent decrees and orders to redress antitrust violations. These measures memorialize settlements of imminent or actual litigation between the government and the defendants. Typically, consent decrees are filed with the court along with a complaint, fully resolve the litigation, and are thereafter as enforceable as any other court or agency order. It should also be noted, however, that as compromises, consent decrees do not have precedential value and do not necessarily reflect the state of the law.

A special set of procedures applies to the settlement of litigation by the Antitrust Division of the Department of Justice. The Antitrust

Procedures and Penalties Act of 1974 (also known as the "Tunney Act") requires the Justice Department to give public notice of proposed settlements 60 days before the entry of a consent decree and to solicit public comments. The Department also must file a "competitive impact statement" with the court, which may enter the consent decree as a judgment only if it finds that the decree is in the "public interest." 15 U.S.C. § 16(a). FTC consent orders must be published in the Federal Register for sixty days to obtain public comments, but do not require judicial approval. 16 C.F.R. § 16.

The Tunney Act was drafted in response to the alleged use of political influence by the White House during the Nixon Administration to induce the settlement of an antitrust action by the Department of Justice. It functions in part as a "sunshine law" by requiring that government settlements be scrutinized on the public record. But by assigning the district court the role of evaluating whether the settlement is in the "public interest," a term the Act did not originally define, the Act also contemplates a more substantive review of proposed settlements. The Act's provisions were amended in 2004, in theory to permit a more searching review by the district court. See Title II, Subtitle B of Pub. L. No. 108–237, "Tunney Act Reform," codified at 15 U.S.C. §§ 16 (e)-(f). The amendments appeared to expand upon the definition of the district court's "public interest" charge, but have already been read narrowly by the first court to evaluate their import. See United States v. SBC Communications, Inc., 489 F. Supp. 2d 1 (D.D.C. 2007).

The court's mandated role in approving settlements under the Tunney Act, however, has given rise to some significant controversy over the years. That controversy has focused on the scope of the court's independent authority to evaluate such settlements and the degree of deference it owes to the Justice Department when a settlement is submitted for approval. Like any decision to settle a civil action, the government's decision to do so may turn on many factors, such as the perceived strength of the case, the likely outcome of trial, the resources it will take to pursue the case, budgetary constraints, enforcement priorities, and the perceived strength of the settlement.

That a district court might second guess the Department of Justice's evaluation of these factors—especially prior to the taking of any evidence and in the absence of any finding of illegality—could give rise to substantial separation of powers concerns. See United States v. AT & T Co., 552 F.Supp. 131 (D.D.C.1982), aff'd mem., Maryland v. United States, 460 U.S. 1001 (1983) (Rehnquist, J., dissenting from Court's per curiam approval of AT & T consent decree); United States v. Microsoft Corp., 56 F.3d 1448 (D.C. Cir.1995). Moreover, it is unclear what would in fact happen if a settlement was rejected—how could a court compel the Justice Department to continue prosecuting a case that it prefers to settle? On the other hand, it is clear from both the language and legislative history of the Tunney Act that Congress did not intend for the court to merely "rubber stamp" federal settlements. Id. at 1458.

On two occasions, government litigation with Microsoft produced important decisions interpreting the Tunney Act. In the mid–1990s the Department of Justice sought to resolve its first dispute with Microsoft with a consent decree, which was filed with the U.S. District Court in

Washington, D.C. In response to the filing, Judge Stanley Sporkin demanded extensive additional information from the parties on Microsoft's allegedly ongoing anticompetitive acts. He also sought to assess the government's internal decision-making process in reaching the settlement and ultimately rejected the decree as inadequate—only to be soundly reversed for abuse of discretion by the D.C. Circuit Court of Appeals. *United States v. Microsoft Corp.*, 56 F.3d 1448 (D.C. Cir.1995).

In the court's view, the district court had no authority to in effect conduct its own investigation of Microsoft's conduct, pursuant to which it implicitly and explicitly sought to expand the scope of the government's case. Moreover, it was error to inquire into the internal decision-making processes of the DOJ in the absence of evidence of bad faith or improper behavior. The scope of the relevant Tunney Act inquiry, the court held, is limited to an evaluation of the decree itself, not the actions or behavior of the Department. Finally, the court could not demand remedies based on violations that were not alleged by the government. *Id.* at 1459–60.

Even as it chastised Judge Sporkin, however, the D.C. Circuit instructed district courts applying the Tunney Act to "pay special attention" to the settlement's "clarity," to "pay close attention" to its compliance mechanisms, and to "inquire" into its "purpose, meaning, and efficacy." *Id.* at 1461–62. The appeals court further declared: "[i]f the decree is ambiguous, or the district judge can foresee difficulties in implementation, we would expect the court to insist that these matters are attended to." *Id.* It emphasized that "certainly, if third parties contend that they would be positively injured by the decree, a district judge might well hesitate before assuming that the decree is appropriate." *Id.*

Critics of probing Tunney Act review tend to emphasize the first portion of the D.C. Circuit's opinion, and have contended that the Tunney Act review process should be narrowly construed lest the federal courts invade the province of prosecutorial discretion, posing serious separation of powers problems under the Constitution. They also caution that any other approach may undermine defendants' incentives to reach settlements and hence the Justice Department's ability to secure them. Yet, without exception, the judicial decisions supporting a constrained view of the Act are confined to the most typical Tunney Act situation—settlement achieved before trial. Those same courts, including the D.C. Circuit in the first *Microsoft* proceeding, have made clear that the judge's authority to scrutinize the settlement is more extensive when it follows evidentiary proceedings. *Id.* at 1461. *See also United States v. AT & T*, 552 F.Supp. at 152. Nevertheless, in the second Microsoft proceeding, the court of appeals approved the district court's limited review and approval of the decree. *See Massachusetts v. Microsoft Corp.*, 373 F.3d 1199 (D.C. Cir. 2004) ("Microsoft II").

Another issue that has arisen in connection with consent decrees concerns their impact on subsequent private litigation. As we noted earlier in the Chapter, Section 5(a) of the Clayton Act permits private plaintiffs to use "a final judgment or decree * * * rendered in any civil or criminal proceeding brought by or on behalf of the United States under the antitrust laws" as "prima facie evidence" against the same defendant "as to all matters respecting which said judgment or decree would be an estoppel between" the parties to the original action. But the Act also includes the following proviso: "That this section shall not apply to consent judgments or decrees entered before any testimony has been taken."

If the language of the proviso is read literally, there can be no estoppel when the government reaches settlement with a defendant prior to trial, but there *will* be estoppel once evidence is taken, even though a final decision by the court has yet to be rendered. This makes the proviso a bit more expansive on its face than common law estoppel, which generally is only available once an issue has been "fully litigated," is "necessary to" a prior judgment, and has been "finally decided." What policy reasons might there be for Section 5's estoppel provisions? For its limiting proviso?

First, Section 5 creates an important incentive for follow-on private litigants by providing them with a valuable leg-up in their litigation. For the most part such plaintiffs need not shoulder the significant burden of reestablishing the defendant's antitrust violation. This decided advantage likely leads to more follow-on litigation than might otherwise be the case—and provides a significant tool of deterrence. Of course, it also affects the litigation strategy of the defendant faced with civil or criminal prosecution by the DOJ. By limiting the preclusive effects of the Act prior to the taking of evidence, and giving full preclusive effect after evidence is taken, it provides a powerful incentive for such defendants to settle before any evidence is taken. By doing so, the defendant disarms the would-be future follow-on suit by forcing future private plaintiffs likely to be seeking treble damages to have to fully litigate and prove liability.

What then should be the effect of a consent judgment entered *after* evidence has been taken, or even after a trial on the merits has concluded, as was the case in *Microsoft II*? One would assume that to preserve the statute's balance of incentives, the answer would be that it has full preclusive effects, but the courts have demonstrated surprising flexibility on the issue.

One solution to the problems posed under Section 5 and the common law has been for settling parties to condition their settlements on the district court's agreement to withdraw any findings it has made and expressly to indicate that no conclusion as to liability under the antitrust laws was reached by the court. Some courts have generally endorsed the practice, even when settlement comes after the hearing of evidence. In such circumstances, the court has taken the position that the parties and the district court should be given significant leeway in stating their intentions with respect to the predictable consequences of settlement, lest settlement be discouraged. *See, e.g., S. Pac. Commc'n Co. v. AT & T Co.,* 740 F.2d 1011, 1020–22 (D.C. Cir.1984); *United States v. Nat'l Ass'n of Broadcasters,* 553 F.Supp. 621, 623 (D.D.C.1982).

As noted above, at least in the case of the first district court to interpret them, the 2004 amendments to the Act do not appear to have fundamentally altered the scope of Tunney Act review. It remains to be seen whether other courts might interpret the language of the 2004 amendments more broadly. Any court doing so, however, will have to confront the fundamental structural challenge of Tunney Act review: how can a district court in effect order the Justice Department to continue litigating when it has decided to settle a prosecution.

3. THE PRIVATE TREBLE DAMAGES REMEDY

Incorporated in Section 7 of the original Sherman Act, today's private right of action is contained in Section 4 of the Clayton Act, 15 U.S.C. § 15, which provides:

> * * * [A]ny person who shall be injured in his business or property by reason of anything forbidden in the antitrust laws may sue therefor in any district court of the United States ... and shall recover threefold the damages by him sustained, and the cost of suit, including a reasonable attorney's fee.

In this section of the Chapter we consider several aspects of the private treble damage remedy. First, we briefly survey the policy arguments for and against maintaining the treble damage remedy. Second, we will look at the practical evidentiary question of how a party goes about proving its actual damages, a prerequisite to recovery of treble damages.

a. Why "Treble" Damages?

Much of the debate concerning the private right of action has focused on its authorization of "treble damages." Whereas it is relatively easier to argue in favor of some kind of private right of action that permits recovery of actual damages sustained, it is more challenging to ask "why treble damages"? Indeed, early versions of the Sherman Act proposed only double damages. According to an ABA Antitrust Section survey, the traditional justifications most often cited by the Supreme Court include:

- to provide private relief or compensation;
- to encourage private enforcement of the antitrust laws;
- to deter violations;
- to deprive antitrust violators of the fruits of their illegal acts; and
- to punish violators.

See ABA Antitrust Section, Monograph No. 13, Treble–Damages Remedy 16–21 (1986)("Treble Damages Monograph"). Clearly an assumption was made in 1890 and since that authorizing recovery of mere actual damages would be inadequate to achieve these basic goals. For additional comprehensive studies, see William Breit & Kenneth G. Elzinga, Antitrust Penalty Reform: An Economic Analysis (1986); Lawrence J. White, ed., Private Antitrust Litigation: New Evidence, New Learning (1988)(hereafter "Georgetown Study").

As with many of the other issues we have studied in this Chapter, debates over the wisdom and efficacy of the treble damage remedy often turn on perceptions about the relative tendency of antitrust prohibitions to under or over-deter anticompetitive conduct. Critics argue that the possibility of treble damages unduly encourages parties and their counsel to initiate and pursue civil antitrust actions, and might lead defendants to settle less than fully meritorious cases for fear of treble damage exposure. These arguments have intensified due to the increase in multi-jurisdictional federal and state anti-trust litigation owing to *Illinois Brick* and *ARC America* (Sidebar 9–5, Casebook, *supra*), with some critics asserting that, more than ever, defendants face the prospect of duplicative recoveries owing to the "windfall" gains sought by plaintiffs, themselves spurred on by an active class action bar.

In response to these criticisms, there have been a number of legislative proposals over the years to alter the current scheme. These proposals fall in to three categories: (1) de-treble damages, (2) make treble damages discretionary with the court instead of mandatory; and (3) limit the availability of treble damages to the most severe antitrust violations. *See* ABA TREBLE DAMAGES MONOGRAPH, at 50–65. By and large, these proposals for reform have been unsuccessful, although some statutory exceptions have even been created that limit recovery to actual damages for conduct that has been reviewed and approved by government agencies. *See, e.g.,* 15 U.S.C. § 4016(a)(a) (Export Trading Company Act of 1982, § 306); 15 U.S.C. § 4303 (National Cooperative Research and Production Act of 1993, § 4).

On the other hand, defenders of the treble damage remedy point out that today it is more difficult than ever to prove an antitrust violation. Owing to changes in antitrust rules that have elevated burdens of proof, as well as judicially imposed restrictions on the scope of the private remedy, such as those reflected in *Brunswick*, *Illinois Brick* and *Associated General*, the threat of over-deterrence has been minimized. In part due to these changes, the cost of pursuing antitrust litigation similarly has exploded. Hence, they argue, the greater danger today is under-deterrence: antitrust violations will go unde-tected, unprosecuted and/or unpunished. Treble damages, in their view, remain critical precisely because they provide an incentive for plaintiffs to sue and because they serve to deter serious antitrust violations. Indeed, they point to cases such as *ADM* (Lysine) and *Vitamins*, which we studied in Chapter 1, as evidence that even treble damages and the threat of fines and prison remain insufficient in some cases to deter the most profitable and egregious of antitrust violations.

Our next Sidebar evaluates the economic foundations of this long-running debate.

Sidebar 9–7:
The Economics of Penalties

How large should antitrust law set the penalty for a violation? Are penalties systematically too low—no more than "slaps on the wrist"—leading firms to ignore the antitrust laws? Can penalties be too high? Economists have studied questions like this under the twin assumptions that the primary purpose of antitrust sanctions is deterrence* and that the goal of antitrust is economic efficiency (aggregate wealth maximiza-tion). *This Sidebar sketches how economists think about antitrust penal-ties and the incentive effects of the private treble damages system.*

---

* This assumption rules out other goals of antitrust penalties that may be important in practice, including punishment to wrongdoers, compensation to victims, and the creation of incentives for private parties to bring suit to vindicate the antitrust laws. Some effects of private damages on those other goals are dis-cussed in passing in this Sidebar, however.

Net Harm to Others: An Example

An example will help clarify the economic issues. Suppose that the antitrust violation involves horizontal market division, and the only available remedy involves a fine payable by the violators to the government treasury. How large should that fine be?

To make the problem concrete, refer to Figure 9–4 (which is modeled on Figure 5–1). In the particular example set forth in Figure 9–4, the violation leads to an industry-wide price increase (from P^0 to P^1) and a reduction in industry output (from Q^0 to Q^1). The transfer from buyers to sellers resulting from the violation is 1000. The allocative efficiency loss is 400 and has two parts, because the foregone gains from trade that the market would have achieved had the firms not exercised market power would have been shared by sellers and buyers. In particular, sellers lost the lower rectangle (300 in the example) and buyers lost the upper triangle (100 in the example). The violation leads to production cost savings of 50 (perhaps arising because the firms adopted a territorial market allocation scheme that kept the transportation costs of serving customers low).

Figure 9–4:
The Economics of Penalties: Numerical Example

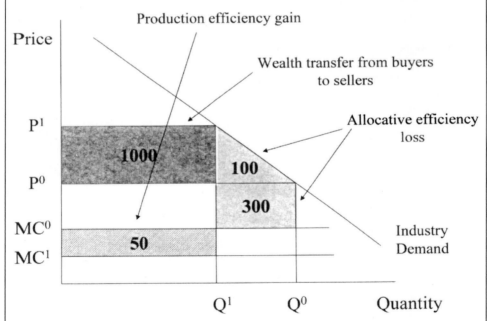

If detection and conviction were certain, the remedial rule that leads to economically efficient outcomes would require that the sellers, as a group, pay 1100: the sum of the transfer from buyers (here 1000) and that portion of the allocative efficiency loss that would have benefitted buyers in the absence of the violation (100). If sellers must give up as a remedy for an antitrust violation an amount equal to the harm they cause others—the transfer plus the portion of the allocative efficiency loss that would have gone to buyers—then the sellers will only go ahead with conduct if that conduct is efficient. Here's why. Absent antitrust enforcement, sellers would be expected to go ahead with their conduct (here the market division arrangement) because it would be profitable to them as a group.** They would benefit from the transfer from buyers (1000) plus the production cost savings (50), less the portion of the allocative efficiency loss that would have gone to sellers (300), for a net profit of 750. Take away the transfer and the portion of the allocative efficiency loss that would have gone to buyers, and sellers would profit if and only if the production cost savings exceeds the collective allocative efficiency loss—that is, if and only if there are efficiency gains to society as a whole from the conduct.

The generalization that can be taken from this example is that the efficient fine for an antitrust violation equals the net harm that the violation causes others (here the transfer plus the allocative efficiency loss to buyers), as that rule will lead prospective violators to consider the welfare of others as well as their own welfare, and take only those actions that are beneficial to society as a whole. The "net harm to others" formulation comes from William Landes, *Optimal Sanctions for Antitrust Violations,* 50 U. CHI. L. REV. 652 (1983), and the approach is implicit in the pioneering economic analysis of legal sanctions in Gary Becker, *Crime and Punishment: An Economic Approach,* 76 J. POL. ECON. 169 (1968).

Why wouldn't the efficient sanction instead set the fine at the profit to sellers (here 750)? A sanction based on disgorgement of seller profits (rather than the net harm to others) would have the virtue of making all violations unprofitable, and thus deterring them. But from an economic efficiency point of view, such a rule goes too far in principle: it deters alike inefficient conduct and efficient conduct (that nevertheless happens to violate an imperfectly-specified legal rule), because it treats the production cost savings (which add to seller profits) as bad, not good.*** *See* A. Mitchell Polinsky & Steven Shavell, *Should Liability Be Based on the Harm to the Victim or the Gain to the Injurer?*, 10 J. L. ECON. & ORG. 427 (1994) (providing general analysis, not focused specifically on antitrust).

Overdeterrence and Underdeterrence

If the rule for determining sanctions for lawbreaking generally leads violators to pay less than the net harm to others, the legal system is said to "underdeter" violations: the harm to society from the violations of law exceeds the cost of preventing them. With underdeterrence, firms will not invest sufficient resources to ensure antitrust compliance, for example.

** This discussion assumes that so long as the arrangement is profitable for the sellers as a group, they can devise a mechanism for sharing the profits among themselves so that each member of the arrangement benefits individually.

*** In the example, suppose that production cost savings were 500 rather than 50. Then the profit from the market division scheme would be 1200 (1000 transfer + 500 cost savings − 300 sellers' share of allocative efficiency loss). A sanction based on seller profits would fine sellers 1200, deterring the practice. But the sanction based on net harm to others (still 1100) would be less than the profit to sellers, so the practice would not be deterred under the efficient sanctions rules—as is appropriate, given a focus on efficiency, since the production cost savings (500) exceeds the total allocative efficiency loss (400). As this example makes clear, the choice of a rule for determining sanctions for violations is tied up with views as to the purposes of antitrust law (economic efficiency or something else?) and the purposes of remedies (deterrence or something else?).

On the other hand, if the rule for determining sanctions imposes a penalty in excess of the efficient remedial rule, more lawbreaking will be prevented, but "overdeterrence" will result. Firms will be led to spend more to stamp out the last violations than those violations cost society (in terms of efficiency). Compliance programs may become so onerous, or executives may become so cautious, that firms will stay away from socially beneficial conduct close to the line of illegality, for fear that they will be found to violate the law and forced to pay a large penalty even though their conduct generates only a small reduction in aggregate social wealth.

For practices that would be challenged as civil violations, and particularly those that would be analyzed under the rule of reason, overdeterrence is likely as serious a concern as underdeterrence. But for criminal violations—naked price-fixing, bid-rigging or market division among rivals—the threat of overdeterrence appears less troublesome, at least as the antitrust laws are enforced today. There is no serious evidence, for example, that firms are limiting joint venture formation or legitimate trade association activity for fear of being charged with price-fixing.

Concealment and the Damage Multiple

Many antitrust violators seek to hide their actions from their victims and the government, finders of fact do not always see all the evidence, and courts do not always reach the correct conclusions from the evidence in the record. For reasons like these, it is by no means certain that antitrust violations will be detected and successfully prosecuted. If a seller thinks that its unlawful actions have only one chance in three of detection and conviction, it will treat the remedy of 1100 as if it were only one third that size (about 367).[****] In order to make sellers act as though the sanction for violation would be 1100 under such circumstances, the penalty must be multiplied by the inverse of what sellers, thinking about whether to violate the law, would consider the likelihood of eventual detection and judicial enforcement. In this example, with the probability of enforcement 1/3, the penalty would need to be multiplied by 3 (the inverse of 1/3), leading to an efficient sanction of 3300. More generally, *under the efficient sanction, the "net harm to others" would be the penalty base, and the full penalty would multiply that base by a multiple set at the inverse of the violator's subjective probability of detection and conviction, as the violator would have evaluated its chances at the time it engaged in the unlawful practices.*

Private Damages: Ideal vs. Reality

The structure of the efficient sanction bears a family resemblance to the private damages remedy in force today. The current remedy begins with a penalty base related to the injury to victims (the overcharge if the victims are buyers, or lost profits if the victims are excluded rivals). A successful private plaintiff recovers triple the penalty base—this is the familiar "treble damages" remedy in private antitrust litigation. *See generally* Steven C. Salop & Lawrence J. White, *Economic Analysis of Private Antitrust Litigation*, 74 Geo. L. J. 1001 (1986) (reporting on

---

[****] This statement assumes that the seller is "risk-neutral:" it would not pay an insurance premium to reduce risks on the one hand, and would not pay to take gambles on the other hand.

empirical study of private antitrust litigation). How does this remedy compare with the efficient sanction suggested by economic theory?

There are many points of difference between the two, some suggesting that the private treble damages remedy is too high, others suggesting it is too low, and still others suggesting it is not set at the efficient level in any case but not clearly too high or too low on average. *See generally* William Breit & Kenneth G. Elzinga, *Private Antitrust Enforcement: The New Learning*, 28 J. L. Econ. 405 (1985).

Too low. The penalty base (and thus the private penalty as a whole) is too low in principle because it only counts the direct injury to the victim (the overcharge if the victim is a buyer) and ignores the portion of the allocative efficiency loss that would have gone to buyers absent the violation. It is also too low because antitrust law systematically understates the penalty base relative to the underlying economic concept by not awarding plaintiffs prejudgment interest and by cutting off recovery of damages for older violations through application of the statute of limitations. Robert H. Lande, *Are Antitrust "Treble" Damages Really Single Damages?*, 54 Ohio St. L.J. 115 (1983).

Moreover, damages may be too low to the extent that some victims, injured by the violation, do not recover—for example, because their lawsuit is deterred by the transactions costs of going to court, by risk aversion, by restrictions on the ability of indirect purchasers to recover damages, or by limitations on the extraterritorial jurisdiction of the U.S. antitrust laws. In addition, the deterrent effects of private damages actions will be reduced to the extent the victims were aware that they may have been dealing with a cartel or other antitrust violator when they were charged a high price by it, and thus knew they might someday blow the whistle on the violator by filing a private lawsuit for damages. When both victim and violator are aware that the victim may sue for damages in the future, the market price will rise to counteract the later damages in an expected sense. If the violator and victim contract around the private treble damages system in this way, the private remedy does not deter violations, no matter how high the multiple. Jonathan B. Baker, *Private Information and the Deterrent Effect of Antitrust Damages Remedies*, 4 J. L. Econ. & Org. 385 (1988); Stephen Salant, *Treble Damage Awards in Private Litigation for Price Fixing*, 95 J. Pol. Econ. 1326 (1987); Daniel F. Spulber, Regulation and Markets § 19.4 (1989).

Too high. Private damages may be too high to the extent that the antitrust violator is subject to other penalties that also provide deterrence. Here the relevant question is not whether any individual sanction is efficient, but whether the collection of penalties, as a group, provides deterrence. Those other penalties can include fines or jail time for executives in a related Justice Department criminal prosecution, disgorgement in a related FTC case, damages in a related case under state law, and injunctive relief in civil cases brought by the DOJ, the FTC or states that raises the costs of doing business. If penalties in any one proceeding are set without consideration of the deterrent consequences of relief in earlier or simultaneous proceedings, they may, in aggregate, end up too high. Moreover, penalties may be too high if, absent proper application of the antitrust injury doctrine, plaintiffs are permitted to recover for harms that are not causally related to the efficiency loss from the violation. *See, e.g.*, William H. Page, *Antitrust Damages and Economic Efficiency: An Approach to Antitrust Injury*, 47 U. Chi. L. Rev. 467 (1980); Phillip Areeda, *Antitrust Violations Without Damage Recoveries*, 89 Harv. L. Rev. 1127 (1976).

Also, some suggest that the private treble damages award leads to excessive litigation, because plaintiffs, attracted by the prospect of a recovery substantially in excess of their injury, do not consider the costs to the judicial system in deciding whether to bring their case. Proposals for "decoupling" the violator's payment from the victim's recovery—splitting the payment between the victim and the government—make clear that the penalty level that best deters violations does not necessarily provide the most appropriate incentive for private antitrust enforcement or the most appropriate level of compensation for victims. *See* A. Mitchell Polinsky, *Detrebling Versus Decoupling Antitrust Damages: Lessons from the Theory of Enforcement*, 74 Geo. L. J. 1231 (1986) (asserting that the same level of deterrence could be achieved at lower social cost by raising the amount paid by the defendant while lowering the amount received by the plaintiff, with the government receiving the difference).

Not correct in individual cases. The economic approach to penalties suggests that the damage multiple in every case should equal the inverse of the violator's subjective probability of detection and conviction, measured as of the time the violator chose to engage in the unlawful practices. Assuming the penalty base were not too high or too low, this means that a multiple of three (treble damages) is correct in every case only if every violator expects that it has one chance in three of eventually being forced to pay damages. Detection and conviction are indeed uncertain, but there is no reason to think that the probability is one in three in every case. In particular, some antitrust violators, like the participants in the lysine and vitamins cartels, take steps to conceal their unlawful conduct from detection, while other violations, including many forms of exclusionary conduct, are not hidden from view. It is possible, therefore, that antitrust law deters (even overdeters) those violations that are the easiest to detect and prosecute, without adequately deterring highly concealed violations. One could imagine a system in which a rough triage is employed to address this possibility: assign a private damages multiple of three in most cases but double the multiple to six if the violators aggressively concealed their conduct and halve it to 1.5 if the violation was particularly open and easy to detect.

Conclusion

The economic approach to penalties provides a way to think about the general level of sanctions for antitrust violations, not a mathematical formula for determining damages in any particular case. Note, too, that the economic approach suggests that the effects of the system of penalties cannot be understood in a vacuum. If government enforcers devote fewer resources to investigating antitrust violations or changes in substantive law reduce the ability of certain classes of plaintiffs to challenge violations, those acts will reduce the likelihood that any particular violator will be detected and convicted. Unless the damages multiple is increased under such circumstances, the level of deterrence will be reduced. In this regard it is interesting to note that over the past thirty years, the courts have restricted the access of certain plaintiffs to the courts (for example through the antitrust injury and indirect purchaser doctrines) while Congress has simultaneously increased the penalties for criminal antitrust violations.

Finally, the relationship between penalties and deterrence also can be affected by legal rules respecting the scope of liability. *See generally* William H. Page, *The Scope of Liability for Antitrust Violations*, 37 STAN. L. REV. 1445 (1985) (scope of liability must be integrated with measurement of damages to achieve the efficient sanction). For example, in *Texas Indus., Inc. v. Radcliff Materials, Inc.*, 451 U.S. 630 (1981), the Supreme Court held that co-conspirators are jointly and severally liable for the entire amount of damages attributable to a conspiracy. In the case of a price-fixing cartel, therefore, each co-conspirator is in theory liable for three times the entire amount of the overcharges attributable to the conspiracy. No right of contribution exists, therefore, whereby one defendant found liable can implead its alleged co-conspirators to collect their share of the damages done. How might this rule affect deterrence under the economic models discussed in this Sidebar?

Note on Disgorgement and the Mylan Litigation

Note that one of the penalties discussed in Sidebar 9–7 is the option of "disgorgement"—requiring as a penalty that the antitrust violator pay over to the government or private parties the ill-gotten gains attributable to its violation, sometimes referred to as the "fruits" of its violation. In a price fixing or monopolization case, those gains might be measured by the additional profits the firm was able to obtain through its anticompetitive conduct.

As noted in the Sidebar, the economic rationale for disgorgement, sometimes also referred to as "restitution," is straight-forward—by extracting the fruits of the unlawful conduct the economic incentive to engage in the conduct in the first place is neutralized, and hence may function as a useful deterrent. That assumes, however, that detection efforts are successful. If a firm discounts the likelihood of disgorgement due to its belief that its illegal conduct will not be detected, the mere possibility that it might lose its ill-gotten gains alone will not deter the conduct. Indeed, if disgorgement were the only remedy, unlawful conduct might be encouraged on the theory that the "worst case" means only giving back the gains.

The legal basis for seeking disgorgement, however, is less clear than the economic. In authorizing suits for damages, Section 4 of the Clayton Act focuses on the harm of the illegal conduct to its victims, typically yielding claims of overcharges from consumers in cases of collusion or monopolization, and claims of lost profits from the prey in exclusionary effects cases. It does not focus on the benefits of the violation to the violator. But what about public enforcement authorities?

In late 1998, the FTC sought to extend its injunctive powers to cover disgorgement in a highly visible case involving the generic prescription drug manufacturer Mylan Laboratories. As a generic drug manufacturer, Mylan typically licensed the information necessary to produce a drug from a specialty chemical manufacturer. In this instance, Mylan had entered into a 10–year exclusive licensing arrangement with the chemical manufacturers of the active pharmaceutical ingredients for two popular prescription drugs, lorazepam and clorazepate.

According to the complaints in the case, Mylan thereafter raised its prices on one of the drugs by between 1,900 and 3200%. On the other, it raised prices 1,900 to 19,000 %.

In a typical FTC proceeding, the FTC would seek to secure an order to "cease and desist" pursuant to its authority to secure "temporary restraining orders" and "preliminary injunctions" under Section 13(b) of the FTC Act, 15 U.S.C. § 53(b). The FTC argued in *Mylan* that its authority permitted it to seek permanent injunctions rescinding the licensing agreements and preventing them from being reinstated, and, as an additional equitable remedy, disgorgement of $120 million in alleged ill-gotten profits. Although the ultimate deterrent value of disgorgement can be debated, compared to a mere order to cease and desist it was clearly a more formidable tool of enforcement.

Three significant issues related to disgorgement arose in the course of the litigation: (1) whether the FTC had the authority under § 13 (b) to seek disgorgement of profits attributable to an antitrust violation; (2) whether the states that had joined in the case pursuing claims under Sections 1 and 2 of the Sherman Act also could seek disgorgement via Section 16 of the Clayton Act; and (3) whether private plaintiffs could pursue treble damages even after the FTC had secured a settlement that included disgorgement. In a series of opinions, the court answered all three of these questions in the affirmative.

Noting that five other circuit courts of appeals had read the FTC Act's grant of equitable authority as sufficient to permit the FTC to pursue monetary relief, the district court denied Mylan's motion to dismiss the disgorgement claims. *See FTC v. Mylan Labs., Inc.*, 62 F. Supp. 2d 25 (D.D.C. 1999). The court concluded that the power to seek monetary relief was consistent with the broad remedial purposes of Section 5 of the FTC Act, pursuant to which the FTC should be permitted to seek "complete relief" against violations. *Id.* at 36–37. The second question proved more challenging. Although the court initially concluded that the states could not seek disgorgement under Section 16 of the Clayton Act, *id.* at 40–42, it later modified that judgment to recognize the states' right to do so under state laws that referenced or were modeled after the FTC Act. *See FTC v. Mylan Labs., Inc.*, 99 F. Supp. 2d 1 (D.D.C. 1999).

The case brought by the FTC and the states was quickly followed by a number of private treble damage class actions initiated by, among others, health care providers and hospitals who were direct purchasers of lorazepam and clorazepate. The cases were transferred and consolidated by the Judicial Panel on Multidistrict Litigation pursuant to the procedures of 28 U.S.C. § 1407. Mylan then moved to dismiss the actions on the ground that the plaintiffs "lacked standing" to pursue their damage claims given the FTC's recovery of disgorged profits through its settlement with Mylan (which followed the district court's ruling that the Commission had the authority to seek disgorgement). *See In re Lorazepam & Clorazepate Antitrust Litigation*, 202 F.R.D. 12 (D.D.C.2001); *see also In re Lorazepam & Clorazepate Antitrust Litigation*, 289 F.3d 98 (D.C. Cir. 2002) (declining interlocutory review of district court's decision to certify class action).

Mylan argued that the rationale of *Illinois Brick* should control, even though the plaintiffs were direct, not indirect purchasers. It urged the court to embrace an "Ultimate Purchase Rule," which, consistent with *Illinois Brick* would only recognize the right to recover damages of a single class of persons—here represented by the FTC. Any further recovery, it urged, would be duplicative. While noting that the defendants' arguments were "creative," the court nevertheless rejected them. Distinguishing *Illinois Brick*, it declined to endorse any general rule of "exclusive standing" based on the policies that animated *Illinois Brick*. Whereas *Illinois Brick* raised the question of how damages could be apportioned among two competing sets of plaintiffs seeking recovery under the same statute— Section 4 of the Clayton Act—in *Mylan* the FTC proceeded under a "wholly separate cause of action," namely Section 13(b) of the FTC Act. In further support of its position, the court cited *ARC America*, where, in rejecting the argument that state indirect purchaser statutes were preempted by *Illinois Brick*, the Supreme Court implicitly endorsed the view that complementary remedial schemes directed at the same or similar conduct can coexist without damaging the overall remedial goals of the antitrust laws (*see* Sidebar 9–5, *supra*.)

The FTC's victory in *Mylan* was deemed significant, solidifying its power to seek monetary relief and introducing the threat of disgorgement into its arsenal of remedial tools. But do you agree with all of the district court's rulings? Might they result in over-deterrence, authorizing as they do disgorgement by the FTC and the states, as well as treble damages by private direct purchasers? Or is it arguable that multiple threats are necessary to achieve adequate deterrence given the challenges of detection and the possibility that potential wrong doers will discount the likelihood of being discovered?

To clarify its enforcement intentions in light of its victory in *Mylan*, the FTC in 2003 issued a policy statement on the use of monetary equitable remedies in antitrust cases. *See* http://www.ftc.gov/os/2003/07/disgorgementfrn.htm. The Policy Statement explained that the agency would consider three factors in deciding whether to seek disgorgement or restitution: (1) whether the underlying violation is clear, (2) whether there is a reasonable basis for calculating the amount of the remedial payment, and (3) the value that the Commission would contribute to effective enforcement by pursuing monetary equitable relief in light of other likely remedies, including remedies in private actions and criminal proceedings. How, if at all, do these conditions reflect the economic theory of penalties discussed in Sidebar 9–7? Responding to concerns raised during the public comment period that preceded the issuance of the policy statement, the Commission said it remains sensitive to potential duplicative recoveries by injured persons or the possibility that defendants might be required to make excessive multiple payments for the same injury.

b. Calculating Antitrust Damages

To justify an award of antitrust damages, a party must overcome several distinct hurdles. First, and most obvious, it must establish an antitrust violation. Second, it must establish the "fact of injury," *i.e.*, that the conduct of the defendant that violated the antitrust laws was the proximate cause of an actual injury to its "business or property." " '[W]here the plaintiff proves a loss, and a violation by defendant of the antitrust laws of such nature as to be likely to cause that type of loss * * * the jury, as the trier of facts, must be permitted to draw from this circumstantial evidence the inference that the necessary causal relation exists.' " *Continental Ore Co. v. Union Carbide and Carbon Corp.*, 370 U.S. 690, 697 (1962). *See also Bigelow v. RKO Radio Pictures*, 327 U.S. 251, 264 (1946). Third, it must establish the amount of its antitrust damages—*i.e.*, the fact of injury alone is distinct from the amount of damages. Accommodating the current complexity of these issues is an important factor in successfully managing treble damage litigation.

All three requirements are evident in the following case excerpt from the Supreme Court's opinion in *J. Truett Payne*.

J. TRUETT PAYNE CO. v. CHRYSLER MOTORS CORP.

United States Supreme Court, 1981.
451 U.S. 557, 101 S.Ct. 1923, 68 L.Ed.2d 442.

[The Court began by noting that the mere fact that a violation of the antitrust laws has occurred does not mean that a private party seeking redress under Section 4 of the Clayton Act has suffered compensable "injury." Quoting *Brunswick Corp. v. Pueblo Bowl–O–Mat, Inc.*, 429 U.S. 477 (1977), the Court reiterated that " 'to recover damages [under § 4] respondents must prove more than that the petitioner violated [a provision of the federal antitrust laws] * * *, since such proof establishes only that injury may result.' " In the excerpt that follows, we will see how the Court integrated the traditional framework for proving fact of injury with the antitrust injury concept from *Brunswick*. Eds.]

II

* * *

Petitioner nevertheless asks us to consider the sufficiency of its evidence in light of our traditional rule excusing antitrust plaintiffs from an unduly rigorous standard of proving antitrust injury. In *Zenith Radio Corp. v. Hazeltine Research, Inc.*, 395 U.S. 100, 123–124, 89 S.Ct. 1562, 1576, 23 L.Ed.2d 129 (1969), for example, the Court discussed at some length the fixing of damages in a case involving market exclusion. We accepted the proposition that damages could be awarded on the basis of plaintiff's estimate of sales it could have made absent the violation:

"[D]amage issues in these cases are rarely susceptible of the kind of concrete, detailed proof of injury which is available in other contexts. The Court has repeatedly held that in the absence of more precise proof, the factfinder may 'conclude as a matter of just and reasonable inference from the proof of defendants' wrongful acts and their tendency to injure plaintiffs' business, and from the evidence of the decline in prices, profits and values, not shown to be attributable to other causes, that defendants' wrongful acts had caused damage to the plaintiffs.' *Bigelow v. RKO Pictures, Inc., supra* [327 U.S.], at 264 [66 S.Ct., at 579]. *See also Eastman Kodak Co. v. S. Photo Materials Co.*, 273 U.S. 359, 377–379 [47 S.Ct. 400, 404, 405, 71 L.Ed. 684] (1927); *Story Parchment Co. v. Paterson Parchment Paper Co.*, 282 U.S. 555, 561–566, 51 S.Ct. 248, 250, 75 L.Ed. 544 (1931)." Ibid.

In *Bigelow v. RKO Radio Pictures, Inc.*, 327 U.S. 251, 66 S.Ct. 574, 90 L.Ed. 652 (1946), relied on in *Zenith*, film distributors had conspired to deny the plaintiff theater access to first-run films. The jury awarded damages based on a comparison of plaintiff's actual profits with the contemporaneous profits of a competing theater with access to first-run films. Plaintiff had also adduced evidence comparing his actual profits during the conspiracy with his profits when he had been able to obtain first-runs. The lower court thought the evidence too imprecise to support the award, but we reversed because the evidence was sufficient to support a "just and reasonable inference" of damage. We explained:

"Any other rule would enable the wrongdoer to profit by his wrong-doing at the expense of his victim. It would be an inducement to make wrongdoing so effective and complete in every case as to preclude any recovery, by rendering the measure of damages uncertain. Failure to apply it would mean that the more grievous the wrong done, the less likelihood there would be of a recovery." 327 U.S., at 264–265, 66 S.Ct., at 580.

Our willingness to accept a degree of uncertainty in these cases rests in part on the difficulty of ascertaining business damages as compared, for example, to damages resulting from a personal injury or from condemnation of a parcel of land. The vagaries of the marketplace usually deny us sure knowledge of what plaintiff's situation would have been in the absence of the defendant's antitrust violation. But our willingness also rests on the principle articulated in cases such a *Bigelow*, that it does not " 'come with very good grace' " for the wrongdoer to insist upon specific and certain proof of the injury which it has itself inflicted.

* * *

———————

If all issues of directness and proximity have been resolved in the plaintiff's favor, there remains the question of how to measure damages. To provide a basis for quantifying harm, the plaintiff must attempt to demonstrate how it would have fared, and if it is a business, what profits it might have gained, were it not for the defendant's misconduct.

Although the traditional case law, reflected in *J. Truett Payne*, established the general principle that once liability is found the standards of proof on damages should not be rigorous, that traditional leniency may be on the wane. More recently, plaintiffs have faced increasingly skeptical courts in presenting their cases for damages. As we observed in Chapter 8 with respect to the economic issues associated with liability, likewise it is true today that plaintiffs almost always turn to expert economic testimony to improve the odds of recovery, which in turn can trigger *Daubert* challenges. *Contrast Concord Boat Corp. v. Brunswick Corp.*, 207 F.3d 1039 (8th Cir.2000) (excluding damages expert's testimony) *with New York v. Julius Nasso Concrete Corp.*, 202 F.3d 82, 88 (2d Cir.2000) (citing *Zenith* in support of its decision reversing district court's exclusion of plaintiff's proposed expert testimony on antitrust damages).

Here, too, the traditional legal framework is important to consider. In the past, courts generally accepted two principal models of antitrust damages: "before and after" and "yardstick." Note how these approaches are reflected in the quotation from *Zenith* in the Court's opinion in *J. Truett Payne*. "Before and after" models could be used in price fixing and other kinds of consumer damage cases, and by injured, although not destroyed, prey in cases of exclusionary conduct. In price fixing cases, "before and after models" seek to compare prices in the non-conspiracy period to prices in the conspiracy period and use the difference as a baseline approximation of overcharges. In cases of exclusionary conduct, in which the prey continued in business, the method could be used to focus on the prey's profitability before and after the alleged predatory conduct. Assuming that the diminution in profits in the period of unlawful conduct could be causally linked to the anti-competitive conduct, it too could produce an approximation of damages.

"Yardstick" models are based on a comparison of the firm or firms most directly involved in or affected by anticompetitive conduct with firms that are not, and can be used in cases of collusive or exclusionary conduct. In cases alleging collusive effects, the "yardstick" method compares the market subject to restraint with another market that is not—the "yardstick" market. A yardstick can also be used in an exclusionary effects case to compare the success of the target of predation against a comparable firm not faced with predation, or with some portion of the same firm in a distinct geographic or product market. In each circumstance, the goal of a yardstick is to seek to evaluate the damages attributable to the anticompetitive conduct by comparing the performance of the firm affected by the conduct with firms that are not. The yardstick method also can be used to establish a "going concern" value for a business that has been totally excluded.

Figure 9–5:
Typical Measures of Damages in Private Antitrust Cases

Collusive Anticompetitive Effects	Exclusionary Anticompetitive Effects	Methodologies for Proving
• overcharges	• lost profits • going concern value	• before-and-after • yardstick • regression • other statistical or econometric means

While these basic models in large part continue to influence damages evidence in antitrust cases, newer, more sophisticated, and more case-specific econometric models and regression analyses are also being employed. Often, however, even those new models are influenced by the traditional methods, as we shall see in our next case.

Conwood Co. v. United States Tobacco Co., 290 F.3d 768 (6th Cir.2002) illustrates what is at stake when a court seeks to quantify the damage done to a firm as a consequence of an antitrust violation. The plaintiff (Conwood) and the defendant (United States Tobacco Co. or USTC) manufactured moist snuff, a smokeless tobacco product. USTC accounted for 77 percent of sales in a relevant market defined as "smokeless moist snuff tobacco in the United States," and Conwood had 13–14 percent. At trial, USTC conceded that it was a monopolist. Conwood alleged that USTC engaged in illegal monopolization by: (1) removing and discarding Conwood's product display racks from stores without the store manager's permission; (2) training its sales agents to deceive store clerks into giving them permission to reorganize the store's moist snuff section, after which the sales agents hid or destroyed Conwood's racks; (3) misusing its position as a "category manager" by providing misleading information to retailers to make them believe that USTC products enjoyed better sales so that retailers would carry USTC products and drop Conwood products; and (4) entering into exclusive agreements with retailers to exclude Conwood's products.

The case was tried before a jury, which found USTC guilty of monopolization and returned a verdict of $350 million. The trebled award was $1.05 billion—one of the largest treble damage verdicts in the history of the U.S. antitrust laws. USTC appealed, challenging the trial court's denial of several of its motions, pre and post-verdict, as well as its refusal to exclude the damages study and testimony of Conwood's damage expert. The court of appeals affirmed. Concluding that USTC had engaged in improper exclusion, the Sixth Circuit endorsed the district court's rulings on evidence and other matters concerning damages. Passages of the court's opinion concerning damages appear below.

CONWOOD CO. v. UNITED STATES TOBACCO CO.

United States Court of Appeals for the Sixth Circuit, 2002.
290 F.3d 768.

CLAY, Circuit Judge

* * *

Damages

[William Rosson, Conwood's Chairman,] testified that had Conwood not been subjected to USTC tactics, it would have had a national market share of approximately 22 to 23 percent. Rosson testified that he had carefully tracked Conwood's market share over the past 20 years. Conwood's actual market share in its first 10 years in the moist snuff industry was 11 percent. In the next decade, starting from 1990, that figure increased by roughly 2.5 percent. Rosson testified that the lack of growth that occurred during the second decade largely resulted from USTC's tactics. He testified that his numbers are based on his studying markets where the company had a foothold and those in which it did not. In places where the company had a "foothold," *i.e.*, a relatively high market share in a given area, it saw its market share increase during the 1990s to a market share above 20 percent. Rosson testified that each additional point (one percent) of market share translates into approximately $10 million in annual profits.

[Terry Williams, Conwood's national sales manager,] testified concerning Conwood's market share with respect to the ten retail locations for which USTC offered evidence at trial. In those locations where USTC did not have rack exclusivity, Conwood's moist brands market share was well above its national average. For those locations where USTC had rack exclusivity, Conwood's market share was below its national average. Conwood argues that from these figures, a jury could have concluded that in unimpeded competition, Conwood's market share would have been approximately 25 percent instead of 13.5 percent nationally.

Finally, to prove damages, Conwood relied on the expert testimony of Professor Richard Leftwich of the University of Chicago Graduate School of Business, who is recognized as an expert on business valuation and lost profits. Leftwich apparently tested Rosson's hypothesis that Conwood's market share increased in areas in which it did not face USTC exclusivity.

Using a regression analysis, Leftwich found a statistically significant difference between states in which Conwood had a foothold and those in which it did not. Under Leftwich's model, in states where Conwood had a market share in 1990 of 20 percent or more, the market share grew on average an additional 8.1 percent from 1990 to 1997. In states where Conwood's market share in 1990 was at least 15 percent, it grew an additional 6.5 percent. In states below these thresholds, Conwood's growth was considerably lower. As the district court noted:

> Leftwich applied a regression analysis to test Conwood's hypotheses. He determined that Conwood's share in a state in 1990 is statistically related to the change in Conwood's market share between 1990 and 1997. The regression model predicts that where Conwood had a higher market share (*e.g.*, 15–20%) in 1990, Conwood's market share grew during the period 1990 to 1997. In contrast, in states where Conwood had a lower market share, the regression predicts that its share would grow very little.

Leftwich then determined that Conwood's low market growth was due to USTC's behavior. Leftwich's model also found that increases in USTC's exclusionary behavior in a state reduced Conwood's share of sales by a statistically significant amount. He found that Conwood's damages as a result of USTC's actions amounted to a figure between $313 million and $488 million, depending on whether Conwood's market share would have grown by 6.5 percent or 8.1 percent. The jury awarded damages of $350 million.

* * *

V.

USTC challenges the district court's decision to allow Leftwich to testify as to the damages sustained by USTC's conduct. USTC argues that the district court made no findings regarding the admissibility of Leftwich's report under *Daubert v. Merrell Dow Pharm., Inc.,* 509 U.S. 579, 113 S.Ct. 2786 (1993). USTC argues that Leftwich's methodology fails because it was constructed solely for this case. USTC also argues that Leftwich's study did not attempt to segregate the effects of other factors that could have contributed to Conwood's low sales in some states, and it made no attempt to test whether the slow growth in certain states was causally linked to any of USTC's conduct. Thus, USTC argues the study did not and could not fit the case at hand.

* * *

USTC does not challenge Leftwich's qualifications as an expert, but only his testimony and damages study. Pursuant to Rule 702 of the Federal Rules of Evidence, "[i]f scientific, technical, or other specialized knowledge will assist the trier of fact to understand the evidence or to determine a fact in issue, a witness qualified as an expert by knowledge, skill, experience, training, or education, may testify thereto in the form of an opinion or otherwise.* * *" In *Daubert,* the Supreme Court "established a general gatekeeping [or screening] obligation for trial courts" to exclude from trial expert testimony that is unreliable and irrelevant. The district court must determine whether the evidence "both rests on a reliable foundation and is relevant to the task at hand." In assessing relevance and reliability, the district court must examine "whether the expert is proposing to testify to (1) scientific knowledge that (2) will assist the trier of fact to understand or determine a fact in issue." This involves a preliminary inquiry as to whether the reasoning or methodology underlying the testimony is scientifically valid and whether that reasoning or methodology properly can be applied to the facts in issue. Some of the factors that may be used in such an inquiry include: (1) whether the theory or technique has been tested and subjected to peer review and publication, (2) whether the potential rate of error is known, and (3) its general acceptance. "This inquiry is a flexible one, with an overarching goal of assessing the 'scientific validity and thus the evidentiary relevance and reliability' of the principles and methodology underlying the proposed expert testimony." "[A] trial judge must have considerable leeway in deciding in a particular case how to go about determining whether particular expert testimony is reliable." *Kumho Tire Co., Ltd. v. Carmichael,* 526 U.S. 137, 152, 119 S.Ct. 1167 (1999).

USTC presents no reasoned basis for us to find that the district court abused its discretion in determining that Leftwich's methodology was sufficiently reliable or relevant to survive a *Daubert* challenge. USTC asserts two principal challenges to Leftwich's study and testimony. USTC claims that Leftwich did not relate any of Conwood's loss to specific bad acts by USTC and failed to account for other factors that could have had a negative effect on Conwood's sales. Leftwich used a regression analysis to test Rosson's hypothesis that Conwood's growth was suppressed most in states where it had only a small market share when USTC began its exclusionary practices. He also tested whether the intensity of USTC's misconduct increased in or around 1990. Rosson testified that once his company reached a 15 percent market share, USTC's exclusive vending practices were not as effective.

Leftwich employed three methods to test Conwood's claims: regression analyses, a yardstick test and a before-and-after test. All three are generally accepted methods for proving antitrust damages. *See e.g., Petruzzi's IGA Supermarkets, Inc. v. Darling–Delaware Co.,* 998 F.2d 1224, 1238 (3d Cir. 1993) (explaining that if performed properly multiple regression analysis is a reliable means by which economists may prove antitrust damages); *Eleven Line, Inc. v. North Texas State Soccer Ass'n,* 213 F.3d 198, 207 (5th Cir.2000) (noting that the two most common methods of quantifying antitrust damages are the "before and after" and "yardstick" measures of lost profits).[8]

Leftwich found a statistically significant difference in Conwood's market share between those states in which Conwood had a foothold and those in which it did not. In those states in which Conwood enjoyed a market share of 15 and 20 percent or more, Conwood grew in share, between 1990 and 1997, on an average of 6.5 percent and 8.1 percent, respectively. He concluded that but for USTC's exclusionary acts, Plaintiff's market share would have grown by these same amounts in non-foothold states. Contrary to USTC's arguments, the record indicates that Leftwich ruled out the possibility that the statistical relationship was caused by factors other than USTC's conduct. We find particularly relevant the undisputed evidence that Leftwich examined the

---

8. "The before and after theory compares the plaintiff's profit record prior to the violation with that subsequent to it [and] the yardstick test ... consists of a study of the profits of business operations that are closely comparable to the plaintiff's." A regression analysis looks at the relationship between two variables. The point of a regression analysis is to determine whether the relationship between the two variables is statistically meaningful.

possible explanations that USTC's own expert suggested as possible explanations for Conwood's low market share. Leftwich testified that he tested all "plausible explanations" for his results for which he had data. Employing a regression analysis, Leftwich analyzed whether these other factors could explain Conwood's laggard growth in non-foothold states and concluded that they could not.

Leftwich also employed a before-and-after test to investigate Conwood's claims. Specifically, he tested whether the relationship between Conwood's share of moist snuff sales in a state and the rate of growth in Conwood's share of sales in that same state was the same or different for the seven year period before 1990 as it was for the seven year period after 1990. He found that Conwood's moist snuff market share did not grow significantly more in foothold states in the seven year period before 1990. Thus, there was no correlation in the pre–1990 period between Conwood's foothold status and market share growth rate.

Further, Leftwich employed a yardstick test to examine whether in the related loose leaf tobacco market, in which USTC does not participate, Conwood would always grow more in states where they started out with a high market share. He did not find a statistically significant relationship in Conwood's increase in market share in the loose leaf market between 1990 and 1997 and its share in 1990. In other words, where Conwood enjoyed a high market share or foothold in 1990 in the loose leaf market, it did not necessarily grow more in the period between 1990 and 1997.

USTC complains that Leftwich failed to take into account any USTC "bad act." However, this is not completely accurate. Using USTC's expert's own regression model, Leftwich used sworn affidavits compiled from 241 Conwood sales representatives detailing USTC's unethical activity in their areas. He used this information to construct three alternate measures of USTC's bad acts by state. * * * Thus, his damages study was relevant to the issues of this case.

USTC also complains that Leftwich's regression analysis ignored other market variables that could have caused Conwood's harm. However, as explained above, Leftwich ruled out all plausible alternatives for which he had data. Moreover, he accounted for all variables raised by USTC's own expert. In any event, "[i]n order to be *admissible* on the issue of causation, an expert's testimony need not eliminate all other possible causes of the injury." In sum, after reviewing the record and giving due deference to the district court's decision, we believe that the district court did not abuse its discretion in concluding that Leftwich's study satisfied *Daubert* and allowing him to testify, subject to vigorous cross examination and an opportunity for Defendant to introduce countervailing evidence of its own.

Finally, USTC contends that Rosson's testimony regarding damages and Leftwich's study were speculative and failed to support the damages awarded. We disagree. USTC essentially argues that a more rigorous standard of proof of damages was warranted. However, it is undisputed that USTC did not object to the jury instructions regarding damages. The jury was instructed that it could not award damages for injuries caused by other factors. As juries are presumed to follow the instructions given, we reject USTC's argument that Conwood failed to disaggregate the injury caused by USTC as opposed to that caused by other factors.

In addition, an award of damages may be awarded on a plaintiff's estimate of sales it could have made absent the antitrust violation. *J. Truett Payne Co. v. Chrysler Motors Corp.*, 451 U.S. 557, 565, 101 S.Ct. 1923 (1981). While USTC demands a more exacting standard, "[t]he vagaries of the marketplace usually deny us sure knowledge of what plaintiff's situation would have been in the absence of the defendant's antitrust violation." *Id.* at 566. "The antitrust cases are legion which reiterate the proposition that, if the fact of damages is proven, the actual computation of damages may suffer from minor imperfections."

We believe that there was sufficient evidence to support the jury's award of damages in this case. There was testimony that absent USTC's unlawful conduct, Conwood would have achieved market share in the mid–20s. For instance, Rosson testified that had Conwood not been subjected to USTC tactics, it would have had a national market share of approximately 22 to 23 percent. Rosson testified that he had carefully tracked the growth of Conwood's market share over the past 20 years, and its sharp decline in the 1990s was largely due to USTC's tactics. Williams, Conwood's national sales manager, also testified that in those stores where USTC practiced rack exclusivity, Conwood's market share was well below its national average. Such evidence supported Leftwich's damages analysis, and he estimated that Conwood's damages ranged between $313 million and $488 million. The jury awarded damages well within that range. Although USTC argues that there was evidence that undermined Rosson's testimony regarding whether USTC's conduct caused Conwood's injury, the jury heard all of the evidence presented to it, and apparently found other testimony supporting the award of damages more credible. In sum, we believe that there was sufficient evidence to sustain the award in this case.

* * *

Conwood highlights two important elements of calculating damages in private antitrust litigation. The first is the need to select an analytical model that best captures the results that plaintiff would have achieved had it not been for the defendant's misconduct. The second is the centrality of expert testimony—typically, by accountants and economists—in supplying a model for computing damages and in applying the model to the facts at hand

As noted above, in accordance with Section 4 of the Clayton Act, the $350 million in "actual" damages proved by Conwood was trebled to $1.05 billion. In addition, as a prevailing plaintiff, Conwood received an award of attorney's fees and costs pursuant to § 4 of the Clayton Act. What might justify this seeming windfall to Conwood?

For another illustration of the interplay of damages, economic models, and the role of expert testimony, see *LePage's Inc. v. 3M Company*, 324 F.3d 141 (3d Cir. 2003). In *LePage's*, the court rejected arguments by 3M that the plaintiff's damage expert's testimony should have been excluded. 3M asserted that the testimony was flawed in two general respects: (1) the "lost market share" model that the plaintiff's expert constructed as a yardstick to evaluate the "but for" world, *i.e.*, LePage's' likely success but for 3M's conduct, rested upon improper assumptions, and (2) that it failed to disaggregate damages based on lawful and unlawful conduct by 3M. The court rejected both arguments, sustaining the district court's treble damage award of nearly $70 million.

Sidebar 9–8:
Legal Procedure and Settlement

Notwithstanding all the attention casebook authors give to judicial decisions, most antitrust cases are resolved through settlement. This Sidebar asks why all cases are not settled. It also discusses the concern raised by some critics of private enforcement that private plaintiffs can coerce inappropriate settlements in frivolous cases. For further discussion of these issues, see Bruce L. Hay & Kathryn E. Spier, *Settlement of Litigation, in* THE NEW PALGRAVE DICTIONARY OF ECONOMICS AND THE LAW 442 (Peter Newman, ed., 1998).

Why Don't All Cases Settle?

Most court complaints between private parties, antitrust included, are settled rather than tried. A mid–1980s study found that between 70% and 88% of private antitrust damages cases that reached a final disposition (judgment or settlement) were settled. Steven C. Salop & Lawrence J. White, *Economic Analysis of Private Antitrust Litigation*, 74 GEO. L.J. 1001, 1010 (1986) (table 9). The range arises because dismissals may have been settlements or judgments for defendants. Both figures may understate the settlement rate, if many disputes are settled before trial or if private injunctive cases are more likely to settle than private damages cases.

In most private cases, settlement has substantial advantages for both sides. It saves on litigation costs, which can be substantial, avoids business harms that may be associated with delay in resolving the dispute or the public airing of trial testimony, and allows risk averse parties to avoid the uncertainty of trial. Even if the parties disagree to some extent about the likely judicial resolution or the likely remedy in the event plaintiff prevails, there will typically be a range of possible settlements that make both sides better off than they would be in going to trial. In a damages case, the minimum plaintiff will take to settle is the expected damage award (its assessment of the prospects of success, times the damage payment it expects to receive if it prevails) less the future costs of continued litigation (including court costs, attorney and expert fees, the diversion of executive time, and the costs of uncertainty and delay). The maximum the defendant will pay in a settlement is its expected damage payment plus the future costs of litigation. If the maximum a defendant will pay exceeds the minimum plaintiff will accept, there is room for a deal, and the parties can usually be counted on to reach a settlement in that range. Under such circumstances, why don't all private cases settle?

The economics literature suggests two main reasons. First, the two sides may have such different beliefs or expectations about the likelihood of prevailing or the nature of the remedy as to leave no room for settlement. If one or both of the parties is overly-optimistic about its prospects for success at trial, or if defendant thinks it would not have to pay much in damages should it lose while plaintiff expects a very large award if it prevails, the maximum defendant will pay may be less than the minimum plaintiff will accept, leaving no possibility for settlement.

Second, when two sides bargain rationally with private or incomplete information, they might miss a mutually beneficial deal simply because it may rationally take a tough bargaining stance. If one side reasonably but wrongly thinks it can get a better deal by holding out for more, for example, the parties may reach an impasse even if there is room for a deal that would benefit both. Or if a plaintiff expects to bring a series of similar actions, and can't tell which defendants have particularly strong cases, it may do best by making an offer that defendants with weak cases will take and going to trial with the rest, even if it could have reached a deal with the latter defendants if it could have sorted them in advance. In this story, the plaintiff cannot make such a deal later; otherwise the defendants with weak cases will pretend to have strong ones to get the same settlement. Nor can a defendant with a strong case convincingly prove that fact in any other way than by going to trial, even through discovery.

These explanations for the failure of litigating parties to reach a negotiated deal suggest that the prospects for settlement go up if expected trial costs rise (increasing the settlement range), if the parties engage in additional discovery (reducing information differences between the sides and bringing their beliefs and expectations closer together), or through the use of alternative dispute resolution techniques like mock trials and mediation (again bringing the beliefs and expectations of the parties closer together).

Terms of Settlement

Some critics of private antitrust enforcement have expressed concern about the influence of extensive discovery and the threat of treble damages on the terms of settlement in antitrust cases. They raise the possibility that plaintiffs with weak cases could nevertheless extract substantial settlements from defendants because of these procedural aspects of antitrust litigation, encouraging the filing of frivolous claims. To understand this argument it is necessary to explore what influences the terms of settlement.

A settlement of a case would be expected to fall between the minimum plaintiff would accept and the maximum defendant would pay. But the difference will not be split 50–50 if one party has greater bargaining power than the other. In the economic literature, bargaining power depends importantly on what happens if firms do not reach a deal.* In the most basic analysis, if litigation is very costly for defendant, and not so costly for plaintiff, then the plaintiff has the stronger bargain-

---

* The economic theory of bargaining suggests that in a negotiation, the lion's share of the joint benefits will go to the party that has the least to lose if no deal is reached. *See, e.g.,* Avinash Dixit & Susan Skeath, GAMES OF STRATEGY 521–47 (1999).

ing position—it can threaten to impose large costs by litigating—so a settlement will likely favor plaintiff. This simple bargaining power story may be complicated, though, by differences between the parties in their desire to avoid risk, by a party's concern that it will be adversely affected in other cases if it accedes to a weak settlement in this one, or by the possibility that lawyers with somewhat different interests than the parties they represent may control settlement talks on their side of the table.

In the picture of private antitrust litigation offered by the critics, the prospect of a treble damage award and the likelihood that discovery will be much more expensive for the defendant than the plaintiff lead systematically to settlements that favor plaintiffs, even when cases are weak. The prospect of pro-plaintiff settlements, in turn, may encourage plaintiffs to bring more cases. This theory is difficult to evaluate, however, because there is little evidence from which to gauge the social value of weak cases. If most are frivolous, then there is reason for concern. But cases may be difficult for plaintiffs to win even if they are meritorious— for example, if the substantive legal rules make it difficult for plaintiffs to succeed even when competition is harmed, if plaintiffs who would end up victorious were all the facts known frequently cannot surmount the burden they must meet to justify more complete discovery, or if standing rules exclude from the courthouse plaintiffs with knowledge of violations and the resources to litigate. Put differently, rules that encourage plaintiffs to bring antitrust lawsuits can benefit the economy by increasing the deterrent effect of the antitrust laws, or harm the economy by imposing litigation costs on wrongly accused defendants and discouraging procompetitive conduct likely to prompt a complaint. The value of private treble damage actions and easy access to discovery must be evaluated with both possibilities in mind.

G. CONCLUSION

In this Chapter, we have seen that, to assess the antitrust significance of an episode of business conduct, one must ask a series of interrelated questions about the enforcement process. Who is likely to challenge the behavior in question? For example, is there a risk of criminal enforcement by the Justice Department, or might the FTC use Section 5 of the FTC Act to reach behavior not condemned by the Sherman or Clayton Acts? Suppose the federal agencies decline to attack a merger. Will a state intervene? If a competitor or customer sues, can she satisfy the threshold requirements of standing, antitrust injury, and directness? Can the plaintiff bear evidentiary burdens essential to establishing liability, or are there evidentiary ambiguities or analytical weaknesses (*e.g.*, economic implausibility) that may warrant summary judgment? Will a foreign government assert jurisdiction? Will foreign plaintiffs sue abroad?

As you may recall from the Chapter's introduction, we noted that in answering these questions, decision makers often are influenced by their tendency to view the antitrust laws as over or under deterring anticompetitive conduct. This was so even though they shared a common goal of striking an "optimal" balance. How was that evident in the material on jurisdiction, both domestic and foreign? Was it also evident in the material on antitrust injury,

Illinois Brick and standing? And finally, how was it evident in the material on remedies?

H. PROBLEMS AND EXERCISES

Problem 9–1:
Sweet Co.

a. *The Facts*

Sweet Co. is one of four principal manufacturers of artificial sweeteners in the world. Like other artificial sweeteners, Sweet Co.'s main product, SweetStuff, is used as an additive in a variety of foods, such as cereals, soda pop, juices, cookies, and cakes. Sweet Co.'s principal customers, therefore, are food manufacturers, who account for more than 75% of its sales. SweetStuff is also sold through supermarkets to consumers, who use it in place of sugar for cooking purposes and as a drink sweetener for hot drinks (coffee and tea), as well as cold drinks (lemonade and iced tea). Worldwide sales of artificial sweeteners have been growing steadily for the last decade, and are now roughly $10 billion/year. Sweet Co.'s annual sales are roughly $3 billion.

Following a two year grand jury investigation, the Antitrust Division of the Department of Justice sought and secured criminal indictments against Sweet Co. and its two largest rivals for engaging in a worldwide conspiracy to fix the prices of artificial sweeteners. Sweet Co. denied that it had conspired with its rivals and vowed to vigorously contest the government's charges. After the close of the government's case in chief at trial, a settlement agreement was reached, pursuant to which Sweet Co. agreed to pay fines of $250 million.

Shortly after the indictments were announced, a number of private parties filed suit against Sweet Co., both as individuals and, in many cases, as purported class representatives. By the time the settlement agreement was reached with the government, over three dozen such suits had been filed. Four of these are summarized below.

Suit No. 1: *Drink Manufacturers vs. Sweet Co. (Federal Court).* In this action, filed in the United States District Court, several of the major manufacturers of soda pop and juices have joined to sue Sweet Co. for its alleged violations of Section 1 of the Sherman Act. Pursuant to Section 4 of the Clayton Act, the plaintiffs seek to recover three times the alleged overcharges they incurred as purchasers of SweetStuff during the period of the alleged conspiracy.

Suit No. 2: *Consumers of SweetStuff v. Sweet Co. (Federal Court).* This is a consumer class action also filed in a United States District Court, but in a different district than Suit No. 1. It too alleges violations of Section 1 of the Sherman Act and seeks three times the alleged overcharges paid by the class for SweetStuff. The complaint purports to be brought on behalf of a class of consumers who purchased SweetStuff at supermarkets and groceries for their own use as a sweetener.

Suit No. 3: *Consumers of SweetStuff Products v. Sweet Co. (State Court).* This too is a consumer class action, but it was filed in state court under state antitrust laws. The complaint alleges violations of state antitrust provisions that parallel those of Section 1 of the Sherman Act, and seeks to recover three times the actual damages sustained by consumers who purchased cereals, soda pop, juices, and cookies that contained SweetStuff at their local supermarkets.

Suit No. 4: *Foreign Supermarkets vs. SweetCo. (Federal Court).* This is a federal antitrust action filed in U.S. District Court by two of the largest supermarket chains in Europe, who allegedly purchased packaged SweetStuff from Sweet Co. during the period of the alleged conspiracy. The SweetStuff purchased was for resale to consumers in their stores in Europe, as well as in the United States. The two supermarket chains seek treble damages for the overcharges they paid for all of their purchases of SweetStuff.

b. The Problems

You are the principal deputy general counsel for litigation and antitrust at Sweet Co. In response to the four described actions, you have been asked to prepare a "Litigation Plan" detailing the company's initial procedural strategy for defending against these actions. In particular, consider the following issues with respect to each suit:

(1) What motion or motions might you file challenging any of the actions on grounds of lack of jurisdiction, standing or antitrust injury?

(2) What procedural steps might you recommend to combine any of these actions, as through removal, transfer and/or consolidation?

(3) Which, if any, of the class actions strikes you as vulnerable with respect to class certification? Why?

c. Skills Exercise

Select one or two of the issues you identified in your answers to the immediately preceding Problems, and draft a motion of no more than three (3) pages asking the court to consider the issue. To accompany the motion, draft a brief of no more than five (5) pages setting forth the arguments in support of the motion.

Problem 9–2:
Maverick Motors

a. The Facts

In response to shortages of gasoline and consequently higher gasoline prices in the early 1970s, federal government regulators imposed minimum fuel economy standards on all of the major automobile manufacturers. These standards, known as Corporate Average Fuel Economy ("CAFÉ") standards, applied to cars and light trucks, although different standards were established for each. Around the same time, federal regulators also responded to increased levels of automotive air pollution by developing standards to control and reduce vehicle emissions. Moreover, California adopted uniquely strict emissions standards that required the producers to make significant changes to engine design. Other states followed suit and adopted similarly strict standards.

Since that time, CAFÉ and low emission standards have been controversial features of government regulation of the automobile industry. Environmentalists and others urge increases in the CAFÉ standards and stricter regulation of vehicle emissions, while most automobile manufacturers oppose government-mandated increases in fuel economy and decreases in emissions, particularly at a time when consumers have made clear their preference for performance cars and larger vehicles, especially minivans and sport utility vehicles. These larger vehicles tend to be far more profitable for the automobile producers than are passenger cars, but they are also less fuel efficient and more polluting. Indeed, although the major manufacturers publicly maintain that they are interested in and diligently working to produce more fuel efficient and lower polluting vehicles, the pace of innovation to accomplish those goals has remained slow in much of the industry.

In response to renewed calls for increased CAFÉ standards for both passenger vehicles and light trucks, as well as even stricter emissions standards, five of the six largest automobile manufacturers (measured by their shares of U.S. domestic passenger vehicle sales) formed the Coalition of Car Producers ("CCP"). CCP funds studies of automotive safety, pollution and fuel economy, and lobbies at the state and federal level to oppose regulation of both fuel economy and automotive emissions. CCP has successfully lobbied to stall legislative efforts in several states to impose stricter emissions standards and has persuaded federal regulators to delay higher CAFÉ standards, which although adopted in 2007, will not take full effect until 2020.

Maverick Motors is the only major automobile producer that has refused to join the Coalition. Indeed, it has frequently opposed CCP at both state and federal hearings, attempting to refute its charges that technology is either unavailable or too costly to meet more stringent fuel economy and emissions standards. Maverick has been an industry leader for almost three decades with respect to "green" technology that lowers fuel consumption *and* engine emissions, without reducing engine horsepower or acceleration. It also is an industry leader in passenger car production techniques, and traditionally enjoys a significant cost advantage over its rivals, producing high quality cars at lower cost. Maverick's ability to offer more fuel efficient and "ultra low emission" vehicles at prices that remain competitive with its rivals is a function of these production cost advantages, as well as its persistent investment in engine technology research and development.

b. The Problem

Maverick has filed suit against CCP and its members claiming that their collective actions constitute violations of Section 1 of the Sherman Act. In particular, the complaint alleges that its legitimate competitive advantage—a function of its efforts to develop new technologies and cut production costs—is being neutralized by the successful efforts of CCP and its members to preclude more stringent fuel economy and emissions standards. Indeed, Maverick alleges, it would be uniquely situated to meet more stringent fuel economy and emissions standards if the federal government and the states were to impose them, and could quickly gain market share from its rivals.

Maverick further alleges that the coordination among members of CCP goes beyond simple lobbying and includes joint efforts to slow the pace of innovation in the industry in order to maintain current levels of profitability and deny Maverick a larger share of sales. As a consequence, consumers have been deprived of the benefits of cleaner air, reduced CO_2 emissions associated with global warming, and more fuel efficient automobiles at competitive prices.

In its complaint, brought under Sections 4 and 16 of the Clayton Act, Maverick prays for an order enjoining the defendants from continuing to engage in violations of Section 1 of the Sherman Act. It also asserts claims for treble damages, attorneys fees, and costs, alleging that but for the defendants' conduct its market share and consequent profitability would have substantially grown.

c. *Skills Exercise*

You are a law clerk to the Hon. Justice B. Dunn, the federal district court judge to which Maverick's civil action has been assigned. In response to the action, CCP has filed a motion to dismiss, arguing that Maverick: (1) lacks standing to bring its suit; (2) has not suffered any antitrust injury; and (3) that in any event, CCP's activities constitute petitioning conduct that is immune from Sherman Act scrutiny. Draft a memorandum for Judge Dunn of no more than five (5) pages advising the court as to the proper disposition of each of the three asserted bases for CCP's motion.

Chapter 10

INNOVATION, INTELLECTUAL PROPERTY, AND THE "NEW ECONOMY"

INTRODUCTION

Antitrust doctrine to a significant extent is a product of its times—and times change. Industries and industry practices change, economic learning changes, and attitudes about government regulation change. Such changes can spark antitrust scrutiny, particularly when they affect consumers and rivals, which they often do. It is no accident, for example, that in its formative years, antitrust enforcement focused on industries such as steel, oil, tobacco, and railroads—the high-tech markets of the 19th century—whereas attention now has turned to industries such as health care and the information and other technology industries of today's "new economy."

This Chapter explores the relationship between antitrust and "new economies." Although when we speak of today's "new economy" we refer broadly to the information-age typified by the rise of computers, telecommunications, and the Internet, in truth, today's "new economy" is but one example of a broader phenomenon. At least since the dawn of the industrial age, some sectors of the economy are almost always undergoing significant change as a consequence of technological evolution and revolution. "New" economies are almost always being created and destroyed in various industries at various times.

The birth of new economies is triggered by "innovation." Innovation can take the form of new products and services, new processes for producing products, and new methods of assembling and distributing those products. It can lead to the emergence of entirely new industries and the demise of others. Innovation also can take the form of new relationships among rivals, and can spawn new strategies by entrants and incumbents alike. Finally, innovation can take the form of "intellectual property" ("IP")—patents, copyrights, know-how, and to a lesser extent, trademarks and trade names. Indeed, IP laws exist to reward innovation, thereby creating an incentive to its creation. They reflect a philosophy that associates innovation through the creation of IP with progress and the public good. IP laws confer on the owners of IP certain "intellectual property rights" ("IPRs"), the most critical of which is the right to exclude others from using the IP.

Dynamic economies demand adaptable principles and rules of competition and intellectual property. The constant clash of old and new has persistently triggered antitrust challenges and ensured that antitrust plays a critical role in protecting the process of innovation. But has antitrust proved adaptable enough to changing times? Today, the information age challenges antitrust doctrine and institutions to adapt to the hastening pace of change.

A comprehensive examination of the interaction of antitrust and innovation, technology and intellectual property, however, could fill an entire volume. Our goal in this Chapter is more modest: to use a limited selection of illustrative issues and topics to introduce some of the many ways in which antitrust laws and institutions have adapted to change. We begin in Sidebar 10–1 with an overview of the economic principles that distinguish today's "new economy."

Sidebar 10–1:
Antitrust Principles and the "New Economy"*

The term "new economy" lost some of its cachet after the boom years of the 1990s ended with a technology bust. Still, one can point to a number of distinct features common to many high-technology markets in the information age. In short, new economies can be characterized by new economics. These features affect how virtually all of the core concepts of antitrust, including market power, entry, efficiency, and anticompetitive effects, apply in information-based sectors of the economy. Moreover, as this Sidebar will explain, the application of antitrust to high-technology markets today can be rationalized around a handful of core principles.

What Makes the "New Economy" New?

Relationship of Marginal and Fixed Costs. First, marginal costs are often low relative to fixed costs of production (in the sense that most of the costs of production are fixed and marginal costs are not increasing with output). A new software product may cost millions of dollars to develop, but each additional unit sold may cost only cents to produce if distributed by disk, and even less if distributed over the Internet. In such industries, firms would lose money if they were led by rivalry to reduce prices across-the-board and permanently to marginal cost. Accordingly, marginal cost pricing cannot be the competitive equilibrium in such markets—the competitive price must be higher—if firms are to be induced to enter and remain in the industry. In contrast, perfect competition leads to marginal cost pricing in other industries, in which marginal costs are increasing with output and variable costs are substantial relative to fixed costs.

New economy industries are not unique in having this type of cost structure. The cost of filling an otherwise empty seat in a movie theater

---

* This Sidebar was adapted in part from *Competition Policy in High–Tech Markets*, Jonathan B. Baker, *Can Antitrust Keep Up?* Brookings Rev. 16 (Winter 2001).

may be very small, and the cost of adding a passenger to an aircraft to fill a seat that would otherwise go empty might literally be peanuts. But low marginal costs of expanding output form a particularly distinctive feature of information industries, which are mainstays of the high-technology sector today.

As you will recall, "market power" is the power profitably to raise or maintain price above the competitive level for a significant period of time. Often, as we have generally assumed in this casebook, "the competitive level" is best understood as referring to the marginal cost of expanding output by industry participants. To facilitate the evaluation of allegedly anticompetitive conduct in information industries, however, it is necessary to recognize that in such settings, "competitive price" must be defined differently.

What should we think of as the "competitive" price in a high-fixed cost, low-marginal cost industry? Economists most often suggest thinking of competition in such settings as a hypothetical market with "free entry," by which a new rival would enter so long as price exceeds its *average* cost. (Under the free entry assumption, the entrant does not worry about the issues raised by the entry "likelihood" analysis of committed entry in the merger setting. It does not fear that its additional output will depress the market price, making it unable to cover its sunk expenditures, nor worry about aggressive incumbent reactions to its entry depressing price further.) From this perspective, the competitive price in a high fixed cost, low marginal cost industry may be equated with *entrant average cost*, for an entrant with a reasonable and practical entry plan, likely to be sufficient to keep price from rising. With free entry, after all, price could not rise above the entrant's average cost without attracting new competition.** Entrant average cost will generally exceed incumbent firm marginal cost in industries in which firms experience high fixed costs and low marginal costs.

Of course, many firms sell multiple products, charge different prices to different customers, or allow prices to vary over time. In markets where these practices are common, it is difficult to speak of a single competitive "price." Firms cover the fixed costs for their operations as a whole, but do so with high prices to some customers, on some products or at some times, and low prices in other cases. The definition of competition set forth above generalizes naturally. Under such circumstances— high fixed-cost, low marginal cost sellers in industries with multi-product sellers, firms that discriminate in price, or price promotions—prices can be thought of as competitive if *on average* they do not exceed entrant average cost. We employed a similar analysis in describing what competition might mean among firms that discriminate in price in Chapter 7. (*See* Sidebar 7–8, *supra*.)

Shifting Market Boundaries. The second feature common to many high-technology industries is that product boundaries change rapidly. Product upgrades may be common, both to improve quality and add features, and new generations may be sold before old generations have

---

** The entrant's average cost can be understood as the industry's marginal cost of expanding output when the industry performs competitively by virtue of free entry. In this sense, "the competitive price" defined for a high-fixed cost, low-marginal cost industry continues to be a form of marginal cost pricing.

been withdrawn. These settings may well add complexity to market definition in practice, but they do not change the conceptual task: to identify a collection of products and locations that would constitute a valuable monopoly, notwithstanding buyer incentives to substitute alternatives in the event price were to rise. Moreover, innovation may come from unlikely sources. Which telephone wire manufacturers would have predicted that their product would be challenged by new fiber optic lines developed by the glass industry? Possibilities such as these may make entry analysis less certain, but courts are unlikely to presume that entry is easy in high-technology markets without analysis of the best available evidence.

Rapid product and process innovation creates another dilemma for antitrust enforcement: high-technology industries can be highly innovative sectors important to economic growth. As we will see later in this chapter, courts have often been reluctant to interfere with markets that are producing new and better products, even when confronted by serious arguments that the dominant firms have improperly acted to exclude rivals that seek to supplant the leading firm with better products. Might this attitude explain the deference often given by the courts to firms said to have harmed competition through exclusionary new product design?

Network Effects. Third, many high-technology markets are characterized by *network effects* (also termed "network externalities" or "demand-side scale economies"). When a product or service exhibits network effects, its value to a buyer is greater when some other buyer also purchases the product or service—and the more buyers there are, the more significant the network effect. Network effects are often especially important in communications or computer operating system software. The value of a particular long-distance telephone service, for example, would be very limited if it only facilitated calls to other subscribers of the same service. But as the number of subscribers increases, the value of the service to *all* subscribers increases, as well. The more subscribers there are on the "network," the more valuable it becomes to join, and the more likely it is that others will subscribe, as well. Network effects can also be indirect. The value of particular software programs for word processing or spreadsheets, for example, increases for a firm if its suppliers and customers use similar software, making it easier to share information and for new employees to be trained to use it.

Markets with strong network effects are frequently characterized by "tipping." A firm that is expected to become dominant, perhaps after it achieves a small advantage in early competition, may find that new buyers disproportionately select its product. The market may quickly establish such a firm as the winner of what is effectively a standard-setting competition. Such competition is typically winner-take-most or winner-take-all, and for good reason: buyers benefit from joining the network of buyers patronizing the winner.

Once a market tips, however, it becomes harder for a rival to compete, even with a better product. Some losers nevertheless may remain in the market, profitably serving small groups of buyers whose preferences for variety or the rival's unique features are so strong as to justify the sacrifice of not joining the network. To dislodge an industry leader in a market with strong network effects, however, the entrant may need to develop a dramatically improved new product that "leapfrogs" the market leader's technology. Recognizing this, firms often compete very aggressively to become the winner—even giving away their products, as Microsoft and Netscape were led to do with their Internet browsers.

The possibility that a market may quickly tip, and the difficulty of dislodging a winner once it does so, create special problems for antitrust enforcement. Anticompetitive practices during the period in which firms are competing aggressively to become the winner may lead the market to tip to the violator, not because it has better or cheaper products, but because it found a way to significantly impair or exclude its rivals through exclusionary conduct. By the time a court reaches a verdict, however, it may be too late to restore the lost competition. Buyers have selected a dominant product or standard, and have made investments to join the winner's installed base that may be costly and difficult to dislodge. How can competition be restored after the market has tipped, without harming the buyers that a remedy aims to help? It is useful to reconsider the *Microsoft* settlement with this issue in mind.

Five Antitrust Principles for Addressing Competition in High–Technology Markets

Antitrust's contemporary engagement with high-technology markets can be understood as based upon five core principles that arguably define an emerging intellectual consensus. As you read the materials in this chapter, consider whether these five principles are reflected in the modern cases, and whether they are (or should be) more contested than the claim of intellectual consensus we make here would suggest.

1. Intellectual Property is Property. The first principle is that for antitrust purposes, intellectual property is just another form of property. A high-technology firm's patents and copyrights are no different from its physical property, its plants and equipment. That it may be easier to misappropriate many forms of intellectual property than to steal physical products is no reason to make intellectual property more or less suspect under the antitrust laws than any other form of property.

Mergers provide an example. If Coke were to acquire Pepsi, or United Airlines were to acquire American, the transaction would surely trigger an antitrust investigation, because the products and services sold by the acquired firm are likely important substitutes to customers of the acquiring firm. The analysis is similar when the key assets of the firms are intellectual property rights. Antitrust enforcers would also be skeptical if a firm that owns the rights to one drug for treating a disease were to acquire a firm with the rights to the only other drug with a similar use, for example, or if the merging firms were among a small number of rivals in an "innovation market." Moreover, as this Chapter makes clear, the examples extend throughout antitrust law. The Justice Department's analysis of a "patent pool" among owners of competing patents follows the general template for the antitrust analysis of collaboration among competitors. The D.C. Circuit's analysis in *Microsoft* of exclusionary conduct involving high-technology products like Internet browsers resembled the Supreme Court's analysis of exclusionary conduct involving lower-tech advertising in *Lorain Journal* (Casebook, Chapter 6, *supra*).

2. Competition Promotes Innovation. The second principle, that competition promotes innovation, recognizes that firms have a powerful incentive to gain an advantage on their rivals by cutting costs or being first with new products or product improvements. Just as competition encourages firms to increase output and lower prices, it also leads firms to improve product quality and service, develop new products, and introduce new methods of production that lower cost. In many of the leading oligopolistic sectors of the economy, including the computer industry, innovation competition, not price competition is the "prime competitive weapon" and that competition is an enormous engine for economy-growth. WILLIAM J. BAUMOL, THE FREE-MARKET INNOVATION MACHINE: ANALYZING THE GROWTH MIRACLE OF CAPITALISM 4 (2002).

The extent of pre-innovation competition is not the only determinant of innovation, however. *See generally* Richard Gilbert & Steven Sunshine, *Incorporating Dynamic Efficiency Concerns in Merger Analysis: The Use of Innovation Markets,* 63 ANTITRUST L.J. 569 (1997); LUÍS M.B. CABRAL, INTRODUCTION TO INDUSTRIAL ORGANIZATION 292–302 (2000). Moreover the extensive economic literature relating market structure to investments in research and development ("R & D") and the prospects for innovation, while arguably consistent with the view that competition promotes innovation, also suggests ways in which non-competitive market structures promote innovation. Accordingly, there may be greater consensus on the view that innovation can be fostered by policies that promote competition in the antitrust community than in the economic literature. *See generally* ANTITRUST, INNOVATION AND COMPETITIVENESS (Thomas M. Jorde & David J. Teece, eds. 1992).

The question related to the importance of competition for innovation most studied by economists asks whether innovation tends to increase or decrease as the number of firms decline. Competing theoretical arguments were framed decades ago. On the one hand, a monopolist may have less incentive to innovate than would competitors, because the monopolist may have more to lose. A monopolist could spend a great deal of money to lower cost, improve quality, or add a product line only to find that it does not get much additional business as a result—because, unlike a competitor, it already has most of the business there is to get. Kenneth J. Arrow, *Economic Welfare and the Allocation of Resources for Innovation*, in THE RATE AND DIRECTION OF INVENTIVE ACTIVITY 609–25 (Nat'l Bureau of Econ. Research ed., 1962). Put differently, competition encourages innovation because firms have a strong incentive to develop new, better, or cheaper products in order to escape competition. Monopoly may also discourage innovation because a monopolist's employees may resist innovations that would threaten the existing organizational structure.

On the other hand, some argue that monopoly may instead encourage innovation, as a monopolist may have greater access to low-cost internal finance, and may be better able to take advantage of scale economies in research and development and to appropriate the full value of its new ideas. *See* JOSEPH SCHUMPETER, CAPITALISM, SOCIALISM, AND DEMOCRACY 81–106 (1942); 1 MORTON I. KAMIEN, MARKET STRUCTURE AND INNOVATION REVISITED: JAPAN AND THE WORLD ECONOMY 331 (1989). Note, however, that the first two of these three counter-arguments are potential advantages of all large firms, regardless of the extent to which they face competition. And the third, the monopolist's possible advantage in appropriating the gains from innovation, matters most when other means of assuring reasonable appropriability, such as intellectual property protection, are weak. Put differently, the prospect of post-innovation competition discourages innovation, but pre-innovation monopoly is not the only way, or necessarily the best way, to alleviate that disincentive. One way to harmonize a monopolist's incentive to innovate with the monopolist's disincentive to innovate resulting from its pre-innovation profits is to suppose that many industries exhibit a form of Schumpeterian "creative destruction," by which a temporary monopolist is supplanted by another, which has developed an improved product or production process. LUÍS M.B. Cabral, INTRODUCTION TO INDUSTRIAL ORGANIZATION 295 (2000).

Empirical researchers have sought to determine which of these theories are in practice the most important. For a time, there was a consensus that oligopoly market structures (a handful of firms) would be more conducive to innovation than either monopoly or a large number of firms. But some more recent studies have highlighted methodological problems with the earlier works that may have led earlier studies incorrectly to suggest that greater seller concentration promotes innovation. *See generally* Wesley M. Cohen & Richard C. Levin, *Empirical Studies of Innovation and Market Structure, in* 2 HANDBOOK OF INDUSTRIAL ORGANIZATION 1059, 1074–79 (Richard Schmalensee & Robert D. Willig, eds. 1989); WILLIAM L. BALDWIN & JOHN T. SCOTT, MARKET STRUCTURE AND TECHNOLOGICAL CHANGE 63–113 (1987), P.A. Geroski, *Innovation, Technological Opportunity, and Market Structure*, 42 OXFORD ECON. PAPERS 586 (1990); Richard C. Levin, et al., *R & D Appropriability, Opportunity and Market Structure: New Evidence on Some Schumpeterian Hypotheses*, 75 AM. ECON. REV. 20 (Papers and Proceedings, May 1985). This evidence is arguably consistent with the view that competition promotes innovation, once the degree of appropriability across industries is controlled for. *But see* Philippe Aghion et al., *Competition and Innovation: An Inverted U Relationship* (Institute for Fiscal Studies Working Paper No. 02/04, 2002) (providing evidence that oligopoly market structures maximize innovation).

Recent theoretical work about the determinants of innovative effort and the prospects for innovation success has begun to consider the significance of strategic behavior in market structures not at the extremes of monopoly or competition. From this work, four important principles relating competition and innovation have emerged. These principles do not encompass every aspect of economic research on the determinants of innovation—far from it—but they do describe important aspects that are particularly relevant to antitrust. First, competition in innovation itself—that is, competition among firms seeking to develop the same new product or process—encourages innovation. Second, competition among rivals producing an existing product encourages those firms to find ways to lower costs, improve quality, or develop better products. Firms engage in research and development because innovation may allow them to escape competition, and so earn greater profits. By contrast, a firm that faces less competition has less need to work hard to escape competition. Third, firms that expect to face more product market competition after innovating have less incentive to invest in R & D. A firm has less incentive to innovate in the first place if doing so would not allow it to profit by escaping competition, but would instead be expected to throw it into a pool with sharks, causing it to profit less from R & D. This incentive may encourage firms introducing new products to seek to differentiate them from those of their rivals, as differentiated products often face less post-innovation product market competition than do products similar to those sold by other firms. Fourth, a firm will have an extra incentive to innovate if in doing so it can discourage potential rivals from investing in R & D. This preemption incentive arises because an innovating firm may be able to benefit from its investments in R & D not simply through its ability to offer buyers better or cheaper products, but also by discouraging potential rivals from innovating. *See generally*, Jonathan B. Baker, *Beyond Schumpeter vs. Arrow: How Antitrust Fosters Innovation*, 74 ANTITRUST L.J. 575 (2008); Richard Gilbert, *Looking for Mr. Schumpeter: Where Are We in the Competition–Innovation Debate?*, *in* 6 INNOVATION POLICY AND THE ECONOMY 159 (Adam B. Jaffe, Josh Lerner & Scott Stern, eds. 2006).

Accordingly, as a matter of economic theory, it is impossible to say whether antitrust enforcement that would restrict the conduct of a dominant firm would, on balance, enhance or reduce aggregate industry innovation in general. The most direct effects likely go in opposite ways: lessening the incentive of the dominant firm to innovate, while increasing the incentive of fringe firms to innovate. However, it has been suggested that when innovation competition is winner-take-most or winner-take-all, as when network effects are important or the first to invent obtains broad intellectual property protection, it is unlikely that the dominant firm's innovation incentives would decline substantially as a result of antitrust intervention against the dominant firm—as the prize to innovation, from the point of view of the dominant firm, is likely to be large whether or not the antitrust laws prohibit monopolization. If so, antitrust enforcement could on balance promote industry innovation in the aggregate in winner-take-most markets characterized by a dominant firm and competitive fringe. For an argument that antitrust rules and enforcement today are appropriately focused to promote innovation, see Jonathan B. Baker, *Beyond Schumpeter vs. Arrow: How Antitrust Fosters Innovation*, 74 ANTITRUST L.J. 575 (2008).

Moreover, broad intellectual property rights can offer rich rewards to initial innovation, but they may also impede follow-on innovation. For this reason, some might seek to justify a policy of fostering competition among owners of intellectual property solely in terms of its benefits in encouraging innovation, even ignoring consumer benefits from limiting the exercise of monopoly power.

3. *Network effects heighten the concern with exclusion.* The third core principle is that network effects increase the antitrust concern with anticompetitive exclusion. When network effects are important, the market may quickly tip to select a winner of what is effectively a winner-take-most or winner-take-all standard-setting competition, and that winner may be difficult to dislodge. Accordingly, in markets with network effects, antitrust enforcers must try to move rapidly once they identify a competitive problem in order to make relief meaningful.

But enforcement agencies, cognizant of this difficulty, may be led to take action before all the facts are clear, raising the risks of error. Moreover, if competition problems are not identified until after buyers have committed to the winning standard, it may be difficult to restore competition through an antitrust remedy. For an argument that antitrust enforcement is unnecessary in markets where network effects are important, see Daniel F. Spulber, *Consumer Coordination in the Small and in the Large: Implications for Antitrust in Markets with Network Effects,* 4 J. COMPETITION L. & ECON. ___ (forthcoming 2008), *available at* http://jcle. oxfordjournals.org/cgi/content/abstract/nhm031v1.

4.   *Rapid information exchange could benefit or harm competition.* The fourth key principle underlying contemporary antitrust enforcement in high-technology markets is that rapid information exchange need not create a perfectly competitive market. The vision of "frictionless competition" from rapid information exchange is a powerful one. What could be more procompetitive than the instant and universal exchange of enormous amounts of market and product information? Information exchange can dramatically reduce a buyer's transactions costs of search and help firms make better production and pricing decisions. In addition, Internet access and advertising could reduce the sunk costs of entry, also making markets more competitive. For these reasons, the rapid information exchange made possible by the Internet is likely, in general, a strongly procompetitive force, helping buyers obtain better and cheaper products.

But not always. Entry in the world of electronic commerce is not necessarily as easy as going online to create a web site. The entrant must establish a reputation, both for high-quality products and for fair business practices. Furthermore, rapid information exchange could lead to higher-than competitive prices if it gives sellers a better way to reach an anticompetitive consensus on prices and market shares, or if it makes it easy for price-fixing rivals to detect cheating on that consensus. *See* Jonathan B. Baker, *Identifying Horizontal Price Fixing in the Electronic Marketplace,* 65 ANTITRUST L.J. 41 (1996).

5.   *Most business conduct involving innovation does not harm competition.* The final core principle shaping antitrust's perspective on competition in the high-technology sector is that most business conduct involving innovation by high-technology firms is procompetitive or competitively benign. To be sure, antitrust enforcers pay attention to emerging markets. When today's Old Economy industries like oil refining, steelmaking, and aluminum production were high-technology, they too were an appropriate focus for federal antitrust activity. But relative to the scope of high-technology markets in the economy, both yesterday and today, antitrust enforcement in the high-technology sector has been both measured and infrequent. Indeed, the antitrust enforcement agencies and the courts have long recognized the importance of innovation, the procompetitive benefits of most R & D collaborations, and the strong innovation record of many firms with large market shares. There are many market leaders whose market conduct does not seem to attract antitrust litigation.

In summary, under the contemporary perspective on competition and antitrust enforcement in high-technology markets—the five principles highlighted above—antitrust enforcement does not supplant the market. The principles support the market by enlisting competition in the service of promoting innovation. Under this view, antitrust is far from irrelevant to high-technology industries. Competition is vital to ensuring the continued rapid pace of innovation, and antitrust remains as essential as it always has been to preserving competition.

How did the issues raised in this sidebar play out in the *Microsoft* litigation, which we studied in Chapters 6, 7 and 8? Is software a high-fixed cost, low-marginal cost industry? If so, did the nature of the industry make it difficult for the economic experts and the court to identify the competitive price, and determine whether Microsoft exercised market power? Did the speed of product upgrades and innovations in the software industry make it hard for the experts and the court to define the boundaries of the product market? Were the software products at issue in the case, including computer operating systems and Internet browsers, characterized by strong network effects? If so, did the network effects increase the antitrust concern with exclusion? Make relief more difficult? Did the outcome in *Microsoft* suggest that courts and antitrust enforcers will scrutinize business conduct involving innovation closely in the future, or that antitrust's engagement with the high-technology sector will continue to be both measured and infrequent?

A. ANTITRUST AND INNOVATION

INTRODUCTION

Competition in most product markets is rarely static. Even in markets featuring products with relatively stable designs and quality characteristics, existing producers continue to offer refinements to the state of the art, and other firms attempt to devise new approaches to satisfying the same consumer needs. Innovation in developing and improving products supplies an unequaled source of vitality to the market system. In perhaps the most famous statement of this view, Joseph Schumpeter in 1942 declared that the "competition that counts" is "the competition from the new commodity, the new technology, the new source of supply, the new type of organization * * *— competition which commands a decisive cost or quality advantage and which strikes not at the margins of the profits and the outputs of the existing firms but at their foundations and their very lives." To survive in a capitalist system, he argued, incumbent firms must withstand a "perennial gale of competition" in the form of "the new consumers' goods, the new methods of production or transportation, the new markets, the new forms of industrial organization." JOSEPH A. SCHUMPETER, CAPITALISM, SOCIALISM AND DEMOCRACY 83–84 (1942).

In this section we focus on the treatment of efforts to suppress innovation. As Schumpeter observed, "innovation," whether in products, services or processes of production and distribution, can be a substantial source of competitive vigor. Current markets for research and development can be vital and characterized by intense rivalry. Conduct that impairs or compromises that rivalry, therefore, can pose a significant competitive threat to current markets.

But not all innovation concerns current markets. Some innovation will be directed at developing future products or processes in either existing markets or markets yet to emerge. As one court has observed:

When an established producer of conventional products enters into a conspiracy to suppress a competitor's new and innovative product, that conspiracy will give rise to liability under sections 1 and 2 [of the Sherman Act]—assuming all of the other elements of the causes of action under those sections are present.

Impro Products, Inc. v. Herrick, 715 F.2d 1267, 1273 (8th Cir. 1983). Note the court's qualification, however, that prohibition of efforts to suppress innovation assumes that "all of the other elements of the causes of action under those sections are present." But for several reasons, it can be difficult to predict the future effects of innovation-inhibiting conduct on these kinds of potential or nascent markets. Innovation often represents future competitive potential only. Some, perhaps most, innovations fail or have little competitive effect. If development of a future product is somehow suppressed before those effects can be observed, how can courts or agencies accurately predict whether the product would have succeeded, or even have made it to the market at all?

Moreover, private plaintiffs may be hard pressed to establish antitrust injury when the threat to competition is deemed speculative. Although that might portend a greater role for government enforcement, the government too can face difficult questions of proof when it seeks to demonstrate that consumers have been deprived of the possibility of future products never born due to allegedly anticompetitive conduct. How certain must the prediction be that the new technology would have overtaken the old before this standard can be satisfied?

Although there are a number of cases involving alleged efforts by a firm or firms to suppress innovation, comprehensive discussions of it are notably lacking. We will explore the phenomenon, therefore, by looking at several areas of concern suggested by the cases. Later in this Chapter, we will look more specifically at the relationship between intellectual property rights, such as patents and copyrights, which often embody innovation, and antitrust. Before proceeding, however, we need to more carefully consider the relationship of innovation to competition and to IP.

Note on Innovation and the Scope of Intellectual Property Protection

As should already be apparent, innovation is an extremely important economic activity. Because of new products and improvements to production processes and product design, people in the most developed nations of the world are dramatically healthier and wealthier than their ancestors. Think, for example, of auto and air travel; consumer electronics; air conditioning and refrigeration; the food for sale year round in the supermarket; antibiotics and medical imaging; and the goods and services available in department stores, catalogs, and on the Internet. All these are the product of innovation over time. If anything, moreover, innovation likely occurs less frequently than would be socially optimal given its costs and the opportunities for doing so. Studies of the return to research and development ("R & D") find that the return to society is more than double the return to the firms making the investment, suggesting that private markets provide less than the optimal incentive to innovate. *See, e.g.,* Edwin Mansfield, *Microeconomics of Technological Innovation, in* TECHNOLOGY AND GLOBAL INDUSTRY 311 (Bruce R. Guile & Harvey Brooks eds., 1987); Jeffrey Bernstein & M. Ishaq

Nadiri, *Interindustry R & D Spillovers, Rates of Return, and Production in High–Tech Industries*, 78 AM. ECON. REV. 429 (1988); Charles I. Jones & John C. Williams, *Measuring the Social Return to R & D*, 113 Q. J. ECON. 1119 (1998).

From an economic perspective, the benefits of intellectual property protection come from their encouragement to innovation. Absent intellectual property rights, a free rider problem would inhibit much innovative effort. An inventor or firm would not be expected to put much effort into R & D if the new ideas that result could be copied quickly and inexpensively by rivals. Intellectual property rights, including patents and trade secrets, address this possible market failure, and so enhance incentives to innovate by protecting the inventor's ability to appropriate the benefits of new inventions.

Intellectual property rights are not the only way to ensure that an innovator can appropriate the benefits of its new ideas, however. When intellectual property protections are imperfect, a firm with a monopoly in existing products may be able to exploit that position to protect its gains from innovation:

> Knowledge, which cannot be directly protected by intellectual property laws, diffuses to competitors and allows them to share in the benefits of an innovation when intellectual property regimes fail to provide complete protection against innovation. Under these circumstances, a large share of the markets in which an innovation would be used may enable a firm to appropriate more fully the value of its innovative efforts. A monopolist may thus have a greater incentive to innovate than competitive firms, even if the monopolist suffers from the problem of eroding its own profit base or inducing the obsolescence of its existing products.

Richard J. Gilbert & Steven C. Sunshine, *Incorporating Dynamic Efficiency Concerns in Merger Analysis: The Use of Innovation Markets*, 63 ANTITRUST L.J. 569, 576–77 (1995).

Moreover, even when intellectual property protections are critical for protecting an innovator's ability to profit from its new ideas, more extensive intellectual property rights would not necessarily generate more new products or other innovation. A potential problem arises because much, if not all innovation is cumulative. Policies that broaden intellectual property protections might enhance the incentives for initial innovation, but in doing so they may discourage follow-on innovation. When intellectual property protections are broad, an owner of the intellectual property rights may have strong incentives to develop product improvements, but others may not. For anyone else, the only way to profit from a product enhancement is to sell it to a single buyer, the initial innovator. In order to avoid placing themselves in a disadvantageous bargaining situation, third parties may prefer to channel their innovation efforts elsewhere.

The resulting tradeoff has been described succinctly in testimony by Nobel Prize-winning economist Joseph E. Stiglitz, then a member of President Bill Clinton's Council of Economic Advisers:

> We often talk about how important patents are to promote innovation, because without patents, people don't appropriate the returns to their innovation activity, and I certainly very strongly subscribe to that. The key importance of intellectual property rights is [that they are] part of the mechanism that the market economy has to stimulate [innovation]. * * * On the other hand, some people jump from that to the conclusion that the broader the patent rights are, the better it is for innovation, and that isn't always correct, because we have an innovation system in which

one innovation builds on another. If you get monopoly rights down at the bottom, you may stifle competition that uses those patents later on, and so * * * the breadth and utilization of patent rights can be used not only to stifle competition, but also have adverse effects in the long run on innovation. We have to strike a balance.

FTC Hearings on Global and Innovation–Based Competition, Day 1, at 11 (Oct. 12, 1995), *available at* http://www.ftc.gov/opp/global/GC101295.htm.

Striking the right balance is in part an issue for the intellectual property system, for example in determining the breadth of patent grants. But it is also an issue for antitrust, as discussed in Sidebar 10–1. The prospect of a large future prize for successful innovation—in the form of the profits that arise from the intellectual property rights owner's ability to exclude others—is undoubtedly a spur to innovation. But competition also promotes innovation. Firms have a powerful incentive to gain a march on their rivals by cutting cost or being first with new products or product improvements. Overly-broad intellectual property rights discourage innovation because they discourage successive innovators from improving, and seeking the returns from supplanting, existing approaches.

As we shall see in this chapter, antitrust rules have, to varying degrees in different eras, restricted what an intellectual property owner can do with its intellectual property rights. In this broad sense, therefore, the antitrust rules operate as another limit on the scope of intellectual property rights, just as they limit the use of other property if it would significantly harm competition.

1. MANIPULATION OF PRODUCT STANDARDS AND CERTIFICATIONS

Standards are used in many industries to certify products as safe and effective for specified uses. For example, local building codes normally specify in great detail the kind of plumbing, electrical and general material requirements of residential and commercial construction. Often these codes are the product of efforts by industry to develop codes themselves through trade associations. Independent testing labs such as Underwriters Laboratories and the National Science Foundation also test and certify products. States, counties, and municipalities adopt these codes as public law.

Products and safety standards evolve over time, which necessitates a continual process of reevaluating codes. New products that could not have even been imagined at the time a code was drafted may necessitate redrafting or amending the code to account for new technology and new designs. Safety may dictate use of a certain material today, but the advent of a different, safer material may lead to changes in code. Asbestos insulation, for example, may at one time have been viewed as "state of the art" and approved by many building codes, but that clearly is no longer the case.

A supplier of a product that "does not meet code" will at best have a difficult time selling the product. For example, if a building code specifies that only steel electrical conduit can be used for certain purposes, the use of polyvinyl chloride ("PVC") conduit will in effect be prohibited, and suppliers of PVC conduit may find that there is no market for their product in a particular locale. *See, e.g., Allied Tube & Conduit Corp. v. Indian Head, Inc.,* 486 U.S. 492 (1988). This possibility—that a code or industry standard could in effect bar a substitute product—may in some circumstances create an incentive for rivals to attempt to influence the drafting of the code or standard. This incentive may be heightened when a new, innovative product threatens to displace an old one. Producers of the incumbent technology may try to delay or even totally preclude the emergence of the new technology by maintaining out-dated codes, or advocating more restrictive ones. In doing so, they may prevent price erosion and/or forestall improvements in product quality or choice—all to the detriment of consumers.

Am. Soc'y of Mech. Eng'rs, Inc. v. Hydrolevel, Corp., 456 U.S. 556 (1982) illustrates such a scenario. Although the narrow legal issue in the case concerned the Society's vicarious liability for the acts of its agent—an industry participant that had used its role as an ASME member to interpret an ASME promulgated code to exclude the product of one of its nascent rivals— the Court assumed that the activities described in the following excerpt violated the Sherman Act.

AMERICAN SOCIETY OF MECHANICAL ENGINEERS, INC. v. HYDROLEVEL CORP.

Supreme Court of the United States, 1982.
456 U.S. 556, 102 S.Ct. 1935, 72 L.Ed.2d 330.

Justice BLACKMUN delivered the opinion of the Court.

Petitioner, the American Society of Mechanical Engineers, Inc. (ASME), is a nonprofit membership corporation organized in 1880 under the laws of the State of New York. This case presents the important issue of the Society's civil liability under the antitrust laws for acts of its agents performed with apparent authority. Because the judgment of the Court of Appeals upholding civil liability is consistent with the central purposes of the antitrust laws, we affirm that judgment.

I

ASME has over 90,000 members drawn from all fields of mechanical engineering.* * * It employs a full-time staff, but much of its work is done through volunteers from industry and government. * * *

* * * ASME promulgates and publishes over 400 separate codes and standards for areas of engineering and industry. These codes, while only advisory, have a powerful influence: federal regulations have incorporated many of them by reference, as have the laws of most States, the ordinances of major cities, and the laws of all the Provinces of Canada. Obviously, if a manufacturer's product cannot satisfy the applicable ASME code, it is at a great disadvantage in the marketplace.

Among ASME's many sets of standards is its Boiler and Pressure Vessel Code. This set, like ASME's other codes, is very important in the affected industry; it has been adopted by 46 States and all but one of the Canadian Provinces. Section IV of the code sets forth standards for components of heating boilers, including "low-water fuel cutoffs." If the water in a boiler drops below a level sufficient to moderate the boiler's temperature, the boiler can "dry fire" or even explode. A low-water fuel cutoff does what its name implies: when the water in the boiler falls below a certain level, the device blocks the flow of fuel to the boiler before the water level reaches a dangerously low point. To prevent dry firing and boiler explosions, ¶ HG–605 of Section IV provides that each boiler "shall have an automatic low-water fuel cutoff so located as to automatically cut off the fuel supply when the surface of the water falls to the lowest visible part of the water gage glass."

For some decades, McDonnell & Miller, Inc. (M&M), has dominated the market for low-water fuel cutoffs. But in the mid–1960's, respondent Hydrolevel Corporation entered the low-water fuel cutoff market with a different version of this device. The relevant distinction, for the purposes of this case, was that Hydrolevel's fuel cutoff, unlike M&M's, included a time delay.

In early 1971, Hydrolevel secured an important customer. Brooklyn Union Gas Company, which had purchased M&M's product for several years, decided to switch to Hydrolevel's probe. Not surprisingly, M&M was concerned.

Because of its involvement in ASME, M&M was in an advantageous position to react to Hydrolevel's challenge. ASME's governing body had delegated the interpretation, formulation, and revision of the Boiler and Pressure Vessel Code to a Boiler and Pressure Vessel Committee. That committee in turn had authorized subcommittees to respond to public inquiries about the interpretation of the code. An M&M vice president, John W. James, was vice chairman of the subcommittee which drafted, revised, and interpreted Section IV, the segment of the Boiler and Pressure Vessel Code governing low-water fuel cutoffs.

After Hydrolevel obtained the Brooklyn Union Gas account, James and other M & M officials met with T. R. Hardin, the chairman of the Section IV subcommittee. The participants at the meeting planned a course of action. They decided to send an inquiry to ASME's Boiler and Pressure Vessel Committee asking whether a fuel cutoff with a time delay would satisfy the requirements of ¶ HG–605 of Section IV. James and Hardin, as vice chairman and chairman, respectively, of the relevant subcommittee, cooperated in drafting a letter, one they thought would elicit a negative response.

The letter was mailed over the name of Eugene Mitchell, an M&M vice president, to W. Bradford Hoyt, secretary of the Boiler and Pressure Vessel Committee and a full-time ASME employee. Following ASME's standard routine, Hoyt referred the letter to Hardin, as chairman of the subcommittee. Under the procedures of the Boiler and Pressure Vessel Committee, the subcommittee chairman—Hardin—could draft a response to a public inquiry without referring it to the entire subcommittee if he treated it as an "unofficial communication."

As a result, Hardin, one of the very authors of the inquiry, prepared the response. Although he retained control over the inquiry by treating the response as "unofficial," the response was signed by Hoyt, secretary of the Boiler and Pressure Vessel Committee, and it was sent out on April 29, 1971, on ASME stationery. Predictably, Hardin's prepared answer, utilized verbatim in the Hoyt letter, condemned fuel cutoffs that incorporated a time delay * * *.

* * *

As anticipated, M&M seized upon this interpretation of Section IV to discourage customers from buying Hydrolevel's product. It instructed its salesmen to tell potential customers that Hydrolevel's fuel cutoff failed to satisfy ASME's code. And M&M's employees did in fact carry the message of the subcommittee's response to customers interested in buying fuel cutoffs. Thus, M & M successfully used its position within ASME in an effort to thwart Hydrolevel's competitive challenge.

* * *

What was the nature of the anticompetitive effects being alleged in *Hydrolevel*? Are there predictable dangers to providing industry-run trade or membership organizations the authority to establish industry product standards? What might the advantages be? How would you counsel a client interested in participating in an industry run standard-setting effort based on what you just learned in *Hydrolevel*? For another illustration of the threat to research, development, and innovation that can arise when rivals cooperate in the context of product development, see *United States v. Automobile Manufacturers Ass'n.*, 307 F.Supp. 617 (C.D. Cal.1969) (approving consent decree where automobile manufacturers were accused of conspiring to suppress research and development of automotive air pollution control equipment). An anticompetitive manipulation of standard setting also can arise in the context of intellectual property, which we will discuss in greater depth later in this Chapter.

2. SUPPRESSION OF RIVAL INNOVATION BY A DOMINANT FIRM OR FIRMS

Dominant firms may also use a variety of strategies to impede or forestall competition from new and innovative products. One such strategy involves product design. IBM was accused in a series of cases in the 1970s of intentionally designing its hardware to be incompatible with the hardware of other manufacturers of peripheral devices, such as hard drives and other information storage devices. *See, e.g., California Computer Prods., Inc. v. IBM Corp.*, 613 F.2d 727, 744 (9th Cir.1979) (IBM's product design decisions upheld where evidence indicated that the redesign lowered costs and improved product performance). Similar accusations were rejected in *Berkey Photo, Inc. v. Eastman Kodak Co.*, 603 F.2d 263 (2d Cir.1979), where Kodak was accused of exploiting its monopoly of amateur photographic film by producing new films in different formats that would only function with Kodak cameras. The court rejected the plaintiff's assertion that Kodak had a duty to pre-disclose information on its product developments to rival camera manufacturers in order to facilitate their design and production of equipment capable of utilizing the new formats.

More broadly, *Berkey* suggests standards for judging whether and when a dominant firm's investment in new products might be scrutinized as an instrument of strategic entry deterrence. Antitrust's fundamental task here is to find ways to challenge those R & D and marketing strategies involving new products that deter competition by rivals without producing benefits to buyers, and it is a tough assignment. One reason it is difficult is that firms will often not know how their R & D efforts will work out. Thus, both the buyer benefits and the rival deterrent effects of R & D must be assessed from an *ex ante* perspective, focusing on what would be reasonable to expect at the time of innovation—a question related to, but not identical with, asking whether the R & D actually benefitted buyers or harmed competitors.

One approach to this task was suggested by *Berkey*, which explained that Kodak's introduction of a new film format and simultaneous withdrawal of an old format, forcing photographers to buy photofinishing from Kodak rather than Berkey, could have supplied the "bad act" necessary to support a charge of monopolization—but only if the new format had not been better or cheaper than the old. *Berkey Photo*, 603 F.2d at 287 n.39. *See* Jonathan B. Baker, *Product Differentiation Through Space and Time: Some Antitrust Policy Issues*, 42 ANTITRUST BULL. 177, 190–96 (1997).

The use of strategies targeted at impeding competition from new and innovative products also was at the heart of the 1998 prosecution of Microsoft for monopolization, which we studied in Chapters 6, 7, and 8. As we learned, the federal government and a group of states alleged that Microsoft, perceiving a threat to its monopoly in Intel-compatible PC desktop operating systems, set out to impede competition from what was termed "middleware," such as Netscape's Navigator Internet browser and Sun Microsystems' Java programming language. Although middleware did not itself constitute an alternative to Intel-compatible PC desktop operating systems, such as Microsoft's Windows and Apple's Mac OS, the prosecution's theory—ultimately endorsed by both the district and the court of appeals—was that middleware had the potential to become an operating system alternative. Microsoft was accused of attempting to quell that threat through a range of exclusionary conduct, including exclusive dealing arrangements, tying, pricing, and other anticompetitive strategies.

The competitive threat of middleware as an operating system substitute, however, was at best nascent—it had yet to coalesce into a true alternative to Windows. Relying on that fact, Microsoft maintained that the government had failed to demonstrate any causal link between Microsoft's allegedly anticompetitive conduct and its maintenance of monopoly power—the emerging technologies never coalesced into a true threat to its monopoly. According to Microsoft, the elimination of Netscape and Sun, therefore, was competitively inconsequential. In the following brief excerpt from the case, the court responded in strong terms.

UNITED STATES v. MICROSOFT CORP.

United States Court of Appeals for the District of Columbia Circuit, 2001.
253 F.3d 34.

PER CURIAM

* * *

II

* * *

* * * To require that § 2 liability turn on a plaintiff's ability or inability to reconstruct the hypothetical marketplace absent a defendant's anticompetitive conduct would only encourage monopolists to take more and earlier anticompetitive action.

We may infer causation where exclusionary conduct is aimed at producers of nascent competitive technologies as well as when it is aimed at producers of established substitutes. Admittedly, in the former case there is added uncertainty, inasmuch as nascent threats are merely *potential* substitutes. But the underlying proof problem is the same—neither plaintiffs nor the court can confidently reconstruct a product's hypothetical technological development in a world absent the defendant's exclusionary conduct. To some degree, "the defendant is made to suffer the uncertain consequences of its own undesirable conduct." 3 Areeda & Hovenkamp, Antitrust Law ¶ 651c, at 78.

Given this rather edentulous test for causation, the question in this case is not whether Java or Navigator would actually have developed into viable platform substitutes, but (1) whether as a general matter the exclusion of nascent threats is the type of conduct that is reasonably capable of contributing significantly to a defendant's continued monopoly power and (2) whether Java and Navigator reasonably constituted nascent threats at the time Microsoft engaged in the anticompetitive conduct at issue. As to the first, suffice it to say that it would be inimical to the purpose of the Sherman Act to allow monopolists free reign to squash nascent, albeit unproven, competitors at will—particularly in industries marked by rapid technological advance and frequent paradigm shifts. As to the second, the District Court made ample findings that both Navigator and Java showed potential as middleware platform threats.

* * *

———

The D.C. Circuit was unequivocal in its conclusion that the antitrust laws should be able to reach conduct that threatens to forestall or completely impede emerging competitive threats. But how developed and concrete must those threats be? Would the court's conclusion have been altered had Navigator and Java never actually made it to market? In other words, how "nascent" and how "imminent" must the competitive threat be before the plaintiff can satisfy the Sherman Act's threshold requirements of substantiality?

More broadly, what are the permissible boundaries of a dominant firm's responses to new competition? Must it sit back and avoid aggressive responses for fear that it will cross the line of legality? Will the cost in terms of diminished competitive vigor outweigh the value of too strict a standard? Given what we have read about Microsoft's conduct, would you agree with Microsoft's position that its hands were being tied unfairly by the court, impeding Microsoft's own ability to innovate without promoting innovation by its rivals?

3. SUPPRESSION OF RIVAL INNOVATION THROUGH ACQUISITION

One final scenario concerns the acquisition and subsequent suppression of an innovative rival, or perhaps its intellectual property. Intellectual property, of course, is an "asset," and so acquisitions of intellectual property can be subject to scrutiny under Section 7 of the Clayton Act. What if the acquisition itself appears lawful, but the acquiring firm's sole purpose is to acquire the new technology for the purpose of suppressing it?

Those were the allegations in *McDonald v. Johnson & Johnson*, 722 F.2d 1370 (8th Cir.1983), a case brought under Sections 1 and 2 of the Sherman Act, as well as Section 7 of the Clayton Act, by the former shareholders of an electronic pain-relieving device called "TENS" ("transcutaneous electronic nerve stimulator"). The plaintiffs had sold their interests in their firm to Johnson & Johnson, a pharmaceutical company, and alleged that in violation of the sale agreement, Johnson & Johnson suppressed rather than promoted their TENS device in order to protect its popular pain relieving pharmaceuticals from competition.

The case proceeded on fraud and breach of contract grounds, but the antitrust claims were dismissed for lack of antitrust injury, with the court relying on *Brunswick*. Why would the court so hold? Could former shareholders suffer injury of the kind the antitrust laws were designed to prevent? According to the Eighth Circuit, because the plaintiffs had sold their interests in toto, voluntarily withdrawing from the TENS market, they were no longer competitors of Johnson & Johnson, hence they could not have suffered the effects of any exclusionary conduct. Moreover, since they were not consumers of TENS either, they were not damaged by any collusive effects of Johnson & Johnson's conduct. Their injuries though real were contractual, not competitive in nature. 722 F.2d at 1374–79.

But the underlying scenario may nevertheless raise legitimate antitrust concerns. Under what circumstances should the acquisition for purposes of suppression of new emerging technologies constitute an antitrust violation? Should it matter that the technology is intellectual property? Should the new owner of property be free to decide not to exploit the technology? What problems can you see in trying to remedy a failure adequately to promote acquired technology?

Johnson & Johnson is the relatively rare case. The obvious intent to *suppress* innovation through acquisition makes it akin to other exclusionary effects cases, such as a firm's efforts to manipulate standards or preclude entry by a new rival. Acquisitions can also have collusive anticompetitive effects by reducing competition for innovation. As would any anticompetitive merger between competing firms, the analysis will focus on whether the merger will have unilateral or coordinated anticompetitive effects.

As we learned in Chapter 5, however, to complete that analysis, it is first necessary under the Merger Guidelines and the case law to define a relevant market. A number of issues, some quite controversial, have arisen in that regard, and we turn to them in our next section. We will also revisit suppression of innovation through acquisition later in this Chapter, when we look more particularly at mergers of firms with competing patents.

Before we turn to market definition issues, however, consider Figure 10–1, which summarizes some of the theories of innovation-related anticompetitive effects we have just reviewed. In evaluating the list, also consider: (1) the statutory basis most likely to be invoked to challenge the conduct in each instance; (2) the traditional elements required to establish each such offense; (3) the proof problems likely to arise in each case; and (4) whether rivals or consumers could adequately demonstrate antitrust injury in challenging conduct falling into any of the categories.

Figure 10–1:
Some Antitrust Theories for Challenging Innovation–Based Anticompetitive Effects

- manipulation of product standards or certifications
- suppression of rival innovation by a dominant firm
- suppression of rival innovation through acquisition

The scenarios discussed in this section are just a sampling of the kinds of innovation-suppressing conduct courts have examined. While there appears to be a consensus that the successful suppression of a new product or innovation should constitute an "anticompetitive effect" cognizable under the antitrust laws, as you can see, there may be challenging questions of fit and proof in such cases.

B.   NEW TECHNOLOGIES, NEW CONDUCT AND THE ADAPTABILITY OF ANTITRUST

In Section A we examined how courts and antitrust enforcement agencies have come to value and protect innovation. Note how that protection can cover new products as well as the competitive processes that produce them, and how a variety of antitrust provisions were at issue—Section 1 of the Sherman Act and Section 5 of the FTC Act in the standard setting cases, Section 2 of the Sherman Act in the dominant firm cases, and Section 7 of the Clayton Act in the merger and acquisition cases. In this Section we will examine a sampling of instances in which the presence of innovation, new products or technologies affected the traditional approach to analyzing allegedly anticompetitive conduct.

1.   CHANGING TECHNOLOGIES AND MARKET DEFINITION

The "perennial gales" of which Schumpeter spoke can greatly complicate the process of defining relevant markets and measuring market power in antitrust cases. The problem is greatest in markets featuring significant, technologically-driven change. A common scenario involves the response of a dominant firm that produces a relatively mature product to competition from a new product that has emerged with the potential to displace the incumbent one. The new product often enjoys only a small share of total sales, and the possibilities for its growth are somewhat uncertain.

Consider an example from the aerospace industry. In the mid to late 1950s, jet propulsion held out prospects for a revolution in commercial air travel. Aircraft producers varied substantially in their capability to make the transition from building propeller-driven airliners to making jet aircraft. From 1955 until 1970, jet transports gradually displaced propeller-driven airliners, although commercial airlines treated the two types of aircraft as substitutes for certain routes. An effort to define relevant markets in, say, 1960, that focused solely on sales of propeller-driven aircraft would have erred by ignoring the competitive potential of jets. For long-distance routes such as the trans-Atlantic trade, one could have justified the design and production of jet transports as its own relevant market.

In industries experiencing significant technological change, the court must confront a number of especially vexing questions: Should it define the market narrowly, limited to the mature product or technology? If the new product or technology promises dramatic improvements in quality or might confer a decisive cost advantage, should the court treat the innovation as its own product market? Must the court use a hybrid methodology that assigns differing weights to the old and the new, and attributes market shares to industry participants according to their capability to offer both?

The petroleum industry provided an important early test of the judiciary's ability to answer these questions. In 1924, the Justice Department sued 50 petroleum companies for illegally combining to create a monopoly in a new technology for refining crude petroleum. The principal defendants were four petroleum refiners, Standard Oil Company of Indiana (a remnant of the original Standard Oil trust that was later known as Amoco), the Texas Company (later known as Texaco), Standard Oil Company of New Jersey (also a remnant of the Standard Oil trust, later known as Exxon), and the Gasoline Products Company. These four refiners held patents for extracting gasoline from crude oil by the process of "cracking." Developed in 1913 by Standard of Indiana, cracking enabled refiners to extract a larger amount of gasoline (a higher valued product) from each barrel of crude oil.

The government alleged that the defendants violated Sections 1 and 2 of the Sherman Act by creating a patent pool to share and license rights to use cracking technology that each company had developed. The companies argued that the pool was necessary to avoid infringement actions that would impede any one firm's use of cracking technology. The focus of the government's concerns was a provision in the pooling agreements by which the firms collectively set the royalties that each could charge for licensing patents covered by the pool and created a formula for distributing royalty payments among themselves.

The district court sustained the government's complaint against the defendants, and the Supreme Court reversed in a unanimous opinion by Justice Louis Brandeis. Crucial to the Court's assessment of the challenged pooling arrangement was its evaluation of the primary defendants' collective position in the market for petroleum refining.

STANDARD OIL COMPANY (INDIANA)
v. UNITED STATES

United States Supreme Court, 1931.
283 U.S. 163, 51 S.Ct. 421, 75 L.Ed. 926.

Mr. Justice BRANDEIS delivered the opinion of the Court:

* * *

* * * The main contention of the Government is that even if the exchange of patent rights and division of royalties are not necessarily improper and the royalties are not oppressive, the three contracts are still obnoxious to the Sherman Act because specific clauses enable the primary defendants to maintain existing royalties and thereby to restrain interstate commerce. The provisions which constitute the basis for this charge are these. The first contract specifies that the Texas Company shall get from the Indiana Company one-fourth of all royalties thereafter collected under the latter's existing license agreements; and that all royalties received under licenses thereafter issued by either company shall be equally divided. Licenses granting rights under the patents of both are to be issued at a fixed royalty—approximately that charged by the Indiana Company when its process was alone in the field. By the second contract, the Texas Company is entitled to receive one-half of the royalties thereafter collected by the Gasoline Products Company from its existing licensees, and a minimum sum per barrel for all oil cracked by its future licensees. The third contract gives to the Indiana Company one-half of all royalties thereafter paid by existing licensees of the New Jersey Company, and a similar minimum sum for each barrel treated by its future licensees,— subject in the latter case to reduction if the royalties charged by the Indiana and Texas companies for their processes should be reduced. The alleged effect of these provisions is to enable the primary defendants, because of their monopoly of patented cracking processes, to maintain royalty rates at the level established originally for the Indiana process.

The rate of royalties may, of course be a decisive factor in the cost of production. If combining patent owners effectively dominate an industry, the power to fix and maintain royalties is tantamount to the power to fix prices. Where domination exists, a pooling of competing process patents, or an exchange of licenses for the purpose of curtailing the manufacture and supply of an unpatented product, is beyond the privileges conferred by the patents and constitutes a violation of the Sherman Act. The lawful individual monopolies granted by the patent statutes cannot be unitedly exercised to restrain. But an agreement for cross-licensing and division of royalties violates the Act only when used to effect a monopoly, or to fix prices, or to impose otherwise an unreasonable restraint upon interstate commerce. In the case at bar, the primary defendants own competing patented processes for manufacturing an unpatented product which is sold in interstate commerce; and agreements concerning such processes are likely to engender the evils to which the Sherman Act was directed. We must, therefore, examine the evidence to ascertain the operation and effect of the challenged contracts.

No monopoly, or restriction of competition, in the business of licensing patented cracking processes resulted from the execution of these agreements. Up to 1920 all cracking plants in the United States were either owned by the Indiana Company alone, or were operated under licenses from it. In 1924 and 1925, after the cross-licensing arrangements were in effect, the four primary defendants owned or licensed, in the aggregate, only 55 percent of the total cracking capacity, and the remainder was distributed among twenty-one independently owned cracking processes. This development and commercial expansion of competing processes is clear evidence that the contracts did not concentrate in the hands of the four primary defendants the licensing of patented processes for the production of cracked gasoline. Moreover, the record does not show that after the execution of the agreements there was a decrease of competition among them in licensing other refiners to use their respective processes.

No monopoly, or restriction of competition, in the production of either ordinary or cracked gasoline has been proved. The output of cracked gasoline in the years in question was about 26 percent of the total gasoline production. Ordinary or straight run gasoline is indistinguishable from cracked gasoline and the two are either mixed or sold interchangeably. Under these circumstances the primary defendants could not effectively control the supply or fix the price of cracked gasoline by virtue of their alleged monopoly of the cracking processes, unless they could control, through some means, the remainder of the total gasoline production from all sources. Proof of such control is lacking. Evidence of the total gasoline production by all methods, of each of the primary defendants and their licensees is either missing or unsatisfactory in character. The record does not accurately show even the total amount of cracked gasoline produced, or the production of each of the licensees, or competing refiners. Widely variant estimates of such production figures have been submitted. These were not accepted by the master and there is no evidence which would justify our doing so.

No monopoly, or restriction of competition, in the sale of gasoline has been proved. On the basis of testimony relating to the marketing of both cracked and ordinary gasoline, the master found that the defendants were in active competition among themselves and with other refiners; that both kinds of gasoline were refined and sold in large quantities by other companies; and that the primary defendants and their licensees neither individually or collectively controlled the market price or supply of any gasoline moving in interstate commerce. There is ample evidence to support these findings.

Thus it appears that no monopoly of any kind, or restraint of interstate commerce, has been effected either by means of the contracts or in some other way. In the absence of proof that the primary defendants had such control of the entire industry as would make effective the alleged domination of a part, it is difficult to see how they could by agreeing upon royalty rates control either the price or the supply of gasoline, or otherwise restrain competition. By virtue of their patents they had individually the right to determine who should use their respective processes or inventions and what the royalties for such use should be. To warrant an injunction which would invalidate the contracts here in question, and require either new arrangements or settlement of the conflicting claims by litigation, there must be a definite factual showing of illegality. Chicago Board of Trade v. United States, 246 U.S. 231, 238, 38 S.Ct. 242.

* * *

* * * The District Court accepted the Government's estimates of cracked gasoline production; found that the primary defendants were able to control both supply and price by virtue of their control of the cracking patents; held that although these patents were valid consideration for the cross-licenses, the agreement to maintain royalties was in effect a method for fixing the price of cracked gasoline; and concluded that a monopoly existed as a result of such agreements. This appears to be the only basis for the relief granted. But the widely varying estimates, relied upon to establish dominant control of the production of cracked gasoline were insufficient for that purpose. And the court entirely disregarded not only the fact that the manufacture of gasoline by the cracking process constituted only a part of the total gasoline production, but also the evidence showing active competition among the defendants themselves and with others. Its findings are without adequate support in the evidence. The bill should have been dismissed.

* * *

———

The Supreme Court's evaluation of the patent pooling arrangement in *Standard Oil (Cracking)* rested heavily on whether the principal defendants had substantial market power. If the relevant market consisted of the output of gasoline from cracking technology, the principal defendants' market share was 55 percent. If the relevant market included gasoline produced from both cracking technology and the older distillation method of refining, their share was 26 percent. By choosing to treat cracking technology and distillation technology as fungible, *i.e.*, as part of an indivisible product market, the Court decided that the firms controlled only 26 percent of total gasoline output. They therefore did not threaten to suppress competition unduly by jointly setting the royalties to be charged for patents included in the pooling arrangement.

But was the Court correct in combining in a single product market the old and new technologies? The argument against such an approach is that by doing so the Court underestimated the significance of cracking technology. By allowing refiners to extract a greater amount of gasoline from each barrel of crude oil, cracking conferred a significant cost advantage upon its users. Broad application of cracking technology throughout the industry promised to reduce the industry's cost of producing gasoline, and the pooling arrangement at issue in *Standard Oil (Cracking)*, by raising the price that companies had to pay to license the cracking patents, may have retarded that development.

As we have observed at many points in the Casebook, the reliability of market shares as a proxy for market power largely depends on the accuracy of relevant product market definition. In the case of industries that involve competing production processes, defining a product market may require difficult judgments about which industrial processes to include and which to leave out. By declining to identify control of cracking technology as its own relevant product market, the Court generated a market share for the defendants (26 percent) that may have obscured the true significance of a new process in petroleum refining.

It is also apparent that a court cannot calculate market shares accurately without sound data. The Supreme Court's reluctance to accept the government's suggested approach to defining the relevant market in terms of cracking technology seems to have stemmed partly from its concerns about the reliability of the prosecution's data on gasoline production. This underscores an additional basic point about the use of market shares as proxies for market power: the reliability of market shares as measures of market power is largely a function of the quality of data concerning the industry activity to be analyzed.

But is there an argument to be made that *Standard Oil* could have been decided in favor of the government even with a broad market definition? If the defendants' practices prevented prices from falling, *i.e.*, had actual anticompetitive effects, should the choice of market definition be outcome determinative? Recall cases like *NCAA* from Chapter 2 and *Staples* from Chapter 5. What importance should be assigned to such actual effects evidence and how might it affect the role of market definition?

Finally, *Standard Oil* serves as a reminder that "new economies" are a persistent feature of markets over time. Although the locus of innovation may change, the fact of it and its power to transform industries does not. In the 1920s, the emergence of cracking technology was transforming oil refining.

What factors should influence the decision to isolate "new" technologies as a distinct relevant market? In its 2002 consent decree in connection with the proposed acquisition by Bayer AG of Aventis Crop Science Holding S.A., the FTC concluded that "*New Generation* Chemical Insecticide Active Ingredients" and "*New Generation* Chemical Insecticide Products" were distinct relevant product markets. *See In the Matter of Bayer AG and Aventis S.A.*, Dkt. No. C–4049, 2002 WL 1151015 (FTC May 30, 2002). Figure 10–2 summarizes the factors the Commission relied upon to support those markets in its Analysis to Aid Public Comment. Were any of these factors, or perhaps analogous ones, also present in *Standard Oil*?

Figure 10–2:
Factors Relied Upon by the FTC in *Bayer/Aventis* to Justify Market for "New Generation" Products

Product Advantages Relative to "Old Generation"

- reductions in the amount of insecticides used, resulting in reduced negative consequences for health and environment

- reduced risk to humans and beneficial insects due to use of safer chemicals

- superior control of undesirable pests

- eligibility for regulatory approval under elevated EPA standards

Characteristics of Merging Firms and Industry

- merging firms are two of only three firms that have successfully developed and commercialized "next generation" products

- the merging firms have unique product development and commercialization skills

- rivals, through licensing, seek out and utilize expertise of the merging firms to develop their own new products

The antitrust analysis in both *Standard Oil (Cracking)* and *Bayer/Aventis* concerned existing markets, which were in the process of being transformed by new technologies. In *Standard Oil*, the Court chose to treat the new and the old as part of a single relevant market, whereas the Commission in *Bayer/Aventis* viewed the "New Generation" technology as a distinct market. But how should antitrust treat efforts to innovate that have yet to yield any marketable product? In other words, can there be "innovation markets"?

The idea that current research and development efforts could constitute a distinct relevant market for antitrust purposes—even though they have yet to produce a marketable product—began to take hold in the early 1990s, but it has engendered a great deal of discussion at the enforcement agencies and in the literature. Consider the implications of the following scenarios, some of which we have already observed:

- a merger is proposed between two firms that are both leaders in R & D for a particular *future* product or process;

- a dominant firm undertakes conduct that delays or otherwise impairs the emergence of a new product or technology that may in the *future* develop into a serious challenge to its own, currently dominant product or process;

- a group of rivals agrees to limit the access of another one of their rivals to a product or process necessary to the development of "next generation" products.

The next Sidebar explores some of the commentary that has focused on the pluses and minuses of seeking to protect "innovation" markets in these sorts of circumstances and others.

Sidebar 10–2:
Innovation Markets

In 1997, the Federal Trade Commission accepted a final a consent order growing out of its review of the merger of Ciba–Geigy and Sandoz, two pharmaceutical firms that combined to create Novartis. *In re Ciba-Geigy*, 123 FTC 842 (1997). *See generally* Richard J. Gilbert & Willard K. Tom, *Is Innovation King at the Antitrust Agencies? The Intellectual Property Guidelines Five Years Later*, 69 ANTITRUST L.J. 43, 55–58 (2001). The settlement addressed several FTC concerns involving "gene therapy" treatments for medical conditions, which would work by modifying the genes in patients' cells. At the time of the merger, this industry did not actually exist—no gene therapy product had been marketed or even approved by the Food and Drug Administration—but some such products were in clinical trials and pharmaceutical firms were investing heavily in their development and commercialization.

The FTC's complaint alleged harmful competitive effects in markets for the "research, development, manufacture and sale" of gene therapy products for treating various diseases, including cancer. *In re Ciba-Geigy*, 123 F.T.C. at 844. According to the Commission, only the merging firms and one other, Chiron, controlled the substantial property rights necessary to commercialize gene therapy products. The adverse competitive effects would include:

> (1) a reduction in innovation competition among firms developing gene therapy products, resulting in delay or redirection of R & D tracks;

> (2) market power in various gene therapy markets, exercised either unilaterally or through coordinated interaction with Chiron;

> (3) a reduction in potential competition by prospective entrants, who would be required to invent around a broader portfolio of patents in order to succeed; and

> (4) a disincentive for the merged firm to license intellectual property rights or collaborate with other firms as compared with premerger incentives. *Id.* at 851–52.

One of these allegations, the fourth, involves harm to competition in markets for the sale of *current* products, namely various intellectual property rights. This kind of product market is termed a "technology market" in the Intellectual Property Guidelines. U.S. Dep't of Justice and Federal Trade Comm'n, *Antitrust Guidelines for the Licensing of Intellectual Property* § 3.2.2 (April 6, 1995) (hereinafter "*IP Guidelines*"). But the other three allegations do not. The second and third allege harm to competition in markets for the sale of *future* products, involving collusive and exclusionary effects respectively. The first allegation involves the loss of competition in what the IP Guidelines term an "innovation market"— a market for research and development directed to particular new or improved goods or processes, and the close substitutes for that research and development. *IP Guidelines*, § 3.2.3. Innovation markets may be defined in merger analysis, but also to analyze the full range of possible antitrust offenses, including licensing of intellectual property (the subject of the Intellectual Property Guidelines), collaborations among rivals, and alleged monopolization.

Why do the enforcement agencies seek to define innovation markets and future product markets? Why not merely plead harmful competitive effects involving innovation in existing product markets? One reason is that many forms of conduct under review, especially mergers, are analyzed prospectively, before the possible harms appear. If, as a result, the competitive harms would arise in future product markets, or through a reduction in the prospects for innovation that would lead to new products, they would not necessarily fall on the customers of current products. *See generally* Richard J. Gilbert & Steven C. Sunshine, *Incorporating Dynamic Efficiency Concerns in Merger Analysis: The Use of Innovation Markets*, 63 ANTITRUST L.J. 569 (1995); Richard J. Gilbert & Steven C. Sunshine, *The Use of Innovation Markets: A Reply to Hay, Rapp, and Hoerner*, 64 ANTITRUST L.J. 75, 80–82 (1995).

A key problem for defining innovation markets is that new products and processes that supplant existing goods and methods can be developed in unrelated industries. As one critic puts it, "the capacity to innovate is hard to monopolize." Richard T. Rapp, *The Misapplication of the Innovation Market Approach to Merger Analysis*, 64 ANTITRUST L.J. 19, 36–37 (1995). The IP Guidelines anticipate this criticism, and explain that "The Agencies will delineate an innovation market only when the capabilities to engage in the relevant research and development can be associated with specialized assets or characteristics of specific firms." *IP Guidelines* § 3.2.3. Under such circumstances, the enforcement agencies contend, they can identify the particular research and development tracks directed at a particular new product or process, and in competition. Thus, many of the FTC's innovation market cases have involved the development of new pharmaceuticals; for these products, it may be easy to determine how far along each firm has come in the Food & Drug Administration approval process. Perhaps because of this limitation, innovation markets are not commonly defined.

Buyers or excluded rivals who allege that they are victims of anti-competitive conduct in innovation markets may face an additional hurdle: proof of injury and causation sufficient to ground standing to sue. *See generally* 1 HERBERT HOVENKAMP, MARK D. JANIS & MARK A. LEMLEY, IP AND ANTITRUST: AN ANALYSIS OF ANTITRUST PRINCIPLES APPLIED TO INTELLECTUAL PROPERTY LAW ¶ 4.3d (2002). Should that also be a concern in a government prosecution?

The analysis of firm conduct within future product markets or innovation markets does not end at market definition. Firms merging their research and development activities, or collaborating in R & D, for example, may often achieve substantial efficiencies by doing so, and these efficiencies should be accounted for in assessing the reasonableness of the practice. The firms may be able to achieve scale economies in R & D, for example, or improve their prospects for innovation success by pooling complementary knowledge or skills. Here, as elsewhere in antitrust, indirect evidence of market power, derived from market definition and market shares, may not capture all aspects of competitive harm that might be relevant under the rule of reason. Reconsider the *Standard Oil (Cracking)* case from this perspective. Would the Court's analysis have differed had the product market been limited to production (or innovation) using the new technology? Should the market definition matter to the competitive effects analysis?

The definition and competitive significance of innovation markets has continued to spawn differences of opinion and debate. In January 2004, by a divided vote, the FTC closed its investigation into the 2001 acquisition by Genzyme Corporation of Novazyme Pharmaceuticals, Inc. Novazyme was engaged primarily in conducting early pre-clinical studies relating to enzyme-replacement treatment (ERT) for Pompe disease, a rare and often fatal early childhood disease. Genzyme was also engaged in preclinical animal testing of ERTs. The Commission's investigation focused on the transaction's potential impact on the pace and scope of research into the development of a treatment for Pompe disease, given that the two firms appeared to be the only active sources of R & D into therapies for Pompe disease.

The Commission voted 3–1–1 to close the investigation. Three separate statements were filed, one by then Chairman Muris for the majority, a dissenting statement by Commissioner Thompson, and a separate statement by Commissioner Harbour. All focused on and discussed the analysis of innovation markets in the context of mergers. *See* http://www.ftc.gov/opa/2004/01/genzyme.htm.

As you continue with your readings in this Chapter, consider how the use of "innovation markets" might enhance understanding of the competitive effects of the conduct being challenged.

2. NEW FORMS OF COOPERATION, COLLABORATION AND EXCLUSION: THE INTERNET AS A MARKETPLACE

a. Internet Free Riding

In Chapter 4 we first learned of the Supreme Court's acceptance of the prevention of "free-riding" as a legitimate rationale for a manufacturer to impose vertical, intrabrand restraints on its dealers or franchisees in *Sylvania* and *Leegin*. Recall from *Leegin*, that although the Supreme Court dropped the per se rule, it noted that dealer-instigated minimum resale price maintenance could still be anticompetitive, because it could be used to facilitate a dealer cartel. Although the following excerpt from an FTC Aid to Public Comment arose before *Leegin*, note how the Commission applied *Sylvania*, the previous cases on minimum resale price maintenance that addressed the dealer cartel problem (especially *Business Electronics*), and the boycott cases discussed in Chapters 2 and 7 to Internet sales. Note too that it found a competitive problem given the nature of the free-riding complaints from a group of Chrysler new car dealers.

IN RE FAIR ALLOCATION SYSTEM, INC.
Federal Trade Commission, 1998.
63 Fed. Reg. 43182.

* * *

ANALYSIS OF PROPOSED CONSENT ORDER TO AID PUBLIC COMMENT

The Federal Trade Commission has accepted a proposed consent order from Fair Allocation System, Incorporated ("FAS"). FAS is an organization of twenty-five automobile dealerships from five Northwest states that was formed to address dealer concerns over the marketing practices of automobile manufacturers. In particular, FAS members were concerned about an automobile dealership—Dave Smith Motors of Kellogg, Idaho—which was attracting customers from around the Northwest and taking substantial sales from FAS members by selling cars for low prices and marketing them on the Internet.

According to the complaint, because of these concerns, the members of FAS collectively attempted to force Chrysler to change its vehicle allocation system. Chrysler allocates vehicles based on the dealer's total sales; FAS members wanted Chrysler to allocate vehicles based on the expected number of sales from a dealer's local area, which would have substantially reduced the number of cars available to a dealership like Dave Smith Motors that drew customers from a wider geographic area. According to the complaint, the members of FAS threatened to refuse to sell certain Chrysler vehicles and to limit the warranty service they would provide to particular customers unless Chrysler changed its allocation system so as to disadvantage dealers that sold large quantities of vehicles outside of their local geographic areas.

The compliant charges that FASs' agreements or attempts to agree with its dealer members to coerce Chrysler violate Section 5 of the FTC Act, as amended, 15 U.S.C. 45. According to the complaint, FAS members constitute a substantial percentage of the Chrysler, Plymouth, Dodge, Jeep and Eagle dealerships in eastern Washington, Idaho, and western Montana, and FASs' threats would have harmed competition and consumers in those areas. In particular, FASs' efforts would have deprived consumers of local access to certain Chrysler models and to warranty service, and would have reduced competition among automobile dealerships, including rivalry based on price or via the Internet.

The goal of the boycott was to limit the sales of a car dealer that sells cars at low prices and via a new and innovative channel—the Internet. FASs' threatened action against Chrysler is a per se illegal group boycott. In *United States v. General Motors*, 384 U.S. 127 (1966), the Supreme Court held per se illegal a comparable dealer cartel in Los Angeles that sought to prevent other area dealers from selling automobiles through discount brokers. Since General Motors, the Supreme Court has twice cited its per se condemnation of dealer cartels with approval. See *Continental T.V., Inc. v. GTE Sylvania Inc.*, 433 U.S. 36, 58 n. 28 (1977); *Business Electronics v. Sharp Electronics*, 485 U.S. 717, 734 n. 5 (1988). Such dealer cartels are "characteristically likely to result in predominantly anticompetitive effects," *Northwest Wholesale Stationers v. Pacific Stationery & Printing Co.*, 472 U.S. 284, 295 (1985), because they aim to limit competition while producing no plausible efficiencies.

Even where an agreement otherwise appears to fall in a category traditionally analyzed under a per se rule, a more extensive, rule-of-reason analysis may be necessary if there are plausible efficiency justifications for the conduct. *Broadcast Music, Inc. v. Columbia Broadcasting System*, Inc., 441 U.S. 1 (1979). Here, however, there appear to be no plausible efficiencies that would justify the dealers' conduct. Even if there were reason to believe that Dave Smith Motors, or similarly operated dealerships, were free-riding[1] on the efforts of more traditional dealers, no boycott would be needed to deal with the problem. Manufacturers have strong incentives to prevent free-riding by a few of their dealers at the expense of the rest, and can be expected to be responsive to complaints from their dealers acting individually if the free-riding concerns are genuine. In the absence of an efficiency justification that plausibly explains why concerted action is necessary, extensive searches for and investigations of justifications for such conduct would be unwarranted, and would only add a layer of complication and delay.

In this case, the absence of a justification is especially clear. Chrysler has previously rejected demands that it change its allocation system and publicly lauded Dave Smith Motors. Indeed, Chrysler's Vice President of Sales and Marketing has flatly stated that Chrysler believes the best way to increase its

---

1. "Free-rider" concerns may arise where two distributors sell the same product, but provide different levels of service in connection with the sale of that product. For example, one distributor may have a full-service showroom and the other may sell out of a warehouse that offers no service. Consumers may visit the showroom, learn all they need to know about the product, and then purchase the produce from a "no-service" discounter. The problem is that over time the full-service distributor may lose its incentive or financial ability to provide the services, to the detriment of both the manufacturer and the consumers who value those services. Free-rider concerns generally do not exist if the full-service distributor is compensated for its services.

sales penetration is to provide dealers as much product as they can sell, no matter where the customer comes from. Even if Chrysler had acceded to the boycotters' demands, however, that would not have justified a horizontal boycott by the dealers.

The proposed consent order would prohibit FAS from participating in, facilitating, or threatening any boycott of or concerted refusal to deal with any automobile manufacturer or consumer. There is nothing in the proposed order, however, that would prohibit FAS from informing automobile manufacturers about the views and opinions of FAS members.

* * *

By direction of the Commission.

* * *

———

What competitive concerns gave rise to the FTC's challenge to the activities of FAS? How, if at all, did the use of the Internet as an alternative distribution channel affect the analysis of the ostensibly vertical restraints FAS sought from Chrysler? Should it have altered it at all? Can you hypothesize circumstances under which a manufacturer might want to impose vertical non-price restraints on its dealers in order to forestall true free-riding by Internet retailers? Would the case be analyzed any different since *Leegin* decided that resale price maintenance should be analyzed under the rule of reason? For a successful invocation of a free-riding rationale in connection with limitations in Internet sales, see *Morris Communications Corp. v. PGA Tour, Inc.*, 364 F.3d 1288 (11th Cir. 2004) (affirming summary judgment on Section 2 monopolization claim based on defendant's evidence that challenged distribution restrictions were adopted to address legitimate concerns about Internet free riding).

b. Cyberspace Joint Ventures: Two Case Studies

With the growth of the Internet as a marketplace in the mid–1990s, businesses began to explore how cyberspace markets could be utilized to achieve greater efficiencies in the process of supplying inputs to the production process. One result was the advent of the "Business-to-Business" ("B2B") exchange. B2B exchanges are designed to facilitate transactions among and between businesses (as opposed to among and between business and consumers), and typically involve the creation of a limited access web site. They can take a number of forms and there are several typical models:

- *Simple Sale or "Catalog" Model*. A firm offers to sell to other firms from its own Internet web site, often through on-line "catalog" offerings.

- *Exchange Model*. A web site is created for the exchange by multiple sellers and buyers of a category of goods or services. The web site might be owned and operated by an industry participant, or it might be the product of a joint venture created by industry participants and run by a newly created entity.

- *Auction Model.* Drawing from consumer examples such as E–Bay, a B2B can also be constructed around an auction model, in which sellers and buyers bid for products and services.

- *Negotiation Model.* Under a "negotiation" model, which can take many forms, a seller or prospective buyer might as a prelude to individual negotiations post a "request for proposal" ("RFP") on a web site, inviting bids or proposals from potential business partners.

For a more thorough discussion of the various forms B2Bs can take, see FTC Staff Report, *Entering the 21st Century: Competition Policy in the World of B2B Electronic Marketplaces* (October 2000), *available at* http://www.ftc.gov/os/2000/10/b2breport.pdf (hereinafter *"FTC Staff Report on B2Bs"*).

Of course, these models are illustrative and not limiting. A B2B web site can combine a number of features of any of the four, and both their form and operation remain in flux. A typical B2B exchange web site, however, might create a cyberspace based marketplace in which input suppliers and finished good producers can meet, bid and contract for the supply of inputs.

Another generally more familiar variant is the "Business-to-Consumer" ("B2C") web site. Although similarly diverse in design, B2C web sites also tend to take the form of a simple sale, exchange or auction model. Popular examples include Amazon (an Internet only simple sale model) and E–Bay (an auction model, although it can be viewed as a "C2C"). Of course, there are literally thousands of other examples of firms that sell through traditional distribution channels, but also sell from web sites over the Internet.

As with the creation of any marketplace, the principal economic attraction of Internet web sites, especially B2B sites, are their tendency to reduce transaction costs compared to paper transactions. In the place of individual negotiations with multiple suppliers, the B2B facilitates a new method of communicating among businesses that allows for almost instantaneous, and relatively low cost, offer, acceptance, bidding and sales. Costs associated with soliciting, processing, and handling transactions can be reduced. Moreover, B2B based transactions, through improved inventory management, can reduce inventory costs and, by facilitating rivalry, lead to lower costs overall. They can also reduce software development and operation costs, producing a single, jointly developed and managed, secure exchange. *See generally* Symposium, *Inside the Internet Bazaar: B2B Exchanges*, ANTITRUST, Fall 2000, at 6–49; *FTC Staff Report on B2Bs*, Part 2.

Internet web sites can also raise antitrust concerns, some significant. As with any anticompetitive scenario, those associated with Internet web sites fall broadly into two categories: collusive and exclusionary, and as with any joint venture, issues can arise in connection with the formation or the operation of the site. By facilitating the exchange of information on prices and costs among rivals, Internet web sites can lead to price fixing, bid rigging, division of markets or other horizontal concerns. By providing solutions for "cartel problems" they might also facilitate *tacit* collusion, which might not rise to the level of "agreement," but which could lead to higher prices, especially if a significant portion of an industry's capacity is funneled through a single web site. Because by their very nature web sites involve limited access, they can also lead to exclusionary effects when by either design or operation participants are limited and participation becomes critical for industry members.

As a way of focusing our consideration of the competition issues raised by Internet web sites, we first profile two examples of the genre: (1) Covisint, a B2B web site created by a group of automotive manufacturers and suppliers; and (2) Orbitz, a B2C web site created by some of the Nation's major airlines as a one-stop travel service portal. After doing so, in Sidebar 10–3, we examine the antitrust issues that Internet web sites can pose.

COVISINT

Covisint was the first B2B web site to be analyzed—and approved—by the FTC. Formed in 2000 by five automotive manufacturers who at the time together accounted for about 50% of total worldwide automobile production (General Motors, Ford, DaimlerChrysler, Renault, and Nissan), and two information technology firms (Commerce One and Oracle), Covisint was presented to the FTC for review through a Hart–Scott–Rodino Premerger notification filed in June 2000. Illustrating the trend towards transnational cooperation in the investigation of global antitrust matters, the FTC cooperated in its investigation with the German Cartel Office (Bundeskartellamt), which also cleared the creation of Covisint shortly thereafter. Approval from the EU followed in August 2001.

Covisint was designed to operate as an Internet-based B2B exchange providing services to firms operating at various levels in the automotive industry supply chain worldwide. According to the FTC, its "core offerings" included "services to assist in product design, supply chain management and procurement functions performed by auto manufacturers and their direct and indirect suppliers." Press Release, *FTC Terminates HSR Waiting Period for Covisint B2B Venture*, September 11, 2000, *available at* http://www.ftc.gov/opa/2000/09/covisint.shtm. It appeared, therefore, that its goal was to modernize and streamline the operation of the automotive supply chain in the hope of achieving very significant efficiencies.

In terminating the HSR waiting period, the FTC provided little in the way of an antitrust analysis. At the time early termination was sought, however, Covisint was not yet operational. In fact, as the FTC noted, it was still in its early stages of development, and had yet to adopt any bylaws, operating rules or terms for participant access. That fact, coupled with the founding members' "large share" of the auto production market, led the FTC to indicate that its green light was provisional, and that it reserved the right to revisit the venture once its true dimensions and methods of operation had taken shape. Noting the significant efficiency potential of B2B ventures in terms of increased productivity and lower costs, the then FTC Chairman also observed:

> * * * [A]s is the case with any joint venture, whether in the traditional or new economy, B2Bs should be organized and implemented in ways that maintain competition. The antitrust analysis of an individual B2B will be specific to its mission, its structure, its particular market circumstances, procedures and rules for organization and operation, and actual operations and market performance.

Id.

Why would the antitrust analysis of a B2B venture be just like that of "any joint venture"? Are there any factors unique to the B2B setting that require new antitrust rules? Or is the analysis of joint ventures in new settings, such as the Internet, merely a matter of adapting the applicable legal rules to the particular facts, including Internet-specific facts? What do you suppose the Chairman means in the last quoted sentence, when he lists a number of factors as relevant to the antitrust assessment of a B2B venture? How would those factors affect the antitrust analysis of a B2B venture? How could such a venture appear to be permissible at the formation stage, but potentially raise more serious antitrust issues in operation? We will revisit some of these questions in Sidebar 10–3.

Covisint is now operational (*see* www.covisint.com). It has expanded to include the health care as well as the automotive industry, as well as a range of additional web-based services.

Orbitz

Orbitz is an Internet web site created by the five largest domestic U.S. airlines (American, Continental, Delta, Northwest, and United) and launched in June 2001. Whereas Covisint focused on establishing a market place where producers and suppliers could stream-line the process of supplying inputs among themselves, Orbitz was conceived of as a vehicle for putting suppliers in direct contact with consumers—a "Business-to-Consumer" ("B2C") web site. Since it became operational, most of the remaining airlines have become associate members of Orbitz, which may have already surpassed its major rivals Expedia and Travelocity in terms of on-line air line ticket sales. Subject to the "most-favored nation" (MFN) clause discussed below, neither the founding nor the associate members of Orbitz are formally required to offer Internet tickets exclusively through Orbitz; hence, each can in theory offer on-line air fares either through its own web site or through another on-line travel service. Moreover, although Orbitz's founding members cooperated in the creation of Orbitz, and continue to cooperate in connection with its operation, sales of airline tickets through Orbitz reportedly only account for about 10% of all members' ticket sales, and each continues to compete in the sale of air travel, although those facts may be evolving over time. *See* William F. Adkinson, Jr. & Thomas M. Lenard, *Orbitz: An Antitrust Assessment*, Antitrust, Spring 2002, at 76.

Just as the FTC initially granted clearance to Covisint, in April 2001 the Department of Transportation concluded that it would not seek to prevent Orbitz from becoming operational. After that, however, additional scrutiny was directed at Orbitz and its operation, much of it in response to the urging of other airlines, as well as travel agents and industry groups, and industry rivals Expedia and Travelocity. Principal among the accusations directed at Orbitz was that certain features of its operating agreements may encourage and facilitate uniformity of air fares (collusive effects), that through the use of "MFN" clauses its members confined their best fares to Orbitz, placing other Internet travel services at a distinct disadvantage (exclusionary effects), and that its members imposed uniform commission rates (collusive effects). In response, Orbitz claimed a number of competitive benefits and efficiencies, including: (1) superior search engine and software; (2) unbiased flight displays; (3) reduced distribution costs; (4) reduced consumer search costs (a benefit of "one-stop" shopping); and (5) increased competition in on-line travel. *Id.*

The Department of Justice announced the closing of its investigation of Orbitz on July 31, 2003. *See* http://www.usdoj.gov/atr/public/press_releases/2003/201208.htm. According to the press release:

> The Division considered several theories of harm none of which was ultimately borne out by the information collected by the Antitrust Division. These concerns included whether certain Orbitz contract terms would facilitate coordination among the participating airlines or reduce their incentives to discount resulting in higher fares and whether those contract terms would make the Orbitz joint venture dominant in online air travel distribution. The Division found that those terms did not result in higher fares or make Orbitz dominant in online air travel distribution.

On December 23, 2003, the Antitrust Division also closed its investigation of two B2C internet joint ventures, PressPlay and MusicNet, which were established by major record labels to sell digital music to consumers from Internet web sites. As in the case of Orbitz, the Department stated that it had looked at several theories of anticompetitive harm, both collusive and exclusionary, but that none ultimately were supported by the facts. *See* http://www.usdoj.gov/atr/public/press_releases/2003/201946.htm.

As you read through the next Sidebar, consider how you would go about conducting an antitrust analysis of a venture like Covisint or Orbitz. What kinds of information would you need? How would the government's *Guidelines for Collaborations Among Competitors* apply? Which of the cases we have studied would be relevant to your analysis?

Sidebar 10–3:
Competitive Analysis of Internet
Joint Ventures

As is no doubt evident from the foregoing discussion, commerce organized around Internet web sites, especially B2B web sites, may have the potential to achieve very substantial efficiencies. On the other hand, as with any joint venture that brings together rivals in cooperation, they may also present antitrust risks. In this Sidebar, we take a closer look at how these countervailing possibilities are evaluated in the antitrust analysis of B2B web sites.

Analytical Framework

New Rules or New Setting. A threshold issue that has arisen is whether contemporary antitrust rules can provide an adequate basis for assessing the anticompetitive impact of New Economy industries and conduct. For the most part, the answer has been "yes." As we shall see, although the setting and facts surrounding B2B web sites may be new, the basic framework for analyzing them is derived from traditional joint venture cases and the government's *Antitrust Guidelines for Collaboration Among Competitors. See FTC Staff Report on B2Bs*, Part 3. The more substantial challenge to antitrust's adaptability may lie instead with the limits of its institutions. As one commentator has argued more broadly with respect to the application of antitrust rules to the new economy:

> * * * [A]ntitrust doctrine is supple enough, and its commitment to economic rationality strong enough, to take in stride the competitive issues presented by the new economy. The real problem lies on the institutional side: the enforcement agencies and the courts do not have adequate technical resources, and do not move fast enough, to cope effectively with a very complex business sector that changes very rapidly.

Richard A. Posner, *Antitrust in the New Economy*, 68 ANTITRUST L.J. 925 (2001).

Applicability of Rule of Reason. As noted above, B2B web sites can achieve a number of significant efficiencies. According to the *FTC Staff Report on B2Bs*, "[t]hey can help reduce administrative costs, cut search costs, open new markets, check unmonitored corporate spending, aid efficient joint purchasing, facilitate supply chain management, and facilitate efficient collaborations for such projects as joint product design. * * * "*FTC Staff Report on B2Bs*, Part 3.

Absent evidence that the B2B is a mere facade for a price-fixing or market division arrangement, therefore, they will be evaluated by government enforcement agencies under the *Antitrust Guidelines for Collaboration Among Competitors* for their reasonableness, taking into account their potential efficiencies and anticompetitive effects. Relevant factors might include: (1) the structure of the B2B joint venture entity; (2) the provisions of its bylaws; (3) its operating rules; (4) contracts with participants; (5) the nature of its ownership and management; and (6) the characteristics of the markets in which it operates, including such factors as the market shares of the participants, conditions of entry, and the presence of network effects. *Id*. According to the *FTC Staff Report*, most competitive problems that arise in the context of B2B web sites can be addressed through "well-crafted operating rules." *Id*. Addressing those competitive concerns, however, may also require familiarity with the technical aspects of B2B commerce. *See, e.g.*, David H. Evans, *B2Bs–A Technical Perspective*, ANTITRUST, Spring 2000, at 45.

Markets Affected. What is the "relevant market" in which to assess a B2B joint venture? In part, answering that question turns on an assessment of the kinds of anticompetitive effects that can flow from the formation and/or operation of B2B joint ventures. The *FTC Staff Report* divided those possible effects into two categories: (1) effects in the markets for goods traded on B2Bs; and (2) effects on the "market for marketplaces." Although the first category is self-evident, the second may not be—it asks "how can the formation or operation of this B2B joint venture affect competition *among and between* rival B2B joint ventures in the same goods markets"? Over-inclusive membership, for example, may significantly diminish the likelihood that other B2B joint ventures will be formed. If B2B marketplaces for a particular category of goods constitute a relevant market distinct from the general market for the sale of the affected goods or services, joint ventures must be evaluated not only for their effects on the underlying goods markets, but for their effects on competition either among existing B2Bs, or for the creation of future B2Bs.

Competitive Analysis

As noted earlier, as with any joint venture, competitive analysis of B2Bs will focus on collusive and exclusionary anticompetitive effects. Each is discussed below, with reference to the B2B goods markets, as well as the market for B2B marketplaces.

1. *Competition in the Relevant Goods and/or Services Market*

Collusive Effects Associated With Information Sharing. One of the principal concerns that has arisen in connection with the antitrust evaluation of B2B joint ventures is their potential to facilitate coordinated pricing and output decisions. Almost by definition, a B2B involves some sharing of information. Indeed, to operate effectively, and to achieve its hoped for efficiencies, a B2B web site must enable its participants to exchange information, often information on price. Other competitively sensitive information might also be exchanged, such as information on output, costs, design, features, and future product plans.

Information exchanges among rivals, of course, have a long history under the antitrust laws. (Chapter 3C4, *supra*). Indeed, Section 3.34(e) of the *Antitrust Guidelines for Collaborations Among Competitors* specifically addresses the "Likelihood of Anticompetitive Information Sharing," emphasizing the role that contractual safeguards can play in insulating rivals from exchanging the kinds of information that may allow them to solve their cartel problems. Similarly, and with reference to the *Guidelines*, the *FTC Staff Report on B2Bs* discusses information exchanges at length, noting their two-edged character: information exchange can at once give rise to the efficiencies that drive the venture and raise anticompetitive concerns. *See also United States v. Airline Tariff Publ'g Co.*, 58 Fed. Reg. 3971 (Jan. 12, 1993) (proposed final judgment concerning alleged use of computerized airline reservation systems to facilitate collusion).

The potential for anticompetitive effects is most acute (1) in concentrated markets; and (2) when the participants in the joint venture account for a very significant percentage of industry capacity. Under these circumstances, information exchanges are relatively more likely to facilitate reaching consensus as well as the detection of cheating, and thus more likely to lead to coordinated anticompetitive effects. Increases, as well as decreases, in price can instantaneously be communicated to all rivals. What information is shared, how that information is shared, and who has access to that information, therefore, are typically critical questions. *See generally* Gail F. Levine & Hillary Greene, *Antitrust Guideposts for B2B Electronic Marketplaces*, ANTITRUST, Fall 2000, at 26; Jonathan B. Baker, *Identifying Horizontal Price Fixing in the Electronic Marketplace*, 65 ANTITRUST L.J. 41 (1996). According to the *FTC Staff Report on B2Bs*, Part 3A1, factors relevant to assessing the risk that information sharing will lead to anticompetitive collusion include:

> (1) the overall susceptibility of the market to collusion—*i.e.*, the structure of the market served by the B2B, including the degree of concentration and conditions of entry, the homogeneity of products, the characteristics of buyers and sellers and of typical transactions;

(2) whether information is being shared by *competitors*;

(3) the nature of the information being shared, *i.e.*, is it information concerning competitively sensitive subjects, such as price, output, costs or strategic planning;

(4) whether the shared information is historic or prospective, with prospective raising more serious concerns; and

(5) the availability and accessibility of the information from sources other than the B2B.

In addition, the *FTC Staff Report* inquires "Is the information-sharing practice reasonably necessary to promote certain efficiencies?", and "How might information sharing enhance competition?" Efficiencies, too, would have to be evaluated under the "cognizable" and "verifiable" test of the *Collaboration Guidelines*, as would the availability of less restrictive means of achieving the same efficiencies. *Id. See also Antitrust Guidelines for Collaborations Among Competitors*, § 3.36.

Monopsony. A second collusive effects concern that has been voiced in connection with B2B web sites is their potential to facilitate the exercise of monopsony power. The flip side of monopoly power, "monopsony power," as defined by the *FTC Staff Report*, arises when "a single buyer (or a group of firms acting as a single buyer) in the market seeks to lower the price it must pay for a given input through the means of reducing its purchases of that input." *FTC Staff Report on B2Bs*, Part 3A2. In evaluating the risk that a B2B joint venture could lead to the exercise of monopsony power, the Report suggests that several factors are critical:

(1) Does the B2B facilitate joint purchasing? Related questions include: Does it directly, or indirectly, as through the use of an agent or consulting service, make coordinated purchases? Do the organic documents of the B2B include exclusivity provisions that require all or specified quantities of purchases to be made through the web site?

(2) Does the B2B involve joint purchasing of direct or indirect inputs?

(3) Does the buying group account for a sufficient enough share of the buying market for direct inputs such that its purchases can influence price and output?

Of course, the analysis of alleged monopsony situations must be sensitive enough to distinguish between lower prices that are the consequence of realized efficiencies and those attributable to the exercise of monopsony power.

Exclusionary Effects. As we observed in connection with Covisint and Orbitz, B2B web sites frequently are established by a group of "founding" or "equity" members, who can be very significant players in their respective industries. These members provide industry expertise, underwrite the costs of establishing the web site, are responsible for obtaining any needed regulatory approvals, and typically select the management structure for the venture. In addition, the organic documents of the organization establish other categories of members, such as "associates" and "affiliates." Membership may be very open ended; it can also be subject to limitations. If a B2B substantially succeeds, but limits its membership, those firms denied access may find themselves at a competitive disadvantage. On the other hand, if membership is not limited, distinct competitive problems associated with "over-inclusiveness" can also arise. Those issues are discussed separately below.

As was the accusation in the case of Orbitz, exclusionary effects might also be attributed to the operation of the web site, as opposed to its formation. Recall that in Orbitz's case, competing web sites asserted that Orbitz's use of "most-favored nation" clauses, which required its members to offer their best fares through Orbitz, discouraged Orbitz members from making equivalent fares available through other, competing on-line travel services. Given the degree of continuing competition among airlines through other channels of distribution, however, could these sorts of effects on rivals be sufficient to lessen competition?

Exclusionary effects are likely to be evaluated much as any exclusionary conduct, particularly exclusive dealing. (*See* Casebook, Chapter 7B2). Critical questions will include:

(1) How significant is the competitive advantage conferred by B2B membership? Has exclusion significantly raised the excluded rivals' costs such that the B2B members have obtained power over price? Are there counter-strategies that the excluded rival can employ to neutralize these effects?

(2) Are there factors inhibiting entry into the B2B marketplace? In other words, can the excluded rivals realize similar cost savings through alternative means, such as the establishment of competing web sites? Can comparable savings be realized by other, non-Internet methods? Or do network effects make alternatives unsatisfactory?

(3) Are there efficiencies related specifically to the exclusion?

FTC Staff Report on B2Bs, Part 3A3. From this list of factors, as well as the material we studied in our discussion of exclusionary conduct in Chapters 6 and 7, it should be apparent that under current case law it may be difficult to establish viable cases of both significant exclusionary effects and antitrust injury to rivals. That may change, however, if markets become increasingly dependent on B2Bs.

2. *Marketplace Competition*

A final area of concern is a B2B web site's tendency to impair competition for the creation of competing web sites, *i.e.*, "competition in the market for marketplaces." This might occur if a single B2B becomes the dominant Internet portal for Internet-based sales of a particular good or service. Such a result might obtain if (1) membership requires some degree of exclusivity in terms of purchases, and/or (2) membership is over-inclusive, *i.e.*, if a very substantial share of all market participants are members. Wholly aside from price or other effects in the markets for the underlying goods and services sold through an Internet portal, the dominance of a single portal could have price and other anticompetitive effects on the services or products offered exclusively by or through the portal. These concerns apply equally to B2B and B2C web sites.

The FTC Staff Report highlights a variety of means whereby a B2B could create disincentives for its members to participate in any other Internet portal.

> * * * B2Bs may use a variety of carrots (profit interests or rebates
> or revenue-sharing devices in return for commitments to achieve
> certain volume levels) or sticks (minimum volume or minimum per-
> centage requirements, bans on investment in other B2Bs, up-front
> membership fees or required software investments, or pressure on
> suppliers and buyers) to capture business. These exclusivity prac-
> tices impose switching costs in terms of benefits to forgo or penalties
> to pay if a participant chooses to support another B2B. In light of
> the potentially powerful network effects at work in B2B contexts
> * * * exclusivity practices warrant close attention as potential cata-
> lysts for market domination. Of course, to the extent they also give
> rise to efficiencies, the practices may prove procompetitive overall,
> but that merely highlights the need for taking a close look.

FTC Staff Report on B2Bs, Part 3B1. Divining the right balance between
under and over-inclusiveness has long been a challenge of joint venture
analysis, and may be especially challenging in the case of Internet
commerce. Over-inclusiveness could lead to either exclusionary or collusive anticompetitive effects. Exclusionary concerns may arise if remaining
industry participants who are denied access to the portal compete less
aggressively or exit the market, allowing the B2B participants to raise
price or reduce service. Collusive effects also could arise if the participants raise the price of goods or services sold through the portal.
Concerns such as these were raised, but ultimately rejected, with respect
to Orbitz.

Conclusion

As should be evident from this Sidebar, the basic framework for
evaluating Internet-based web site joint ventures such as B2Bs and B2Cs
is the same as that used with any competitor collaboration. However, the
technology behind Internet joint ventures, and some of the economic
realities of the new economy, may require new, fact-specific inquiries that
in large part will be driven by the legal and technical characteristics of
the particular venture.

C. ANTITRUST AND INTELLECTUAL PROPERTY: PERSPECTIVES

INTRODUCTION

In the United States, the existence of a system for granting intellectual
property rights ("IPRs") derives from Article I, Section 8, Clause 8 of the
Constitution, which confers upon the Congress authority to "[t]o promote the
Progress of Science and useful Arts, by securing for limited Times to Authors
and Inventors the exclusive Right to their respective Writings and Discoveries. * * * " Pursuant to that grant of authority, Congress has provided by
statute for the recognition and protection of patents and copyrights.

The principal legal feature of intellectual property as property is the *right
to exclude*. Subject to certain conditions and limitations, the statutory grant of
exclusivity lasts: "for a term beginning on the date on which the patent issues

and ending 20 years from the date on which the application for the patent was filed in the United States or, if the application contains a specific reference to an earlier filed application * * * from the date on which the earliest such application was filed." 35 U.S.C. § 154(a)(2). *See also* 35 U.S.C. §§ 155–56. Because the 20–year term commences with "filing," as a practical matter the 20–year term is shortened based on the amount of time it takes the PTO to process the application. Also subject to various conditions and limitations, for works created since January 1, 1978, a copyright "endures for a term consisting of the life of the author and 70 years after the author's death." 17 U.S.C. § 302(a). These federal, statutory rights are intended to provide an incentive for entrepreneurs to innovate by rewarding those efforts with a period during which they can exclude others from making use of the fruits of their efforts.

A comprehensive examination of the patent and copyright laws is, of course, beyond the scope of this section of the Chapter. Our more modest goal is to introduce the student new to antitrust to a sampling of the range of issues that have arisen as a consequence of a long-standing perceived tension between the IP laws and the antitrust laws.

With the exception of a brief period early in the twentieth century, intellectual property was viewed with suspicion by antitrust enforcers and courts applying the antitrust laws until the early 1980s. In some instances, both presumed that the legal monopoly created by intellectual property was the equivalent of economic monopoly. The "right to exclude" that is the hallmark of intellectual property rights, therefore, was viewed as antithetical to antitrust's goal of preserving and promoting competition. By using antitrust to constrain intellectual property rights, antitrust law was viewed as a means of ameliorating the potential threat of intellectual property in the interest of competition. *See generally* Mark A. Lemley, *A New Balance Between IP and Antitrust*, 8 Sw. J. L. & Trade Am. 237 (2007); Michael A. Carrier, *Resolving the Patent–Antitrust Paradox Through Tripartite Innovation*, 56 Vand. L. Rev. 1047 (2003); Willard K. Tom & Joshua A. Newberg, *Antitrust and Intellectual Property: From Two Separate Spheres to Unified Field*, 66 Antitrust L.J. 167 (1997); Louis Kaplow, *The Patent–Antitrust Intersection A Reappraisal*, 97 Harv. L. Rev. 1813 (1984). For a more comprehensive resource, see Herbert Hovenkamp, Mark A. Lemley & Mark D. Janis, IP and Antitrust: An Analysis of Antitrust Principles Applied to Intellectual Property law (2002).

Starting in the early 1980s, however, courts and enforcers increasingly came to view competition for new innovation as a critical engine driving the new economy, and a very pro-competitive one at that. With that change of attitude came greater recognition of the pro-competitive potential of intellectual property protections, and a decided turn away from aggressive use of the antitrust laws to constrain intellectual property rights. Although to some degree the courts appeared to lag behind these changes, they became formalized in 1995, at least with respect to federal government enforcement policy, when the Department of Justice and the Federal Trade Commission issued their first Antitrust Guidelines for the Licensing of Intellectual Property.

Nevertheless, the linkage between intellectual property and technological progress, as well as the increasing globalization of world markets for technology, have spawned renewed debate about the optimal relationship between antitrust and intellectual property. In 1995 and again in 2002, those debates led the FTC and the DOJ to convene extensive hearings on the relationship of antitrust and intellectual property. The 2002 hearings explored a broad range of issues, such as the proliferation of patents, the scope and duration of patent rights, the substantive constraints that antitrust should impose on specific kinds of conduct that involve the exercise of IP rights, and the role of the Federal Circuit in formulating antitrust rules affecting IP rights. As a consequence of the hearings, the two agencies produced an extensive report. *See Antitrust Enforcement and Intellectual Property Rights: Promoting Innovation and Competition* (Apr. 2007), *available at* http://www.ftc.gov/reports/innovation/P040101PromotingInnovationandCompetitionrpt0704.pdf. *See also* FTC Report, *To Promote Innovation: The Proper Balance of Competition and Patent Law and Policy* (Oct. 2003), *available at* http://www.ftc.gov/os/2003/10/innovationrpt.pdf.

Few courts or commentators today would embrace the view that intellectual property rights and antitrust principles are inherently antagonistic, but courts and commentators do disagree on the degree of intellectual property protection that is appropriate and necessary to spur innovation. Some favor broader protections and less stringent antitrust constraints; others view expansive patent grants and over-protection of intellectual property as a real threat to competition. The core question has become: "what level of IP protection is sufficient to create a substantial incentive to innovate, without creating rights to exclude so broad as to seriously impair competition?" Because the scope of IPRs is affected by both patent and antitrust doctrines, answering this core question requires a harmonization of the two enforcement systems.

The task of reconciling these two opposing views has become more complex due to a division of jurisdiction in the federal courts. Federal courts have always had exclusive jurisdiction over both patent and copyright and antitrust disputes. Starting in the early 1980s, however, the United States Court of Appeals for the Federal Circuit was created and authorized to exercise exclusive jurisdiction over appeals of patent disputes from the federal district courts. 28 U.S.C. § 1295. Because patent infringement actions frequently trigger antitrust counterclaims, the Federal Circuit also has assumed a prominent role in shaping the intersection of antitrust and patent rights. As we shall see, that has given rise to a kind of institutional tension that has amplified the underlying doctrinal one.

We begin our introductory examination of the patent-antitrust relationship with a brief survey of the evolution of attitudes towards the use of antitrust laws to regulate the conduct of IPR holders, particularly patent holders, from one of great skepticism to one of more relative permissiveness.

1. THE RISE AND FALL OF THE "NINE NO–NOS"

Today's tensions arise after a century of evolution in attitudes about the competitive consequences of various practices associated with the exercise of intellectual property rights. Perhaps best illustrated by some of the early tying cases, the Supreme Court associated IPRs with "monopoly." *See, e.g., Int'l Bus. Machs. Corp. v. United States*, 298 U.S. 131 (1936); *Int'l Salt Co. v.*

United States, 332 U.S. 392 (1947); *United States v. Loew's, Inc.*, 371 U.S. 38 (1962). Indeed, as recently as 1984, the Court continued to rely on these and other cases for the proposition that patents confer market power. *See Jefferson Parish Hosp. Dist. No. 2 v. Hyde*, 466 U.S. 2, 16–17 (1984). The coupling of the presumption of market power with the right to exclude inherent in IP rights led the Court to view with great suspicion a variety of practices that went beyond the mere act of licensing or refusing to license IP rights. That view formally came to an end in 2007, when the Supreme Court expressly rejected the long-standing presumption that patent rights confer market power. *See Illinois Tool Works Inc. v. Independent Ink, Inc.*, 547 U.S. 28 (2006).

Antitrust's hostility to intellectual property rights eventually coalesced into what became known as the "Nine No–Nos." In an address delivered by a former official of the Antitrust Division in 1970,* the Justice Department articulated nine practices associated with the exercise of intellectual property that the Division would view not only as suspect, but as per se violations of the Sherman Act.

Figure 10–3:
The Now Outmoded Nine No–Nos

(1) tying of unpatented to patented products;

(2) mandatory know-how grantbacks from the patent licensee to the patent licensor;

(3) post-sale resale restrictions on purchasers of patented products;

(4) "Tie-out" agreements, whereby the purchase of a patented product was conditioned on the purchaser's agreement not to purchase another product not covered by the patent, typically one supplied by the patent holder's rivals;

(5) exclusive licensing—particularly, a guarantee by the licensor that it will not grant any other licenses without the consent of the licensee;

(6) mandatory package licensing;

(7) compulsory payment of royalties in amounts not reasonably related to sales of the patented product;

(8) restrictions on sales of unpatented products made by a patented process; and

(9) utilizing resale price maintenance in connection with the licensing of patented products.

In large part, these restrictions reflected the state of antitrust law that prevailed at the time. Recall from Chapters 2, 4, and 7, especially, that in 1970, all manner of vertical intrabrand agreements, and many kinds of horizontal agreements were more readily condemned as per se unlawful before *Sylvania* and *Broadcast Music* established the modern trend. But the

---

* Bruce B. Wilson, *Patent and Know–How License Agreements: Field of Use, Territorial, Price and Quantity Restrictions*, Address Before the Fourth New England Antitrust Conference (Nov. 6, 1970).

Nine No–Nos were also rooted in a long line of Supreme Court and lower court decisions that evidenced great suspicion of the impact intellectual property could have on competition. Consider each in turn. What would the rationale be for prohibiting them? For making them per se unlawful? What assumptions are they based upon, particularly with respect to the market power associated with intellectual property? Can you imagine pro-competitive benefits of any of them? Consider these questions in reviewing the following excerpt from the complaint and consent order entered in 1975 by the FTC and Xerox Corporation.

IN THE MATTER OF XEROX CORPORATION

Federal Trade Commission, 1975.
86 F.T.C. 364.

COMPLAINT

* * *

IV NATURE OF TRADE AND COMMERCE

PAR. 8. The relevant market is the sale and lease of office copiers in the United States, hereinafter referred to as the office copier market. This market includes as a relevant submarket the sale and lease of plain paper office copiers in the United States, hereinafter referred to as the plain paper submarket. The office copier market is dominated by the plain paper submarket and Xerox dominates the plain paper submarket.

PAR. 9. (a) In 1971, revenues from the sale and lease of office copiers were approximately $1.1 billion and total revenues from the sale and lease of office copiers and supplies were approximately $1.7 billion; Xerox accounted for approximately 86 percent of the former and 60 percent of the latter. In 1971, revenues from the sale and lease of plain paper copiers and supplies were approximately $1.0 billion; Xerox accounted for approximately 95 percent of said revenues.

(b) Approximately 25 firms are presently engaged in the office copier market. Of these 23 sell or otherwise distribute coated paper copiers and three sell or otherwise distribute plain paper copiers. After Xerox, the next largest firm in the office copier market accounted for approximately 10 percent of 1971 revenues from the sale or lease of office copiers and the sale of supplies therefor.

PAR. 10. The office copier market has had and continues to have high barriers to entry and barriers to effective competition among existing competitors.

* * *

VI. VIOLATIONS

PAR. 12. (a) Xerox has monopoly power in the relevant market and submarket.

(b) Xerox has the power to inhibit, frustrate, and hinder effective competition among firms participating in the relevant market and submarket.

* * *

PAR. 14. Xerox has engaged in acts, practices and methods of competition relating to patents including, but not limited to,

(a) monopolizing and attempting to monopolize patents applicable to office copiers,

(b) maintaining a patent barrier to competition by attempting to recreate a patent structure which would be equivalent in scope to expired patents,

(c) developing and maintaining a patent structure of great size, complexity, and obscurity of boundaries,

(d) using its patent position to obtain access to technology owned by actual or potential competitors,

(e) entering into cross-license arrangements with actual or potential competitors,

(f) including in licenses under United States Patent Number 3,121,006 provisions having the effect of limiting licensees to the manufacture and sale of only coated paper copiers,

(g) offering patent licenses applicable to plain paper copiers with provisions which, in effect, limit the licensee to the manufacture or sale of low speed copiers,

(h) including in patent licenses provisions having the effect of precluding the licensee from utilizing Xerox patents in the office copier market,

(i) entering into and maintaining agreements with Battelle Memorial Institute, Inc. and Battelle Development Corporation, Delaware corporations with principal offices at Columbus, Ohio, hereinafter referred to collectively as Battelle, pursuant to which Battelle is required to convey to Xerox all patents, patent applications, and know-how coming into its possession relative to xerography.

(j) preventing actual and potential competitors from developing plain paper copiers while permitting them to develop coated paper copiers.

* * *

The influence of the Nine No–Nos is of course evident in the list of violations alleged by the Federal Trade Commission in the *Xerox* complaint, which included pricing, licensing, grantback, and acquisition practices. It was also evident in the elaborate remedial order that followed, which, in addition to prohibiting the alleged practices, compelled Xerox to license its patents at what was arguably a minimal royalty. The breadth of the prohibitions and remedies in *Xerox* is extraordinary by contemporary standards, but it reflected the law and attitudes of the time about dominant firm conduct, particularly with respect to patents.

Nevertheless, evaluating Xerox with the benefit of hindsight, is not a simple matter. As one commentator has written:

> At the most superficial level, the *Xerox* case fascinates in the way that a previously undiscovered ancient culture would draw the attention of an anthropologist, or a car crash would attract that of a

rubbernecker. This is so, first, because so many of the practices alleged in the complaint or prohibited by the order seem innocuous to modern eyes and thus suggest an entirely foreign way of looking at the world, and second, because the subsequent judicial backlash in *SCM Corp. v. Xerox Corp.* [the next case in this Chapter] led to contortions in reasoning that were unnecessary and could impede appropriate antitrust enforcement. More deeply, the case is unsettling because, for all the case's flaws, the FTC's remedy actually seems to have done quite a bit of good, by breaking up a "killer patent portfolio" that threatened to insulate Xerox from competition, not for seventeen years, but forever, bringing with it the sluggish unimaginativeness long thought characteristic of a monopoly. In this respect, *Xerox* provides a window into some tensions—not yet resolved and perhaps unresolvable by antitrust principles—between the reward system created by the intellectual property laws and the very innovation those laws are intended to foster. The extent to which any progress can be made in reducing those tensions is one of the more interesting issues to be addressed in the coming years.

Willard K. Tom, *The 1975* Xerox *Consent Decree: Ancient Artifacts and Current Tensions*, 68 Antitrust L.J. 967 (2001). *See also* Timothy F. Bresnahan, *Post-Entry Competition in the Plain Paper Copier Market, in* Issues in the Economics of R & D, 75 Am. Econ. Rev. 15 (1985) (Papers and Proceedings).

The core concern in *Xerox*, was the firm's ability to assemble what has been termed a "killer patent portfolio." Tom reasons persuasively, however, that just as we distinguish between monopoly achieved through skill, industry, and foresight, on the one hand, and exclusionary practices on the other, there may be grounds to distinguish between the internally generated "killer portfolio," which may cause "no concern at all," and the portfolio assembled through other, externally directed and more debatable means, such as:

Conduct/Effects Involving Substitutes:

- acquisitions of emergent substitutes, by assignment, license or purchase
- "predatory patenting," a kind of patent proliferation strategy designed more to block others from entering a market than to develop new products or processes

Conduct/Effects Involving Complements:

- creating bottlenecks through acquisition
- network effects and the extension of monopoly power across generations
- incomplete information about the scope of patents as an entry barrier

Tom, *The 1975* Xerox *Consent Decree*, 68 Antitrust L.J. at 981–89. Tom does not suggest that each of these scenarios should necessarily be regulated by antitrust remedies, but he does point out through these examples how *Xerox* can be used to inform a more contemporary perspective.

As we move forward in this Section of the Chapter, consider the reasons why the attitude about intellectual property that is reflected in *Xerox* might lead to inadequate protections for IPRs, even though in *Xerox*, itself, they perhaps led to a significantly more competitive market.

As we noted earlier in the Chapter, economists have long recognized that innovation is critical to growth in productivity and ultimately to economic progress. But what kind of economic ordering is most conducive to innovation? Will competition maximize innovation? Monopoly? Will small or large firms prove more adept at innovation?

In addition to these basic choices of how economic decisions are to be made in a society and within firms, IPRs greatly impact the course of innovation. If antitrust imposes extensive constraints on intellectual property rights, they will fail to generate adequate incentives to innovate. Without the promise of reward, innovators will focus their creative energies elsewhere. On the other hand, if IPRs are defined too broadly, initial innovators may be over-compensated at the expense of subsequent innovators, who may suffer exclusion. Because striking that balance may prove difficult and may vary by industry and innovation, the convention of using unitary statutory rules to define the scope of IPRs necessarily risks instances of over and under-protection—of too much and too little innovation.

Whether antitrust laws can serve as an effective method for identifying and correcting instances of "over-protection" is at the heart of current debates over the relationship of antitrust and intellectual property. If innovation is a critical plane of competition that drives economic progress—especially in the new economy—then antitrust would seem a natural policing device for attempts to exclude competition that cannot be justified in terms of the incentive to innovate. Critics argue, however, that striking the balance should be accomplished within the parameters of intellectual property laws, themselves, and not by subjecting IP owners to the vagaries of antitrust regulation.

Note how these issues were framed up by the court in the following excerpt from a private challenge directed at Xerox that followed on the heels of the government's 1975 prosecution.

SCM CORPORATION v. XEROX CORP.
United States Court of Appeals for the Second Circuit, 1981.
645 F.2d 1195.

[SCM accused Xerox of acquiring, then refusing to license, patents relating to plain paper copying machines. According to SCM's complaint, Xerox's refusal to license precluded SCM from "competing effectively" in the market for plain paper copiers, and constituted violations of Sections 1 and 2 of the Sherman Act, as well as Section 7 of the Clayton Act. The district court had set aside the jury's treble damage verdict of $111.3 million holding that monetary damages under the antitrust laws could not be recovered for Xerox's patent related conduct. Eds.]

Before WATERMAN, FRIENDLY and MESKILL, Circuit Judges.

MESKILL, Circuit Judge.

* * *

I

The patent laws were enacted pursuant to Congress' authority to "promote the Progress of Science and useful Arts, by securing for limited Times to

Inventors the exclusive Right to their Discoveries." U.S. Const., Art. I, § 8, cl. 8. That the first patent laws were enacted at the second session of our first Congress manifests the importance our founding fathers attached to encouraging inventive genius, a resource that proved to be bountiful throughout this nation's history. The patent laws reward the inventor with the power to exclude others from exploiting his invention for a period of seventeen years. 35 U.S.C. § 154 (1976). In return, the public benefits from the disclosure of inventions, the entrance into the market of valuable products whose invention might have been delayed but for the incentives provided by the patent laws, and the increased competition the patented product creates in the marketplace. The antitrust laws, on the other hand, were enacted to protect competition in the market. The antitrust laws are based upon the fundamental premise that the public benefits most from a competitive marketplace. *Standard Oil Co. v. United States*, 221 U.S. 1, 58, 31 S.Ct. 502, 515, 55 L.Ed. 619 (1911); *United States v. Aluminum Co. of America*, 148 F.2d 416, 428–29 (2d Cir.1945).

The conflict between the antitrust and patent laws arises in the methods they embrace that were designed to achieve reciprocal goals. While the antitrust laws proscribe unreasonable restraints of competition, the patent laws reward the inventor with a temporary monopoly that insulates him from competitive exploitation of his patented art. When the patented product, as is often the case, represents merely one of many products that effectively compete in a given product market, few antitrust problems arise. When, however, the patented product is so successful that it evolves into its own economic market, as was the case here, or succeeds in engulfing a large section of a preexisting product market, the patent and antitrust laws necessarily clash. In such cases the primary purpose of the antitrust laws to preserve competition can be frustrated, albeit temporarily, by a holder's exercise of the patent's inherent exclusionary power during its term.

II

The law is unsettled concerning the effect under the antitrust laws, if any, that the evolution of a patent monopoly into an economic monopoly might have upon a patent holder's right to exercise the exclusionary power ordinarily inherent in a patent. Indeed, implicit in Judge Newman's decision below is a deep concern over the uncertain antitrust law implications just such an event might have had in this case. His thoughtful analysis of the relationship between the patent and antitrust laws led him to conclude that "the need to accommodate the patent laws with the antitrust laws precludes the imposition of damage liability for a unilateral refusal to license valid patents." 463 F.Supp. at 1012–13. * * *

SCM has contended that a unilateral refusal to license a patent should be treated like any other refusal to deal by a monopolist, *see generally Otter Tail Power Co. v. United States*, 410 U.S. 366, 93 S.Ct. 1022, 35 L.Ed.2d 359 (1973); *Lorain Journal Co. v. United States*, 342 U.S. 143, 72 S.Ct. 181, 96 L.Ed. 162 (1951); *Eastman Kodak Co. v. S. Photo Materials Co.*, 273 U.S. 359, 47 S.Ct. 400, 71 L.Ed. 684 (1927), where the patent has afforded its holder monopoly power over an economic market. While, as SCM suggests, a concerted refusal to license patents is no less unlawful than other concerted refusals to deal, in such cases the patent holder abuses his patent by attempting to enlarge his monopoly beyond the scope of the patent granted him. Where a patent holder, however, merely exercises his "right to exclude others from making, using, or selling the invention," 35 U.S.C. § 154 (1976), by refusing unilaterally to license his patent for its seventeen-year term, such conduct is expressly permitted by the patent laws. * * * Simply stated, a patent holder is permitted to maintain his patent monopoly through conduct permissible under the patent laws.

No court has ever held that the antitrust laws require a patent holder to forfeit the exclusionary power inherent in his patent the instant his patent monopoly affords him monopoly power over a relevant product market. In *Alcoa* this Court never questioned the legality of the economic monopoly *Alcoa* maintained by virtue of the two successive patents it had acquired. Indeed, Judge Learned Hand termed Alcoa's economic monopoly during the terms of those patents "lawful." We do not interpret Judge Wyzanski's decision in *United States v. United Shoe Machinery Corp.*, 110 F.Supp. 295 (D.Mass.1953), *aff'd per curiam*, 347 U.S. 521, 74 S.Ct. 699, 98 L.Ed. 910 (1954), as supporting SCM's argument to the contrary. In *United Shoe*, the primary vehicle found to have been employed by United Shoe in achieving and maintaining its monopoly was its lease-only system of distributing its machines. The patent acquisitions scrutinized by Judge Wyzanski occurred after United Shoe possessed substantial market power and were not "one of the principal factors enabling (United Shoe) to achieve and hold its share of the market." 110 F.Supp. at 312. Thus, contrary to appellant's contention, the *United Shoe* case stands in stark contrast to the one at bar where the patents were acquired prior to the appearance of the relevant product market and where the patents themselves afforded Xerox the power to achieve eventual market dominance.

In *Alcoa* Judge Learned Hand stated that the "successful competitor, having been urged to compete, must not be turned upon when he wins." 148 F.2d at 430. And while that statement was made in regard to a hypothetical situation where only one of a group of competitors ultimately survives, it at least indicates a concern Judge Hand had for preserving those economic incentives that provide the primary impetus for competition. * * *

* * *

The tension between the objectives of preserving economic incentives to enhance competition while at the same time trying to contain the power a successful competitor acquires is heightened tremendously when the patent laws come into play. As the facts of this case demonstrate, the acquisition of a patent can create the potential for tremendous market power.

III.

Patent acquisitions are not immune from the antitrust laws. Surely, a [section] 2 violation will have occurred where, for example, the dominant competitor in a market acquires a patent covering a substantial share of the same market that he knows when added to his existing share will afford him monopoly power. That the asset acquired is a patent is irrelevant; in such a case the patented invention already has been commercialized successfully, and the magnitude of the transgression of the antitrust laws' proscription against willful aggregations of market power outweighs substantially the negative effect that the elimination of that class of purchasers for commercialized patents places upon the patent system.

The patent system would be seriously undermined, however, were the threat of potential antitrust liability to attach upon the acquisition of a patent at a time prior to the existence of the relevant market and, even more disconcerting, at a time prior to the commercialization of the patented art. As SCM itself admits, the procurement of a patent by the inventor will not violate § 2 even where it is likely that the patent monopoly will evolve into an economic monopoly; yet SCM would deny the same reward to anyone but the patentee.

If the antitrust laws were interpreted to proscribe the natural evolution of a patent monopoly into an economic monopoly, then Judge Newman's concern would be well founded. If the threat of treble damage liability for refusing to license were imbedded in the minds of potential patent holders as a likely prospect incident to every successful commercial exploitation of a patented invention, the efficacy of the economic incentives afforded by our patent system might be severely diminished.

Nevertheless, it is especially clear that the economic incentives provided by the patent laws were intended to benefit only those persons who lawfully acquire the rights granted under our patent system. *Cf. Walker Process Equipment, Inc. v. Food Mach. & Chem. Corp.*, 382 U.S. 172, 86 S.Ct. 347, 15 L.Ed.2d 247 (1965) (patent obtained by fraud on Patent Office as basis for monopolization claim). Where a patent in the first instance has been lawfully acquired, a patent holder ordinarily should be allowed to exercise the patent's exclusionary power even after achieving commercial success; to allow the imposition of treble damages based on what a reviewing court might later consider, with the benefit of hindsight, to be too much success would seriously threaten the integrity of the patent system. Where, however, the acquisition itself is unlawful, the subsequent exercise of the ordinarily lawful exclusionary power inherent in the patent would be a continuing wrong, a continuing unlawful exclusion of potential competitors.

Without passing upon the validity of Judge Newman's theory to preclude antitrust damage liability in all cases where the injury is predicated upon a patent holder's refusal to license, we hold that where a patent has been lawfully acquired, subsequent conduct permissible under the patent laws cannot trigger any liability under the antitrust laws.[10] This holding, we believe, strikes an adequate balance between the patent and antitrust laws.
* * *

* * *

———

Do you agree with the Second Circuit's premise that the patent laws and the antitrust laws serve different goals and are in "conflict"? If they are, how can a court know whether in any given case the policies of the antitrust or

10. We leave for an appropriate case the resolution of the question whether damage liability can accrue to a holder for refusing to license patents that he subsequently abuses through pooling or otherwise.

patent laws should be given precedence? Does the court suggest any guidelines for making that choice? *SCM* concerned the scope of a firm's right to unilaterally refuse to license its IP, an issue we studied in Chapter 6C5, *supra*. Is *SCM* in conflict with the modern view? Is that view still forming in part because of the complexity of the issues developed in SCM?

2. CHANGING TIMES, CHANGING ATTITUDES: THE INTELLECTUAL PROPERTY GUIDELINES (1995)

By the early 1980s, government attitudes, building on the sea-change in the case law, specifically disavowed the Nine No–Nos in favor of a decidedly more permissive attitude towards intellectual property licensing and sales practices. That new attitude recognized the complex nature and pro-competitive potential of IPRs and conduct related to the exercise of those rights.[*] These changes in enforcement policy paralleled a similar evolution in the courts, reflected in cases like *SCM* and *Dawson Chem. Co. v. Rohm & Haas Co.*, 448 U.S. 176 (1980).

Movement away from the Nine No–Nos continued for more than a decade. At the enforcement agencies, it culminated in the 1995 adoption of *Antitrust Guidelines for the Licensing of Intellectual Property*. See http://www. usdoj.gov/atr/public/guidelines/0558.htm. Much as did the court in *SCM*, the Guidelines opened with a discussion of the characteristics of antitrust and IPRs. After briefly summarizing the "right to exclude" provided by both the patent and copyright laws, however, they offer the following observation, which is suggestive of quite a different philosophy from that embraced in *SCM*:

> The intellectual property laws and the antitrust laws share the common purpose of promoting innovation and enhancing consumer welfare.[8] The intellectual property laws provide incentives for innovation and its dissemination and commercialization by establishing enforceable property rights for the creators of new and useful products, more efficient processes, and original works of expression. In the absence of intellectual property rights, imitators could more rapidly exploit the efforts of innovators and investors without compensation. Rapid imitation would reduce the commercial value of innovation and erode incentives to invest, ultimately to the detriment of consumers. The antitrust laws promote innovation and consumer welfare by prohibiting certain actions that may harm competition with respect to either existing or new ways of serving consumers.

IP Guidelines, § 1.0. Note how the Guidelines thus appear to propose that the promotion of "innovation" can serve as the unitary and harmonizing goal for both antitrust and IP. Why might that be so? How might it operate in practice? How might it have affected the court's analysis in *SCM*?

---

[*] *See* Abbott B. Lipsky, Deputy Assistant Attorney General, Antitrust Division, Remarks before the American Bar Association, Antitrust Section, (Nov. 5, 1981).

8. "[T]he aims and objectives of patent and antitrust laws may seem, at first glance, wholly at odds. However, the two bodies of law are actually complementary, as both are aimed at encouraging innovation, industry and competition." *Atari Games Corp. v. Nintendo of America, Inc.*, 897 F.2d 1572, 1576 (Fed. Cir.1990).

The Guidelines then proceed to state three baseline principles for implementing that goal:

2.0   These Guidelines embody three general principles:

a.   for the purpose of antitrust analysis, the Agencies regard intellectual property as being essentially comparable to any other form of property;

b.   the Agencies do not presume that intellectual property creates market power in the antitrust context; and

c.   the Agencies recognize that intellectual property licensing allows firms to combine complementary factors of production and is generally procompetitive.

What is the significance of these three principles? What is the *antitrust* significance of the Guidelines' assertion that IP is "essentially comparable to any other form of property"? How is it related to the second assertion, that IP rights do not necessarily confer market power? Of course, that assertion, which was at the time contrary to a long line of Supreme Court cases, is pivotal in terms of re-connecting the analysis of conduct involving IP to the analysis of any allegedly anticompetitive conduct.

To illustrate the third, and also critical principle, the Guidelines offer the following hypothetical:

EXAMPLE 1

Situation:

ComputerCo develops a new, copyrighted software program for inventory management. The program has wide application in the health field. ComputerCo licenses the program in an arrangement that imposes both field of use and territorial limitations. Some of ComputerCo's licenses permit use only in hospitals; others permit use only in group medical practices. ComputerCo charges different royalties for the different uses. All of ComputerCo's licenses permit use only in specified portions of the United States and in specified foreign countries. The licenses contain no provisions that would prevent or discourage licensees from developing, using, or selling any other program, or from competing in any other good or service other than in the use of the licensed program. None of the licensees are actual or likely potential competitors of ComputerCo in the sale of inventory management programs.

How would you go about analyzing this problem in the absence of the Guidelines's three stated principles? How would that analysis change once those principles are taken into account? How would you go about analyzing Example 1 based on what we have learned in the course, taking into account the issues raised in this Chapter concerning the need to accommodate intellectual property rights and the Guidelines's premise that we should interpret IP and antitrust law as to promote innovation? Here's an excerpt from the Guidelines' discussion:

Discussion:

The key competitive issue raised by the licensing arrangement is whether it harms competition among entities that would have been actual or likely potential competitors in the absence of the arrangement. Such harm could occur if, for example, the licenses anticompetitively foreclose access to competing technologies (in this case, most likely competing computer programs), prevent licensees from developing their own competing technologies (again, in this case, most likely computer programs), or facilitate market allocation or price-fixing for any product or service supplied by the licensees. * * * If the license agreements contained such provisions, the Agency evaluating the arrangement would analyze its likely competitive effects as described in parts 3–5 of these Guidelines. In this hypothetical, there are no such provisions and thus the arrangement is merely a subdivision of the licensor's intellectual property among different fields of use and territories. The licensing arrangement does not appear likely to harm competition among entities that would have been actual or likely potential competitors if ComputerCo had chosen not to license the software program. The Agency therefore would be unlikely to object to this arrangement. Based on these facts, the result of the antitrust analysis would be the same whether the technology was protected by patent, copyright, or trade secret. The Agency's conclusion as to likely competitive effects could differ if, for example, the license barred licensees from using any other inventory management program.

After discussing these three foundation principles, the IP Guidelines go on to address the kinds of markets that can be affected by intellectual property licenses, and the framework for analysis that the agency will use in evaluating the anticompetitive potential of particular licenses. At this point, you should review Sections 3 and 4 of the Guidelines. As you do so, consider the extent, if any, to which the conceptual framework we have discussed throughout the Casebook, which focuses on the need to identify a theory of anticompetitive effects—collusive and/or exclusionary—as a prerequisite to any antitrust challenge is imbedded in the IP Guidelines.

With basic principles set, and a framework for analysis in place, the IP Guidelines establish a "Safety Zone" or safe harbor for IP licensing arrangements that (1) are not facially anticompetitive; and (2) involve a licensor and licensees who together account for "no more than twenty percent of each relevant market significantly affected by the restraint." *IP Guidelines*, § 4.3. They then turn to seven particular categories of conduct that have traditionally given rise to antitrust concerns: (1) horizontal restraints; (2) resale price maintenance;* (3) tying; (4) exclusive dealing; (5) cross-licensing and pooling arrangements; (6) grantbacks; and (7) acquisition of intellectual property rights. Note how many of these also were addressed—albeit far more harshly—by the Nine No–Nos, and surfaced in *Xerox*.

Many of these same issues have garnered attention in the European Union. To address them and update previous regulations, the EU adopted a

---

* The Guidelines' discussion of resale price maintenance pre-dates and therefore does not reflect the Supreme Court's decision in *Leegin*   *Creative Leather Products, Inc. v. PSKS, Inc.*, ___ U.S. ___, 127 S.Ct. 2705 (2007).

revised block exemption pursuant to Article 81(3), as well as its own set of Guidelines. *See* Commission Regulation (EC) No 772/2004 of 27 April 2004 on the application of Article 81(3) of the Treaty to categories of technology transfer agreements, OJ L 123, 27.04.2004, *available at* http://ec.europa.eu/comm/competition/antitrust/legislation/transfer.html; *Guidelines for the assessment of technology transfer agreements*, *available at* http://ec.europa.eu/comm/competition/antitrust/legislation/guidelines_index_en.pdf.

In the next section we turn to some specific practices addressed in the U.S. Guidelines, and which have continued to attract significant attention from commentators, government enforcement agencies and the courts. First, we provide a brief overview of single firm IP licensing practices, including bundling, exclusive dealing, grantbacks and various kinds of restrictions, and the acquisition of IP rights. (Recall again that unilateral refusals to license were addressed in Chapter 6). We then turn to more in depth treatment of:

- patent pools, such as the one at issue in the *Standard Oil (Cracking)* case;
- standard setting practices;
- antitrust counterclaims that attack the validity of patents; and finally
- patent infringement settlement agreements between actual or potential rivals.

In each instance, consider two issues: (1) how does each court approach the problem of defining the scope of IP rights through its relationship to competition law principles?; and (2) to what extent might the decision-makers be utilizing distinct institutional perspectives in answering that question?

3.   CONTEMPORARY ISSUES AT THE CROSSROADS OF IP AND COMPETITION POLICY

a.   *Single Firm Licensing Practices*

Perhaps the most common practice associated with patents and copyrights is "licensing." Although many patents are utilized by the patent owner, many more are licensed to others, be they process or product patents. Copyrights, of course, by their nature are almost all the subject of licensing.

Anticompetitive issues associated with licensing practices parallel to a degree the full range of horizontal and vertical relationships we have studied. A critical threshold issue, therefore, is whether the patent holder and the licensee produce substitutable products. If not, the license will be analyzed as "vertical." *See Antitrust Guidelines for the Licensing of Intellectual Property*, § 3.3 & accompanying problem. "Cross-licensing" and "patent pooling," two kinds of licensing that often involve rival patent holders, are discussed below.

Many typical patent and copyright licensing practices, however are "vertical"—the IP owner and the licensee do not compete, at least not in the market for the IP protected product. Vertical IP licensing can mirror virtually all of the vertical intrabrand and interbrand restrictions we studied in Chapters 4 and 7. For example, a patent holder might negotiate territorial, customer, or "field of use" restrictions with its licensees in order to best develop and exploit its IP rights, or seek to use minimum or maximum resale price restrictions. Similarly, it might agree to grant the equivalent of an exclusive distributorship to a single licensee. The patent holder might also seek to limit its licensees through exclusive dealing, as well as bundling or tying, either multiple patented products or a mix of patented and unpatented ones.

The IP Guidelines focus their attention on four vertical licensing practices: (1) resale price maintenance ("RPM")(§ 5.2); (2) tying (§ 5.3); (3) exclusive dealing (§ 5.4); and (4) grantbacks (§ 5.6). We describe each here only briefly. For a more in-depth treatment, see the respective sections of the IP Guidelines.

RPM. At the time the IP Guidelines were issued, both minimum and maximum RPM were still per se illegal. As we learned in Chapter 4, however, since that time the Supreme Court has reversed course and abandoned the per se rule in *Leegin* (minimum RPM) and *Khan* (maximum RPM). Although the IP Guidelines still discuss minimum RPM as per se illegal, the agencies would likely take those newer decisions into account and analyze any use of RPM under the rule of reason.

Tying. As we noted at the beginning of our discussion of IP rights, tying was among the earliest of IP practices to command severe antitrust scrutiny. That level of scrutiny followed largely from the Supreme Court's assumption that IP rights conferred market power. Recall, however, that one of the IP Guidelines' first principles is that such a presumption is unwarranted (and the Supreme Court endorsed that view in *Illinois Tool Works Inc. v. Independent Ink, Inc.*, 547 U.S. 28 (2006)).

Hence, the Guidelines, without focusing on the per se past of the prohibition of tying, indicate that tying would only be challenged in the context of IP licensing if (1) the seller (whether licensor or licensee) has market power; (2) the arrangement will have an adverse effect on competition in a relevant market; and (3) "efficiency justifications * * * do not outweigh the anticompetitive effects." *IP Guidelines*, § 5.3.

Section 5.3 of the Guidelines also discuss "package licensing," "the licensing of multiple items of intellectual property in a single license or in a group of related licenses." Noting the efficiency potential of package licenses, the IP Guidelines indicate that they will be evaluated like all other tying arrangements, through an evaluation of their anticompetitive effects and efficiencies.

Exclusive Dealing. Tracking traditional case law, the IP Guidelines' discussion of exclusive dealing notes that it has been evaluated under a rule of reason analysis. Two steps are set forth as critical:

> In determining whether an exclusive dealing arrangement is likely to reduce competition in a relevant market, the Agencies will take into account the extent to which the arrangement (1) promotes the exploitation and development of the licensor's technology and (2) anticompetitively forecloses the exploitation and development of, or otherwise constrains competition among, competing technologies.

IP Guidelines, § 5.4. Relevant factors include:

> * * * the degree of foreclosure in the relevant market, the duration of the exclusive dealing arrangement, and other characteristics of the

input and output markets, such as concentration, difficulty of entry, and the responsiveness of supply and demand to changes in price in the relevant markets.

Id. Note that the approach reflects some of the uncertainty in this area that we explored in Chapter 7, by combining consideration for "foreclosure" with consideration of other factors that might constrain competition.

Grantbacks. Grantbacks can arise in the context of horizontal or vertical licensing. According to the *Guidelines*, a grantback is "an arrangement under which a licensee agrees to extend to the licensor of intellectual property the right to use the licensee's improvements to the licensed technology." *IP Guidelines*, § 5.6. The IP Guidelines recognize that grantbacks can have procompetitive effects, "especially if they are nonexclusive." "Such arrangements provide a means for the licensee and the licensor to share risks and reward the licensor for making possible further innovation based on or informed by the licensed technology, and both promote innovation in the first place and promote the subsequent licensing of the results of the innovation." Grantbacks can also pose competitive risks, however, "if they substantially reduce the licensee's incentives to engage in research and development and thereby limit rivalry in innovation markets."

Because grantbacks can diminish the incentive to innovate, the analysis of grantbacks can be linked to an evaluation of innovation and technology markets. Hence, an "important factor in the Agencies' analysis of a grantback will be whether the licensor has market power in a relevant technology or innovation market." *IP Guidelines*, § 5.6. The Guidelines continue:

> If the Agencies determine that a particular grantback provision is likely to reduce significantly licensees' incentives to invest in improving the licensed technology, the Agencies will consider the extent to which the grantback provision has offsetting procompetitive effects, such as (1) promoting dissemination of licensees' improvements to the licensed technology, (2) increasing the licensors' incentives to disseminate the licensed technology, or (3) otherwise increasing competition and output in a relevant technology or innovation market. *See* section 4.2. In addition, the Agencies will consider the extent to which grantback provisions in the relevant markets generally increase licensors' incentives to innovate in the first place.

Id.

We will revisit some of these various licensing practices at the end of the Chapter when we look at some of the related problems presented in the IP Guidelines. It may also be productive for you to consider them at this point.

b. *Acquisition of IP Rights ("IPRs") and the Role of "Blocking Patents"*

Although many IP related practices are policed under Sections 1 and 2 of the Sherman Act, the acquisition of IP rights, like the acquisition of any "asset," also can be analyzed under the provisions of Section 7 of the Clayton Act. As we noted earlier in this Chapter, innovation can be suppressed through acquisition. In the case of IPRs, acquisitions could lead to exclusionary or collusive anticompetitive effects. Acquisitions could be exclusionary, for example, if the acquired technology is totally suppressed, or if its introduction to the market is delayed. Acquisitions can also lead to coordinated or unilateral collusive effects, such as restricted output and higher prices. Examples might include the merger of two firms that own competing IPRs, or the acquisition by one firm of the IPRs of another. Section 5.7 of the IP Guidelines declares the government's intention to examine IPR acquisitions under all of the relevant antitrust provisions, including Section 7, and to analyze a merger or acquisition under the Merger Guidelines, when appropriate.

One of the issues that has garnered significant attention in recent years is the role in merger review of "blocking patents." A blocking patent is one so broad in scope that no potential rival can compete in the relevant market without infringing the patent. Blocking positions are most often asserted in merger analysis by an acquiring firm, which asserts that its IPRs are broad enough to block competition from any rival, including the acquired firm. Hence, the acquisition can not substantially lessen competition. The acquired firm poses no threat to competition owing to the fact that the acquired firm could only compete with it by infringing its IPRs.

If it is true that the acquired firm can only compete by infringing on the blocking patents, the argument may hold some merit. However, the assertion of a blocking position may depend upon the validity of and broad scope of the patent—either or both of which may be contestable. Moreover, there may be evidence that the acquiring firm indeed faces competition, either from the acquired firm, or other firms, that has not led to infringement. Does that necessarily defeat the claim of a blocking position? How should the agencies evaluate entry if the threat of an infringement action is genuine? In such circumstances, the agencies can be faced with difficult choices between the acquiring firm's assertion of validity and broad scope, and the acquired firm's view that competition without infringement is possible. If the latter is true, the acquisition might indeed prove anticompetitive, and might pose serious threats to innovation.

c. Patent Pools and Cross–Licensing

As was evident from the underlying conduct in *Standard Oil* (Cracking), "patent pooling," or the licensing of patent portfolios is not a particularly new category of conduct in the IP area. But in contrast to the time of the *Cracking* case, today the enforcement agencies recognize the potential procompetitive benefits of such agreements. As noted in § 5.5 of the IP Guidelines:

> Cross-licensing and pooling arrangements are agreements of two or more owners of different items of intellectual property to license one another or third parties. These arrangements may provide procompetitive benefits by integrating complementary technologies, reducing transaction costs, clearing blocking positions, and avoiding costly infringement litigation. By promoting the dissemination of technology, cross-licensing and pooling arrangements are often procompetitive.

But patent pools and cross licensing also can have collusive or exclusionary anticompetitive consequences.

In our next reading, we will examine the response of the Antitrust Division of the Justice Department to a request for a Business Review letter regarding a proposed patent pooling and licensing arrangement relating to digital audio and visual compression technology. Under 28 C.F.R. § 50.6, the parties to a proposed transaction that raises antitrust concerns can request a statement of the Department's current "enforcement intention" with respect to the transaction. Although a positive response neither permanently binds the agency nor any private party, it generally does indicate that the practice can proceed without fear of government challenge in the near term. It also serves as a useful source of guidance for the immediate parties, as well as the members of the antitrust bar and their clients.

In this instance the request was made by nine companies and one university, who sought to create a "one-stop-shopping" clearinghouse, by pooling all of their patents. Firms interested in manufacturing equipment that stores or transmits compressed video technology could not do so without infringing one or more of the many patents that covered the compression technology, which would require individual negotiations and potentially prohibitive royalties. The pool was intended to solve those problems and permit cost-effective, widespread exploitation of the technology.

PATENTS FOR MPEG–2 TECHNOLOGY

United States Department of Justice, 1997.
1997 WL 356954 (D.O.J.).

VIA FAX

Gerrard R. Beeney, Esq.
Sullivan & Cromwell
125 Broad Street
New York, NY 10004–2498

Dear Mr. Beeney:

This is in response to your request on behalf of the Trustees of Columbia University, Fujitsu Limited, General Instrument Corp., Lucent Technologies Inc., Matsushita Electric Industrial Co., Ltd., Mitsubishi Electric Corp., Philips Electronics N.V., Scientific–Atlanta, Inc., and Sony Corp. (collectively the "Licensors"), Cable Television Laboratories, Inc. ("CableLabs"), MPEG LA, L.L.C. ("MPEG LA"), and their affiliates for the issuance of a business review letter pursuant to the Department of Justice's Business Review Procedure, 28 C.F.R. § 50.6. You have requested a statement of the Department of Justice's antitrust enforcement intentions with respect to a proposed arrangement pursuant to which MPEG LA will offer a package license under the Licensors' patents that are essential to compliance with the MPEG–2 compression technology standard, and distribute royalty income among the Licensors.

I. THE PROPOSED ARRANGEMENT

A. *The MPEG–2 Standard*

The MPEG–2 standard has been approved as an international standard by the Motion Picture Experts Group of the International organization for Standards (ISO) and the International Electrotechnical Commission (IEC) and by the International Telecommunication Union Telecommunication Standardization Sector ("ITU–T"). It contains nine operative parts. Only Parts 1

(ISO/IEC 13818–1) and 2 (ISO/IEC 13818–2), which deal with systems and video, are relevant to the proposed activity. * * *[1]

The video and systems parts of the MPEG–2 standard will be applied in many different products and services in which video information is stored and/or transmitted, including cable, satellite and broadcast television, digital video disks, and telecommunications. However, compliance with the standards will infringe on numerous patents owned by many different entities. Consequently, a number of firms that participated in the development of the standard formed the MPEG–2 Intellectual Property Working Group ("IP Working Group") to address intellectual property issues raised by the proposed standard. Among other things, the IP Working Group sponsored a search for the patents that covered the technology essential to compliance with the proposed standard and explored the creation of a mechanism to convey those essential intellectual property rights to MPEG–2 users. That exploration led ultimately to an agreement among the Licensors, CableLabs and Baryn S. Futa establishing MPEG LA as a Delaware Limited Liability Company.

Each of the Licensors owns at least one patent that the IP Working Group's patent search identified as essential to compliance with the video and/or systems parts of the MPEG–2 standard (hereinafter "MPEG–2 Essential Patent" or "Essential Patent"). Among them, they account for a total of 27 Essential Patents, which are most, but not all, of the Essential Patents. Pursuant to a series of four proposed agreements, the Licensors will combine their Essential Patents into a single portfolio (the "Portfolio") in the hands of a common licensing administrator that would grant licenses under the Portfolio on a nondiscriminatory basis, collect royalties, and distribute them among the Licensors pursuant to a pro-rata allocation based on each Licensor's proportionate share of the total number of Portfolio patents in the countries in which a particular royalty-bearing product is made and sold.

* * *

B. MPEG LA

* * * MPEG LA will: (1) grant a worldwide, nonexclusive sublicense under the Portfolio to make, use and sell MPEG–2 products "to each and every potential Licensee who requests an MPEG–2 Patent Portfolio License and shall not discriminate among potential licensees"; (2) solicit Portfolio licensees; (3) enforce and terminate Portfolio license agreements; and (4) collect and distribute royalties. For this purpose, each MPEG–2 Licensor will grant MPEG LA a nonexclusive license under its Essential Patents, while retaining the right to license them independently for any purpose, including for making MPEG–2–compliant products.

The Licensing Administrator Agreement places the day-to-day conduct of MPEG LA's business, including its licensing activities, under the sole control of Futa and his staff. The other owners retain some control, however, over "major decisions," including approval of budgets and annual financial state-

---

1. Notably, neither Part 1 nor Part 2 dictates a particular method for encoding video or programs into the specified syntax and semantics. Users of the standard are thus free to develop and use the encoding method they find most advantageous, while preserving the compatibility necessary to the integrity of the standard.

ments, extraordinary expenditures, entry into new businesses, mergers and acquisitions, and the sale or dissolution of the corporation.

C.   The MPEG–2 Portfolio

As noted above, the Portfolio initially will consist of 27 patents, which constitute most, but not all, Essential Patents. These 27 patents were identified in a search carried out by an independent patent expert under the sponsorship of the IP Working Group. Once the MPEG–2 standard was largely in place, the IP working Group issued a public call for the submission of patents that might be infringed by compliance with the MPEG–2 standard. CableLabs, whose COO Futa was an active participant in the IP Working Group, retained an independent patent expert familiar with the standard and the relevant technology to review the submissions. In all, the expert and his assistant reviewed approximately 8000 United States patent abstracts and studied about 800 patents belonging to over 100 different patentees or assignees. No submission was refused, and no entity or person that was identified as having an essential patent was in any way excluded from the effort in forming the proposed joint licensing program.

The proposed agreement among the Licensors creates a continuing role for an independent expert as an arbiter of essentiality. It requires the retention of an independent expert to review patents submitted to any of the Licensors for inclusion in the Portfolio and to review any Portfolio patent which an MPEG–2 Licensor has concluded is not essential or as to which anyone has claimed a good-faith belief of non-essentiality. In both cases, the Licensors are bound by the expert's opinion.

* * *

D.   The Portfolio License

The planned license from MPEG LA to users of the MPEG–2 standards is a worldwide, nonexclusive, nonsublicensable license under the Portfolio patents for the manufacture, sale, and in most cases, use of: (1) products and software designed to encode and/or decode video information in accordance with the MPEG–2 standard; (2) products and software designed to generate MPEG–2 program and transport bitstreams; and (3) so-called "intermediate products," such as integrated circuit chips, used in the aforementioned products and software. The license grant to use encoding-related products and software for recording video information on a "packaged medium," *e.g.*, encoding a motion picture for copying on digital video disks, is separate from the other grants for the same products and software.

The Portfolio license expires January 1, 2000, but is renewable at the licensee's option for a period of not less than five years, subject to "reasonable amendment of its terms and conditions." That "reasonable amendment" may not, however, increase royalties by more than 25%. Each Portfolio licensee may terminate its license on 30 days' written notice. The per-unit royalties are those agreed upon in the Agreement Among Licensors, but they are subject to reduction pursuant to a "most-favored-nation" clause. The royalty obligations are predicated on actual use of one or more of the licensed patents in the unit for which the royalty is assessed. The Portfolio license imposes no obligation on the licensee to use only the licensed patents and explicitly leaves the licensee free independently to develop "competitive video products or video services which do not comply with the MPEG–2 Standard."[25]

The Portfolio license will list the Portfolio patents in an attachment. It also explicitly addresses the licensee's ability, and possible need, to obtain Essential Patent rights elsewhere. The Portfolio license states that each Portfolio patent is also available for licensing independently from the MPEG–2 Licensor that had licensed it to MPEG LA and that the license may not convey rights to all Essential Patents.

The license's grantback provision requires the licensee to grant any of the Licensors and other Portfolio licensees a nonexclusive worldwide license or sublicense, on fair and reasonable terms and conditions, on any Essential Patent that it has the right to license or sublicense. The Licensors' per-patent share of royalties is the basis for determining a fair and reasonable royalty for the grantback. Alternatively, a licensee that controls an Essential Patent may choose to become an MPEG–2 licensor and add its patent to the Portfolio. * * *

A separate provision allows for partial termination of a licensee's Portfolio license as to a particular MPEG–2 Licensor's patents. Pursuant to Section 6.3, an MPEG–2 Licensor may direct MPEG LA to withdraw its patents from the Portfolio license if the licensee has (a) brought a lawsuit or other proceeding against the MPEG–2 Licensor for infringement of an Essential Patent or an MPEG–2 Related Patent ("Related Patent") and (b) refused to grant the MPEG–2 Licensor a license under the Essential Patent or MPEG–2 Related Patent on fair and reasonable terms and conditions.[33] As with the grantback, the per-patent share of Portfolio license royalties is the basis for determining a fair and reasonable royalty for the licensee's patent. * * *

II. ANALYSIS

A.   *The Patent Pool in General*

* * *

A starting point for an antitrust analysis of any patent pool is an inquiry into the validity of the patents and their relationship to each other. A licensing scheme premised on invalid or expired intellectual property rights will not withstand antitrust scrutiny.[39] And a patent pool that aggregates

25.   * * * We understand this to mean that licensees are free also to develop technological alternatives to the MPEG–2 compression standard.

33.   * * * The Portfolio license, like several of the relevant documents, defines "MPEG–2–Related Patent" as "any Patent which is not an MPEG–2 Essential Patent but which has one or more claims directed to an apparatus or a method that may be used in the implementation of a product or a service designed in whole or in part to exploit the MPEG–2 Standard under the laws of the country which issued or published the Patent." Read literally, this definition could encompass any patent capable of being employed in a product or service that exploits the MPEG–2 standard. At the extreme, it would take in any patent relevant not only to MPEG–2 applications but also to unrelated products, as well as patents on products or services that someone might build into an MPEG–2 Royalty Product—for example, a patented informational display on a DVD player.

You have informed the Department, however, that such a broad, literal interpretation was not the intent of the drafters of the Patent Portfolio License and that your clients would construe the term "MPEG–2 Related Patents" to encompass only patents which, as applied, constitute implementations of the MPEG–2 standard. Further, you have told the Department that it is exceedingly unlikely that any Related Patent would have any utility for any application other than MPEG–2.

39.   *See, e.g., United States v. Pilkington Plc*, 1994–2 Trade Cas. (CCH) ¶ 70,842 (D.Ariz.

competitive technologies and sets a single price for them would raise serious competitive concerns. On the other hand, a combination of complementary intellectual property rights, especially ones that block the application for which they are jointly licensed, can be an efficient and procompetitive method of disseminating those rights to would-be users.

Based on your representations to us about the complementary nature of the patents to be included in the Portfolio, it appears that the Portfolio is a procompetitive aggregation of intellectual property. The Portfolio combines patents that an independent expert has determined to be essential to compliance with the MPEG–2 standard; there is no technical alternative to any of the Portfolio patents within the standard. Moreover, each Portfolio patent is useful for MPEG–2 products only in conjunction with the others.[40] The limitation of the Portfolio to technically essential patents, as opposed to merely advantageous ones, helps ensure that the Portfolio patents are not competitive with each other and that the Portfolio license does not, by bundling in non-essential patents, foreclose the competitive implementation options that the MPEG–2 standard has expressly left open.

The continuing role of an independent expert to assess essentiality is an especially effective guarantor that the Portfolio patents are complements, not substitutes. The relevant provisions of the Agreement Among Licensors appear well designed to ensure that the expert will be called in whenever a legitimate question is raised about whether or not a particular patent belongs in the Portfolio; in particular, they seem designed to reduce the likelihood that the Licensors might act concertedly to keep invalid or non-essential patents in the Portfolio or to exclude other essential patents from admission to the Portfolio.

B. Specific Terms of the Agreements

Despite the potential procompetitive effects of the Portfolio license, we would be concerned if any specific terms of any of the contemplated agreements seemed likely to restrain competition. Such possible concerns might include the likelihood that the Licensors could use the Portfolio license as a vehicle to disadvantage competitors in downstream product markets; to collude on prices outside the scope of the Portfolio license, such as downstream MPEG–2 products; or to impair technology or innovation competition, either within the MPEG–2 standard or from rival compression technologies. It appears, however, that the proposed arrangement will not raise any significant competitive concerns.

1. Effect on Rivals

There does not appear to be any potential for use of the Portfolio license to disadvantage particular licensees. The Agreement Among Licensors commits the Licensors to nondiscriminatory Portfolio licensing, and the Licensing Administrator agreement both vests sole licensing authority in MPEG LA and

---

1994) (consent decree resolving antitrust suit against exclusive licenses premised on technology covered by expired patents).

40. The Department presumes from the information you have provided us that the Portfolio patents are valid. Should this prove not to

be so, the Department's analysis and enforcement intentions would likely be very different. As noted above, the Agreement Among Licensors provides for the deletion from the Portfolio of licenses held invalid or unenforceable.

explicitly requires MPEG LA to offer the Portfolio license on the same terms and conditions to all would-be licensees. Thus, maverick competitors and upstart industries will have access to the Portfolio on the same terms as all other licensees. The Portfolio license's "most-favored-nation" clause ensures further against any attempt to discriminate on royalty rates.

Although it offers the Portfolio patents only as a package, the Portfolio license does not appear to be an illegal tying agreement. The conditioning of a license for one intellectual property right on the license of a second such right could be a concern where its effect was to foreclose competition from technological alternatives to the second. In this instance, however, the essentiality of the patents—determined by the independent expert—means that there is no technological alternative to any of them and that the Portfolio license will not require licensees to accept or use any patent that is merely one way of implementing the MPEG–2 standard, to the detriment of competition. Moreover, although a licensee cannot obtain fewer than all the Portfolio patents from-MPEG LA, the Portfolio license informs potential licensees that licenses on all the Portfolio patents are available individually from their owners or assignees. While the independent expert mechanism should ensure that the Portfolio will never contain any unnecessary patents, the independent availability of each Portfolio patent is a valuable failsafe. The list of Portfolio patents attached to the Portfolio license will provide licensees with information they need to assess the merits of the Portfolio license.

2. Facilitation of Collusion

From what you have told us, there does not appear to be anything in the proposed agreements that is likely to facilitate collusion among Licensors or licensees in any market. Although MPEG LA is authorized to audit licensees, 42 confidentiality provisions prohibit it from transmitting competitively sensitive information among the Licensors or other licensees. Further, since the contemplated royalty rates are likely to constitute a tiny fraction of MPEG–2 products' prices, at least in the near term, it appears highly unlikely that the royalty rate could be used during that period as a device to coordinate the prices of downstream products.

3. Effect on Innovation

It further appears that nothing in the arrangement imposes any anticompetitive restraint, either explicitly or implicitly, on the development of rival products and technologies. Nothing in the Agreement Among Licensors discourages, either through outright prohibition or economic incentives, any Licensor from developing or supporting a rival standard. As noted above, the Portfolio license explicitly leaves licensees free independently to make products that do not comply with the MPEG–2 standard and premises royalty obligations on actual use of at least one Portfolio patent.[44] Since the Portfolio includes only Essential Patents, the licensee's manufacture, use or sale of MPEG–2 products will necessarily infringe the Portfolio patents. By weeding out non-essential patents from the Portfolio, the independent-expert mechanism helps ensure that the licensees will not have to pay royalties for making MPEG–2 products that do not employ the licensed patents.

---

44. Cf. United States v. Microsoft Corp., 1995–2 Trade Cas. (CCH) ¶ 71,096 (D.D.C. 1995) (consent decree resolving suit against, among other things, use of per-processor royalty for license of dominant operating system).

The license's initial duration, to January 1, 2000, does not present any competitive concern. While the open-ended renewal term of "no less than five years" holds open the possibility of a perpetual license, its competitive impact will depend substantially on whether any of the "reasonable amendments" made at that time increase the license's exclusionary impact. While the term "reasonable" is the Portfolio license's only limitation on the Licensors' ability to impose onerous non-royalty terms on licensees at renewal time, the 25% cap on royalty increases and the "most-favored-nation" clause appear to constrain the Licensors' ability to use royalties to exploit any locked-in installed base among its licensees.

Nor does the Portfolio license's grantback clause appear anticompetitive. Its scope, like that of the license itself, is limited to Essential Patents. It does not extend to mere implementations of the standard or even to improvements on the essential patents.[45] Rather, the grantback simply obliges licensees that control an Essential Patent to make it available to all, on a nonexclusive basis, at a fair and reasonable royalty, just like the Portfolio patents. This will mean that any firm that wishes to take advantage of the cost savings afforded by the Portfolio license cannot hold its own essential patents back from other would-be manufacturers of MPEG–2 products. While easing, though not altogether clearing up, the holdout problem,[46] the grantback should not create any disincentive among licensees to innovate. Since the grantback extends only to MPEG–2 Essential Patents, it is unlikely that there is any significant innovation left to be done that the grantback could discourage.[47] The grantback provision is likely simply to bring other Essential Patents into the Portfolio, thereby limiting holdouts' ability to exact a supracompetitive toll from Portfolio licensees and further lowering licensees' costs in assembling the patent rights essential to their compliance with the MPEG–2 standard.

In different circumstances, the right of partial termination set forth in Section 6.3 of the Portfolio license could raise difficult competition issues. That section provides that, on instruction from any Licensor, MPEG LA, pursuant to its obligations under the Licensing Administrator Agreement, shall withdraw from a particular licensee's portfolio license that Licensor's patent or patents if the licensee has sued the Licensor for infringement of an Essential Patent or a Related Patent and refused to grant a license on the allegedly infringed patent on "fair and reasonable terms."

Of course, a licensee's refusal to license an Essential Patent on fair and reasonable terms, as required by Section 7.3 of the Portfolio License, is grounds for termination of the Portfolio license altogether. Even though MPEG LA may choose not to exercise its right to terminate, a Licensor that has been denied a license may invoke the less drastic partial termination provision, which is mandatory on MPEG LA. Partial termination would force

45. Consequently, much of the section on grantbacks in the IP Guidelines is not directly applicable to this provision. The ultimate question, though, is the same: whether, by reducing licensees' incentives to innovate, the grantback causes competitive harm that outweighs its procompetitive effects. *See* IP Guidelines, § 5.6.

46. Any non-manufacturing owner of an Essential Patent, in contrast, can still be a holdout, having no need for the Portfolio license.

47. Improvements on MPEG–2 Essential Patents and technological alternatives to the Essential Patents would not be Essential Patents themselves and would not be subject to the grantback. Therefore, the grantback should not discourage their development.

the licensee to negotiate with the Licensor as if the pool had never existed. Thus, while the partial termination right leaves the licensee no worse off than it was in the absence of the pool, it enforces the Essential Patent grantback, which, as discussed above, appears procompetitive.

The right of partial termination could have a very different impact on a Portfolio licensee that owns a Related Patent. No matter how attractive the licensee's patented implementation of the MPEG–2 standard may be, by definition the Related Patent will not be essential to compliance with the standard. And, not being essential, the patent is not subject to the Section 7.3 grantback. If the Portfolio licensee that owns a Related Patent chooses not to license others to use its technology, those others may still have alternatives to choose from. But if a Licensor chooses to infringe the Portfolio licensee's Related Patent after having been denied a license, the Portfolio licensee's decision to sue for infringement could cause it to become unable, at least temporarily, to comply with the MPEG–2 standard.[48]

The MPEG–2 Licensor is not entirely unconstrained: Importantly, as you have pointed out, its undertakings to the ISO and/or the ITU–T obligate it to license on fair and reasonable terms. However, it is not clear that this general commitment alone deprives the Licensor of the ability to impair competition. The partial termination right may enable Licensors to obtain licenses on Related Patents at royalty levels below what they would have been in a competitive market. Consequently, the partial termination right may dampen licensees' incentives to invest in research and development of MPEG–2 implementations, undercutting somewhat the benefits of the openness of the MPEG–2 standard and the prospects for improvements on the Essential Patents.

This impact on the incentive to innovate within the MPEG–2 standard would be of particular concern were the partial termination right designed to benefit all portfolio licensees. In that event, the partial termination right would function much like a compulsory grantback into the Portfolio. Licensees that owned Related Patents would not be able to choose among and negotiate freely with potential users of their inventions. The licensees' potential return from their R & D investments could be curtailed drastically, and the corresponding impact on their incentive to innovate could be significant.

Here, however, the partial termination right, unlike the grantback, protects only the Licensors. Other portfolio licensees have no right under the pool license to practice fellow licensees' inventions. And the Licensors are likely to be restrained in exercising their partial termination rights because the development of Related Patents will enhance MPEG–2 and, thus, the value of the Portfolio. The long-term interest of the Licensors is generally to encourage innovation in Related Patents, not to stifle it.

Moreover, the partial termination right may have procompetitive effects to the extent that it functions as a nonexclusive grantback requirement on licensees' Related Patents. It could allow Licensors and licensees to share the

---

48. Since, as noted in note 33 above, it is exceedingly unlikely that a Related Patent would ever have any utility outside the MPEG–2 standard, it is correspondingly unlikely that an owner of a Related Patent would ever have cause to sue an MPEG–2 Licensor for infringe- ment of that patent in connection with the manufacture, use or sale of anything other than MPEG–2–related products or services. If Section 6.3 were used in response to such an infringement action, we could have serious concerns.

risk and rewards of supporting and improving the MPEG–2 standard by enabling Licensors to capture some of the value they have added to licensees' Related Patents by creating and licensing the Portfolio. In effect, the partial termination right may enable Licensors to realize greater returns on the Portfolio license from the licensees that enjoy greater benefits from the license, while maintaining the Portfolio royalty at a level low enough to attract licensees that may value it less. This in turn could lead to more efficient exploitation of the Portfolio technology.

Therefore, in light of both its potentially significant procompetitive effects and the limited potential harm it poses to Portfolio licensees' incentives to innovate, the partial-termination clause appears on balance unlikely to be anticompetitive.

III.   CONCLUSION

Like many joint licensing arrangements, the agreements you have described for the licensing of MPEG–2 Essential Patents are likely to provide significant cost savings to Licensors and licensees alike, substantially reducing the time and expense that would otherwise be required to disseminate the rights to each MPEG–2 Essential Patent to each would-be licensee. Moreover, the proposed agreements that will govern the licensing arrangement have features designed to enhance the usual procompetitive effects and mitigate potential anticompetitive dangers. The limitation of the Portfolio to technically essential patents and the use of an independent expert to be the arbiter of that limitation reduces the risk that the patent pool will be used to eliminate rivalry between potentially competing technologies. Potential licensees will be aided by the provision of a clear list of the Portfolio patents, the availability of the Portfolio patents independent of the Portfolio, and the warning that the Portfolio may not contain all Essential Patents. The conditioning of licensee royalty liability on actual use of the Portfolio patents, the clearly stated freedom of licensees to develop and use alternative technologies, and the imposition of obligations on licensees' own patent rights that do not vitiate licensees' incentives to innovate, all serve to protect competition in the development and use of both improvements on, and alternatives to, MPEG–2 technology.

For these reasons, the Department is not presently inclined to initiate antitrust enforcement action against the conduct you have described. This letter, however, expresses the Department's current enforcement intention. In accordance with our normal practices, the Department reserves the right to bring an enforcement action in the future if the actual operation of the proposed conduct proves to be anticompetitive in purpose or effect.

This statement is made in accordance with the Department's Business Review Procedure, 28 C.F.R. § 50.6. Pursuant to its terms, your business review request and this letter will be made publicly available immediately, and any supporting data will be made publicly available within 30 days of the date of this letter, unless you request that part of the material be withheld in accordance with Paragraph 10(c) of the Business Review Procedure.

Sincerely,

Joel I. Klein

[then Assistant Attorney General, Antitrust Division, Department of Justice. Eds.]

————

There are many important aspects to the DOJ's 1997 Business Review letter in *MPEG*. On a basic level, first note how the Department used the IP Guidelines to shape its analysis. Note, too, that as we have emphasized throughout the book, its inquiry focused on the arrangement's potential to lead to collusive or exclusionary anticompetitive effects. But it devoted a considerable portion of its analysis to whether the arrangement would more particularly have a negative effect on *innovation*. What explains that emphasis?

MPEG also illustrates the many kinds of antitrust issues that can arise in the context of patent pooling or cross licensing. Note how the DOJ touched upon and evaluated the possibility that the pooling plan would lead to horizontal price fixing, exclusionary boycotts, exclusive dealing, and tying. What elements of its analysis could you tie to cases we have studied? Consider how cases like *Broadcast Music, Northwest Wholesale Stationers, Jefferson Parish,* and *Omega Environmental* provide a backdrop for the Department's analysis. For other examples of the Department's approach to evaluating patent pools, see *Request for Business Review Letter Regarding the Licensing of Patents for DVD Technology*, 1999 WL 392163 (D.O.J. 1999); *Business Review Letter Regarding the Licensing of Patents Essential to DVD–Video and DVD–Rom*, 1998 WL 890334 (D.O.J. 1998). *See also U.S. IP Guidelines*, § 5.5; *Canadian IP Guidelines*, Example 6.

More substantively, what was the "problem" the *MPEG* parties were trying to solve? How did cross-licensing and pooling patents provide an efficient resolution of their problem? What were the specific features and characteristics of the agreements that were negotiated by the *MPEG* parties? How clear of a road map does the government's analysis provide to others who might want to propose similar arrangements? Were there features that were indispensable from the DOJ's view, in terms of ensuring that the pooling arrangement would not be anticompetitive?

What might have caused "the problem"? How could there have been 8000 related patents? Twenty-seven that were "essential"? In the following Note, we explore how patent pools have emerged as a solution for what one commentator has termed the "patent thicket"—the apparent proliferation of patent applications that are approved by the Patent & Trademark Office ("PTO")—which, he argues is a consequence of overly lenient standards for issuing patents.

Note on The Role of the PTO in Defining the Scope of Patent Protection

As we discussed at the outset of our treatment of IPRs, their essential characteristic is the "right to exclude." That right to exclude, of course, generates both the incentive to innovate that is the point of IPRs, as well as concern for their possible negative impact on competition. As a general matter, if IPRs are defined very broadly by the Patent & Trademark Office ("PTO"), and if it grants a lot of applications for IPRs, the greater the possibility that the IPRs system will (1) confer greater power to exclude than is necessary to spur innovation; and (2) diminish competition for innovation by facilitating unjustifiable and unnecessary exclusion. The equilibrium of the IP rights system can also be disrupted by granting IP rights that endure longer than is necessary to attract the investment and effort to innovate.

These three fundamental aspects of patent rights—scope, duration and proliferation of patents, therefore, have taken center stage in the ongoing public debate about the interface of antitrust and IP, and were extensively addressed in the 2002 FTC/DOJ IP hearings and reports issued in 2003 and 2007. According to Timothy J. Muris, the then FTC Chairman, the number of patents granted by the PTO has increased from approximately 60,000 per year in 1980 to more than 175,000 in 2000. *See* Timothy J. Muris, *Competition and Intellectual Property Policy: The Way Ahead* (Nov. 15, 2001) (http://www.ftc.gov/speeches/muris/intell ectual.htm). As in *MPEG*, this proliferation of patents may necessitate greater degrees of cooperation among rivals, who may find themselves unable to utilize a process or produce a product because of the presence of multiple patents and the threat of infringement actions, and consequently higher risks of anticompetitive coordination. *See* Carl Shapiro, *Navigating the Patent Thicket: Cross–Licenses, Patent Pools, and Standard Setting, in* 1 INNOVATION POLICY AND THE ECONOMY (Adam Jaffe, Joshua Lerner & Scott Stern, eds. 2001), *available at* http://faculty.haas. berkeley.edu/shapiro/thicket.pdf. As Chairman Muris inquired:

> We need to understand the recent trend of patent proliferation: What are the factors underlying the trend—an explosion of innovation, changes in business approaches to intellectual property, patent procedures at the PTO, or other causes? How does this trend affect the commercialization of new technology? If the central approaches to navigating a patent thicket involve cross-licenses and patent pooling, how should antitrust enforcement react to these practices? To the extent that such a patent thicket exists, how does it affect standard setting, for example when access to multiple patents in the hands of different patentees may be required to develop and implement a technological standard?

As should be apparent, resolving many of the issues posed in this Chapter may turn on the answers to these questions. In short, the antitrust response to IP rights will ultimately be a function of the scope of those rights, themselves.

d. Standard Setting and IP Rights

As we observed earlier in this Chapter, standard setting can be effectively manipulated to achieve significant exclusionary effects even in the absence of IPRs. But can the introduction of IPRs to the scenario amplify that effect? For example, what if the owner of a patented product or process persuades a standard setting organization to specify the patented product or process as the industry standard? Obviously, in such a situation, the patent owner may find itself in a very advantageous situation: not only will all industry participants effectively be forced to license the product/process from the patent holder, but owners of competing products or processes, be they patented or not, may be effectively excluded. Is it likely, therefore, that the standard setting organization would specify a patented or otherwise proprietary product/process as an industry standard? Perhaps so, but only if it either: (1) did not know that the product or process being specified was patented; or (2) it received assurances that the patent holder would freely license it on reasonable terms. In our next case we examine the FTC's 1995 consent decree with Dell Computer Corporation, which illustrates this scenario.

IN THE MATTER OF DELL COMPUTER CORPORATION

Federal Trade Commission, 1996.

121 F.T.C. 616.

* * *

STATEMENT OF THE FEDERAL TRADE COMMISSION

* * *

The outcome of any Commission enforcement action depends on the facts of the particular case. The Dell case involved an effort by the Video Electronics Standards Association ("VESA") to identify potentially conflicting patents and to avoid creating standards that would infringe those patents. In order to achieve this goal, VESA—like some other standard-setting entities—has a policy that member companies must make a certification that discloses any potentially conflicting intellectual property rights. VESA believes that its policy imposes on its members a good-faith duty to seek to identify potentially conflicting patents. This policy is designed to further VESA's strong preference for adopting standards that do not include proprietary technology.

This case involved the standard for VL-bus, a mechanism to transfer instructions between a computer's central processing unit and its peripherals. During the standard-setting process, VESA asked its members to certify whether they had any patents, trademarks, or copyrights that conflicted with the proposed VL-bus standard; Dell certified that it had no such intellectual property rights. After VESA adopted the standard—based, in part, on Dell's certification—Dell sought to enforce its patent against firms planning to follow the standard.

We believe that in the limited circumstances presented by this case, enforcement action is appropriate. In this case—where there is evidence that the association would have implemented a different non-proprietary design had it been informed of the patent conflict during the certification process, and where Dell failed to act in good faith to identify and disclose patent conflicts—enforcement action is appropriate to prevent harm to competition and consumers.[2]

The remedy in this case is carefully circumscribed. It simply prohibits Dell from enforcing its patent against those using the VL-bus standard.[3] This relief assures that the competitive process is not harmed by the conduct

---

2. The Commission has reason to believe that once VESA's VL-bus standard had become widely accepted, the standard effectively conferred market power upon Dell as the patent holder. This market power was not inevitable: had VESA known of the Dell patent, it could have chosen an equally effective, non-proprietary standard. If Dell were able to impose a royalty on each VL-bus installed in 486–generation computers, prices to consumers would likely have increased.

The dissent speculates that computer manufacturers could have readily shifted to a new standard. Although that alternative might be possible in some settings, it was not in this case where the market had overwhelmingly adopted the VL-bus standard.

3. It also prohibits Dell from enforcing patent rights in the future when it intentionally fails to disclose those rights upon request of any standard-setting organization during the standard-setting process.

addressed in the Commission's complaint. Moreover, the remedy in this case is consistent with those cases, decided under the concept of equitable estoppel, in which courts precluded patent-holders from enforcing patents when they failed properly to disclose the existence of those patents. In this case, Dell is precluded from enforcing the patent only against those implementing the relevant standard.[5]

Some of those who commented on the Agreement Containing Consent Order suggested that this matter expresses an endorsement of certain types of standards (*i.e.*, those including only non-proprietary technology versus those including proprietary technology) or of a certain form of standard-setting process. On the contrary, the Commission's enforcement action does not address, and is not intended to address, any of these broader issues.

Other commenters asked whether the Commission intended to signal that there is a general duty to search for patents when a firm engages in a standard-setting process. The relief in this matter is carefully limited to the facts of the case. Specifically, VESA's affirmative disclosure requirement creates an expectation by its members that each will act in good faith to identify and disclose conflicting intellectual property rights. Other standard-setting organizations may have different procedures that do not create such an expectation on the part of their members. Consequently, the relief in this case should not be read to impose a general duty to search.

Others suggested that the theory supporting this enforcement action could impose liability for an unknowing (or "inadvertent") failure to disclose patent rights. Again, the Commission's enforcement action is limited to the facts of this case, in which there is reason to believe that Dell's failure to disclose the patent was not inadvertent. The order should not be read to create a general rule that inadvertence in the standard-setting process provides a basis for enforcement action. Nor does this enforcement action contain a general suggestion that standard-setting bodies should impose a duty to disclose.

Finally, some commenters suggested that private litigation is sufficient to address this type of controversy. Although there has been private litigation for failure to disclose patent rights under equitable estoppel theories, enforcement of Section 5 of the Federal Trade Commission Act also serves an important role in this type of case, where there is a likelihood of consumer harm. Moreover, unlike other antitrust statutes, Section 5 provides only for prospective relief. In fact, the judicious use of Section 5—culminating in carefully tailored relief—is particularly appropriate in this type of case, in which the legal and economic theories are somewhat novel.

---

5. The dissent seems to suggest that relief should be limited to those firms that relied on Dell's certification. The equitable estoppel doctrine, which seeks to remedy harm to the aggrieved companies, would support such a limited remedy. But from the Commission's perspective, based on our responsibility to protect the competitive marketplace, broader relief is warranted.

Here the market adopted the VL-bus standard. Both those who relied on Dell's represen-

tation, and others who had to adopt the industry standard, were faced with potential harm. Absent our enforcement action, Dell could have required royalties from all firms that adopted the standard. Where the market has chosen a particular technology believed to be available to all without cost, limiting the order solely to those companies that relied on Dell's certification might not fully protect the competitive process or consumers.

* * * The Commission recognizes that enforcement actions in this area should be undertaken with care, lest they chill participation in the standard-setting process. Nevertheless, a standard-setting organization may provide a vehicle for a firm to undermine the standard-setting process in a way that harms competition and consumers.[8] We believe that the commission's enforcement action in Dell strikes the right balance between these important objectives.

DISSENTING STATEMENT OF COMMISSIONER MARY L. AZCUENAGA

* * *

The complaint against Dell does not articulate a violation of Section 5 of the FTC Act under any established theory of law. Under any novel theory, the competitive implications of the conduct alleged remain unclear. As confirmed by the comments we have received, a host of questions needs to be resolved before the Commission creates a new antitrust-based duty of care for participants in the voluntary standards-setting process.

The statement of the majority appears intended to respond to the concerns raised in the comments. Unfortunately, it does not resolve those concerns. Instead, by failing to take a clear stand on what legal standard it intends to apply, the majority creates more confusion. In its explanatory statement, the majority tries to have it both ways: it manages at once to suggest that this case is based on a traditional theory, which requires a showing of intent, and at the same time to say that this case is based on a novel theory, apparently to explain the absence of any showing or allegation of intent. The complaint and order combined with the explanatory statement of the majority give rise to troubling implications about the duty of care in the standards-setting process.

I. FACTUAL BACKGROUND

This is a case about alleged abuse of the standards-setting process by a patent holder. The facts alleged in the complaint are not complex. The Video Electronics Standards Association ("VESA") is a private standards-setting organization, including as members both computer hardware and software manufacturers. In 1991 and 1992, VESA developed a standard for a computer bus design, called the VESA Local Bus ("VL-bus"). The bus carries information and instructions between the computer's central processing unit and peripheral devices. In August 1992, VESA conducted a vote to approve its VL-bus standard. The VESA ballot required each member's authorized voting representative to sign a statement that "to the best of my knowledge," the proposal did not infringe the member company's intellectual property rights.

According to the Commission's complaint, after adoption of the standard, the VL-bus design was incorporated in many computers. The complaint alleges that Dell subsequently asserted that the "implementation of the VL-bus [by other computer manufacturers] is a violation of Dell's exclusive [patent] rights." For purposes of antitrust analysis, it is important to note that the complaint does not allege that Dell's representative to VESA had any knowledge of the coverage of Dell's relevant patent (known as the " '481"

---

8. *See, e.g., Allied Tube & Conduit Corp. v. Indian Head, Inc., 486 U.S. 492 (1988).*

patent) or of the potential infringement by the VL-bus at the time he cast the ballot.

Nothing in the limited information available to the Commission suggests that Dell had any greater role in the development and promulgation of the VESA VL-bus standard than that described in the minimal factual allegations in the complaint. For example, the complaint does not allege that Dell proposed or sponsored the standard, that Dell urged others to vote for the standard, that Dell employees participated in drafting the standard, that Dell employees were present, in person or online, during the committee drafting sessions, that Dell steered the VESA committee toward adopting a standard that incorporated Dell technology, or that Dell had any hand whatsoever in shaping the standard.

The sole act for which Dell is charged with a violation of law is that Dell's voting representative, in voting to adopt the standard, signed a certification that to the best of his knowledge, the proposed standard did not infringe on any relevant intellectual property.

[Here Commissioner Azcuenaga took issue with the majority's decision to treat the signed certification as sufficient to meet the traditional intent standards of the antitrust laws, arguing that it was insufficient under the standards used in cases of alleged fraudulent procurement of patents. Eds.]

* * *

III. ANTICOMPETITIVE EFFECTS

A second notable omission from the Dell complaint is any allegation that the company acquired or extended market power.[9] Instead, paragraph nine of the complaint alleges that Dell unreasonably restrained competition in four ways: (1) industry acceptance of the VL-bus "was hindered"; (2) systems using the VL-bus "were avoided"; (3) uncertainty concerning the acceptance of the VL-bus design standard "raised the costs of implementing the VL-bus design" and "of developing competing bus designs"; and (4) "willingness to participate in industry standards-setting efforts have [sic] been chilled." Assuming the allegations are true, none of them suggests that Dell acquired the power to control price and output in a relevant antitrust market. Indeed, if, as appears from the allegations to be the case, computer producers readily could switch to bus designs that do not incorporate Dell's technology, no monopoly seems possible. The first three allegations regarding delay in acceptance of the standard, avoidance of systems using the VL-bus, and uncertainty about the bus standard, all relate to the speed and breadth of industry acceptance of the standard. Assuming that industry acceptance of the bus was slower or less extensive than it otherwise would have been, those effects do not necessarily translate into higher prices of computers for consumers, restricted output of computers in any relevant geographic market, or any other harm to consumers or competition.

Although the complaint does not allege that Dell acquired market power, the majority asserts in its explanatory statement that "once VESA's VL-bus

---

9. The complaint does not identify or allege any relevant product or geographic market. Usually, the antitrust analysis of particular practices begins with the identification of relevant product and geographic markets.

standard had become widely accepted, the standard effectively conferred market power upon Dell as the patent holder." It is worth noting that even here the majority does not allege that Dell did anything to acquire market power. In addition, the majority fails to identify the relevant market in which market power assertedly was "conferred." Dell is a producer of computers, and the press release announcing that the order had been accepted for public comment stated that Dell restricted competition "in the personal computer industry." Perhaps the majority actually does mean to find that Dell has market power in the personal computer industry; if so, some explanation is needed to make the finding more plausible, and an allegation to that effect in the complaint would seem to be in order.

The fourth allegation in the complaint, that Dell "chilled" willingness to participate in standards-setting, is particularly odd. Under the Dell order, a participant in a VESA-like standards process would be well advised not only to review its patent portfolio carefully before permitting its voting representative to sign a ballot, but if it has valuable intellectual property to protect, it might well consider not voting at all. The danger that voting on a standard might result in the loss of a company's intellectual property rights may dissuade some firms from participating in the standards-setting process in the first place. That would be a curious result indeed for an order resting on a complaint that alleges, as an anticompetitive effect, that "[w]illingness to participate in industry standard-setting efforts ha[s] been chilled."

IV. REMEDY

The relief imposed by the majority seems unnecessarily harsh. The order prohibits Dell from enforcing its '481 patent against any firm using the patented technology to implement the VL-bus design for the life of the patent. In effect, the order requires Dell to provide a global royalty-free license to any firm that may have used the technology in the past, or may use it in the future, to implement the standard. The explanatory statement of the majority indicates that the relief is "carefully limited to the facts of the case," because VESA's disclosure requirement "creates an expectation by its members" that intellectual property rights will be disclosed. This emphasis on an "expectation" sounds like a private patent estoppel case, not a competition case brought in the interest of the public. In any event, the complaint did not allege an "expectation" by VESA members as an element of the offense or of the competitive effects.

The private remedy of patent estoppel should suffice to remedy expectations based on Dell's conduct by barring inappropriate enforcement of a patent claim. * * * If Dell's vote with its accompanying certification was misleading, and if another VESA member relied on the certification to its material prejudice, then the other firm may assert estoppel as a bar to any claims under the patent. The Commission order, however, bars Dell from enforcing its patent without regard to whether the infringer relied on the miscommunication or whether the infringer would be materially prejudiced. If, as the majority suggests in its explanatory statement, an "expectation" is a critical underpinning of the remedy, it seems curious to bar enforcement of the patent without some better proof of expectation.

The anticompetitive effects alleged in the complaint were all highly ephemeral; they involved a delay in industry acceptance of the VL-bus design standard, avoidance of systems using the standard, and increased costs due to uncertainty about acceptance of the VL-bus and development of competing bus designs. As a practical matter, a Commission order, entered in 1996, can do little to correct any uncertainty and delay that might have occurred in early 1993, when Dell asserted the claim. Presumably, companies have long since decided what bus design to select. In a "precedent-setting" matter such as this one, the Commission should attempt to identify the relevant competitive interests and strike a fair balance among them. An order limiting enforcement of an undisclosed patent for an ample period of time to permit modification of the standard to eliminate the patent conflict would be less draconian than the majority's permanent ban on enforcement and seems more proportional to the alleged harm.

* * *

I dissent.

———

What provision of the antitrust laws did Dell violate? What specific conduct constituted the violation? How did the Commission justify its rationale for prohibiting that conduct? Do you agree with the dissent that the remedy was unduly broad?

Would Dell's conduct have posed any serious antitrust problem if its patent rights were not implicated by the VL-bus design standard? Should the matter have been analyzed as a problem of "patent misuse" as opposed to an antitrust violation? In the next Sidebar, we look at some other implications of the issues posed in *Dell*.

Sidebar 10–4:
Open vs. Closed Access to Industry Standards

The problem enforcers and courts face in distinguishing between harmful and beneficial conduct can be particularly difficult when investment in research and development does not merely lead to new products, but also sets a proprietary industry standard. Then competition may involve rivalry over the opportunity to create the next standard even more than rivalry among the products within the standard. A standard-setter with intellectual property protection might deter competition or control access to the industry, thus inhibiting existing rivals employing the existing standard as well as potential rivals with a potentially better one.

On the other hand, standards often amplify the consumer benefits from innovation, and intellectual property protection may be necessary to induce firms to invest in developing and promoting potential standards. Both the scope of the potential harm to competition and the range of potential efficiency benefits are likely further increased if, as often occurs, adopting the standard facilitates the growth of network externalities. Moreover, the competitive analysis of industry standards may also depend on whether access to the standard is "open" or "closed." This Sidebar explains that distinction, and its relationship to "component" versus "systems" competition.

The development of many services—from stereo components to computer software—requires collaboration among the sellers of the complementary services involved. One possible framework for that collaboration is an "open" access regime, in which the service providers at each level receive and grant non-discriminatory access to all complementary services, for free or for a reasonable licensing fee. This regime can allow "component" competition, in both price and innovation. The home stereo market largely evolved this way. Music storage technologies, such as records, tapes and CDs, and music access technologies, such as phonographs, tuners, amplifiers, tape players, and CD players, interconnect in a host of ways—from plug interfaces between components to CD formats and electronic signal interface conventions. This interoperability allows consumers to mix and match components from different manufacturers according to their preference.

The interconnection standards may have emerged through competition in the marketplace or by agreement among some or all industry participants, as the industry association attempted to achieve in *Dell*. Although an open access regime does not preclude the development of integrated "systems"—even in the stereo market, some manufacturers have packaged multiple components under a common brand name— component competition is more likely to arise with open access than with closed access.

At the other extreme lies the "closed" access regime, in which firms can limit compatibility to specified sellers of complements. They may do so through proprietary interconnection standards, for example. Competition in the personal computer market took this form to some extent in the 1980s rivalry between the Apple and IBM operating systems. Although firms controlling access may prefer to permit component competition to some extent, as IBM did to a greater extent than Apple, systems competition—in which a collection of complements working together offers a product or service in competition with another collection of complements—is probably more likely to arise with closed access than with open access. It is also possible to imagine intermediate access regimes, in which a firm permits favored providers of complements to have superior access than less favored providers.

Both open access regimes and closed access regimes can be competitive, and systems competition is not necessarily more or less competitive than component competition. *See generally* Catherine Fazio & Scott Stern, *Innovation Incentives, Compatibility, and Expropriation as an Antitrust Remedy: The Legacy of the Borland/Ashton–Tate Consent Decree*, 68 ANTITRUST L.J. 45 (2000); CARL SHAPIRO & HAL VARIAN, INFORMATION RULES: A STRATEGIC GUIDE TO THE NETWORK ECONOMY (2000); Joseph Farrell & Michael Katz, *The Effects of Antitrust and Intellectual Property Law on Compatibility and Innovation*, 43 ANTITRUST BULL. 609 (1998).

Sometimes, a firm competing in an open access regime may develop and insist upon a proprietary standard. As a consequence, the industry may move to a closed access regime. Some of the exclusionary conduct in

Microsoft can be understood in such terms. This kind of industry evolution may occur in high-technology markets where product innovation leads to frequent modification of interfaces or interconnection standards. If a switch from open access to closed access leads to the end of component competition, that outcome is not necessarily harmful to competition, as systems competition may instead develop. But if the development of proprietary standards has the effect of preventing the development of systems competition, the result may instead be a reduction in industry competition, and perhaps the creation of a systems monopoly. For example, the excluded components may have difficulty working together to develop a rival system. *See* DENNIS W. CARLTON & ROBERT H. GERTNER, INTELLECTUAL PROPERTY, ANTITRUST AND STRATEGIC BEHAVIOR (Nat'l Bureau of Econ. Research, Working Paper No. 8976, 2002).

In *Dell*, a standard-setting process intended to lead to an open access regime, with component competition, was allegedly hijacked by one participant, whose assertion of intellectual property rights could lead to a closed access regime. Could the excluded firms have gone back to the drawing board, and developed a competing standard? Or was this impractical given the head start that the assertion of intellectual property rights would have given Dell, and the investments in new product development the rival firms had made under the expectation that the standard would permit open access? In short, would the practice challenged in *Dell* have led, absent antitrust enforcement, to systems competition or systems monopoly?

Note on Abuse of Standard Setting: The Rambus and Unocal Litigations

In June 2002, the Federal Trade Commission voted 5–0 to issue an administrative complaint against Rambus, Inc., for "deliberately" trying to deceive an industry-wide standard-setting organization. *See In re Rambus, Inc.*, File No. 011 0017, Docket No. 9302, www.ftc.gov/opa/ 2002/06/rambus.htm. According to the complaint, over a four year period, Rambus actively participated in an industry standard-setting organization's efforts to develop a common industry technical standard for synchronous dynamic ram access memory ("SDRAM"), which is used on memory chips in many kinds of computers and other memory equipped electronic products, such as fax machines, printers and PDAs. Even as it sought to influence the content of the standard, Rambus is alleged to have been covertly working to develop patents for technologies that were specifically incorporated into the standards. Concealing that information was in direct contravention of the organization's operating rules and procedures.

On August 2, 2006, the full Commission unanimously reversed the ALJ's initial decision in favor of Rambus, concluding that the firm had in fact engaged in unlawful monopolization. *See In the Matter of Rambus*, Inc., Dkt. No. 9302, *available at* http://www.ftc.gov/os/adjpro/d9302/060802commissionopinion.pdf. Following a subsequent round of briefing, a more divided Commission issued a separate order on remedy. *See* http://www.ftc.gov/os/adjpro/d9302/070205opinion. pdf. Commissioners Thomas Rosch and Pamela Jones Harbour both dissented in part. On April 22, 2008, the FTC's decision was reversed and remanded. *See Rambus, Inc. v. FTC*, ___ F.3d ___, 2008 WL 1795594 (D.C. Cir. 2008).

Note that two allegations in *Rambus* were also present in *Dell*: (1) that the industry organization had a policy against utilizing IP protected technology in its standards, and (2) the firm accused of the antitrust violation concealed the fact that it was urging the inclusion in the standards of its patented technology. For antitrust purposes, how much weight, if any, should be accorded to proof that a firm participating in standard setting concealed its IP rights, and perhaps its anticompetitive intentions?

The FTC complaint parallels a private civil action that was dismissed by the Federal Circuit. *See Rambus, Inc. v. Infineon Technologies*, 164 F. Supp.2d 743 (E.D. Va.2001), *vacated in part, reversed in part, affirmed in part, and remanded, Rambus Inc. v. Infineon Technologies AG*, 318 F.3d 1081 (Fed. Cir. 2003). The Federal Circuit concluded that, as a matter of law, the evidence did not support a finding that Rambus breached its duty to disclose pending patent applications to fellow members of the open standards committee.

The FTC challenged another abuse of standard setting in *In the Matter of Union Oil Co. of Calif.*, Dkt N. 9305 (July 6, 2004) (*"Unocal"*), which reversed an ALJ's dismissal of the FTC's complaint (*available at* http://www.ftc.gov/os/adjpro/d 9305/040706commissionopinion.pdf). In a March 4, 2003 administrative complaint, the FTC accused Unocal of making false and misleading statements to a state regulatory body—the California Air Resources Board ("CARB")—for the purpose of inducing it to issue regulatory standards that would incorporate Unocal's patented technology. Specifically, Unocal allegedly failed to disclose its patent rights in certain reformulated gasoline standards, which it was urging CARB to adopt. According to the complaint, Unocal (1) induced CARB to adopt reformulated gasoline standards that substantially overlapped Unocal's patent claims and (2) induced other refiners to reconfigure their refineries in ways that subsequently exposed them to Unocal's patent claims. The FTC alleged that in so misleading CARB and its rivals, Unocal sought to secure market power by having the state regulations incorporate its patents. Finally, the complaint alleged that Unocal was claiming to be entitled to hundreds of millions of dollars in royalties.

The case was remanded to the ALJ for trial, but was settled in connection with Chevron's acquisition of Unocal in 2005. As part of that consent decree, Chevron agreed not to enforce the patents at issue in the FTC Unocal administrative case, in effect giving the FTC the relief it sought in the Unocal administrative case. *See* Decision and Order, *In the Matter of Chevron Corp. and Unocal Corp.*, *available at* http://www.ftc.gov/os/adjpro/d9305/050802do.pdf.

e.   *Antitrust Counterclaims that Attack the Validity of Patents*

One way a patent holder might seek to exercise its right to exclude is by initiating civil actions for infringement against its rivals. The alleged infringers in such cases often respond by asserting an antitrust counterclaim directed at, among other things, the initiation of the infringement lawsuit. As you read *Walker Process*, and *Nobelpharma* which follows it, consider how such a scenario is likely to raise questions about IP, antitrust, and, as we learned in Chapter 9, the *Noerr-Pennington* doctrine as it applies to petitioning of the courts.

WALKER PROCESS EQUIPMENT INC. v. FOOD MACHINERY AND CHEMICAL CORP.

Supreme Court of the United States, 1965.
382 U.S. 172, 86 S.Ct. 347, 15 L.Ed.2d 247.

Mr. Justice CLARK delivered the opinion of the Court.

The question before us is whether the maintenance and enforcement of a patent obtained by fraud on the Patent Office may be the basis of an action under § 2 of the Sherman Act, and therefore subject to a treble damage claim by an injured party under § 4 of the Clayton Act. The respondent, Food Machinery, & Chemical Corp. (hereafter Food Machinery), filed this suit for infringement of its patent No. 2,328,655 covering knee-action swing diffusers used in aeration equipment for sewage treatment systems. Petitioner, Walker Process Equipment, Inc. (hereafter Walker), denied the infringement and counterclaimed for a declaratory judgment that the patent was invalid. After discovery, Food Machinery moved to dismiss its complaint with prejudice because the patent had expired. Walker then amended its counterclaim to charge that Food Machinery had "illegally monopolized interstate and foreign commerce by fraudulently and in bad faith obtaining and maintaining * * * its patent * * * well knowing that it had no basis for * * * a patent." It alleged fraud on the basis that Food Machinery had sworn before the Patent Office that it neither knew nor believed that its invention had been in public use in the United States for more than one year prior to filing its patent application when, in fact, Food Machinery was a party to prior use within such time. The counterclaim further asserted that the existence of the patent had deprived Walker of business that it would have otherwise enjoyed. * * *

* * *

I

* * *

Both Walker and the United States, which appears as amicus curiae, argue that if Food Machinery obtained its patent by fraud and thereafter used the patent to exclude Walker from the market through "threats of suit" and prosecution of this infringement suit, such proof would establish a prima facie violation of § 2 of the Sherman Act. On the other hand, Food Machinery says that a patent monopoly and a Sherman Act monopolization cannot be equated; the removal of the protection of a patent grant because of fraudulent procurement does not automatically result in a § 2 offense. Both lower courts seem to have concluded that proof of fraudulent procurement may be used to bar recovery for infringement, but not to establish invalidity. * * *

II

We have concluded, first, that Walker's action is not barred by the rule that only the United States may sue to cancel or annul a patent. It is true that there is no statutory authority for a private annulment suit and the invocation of the equitable powers of the court might often subject a patentee "to innumerable vexatious suits to set aside his patent." But neither reason applies here. Walker counterclaimed under the Clayton Act, not the patent laws. While one of its elements is the fraudulent procurement of a patent, the action does not directly seek the patent's annulment. The gist of Walker's claim is that since Food Machinery obtained its patent by fraud it cannot enjoy the limited exception to the prohibitions of § 2 of the Sherman Act, but must answer under that section and § 4 of the Clayton Act in treble damages to those injured by any monopolistic action taken under the fraudulent patent claim. Nor can the interest in protecting patentees from "innumerable vexatious suits" be used to frustrate the assertion of rights conferred by the antitrust laws. It must be remembered that we deal only with a special class of patents, *i.e.*, those procured by intentional fraud.

Under the decisions of this Court a person sued for infringement may challenge the validity of the patent on various grounds, including fraudulent procurement. In fact, one need not await the filing of a threatened suit by the patentee; the validity of the patent may be tested under the Declaratory Judgment Act. At the same time, we have recognized that an injured party may attack the misuse of patent rights. To permit recovery of treble damages for the fraudulent procurement of the patent coupled with violations of § 2 accords with these long-recognized procedures. It would also promote the purposes so well expressed in *Precision Instrument, supra*, 324 U.S. at 816, 65 S.Ct. at 998:

> "A patent by its very nature is affected with a public interest. * * * (It) is an exception to the general rule against monopolies and to the right to access to a free and open market. The far-reaching social and economic consequences of a patent, therefore, give the public a paramount interest in seeing that patent monopolies spring from backgrounds free from fraud or other inequitable conduct and that such monopolies are kept within their legitimate scope."

III

Walker's counterclaim alleged that Food Machinery obtained the patent by knowingly and willfully misrepresenting facts to the Patent Office. Proof of this assertion would be sufficient to strip Food Machinery of its exemption from the antitrust laws.[5] By the same token, Food Machinery's good faith would furnish a complete defense. This includes an honest mistake as to the effect of prior installation upon patentability—so-called "technical fraud."

To establish monopolization or attempt to monopolize a part of trade or commerce under § 2 of the Sherman Act, it would then be necessary to appraise the exclusionary power of the illegal patent claim in terms of the relevant market for the product involved. Without a definition of that market there is no way to measure Food Machinery's ability to lessen or destroy competition. It may be that the device—knee-action swing diffusers—used in sewage treatment systems does not comprise a relevant market. There may be effective substitutes for the device which do not infringe the patent. This is a matter of proof, as is the amount of damages suffered by Walker.

* * *

* * * Fairness requires that on remand Walker have the opportunity to make its § 2 claims more specific, to prove the alleged fraud, and to establish the necessary elements of the asserted § 2 violation.

Reversed and remanded.

---

5. This conclusion applies with equal force to an assignee who maintains and enforces the patent with knowledge of the patent's infirmity.

Mr. Justice HARLAN (concurring).

* * *

We hold today that a treble-damage action for monopolization which, but for the existence of a patent, would be violative of § 2 of the Sherman Act may be maintained under § 4 of the Clayton Act if two conditions are satisfied: (1) the relevant patent is shown to have been procured by knowing and willful fraud practiced by the defendant on the Patent Office or, if the defendant was not the original patent applicant, he had been enforcing the patent with knowledge of the fraudulent manner in which it was obtained; and (2) all the elements otherwise necessary to establish a § 2 monopolization charge are proved. * * *

It is well also to recognize the rationale underlying this decision, aimed of course at achieving a suitable accommodation in this area between the differing policies of the patent and antitrust laws. To hold, as we do, that private suits may be instituted under § 4 of the Clayton Act to recover damages for Sherman Act monopolization knowingly practiced under the guise of a patent procured by deliberate fraud, cannot well be thought to impinge upon the policy of the patent laws to encourage inventions and their disclosure. Hence, as to this class of improper patent monopolies, antitrust remedies should be allowed room for full play. On the other hand, to hold, as we do not, that private antitrust suits might also reach monopolies practiced under patents that for one reason or another may turn out to be voidable under one or more of the numerous technicalities attending the issuance of a patent, might well chill the disclosure of inventions through the obtaining of a patent because of fear of the vexations or punitive consequences of treble-damage suits. Hence, this private antitrust remedy should not be deemed available to reach § 2 monopolies carried on under a nonfraudulently procured patent.

* * *

Today, a case like *Walker Process* very likely would make its way to the Supreme Court via the Federal Circuit. As a patent infringement action, even though followed by a significant antitrust counterclaim, it would have in the first instance been appealed from the district court to the Federal Circuit. Given what we learned earlier in this Section, how might the Federal Circuit apply *Walker Process's* "fraud on the patent office" standard? The answer to that question came in our next case, *Nobelpharma*.

NOBELPHARMA AB v. IMPLANT INNOVATIONS, INC.
United States Court of Appeals for the Federal Circuit, 1998.
141 F.3d 1059.

Before RICH, PLAGER, and LOURIE, Circuit Judges.

LOURIE, Circuit Judge.

[Nobelpharma AB and its American affiliate (collectively "NP") sued Implant Innovations, Inc. ("3I") for patent infringement in the United States

District Court for the Northern District of Illinois. After a trial, that court held that NP's patent was invalid and infringed by 3I. The court also sustained 3I's antitrust counterclaim, which focused on NP's initiation of patent litigation against 3I and was based on *Walker Process*. The jury returned a verdict for 3I on that counterclaim, and the district court denied NP's motion for judgment as a matter of law. In its motion, NP unsuccessfully challenged 3I's *Walker Process* claim of fraud on the patent office and also asserted *Noerr* petitioning immunity in connection with the filing of the initial action for infringement. NP then appealed to the Federal Circuit.

After initially affirming in part and reversing in part, upon reconsideration and after consultation with the en banc court with respect to a critical choice of law question, the Court of Appeals for the Federal Circuit concluded that Federal Circuit law, not the law of the Circuit from which a patent infringement action is appealed, applies to determine whether a patentee's conduct in procuring a patent is sufficient to strip it of its immunity from antitrust liability. Eds.]

*　*　*

Discussion

B.　Antitrust Liability

*　*　*

II.

As a general proposition, when reviewing a district court's judgment involving federal antitrust law, we are guided by the law of the regional circuit in which that district court sits. However, we apply our own law, not regional circuit law, to resolve issues that clearly involve our exclusive jurisdiction.

Whether conduct in the prosecution of a patent is sufficient to strip a patentee of its immunity from the antitrust laws is one of those issues that clearly involves our exclusive jurisdiction over patent cases. It follows that whether a patent infringement suit is based on a fraudulently procured patent impacts our exclusive jurisdiction.

Moreover, an antitrust claim premised on stripping a patentee of its immunity from the antitrust laws is typically raised as a counterclaim by a defendant in a patent infringement suit. *See Argus Chem. Corp. v. Fibre Glass–Evercoat Co.*, 812 F.2d 1381, 1383, 1 USPQ2d 1971, 1973 (Fed.Cir. 1987) ("*Walker Process*, like the present case, was a patent infringement suit in which an accused infringer filed an antitrust counterclaim."). Because most cases involving these issues will therefore be appealed to this court, we conclude that we should decide these issues as a matter of Federal Circuit law, rather than rely on various regional precedents. We arrive at this conclusion because we are in the best position to create a uniform body of federal law on this subject and thereby avoid the "danger of confusion [that] might be enhanced if this court were to embark on an effort to interpret the laws" of the regional circuits. Accordingly, we hereby change our precedent and hold that whether conduct in procuring or enforcing a patent is sufficient to strip a patentee of its immunity from the antitrust laws is to be decided as a question of Federal Circuit law.[5] This conclusion applies equally to all antitrust claims premised on the bringing of a patent infringement suit.* * * However, we will continue to apply the law of the appropriate regional circuit to issues involving other elements of antitrust law such as relevant market, market power, damages, etc., as those issues are not unique to patent law, which is subject to our exclusive jurisdiction.

III.

A patentee who brings an infringement suit may be subject to antitrust liability for the anti-competitive effects of that suit if the alleged infringer (the antitrust plaintiff) proves (1) that the asserted patent was obtained through knowing and willful fraud within the meaning of *Walker Process Equipment, Inc. v. Food Machinery & Chemical Corp.*, 382 U.S. 172, 177, 86 S.Ct. at 350, 147 USPQ 404, 407 (1965), or (2) that the infringement suit was "a mere sham to cover what is actually nothing more than an attempt to interfere directly with the business relationships of a competitor," *Eastern R.R. Presidents Conference v. Noerr Motor Freight, Inc.*, 365 U.S. 127, 144, 81 S.Ct. 523, 533, 5 L.Ed.2d 464 (1961); *California Motor Transp. Co. v. Trucking Unlimited*, 404 U.S. 508, 510, 92 S.Ct. 609, 611–612, 30 L.Ed.2d 642 (1972) (holding that *Noerr* "governs the approach of citizens or groups of them ... to courts, the third branch of Government"). *See Professional Real Estate Investors, Inc. v. Columbia Pictures Indus., Inc.*, 508 U.S. 49, 62 n. 6, 113 S.Ct. 1920, 1929 n. 6, 123 L.Ed.2d 611, 26 USPQ2d 1641, 1646–47 n. 6 (1993) (*PRE*) (declining to decide "whether and, if so, to what extent *Noerr* permits the imposition of antitrust liability for a litigant's fraud or other misrepresentations").

In *Walker Process*, the Supreme Court held that in order "to strip [a patentee] of its exemption from the antitrust laws" because of its attempting to enforce its patent monopoly, an antitrust plaintiff is first required to prove that the patentee "obtained the patent by knowingly and willfully misrepresenting facts to the [PTO]." The plaintiff in the patent infringement suit must also have been aware of the fraud when bringing suit. The Court cited prior decisions that involved the knowing and willful misrepresentation of specific facts to the Patent Office * * *. These cases indicate the context in which the Court established the knowing and willful misrepresentation test.

Justice Harlan, in a concurring opinion, emphasized that to "achiev[e] a suitable accommodation in this area between the differing policies of the patent and antitrust laws," a distinction must be maintained between patents procured by "deliberate fraud" and those rendered invalid or unenforceable for other reasons. *Walker Process*, 382 U.S. at 179–80, 86 S.Ct. at 351–52, 15 L.Ed.2d 247, 147 USPQ at 408. He then stated:

> [T]o hold, as we do not, that private antitrust suits might also reach monopolies practiced under patents that for one reason or another may turn out to be voidable under one or more of the numerous technicalities attending the issuance of a patent, might well chill the disclosure of inventions through the obtaining of a patent because of fear of the vexations or punitive consequences of treble-damage suits.

5. Because precedent may not be changed by a panel, the issue of "choice of circuit" law set forth in this Section B.II. has been considered and decided unanimously by an *in banc* court consisting of MAYER, Chief Judge, RICH, NEWMAN, MICHEL, PLAGER, LOURIE, CLEVENGER, RADER, SCHALL, BRYSON, and GAJARSA, Circuit Judges.

Hence, this private antitrust remedy should not be deemed available to reach [Sherman Act] § 2 monopolies carried on under a nonfraudulently procured patent.

Id. at 180, 86 S.Ct. at 352, 147 USPQ at 408.

Consistent with the Supreme Court's analysis in *Walker Process*, as well as Justice Harlan's concurring opinion, we have distinguished "inequitable conduct" from *Walker Process* fraud, noting that inequitable conduct is a broader, more inclusive concept than the common law fraud needed to support a *Walker Process* counterclaim. Inequitable conduct in fact is a lesser offense than common law fraud, and includes types of conduct less serious than "knowing and willful" fraud.

* * *

Inequitable conduct is thus an equitable defense in a patent infringement action and serves as a shield, while a more serious finding of fraud potentially exposes a patentee to antitrust liability and thus serves as a sword. Antitrust liability can include treble damages. In contrast, the remedies for inequitable conduct, while serious enough, only include unenforceability of the affected patent or patents and possible attorney fees. *See* 35 U.S.C. §§ 282, 285 (1994). Simply put, *Walker Process* fraud is a more serious offense than inequitable conduct.

In this case, the jury was instructed that a finding of fraud could be premised on "a knowing, willful and intentional act, misrepresentation or omission before the [PTO]." This instruction was not inconsistent with various opinions of the courts stating that omissions, as well as misrepresentations, may in limited circumstances support a finding of *Walker Process* fraud. We agree that if the evidence shows that the asserted patent was acquired by means of either a fraudulent misrepresentation or a fraudulent omission and that the party asserting the patent was aware of the fraud when bringing suit, such conduct can expose a patentee to liability under the antitrust laws. We arrive at this conclusion because a fraudulent omission can be just as reprehensible as a fraudulent misrepresentation. In addition, of course, in order to find liability, the necessary additional elements of a violation of the antitrust laws must be established. *See Walker Process*, 382 U.S. at 178, 86 S.Ct. at 351, 147 USPQ at 407.

Such a misrepresentation or omission must evidence a clear intent to deceive the examiner and thereby cause the PTO to grant an invalid patent. In contrast, a conclusion of inequitable conduct may be based on evidence of a lesser misrepresentation or an omission, such as omission of a reference that would merely have been considered important to the patentability of a claim by a reasonable examiner. A finding of *Walker Process* fraud requires higher threshold showings of both intent and materiality than does a finding of inequitable conduct. Moreover, unlike a finding of inequitable conduct, a finding of *Walker Process* fraud may not be based upon an equitable balancing of lesser degrees of materiality and intent. Rather, it must be based on independent and clear evidence of deceptive intent together with a clear showing of reliance, *i.e.,* that the patent would not have issued but for the misrepresentation or omission. Therefore, for an omission such as a failure to cite a piece of prior art to support a finding of *Walker Process* fraud, the withholding of the reference must show evidence of fraudulent intent. A mere failure to cite a reference to the PTO will not suffice.

IV.

The district court observed that the Supreme Court, in footnote six of its *PRE* opinion, "left unresolved the issue of how '*Noerr* applies to the *ex parte* application process,' and in particular, how it applies to the *Walker Process* claim." The court also accurately pointed out that we have twice declined to resolve this issue. Therefore, after reviewing three opinions from the Ninth and District of Columbia Circuit Courts of Appeals, the district court made its own determination that *PRE's* two-part test for a sham is inapplicable to an antitrust claim based on the assertion of a patent obtained by knowing and willful fraud. We do not agree with that determination. *PRE* and *Walker Process* provide alternative legal grounds on which a patentee may be stripped of its immunity from the antitrust laws; both legal theories may be applied to the same conduct. Moreover, we need not find a way to merge these decisions. Each provides its own basis for depriving a patent owner of immunity from the antitrust laws; either or both may be applicable to a particular party's conduct in obtaining and enforcing a patent. The Supreme Court saw no need to merge these separate lines of cases and neither do we.

Consequently, if the above-described elements of *Walker Process* fraud, as well as the other criteria for antitrust liability, are met, such liability can be imposed without the additional sham inquiry required under *PRE*. That is because *Walker Process* antitrust liability is based on the knowing assertion of a patent procured by fraud on the PTO, very specific conduct that is clearly reprehensible. On the other hand, irrespective of the patent applicant's conduct before the PTO, an antitrust claim can also be based on a *PRE* allegation that a suit is baseless; in order to prove that a suit was within *Noerr's* "sham" exception to immunity, an antitrust plaintiff must prove that the suit was both *objectively* baseless and *subjectively* motivated by a desire to impose collateral, anti-competitive injury rather than to obtain a justifiable legal remedy. *PRE*, 508 U.S. at 60–61, 113 S.Ct. at 1929, 26 USPQ2d at 1646. * * * Thus, under *PRE*, a sham suit must be both subjectively brought in bad faith and based on a theory of either infringement or validity that is objectively baseless. Accordingly, if a suit is not objectively baseless, an antitrust defendant's subjective motivation is immaterial. In contrast with a *Walker Process* claim, a patentee's activities in procuring the patent are not necessarily at issue. It is the bringing of the lawsuit that is subjectively and objectively baseless that must be proved.

* * *

Is *Walker Process* properly thought of as a patent case or an antitrust case? Do you concur with the Federal Circuit's conclusion in *Nobelpharma* that the scope of *Walker Process's* "fraud on the patent office" exception to IP rights is properly a question of Federal Circuit law? *See* Ronald S. Katz & Adam J. Safer, *Should One Patent Court Be Making Antitrust Law for the Whole Country?*, 69 ANTITRUST L.J. 687 (2002).

Is *Nobelpharma* consistent with *Walker Process*? Does it narrow the utility of the "fraud on the patent office" idea by elevating the standard for establishing it? Can *Nobelpharma* fairly be criticized on the ground that it makes a *Walker Process* claim more difficult to prove than virtually any other antitrust claim? If so, is it a reasonable accommodation to the protection of IP rights? Does it denigrate the values of competition policy?

The Federal Circuit's *Walker Process* jurisprudence, including *Nobelpharma*, was criticized by the then-FTC Chairman. *See* Robert Pitofsky, *Challenges of the New Economy: Issues at the Intersection of Antitrust and Intellectual Property*, 68 ANTITRUST L.J. 913 (2001). As discussed in Sidebar 6–5, Chairman Pitofsky argued that the Federal Circuit's approach tends to undermine the longstanding balance between antitrust and intellectual property in a way that exalts intellectual property. Do you agree? Notwithstanding this criticism, and in what some viewed as a surprising turn of events, the Federal Circuit has expanded the scope of *Walker Process*-based antitrust claims to include threatened, as well as actually instituted claims of patent infringement. *See Hydril Co. LP v. Grant Prideco LP*, 474 F.3d 1344 (Fed. Cir. 2007). For a discussion of the case see Christopher R. Leslie, *New Possibilities for Asserting* Walker Process *Claims*, ANTITRUST, Summer 2007, at 48.

> *f. The Settlement of Patent Infringement Actions Between Actual or Potential Rivals*

An especially thorny issue that has arisen in the context of patent licensing concerns the ability of rivals to settle patent infringement actions, either through cross-licensing of patents, or through payments designed to keep a competing, and allegedly infringing product, from being marketed.

These kinds of settlements are sometimes referred to as "reverse payment" settlements, because instead of the compensation flowing from the alleged infringer to the patent holder, it flows from the patent holder to the alleged infringer. A group of such cases arose in the prescription drug industry, where competition from generic versions of popular prescription drugs posed a competitive threat to the branded and patented drug as its patent life came to an end. These cases also involve the intricacies of the Hatch–Waxman Act, which is explained in the next case.

ANDRX PHARMACEUTICALS, INC. v. BIOVAIL CORP.

United States Court of Appeals for the District of Columbia Circuit, 2001.
256 F.3d 799.

Before: HENDERSON, RANDOLPH and GARLAND, Circuit Judges. Opinion for the court filed by Circuit Judge HENDERSON.

* * *

I. Statutory Background

A company wishing to market a new drug must seek the approval of the United States Food & Drug Administration (FDA) by completing a "New Drug Application" (NDA). An NDA is time consuming and costly to prepare because it must include data from studies showing the drug's safety and effectiveness. In 1984 the Congress enacted the Hatch–Waxman Amendments to the Food, Drug and Cosmetic Act (Amendments) to, *inter alia*, simplify the procedure for FDA approval. *See* Drug Price Competition and Patent Term Restoration Act of 1984, Pub. L. No. 98–417, 98 Stat. 1585 (1984) (codified in various sections of titles 21, 35 & 42 U.S.C.). Under the Amendments, the original applicant for FDA approval (the "pioneer" applicant) must still prepare an NDA. Subsequent applicants who wish to manufacture generic versions[1] of the pioneer drug, however, need only complete an Abbreviated New Drug Application (ANDA) that relies on the FDA's previous determination that the drug is safe and effective. The generic drug share of the prescription drug market has grown from 19 per cent in 1983 to over 40 per cent in 1995. In addition, almost all of the most popular pioneer drugs with expired patents now have generic versions available.

Although the Congress was interested in increasing the availability of generic drugs, it also wanted to protect the patent rights of the pioneer applicants. The Amendments, therefore, require that an NDA contain a list of any patents "which claim[ ] the drug . . . or which claim[ ] a method of using such drug and with respect to which a claim of patent infringement could reasonably be asserted if a person not licensed by the owner engaged in the manufacture, use, or sale of the drug." 21 U.S.C. § 355(b)(1). The FDA maintains a record of such information in its publication entitled *Approved Drug Products with Therapeutic Equivalence*, commonly known as the Orange Book. *See* 21 U.S.C. § 355(j)(7)(A). For each patent applicable to the pioneer drug listed in the Orange Book, an ANDA applicant must certify whether the proposed generic drug would infringe that patent and, if not, why not. An ANDA applicant has four certification options. It may certify (1) that the required patent information has not been filed, (2) that the patent has expired, (3) that the patent has not expired but will expire on a particular date or (4) that the patent is invalid or will not be infringed by the drug for which the applicant seeks approval. *See* 21 U.S.C. § 355(j)(2)(A)(vii). The last of these options, and the one relevant here, is the Paragraph IV certification. After an applicant makes a Paragraph IV certification, the statute provides a 45–day window during which the patent holder may bring suit against the applicant. If the patent holder brings a timely suit, the statute bars the FDA from approving the applicant's ANDA, or any subsequent ANDA, for thirty months or until the successful resolution of the patent infringement suit, whichever is earlier, at which time the first ANDA applicant is eligible for FDA approval and upon such approval is awarded a 180–day exclusivity period in which to market its generic version. *See* 21 U.S.C. § 355(j)(5)(B)(iii). The statute permits the court to lengthen or shorten the 30–month waiting period if it determines that either party has failed to "reasonably cooperate in expediting the action." *Id*.

II. Background

Hoechst Marion Roussel, Inc. (HMRI) is the manufacturer, marketer and patent holder of the brand name prescription drug Cardizem CD. * * * Cardizem CD is widely prescribed for the treatment of chronic chest pains

---

1. A generic version of a pioneer drug (often described as a brandname drug) contains the same active ingredients, but not necessarily the same inactive ingredients, as the pioneer drug. A generic drug, as the name implies, is ordinarily sold without a brand name and at a lower price.

(angina) and hypertension and for the prevention of heart attacks and strokes. On September 22, 1995 Andrx filed an ANDA with the FDA seeking approval to manufacture and sell a generic form of Cardizem CD. On December 31, 1995 it made the Paragraph IV certification with regard to all unexpired patents included in the Orange Book's Cardizem CD entry and certified that its generic form of Cardizem CD did not infringe the patents owned or controlled by HMRI or its affiliates. In early 1996 HMRI filed a timely suit against Andrx for patent infringement. The filing of the suit triggered the statutory 30–month waiting period during which any subsequent ANDA applicant, including Biovail, could not receive final approval of its generic version of Cardizem CD.

In June 1997 Biovail filed an ANDA with the Paragraph IV certification for its generic version of Cardizem CD but HMRI filed no patent infringement suit against it. On September 15, 1997 the FDA issued its tentative approval of Andrx's ANDA.[5] Nine days later, on September 24, 1997, HMRI and Andrx entered into an agreement (Agreement or HMRI–Andrx Agreement) purporting to maintain the status quo pending the outcome of HMRI's patent infringement suit against Andrx. Under the terms of the Agreement, Andrx agreed not to sell its generic version of Cardizem CD until a specific time agreed upon by the parties. It also agreed to diligently prosecute its ANDA and not to relinquish or otherwise compromise any right accruing thereunder. HMRI agreed to make interim payments to Andrx in the amount of $40 million per year, payable quarterly, beginning on the date Andrx's generic version of Cardizem CD received FDA approval and ending on the date Andrx either began to sell its generic version or was adjudged liable for patent infringement.

In early 1998 Andrx filed suit against the FDA and certain ANDA applicants (including Biovail) to clarify its right as the first to file an ANDA for Cardizem CD. The suit sought injunctive relief requiring the FDA to provide Andrx with "a period of 180 days of marketing exclusivity for its controlled release generic formulations of the drugs Dilacor XR and Cardizem CD." It also requested injunctive relief prohibiting the FDA "from approving any ANDA submitted by defendant Biovail ... for a generic version of Cardizem CD that contains a paragraph 4 certification until 180–days after Andrx begins marketing its generic formulation of Cardizem CD or a court enters a judgment in the patent litigation brought by HMRI. * * * Biovail counterclaimed, alleging that Andrx had violated sections 1 and 2 of the Sherman Act as well as New Jersey common law.[6]

On July 3, 1998 the FDA granted final approval to Andrx's ANDA for a generic version of Cardizem CD. By then, the 30–month waiting period had

---

5. The FDA issued tentative, as opposed to final, approval due to the pending infringement suit and the resulting 30–month statutory waiting period.

6. On July 14, 1998 the FDA published a notice entitled "Guidance for Industry on 180–Day Generic Drug Exclusivity Under the Hatch–Waxman Amendments to the Federal Food, Drug, and Cosmetic Act; Availability," interpreting the Hatch–Waxman Amendments so as to give Andrx the relief it sought in its

complaint. The Guidance explained that the FDA intended to delete the "successful defense" provisions from § 314.107(c)(1) and that the FDA would not enforce the "successful defense" provisions in the interim. Accordingly, the district court subsequently dismissed the complaint. Andrx had earlier moved to dismiss Biovail's counterclaim for failure to state a claim upon which relief may be granted because, *inter alia*, Biovail lacked standing to assert an antitrust violation.

expired and Andrx was no longer restricted under the statutory scheme from marketing and selling its generic drug. Andrx, however, did not do so and on July 9, 1998, pursuant to the Agreement, HMRI began making quarterly payments of $10 million to Andrx. By not marketing its generic version of Cardizem CD, Andrx did not trigger the 180–day market exclusivity period, which in turn prevented the FDA from giving final approval to any subsequently filed applications for competing generic versions of Cardizem CD.

Approximately one year later, HMRI and Andrx terminated their Agreement and entered into a stipulation settling the patent litigation. On June 23, 1999, Andrx then began to market its generic version and its 180–day exclusivity period began to run. In October 1999 the FDA gave tentative approval to Biovail's ANDA and final approval on December 23, 1999.[7] Neither Andrx nor Biovail, however, informed the district court of these developments. On January 6, 2000 the district court granted Andrx's Rule 12(b)(6) motion to dismiss Biovail's counterclaim, the federal antitrust counts with prejudice and the state law claims without prejudice. The court concluded that Biovail did not, and in fact could not, plead an antitrust injury causally linked to Andrx's alleged anticompetitive behavior. * * *

III. ANALYSIS

* * *

A. *Injury-in-Fact and Causation*

As in any civil action for damages, the plaintiff in a private antitrust lawsuit must show that the defendant's illegal conduct caused its injury. The plaintiff's first step is to plead an injury-in-fact or, in a suit for equitable relief, a threatened injury-in-fact to business or property. The "burden of proving the fact of damage under § 4 of the Clayton Act is satisfied by [ ] proof of *some* damage flowing from the unlawful conspiracy; inquiry beyond this minimum point goes only to the amount and not the fact of damage." *Zenith Radio Corp. v. Hazeltine Research, Inc.,* 395 U.S. 100, 114 n. 9, 23 L. Ed. 2d 129, 89 S.Ct. 1562 (1969) (emphasis original). The district court held that Biovail not only failed to plead an injury or a threatened injury but also was unable to do so because Biovail had yet to receive FDA approval for its generic version of Cardizem CD and gave no assurance that it would have entered the market had it gained approval.

When competitors violate the antitrust laws and another competitor is forced from a market, the latter suffers an injury-in-fact. A competitor that has not yet entered the market may also suffer injury but courts require a "potential" competitor to demonstrate both its intention to enter the market and its preparedness to do so. "Indicia of preparedness include adequate background and experience in the new field, sufficient financial capability to enter it, and the taking of actual and substantial affirmative steps toward entry, 'such as the consummation of relevant contracts and procurement of necessary facilities and equipment.' " Thus, in evaluating whether Biovail sufficiently pleaded or *can* sufficiently plead an injury or threatened injury, we must examine its intent and preparedness to enter the market from which

---

7. In a letter dated October 22, 1999 the FDA explained to Biovail that it had "completed review" of its ANDA and found its generic "safe and effective." It gave tentative, rather than final, approval because of "the exclusivity granted by the agency to Andrx."

it alleges it was excluded, that is, the Cardizem CD, or controlled-release dilitiazem-based drug, market.

In the pharmaceutical industry, FDA approval is a prerequisite to enter *any* drug market. The district court concluded that Biovail suffered no injury as a result of the HMRI–Andrx Agreement "because *even today*, Biovail *could not go to market with a generic version of Cardizem*, because it had not received FDA approval."[10] The only facts Biovail alleged to support its claim of injury were that the Agreement "prevented generic Cardizem CD products by Biovail and others from reaching the market as soon as they would otherwise be allowed," and that Biovail had filed an ANDA for a generic version of Cardizem CD. Biovail did not explicitly allege that it was prepared to bring a generic version of Cardizem CD to market or that it anticipated FDA approval. In addition, when the FDA eventually approved its ANDA, Biovail inexplicably failed to inform the district court. Based on Biovail's failure to plead sufficient intent and preparedness to enter the market, the district court dismissed Biovail's antitrust counterclaim.[11]

The district court, however, went beyond dismissing the counterclaim based on the pleading's insufficiency. It dismissed Biovail's antitrust counterclaim *with prejudice*. In so doing it decided, as a matter of law, that Biovail was unable to set forth any set of facts that would entitle it to the relief it sought. * * * The district court did not conclude that Biovail did not intend to enter the market or that it was not sufficiently prepared to do so but instead that it had not sufficiently alleged its intent and capacity to enter the market. Its statement that the FDA had not yet approved Biovail's ANDA as of the date of its ruling was understandable in light of the parties' failure to inform the court to the contrary but the statement was nonetheless erroneous and not a ground to dismiss with prejudice.

* * * Biovail *can* allege facts sufficient to indicate its intent and preparedness. And even before the FDA approved Biovail's ANDA, Biovail could have alleged its intent and preparedness to enter the market by claiming that FDA approval was probable. Andrx's original suit, which sought to enjoin the FDA from approving Biovail's ANDA, suggests that Biovail (or so Andrx believed) may have intended and been sufficiently prepared to enter the market. *See Zenith Radio,* 395 U.S. at 130. * * * Because Biovail may be able to cure its pleading deficiency, we conclude that dismissal with prejudice was erroneously granted.

Andrx responds, however, that an independent legal ground supports dismissal with prejudice. It argues Biovail is unable to allege causation. To sufficiently plead causation, a plaintiff must allege that the defendant violated the antitrust laws, that the defendant's alleged violation "had a tendency to injure" the plaintiff's business or property, and that the plaintiff suffered a decline in its business or property "not shown to be attributable to other causes." The Supreme Court has explained "it is enough that the illegality is

10. By the time of the district court's decision, however, the FDA had approved Biovail's ANDA for its generic version of Cardizem CD although the court was not apprised of that development.

11. The issues of injury-in-fact and causation are closely linked on this point. By not alleging facts indicating its intent and preparedness to enter the Cardizem CD market, Biovail failed to allege both an injury (no loss of profits because not prepared to enter market) and causation (any damages not related to HMRI–Andrx Agreement because Agreement did not cause loss of profits).

shown to be a material cause of the injury; a plaintiff need not exhaust all possible alternative sources of injury in fulfilling his burden of proving compensable injury under [section 4 of the Clayton Act]." *Zenith Radio*, 395 U.S. at 114 n.9.

The district court found that Biovail failed to establish the requisite causal connection between its injury and the alleged anticompetitive conduct. It concluded that any injury Biovail may have suffered was caused not by the HMRI–Andrx Agreement but instead by the lack of FDA approval of its generic version of Cardizem CD and by the delay period prescribed by the Hatch–Waxman Amendments. We disagree. Although we affirm the district court's dismissal to the extent Biovail failed to allege an injury-in-fact, we disagree with its conclusion that any injury Biovail might plead would be caused by "the existence of a troublesome statutory scheme that prohibits it from marketing a drug until the first ANDA recipient goes to market, and which places no restrictions on when, or even whether, that applicant must to *[sic]* go to market." We also reject Andrx's argument that any rational actor like itself would not market its generic drug until the patent infringement suit against it was resolved, making any loss of profits caused by Biovail's exclusion from the market a result of the statutory scheme, not Andrx's conduct. A reasonable juror could conclude that Andrx's argument contradicts the very premise of the HMRI–Andrx Agreement. Under the Agreement, HMRI paid Andrx 10 million dollars per quarter effectively not to enter the market. One can fairly infer from these facts, which were alleged in the counterclaim, that but for the Agreement, Andrx would have entered the market. As one commentator has noted, "[a] payment flowing from the innovator to the challenging generic firm may suggest strongly the anticompetitive intent of the parties in entering the agreement and the rent-preserving effect of that agreement."

Andrx, however, argues that it "did nothing other than to act in accordance with rights granted to it under the Hatch–Waxman [Amendments]. The exercise of these statutory rights, exclusionary though they may be, cannot support a claim under the antitrust laws." Andrx may be correct that "[a] plaintiff cannot be injured in fact by private conduct excluding him from the market when a statute prevents him from entering that market in any event." Although the Hatch–Waxman Amendments provide a 180–day period of market exclusivity to the first applicant to file an ANDA for a generic version of a pioneer drug, through the Amendments, "Congress sought to get generic drugs into the hands of patients at reasonable prices—fast." We disagree with Andrx that "its conduct was not only permitted under but clearly contemplated by the Hatch–Waxman" Amendments. Although it is true that the first to file an ANDA is permitted to delay marketing as long as it likes, the statutory scheme does not envision the first applicant's agreeing with the patent holder of the pioneer drug to delay the start of the 180–day exclusivity period.

By accepting payments from HMRI, Andrx received the benefit of the 180–day exclusivity period without starting the clock. By agreeing with HMRI to share HMRI's profits from the sale of Cardizem CD, it was able to exclude other competitors from entering the market. Andrx's commitment not to trigger the running of the 180–day exclusivity period could have caused Biovail's injury (assuming FDA approval was probable and it was sufficiently prepared to enter the market) by denying it the ability to proceed to market with its own generic version. Although the 180–day provision of the Hatch–Waxman Amendments legally barred it from selling its product, Andrx's manipulation of the exclusivity period trigger date extended the legal bar.

* * *

Andrx * * * relies on the holding in *Polk Bros., Inc. v. Forest City Enters., Inc.*, 776 F.2d 185 (7th Cir.1985). In *Polk Bros.*, two companies, one that sold appliances and home furnishings and the other that sold building materials, lumber, tools and related products, reached an agreement to build on a large parcel of land one building, partitioned on the interior, to house both stores. The arrangement was attractive to both firms due to the complementary nature of their products. They feared, however, that one day competition might replace cooperation so they negotiated a covenant restricting the products each could sell. Years later one of the firms wanted to sell certain products in violation of the covenant and challenged the covenant on antitrust grounds when the other firm sought to enforce it. * * * The Seventh Circuit upheld the validity of the covenant on the ground that, although "naked" restraints on trade are unlawful *per se*, ancillary restraints that facilitate productive activity are not. * * * [E]ven were we to adopt Andrx's characterization of the Agreement as "designed to preserve the *status quo* by duplicating relief that the court could have ordered had HMRI proceeded with" its motion for a preliminary injunction in the patent infringement litigation, the Agreement's allegedly anticompetitive provisions, including Andrx's pledge to continue to pursue its ANDA so as to forestall other applicants from receiving final FDA approval, were not necessarily ancillary restraints but rather could reasonably be viewed as an attempt to allocate market share and preserve monopolistic conditions.

* * *

B. Antitrust Injury

* * *

In asserting that Biovail cannot assert an antitrust injury, Andrx compares it to the *Brunswick [Corp. v. Pueblo Bowl–O–Mat, Inc.*, 429 U.S. 477 (1977)] plaintiffs. * * * Unlike the *Brunswick* plaintiffs' injury, Biovail's alleged injury is the type the antitrust laws were designed to prevent. If Biovail's allegations are correct, the Andrx–HMRI Agreement neither enhanced competition nor benefitted consumers; if anything, it accomplished just the opposite by preserving HMRI's monopoly. Moreover, Biovail alleged that its exclusion from the market occurred not only by reason of the unlawful Agreement but also by reason of that which made the Agreement unlawful, that is, an illegal restraint of trade.

Andrx next argues that it could have lawfully excluded Biovail from the Cardizem CD market by deciding, on its own, to delay marketing of its generic version of Cardizem CD and therefore Biovail's alleged injury does not constitute an antitrust injury. It contends that because its underlying conduct was legal, the fact that it combined to act that way cannot give rise to an antitrust violation. Under the Hatch–Waxman Amendments, Andrx was lawfully entitled to unilaterally delay marketing its product until the patent infringement claims against it were resolved. Although its *unilateral* decision not to market its generic version of Cardizem CD would have prevented others, including Biovail, from entering the market, the counterclaim alleges that Andrx entered into an anticompetitive *agreement* with HMRI in order to exclude others; HMRI's ten million dollar quarterly payments were presumably in return for something that Andrx would not otherwise do, that is, delay marketing of its generic. Andrx's argument that any rational actor would wait for resolution of the patent infringement suit is belied by the *quid* of HMRI's *quo*.[15]

Antitrust law looks at entry into the market as one mechanism to limit and deter exploitation of market power by those who may temporarily possess it. "Existing firms know that if they collude or exercise market power to charge supracompetitive prices, entry by firms currently not competing in the market becomes likely, thereby increasing the pressure on them to act competitively." *FTC v. H.J. Heinz Co.*, 246 F.3d 708, 717 n. 13 (D.C.Cir.2001). The FDA acknowledges that "under current regulatory provisions, the first generic applicant to file a substantially complete ANDA with a paragraph IV certification can delay generic competition by entering into certain commercial arrangements with an innovator company." Such an arrangement can manipulate the statutory grant of a monopoly to bar competitive entries. Andrx argues that the Agreement merely preserved the status quo—in effect a stipulated preliminary injunction—until the conclusion of the patent infringement suit. When the court grants preliminary injunctive relief, however, it does so only after considering the public interest and the likelihood of success on the merits.[17] Moreover, even if Andrx's agreement to maintain the status quo was lawful, its commitment to continue to prosecute its ANDA and do nothing to jeopardize its 180–day exclusivity period went beyond preserving the status quo. "To be ancillary, and hence exempt from the per se rule, an agreement eliminating competition must be subordinate and collateral to a separate, legitimate transaction.... If [the restraint] is so broad that part of the restraint suppresses competition without creating efficiency, the restraint is, to that extent, not ancillary." *Rothery Storage & Van Co. v. Atlas Van Lines, Inc.*, 253 U.S. App. D.C. 142, 792 F.2d 210, 224 (D.C.Cir.1986). As Biovail has pleaded the facts, HMRI and Andrx combined to achieve an unlawful objective, namely, the extension of the exclusivity period granted under the Hatch–Waxman Amendments. Accordingly, we conclude that Biovail can allege an antitrust injury, that is, one the antitrust laws were

---

15. The statutorily granted monopoly of patent rights is similar. Like a drug's 180–day exclusive market period, a patent grant in and of itself is "an exception to the general rule against monopolies and to the right to a free and open market." But even a patent-right holder is not immune from antitrust liability. In *United States v. Singer Mfg. Co.*, 374 U.S. 174, 10 L. Ed. 2d 823, 83 S.Ct. 1773 (1963), two competitors, Singer and Gegauf, entered into a cross-licensing agreement to settle a Patent Office interference proceeding involving their conflicting patent claims. Although Singer (like Andrx) had no obligation to pursue a

patent grant and could have, on its own, withdrawn from the interference proceeding, it nevertheless acted unlawfully when it agreed with a competitor to settle the dispute, suppress information and exclude others from the market. *See id.* at 196; *see also American Cyanimid Co.*, 72 F.T.C. 623 (1967), *aff'd sub nom. Charles Pfizer & Co. v. FTC*, 401 F.2d 574 (6th Cir.1968) (Tetracycline case).

17. By contrast, a private agreement purporting to maintain the status quo may not be in the public interest or may have little likelihood of success on review.

designed to prevent and that flows from that which makes the defendant's conduct unlawful.

* * *

[The court went on also to reject Andrx's arguments under *Associated Gen'l Contractors of Calif., Inc. v. California State Council of Carpenters*, 459 U.S. 519 (1983) (discussed in Chapter 9, *supra*), that Biovail's claim of harm was "speculative" and that consumers of Cardizem were more appropriate plaintiffs to pursue the case. It also rejected Andrx's attempt to analogize the case to *Illinois Brick* (Also discussed in Chapter 9, *supra*). The court found no danger that awarding damages to consumers for overcharges as well as damages to Biovail for lost profits would raise the kinds of concerns about duplicative recovery and apportionment problems that animated *Illinois Brick*. Finally, the court rejected Andrx's assertion of *Noerr-Pennington* petitioning immunity (discussed in Chapter 9, *supra*). Eds.]

————

The agreement between Hoechst and Andrx also drew the attention of the FTC, which issued an administrative complaint against them in April 2000. That complaint was resolved by a consent order, agreed to the following year. *See In the Matter of Hoechst Marion Roussel, Inc.*, 66 Fed. Reg. 18636 (FTC 2001). According to the Statement to Aid Public Comment that accompanied the consent order, the Hoechst–Andrx agreement "was not justified by countervailing efficiencies" and was instead designed to permit Hoechst "to preserve its dominance by delaying the entry of Andrx and other generic companies into the market." The Commission went on to discuss its proposed ten (10) year remedial order:

> * * * Private agreements in which the brand name drug company (the "NDA Holder") pays the first generic to seek FDA approval (the "ANDA First Filer"), and the ANDA First Filer agrees not to enter the market, have the potential to delay generic competition and raise serious antitrust issues. Moreover, the FDA has observed that the incentives for companies to enter into such arrangements are becoming greater, as the returns to a brand name company from extending its monopoly increasingly exceed the potential economic gains to the generic applicant from its 180 days of market exclusivity.

> The proposed order strikes an appropriate balance, on a prospective basis, between the legitimate interests of the Respondents and the Commission's concerns with the possible competitive effects of agreements between NDA Holders and ANDA First Filers. By not imposing any broad prohibitions on the Respondents' ability to compete, the order maintains HMR's incentive to develop and sell new drug products and Andrx's incentive to develop and sell generic products that do not infringe valid intellectual property rights held by others. In addition, the order preserves Andrx's ability to decide for itself whether to market a product in the face of a claim of patent infringement, so long as such decision is otherwise lawful.

> * * * [T]he proposed order:

—Bars (except in certain licensing arrangements) two particular types of agreements between brand name drug companies and potential generic competitors—restrictions on giving up Hatch–Waxman 180–day exclusivity rights and on entering the market with a non-infringing product;

—Requires that interim settlements of patent litigation involving payments to the generic company in which the generic company temporarily refrains from bringing its generic product to market, be approved by the court, with notice to the Commission to allow it time to present its views to the court; and

—Requires the Respondents to give the Commission written notice 30 days before entering into such agreements in other contexts.

The settlement of patent disputes, especially those arising in the context of generic drug approval, have led to considerable discussion owing in part to the apparent susceptibility of Hatch–Waxman to anticompetitive manipulation. *See, e.g.,* C. Scott Hemphill, *Paying for Delay: Pharmaceutical Patent Settlement as a Regulatory Design Problem*, 81 N.Y.U. L. Rev. 1553 (2006). Settlements of patent disputes between rivals also can arise, however, outside of the pharmaceutical context, and can present a variety of significant competition issues. For one view that patent settlements may warrant limitations imposed by antitrust laws, *see* Carl Shapiro, *Antitrust Limits to Patent Settlements*, 34 Rand J. Econ. 391 (2003), *available at* http://faculty.haas.berkeley.edu/shapiro/settle.pdf. *See also* David A. Balto, *Pharmaceutical Patent Settlements: The Antitrust Risks*, 55 Food & Drug L.J. 321 (2000) (cited with approval in *Andrx*).

Note on the FTC's Litigation Against Schering–Plough

The settlement of patent disputes between generic and branded pharmaceutical suppliers—particularly the use of reverse payments—was again challenged by the FTC in *In the Matter of Schering–Plough Corp.*, Dkt. No. 9297 (F.T.C. 2003) (reversing ALJ and finding liability), *available at* http://www.ftc.gov/os/adjpro/d9297/031218commissionopinion.pdf. *See also In the Matter of Bristol–Myers Squibb Company*, Dkt. No. C–4076 (consent order), *available at* http://www.ftc.gov/os/caselist/c4076.htm. Much of the debate concerns the weight that should be accorded the very fact of a reverse payment for antitrust purposes.

In *Schering-Plough Corp. v. FTC*, 402 F.3d 1056 (11th Cir. 2005), the U.S. Court of Appeals for the Eleventh Circuit set aside the decision of the Commission and vacated its order. As the conclusion to its opinion suggests, the court of appeals disagreed with the FTC's assessment of the proper role of antitrust enforcement in policing "reverse payment" settlements between branded pharmaceutical producers and generic manufacturers seeking to offer generic equivalents in the framework established by the Hatch–Waxman Act:

> Simply because a brand-name pharmaceutical company holding a patent paid its generic competitor money cannot be the sole basis for a violation of antitrust law. This alone underscores the need to evaluate the strength of the patent. Our conclusion, to a degree, and we hope the FTC is mindful of this, reflects policy. Given the costs of lawsuits to the parties, the public problems associated with overcrowded court dockets, and the

correlative public and private benefits of settlements, we fear and reject a rule of law that would automatically invalidate any agreement where a patent-holding pharmaceutical manufacturer settles an infringement case by negotiating the generic's entry date and, in an ancillary transaction, pays for other products licensed by the generic. Such a result does not represent the confluence of patent and antitrust law.

Schering-Plough, 402 F.3d at 1076. *But see* Herbert Hovenkamp, *Sensible Antitrust Rules for Pharmaceutical Competition,* 39 U.S.F. L. Rev. 11 (2004) (making argument for more active antitrust intervention to police, among other practices, settlements involving disputes between producers of branded pharmaceutical producers and manufacturers of generics; generally endorsing FTC decision in *Schering*).

As noted above, the court of appeals quarreled with two principal features of the Commission's decision. First, the court rejected the FTC's interpretation of the evidence bearing upon the motive for Schering's decision to pay two generic entrants ($60 million to Upsher and $15 million to ESI) to delay the introduction of generic equivalents for Schering's K–Dur 20, an extended-release, potassium chloride product taken in conjunction with prescription medicines for the treatment of high blood pressure and congestive heart disease. While reciting the traditional standard of administrative law that the FTC's decision must be upheld if supported by substantial evidence, the court displayed little deference to the Commission's interpretation of the record. Instead, the court found persuasive the findings of the FTC's administrative law judge (ALJ), who had grounded his decision to reject liability significantly upon the conclusion that Schering had paid the settlements for legitimate reasons and not simply to delay entry by its rivals. The court characterized the Commission's evaluation of the evidence as "somewhat forced," "meretricious," and "somewhat myopic." *Id.* at 1070, 1073. While chastising the Commission for failing to embrace the ALJ's analysis of the record, the court did not discuss the Commission's 40 pages of factual findings nor did it recount the specific rationales that the Commission offered in its narrative of the facts for displacing the ALJ's assessment of the facts.

As its second major ground for vacating the FTC's order, the court of appeals rebuked the agency for not adhering to the analytical approach and policy perspective that the Eleventh Circuit had endorsed in *Valley Drug Co. v. Geneva Pharm., Inc.,* 344 F.3d 1294 (11th Cir. 2003). In particular, the court stated that the Commission had failed to give adequate weight to "the exclusionary power of [Schering's] patent" in evaluating the competitive effects of the settlement agreement. *Schering-Plough,* 402 F.3d. at 1072–76. The court of appeals explained that "[b]y virtue of its '743 patent, Schering obtained the legal right to exclude Upsher and ESI from the market until they proved either that the '743 patent was invalid or that their products * * * did not infringe Schering's patent." *Id.* at 1066–67. The court seemed to assume that, without the settlements at issue in the case, Schering would have been able to forestall entry by Upsher and ESI for the full term of the Schering patent. Thus, the court rejected the Commission's conclusions that Upsher and ESI could have entered at a time earlier than the dates agreed to in the challenged settlements and that the payments at issue were simply and directly tied to a delay in entry. As suggested in the extended passage quoted above, the court viewed the settlements as compromises of legitimate patent validity uncertainties and attached great weight to the value of settlements in resolving contentious disputes concerning patent infringement issues. The Commission's experience since the mid–1990s in studying settlement issues in the Hatch–Waxman context, and its role in this decade in performing empirical research on the entry of generics and monitoring settlement developments, did not appear to influence the Eleventh Circuit's analysis.

The FTC exercised its independent statutory authority to seek review of the court of appeals decision in the Supreme Court, but that effort failed when the Court sought the views of the Solicitor General, who opposed granting the petition for certiorari. Shortly thereafter the Court denied the petition. *See F.T.C. v. Schering–Plough Corp.*, 126 S. Ct. 2929, 74 U.S.L.W. 3130, 74 U.S.L.W. 3714, 74 U.S.L.W. 3722 (U.S. Jun. 26, 2006) (No. 05–273). For a criticism of the Solicitor General's position, see Harry First, *Controlling the Intellectual Property Grab: Protect Innovation, Not Innovators*, 38 Rutgers L.J. 365, 394–95 (2007).

D. CONCLUSION

In this Chapter we have explored some of the competitive ramifications of innovation, in its various forms, and how antitrust has adapted to them. As we observed, increasingly enforcement agencies, commentators and courts recognize that innovation may often be a critical source of competitive vigor that requires protection under competition laws.

Particularly difficult issues emerged, however, in connection with innovation that takes the form of intellectual property rights. These issues are the "cutting edge" of antitrust in the new economy, and are likely to become even more prominent in the 21st century. They will continue to spur economic thought and doctrinal development, as well as debates over the efficacy of antitrust institutions.

E. PROBLEMS AND EXERCISES

All of the Problems in this Section are taken from the U.S. IP Guidelines. In each instance, consider how you would approach the analysis. What cases, principles and policies would be relevant? What accommodation, if any, would you have to make to non-IP precedent to apply it to these situations? What questions would you ask?

After initially working through each problem, consult the discussions of each that can be found in the corresponding section of the relevant Guidelines. The U.S. IP Guidelines can be accessed on the Internet at http://www.usdoj.gov/atr/public/guidelines/ipguide.htm. Additional problems are analyzed in the Canadian IP Guidelines at http://strategis.ic.gc.ca/SSG/ct01992e.html. Do there appear to be differences in the competition statutes of the two jurisdictions? Do those differences appear to affect the analysis of the problems? Are the differences, if any, a function of differing enforcement philosophies? Other factors?

Problem 10–1:
U.S. IP Guidelines Problem 5
("Distinguishing Horizontal from
Vertical Arrangements")

EXAMPLE 5

Situation:

AgCo, a manufacturer of farm equipment, develops a new, patented emission control technology for its tractor engines and licenses it to

FarmCo, another farm equipment manufacturer. AgCo's emission control technology is far superior to the technology currently owned and used by FarmCo, so much so that FarmCo's technology does not significantly constrain the prices that AgCo could charge for its technology. AgCo's emission control patent has a broad scope. It is likely that any improved emissions control technology that FarmCo could develop in the foreseeable future would infringe AgCo's patent.

Problem 10–2:
U.S. IP Guidelines Problem 8
("Exclusive Dealing")

EXAMPLE 8

Situation:

NewCo, the inventor and manufacturer of a new flat panel display technology, lacking the capability to bring a flat panel display product to market, grants BigCo an exclusive license to sell a product embodying NewCo's technology. BigCo does not currently sell, and is not developing (or likely to develop), a product that would compete with the product embodying the new technology and does not control rights to another display technology. Several firms offer competing displays, BigCo accounts for only a small proportion of the outlets for distribution of display products, and entry into the manufacture and distribution of display products is relatively easy. Demand for the new technology is uncertain and successful market penetration will require considerable promotional effort. The license contains an exclusive dealing restriction preventing BigCo from selling products that compete with the product embodying the licensed technology.

Problem 10–3:
U.S. IP Guidelines Problem 9
("Horizontal Restraints")

EXAMPLE 9

Situation:

Two of the leading manufacturers of a consumer electronic product hold patents that cover alternative circuit designs for the product. The manufacturers assign their patents to a separate corporation wholly owned by the two firms. That corporation licenses the right to use the circuit designs to other consumer product manufacturers and establishes the license royalties. None of the patents is blocking; that is, each of the patents can be used without infringing a patent owned by the other firm. The different circuit designs are substitutable in that each permits the manufacture at comparable cost to consumers of products that consumers consider to be interchangeable. One of the Agencies is analyzing the licensing arrangement.

Problem 10–4:
U.S. IP Guidelines Problem 11
("Acquisitions of Intellectual
Property Rights")

EXAMPLE 11

Situation:

Omega develops a new, patented pharmaceutical for the treatment of a particular disease. The only drug on the market approved for the treatment of this disease is sold by Delta. Omega's patented drug has almost completed regulatory approval by the Food and Drug Administration. Omega has invested considerable sums in product development and market testing, and initial results show that Omega's drug would be a significant competitor to Delta's. However, rather than enter the market as a direct competitor of Delta, Omega licenses to Delta the right to manufacture and sell Omega's patented drug. The license agreement with Delta is nominally nonexclusive. However, Omega has rejected all requests by other firms to obtain a license to manufacture and sell Omega's patented drug, despite offers by those firms of terms that are reasonable in relation to those in Delta's license.

Appendix A

SELECTED ANTITRUST STATUTES

---

*Excerpts from the Principal U.S. Antitrust Statutes**

A. The Sherman Act

§ 1   Sherman Act, 15 U.S.C. § 1—Trusts, etc., in restraint of trade illegal; penalty

Every contract, combination in the form of trust or otherwise, or conspiracy, in restraint of trade or commerce among the several States, or with foreign nations, is declared to be illegal. Every person who shall make any contract or engage in any combination or conspiracy hereby declared to be illegal shall be deemed guilty of a felony, and, on conviction thereof, shall be punished by fine not exceeding $100,00,000 if a corporation, or, if any other person, $350,000, or by imprisonment not exceeding three years, or by both said punishments, in the discretion of the court.

§ 2   Sherman Act, 15 U.S.C. § 2—Monopolizing trade a felony; penalty

Every person who shall monopolize, or attempt to monopolize, or combine or conspire with any other person or persons, to monopolize any part of the trade or commerce among the several States, or with foreign nations, shall be deemed guilty of a felony, and, on conviction thereof, shall be punished by fine not exceeding $100,000,000 if a corporation, or, if any other person, $1,000,000 or by imprisonment not exceeding ten years, or by both said punishments, in the discretion of the court.

§ 3   Sherman Act, 15 U.S.C. § 3—Trusts in Territories or District of Columbia illegal; combination a felony

(a) Every contract, combination in form of trust or otherwise, or conspiracy, in restraint of trade or commerce in any Territory of the United States or of the District of Columbia, or in restraint of trade or commerce between any such Territory and another, or between any such Territory or Territories and any State or States or the District of Columbia, or with foreign nations, or between the District of Columbia and any State or States or

* For a comprehensive collection of the antitrust statutes enforced by the Department of Justice, *see* http://www.usdoj.gov/atr/foia/divisionmanual/ch2.htm; for a compilation of the statutes enforced by the Federal Trade Commission, *see* http://www.ftc.gov/ogc/stats.shtm.

foreign nations, is declared illegal. Every person who shall make any such contract or engage in any such combination or conspiracy, shall be deemed guilty of a felony, and, on conviction thereof, shall be punished by fine not exceeding $100,000,000 if a corporation, or, if any other person, $1,000,000, or by imprisonment not exceeding 10 years, or by both said punishments, in the discretion of the court.

(b) Every person who shall monopolize, or attempt to monopolize, or combine or conspire with any other person or persons, to monopolize any part of the trade or commerce in any Territory of the United States or of the District of Columbia, or between any such Territory and another, or between any such Territory or Territories and any State or States or the District of Columbia, or with foreign nations, or between the District of Columbia, and any State or States or foreign nations, shall be deemed guilty of a felony, and, on conviction thereof, shall be punished by fine not exceeding $100,000,000 if a corporation, or, if any other person, $1,000,000, or by imprisonment not exceeding 10 years, or by both said punishments, in the discretion of the court.

§ 4 Sherman Act, 15 U.S.C. § 4—Jurisdiction of courts; duty of United States attorneys; procedure

The several district courts of the United States are invested with jurisdiction to prevent and restrain violations of sections 1 to 7 of this title; and it shall be the duty of the several United States attorneys, in their respective districts, under the direction of the Attorney General, to institute proceedings in equity to prevent and restrain such violations. Such proceedings may be by way of petition setting forth the case and praying that such violation shall be enjoined or otherwise prohibited. * * *

§ 7 Sherman Act, 15 U.S.C. § 6a (Foreign Trade Antitrust Improvements Act of 1982)—Conduct involving trade or commerce with foreign nations

Sections 1 to 7 of this title shall not apply to conduct involving trade or commerce (other than import trade or import commerce) with foreign nations unless—

(1) such conduct has a direct, substantial, and reasonably foreseeable effect—

(A) on trade or commerce which is not trade or commerce with foreign nations, or on import trade or import commerce with foreign nations; or

(B) on export trade or export commerce with foreign nations, of a person engaged in such trade or commerce in the United States; and

(2) such effect gives rise to a claim under the provisions of sections 1 to 7 of this title, other than this section.

If sections 1 to 7 of this title apply to such conduct only because of the operation of paragraph (1)(B), then sections 1 to 7 of this title shall apply to such conduct only for injury to export business in the United States.

B. The Clayton Act

§ 2   Clayton Act, 15 U.S.C. § 13—Discrimination in price, services, or facilities

(a) *Price; selection of customers*

It shall be unlawful for any person engaged in commerce, in the course of such commerce, either directly or indirectly, to discriminate in price between different purchasers of commodities of like grade and quality, where either or any of the purchases involved in such discrimination are in commerce, where such commodities are sold for use, consumption, or resale within the United States or any Territory thereof or the District of Columbia or any insular possession or other place under the jurisdiction of the United States, and where the effect of such discrimination may be substantially to lessen competition or tend to create a monopoly in any line of commerce, or to injure, destroy, or prevent competition with any person who either grants or knowingly receives the benefit of such discrimination, or with customers of either of them: *Provided,* That nothing herein contained shall prevent differentials which make only due allowance for differences in the cost of manufacture, sale, or delivery resulting from the differing methods or quantities in which such commodities are to such purchasers sold or delivered * * *.

(b) *Burden of rebutting prima-facie case of discrimination*

Upon proof being made, at any hearing on a complaint under this section, that there has been discrimination in price or services or facilities furnished, the burden of rebutting the prima-facie case thus made by showing justification shall be upon the person charged with a violation of this section, and unless justification shall be affirmatively shown, the Commission is authorized to issue an order terminating the discrimination: *Provided, however,* That nothing herein contained shall prevent a seller rebutting the prima-facie case thus made by showing that his lower price or the furnishing of services or facilities to any purchaser or purchasers was made in good faith to meet an equally low price of a competitor, or the services or facilities furnished by a competitor.

(c) *Payment or acceptance of commission, brokerage, or other compensation*

It shall be unlawful for any person engaged in commerce, in the course of such commerce, to pay or grant, or to receive or accept, anything of value as a commission, brokerage, or other compensation, or any allowance or discount in lieu thereof, except for services rendered in connection with the sale or purchase of goods, wares, or merchandise, either to the other party to such transaction or to an agent, representative, or other intermediary therein where such intermediary is acting in fact for or in behalf, or is subject to the direct or indirect control, of any party to such transaction other than the person by whom such compensation is so granted or paid.

(d) *Payment for services or facilities for processing or sale*

It shall be unlawful for any person engaged in commerce to pay or contract for the payment of anything of value to or for the benefit of a customer of such person in the course of such commerce as compensation or in consideration for any services or facilities furnished by or through such customer in connection with the processing, handling, sale, or offering for sale of any products or commodities manufactured, sold, or offered for sale by such person, unless such payment or consideration is available on proportionally equal terms to all other customers competing in the distribution of such products or commodities.

(e) *Furnishing services or facilities for processing, handling, etc.*

It shall be unlawful for any person to discriminate in favor of one purchaser against another purchaser or purchasers of a commodity bought for resale, with or without processing, by contracting to furnish or furnishing, or by contributing to the furnishing of, any services or facilities connected with the processing, handling, sale, or offering for sale of such commodity so purchased upon terms not accorded to all purchasers on proportionally equal terms.

(f) *Knowingly inducing or receiving discriminatory price*

It shall be unlawful for any person engaged in commerce, in the course of such commerce, knowingly to induce or receive a discrimination in price which is prohibited by this section.

§ 3   Clayton Act, 15 U.S.C. § 14—Sale, etc., on agreement not to use goods of competitor

It shall be unlawful for any person engaged in commerce, in the course of such commerce, to lease or make a sale or contract for sale of goods, wares, merchandise, machinery, supplies, or other commodities, whether patented or unpatented, for use, consumption, or resale within the United States or any Territory thereof or the District of Columbia or any insular possession or other place under the jurisdiction of the United States, or fix a price charged therefor, or discount from, or rebate upon, such price, on the condition, agreement, or understanding that the lessee or purchaser thereof shall not use or deal in the goods, wares, merchandise, machinery, supplies, or other commodities of a competitor or competitors of the lessor or seller, where the effect of such lease, sale, or contract for sale or such condition, agreement, or understanding may be to substantially lessen competition or tend to create a monopoly in any line of commerce.

§ 4   Clayton Act, 15 U.S.C. § 15—Suits by persons injured

(a) *Amount of recovery; prejudgment interest*

Except as provided in subsection (b) of this section, any person who shall be injured in his business or property by reason of anything forbidden in the antitrust laws may sue therefor in any district court of the United States in the district in which the defendant resides or is found or has an agent, without respect to the amount in controversy, and shall recover threefold the damages by him sustained, and the cost of suit, including a reasonable attorney's fee. * * *

§ 4A   Clayton Act, 15 U.S.C. § 15a—Suits by United States; amount of recovery; prejudgment interest

Whenever the United States is hereafter injured in its business or property by reason of anything forbidden in the antitrust laws it may sue therefor in the United States district court for the district in which the defendant resides or is found or has an agent, without respect to the amount in controversy, and shall recover threefold the damages by it sustained and the cost of suit. * * *

§ 4B   Clayton Act, 15 U.S.C. § 15b—Limitation of actions

Any action to enforce any cause of action under sections 15, 15a, or 15c of this title shall be forever barred unless commenced within four years after the cause of action accrued. * * *

§ 4C   Clayton Act, 15 U.S.C. § 15c—Actions by State attorneys general

(a) *Parens patriae; monetary relief; damages; prejudgment interest*

(1) Any attorney general of a State may bring a civil action in the name of such State, as parens patriae on behalf of natural persons residing in such State, in any district court of the United States having jurisdiction of the defendant, to secure monetary relief as provided in this section for injury sustained by such natural persons to their property by reason of any violation of sections 1 to 7 of this title. The court shall exclude from the amount of monetary relief awarded in such action any amount of monetary relief (A) which duplicates amounts which have been awarded for the same injury, or (B) which is properly allocable to (i) natural persons who have excluded their claims pursuant to subsection (b)(2) of this section, and (ii) any business entity.

(2) The court shall award the State as monetary relief threefold the total damage sustained as described in paragraph (1) of this subsection, and the cost of suit, including a reasonable attorney's fee. * * *

§ 4D   Clayton Act, 15 U.S.C. § 15d—Measurement of damages

In any action under section 15c(a)(1) of this title, in which there has been a determination that a defendant agreed to fix prices in violation of sections 1 to 7 of this title, damages may be proved and assessed in the aggregate by statistical or sampling methods, by the computation of illegal overcharges, or by such other reasonable system of estimating aggregate damages as the court in its discretion may permit without the necessity of separately proving the individual claim of, or amount of damage to, persons on whose behalf the suit was brought.

§ 5   Clayton Act, 15 U.S.C. § 16 (Tunney Act)—Judgments

(a) *Prima facie evidence; collateral estoppel*

A final judgment or decree heretofore or hereafter rendered in any civil or criminal proceeding brought by or on behalf of the United States under the antitrust laws to the effect that a defendant has violated said laws shall be prima facie evidence against such defendant in any action or proceeding brought by any other party against such defendant under said laws as to all matters respecting which said judgment or decree would be an estoppel as between the parties thereto: *Provided,* That this section shall not apply to consent judgments or decrees entered before any testimony has been taken. Nothing contained in this section shall be construed to impose any limitation on the application of collateral estoppel, except that, in any action or proceeding brought under the antitrust laws, collateral estoppel effect shall not be given to any finding made by the Federal Trade Commission under the antitrust laws or under section 45 of this title which could give rise to a claim for relief under the antitrust laws.

* * *

§ 7   Clayton Act, 15 U.S.C. § 18—Acquisition by one corporation of stock of another

No person engaged in commerce or in any activity affecting commerce shall acquire, directly or indirectly, the whole or any part of the stock or other share capital and no person subject to the jurisdiction of the Federal Trade Commission shall acquire the whole or any part of the assets of another person engaged also in commerce or in any activity affecting commerce, where in any line of commerce or in any activity affecting commerce in any section of the country, the effect of such acquisition may be substantially to lessen competition, or to tend to create a monopoly.

No person shall acquire, directly or indirectly, the whole or any part of the stock or other share capital and no person subject to the jurisdiction of the Federal Trade Commission shall acquire the whole or any part of the assets of one or more persons engaged in commerce or in any activity affecting commerce, where in any line of commerce or in any activity affecting commerce in any section of the country, the effect of such acquisition, of such stocks or assets, or of the use of such stock by the voting or granting of proxies or otherwise, may be substantially to lessen competition, or to tend to create a monopoly.

This section shall not apply to persons purchasing such stock solely for investment and not using the same by voting or otherwise to bring about, or in attempting to bring about, the substantial lessening of competition. * * *

§ 11   Clayton Act, 15 U.S.C. § 21—Enforcement provisions

* * *

(c) Review of orders; jurisdiction; filing of petition and record of proceeding; conclusiveness of findings; additional evidence; modification of findings; finality of judgment and decree

Any person required by such order of the commission * * * to cease and desist from any such violation may obtain a review of such order in the court of appeals of the United States for any circuit within which such violation occurred or within which such person resides or carries on business * * *. The findings of the commission * * * as to the facts, if supported by substantial evidence, shall be conclusive. * * * The judgment and decree of the court shall be final, except that the same shall be subject to review by the Supreme Court upon certiorari, as provided in section 1254 of Title 28.

* * *

(*l*) Penalties

Any person who violates any order issued by the commission * * * under subsection (b) of this section after such order has become final, and while such order is in effect, shall forfeit and pay to the United States a civil penalty of not more than $5,000 for each violation, which shall accrue to the United

States and may be recovered in a civil action brought by the United States. Each separate violation of any such order shall be a separate offense, except that in the case of a violation through continuing failure or neglect to obey a final order of the commission * * * each day of continuance of such failure or neglect shall be deemed a separate offense.

§ 12   Clayton Act, 15 U.S.C. § 22—District in which to sue corporation

Any suit, action, or proceeding under the antitrust laws against a corporation may be brought not only in the judicial district whereof it is an inhabitant, but also in any district wherein it may be found or transacts business; and all process in such cases may be served in the district of which it is an inhabitant, or wherever it may be found.

§ 15   Clayton Act, 15 U.S.C. § 25—Restraining violations; procedure

The several district courts of the United States are invested with jurisdiction to prevent and restrain violations of this Act, and it shall be the duty of the several United States attorneys, in their respective districts, under the direction of the Attorney General, to institute proceedings in equity to prevent and restrain such violations. Such proceedings may be by way of petition setting forth the case and praying that such violation shall be enjoined or otherwise prohibited. When the parties complained of shall have been duly notified of such petition, the court shall proceed, as soon as may be, to the hearing and determination of the case; and pending such petition, and before final decree, the court may at any time make such temporary restraining order or prohibition as shall be deemed just in the premises. Whenever it shall appear to the court before which any such proceeding may be pending that the ends of justice require that other parties should be brought before the court, the court may cause them to be summoned whether they reside in the district in which the court is held or not, and subpoenas to that end may be served in any district by the marshal thereof.

§ 16   Clayton Act, 15 U.S.C. § 26—Injunctive relief for private parties; exception; costs

Any person, firm, corporation, or association shall be entitled to sue for and have injunctive relief, in any court of the United States having jurisdiction over the parties, against threatened loss or damage by a violation of the antitrust laws, including sections 13, 14, 18, and 19 of this title, when and under the same conditions and principles as injunctive relief against threatened conduct that will cause loss or damage is granted by courts of equity, under the rules governing such proceedings, and upon the execution of proper bond against damages for an injunction improvidently granted and a showing that the danger of irreparable loss or damage is immediate, a preliminary injunction may issue: *Provided,* That nothing herein contained shall be construed to entitle any person, firm, corporation, or association, except the United States, to bring suit for injunctive relief against any common carrier subject to the jurisdiction of the Surface Transportation Board under subtitle IV of Title 49. In any action under this section in which the plaintiff substantially prevails, the court shall award the cost of suit, including a reasonable attorney's fee, to such plaintiff.

C. Federal Trade Commission Act (15 U.S.C. §§ 41–58, as amended)

§ 1   FTC Act, 15 U.S.C. § 41—Federal Trade Commission established; membership; vacancies; seal

A commission is created and established, to be known as the Federal Trade Commission (hereinafter referred to as the Commission), which shall be composed of five Commissioners, who shall be appointed by the President, by and with the advice and consent of the Senate. Not more than three of the Commissioners shall be members of the same political party. * * * The President shall choose a chairman from the Commission's membership. * * *

§ 5   FTC Act, 15 U.S.C. § 45—Unfair methods of competition unlawful; prevention by Commission

(a) Declaration of unlawfulness; power to prohibit unfair practices; inapplicability to foreign trade

(1) Unfair methods of competition in or affecting commerce, and unfair or deceptive acts or practices in or affecting commerce, are hereby declared unlawful.

* * *

(2) The Commission is hereby empowered and directed to prevent persons, partnerships, or corporations * * * [with some specified exceptions] from using unfair methods of competition in or affecting commerce and unfair or deceptive acts or practices in or affecting commerce.

(b) Proceeding by Commission; modifying and setting aside orders

Whenever the Commission shall have reason to believe that any such person, partnership, or corporation has been or is using any unfair method of competition or unfair or deceptive act or practice in or affecting commerce, and if it shall appear to the Commission that a proceeding by it in respect thereof would be to the interest of the public, it shall issue and serve upon such person, partnership, or corporation a complaint stating its charges in that respect and containing a notice of a hearing upon a day and at a place therein fixed at least thirty days after the service of said complaint. The person, partnership, or corporation so complained of shall have the right to appear at the place and time so fixed and show cause why an order should not be entered by the Commission requiring such person, partnership, or corporation to cease and desist from the violation of the law so charged in said complaint. * * *

(c) Review of order; rehearing

Any person, partnership, or corporation required by an order of the Commission to cease and desist from using any method of competition or act or practice may obtain a review of such order in the court of appeals of the United States, within any circuit where the method of competition or the act or practice in question was used or where such person, partnership, or corporation resides or carries on business, by filing in the court, within sixty days from the date of the service of such order, a written petition praying that the order of the Commission be set aside. * * *

(d) Jurisdiction of court

Upon the filing of the record with it the jurisdiction of the court of appeals of the United States to affirm, enforce, modify, or set aside orders of the Commission shall be exclusive.

* * *

(*l*) Penalty for violation of order; injunctions and other appropriate equitable relief

Any person, partnership, or corporation who violates an order of the Commission after it has become final, and while such order is in effect, shall forfeit and pay to the United States a civil penalty of not more than $10,000 for each violation, which shall accrue to the United States and may be recovered in a civil action brought by the Attorney General of the United States. Each separate violation of such an order shall be a separate offense, except that in a case of a violation through continuing failure to obey or neglect to obey a final order of the Commission, each day of continuance of such failure or neglect shall be deemed a separate offense. In such actions, the United States district courts are empowered to grant mandatory injunctions and such other and further equitable relief as they deem appropriate in the enforcement of such final orders of the Commission.

* * *

(n) Standard of proof; public policy consideration

The Commission shall have no authority under this section * * * to declare unlawful an act or practice on the grounds that such act or practice is unfair unless the act or practice causes or is likely to cause substantial injury to consumers which is not reasonably avoidable by consumers themselves and not outweighed by countervailing benefits to consumers or to competition. In determining whether an act or practice is unfair, the Commission may consider established public policies as evidence to be considered with all other evidence. Such public policy considerations may not serve as a primary basis for such determination.

§ 13 FTC Act, 15 U.S.C. § 53—False advertisements; injunctions and re- straining orders

* * *

(b) Temporary restraining orders; preliminary injunctions

Whenever the Commission has reason to believe—

(1) that any person, partnership, or corporation is violating, or is about to violate, any provision of law enforced by the Federal Trade Commission, and

(2) that the enjoining thereof pending the issuance of a complaint by the Commission and until such complaint is dismissed by the Commission or set aside by the court on review, or until the order of the Commission made thereon has become final, would be in the interest of the public—

the Commission by any of its attorneys designated by it for such purpose may bring suit in a district court of the United States to enjoin any such act or practice. Upon a proper showing that, weighing the equities and considering the Commission's likelihood of ultimate success, such action would be in the public interest, and after notice to the defendant, a temporary restraining order or a preliminary injunction may be granted without bond * * *. Provided further, That in proper cases the Commission may seek, and after proper proof, the court may issue, a permanent injunction. Any suit may be brought where such person, partnership, or corporation resides or transacts business, or wherever venue is proper under section 1391 of Title 28. In addition, the court may, if the court determines that the interests of justice require that any other person, partnership, or corporation should be a party in such suit, cause such other person, partnership, or corporation to be added as a party without regard to whether venue is otherwise proper in the district in which the suit is brought. In any suit under this section, process may be served on any person, partnership, or corporation wherever it may be found.

Sample State Antitrust Statute—New York's Donnelly Act

Art. 22, § 340, N.Y. Gen. Bus. § 340. Contracts or agreements for monopoly or in restraint of trade illegal and void

1. Every contract, agreement, arrangement or combination whereby A monopoly in the conduct of any business, trade or commerce or in the furnishing of any service in this state, is or may be established or maintained, or whereby Competition or the free exercise of any activity in the conduct of any business, trade or commerce or in the furnishing of any service in this state is or may be restrained or whereby For the purpose of establishing or maintaining any such monopoly or unlawfully interfering with the free exercise of any activity in the conduct of any business, trade or commerce or in the furnishing of any service in this state any business, trade or commerce or the furnishing of any service is or may be restrained, is hereby declared to be against public policy, illegal and void.

* * *

5. An action to recover damages caused by a violation of this section must be commenced within four years after the cause of action has accrued. The state, or any political subdivision or public authority of the state, or any person who shall sustain damages by reason of any violation of this section, shall recover three-fold the actual damages sustained thereby, as well as costs not exceeding ten thousand dollars, and reasonable attorneys' fees. At or before the commencement of any civil action by a party other than the attorney-general for a violation of this section, notice thereof shall be served upon the attorney-general. Where the aggrieved party is a political subdivision or public authority of the state, notice of intention to commence an action under this section must be served upon the attorney-general at least ten days prior to the commencement of such action. This section shall not apply to any action commenced prior to the effective date of this act.

6. In any action pursuant to this section, the fact that the state, or any political subdivision or public authority of the state, or any person who has sustained damages by reason of violation of this section has not dealt directly with the defendant shall not bar or otherwise limit recovery; provided,

however, that in any action in which claims are asserted against a defendant by both direct and indirect purchasers, the court shall take all steps necessary to avoid duplicate liability, including but not limited to the transfer and consolidation of all related actions. In actions where both direct and indirect purchasers are involved, a defendant shall be entitled to prove as a partial or complete defense to a claim for damages that the illegal overcharge has been passed on to others who are themselves entitled to recover so as to avoid duplication of recovery of damages.

Principal E.U. Treaty Provisions **

Article 81 (formally Article 85)

1. The following shall be prohibited as incompatible with the common market: all agreements between undertakings, decisions by associations of undertakings and concerted practices which may affect trade between Member States and which have as their object or effect the prevention, restriction or distortion of competition within the common market, and in particular those which:

    (a) directly or indirectly fix purchase or selling prices or any other trading conditions;

    (b) limit or control production, markets, technical development, or investment;

    (c) share markets or sources of supply;

    (d) apply dissimilar conditions to equivalent transactions with other trading parties, thereby placing them at a competitive disadvantage;

    (e) make the conclusion of contracts subject to acceptance by the other parties of supplementary obligations which, by their nature or according to commercial usage, have no connection with the subject of such contracts.

2. Any agreements or decisions prohibited pursuant to this Article shall be automatically void.

3. The provisions of paragraph 1 may, however, be declared inapplicable in the case of:

    —any agreement or category of agreements between undertakings;

    —any decision or category of decisions by associations of undertakings;

    —any concerted practice or category of concerted practices,

    which contributes to improving the production or distribution of goods or to promoting technical or economic progress, while allowing consumers a fair share of the resulting benefit, and which does not:

    (a) impose on the undertakings concerned restrictions which are not indispensable to the attainment of these objectives;

** For a comprehensive collection of the relevant provisions of the E.U. Treaty, as well as the various regulations, exemptions and guidelines, *see* http://europa.eu.int/comm/competition/antitrust/legislation/.

(b) afford such undertakings the possibility of eliminating competition in respect of a substantial part of the products in question.

Article 82 (formally Article 86)

Any abuse by one or more undertakings of a dominant position within the common market or in a substantial part of it shall be prohibited as incompatible with the common market insofar as it may affect trade between Member States.

Such abuse may, in particular, consist in:

(a) directly or indirectly imposing unfair purchase or selling prices or other unfair trading conditions;

(b) limiting production, markets or technical development to the prejudice of consumers;

(c) applying dissimilar conditions to equivalent transactions with other trading parties, thereby placing them at a competitive disadvantage;

(d) making the conclusion of contracts subject to acceptance by the other parties of supplementary obligations which, by their nature or according to commercial usage, have no connection with the subject of such contracts.

Appendix B

SELECTED ANTITRUST RESOURCES ON THE INTERNET

Principal Guidelines and Policy Statements Issued by the Federal Trade Commission and the United States Department of Justice

A. Cartels and Criminal Antitrust Offenses

U.S. Department of Justice, Antitrust Division,
Criminal Enforcement Resources
http://www.usdoj.gov/atr/public/criminal.htm

U.S. Department of Justice, Leniency Policy for Individuals (1993)
http://www.usdoj.gov/atr/public/guidelines/lenind.htm

U.S. Department of Justice, Corporate Leniency Policy (1993)
http://www.usdoj.gov/atr/public/guidelines/0091.htm

U.S. Department of Justice, Antitrust Grand Jury Practice Manual
http://www.usdoj.gov/atr/public/guidelines/4371.htm

U.S. Sentencing Guidelines Manual (Section 2R1.1 addresses
criminal antitrust offenses)
http://www.ussc.gov/GUIDELIN.HTM

B. Mergers

Horizontal Merger Guidelines (1982, as revised through 1997)
http://www.usdoj.gov/atr/public/guidelines/hmg.htm

Commentary on the Horizontal Merger Guidelines (2006)
http://www.usdoj.gov/atr/public/guidelines/215247.htm

Pre–Merger Notification Under the Hart–Scott–
Rodino Act—Resources
http://www.ftc.gov/bc/hsr/hsr.shtm

U.S. Department of Justice, Antitrust Division,
Policy Guide to Merger Remedies (2004)
http://www.usdoj.gov/atr/public/guidelines/205108.htm

Non–Horizontal Merger Guidelines (1984)
http://www.usdoj.gov/atr/public/guidelines/2614.htm

Protocol for Coordination in Merger Investigations
Between the Federal Enforcement Agencies and
State Attorneys General (1998)
http://www.usdoj.gov/atr/public/guidelines/1773.htm

National Association of Attorneys General, Horizontal
Merger Guidelines (1993)
http://www.naag.org/assets/files/pdf/
at-hmerger_guidelines.pdf

C.   Other Enforcement Policy Guidelines and Related Material

Antitrust Guidelines for the Licensing of
Intellectual Property (1995)
http://www.usdoj.gov/atr/public/guidelines/0558.htm

Antitrust Enforcement Guidelines for International Operations (rev. 1995)
http://www.usdoj.gov/atr/public/guidelines/internat.htm

Statements of Antitrust Enforcement Policy in Health Care (1996)
http://www.usdoj.gov/atr/public/guidelines/0000.htm

Antitrust Guidelines for Collaborations Among Competitors (2000)
http://www.ftc.gov/os/2000/04/ftcdojguidelines.pdf

Guides to Advertising and Promotional Allowances
(*"Fred Meyer* Guides")
http://www.ftc.gov/bc/docs/16cfr240.htm

U.S. Department of Justice, Antitrust Division Manual
http://www.usdoj.gov/atr/foia/divisionmanual/
table_of_contents.htm

Selected Other Antitrust Internet Resources of Interest

U.S. Department of Justice, Antitrust Division
http://www.usdoj.gov/atr/

U.S. Federal Trade Commission
http://www.ftc.gov/

National Association of Attorneys General, Antitrust Project
http://www.naag.org/antitrust.php

Links to Antitrust Enforcement Agency Web Sites Worldwide
http://www.usdoj.gov/atr/contact/otheratr.htm

American Bar Association, Section on Antitrust Law
http://www.abanet.org/antitrust/

American Antitrust Institute
http://www.antitrustinstitute.org/

Antitrust Modernization Commission
http://www.amc.gov/index.html

European Commission, Directorate General for Competition
http://europa.eu.int/comm/competition/index_en.html

Index

References are to Pages

1265